Wisconsin Birdlife

*Publication of this book
is sponsored in part by
Friends of the Museum, Inc.,
of the Milwaukee Public Museum*

Pileated Woodpecker. Portrait by Owen J. Gromme

Wisconsin Birdlife

Population & Distribution
Past & Present

Samuel D. Robbins, Jr.

The University of Wisconsin Press

The University of Wisconsin Press
114 North Murray Street
Madison, Wisconsin 53715

3 Henrietta Street
London WC2E 8LU, England

Printed in the United States of America

Publication of this book has been assisted by grants from the
Badger Meter Foundation, Inc., Milwaukee, Wisconsin,
and the Chapman Foundation, Milwaukee, Wisconsin.

Inclusion of the frontispiece portrait of the
Pileated Woodpecker by Owen J. Gromme
was made possible by the generosity of the
Marshall & Ilsley Corporation, Milwaukee, Wisconsin,
and Stanton & Lee, Madison, Wisconsin.

The maps were prepared by the University of
Wisconsin–Madison Cartographic Laboratory
and by R. A. Robbins.

Library of Congress Cataloging-in-Publication Data
Robbins, Samuel D.
Wisconsin birdlife: population & distribution past & present /
Samuel D. Robbins.
720 pp.   cm.
Includes bibliographical references and index.
1. Birds—Wisconsin.   2. Bird populations—Wisconsin.
3. Ornithology—Wisconsin—History.   I. Title.
QL684.W6R63   1990
598.29775—dc20   90-50095
ISBN 0-299-10260-2   CIP

To
Owen J. Gromme
whose vision, vigor, and determination
first gave impetus to this volume

Contents

Preface   ix

Acknowledgments   xi

Introduction   xiii

Abbreviations and Nomenclature   xviii

Part I The Background

The Development of Wisconsin Ornithology   3

    Recording Wisconsin's Birds   3

    Avifaunal Changes   12

    Appraisals of Avian Population Changes   16

    Combatting Bird Losses   19

The Landscape and the Birds

    James Hall Zimmerman   35

    Wisconsin's Environmental Setting   38

    The History of Wisconsin Bird Habitats   70

Part II The Birds

Introduction to Part II   93

List of Wisconsin Species, Showing Status and Seasonal Distribution   101

Accounts of Individual Species   113

    Loons through Ducks   113

    Hawks through Cranes   198

    Plovers through Doves   251

    Cuckoos through Swallows   329

    Jays through Wrens   402

    Kinglets through Warblers   428

    Tanagers through Finches   524

    Species of Hypothetical Status   607

    Possible Escapes   613

Habitat Preferences
    James Hall Zimmerman   615
  Habitat Descriptions   615
    Table 1. Habitat Types   616
  Breeding Bird Habitats   633
    Table 2. Habitat Preferences of Wisconsin Breeding Birds   634
  Wintering Bird Habitats   645
    Table 3. Habitat Preferences of Wisconsin Wintering Birds   646
  Migrating Bird Habitats   648
    Table 4. Habitat Preferences of Birds Found in Wisconsin
      Only during Migration   649

Bibliography
  Walter E. Scott and Gertrude M. Scott   653
List of Observers   689
Index of Species   696

Preface

This book is written with three types of readers in mind. First, there are serious-minded amateurs engaged in active fieldwork in bird study, either as a hobby or as related peripherally to professional work, who are constantly observing birds and asking questions about the significance of their observations. This work is intended to help them to appraise the usual and the unusual in terms of when and where birds are found in Wisconsin.

Second, there are professional ornithologists, engaged in teaching, research, compilation of data, and writing, who need a carefully documented historical record of every species reliably recorded in the state, with evidence to show historical changes in abundance. This book is intended to summarize the essential facts of status for each species as a migrant, a breeder, and a winter resident.

Third, there is a growing number of bird-appreciators, interested in birds but not necessarily involved in ornithological activity beyond feeding birds in winter and providing nesting habitat in summer. These enthusiasts are interested in learning about the birds with which acquaintance has already been made and species with which acquaintance could be developed in the future. Such people will need pocket-sized field guides, picture volumes (such as O. J. Gromme's *Birds of Wisconsin*), and recordings to enable them to recognize the plumage and sounds of the various species and to learn their continental summer and winter ranges. This volume makes no attempt to duplicate in those areas. But it is meant to enlarge the reader's knowledge and appreciation of the statewide history, abundance, and habitat preferences for each Wisconsin species.

Much of the information in this book was obtained from cooperative volunteers. Numerous organizations now exist to enable bird-enthusiasts of all kinds to pool their interests and resources.

Much remains to be learned about Wisconsin birds. Prompted by the many unanswered questions I encountered in preparing this manuscript, I developed a list of suggested research projects. I gave this list to the heads of local bird clubs, to ornithology teachers on Wisconsin college and university campuses, to the Wisconsin Department of Natural Resources Bureau of Research, and to the Wisconsin Society for Ornithology Research Committee, hoping that an expanding task force of observers will help roll back the frontiers of the unknown. This is crucial. In the face of an increasing population and sharpening controversy over competing land use, the preservation of many of our birds can no longer be taken for granted.

Acknowledgments

Hundreds of people have contributed to this book, knowingly or unknowingly. Whether or not their names appear beside a particular record mentioned in this volume, the hundreds of contributors to the Wisconsin Society for Ornithology field note program during the past 50 years have been supplying essential information for this book. The same can be said of every Christmas Bird Count and Breeding Bird Survey participant. Without these myriad bits of data, it would not have been possible to determine the distribution and migration patterns of 400 species in a state that encompasses 56,184 square miles.

More specifically, I must begin by expressing gratitude to those who helped guide this project from beginning to end. This includes O. J. Gromme, who initiated this work and guided it through its early stages, then encouraged me to pick up where he left off. It includes F. L. Ott, Jr., and the other officers of the Friends of the Museum, Inc., of the Milwaukee Public Museum, who gave the necessary financial support and exercised such great patience when the project experienced one delay after another. It includes T. Webb, Jr., and E. Steinberg and their associates at the University of Wisconsin Press, whose counsel about publication problems was of inestimable value. It includes the late W. E. Scott, who not only was principally responsible for the bibliography, but also brought to my attention hundreds of historical references to Wisconsin birds and helped greatly with the development chapter. It includes J. H. Zimmerman, who wrote the chapters on bird habitats and compiled the tables of habitat types, and who did much to broaden my understanding of birds and their related habitats. It includes R. A. Robbins, who assisted throughout the project by culling field notes from *The Passenger Pigeon*, by analyzing the BBS results and producing the data for range maps, and by drawing most of the maps.

As I visited museums and wildlife refuge headquarters in search of raw data, I invariably received wholehearted cooperation and assistance. Thanks are tendered to W. N. MacBriar, Jr., and N. Kraucunas of the Milwaukee Public Museum,

G. Stieg of the Racine County Historical Museum, F. A. Iwen of the University of Wisconsin Zoological Museum, Madison, W. D. Carter and J. R. Toll of the Horicon National Wildlife Refuge, G. A. Clawson of the Necedah National Wildlife Refuge, K. H. Krumm and W. E. Green of the Upper Mississippi River National Wildlife Refuge, and N. R. Stone and J. O. Evrard of the Crex Meadows State Wildlife Area.

For furnishing additional unpublished data, I thank R. K. Anderson, F. M. Baumgartner, M. H. Baumgartner, D. D. Berger, B. N. Brouchoud, M. F. Donald, K. Dueholm, A. C. Epple, T. C. Erdman, L. W. Erickson, C. A. Faanes, V. A. Heig, J. J. Hickey, M. B. Hickey, R. L. Hine, C. S. Jung, J. L. Kaspar, C. A. Kemper, K. I. Lange, S. W. Matteson, M. J. Mossman, M. E. Olson, L. R. Petersen, C. H. Richter, D. D. Tessen, R. P. Thiel, D. R. Thompson, P. V. Vanderschaegen, C. M. Weise, and H. C. Wilson.

Information on the recovery of banded birds was graciously given by R. R. Adams, K. E. Bartel, R. K. Bell, D. D. Berger, B. N. Brouchoud, J. T. Emlen, T. C. Erdman, W. H. Erickson, D. G. Follen, A. F. Gauerke, O. J. Gromme, R. Gysendorfer, F. Hamerstrom, R. A. Hasterlik, R. S. Huff, T. N. Ingram, C. A. Kemper, K. H. Kuhn, R. J. Lukes, J. F. Lund, W. N. MacBriar, H. A. Mathiak, M. T. Maxson, H. C. Mueller, E. W. Peartree, R. H. Pough, V. C. Rossman, D. F. Rupert, E. G. Schluter, D. A. Seal, C. R. Sindelar, N. F. Sloan, M. K. Stocking, and H. C. Wilson. Thanks are given to them, and to Brian Sharp of the U.S. Fish and Wildlife Service Bird Banding Laboratory.

For furnishing the photographs used in this volume, I wish to thank D. W. Anderson, J. L. Baughman, D. Bolduc, G. A. De Boer, M. E. Decker, T. C. Erdman, C. A. Faanes, F. N. Freese, J. F. Fuller, A. Gauger, L. E. Gregg, J. Hager, D. Hanbury, D. Haugen, J. H. Idzikowski, C. A. Kemper, L. Kranich, S. J. Lang, K. F. Legler, O. R. Lemke, F. Z. Lesher, H. G. Liebherr, H. L. Lindberg, M. L. Lound, R. J. Lukes, R. A. McCabe, M. T. Maxson, S. C. Meyer, E. B. Prins, W. H. Pugh, J. Rankl, E. E. Schumann, G. M. Scott, J. Smith, N. G. Tilghman, T. J. Underwood, R. L. Verch, C. Vig, the State Historical Society of Wisconsin, Department of Wildlife Ecology of the University of Wisconsin–Madison, Racine County Historical Museum, and Milwaukee Public Museum. Valuable assistance in evaluating photographs and documentation was given by G. W. Foster, J. J. Hickey, W. L. Hilsenhoff, and D. D. Tessen.

Particularly helpful were the efforts of those who reviewed portions of the manuscript, pointing out errors, and offering constructive criticism: D. D. Berger, T. C. Erdman, F. Hamerstrom, F. N. Hamerstrom, R. A. Hunt, J. R. March, L. R. Petersen, C. S. Robbins, C. R. Sindelar, H. C. Wilson, E. H. Zimmerman, and J. H. Zimmerman.

Finally there are the typists who manipulated magic fingers for untold hours: J. Chuba, E. A. Robbins, R. A. Robbins, S. T. Robbins, and G. M. Scott. All played important roles in producing this volume.

Introduction

Wisconsin Birdlife has been nearly 70 years in the making. It was first envisioned by Herbert Stoddard when he worked for the Milwaukee Public Museum near the end of World War I, but remained nothing more than a dream when Stoddard moved away from Wisconsin in 1921. It remained the dream of the Milwaukee museum personnel in the 1930s, but those were hard years—depression years—when the serious prospects of funding an ambitious research and publication project seemed out of the question.

To Owen J. Gromme, then curator of birds at the Milwaukee Public Museum, goes much of the credit for clothing with reality this skeletal dream of a few visionaries. Inspired by such monumental works as E. H. Forbush's *Birds of Massachusetts and Other New England States* (3 vols., Boston: Mass. Dep. Agric., 1925–1929), R. H. Eaton's *Birds of New York* (2d ed., 2 vols., Albany: N.Y. State Mus., Memoir 12, 1923), and T. S. Roberts' *Birds of Minnesota* (2d rev. ed., 2 vols., Minneapolis: Univ. of Minn. Press, 1937), Gromme developed a plan for a major volume for Wisconsin. It would not only describe and document every species of bird known to have visited this state, but also depict each species with his own original paintings. Staunch support in both enthusiasm and financial undergirding came from the then recently organized Friends of the Museum, Inc. The green light was given in 1939 by the museum board of directors. A magnificent, ambitious undertaking!

Gromme immediately plunged ahead with the paintings and assembling information. He contacted individuals, museums, colleges, and universities to obtain listings of state specimens. This required some detective work, for several nineteenth-century collections had been passed from one individual to others or to institutions. Eventually catalogues were obtained from the collections of P. R. Hoy (now housed at the Racine County Historical Museum), Thure and Ludwig Kumlien (mainly at the Milwaukee Public Museum), J. N. Clark (University of Wisconsin–Eau Claire), A. J. Schoenebeck (University of Wisconsin–Stevens

Point), C. H. Richter (University of Wisconsin–Green Bay), A. W. Schorger (University of Wisconsin–Madison), E. G. Wright (Neville Public Museum, Green Bay), W. E. Snyder (Dodge County Historical Society, Beaver Dam), and J. F. Stierle (Marshfield Public Library). These collections had been augmented by the contributions of numerous more recent specimen-takers. Unfortunately, an extensive collection at the Oshkosh Public Museum was destroyed by fire in 1916. Additional specimens were located out of state in Chicago, Minneapolis, and Washington, D.C.

Catalogues of egg collections were obtained. Three major egg collections are the well-known B. F. Goss assemblage (Milwaukee Public Museum), containing many sets from Waukesha and Dodge counties, the 11,000 sets of C. H. Richter (University of Wisconsin–Green Bay), and the varied collection of A. J. Schoenebeck (University of Wisconsin–Stevens Point). Richter's and Schoenebeck's collections were largely assembled in northeastern Wisconsin.

Gromme solicited personal field notes from dozens of observers. Notable among these contributors were F. S. Dayton (1916–1938, Winnebago and Waupaca counties), Francis Zirrer (1924–1940, Sawyer and Rusk counties), J. H. Evans (1925–1944, Winnebago County), George vos Burgh (1910–1935, Columbia County), Gilbert Raasch (1920–1940, scattered southern Wisconsin counties), and C. A. Kemper (1940–1958, Chippewa County). Gromme's own field notes, covering 1915–1960 and including many field trips to widely scattered parts of the state, provided valuable raw data. Nearly all of this material was previously unpublished.

The published literature was examined, starting with Wisconsin's one previous state bird book: Kumlien and Hollister's *The Birds of Wisconsin* (1903). From such periodicals as the *Auk, Wilson Bulletin, Oologist, Wisconsin Naturalist,* and *Transactions of the Wisconsin Academy of Sciences, Arts and Letters* came many brief references of unusual bird sightings, plus the extended commentaries of P. R. Hoy (1853b, 1885b), A. C. Barry (1854), F. L. Grundtvig (1895), A. J. Schoenebeck (1902), A. R. Cahn (1913), H. L. Stoddard (1917, 1922a), H. H. T. Jackson (1923, 1927, 1943), and A. W. Schorger (1929b, 1931a). Buss and Mattison's *A Half Century of Change in Bird Populations of the Lower Chippewa River, Wisconsin* (1955) combined the observations of J. N. Clark (1886–1902) with their own (1935–1955).

The organization of the Wisconsin Society for Ornithology and the inception of its publication *The Passenger Pigeon* (1939) opened up new possibilities for ornithological knowledge. Gromme and his assistants painstakingly copied all field notes from every issue and every article that had some bearing on the history and distribution of Wisconsin birds. All this was filed according to species—the files gradually growing from 1940 to 1960 while Gromme concentrated on the paintings.

By 1960 it became apparent that the paintings should be published separately. The result was Gromme's book *Birds of Wisconsin* (1963). In addition to his superb paintings, Gromme included simple range maps and brief statements of the status of each Wisconsin species. The pressure of other commitments then led him to turn over the writing of the present volume to other hands.

My involvement with this book began in 1969. A first step was the upgrading of my personal knowledge of Wisconsin birdlife from Superior to Kenosha, from Pembine to Potosi. Perusing my own field notes sufficed for part of this. Since 1939 I have lived 10 years in Dane County, 9 in Adams, 2 in Clark, 9 in Taylor, 10 in Chippewa, and 8 in St. Croix. In addition, I had preserved records from dozens of field excursions to other parts of the state. My knowledge of some areas, however, left much to be desired, so throughout the 1970s I took numerous trips to familiarize myself more thoroughly with some of the lesser-known regions.

A second step was the collection and examination of additional field observation material. Some material consisted of other observers' unpublished notes. Volumes of records were examined at the Horicon Marsh, Necedah, and Upper Mississippi River National Wildlife refuges, and at the Crex Meadows Wildlife Area. Much information—only part of it published—was received from the University of Wisconsin–Milwaukee Field Station at Cedarburg and the ornithological research stations at Little Suamico, Woodland Dunes, and Cedar Grove.

The field notebooks of A. W. Schorger (primarily Dane County, 1920–1958) contain much valuable data beyond those published in his "Birds of Dane County, Wisconsin" (1929, 1931). I also examined the collected notes of C. S. Jung (Milwaukee County, 1918–1960), the journals of S. P. Jones (Waukesha County, 1922–1956), the compiled records of the Kumlien Club (Dane County, 1940–1955), the highlights of M. E. Olson's observations (Pierce County, 1952–1958), R. A. Knuth's unpublished summary of Fond du Lac County birds (1956–1970), and C. A. Kemper's television tower kill data (Eau Claire County, 1957–1972).

Published sources, in addition to those identified by Gromme, include the various technical bulletins put out by the Wisconsin Department of Natural Resources and its predecessor Conservation Department, T. S. Roberts' *Logbook of Minnesota Field Observations* (1938, including records from western Wisconsin), E. W. Beals's "Notes on the Summer Birds of the Apostle Islands" (1958), R. F. Bernard's "Birds of Douglas County, Wisconsin" (1967), C. A. Kemper's "Birds of Chippewa, Eau Claire, and Neighboring Counties" (1973), C. A. Faanes and S. V. Goddard's "Birds of St. Croix and Pierce Counties" (1976), H. Young and R. F. Bernard's "Spring and Summer Birds of the Pigeon Lake Region" (1978), J. T. Harris and M. J. Jaeger's "Annotated List of Spring Birds Observed in the Apostle Islands, 1976 and 1977" (1978), *Brown County Birds* (Strehlow et al. 1978), C. A. Faanes's *Birds of the St. Croix River Valley: Minnesota and Wisconsin* (1981), P. V. Vanderschaegen's "Birds of Forest, Oneida and Vilas Counties, Wisconsin" (1981), M. J. Mossman and K. I. Lange's *Breeding Birds of the Baraboo Hills, Wisconsin* (1982), and S. A. Temple and J. T. Harris' *Birds of the Apostle Islands* (1985). Continuing where Gromme left off in 1960, I examined all field notes listed in *The Passenger Pigeon* as observed through May 1989 (Vol. 51, No. 4), and all Wisconsin observations published in *Audubon Field Notes* and *American Birds* as observed through May 1989 (Vol. 43, No. 3).

I obtained wintering information by analyzing the results from over 2,500 Christmas Bird Counts, taken between 1900 and 1989, published in *Bird-Lore, Audubon Field Notes, American Birds,* and *The Passenger Pigeon*. For summer information, I made widespread use of the 257 Summer Bird Counts made by the WSO between 1961 and 1965 and the 1,520 Breeding Bird Surveys conducted from 1966 through 1989 as Wisconsin's part of the North American survey conducted by the U.S. Fish and Wildlife Service. This information was augmented by examination of 5,000 nest record cards collected from Wisconsin observers, processed by University of Wisconsin–Stevens Point personnel, and forwarded to the North American Nest Record Card program at Cornell University. Breeding data (egg dates, clutch size, etc.) came from this source, from the information accompanying the museum egg collections, and from the field notes of many observers, primary among them being O. J. Gromme, S. P. Jones, C. H. Richter, and A. W. Schorger.

Undertaking to determine the whereabouts of Wisconsin birds when they are not within the confines of this state led me to consult the records of the Bird Banding Laboratory of the U.S. Fish and Wildlife Service. Over 4,000 out-of-state banding recovery cards were studied. Most of the banding information quoted in this book refers to recoveries made within 12 months of date of banding.

My third step in preparing this book was developing a format to present the material that had been gathered. As an artist selects a frame to provide the optimum setting for a painting, I felt the need to provide a frame to give background and perspective for my word-pictures of Wisconsin's birds. Actually two frames are presented in Part I of this book.

The first frame is the perspective of history. The first chapter, "The Development of Wisconsin Ornithology," begins with the pioneer efforts to determine what species were found in the state. As these efforts proceeded, there came an increasing realization that marked changes in the avifauna were occurring as a result of the expanding human population, expanding agriculture, timber harvest, dam construction, and wetland drainage. The chapter sketches human efforts to respond to these changes in bird populations, leading to the present-day emphasis on habitat preservation.

The second frame is ecological. In "The Landscape and the Birds" James Hall Zimmerman describes the underlying rocks, soils, and climate of the state, and discusses the vegetation that develops from the interaction of climate on soil. For most birds, the primary interest is the vegetation; but as Zimmerman points out, the vegetation depends on the soil, which in turn relies on the rock and water formations.

Part II of this book offers detailed information for every species known to Wisconsin. It deals with 394 species deemed to merit a place on the list of Wisconsin birds, plus an additional 13 species considered hypothetical, and 6 that may have escaped from captivity. In the preparation of this material a cutoff date of 31 May 1989 was used, except for the inclusion of the Anna's Hummingbird, observed between late August and 3 December 1990. Of the 394, 358 have been substantiated by specimens, 31 by identifiable photographs, 1 by recorded sound (Chuck-will's-widow), and 4 by written documentation. The assignment of a species to confirmed or hypothetical status was done by an ad hoc "records evaluation committee" (G. W. Foster, J. J. Hickey, W. L. Hilsenhoff, and D. D. Tessen), which I selected to help determine the status of the rarest Wisconsin species. This committee gave serious consideration to written documentation whenever neither specimen nor photograph was available. If there were two or more independent observations of a rarity, each supported by thorough and definitive written documentation, the record was granted full acceptance. If there was but one sighting with written details deemed definitive by the committee, the record was considered hypothetical. A shadow of doubt in a committee member's mind led to rejection of the record.

The extensive bibliography which this book contains was painstakingly prepared by Walter and Gertrude Scott. The Scotts spent many hours paging through early issues of state and national periodicals, procured lists of publications—everything from major books to minor paragraphs in newspapers and magazines—from scores of Wisconsin authors, and scoured the card catalogues of several libraries. From these the Scotts selected those titles that dealt in some way with the presence, distribution, migration, and biology of Wisconsin birds. The bibliography printed here is an abridged version of an even larger listing prepared by the Scotts. Copies of the unabridged version, listing over 4,700 titles, are filed in the libraries of the Milwaukee Public Museum, the University of Wisconsin–Stevens Point, and the University of Wisconsin–Madison. I have added a few recent entries, following the completion of the Scotts' work in 1981.

Abbreviations and Nomenclature

In addition to the customary abbreviations for geographical subdivisions (E = East, N = North, W = West, S = South, C = Central), the following abbreviations are frequently used:

AB:	*American Birds*
AFN:	*Audubon Field Notes*
AOU:	American Ornithologists' Union
BBS:	Breeding Bird Survey
CBC:	Christmas Bird Count
DNR:	Department of Natural Resources (Wisconsin)
FWS:	Fish and Wildlife Service (United States)
MPM:	Milwaukee Public Museum
NWR:	National Wildlife Refuge
WCD:	Wisconsin Conservation Department
WSO:	Wisconsin Society for Ornithology

The English and scientific names of birds conform to the nomenclature used in the American Ornithologists' Union *Check-list of North American Birds*, sixth edition (1983), and in supplements 35 (1985), 36 (1987), and 37 (1989).

Part I. The Background

The Development of Wisconsin Ornithology

Wisconsin's first ornithologists were the American Indians. When Europeans first arrived in Wisconsin in the seventeenth century, the Fox, Kickapoo, Menominee, Ojibwa, Ottawa, Potawatomi, Sauk, Santee Sioux, and Winnebago Indian bands inhabited the lands between the Mississippi River and Lakes Michigan and Superior, and birds played an important part in their culture. These people had to be astute observers of bird behavior and migration to harvest game birds for food. Traditional head-dresses required feathers. Ceremonial dances were sometimes patterned after the courtship dances of birds such as the Sharp-tailed Grouse.

Hundreds of effigy mounds, constructed long before the arrival of white settlers (primarily from about A.D. 700 or 800 to A.D. 1100 or 1200), suggest that American Indians regarded many birds with wonder and respect. Mounds have been discovered with shapes resembling hawks, ducks, and geese, presumably testifying to the presence of these birds as part of the state's avifauna of past centuries.

Recording Wisconsin's Birds

Pioneer Bird Lists
With the start of exploration by the French and English in the seventeenth and eighteenth centuries, observers began a long process of determining which species were present. While traveling up the Mississippi River in the 1660s, Nicolas Perrot (1911) mentioned in his journal the presence of turkeys, "pheasants," quails, pigeons, curlews, swans, "bustards," wild geese, and ducks. He remarked, "Pelicans are very common, but they have an oily flavor, whether alive or dead, which is so disagreeable that it is impossible to eat them."

3

A century later Jonathan Carver started at what is now Green Bay, proceeded up the Fox River past Lake Winnebago to the "Carrying Place" (Portage), down the "Ouisconsin River" to Prairie du Chien, and up the Mississippi to what is now Minnesota. In his journal (Carver 1779) he mentioned large flocks of ducks and geese on Lake Winnebago. On and near Lake Pepin he found "great numbers of fowl . . . such as storks, swans, geese, brants and ducks; and in the groves are found great plenty of turkeys and partridges." Other birds mentioned by Carver included what we now call the Common Loon, Bald Eagle, Osprey, Common Nighthawk, Ruby-throated Hummingbird, Northern Flicker, Blue Jay, and Red-winged Blackbird. The Whip-poor-will held special meaning for the Indians Carver visited. The song of the first birds returning in the spring was the signal that the weather was now warm enough to plant corn.

Further bird lists were contributed by Henry Schoolcraft between 1820 and 1832. As agent for the northwestern Indians during most of that interval, stationed near Sault Ste Marie, Schoolcraft made several expeditions through parts of "Michigan Territory" that later became part of Wisconsin. On one trip along the Mississippi River near Prairie du Chien, he recorded the presence of the White Pelican, Turkey Vulture, Wild Turkey, Passenger Pigeon, Common Raven, and Blue Jay. Between Prairie du Chien and Portage he noted the American Woodcock, Belted Kingfisher, Wood Duck, Canada Goose, and Song Sparrow. Wild rice beds along the Fox River held enormous numbers of ducks and Red-winged Blackbirds. Large numbers of Passenger Pigeons were found washed ashore near the mouth of the Manitowoc River, apparently victims of inclement weather. On a trip down the Namekagon River, he listed the American Robin, Gray Catbird, Red-headed Woodpecker, and "yellow-hammer." On an expedition across the southern prairies between Portage and Galena, Illinois, he often encountered Prairie-Chicken flocks. Schoolcraft referred to "brant," "snipe," "plover," and "grouse" but did not leave sufficient clues to indicate exactly which species were meant.

Once Wisconsin achieved statehood in 1848, a more thorough inventory of all forms of wildlife was needed. In 1851 "A Systematic Catalogue of the Animals of Wisconsin" (1852) was prepared for the University of Wisconsin by I. A. Lapham. His list of mammals, birds, reptiles, fish, and mollusks was subsequently published as an appendix to the Journal of the Wisconsin Senate the following year. Lapham contributed little to the state bird list personally, but relied heavily on an 1848 list of Milwaukee birds by S. R. Sercomb, augmented by the Racine observations of P. R. Hoy.

Sercomb was a taxidermist, whose list of 119 species consisted largely of birds he collected between 1837 and 1848. In 1853 he moved to Madison, where he had charge of the museum begun by the Wisconsin Natural History Association.

Hoy combined his ornithological hobby with his work as a physician from the time of his arrival at Racine in 1846 until near the time of his death in 1892. Not content with simply making additions to Lapham's list, Hoy published his own annotated list in 1853. "Notes on the Ornithology of Wisconsin" listed 283 "species," several of which are now recognized as subspecies, color phases, or variant plumages. Most were birds he had observed (many of which he collected) within 15 miles of Racine. Hoy recognized that he was at an exceptionally fine vantage point. "This city," he wrote, "is situated on the western shore of Lake Michigan, at the extreme southern point of the heavy timbered district where the great prairies approach near the lake from the west, . . . a grand point, a

P. R. Hoy, 1816–1892 (Racine County Historical Museum photo)

kind of rendezvous, that birds make during their migrations." In winter he recorded such northern species as the Golden Eagle, Northern Hawk Owl, Great Gray Owl, Boreal Chickadee, "pine bull finch" (Pine Grosbeak), Evening Grosbeak, White-winged Crossbill, Gray Jay, and Black-backed and Three-toed Woodpeckers. In summer there were such southerners as the Swallow-tailed Kite, Yellow-breasted Chat, Northern Mockingbird, Carolina Wren, and Cerulean and Worm-eating Warblers.

Lapham was apparently unaware of the work of another promising young naturalist who lived near Lake Koshkonong. Thure Kumlien arrived from Sweden in 1843, settled on a farm near Busseyville in southwestern Jefferson County, and for the next 45 years supplemented the meager income from his farm by

Thure Kumlien, 1819–1888 (State Historical Society of Wisconsin photo; WHi(X3)41293)

selling bird eggs and specimens that he collected. Although Kumlien lived but 60 miles west of Racine, he found the habitat quite different—more dominated by the prairies and the rich Rock River valley. Upland Sandpipers and Long-billed Curlews bred in great abundance. Golden-Plovers staged phenomenal migrations. Waterfowl were plentiful. Kumlien published no lists. His records of collected specimens often mentioned the month but not the exact date of collection. Little is known of his sight observations. But he made enormous contributions to knowledge of the birds of Wisconsin, which eventually appeared in the writings of his son.

In 1859 Lapham attempted to persuade the legislature to authorize a full-fledged inventory of the state's natural resources. A statewide survey done while vast portions of the state were still relatively undisturbed would have been of inestimable value. Unfortunately, the legislation did not pass.

Without an organized statewide survey, answers to the question, What birds come to Wisconsin? have been forthcoming only in occasional fits and starts. A. C. Barry, clergyman and educator, contemporary and companion of Hoy, published his own list of Racine-area birds in 1854. A list of Sauk County birds, authored by W. H. Canfield, appeared in the *Baraboo Republic* in 1866. In 1885 S. W. Willard published a list of birds he found in Brown and Outagamie counties. Another Outagamie County list appeared 10 years later, when F. L. Grundt-vig documented his 1881–1883 observations in the Shiocton area. In Dunn

Ludwig Kumlien, 1853–1902 (State Historical Society of Wisconsin photo; WHi(X3)45495)

County J. N. Clark did extensive fieldwork and collecting, mainly between 1886 and 1902. Although his plans for publication never materialized, his collection is now housed at the University of Wisconsin–Eau Claire. The year 1902 also saw the publication of A. J. Schoenebeck's *Birds of Oconto County* and W. E. Snyder's "Brief Notes on Some of the Rarer Birds of Dodge County."

These were regional lists. Near the turn of the century Ludwig Kumlien and Ned Hollister began to piece together the information from these sources, along with their personal records. The result was the landmark publication of *Birds of Wisconsin* in 1903. Ludwig grew up under the tutelage of his father, Thure. At the age of 16 he prepared a list of migrating birds, and he spent nearly all of his 49 years observing, collecting, teaching, writing, and drawing the birds of southeastern Wisconsin. Hollister, 23 years Kumlien's junior, began keeping records at the age of 12 and accumulated 15 years of observation—mainly in the Delavan area—before moving to Washington, D.C., for lifetime work with the U.S. Biological Survey, the U.S. National Museum, and the National Zoological Park. Drawn together were the fruits of 45 years of collecting and observation by Thure Kumlien, 35 by Ludwig Kumlien, and 15 by Hollister. In the preface the authors wrote:

> In this time work has been done, more or less thorough, over a large portion of the state. While the greater part by far of the time has been spent in the southeastern counties of Jefferson, Rock, Dane, Milwaukee, Waukesha and Walworth, trips have been made, allowing of extended observations and collections, along the entire length of the shores of Lake Michigan and Lake Superior, the Michigan border, and to different points along the Mississippi River, as well as in a goodly number of the central counties.

The appraisal of the state's avifauna did not stop with the publication of *Birds of Wisconsin*. Kumlien and Hollister acknowledged: "Notwithstanding the vast amount of work which has been done in the state, the long period of years represented, and the pleasing results obtained, there are still many points on which the information obtainable is entirely inadequate. . . . Many sections, in fact, whole counties and groups of counties have been but little worked."

Regional Bird Lists

Some of the gaps have been filled in as other ornithologists worked their local areas. Regional lists were published for Waukesha County in 1913 (A. R. Cahn), Green Lake County in 1915 (J. L. Lowe), Dane County in 1929 and 1931 (A. W. Schorger), the lower Chippewa River region in 1955 (I. O. Buss and H. M. Mattison), Douglas County in 1967 (R. F. Bernard), Fond du Lac County in 1970 (R. A. Knuth), Chippewa and Eau Claire counties in 1973 (C. A. Kemper), Pierce and St. Croix counties in 1976 (C. A. Faanes and S. V. Goddard), Brown County in 1978 (E. W. Strehlow et al.), the St. Croix River valley in 1981 (C. A. Faanes), and the Apostle Islands in Ashland County in 1985 (S. A. Temple and J. T. Harris). In a more limited sense, lists of species have been issued for the Necedah, Horicon, and Upper Mississippi River National Wildlife refuges, and the Chequamegon National Forest (available at the various headquarters). Spring and summer birds of the Pigeon Lake region in Bayfield County were summarized by Young and Bernard (1978).

Partial glimpses of the less-studied areas have been obtained by museum-sponsored expeditions. The Milwaukee Public Museum, for instance, sent H. L. Ward on visits to Waukesha, Brown, Door, Grant, and Ashland counties in the

1850-1900

1 F. H. King
2 J. N. Clark
3 A. J. Schoenebeck
4 S. W. Willard
5 F. L. Grundtvig
6 W. H. Canfield
7 W. E. Snyder
8 W. W. Cooke
9 T. L. Kumlien
10 A. L. Kumlien
11 N. Hollister
12 B. F. Goss
13 S. R. Sercomb
14 H. Nehrling
15 P. R. Hoy
16 A. C. Barry

1900-1940

17 H. H. T. Jackson
18 K. H. Kahmann
19 F. Zirrer
20 I. O. Buss
21 J. W. Stierle
22 W. B. Grange
23 F. N. and F. Hamerstrom
24 F. S. Dayton
25 C. H. Richter
26 E. G. Wright
27 H. C. Wilson
28 R. M. Strong
29 J. L. Lowe

30 A. Leopold
31 H. L. Stoddard
32 A. W. Schorger
33 W. Taylor
34 J. S. Main
35 A. S. Hawkins
36 A. R. Cahn
37 S. P. Jones
38 O. J. Gromme
39 C. Jung
40 I. N. Mitchell
41 H. L. Ward

Locations of major Wisconsin ornithologists, 1850–1940

first decade of the twentieth century. Soon after World War I, this museum sponsored investigations by H. L. Stoddard to Columbia, Dodge, Lafayette, Sheboygan, Kenosha, Buffalo, and Pierce counties. While these expeditions were designed partly to obtain specimens and photographs for museum exhibits, they also produced general notes that added significant knowledge about the avifauna in these areas. A particularly extensive expedition, from May to September of 1919, sent H. H. T. Jackson, H. H. Sheldon, and A. J. Poole through much of northwestern Wisconsin under the auspices of the U.S. Biological Survey, the Wisconsin Geological and Natural History Survey, and the University of Wisconsin. Again, it was the Milwaukee museum that underwrote trips by O. J. Gromme, I. J. Perkins, J. L. Diedrich, and others to Fond du Lac, Oconto, Vilas, Price, Douglas, and Burnett counties between World Wars I and II. The American Museum of Natural History helped underwrite Edward Beals's survey of summer birds on the Apostle Islands in 1958.

Further information about the avifauna in poorly canvased regions was furnished by ornithologists on side trips of their own. H. H. T. Jackson published extensive notes on summer birds in Vilas (1923) and Door (1927) counties. A. R. Cahn listed summer birds in Vilas County in 1927. A. W. Schorger took extensive notes on the avifauna in Grant (1925), Bayfield (1925), Vilas (1945), and Sawyer (1947) counties.

When the Wisconsin Society for Ornithology was organized in 1939, a network of observers was developed, with monthly (quarterly since 1943) field reports summarized in *The Passenger Pigeon*. The network was small at first, limited largely to bird-watchers in the "Madison–Racine–Green Bay triangle." By 1946 the network had enlarged significantly both in size and scope, and records were transferred to permanent file cards. Most areas of the state are now included, and the records are stored permanently in computer files at the University of Wisconsin–Stevens Point.

As O. J. Gromme worked on his *Birds of Wisconsin* in the 1940s and 1950s, he collected bird observation data from over 30 volunteers. Many of these records came from the 1920–1940 era and had not been previously published anywhere. Of particular value were the records of F. S. Dayton in Winnebago, Outagamie, and Waupaca counties, those of F. Zirrer in Rusk and Sawyer counties, those of C. H. Richter in Oconto County, and the nest observations of J. F. Stierle in Wood County. These records are stored at the Milwaukee Public Museum.

Three relatively recent efforts have addressed the question, Which species come to Wisconsin? First came a pocket-sized *Wisconsin Birds—A Preliminary Checklist with Migration Charts* prepared for the Wisconsin Society for Ornithology by N. R. Barger, E. E. Bussewitz, E. L. Loyster, S. D. Robbins, and W. E. Scott in 1942. This checklist was revised in 1950 by the same authors, in 1960 and 1975 by Barger, R. H. Lound, and Robbins, and in 1988 by Barger, Robbins, and S. A. Temple. Second was the republication in 1951 of Kumlien and Hollister's *Birds of Wisconsin*, together with an updating commentary by A. W. Schorger. Third was the completion of Gromme's *Birds of Wisconsin* in 1963.

Nesting Data

Which species nest in Wisconsin? Several of the nineteenth-century ornithologists were egg collectors. Most notable was B. F. Goss of Pewaukee, who collected extensively in southeastern Wisconsin between 1876 and 1892. While he traveled widely on oological expeditions to southern United States and eastern

Canada, the bulk of his collecting was done near Pewaukee and Horicon. When Goss's collection was donated to the Milwaukee Public Museum in 1885, it was one of the largest accumulations in North America, numbering 2,305 eggs of 471 species.

An annotated list of species known to breed in Wisconsin was begun in 1890 by C. F. Carr and continued the following year by A. L. (Ludwig) Kumlien. Unfortunately, this undertaking was never completed. Kumlien's information about native breeding species appeared in his *Birds of Wisconsin* 12 years later.

Two outstanding egg collections came from the Oconto area. A. J. Schoenbeck collected eggs mainly in Oconto and Shawano counties between 1885 and 1910. By trading extensively with other oologists, he developed one of the more extensive North American collections. It was donated first to the St. Joseph's Academy Museum in Stevens Point and subsequently to the University of Wisconsin–Stevens Point. C. H. Richter collected extensively in northeastern Wisconsin from 1912 to 1971, purchased and traded considerably, then donated over 10,000 egg sets to the University of Wisconsin–Green Bay.

Oology no longer flourishes as a branch of ornithological science, as it did in the nineteenth century, and the taking of eggs is now solely the realm of the research scientist under federal permit. But nest observations continue. Since 1965 Wisconsin observers have cooperated in the North American Nest Record Card Program under the auspices of the Cornell University Laboratory of Ornithology. Data on over 5,000 nests of 160 species are on file at the University of Wisconsin–Stevens Point, as well as at Ithaca, New York.

Migration Data

One of the first researchers to study migration dates was W. W. Cooke. Beginning in 1882 from his home in Jefferson, Cooke attempted to develop a line of observers who would record arrival and departure dates of birds at various points along the Mississippi River valley. From early January to late May 1883 Cooke hiked near his home for 2 hours a day 5 days a week, documenting weather conditions and birds observed. One January morning was registered at −32°F, and his journal indicated that on some mornings the birds were "hardly thawed out" by the time the daily hike ended. The 1883 "network" consisted of observation points only in Jefferson, Wisconsin, and St. Louis, Missouri. It enlarged significantly in the next 2 years, with several observers in Illinois, Iowa, and Minnesota joining in.

Another cooperative enterprise involved a statewide network recruited by I. N. Mitchell between 1907 and 1913. The number of observers reporting each year varied from 30 to 90, stretching from Superior, Ashland, and Tomahawk in the north to South Wayne, Albany, and Lake Geneva in the south. Contributed data were limited to the first spring arrival date for each species, and were published annually in the *Wisconsin Arbor and Bird Day Annual*. The results were of limited value, partly because reports were apparently based on very limited fieldwork, and partly because some rather obvious instances of misidentifications crept in, casting doubt on many other records. But this effort proved that volunteer observers could yield important information about the timing of migration.

By far, most of our information on the timing of migration has come through the network of observers recruited by the Wisconsin Society for Ornithology since 1939. From 50 to 100 participants report quarterly, listing arrival and departure dates, detailed descriptions of rarities, comments on weather, and sometimes dates and size of peak abundance. When I published a list of earliest arrival and latest departure dates for each Wisconsin species (1970), I found that 618 of the 714 listed dates were noted since 1939. Surely, many more exceptional migration dates occurred in the pre-1939 era, but most went unrecorded or unpublished. Much of the migration information amassed by the WSO has been passed on to *American Birds* (formerly *Audubon Field Notes*) for use in continental seasonal summaries. The information has been used for various research projects and provided the basis for the month-by-month graphs in *Wisconsin Birds—A Checklist with Migration Graphs* (Barger, Lound, and Robbins 1975). Between 1982 and 1989, WSO members carried out the Checklist Project under the direction of S. A. Temple, submitting weekly field note reports that help us understand the timing and population levels of bird migration.

Avifaunal Changes

As Wisconsin evolved from a sparsely populated wilderness of forest, savanna, and prairie to a land of 4.7 million people and 1.8 million cows, significant changes in bird populations were inevitable. One major change involved the development of agriculture. The conversion of unbroken sod to plowed land proceeded rapidly throughout most of southern and eastern Wisconsin and parts of the western region. Prairie fires were common in the 1840s and 1850s, and it was not uncommon for pioneer farmers to protect against these fires the acres they intended to plow the following summer. The dry grass of the unburned acres provided especially favored nesting habitat in May for the hordes of Upland Sandpipers, Long-billed Curlews, and other grassland species. But the pioneers considered the period from late May through July the best time for "firing" and plowing the marked fields, with disastrous results for these birds. As a small lad in the early 1850s, H. L. Skavlem (1912b) witnessed some of this land-clearing near Lake Koshkonong, and was so deeply impressed by the tragedy of the destruction of bird nests that he was able to reminisce 60 years later:

But what of our bird friends, the old habitants of the land, Bobwhite and his interesting family, the Prairie Snipe and their big eggs or their curious odd-looking long-billed babies, the Brown Thrashers, Catbird, Bobolink and Lark? All are gone. A black, scorched and desolate scar profusely sprinkled with wrecks of nests, scorched eggs and charred bodies of little baby birds, disfigure the face of Mother Earth. . . . It was not until the next day that the little boy realized the loss of his flowery playground and the many bird nests that he had spotted with boyish ingenuity. . . . here comes the big snipe, with silent but graceful motion she sails a circle around the distracted child, then utters her harsh call, indicating both anger and distress. Soon her fellow sufferers respond from all points of the compass, and the air is full of the big long-billed birds angrily screaming and scolding, now and then making threatening dives at the thoroughly scared and crying lad.

Where there were 400,000 acres of cropland in 1830, there were nearly 3 million by 1850 and over 15 million by 1880. Brush was cleared from much of the southern and central savanna land by 1880, but in many instances patches were left to develop into farm woodlots. Prairie fires were largely eliminated.

Developing agriculture has continued to have a significant impact on birdlife in the twentieth century. More land has been cleared for crops in central areas and in some northern ones. The development of fast-maturing seed encouraged

Franklin Hiram King, 1848–1911 (State Historical Society of Wisconsin photo; WHi(X3)5609)

agricultural development in parts of northern Wisconsin where short growing seasons were previously considered a deterrent. Mechanization has led to "clean farming" and the removal of brush and hedgerows that once provided important cover for wildlife. New techniques developed since 1950 have led to conversion of swamp forest and sedge meadow into muck farms.

A second major environmental change has come about through the extensive harvest of timber. Maps based on original surveys in the 1850s indicate that forests blanketed nearly all lands north of a line from Hudson to Manitowoc. South of this line sizable forested tracts existed—especially in the west and east—with smaller acreages scattered through the prairie and savanna regions. The state's first sawmill was erected near De Pere in 1809. For the next 55 years the business of harvesting virgin timber gathered momentum with few controls and few protests. In 1867 the legislature appointed I. A. Lapham, J. G. Knapp, and H. Krocker to a forestry commission. Their published report, "The Disastrous Effects of the

Destruction of Forest Trees Now Going On So Rapidly in the State of Wisconsin"
(in Scott 1967), warned of dangers of ensuing erosion and potential flooding, and
recommended stricter control of lumber harvesting. But the report went un-
heeded. Not until 1900 did the harvest decline markedly. By then, precious little
virgin woodland remained.

Many portions of the original northern forest, as well as extensive acreages in
the central region, have become reforested in the past 75 years, partly by natural
reseeding, partly by deliberate commercial replanting. The giant red and white
pines have been replaced by more modest-sized maples and by extensive spreads
of aspen and jack pine that are selectively cut for pulpwood. The forests that
once proved attractive to Spruce Grouse are now better adapted to Ruffed Grouse.
No one knows how many Blackburnian and Black-throated Green Warblers once
inhabited the virgin timber; but while they may have decreased significantly, the
Chestnut-sided Warbler and Red-eyed Vireo have found the emergent cutover
forests to their liking.

A third significant environmental development was the alteration of wetlands.
At first this meant chiefly the drainage of marshes and swamps, and it went
hand in hand with the clearing of land for agriculture. Legislation in the 1850s
not only encouraged drainage but even required landowners to "show cause" if
they did not want ditches dug across their property. In a few instances, such as
at Horicon in the east and Crex Meadows in the west, the decision to drain was
subsequently reversed, with land eventually reverting to moist conditions. But
in most regions drainage has proceeded intermittently through much of the twentieth century. Even today, muck farmers are looking longingly at portions of the
sparsely populated wet areas of Jackson, Juneau, Wood, and Adams counties.

Even as farmers were draining the marshes and swamps, industrial entrepre-
neurs began damming Wisconsin's streams, deepening channels here, creating
lakes there. Dams were erected on the Wisconsin, Wolf, Chippewa, and Red
Cedar rivers by timber harvesters to help transport logs to the sawmills. Paper
mills and other industries sprang up, especially along the Fox and Wisconsin
rivers. Between 1935 and 1939 a series of locks and dams were erected along the
Mississippi River both to control spring floods and to facilitate boat traffic north
to St. Paul, Minnesota, creating extensive "pools." On the Wisconsin River,
Castle Rock and Petenwell flowages, two of the state's three largest inland water
surfaces, were created in 1950 by dams erected for power generation.

The landscape of Wisconsin has been altered further by the sheer expansion of
our human population. Land once the exclusive domain of wildlife has been
claimed in ever-increasing quantities by people. As the number of Wisconsin
citizens grew from 300,000 in 1850, 2 million in 1900, 3.4 million in 1950, to 4.7
million in 1980, huge acreages were appropriated for residents, industry, and
transportation. First to be severely affected was the Lake Michigan shore around
Kenosha, Racine, and Milwaukee. Hoy was beginning to detect the impact of
human expansion on birds at Racine in 1885 (Hoy 1885b), and Milwaukee Public
Museum personnel noted significant changes in the Milwaukee region from 1900
on. The process has continued throughout the twentieth century, engulfing
even more of the Lake Michigan region, and spreading to other urban centers:
Madison, Green Bay, the Lake Winnebago region, and La Crosse. Around the
numerous smaller cities scattered throughout the state, human demands for
land have forced at least minor adjustments by uprooted birds. Even in the relatively sparsely populated north, lakes that once were undisturbed now have

motorboats on them; and woods that were quietly being regenerated after the demise of the logging industry now experience the visits of snowmobiles in winter and trail-bikes in summer. Many bird species have adjusted to such human disturbances. Some not only adjust but profit from human expansion. Others cannot adjust, and are decreasing.

The gun must also be mentioned as an environmental factor. Following the Civil War, professional market hunters were drawn to Wisconsin by the nesting hordes of Passenger Pigeons. Using recently installed railroad lines, they could travel easily to the most favorable spots and ship to eastern markets the products of their "harvest." How many hundreds of thousands (millions?) of pigeons left Wisconsin in crates and barrels will never be known.

When the decline in pigeons set in after 1871, market hunters turned to shorebirds. Typical is the 1890 record of 40 barrels of shorebirds reaching Boston merchants from the West "crammed with ten thousand Golden Plovers and four thousand Eskimo Curlews, the interstices being stuffed with the bodies of Upland Plovers. The merchants had a standard formula: 25 dozen Eskimo Curlew or 60 dozen Golden Plover to the barrel." (Hall 1960, p. 62). How many of these came from Wisconsin, and how many barrels from Wisconsin made their way to other merchants before and after that date, will forever be a matter of guesswork. But in the 1870–1890 era Wisconsin shorebird populations plummeted.

Waterfowl numbers dropped seriously at the same time, partly because of the organized slaughter by market hunters, and partly because of the excessive eagerness of the members of private hunting clubs at Lake Koshkonong and Horicon. Both areas were widely known as duck concentration points, attracting hunters from several states. Daily bags of 80 were not uncommon. Frautschi (1945) described how some of the most zealous hunters pursued their sport:

The original Koshkonong flatboat was built nearly in the shape of a pumpkin seed about sixteen feet long and six feet wide. The shooter lay in a long pit projecting below the bottom of the boat and under the water line. The rest of the craft was all wings tapering gradually from the cockpit to the outer circumference. When towed to location, the waters lapped over the flat edges, and the hunter, concealed in his central nest, was hardly discernible above the surface. With decoys placed on the boat and just beyond its periphery, the set-up was ideal for slaughtering ducks.

Club members eventually realized that the waterfowl population could not stand this pressure indefinitely, and helped curtail the excesses. But in the meantime waterfowl numbers dwindled seriously. Strict limits on hunting have been a part of the Wisconsin scene since 1910.

By 1880 the traffic in bird feathers for women's hats had also reached serious proportions. There is no evidence that alarming numbers of birds were killed in Wisconsin to supply feathers for the millinery trade. But the showy display of hats decorated with shafts from Barn Swallows, American Robins, Mourning Doves, and other birds occurring in Wisconsin indicated that there was some slaughter. Much more serious was the collection of egret plumes in the southern states, which severely affected the number of birds migrating to Wisconsin. "White herons" were so severely threatened in the early years of the twentieth century that Wisconsin experienced an almost complete dearth of these species between 1900 and 1930.

A new danger to birds emerged at the conclusion of World War II in the form of powerful new pesticides: broad-spectrum, persistent chemicals, such as the chlorinated hydrocarbons. On the one hand, these chemicals effectively controlled insects that were endangering forests and residential shade trees, interfering with agricultural crop production, and spreading some human disease organisms. On the other hand, these pesticides were directly lethal to birds in some instances and interfered seriously with reproduction in many others. Their long-term effect on changes in the ecological balance of nature is still not fully understood.

Organophosphates, which interfere with water quality and emergent vegetation, entered the environment through newly developed laundry detergents. Storm runoff from disturbed urban and rural land has caused siltation, turbidity, and eutrofication of waters and wetlands. There are suspicions that these conditions, in turn, have reduced the population of frogs, fish, and other bird foods. Contamination of water wells is showing up in areas where aldecarb is widely used by commercial potato growers. All these issues of water quality are being debated in the courts and the legislature. The full effects on water and marsh birds are not yet clear. Still less is known about the ultimate effect of nuclear energy plants operating in Vernon, Manitowoc, and Kewaunee counties, and the underground electric field that has been installed experimentally in Ashland County (Project ELF).

Appraisals of Avian Population Changes

One of the first ornithologists to comment on changes in Wisconsin's avifauna was P. R. Hoy. In his "Man's Influence on the Avifauna of Southeastern Wisconsin" (1885), he reflected on his observations near Racine over a 39-year interval. Wild Turkeys disappeared entirely in the 1840s, followed in the 1850s by the Swallow-tailed Kite and the Sharp-tailed Grouse. Ruffed Grouse, Prairie-Chickens, Northern Bobwhites, Passenger Pigeons, and Sandhill Cranes were greatly diminished. Before 1860 such northern species as the Northern Hawk-Owl, Great Gray Owl, Common Raven, and Evening Grosbeak were frequently encountered in winter; not so in more recent years. In Hoy's earlier years he found such southern species as the Turkey Vulture, Carolina Wren, Northern Mockingbird, Yellow-breasted Chat, and Northern Cardinal; few if any were recorded after 1855. "[It has been] twenty or thirty years since the cheerful chattering song of the Short-billed Marsh Wren was heard in every low prairie covered with fine carex. . . . I have seen or heard scarcely a bird of this kind for fifteen or twenty years. Their song has been silenced by the click of the mower. . . . They have gone, I hope, somewhere carex abounds and mowers do not" (Hoy 1885b). But the wren had been replaced by increasing numbers of Vesper and Field Sparrows. The Common Raven was replaced by the American Crow. Although other warblers had declined, Yellow Warblers were on the gain. American Woodcocks were increasing.

Kumlien and Hollister (1903) included many comments about changes in bird populations, based not only on Ludwig Kumlien's 35 years' experience, but also on the records of his father, Thure, going back an additional 25 years. They marked the virtual extirpation of the Trumpeter Swan, Whooping Crane, Long-billed Curlew, and Passenger Pigeon in the 1880s and 1890s. Drastic declines were noted for several ducks (the Gadwall, American Wigeon, Blue-winged

Teal, Wood Duck, Redhead, Bufflehead, and Ruddy Duck), the White Pelican, Lesser Golden-Plover, several sandpipers (especially dowitchers, Lesser Yellow-legs, and Upland and Pectoral Sandpipers), and Snow and White-fronted Geese. The loss of heavy timber reduced the ranges for the Great Horned Owl and Pileated Woodpecker. The loss of unbroken prairie sod meant fewer Eastern Meadowlarks and Lark Sparrows.

To some extent, losses in some species were balanced by gains in others. Western Meadowlarks increased as their eastern relatives receded. The Prairie-Chicken gradually replaced the Sharp-tailed Grouse in southern Wisconsin. The spread of the House Sparrow was blamed for a decline in the Purple Martin. Others that showed considerable increases include the Chimney Swift, Cliff Swallow, Brown-headed Cowbird, Yellow-headed Blackbird, King Rail, and Black-crowned Night-Heron.

In 1919 Ned Hollister revisited his old Delavan stamping grounds, and was impressed with further changes. Noticeably more numerous were the Yellow-billed Cuckoo and Red-headed Woodpecker. The Forster's Tern had virtually disappeared. The Barn Swallow and Brown Thrasher seemed less numerous.

Twenty miles north of the Kumliens' Lake Koshkonong, A. S. Hawkins made a limited then-and-now study of the Faville Grove area near Lake Mills between 1936 and 1938. His report (1940) summarized the major changes in game species between 1838 and 1938, as the region evolved from woodland and prairie to cultivated cropland, pinpointing the years of disappearance for the Passenger Pigeon, Prairie-Chicken, and Ruffed Grouse, and for the appearance of the Ring-necked Pheasant, Gray Partridge, European Starling, House Sparrow, Dickcissel, Northern Cardinal, and Red-bellied Woodpecker.

Between 1948 and 1951, A. W. Schorger prepared some supplementary notes to accompany the 1951 reprinting of Kumlien and Hollister's *Birds of Wisconsin*. Schorger commented on the complete extinction of the Passenger Pigeon, serious declines for the Hudsonian Godwit and Prairie-Chicken, and a growing trend in the Yellow-bellied Sapsucker, Nashville Warbler, and American Redstart to restrict breeding range to the northern two-thirds of the state. He mentioned the introduction of the Gray Partridge, Ring-necked Pheasant, and European Starling, and the spread of the Northern Cardinal, Blue-winged Warbler, Tufted Titmouse, Western Meadowlark, and Brewer's Blackbird. He pointed to the initial appearances of the Yellow-crowned Night-Heron, Acadian Flycatcher, Bewick's Wren, and Bell's Vireo—birds that have subsequently become nearly annual breeders.

Unfortunately, no such careful contrasts are possible for the central and northern regions spanning the years of heavy lumbering. No records have been found that give an adequate picture of the avian population before the virgin forests were cut. J. N. Clark was active in southern Dunn County between 1884 and 1902, but he lived near the end of the major timber-cutting era. He concentrated more on the prairie region than on the forested portion that terminated just to the north of his Meridean study areas, and confined his records largely to his collection efforts.

Nevertheless, when Buss and Mattison (1955) compared their records of the 1930s and 1940s with those of Clark a half century earlier, they pinpointed several significant changes. The disappearance of virgin forests was correlated with decreases in Northern Goshawks, Whip-poor-wills, Red-breasted Nuthatches, and Pileated, Black-backed, and Three-toed Woodpeckers. Tied in with the in-

A. W. Schorger, 1884–1972 (courtesy of the Department of Wildlife Ecology, University of Wisconsin–Madison)

crease in cropland were noticeable gains in Eastern and Western Meadowlarks, Brown-headed Cowbirds, Brewer's Blackbirds, and Vesper and Clay-colored Sparrows. Responding favorably to the spreading human population were such residential dwellers as Purple Martins, House Wrens, and Northern Orioles. Buss and Mattison called attention to such southern species as the Red-bellied Woodpecker, Red-shouldered Hawk, Blue-gray Gnatcatcher, Blue-winged Warbler, and Northern Cardinal—scarce or absent in Clark's day, now moving northward.

The most recent past-present comparison is a brief 1939–1964 summary I prepared for the Wisconsin Society for Ornithology's silver anniversary (Robbins 1964a). Most alarming were sharp declines in the Double-crested Cormorant, Peregrine Falcon, Cooper's Hawk, Northern Harrier, and nesting Bald Eagle and Osprey, with heavy use of chlorinated hydrocarbon pesticides suspected as a major cause. American Robins were also heavy losers in southern Wisconsin cities that used DDT to combat Dutch elm disease. Eastern Bluebird populations dropped alarmingly, while numbers of King Rails and Piping Plovers also dwindled. European Starlings and House Sparrows completed their spread throughout the state, and reached pest proportions in several cities. The Redthroated Loon, Eared and Red-necked Grebes, Swainson's Hawk, Stilt Sandpiper, Bell's and White-eyed Vireos were noted increasingly as annual visitants. Great Egrets and Common Ravens spread.

Following the 1969 ban on the use of DDT in the United States, such raptors as the Cooper's Hawk, Osprey, and Bald Eagle have shown increases. The Department of Natural Resources Bureau of Endangered Resources now monitors closely the population levels of these and all other endangered and threatened species.

Wisconsin DNR personnel make frequent checks on population levels of all game species, partly through research, partly through gathering data on hunter kills. They make recommendations about hunting regulations, designed to help maintain adequate populations of ducks, geese, grouse, pheasants, and so on.

The June Breeding Bird Survey helps keep tabs on all Wisconsin breeding species—especially passerines. The 5-year summaries (Robbins 1971, 1977, 1982b) show that most species are holding their own. There have been modest increases in Killdeers, Barn Swallows, American Crows, American Robins, and Common Grackles, and decreases in Black Terns, Northern Flickers, Eastern Bluebirds, and Warbling Vireos. Most pronounced have been declines since 1975 in such grassland species as Eastern and Western Meadowlarks, Dickcissels, and Grasshopper and Vesper Sparrows.

The analysis of the quarterly field notes in *The Passenger Pigeon* reveals other trends. Common and Forster's Terns and Black-crowned Night-Herons have experienced noticeable declines as breeding species. Populations of several southern species at the northern fringe of their breeding range—notably the Bewick's Wren, Bell's Vireo, Loggerhead Shrike, and Yellow-breasted Chat—have shown a definite drop since 1965. Other southerners—the Tricolored Heron, Cattle Egret, White-eyed Vireo, Worm-eating and Prairie Warblers, and Laughing Gull—have appeared more regularly. Moving westward through the Great Lakes area have been several gulls: the Ring-billed as a common breeder, the Little as a localized breeder, and such European vagrants as the Lesser Blackbacked, Common Black-headed, and Mew. The expected House Finch influx has begun. Common Grackles and Brown-headed Cowbirds have spread to the extent that they have been recommended for pest-control. After years of decline, the Common Loon, Peregrine Falcon, Double-crested Cormorant, and Eastern Bluebird have shown encouraging increases in the 1980s.

Combatting Bird Losses

Before the end of the nineteenth century, the loss of birdlife had become a source of great consternation. When various Wisconsin ornithologists were asked in 1898 to comment on declining bird populations, alarming notes were sounded (in Hornaday 1898, p. 39): "Birds have decreased very greatly" (R. M. Strong, Milwaukee); "One half as many birds as formerly" (G. A. Morrison, Fox Lake); "Where in the days of my boyhood thirty-five years ago, orchards and woodlands were ringing with bird music, silence seems to reign supreme" (H. Nehrling,

Milwaukee); "I could not give the percentage of decrease for the state as greater than 30% in fifteen years; locally it seems greater" (A. L. Kumlien, Milton).

How could these losses be stemmed? One answer: legislation to limit killing. Some beginning steps in this direction had been taken nearly 50 years earlier, when an 1851 law was adopted to prohibit spring and summer hunting of the Greater Prairie-Chicken, Ruffed Grouse, Northern Bobwhite, and American Woodcock. By 1870, spring and summer protection was extended to the main breeding waterfowl: Mallards, Wood Ducks, and Green- and Blue-winged Teal. A more inclusive law in 1899 outlawed spring shooting of waterfowl entirely. The drastic reduction of the Passenger Pigeon in the 1870s stimulated legislation in 1877 to protect nesting populations; but this action proved to be too little, too late.

Setting game laws became an annual concern for the state legislature, often stimulating heated debate. Laws dealt with the species that could be hunted, the length of the seasons, the kinds of boats that could be used in duck-hunting, weapons, bag limits, and the penalty to be assessed against violators. The more complex the laws, the more necessary it was to have professional personnel for enforcement. Game wardens were first authorized in 1887. At first the task of the warden was an exasperating one. Salary and travel allowance were grossly inadequate. Public antagonism was great. Justice officials were often uncooperative. An article by Emerson Hough (1890a) in *Forest and Stream* quoted Warden W. Y. Wentworth:

I am State Game Warden for twenty counties . . . Waukesha County alone has eighty-six lakes within its boundaries, on almost any one of which there is temptation for a law-breaker. . . . My territory also covers Lake Winnebago . . . well known to be infested with illegal nets. My salary is $600 a year, and I am allowed $250 a year for travel expenses. I have a deputy in every county, whose sole pay rests in half of the fines imposed under actual convictions. Many of these deputies are timid and afraid to act without my help. I ought to be traveling all the time. How can I be on $250 a year? I am a good deal out of pocket on traveling expenses for the past year, and yet I have felt that I was slighting the work.

The process of upgrading the warden's job, with public acceptance and cooperation, was long and arduous. In time, a full-fledged force of state and county wardens evolved. The responsibility for setting annual game regulations remained the province of the legislature until 1933, when it passed to the Conservation Commission, and eventually to the Department of Natural Resources.

Nongame birds needed protection too. A first step was taken in 1857 with a law prohibiting the taking of birds and their eggs in cemeteries. This was followed 12 years later by legislation protecting all "insect-eating birds" within 2 miles of an incorporated city. Similar protection was broadened to encompass the entire state in 1877.

Stimulated by the heavy kill of herons, gulls, and various passerines by plume-hunters, Audubon societies sprang up in many states in the 1890s, and worked for protective legislation. The Wisconsin Audubon Society was organized in 1897. In an explanatory brochure, General Secretary Mrs. George Peckham (1897) wrote: "This Society appeals to women to refrain entirely from the use of wild birds' feathers, and to men to secure, by all possible means, the preservation and protection of our native birds." By 1898 Wisconsin had a law that stated: "Any person who shall catch or kill at any time, or for any purpose whatever, except as authorized by law, any whip-poor-will, nighthawk, bluebird, finch, thrush, robin, lark, turtle dove, or any other harmless bird shall be punished by a fine of not more than fifty dollars or by imprisonment in the county jail for not more than thirty days, provided that this section shall not apply to blackbirds, crows, English sparrows or pigeons for trapshooting."

Conservation received a tremendous boost nationwide with the strong support of President Theodore Roosevelt in the early years of the twentieth century, the enactment of the Weeks-McLean bill in 1913, which established the principle of federal control of migratory birds, and the 1918 passage of the Migratory Bird Treaty Act. But fishermen were concerned over the loss of fish to kingfishers, bitterns, and herons. Rules were relaxed in 1920 to allow killing of these birds and were not tightened again until 1972.

Environmental pollution became a matter of major legal concern in the 1960s, as the serious effects of chlorinated hydrocarbon pesticides became increasingly apparent. This led to administrative rules restricting the use of various chemicals, and to the ban on DDT in 1969. Further bans or restrictions on chemicals are presently being debated. Acid rain has been identified as a potentially harmful influence on water bird habitat, but its long-term effect on birds is not yet known.

Restocking

Not content merely to try to slow the decline of birds by legislation, conservationists have attempted to replenish the supply of game birds by restocking. The first recorded venture was the private release of Northern Bobwhite in 1884. Quail had been abundant 30 years earlier, then dropped off precipitously. But a succession of plantings in the next 20 years did not fare well. Nor did more recent plantings by the Wisconsin Conservation Department in the 1950s.

Various attempts have been made to restock Wild Turkeys following their drastic reduction in 1843 and subsequent extirpation. Between 1929 and 1939, the Wisconsin Conservation Department planted substantial numbers in the wooded hills of Grant and Sauk counties. The last of these (or their descendants) perished in 1958. A few individuals remain from releases in Juneau County between 1954 and 1957. New plantings were made at several sites in Vernon and Buffalo counties in the 1970s and early 1980s. These have been sufficiently successful to permit limited hunting beginning in 1983. By 1989 restocking had taken place in 34 counties, with conspicuous success.

Small numbers of Greater Prairie-Chickens have been released in Burnett County on several occasions since 1975. It is hoped that Wisconsin can thus establish some new flocks in addition to the few groups struggling for survival in and near the Buena Vista Marsh in Portage, Wood, Adams, and Marathon counties.

The most extensive stocking program has been the introduction of the Ring-necked Pheasant. Private plantings were spasmodic from 1895 on, then became more extensive after 1911. State conservation agencies joined the stocking program in 1928, enlarged it with the establishment of the Poynette Game Farm 5 years later, and have provided birds for release in many parts of the state ever since. Stocking was moderately successful, especially in the south and east, until the 1970s. But with farmers now beginning hay harvest in early June (before young are capable of survival), and with undisturbed habitat continually dwindling, pheasant stocking now results in little carry-over of birds from one year to the next. Chainsaw attacks on hedgerows have eliminated favorable habitat. Hunter success figures in the 1980s are far below those of the 1960s.

The introduction of the Gray Partridge, begun privately in 1910, developed into a public conservation program 20 years later. The spread has been modest but encouraging. Conspicuously unsuccessful were the releases of the California Quail (1932), Chukar (1932–1945), Willow Ptarmigan (1941), Reeves' Pheasant (1947), Capercaille (1949–1950), Black Grouse (1949–1950), and Red-legged Partridge (1950–1952).

To rebuild the nesting population of Wood Ducks, seriously diminished in the first half of the twentieth century, the Wisconsin Conservation Department oversaw the release of 855 birds in 1958 and 1960. Since 1950 the state has also established captive flocks of Canada Geese, and has been successful in reestablishing this as a breeding species at several locations. Canada Geese bred in over half of Wisconsin's counties in the 1980s, and were beginning to be looked on as summer pests in Milwaukee.

The early 1980s saw beginning efforts to release a few Peregrine Falcons in Wisconsin and southeastern Minnesota. Great Horned Owl predation interfered with initial efforts along the bluffs overlooking the Mississippi River, but releases among the tall buildings in Milwaukee and Madison show promise of success. Personnel from the DNR Bureau of Endangered Resources have begun a program of reestablishing the Trumpeter Swan, using Mute Swans as foster parents.

Public Education

Some of the same voices that pleaded for legislation to curb the killing of birds were also raised to encourage widespread education about the aesthetic and economic values of birds. The Wisconsin Audubon Society, organized in 1897 and active in promoting protective legislation by 1900, soon developed local school chapters that enrolled over 20,000 children. Victor Kutchin, secretary of this society, sounded a clarion call in the 1915 *Wisconsin Arbor and Bird Day Annual:* "Our battle cry is 'educate, educate, educate.'" This society promoted the annual observance of Wisconsin Arbor and Bird Day and disseminated avian lore through its publication *By the Wayside.*

Some educational work had begun nearly 50 years earlier, in the form of museum exhibits of birds along with other forms of wildlife. When the Wisconsin Natural History Association was organized in 1853, a first step was the purchase of the Samuel Sercomb collection, previously on display in Milwaukee. The collection included birds, mammals, reptiles, plants, and rocks. The announcement of this accession read: "Mr. Sercomb has the charge of the room, and we must say, that for tasty arrangement, we have seldom if ever seen the 'Madison Museum' equaled in our larger cities" (L. J. Farwell in the *Madison State Journal*, 23 March 1853).

Four years later Der Naturhistoriche Verein für Wisconsin got started in Milwaukee, eventually being incorporated as the Wisconsin Natural History Society. From this beginning came the Milwaukee Public Museum, a prime repository for bird specimens, and a vital force in promoting ornithological education.

In the earliest years of Wisconsin's statehood, A. C. Barry—noted both as an ornithologist and an educator—recommended in his 1855 report as state superintendent of public instruction, "If the study of Natural History were introduced into our schools, it could not fail, I think, of becoming one of the most grateful and efficient of the formative powers in education." He had birds partly in mind as he continued: "It is of great practical utility, and is of essential advantage to the farmer, dairyman and gardener in particular. It promotes health and cheerfulness—frees the mind from the dread and apprehension of supernatural power—brings the moral affections into communion with the harmonies of nature and opens new sources of the purest happiness."

Such natural history study gradually became an important part of the curriculum of primary and secondary schools. Wisconsin Arbor and Bird Day was widely observed in schools in the earliest years of the twentieth century, with a wide variety of related outdoor projects. Eventually, in 1935, legislation was enacted requiring the teaching of courses in the conservation of natural resources.

In the meantime, the state made education about birds an important phase of the game warden's job. By 1912, Warden E. A. Cleasby was writing and speaking vigorously about the value of birds in the total environment. Typical was this explanation in the *Wisconsin Farmers' Institute Bulletin* (1912):

Each bird family plays its part in the never-ending warfare and the number of insects annually consumed by the combined hosts is simply incalculable. It is well that this is so, for so vast is the number of insects and so great is the quantity of vegetation required for their subsistence that the existence of every green thing would be threatened were it not for birds and other agents especially designed to keep them in check.

The Wisconsin Conservation Department soon entered the educational field more broadly by means of various publications, beginning with *The Wisconsin Conservationist* (1919–1922), and continuing with *Monthly Survey* (1928–1936) and *Wisconsin Conservation Bulletin* (1936–1977). Although aimed largely at hunters and fishermen, the *Conservation Bulletin* had wide appeal for nature-lovers in general. One of its regular features for over 22 years was N. R. Barger's verbal portraits of many of Wisconsin's nongame birds: brief paragraphs describing life history features, plumage description, and comments on where and when each species could be found in the state. Since 1977 the DNR has continued a more lavishly illustrated publication: *Wisconsin Natural Resources.*

Independent organizations have played an important role in ornithological education ever since the advent of the Wisconsin Audubon Society. Many a public or private school has had a local Audubon chapter at one time or another in the past 90 years. Interest in birds helped develop the Wisconsin Natural History Society (1899), the Friends of Our Native Landscape (1920), the Izaak Walton League (1922), the Wisconsin Wildlife Federation (1936), the Wisconsin Federation of Conservation Clubs (1948), and the Citizens Natural Resources Association (1959).

Local bird clubs began to spring up in some major cities in the 1930s. Madison had its Madison Bird Club and Kumlien Club, Green Bay its Green Bay Bird Club, and Waukesha its Benjamin F. Goss Club. In the 1940s and 1950s, there developed the John Muir Club (Milwaukee), Wausau Bird Club, P. R. Hoy Bird Club (Racine), Appleton Bird Club, Roger Tory Peterson Bird Club (Manitowoc), Wild Wings Bird Club (Kenosha), Chippewa Wildlife Society (Chippewa Falls), Ned Hollister Bird Club (Beloit), S. Paul Jones Bird Club (Oconomowoc), Owen J. Gromme Bird Club (Fond du Lac), Chequamegon Bird Club (Medford) and Audubon chapters in Appleton, Barron, Green Bay, Madison, Milwaukee, La Crosse, Wausau-Merrill, Stevens Point, and Platteville. In several of these cities, Audubon screen tours have brought nationally known lecturer-photographers in the field of ornithology to the attention of thousands.

The organizers of the Madison Bird Club were also prime movers in the formation of the Wisconsin Society for Ornithology in 1939. Throughout a colorful 50-

Aldo Leopold, 1887–1948 (courtesy of Robert A. McCabe)

year history, the WSO has reached out to people in all parts of the state through its publication *The Passenger Pigeon*, its annual conventions and paper sessions, its camp-outs and field trips, its field note program and cooperative research projects, its supply department, and its land preservation efforts.

The Wisconsin Audubon Camp, founded near Sarona (Washburn County) in 1955, brought another strong educational force to Wisconsin. The only camp maintained by the National Audubon Society in the Midwest, it attracted hundreds of students each year through 1986. Many—if not most—of these campers have returned to their home communities and been instrumental in teaching others about nature in general, and birds in particular.

The teaching of ornithology and related conservation subjects on the college level received a tremendous boost in 1933 when the University of Wisconsin–Madison appointed Aldo Leopold to develop a Department of Wildlife Management. This was a pioneer effort. For the training of wildlife specialists Leopold developed a program that drew worldwide acclaim and respect; in addition, he stimulated a deep understanding and respect for ecology in many students majoring in other fields. The University of Wisconsin furthered its program of training biologists with the presence of John Emlen on its faculty from 1946 to 1974. The development of the College of Natural Resources at the University of Wisconsin–Stevens Point in the 1960s was also widely acclaimed. Since 1950, courses in ornithology have been added to the curriculum of at least 10 other Wisconsin colleges and universities.

The 1970s and 1980s have seen the development of privately sponsored nature centers at Milwaukee (Schlitz Audubon Center and Wehr Nature Center), Green Bay (Bay Beach Sanctuary), and Manitowoc (Woodland Dunes Nature Center). These centers maintain libraries and nature exhibits of various types and sponsor field trips for adults and children. So also does the Sigurd Olson Environmental Institute at Northland College in Ashland and the Natural History Museum at Cable.

Research

While Leopold was keenly aware of the need for education to help in bird preservation, he was equally convinced that any sound program for maintaining strong representative bird populations had to be based on solid basic research. His own research on appraising wildlife populations, done shortly before the beginning of his teaching career, was an outstanding example of what should be undertaken (Leopold 1929).

One of the earliest research efforts in Wisconsin was Franklin H. King's inquiry into the feeding habits and requirements of birds. Between 1873 and 1877, he examined the stomach contents of 1,608 birds, dissecting and identifying plant and animal matter. From these and the findings of others, he documented the types of food preferred by most Wisconsin species. The result was the landmark publication of King's "Economic Relations of Wisconsin Birds" (1883).

Night studies of migrants were carried on by H. A. Winkenwerder and O. G. Libby between 1898 and 1900, at a time when theories about migration were in their infancy. Manning telescopes at Madison and Beloit, Winkenwerder took detailed notes on birds silhouetted against a full moon, noting the size and direction of migratory flight, and estimating the altitude at which birds were flying. On nights of heavy migration, data were collected on as many as 121 birds in 2 hours (Winkenwerder 1902a,b).

Migration studies of a different type received strong impetus in 1910 when Leon J. Cole joined the faculty of the University of Wisconsin at Madison. Cole had previously developed methods of trapping and banding birds in Michigan and Connecticut, and was instrumental in the formation of the American Bird Banding Association in 1909. He served as the association's first president, setting it on a course that led to its incorporation into the U.S. Bureau of Biological Survey 10 years later.

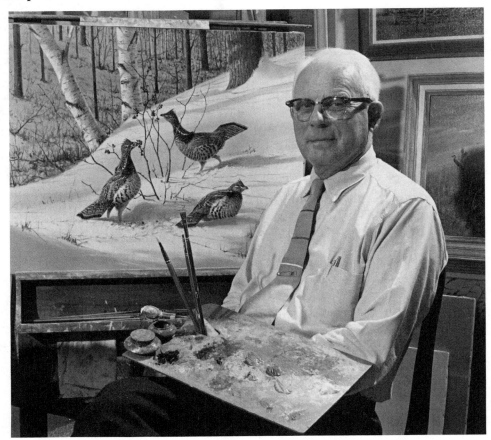

Owen J. Gromme, 1896— (Milwaukee Public Museum photo)

Banding thereafter became one of the basic tools of ornithological research. Harold C. Wilson began banding Herring Gull nestlings on the Door County islands in 1924 and contributed greatly to our understanding of this species through over 50 years of work. In a wide variety of research projects centered at University of Wisconsin campuses at Madison, Milwaukee, and Stevens Point, banding has played a major role.

Extensive raptor-trapping began at Cedar Grove in Sheboygan County in 1937 by Owen J. Gromme, Clarence S. Jung, and others on the Milwaukee Public Museum staff. Later, the Cedar Grove Ornithological Station was established. Similar banding of hawks and owls has been carried on at the Little Suamico Ornithological Station in Oconto County since 1971, at Woodland Dunes Nature Center in Manitowoc County since 1965, and at the Wisconsin Foundation for Wildlife Research in the Marshfield area since 1984.

The formation of a research bureau by the Wisconsin Conservation Commission in 1927 led to extensive studies of game birds that still continue. Beginning with the Greater Prairie-Chicken and Sharp-tailed Grouse investigation by A. O. Gross and F. J. W. Schmidt (Gross 1930a), early researchers inquired into food habits, habitat requirements, disease problems, population densities, predator relationships, and cyclic phenomena of the Ring-necked Pheasant, Northern Bobwhite, Ruffed Grouse, and Gray Partridge. Concurrent with these beginnings was Aldo Leopold's (1931a) game survey for the Sporting Arms and Ammunition Manufacturers' Institute.

The work of the WCD Research Bureau, expanded subsequently by DNR personnel, has been crucial to the survival of Wisconsin's Prairie-Chicken and Sharp-tailed Grouse. Frederick and Frances Hamerstrom, instrumental in this work, also contributed an important Sandhill Crane study (F. N. Hamerstrom 1938) at a time when this bugler was dangerously close to extirpation in Wisconsin. Under Fred Zimmerman, Laurence Jahn, and Richard Hunt, researchers turned to waterfowl management in the 1940s as birds attempted to recoup from the drought of the 1930s and from dwindling habitat. In the 1970s and 1980s, DNR personnel have continued to monitor populations of waterfowl and other game species. Each year new technical bulletins are issued, some dealing with fish, mammals, and water quality, some dealing with birds (e.g., the Woodcock, Ruffed Grouse, Northern Bobwhite, Double-crested Cormorant, and breeding ducks). There is increasing concern over several nongame species—especially such grassland nesters as Dickcissels, Bobolinks, Grasshopper and Vesper Sparrows, and the meadowlarks.

The formation of the Wisconsin Society for Ornithology led to a series of research-oriented range and population studies, in which dozens of volunteers contributed sight observations, and project leaders analyzed and summarized data. At first, particular attention was given to species that were most noticeably expanding their Wisconsin range: the Northern Cardinal, Red-bellied Woodpecker, Great Egret, and Yellow-headed Blackbird. Increasingly, studies have also dealt with declining species: the Bald Eagle, Osprey, Great Blue Heron, Double-crested Cormorant, Common Loon, Loggerhead Shrike, and Black Tern.

The WSO has also been instrumental in developing Wisconsin's part in two major continent-wide population measurement ventures: the National Audubon Society–sponsored Christmas Bird Count (CBC) and the U.S. Fish and Wildlife Service's Breeding Bird Survey (BBS). Both are designed to measure bird populations through representative sampling at times of the year when migration is minimal.

The CBC is conducted between 15 December and 5 January, when winter populations are static, except for lingering waterfowl in southeastern Wisconsin. Each count area consists of a circle 15 miles in diameter, with from 1 to 80 observers spending a full day afield. Although the CBC was begun in 1900, Wisconsin's participation was limited to 1–3 counts per year until the WSO was organized in 1939. Through the 1940s Wisconsin observers conducted an average of 12 counts per year. This swelled to 34 counts per year in the 1950s, 63 in the 1960s, and 68 in the 1970s. By 1982 over 1,300 observers were participating in 85 counts covering portions of 67 counties.

The BBS is conducted in June when breeding populations are static and bird song is at its peak. Wisconsin was assigned 70 count areas when the project was begun in 1966, and has maintained an 89% completion record ever since—thanks to 80–90 volunteer observers. Each count area consists of 50 look-and-listen stops at 0.5-mile intervals along an assigned 24.5-mile road transect.

Both counting projects are providing normative bases of population levels for each species, from which researchers can detect substantial fluctuations when they occur. CBC summaries appear annually in the spring issues of *The Passenger Pigeon*. BBS summaries appear at approximate 5-year intervals (Robbins 1971, 1977, 1982) in *The Passenger Pigeon*.

The International Crane Foundation, headquartered near Baraboo (Sauk County), has earned a worldwide reputation for research on the habits of the

Carl Richter, 1903–1977 (photo by M. Lound)

world's cranes. This research has contributed greatly to understanding the food and habitat requirements of each of the 15 species of cranes, exerted tremendous international influence toward habitat preservation, and developed unique methods of raising captive young of endangered crane species. If, in time to come, several presently endangered crane species survive, it will be largely due to the work of George Archibald, Ronald Sauey, and their associates at the Foundation.

Endangered Species
Since 1971 the DNR has given increasing attention to research surrounding Wisconsin's endangered species. In 1972 an Endangered Species Committee headed by Ruth Hine prepared a list of Wisconsin's plants, mammals, birds, reptiles,

amphibians, fishes, and mollusks deemed "endangered"—in danger of becoming extirpated (Hine 1973b). Three birds were listed: the Double-crested Cormorant, Bald Eagle, and Osprey. The Peregrine Falcon was added in 1975.

An expanded list in 1979 (Les) added the Piping Plover, Forster's Tern, Common Tern, and Barn Owl. The 1979 list also categorized as "threatened"—appearing to be on the decline, possibly becoming endangered within the foreseeable future—the Great Egret, Cooper's Hawk, Red-shouldered Hawk, Greater Prairie-Chicken, and Loggerhead Shrike. By 1983 the Double-crested Cormorant had recovered sufficiently to be transferred from the endangered list to the threatened roster. The Red-necked Grebe was also added to the threatened category.

Walter E. Scott, 1911–1983 (photo by Edward E. Schumann and Associates)

Research dealing with some of these species has been proceeding at an increased pace. Declining populations of gulls and terns prompted surveys of breeding colonies of Herring Gulls and Common Terns on Lake Superior (Harris and Matteson 1975a,b), Forster's and Common Terns and Herring Gulls on upper Green Bay and Lake Michigan (T. C. Erdman 1977, pers. comm.), Forster's Terns on the upper Mississippi River (D. H. Thompson 1977), Black Terns on all Wisconsin wetlands (Tilghman 1980), and surveys of nesting colonies of Forster's, Common, and Black Terns (Mossman 1981, unpublished reports to the DNR). L. R. Petersen (1980) coordinated an important Barn Owl survey.

By the late 1970s the DNR Office of Endangered and Nongame Species, under the leadership of J. B. Hale, was coordinating a series of activities designed to enhance nesting success of threatened and endangered species. Artificial nest platforms were erected for Ospreys, Bald Eagles, Double-crested Cormorants, Common Terns, and Forster's Terns.

In 1984 with a new name (Bureau of Endangered Resources) and a new director (Ronald Nicotera), this DNR agency began gathering information about some additional species that may be declining: Yellow-crowned and Black-crowned Night-Herons and such grassland species as Upland Sandpiper, Dickcissel, Western Meadowlark, and Grasshopper Sparrow. A revised list of endangered species (1989) includes the Trumpeter Swan (assisted with high-priority reintroduction efforts) and Worm-eating and Yellow-throated Warblers (marginal breeders in Wisconsin). The DNR policy is to list as endangered only those species known to breed in Wisconsin.

Federal and state wildlife specialists are working together to monitor populations of Ospreys and Bald Eagles, to band their young, and to protect their nesting habitat. Through Wisconsin Project Loon Watch, the Sigurd Olson Environmental Institute at Ashland is making yeoman efforts to provide protection for nesting Common Loons throughout northern Wisconsin.

In many of the above investigations, inquiry has gone beyond population inventories. Studies of food requirements, water quality, nesting habitat preferences, and effects of human encroachment have been a basic part of this research. It has become increasingly clear that Wisconsin's migrant species are affected not only by environmental factors within Wisconsin during the breeding and migration seasons, but also by the environmental features encountered by each species on its wintering grounds. Are water birds and hawks continuing to ingest DDT outside the United States? Are forest species likely to suffer from the widespread destruction of rain forest currently taking place in Mexico and Central America? Wisconsin researchers need to tie in with federal research now being carried on "south of the border."

Habitat Preservation

As some of Wisconsin's earliest residents began to detect decreasing populations of certain species, thoughts of preserving habitat started to take shape. Perhaps it was inspired as much by concerns for human protection as for bird protection, but in 1869 the legislature passed a law forbidding the killing of "all insect eating birds" within 2 miles of an incorporated city. Did this cover all "song birds"? All "passerines"? The law did not clearly specify, but an offender could be fined from $5 to $25. How much effort was made to enforce the law is not known, but one intent of the law was to establish some type of limited sanctuary to assist in the preservation of birds.

Birds were beneficiaries also in the development of state parks and forests. Undoubtedly, in the minds of park proponents the desire to protect forests and mammals was as great as the need to create bird sanctuaries. Conversations between Wisconsin and Minnesota residents led to the decision in 1900 to create the Interstate Park at St. Croix Falls–Taylors Falls. The appointment of a State Park Commission in 1907 led to the development of Peninsula State Park near Ephraim, Devil's Lake State Park near Baraboo, and Wyalusing State Park near Prairie du Chien in the next 10 years. This trend has expanded through the years. By 1980 Wisconsin had 66 state parks, 5 designated state forests, and an additional 450 parks set aside by individual counties.

It was more specifically with birds in mind that lands were set aside as part of the national wildlife refuge system. The late 1920s saw the development of the Upper Mississippi River NWR, incorporating significant areas of marshes and wooded bottomlands along the western Wisconsin border. Migrating and nesting waterfowl received additional assistance with the establishment of national refuges at Necedah (1939) and Horicon (1941). Birds have benefited from the establishment of two national forests (Chequamegon, Nicolet) between 1928 and 1933.

Through its conservation agencies (WCD, DNR), the Wisconsin state government set aside additional land for wildlife. Among the largest parcels are Horicon Marsh in Dodge County, Central Wisconsin Conservation Area in Juneau and Wood counties, Crex Meadows in Burnett County, Mead Wildlife Area in Marathon, Portage, and Wood counties, Powell Marsh in Vilas and Iron counties, Grand River Wildlife Area in Green Lake and Marquette counties, Sandhill Wildlife Area in Wood County, Collins Marsh in Manitowoc County, Tiffany Bottoms in Buffalo and Pepin counties, and Navarino Wildlife Area in Shawano County. This land acquisition program started slowly in 1927, proceeded at a modest rate throughout the 1950s, then received a substantial boost in 1961 with the enactment of the Outdoor Recreation Act Program, with impetus from Governor Gaylord Nelson and financed largely by a tax on cigarettes. By 1979 the number of state-owned or -leased lands for public hunting and fishing grounds and other habitat protection purposes had grown to 280, embracing over a half million acres.

Increasingly in the 1940s and 1950s additional lands were purchased by private individuals and organizations. A particularly ambitious private project was the effort to preserve Prairie-Chicken habitat in the Plainfield-Bancroft region. The combined efforts of the Prairie Chicken Foundation, the Society of Tympanuchus Cupido Pinnatus, Ltd., and other supportive organizations and individuals resulted in the setting aside of over 10,000 acres of prime chicken habitat, which is being managed by DNR personnel.

Since 1960 the Wisconsin Chapter of The Nature Conservancy has been a vital factor in preserving habitat. Through a national loan fund replenished by ambitious local fund-raising efforts, this group is able to act quickly when a desirable piece of wildlife property becomes available. Sometimes reselling the property to other state conservation groups, sometimes retaining title itself, The Nature Conservancy has had a hand in preserving over 35,000 acres scattered over 40 counties. This is done not only with birds in mind, but also in the interest of preserving valuable areas for a variety of native plants and mammals.

For similar reasons the Wisconsin legislature established a state board for the Preservation of Scientific Areas in 1951. Later renamed the Scientific Areas Pres-

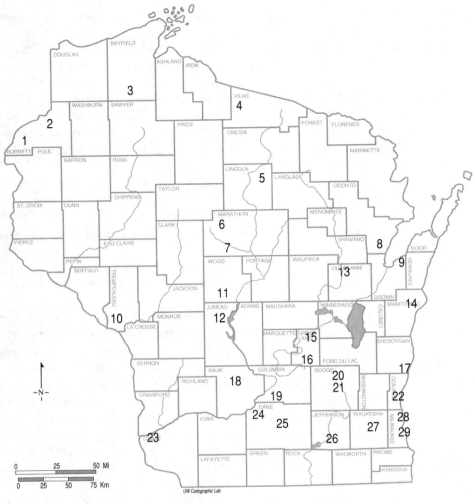

1	Fish Lake Wildlife Area
2	Crex Meadows Wildlife Area
3	Pigeon Lake Biological Research Station
4	Powell Marsh Wildlife Area
5	Treehaven Biological Research Station
6	Wisconsin Foundation for Wildlife Research Station
7	Mead Wildlife Area
8	Little Suamico Ornithological Station
9	Bay Beach Wildlife Sanctuary
10	Upper Mississippi River National Wildlife Refuge
11	Sandhill Wildlife Area
12	Necedah National Wildlife Refuge
13	Mosquito Hill Nature Center
14	Woodland Dunes Nature Center
15	White River Marsh Wildlife Area

16	Grand River Marsh Wildlife Area
17	Cedar Grove Ornithological Station
18	Honey Creek Natural Area
19	Goose Pond Wildlife Sanctuary
20	Horicon Marsh National Wildlife Refuge
21	Horicon Marsh Wildlife Area
22	University of Wisconsin-Milwaukee Field Station
23	Wyalusing State Park
24	Mazomanie Wildlife Area
25	University of Wisconsin-Madison Arboretum
26	Prince's Point Wildlife Area
27	Vernon Marsh Wildlife Area
28	Schlitz Audubon Nature Center
29	Wehr Nature Center

Locations of national wildlife refuges, major state wildlife areas, and major ornithological research stations ervation Council, this group has examined hundreds of land parcels. By the end of 1984, the number of parcels designated worthy of preservation had reached 194. They are representative of relatively unspoiled samples of varied types of biotic communities. A county-by-county inventory is progressing as this movement gathers momentum.

The habitat preservation movement has commanded increasing attention since the first formal listing of endangered species in 1972. Even before the Bald Eagle was added to this list, the Eagle Valley Environmentalists began raising funds to purchase suitable eagle wintering territory in Grant County. Although this group has now disbanded, it did much to raise public consciousness and was also instrumental in preserving part of Ferry Bluff in Sauk County as prime eagle wintering habitat.

Amid all these activities of private and public organizations, there have been persistent voices reminding individual landowners of their habitat preservation responsibilities. By 1979 the National Wildlife Federation's Backyard Wildlife program had enlisted 80 Wisconsin cooperators. A far-sighted landowner landscapes his home and surroundings not only from the standpoint of neatly groomed lawns and elegantly trimmed shrubbery, but also with an eye to the natural food requirements of birds and animals and the value of undisturbed thickets that offer food and shelter for wildlife. A farmer votes for or against the preservation of varied plant and animal life (including birds) by the decisions he makes about maintenance of woodlots, preservation of brushy edges, and rotation of crops.

No one understood this better than Aldo Leopold. Patiently but persistently he taught this in the classroom, lobbied for this in state agencies, wrote of this for farmers. In *Wildlife Conservation on the Farm* (1941) Leopold offered these "Recipes for Rural Conservation":

Don't graze the whole woodlot. Fence off a part for the birds and wildflowers.

Don't burn, mow, or graze the whole marsh. Protect a part as winter shelter for birds, and as a refuge for bog flowers and tamaracks.

Leave some fencerows or plant windbreaks to check the wind, catch snow, and shelter wildlife.

Leave corn or spread manure to feed the birds in winter.

Den-trees, dead snags, fencerows, bird houses, and feeding stations are the visible evidences of your hospitality toward wild things.

A remnant of each of the plants and animals originally native to your farm is visible evidence that it grows historical perspective as well as butter fat or cheese. He who knows what his land was is a safe custodian of its future.

Habitat preservation becomes increasingly vital for the maintenance of bird populations. Each passing year, we see an increase in human population, with no increase in area. Pressures inevitably build as various segments of our society vie for land for purposes of agriculture, industry, transportation, residential living, and recreation of various types. Wisconsin's prospects for an avifauna in the twenty-first century, comparable with that described in this volume for the nineteenth and twentieth centuries, are destined to rise or fall depending on present and future land-use patterns.

The Landscape and the Birds
James Hall Zimmerman

The preceding chapter traces the development of human perceptions of and attitudes toward our birdlife. Here we complement that historical account by viewing the landscape from the birds' perspective. A consideration of the natural setting of Wisconsin can help answer questions such as: Why are there so many kinds of birds found in Wisconsin? Where do particular bird species meet their needs for food, shelter, social life, warmth, and protection? How do we read the landscape to locate birds and to assess their present status and future prospects for survival? We look for habitats.

First of all, what is habitat? It is the particular physical and biological environment experienced by an organism in a given place: the combination of factors such as climate, topography, soil, moisture, vegetation, and animal life. Habitat can refer to the conditions in a given place, or it can refer to the needs of a particular bird species or other form of life. Where the conditions coincide with a particular species' needs, we may expect that species to be able to live there. A living organism responds to its environment by adaptation. Some adaptations are long-term and largely genetic, that is, inherited. The long bill of a heron is designed for spearing fish, while the feet, unlike those of most water birds, can grasp a limb and enable herons to perch in trees. Other adaptations may be temporal, and so are physiological or behavioral. A good example of the latter—whether genetic or learned—is the response to seasonal change in the environment such as migration or a change in diet.

While we do address migratory and wintering habitats here and there in this chapter and again in the chapter on habitat preferences in Part II, the emphasis here is on breeding habitat. That is the most distinct and easiest kind to pin down, as well as being the most critical for bird conservation and management in Wisconsin. We must not forget, however, that migration and wintering habitats are equally vital to the survival of the species.

The importance of the habitat approach is illustrated by the present status of our cranes and geese as contrasted with that of our herons and ducks. In the years since hunting has been regulated, the numbers of our geese and cranes have increased spectacularly. They have joined the blackbirds as a cause of crop damage in localized areas near wetlands. The habitats of these birds are ample, and they are maintained and protected, at present, in all three types of sites necessary for survival: summer breeding grounds, migration stops, and wintering landscapes. Many geese breed in the Arctic and winter in refuges or in inaccessible coastal marshes; many of our cranes take advantage of the wetlands restored in central Wisconsin after farm failures in the 1930s, and still find sufficient acreages of undrained wetlands in Florida, while artificial feeding sustains them in their northern Indiana migratory refuge.

On the other hand, most of our ducks are still declining in numbers today, because all three types of their habitat—breeding sites, migration stops, and wintering grounds—happen to be wetlands, which are in demand by expanding agriculture. The herons and bitterns appear to be suffering as well, perhaps in their case because of the loss of wild places for rookeries and possibly because of pollution of waters affecting the fish and frogs on which they must feed.

The fact that the environment is not uniform enables a variety of birds to inhabit the same area. Each species is confined by its adaptations to specific habitats. Different bird species can coexist by specializing for certain nest sites and foods, thereby avoiding competition for the limited supply of resources. How do birds recognize the habitat they need? First, it is helpful to note that there are three elements in habitat. One is the provision, in combination, of the appropriate essentials—food, water, cover, and sites for nests, song perches, resting or roosting, and so on. All these needs must be provided within a convenient distance from a nesting site, or within a "home range." The second element is the landscape design—the arrangement of the essentials. Just as the abundance and arrangement of furniture determines how a room may be used, so in nature the size or spacing of trees or the gradualness of a shoreline must be suited to the way a bird makes its living—or its life style. Finally, there is the general landscape on a grand scale. Is it mountainous or flat, open or cluttered with vegetation, and is the vegetation and topography patterned in any way? Even on this scale, human activity can be as influential in determining habitat as the climatic influences are—for instance, by replacing forests with prairielike alfalfa fields.

Birds probably recognize suitable habitat by a combination of three sets of programming. One is genetic, or instinctive, molded in a species over very long periods of time. The second is early individual experience; birds, like people, can become imprinted on a particular place that was their home while they were very young. Just as we may long for the scene of our youth, the bird may seek the exact scene of its rearing, and not rest until it finds it or a similar place. Finally, a bird blundering into unsuitable habitat must be frustrated at not finding needed food or other resources or at not being able to satisfy its urge to display or nest, and presumably remains restless until its searches bring it to suitable habitat. By this search-and-compare technique, birds are sooner or later able to find the right place to live, even if they become temporarily lost during migration. As seen below, however, they may be able to find home simply by accurate navigation, for which the urge is strong and the ability phenomenal.

Many examples of fidelity to habitat can be given. Western and Eastern Meadowlarks seldom nest together. Easterns will inhabit grassy fields even when surrounded by trees, while Westerns prefer more open, treeless, drier landscapes with shorter vegetation or bare patches of soil. Knowledge of such fidelity to landscape pattern is a powerful tool for finding birds and for managing habitat. Bluebird trails provide a practical application of appropriate landscape design to maximize habitat for a desired species. A bluebird house may be usurped by Tree Swallows if near water, or by House Wrens if near shrubbery; and it may not be used by bluebirds if other bluebirds nest within 300 feet. Bluebirds will use the forest edge if near to open fields, but are deterred by too much forest or too much open country, and by traffic disturbance as well. Someday we may be able to maximize bird diversity by observing habitats more closely and dovetailing the various elements on the same property.

On the state as a whole, of course, this is already the case. The habitat diversity across Wisconsin, which accounts for its bird diversity, can be explained as the legacy of its geologic, climatic, and biological history. But before going into this history in detail, we need to look at two other factors that affect the distribution of birds: chance and the homing tradition. Accidents of history and of accessibility can establish or remove a population. An example is the Kirtland's Warbler, which breeds regularly only in central Michigan. We do not know whether the strays we see in similar jack pine scrub habitat in central Wisconsin are relics of a former breeding range or invaders that might someday establish a breeding population. We may guess that some historical events or factors, reinforced by tradition, caused the present situation.

As an example of possibly recent spreading of ranges where suitable habitat is accessible may be the Wolf River, where I heard songs from both Northern and Louisiana Waterthrushes at the same site one summer a decade ago. Perhaps this river forms a corridor of transition between the northern swamps and southern valley forest which, respectively, attract these species. Various blackbird species well illustrate how logging, farming, and urbanization can enable a species to extend its range and sometimes become a pest—but ironically, only because we have enabled their presence with our own changes to the environment.

The other factor, homing tradition, is equally easy to observe and understand. The strong tendency to return to the exact site where a bird was raised is the result of natural selection favoring conservatism in breeding sites. The best chance of success exists where success was enjoyed before; so in the long run those that return faithfully are more likely to pass on their homing traits than those who experiment with new sites. Occasionally this conservatism is an obstacle to maximum utilization of breeding habitat. For example, after a local family of breeding Red-headed Woodpeckers was shot in 1936 by a neighbor concerned about damage to a house, this species has failed to summer in my neighborhood for the ensuing 53 years, despite annual visitation by spring and fall migrants, including immature Redheads. My island of trees (University Heights in Madison) has provided suitable habitat—partly dead oaks—during all that time. The nearest occupied habitats (Hoyt Park, Eagle Heights, and the shores of Lake Wingra, all about a mile away) are evidently too far away for my island to be included in their concept of home. Perhaps, of course, there have never been enough young birds to overflow from the other sites during this period, so there has been no need to search farther away for new housing.

The years of frustration often experienced by people who erect Purple Martin houses in new areas to no avail provide another case which may strengthen the argument for the power of homing tradition. Again, however, the population might be suffering a decline or barely holding its own in numbers at present. One may speculate, at any rate, that the isolated breeding populations of Winter Wrens and various southern and northern warbler species in the forested Baraboo hills, which are isolated from the rest of their habitats by dozens or even hundreds of miles of open farmlands, could represent unbroken traditions of nesting spanning hundreds, perhaps thousands, of years—or even going back to preglacial times, since most of these hills escaped being covered by ice. Certainly of late we have experienced evidence of the strength of these traditions in the attempts of Sandhill Cranes to nest in marshes being drained or filled, and of Western and Eastern Meadowlarks to return to sites that had been farmland but were recently converted to housing developments.

Along this same line of argument are what might be called the fringe effects of corridors of heavy bird use, namely the spilling over of birds into marginal habitat when there seems to be a surplus of birds or a scarcity of habitat along a much-frequented corridor of migration or breeding. We see water birds utilize every inch of marsh on the Yahara River in Madison and on the upper Rock near Horicon Marsh, as well as in the vicinity of Green Bay. In the tiny 7-acre Nielsen Marsh by University Bay on the University of Wisconsin campus at Madison, many bird species of cattail and bulrush beds have bred or attempted to breed in those years since its creation in 1969, when water levels and vegetation were suitable. These species include the Black Tern, Yellow-headed Blackbird, Least Bittern, Common Moorhen, Sora, Virginia Rail, Pied-billed Grebe, Marsh Wren, and American Coot, along with the Mallard, Blue-winged Teal, and Wood Duck. It is of interest that in the 1950s successful experiments with foster-rearing in the nests of Robins and Redwings to reestablish a breeding tradition at University Bay did not result in restoration of nesting by Yellowheads in the adjacent main bay when its only available cattails and bulrushes were no longer in deep enough water to suit this species. It appears that for them the restoration needed was habitat rather than tradition!

Wisconsin's Environmental Setting

Despite the uncertainties created by accidents, tradition, and incomplete information, we can make a start toward relating the occurrence of birds to the forces that shaped Wisconsin's landscape and created its bird habitats. This can be done by thinking of our environment from several different perspectives, namely the interacting factors of geography, climate, topography, geology and soils, vegetation, and human land use. In each case, Wisconsin proves to be a varied landscape with a concomitant diversity of birds.

Geographic Location
Wisconsin is located in the heartland of North America, about midway between the frozen tundra and the tropical regions. Although lying over 1,000 miles from the Pacific Ocean and 900–1,000 from the Atlantic Ocean, Wisconsin is uniquely bordered by two different sorts of major waterways—the Mississippi River and the Great Lakes. These water frontages not only diversify its habitats but provide immigration corridors for both plant life and birdlife. By influencing the movements of migrants and strays, Lakes Michigan and Superior and the Mississippi and Wisconsin river corridors bring us sightings, and sometimes breeding popu-

lations, of species whose main ranges are to the west, south, north, or east. Some examples of strays are the American Avocet and the American White Pelican from the West, several herons and formerly the Swallow-tailed Kite from the South, and various scoters and eiders and once even a Dovekie from the Atlantic. Breeding birds whose ranges might be influenced by these corridors include southerners like the Bewick's Wren, Orchard Oriole, and Great Egret. It is tempting, at least, to see these birds following the Mississippi and Rock rivers northward and missing the Wisconsin River valley. In May I once observed a Great Egret circling over Madison and then heading northeast to Horicon—as if it had taken the "wrong" Yahara branch of the Rock River and chose to reset its bearings northeast to Horicon rather than course northwest over the short upland barrier to the Wisconsin River at Sauk City.

It is risky to make generalizations based on limited observations and circumstantial evidence. Certainly there are migratory routes that do not follow rivers or lake coasts. For example, in spring our Sandhill Cranes come northwest from Florida through northern Indiana, and our Tundra Swans fly almost due west from the Atlantic Coast before turning northwest toward the Yukon. According to Bellrose (1976), at least 10 species of ducks follow this pattern, too, rather than following the north-south Mississippi corridor. One may speculate that these water birds are following a tradition begun when the glacier occupied Canada and created an east-west chain of waters and wetlands along its southern borders; but it is also important to note that these more southern marshes are the first to open in spring, allowing the birds to fatten up in migratory habitat that would be unavailable were they to fly directly northward ahead of spring. Another unexpected circumstance is the likelihood that our breeding Yellow-headed Blackbirds and Dickcissels and perhaps some of our migrating White-crowned Sparrows come northeastward from the southern plains, while our Cape May and Connecticut Warblers seem to reach us—following the cranes—from wintering grounds in Florida and the Bahamas. In general, there is insufficient banding evidence to establish migration routes; and although many returns have been plotted, such as for American Robins, Mourning Doves, and Red-tailed Hawks, the results are confusing; recoveries from Wisconsin may be found anywhere from the Carolinas to Texas! In the species accounts, pertinent tidbits of banding recovery data have been included.

Perhaps more important than its water corridors is the fact that Wisconsin is located at the junction of three major vegetational provinces: the southeastern broad-leaved (deciduous, or hardwood) forests, the northern, or boreal (mostly coniferous, evergreen, needle-leaved, or softwood), forests; and the dry prairie grasslands, or plains, to the west. So it is of interest to see how their respective species—responding to the large-scale landscape features of habitat—spill over into Wisconsin from these different sides.

Of the more than 200 bird species that nest in Wisconsin every year (or nearly every year), 80 or so species range so far both east and west of our state that they are not readily attributed to any one of the three vegetational provinces. A glance at the range maps of any of the popular field guides shows that such species as the Mourning Dove, Eastern Kingbird, Barn Swallow, American Robin, Common Yellowthroat, and Red-winged Blackbird are continent-wide in summer distribution.

A second group of about 50 species is associated with the eastern broad-leaved forest region, in whose northwestern fringe we are located. The summer range of many of these species encompasses all of Wisconsin, as well as most of the northeastern United States. Included are some favorite woodland birds such as the Whip-poor-Will, Eastern Phoebe, Ovenbird, Scarlet Tanager, and Rose-breasted Grosbeak, and those drawn to wetland and meadow habitat found near woodlands, such as the Wood Duck, American Woodcock, Sedge Wren, and Swamp Sparrow.

Also related to the eastern forest region are a number of birds whose summer range reaches only partly into Wisconsin, and whose main range centers in the southeastern United States. These will be referred to as the *southern contingent* in later discussion in this chapter. Examples include such woodland species as the Red-bellied Woodpecker, Acadian Flycatcher, Blue-gray Gnatcatcher, Prothonotary and Kentucky Warblers, and such wetland habitués as the Great and Cattle Egrets, King Rail, and Common Moorhen. Representatives such as the Green-backed Heron, Turkey Vulture, Yellow-throated Vireo, and Northern Cardinal have expanded their northern range limits in recent years, and may become statewide in range before long. Others, including the Barn Owl, Carolina and Bewick's Wrens, Bell's Vireo, and Yellow-breasted Chat, have pulled back somewhat from formerly more northern range limits.

A third group consists of approximately 65 species whose breeding range is primarily north of our borders. In a few instances they actually nest sparingly across southern Wisconsin, for example, the Alder and Least Flycatchers, Nashville and Mourning Warblers, White-throated Sparrow, and Common Snipe. However, the majority of northerners are closely tied to the coniferous forests and associated lakes, rarely nesting south of the three northernmost tiers of counties in our state. Waterfowl in this group include the Common Loon and Red-breasted and Common Mergansers. In the evergreen forests and bogs one finds Gray Jays, Winter Wrens, Northern Goshawks, Northern Saw-whet Owls, Olive-sided and Yellow-bellied Flycatchers, Hermit and Swainson's Thrushes, Golden-crowned Kinglets, Lincoln's Sparrows, and several species of wood warblers, including the Yellow-rumped. These birds will be referred to as the *boreal contingent.*

Other species which we associate with the north country today actually range far south or east or west of Wisconsin as well. They need undisturbed waters and/or large forests with big trees to nest, feed, or display on. Examples are the Pileated Woodpecker, Osprey, Bald Eagle, and Ruffed Grouse. Along with these the Common Raven has been pushing southward as more forests mature in the southern counties, beginning with river corridors like the Black, Wisconsin, and Mississippi.

A fourth group of about 20 species nests primarily west and north of Wisconsin. Several of these inhabit open wetlands, for example, the Red-necked Grebe, Northern Shoveler, Ruddy Duck, Wilson's Phalarope, Forster's and Black Terns, and Yellow-headed Blackbird. Those that are attracted to open fields, low shrubs, or saplings and are similarly scattered over much of Wisconsin, but only in suitable habitat, are the Western Meadowlark, Brewer's Blackbird, and Clay-colored Sparrow. More restricted to the western portion of the state are the Western Kingbird, Dickcissel, and Lark Sparrow. These birds form the *prairie contingent.* Undoubtedly this group was larger in presettlement days, when Long-billed Curlews roamed the virgin prairies, and when the Upland Sandpipers, Sharp-tailed Grouse, and Greater Prairie-Chickens were far more numerous than they are today.

Climate

Wisconsin enjoys a true four-season climate, with cold winters, warm summers, and cool springs and falls. Since air masses moving eastward off the plains dominate the weather, our region has midcontinental extremes and irregularity, and tends to be on the dry side. Arctic air brings the worst wintry blasts, and when colliding with warmer subtropical air masses from the Gulf of Mexico, causes most of our precipitation. The Caribbean maritime air is responsible for our warm sultry summers. Precipitation varies little across the state (about 33 inches annually) and generally supports lush vegetation during the summer months. However, with cooler temperatures prevailing, northeastern Wisconsin tends to have the steadier, moister climate of the more maritime eastern forest regions, favoring continuous forest; but the stabilizing effect of Lake Michigan gives it a longer and milder autumn. An interesting illustration of the way climatic factors limit a bird's distribution is provided by the Northern Bobwhite (in the southern contingent). In the north, there is plenty of vegetation for roost cover, but deep snow hides seeds which these birds need for winter food. In our southern counties, intensive agriculture leaves too little cover for the birds to endure winter despite plenty of weed seeds and grain to eat. In central Wisconsin, with some of the harshest and most variable weather, quail survive because farming is less intensive, leaving an abundance of both fencerow cover and waste foods to eat. The farming there is low-key because of a combination of poor soils and unfavorable climatic factors, explained in more detail later.

The first and most drastic general climatic influence is, of course, seasonal change. Summer provides good nesting habitat for many species of birds, whereas the severity of winter makes migration routine for most species. Wisconsin's winter birdlife is but a trace of its summer abundance and variety. The capricious, changeable weather in fall and spring makes migration variable and interesting for the observer. Frequent but irregular warm and cold fronts provide many opportunities for lift and tail winds. Despite this variability in the numbers of migrating birds and their locations, however, migration is surprisingly punctual year after year, on account of the solar clock by which birds schedule their lives.

The second general influence of climate—on vegetation—may be thought of as a "rainbow" of gradually varying conditions. This rainbow is formed by Wisconsin's gradients of moisture conditions from west to east and of temperature from north to south. These two gradients explain the proximity to Wisconsin of boreal vegetation and its birds and of the grasslands with prairie-plains species to the west. Superimposed on these gradients, local topographic peculiarities act like many islands of a different "color"—combinations of climatic factors beyond the main geographic reach of such weather. They explain in large part how Wisconsin can attract birds beyond their main geographic province. Figure 1 suggests some general differences among regions of Wisconsin, each with its special local influences modifying the general climate. Let's look at the gradual rainbow effect first, and then take up the local exceptions under topography.

The effect of climate on evergreen trees illustrates how environmental factors reinforce each other. Evergreens risk drying out in winter when they can't replenish water lost from their leaves. As noted above, some consequences of the generally lower temperatures in the north (Figs. 2 and 3) make precipitation more effective there: (1) lower evaporation rates, enhanced by the forest cover, conserve soil moisture by favoring total penetration and soil storage; (2) more of

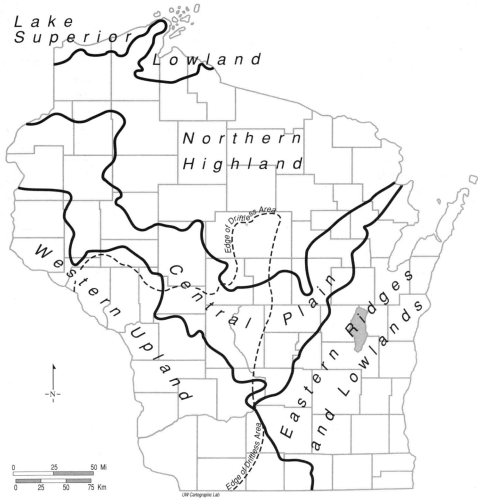

Figure 1. The five major geographical provinces of Wisconsin: Lake Superior Lowland, Northern Highland, Central Plain, Western Upland, and Eastern Ridges and Lowlands. Also, enclosed by the dashed line is the unglaciated area, or Driftless Area. (After Martin 1965, p. 33.)

the precipitation falls as snow, again favoring gradual (effective) penetration and less loss to the air from the blanketed ground and from snow-covered evergreen leaves; and (3) since the northern snow cover tends to precede cold weather, the soil frost may be minimal and actually go less deep than it does farther south (Fig. 4). As a result, trees, especially the evergreen conifers, are favored, since they can pump water in warm or windy spells and even carry on photosynthesis during the cool seasons.

Central Wisconsin is an exception to this rule—proving it not to be infallible! The Central Plain has our most severe climate, with deep soil frost, summer frosts from cold air settling at night, and hot dry spells accentuated by the drouthy sandy soil. This region distorts the rainbow because it is hostile to most kinds of vegetation. However, that circumstance allows two rugged species to dominate—the jack pine, a cousin of the lodgepole pine of dry western mountains, and the scrub oak, a cousin of the tolerant black oak of southern sand barrens. These trees specialize in water conservation and the capacity to regrow or reseed after fire and frost damage.

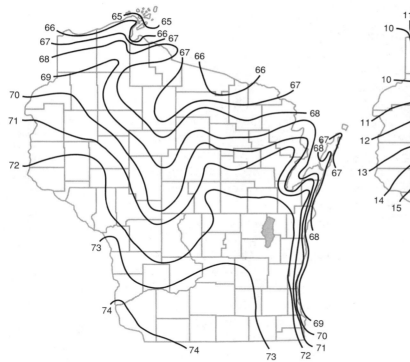

Figure 2. Average July air temperatures (°F), 1931–1960. August exhibits a similar pattern. (After "Wisconsin Weather," Wis. Stat. Rep. Serv., Madison, Aug. 1967.)

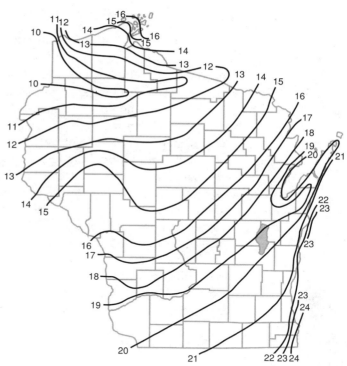

Figure 3. Average January air temperatures (°F), 1931–1960. February exhibits a similar pattern. (After "Wisconsin Weather," Wis. Stat. Rep. Serv., Madison, Aug. 1967.)

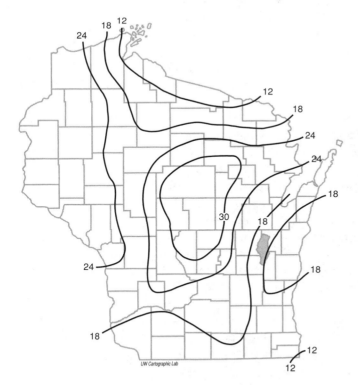

Figure 4. Average depth of soil frost (inches below surface) in late February, 1961–1968. (After "Snow and Frost in Wisconsin," Wis. Stat. Rep. Serv., Madison, June 1970.)

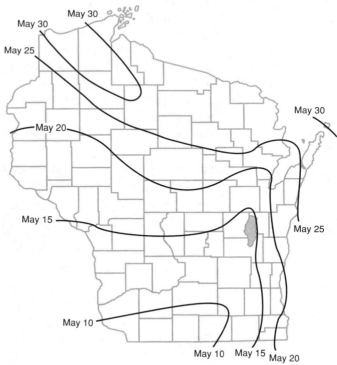

Figure 5. Progress of spring across Wisconsin, exemplified by average dates of first flowering of purple common lilac, 1961–1968. Lilacs usually bloom after the last frost. (After "Manual for observers," Wis. Phenological Soc., Madison, 1977.)

Wisconsin temperatures do not follow the same patterns in winter as in summer (compare Figures 2 and 3). As a result, not all plants follow the same distribution trends. White oak and hemlock seem to be as sensitive to western Wisconsin's winter drought and cold as to the gradient of summer warmth which governs a large share of the vegetation in our state. Probably the most important reason for tree sensitivity in our prairie-forest border region is the irregularity of our continental climate. Not only do we have prolonged dry spells once in a while, but also sudden changes in weather that stress vegetation, especially trees. An example of what can happen was experienced in 1984 in Jefferson County. An unusually early November snow prevented soil frost, and an unusually warm January thaw started trees growing. Then a return of very cold weather in February froze the soil deeply and killed the swelling buds. Since some century-old white oaks were severely damaged, we know that these events are rare; yet it takes only one "killer" season to eliminate a species for a long time. Thus, it is possible for rare events to control the distribution of a forest species and in turn the birds dependent on it, such as Wood Ducks feeding on acorns or Black-throated Green Warblers nesting in hemlocks.

The gradients of summer heat and of the length of the growing season (Figs. 2 and 5) seem to coincide. One or both of them seem to determine the border between Wisconsin's two major regions of presettlement vegetation (see Figure 8). In southwestern Wisconsin was the province of fire-swept prairies with scattered oak groves and savannas (widely spaced trees). In the northeast was the province of more-or-less continuous, cool, damp conifer-hardwood forest. The rather sharp line demarking these regions is testimony to the effect of vegetation reinforcing its own environment: forests hold moisture and shade out grasses, while grasses favor fires and exclude fungi needed by trees. Some soil effects (seen later) also reinforce this boundary.

The prairie and oak region is a blend of species of plants and birds of both the plains and the eastern forest, while the conifer-hardwood forest region is a blend of the two eastern forest types—conifers to the north and deciduous trees to the south. This mixed forest extends eastward around the Great Lakes to New England and southward in the Allegheny and Appalachian mountains.

The respective birdlife of these two major Wisconsin vegetation regions—prairie groves and mixed forest—still differs in flavor despite the fact that civilization for 150 years has made these regions more uniform and less distinct with regard to vegetation and openness of the landscape (Fig. 6). Since life-forms are important to birds, the fact that all of our native conifer trees, except the red cedar, are generally confined to the northeastern region may be the most important reason for the difference in birdlife in the two regions. Whereas the southern contingent includes fewer than half of our eastern broad-leaved forest birds, the northern contingent (mostly of conifer forest) accounts for nearly all of our birds that range north of Wisconsin.

The northward migration of songbirds appears to accelerate as the season advances, so that it outstrips the seasonal warming. By May, at least, migration across the state is relatively rapid, while the northward progression of spring (averaged in Figure 5) can be rather slow in some years. Therefore, when spring starts early in the southern counties of Wisconsin, tree leafing may get underway there before the arrival of the later-migrating bird species, whereas leafing of the northern forests is less likely to be ahead of the birds and may be only in the budding stage when most of the warblers arrive. This situation makes spring

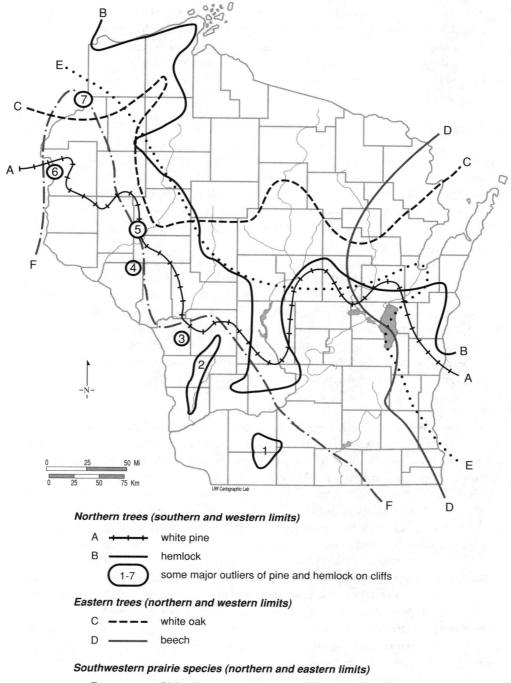

Northern trees (southern and western limits)

    A ┝━┿━┿━┥   white pine

    B ━━━━━   hemlock

    (1-7)   some major outliers of pine and hemlock on cliffs

Eastern trees (northern and western limits)

    C ━ ━ ━ ━   white oak

    D ━━━━━   beech

Southwestern prairie species (northern and eastern limits)

    E • • • • •   Bicknell's sedge – typically present on most prairies

Sphagnum bog species (southwestern limit)

    F ━ · ━ · ━   pitcher plant – a typical species found in most bogs

Figure 6. Some generalized plant ranges in Wisconsin, excluding most small outlying relic populations. (Plant ranges estimated by author from various sources.)

birds of the forest easier to observe in the north, especially in Door County, than they are in Milwaukee or Madison or even Green Bay. This anomaly doesn't seem to hurt the birds, and in fact it may place the peak of insect abundance (when leafing is just completed) right at the onset of nesting, when it is most needed. However, the short northern summer may place a premium on the first nesting attempt.

Topography

Wisconsin may be thought of as a gentle dome, with a total range of elevation of only about 1,000 feet. Except for the deeply dissected valley, or coulee, region of southwestern Wisconsin, the topography is gently rolling to almost flat. Figure 7 shows the state in low relief as it might appear if viewed with a telescope from the moon at sunrise or sunset so the shadows would highlight the small local differences in elevation of up to 400 feet. (Compare Figures 1 and 7 to see why each region is so named.)

In spite of Wisconsin's generally flat nature, the fine details of topography are as important to bird habitat as is general climate, especially in assuring a diversity of species in each local region. Certain outstanding local topographic features deserve attention: water features, water-associated uplands, sharp topography, and patterned landscapes. While attracting people by offering aesthetic and recreational opportunities, such places do discourage intensive agriculture, to the birds' benefit. At the end of this section we shall look briefly at microclimates as they contribute to the diversity of birdlife.

Water Features

We are blessed with an unusual abundance of glacial lakes and wetlands. Coasts, shores, and rivers trending north-south may aid migrants in navigation, as noted above, since some flyways do seem to follow them. The rugged river coulee country of southwestern Wisconsin (Figs. 1 and 7) may appeal to birds of the southern contingent because it resembles the unglaciated terrain of states farther south and harbors southern vegetation that may look familiar. Valleys provide a steadier, moister, milder climate because of air mixing as well as open water, possibly favoring plants and animals sensitive to harsh weather.

The humidity and available water of lowlands in general may be an important attractant for many upland travelers, as well as for wetland species. The wooded shores of Madison's lakes, for example, concentrate spring warblers and other forest birds to densities not often encountered away from lakes and rivers. Water is essential for drinking, bathing, and enhancing the availability of invertebrate foods, even in trees and the air. In this regard, water may be equally important during the nesting season, as we see next.

Water-associated Uplands

The surprising density and variety of birds nesting close to, but not on, the water is beginning to be appreciated. Water birds, of course, are mostly found near shores, where the various types of wetland occur. In addition, while censusing upland birds (in 1982–1985) I began to notice what I believe to be a definite fringe effect of larger water bodies. In western Jefferson County, one lakeshore property of only 3 acres of brushy abandoned pasture with oak savanna had 34 resident species of upland birds in summer and a density of up to 18 singing males, nests, or pairs per acre; that is over three times the density usually

Figure 7. Landforms (relief) of Wisconsin. Notice especially the steep, deeply dissected terrain of the Mississippi drainage in southwestern Wisconsin; the outline of the Green Bay lobe of the Wisconsin glacier (see Figure 12); and the Central Plain (Glacial Lake Wisconsin) with its modern agricultural ditches. The diversity of landscape in different segments of the Wisconsin River valley is typical of the state. (Map by D. A. Woodward, U.S. Geol. and Nat. Hist. Surv. and Univ. Wis. Ext., Madison, 1971.)

reported away from water even for this generally rich avian habitat. The same habitat only a mile away had the usual average of one or slightly more than one pair or nest per acre despite the diversity created by a small pond and bog nearby. In northern Door County, one of the boreal forest relics sported over 40 species of upland birds at a density of over 140 pairs or nests along a mile of Lake Michigan shoreline (in 61 acres, or over two pairs or nests per acre). The same forest of spruce, pine, birch, fir, and white cedar only 500 feet farther inland had barely one pair per several acres.

The reasons for these differences are not fully clear. Some possibilities in these particular cases are: a total absence of pesticides in these nonagricultural sites; the availability of larger areas of each kind of habitat nearby; the greater fertility of waters (as compared with land), which may nourish nearby plants; the low-key land use (in preserves and large or undeveloped recreation properties); and the attractiveness of water to birds for drinking and bathing. In addition, the open edge may provide a permanent diversity of landscape structure and foliage heights. This permanence, allowing traditions of nesting to build up, could favor a large and diverse breeding population. Furthermore, higher humidity near open water may favor lush plant growth and better insect survival. Perhaps most important of all is the added food supply provided by the abundance of small flying insects from a relatively large body of water. The density and diversity of spiders near such shores are very much higher than elsewhere; spiders may be a means of translating the swarms of very small midges, mayflies, and microlepidoptera into morsels large enough for birds. Also, Cedar Waxwings, Eastern Kingbirds, and other birds may take directly the larger lake insects including some mayflies, caddis flies, and damsel flies.

Rivers, too, may be expected to have such richness. An incomplete June sample taken while I was escorting a class by canoe through the Kickapoo Dells below Ontario (Vernon County) in 1972 yielded a minimum count of 60 species of birds—mostly upland songbirds—and at least 300 singing males or pairs on a stretch of less than 10 river miles. This high density is due only in part to high numbers in species which like to be near water, for example, the American Redstart, Song Sparrow, and several swallows.

Sharp Topography

Escarpments, bluffs, dells, cliffs, buttes, high moraines and dunes, and monadnocks (isolated remnants of mountains) also create special habitats. Directly they provide important special and secluded nesting sites, such as eyries for falcons, ravens, and vultures, and nooks or dens for swallows, phoebes, and kingfishers. The dolomite cliffs in Door County, sandstone cliffs in the Apostle Islands and at the Wisconsin Dells, and cliffs of igneous rock on the St. Croix River are all important examples. Secondly, the isolating effect of islands in rivers, lakes, and wetlands has long been known to favor breeding sites for "touchy" species such as herons (which nest, for example, in the Horicon Marsh in Dodge County and on the Wisconsin and Mississippi rivers), Bald Eagles and Ospreys in the northern forests and lakes, and Common Terns and Double-crested Cormorants on the Great Lakes islands. The value of combinations of inaccessible vertical faces and isolation of the forested tops of the sandstone buttes in west-central Wisconsin remains to be assessed.

Sharp topography also creates a very important migration effect, especially along bodies of water, sometimes enhanced by peninsulas such as Bayfield and

Door. Local atmospheric circulation at these places facilitates concentrated migration, providing for easy and sometimes spectacular observations. One of the causes of these concentrations is the presence of thermals (updrafts of warm air), favoring the soaring of hawks, gulls, and cranes and giving lift for the migration of many other species. The high bluffs of the Wisconsin, St. Croix, and Mississippi rivers and of the Baraboo hills are outstanding in this regard. Another cause is the lack of these thermals over large, open bodies of water, making them areas which migrants try to avoid. In autumn, hawks, nighthawks, and other migrating birds sail southward from thermal to thermal. The prevailing westerly winds associated with cold fronts, which spur the birds' departure, tend to cause these lines of thermals (visible because they are topped by cumulus clouds) to drift eastward or southeastward across the Midwest, taking the birds along. Whenever the soaring migrants are carried toward a coast, the birds accumulate. Thus, we find good hawk-watching and banding stations at Duluth-Superior, Green Bay, and the Cedar Grove Ornithological Station in Sheboygan County.

Actual elevation has only minor effects on vegetation and birds in Wisconsin, since we lack mountains. The tops of Blue Mounds, Rib Mountain, Baraboo Bluffs, major glacial moraines, and the drumlin hills in the northern forest may receive significantly higher precipitation, but the occurrence of forest caps is probably due more to soil effects (see Geology and Soils section). In contrast, the bluffs of the Mississippi and lower Wisconsin rivers and associated dolomite-capped hills tend to be open on top (supporting prairie grassland), despite fertile soils, because of exposure to wind and sun in the large, open valley. Steep rapid streams and waterfalls are absent from southeastern Wisconsin, but in the southwestern coulees their presence favors Louisiana Waterthrushes. In the north, where such streams and falls are the most abundant, we have no birds specifically attracted to moving water.

The isolated 17-square-mile Baraboo Range in Sauk County deserves special mention as an outstanding example of topographic influence on birdlife. First, it is a rugged series of hills (an ancient monadnock) of hard rock (quartzite) which was deeply cut to a relief of up to 400 feet by a long series of unusual geological events. Many wooded valleys were formed which retain open steep rock slopes and faces, of which those at Devil's Lake are the most spectacular. Resistant rock has prevented millennia of erosion from dulling the diversity of landscape. The only way the rock can weather is by occasional splitting from the strain of temperature differences. Below each bluff lies a huge pile of rubble (some pieces as big as houses) which forms extensive loose talus slopes of open or only partly vegetated rock. From within the talus, cold air issues below in summer to provide boreal environments, while at the cliff tops hot rising air keeps oaks from invading the prairie relics and molds the pines into picturesque flag shapes.

The open slopes favor pines, in which occasional lightning-set fires stimulate replacement of these sun-loving trees. Thin soils perpetuate prairie savanna and unusual dwarf hickory forest on at least one blufftop, while other tops form large expanses of normal oak forest. North-facing talus and some valleys harbor acid-loving hemlock and pine forests, while more fertile valleys protect old sugar maple and even floodplain forests. Valleys contain bubbling, bouldery "New England" streams—unusual for southern Wisconsin. This perpetuated diversity is extensive enough to harbor viable relic populations of many bird species beyond their main ranges today.

Rugged topography and often thin soils have discouraged intensive agricultural use, and early recognition of the scenic, geological, and recreational value of Devil's Lake made it one of Wisconsin's first state parks, thereby discouraging further cottage and quarry intrusions. In recent years many dedicated people, including members of the Wisconsin Society for Ornithology and The Nature Conservancy, have worked to protect more and more of the Baraboo Range as a preserve for wildlife and rare vegetation. This range is located centrally in Wisconsin's climatic and vegetation gradient, and is on the Wisconsin River corridor of species spread and migration. Small wonder, then, that it boasts over 600 species of flowering plants and 12 of the southern contingent and 10 of the boreal contingent of birds as part of its total breeding-bird list of some 100 species (Mossman and Lange 1982). Of special note are the Broad-winged Hawk, Pileated Woodpecker, Ruffed Grouse, Winter Wren, Turkey Vulture, and many warblers. Peregrine Falcons nested at Devil's Lake until 1948.

Except for those in the Baraboo hills, the relics of pine and hemlock on north-facing bluffs and talus slopes, although numerous in southwestern Wisconsin (see Figure 6 for a few), are often too small and isolated to harbor many northern birds. However, it must be noted that no systematic bird census has been conducted on any of our scores of rivers, north or south. Some remarkable wildernesses await exploration by the modern voyager with canoe and binoculars—from the Bois Brule to the Sugar, and the Chippewa and Black to the Root and "Little" Fox, and even the streams of the Door Peninsula.

Patterned Landscapes

Landscape patterns (with repeat designs) are especially important in maintaining many species requiring different habitats and, in conjunction with territoriality, enabling birds of the same species to occur in extensive populations without crowding. Birds have very keen vision and can see color. They can recognize landscape elements from the air: hills, valleys, plains, hollows, cliffs, shores, marshes, water, trees, shrubs, grassy expanses. Apparently, too, they can remember specific parts of a repeat design, enabling their faithful return. For our purpose here, then, topography is defined as including gross vegetation as well as waters and variations in altitude of rock and soil. The hills of the Baraboo Range have a unique repeat design. Some other repeat patterns are coulees, drumlins, potholes, plains, beach ridges, and peatlands.

Coulee Country. The scenic, deeply dissected, and presumably unglaciated high land in southwestern Wisconsin, extending from Dane and Sauk counties westward and from Pepin and Monroe counties southward, creates a repetition of many deep valleys cut into dolomite and sandstone. In each valley are zones of sedge meadow and floodplain forest along the streams, sugar maple forest on lower slopes, oak on upper slopes, virgin dry prairie on the ridges and sunny ledges, and conifers on steep faces.

For a long time, low-key farming in this rugged terrain maintained diverse birdlife, because lowland corn-growing took only part of the floodplain, pastures took only part of the floodplains and slopes, and corn and alfalfa fields on the ridges took only the deeper soils. Recent demand for more firewood and corn has degraded all these zones, causing forest losses, more soil erosion, and decreased quality of wetlands and waters. Near the Mississippi River, the Rush Creek preserve in Crawford County has been restoring its vegetation to original conditions; the Wyalusing State Park in Grant County maintains the original condition of its land. Birdlife has prospered with recent federal ownership of the

Kickapoo Valley north from La Farge (Vernon County), and with private efforts at Eagle Valley (Grant County).

Fields of Drumlins and Latticed Lowlands. Toward the edges of each glacial lobe (see Figure 12), and especially of the large Green Bay lobe between Horicon, Waukesha, and Madison, the thinning ice built hundreds of drumlins—elongate, streamlined hills. Shaped like an inverted teaspoon and up to a mile long, these deposits all trended in the same direction and blocked the drainage between. The flat matrix between the drumlins was originally covered with peaty sedge meadows and tamarack swamps, connecting like a lattice and fed by seeping groundwater stored between rainfalls in the drumlins. With settlement, these gravelly steep hills, seldom plowable, went to forest, which now accentuates their height. Today, the extensively but imperfectly drained lowland is partly cropped, partly pastured, and partly unused but altered meadows with weeds and shrubs. Thus, these lowlands remain treeless and still support large populations of meadow mice. As a consequence of the interspersion of wooded slopes for nests and good feeding habitat, this region supports an excellent breeding population of Red-tailed Hawks (one pair per 1½ square miles) and Great Horned Owls (one pair per 3 square miles), according to a recent Wisconsin Department of Natural Resources study (Petersen 1979). These densities are as great as, if not greater than, those in the coulee country, and they may be among the continent's highest for these raptors. A typical example, the Goose Lake Wildlife Area in Dane County, is largely in the presettlement condition, supporting Sandhill Cranes and several species of raptors among 12 drumlins and diverse wetlands in 3 square miles.

Prairie Pothole Country. Potholes (technically kettles) mark much of Wisconsin's rolling glaciated landscape, and they form three types of repeating habitat that greatly diversify the terrain. One type is open grassland with small marshes and ponds—prairie pothole country. Our relatively few places resembling the major duck breeding region of the Dakotas and the prairie provinces of Canada are located mostly in southeastern central Wisconsin (Dane, Rock, Jefferson, and Columbia counties) and in the northwestern counties (Burnett, Polk, and St. Croix). They harbor most of our prairie contingent of breeding bird species.

Presettlement fires and now farming have kept the forest down to a very few woodlots in these regions. While many of the pothole wetlands are drained or polluted with silt, a few excellent small, wet marshes attractive to many waterfowl persist, and some are being restored. Their advantages over large wetlands like Horicon Marsh include their diversity of size and depth. Furthermore, the separation prevents competition by territorial pairs of birds, the surrounding forage fields are suitable for upland nesting such as by Blue-winged Teal and Mallards, and the isolation prevents the spread of disease. Examples of prairie potholes are the Harvey's Marsh complex in Dane County, Grassy Lake, Mud Lake, and Goose Pond, all in Columbia County, and of course the Crex Meadows State Wildlife Area in Burnett County. The latter, isolated from farming and kept open with fires, also has a large diversity of herons, raptors, and upland prairie birds.

Northern Lake Districts. The second kettle terrain includes the abundant lakes and bogs in the central and western sectors of northern Wisconsin (and parts of Minnesota and Michigan). The larger kettles have open lakes with boggy bays, supporting Common Loons, Ospreys, Bald Eagles, and Common and Red-breasted Mergansers. The lakeshores, often protected from fires and logging by the early wealthy lodge owners and now often dotted with many small cottages, maintain our largest pines and other forest trees, favoring raptors' nests, but only when not disturbed. Some undeveloped lakes in the state and national forests, by virtue of their remoteness, favor these birds. Small kettles have mossy floating "cat's eye" bogs with Olive-sided Flycatchers, Lincoln's Sparrows, Palm and Nashville Warblers, and other distinctive wetland species of the boreal contingent. (A cat's eye is a small area of open water at the center of a floating bog that hasn't quite closed over a small lake.) Among the smallest kettles, the dry ones ("sags") have no trees because of summer frost injury; they form openings in otherwise dense forests, as do the sedgy wet kettles. Dry and wet kettles may favor some forest-edge birds, but they have not been studied as such. Most of the streams crossing the northern counties run from kettle to kettle and have similar birds to those of the lakes, marshes, and bogs, to the delight of anyone who "birds" from the canoe.

Southern Tamarack Swamps. The third kettle district accounts for most of our tamarack swamps in southeastern Wisconsin, persisting in today's warmer climate on cold bog and fen peats in frost pockets, especially in the kettle moraine near Waukesha and from there distributed westward and southward. A recent attempt to census breeding birds in these tamarack swamps (J. E. Bielefeldt in DNR Endangered Resources files) has revealed that only a few of the northern bog species use them (the White-throated Sparrow, Nashville and Canada Warblers, Northern Waterthrush, Veery), that many birds of the deciduous forest edge use them (the Rufous-sided Towhee, Indigo Bunting, American Robin, House Wren) and that they may be important for certain raptors (the Sharp-shinned Hawk, Long-eared Owl, Great Horned Owl, and possibly the Northern Saw-whet Owl). More census work is needed in these highly inaccessible swamps replete with poison sumac!

The larger southeastern Wisconsin kettles have lakes, now heavily populated with cottages, but certain quaky shores that have discouraged agriculture near them keep some portions in natural peatland vegetation. The abundance of springs in and near the kettle moraine offers hope of some habitat restoration because of the steady source of clean water. Some of this land is quite wild, and it is protected in the Kettle Moraine State Forest and several associated smaller wildlife areas tucked among the high gravel hills.

Plains. Large plains, especially Wisconsin's Central Plain (an old glacial lake bed), consist of a checkerboard of low dunes and a network of small sluggish waterways, producing a seemingly endless alternation of dry and wet habitats. They supported a presettlement interspersion of open wiregrass meadows, mossy bogs, and tamarack swamps, with grassy prairies and pine islands on the dunes. After logging, drainage, and peat fires, the abandoned lowland sectors are now mostly covered with aspen, but some nonintensive agricultural operations maintain the treeless skyline attractive today to Greater Prairie-Chickens and other plains species.

Where the wetlands persist or are restored, Common Snipe, Northern Harriers, Short-eared Owls, and Sandhill Cranes nest along with the upland birds of open prairies—Horned Larks, Eastern and Western Meadowlarks, Bobolinks, Upland Sandpipers, Sedge Wrens, and Lark Sparrows. Along the drier edges of the central glacial lake bed, extensive scrub oak and jack pine barrens used to be and still are the rule because of the dry sandy soil and the ease with which fires sweep level areas. These barrens resemble the northern forest from the point of view of Northern Ravens, Hermit Thrushes, and Nashville Warblers, which represent the boreal contingent inhabiting areas adjacent to the hot, dry prairies. Examples of the wetter landscapes in this Wisconsin sand plain have been restored in several places such as the Sandhill and Meadow Valley State Wildlife areas in Wood County, whereas the soggy Summerton Bog preserve in Marquette County may maintain its original state.

Beach Ridges. Former higher levels of Lake Michigan created another sort of patterned sand plain. The many very low ridges in the treeless expanse of Chiwaukee Prairie and Carol Beach south of Kenosha vastly diversify the plant life. Efforts to justify its preservation have been largely based on its rare plants. However, the subtle repeat pattern of wet to dry habitats deserves consideration in regard to birds of the prairie contingent, including such interesting species as the Upland Sandpiper, Brewer's Blackbird, and several rails. In Door County, likewise, rare plants have received the bulk of attention at sanctuaries occupying ridge complexes at Bailey's Harbor and Jackson Harbor. The very large boreal contingent of birdlife in these coniferous landscapes may likewise depend in part on the diversity of habitats maintained by the series of many rather high sand ridges (up to 6 feet) separated by swales which interrupt the pine, spruce, and white cedar forest with open dunes, ponds, bogs, and shrubby tangles. Unfortunately, as at Chiwaukee, some of the best bird habitat toward shore is in great demand for intensive real estate development.

Patterned Peatlands. We lost our largest peatlands to fires accompanying early attempts to farm our Central Plain and Horicon Marsh. However, certain other large expanses of peat are now receiving ornithological as well as botanical attention, for they are unique landscapes created by the peat itself as it builds up irregularly or slips down gentle slopes. Called string bogs, they consist of repeated forested islands and strands in a gradually creeping matrix of peat thrown into regularly spaced wrinkles at right angles to the direction of flow. The ridges are forested, and the swales are composed of wet, open, mossy bogs and sedge fens. Some major United States string bog regions occur in northwestern Minnesota and parts of the Upper Peninsula of Michigan; but we have almost 1 square mile of string bog in Ozaukee County at the University of Wisconsin–Milwaukee Field Station and Scientific Area near Saukville. Bird studies there are revealing a good diversity of northern species as well as general wetland birds.

Microclimates

Major topographic features can modify the climate locally, producing microclimates. Most important are large bodies of water that are slow to warm or freeze. Water exerts a stabilizing effect on the extremes of heat and cold, while keeping the humidity more even, if not actually higher. The southward dipping of northern forest with its birds along Lake Michigan (Fig. 8) is a conspicuous example of the cooler summer effect along even the west shore of this lake, despite prevailing offshore winds. A corresponding reverse effect is noted on the east shore in Michigan, where highbush blueberry and cherry and peach orchards take advantage of the milder climate there, as do certain southern trees. The cool summer is apparently less important than the combination of cooler springs and milder falls, for the problem for tender plants in the north is frost damage. In such places, leafing is retarded, lowering the risk of spring setback, while autumn is prolonged, enabling buds to become winterized before freezing. We see this same effect in Door County on the Green Bay side where most of our cherry and apple orchards are located.

However, on the Lake Michigan side of Door County a peculiarity of water circulation makes for very cold summers in several bays facing south, enabling our best examples of boreal forest to persist. (Most of our upland spruce-fir forests, near Lake Superior, succumbed a century ago to logging and devastating fires.) When winds from the south or southwest bring our hottest summer weather, the lake's water twists clockwise as it is carried northward. It veers off at the surface toward the Michigan shore, because its greater eastward momentum is maintained as it moves northward into latitudes where the earth has a shorter turning radius. This eastbound drift of warm surface water causes upwelling of very cold deep water off our coast, over which the hot winds must pass and are cooled as they drive the cold water and fog into the south-facing bays of Door County and the shore down to Sheboygan. These boreal microclimates, of which the most extensive is at Bailey's Harbor, present to the eye of bird and bird-watcher alike an Alaskan scene of somber spires of white spruce and balsam fir. The birdlife here has as large a boreal contingent as that of our other main boreal environment, the large black spruce and tamarack swamps, such as those near Three Lakes in Oneida County.

The effect of open water in creating habitat also gives us our wintering waterfowl, such as geese in the giant Turtle Creek springs of Rock County, the Oldsquaws and scoters near Milwaukee on Lake Michigan, and the wintering Bald Eagles on the lower Wisconsin and Mississippi rivers.

A second major microclimatic influence on the landscape is the result of the aspect (direction of exposure) of steep slopes and the effect of the slopes themselves. Throughout southwestern Wisconsin, the cool, damp, northeastern exposures favor pine, yellow birch, and hemlock on poor soil and fire-free sugar maple forest on fertile soil. The hot, dry, southwestern exposures, with the aid of recurrent fires, maintain prairies, red cedars, or oaks, seen throughout southwestern Wisconsin. In addition, we have some valley effects. In two places the settling of cold night air is thwarted, which gives plant life of more southern affinities a chance: near open flowing water in winter, and on midslopes where air circulates and enables spring to come early without setback. Thus, the overlapping of the southern contingent, such as Red-bellied Woodpeckers and Red-shouldered Hawks, with the boreal contingent, such as Yellow-bellied Sapsuckers and Brown Creepers, up and down the Wisconsin and Mississippi river corridors may reflect a continuity of their respective favorable microclimates and associated vegetation.

A final type of microclimate that diversifies the landscape is the containment of settling cold night air in basins called frost pockets. These include the open sedgey or grassy "sags" of northwestern Wisconsin (and some forest clearings that have become "sod-bound"), the kettle bogs of southeastern Wisconsin, and the low Central Plain. This plain, whose recurrent frosts even the cranberry growers must battle, retains large wild habitats now protected in part as wildlife areas and state forests. An example of the result is the enduring raven population in the Black River State Forest in Jackson County.

Vegetation
With over 2,000 species of seed plants and ferns, including nearly 200 kinds of trees and shrubs, our flora is relatively diverse for our latitude. This floral

richness is due to the combination of diverse topography, waterway migration corridors on both sides and up the middle, the glacial legacy, and the nearness to three different vegetation regions—boreal coniferous forest, eastern broad-leaved forest, and the prairies of the western plains. We take up vegetation before considering soils in order to introduce concepts which will be useful in translating geologic influences into environments for birds. We need to see how plants accommodate themselves to the environment. The interactions occur on three scales—the plant community, the successional stage, and the regional vegetation zone or province.

Plant Communities

Green plants are highly competitive for a place in the sun, since they all must get their light, as well as minerals and water, in the same way in the same places, in contrast to the diverse feeding specializations available to mobile animals, especially birds. The vegetation at a given point results from the playing of two games: "musical chairs" and "king-of-the-hill." A bare unvegetated site is soon invaded by those plant species that can get there (seed availability), can grow there (adaptation to the climate and site), and can compete successfully. The winners are those that have the earliest start, can grow fastest, can outlast the others, or can alter the site in their favor. Once established, the winners can keep out all other plants until the next disturbance devegetates the site and gives all species a chance anew. Among the winners, the site is shared by avoidance of competition. Just as the Red-eyed Vireo shares the same woods with the Ovenbird by one feeding high and the other low, so the plant associates of a forest share the space, materials, and energy by getting them in different vertical zones or at different times during the year.

Thus, vegetation consists of winning combinations of "bedfellow" plants called associations or plant communities. These communities are quite distinct botanically; but birds, in choosing habitat, probably recognize them not as vegetation types but as landscape features. For example, most deciduous-forest birds such as vireos and orioles occur throughout the dry (oak), mesic (neither wet nor dry, e.g., sugar maple), and damp (floodplain swamp) types of broad-leaved forest. A few, however, seem to recognize and prefer only one of these: Ovenbirds avoid brushy forest, perhaps requiring a clean view and flight lane for their twilight sky-dance, placing most of them in sugar maple forest whose dense shade eliminates shrubs. However, the Madison School Forest at Verona, with damp tangles that attract the Veery, also has Ovenbirds on dry slopes where poor soil discourages the usual shrubs of the relatively sunny oak forest. When robins nest in wild forest, it is usually near water, whose floods probably clean off the ground litter so worms can be found more easily. Robins also like to bathe often, and use mud in constructing the nest, again requiring access to water. Red-tailed Hawks like oak forests, perhaps because these often occur on exposed hilltops, bluffs, and slopes, giving these birds both vantage and updrafts on which to soar down easily in search of prey and ride the elevators back to the nest. Here we see the interaction of plant life-form and landscape pattern in favoring certain birds.

For whatever reasons birds choose certain plant communities, it is useful to think of vegetation in these terms of winning combinations of plant competitors. They exist as very distinct plant groupings—cattail-bulrush marsh, sugar maple–basswood or spruce-fir forest, Eurasian grassy fields or native relic prairie species or wet sedge meadows, brushy landscapes (carrs) dominated by shrubs, tamarack-leatherleaf bogs, and so on. The distinct, easily recognized plant community and its life-form is one of the three vegetation concepts useful as tools for translating climate and soil into bird habitat. As seen in the chapter on habitat preferences, plant communities, grouped by life-form, are important, although not always sufficient alone, for describing the habitats for breeding and migration; for total landscapes are what count most. Boreal birds like Yellow-rumped Warblers and Gray Jays choose coniferous skylines; prairie birds such as most waterfowl, Greater Prairie-Chickens, and Upland Sandpipers like treeless expanses and accept any short grass whether Eurasian or native prairie; Piping Plovers like bare sand near water, irrespective of plant species; and shrubs whether wet or dry favor Gray Catbirds, while Sedge Wrens like grasses or sedges whether in hayfield or marsh.

For the curious person—professional or amateur—who would further investigate the botanical and landscape interaction in bird habitat, several important places in Wisconsin provide an accumulation of information from past studies. These include the field stations and arboreta of colleges and the state university, many private nature centers and sanctuaries, state and county parks and forests, and the lands protected through the efforts of the Wisconsin Chapter of The Nature Conservancy and the state Natural Areas Preservation Council, which advises the state Department of Natural Resources. For locating them the reader is directed to the Wisconsin DNR's Bureau of Endangered Resources at Madison and the Wisconsin Society for Ornithology.

Successional Stages

When the vegetation is removed, how do plants restore themselves? Devegetation entails a disturbing force. Our most familiar examples are tilling of the land, abundant grazing by livestock, or clear-cutting of forest. Before man was on the scene, natural disturbances included severe fires, prolonged summer floods, and the constant digging of animals; for example, woodland foxes and woodchucks dig dens, skunks and badgers rip up extensive patches of grass sod in their respective hunts for turtle eggs and ground squirrels, ants incessantly create volcanoes of subsoil, and bison wallow in muddy places. Beavers and muskrats, through their eating and flooding activities, destroy the vegetation in wet habitats, as do occasional dry spells that kill aquatic plants.

Most people have noticed that, following disturbances, the vegetation may come back in several stages, rather than immediately resembling the type that was destroyed. Following abandonment of farming in northern and eastern Wisconsin, there is a sequence of stages: annual weeds, grassy old field, invading shrubs and saplings (brush or carr), pioneer (light-demanding) forest of oak, aspen, white birch, pine, etc., and finally a "climax" forest stage of crowding-tolerant (shade-tolerant) trees such as red and sugar maples, hemlock, and beech. When set back by fire or windthrow, all forests go through at least the last two stages. After a drawdown, wet marshes go through a transitory stage of shore annuals such as bidens, cutgrass, and smartweed before the deepwater aquatic plants win out as the water returns. When a flood occurs during the growing season, caused perhaps by summer rains or a new beaver dam, lowland forests die and are replaced by a series of wetland types, depending on ensuing water depths; forest may or may not return. If water depths change gradually toward shore, different stages may persist; and if the frequency and severity of fire, storm damage, or animal digging vary from place to place, the vegetation of uplands likewise may freeze into a gradient of types, as long as the pattern of disturbance remains steady. These stages or phases of the vegetation are one way plant species can avoid competition and utilize the same site—by taking turns. This temporal dovetailing of vegetation—whether or not frozen in space as well as time—is called plant succession.

Since many plants and many animals, including a large share of our birds, are specialized for or adapted to one or more of the transitory (nonclimax) stages of succession, we can assume that succession has been renewed or recycled many times and in many places over very long periods of time. Wildlife managers know that nonclimax stages often produce the greatest abundance and diversity of game. One reason is that the various pioneering vegetation types create a diversity of life-forms during their mad scramble to get "in" with the game of musical chairs. Successional life-forms are not as uniform as those of climax forest, nor need the types invade in a uniform sequence, since small variations in soil and chance factors vary the vegetation during these periods of rapid change. This foliage-height diversity and patterning of plant spacing provides a variety of foods—plant and insect—and of feeding, nesting, and song perch sites, so many bird species can dovetail their needs. Climax forest (or grassland or wetland), on the other hand, tends to be more monotonous in aspect, because the relatively few final plant winners crowd out some of the diversity.

A second reason why wildlife prospers during succession is that pioneering plants can exploit, and produce abundantly from, the incompletely utilized sources of energy (light), minerals, and water, until the site is again fully occupied by dense competition-tolerant vegetation. The climax plants tend to lock up minerals, water, and energy for use by themselves alone, for they can barely hold their own against each other. For this reason the production of seeds and even foliage tends to be highest among pioneering plants, including herbs (ragweeds and smartweeds), shrubs and vines (berries), and trees (cherries, oaks, and other nut trees), in contrast to those of climax or at least stable stages, which don't need to reproduce much anyway and so can get along on limited resources under conditions of crowding. Thus, during the new scrambling following each disturbance, foods for birds and other animals may well be more abundant as well as more diverse—and possibly even more nutritious. Examples of climax (or at least crowded and stable) communities are the thick sod grasses and sedges of prairies and wet meadows and the dense stands, especially when not mixed, of sugar maples, beeches, ashes, hemlocks, or pines in certain situations.

In looking for or managing wildlife, including birds, it is therefore important to seek a moderate amount of recurrent disturbance to recycle or maintain the needs of pioneer or intermediate (unstable or transient) stages of plant succession—either by periodic staggered setbacks or by some sort of environmental gradient or edge mechanism that spreads out the stages in space, such as the wetland border. Windthrow and fires used to keep parts of forest regions—both north and south—in brushy early stages of regeneration to the benefit of towhees, grouse, and many other birds that feed or nest in openings, shrubby tangles, or groups of young trees. In fact, it appears that most forest birds like to be near an opening or edge; only a few vireos, woodpeckers, warblers, flycatchers, and thrushes are more numerous in the centers of dense uniform forests. In this regard we should take notice that many birds actually use several plant communities or at least several successional stages in their habitat: Red-tailed Hawks feed in meadows but nest in forest; Ruffed Grouse eat male buds of pioneering aspens in winter but drum on old forest logs in spring. Hence, we must stress the importance of "edge" habitat, meaning the interspersion of plant communities whether climax or pioneer. The dynamic succession and associated edge concepts are the second important tool for using vegetation to translate landscape and its history into bird habitats.

Vegetation Zones and Provinces

A final area of interest is the behavior of plants near the borders of their geographic ranges, where the climate begins to be marginal for them. Then the game of king-of-the-hill among different plant species is like the game of territoriality between two rival males of the same species of songbird. Each one is secure on its own ground but is easily discouraged when challenged in the territory of the other. In Wisconsin, two floras with very different requirements reach a sort of territorial boundary along a narrow zone running between the Twin Cities and Milwaukee. Figure 8, generalized from the notes of the early land surveyors (circa 1840), shows a definite change in the vegetation along this zone. The southern element that drops out here is chiefly composed of plant species of the prairie and oak-grove province, which need long warm summers and lots of light. The northern species that stop in this zone are chiefly conifers and associated boreal plants which abhor hot summer weather. South of this zone, recurrent drought and fire have favored prairies and oaks over dense climax forest, while the northern plants survive only in cool damp microclimates such as on north-facing cliffs. North of the zone, tree invasion can be very rapid in the cool damp summers, and dense persistent forest growth tends to shade out young oaks (except the midsuccession red oak) and prairie species, which persist only in dry sandy places kept open by frequent fires and suitable for only scrub oaks and jack pines.

In his *Vegetation of Wisconsin*, John Curtis (1959) shows that the counties in this transition zone contained more range limits of plant species (excluding isolated relic populations) than other Wisconsin counties. So this zone of conflict and rapid geographic change has come to be known to botanists as the *tension zone* (Fig. 9). Our conspicuous and scenic white pine is the easiest marker of this zone for the northbound traveler today; south of the zone it ceases to be a prevalent forest tree and is found only as local relics or in plantings. Maize used to be the best warm-season marker that faded out in this zone; but since the 1960s, short-season varieties have enabled farmers to grow it two counties farther north, overlapping the natural range of the white pine. You can see the correspondence between the limits of the range of white pine (Fig. 6), the change in vegetation (Fig. 8), and the location of the tension zone (Fig. 9). They all are located along the middles of the gradients of summer heat and length of growing season (Figs. 2 and 5).

The tension zone is a very useful tool for describing Wisconsin's vegetation, because it brings out the local factors that counteract or reinforce the climatic influences on each side of it. It is equally useful for characterizing birdlife, because most microclimates north or south of this zone do not support large enough examples of anomalous vegetation to influence the birds. Exceptions among northern forest relics are a few pine and hemlock groves in southwestern Wisconsin harboring Red-breasted Nuthatches and certain warblers, and some of the southeastern tamarack bogs in which a few Nashville Warblers and

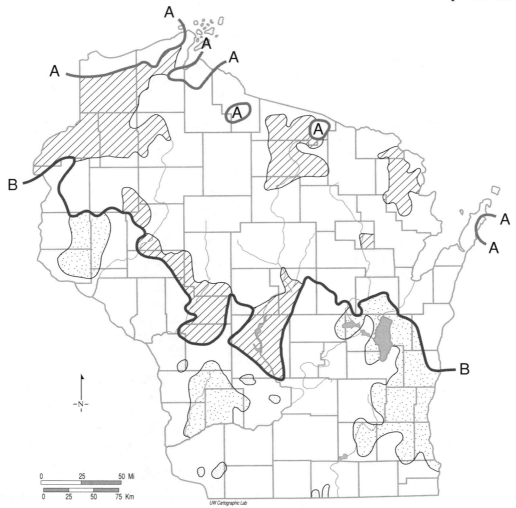

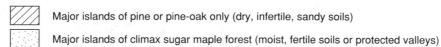

A ━━━━━ Southern limits of boreal spruce-fir forest outliers in Wisconsin (excluding spruce-tamarack bogs)

B ━━━━━ Boundary between NE conifer-hardwood forest province and SW prairie-oak grove and savanna province

Exceptions

▨ Major islands of pine or pine-oak only (dry, infertile, sandy soils)

▦ Major islands of climax sugar maple forest (moist, fertile soils or protected valleys)

Figure 8. Major regions of Wisconsin vegetation at the time of European settlement (circa 1840–1850). (Adapted by Finley, Cottam, and Loucks from land survey maps, Wis. Geol. and Nat. Hist. Surv., map in color, in DNR files, Madison, 1965.)

White-throated Sparrows breed. And abandoned farms sport prairie birds in Door County!

The southward dip in the tension zone in central Wisconsin, bringing with it associated pines and other northern plants (Figs. 8 and 9), is partly due to the poor soil and partly to the settling of cold air at night in the central basin. Most conifers are accustomed to poor soil, and they are less seriously affected than

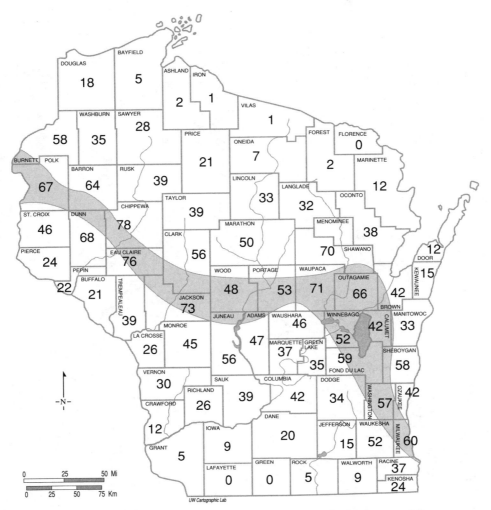

Figure 9. The tension zone of Wisconsin vegetation (after Curtis 1959, p. 20); summary of range limits for 182 native plant species. The figure in each county indicates the number of species attaining a range boundary there. The shaded band is the tension zone, based on the densest concentration of individual range boundaries (compare this figure with Figures 2, 5, 6, and 8).

deciduous trees by cool weather in spring and late frosts, because the old tough needles can continue to function while the new growth tardily emerges. The low places and some rises with very cold nights cause enough dewfall to enable some of the more sensitive northern conifers like spruce and pine, along with the tough jack pine, to endure the sudden windy or hot spells.

The tension zone in central and northwestern Wisconsin is blurred when you look at birdlife. There is a mixture of birds of southern and northern distribution. Species like the Hermit Thrush and Nashville Warbler favor the coniferous landscape of pines on sands and spruces in bogs, while open-country birds such as meadowlarks and several sparrows use the open sandy prairies. Into these regions the Red-bellied Woodpecker, Red-shouldered Hawk, and other deciduous forest birds push northward along the relatively fertile river corridors with their deciduous (hardwood) floodplain forests. Thus, the Wisconsin Audubon Camp at Sarona (Washburn County) can teach students about bird ecology of all parts of the Midwest. In eastern Wisconsin, the tension zone turns north, then south, finally narrowing to isolate a very thin strip of cool northern forest along Lake Michigan (Fig. 9). The tongue of warmer summers running up the "Big" Fox Valley to Green Bay, reinforced perhaps by presettlement fires in the open sedge peatlands and the sandy prairies on the flat glacial lake beds, kept that landscape open past Lake Winnebago to Green Bay for open-marsh and grassland birds of the prairie contingent. East of Green Bay the change to northern forest is very abrupt, probably because of the firebreak effect of the cliffs of the Niagara cuesta (see Figure 13).

The tension zone across Wisconsin does, in a general way, form a break in birdlife, at least in relative abundance of different species (see analysis of BBS's). The boreal contingent of Wisconsin's birds is attracted to coniferous landscapes and tends to stop at or north of the tension zone where the conifers do. Birds breeding chiefly south of the tension zone are the southern contingent. In contrast, most birds of the eastern broad-leaved (deciduous) forest breed throughout Wisconsin, for example, the Northern Oriole, Ovenbird, and several flycatchers and vireos, as noted earlier.

There is a further effect in winter, favoring, in some years at least, more birdlife south of the tension zone than north of it. The climate south and west of the tension zone is more continental, more variable, and sometimes temporarily colder, but often with less snow. Wintering birds needing open water stay in mild years, while those feeding on bare ground may stay in the snowless years, regardless of temperature. Thus, southern and western Wisconsin may have wintering Bald Eagles, several hawks (Red-tailed, Cooper's, Kestrel), Northern Flickers, Red-headed Woodpeckers (in good acorn years), several blackbirds (Red-winged, Rusty, Common Grackle), both meadowlarks, Horned Larks, Belted Kingfishers, and some waterfowl.

This third vegetation tool—the tension zone—along with the geological influences discussed next, forms the basis for dividing the state for interpreting the breeding bird surveys (BBS's) mapped in Part II.

Geology and Soils

Local bedrock, glacial deposits, and soils have a profound effect on both vegetation and land use, and so on birdlife as well. For the most part, soils covering Wisconsin are a direct expression of the underlying geology of various parts of the state. Our three major soil regions reflect the concentric exposures of bedrock (compare Figures 10 and 11): (1) the often coarse, rather acid, and often not very fertile soils derived from igneous and metamorphic rock of the central Northern Highland; (2) the generally very acid and infertile sands from the central crescent of sandstones; and (3) the fine-grained, fertile, limy "outer necklace" derived from dolomite. Locally, of course, you can find almost any type of soil, since wind, water, and ice have moved the soil about.

The glaciers had a very important, in fact crucial, influence on our landscape—on topography, on soils, on water—so much so that Wisconsin was chosen by the National Park Service as the site for the Ice Age National Reserve. Trails now being laid across the state to demonstrate many glacial features will provide access for students of birdlife as well. The major glacial features are shown in Figure 12. Most of our soils were not only moved about but were actually created by glacial action. Five major types of soil resulted: clay, gravel, sand, silt, and peat.

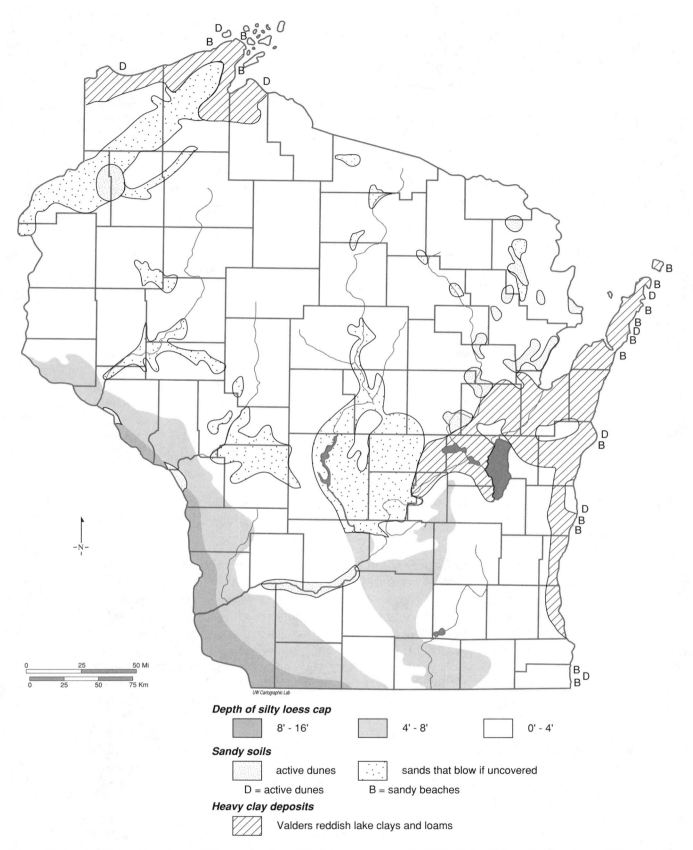

Depth of silty loess cap

█ 8' - 16'   ▒ 4' - 8'   ☐ 0' - 4'

Sandy soils

▒ active dunes   ⋰ sands that blow if uncovered

D = active dunes   B = sandy beaches

Heavy clay deposits

▨ Valders reddish lake clays and loams

Figure 10. Some major soil regions of Wisconsin. (Simplified from two maps by F. D. Hole, "Major Soil Regions of Wisconsin" and "Areas Having Aeolian Silt and Sand Deposits in Wisconsin," Soils Div., Wis. Geol. and Nat. Hist. Surv., Madison, 1950.)

Fine Dense Clays

These soils were laid down where quiet water stood over a considerable length of time. Our chief clay regions are near the Great Lakes. Since some interglacial levels were higher than those today, the Great Lakes overlapped adjacent parts of Wisconsin (compare Figures 10 and 12). The most recent deposit (Valders) is of reddish clays found in Manitowoc County, the Green Bay area, the east half of the Bayfield Peninsula, the Apostle Islands, and the Lake Superior lowlands. Today, this deposit favors green ash, elm, and aspen where once there had been spruce, at least in glacial times. An old spruce forest buried under the Valders clay is now exposed in the eroding lake bluff at Two Rivers (Manitowoc County).

The convenient location of clay, needed for nest construction, atop the low sandstone cliffs on Lake Superior and the dolomite in Door County—both near water with its abundant insects—may explain the high density of cliff and other swallows in the Apostles, Bayfield, and Door County areas. Heavy clays are slow to drain and warm up in spring; so even on uplands they are difficult to farm despite their fertility. They often lie unplanted for a time, carrying puddles into late spring. These puddles provide mud sources for the nesting swallows, and they also provide appropriate open wet landscapes, worms, and other mud invertebrates needed by migrant plovers and other shorebirds on their long journey northward through eastern Wisconsin. Thus, clay maintains a unique, essential habitat for birds and bird-watchers alike.

Coarse Gravelly to Sandy Soil

These soils are at the opposite extreme from clay in particle size. Derived from igneous and metamorphic as well as sedimentary rocks and washed out near the retreating ice by fast, temporary streams across Wisconsin, these soils make up many terminal, recessional, and interlobate moraines and even some drumlins. They prevail in much of the Northern Highland and the eastern kettle moraine regions (Figs. 1, 12, and 13). Favoring pines and hemlocks in the north, these soils cause our northern forests to harbor the many boreal-contingent birds that like coniferous landscapes and consume seeds or insects provided by pines, spruces, hemlocks, and their associated birches, red maples, and aspens. In the kettle moraine the nonplowable, dry, gravelly or sandy hills with their red cedars and oaks with small clearings went from subsistence farms to recreation properties and state forest. Some still support a diverse array of deciduous forest and old-field birds today, including sometimes the bluebird. However, brush and forest invasion, including masses of alien cathartic buckthorns favored by livestock disturbances, threaten to create dark thorny monotypes unless restrained by management.

Fine Sands

The uniformly fine sands were sorted by wave action and accumulated in many temporary shallow lakes near the ice front. Our two largest sand regions are northwestern Wisconsin and the low Central Plain (Figs. 1, 10, and 12). When the glacial lakes emptied, the sand was thrown by wind into many low dunes, resulting in contrasting dry and wet habitat (because sand is either very wet or very dry) in both prairie and conifer forest. Sands concentrated by wave action on the Great Lakes shores were whipped by stronger and longer wave and wind action into high dunes behind a broad band of sand beach (see symbol B on Figure 10). These are dry, but minerals, including lime, and the humidity from the lake enable various forest types to invade some of them, forming highly diverse landscapes.

Sand was also washed down the Wisconsin, the Mississippi, and even small rivers like the Sugar (Figs. 10 and 12), to give us many terraces and islands today. These moving deposits provided the bare sand needed by Horned Larks, Common Nighthawks, and Piping Plovers that probably nested there before human disturbance, as they also did until recently on the Great Lakes beaches. Stable deposits support floodplain forest, whose mosquitoes, nettles, and rampant poison ivy may keep people away from their forest birds and secluded heron rookeries. Along the Mississippi and the lower Wisconsin, a few roadless, windswept barren dunes and sand terraces still maintain our only "deserts." In these warm loose sands rare turtles, lizards, and snakes make their last stand, aided by the activity of pocket gophers and in turn providing easy food for the Red-shouldered Hawks and Barred Owls that nest in the nearby forests. Barren river and Central Plain sands maintain our few populations of Lark Sparrows, but pine plantations, cottage development, and irrigation farming now threaten most of them. When young, the pine and spruce plantations favor another interesting bird, the Clay-colored Sparrow; and when older, they may winter some owls or become roosts for crows or blackbirds. Most of our southern Wisconsin pine plantings are not large enough or allowed to mature to the point where they might attract our boreal contingent of birds, with a few possible exceptions such as the University of Wisconsin–Madison Arboretum.

Sands, like the gravelly soils, are generally infertile and hold water poorly. They, too, have for a long time retarded succession and forced land use to be less intensive than regions of better soils. Nonintensive farming is still the rule in parts of the central and northwestern regions, thus resembling the early settlement times when a mix of cropland, pasture, woodlot, fallow fields, fencerows, and incompletely used wetlands maintained what may well have been the maximum variety of birds possible on any landscape. Before intensive land use for recreation and high-tech farming began to move into our sands, several large areas were set aside, such as the Meadow Valley and Sandhill State Wildlife areas in Wood County. Emphasis there has usually been on wetland restoration; but at the Crex Meadows State Wildlife Area in Burnett County and Necedah National Wildlife Refuge in Juneau County, management to maintain open prairies and savannas, through the use of fires, will benefit water, grassland, and barrens birds alike of the prairie contingent, since all these species need treeless skylines. State acquisition of and recreation-corridor planning now in progress for the lower Wisconsin River holds hope for maintaining some of the prairie contingent there as well. Perhaps the growing groundwater problems in the Central Plain will set a limit on irrigation farming before all the special habitats there are gone.

Smaller patches of sandy soils have a number of subtle effects statewide, mainly in diversifying the local vegetation and probably the birdlife in some cases. North of the tension zone, sandy areas, of which Figures 8 and 10 show only a few, have maintained pine dominance—both red-white pine stands and jack pine–scrub oak barrens—usually with prairie grass understory. These numerous coniferous islands sharpen the transition to northern forest and its birds as one travels north of the tension zone. South of the tension zone, drought, low fertility, and fire on sands have likewise maintained oaks and prairies against invasions of denser, more monotypic forest. In the coulee country especially, sandstone outcrops and their associated infertile acid soils have maintained local open barren sites on hot south exposures, while they account for most of the pine and hemlock relics on cool, damp east or north faces. Wet sites on poor sandy soils favor low-nutrient peats, with either open or forested bogs, of which the largest, but by no means the only, group is in the Northern Highland of Vilas and Oneida counties. On the other hand, near Lakes Superior and Michigan and Green Bay, the sands are more limy from recent glacial or lake action, and their bogs have more vegetation complexity. White cedars are characteristic on these limy sands as well as on exposed dolomite bedrock. Influences on birds are certain to be found with detailed studies. White cedars, for example, are especially secure nest sites, but offer meager insect fare.

Fine Silty Soils

These soils have a special history and a special significance for us. First, they were ground off the Canadian Shield by the ice, making the streams milky with "rock flour," like that which colors the brooks we see today running down glacier-topped mountains. Next, the silts were deposited in alluvial fans and shallow puddles all across the northern plains and into Missouri, Illinois, Iowa, and Wisconsin. Finally, before vegetation could stabilize them, they blew about in giant dust storms both over and in front of the ice fields. Not quite so fine in particle size as clay, they loosen up and blow easily.

These windblown silts, called loess (the German term), are our fertile agricultural soils. They contain many minerals and hang onto and store many more minerals as well as much water. They are free of boulders and pebbles, making them ideal to plow. And they don't exclude air by packing too much, as the clays do. Although they support our wheat, corn, soybean, and dairy agriculture, they erode by water and wind so readily that we have already lost approximately half of what the glacier gave us, in just the century and a half since intensive farming began. The fertile loess causes much of our upland landscape to be used for intensive farmland today, and the loess cap makes farming possible even on our dolomitic ridges in southwestern Wisconsin. These farmlands are avoided by birds for nesting purposes. However, in the quartzite Baraboo hills, loess deposits on the infertile rock enable sugar maples to grow next to the pines and oaks.

Even before farming vastly accelerated erosion, accumulating loess had begun to form deposits in river valleys. As a result, even our valleys have a diversity of soils, ranging from dry to damp, and from nutrient-poor glacial sand to fertile alluvium—diversifying the vegetation and so the birds. On the Wisconsin River, for example, the silty alluvium favors deciduous forest and cattail marshes even as far north as conifer-dominated Vilas County, while in the south along the river the sands bring pines down past Sauk County, along with the warm open "deserts" noted above.

Even our productive northern forests enjoy the benefits of a small amount of loessial soils. There they occur chiefly atop the drumlins, which seems strange because you would expect that the loess would have been washed off into the lowlands. Some was, but apparently some of the dust storms occurred *during* the glacial retreat, while the lowlands between hills still had rushing streams that took all but coarser soils away. Thus, the "fussy" sugar maple forest type on the hilltops can diversify the northern forest to the benefit of the eastern broad-leaved forest birds, whereas most low or level land is plagued by summer frosts, waterlogging, or low fertility tolerated chiefly by conifers.

The diverse soil types within the Menominee Reservation illustrate beautifully how soil differences influence vegetation. Here, the climate is uniform, and human alteration has been minimal. Logging has never been intensive on a large scale, and only one sector has had a severe postsettlement fire. Until recently the deer population was kept down to presettlement levels by year-round hunting. Consequently, the full diversity of conifers and broad-leaved trees remains in all age classes from saplings to very old trees, in various checkerboards and mixtures of foliage heights and groupings. Birdlife is very diverse, but it is difficult to study because of limited access and very tall trees. This block of forest even shows up in satellite photographs, revealing the extent of general forest destruction elsewhere on all sides and the northward expansion of agriculture along the tension zone.

The western zone of the Menominee forest, consisting of fertile silty drumlins, supports primarily climax hardwoods (sugar maple, basswood, white ash) typical of eastern Wisconsin. The central zone, mostly composed of gravelly and sandy outwash of intermediate fertility and moisture retention, has white pine–hemlock–yellow birch–red maple forest typical of much of the central Northern Highland region but with the addition of beech, as in Door County. The southeastern Menominee zone, composed of sandy outwash, is droughty, acid, and infertile like much of northwestern and central Wisconsin; it supports scrub oak and jack pine with an understory of prairie plants and blueberries.

The typical upland early successional stages of each zone are, respectively, red oak, aspen–white birch–red pine–white pine, and resprouting scrub (Hill's and black) oak. The typical later successional scenes are, respectively, sugar maple under oak, red maple and/or hemlock under white and red pine, and red pine under jack pine and scrub oak. "Habitat Preferences" in Part II will indicate some of the differences in birdlife to be expected in these different forest mixtures.

The three distinct soils of the relatively small Menominee Reservation, supporting three very distinct upland forest types, typify soil effects statewide. The trees present on these soils accentuate these differences in forest types, the pines making acid soils poorer while the sugar maples make rich soils richer. The adjacent lowlands, getting water from slopes above, reflect this difference—again, typical throughout our northern forest region: white cedar occurs downhill from sugar maple, black spruce below pine, and tamarack, fir, black ash, elm, and red maple in intermediate low sites. Away from water, the cedars, firs, and spruces seem to have few birds, perhaps because these trees resist attack by most insects; but among these coniferous spires you may seek the elusive Boreal Chickadee, Gray Jay, and Spruce Grouse.

Peats

Created by acid bog mosses, limy fen sedges, and various swamp trees, peats compose our fifth major type of soil. Laid in soggy places and hence deficient in oxygen, these organic plant deposits fail to decay, so they accumulate. The fertile peats of sedges and fen plants of southeastern and east-central Wisconsin, where the Green Bay lobe of the glacier (Fig. 12) provided a source of lime from the Niagara dolomite, have been intensively used as muck farms, but the peats have not yet been exhausted. The more acid bog peats, found especially in sandy regions, are mostly too infertile and localized to be useful, except for the cranberry industry in north-central and northern Wisconsin. Cranberry operations displace bird habitats just as muck farming does, but the extensive impoundments needed to flood cranberries for frost protection do maintain high water tables for wetland species outside of the small cranberry beds.

The "mud lakes" so frequent almost everywhere on old maps are the bog and fen lakes with a "false bottom" of peat instead of an exposed sand or gravel floor. These small lakes often maintain undisturbed habitats today, since peaty shores are hard to farm or put cottages on, and lake levels can't be altered as easily under Wisconsin's laws as could wetlands away from waters. Furthermore, such peatlands must have a very steady water supply or they would have burned or decayed out periodically; their water supply is often underground and therefore is not so likely to be interrupted or polluted by accelerated surface drainage from urban or rural landscapes. Some of the small peaty lakes in southeastern Wisconsin and many bog lakes in the north have yet to be thoroughly censused for birdlife. Unless they are traversed by a stream, their access is usually difficult.

In summary, Wisconsin's soils are important in causing our rich birdlife, first because of the general presence of fertile soils and waters, and second because a high diversity of soils in each region makes for a diversity of vegetation cover. Thirdly, although possibly the least productive of total biomass, the "poorer" sandy, gravelly, and peaty soils have protected many bird habitats from loss both to natural succession and more recently to intensive land use. (This effect may help explain why some studies elsewhere indicate highest wildlife values where soils are relatively infertile.) As a possible example, the seemingly monotonous central sands have a relatively high density of Mourning Doves and Vesper Sparrows (see the BBS's)—species which do well enough on prosperous farms. Only the acid bog peats may actually have a low abundance and diversity of birds; but these of course include some unusual boreal species.

Land Use

Human land use has had drastic effects on bird habitats, for both better and worse. What land use patterns are characteristic of Wisconsin's landscape? Wisconsin is a moderately populated state, with 4.9 million people today, and most of them are concentrated in urban complexes near Milwaukee and Green Bay. In the rural areas, three additional accidents of Wisconsin history have tended to lower overall human impact and maintain bird habitats up to the present. First, the central and northern Wisconsin regions, characterized by rugged climate and generally poor soils, have had especially low human density; land has been used primarily for forestry and recreation. Where profitable industry is difficult to sustain, the land must be accepted as it is and its products harvested without much expenditure on alteration of the landscape. Under such circumstances, people can agree on certain cooperative aspects of land husbandry, such as fire protection and pollution control. Wisconsin's public trust doctrine and shoreland zoning to protect all navigable waters grew out of that cooperative spirit. So, too, has this spirit fostered protection of extensive areas containing important forest and wetland habitats in national and state forests, wildlife areas, Indian reservations, and the Apostle Islands National Lakeshore on Lake Superior.

The second accident of history, partly related to the first, was the settlement of much of Wisconsin by dairy farmers. The boulders, gravels, and sands left by the glacier, the thinner loessial deposits than those in states farther west and south, and the hilly drumlin, moraine, and coulee regions all contributed to this result by attracting settlers from poor or hilly land suitable chiefly for pasturing, rather than people used to the richer flat farmland needed for cultivated crops. Tradition and the state's central location for marketing milk and cheese has maintained a predominance of dairy industry to the present. So we have remaining an unusually high percentage of that endangered breed of agriculturist, the relatively small family farm.

To be sure, as dairying became more efficient, livestock was placed in feedlots, which may have polluted the nearby waters. But along with the feedlot, a typical dairy farm supported considerable acreage of unpastured alfalfa-grass mixture maintained for 2–4 years; this mixture was alternated with oats and corn in only 1- or 2-year rotations. These untrampled and ungrazed forage fields supported a variety of both prairie and forest-region songbirds of open places, and these farms also retained the rest of the eastern birds in the typical woodlot, which the dairyman needed for a source of fuel. Thus, dairying—with at least four farms per square mile—maintained samples of both forest and "prairie." In moderation, the cornfield was an asset to wildlife as well, providing important waste grain and weed seeds around the edge for migrating and wintering birds and possible spring nesting of larks. The alfalfa, when not mowed too often or at the wrong time, also served importantly as nesting sites for pheasants and ducks. Some farmers even put a flushing bar on the cutting machine to spare the hens for a renesting attempt.

The third accident of Wisconsin's history, related to both of the others, was the significantly lower number of drainage projects in Wisconsin than in all the adjacent states. South of our tension zone we may have lost 75% of our wetlands, while the five states we touch have lost nearly 90% in their agricultural regions. This lack of drainage began as a practical matter. Many low areas were not suitable for intensive farming, but could be used without much costly drainage as pastures or feedlots. Later, the public trust doctrine led to floodplain and shoreland zoning that now helps protect those wetlands located on waters in agricultural southern as well as in recreational northern Wisconsin. Although many protected wetlands are at present degraded, especially from poor water quality, they could be restored if upland management were to become wiser, as it must if soils, fertilizers, and groundwaters are to be conserved, and excrement recycled.

Today, of course, we face a trend toward intensive land use which is placing severe economic pressures on the land and so also on its bird habitats. For example, the old-time hayfields favored grassland birds, because these fields were harvested only once, in June or July. Today, alfalfa–brome grass mixtures are cut two or three times, starting as early as Memorial Day, leaving no interval long enough for a nest and brood to succeed. On top of this, dairy farming is now giving way to cash cropping, family farms are yielding to larger commercial operations with large machinery and actual abandonment of soil conservation practices, and marginal lands like the central sands (both dry and wet) are being converted to irrigation projects and beef cattle raising.

Meanwhile, the northern forests are being managed more and more intensively as monotypic short-rotation pine and aspen pulp farms. "Cheater strips" of tall trees are left along roads and waterways, but they may be too narrow to support much birdlife. Rights-of-way of roads, railroads, power lines, and pipelines, whose clearings once broke up the forest's monotony, are now managed so intensively that birds find little habitat there either. Perhaps worst of all, even if the human population does not increase much further, the demand for real estate development on wild lands continues to intensify as people seek cottage retreats and second homes in attractive landscapes. While a few clearings often increase birdlife, even along shores and in unbroken forests and barrens, the usual result of intense pressure for development is very small lots at very high prices. Thus, most vegetation must be removed for the house, and no one can afford to buy two or three lots to protect the very amenities that attracted buyers to the wild country in the first place. Larger private and public recreation lands are often planted to pines or left to grow up to forest, eliminating the vital openings and early stages of succession that presettlement fires and low-key farming had maintained.

Two trends, it is hoped, may help soften this blow if guided by educational efforts toward appreciation of natural resources accompanied by an understanding of ecology. One is that, while full-time farms both big and little are declining in number, small part-time farms are on the rise in number and political influence. Such farmers are resource-oriented, and since they are supported by a job in town, they do not need to beat up the land to eke out their living. They tend to have a more diversified education and the highest interest in better management of soil, water, and wildlife. The second trend is the gradual tightening of restrictions on developers of land near both lakes and urban centers, for example in the protection of prime farmland, prevention of soil erosion, and preservation of natural resources of recognized public benefit. As the temporary zone of abandoned farms held by land speculators around growing municipalities comes to be appreciated for its abundant returning American Kestrels and many other interesting birds, efforts will intensify to maintain this open space in the form of greenways, recreation corridors, resource protection areas, and natural "conservation" parks. After all, these are the only places where urban dwellers—90% of the population, including most children—will have any chance of significant access to their heritage of wildlife today.

A final accident of human settlement of America is only beginning to be appreciated as a threat to bird habitats and resource conservation in general. That is the escape into natural lands of certain alien species that become pests by altering habitats and species balances. *Alien* means native in another part of the world, whether on our continent or another. The first organisms that come to mind are parasites to which the native plants and animals are vulnerable. Dutch elm disease fungus is an example of an alien parasite that has had drastic effects on our forests—and urban environments, as well. Among alien animals, cats, rats, house mice, European Starlings, House Sparrows, and Rock Doves seem, in most situations, to be a liability from the standpoint of predation on desirable birds and/or competition for their food. In the water, there is little dispute over the harm to fish and bird habitats from a single alien fish species—the carp—which disrupts vegetation and water quality in marshes, lakes, and rivers.

Birdlife also suffers from certain invading alien plant species which reduce habitat and vegetation diversity, forming monotypes of little wildlife value. While most plants taken to new parts of the world do poorly except under the gardener's care, a few species hit it off and overpopulate areas having climates analogous to their own—perhaps because they lack the consumers (animals or diseases) that controlled them in their native land. The legacy of abandoned farms and drained peatlands often set the stage for alien plants to get a quick foothold in the scramble for revegetation. Today their seeds are everywhere, making spread much easier whenever a new opportunity arises. Some of these invaders have become only mildly obnoxious and seem, on balance, to benefit birds. About half of our crop and garden weeds are Eurasian, and some, like the lamb's quarters (pigweed), certainly have benefited birds while not endearing themselves to the farmer. Examples of woody aliens which favor wildlife include the Russian mulberry, Eurasian crabs and apples, and the American box elder. These have spread widely yet are not a threat to native species. On the other hand, there may be more harm than good from two thorny species once widely planted and now stubbornly persistent—the Chinese multiflora rose and the Tennessee black locust. Today our worst upland threats seem to be bella honeysuckle (a hybrid between Siberian Tartarian honeysuckle and Japanese Morrow honeysuckle) and the European cathartic buckthorn (*Rhamnus cathartica*). A further potential menace is the Norway maple, so welcomed in dry, hot, paved cities where this tough tree provides dark, pest-resistant shade under trying conditions for plants and people. However, it has now begun to infiltrate our wild forests from Minnesota to the Atlantic Coast and thrives in all kinds of soils. Along with the similarly shade-tolerant cathartic buckthorn, the Norway maple may threaten forestry as well as wildlife, because neither ground plants nor saplings grow under these species, which themselves may be of low economic value.

In wetlands we are seeing four monotypic invaders threatening bird habitats by displacing food plants and vegetation diversity. The marsh nettle, native on our river floodplains, has taken over many drained and burned peatlands and now is difficult to dislodge. The robust Eurasian strain of reed canary grass, once planted for cattle forage as a hoped-for improvement over wild sedges in peatlands, is still widely planted as a bank stabilizer, furthering the monotony and sterility of the landscape as it spreads. European purple loosestrife, a handsome garden flower and favorite bee plant (honeybees came from Europe too) but of little wildlife value, is now rapidly seizing acreage in three types of wetlands— river floodplains, cattail marshes, and peaty sedge meadows. Like reed canary, it is a long-lived perennial that spreads chiefly when the wetland is disturbed, but disturbances today are the rule. The seeds, as well, are long-lived and blow or float everywhere by the millions. The fourth lowland pest is another European buckthorn, *Rhamnus frangula*, which seems to be abundantly invading even undisturbed swamps and fens, including the Cedarburg Bog Wildlife Refuge in Ozaukee County. These pests and others will challenge the manager of natural lands and the bird conservationist for all time to come.

Some further recent trends both good and bad for bird habitat will be summarized at the end of the chronology which follows.

The History of Wisconsin Bird Habitats

The scene is never static. To appreciate the sequence of historic factors that have shaped Wisconsin's birdlife habitats, influential events can now be set in three frames of time reference. Geologic forces acted on the earth's crust through long periods of time measured in hundreds of millions of years. Climatic forces are interrelated with those of the earth's crust, but they can change and influence wildlife on much shorter scales measured in thousands of years, and sometimes only centuries or decades (witness the droughts of the 1930s). Finally, the advent of man and his effects on the landscape, although equally influential, must now be monitored on an annual basis, for in today's world they can change overnight. Understanding these time scales is important not just for better enjoyment of the landscape but also for reading it and perceiving trends that can affect birdlife in time for corrective action.

Geological Forces

Four spans of geological time shaped our substrate. The vast Precambrian era, largely devoid of life and composing most of the earth's history, ended some 500 million years ago. During that era, mountains in our region rose and weathered completely away again. Here and there today we see at the surface a few glimpses of rock formed during this time—hard igneous granites, lava flows, and sandstones warped and metamorphosed into resistant infertile quartzite by heat and pressure. These show up as monadnocks—resistant ridges and knobs like the Gogebic, Rib, Blue, and Baraboo ranges—and create most of the dells and waterfalls in the northern half of the state. In the center of the Northern Highland region (Fig. 1) only the recent glacial deposits cover our portion of the vast igneous peneplain called the Canadian Shield. (In a peneplain, leveling is nearly complete.) Elsewhere in Wisconsin the Shield is bent or faulted downward and buried under softer sedimentary rocks of more recent age. For example, at Madison it lies nearly 1,000 feet down.

The second span of time—for us an age of deposition—was the early part of the Paleozoic era. In its first 200 million years, shallow seas came and went several times across the Midwest. Thus, between 500 and 300 million years ago, Wisconsin received, first, mostly deposits of sand (evidently near shore) and, later, mostly limy mud formed by algae and corals farther offshore in shallow clear water. As the shorelines and water depths shifted about, these sediments varied in depth and extent. They later hardened, respectively, into various thicknesses of sandstone and limestones, with some intermediate shaly rocks from deposits of fine silt. The result is a somewhat marbled "layer cake" reaching a maximum thickness of some 1,600 feet (Figs. 11a and b).

The third geologic interval (from the Devonian period of the Paleozoic era, through all of the Mesozoic era and most of the Cenozoic era), in all spanning another 300 million years and the evolution of vertebrates from fishes to man, was one of almost continuous erosion in our region. Wisconsin was warped gently upward into a dome, while what is now southern Michigan, Illinois, and Iowa, sank for awhile and continued to bury fossils in sediments up through the Coal Age. Then Wisconsin was peneplained again, but because of the warping, the sediments were unevenly removed. The igneous central Northern Highland, the top of the dome, was fully exposed again; at Madison, 800–1,000 feet of the "layer cake" were removed; along Lake Michigan, the down-warped layers were preserved in entirety (Fig. 11b). The buried monadnocks were fully or partly exhumed as hills or as barriers to river flow. Southwestern Wisconsin was bent down less far than the southeastern quarter, allowing deep dissection of the Western Upland by the Mississippi's tributaries, exposing most of the sedimentary layers in each coulee. Most of the erosion probably occurred before the evolution of modern, efficient, dense vegetative cover that stabilized the soil as early as 60 million years ago.

The resulting carved surface determines to a large extent the major geographic regions seen today (Figs. 1 and 7). As the edges of the tilted layers of the "cake" eroded back, the layers stood out as shinglelike cliff edges (cuestas) with occasional mesas or buttes out in front of these cliffs remaining as outliers. These

Canadian Shield (Precambrian); hard, ancient, igneous and metamorphic rocks

Sandstones (Cambrian and Ordovician); sedimentary rocks

Dolomites and associated shales (Ordovician, Silurian, and Devonian); sedimentary rocks

Figure 11a. Simplified map of bedrock geology of Wisconsin as the surface would look if soils and glacial deposits could be removed. (After map by F. D. Hole, Soils Div., Wis. Geol. and Nat. Hist. Surv., Madison, 1950.)

cuestas show up across the state as the two concentric arcs of differing rock exposures (Figs. 11a and b).

Most of the lower (Cambrian) rocks are sandstones (inner arc) while most of the upper (Ordovician and Silurian) rocks are of dolomite (outer arc). Dolomite is limestone containing a significant complement of magnesium as well as calcium carbonate.

Our most spectacular dolomite cliffs (Niagara formation) occur along the Green Bay shore of Door County, gradually waning toward Waukesha. Our best sandstone cliffs include the dells of the Kickapoo and Wisconsin rivers and the central Wisconsin sandstone buttes, concentrated in the Camp Douglas area (Juneau County), which were left behind as the Cambrian sandstone cuesta retreated southward. Our highest bluffs—along the Mississippi—are capped by Silurian dolomite but extend down to the sandy Cambrian layers where the river has scoured their bases. (See Figure 13 for reference to some special Wisconsin features.)

The final geologic span of importance to us—the Pleistocene era, or Ice Age—was so recent that despite its geologically short duration (only 1 million years) its modest influence is still strongly felt. Although its deposits and sculptures are fragile in a geological sense, there has not been time for wind and water to obliterate them from our landscape. Whereas the basic topographic and drainage pattern has remained much the same, vegetation and human land use have been profoundly influenced by the glaciers. They modified and refined our soils and created most of our numerous lakes and wetlands. The ice probably even carried boreal vegetation on its back and along its drainageways, washing these plants onto cool cliffs in southwestern Wisconsin and dropping them into soggy sphagnum bogs in southeastern Wisconsin.

Many of the glacial influences we know about were due to the last of the four major ice advances, called the Wisconsin stage of glaciation (because it stopped

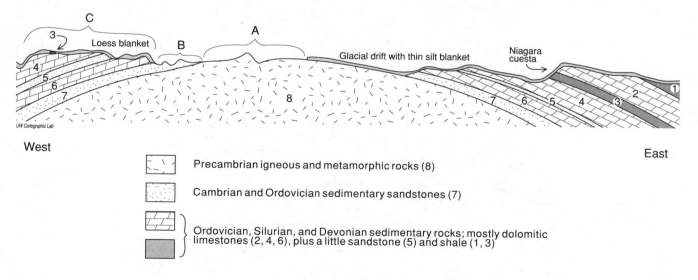

Figure 11b. Imaginary cross section of Wisconsin bedrock from the Mississippi River to Lake Michigan. Concentric zones A, B, and C (Fig. 11a) are cut through to show the doming of rocks after they were deposited and the resulting cuestas (where after erosion one rock overlaps the next layer beneath). The cuestas form the concentric zones shown in Figure 11a and correspond to the "layer cake" of sedimentary rocks. (After map by F. D. Hole, Soil Surv. Div., Wis. Geol. and Nat. Hist. Surv., Madison, undated, adapted from Martin 1965.)

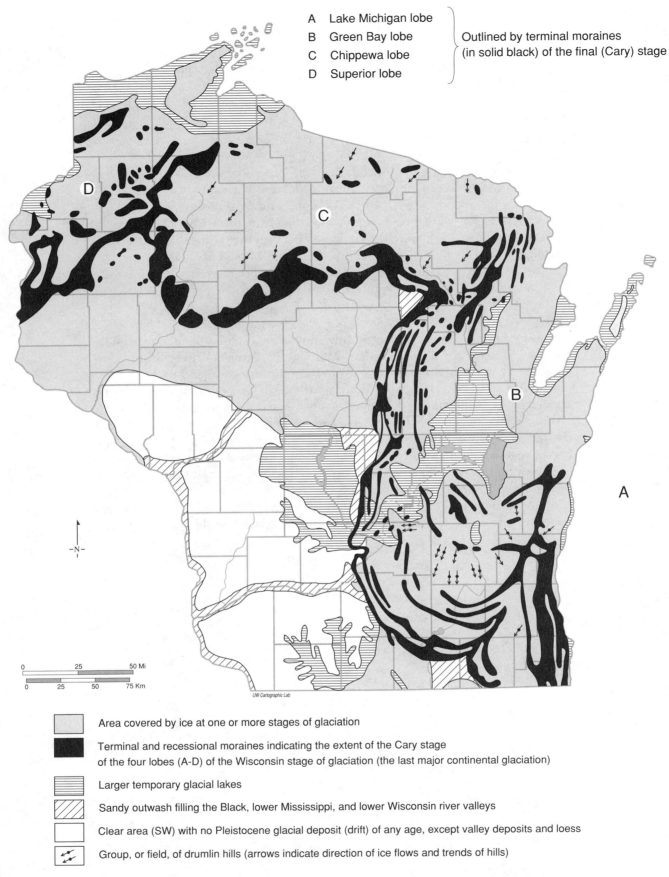

A   Lake Michigan lobe
B   Green Bay lobe
C   Chippewa lobe
D   Superior lobe

Outlined by terminal moraines (in solid black) of the final (Cary) stage

☐ Area covered by ice at one or more stages of glaciation

■ Terminal and recessional moraines indicating the extent of the Cary stage of the four lobes (A-D) of the Wisconsin stage of glaciation (the last major continental glaciation)

▤ Larger temporary glacial lakes

▨ Sandy outwash filling the Black, lower Mississippi, and lower Wisconsin river valleys

☐ Clear area (SW) with no Pleistocene glacial deposit (drift) of any age, except valley deposits and loess

↙ Group, or field, of drumlin hills (arrows indicate direction of ice flows and trends of hills)

Figure 12. Some major glacial features of Wisconsin. (Simplified from map by F. D. Hole [after Thwaites 1956], Soils Div., Wis. Geol. and Nat. Hist. Surv., Madison, 1950.)

74

in Wisconsin, where many of its deposits are conspicuous, making for easy study). It lasted perhaps 250,000 years, and most of its deposits occurred as it retreated during its last 4,000 years, ending some 10,000 years ago.

The most conspicuous glacial "footprints" are the system of terminal and interlobate moraines which outline the farthest advance of the four lobes of Wisconsin ice (Fig. 12). These moraines were formed by rock and soil carried in, on, and under the ice as it flowed outward from the center of each lobe. Located at the melting edges of the ice, these irregular, ice-contact deposits were coarse (gravelly) because the gushing meltwaters carried all finer particles farther away from the ice front. Wisconsin's highest moraine, called the kettle moraine, is an interlobate moraine pushed up between the Green Bay and Lake Michigan lobes (see Figures 12 and 13). Kettles, which also occur in all terminal and ground moraines and in outwash, are steep-sided hollows where buried blocks of ice eventually melted, leaving pits which the slumping sides could not fill.

Terminal and interlobate moraines are easy to spot once one understands where to find them. The Niagara cuesta (Fig. 13) separated the Green Bay and Lake Michigan lobes and provided the limy rubble that was piled up between them. This rubble formed the kettle moraine and associated deposits that continue southward into southeastern Wisconsin. Therefore, the adjacent peatlands are fed by limy groundwater, which makes them fertile. As a result, most have suffered agricultural drainage.

U.S. Highway 51 follows near to or on the Green Bay lobe's western terminal moraine all the way from Portage to Stevens Point (see Figures 12 and 13). One must go off on side roads east and west to see it loom up in contrast to ground moraine (east), outwash (west), and old glacial lake beds (both sides). Much of this moraine is sandy because of the prevalent local sandstone. However, in places it contains both lime and sand, and especially so in the south between Madison and Lake Geneva (Walworth County), where it courses southeastward near Highways 14, 12, and I-90.

Most of the glaciated parts of the state are covered with a more subtle, irregular mantle of unsorted material (everything from boulders to fine clay) called till or ground moraine. It was simply dropped by the final stagnant ice. Although much of it is local bedrock ground up and moved but a short distance, you usually can find a few igneous and metamorphic boulders and pebbles that could have come from as far as central Canada. The Chippewa lobe brought igneous and metamorphic gravel and sand from northern Michigan to the central Northern Highland, whereas the Superior lobe ground up the Cambrian sandstone near Lake Superior and moved the sand about in northwestern Wisconsin (Figs. 1, 10, 11, and 12). These infertile substrates (and the cool climate) favor acid boggy shores, in contrast to the influence of the Green Bay lobe.

A special glacial feature is the drumlin—a hill ridden over and streamlined by ice flow. Some drumlins have bedrock cores; others are built entirely of gravel, sand, and clay. Drumlins often occur abundantly in "families" or "fields"; the largest field extends between Madison, Waukesha, and Horicon (Figs. 12 and 13). It contains hundreds of elongate hills whose trends (southwest, south, or southeast) indicate the direction of ice movement in the spreading Green Bay lobe. Such fields occur in low flat areas (near the front) where ice thickness was lessening, allowing maximum deposition of glacial materials and little scouring.

Glacial action also produced or altered water features. Some waters and wetlands resulted from moraines blocking preglacial streams cut into the bedrock, such as in the Yahara River valley at Madison, and on the Rock River from Hori-

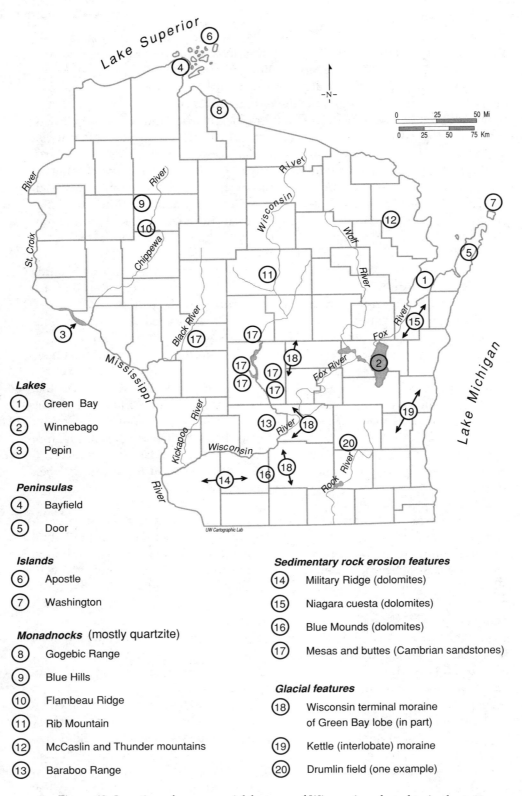

Lakes

① Green Bay
② Winnebago
③ Pepin

Peninsulas

④ Bayfield
⑤ Door

Islands

⑥ Apostle
⑦ Washington

Monadnocks (mostly quartzite)

⑧ Gogebic Range
⑨ Blue Hills
⑩ Flambeau Ridge
⑪ Rib Mountain
⑫ McCaslin and Thunder mountains
⑬ Baraboo Range

Sedimentary rock erosion features

⑭ Military Ridge (dolomites)
⑮ Niagara cuesta (dolomites)
⑯ Blue Mounds (dolomites)
⑰ Mesas and buttes (Cambrian sandstones)

Glacial features

⑱ Wisconsin terminal moraine of Green Bay lobe (in part)
⑲ Kettle (interlobate) moraine
⑳ Drumlin field (one example)

Figure 13. Location of some special features of Wisconsin referred to in the text.

con to Koshkonong, and Devil's Lake in the Baraboo hills. Many others are in steep-sided kettles, where buried ice blocks melted. Kettles in ground moraine and outwash resulted when a second minor ice advance buried a mixture of ice and soil under more fill, or when meltwaters from receding ice buried unmelted outliers under new gravel or sand. Our two major kettle lake districts in the north were created by the Superior and Chippewa lobes and have, as noted above, somewhat different substrates. The third kettle lake district, in end moraines and outwash, extends southward from Waukesha and Milwaukee into northeastern Illinois. These lakes, too, often have peaty shores and floors, but the peat is more often limy (fen) than acid (bog) because of the generally fertile substrate. The especially large number of springs in southeastern Wisconsin is due to the massive groundwater reservoirs in the porous ground moraines as well as in the interlobate and recessional moraines.

The beds of temporary glacial lakes, created wherever the ice retreated behind its terminal or recessional moraine, produced numerous wetlands, because flat land drains out with difficulty. A series of glacial lake beds extend from central Wisconsin to Green Bay and Lake Winnebago (Figs. 1, 7, and 12). The largest even plain, the bed of Glacial Lake Wisconsin, covers parts of five counties in the central sand district. Waves of this lake carved the vertical cliffs of the sandstone buttes near Camp Douglas. Because the sands have been easily washed of their relatively low lime content, they are acid.

Rivers were altered in several ways. Parts of the preglacial Rock River were filled with mixtures of gravel and ice to form the chain of wetlands and lakes in Jefferson County from Lake Mills to Lake Koshkonong. The low terminal moraine at Portage (Columbia County) was sufficient to block off the Fox-Wolf system from the Wisconsin-Mississippi, forcing the "Big" Fox to reverse its flow via Green Bay to the St. Lawrence. The resultant low grade in east-central Wisconsin created the vast peaty wetlands of the "Big" Fox Valley. Meanwhile, sand washed from the Wisconsin Dells and from Glacial Lake Wisconsin filled the lower Wisconsin River valley up to a depth of 300 feet and altered other drainage patterns. For example, Honey Creek was backed up temporarily so that waves cut its sandstone buttes and distributed sand to form the extensive Sauk Prairie. Before revegetation, all the sands (Fig. 10) were blown into low dunes, which show up today as numerous forest islands in the vast wetlands of central Wisconsin and down the Wisconsin River to its mouth. Similar sand islands and dunes were deposited up and down the Mississippi. In the northern forest, pines mark the old sandy dunes and glacial lake shores.

Many wetlands, meanders, and oxbow lakes were created along the Sugar, Lemonweir, Yellow, Black, Wisconsin, Mississippi, and other rivers. These resulted from widening of the valleys by meltwaters, filling of the valleys with sand, and tardy rising of the land as the glacier's weight shifted northward, creating a temporary low grade so that much of the sand has remained.

As a result of these glacial actions on water features, we have in the central part of the state a continuous wilderness corridor still only moderately affected by human actions; it includes the Glacial Lake Wisconsin lake bed (wet acid sand, formerly with bogs and pine islands, now partly drained, with mostly aspen), the "Big" Fox Valley (more fertile, with sedge meadows and bogs, partly farmed), and the Wisconsin River valley (with everything from cactus desert to floodplain hardwoods, surrounded by high wooded bluffs). This low-impact corridor, connecting southwestward to the Mississipi River valley and northeastward to the northern forest and Great Lakes regions, maintains much of our birdlife.

The largest damming project of the Ice Age was, of course, the Great Lakes themselves, although these basins were also partly created by preglacial erosion, bedrock faulting and tilting, cuestas like the resistant dolomitic ledge at Niagara Falls, and glacial scouring. When the last Wisconsin ice retreated toward its center northeast of us, it held Lakes Superior and Michigan at a higher level (stage) for awhile by blocking the Straits of Mackinac and Sault Ste Marie. This happened a second time when a small re-advance again blocked the outlet of our Great Lakes, causing burial of a spruce forest between two layers of clay (visible today in Manitowoc County). The carbon 14 content of the buried spruces gives us an accurate date for final minor glacial advances: 11,200 years ago (give or take a few hundred).

The clay deposits and sand-beach ridges created by the temporarily higher Great Lake levels were shown earlier to have profoundly influenced our vegetation and land use in eastern Wisconsin. Even that remarkable area, unglaciated southwestern Wisconsin (Figs. 1 and 12), was strongly influenced by the ice via river-sand deposits, wind-blown loess, and probable transplants of northern vegetation.

Climates and Fires

We could delve in great detail into the 11,000 years of postglacial history; but since much of it is still speculative, only the high points will be given here. Our best history books are the lake sediments and the bog peats, in which animal fossils, plant remains, pollen deposits, traces of soil, ash, and charcoal, and even human artifacts are preserved. In general, the climate seems to have warmed up gradually, up to the period called the Xerothermic, which ended about 3,000 years ago. By that time, the pollen of spruce and firs had been replaced in successive layers of sediments by oak and grass southward and by pine and oak northward. However, there is some evidence that the spruce grew chiefly on the ice or in the bogs, while deserts or prairies actually existed just in front of the ice, where cold air pouring off the ice became dry as it warmed up. As the ice retreated, the prairie plants could have populated what became our drier-soil prairies, sandy inland and coastal dunes, and our jack pine–scrub oak barrens of central and northern Wisconsin. These grasslands then may have spread farther during the Xerothermic. After the Xerothermic period, the climate seems to have become somewhat cooler and moister again, according to the pollen record, favoring a wider diversity of trees.

We cannot bring climatic influences up to the present without considering storms and fires. The incidence of fires is correlated with soil, climate, weather, and human actions. Recent studies of lake sediments suggest that, at any given time, one-third of the presettlement northern forest area was recovering from fire, and another third was regrowing after windthrow. But fires were unequally distributed. Climax hemlock or sugar maple forests, as well as hardwood swamps and coniferous bogs, are usually too damp to burn. Droughty sandy soils are the most fire prone, especially because they foster scrub (low) or savanna (open groves) types of vegetation, which dry out more easily with their greater accessibility to wind and sun. In addition, the drought-tolerant pines and prairie plants are highly resinous and hence highly flammable. In intermediate sites, the tall old pines invited lightening; but unless storms had opened up large acreages allowing the area to dry out, fires would have been localized, creating small clearings of only a few acres.

Several lines of evidence point to one or more short but severe droughts which occurred not long before European settlement and could have induced very destructive fires. One such clue was the prevalence of groves of large pines (the "pineries" that attracted land speculators and loggers in the late 1800s) in and northeast of the tension zone. Pines are pioneer trees, reproducing best after forest destruction, and they are tolerant of drought. Another clue was the prevalence of brushy oak savanna with prairie understory on relic forest soil types southwest of the tension zone. Oaks, too, are pioneer species, favored by fire; but to have influenced the soil, they would have required several relatively fireless centuries to do so. Many local variations in vegetation, suggesting burned areas, show up in detailed analyses of presettlement vegetation interpreted from the notes of the land surveyors in the 1840s. (Figure 8 is too general to show most of the local pine and prairie areas frequently encountered in those days.)

Still another clue is found in studies of midwestern Indian food dumps, which pinpoint a sudden shift in our climate to drier conditions around A.D. 1180 (Bryson and Murray 1977). A cosmic event, such as an asteroid's near miss of earth, is a possible cause of such a sudden temporary climatic change. Once widely established as a seed source, both prairies and pineries could have perpetuated themselves over the next 7 centuries, because they invited more fires (and also windthrow in the case of the tall, emergent white and red pines).

In addition, American Indians probably had by then been using fire in vegetation management (they certainly were doing so by the time of European settlement) to enhance the hunt and hasten the greening of forage. In some northern forests, there is evidence that frequent human-set ground fires actually saved the large pines from fatal crown fires by continually clearing out flammable fallen slash and underbrush that could have kindled the upper branches.

A final clue pointing to the influence on vegetation of one or more sudden fiery periods only a few centuries before settlement, rather than a long drought over thousands of years, was the persistence of small relic stands of fire-sensitive sugar maple and basswood forests on the east sides of hills and waters throughout Wisconsin's prairie-oak region. Examples are still found in Dane and Jefferson counties.

On the other hand, in the Driftless Area's larger regions of deep valleys—such as Dunn, Pierce, Vernon, Richland, and southern Green counties, and the Baraboo hills—extensive dense forest already appeared in 1840 much as it does today (see Figure 8). But even in these regions at that time, prairies covered the ridges and oaks grew on the west sides of valleys and hills, which today are being invaded by sugar maples. Evidently, then, fires had occurred here, but were not so frequent or so severe, despite drought, where large areas of forest prevailed. Some of these forested regions today enjoy a locally higher summer rainfall than do the surrounding lands. Whether a cause or an effect of the trees, especially the maples, the damper summers could help exclude ordinary fires. In eastern Wisconsin, the Rock River as well as the kettle moraine and Niagara cuesta (Fig. 13) helped form a final firebreak for even exceptional conflagrations fanned by dry westerly winds, favoring to their east sides a fire-free climax forest along with the provision of lime needed by the sugar maples.

It appears, then, that for the past 11,000 years, since the glaciers melted, the same bird habitats have been present in Wisconsin. Their relative abundance and distribution may have changed from time to time. Especially important in maintaining a diversity of bird habitats have been the prairie and brushy openings and early stages of forest succession (oak, aspen, pine) in a patchwork of burns and storm blowdowns across the state.

Impacts of Settlement

In the final settlement period of barely a century and a half, bird habitats have been as drastically affected as in the much longer climatic and geologic time spans. Eyewitness accounts give us a much more detailed set of clues. Here we are concerned mainly with the undesirable effects of settlement on birdlife. The first major impact had to do with changes in the amount of fire. The start of settlement tipped the balance in Wisconsin back to dense broad-leaved (deciduous) forests, in the north by too much fire and in the south by too little. The second major impact had to do with agriculture. At first farming was attempted everywhere; later it became increasingly intensive south of the northern forest region, first in the better soils and finally spreading to the marginal lands not usurped for recreation. We can trace the fate of specific habitat types and their bird contingents in a number of cases, both north and south of the tension zone.

Impacts on Birdlife in Northern Wisconsin

The logging boom that intensified to a frenzied pace in the late 1800s was careless and greedy. So the pineries were lost, and the climax maples and hemlocks as well. Most of the seed trees were either cut down or burned up in the slash-fed holocausts in the dry opened-up landscape. The fires even destroyed several towns. Today it is hard to imagine the near total destruction of so much of the northern forest in the northern lake states. But photographs don't lie, nor did the temporary invasion of the north country by the Greater Prairie-Chicken. This bird showed up in nearly every county, telling us that the skyline was actually treeless, and that this species is able to "explode" into suitable habitat when it becomes available. As early attempts to reclaim the land with farming failed in the cold forest climate, the old fields and pastures soon were invaded (as were the unfarmed burns) by monotonous landscapes of aspen and white birch, whose seeds are widely dispersed by the wind. These pioneer forests led to a paper industry largely dependent on these fast-growing species and a vested interest in aspen-birch farming today.

Our regenerating forest still exhibits in places the "generation gap"—the missing white pine and red oak stages between the pioneering aspen and birch and the gradually returning shade-tolerant red and sugar maples (the maples, respectively, of poor and fertile soils), fir, and hemlock. When the few surviving young oaks and pines reached reproducing age, the forest was already too shady for them to invade.

Today much of the northern forest is managed more and more intensively for short-rotation monotypes of aspen or planted pines for paper, while climax hardwoods under selective timber logging enable the sugar maple to become more uniformly dominant. Mounting demand for wood products is causing "cleaner" forests, while mechanization favors management in large uniform blocks. Despite the commercial emphasis on pioneer types of trees, the loss of the interspersion of conifers and hardwoods and the uniformity in tree size presumably mean lower bird diversity if not also lower abundance. Ruffed Grouse and some others may prosper in young aspen but studies of the requirements of all bird species are needed. These studies may now be possible by comparing the managed and natural forests. Because nature isn't static, studies must be of trends. For example, ravens have lost their wilderness but seem to have taken advantage of waste dumps and road-killed carrion. Lowland forests are being left alone by loggers today, because they tend to get wetter and colder when trees are removed. Powell Marsh in Vilas County, reverting to wet meadow after the big fires, may be a good place to manage for Sharp-tailed Grouse.

The growing use of herbicides to remove hardwoods on land planted to young pines, as well as on rights-of-way, is a matter of controversy, along with the width of the "cheater strips," now that scenery is so important to the tourist industry. Group-selection forestry—an alternative to monotypic large-block management that attempts to simulate the small openings and diverse age groups created by windthrow or local fires in the old days—would seem to be the ideal way to mesh forest utilization with bird habitat maintenance. Such fine-tuned landscape design will not win favor until there is pressure to try it. One possible form of pressure is present in the vulnerability of uniform tree crops to the spread of insect or disease pests, as is the case in our agricultural crops. The resulting likelihood is large-scale chemical application of pesticides, which may be even more harmful to wildlife than the monotypes and may cause backlashes in both pests and public opinion. A possible case in point is the recent Wisconsin outbreak of budworms on spruce and tamarack. It may just be part of the insect's natural cycle; but another suspected cause is the buildup of numbers of firs, which the budworm favors, because the fir has suffered comparatively little from logging and deer.

The complex deer problem may become as serious for bird habitats as is intensive forestry management. Many places today have 3–10 times the deer population they had when wolves and Indians (and their dogs) were hunting them the year round, and before widespread logging provided so much young palatable growth to eat. Today, the combined toll of hunting, road mortality, and periodic winter starvation, although considerable and growing, still seems insufficient to restore the deer to moderate levels. Unfortunately, there are also many vested interests who favor excessive numbers of deer so they can be easily seen or harvested. Already we have lost our American yew and much of the natural reproduction of pine, yellow birch, white cedar, and hemlock that could be important elements in the forest's natural habitat for birds (as well as deer) and economic flexibility. These effects are now showing up, especially in public forests, parks, reservations, and scientific areas.

We do have near-virgin forests in certain places today, especially around our many northern lakes and boggy wetlands, which often served as firebreaks. There, wealthy estates and recreation interests reduced logging activity, and fires as well. Now some of the pines and other trees that were only half-grown in Paul Bunyan's day are fully mature, to the evident benefit of certain boreal-contingent warblers, fringillids, and birds of prey. The future of these attractive shorelines, made so much of by the recreation industry, is in doubt, however. For one thing, the deer prosper here most of all, since hunting is discouraged near dwellings. And these dwellings are multiplying so rapidly that cottage and second-home development may rival the logging boom in devastation of bird habitat—this time with permanent consequences. On small lots there is very little room between houses, lawns, and roads for new trees to grow. Old trees are taken down for utility lines and to reduce hazard to people and structures as they become half-dead snags, which are of special value to birds. On the sand beaches, heavy human use has eliminated nearly all nesting species, including most breeding sites of the Piping Plover on our Great Lakes coasts.

While small birds may prosper at present in the incompletely developed, diverse, mature shore forests, our Bald Eagles may not remain where the wilderness solitude is shattered by the chain saw and the motorboat. Pervasive fishing and recreation boating threaten shore erosion, fish habitat, and the reproduction of loons and mergansers as well. A small start is being made to zone certain lakes and forests for eagle sanctuaries, and perhaps this approach for water-bird protection will follow. For Double-crested Cormorants, Ospreys, and Great Blue Herons, the early snag-filled impoundments for log rafting and power generation were larger than—and so an improvement on—beaver flowages. But later, the beavers were trapped to spare trout, and laws required snag removal on flowages for boating safety. Now these birds must depend on artificial platforms for a comeback. The northern boggy wetlands and streams are generally in very good condition, with natural shores and good water quality, since their watersheds are still forested, at least with young trees. But control of the beaver has lowered the frequency of flooded dead spruces that evidently favored Black-backed Woodpeckers.

Serious, but not yet fully understood, are the environmental impacts of acid rain, expanded mining, road and communications development, and increased waste disposal. Nor is it yet known to what extent our warblers and other northern (as well as southern) forest birds will be affected by accelerated forest destruction in Latin America, where many of our insect-eating species overwinter.

Impacts on Birdlife in Southern Wisconsin

South of the tension zone, the patchwork of prairies and brushy oak groves has been replaced by a patchwork of cultivated fields, pastures, and maturing woodlots. The species of the eastern contingent that suffered most were some upland edge and shrub nesters such as the Rufous-sided Towhee. (See the tables in the chapter on habitat preferences.) Among nonforest species, the impact of farming on birds in southern Wisconsin has been at least one order of magnitude greater than it has been in the north. It can only be described as drastic. Fire stoppage, farming, and drainage have altered most of the landscape. Right after settlement in the 1840s the Greater Prairie-Chicken and perhaps other prairie species enjoyed a temporary boom as cropland began to diversify the available winter food, only to succumb to loss of brood cover as farming intensified. As savanna and fencerow grew up to brush, the Rufous-sided Towhee prospered, while the Eastern Bluebird expanded its numbers in hollow fenceposts and orchard trees, and the Red-headed Woodpecker capitalized on the utility poles of rural electrification.

Today, however, the roadside has generally become a biological desert rivaling the cornfield, with the advent of regrading for fast traffic, brush removal, metal fences, repellents on poles, wide use of herbicides, and frequent right-of-way mowing. The result of recent efforts to delay right-of-way mowing awaits study. The American Crow and possibly the Turkey Vulture have prospered by feeding on car-killed mammals, but traffic is a hazard to hawks and owls alighting on pavement. The Passenger Pigeon was lost to hunting before the oak forests could make a postfire comeback on unplowed, ungrazed hills, and before intensive farming would have branded this bird a pest. The forestation of bluffs began to foreclose falcon eyries before poaching and pesticides extirpated Wisconsin Peregrines. But the abundant red cedars invading unburned bluffs and pastures today are a boon to nesting doves, grackles, and other small birds.

Impacts on Forest Birds in Southern Wisconsin. Forest birds have suffered the least, because our southern woodlots have gone through only a mild rise and fall as favorable habitats. First, the unfarmed brushy savannas became dense, even-aged oak woodlots, because fire protection and the cessation of grazing by bison and early livestock enabled oak "grubs" and new seedlings to grow up. The number of birds of dense forest must have increased significantly at the expense of those of grassland, savanna, and brush. For a parallel, we know that our fox squirrel—favored by open savannas and large trees—was largely replaced by the gray squirrel between 1940 and 1960. By the 1960s many useful den trees—open-grown oaks of the former savanna (and large maples, basswoods, elms, and beeches in their fire-protected regions)—had succumbed to rot, shading, storms, and timber-stand improvement. Thus, woodpeckers and other hole-nesters, possibly including several owls, have probably declined somewhat again.

Modern woodlots lack a gradual edge near cropland, are shrinking in acreage and tree size because of demand for crops and fuel, and are still being pastured in many cases to the detriment of soil, trees, and birds. Some woodlots are succeeding to more uniform trees by invasion or plantings of sugar maples and walnuts. Many woodlots, especially in southeastern Wisconsin, are experiencing an invasion of alien species—honeysuckle, buckthorn, and the Norway maple—that form a green wall in autumn after the native shrubs have dropped their leaves. In winter, rabbits and deer give the aliens the edge by preferring to eat the native shrub and sapling species. Thus, as in the north but for different reasons, forest reproduction is hindered, and habitat monotony is on the rise.

This loss of diversity of plant species and life-form can have many consequences for specific bird species. For example, with fire protection, the light-demanding oaks are able to reproduce today only in recently abandoned pastures and in open sandy country. With so little opportunity for their renewal, oaks, whose abundance we take for granted today, will experience a major decline caused by logging, old age, and diseases like oak wilt. Oaks are important trees, providing much insect food and both acorns and enduring den sites for a number of our birds as well as several mammals. On the other hand, the loss to Dutch elm disease of most of our elms in both the river floodplains and climax upland maple forests, as well as in cities, during the past 25 years has had little noticeable effect on birds. Warbling Vireos may have declined, but the Northern Oriole has maintained its numbers where mature cottonwoods, oaks, and maples have been available for nest sites. The era of hard pesticides used in the early years in control of elm disease was cut short because of obvious damage to bird-life and growing awareness of danger to people as well. Therefore, most urban birds, from robins to screech-owls, have recovered, although some scars remain, such as the continuing absence of the traditional Yellow-throated Vireo from the University of Wisconsin–Madison campus. Woodpeckers did not increase as significantly as might have been expected from the abundance of dying elms. Possibly one reason is that, unlike oaks, elms rot and fall too soon after dying for their woodpecker habitat to build up.

More emphasis on specific habitat requirements will be needed to assess the causes of peculiarities—new or continuing—in our birds' populations. Why, for instance, are the Broad-winged Hawk, Pine Warbler, and Black-and-white Warbler virtually absent in southern Wisconsin in summer, although widely present both in northern Wisconsin and in the southern states? (Only the Pine Warbler seems to be confined to pine trees, which are scarce in southern Wisconsin, except for uniform young plantations.) The case of the Parula Warbler is clearer; for its special nest site it chooses Spanish moss (*Tillandsia*) of the southern coastal plain on this continent and the similar "old man's beard" lichen (*Usnea*) of the boreal forest, of which Wisconsin has a few remnants today. For many birds—such as the Wood Thrush, Great Crested Flycatcher, and Hairy Woodpecker—the higher BBS numbers in the northern counties may simply reflect the higher amounts of forest habitat in the transects. But there is the likelihood that some species require larger tracts of unbroken woodland than do others. Larger species—the Ruffed Grouse, Barred Owl, Pileated Woodpecker—need large wooded feeding areas, which are rarer south of the tension zone.

Perhaps, too, there are preferences by races (or local learned traditions) that cause some populations to favor different habitats in parts of a species' overall range. A possible example is that Rose-breasted Grosbeaks nest in white oaks near Verona but in box elders near Madison (pers. obs.), although both trees occur in both forests. The higher transect density noted for the Scarlet Tanager in the north-central zone of Wisconsin can be laid to the prevalence of this species' preferred oaks in large tracts in this sandy region. Some birds of the southern contingent seem to favor the unglaciated coulee country of southwestern Wisconsin for reasons cited earlier, or possibly even because of the continuation of preglacial traditions.

The partly unglaciated "island" of forest composing the Baraboo Range may be such a case for both its southern- and boreal-contingent birds. Certain plants found there are likewise isolated far from their primary ranges to the south and north. Today there is concern over the threat to some of the rarer isolated warbler species due to increasing Brown-headed Cowbird parasitism caused by or coupled with the opening or cutting up of the Baraboo hills' extensive woodlots into smaller isolated tracts. In fact, recent studies (Terborgh 1989) suggest that songbirds in all areas of the continent are threatened by a cowbird population explosion triggered by waste-grain abundance and fragmentation of forested tracts everywhere by development which permits cowbird entry.

Impacts on Grassland Birds—Primarily in Southern and Western Wisconsin. The populations of most grassland birds, in contrast to those of the forest, have been severely depleted by intensive land use. While many of them still thrive in the sparsely settled dry plains and badlands of the western United States, prairie species have been virtually eliminated from much of the corn, soybean, and wheat belt. (The outstanding exception is the versatile Red-winged Blackbird, of course.) Even dairy country has made poor prairie habitat; for after settlement, livestock enclosures, having evolved from intensively grazed fields to thoroughly trampled feedlots, have never been a substitute for wild grasslands. However, the advent of the dairy feedlot has required maintenance of large acreages of cropland planted in untrampled perennial alfalfa-grass mixtures. At first these dairyland hayfields continued to support an abundance of not only nesting Red-winged Blackbirds and Savannah Sparrows but also Bobolinks, Eastern and Western Meadowlarks, Dickcissels, and Vesper and Grasshopper Sparrows, their breeding squeezed in between snowmelt and the first or second mowing each summer. However, as noted above, recent, more intensive hay-mowing schedules, if not outright conversion to cash crops, is seriously reducing grassland bird-breeding habitat. The Dickcissel has declined in Wisconsin since 1968, with both meadowlarks and Grasshopper Sparrows more recently following suit. Horned Larks and Killdeers still persist on open barren landscapes such as late-plowed fields, pastured ponds, and large muck farms.

The Greater Prairie-Chicken's replacement, the Ring-necked Pheasant, thrives in cornland; the pheasant, however, prospers only where it has access to some grassy or marshy winter and nest cover, while the "chickens" are now artificially and very locally maintained on lands managed for unmowed grass that were once bog and forest. Only a few unforested Wisconsin prairie preserves such as the Chiwaukee Prairie Scientific Area in Kenosha County are large enough to support still today a few of the once-abundant Upland Sandpipers. But this species has invaded and persisted in fields near the shore of Lake Michigan, where cooler summers have favored a prevalence of perennial forage crops, and in vacant lands that once were cherry orchards (especially in Door County). This bird and its dozen prairie associates, including the American Kestrel, also persist on a few treeless ridges in the Driftless Area, such as that south of Blue Mounds in Dane County, a few undrained southeastern low meadows, a few poor central Wisconsin sand farms and lowlands, several large airports, the Bong State Recreation Area in Racine County, and certain temporarily open, idle lands slated for urban development. Some of these unmowed grassy fields and meadows have Henslow's Sparrows and Sedge Wrens as well.

Most true prairie vegetation relics—scattered along railroads and steep bluffs—are too small to support birds except sometimes a territory or two for the Grasshopper Sparrow. Moreover, pesticide use on surrounding cropland may drastically reduce insect supplies, making these areas even less likely to attract and hold birds. However, parts of hilly southwestern and flat, sandy, central Wisconsin retain a tradition of intermittent pasturing on unimproved sands, slopes, and rocky ridges, even with actual fallowing of some fields, favoring a variety of open-country species. These regions also have partly open land favoring Field Sparrows, Red-headed Woodpeckers, Mourning Doves, and Vesper Sparrows. Both the central and southwestern regions maintain the bobwhite, because abundant fencerow cover has been incidentally retained. Unfortunately, drained and irrigated cropland, pine plantations, and beef feedlots continue to encroach on the central sandy glacial lake bed and riverine sand barrens, which have, until recently, maintained much prairie wildlife.

Most of the interest in prairie restoration has been purely botanical; hence, most areas of attempted restoration are too small to harbor viable breeding populations of prairie birds. But an exciting possibility would be to upgrade a few prairie preserves to make them as large and complete as possible, favoring birds ranging from Bobolinks and Northern Harriers to Sedge Wrens and Greater Prairie-Chickens, and other animals ranging from lizards, snakes, and pocket gophers to badgers and bison. Possibly suitable sites to consider include open lands of a square mile or more near Plainfield, Grantsburg, Rush Lake (see Impacts on Peatland Birds section, below), Blue Mounds, the Bong area, and several sites along the lower Wisconsin River such as at Spring Green. It is not too soon to explore such possibilities, for agricultural practices could suddenly intensify further, while all open space continues to shrink under mounting pressures of human population.

Impacts on Water Birds—Primarily in Southern and Western Wisconsin. The birds of wetlands and lakes have suffered losses as great as those of the prairies, despite Wisconsin's relatively low drainage effort among states in the Midwest. Even in the prairie states and Canadian provinces, shorebird and duck habitat is still succumbing at a rapid rate to expanding agriculture. Efforts of organizations like Ducks Unlimited to counteract this trend have until recently been confined to Canada. Of Wisconsin's wetlands south of the tension zone, most of those remaining (about one-quarter by acreage) have suffered a decline in quality and extent of habitat, especially in recent years. For example, deep and shallow marshes and waters have been largely eliminated as bird habitat by three stark impacts: (1) permanent or seasonal water level alteration, up or down, too fast or too slow, too often, or at the wrong season; (2) deterioration of water quality (turbidity and loss of oxygen from siltation and eutrophication); and (3) alteration of edges and shorelines (silt deltas, steepening of gradient by filling or digging, loss of buffer strips). Motorboat wakes, too, alter shores and disturb waterbirds (not just loons).

Many river corridors are still relatively wild. But except for the lower Wisconsin and a few sections of other rivers, they suffer from turbid green or brown water, exaggerated floods, dammed-up flowages, levees, channelization, and dredge spoil deposits, which have eliminated much of the floodplain's natural wetland diversity and quality. Plant life and small animal life have suffered, and so have the birds that used to characterize the complex networks of natural meanders and shallow marshy sloughs associated with rivers. Loss of major water-bird habitats on much of the Mississippi corridor is a matter of special concern but not without hope of reversal.

Since wetlands receive and concentrate pollutants, wetland birds may be injured through the foods they eat. Deformities in and a recent decline in numbers of some herons, bitterns, cormorants, and terns are suspected of being caused partly by exposure to the same pollutants and pesticides that have decimated some raptors. Green Bay is a prime example of this effect. In addition, poisoning from accumulating lead shot may be a problem for eagles feeding on sick waterfowl as well as for the ducks and geese themselves. On the other hand, with sensitive management, sludge ponds for recycling sewage and canning wastes can be a gold mine for breeding and migrating shorebirds and waterfowl, for example, at Madison and Arlington (Columbia County), respectively. Thermal pollution and water disturbance at power plants and dams have had at least a "bird feeder" effect, attracting fish and maintaining open water for wintering populations of waterfowl and eagles where we can have access to them. Examples are at Portage, Madison, Cassville, Sauk City, and Milwaukee.

Atkinson's Marsh at Green Bay is a rare case of outright filling of a large valuable wetland. Duschak's Marsh in Dane County is a rare case of outright drainage of another high-quality waterfowl marsh. More typically, a gradual sequence of alterations has modified and progressively simplified complex wetland systems as a result of conflicting pressures by special interest groups. Often, successive causes and effects overlap, confusing the issue for the lay person as well as frustrating the scientist and manager.

An example of such a confused issue centers on the Rock River, whose Koshkonong and Horicon marshes (the history of the latter having been partly documented in Gard 1972 and Hanson 1977) were once famous for all kinds of water birds.

Koshkonong in Jefferson County was first dammed to run a mill, eliminating the wild rice with higher water. Then it was impounded even higher for a small power-generating station still operating today. Resulting shoreline erosion along with accumulated silt from poor upstream land use has made the lake shallow and muddy, and has led to an infestation of carp. The surrounding low prairies, sedge meadows, and river-mouth levees became, respectively, shallow marshes, deep marshes, and floodplain forest, supporting today's breeding waterfowl and heron rookeries. But certain invertebrate, fish, and duck populations are low because of a loss of suitable plant or animal food. The causes of the loss include turbidity from agricultural and shore erosion; algal blooms caused by eutrophication from sewage effluent, eroding soil, and feedlots; wave action from boats; and bottom feeding by carp. If unenlightened cottagers and boaters had their way, water levels would be kept higher in summer, eliminating the remaining wetlands, and causing further septic system failures.

A parallel case is that of Horicon Marsh in Dodge County, which was originally shallower than Koshkonong, apparently mostly in giant peaty sedge meadow with meandering shallow, marshy river channels. It was likewise dammed at first for mill power, boat traffic, and recreation. Later, when it was ditched and drained, expanding agriculture clashed with the duck-shooting and fishing interests, whose growth indicated that the clean shallow water had become ideal habitat. Later, unrestrained hunting, combined with drainage, endangered the waterfowl, and pressure to restore Horicon resulted in federal and state acquisitions. It was impounded a second time, but by then the water quality had deteriorated. Many of the huge buffering low prairies and peat meadows had been drained and burned and were being intensively farmed. Ditches and upland erosion (and sewage plants) were now contributing flash floods, abundant silt and nutrients, and possibly toxic pesticides. Algal blooms and muddy waters helped lower oxygen levels and favored carp, which further deterred desirable water plants, small animals, fish, and birds. Gone were the rice and waterweeds that ducks feast upon, except for small pockets.

Although its diversity of birds remains high, Horicon's production of fish and fowl seems to be much too low for its large acreage. One factor is the halting and piecemeal approach to problem remediation as a result of conflicting special-interest pressures. Here, as on the Mississippi River refuges, four needs must be met if habitat restoration is to succeed: (1) clarifying the needs of water birds through both research and better public education; (2) establishing a consistent but flexible management policy and strategy through time; (3) reducing flood and pollution problems through effective waste and soil management on the *entire* watershed; and (4) restoring natural diversity in the marsh with subtle management of substrate, waters, shores, vegetation, and muskrats. The potential is there. With the lack of upland runoff during the dry 18 months ending in August 1977, the waters cleared and the diverse waterweeds made a brief comeback in parts of both Horicon and Koshkonong (pers. obs.). At Horicon, management is at the present time succeeding with an expensive program of dikes and pumps to isolate sections from the polluted river water. Koshkonong still has good fishery where springs issue clean water. Treating a wetland, including its entire upland watershed, as an integral unit is a new concept. But the recent emphasis on improving our water quality cannot fail to help the aquatic birds as an unintentional by-product of better land, water, and waste management.

Impacts on Peatland Birds—Primarily in Southeastern and Central Wisconsin. Turning to the peatlands remaining today, we again find changes which drastically contrast the natural cycles of succession. Fire stoppage followed by partial drainage for use of adjacent farmland, along with temporary disturbances such as haying and grazing, have caused vast natural acreages of formerly open peatlands to succeed to shrub carrs and forest, which have acquired a new permanence. The invading shrubs include the same alien honeysuckles and buckthorns that now choke so many upland woodlots. Changes in the birds have closely followed this succession.

An example of peatland bird changes following drainage can be seen near Lake Wingra in Madison. Around 1912, the area supported Northern Harriers, Short-eared Owls, American Bitterns, and Sedge Wrens. Schorger (1931a) even cited one sighting of a Greater Prairie-Chicken; and an old photograph in Cahn's (1916a) paper shows an almost total absence of shrubs and trees. However, by 1965, as shrubs filled the open areas, Common Snipe and persisting Ring-necked Pheasants were yielding territory to the American Woodcock (J. H. Zimmerman 1969). Abundant shrub-nesters included the Yellow Warbler, Common Yellowthroat, Swamp Sparrow, Willow Flycatcher, Song Sparrow, American Goldfinch, and Gray Catbird. An occasional Bell's Vireo, Yellow-breasted Chat, and Mourning Warbler were seen. The population of cottontail rabbits mushroomed in the abundant brush. By 1980, species of the forest edge were becoming more common (pers. obs.): the Indigo Bunting, Northern Cardinal, American Robin, Black-capped Chickadee, Downy Woodpecker, Blue Jay, and House Wren. And an overpopulation of white-tailed deer were trampling everywhere.

Drainage and disturbance of peatlands have often brought in weedy herbs instead of shrubs. These nonshrubby drying peatlands maintain far less wildlife, and they support four kinds of monotypes that keep shrubs from invading. These are reed canary grass (often planted), marsh nettle (especially on burned peat), giant ragweed (favored by siltation), and lowland and upland asters and goldenrods. The Red-winged Blackbird feeds heavily on ragweed seed in fall, American Tree Sparrows like aster and goldenrod seeds in winter, and the carr shrubs including the alien species provide blackbird roosts and berries for American Robins. But few true wetland birds benefit from any of these invading herbaceous and shrubby vegetation types so commonly found today on public hunting grounds that have been acquired or leased by the state after alteration by drainage (primarily agricultural).

Now, a new wave of alien (nonnative) species may pose further problems. On the Rock River, the yellow iris and pink flowering rush bear watching. The similarly handsome but very aggressive purple loosestrife, another Eurasian, has already abundantly invaded many wetlands in eastern Wisconsin during the past decade. Like its related native water willow, a peatland-edge species which increases under eutrophication, the purple loosestrife has little wildlife value. It seems to be crowding out native vegetation and forming persistent monotypes both in silted or pastured sedge meadows and in deeper (cattail) marshes, especially when altered by water-level manipulation or dike construction. In the Horicon Marsh National Wildlife Refuge, its invasions may bring an end to the drawdown technique used to restore lost cover.

Thus, in the lowlands as in the uplands, we are losing the bird diversity dependent on vegetation diversity. Species which are difficult to observe and not economically important, such as the LeConte's Sparrow and the various rails, have not been sufficiently monitored; but they may have declined like the Greater Prairie-Chicken, Sharp-tailed Grouse, American Bittern, and Ring-necked Pheasant.

It is worth recalling that many open-country birds use both dry and wet sites (see "Habitat Preferences" in Part II), indicating that an open skyline is more important to them than moisture conditions or specific plant species. Even our Greater Prairie-Chicken thrives on certain Eurasian grasses. Except at the Crex Meadows State Wildlife Area, little attention has been given so far to the concept of a prairie pothole complex with spacious gradual transitions from upland to wetland, like those described by Thure Kumlien at and near Lake Koshkonong over 100 years ago. Our now-scarce shorebirds and waterfowl probably depended on puddles in the undrained midwestern prairies for migration stops as well as for breeding, but this concept has been neglected for study because so few unaltered benchmark areas remain in the Midwest. Possibly one of the least disturbed natural examples we still have is Rush Lake in Winnebago County with its associated extensive shallow marshes and open sedge meadows. Perhaps it is significant that Wisconsin's breeding Red-necked Grebes choose Rush Lake, along with Grassy Lake in Columbia County and a few prairie potholes in St. Croix and southern Polk counties.

Beneficial Human Actions

Human impacts have a bright side; we must take note of the "non-nuisance" bird species that human actions have benefited. We have supplied the American Robin with the European night crawler, and we keep an incredibly large acreage closely mowed so it can easily hunt this bigger and better worm. Our chimneys and flat roofs far outnumber the hollow forest giants and burned barrens where, respectively, raccoons used to consume the eggs of Chimney Swifts and Common Nighthawks. We build thousands of barns for Barn and Cliff Swallows and countless smaller houses for Eastern Bluebirds, Purple Martins, Wood Ducks, and Tree Swallows. Lighthouses are located conveniently near water for Cliff Swallows, while, happily, the I-beam supports both the highway bridge and the Eastern Phoebe's nest (and more Barn and Cliff Swallows). Islands of dredge spoils in Green Bay are sometimes used by terns, gulls, and cormorants as safe nesting sites.

The once-southern Northern Cardinal now flocks in winter to Wisconsin corncribs and, together with many wintering finches and bark-feeders, flourishes at innumerable bird feeders. Planted ornamental conifers furnish ideal roost and nest sites for the cardinals as well as for Chipping Sparrows, Mourning Doves, Blue Jays, and an uncommonly large number of Common Grackles.

Sanctuaries, refuges, natural and scientific areas, parks, duck stamps, shore and floodplain zoning, the Environmental Impact Statement, and the Endangered Species Act all do their part, with cranes and geese responding magnificently. Wisconsin's recently upgraded requirements for school teacher certification in ecology and resource management could accomplish much. Most important of all is the conservation-minded private landowner.

Research on bird behavior, starting with egg and chick transplants to restore breeding Wood Ducks half a century ago, has flowered with the perfection of captive rearing, outdoor foster-parenting, and hacking procedures, to the eventual benefit, we can hope, of Trumpeter Swans, Greater Prairie-Chickens, Peregrine Falcons, and Barn Owls. And this is the era of the artificial nest platform for herons, Ospreys, cormorants, and terns. Attempts to restore Wild Turkeys, especially in the hilly unglaciated coulee area, may at last succeed, if a second wave of timber denudation does not again evict these birds from an area which may have harbored them through times troubled by glaciers elsewhere.

Intentional and accidental establishment of new breeding populations of birds, for example, today's restoration of Canada Geese to many former nesting places in Wisconsin, enriches the local birdlife as well. However, when the established species is not native, such as the Mute Swan and the House Finch, the implications may be complex and the situation bears watching. Introduced Rock Doves, European Starlings, and House Sparrows are generally considered nuisances, yet may provide important winter food, along with the Ring-necked Pheasant, for some owls and hawks. House Sparrows can displace or evict nesting bluebirds, Purple Martins, Black-capped Chickadees, and other native species, while starlings are notorious for destroying the nests of woodpeckers. Yet, one study of Northern Flickers indicated that in summer, when these birds renested, their food (ants) was more abundant and territories were smaller, resulting in more young produced per unit area, than the first broods would have produced had starlings not interfered!

The urban scene could, through habitat management, harbor a much wider variety of birds, especially of breeding forest songbirds. As a useful offset to high mortality due to picture windows, television towers, and feral cats, the National Wildlife Federation's Backyard Wildlife Program is off to a good start, stressing shrubby tangles for nests and privacy, access to fresh water, and a variety of food plants. Wisconsin is near the top in the number of cooperators. Leaving dead or partly dead trees standing (where not a hazard) and removing (and not replanting) alien pest plants should be added to the National Wildlife Federation's list of techniques, along with the increasing popularity of unmowed areas of native flowers, native grasses, or fallen leaf litter. The major obstacles to these developments are disagreements among neighbors over values, and city officials' conservatism on the management of lawns, street trees, parks, greenways, and school grounds. When the need to have additional trees (for summer air conditioning) and larger runoff catchment areas (for better soil and water management) becomes as familiar as the concepts of waste recycling and natural heating and cooling through redesign of urban landscapes, the birds will chorus their approval. Better soil conservation on farms and roadside management with wildlife in mind will likewise certainly benefit birds.

An important concept for habitat restoration is time. In Europe, civilization developed so slowly that storks could adapt to chimneys for nest sites, and people could assimilate them into their culture as good omens. If we maintain our wildlife for a while longer, perhaps herons and other wild water birds and raptors will tolerate human activity, as the Peregrine Falcons and Sandhill Cranes seem to have begun to do, with a reciprocal acceptance by our public.

It is clear that many past losses of wildlife were the unnecessary result of ignorance. But as long as the technology was limited to the gun, reversal of impact was relatively easy. Today we have much more power, worldwide, over that crucial element in bird conservation—habitat. However, our modern technology can also be turned to the benefit of birds, in education and management of both birds and landscape. The needed monitoring of bird populations, becoming ever more popular (such as the breeding bird surveys, censuses, and state atlases) will give future bird study the pleasurable added dimension of the amateur's personal involvement in ecology. The recent developments documented in the preceding chapter give hope that this will be so.

Part II. The Birds

Introduction to Part II

Part II directs attention to the bird species known to have been observed in Wisconsin. In the first section, it presents a chart which lists all of the 394 confirmed species plus the 13 species granted hypothetical status, shows at a glance the seasons of the year and the parts of the state in which each species is normally present and the frequency (annual or otherwise) with which each species has been observed, and gives the page number of the species account in this volume.

In the next section, more complete accounts of the species are given. The information they contain deals with such key questions as, When is the bird to be found in Wisconsin? In what parts of the state can it be found? What type of habitat does it favor? Has its range or abundance changed perceptibly within the last 50–100 years? Are there significant differences in abundance in different parts of the state?

Two supplemental lists follow the accounts of confirmed species. One, listing species of hypothetical status, describes sight observations of 13 species for the presence of which there is strong but inconclusive evidence. Several species now on the confirmed list started out on a hypothetical list and subsequently attained full status. In all likelihood several "hypothetical" species will again visit Wisconsin, and—if conditions are right—may be granted full acceptance. A list of "possible escapes" documents six species observed in the state, but under conditions that suggest possible escape or release in or near Wisconsin's borders.

A section delineating habitat preferences of various species concludes Part II. A breeding season table matches 229 species with 29 habitat types. A more limited winter season table lists 144 species under 10 habitat types. For an additional 79 species, present in neither winter nor summer, a table lists habitat preference for woodland, shrub, open land, wetland, and lakes and streams. Acceptable habitat for many species is not as narrowly defined for winter and for spring and fall migration as it is for the breeding season.

The species accounts form the bulk of Part II. Each is introduced by a succinct summary of information about the bird, a data block, which includes its status in

Wisconsin during spring and fall migration, summer, and winter; a brief notation of habitat preference; migration dates where applicable; breeding data, listing extreme egg dates where known, clutch size, and related evidence; winter information, pinpointing those portions of the state where a species regularly and/or occasionally occurs, if the distribution is not statewide; and the plate number of the bird's portrait if it is pictured in O. J. Gromme's *Birds of Wisconsin*.

In describing the Wisconsin status for each species, I have used four terms for birds that occur regularly every year (*abundant, common, fairly common, uncommon*), and three for birds whose occurrence is occasional and cannot be expected each year (*rare, casual, accidental*).

Abundant, Common, Fairly Common, Uncommon. These terms are necessarily subjective. To apply objective, numerical values, one would need to measure (1) the number of birds present per unit of a species' favored habitat, and (2) the amount of favored habitat as related to the state's total acreage. Available data are far too fragmentary to make such judgments. Before assigning one of these four terms to a given species, I appraised an entire family of species and made a preliminary judgment about which members of the family were most numerous (*abundant*), least numerous (*uncommon*), and in between (*common* and *fairly common*). Then I compared these preliminary judgments with figures from the Breeding Bird Survey, the Christmas Bird Count, and numbers recorded in my personal journals. Refinements were then made. Species such as the Chimney Swift, Blue-gray Gnatcatcher, and Brown Thrasher, belonging to families poorly represented in Wisconsin, were compared with species of similar abundance in the larger families, and are given a similar designation.

Rare, Casual, Accidental. Species that occur in from 1 to 9 years in a 10-year interval, but are not observed every year, are designated as *rare*. Species that have been recorded at least six times, but not necessarily in every decade, are designated as *casual*. Species that have been reported on from one to five occasions are designated as *accidental*.

Certain terms were also needed to describe seasonal residence status. *Residents* are essentially nonmigratory species (e.g., the Ruffed Grouse, House Sparrow, Northern Cardinal). Most other birds are classed as *summer residents* (confirmed or presumed breeders), *winter residents* (presumably tied to a limited territory during the period of winter residency), and *migrants* (transient visitants in spring and fall). In a few instances, the terms *winter visitant* and *summer visitant* are used to indicate relatively brief appearances in winter and summer. The lines separating these seasonal categories are not clearcut. How many of our Great Egrets and Great Blue Herons are summer residents, and how many are postbreeding or nonbreeding visitants? How many of our Mallards, Great Horned Owls, Blue Jays, and Black-capped Chickadees are permanent residents, and how many are summer or winter residents? Are flocks of Evening Grosbeaks winter residents at a given location, or are they visitants moving in and out and being replaced by others of the same species? My assignments involved some arbitrary guesswork that may well require future revision when more information becomes available.

Migration dates are important in showing each species' own seasonal timetable. For what may be considered a species' "normal" migration dates I have made use in the data block and map legends of the following generalizations: dates from 1 to 10 in a month are designated as *early*; dates from 11 to 20, *mid*; dates from 21 to 31, *late*. And, for birds absent in summer and/or winter, extreme arrival and departure dates are given in the data block. While some extreme dates coincide with the normal migration period, others are a month or more removed, representing accidental occurrences unlikely to be repeated.

In referring to geographical subdivisions of Wisconsin, I have used terms such as eastern, central, western, southern, and northern loosely. Arbitrarily, I have chosen Highways 33 (La Crosse–Baraboo–Port Washington) and 64 (New Richmond–Merrill–Marinette) to delineate a three-way south-north division of the state. This system places most of the three southernmost tiers of counties in "southern Wisconsin," most of the three northernmost tiers in "northern Wisconsin," and the intervening region in "central Wisconsin." For a three-way west-east division, I drew a hypothetical line south from Ashland to Black River Falls, then south-southeast to Monroe, and another line from Florence south through Oshkosh to Walworth (see the accompanying map). Thus, "eastern Wisconsin" refers generally to the two easternmost tiers of the counties, while "western Wisconsin" embraces the two westernmost tiers plus a third tier in the "Indianhead Bulge."

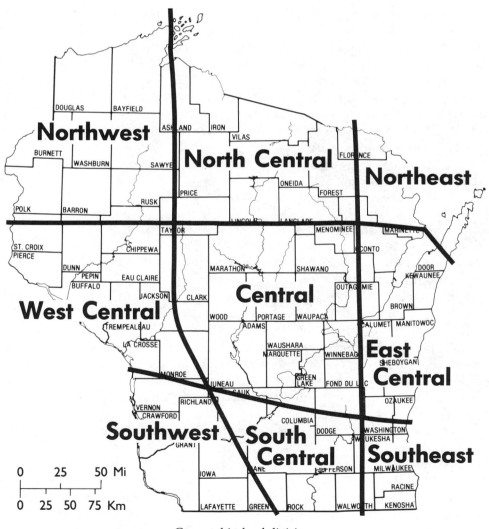

Geographical subdivisions

Anyone familiar with Wisconsin geography knows the confusion that can exist over place-names. "Milwaukee" could refer to the city of Milwaukee or Milwaukee County. The city of Portage is far removed from Portage County. The city of Monroe is 85 miles from Monroe County. In the species accounts, the place-names within parentheses designating locations of sightings refer to the county, unless specifically designated otherwise. County names are not included with place-names used to demarcate a line, with cities from the first through the second class, or with cities whose county names are virtually identical.

Documentation of the sources used in the preparation of the species accounts falls into two main categories:

Unpublished records. I drew heavily from personal communication with Wisconsin ornithologists, most of whom are cited in the general introduction to this volume, and from unpublished records and field notes that were made available to me. For data which exist in my possession only and not on file elsewhere as well, no documentation is provided. If the unpublished data can be found publicly—in the Milwaukee Public Museum files, the Racine County Historical Museum files, the files of the national refuge headquarters located in Wisconsin, or the Wisconsin Society for Ornithology Records Committee files—documentation is provided.

Published records. Records that are taken from *The Passenger Pigeon* field notes, including the "By the Wayside" column, are cited in the text with date (year), county, and observer's name. For these and for the records gleaned from the annual summaries of the Christmas Bird Counts and the 5-year summaries of the Breeding Bird Surveys, specific references to *The Passenger Pigeon* are provided in the text only for species of accidental or casual occurrence. For records published in such other journals as *The Auk, American Birds,* and the *Wilson's Bulletin,* citations are given in the text to title, volume, and page of the publication. If a record or other comment in the text has been the subject of a formal signed article, the citation is given in the standard reference form of author's name and date.

The bird photographs included in Part II were all taken in Wisconsin, and were selected to help document the presence of rare species. For 31 of Wisconsin's species, specimens are lacking. These photos provide much of the evidence validating the presence of these 31 species in this state. The original photographs, in most instances, have been preserved in the photo file of the Wisconsin Society for Ornithology.

Maps, more than photographs, are used here to tell the story of Wisconsin birds. There are four main types: (1) summer density maps describing relative abundance for species present annually throughout the state; (2) maps showing resident, summer, and/or winter range for species present in only parts of the state, or throughout the state in very limited numbers; (3) maps of rarities, showing the locations of confirmed sightings; and (4) maps documenting the spread or decline of species whose status has changed significantly in the past 50–100 years.

The summer density maps evolved from 1966–1980 Breeding Bird Survey data. While Wisconsin's BBS routes are based on latitude-longitude lines, it is recognized that birds select their summer homes more on the basis of topography, related soil and vegetation types, and available food supply. This realization led me to construct a plan for these maps based on geography and vegetation.

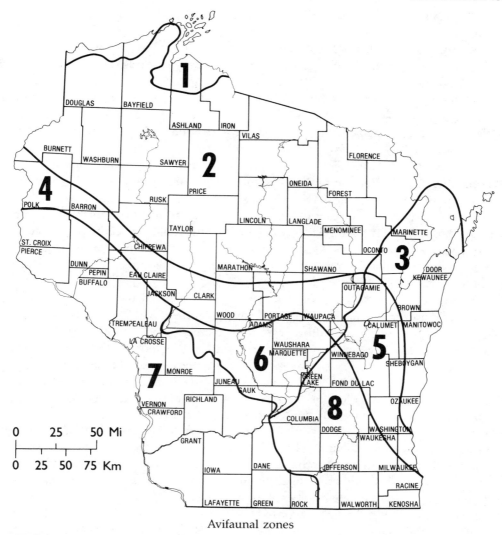

Avifaunal zones

In Lawrence Martin's *The Physical Geography of Wisconsin* (1932), five geographical provinces are described: Lake Superior Lowland, Northern Highland, Central Plain, Western Upland, and Eastern Ridges and Lowlands. In *The Vegetation of Wisconsin* (1959), J. T. Curtis developed the concept of a "tension zone,"—a transition zone—a band roughly 30–60 miles wide, extending in a general northwest-southeast direction from St. Croix Falls to Racine, which contains both the northern range limit of significant numbers of southern plant species and the southern limit for numerous northern plants. By superimposing the tension zone on Martin's five regions, I have identified eight areas that show distinctive avifaunal features (see the accompanying map).

1. *Lake Superior Lowland:* Lake Superior shore, interspersed with north-flowing streams; features young birch and aspen, alder thickets, bracken grasslands, and occasional sedge meadows.

2. *Northern Upland Forest:* Most of northern Wisconsin, dominated by extensive deciduous and coniferous forests, with occasional agricultural openings and numerous lakes; features sugar maple, basswood, white and yellow birch, white

and red pine, hemlock, balsam fir, white and black spruce, black ash, and numerous other tree species.

3. *Lake Michigan Upland:* Lake Michigan and Green Bay region, alternating mixed woods with agricultural clearings; features sugar maple, beech, hemlock, and basswood.

4. *Tension Zone West and Central:* Tension zone from the Minnesota border to the edge of the Fox River valley, deciduous forests with extensive dairy farm clearings; features aspen, birch, pine, red and white oak, and red and sugar maple.

5. *Tension Zone East:* Lake Winnebago, northern unit of Kettle Moraine State Forest, with glacial remnant hills surrounded by cleared farmland and urban development; features sugar maple, red oak, basswood, beech, and slippery elm.

6. *Central Sand Plain:* Roughly a triangular region anchored by Black River Falls, Berlin, and Portage, relatively level with light soil, bisected by the Wisconsin River; features jack pine, Hill's and white oak, plus American elm, sugar maple, black willow, and cottonwood near the Wisconsin River and its tributaries.

7. *Western Hill Zone:* Hills and valleys closely associated with the Mississippi River and lower portions of the St. Croix, Chippewa, Black, and Wisconsin rivers, with extensive agricultural clearings; features black, white, and red oak on the uplands, American elm, river birch, and cottonwood on the lowlands.

8. *Southeastern Zone:* Extensive areas of cleared cropland and marshes associated with the Rock and Fox rivers, with woodlands limited largely to the southern unit of the Kettle Moraine State Forest and to remnant farm woodlots; features silver maple, American elm, basswood, green ash, and willow thickets.

The zonal averages on the summer density maps were derived by converting BBS data to these eight avifaunal zones. While it is true that lines marking zonal boundaries are gradual rather than abrupt, each of the 70 BBS transects can logically be assigned to one of the eight avifaunal zones. For a given species on a given transect, the average number of individuals per year was obtained by totaling the number of individuals recorded each year and dividing by the number of years the transect was run during the 1966–1980 interval. This average figure was added to similar figures for the same species on all other transects within the same avifaunal zone, then divided by the number of transects falling within that zone to obtain the zonal average for that species.

The maps that show the resident, summer, and/or winter range make use of three patterns and four symbols:

	Resident range
	Summer range
	Winter range
△	Spring observation
○	Summer observation
▽	Fall observation
□	Winter observation

For most species I have used the 1960–1989 period to give a picture of present-day range. Summer and winter symbols indicate sightings outside the usual range of the species. Occasional spring and fall observations are indicated by migration symbols. Migration symbols have generally not been used in counties where summer and/or winter symbols or range patterns appear. It can be presumed that birds had to migrate to reach their summer and winter locations. For a few species, such as the Mallard and the Red-tailed Hawk, range is indicated without the detail of the summer density maps.

Maps of rarities use the four seasonal symbols to delineate known records. Normally, migration symbols do not appear in counties with summer and/or winter symbols, but when the designation "All records" appears, all appropriate symbols are included. For species recorded fewer than five times, maps have not been provided.

The map legends make use of generalized dates to portray the normal seasonal occurrence of a species; specific dates are given only for records of occurrences considered accidental or casual.

For 11 species whose spread across the state has been well documented, the maps show the years of initial sightings for each county where known. The decline of the Greater Prairie-Chicken is indicated on a map which lists the last year of observation known for each county.

No maps have been provided for species, such as the Pectoral Sandpiper, the Black-bellied Plover, and the Gray-cheeked Thrush, whose presence in Wisconsin is strictly migratory, covering the entire state.

List of Wisconsin Species
Showing Status and Seasonal Distribution

To the left of each species is the notation of the times of year when each bird is normally present. "All" appears when a species is present throughout the state in summer and/or winter. Designations for north (N), east (E), south (S), west (W), and central (C) are used for species whose distribution in summer or winter is not statewide. A mark (•) in the "Migration Only" column indicates the bird's presence essentially as a transient, usually during spring and fall migration, sometimes as a winter or summer wanderer, observed on exceptional occasions.

To the right of each species is a designation based on frequency of observation: Regular (present every year), Rare (found at least once every 5 years), Casual (six or more sightings), Accidental (one to five records), Former (once present in some numbers, now extinct or extirpated), and Hypothetical (strong but inconclusive evidence).

The number in parentheses following the bird's name is the page number of the species account in this volume.

Seasonal Distribution				Status					
Summer	Winter	Migration Only	Species	Regular	Rare	Casual	Accidental	Former	Hypothetical
		•	Red-throated Loon (113)	•					
		•	Pacific Loon (114)			•			
N, C			Common Loon (115)	•					
All	All		Pied-billed Grebe (117)	•					
W, E	E		Horned Grebe (118)	•					

Seasonal Distribution			Species	Status					
Summer	Winter	Migration Only		Regular	Rare	Casual	Accidental	Former	Hypothetical
W, E			Red-necked Grebe (119)	•					
		•	Eared Grebe (120)	•					
		•	Western Grebe (122)		•				
		•	Clark's Grebe (607)						•
		•	American White Pelican (123)		•				
		•	Brown Pelican (124)				•		
N, C			Double-crested Cormorant (125)	•					
		•	Anhinga (127)				•		
		•	Magnificent Frigatebird (129)				•		
All	S, C		American Bittern (130)	•					
All			Least Bittern (131)	•					
All	S, C		Great Blue Heron (132)	•					
W, S, E			Great Egret (134)	•					
		•	Snowy Egret (135)	•					
		•	Little Blue Heron (136)		•				
		•	Tricolored Heron (137)		•				
E			Cattle Egret (138)	•					
All			Green-backed Heron (140)	•					
All	S, C		Black-crowned Night-Heron (141)	•					
S, C			Yellow-crowned Night-Heron (142)	•					
		•	White Ibis (607)						•
		•	Glossy Ibis (144)		•				
		•	White-faced Ibis (145)				•		
		•	Roseate Spoonbill (146)				•		
		•	Wood Stork (147)				•		
		•	Fulvous Whistling-Duck (148)				•		
	W, E		Tundra Swan (148)	•					
		•	Trumpeter Swan (149)					•	
N, E, S	N, E, S		Mute Swan (151)	•					
		•	Greater White-fronted Goose (152)		•				
	S, C		Snow Goose (153)	•					
		•	Ross' Goose (154)				•		
		•	Brant (155)		•				
All	S, C		Canada Goose (156)	•					
All	S, C		Wood Duck (158)	•					
S, C	S		Green-winged Teal (159)	•					
N, C	All		American Black Duck (160)	•					
All	All		Mallard (162)	•					
		•	White-cheeked Pintail (163)				•		
W, C, E	All		Northern Pintail (164)	•					

| Seasonal Distribution | | | Species | Status | | | | | |
Summer	Winter	Migration Only		Regular	Rare	Casual	Accidental	Former	Hypothetical
All	E		Blue-winged Teal (165)	•					
		•	Cinnamon Teal (166)		•				
W, E	S, E		Northern Shoveler (167)	•					
W, E	S		Gadwall (169)	•					
		•	Eurasian Wigeon (170)		•				
All	S, E		American Wigeon (171)	•					
W, E	S, C		Canvasback (173)	•					
W, E	S, C		Redhead (175)	•					
N, C, E	S, C		Ring-necked Duck (176)	•					
	E		Greater Scaup (178)	•					
N, E	All		Lesser Scaup (179)	•					
		•	Common Eider (180)				•		
		•	King Eider (181)			•			
	S, E		Harlequin Duck (182)		•				
	E		Oldsquaw (183)	•					
		•	Black Scoter (184)	•					
		•	Surf Scoter (185)	•					
	E		White-winged Scoter (186)	•					
N, E	All		Common Goldeneye (188)	•					
	S, E		Barrow's Goldeneye (189)		•				
N, E	All		Bufflehead (190)	•					
N, C, E	All		Hooded Merganser (191)	•					
N	All		Common Merganser (193)	•					
N	E		Red-breasted Merganser (194)	•					
W, S, E	S, E		Ruddy Duck (196)	•					
		•	Masked Duck (197)				•		
		•	Black Vulture (198)				•		
All			Turkey Vulture (199)	•					
N, C			Osprey (201)	•					
		•	American Swallow-tailed Kite (202)				•		
		•	Black-shouldered Kite (203)				•		
		•	Mississippi Kite (204)			•			
W, N, C	W, N, C		Bald Eagle (205)	•					
All	S		Northern Harrier (207)	•					
N, C	All		Sharp-shinned Hawk (208)	•					
All	S, C		Cooper's Hawk (210)	•					
N, C	All		Northern Goshawk (211)	•					
All	S, C		Red-shouldered Hawk (213)	•					
W, N, C			Broad-winged Hawk (214)	•					
		•	Swainson's Hawk (216)		•				

Seasonal Distribution			Species	Status					
Summer	Winter	Migration Only		Regular	Rare	Casual	Accidental	Former	Hypothetical
All	S, C		Red-tailed Hawk (217)	•					
		•	Ferruginous Hawk (219)		•				
	All		Rough-legged Hawk (220)	•					
	All		Golden Eagle (221)	•					
All	S, C		American Kestrel (222)	•					
N	S, C		Merlin (224)	•					
S	S, C		Peregrine Falcon (225)	•					
	All		Gyrfalcon (227)		•				
		•	Prairie Falcon (607)						•
S, C	S, C		Gray Partridge (229)	•					
S, C	S, C		Ring-necked Pheasant (230)	•					
N	N		Spruce Grouse (231)	•					
		•	Willow Ptarmigan (232)				•		
All	All		Ruffed Grouse (233)	•					
W, C	W, C		Greater Prairie-Chicken (234)	•					
N, C	N, C		Sharp-tailed Grouse (235)	•					
W, C, E	W, C, E		Wild Turkey (237)	•					
S, C	S, C		Northern Bobwhite (238)	•					
N, E			Yellow Rail (240)			•			
		•	Black Rail (608)						•
S, C			King Rail (241)	•					
All	W		Virginia Rail (242)	•					
All	W		Sora (244)	•					
		•	Purple Gallinule (245)				•		
W, E			Common Moorhen (246)	•					
All	S, C		American Coot (247)	•					
All	E		Sandhill Crane (249)	•					
		•	Whooping Crane (250)					•	
		•	Black-bellied Plover (251)	•					
		•	Lesser Golden-Plover (252)	•					
		•	Snowy Plover (253)				•		
		•	Semipalmated Plover (253)	•					
N			Piping Plover (254)		•				
All	S		Killdeer (255)	•					
		•	Black-necked Stilt (256)				•		
		•	American Avocet (257)	•					
		•	Greater Yellowlegs (258)	•					
		•	Lesser Yellowlegs (259)	•					
		•	Spotted Redshank (609)						•
		•	Solitary Sandpiper (260)	•					

Seasonal Distribution			Species	Status					
Summer	Winter	Migration Only		Regular	Rare	Casual	Accidental	Former	Hypothetical
		•	Willet (261)	•					
All			Spotted Sandpiper (262)	•					
All			Upland Sandpiper (263)	•					
		•	Eskimo Curlew (264)					•	
		•	Whimbrel (265)	•					
		•	Long-billed Curlew (266)			•			
		•	Hudsonian Godwit (267)	•					
		•	Marbled Godwit (268)	•					
		•	Ruddy Turnstone (269)	•					
		•	Black Turnstone (270)				•		
		•	Red Knot (270)	•					
		•	Sanderling (271)	•					
		•	Semipalmated Sandpiper (272)	•					
		•	Western Sandpiper (273)	•					
		•	Least Sandpiper (274)	•					
		•	White-rumped Sandpiper (275)	•					
		•	Baird's Sandpiper (275)	•					
		•	Pectoral Sandpiper (276)	•					
		•	Purple Sandpiper (277)			•			
		•	Dunlin (278)	•					
		•	Curlew Sandpiper (279)				•		
		•	Stilt Sandpiper (280)	•					
		•	Buff-breasted Sandpiper (281)		•				
		•	Ruff (282)		•				
		•	Short-billed Dowitcher (283)	•					
		•	Long-billed Dowitcher (284)	•					
N, C, E	S, C		Common Snipe (285)	•					
	All		American Woodcock (286)	•					
W, N, E			Wilson's Phalarope (288)	•					
		•	Red-necked Phalarope (289)	•					
		•	Red Phalarope (290)			•			
		•	Pomarine Jaeger (292)				•		
		•	Parasitic Jaeger (293)			•			
		•	Long-tailed Jaeger (294)				•		
		•	Laughing Gull (294)			•			
		•	Franklin's Gull (296)	•					
E			Little Gull (297)	•					
		•	Common Black-headed Gull (298)				•		
N, E	E		Bonaparte's Gull (299)	•					
		•	Mew Gull (300)				•		

Seasonal Distribution			Species	Status					
Summer	Winter	Migration Only		Regular	Rare	Casual	Accidental	Former	Hypothetical
N, E	E		Ring-billed Gull (301)	•					
N, E	N, E, S		Herring Gull (302)	•					
	N, E		Thayer's Gull (304)		•				
	N, E		Iceland Gull (305)		•				
		•	Lesser Black-backed Gull (307)			•			
E	N, E		Glaucous Gull (308)	•					
	N, E		Great Black-backed Gull (309)		•				
		•	Black-legged Kittiwake (310)			•			
		•	Sabine's Gull (311)				•		
	N		Ivory Gull (312)				•		
N, E			Caspian Tern (313)	•					
		•	Royal Tern (314)			•			
		•	Roseate Tern (609)						•
N, E			Common Tern (315)	•					
		•	Arctic Tern (316)		•				
W, N, E			Forster's Tern (317)	•					
		•	Least Tern (318)			•			
		•	Sooty Tern (319)				•		
		•	White-winged Tern (320)				•		
All			Black Tern (320)	•					
		•	Dovekie (322)				•		
		•	Ancient Murrelet (322)				•		
All	All		Rock Dove (324)	•					
All	S, C		Mourning Dove (325)	•					
All			Passenger Pigeon (326)					•	
		•	Common Ground-Dove (328)				•		
		•	Carolina Parakeet (329)					•	
All			Black-billed Cuckoo (330)	•					
S, C			Yellow-billed Cuckoo (331)	•					
		•	Groove-billed Ani (332)			•			
S, C	S, C		Barn Owl (334)		•				
S, C	S, C		Eastern Screech-Owl (336)	•					
All	All		Great Horned Owl (337)	•					
	All		Snowy Owl (338)	•					
	N, C		Northern Hawk Owl (340)		•				
		•	Burrowing Owl (341)			•			
All	All		Barred Owl (343)	•					
N	N, C		Great Gray Owl (344)		•				
N, C	S, C		Long-eared Owl (346)	•					
N, C	S, C		Short-eared Owl (347)	•					

Seasonal Distribution				Status					
Summer	Winter	Migration Only	Species	Regular	Rare	Casual	Accidental	Former	Hypothetical
	N, E		Boreal Owl (348)		●				
N, C	S, C		Northern Saw-whet Owl (350)	●					
All			Common Nighthawk (352)	●					
W, S			Chuck-will's-widow (353)			●			
All			Whip-poor-will (354)	●					
All			Chimney Swift (356)	●					
All			Ruby-throated Hummingbird (358)	●					
		●	Anna's Hummingbird (359)				●		
		●	Rufous Hummingbird (359)				●		
All	S, C		Belted Kingfisher (360)	●					
	N		Lewis' Woodpecker (362)				●		
All	S, C		Red-headed Woodpecker (363)	●					
All	All		Red-bellied Woodpecker (364)	●					
N, C, W	S, C		Yellow-bellied Sapsucker (365)	●					
All	All		Downy Woodpecker (367)	●					
All	All		Hairy Woodpecker (368)	●					
	N		Three-toed Woodpecker (369)			●			
N	N, C, E		Black-backed Woodpecker (370)	●					
All	S, C		Northern Flicker (372)	●					
N, C, W	N, C, W		Pileated Woodpecker (373)	●					
N			Olive-sided Flycatcher (375)	●					
		●	Western Wood-Pewee (609)						●
All			Eastern Wood-Pewee (376)	●					
N			Yellow-bellied Flycatcher (377)	●					
S			Acadian Flycatcher (379)	●					
N, C, E			Alder Flycatcher (380)	●					
S, C, W			Willow Flycatcher (382)	●					
All			Least Flycatcher (383)	●					
All			Eastern Phoebe (384)	●					
		●	Say's Phoebe (385)				●		
		●	Vermilion Flycatcher (610)						●
All			Great Crested Flycatcher (386)	●					
		●	Cassin's Kingbird (610)						●
S, W			Western Kingbird (387)		●				
All			Eastern Kingbird (389)	●					
		●	Scissor-tailed Flycatcher (390)		●				
		●	Fork-tailed Flycatcher (391)				●		
All	S, C		Horned Lark (392)	●					
All			Purple Martin (394)	●					
All			Tree Swallow (395)	●					

Summer	Winter	Migration Only	Species	Regular	Rare	Casual	Accidental	Former	Hypothetical
All			Northern Rough-winged Swallow (397)	•					
All			Bank Swallow (398)	•					
All			Cliff Swallow (399)	•					
All			Barn Swallow (400)	•					
N	N, C		Gray Jay (402)	•					
All	All		Blue Jay (403)	•					
		•	Clark's Nutcracker (404)				•		
		•	Black-billed Magpie (405)			•			
All	All		American Crow (406)	•					
N, C	N, C		Common Raven (408)	•					
All	All		Black-capped Chickadee (410)	•					
N	N		Boreal Chickadee (411)	•					
W, S, C	W, S, C		Tufted Titmouse (412)	•					
N, C	All		Red-breasted Nuthatch (414)	•					
All	All		White-breasted Nuthatch (415)	•					
	W		Brown-headed Nuthatch (416)				•		
W,N,E	All		Brown Creeper (417)	•					
S, C	S, C		Carolina Wren (419)		•				
S, W			Bewick's Wren (420)		•				
All			House Wren (422)	•					
N, C	S, C		Winter Wren (423)	•					
All			Sedge Wren (424)	•					
All			Marsh Wren (426)	•					
N	All		Golden-crowned Kinglet (428)	•					
N	S, C		Ruby-crowned Kinglet (429)	•					
S, C			Blue-gray Gnatcatcher (431)	•					
		•	Northern Wheatear (611)						•
All	S		Eastern Bluebird (432)	•					
		•	Mountain Bluebird (434)				•		
	S, C		Townsend's Solitaire (435)			•			
All			Veery (436)	•					
		•	Gray-cheeked Thrush (437)	•					
N			Swainson's Thrush (438)	•					
N, C	S		Hermit Thrush (440)	•					
All			Wood Thrush (441)	•					
All	S, C		American Robin (442)	•					
	N, C, E		Varied Thrush (444)			•			
All	S, C		Gray Catbird (446)	•					
All	S, E		Northern Mockingbird (447)	•					
		•	Sage Thrasher (448)				•		

| Seasonal Distribution | | | | Status | | | | | |
Summer	Winter	Migration Only	Species	Regular	Rare	Casual	Accidental	Former	Hypothetical
All	S, C		Brown Thrasher (449)	•					
W	W, C		Curve-billed Thrasher (450)				•		
		•	American Pipit (452)	•					
		•	Sprague's Pipit (611)						•
	All		Bohemian Waxwing (453)		•				
All	All		Cedar Waxwing (454)	•					
	All		Northern Shrike (456)	•					
All			Loggerhead Shrike (457)	•					
All	All		European Starling (459)	•					
S			White-eyed Vireo (461)	•					
S, W			Bell's Vireo (462)	•					
		•	Gray Vireo (463)				•		
N, C			Solitary Vireo (464)	•					
All			Yellow-throated Vireo (465)	•					
All			Warbling Vireo (466)	•					
		•	Philadelphia Vireo (467)	•					
All			Red-eyed Vireo (468)	•					
S, C			Blue-winged Warbler (470)	•					
All			Golden-winged Warbler (471)	•					
N			Tennessee Warbler (475)	•					
		•	Orange-crowned Warbler (476)	•					
N, C			Nashville Warbler (477)	•					
N, S			Northern Parula (478)	•					
All			Yellow Warbler (480)	•					
N, C			Chestnut-sided Warbler (481)	•					
N			Magnolia Warbler (482)	•					
N			Cape May Warbler (484)	•					
N			Black-throated Blue Warbler (485)	•					
N, C	S, C		Yellow-rumped Warbler (487)	•					
		•	Black-throated Gray Warbler (488)				•		
		•	Hermit Warbler (489)				•		
N, S			Black-throated Green Warbler (489)	•					
N			Blackburnian Warbler (491)	•					
S			Yellow-throated Warbler (492)		•				
N, C			Pine Warbler (493)	•					
N, C			Kirtland's Warbler (494)			•			
S			Prairie Warbler (496)		•				
N			Palm Warbler (497)	•					
		•	Bay-breasted Warbler (498)	•					
		•	Blackpoll Warbler (500)	•					

Summer	Winter	Migration Only	Species	Regular	Rare	Casual	Accidental	Former	Hypothetical
S, C			Cerulean Warbler (501)	•					
N, C			Black-and-white Warbler (503)	•					
All			American Redstart (504)	•					
S,C,W			Prothonotary Warbler (506)	•					
S			Worm-eating Warbler (507)	•					
All			Ovenbird (508)	•					
N, E			Northern Waterthrush (510)	•					
W, C			Louisiana Waterthrush (511)	•					
S			Kentucky Warbler (513)	•					
N			Connecticut Warbler (514)	•					
N,C,E			Mourning Warbler (516)	•					
All			Common Yellowthroat (517)	•					
S, E			Hooded Warbler (519)		•				
		•	Wilson's Warbler (520)	•					
N, C, E			Canada Warbler (521)	•					
		•	Painted Redstart (612)						•
S, W			Yellow-breasted Chat (522)	•					
		•	Summer Tanager (524)		•				
All			Scarlet Tanager (525)	•					
		•	Western Tanager (526)		•				
All	All		Northern Cardinal (527)	•					
All			Rose-breasted Grosbeak (529)	•					
	S		Black-headed Grosbeak (530)			•			
S			Blue Grosbeak (532)			•			
		•	Lazuli Bunting (533)				•		
All			Indigo Bunting (534)	•					
		•	Painted Bunting (535)		•				
S, C, W			Dickcissel (536)	•					
	S, C		Green-tailed Towhee (538)			•			
All	S, C		Rufous-sided Towhee (539)	•					
	All		American Tree Sparrow (540)	•					
All			Chipping Sparrow (541)	•					
N, C			Clay-colored Sparrow (542)	•					
All	S, C		Field Sparrow (544)	•					
All	S		Vesper Sparrow (545)	•					

Seasonal Distribution				Status					
Summer	Winter	Migration Only	**Species**	Regular	Rare	Casual	Accidental	Former	Hypothetical
S, C, W			Lark Sparrow (546)	•					
	S, C		Black-throated Sparrow (547)				•		
		•	Lark Bunting (549)		•				
All	S		Savannah Sparrow (550)	•					
		•	Baird's Sparrow (551)				•		
All			Grasshopper Sparrow (552)	•					
S, C			Henslow's Sparrow (554)	•					
N, C			Leconte's Sparrow (555)	•					
N			Sharp-tailed Sparrow (556)	•					
	S		Fox Sparrow (558)	•					
All	S, C		Song Sparrow (559)	•					
N			Lincoln's Sparrow (560)	•					
All	S, C		Swamp Sparrow (562)	•					
N, C, E	All		White-throated Sparrow (563)	•					
		•	Golden-crowned Sparrow (565)				•		
	S, E		White-crowned Sparrow (566)	•					
	S, C		Harris' Sparrow (567)	•					
N	All		Dark-eyed Junco (569)	•					
	S, C		Lapland Longspur (570)	•					
		•	Smith's Longspur (572)			•			
		•	Chestnut-collared Longspur (573)				•		
	All		Snow Bunting (574)	•					
All			Bobolink (575)	•					
All	S, C		Red-winged Blackbird (576)	•					
All	S, C		Eastern Meadowlark (578)	•					
All	S, C		Western Meadowlark (579)	•					
All	S, E		Yellow-headed Blackbird (581)	•					
	All		Rusty Blackbird (582)	•					
N, C	S, C		Brewer's Blackbird (583)	•					
All	All		Common Grackle (585)	•					
All	S		Brown-headed Cowbird (586)	•					
W, S, E			Orchard Oriole (588)	•					
All	S		Northern Oriole (589)	•					
		•	Rosy Finch (591)				•		
	All		Pine Grosbeak (592)	•					

Seasonal Distribution			Species	Status					
Summer	Winter	Migration Only		Regular	Rare	Casual	Accidental	Former	Hypothetical
N, C	All		Purple Finch (593)	•					
S, C	S, C		House Finch (594)	•					
N, C	All		Red Crossbill (595)	•					
N	All		White-winged Crossbill (597)	•					
	All		Common Redpoll (598)	•					
	All		Hoary Redpoll (599)		•				
N, C	All		Pine Siskin (600)	•					
		•	Lesser Goldfinch (612)						•
All	All		American Goldfinch (602)	•					
N	All		Evening Grosbeak (603)	•					
All	All		House Sparrow (605)	•					
		•	Eurasian Tree Sparrow (606)				•		

Family **Gaviidae:** Loons

Red-throated Loon (*Gavia stellata*)

STATUS. Uncommon migrant east; rare migrant west and north. Casual summer visitant north.
HABITAT. Great Lakes. Inland lakes.
MIGRATION DATES. *Spring:* early April to early June. *Fall:* late September to mid-November; rarely observed on Lake Michigan until early January. *Extremes:* 24 March; 1 January.
BREEDING DATA. None. Rarely present on Lake Superior until early August.
WINTER. One record since 1940.
PORTRAIT. *Birds of Wisconsin:* Plate 1.

From 5 April to 10 May several of these divers can be seen almost daily from the high bluffs overlooking Lake Michigan in southern Ozaukee County. An area 3 miles north of Virmond Park is known as "Loon Bluff" among ornithologists, because loons—Common and Red-throated, with the latter predominating—can be seen so frequently offshore. No one has ever determined how many pass this area in a season, but 30–40 birds have been counted in a day on several occasions in recent years. An estimated 300 were seen on 11 April 1953 (D. L. Larkin).

At other locations along Lake Michigan, from Kenosha to Sturgeon Bay, spring migrants are occasionally seen, but only one to three birds at a time. Most birds are apparently too far out on the lake to be seen at these other lakeshore points. C. R. Sontag has noted spring arrivals in Manitowoc County as early as 24 March (1984) and 26 March (1983).

Spring sightings away from Lake Michigan were few until 1950, consisting of a bird on 7 June 1916 (Dane, A. W. Schorger [1917]) and one on 12 May 1929 (Waukesha, S. P. Jones; MPM files). Additional inland observations eventually followed. Several were mid-May observations, and one from Adams County on 5 June (1962, S. D. Robbins) suggests that the spring migration sometimes extends through all of May.

Since Lake Superior birding was fragmentary before 1950, it did not become apparent until the 1960s that the Red-throated Loon might be an occasional—if not regular—summer visitant there. Eight were seen in Bayfield County in 1955 (29 May, R. H. Lound), and in 1956 several were seen on 13 July and 9 August (W. E. Southern). The presence of young on the earlier date strongly suggested nesting, but definite proof

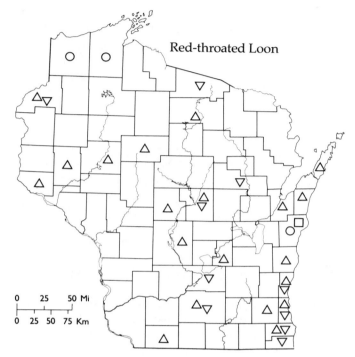

Red-throated Loon

△ Early April to early June
○ Mid-June to mid-August
▽ Late September to early January
□ 7 January to 1 May

Records since 1960

was lacking (*Pass. Pigeon* 18:177). Several additional summer observations between late May and 16 August, both at Superior and near the mouth of the Bois Brule River, led Bernard (1967) to call the Red-throat a "rare transient and summer visitant" in Douglas County.

The only other recent summer record away from Lake Superior was of a fresh-killed bird found at Manitowoc on 25 June 1964 (B. Weber). In the summer of 1881, Ludwig Kumlien (1891a) observed 12 individuals in Door County and published this as a nesting record. Later on Kumlien and Hollister (1903) asserted that the evidence for breeding was inconclusive. C. S. Jung (MPM files) found a dead bird washed up on the beach at Cedar Grove (Sheboygan County) on 27 July 1930.

113

The earliest recorded arrival date for a fall migrant is 26 September (1982, Douglas, D. D. Tessen). As in spring, most fall migrants are found along Lake Michigan, concentrated in greatest numbers off the southern Ozaukee County bluffs. Birds are recorded there mainly between 10 October and 20 November, with peak numbers of 20–30 birds per day.

The latest dates in the north are 17 October (1965, Burnett, N. R. Stone) and 23 October (1973, Bayfield, D. A. Bratley), plus a remarkable straggler on 1 January (1972, Bayfield, A. J. Roy). In the south, a few individuals linger through the CBC period into early January. Several nineteenth-century commentators (Hoy 1853b; Nelson 1876; Kumlien and Hollister 1903) considered the Red-throat a common winter bird along Lake Michigan. According to Kumlien and Hollister, when Lake Michigan was largely frozen near Milwaukee in the severe winter of 1880–1881, "large numbers . . . were seen off that city, and many were caught. They could be seen huddled together on the ice, some dead and others nearly famished."

By no stretch of the imagination can this be called a common winter resident today. The only February–March observation since 1940 is of an individual that remained at Manitowoc from 7 January to 1 May 1987 (C. R. Sontag).

Pacific Loon (*Gavia pacifica*)
Formerly Arctic Loon, Black-throated Loon

STATUS. Casual migrant.

HABITAT. Great Lakes.

MIGRATION DATES. *Spring:* late April to mid-June. *Fall:* late September to early November. *Extremes:* 16 April, 11 June; 25 September, 4 November.

Schoenebeck (1902) listed a male loon shot on Green Bay near Oconto in early November 1893, which he subsequently identified as a Black-throated Loon (Pacific Loon). But this skin evidently did not become a part of his collection, and is now lost.

Two specimens mentioned by Kumlien and Hollister (1903) met a similar fate: an immature said to have been shot near Janesville late in the winter of 1860 and mounted by Thure Kumlien, and one reportedly shot in Milwaukee.

Attempting to follow up on these reports, Hersey (1917) corresponded with H. L. Ward of the Milwaukee Public Museum and Ned Hollister. Ward wrote, "I have been trying to run down the reported Black-throated Loon [Pacific Loon] contained in this museum, but can find no trace of it at all." Hollister commented: "[The Janesville bird] is from the notes of Thure Kumlien and considering the date and circumstances I should not accept it as a real record today. . . . I am prepared to drop the bird from the Wisconsin list." Schorger (1951a), revising Kumlien and Hollister's 1903 work, also advised, "This species must be removed from the list of Wisconsin birds since no specimen for the state is known."

However, a specimen collected by P. R. Hoy has now been rediscovered in the Hoy collection. Although no label is extant, it was collected at Racine,

Pacific Loon

△ 16 April to 11 June
▽ 25 September to 4 November

All records

before 1878, and is now preserved in the Racine County Historical Museum.

Richter (1926b) believed this bird to be at least an occasional visitor in the Green Bay region. In conversations with commercial fishermen in the Oconto area, he learned that on numerous occasions loons had accidentally been trapped in nets set for lake trout 60 feet beneath the surface of the water in Green Bay. "Every fisherman with whom I have ever spoken regarding this peculiar subject said that they had caught numbers of loons in this manner every spring. The Common Loon headed the casualty list, although now and then a Black-throated [Pacific] Loon, but more often the Red-throated Loon were taken."

Carl Richter recalled handling two Pacific Loon skins in the 1920s; but because they were in poor condition and because he believed better specimens would inevitably come along, he did not save the skins. The opportunity to preserve better ones never came.

Five additional sight records were reported in the 1970s: one at the Crex Meadows Wildlife Area in Burnett County on 25 September 1975 by A. H. Grewe; one at Wisconsin Point in Douglas County on 11 June 1977 by C. A. Faanes (*Pass. Pigeon* 40:412–413); and observations at Loon Bluff in Ozaukee County on 22 October 1973 by L. W. Erickson (*Pass. Pigeon* 36:133), 21–25 April 1974 by D. D. Tessen, and 1 November 1978 by Tessen (*Pass. Pigeon* 41:140).

The 1980s added four additional observations: one on 25 May 1980 (Douglas, R. M. Hoffman); two on 16 April 1983 (Ozaukee, D. D. Tessen) with one still present on 21 April (D. K. Gustafson); one from 29 October to 4 November 1984 (Douglas, R. J. Johnson; *Pass. Pigeon* 47:120); and one on 26 October 1988 (Bayfield, S. R. Swengel; *Pass. Pigeon* 51:229).

Common Loon (*Gavia immer*)

STATUS. Fairly common migrant. Uncommon summer resident north; rare summer resident central.
HABITAT. Great Lakes. Inland lakes.
MIGRATION DATES. *Spring:* late March to mid-May. *Fall:* early October to late November. *Extremes:* 3 March; 3 January.
BREEDING DATA. Nests with eggs: 27 May to 12 June. Clutch size: 2 eggs.
PORTRAIT. *Birds of Wisconsin:* Plate 1.

Common Loons are most often seen as April migrants on the larger inland lakes. They do not quite keep up with the Common Goldeneyes and Common Mergansers that appear as soon as sizable openings develop in previously ice-locked lakes. But these loons are not far behind, often appearing before the ice is all gone. First arrivals in the southern counties are usually seen between 25 March and 1 April, but individuals have been recorded as early as 3 March (1983, Dane, A. K. Shea; 1983, Jefferson, K. E. Hale), 9 March (1939, Milwaukee, H. A. Mathiak), and 11 March (1973, Rock, E. Brakefield; 1973, Columbia, W. A. Smith). Farther north, early records exist for 16 March (1961, Washburn, B. A. Bailey), 20 March (1949, Brown, E. O. Paulson), and 23 March (1963, Ashland and Bayfield, J. L. Kozlowski).

In the south the main flight is from 1 to 20 April with a gradual diminishing through 10 May. In the north the greatest buildup is between 15 April and 15 May. Nearly all migrants have moved on by 20 May.

Michael Kohel's study of the 1970 Common Loon migration patterns (Kohel 1972) suggested the possi-

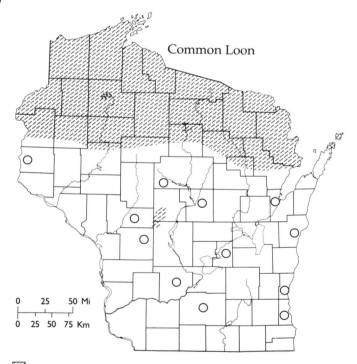

Common Loon

0   25   50 Mi
0 25 50 75 Km

▨ Summer range
○ Late May to late September

Records since 1960

bility that Wisconsin's spring loons come north from southern Lake Michigan, then disperse across the state. But the spring presence of this species in Missouri, Iowa, and Illinois makes it more likely that birds move into Wisconsin across a broad front, including the Mississippi River valley, and go unreported in extreme southwestern Wisconsin because of the paucity of both lakes and observers.

The study by Bielefeldt (1974b) of spring waterfowl in Waukesha County leaves no doubt that Common Loon numbers have dropped significantly since 1950. Before 1950, S. P. Jones frequently found 50–75 birds on the 11 sizable Waukesha County lakes on a typical April day. In 1966 Bielefeldt could find but 12 on his best days.

Breeding populations have declined as well. In the nineteenth and early twentieth centuries, modest numbers—some breeders, some nonbreeders—remained all summer on larger lakes in the Milwaukee-Madison region. No June or July sightings have been reported from Jefferson County since 1942, Waukesha County since 1958, or Green Lake County since 1962.

The current breeding range covers northern Wisconsin south to Polk, Chippewa, Lincoln, and Oconto counties, plus an isolated pocket in Wood and Juneau counties. Since 1970 presumed nonbreeders have been recorded in summer south to St. Croix, Monroe, and Portage counties, plus one on Devil's Lake in Sauk County. Other nonbreeders frequent the Lake Superior region, with individuals occasionally seen on Lake Michigan south to Manitowoc and Ozaukee counties. Lakes chosen for nesting are often smaller than the ones preferred in migration. Suitable nesting lakes need a grassy, shallow area and relatively little human disturbance. Such areas are becoming increasingly scarce.

During fall migration, the loons return to the larger lakes, and more of the birds probably move to Lake Michigan. Inland, migrants are less numerous in fall than in spring. Migration starts in the north by the end of September, peaking in the latter half of October, usually ending when the lakes freeze in mid-November. Exceptionally late records are 21 December (1965, Bayfield, B. F. Klugow), 22 December (1980, Douglas, B. F. Klugow), and 28 December (1963, Lincoln, D. J. Hendrick). In the south, birds start to arrive by 10 October, peak from 20 October to 10 November, and leave by 30 November. Only a few individuals remain for CBCs in Dane, Walworth, Sauk, and Milwaukee counties. The latest record is on 3 January (1960, Ozaukee, W. N. MacBriar).

Since the inception of the Wisconsin Project Loon Watch in 1978, headquartered at the Sigurd Olson Environmental Institute at Northland College (Ashland), much human effort has gone into the monitoring and protection of Loon nests. The 1980s are seeing modest but encouraging population increases.

Family **Podicipedidae:** Grebes

Pied-billed Grebe (*Podilymbus podiceps*)

STATUS. Common migrant. Common summer resident. Rare winter resident.

HABITAT. Inland lakes. Ponds. Shallow marsh.

MIGRATION DATES. *Spring:* mid-March to early May. *Fall:* early September to late December.

BREEDING DATA. Nests with eggs: 22 May to 12 August. Clutch size: usually 5 or 6 eggs; occasionally up to 9.

WINTER. Occasionally present where open water permits, rarely north to Douglas, Bayfield, Price, Marinette, and Door counties.

PORTRAIT. *Birds of Wisconsin:* Plate 2.

I have sometimes wondered, while standing on the road adjacent to the Twin Lakes in St. Croix County, what it would sound like if every Pied-bill on these lakes sounded off at the same time. I have heard five or six going at once and laughed at the ludicrous tomfoolery. Probably 50–100 grebes were present. In Deusing's (1939b, p. 367) summary of nesting studies of this species at Lake Koshkonong in 1938, the call of the male was characterized "wup, pup, pup, pup, kaow, kaow, kaoo, kaoo." The female answered with a soft "whut, hu, hu, hu, hut." On a larger marsh like Horicon, where grebes must number in the hundreds, the sound would be fantastic if all decided to "whup it up" simultaneously.

But this isn't likely. In fact, it is because they sound off so seldom that their numbers are often underestimated. In parts of southern and eastern Wisconsin, east of a line from Monroe through Wisconsin Dells to Marinette, the Pied-bill is abundant as a migrant and common as a summer resident. In parts of western and northern Wisconsin, it is common wherever suitable wetlands exist. Allowing for extensive areas where suitable habitat is absent, this is a common species throughout the state.

A few southern Wisconsin birds are sometimes seen in the first week of March. Whether they are true migrants or overwintering individuals is open to question. Nearly every year a few migrants appear between 15 and 20 March in the south, and reach the northern counties between 1 and 10 April. Birds peak in the south between 15 and 30 April (270 in Dodge, 25 April 1974, T. Sanford), and between 25 April and 10 May in the north.

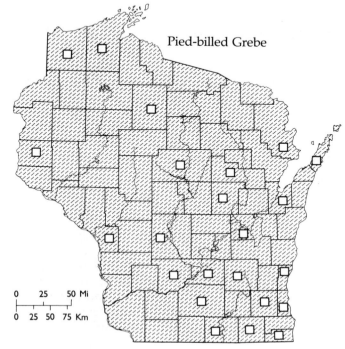

Pied-billed Grebe

0   25   50 Mi
0   25   50   75 Km

▨ Summer range
☐ Early January to early March

Records since 1960

The nesting season is prolonged. Richter found nests with eggs by 22 May and, in one instance, estimated that egg-laying had begun 10 days earlier. At the other extreme, O. J. Gromme's notes show nests with eggs as late as 12 August. Most egg-laying takes place in early June, with young out of the nest by the end of the month.

The start of the fall migration is difficult to pinpoint. Migrating birds tend to use the same wetlands that have already attracted nesting birds. Eau Claire television tower kills on the 5th (1961) and 6th (1965) prove that birds are moving at least by early September. The largest fall numbers have been reported in late September: 300 on Fremont Marsh in Waupaca County on the 23rd (1948, F. Holman King), and 600 in Dodge County on the 30th (1974, T. Sanford). As the hunting season progresses in October, Pied-bills disappear, leaving only individuals and small flocks in early November.

A few linger through December, with individuals showing up on the CBC at from one to seven locations every winter. The Pied-bill is almost a regular on the Lake Geneva CBC, with the surprising total of 36 birds on 2 January (1972, C. O. Palmquist). Some then disappear in early January as the last of the inland lakes freeze. Some may have been hunter-cripples that could not survive a Wisconsin winter. Some do stay through winter, not only in the south, but also as far north as Juneau, Adams, Price, Outagamie, and Winnebago counties.

Horned Grebe (*Podiceps auritus*)

STATUS. Common spring migrant; fairly common fall migrant. Rare summer resident. Rare winter visitant east.
HABITAT. Great Lakes. Inland lakes.
MIGRATION DATES. *Spring:* mid-March to mid-May. *Fall:* early September to early December.
BREEDING DATA. Nests with eggs: 5 and 10 June. Clutch size: 4 or 5 eggs.
WINTER. Occasionally present in the southeast.
PORTRAIT. *Birds of Wisconsin:* Plate 2.

One of the prettiest sights I can remember was the flock of 96 of these diminutive divers, all in bright breeding plumage, swimming in Lake Menomin at Menomonie on 25 April 1967. During spring migration one usually sees from one to five individuals, but birds occasionally stack up in flocks of 50–100. At another Dunn County location, I. O. Buss saw an estimated 300 Horned Grebes at Elk Lake on 17 April 1946. Buss saw an even larger migration, estimated at 500, at Milwaukee on 14 April 1948 (Buss and Mattison 1955).

In the south, the spring flight peaks between 10 and 25 April after a 20–25 March beginning. Early March records such as those for Milwaukee on the 2nd (1973, M. F. Donald) and Pierce County on the 4th (1963, S. D. Robbins) may represent birds wintering in the vicinity. In the north, birds first appear around 10 April, and peak from 20 April to 10 May. Migrants seldom remain beyond 20 May in any part of the state, but there are records of birds lingering until 3 June in Brown County (1957, E. O. Paulson) and until 5 June in Sheboygan County (1949, G. H. Orians).

Most evidence of breeding comes from the nineteenth century. Kumlien and Hollister (1903) stated, "Not infrequently nests in the northern part of the state, as it formerly did even in the southern tier of counties." The only specific instance of breeding listed was in June 1880 when young a few days old were procured at Lake Koshkonong. "The northern part of the state" may refer to the Oconto County area, where Schoenebeck (1902) collected a set of five

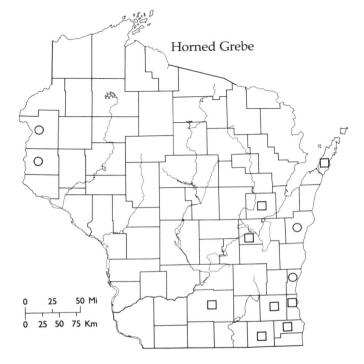

Horned Grebe

0   25   50 Mi
0 25 50 75 Km

○ Late May to late August
□ Mid-December to early March

Records since 1960

eggs on 10 June 1899, and northern Brown County, where H. L. Ward (MPM files) obtained a set of eggs on 5 June 1903. More recently a pair with one small young was seen in Racine County on 15 June 1940 (B. L. von Jarchow), and an adult with four young was observed in Burnett County on 2 July 1951 (N. R. Stone). These latter sightings are presumed to represent nesting birds.

Horned Grebes have also been sighted sporadically during summer months. The summer of 1956 was unusual, with individuals present during June and July in Waukesha (D. R. Bierman), Jefferson (E. W. Peartree), and Dodge (O. J. Gromme) counties. A bird in breeding plumage was discovered in Polk County on 14 June 1974 (C. A. Faanes). Eight individuals were counted on Rush Lake in Winnebago County on 25 June 1953 (R. C. Hopkins), one summered in St. Croix County in 1962 (S. D. Robbins), one was found in Milwaukee on 19 July 1954 (I. N. Balsom), and one was observed in Manitowoc County on 28 July 1983 (C. R. Sontag). One on 3 August (1977, Ozaukee, N. J. Cutright) was very early to be considered a fall migrant.

In most years fall migrants do not appear until 15 September. But field notes in *The Passenger Pigeon* list 18 fall arrivals before that date, the earliest being August arrivals on the 13th (1963, Outagamie, D. D.

Tessen), 14th (1964, Brown, E. O. Paulson), and 18th (1979, Columbia, W. A. Smith). During the peak period, 1 October to 10 November, flocks of 30–40 are sometimes found on Lake Michigan, but inland numbers are far smaller than in spring. By early November, birds have left the northern counties, and by the end of the month most southern birds are gone.

It is not unusual for two or three birds to remain through December scattered along Lake Michigan and Lake Geneva, but most disappear by early January. However, five cases of successful wintering have been reported in recent years from Milwaukee, Waukesha, Winnebago, and Outagamie counties.

Red-necked Grebe (*Podiceps grisegena*)
Formerly Holboell's Grebe

STATUS. Uncommon spring migrant; rare fall migrant. Rare summer resident.
HABITAT. Inland lakes. Shallow marsh.
MIGRATION DATES. *Spring:* mid-April to mid-May. *Fall:* late September to mid-November. *Extremes:* 5 March; 22 December.
BREEDING DATA. Nests with eggs: 9 May to 6 July. Clutch size: usually 4 eggs; rarely 3–6.
PORTRAIT. *Birds of Wisconsin:* Plate 2.

Although considered common in neighboring Minnesota, this bird is deemed a real "find" by most Wisconsin bird enthusiasts. In the mid-nineteenth century, this species and a "Crested Grebe" were thought to be separate species. By 1881 the "Crested Grebe" was recognized as the immature stage of *grisegena*, and from then on the name "Holboell's Grebe" was used. This name was changed to Red-necked Grebe in 1957. The comments of Hoy (1853b) and Barry (1854) are of little value because of the early confusion in identification.

By the late nineteenth century the Red-necked Grebe seemed rare. Schoenebeck (1902) did not list it. Kumlien and Hollister (1903) listed it as "found sparingly" in March and April, from late September to November, and rarely on Lake Michigan in winter. They had no sure evidence of nesting.

In the first third of the twentieth century, Wisconsin sightings averaged one per 5-year period, and these were deemed rare enough to warrant special publication in such journals as *The Auk*. Observations during this period culminated in the state's first positive nesting record: a pair with nest and four eggs on 12 May 1938 (Dane, S. P. Jones [1938]).

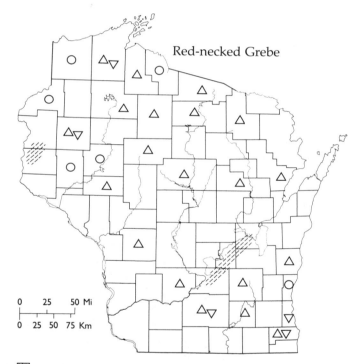

Red-necked Grebe

▨ Summer range
△ Mid-April to mid-May
○ Late May to mid-September
▽ Late September to mid-November

Records since 1960

Between 1938 and 1968, observations became almost an annual event. Of the 68 observations known for that period, 48 were in spring (15 March to 25 May), 5 were in summer (16 July to 5 September), and 15 were in autumn (25 September to 16 November).

Notable are the records from Superior, where this grebe was found to be regular in late April and early May in the 1960s, with as many as 10 present at one time (R. F. Bernard).

In 1969, nesting colonies were discovered at Rush Lake in Winnebago County and at Twin Lakes in St. Croix County. Forty nests were counted at the Winnebago County colony in 1970, with a modest spread into Green Lake and Columbia counties in the 1980s. Though smaller, the St. Croix County cluster appears to be spreading; nesting was reported in northern St. Croix and southern Polk counties in 1977. Aside from these two breeding areas and the harbor at Superior, the Red-necked Grebe remains a rare migrant, with no more than two to six spring and one or two fall observations per year.

Spring records are widely distributed throughout the state. A few are from Lake Michigan, but most are from the shallow edges of small or medium-sized lakes. Only in the southwest, where suitable habitat is scarce, has the Red-necked Grebe gone unrecorded. Most spring records are from 15 April to 10 May. One in Dane County on 5–25 March 1962 (W. L. Hilsenhoff) is exceptional.

By late August, birds have left the nesting areas. Few are seen anywhere in the state in September, but in October and early November observers have occasionally spotted an individual along Lake Michigan near Milwaukee and Racine. There have been November sightings on the 16th (1951, Milwaukee, D. L. Larkin), 20th (1972, Ozaukee, M. F. Donald), and 22nd (1969, Dane, P. Ashman). Two exceptionally late stragglers were found in 1983: on 10 December (Milwaukee, D. D. Tessen) and 22 December (Dane, A. K. Shea).

Eared Grebe (*Podiceps nigricollis*)

STATUS. Uncommon migrant. Casual summer resident.
HABITAT. Inland lakes.
MIGRATION DATES. *Spring:* mid-April to early June. *Fall:* late September to mid-November. *Extremes:* 3 April; 19 December.
BREEDING DATA. One record: pair with young, 6 July.
WINTER. One February record.
PORTRAIT. *Birds of Wisconsin:* Plate 2.

A striking change has come over the status of this western species since 1940. The one twentieth-century record before then was on 30 April 1909, when a hunter shot five of a group of six Eared Grebes north of Prairie du Sac in Sauk County. One of these specimens is now in the Milwaukee Public Museum collection.

Only three indefinite records are known from the nineteenth century. Although Kumlien and Hollister (1903) never met with this bird personally in Wisconsin, they examined two specimens presumably taken near Iron River in Bayfield County, plus the wing of a bird shot near Watertown by H. A. Winkenwerder. Dates are wholly lacking for these early records.

Beginning with A. W. Schorger's sighting of a bird in Dane County on 31 May 1941, a marked increase in observations occurred. There were 10 records in the 1940s, 21 in the 1950s, 22 in the 1960s, 24 in the 1970s, and 19 between 1980 and 1985. One reason for the increase is the better coverage now being given the western counties adjacent to the St. Croix River. Since

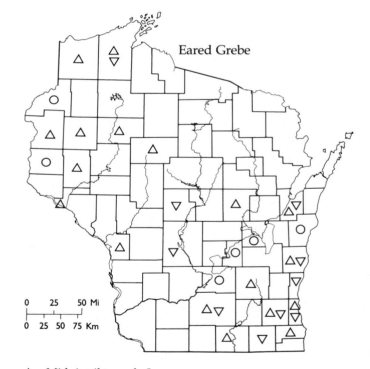

△ Mid-April to early June
O Mid-June to mid-September
▽ Late September to mid-November

Records since 1960

1955 the St. Croix–Polk–Burnett–Douglas County region has produced 17 records.

A second reason may be the closer attention being given shallow ponds in late May. Compared with most waterfowl, the Eared Grebe is a late migrant. Although it has been found as early as 3 April (1949, Racine, L. W. Erickson; 1956, Fond du Lac, R. A. Knuth), the main migration period is between 20 April and 31 May. Spring migrants have been observed as late as 6 June (1976, Dunn, S. D. Robbins; 1977, St. Croix, C. A. Faanes) and 11 June (1968, St. Croix, S. D. Robbins).

Few spring sightings have come from Lake Michigan. This species favors such shallow prairie ponds as Lake Barney in Dane County, Goose Pond in Columbia County, Twin Lakes in St. Croix County, and Crex Meadows in Burnett County. Observers do well to scan the open water of such areas not once but several times per field trip, for the Eared Grebe is a frequent diver, often spending more time submerged than surfaced.

On two occasions individuals have summered at Goose Pond, remaining until at least 29 July (1965, S. D. Robbins) and 5 August (1956, R. G. Wills). One was found in Burnett County on 12 July (1956, A. Sprunt). None showed evidence of breeding. Then on 6 July 1968 in St. Croix County, I located a pair, one carrying two newborn young on its back (*Pass. Pigeon*

31:252). To date, this is Wisconsin's only nesting record. The same area attracted another summer resident in 1977 (3 June–7 August, C. A. Faanes), while two summered in Winnebago County in 1978 (29 June–5 August, T. De Boor). On Lake Maria in Green Lake County, a group of 10 was seen in late June 1981 (B. A. Eichhorst). Two summer 1982 sightings were made in Winnebago (2–17 June, T. Ziebell) and Columbia (9–11 June, M. S. Peterson) counties. Another spent 3 weeks in 1984 in Winnebago County (1–20 June, T. Ziebell). In 1985 one was present in Manitowoc County (9–14 June, C. R. Sontag).

Compared with 69 spring observations between 1941 and 1983, there have been but 21 autumn reports. Most are from Lake Michigan or Madison's Lake Mendota. Only four were in September: the 3rd (1984, Wood, S. R. Swengel), 4th (1967, Waukesha, D. K. Gustafson), 10th (1977, Brown, C. A. Kemper), and 17th (1966, Sheboygan, H. Koopmann). The bulk of the migrants were noted between 10 October and 20 November. Two December dates are known: the 7th (1956, Dane, R. G. Wills) and 19th (1953, Dane, M. A. Walker). As in spring, most observations were single birds, rarely three or four, never more than six.

One remarkable winter record was established on 12 February 1959 when an Eared Grebe was found exhausted in a Rock County cornfield by E. L. Loyster and R. Kyro (*Pass. Pigeon* 21:123).

Western Grebe (*Aechmophorus occidentalis*)

STATUS. Rare migrant. Casual summer visitant. Casual winter visitant east.

HABITAT. Great Lakes. Inland lakes.

MIGRATION DATES. *Spring:* early April to late May. *Fall:* early September to mid-December.

WINTER. Six Lake Michigan records.

PORTRAIT. *Birds of Wisconsin:* Plate 2.

From 2 April to 29 May 1948, Milwaukee observers were treated to an unprecedented influx of Western Grebes along the Lake Michigan shore. As many as 12 could be seen at one time during much of this 2-month span (*Pass. Pigeon* 11:134, 184). In the previous 2 years small flocks of this species had been found along the lakeshore in Door (12 October 1946, P. W. Hoffmann) and Manitowoc (26 November 1946 and 18 November 1947, W. M. Smith) counties. But these were 1-day appearances.

Nothing like this had previously been reported. Before 1946 there were but three twentieth-century records. Four birds were collected near Oconto in September 1924 (Richter 1939a), one was observed in Waukesha County on 6 October 1935 (W. E. Scott; MPM files), and one was found in Racine County on 1 November 1938 (M. Deusing; MPM files). Kumlien and Hollister (1903) described only two nineteenth-century finds: one collected from a group of six in Jefferson County on 4 January 1878 (A. L. Kumlien), and one taken at the same location in October 1881 (A. L. Kumlien). These authors added, "We are positive we have seen others, but they are very rare in Wisconsin." No other dates were mentioned, nor were there additional sightings reported by other nineteenth-century writers.

Nearly every year since 1948, from one to five reports have come from somewhere in Wisconsin. Lone individuals are usually sighted, rarely three or four. Of the 83 observations recorded between 1948 and 1989, 30 were Lake Michigan birds—mainly in Milwaukee and Ozaukee counties, but encompassing most of the shore from Racine to Door counties. Another 20 were in a rectangular area bounded by Walworth, Dane, Brown, and Shawano counties, centered around Lake Winnebago. Another 33 were western Wisconsin birds in St. Croix, Burnett, Douglas, and Ashland counties.

Only 27 of these 83 records were spring birds, spanning the period from 3 April (1978, Ozaukee, L. W. Erickson) to 30 May (1974, Burnett, C. A. Faanes). With the exception of a bird sighted in Milwaukee on 10–21 May 1950, all were individuals on the move—here today, gone tomorrow.

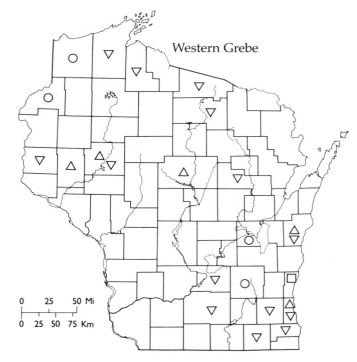

Western Grebe

△ Early April to late May
○ Early June to late August
▽ Early September to mid-December
□ Late December to late March

Records since 1960

Four early summer observations in the northwest indicate a more extended residence: 3–11 June (1979, Burnett, J. O. Evrard), 3–26 June (1981, Douglas, R. J. Johnson), 13–14 June (1981, Burnett, J. E. Hoefler), and 8 June (1976, Burnett, L. Long). Single Western Grebes at Horicon Marsh in Dodge County entertained many birders between 18 June and 1 August 1960, and between 12 June and 5 August 1987. The only late-summer records are of two birds on 23 July (1971, Winnebago, D. D. Tessen) and one on 26 August (1975, Burnett, L. Long).

Autumn is the likeliest time for this species to wander eastward into Wisconsin. Between 9 September (1983, St. Croix, B. R. Bacon) and 8 December (1963, Waukesha, E. W. Peartree), observers have met up with Westerns 42 times since 1948. Two-thirds of these were between 10 October and 10 November. In addition, birds wintered in the Milwaukee area in 1952–1953 and 1954–1955, and one was found in Ozaukee County on 24 January 1976 (J. Bronson).

Family **Pelecanidae:** Pelicans

American White Pelican (*Pelecanus erythrorhynchos*)

STATUS. Rare spring migrant west; rare fall migrant.
Rare summer visitant.
HABITAT. Inland lakes.
MIGRATION DATES. *Spring:* mid-April to late May.
Fall: early October to mid-November. *Extremes:*
9 March; 24 November.
PORTRAIT. *Birds of Wisconsin:* Plate 3.

In "The White Pelican in Early Wisconsin" Schorger
(1954b) gives considerable evidence from newspaper
stories and journal entries of early explorers to show
that this bird was at least moderately common along
the Mississippi before 1850. Thure Kumlien also found
them numerous as April migrants on Lake Koshkonong before 1870, and frequently mentioned them
around the lakes of Dane and Jefferson counties (Kumlien and Hollister 1903).

Migrants reached northeastern Wisconsin in more
limited numbers. Grundtvig (1895) recorded one shot
in Shawano County in 1881, and reported occasional
observations in Outagamie County at that time.
Schoenebeck (1902) referred to this species as an uncommon spring and fall migrant. By then, these birds
had also become decidedly uncommon in southern
Wisconsin. Between 1890 and 1900 there were but two
Lake Koshkonong records.

The pelican has remained a rare migrant and summer visitant throughout the twentieth century. Since
beginning publication in 1939, *The Passenger Pigeon*
has recorded sightings in about 8 of every 10 years,
with from one to four reports per year.

One-fourth of the reports are from late April or
May. The only modern record before 20 April was
10 April (1943, Dane, S. P. Chase). Hoy (1853b) mentioned 10 March as an expected arrival date in his day,
and the 10 March 1866 issue of the *Madison Democrat*
reported a sighting the previous day. But even in the
days of abundance, April and early May were the
chief migration period. In recent times the largest
known flock numbered 48 birds on Cedar Lake in
Polk and St. Croix counties (25 April 1947, L. Hope).

One-fourth of the modern sightings were of summer visitants. Whereas the spring migrants pause
only briefly, birds that turn up in June or July often
linger for weeks. Of four birds that turned up in
Adams County on 15 May 1956, two were still present
on 1 November. Presumably the summer wanderers

American White Pelican

△ Mid-April to late May
○ Early June to late September
▽ Early October to mid-November

Records since 1960

are nonbreeding adults. In no case has breeding been
suspected.

One-half of the recent observations were from October and November. A few were small flocks that
paused for as much as 2 weeks, but most were birds
passing through nonstop. The earliest modern records
of fall migrants are 26 September (1964, Crawford,
E. R. Bierbrauer) and 27 September (1971, Ashland,
A. J. Roy). The latest are in November: the 20th (1975,
Brown, T. C. Erdman), 22nd (1961, Bayfield, B. F. Klugow), and 24th (1958, Dane, R. H. Lound). Fall flocks
have numbered as high as 37, and can be expected
most often between 15 October and 10 November.

While this huge fish-eater may have nested in Wisconsin in the early days, there is no sure evidence
that it did. Kumlien and Hollister (1903) mentioned
an 1883 visit to an abandoned rookery "in the western
part of the state," but offer no further supporting evi-

123

dence to show that this was not a rookery for herons and/or cormorants. The same authors also mentioned secondhand information about breeding "northeast of Merrill" in 1884. Schorger (1954b), pursuing this lead, concluded that the only likely nesting habitat would have been at Pelican Lake in Oneida County, and that older residents could recall this species only as a migrant. He concluded, "Until better information is available, the White Pelican cannot be considered as a formerly breeding bird in Wisconsin."

Brown Pelican (*Pelecanus occidentalis*)

STATUS. Accidental. Four records.
HABITAT. Normally coastal beaches.
MIGRATION DATES. Observed between 22 April and 1 August.
PORTRAIT. *Birds of Wisconsin:* Plate 3.

In the Milwaukee Public Museum is a specimen of a Brown Pelican donated by A. W. Schorger; he had collected the bird in Madison on 1 August 1943 (Schorger 1944a). It was a second-year female, reported first by Mrs. T. E. Coleman on 31 July.

Only after word of the 1943 bird had circulated did it become generally known that a Sauk County specimen had been preserved in the Herman Fuchs home near Blackhawk for the previous 40 years. Two birds had been sighted on the Blackhawk millpond in late May or early June, probably in 1906, and one was collected by S. Fisher. The bird was mounted by Prairie du Sac taxidermist Ed Ochsner, and given to his daughter, Mrs. Fuchs. Schorger visited the Fuchs home 2 weeks after collecting his specimen, and confirmed that this was also a second-year bird (*Pass. Pigeon* 5:47).

An additional sight record is mentioned in personal correspondence from E. J. McKern to O. J. Gromme in 1946. "This is to certify that, in 1929, early in July . . . while walking one morning on the road between Trempealeau and Perrot State Park, I saw a Brown Pelican flying north directly overhead. The low elevation of the flying bird made it quite impossible to make an incorrect identification."

Another unpublished sight record was of two birds flying over the north end of Peninsula State Park in Door County on 22 April 1978. In personal correspondence, Mark Rispens wrote: "At first I thought the birds were herons. . . . As the birds flew almost directly over where I was standing, I noticed that their legs were shorter, and that there was a large flap of skin under their bills." Six weeks later, Michigan obtained its first record for this species.

Accidental sightings have been reported from other midwestern states: North and South Dakota, Nebraska, Iowa, Illinois, and Indiana. In the early 1970s it looked as if Wisconsin's chances of ever having another Brown Pelican visit were slim, for there was nearly catastrophic nesting failure because of the thin eggshells that resulted from the widespread use of pesticides. These mammoth birds are now staging a comeback. Perhaps additional stragglers will wander to this state.

Family **Phalacrocoracidae**: Cormorants

Double-crested Cormorant (*Phalacrocorax auritus*)

STATUS. Uncommon migrant. Uncommon summer
resident.

HABITAT. Great Lakes. Inland lakes. Ponds. Wooded
swamp.

MIGRATION DATES. *Spring:* mid-April to mid-May.
Fall: late September to mid-December.

BREEDING DATA. Nests with eggs: 1 May to 29 July.
Clutch size: 3–6 eggs.

WINTER. Three records.

PORTRAIT. *Birds of Wisconsin:* Plate 3.

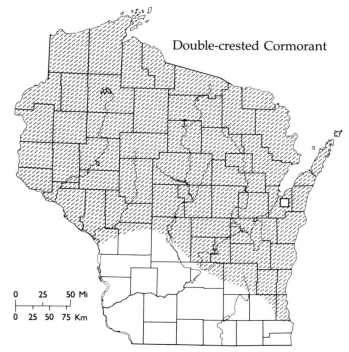

Double-crested Cormorant

0   25   50 Mi

0 25 50 75 Km

▨ Summer range
☐ Mid-December to late March

Records since 1960

There was a time when these birds darkened the sun
as they moved up or down the Mississippi in huge
flocks. A particularly spectacular flight passed La
Crosse on 24 April 1926, and was described by Mark
Byers, editor of the *La Crosse Tribune* (25 April 1926?).
"It continued for two and one-half hours, more or
less intermittently, although there were always from
a dozen to hundreds of large flocks in the air. . . .
The flight was so large that at times it was impossible
to see the sunset sky through the mass. At other
times they would be strung out in long lines and
groups like blackbirds. The number of birds is variously estimated at from 100,000 to 1,000,000 birds."
While this was an exceptional instance, it was not uncommon for substantial flocks of hundreds—if not
thousands—to migrate up the river in April and down
the river in October and early November.

Records from western Wisconsin are so fragmentary before 1940 that it is difficult to know how extensive these flights were. Kumlien and Hollister (1903)
mentioned this species as being common along the
Mississippi and indicated that J. N. Clark considered
it rare along the Chippewa River in Dunn County. It
seems probable that this fish-eater was abundant
along the Mississippi, but only moderately common
in suitable habitat elsewhere in the state.

As recently as 1949, migrating flocks totaling 5,000
were being seen at La Crosse. Morse (1954) described
Genoa as "one of the best places to watch large concentrations" in spring and fall. But even as those
words were being written, a precipitous decline had
begun. Believing the cormorants to be a threat to their
industry, commercial fishing interests systematically
tried to thwart the nesting efforts of cormorants. Part
of the Lac Du Bay colony in Marathon County was

devastated by illegal poaching (Anderson and Hamerstrom 1967). Several colonies in the Green Bay region
were similarly raided.

Numbers plummeted. By 1960 only three to five
birds were observed per season outside the few remaining breeding colonies. Habitat deterioration also
played a part. For many years colonies have come and
gone, as large areas of dead trees appeared with the
creation of new flowages and disappeared with the
decay and removal of these trees. Substantial colonies
in Lafayette and Columbia counties disappeared in
the 1930s. Colonies in Adams and Juneau counties
emptied in the 1950s. The Crex Meadows region in
Burnett County was cormorant-less in the 1960s.

In the late 1960s active rookeries were limited to
Marathon and Trempealeau counties, and the Double-
crest became a prime candidate for the endangered
species list established in 1973. With needed protec-

tion thus afforded, a modest comeback is now evident. New nesting areas have developed in the 1970s in Green Lake, Dodge, Brown, Door, and Burnett counties. But flocks of over 30 are rarely reported except where nesting occurs.

Outside the breeding areas, spring migrants are generally seen between 15 April and 10 May, occasionally between 5 April and 20 May. A few late-March arrivals were reported in the 1940s and 1950s, and a remarkably early flock of nine reached Bayfield County on 16 March 1973 (A. J. Roy). Years ago, however, arrivals were somewhat earlier. Kumlien and Hollister (1903) commented that the cormorant "arrived as soon as the ice began to loosen in the small lakes, varying with the season from early in March until April."

While nesting takes place between mid-May and mid-July in most areas, it is delayed until July in the Green Bay region, where gulls are competitors. Cormorant nesting success is better after gull nesting is finished.

A few fall migratory flocks are seen between 25 September and 10 November. Rarely, the departure period has extended beyond 25 November. December dates beyond the 5th include the 7th (1941, Brown, E. G. Wright), 11th (1948, Milwaukee, H. C. Mueller), 13th (1980, Milwaukee, J. H. Idzikowski), 14th (1957, Manitowoc, J. Kraupa), and 15th (1984, Ashland, R. L. Verch). Single individuals have overwintered in Brown County three times since 1980 (E. D. Cleary).

Cormorants are responding favorably to the placing of artificial platforms in suitable nesting habitat. T. C. Erdman (pers. comm.) reported that 34 of a possible 45 platforms in the Green Bay area were used in 1978. Known breeding pairs in his northeastern Wisconsin study area increased from 37 in 1976 to 64 in 1978. A nestling he banded in July 1976 was recovered in Louisiana the following December.

Meier (1981) also noted promising response by Double-crested Cormorants and Great Blue Herons to artificial platforms he erected on the Mead Wildlife Area in Marathon County between 1974 and 1976. In the 1970s, nesting areas expanded, as shown on the accompanying map. By 1985 the recovery was sufficient to allow the cormorant's removal from the endangered species list. To continue its comeback, this species must be protected from undue human interference, and it must have suitable nesting habitat.

Family **Anhingidae:** Darters

Anhinga (*Anhinga anhinga*)
Formerly Water-Turkey

STATUS. Casual spring migrant; accidental fall migrant.

HABITAT. Wooded swamp.

MIGRATION DATES. *Spring:* observed between 7 April and 22 May. *Fall:* one September record.

Wisconsin's lone specimen was procured by a Dr. Lawrence somewhere along the Green Bay shore in the spring of 1889. The skin was brought to A. J. Schoenebeck, who thought it to be a male because of its glossy black upper parts. But the skin remained in Lawrence's possession, not in the best of condition, and its present whereabouts is unknown. Kumlien and Hollister (1903) did not list this record, and nine years later Hollister (1912, p. 397) commented, "It is possible that the Anhinga might wander some three hundred miles out of its regular range, but until this specimen comes to light and proves not to be a Cormorant, I do not think it should stand for the only authentic state record."

Anhinga

△   7 April to 22 May
▽   27 September

All records

Anhinga, 7 April 1966, Milwaukee County (photo by O. R. Lemke)

Not until 1965 was another "water-turkey" reported. On 11 May at the Cedar Grove Ornithological Station in Sheboygan County, K. Stoll, H. C. Mueller, and D. D. Berger trained their binoculars on a bird soaring in wide circles high overhead. Although it was barely visible to the naked eye, the observers were able to detect a long neck and a fairly long rounded tail that convinced them the bird was not a cormorant. The bird was behaving just as they had seen the Anhinga behave in its normal range (*Pass. Pigeon* 28:10–11). But this, too, hardly qualified as sure-fire evidence for admitting a new species to the state list.

The right kind of evidence came the following year when a bird was discovered in Whitnall Park in Milwaukee County on 7 April 1966 by Dorothy and Russell Bednarek. It was photographed later that day by O. R. Lemke and watched under ideal conditions for nearly 90 minutes (*Pass. Pigeon* 28:112–113).

Another Anhinga put on a command performance for seven raptor-banders at Cedar Grove in Sheboygan County on 27 September 1980. Two of the seven observers (H. C. Mueller, D. D. Berger) had also viewed the 1965 wanderer. They witnessed the same distinctive behavior of flapping and soaring in circles (*Pass. Pigeon* 44:125–126).

On 2 May 1982 an individual soared over Anita Carpenter's head as she bicycled under sunny skies along an Oshkosh road near Lake Winnebago. The long slender neck and long fanned tail were obvious as the bird circled at ever-increasing altitude (*Pass. Pigeon* 45:39–40).

D. G. Follen studied an Anhinga on 22 May 1983 as it swam and dove in a drainage ditch in the Wood County public hunting grounds west of Wisconsin Rapids. Six hours later, 20 miles northeast in the Mead Wildlife Area in southern Marathon County, Ken and Jan Luepke saw what was probably the same bird (*Pass. Pigeon* 46:39–41).

Family **Fregatidae:** Frigatebirds

Magnificent Frigatebird (*Fregata magnificens*)
Formerly Man-O'-War Bird

STATUS. Accidental. Two records.
HABITAT. Normally oceanic.

Along the Milwaukee River at what used to be called Humboldt (now a part of the north side of Milwaukee), a wandering boy noticed a strange bird perched on a rock projecting out of the river. It was an August day in 1880, and the bird was a fair target for the boy's pistol. The boy's name is unknown; the exact date is unknown. But the specimen now resides in the Milwaukee Public Museum as one of the strangest and most remarkable birds in its collection.

Normally a southern oceanic species, the Magnificent Frigatebird is known to do some occasional far-ranging wandering. The AOU *Check-list of North American Birds* mentions accidental records for Ohio, Indiana, Illinois, Iowa, Kansas, and Oklahoma, along with several Atlantic coastal states.

Wisconsin had no subsequent record until 1988. On 28 September at Superior, Donald Swedberg and three fishing associates spotted a large black bird with a deeply forked tail, also engrossed in a fishing expedition. The size and coloration reminded the observers of a cormorant; the behavior reminded them of a large tern (*Pass. Pigeon* 51:229–230). This was accepted by the WSO Records Committee as a "Frigatebird sp.?". There is little doubt that this was a Magnificent Frigatebird blown off course by Hurricane Gilbert that struck the Texas coast on 16 September 1988. Other frigatebirds were reported from Arkansas, Tennessee, Virginia, West Virginia, Oklahoma, Kansas, Missouri, Illinois, and Minnesota.

Family **Ardeidae:** Bitterns, Herons

American Bittern (*Botaurus lentiginosus*)

STATUS. Common migrant. Common summer resident north and central; uncommon summer resident south. Rare winter resident south and central.
HABITAT. Wooded swamp. Shallow marsh. Sedge meadow.
MIGRATION DATES. *Spring:* mid-April to mid-May. *Fall:* early September to early November.
BREEDING DATA. Nests with eggs: 13 May to 14 July. Clutch size: usually 4 or 5 eggs; occasionally 3 or 6.
WINTER. Occasionally present north to Wood and Brown counties.
PORTRAIT. *Birds of Wisconsin:* Plate 5.

This is the only heron more numerous and widespread in the northern half of the state than in the southern. The wet meadows and grass marshes preferred by the "stake-driver" were always few and far between in the hilly regions of the southwest. In the southeast, this formerly widespread habitat has been altered by drainage, mechanized agriculture, and the transformation of reedy lakeshores into residential developments, leaving only relatively isolated areas such as Horicon Marsh in Dodge County. It is in the central and northern counties, north of a line from La Crosse to Sheboygan, that suitable habitat is more widespread. On several occasions, I have heard 10 or more "pumpers" on June BBS transects in Jackson, Juneau, Rusk, and Sawyer counties. A triangular area anchored by Grantsburg, Marinette, and Horicon showed the greatest density. Of the 33 BBS routes located within this triangle, 29 have recorded this species.

First arrivals usually appear around 10–15 April, spreading rapidly to the northern counties. After a 25 April to 15 May peak, migrants move on, and residents busy themselves with nesting activities. However, since 1940, there have been nine published arrival dates during the last week of March, plus an exceptionally early bird on 17 March (1968, Waushara, I. Chipman). Also exceptional are early April birds in the north on the 2nd (1963, Oconto, C. H. Richter) and 4th (1974, Burnett, J. O. Evrard).

Between 1922 and 1947, C. H. Richter collected information on 28 Oconto County nests. Of these, 9 contained five eggs, 15 had four, and 4 held three. Most eggs were laid between 20 May and 1 June, with

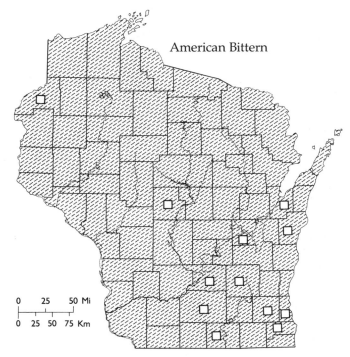

American Bittern

0   25   50 Mi
0 25 50 75 Km

▨ Summer range
☐ Mid-November to late March

Records since 1960

fresh eggs found between 13 May and 26 June. Most nests were found in thick marsh grass, sometimes adjacent to stands of willow and tamarack, within 20 feet of water. One nest was in a burned-over marsh area, with no suitable nesting material nearby, compelling the birds to carry dry grasses from a considerable distance.

Autumn birds are so quiet and inconspicuous that migration goes unnoticed. Presumably most birds leave by early October, with a few lingering into November in mild years, and some attempting to spend the winter.

Listing late-fall departure records is difficult because of the number of birds that have attempted to spend the winter. The bird that flopped down exhausted on the school playground at Cadott (Chippewa County) on 7 December 1970 (S. D. Robbins) apparently remained later than usual because of the presence of open water. It belatedly tried to migrate as sources of food became covered with ice and snow, but was too emaciated to survive. Other wintering birds have been more fortunate. Since 1940, 12 records

have been published for December, 12 for January, and 5 for February: the 6th (1961, Waukesha, E. W. Peartree), 14th (1955, Rock, M. T. Maxson), 17th (1953, Dodge, L. F. Gunther), 24th (1956, Columbia, T. Deerwester), and 28th (1965, Wood, D. G. Follen).

Least Bittern (*Ixobrychus exilis*)

STATUS. Common migrant south; uncommon migrant central and north. Common summer resident south; uncommon summer resident central and north.

HABITAT. Shallow marsh.

MIGRATION DATES. *Spring:* late April to late May. *Fall:* late August to early October. *Extremes:* 17 April; 15 December.

BREEDING DATA. Nests with eggs: 14 May to 2 August. Clutch size: usually 4 or 5 eggs; occasionally 3 or 6.

PORTRAIT. *Birds of Wisconsin:* Plate 5.

If you walk along a path or roadway adjacent to a cattail marsh and pause now and then to examine the vegetation with binoculars, you are likely to conclude that the Least Bittern is a rare species anywhere in Wisconsin. This diminutive heron rarely perches in conspicuous spots. When it flies, it is quick-up-quick-down as it moves from one part of the marsh to another. If you listen attentively as you walk—particularly in early morning or early evening—you may hear the unobtrusive hollow-sounding "bup-bup-bup" or the rhythmic "cu-cu-cu-cu-cu" often enough to conclude that the species is uncommon rather than rare. E. H. Zimmerman (pers. comm.) told of hearing five individuals singing between 12:30 and 2:00 A.M. on 2 June 1972 in Dane County, perhaps preferring to vocalize in the cool of the night rather than the heat of the day. If you explore the marshes with a small boat, you will discover that this is indeed a common species south and east of a line from La Crosse to Marinette. North and west of that line there are records from nearly every county, but in small numbers.

In most years first spring reports come between 5 and 10 May. But there have been enough April sightings (12 between 1952 and 1981) to suggest that birds of this species may be found fairly regularly from 25 April on if observers take the pains to search for them. The earliest April records for the south are on the 17th (1952, Dodge, O. J. Gromme) and 24th (1954, Jefferson, E. Degner; 1962, Dane, K. Brown). In the central counties, records are known for the 20th (1957,

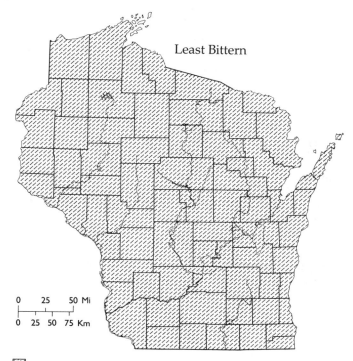

Least Bittern

0 25 50 Mi
0 25 50 75 Km

▨ Summer range

Records since 1960

Winnebago, N. M. Rogers), 22nd (1953, Winnebago, J. H. Evans), and 25th (1962, Portage, K. Brown; 1974, St. Croix, P. A. Tweet). Farther north, sightings occurred on the 27th (1982, Iron, M. E. Butterbrodt) and the 29th (1973, Langlade, B. Pickering). Between 10 and 25 May, birds become well distributed around the state.

Few nests are occupied before June. Between 1927 and 1949, C. H. Richter (pers. comm. to O. J. Gromme) found 37 nests in Oconto County. All were found with eggs between 3 June and 13 July, the majority between 20 June and 10 July. Commenting on the lateness in nesting, he wrote, "This species often must await a growth in weed and rushes suitable to support their nests—this in event that the ice or heavy snows have broken down or carried away old stands of rushes and weed beds." T. C. Erdman (pers. comm.) observed, "They only nest in the current year's growth, never in last year's." Nero (1951) indicated that July nests may also be the result of earlier nests being washed out by high water following heavy rains. In another study, Nero (1950) found that birds learn the typical "freezing" bill-up posture by the age of 4 days and are capable of leaving the nest by the eighth day.

Nesting has been observed as far north as Douglas and Bayfield counties (1971, D. A. Bratley). My own mid-June listening records in Vilas and Iron counties in 1973 suggest probable breeding in the Powell Marsh area. In 1962 the population on the Horicon National Wildlife Refuge in Dodge County was estimated at 200 on 15 August (J. Kurtz; NWR files).

Because of its late nesting season, the Least Bittern probably delays its fall migration to the end of August and the first half of September. No peak has been reported. The migration consists of a general exodus, which is nearly complete by 20 September, with most stragglers gone by 5 October. In addition to late dates on 8 October (1939, Green Lake, E. L. Loyster) and 9 October (1943, Sheboygan, W. C. Pelzer), there is a record of a straggler on 15 November (1957, Dodge, R. M. Russell) and one on 12 December (1940, Oconto, C. H. Richter). On 15 December 1982 an emaciated bird found in Monroe County was brought to Kim Mello, who tried unsuccessfully to rehabilitate the victim.

Great Blue Heron (*Ardea herodias*)

STATUS. Fairly common migrant. Fairly common summer resident northwest; uncommon summer resident northeast, central, and south. Rare winter resident south and central.

HABITAT. Great Lakes. Inland lakes. Ponds. Wooded swamp.

MIGRATION DATES. *Spring:* mid-March to early May. *Fall:* early August to mid-November.

BREEDING DATA. Nests with eggs: 18 April to 23 May. Clutch size: usually 4 or 5 eggs; rarely 3 or 6.

WINTER. A few regularly present north to Buffalo, Adams, and Manitowoc counties.

PORTRAIT. *Birds of Wisconsin:* Plate 25.

This is a hardy bird, capable of withstanding the rigors of a Wisconsin winter, provided it has access to running water that will not freeze in subzero temperatures. Considerable open water prevails just below Petenwell Dam in Adams and Juneau counties. From one to six Great Blues have wintered there nearly every year from 1953 to 1980. These large fish-eaters have been less regular at other locations, but have been recorded on the CBC at one to four locations nearly every year. The northernmost observations between 15 December and 1 March have been in Douglas (19 December 1963, B. F. Klugow), Sawyer (23 December 1965, B. F. Klugow), and Langlade (22 January 1948, B. J. Bradle) counties.

Migrants further show this species' hardy character by arriving in March before the snow has melted and before the lakes are free of ice. The Great Blue Heron is one of the first spring migrants, usually appearing

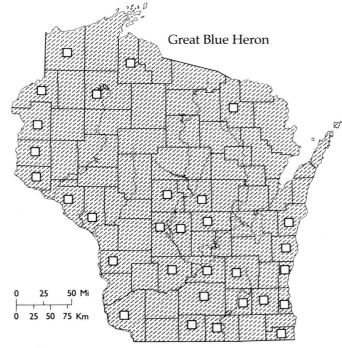

Great Blue Heron

0   25   50 Mi

0 25 50 75 Km

▨ Summer range
☐ Mid-December to late February

Records since 1960

in the southern counties by the 20th, with records of nonwintering birds by the 2nd (1959, Outagamie, A. S. Bradford), 4th (1956, Lafayette, E. Olson), and 7th (1974, La Crosse, F. Z. Lesher; 1974, Portage, F. M. Baumgartner). The northern counties are usually reached by the 30th of March, occasionally by the 14th (1971, Burnett, N. R. Stone), 16th (1964, Oconto, C. H. Richter), and 21st (1966, Oneida, E. Fell). By 15 April distribution throughout the state is general, and by 5 May the spring migration is completed.

Nesting activities begin almost immediately. Birds often use the same rookeries as in previous years, repairing old nests instead of constructing new ones. Most eggs are laid between 20 April and 10 May. Nestlings have been observed by 20 May, with some young on the wing by mid-June.

When Williams (1957) conducted an extensive survey of Wisconsin rookeries, he determined that Great Blues nested at one time or another in nearly all 72 counties. Sometimes only one or two pairs nested in an area; sometimes 600–800 pairs nested together in major rookeries.

Subsequent surveys of Great Blue Heron nesting colonies were carried out in 1969–1972 (Wisconsin Society for Ornithology) and 1973–1974 (Department of Natural Resources). Comparing these results with those summarized by Williams, T. C. Erdman (pers. comm.) pointed to a significant increase in heronries in northwestern counties, and a significant decrease in the northeast and throughout the south. Erdman estimated that between 1956 and 1974 there had been a statewide drop from about 50 nests per rookery to 40.

Some shifting and relocation of heron nesting colonies is natural, as dying trees fall in some flooded areas and new areas develop. However, the decline of Great Blue Herons goes beyond this. Some place the blame on the loss of habitat; others point to needless slaughter by humans; others raise the possibility that the pesticides known to harm other fish-eaters, such as the Bald Eagle and Osprey, in the 1960s are partly responsible. None of these theories has been proved. In the meantime, legislation affording protection for the "blue crane" was finally passed in the 1960s. Some teeth were added to the law in 1975 when two men were convicted and fined for shooting herons near Wisconsin Rapids.

Banding recovery data indicate that at least a few birds move from Illinois into southern Wisconsin in late summer. Beyond that, little is known about the extent of postbreeding wandering in July and August. Sizable numbers can be found feeding in shallow waters along the Mississippi and at many other locations. But it is not known how many of these nested nearby and how many wandered in from more distant locations.

No pronounced flocks of fall migrants have been reported beyond the expanded gatherings of late summer. Numbers diminish gradually in September and early October. By mid-October most are gone, except a few lingering on extensive marshes like Horicon, or along the Mississippi River. An occasional stray bird may remain into November until lakes and swamps freeze up. Some stay even longer where open water permits.

Some of the birds banded as nestlings in Wisconsin spend the following winter in Mississippi. Others move in a southwesterly direction, as recoveries in Arkansas, Texas, Mexico, Belize, and Costa Rica have shown. One individual was recovered in Cuba.

Great Egret (*Casmerodius albus*)

Formerly Common Egret, American Egret

STATUS. Fairly common migrant south; uncommon migrant central; rare migrant north. Uncommon summer resident west, south, and east; rare summer resident central.

HABITAT. Inland lakes. Ponds. Wooded swamp. Shallow marsh.

MIGRATION DATES. *Spring:* late March to late May. *Fall:* late July to mid-November. *Extremes:* 11 March; 27 November.

BREEDING DATA. Nests with eggs: 7 May to 23 June. Clutch size: 2–5 eggs.

WINTER. One January record.

PORTRAIT. *Birds of Wisconsin:* Plate 4.

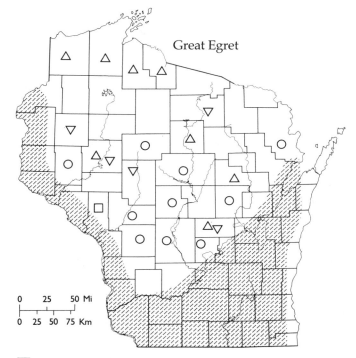

Great Egret

```
0    25    50 Mi
|--|--|--|
0  25  50  75 Km
```

▨ Summer range
△ Late March to late May
○ Early June to mid-July
▽ Late July to mid-November
□ 24 December to 18 January

Records since 1960

In 1900 the outlook was dim for this showy wader, not only in Wisconsin but also throughout the United States. In the 1850s and 1860s, the Great Egret was common in parts of southeastern Wisconsin. Hoy (1853b) did not find it common near Lake Michigan, mentioning but one June 1851 record. But Kumlien and Hollister (1903) found it common at Lake Koshkonong as a late summer visitant, and listed evidence of nesting in Jefferson (1863), Waukesha (1866), and Manitowoc (1880) counties. These authors commented, "Of late years, thanks to the barbarous plume hunters, rare, so rare at the present time that three or four individuals only visit Lake Koshkonong each year where hundreds were found years ago during August and September."

The plume hunters were active in the main breeding grounds in Florida and adjacent states. F. Holman King (1949), summarizing the changing status of this species through the 1940s, wrote, "Many accounts tell of the cruel destruction of these birds in the Gulf States rookeries during the late 1800s when colonies of thousands were reduced to a few individuals in just a few years."

Yeoman conservation efforts by the National Audubon Society were instrumental in outlawing the egret slaughter, and, soon after 1900, populations in the southern states began to show an increase. Wisconsin's egrets were reduced to virtually none through the 1920s (single observations in 1912, 1913, 1924, 1925).

An Oconto County bird in 1929 marked the beginning of a new trend that found at least an occasional individual or small flock showing up somewhere in the state every year. In 1937 groups were found in the southeast in Racine, Walworth, Rock, Jefferson, and Dane counties, and along the Mississippi River in Grant and La Crosse counties. The following year a tremendous influx brought an estimated 2,500 birds

to 42 counties (F. Holman King 1949). The first modern nest records for Wisconsin were obtained in Trempealeau County in 1939 by R. C. Steele (Gabrielson 1939), followed by records of a nesting colony in Dodge County in 1943 (E. T. Mitchell).

These two colonies have since increased and expanded. The Dodge County (Horicon) colony has grown to 225–275 nesting pairs, and a late summer population approaching 800. Along the Mississippi, groups are found all summer long at various locations north to Pierce County. Breeding has been confirmed north to Burnett County (1974, J. O. Evrard [1975a]) and seems probable in Brown and Oconto counties.

Considerable wandering now takes place in spring as well as late summer. First arrivals generally appear along the Mississippi by 30 March. Earlier March dates include the 11th (1955, Waukesha, S. P. Jones), 17th (1971, Vernon, J. R. Rosso), and 19th (1977, La Crosse, J. R. Rosso). Horicon birds arrive soon after 1 April. The biggest movement is between 10 April and 10 May. In the 1960s and 1970s, individuals overshot breeding area limits and appeared briefly in Douglas, Bayfield, Ashland, Lincoln, and Marinette counties between 25 April and 20 May.

Surveys along the Mississippi River (Thompson 1978) indicate that this species shares heronry space with the Great Blue Heron, usually on islands or peninsulas close to shallow-water feeding areas. At Horicon, egg-laying has been observed by 7 May. Eggs have been observed as late as 23 June, and doubtless occur later, for young have been seen in nests as late as 31 July. In most instances young are on the wing before 30 June.

Northward wandering after nesting occurs, but it has been much less pronounced in the 1970s than in the 1940s. There is some dispersal into new areas, but the main concentrations remain close to the breeding

territories. It is not uncommon to find 150–200 birds along the Mississippi in Vernon, La Crosse, Trempealeau, and Buffalo counties, or 200–400 at Horicon. The peak wandering period is between 20 July and 15 September.

Although a general exodus occurs in late September, small numbers often remain well into October, even through mid-November. The latest November departures were recorded on the 21st (1978, La Crosse, F. Z. Lesher), 24th (1948, Vernon, M. E. Morse; 1965, Columbia, W. L. Hilsenhoff), 26th (1948, Rock, C. A. Skelly), and 27th (1979, Oconto, T. C. Erdman).

An astonishingly late bird was discovered in Trempealeau County on 24 December 1980, and was photographed and observed in the area intermittently through 18 January 1981 (W. J. Drazkowski).

Snowy Egret (*Egretta thula*)

STATUS. Uncommon migrant. Rare summer resident east.

HABITAT. Ponds. Wooded swamp. Shallow marsh.

MIGRATION DATES. *Spring:* late April to late May. *Fall:* mid-July to mid-September. *Extremes:* 16 April; 3 November.

BREEDING DATA. Nests with eggs: 15 June to 9 July.

PORTRAIT. *Birds of Wisconsin:* Plate 4.

This has always been a rare Wisconsin species. Hoy (1853b) listed it as "not an uncommon species along the borders of small lakes," but Kumlien and Hollister (1903) believed this to be a case of mistaken identity. These observers mentioned but one spring or early summer record: a specimen collected at Lake Koshkonong in Jefferson County in June 1860. The collection of six birds at Lake Koshkonong in August 1886 (H. L. Skavlem) was the last instance of a modest-sized flock known to Kumlien and Hollister. These writers summarized, "Of late years very rare."

Like the Great Egret, the Snowy was endangered in the early years of the twentieth century, as plume-hunters ransacked the rookeries in the southern states. Until 1947 the only twentieth-century observances known for Wisconsin were a Jefferson County bird on 24 August 1932 (B. Andrews; MPM files) and an astonishingly late Milwaukee wanderer on 3 November 1943 seen by R. A. Bub.

Between 1946 and 1956, when Great Egrets and Little Blue Herons were staging their most pronounced late-summer wanderings, alert observers occasionally found a few Snowies along with them—presumably

Snowy Egret

△ Late April to late May
○ Early June to early July
▽ Mid-July to mid-September

Records since 1960

because of a northward movement of birds whose normal range lies south of Wisconsin. Wisconsin had 14 published occurrences during that stretch, all in the southeast except for a Crawford County bird. All but one (21 May 1950, Milwaukee, R. Jankowski) were seen between 21 July and 24 September.

When the late-summer movements of the other "white herons" declined, they also diminished for the "heron with the golden slippers." Since 1956 the only late-summer visitants were recorded on 29–31 July (1962, Dodge, E. W. Peartree), 6 August (1963, Grant, W. Bair; 1978, Dodge, R. M. Hoffman), 12–16 August (1971, Green Lake, D. D. Tessen), plus three 1981 wanderers: 3–14 July (Dodge, W. A. Cowart), 11 July (Fond du Lac, D. D. Tessen), and 18 July (Green Lake, T. Ziebell).

Spring wandering has increased since 1956. Spring migrants overshot their normal range limits on 20 known instances between 1959 and 1985. Twelve of these were in the southeast, north to Fond du Lac and Sheboygan counties. The other eight were far-reaching birds in Burnett, Bayfield, Ashland, Mari-nette, Manitowoc, Adams, La Crosse, and Crawford counties. The inclusive dates for these spring visitants were 16 April (1976, Fond du Lac, R. A. Knuth) and 2 June (1964, Marinette, H. L. Lindberg).

On 15 June 1975, T. C. Erdman discovered two pairs nesting with Cattle Egrets in a large colony of Black-crowned Night-Herons in Oconto County. The following month he banded five young in one nest. Two pairs returned to nest in 1976. On 9 July there were three eggs in one nest, three eggs and one young in the other. In each succeeding year birds have nested in the Brown-Oconto County area. In no other area in the state has nesting been reported.

A few individuals remain in the Brown-Oconto County area until 10 September. One lingered in Brown County until 30 September (1977, E. D. Cleary), and three until 1 October (1982, W. A. Cowart).

Little Blue Heron (*Egretta caerulea*)

STATUS. Rare spring migrant. Rare summer visitant.
HABITAT. Ponds. Wooded swamp. Shallow marsh.
MIGRATION DATES. *Spring:* late April to late May. *Late summer:* mid-July to mid-September. *Extremes:* 1 April; 27 September.
PORTRAIT. *Birds of Wisconsin:* Plate 4.

These southern wanderers caused a great stir in ornithological circles in the summer of 1930 when dozens turned up in southeastern Wisconsin. Nineteen birds were counted at one Racine County location, and scattered individuals or flocks of from three to six were sighted as far north as Oconto County and as far west as Dane County. There were 10 locations in all, with all records falling into a 5-week span: 29 July to 1 September.

Until that year Wisconsin had but two records: one bird collected in Racine County on 28 August 1848 (Hoy 1853b) and fragments of a partly decomposed specimen at Lake Koshkonong in Jefferson County in the early 1850s (T. L. Kumlien [Kumlien and Hollister 1903]). Kumlien and Hollister never found this species in their many years of observation and considered the species "purely accidental" on the basis of those two early-day records. What would they have thought had they been able to return 50 years later and find that the state had upwards of 40 occurrences totaling over 300 individuals?

The 1930 invasion was followed by an influx of 18 birds in Waukesha County and 5 in Dane County in late July and early August 1934. Following single ob-

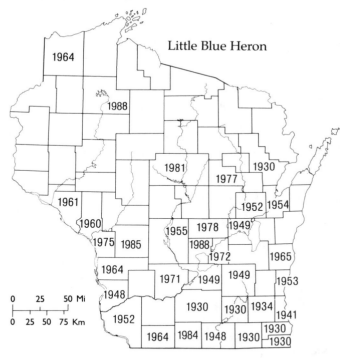

Little Blue Heron

Years of first county records

servations in 1938, 1941, and 1947, a succession of late-summer invasions again occurred: 14 birds in six locations in 1948, 26 in eight areas in 1949, and 15 in two spots in 1950. This reached a climax with a Dodge County congregation estimated at 200 observed on 24 August 1952 by N. R. Barger. Small flocks continued to be seen annually through 1956 north to Crawford, Adams, Outagamie, and Brown counties. Almost without exception these were birds in immature plumage, appearing in the latter half of July, disappearing by mid-September. The latest were on 19 September (1954, Dodge, M. A. Walker), 23 September (1955, Dodge, M. F. Donald), and 27 September (1948, Crawford, M. E. Morse). It appeared at that time that a late-summer northward wandering had become a fixed annual pattern for egrets and immature Little Blues.

With them was an occasional individual in adult plumage. Rarely, adults also began to appear in spring and early summer: one on 10 June 1941 (Milwaukee, C. S. Jung), one on 29 April 1951 (Winnebago, J. H. Evans), and one on 7 June 1955 (Dodge, R. A. Hunt).

After 1956 there was a sudden drop in sightings of late-summer immatures, with only two such records in the 1960s. But the number of April-May-June observations of adults increased, with from one to three birds observed annually since 1963. In most instances, birds appeared one day and were gone the next. Exceptions occurred in 1963 (Racine, 20 April–6 May, B. Weber) and 1972 (Kenosha, 14 April–18 May, R. R. Hoffman).

These spring adults have appeared most frequently between 20 April and 31 May. Unusually early April sightings have come on the 1st (1967, Milwaukee, D. K. Gustafson), 2nd (1960, Trempealeau, W. E. Green), and 6th (1968, Milwaukee, M. F. Donald).

Beginning in 1973, one or more became summer residents in the Oconto–Green Bay area. Three free-flying young in June 1974 suggested probable breeding, and nesting has been suspected several times since; but positive nesting evidence is lacking.

It is in the Green Bay area, where breeding is probably an annual event, that birds are sometimes sighted in September. Steven Krings counted 10 immatures on 17 September 1978. The late-summer wanderers seen at other locations have usually departed by the end of August. Exceptional is the adult spotted on 16 September 1975 (Milwaukee, M. F. Donald).

Tricolored Heron (*Egretta tricolor*)
Formerly Louisiana Heron

STATUS. Rare spring migrant; casual fall visitant. Casual summer visitant east.
HABITAT. Ponds. Wooded swamp. Shallow marsh.
MIGRATION DATES. *Spring:* late April to early June. *Fall:* mid-August to mid-September. *Extremes:* 23 April; 20 September.

Before 1976 Wisconsin had one record of this coastal marsh resident. It was a surprised Mr. and Mrs. Walter Peirce who watched a strange slim heron wading in Horicon Marsh in Dodge County on 19 September 1955. It was too small for a Great Blue, too large for a Green-backed, and with a peculiar form of active behavior that made the observers think of "a drunken ballet dancer." Mrs. Peirce returned the next morning with Edward Prins, and after a day-long search they saw the bird again, identified it as the state's first "Louisiana Heron," and photographed it. Other observers made subsequent efforts to find the bird but without success.

A sudden incursion in 1976 brought 10 individuals to five widely separated areas. First there was a bird at La Crosse, discovered on 23 April by H. F. Young and a group of university students, and seen by several others during the next 2 days. I had the pleasure of seeing this bird on the 24th, viewing the giant strides it used to pace back and forth through the

Tricolored Heron

△ Late April to early June
○ Mid-June to early August
▽ Mid-August to mid-September

All records

shallow water—reminiscent of a nervous expectant father in a hospital waiting room. The bird was photographed by F. Z. Lesher.

The scene then shifted to Ashland on 3 May. In the morning R. L. Verch and a group of Northland College students found a bird in Prentice Park. In the afternoon the visitor had moved a quarter of a mile west into the Fish Creek Marsh in Bayfield County, where it was studied for over an hour by D. A. Bratley.

On 15 May two birds were spotted in southwestern Winnebago County south of Waukau by T. Ziebell. Between then and the 23rd, one or two were seen daily by many observers, and were photographed by B. Parfitt. A third bird was present on the 17th.

Three weeks later an individual was found in Sauk County (3 June, M. F. Donald and R. H. Sundell). By 28 June one had wandered to Oconto Marsh, one of the most favored spots for herons in Wisconsin. Four were counted there on 8 July (D. K. Gustafson), and at least one remained until 4 September (H. L. Lindberg).

No one can say with certainty if these sightings all represent different birds, or if some represent birds that moved from one part of the state to another. But this sudden influx corresponded well with similar wanderings to North Dakota, Manitoba, Illinois, Michigan, Pennsylvania, Quebec, and Massachusetts.

Two additional sightings were made in 1977. One heron returned to the same Oconto County location on 14 May (D. K. Gustafson). Another was found in Burnett County on 7 July by R. Crete and J. E. Toepfer (*Am. Birds* 31:1143).

On 28 May 1978 one was observed in Winnebago County (T. Ziebell). At Green Bay, J. Trick found a Tricolored in one area on 18 June 1978 and two in a different spot 4 days later. One bird remained in the area through 11 August (D. D. Tessen).

After a 2-year absence, birds again wandered to Wisconsin and were seen on three occasions in 1981: 8 May (Sheboygan, H. Koopmann), 27–30 May (Winnebago, T. Bett), and 31 July (Dodge, J. Haseleu). Single sightings followed in 1982 (25 May, Fond du Lac, J. L. Polk) and 1983 (10 July, Winnebago, M. J. Mossman).

Cattle Egret (*Bubulcus ibis*)

STATUS. Uncommon migrant south and central; rare fall visitant north. Uncommon summer resident east.

HABITAT. Ponds. Wooded swamp. Shallow marsh. Grassland.

MIGRATION DATES. *Spring:* mid-April to late May. *Fall:* mid-September to early November. *Extremes:* 3 April; 30 November.

BREEDING DATA. Nests with eggs: 2 June to 23 July. Clutch size: 3–6 eggs.

PORTRAIT. *Birds of Wisconsin:* Plate 89.

This Old World species was first photographed in Florida in 1952. It had colonized Gulf and Atlantic coastal states so rapidly by 1955 that Wisconsin ornithologists began to wonder when it would first be found in the Badger State. That moment came on the afternoon of 24 April 1960. J. H. Evans discovered the bird near Janesville (Rock County) and spread the word so that other birdwatchers could share the excitement in the next four days. A second record followed later the same year when an individual remained on the C. E. Nelson farm near Dousman (Waukesha County) from the 7th to the 19th of November.

The first specimens, procured in the spring of

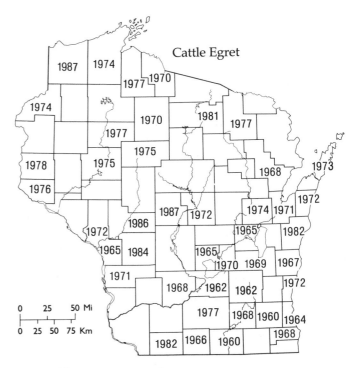

Years of first county records

1962, came from a flock of 12 birds that appeared at a Dodge County farm around 1 May; by early June 5 birds were still present. Two were collected on 3 June and donated to the Milwaukee Public Museum by R. A. Hunt.

Although birds were present in the Horicon region throughout June in both 1962 and 1964, no evidence of nesting was discovered. T. C. Erdman provided the first positive evidence of breeding in 1971 in Brown County, where two nests were found in a large Black-crowned Night-Heron colony on Willow Island (*Pass. Pigeon* 34:108). Five young were produced that year. Nesting pairs returned in 1972. In 1973, because of high water and heron competition, the colony moved to Oconto Marsh. By 1975 a major nesting area had developed near Oconto, where Erdman counted 6 nests, banded 15 young, and estimated that another 10 young were produced. There were 12 nests and 37 young produced (24 were banded) in 1976.

It is likely that breeding also began in the Grand River Marsh area in Green Lake and Marquette counties in 1971. On 16 August, 5 adults and 25 young were counted (D. K. Gustafson). By 1978 another breeding colony had become established at the Horicon National Wildlife Refuge.

Counting each nesting area as a single observation per year, the period from 1960 to 1980 yielded over 70 April-July observations. If a line were drawn from Be-

loit to Oconto, over 70% of the observations would have been located within 20 miles of this line. This puts the main line of travel roughly in the Rock and Fox River valleys with a northward extension up the west Green Bay shore. Small numbers have been observed near the Lake Michigan shore north to Sheboygan and along the Mississippi River north to La Crosse. There also have been sporadic spring sightings in Trempealeau, Pierce, Burnett, Rusk, Ashland, and Forest counties.

Birds are most often seen during spring in flocks of 3–12 between 15 April and 20 May; occasionally, single birds are sighted. The earliest recorded April arrivals are on the 3rd (1977, Ashland, R. L. Verch), 7th (1974, Dodge, M. F. Donald), 8th (1976, La Crosse, J. R. Rosso), and 13th (1974, La Crosse, J. R. Rosso).

Outside the breeding areas in Oconto, Brown, Green Lake, and Dodge counties, there have been few observations between 1 June and 25 September. Between 1960 and 1980 there were 18 October-November records outside the breeding areas, widely dispersed over the state. The latest recorded observation involved a bird found dead in Iron County on 27 November 1970 (H. Schmide). Barely 3 weeks earlier three individuals were sighted in Price County (L. E. Gregg); in 1981 one bird was seen as late as 30 November in Bayfield County (S. Hulse).

Green-backed Heron (*Butorides striatus*)

Formerly Green Heron

STATUS. Common migrant. Common summer resident south and central; uncommon summer resident north.

HABITAT. Inland lakes. Ponds. Wooded swamp. Shallow marsh.

MIGRATION DATES. *Spring:* mid-April to late May. *Fall:*
mid-August to mid-October. *Extremes:* 26 March; 20
December.

BREEDING DATA. Nests with eggs: 11 May to 20 July.
Clutch size: usually 4 or 5 eggs; rarely 3 or 6.

PORTRAIT. *Birds of Wisconsin:* Plate 4.

Green-backed Heron

0   25   50 Mi

0   25 50 75 Km

▨ Summer range
— Northern range limit, 1980
--- Northern range limit, 1963 (after Gromme)

Wisconsin lies on the northern fringe of this species'
normal range, and there are suspicions that this range
is creeping ever so slightly northward. Schoenebeck
(1902) listed only two records for Oconto County, but
Richter (1939a) called it "fairly common." Kumlien
and Hollister (1903) listed it as being found "as far
north as the shores of Lake Superior," but listed no
specific evidence for this and often depended on
hearsay for information about northern Wisconsin
birds. When Mr. and Mrs. I. N. Mitchell (1906–1913)
were collecting spring arrival dates from all parts of
the state from 1907 to 1913, their most northerly reports came from Dunn, Chippewa, Marathon, and
Lincoln counties. Between 1940 and 1960 *The Passenger
Pigeon* listed records north only to Washburn, Sawyer,
Lincoln, Marinette, and Door counties. Gromme
(1963) showed a summer range that excluded nearly
all of the two northernmost tiers of counties.

In 1967 Bernard referred to the bird as a rare summer resident in Douglas County, commenting, "This
species appears to be extending its range north as few
were noted in this county until recent years." Since
1968 I have seen the species in Douglas, Bayfield,
Sawyer, Forest, and Marinette counties. Since 1965
there have been BBS sightings in Oneida and Florence counties. T. C. Erdman (pers. comm.) estimated
that 100 pairs nested in Oconto Marsh in 1976.

This heron has been changing its spring migration
timetable. Schorger (1929b) listed 25 April as the earliest known arrival date for Dane County. In O. J.
Gromme's diaries for the 1912–1961 span, only two
dates preceding 27 April are mentioned: 22 April
(1915, Fond du Lac) and 18 April (1930, Waukesha).
Only rarely before the 1960s did *The Passenger Pigeon*
list arrival dates earlier than the 20th.

Since 1963 April arrival dates have become commonplace. The earliest dates recorded include 26 March
(1988, Dane, S. Thiessen), 31 March (1975, Juneau, B.
Ehlers), 1 April (1978, Brown, E. D. Cleary), and 2

April (1975, Waukesha, T. Bintz). In 1977 one bird
reached Ashland County by 4 April (R. L. Verch).

Even with these changes, this heron should be considered primarily a May migrant. General arrivals
spread over the state during the 1–20 May period.
The birds begin nesting almost immediately after arriving. Gromme collected information from various
sources on 51 nests in the first half of the twentieth
century. These sources indicated that 28 nestings in
May began with clutches on 11 and 13 May. Starting as
early as mid-May, a pair can produce two broods.
Young have been seen by 8 June. Eggs in late June are
probably second nestings. The latest recorded incubation date is 20 July (1939, Racine, E. B. Prins).

This bird does not necessarily nest in wet areas. In
1977 I observed two pairs nesting in a grove of dense
spruces hardly 20 feet from a farm dwelling. The
nearest water was a quarter of a mile distant. The
birds evidently found the density of the trees more
important than proximity to water in selecting the
nest site. C. H. Richter found the species nesting in
aspens and jack pines. Other observers have recorded
nests in willows, oaks, birches, and hawthorns.

Numbers start to diminish in the central region by

late August, indicating that fall migration has begun. By mid-September most birds are gone from the northern and central counties. Until recently it was unusual to find a bird in southern Wisconsin after 30 September, and a 30 October date was considered exceptional. But since 1963 there have been eight November records: the 2nd (1971, Milwaukee, D. K. Gustafson; 1985, Marathon, K. J. Luepke), 4th (1973,

Ozaukee, T. Bintz), 6th (1974, Juneau, B. Ehlers), 8th (1969, La Crosse, J. R. Rosso), 10th (1974, Milwaukee, E. L. Basten), 11th (1977, Dodge, R. L. Drieslein), and 25th (1964, Racine, R. E. Fiehweg). A phenomenal bird looked healthy when seen flying on 20 December (1979, Adams, D. G. Follen), but one wonders if it was healthy when the usual migration period ended.

Black-crowned Night-Heron (*Nycticorax nycticorax*)

STATUS. Common migrant east; uncommon migrant west and central. Common summer resident east and northeast; uncommon summer resident west and northwest. Rare winter resident south and central.

HABITAT. Ponds. Wooded swamp. Shallow marsh.

MIGRATION DATES. *Spring:* early April to mid-May. *Fall:* mid-September to early November.

BREEDING DATA. Nests with eggs: 2 May to 27 July. Clutch size: usually 4 or 5 eggs; occasionally 3 or 6.

WINTER. Occasionally present north to La Crosse, Juneau, and Outagamie counties.

PORTRAIT. *Birds of Wisconsin:* Plate 4.

The range of this species is peculiar. Godfrey's *Birds of Canada* (1966) depicts a breeding range well to the north of Wisconsin in western (Alberta, Saskatchewan, Manitoba) and eastern (Quebec, New Brunswick, Nova Scotia) Canada but excludes nearly all of Ontario. Gromme (1963) drew a northern range limit line from Hudson through Stevens Point to Green Bay, with a small northward penetration along the west Green Bay shore to Oconto and Marinette counties, and northeastward through Door County. There are a few observations north of that line, including the Lake Superior shoreline. In fact, records are known from 57 of Wisconsin's 72 counties.

But it would be grossly misleading to describe the range as statewide in 1989. Numbers have declined, and nesting colonies have shifted. Breeding is now largely confined to an area in eastern Wisconsin from the islands in Green Bay south through the Fox River valley to the Grand River Marsh and Horicon. At Horicon in the mid-1970s upwards of 500 breeding pairs were counted (R. A. Hunt, pers. comm.), but there has been a more recent decline. In 1976 T. C. Erdman (pers. comm.) estimated 435 breeding pairs in northeastern Wisconsin, 375 of them in the Oconto marshes. These numbers, too, have declined, with many pairs relocating on Green Bay islands.

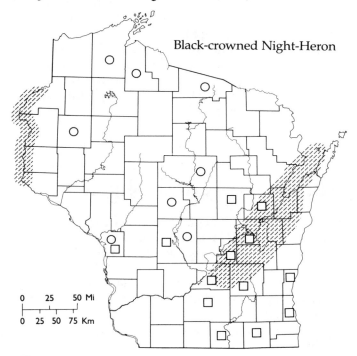

Black-crowned Night-Heron

```
0      25      50 Mi
├──┬──┬──┤
0   25  50  75 Km
```

▨ Summer range
○ Late May to early September
□ Mid-November to late March

Records since 1960

These declines have prompted the DNR to place this species on its watch list. A similar decline throughout the northeastern states has put the bird on the *American Birds* Blue List. In 1977 Erdman (pers. comm.) wrote: "We have found very high levels of PCB and other organochlorines in eggs. Small colonies have been deserting at egg time."

Other nesting areas include Rush Lake in Winnebago County, which once had a substantial colony, and the Mead Wildlife Area in Marathon County, where there is a small colony. Some summer sightings in the lower St. Croix Valley (St. Croix and Pierce counties) probably represent wanderings from heron-ries near St. Paul, Minnesota, but Faanes (1981) knew of three small rookeries in Burnett and St. Croix counties. Summer observations in Bayfield and Ashland counties suggest possible breeding in these regions; but if so, numbers are very small.

First migrants appear in the south between 1 and 10 April, occasionally by 25 March. Unusually early was an observation on 22 March (1956, Jefferson, E. Degner). Farther north, first arrivals usually occur between 10 and 15 April. An unusually early migrant was found dead in Lincoln County on 29 March 1963 (D. J. Hendrick). Typically, however, migration runs from 10 April to 10 May, with some movement until 20 May. People who listen to night migrants will occasionally hear the bird's distinctive "quok" in areas where night-herons are rarely seen in daytime.

The birds build shabby stick nests by the end of April, preparatory to laying eggs between 5 and 15 May. Erdman (pers. comm.) has observed nest construction as early as 20 April. By early July most young have left the nest.

No major northward postbreeding movement is apparent. The likelihood that some northern Illinois birds wander into Wisconsin is suggested by the autumn recovery of four birds banded in northern Illinois in June (Bartel 1975a). Three of the recoveries, 2–4 months after banding, were in southeastern Wisconsin counties. The fourth recovery, 4 months after banding, indicated that the bird had moved 300 miles north to Sawyer County.

Six birds banded in Wisconsin in June or July have turned up the following winter in Mexico, Louisiana, Florida, and Cuba. The fall migration is not conspicuous; it takes the form of birds disappearing from late-summer haunts. A few individuals, no doubt, wander north and west during August and early September. The main southward migration extends from late September through early November. Some birds even attempt to overwinter. Individuals have been recorded on 25 CBC counts since 1939. How many have successfully wintered is not known, but five February records strongly suggest that a few have survived.

Yellow-crowned Night-Heron (*Nyctanassa violacea*)

STATUS. Uncommon migrant south; rare migrant central. Rare summer resident south and central.
HABITAT. Ponds. Wooded swamp. Lowland deciduous forest.
MIGRATION DATES. *Spring:* mid-April to late May. *Fall:* early August to mid-October. *Extremes:* 31 March; 28 November.
BREEDING DATA. Nests with eggs: 13 May to 27 June. Clutch size: 3–5 eggs.
WINTER. One December record.
PORTRAIT. *Birds of Wisconsin:* Plate 4.

Wisconsin's first record came on 15 May 1941, when Martha Wyman and four companions discovered an adult in Kern Park in Milwaukee. O. J. Gromme confirmed the report the next day (Wyman 1941). There was no indication at the time that this was more than an accidental occurrence. Nor was there any hint of what was to develop in the 1950s, when Mr. and Mrs. Martin Paulsen discovered an adult near their home in Sussex (Waukesha County) on 19 May 1949.

But from 1953 on, this distinctive blue-gray heron has been an annual visitor. In 1954, late-summer wanderers were detected in Dodge and Waupaca counties. Then in 1955 the first nest was discovered, in Racine County. Adults had been present since late

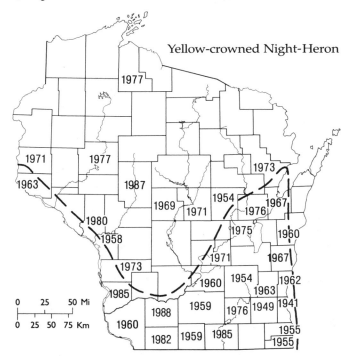

Yellow-crowned Night-Heron

--- Northern limit of 1980 spring and summer range

Years of first county records

April, and when the nest was discovered on 27 June, a broken shell indicated that at least one egg had recently hatched. Five healthy young were observed on 17 July. They left the nest 10 days later after posing for many pictures. Minnesota had its first Yellow-crown nest that same year, and Iowa's first nesting occurred in 1956.

By the end of the 1950s the number of Wisconsin sightings had risen to 26. In the 1960s, published reports averaged over five per year. The first state specimen, collected in Dodge County on 15 May 1962 by R. A. Hunt, went to the Milwaukee Public Museum.

One or more pairs have nested nearly every year in Kenosha, Racine, and/or Milwaukee counties, usually in extensive woodlots close to a stream or a small pond. Nesting is regular near La Crosse, usually on

Yellow-crowned Night-Heron, May 1955, Racine County (photo by W. H. Pugh)

the Minnesota side of the Mississippi River, but birds frequently feed in Wisconsin. A third nesting area has developed along the Wisconsin side of the river near Hager City in Pierce County (R. Behrens).

Since 1969 the number of sight records per year has increased to 8–10. Sightings have spread northward to include St. Croix, Chippewa, Clark, Portage, Outagamie, and Oconto counties.

In areas where this bird does not breed, it should be looked for in spring, primarily between 15 April and 20 May. The earliest recorded sightings are 31 March (1967, Sheboygan, D. K. Gustafson), 9 April (1970, Racine, W. Pugh), 11 April (1970, Dane, R. Monthey) and 12 April (1967, Pierce, R. Behrens; 1978, Chippewa, C. A. Kemper). Apparent late spring migrants occurred as late as 30 May (1968, Columbia, D. K. Gustafson) and 31 May (1971, St. Croix, S. V. Goddard). A lone northern Wisconsin bird appeared at Ashland on 19 May 1977 (R. L. Verch).

The breeding period is from 20 May to 25 July. Nesting birds often leave their home territories in early August. In some years there have been no other autumn reports. In other years there are a smattering of August and September observations, but there is no evidence of a northward postbreeding movement. The latest dates include four observations in October: the 4th (1972, La Crosse, J. R. Rosso), 8th (1969, Wood, E. Hebard), 11th (1970, La Crosse, J. R. Rosso), and 22nd (1954, Dodge, E. Fisher), and two in November: the 15th (1963, Racine, L. W. Erickson) and 28th (1965, Racine, E. B. Prins).

A more remarkable sighting concerns an immature carefully observed in Portage County on 29 December (1971, F. M. Baumgartner).

In the 1980s, the range along the Mississippi River has pulled back somewhat, causing the Bureau of Endangered Resources to add this heron to the list of threatened species.

Family **Threskiornithidae:** Ibises, Spoonbills

Glossy Ibis (*Plegadis falcinellus*)

STATUS. Rare migrant. Casual summer visitor.
HABITAT. Wooded swamp. Shallow marsh.
MIGRATION DATES. Observed between 14 May and 23 August. Indeterminate ibises observed between 25 April and 12 November.
PORTRAIT. *Birds of Wisconsin:* Plate 5.

Dark ibises have been known to wander to this state on 32 occasions through 1988. On two of these occasions the birds were identified as the western White-faced Ibis (*Plegadis chihi*). On the other 30 occasions the birds were listed as either the eastern Glossy Ibis or indeterminate individuals. But in only five instances is the supportive evidence strong enough to assure positive identification of the eastern species.

Even Wisconsin's lone specimen is indeterminate. Ludwig Kumlien collected an ibis at Horicon (Dodge County) on 3 November 1879, and Kumlien and Hollister (1903) identified it as a Glossy. The bird is now on display at the Milwaukee Public Museum. It is in a gray fall plumage characteristic of dark ibises that are now considered virtually identical species.

There is photographic evidence to validate the identification of Glossies at Horicon in 1956 and 1962. In 1956 two birds appeared on 14 May (R. B. Dryer); at least one was still present on 23 August. In the intervening weeks observers reported as many as 12 individuals; one was photographed on 4 August by

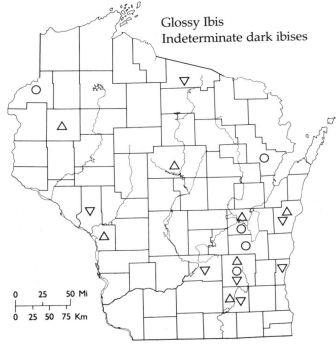

Glossy Ibis
Indeterminate dark ibises

△ Late April to late May
O Early June to late August
▽ Early September to mid-November

All records

Glossy Ibis, 9 May 1962, Dodge County (photo by M. Lound)

Martha Lound. Between 8 and 15 May 1962 three Horicon birds were seen by many observers, and photographed by refuge personnel.

Birds were seen at close range on three separate occasions, and were so well documented that identification as *falcinellus* seems certain. One was another Horicon bird seen on 26 May 1965, and described independently by W. D. Carter and L. D. McMaster. One bird was observed at close range in Winnebago County on 20 May 1966 (R. P. Narf), and another was observed frequently near Oconto between 28 June (D. K. Gustafson) and 20 July (T. C. Erdman) 1976.

The remaining 25 ibis records are indeterminate, either because the conditions of observation precluded the close scrutiny required to see facial markings, or because the documentation was otherwise insufficient.

The first reference to a Wisconsin ibis came from Thure Kumlien in a letter to T. M. Brewer on 25 June

144

1859. Kumlien wrote, "I saw a black ibis" (quoted in *Pass. Pigeon* 8:54). Three years later Kumlien hired a friend to do some collecting at Lake Koshkonong in Jefferson County. When the friend shot a strange dark bird but could not retrieve it, Kumlien hunted for it the next day. He found it and identified it as a Glossy Ibis, but found the specimen to be in poor shape for preservation. Thure and Ludwig Kumlien discovered seven individuals at Lake Koshkonong in September 1872 but were unable to get within collecting range. Kumlien and Hollister (1903) also recalled having "positively seen this bird on the Mississippi near Prairie du Chien in August some twenty years ago."

In addition to the 1956 flock, other Horicon observations of dark ibises were made in 1966 (flock of 10, 25 April–6 May, R. G. Personius), 1967 (29 May, R. G. Personius), and 1982 (17–18 June, D. Haugen).

Additional birds found in spring and early summer in the eastern counties include one at Rush Lake in Winnebago County, 27 June 1958 (H. A. Steinke); eight in Manitowoc County, 29 April 1962 (M. N. Pickett); and one in Jefferson County, 30 April 1962 (many observers). The sole recent spring record from the western edge of the state was an individual at La Crosse on 29 April 1975 (F. Z. Lesher). An adult in breeding plumage was found in Burnett County on 20 July 1977 (B. A. Bailey).

The first of seven recent autumn records of indeterminate ibises was also a Mississippi River valley bird, observed flying in Trempealeau County on 7 October 1971 by waterfowl researchers J. R. March, R. A. Hunt, and J. B. Hale. On 22 September 1973, D. D. Tessen saw a dark ibis fly across a highway in Vilas County. Four birds were seen by many observers in Columbia County, 23–26 September 1976. One bird was flushed in southern Fond du Lac County on 12 November 1978 (R. L. Drieslein). One stood out conspicuously among a large flock of Canada Geese in Dodge County on 5 October 1981 (D. K. Gustafson). Another was glimpsed flying in Manitowoc County on 7 October 1982 (C. R. Sontag). On 20 October 1984 William Cowart observed one flying south along the Lake Michigan shore in Ozaukee County.

Since 1960 the Glossy Ibis has extended its summer range significantly northward along the Atlantic Coast to Massachusetts, Maine, and Nova Scotia, and westward along the Gulf Coast to Louisiana and Texas. There have been increasing extralimital sightings in Ontario, Ohio, Tennessee, Illinois, and Missouri.

There is good reason to believe that most of the indeterminate ibises from the southeastern counties are Glossies. We have to make identifications carefully, however, because the White-faced Ibis is also extending its summer range.

White-faced Ibis (*Plegadis chihi*)
Formerly White-faced Glossy Ibis

STATUS. Accidental. Two records.
HABITAT. Shallow marsh.

Between 23 April and 3 May 1987, three (possibly four) dark ibises showed off their iridescent plumage to numerous observers at the Horicon Marsh National Wildlife Refuge in Dodge County. At times the birds were too distant for positive identification. But J. L. Baughman (*Pass. Pigeon* 50:84) saw one at close range on 23 April, took careful notes, and wrote a full description of the facial and body characteristics of the White-faced Ibis. T. K. Soulen (*Pass. Pigeon* 50: 84–85) had a similar experience at the same location the following day. Two individuals were present when William Miller (*Pass. Pigeon* 50:85) visited the Horicon hotspot on 2 May, with the final sighting by Lawrence Semo occurring on 3 May (*Pass. Pigeon* 50:84–85).

One year later, 19–20 May 1988, another White-faced Ibis showed off its distinctive facial markings for a busload of WSO birders in Waukesha County. M. S. Peterson discovered the bird in Vernon Marsh on the 19th, focused his telescope on it for 40 appreciative observers, and wrote some thorough documentation (*Pass. Pigeon* 50:363–364). The ibis disappeared the following day.

There is strong—albeit inconclusive—evidence that three of the state's indeterminate dark ibises were White-faced. Refuge Manager Lester Dundas (1977, pers. comm.) recollected that an ibis seen at Horicon Marsh (Dodge County) on 18 June 1946 was identified as a White-faced Ibis: "The main thing I remember was the white on the face, which seemed to match the description of the White-faced Glossy Ibis in Peterson's 1937 edition. I cannot remember if the white was in back of the eye and under the chin. During the pursuit of this bird, most of the closer views were from the rear." Dundas believes that this bird was erroneously listed as a Glossy Ibis in the Horicon National Wildlife Refuge narrative report for 1946.

Another individual appeared at Horicon Marsh in 1960. On 6 July Richard Thompson discovered a dark ibis at the north end of the marsh (Fond du Lac County). Refuge Manager Lester Dundas photographed the bird that day, and O. J. Gromme observed it the following day. All believed the stranger to be a White-faced Ibis. So did H. A. Bauers (1961), who observed the ibis on 14 July and wrote a detailed description. Unfortunately the photographs taken by Dundas were never published, and a search for them has proved fruitless.

On 28 April 1983 a dark ibis showed up in central Barron County, which Alta Goff (*Pass. Pigeon* 46:39) described as White-faced. The bird remained through the 29th, and was photographed by Melvin Jensen. But when members of the Wisconsin Society for Ornithology Records Committee examined the photographs minutely, they could find no sure evidence that the bird was a White-faced Ibis instead of a Glossy Ibis. Another hypothetical record.

In the 1970s and 1980s extralimital wanderings have been noted in Manitoba, South Dakota, Minnesota, Iowa, Kansas, and Missouri. Wisconsin observers should not automatically assume that a dark ibis is the eastern Glossy form. They should remember that immatures are probably indistinguishable in the field, that adults are separable only when seen under favorable conditions of light and distance, and that "*Plegadis* sp." may be the most accurate way of reporting a dark ibis.

Roseate Spoonbill (*Ajaia ajaja*)

STATUS. Accidental. One record.
HABITAT. Normally coastal swamp.

In his earliest years in Wisconsin, Thure Kumlien (Kumlien and Hollister 1903) obtained from Indians some fragments—head, wing, and leg—of a Roseate Spoonbill. They were from a bird that had been taken near Janesville in August 1845. These he preserved in his collection, and they constitute the only sure Wisconsin record of this wader. Kumlien and Hollister (1903) never met the spoonbill here, but alluded to "several early references to the peculiar red birds taken or seen in southern Wisconsin" which they assumed were references to this species. No specific references were listed, and none are now known.

Barry (1854) believed this species occurred along the Mississippi "and occasionally about our small lakes in the interior." He offered no supportive evidence.

In the mid-nineteenth century the spoonbill regularly ranged north to southern Illinois. Kumlien and Hollister (1903) reasoned that "it doubtless wandered at times, after the breeding season in late summer, to our southern limits." The typical range now is far more restricted, however, and extralimital wanderings have brought the bird only as far north as Arkansas, Tennessee, and North Carolina.

Family **Ciconiidae:** Storks

Wood Stork (*Mycteria americana*)
Formerly Wood Ibis

STATUS. Accidental. Five records.
HABITAT. Wooded swamp.
MIGRATION DATES. Observed between 3 and 15 May, and in September.
PORTRAIT. *Birds of Wisconsin:* Plate 5.

When Fran Brown discovered a Wood Stork at El-dorado Marsh in Fond du Lac County on 3 May 1973, it constituted the first known Wisconsin visit in over 100 years. In documenting the record, Brown wrote: "The black flight feathers were the first thing I no-ticed, and the shoulders and body were white. The head reminded me of a vulture's at first glance, be-cause it was so ugly, naked, and black with bump knobs. The bill was very long" (*Pass. Pigeon* 36:35). Although the bird flew off almost immediately, and the observation period lasted only 5 minutes, the con-ditions of observation were excellent and the docu-mentation leaves no room for doubt.

Hoy (1853b) recorded the collection of a specimen taken near Milwaukee in September 1852, subse-quently donated to the State Historical Society Mu-seum at Madison. Kumlien and Hollister (1903) re-corded that Hoy procured a second specimen at Racine in September 1868. Kumlien and Hollister also listed a specimen that had been examined by Thure Kumlien but was retained in a private collection. It had been shot "at an early date" along the Rock River in northern Rock County, and mounted by Samuel Sercomb. The present location of the latter two speci-mens is unknown.

On 15 May 1981 a flock of 26 Wood Storks appeared over Sand Lake in Sawyer County, witnessed by De-partment of Natural Resources biologist Frank Pratt and an astonished group of fishermen. Pratt (pers. comm.) recalled the reaction of the fishermen as the birds approached: "None of the fishermen had the foggiest notion what the birds were. Many guessed herons, cranes, geese, etc., while the flock was still

Wood Stork

```
0    25    50 Mi
0  25  50  75 Km
```

△   3 to 15 May
▽   September

All records

off in the distance. But when they came overhead, there was dead silence, followed by a few 'What the———?'" Pratt had seen this species in Florida. He recognized the black-and-white wing pattern, straight neck, and extended legs characteristic of the Wood Stork.

Extralimital wandering is not common, but another 1973 wanderer was recorded in West Virginia. Other recent reports have come from Kansas, Kentucky, Ten-nessee, and New York.

Family **Anatidae:** Swans, Geese, Ducks

Fulvous Whistling-Duck (*Dendrocygna bicolor*)

STATUS. Accidental. One record.
HABITAT. Inland lakes. Shallow marsh.

William Mueller and Dennis Schwartz (*Pass. Pigeon* 52:88–90) were not expecting any unusual waterfowl when they stopped at Goose Pond in Columbia County on 3 July 1989. But there, before their eyes, not 75 yards away, swam a tawny-colored duck with an unusually long neck. Subsequently, when they saw the stranger fly, they noted all the distinctive features of a Fulvous Whistling-Duck. Quickly the word

spread. Several birders had a good chance to observe the bird later that day. I was fortunate enough to join numerous other observers in viewing the wanderer on 4 July, the bird having moved 5 miles east to Schoeneberg's Marsh. Then the duck disappeared, as mysteriously as it had come.

No one can say with certainty that the Fulvous Whistling-Duck was blown northward by a 30 June Texas hurricane. But the brevity of the bird's Wisconsin visit at a time of year when most waterfowl are sedentary is certainly suggestive.

Tundra Swan (*Cygnus columbianus*)

Formerly Whistling Swan

STATUS. Common spring migrant in all but the extreme southwest; sometimes abundant in east central; fairly common fall migrant. Rare summer resident north and central. Rare winter resident west and east.
HABITAT. Inland lakes. Ponds. Shallow marsh. Open cropland.
MIGRATION DATES. *Spring:* mid-March to mid-May. *Fall:* mid-October to late December.
BREEDING DATA. One record.
WINTER. Occasionally present north to Trempealeau, Chippewa, Adams, and Brown counties.
PORTRAIT. *Birds of Wisconsin:* Plate 6.

The sound of what seems like a group of distant barking dogs signals the arrival of the first flocks descending at Horicon Marsh, Lake Winnebago, or Green Bay. Rarely has this occurred as early as 2 March (1968, Brown, E. D. Cleary) and 5 March (1905, Oconto, A. J. Schoenebeck; Schoenebeck collection, University of Wisconsin–Stevens Point), with 15–20 March more likely for first spring arrivals. Between 20 March and 10 April, concentrations from Fond du Lac to Green Bay sometimes exceed 5,000. Late March brings smaller concentrations to the Scuppernong Prairie, Goose Pond, and other shallow-water locations in the south-

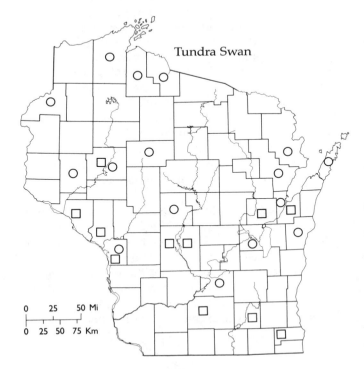

Tundra Swan

0 25 50 Mi
0 25 50 75 Km

○ Late May to early September
□ Early January to early March

Records since 1960

148

eastern counties. Flocks of 10–150 reach the western counties during the 1–10 April period.

These migrants pursue a west-northwesterly direction as they move from their Chesapeake Bay wintering grounds toward their Alaska–western Canada nesting area. They make a brief stopover in Ohio and eastern Michigan before reaching eastern Wisconsin. The migratory path blankets most of the state, but not quite all. South of a line from La Crosse through Madison to Racine swans are rarely seen. The small portion of Wisconsin lying northeast of a line from Hurley to Marinette is also off the beaten track. After a pause of a week or two, most swans move on. Most have left the eastern region by 25 April and the western portion by 1 May. An occasional individual lingers until 15 May.

June and July sightings were very rare before 1960. Among the six known June observations is the state's only nesting record: a pair with four young found in Oneida County during June 1954 by Warden B. H. Popov (*Pass. Pigeon* 16:153). Probably sickness or injury to a parent caused this breeding pair to linger here rather than completing the journey to the tundra. Kumlien and Hollister (1903) reported no nesting in their day.

Although no other known breeding has occurred, 30 published sightings for June and July have turned up since 1960. Most originate from the Green Bay area (from Manitowoc to Marinette) and Chequamegon Bay. Exceptional is the summer of 1974, with brief sightings of one or two birds on 13 June (Chippewa,

C. A. Kemper), 9 July (Columbia, P. Ashman), 28 July (La Crosse, F. Z. Lesher), 6 August (Manitowoc, T. C. Erdman), and 25 August (Winnebago, D. D. Tessen). From early August to early September two adults and three young were present in Brown County (L. Hicks), indicating a probable second nesting record.

For many observers sightings of the fall migration are limited to seeing two or three V-shaped lines passing overhead west-to-east in late October and early November. People living between Marinette and Green Bay, and between Alma and La Crosse, are sometimes treated to the sight of flocks of 1,000 or more birds pausing for from 2 to 4 weeks. Fall flocks usually arrive between 15 and 20 October. Migrants have been noted as early as 24 September (1955, Dodge, R. A. Hunt), 26 September (1971, Waushara, D. E. Greenman), 3 October (1952, Brown, M. H. Staege; 1952, Columbia, A. Cors), and 5 October (1973, Ashland, B. Parfitt). In some years nearly all birds move out of the state by 25 November. In other years, hundreds remain into December—especially along the Mississippi between Alma and La Crosse. The flocks leave by the 15th, but there are numerous instances of individuals remaining through December.

Between 1947 and 1987 there were 20 published records of birds remaining beyond 5 January, including 13 that survived at least into February. Some were injured birds; some appeared to be healthy. Individuals have overwintered successfully in Brown, Outagamie, La Crosse, and Racine counties.

Trumpeter Swan (*Cygnus buccinator*)

STATUS. Formerly uncommon migrant. Formerly a probable breeder. Recently reintroduced.
HABITAT. Inland lakes. Ponds.
MIGRATION DATES. *Spring:* late March to early May. *Fall:* early November.

During the 1930s the United States population of this majestic bird declined below 100, and extinction was forecast. On 5 November 1937 Richter (1939a) observed four of these few birds as they paused near Oconto, first swimming at the mouth of the Pensaukee River, then taking off to join a large flock of Tundra Swans. Richter identified them by sight and by sound: "[I] became familiar with the call of this species when in Yellowstone Park. The call is altogether different from that of the Whistling" (p. 115).

Our only other twentieth-century record is February 1904, when F. S. Crocker shot a bird in Waukesha County. For a time this specimen was "hanging . . . in a local billiard hall in Chicago" (Coale 1915, pp. 88–90).

Records from the nineteenth century are rare, and evidence concerning specific specimens and sightings is tantalizingly indefinite and incomplete. Hoy (1853b) stated, "This larger swan is frequently seen, and occasionally shot in our vicinity." But no dates are mentioned, and no specimens known. Hoy's contemporary at Racine, A. C. Barry, did not list it. Franklin King (1883) referred to this species as "a rather rare migrant," but probably based his information on Hoy and Thure Kumlien. Grundtvig (1895) probably relied on hearsay evidence when he wrote: "Seen at any rate in migration. Is said to breed in the northwest portion of Wisconsin." Reminiscing, vos Burgh (1939) recalled a neighbor in Columbus shooting two or three Trumpeter Swans in the early 1880s; these birds were subsequently mounted and displayed in a hardware store.

Two specimens are located at Lawrence University in Appleton, and one at the Milwaukee Public Museum; they may have been collected in Wisconsin in the nineteenth century, but further information is lacking.

Uncertainty exists concerning the number of specimens procured by Thure Kumlien. He shot one in Jefferson County on 20 April 1880, and sold it to the U.S. National Museum. In the fall of 1857 he procured six specimens from a large flock grounded by a snowstorm east of Stoughton (Dane County). Other hunters shot an additional 14 birds from the same flock. Thure Kumlien obtained a juvenile specimen in Jefferson County sometime between 1842 and 1845. Kumlien and Hollister (1903) described this specimen as having "down on the head and primaries still soft, color a dingy ash." This specimen was known to Kumlien and Hollister in 1900, but its eventual disposition is unknown. Ludwig Kumlien shot "a very large fine male" on the Rock River in March 1892 and mounted one for a hunter the following year. The latter bird was one of three observed at Lake Koshkonong on 6 May 1893. Kumlien and Hollister summarized the bird's status: "At the present day the Trumpeter Swan is surely a very rare bird in Wisconsin, and it is not certain that it could, at any time during the past sixty years, have been called common."

Schorger (1968) presented evidence indicating a high probability of nesting near Madison in 1867. Bellrose (1976) included all of Wisconsin in his map of the "probable former breeding area." This former range is believed to have extended to much of Illinois, northwestern Indiana, and west central Michigan.

This species has made a remarkable comeback since the 1930s. A summer 1968 census indicated there were over 3,000 individuals in Alaska, western Canada, and the northwestern United States. The reintroduction of a flock in Minnesota in 1969 has stirred considerable interest. In 1987, personnel from the Wisconsin Department of Natural Resources began a reintroduction program, hoping to build up to a population of 20 breeding pairs by the year 2000. In 1989, with the release of 24 birds in Burnett County, this species was added to the state's list of endangered species.

Mute Swan (*Cygnus olor*)

STATUS. Uncommon resident north, east, and south.

HABITAT. Great Lakes. Shallow marsh.

BREEDING DATA. Nests with eggs: 4 May to 10 June. Clutch size: 4–7 eggs.

WINTER. Regularly present in Ashland and Waukesha counties.

R. F. Gordon spotted a Mute Swan not yet in adult plumage at Racine on 8 May 1958, arousing suspicions that wild birds might have found their way to Wisconsin. The bird arrived during the morning following 3 days of strong northeasterly winds and flew off to the north later in the day. A check showed no escapes from two local flocks and gave rise to the supposition that this bird had wandered across Lake Michigan from a Michigan colony.

It may have been another Michigan vagrant that appeared in Racine on 3 January 1963 (B. Weber). Three months later, on 14 April, J. F. Fuller photographed one in Columbia County that was accompanied by four Tundra Swans.

The next reports came in 1966: one at the north end of Lake Winnebago at Menasha, 22 January through mid-March (D. D. Tessen), and two in Manitowoc County on 6 March (M. M. Wierzbicki). The year 1970 brought observations of individuals in Rock (12 February, T. R. Ellis), Grant (28 February, F. Z. Lesher), Milwaukee (28 February–31 March, D. D. Tessen), and Waukesha (early May–August, many observers) counties. Since 1970 Wisconsin has had from one to six observations each year.

Considerable mystery surrounds the movements of this species. This bird has popularly been kept in cap-

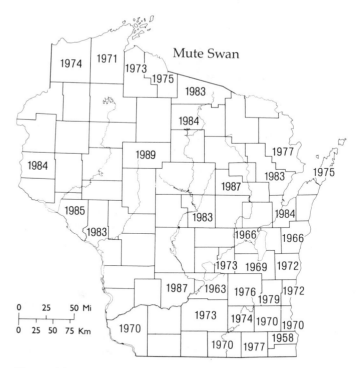

Mute Swan

Years of first county records

tivity, and while it is not normally migratory, it shows a propensity for wandering. How many sightings stem from local escapes? How many birds wandered from wild flocks in Michigan? How many represent multiple sightings of swans moving from one Wisconsin site to another? Of 40 Mute Swans transplanted from Michigan to Illinois in 1971, 4 returned to their Michigan homes within a year. Did others wander to Wisconsin?

A wild population has become firmly established at Ashland. Lake Superior observations began with the detection of two at Bayfield, 26 December 1971—14 January 1972 (D. A. Bratley). During the ensuing 3 years observers reported sightings of from three to five birds from Douglas, Bayfield, Ashland, and Iron counties. On 4 May 1975 five were seen in Iron County, and one bird was photographed on a nest (M. E. Butterbrodt). Nesting is now an annual event at Ashland, and because open water in Prentice Park provides favorable conditions for wintering, the Ashland flock is flourishing. A second wintering area has developed in Waukesha County.

Mute Swan, 13 July 1974, Dane County (photo by K. F. Legler)

Greater White-fronted Goose (*Anser albifrons*)

STATUS. Rare migrant.
HABITAT. Ponds. Shallow marsh. Open cropland.
MIGRATION DATES. *Spring:* late March to mid-May.
  Fall: late September to late October. *Extremes:* 21
  February, 4 June; 13 September, 3 December.
PORTRAIT. *Birds of Wisconsin:* Plate 6.

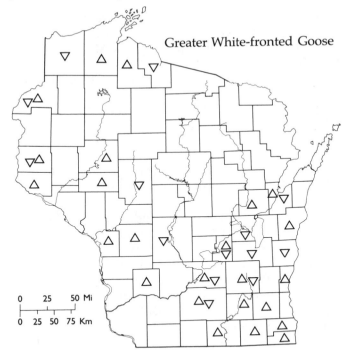

Greater White-fronted Goose

△ Late March to mid-May
▽ Late September to late October

Records since 1960

Although the main migratory pathway for this bird
lies through the Dakotas and the prairie provinces, a
few individuals wander east to Wisconsin nearly
every spring and fall. Sometimes these are solitary individuals; sometimes they are in flocks of 5–20; rarely
are there flocks of 50–100 birds in our state.

This was a much more numerous species in the
nineteenth century. Hoy (1853b) mentioned "large
numbers in spring and fall." Franklin King (1883)
called it "an abundant migrant." Grundtvig (1895), referring to Outagamie County between 1881 and 1883,
described it as "common in migration time." Schoenebeck (1902) called it a common migrant.

Kumlien and Hollister (1903) described it as "formerly an exceedingly abundant spring and fall migrant," but detected a significant decline in the 1890s.
An occasional nonbreeder spent the summer at Lake
Koshkonong in Jefferson County, but there was never
any evidence of nesting. By 1910 this species was decidedly uncommon. Lowe (1915) recorded it but once
in Green Lake County. Between Lowe's 1910 record
and 1938, the only published state observation was
one on 7 April 1929 (Sheboygan, C. S. Jung [1930b]).
Although noted more frequently since 1950 than during the 1900–1940 era, it is still a rare species that cannot be expected in the state every year.

There were from none to four observations per
spring between 1950 and 1974, increasing to eight by
1985. Two-thirds of the spring reports were east of a
line from Prairie du Sac to Green Bay. There are no
spring records for the far southwestern or northeastern counties.

Although a few observations have been of birds
passing overhead, a majority of sightings represent
birds that have paused to rest briefly along the edges
of shallow lakes and ponds. Horicon Marsh in Dodge
and Fond du Lac counties and Goose Pond in Columbia County are favorite stopover points. While stopovers have sometimes lasted 2–3 weeks, most birds
have made their stops very brief: here today, gone
tomorrow.

After the 21 February 1960 sighting of seven birds in
Rock County (J. P. Sipe), the earliest dates for spring
migrants are 3 March (1968, Brown, T. C. Erdman)

and 6 March (1974, Rock, S. R. Craven; 1976, Walworth, D. D. Tessen). The "speckle-belly" has been
found most frequently between 25 March and 15 May.
Observations beyond mid-May have occurred mainly
in the northern counties: 24 May (1977, Ashland,
R. L. Verch), 30 May (1978, Bayfield, D. D. Tessen),
and 2 June (1961, Burnett, N. R. Stone). One lingered
in southern Wisconsin until 4 June (1982, Columbia,
M. S. Peterson).

When a flock of 65 turned up at the Necedah National Wildlife Refuge in Juneau County in mid-
October 1960, followed by a flock of 100 in mid-October
1961 (C. E. Pospichal), conjectures arose that this species might be adding western Wisconsin to its usual
autumn migration route. But such was not the case.
Necedah has had but one autumn record since then,
and observations from other parts of the state have
numbered no more than three per autumn. Fall sightings throughout the state have numbered only 27
during the 1950–1980 interval. Nearly all occurred in
the Canada Goose–concentration areas in Burnett,
Juneau, Fond du Lac, and Dodge counties.

Mid-September arrivals were noted on the 13th (1978, Brown, R. M. Hoffman) and 16th (1964, Burnett, N. R. Stone). Most frequently birds have been found between 25 September and 25 October. One in-

jured bird remained into November in 1974 (Sheboygan, E. Kuhn); in 1964 a bird remained until 10 November (Burnett, N. R. Stone); and in 1968 one was seen on 3 December (Green Lake, J. R. March).

Snow Goose (*Chen caerulescens*)

Formerly Snow Goose and Blue Goose

STATUS. Uncommon spring migrant; fairly common fall migrant. Casual summer visitant. Rare winter visitant south and central.

HABITAT. Inland lakes. Ponds. Shallow marsh. Open cropland.

MIGRATION DATES. *Spring:* mid-March to mid-May. *Fall:* mid-September to early December.

BREEDING DATA. One record.

WINTER. Occasionally present north to St. Croix, Outagamie, Brown, and Door counties.

PORTRAIT. *Birds of Wisconsin:* Plate 6.

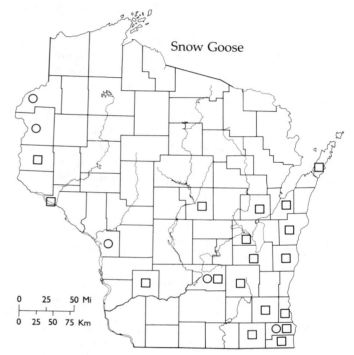

Snow Goose

○ Late May to early September
□ Mid-December to early March

Records since 1960

Wisconsin ornithologists born before 1960 became familiar with the Snow Goose and Blue Goose as distinct species. When a flock was heard or sighted, an observer looked expectantly for both Snows and Blues, for both often traveled in the same flock.

Since 1972, Blues and Snows have been recognized as one species, the Snow Goose. Wisconsin's birds are part of a Mississippi Flyway population that breeds in the eastern Arctic and winters along the Gulf Coast of Louisiana and Texas. Fall hunting statistics indicate that about 70% of the Snows killed each year in this flyway are the blue morphs.

Wisconsin Department of Natural Resources waterfowl specialist R. A. Hunt (pers. comm.) has commented: "Most Snow Geese overfly Wisconsin on a direct flight from James Bay to the Gulf. The number stopping in fall varies widely and is highest in years when the nesting season is late."

The first fall migrants usually appear between 20 and 30 September, and have been viewed as early as the 13th (1961, Sheboygan, H. C. Mueller; 1970, Dodge, R. G. Personius). Exceptional are early September sightings on the 2nd (1980, St. Croix, J. L. Polk) and 4th (1977, Sheboygan, R. M. Hoffman). The main flight occurs between 10 and 25 October. Although large numbers go through the state nonstop, some flocks pause at the major waterfowl resting areas in Burnett, Juneau, Dodge, and Fond du Lac counties. In November 1971 Crex Meadows personnel

estimated numbers at 11,650—double the peak of most years. In 1969 Horicon's peak was 8,000—more than double the usual numbers. Necedah's population usually crests between 1,000 and 3,000; it reached 5,000 in 1959. Another unusually large concentration was the estimated 10,000 passing through Bayfield County on 22 October 1963 (J. L. Kozlowski).

Most birds leave these concentration areas by 15 November, but a few individuals often linger until the first week of December in the southern counties. In recent years a few have overwintered. They first appeared on Wisconsin CBCs in 1948 and have been recorded on from one to three counts virtually every year since 1958. The 15 December–15 February records have been most consistent for Brown and Racine counties, with occasional sightings north to St. Croix, Outagamie, and Door counties.

The spring flight is a prolonged one, sometimes beginning by 24 February (1951, Milwaukee, J. Hoogerheide) and 25 February (1940, Walworth, F. R. Zimmerman). Nonbreeders occasionally linger until mid-June. Observations are most frequent between 25 March and 5 May. Most records indicate flocks numbering 5–20 birds; there have been up to 200–300.

A pair of white morphs nested on a Lake Poygan island in Winnebago County in 1944. When first discovered, the nest contained two eggs, and Charles Koehn (pers. comm.) determined subsequently that the young had fledged successfully. The female was injured, and her mate chose to remain with her rather than completing the migratory journey to Canada (*Pass. Pigeon* 7:21).

Three wild birds remained all summer with a captive goose flock in Racine County in 1974 (L. W. Erickson). Another remained in Columbia County through June and July 1967 (C. A. Wood). N. R. Stone made three additional summer sightings in northwest Wisconsin: 20 June 1951 (Polk), 7 July 1961 (Burnett), and 3 July 1963 (Burnett).

Kumlien and Hollister (1903) treated the Snow Goose and Blue Goose as separate species. They stated that the white bird had been abundant in the nineteenth century, and commented that "a few flocks still regularly pass up the eastern half of the state in spring, but it is a mere fraction of the former numbers." The darker bird was associated more with the Mississippi River valley and was thought to be "of irregular and erratic occurrence" elsewhere.

Kumlien and Hollister (1903) assumed further that the white morphs were almost evenly divided between the "Lesser" and the "Greater" Snow Goose, and reported, "Of the specimens examined, taken during the past sixty years and mostly when the birds were abundant, about one-half are typical of either *hyperborea* (Lesser) or *nivalis* (Greater), and in about equal numbers, and the balance intermediate." Schorger (1951a) commented that no Wisconsin specimens of Greaters are extant. If Kumlien and Hollister were correct, there has been a drastic change, for the Greater is now restricted to Atlantic coastal areas.

Ross' Goose (*Chen rossii*)

STATUS. Accidental. Three records.
HABITAT. Ponds. Shallow marsh. Open cropland.

No Wisconsin specimens are known, but the presence of a Rock County visitor on 1 November 1960 was established from a photograph. Hunter Richard Morehart and his son Gary shot what had been assumed to be an immature Snow Goose in the Milton area, and secured photographs of it. Subsequent examination of a photograph by Wisconsin Conservation Department waterfowl specialist Rusch (1961) raised suspicions that the bird was a Ross' Goose. Fish and Wildlife Service experts H. C. Deignan, J. W. Aldrich, and R. C. Layborne confirmed the finding. The specimen, however, was no longer retrievable (*Pass. Pigeon* 23:49–51).

Predating this record was a sight observation at Horicon Marsh in Dodge County on 31 October 1959 by O. J. Gromme and J. J. Hickey (*Pass. Pigeon* 22:30–31). Twice that day a small white goose was seen flying with a flock of seven Snow Geese. The adult plumage was clearly seen, size comparisons were distinct, and the wing beat of the smaller bird was noticeably more rapid.

Wisconsin's lone spring observation is R. M. Hoffman's thoroughly documented record from Columbia County, 24–26 March 1978. This was an immature bird found at Schoeneberg's Marsh near North Leeds, observed in comparison with nearby Snow Geese with the aid of a 48× spotting scope. The smaller size and more rapid wing beat were clearly visible (*Pass. Pigeon* 41:44–47).

Because the main breeding population in the central Canadian Arctic moves southwestward to wintering grounds in central California, Wisconsin has seemed far outside the bird's migratory range. But there has been a pronounced population increase since 1960, and small breeding areas have been discovered near the west shore of Hudson Bay and on Southampton Island, due north of Wisconsin. Extralimital sightings have increased in the 1960s and 1970s (South Dakota, Nebraska, Oklahoma, Texas, Arkansas, Missouri, Illinois, Quebec, and North Carolina). In 1979 Michigan had its first record, Minnesota its eighth. Although observers should be encouraged to check flocks of Snow Geese carefully for this wanderer in the future, they should also know that identification is difficult.

Brant (*Branta bernicla*)
Formerly Brant and Black Brant

STATUS. Rare migrant.
HABITAT. Inland lakes. Ponds. Shallow marsh. Open cropland.
MIGRATION DATES. *Spring:* early April to late May. *Fall:* early October to late November. *Extremes:* 21 February, 30 May; 2 October, 7 December.
PORTRAIT. *Birds of Wisconsin:* Plate 6.

When Kumlien and Hollister (1903) evaluated purported "brant" records for the nineteenth century, they discounted every report but one: a specimen in the P. R. Hoy collection. "For the past thirty years we have run down 'brant' records innumerable—to find that in every case it proved to be something else, varying from the common Canada Goose to the female Eider Duck." The Hoy specimen was taken from a group of three birds at Racine at an unknown date, and cannot now be located.

Similarly, several twentieth-century "brant" reports have been rejected because of possible confusion with small races of the Canada Goose. Unquestionably authentic are three Wisconsin specimens. A hunter shot an immature female in Dodge County on 17 October 1951. When informed by L. R. Jahn of the identity and rarity of the specimen, he donated the bird to the collection at the University of Wisconsin–Madison. In early November 1959 Ed Mathews shot another on a goose-hunting expedition in Dodge County. When apprised of the bird's rarity, Mathews donated his specimen to the Milwaukee Public Museum. It is possible that this individual had belonged to a small flock that had been present at the Horicon National Wildlife Refuge since 10 October and was photographed by L. H. Dundas. A goose hunter also donated a third specimen, a bird shot in Iron County by W. F. Sievert on 18 October 1970, and given to the MPM. Another bird was shot at Horicon (Dodge County) on 26 October 1966 (*fide* wardens Burhans and Amundsen), with the skin preserved at the Horicon DNR headquarters.

There are seven reliable reports of spring sightings. In 1933 two birds were present in Oconto County for 3 weeks in late April and early May (Richter 1939a). On 10 April 1938 one was discovered among geese near Delavan (Walworth County) (Jones 1938). A flock of five at Sheboygan was independently observed and described on 25 May (A. Quimby) and 26 May (I. K. Lohman) 1950. Another was recorded at the same Sheboygan location on 30 May 1954 (M. Reichwaldt). One appeared in Dane County on 15

Brant

△ Early April to late May
▽ Early October to late November

All records

April 1961 (T. W. Albers), and another in Columbia County on 5 April 1972 (D. D. Tessen). One was spotted among early migrant Canada and Snow Geese in Dane County on 21 February 1981 (J. L. Baughman).

There are an additional 14 sight records in fall, all carefully documented. L. R. Jahn saw a flock of seven pass overhead no more than 20 yards away at Horicon on 3 October 1953. The following year produced three sightings: 3 in Burnett County (2 October, N. R. Stone), 24 in Milwaukee County (12 October, G. Roux, pers. comm. to O. J. Gromme), and 1 in Jefferson County (17 October, L. E. Compton). On four occasions R. A. Hunt discovered this species while checking the goose concentrations in Dodge County: 20 October 1959 (two adults), 30 October 1964 (one adult), 14 November 1967 (one adult), and 23 October 1969 (four adults). Faanes (1981, p. 35) mentioned two additional Burnett County records: 1 bird on 31 October 1959 by N. R. Stone; 10 birds on 6 October 1974 by K. H. Dueholm. On 17 November 1979, R. M. Hoffman observed five birds in Dane County. Chippewa County's first record was established on 7 October

1980 by J. L. Polk. On 19 October 1980 T. C. Erdman encountered a flock of 16 in Oconto County. Unusually late is the individual remaining in Manitowoc County from 21 November through 7 December 1985 (C. R. Sontag).

The Burnett County individual seen on 31 October 1959 was reported as the western race *nigricans*, for- merly granted separate species status as a Black Brant. Remembering this bird 20 years later, Stone (pers. comm.) wrote: "I recall the bird well. It was an adult with the dark breast, much darker than a regular brant. It kept to itself, always about 25 feet at the side of the main group of Canada Geese with which it was feeding."

Canada Goose (*Branta canadensis*)

STATUS. Abundant migrant. Uncommon summer resident. Uncommon winter resident south and central.

HABITAT. Inland lakes. Ponds. Shallow marsh. Open cropland.

MIGRATION DATES. *Spring:* early March to late April. *Fall:* early September to mid-December.

BREEDING DATA. Nests with eggs: 4 April to 30 May. Clutch size: usually 4–7 eggs; occasionally 2–8.

WINTER. Regularly present north to Waushara and Brown counties; occasionally present to St. Croix, Barron, Marathon, Shawano, and Door counties.

PORTRAIT. *Birds of Wisconsin:* Plate 6.

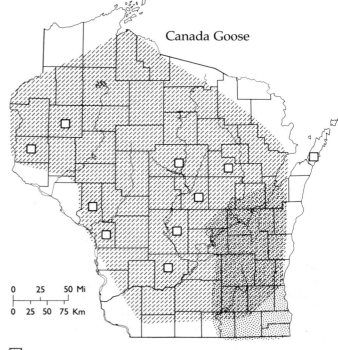

Canada Goose

0   25   50 Mi
0 25 50 75 Km

▨ Summer range
▦ Winter range
☐ Early January to mid-February

Records since 1960

Imagine an assembly of 227,770 honkers! Geese peaked at this figure at Horicon Marsh in Dodge County on 15 November 1971. Records at the Horicon National Wildlife Refuge showed a contrasting peak of 450 birds on 21 October 1942. The population climb was steady through most of the 30-year interval as improving water and food resources attracted more and more birds. This majestic species has increased throughout its North American range since 1945, but perhaps nowhere in the country has this been demonstrated more vividly than at Horicon. No bird-related spectacle in Wisconsin has attracted the attention of the average motorist more than the fall congregation of geese along Highway 49 east of Waupun, at the north end of the marsh.

The huge Horicon concentration sometimes includes more than 70% of the entire Mississippi River valley population that breeds west of James Bay, Ontario, and winters in Missouri, southern Illinois, and western Kentucky.

Wishing to guard against the possibility of a disastrous botulism epidemic, to alleviate crop depredation on neighboring farms, and to distribute fall migrating flocks more evenly between Wisconsin and Illinois, federal and state management specialists began in the early 1970s to take measures to disperse

these birds (Hunt 1971). In the late 1970s, the Horicon numbers were sharply reduced, with larger flocks using satellite areas (Dodge, Columbia, Green Lake, and Fond du Lac counties), and more birds moving on into Illinois. There are other fall stop-over spots in Burnett (Crex Meadows), Vilas (Powell Marsh), Juneau (Necedah NWR), and Brown counties.

Migrants first arrive around 10 September, trickle in through the 20th, then mount rapidly to a 10–25 October peak. Numbers remain high through 15 November, then drop off considerably. Most outlying areas have lost the bulk of their geese by 25 November as many water areas freeze. But Horicon and neighboring lakes often hold thousands of birds through 15 December and sometimes into January.

The CBC has counted Canadas in an average of 10 areas per year since 1960. Late December 1975 was exceptional, with 19 areas harboring over 27,000 individuals. Observers have regularly reported flocks of CBC geese in Rock, Walworth, Waushara, and Brown counties. Irregularly, observers have reported CBC sightings along the Mississippi–St. Croix River valleys north to St. Croix and Barron counties, along the Wisconsin River valley north to Portage and Marathon counties, and in eastern Wisconsin north to Shawano and Door counties. While some are delayed fall migrants that move out in early January, hundreds—sometimes up to 5,000—winter successfully each year.

One favorite wintering area is along Turtle Creek in Rock and Walworth counties. February meanderings of these flocks may prove to be the early spring migrants reported in the southeast. Most of Wisconsin's geese winter in southern Illinois and begin the spring trek northward in late February or early March. Some push right on to the central and northern counties, arriving by 15–20 March. Most arrive in the Rock and Fox River valley regions of southeastern Wisconsin, peaking between 5 and 15 April.

The spring peak at Horicon has reached over 70,000. Birds feed heavily between mid-March and late April as they prepare for the remaining migratory journey. There is a grand exodus, usually between 20 and 25 April, as the well-fed birds take off for their Canadian breeding grounds.

Once a common breeding species, the bird had virtually disappeared as a nester by 1900 (Kumlien and Hollister 1903). Efforts to restore breeding populations experimentally began in Brown County in 1932, in Wood County in 1939, and in Juneau County in 1942 (Hunt and Jahn 1966). A captive flock established at Horicon in 1946 resulted in modest breeding success. In 1957 the Wisconsin Conservation Department relocated some of these nesters at Crex Meadows in Burnett County and Powell Marsh in Vilas County. Private goose-rearing projects were started in La Crosse, Marathon, and Manitowoc counties.

Disease, predation, and seasonal hunting pressure have adversely affected some of these efforts. But free-flying breeders now appear to be fixtures in Burnett, Vilas, Brown, and Dodge counties, and in a Jackson-Juneau-Wood County region. How much summer residency derived from these flocks is not known, but between 1950 and 1980 there were widely distributed observations from 43 counties during June or July.

Some of the efforts to establish breeding populations involved the planting of formerly injured birds. These were presumably hunted birds of the "interior race" (*B. canadensis interior*), and efforts with this subspecies have proved largely unsuccessful. It is the "giant race" (*B. canadensis maxima*) that has provided both the successful breeders and most of the wintering flocks. In both spring and fall there are occasional sightings of small Canadas, variously published as "Hutchins'," "Richardson's," "Lesser Canada," or "Cackling." These are presumably birds that wander somewhat east of their usual route. Unless these birds are carefully weighed and measured in the hand, they are generally not distinguished from one another and are lumped together as "small races." The "cackling race" (*B. canadensis minima*) is highly unlikely to occur here, being essentially a bird of the Far West.

Wood Duck (*Aix sponsa*)

STATUS. Common migrant. Common summer resident. Rare winter resident south and central.

HABITAT. Streams. Wooded swamp. Shallow marsh.

MIGRATION DATES. *Spring:* mid-March to early May. *Fall:* late August to early November.

BREEDING DATA. Nests with eggs: 8 April to 4 July. Clutch size: 8–15 eggs.

WINTER. Occasionally present north to Douglas, Barron, Chippewa, Lincoln, and Marinette counties.

PORTRAIT. *Birds of Wisconsin:* Plate 9.

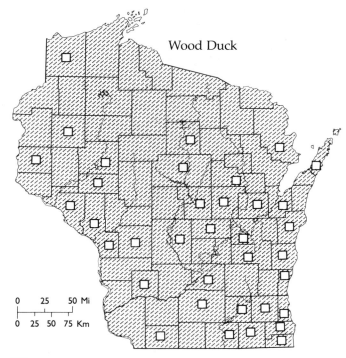

Wood Duck

0   25   50 Mi

0   25 50 75 Km

▨ Summer range
☐ Early December to early March

Records since 1960

It is difficult for birders today to realize that this woodland duck faced extinction 60 years ago. The earliest state ornithologists found them abundant. Barry (1854) wrote, "Found here in great numbers; nearly every wooded stream abounding with them." Grundtvig (1895), reminiscing about the 1882–1883 period, commented, "By far the most common duck at Shiocton. Breeds abundantly in the old maples near the river."

The bird was still quite common in Kumlien and Hollister's day (1903), but had declined noticeably since the early 1870s. Extended hunting, legal and illegal, led to a precipitous decline in the early years of the twentieth century, and only after the adoption of the 1918 Migratory Bird Treaty Act was the trend reversed. A 5 May 1922 record at Madison (Taylor 1923) warranted publication in *The Auk*. Schorger (1931a) described the bird's status in Dane County as "gradually increasing in number, though still one of our rarer species."

Given adequate protection, the Woodie has staged a tremendous comeback. Present-day state populations are difficult to estimate. Substantial numbers reside along streams. A census of these stream-dwellers by means of canoe transects began in 1977. Undoubtedly, the Wood Duck ranks along with the Mallard and Blue-winged Teal as one of Wisconsin's three most numerous breeding ducks.

Spring arrival dates are becoming earlier. In the 1940s most areas had their first birds between 1 and 15 April, with a few early arrivals appearing by 25 March. In the 1970s many southern and central areas had a few birds by 25 March, some by the 15th. Early March arrivals have been recorded on the 4th (1963, Jefferson, E. Degner), 5th (1974, Dodge, J. R. March), 6th (1975, Pierce, D. E. TeRonde), 11th (1966, Juneau, Necedah National Wildlife Refuge personnel), and 15th (1966, Burnett, N. R. Stone). By the end of April nearly all potential breeders are on territory, and those moving farther north are enjoying their last Wisconsin days.

As a summer resident the Wood Duck is present in all parts of the state. The lack of suitable habitat limits numbers in a few areas—in Kewaunee and Door counties, for example—but populations are well distributed throughout the major river systems and most of Wisconsin's lakes.

Nesting activities begin soon after arrival. Exceptionally early was the 8 April 1932 discovery of a nest with 14 fresh eggs (Rusk, E. E. Davison). Normally, clutches are complete from 25 April on. Pileated Woodpecker excavations provide excellent nest sites. C. H. Richter found one such nest in 1970 in Oconto County; in it, a pair had laid six eggs directly on the decaying body of a gray squirrel that had used the same cavity the previous winter. Nest boxes also have served as suitable nesting sites.

Broods appear any time from 10 May on. It challenges the imagination to fathom how tiny chicks are able to descend from nests as high as 45 feet from the ground and then manipulate distances sometimes greater than half a mile to the nearest water. There is additional danger from mammalian predators in the first weeks of life.

Young ducks are ready to fly by 15 August when flocking begins in marshes and on small ponds. These congregations consolidate and enlarge through September. Less wary than other ducks, Woodies suffer considerable loss during the first days of the October hunting season. The largest flocks concentrate in the western half of the state. In late September there are sometimes as many as 1,500 birds at Crex Meadows in Burnett County. After 15 October, numbers drop rap-

idly, with only a few birds remaining into November.

The number of winter stragglers is gradually increasing. Nineteenth-century writers made no mention of wintering individuals. And the CBC would list at most one or two birds per year in the 1940s and 1950s. Only twice in the 1950s was this species recorded on the midwinter waterfowl survey. In the 1970s, however, the CBC recorded 8–35 Woodies per year. Most northerly were sightings in Douglas (1969), Barron (1978), Chippewa (1975), Lincoln (1971), Marathon (1957), Shawano (1967), Marinette (1973, 1980), and Door (1973) counties.

Green-winged Teal (*Anas crecca*)

STATUS. Common migrant south and central; fairly common migrant north. Uncommon summer resident. Rare winter resident south and central.
HABITAT. Inland lakes. Ponds. Shallow marsh.
MIGRATION DATES. *Spring:* mid-March to early May. *Fall:* late August to late November.
BREEDING DATA. Nests with eggs: 29 May to 9 June. Clutch size: 7–12 eggs.
WINTER. Occasionally present north to Burnett, Barron, Portage, Shawano, Brown, and Manitowoc counties.
PORTRAIT. *Birds of Wisconsin:* Plate 8.

In describing the timing of spring migration in their day, Kumlien and Hollister (1903) wrote: "The dates of migration depend entirely on the weather and breaking up . . . of the ice. Of an average season the greenwing arrives early in April, although March records are not infrequent, and large numbers may be found close on to May 1." Interestingly, the timing is the same today, although numbers are below what they were in the nineteenth century.

A few Green-wings are among the earliest vanguard of surface-feeding ducks. Occasionally, observers have seen small flocks by 10 March in the south and by 20 March as far north as St. Croix and Brown counties. It is usually between 1 and 10 April that birds reach the northernmost areas, and by that time the southern lakes and flooded fields are holding peak numbers. In 1974 there were 500 at Necedah (Juneau County) on 1 April, and 1,150 at Horicon (Dodge County) on 5 April. Numbers decline by the 20th in the south and few birds are seen after the 30th. Farther north, modest numbers remain until

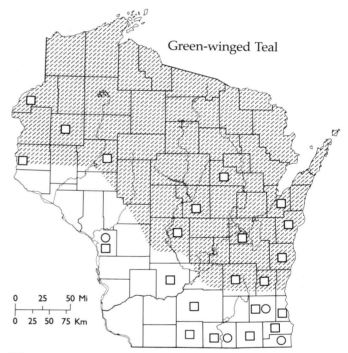

Green-winged Teal

◿ Summer range
○ Early June to late July
□ Early December to late February

Records since 1960

5 May, with nearly all migrants gone by the 15th. Compared with other spring waterfowl using the same type of shallow-water habitat, this species normally outnumbers the Gadwall, is outnumbered by the Mallard and Blue-winged Teal, and is comparable

with the Common Pintail, Northern Shoveler, and American Wigeon.

Only a fraction of the April migrants remain to breed. Kumlien and Hollister (1903) thought regular breeding occurred in modest numbers in the north but intermittently at southern locations such as Lake Koshkonong.

Although the species declined in the first half of the twentieth century, a small increase in summer records has occurred since 1950, mainly north of a line from St. Croix County southeast to Dodge County and northeast to Manitowoc County. A few pairs have bred at Horicon nearly every year since 1970. Although observers have witnessed incubation only from late May on, broods have appeared from 8 June on, suggesting probable egg-laying by 10 May. Present estimates of the average statewide breeding population are 3,000 per year (March, Martz, and Hunt 1973), making this the fourth or fifth most numerous surface-feeding duck in summer.

By 25 August there is a small influx. While this may represent some wandering local birds, others are quite certainly fall migrants. Movement is more pronounced during the first half of September. In 1974 Horicon National Wildlife Refuge personnel estimated that the population that year had swelled from 300 on 26 July to 1,800 on 15 September. There are years when the peak appears to have passed through the state before the hunting season starts in early October. There also are years when the peak does not materialize until the latter half of October. Hunting statistics since 1960 show that 7–8% of the ducks shot each fall are Green-wings. Although most birds leave by 5 November, a few individuals linger until late November.

A few individuals remain to overwinter nearly every year. How many of these are injured or sick birds is not known. CBC figures show from 1 to 12 birds present in late December nearly every year, mainly in Dane, Walworth, and Milwaukee counties. Unusually far north were observations in St. Croix (1971), Barron (1977, 1978), La Crosse (1968, 1975), Portage (1966), Shawano (1970), Brown (1978), Manitowoc (1978), and Sheboygan (1978) counties. Some birds disappear in early January as waters freeze, but at least a few survive through January and February. Most unusual was the report of three birds in Burnett County on 13 February 1950 (N. R. Stone).

American Black Duck (*Anas rubripes*)

STATUS. Common migrant east; fairly common migrant west. Fairly common summer resident north; uncommon summer resident central and southwest. Fairly common winter resident.

HABITAT. Inland lakes. Ponds. Shallow marsh.

MIGRATION DATES. *Spring:* mid-March to early May. *Fall:* mid-September to mid-December.

BREEDING DATA. Nests with eggs: 3 May to 4 July. Clutch size: 6–10 eggs.

WINTER. Regularly present where open water is found.

PORTRAIT. *Birds of Wisconsin:* Plate 7.

The best chance to observe the Black Duck is during winter. Wherever water is kept free of ice, especially at spring-fed lagoons in city parks, a few Blacks are likely to be found among the flocks of wintering Mallards. This is as true for Prentice Park in Ashland as for Juneau Park in Milwaukee. CBC figures show rather small numbers in the north and west, and a near void in the extreme southwest. The highest winter concentrations occur in Green Bay, Neenah (Winnebago County), and Milwaukee, where CBC totals of 200–500 are not uncommon. Total statewide CBC figures were relatively constant between 1960 and 1981, varying from 1,100 to 2,900 per year except for

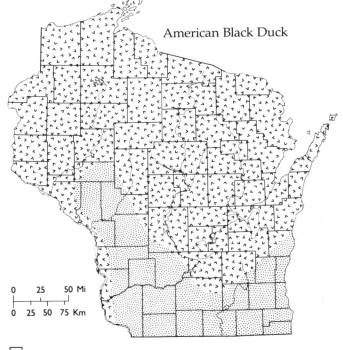

American Black Duck

0   25   50 Mi
0 25 50 75 Km

⌐⌐ Resident range
▪▪ Winter range

Records since 1960

1963 (5,400) and 1965 (4,700). In most winters there are from three to eight times as many Mallards as Black Ducks, but the Black far outnumbers all other surface-feeding ducks.

Spring tells a very different story. As flooded fields appear in March, followed by the opening of previously ice-locked ponds and lakes, ducks appear by the hundreds or thousands, but often there is nary a "Black Mallard" among them. This is especially true in the western counties, close to the western edge of the species' normal continental range. Among the 26,182 surface-feeding ducks counted in St. Croix County in spring 1968–1971, Goddard (1975) tallied but 29 Blacks. The ratio was slightly higher in Barron County in the springs of 1973 and 1974, when Faanes (1975a) found 11 Blacks among 503 "puddlers." Farther east in Waukesha County, spring 1961–1964, Bielefeldt (1974b) rated this species as slightly more numerous than the Pintail and Gadwall, but decidedly less numerous than the Green-winged Teal, American Wigeon, and Northern Shoveler.

The timing of the spring migration parallels that of the Mallard and Pintail. Beginning in mid-March in the south, migration accelerates through late March, with first migrants appearing in the north around 5–10 April. The peak period is 5–20 April in the south and 20–30 April in the north. Most migrants move on by 10 May, with a few lingering until the 20th.

Nowhere in the state is this bird a common breeder. At Horicon National Wildlife Refuge in Dodge County it is estimated that 15–30 young are produced in some years, none in other years. An occasional breeding pair is found in Dane and Columbia counties, along the Mississippi River south to La Crosse and Vernon counties, and along the eastern marshes south to Manitowoc and Sheboygan counties. Most June and July sightings are north of a line from Hudson through Stevens Point to Kewaunee, with highest numbers reported from lakes in northeastern county forests. March, Martz, and Hunt (1973) estimated the state's breeding population to be 7,100 birds, no more than 3% of the summer duck population. Numbers were thought to be declining then, and they have declined still more since then.

Egg-laying has been reported as early as 3 May, and may start in late April some years. Broods of young have been noted from 1 June on. Incubation rarely continues into the first week of July.

Although there is some late-summer wandering in August, fall migration does not commence until mid-September. Even then flights are small until 1 October. The peak occurs between 25 October and 15 November. At Horicon NWR in the 1940s peak numbers were 3,000–5,000. The fall of 1952 was exceptional, with an estimated 22,500 present on 24 November (L. F. Gunther). The Necedah NWR records show a remarkable peak of 12,000 in 1941, with top numbers fluctuating between 500 and 4,000 in other years. Only once since 1965 has the maximum number of birds at one time exceeded 1,000. The main fall concentrations in the 1970s occurred in eastern Wisconsin on Lakes Winnebago, Poygan, and Butte des Morts, and at Horicon NWR and Green Bay.

According to Bellrose (1976), winter populations have declined significantly throughout the Atlantic and Mississippi flyways since 1955.

Mallard (*Anas platyrhynchos*)

STATUS. Abundant migrant. Common summer resident. Common winter resident south and central; uncommon winter resident north.
HABITAT. All wetlands.
MIGRATION DATES. *Spring:* early March to early May. *Fall:* mid-August to mid-December.
BREEDING DATA. Nests with eggs: 2 April to 19 August. Clutch size: 8–11 eggs.
WINTER. Regularly present where open water is found.
PORTRAIT. *Birds of Wisconsin:* Plate 7.

Mallard

0   25   50 Mi

0 25 50 75 Km

⊞ Resident range

Records since 1960

The Mallard is the only duck which is widely present in Wisconsin at all seasons. Other species are primarily winter or summer residents, or common only at times of migration. The American Black Duck is present at all seasons, but in very limited numbers.

As a winter resident the "greenhead" has been holding its own in recent years. The combined tally on CBCs in Madison, Milwaukee, and Green Bay jumped from under 1,000 in 1950 to 5,400 in 1955, and has varied from 4,400 to 11,400 annually since 1962. The more inclusive federal-state midwinter waterfowl inventory showed a low of 3,800 in 1951, but has averaged close to 10,000 every year since then. The largest concentrations exist in the southern and southeastern counties, where there is most open water. But small numbers can be found anywhere in the state where water remains ice-free. Mallards were present on 52 of 76 CBCs in December 1979, when 27,326 individuals were counted, including birds from Douglas, Bayfield, Ashland, Lincoln, and Marinette counties.

Wintering greenheads were common in southern Wisconsin 100 years ago. Kumlien and Hollister (1903) stated, "Large numbers remain on the prairies all winter, feeding in the corn fields and resorting to the open springs and spring runs at night."

The spring migratory flight closely parallels that of the Canada Goose, beginning in early March—sometimes in late February. Mallards move north as quickly as lingering winter ice permits, reaching the northern counties in the last days of March or early April. One rarely sees large concentrations in one place comparable to the huge rafts of Greater and Lesser Scaups. But concentrations of several thousand sometimes appear, and with widely distributed flocks of 50–300 birds adding up, this species rivals the Blue-winged Teal as the most abundant surface-feeding duck in spring. Most migration is completed by 10 May.

March, Martz, and Hunt (1973) estimated that during the 1965–1970 period the annual statewide breed-ing population averaged 125,000 birds. They estimated little change from the 1949–1950 period. During the 1970s, however, significant declines were detected. J. R. March's more recent estimates show the statewide breeding population falling below 60,000 in 1977 (pers. comm.). Until this decline, the Mallard was Wisconsin's most common breeding duck. It now ranks second to the Blue-winged Teal. But broods still are present in all Wisconsin counties, with the highest concentrations in eastern and northwestern regions, and along the Mississippi River.

Part of the Mallard's decline may be due to a loss of suitable wetland habitat for nesting. Although vigorous land acquisition efforts to preserve wetlands have been undertaken and continue to go forward, they have not offset the loss of wetlands to drainage. Also, part of the decline may be due to poor nesting success. March's (pers. comm.) 1973–1977 estimates showed that about 30% of female Mallards normally produce young.

Mallards nesting in swamps and marshes have to contend with fluctuating water levels and mammalian predators. Those nesting in hayfields have the additional hazard of mowers that now operate at progressively earlier dates. Renesting is then required for many pairs, causing the incubation period to extend well into July. A few hens may still be incubating in early August. (Broods have been observed as early as 5 May.) The average size of broods raised to fledging is about 6.0–6.5 young per pair (March, pers. comm.).

Fledglings become increasingly noticeable from 1 August on. The staging flocks swell after 15 August, especially at the Crex Meadows Wildlife Area in Burnett County and at the Horicon National Wildlife Refuge in Dodge County. Some northerly nesters (mainly from western Ontario and Manitoba) arrive in mid-September. But it is only after 10 October that the fall flight picks up momentum, building up through the rest of the month. Peaks usually occur between 10 and 25 October in the north, and 20 October to 5 November in the south. At the Necedah National Wildlife Refuge in Juneau County, personnel have found that the fall peak varies considerably in size, but usually approaches 10,000 to 25,000. At the Horicon NWR the peak numbers sometimes exceeded 20,000 in the 1950s. This number has diminished somewhat since then, probably in part because of the development of more suitable habitat at Grand River Marsh in Green Lake County, Eldorado Marsh in Fond du Lac County, Collins Marsh in Manitowoc County, and the Mead Wildlife Area in Marathon County.

At numerous other points, both along the Mississippi River and on lakes in the central and eastern regions, fall flocks number in the thousands. Soon after 10 November in the north and 20 November in the south, a general exodus takes place. After 10 December only winter residents remain, scattered wherever open water permits.

White-cheeked Pintail (*Anas bahamensis*)
Formerly Bahama Duck

STATUS. Accidental. One record.
HABITAT. Normally Caribbean shallow ponds.

The Milwaukee Public Museum houses the remains of a White-cheeked Pintail found floating dead in Lake Winneconne in Winnebago County on 21 September 1929. Presumably, the bird was originally shot by an unknown hunter who failed to retrieve it. It was then found by a second hunter, Catherine Clark, who recognized it as something unusual and preserved the head, wings, tail, and feet. George Overton of Oshkosh, who was then consulted, forwarded the remains to the Milwaukee Public Museum, where Gromme (1930a) made the identification, constructed a drawing, and wrote the documentation. This species has been variously known as Bahama Pintail, Bahama Duck, and White-faced Pintail.

At that time the only previous United States record involved a bird recorded in Florida. Recent years have brought additional Florida sightings, plus isolated records from Texas, Alabama, Illinois, Virginia, and Delaware. Gromme could find no evidence that the Winneconne bird might have been a released bird or an escape; he wondered if a recent hurricane might have blown it far off course.

Northern Pintail (*Anas acuta*)

STATUS. Common migrant. Uncommon summer resi-
dent west, central, and east. Rare winter resident.
HABITAT. Inland lakes. Ponds. Shallow marsh.
MIGRATION DATES. *Spring:* early March to mid-May.
Fall: late August to late November.
BREEDING DATA. Nests with eggs: 23 May to 1 July.
Clutch size: 8–10 eggs.
WINTER. Occasionally present north to Burnett, Ash-
land, Lincoln, Marinette, and Door counties.
PORTRAIT. *Birds of Wisconsin:* Plate 9.

The faintest suggestion of moderating temperatures
in early March is all it takes to bring the earliest vanguard of "sprigs" to our southern counties. Schorger
(1929b) described their arrival thus: "The sight of a
flock of Pintails flying low over a marsh on a March
morning renders the observer oblivious to chilling
winds. The long neck, long tail and white underparts
of the male produce the mirage of a frigate under full
sail."

Pintails have made occasional appearances in late
February: the 19th (1949, Rock, C. A. Skelly), 26th
(1957, Adams, S. D. Robbins), and 28th (1957, La
Crosse, L. J. Egelberg). There were an estimated 100
individuals on the Scuppernong Prairie in Jefferson
County on 21 February 1954 (L. E. Compton). In
1974 birds reached Barron County by 6 March (C. A.
Faanes).

Usually, sprigs reach most southern areas by 20
March, extend to the central region by 25 March, and
begin to sprinkle the northern counties by 5 April.
There is considerable variation in both the size and
the duration of the spring peak. At Necedah National
Wildlife Refuge in Juneau County the highest spring
counts have sometimes reached 2,000–3,000, but occasionally they are under 100. Peaks occur between 1
and 20 April with the bulk of the migrants gone by
5 May. In 1974, Horicon National Wildlife Refuge personnel in Dodge County tallied over 1,000 individuals
as late as 2 May. Individuals remaining after 15 May
will probably spend the summer.

Wisconsin lies on the extreme southeastern fringe
of the Pintail's breeding range. Bellrose (1976) placed
the annual average North American breeding population for 1955–1973 at 6,193,000, pointing out that next
to the Mallard the Pintail (along with the scaup) may
be the most common nesting duck in North America.
Wisconsin's contribution to this figure is fragmentary
at best. March, Martz, and Hunt (1973) estimated an
annual average of 1,300 breeding birds, probably
under 1% of the state's nesting duck population.

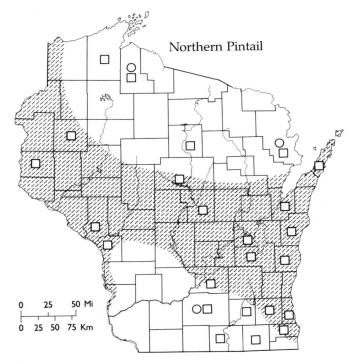

Northern Pintail

▨	Summer range
○	Late May to early August
□	Mid-December to mid-February

Records since 1960

Since 1940 there have been June or July sightings
from nearly half (33) of the state's counties. These
records are well distributed over the state, but are
sparse in the southwestern and north-central counties. In many instances the records document isolated
nesting pairs or nonbreeding individuals. Horicon
Marsh attracts the largest summer population each
year. From 1970 to 1975, federal refuge personnel
found an average of 95 young produced per year.

The fall migration is an extended one, often beginning by 25 August and lasting until waters freeze.
Buss and Mattison (1955) recorded a sharp contrast
between spring (4,762) and fall (618) sightings in Dunn
and adjacent counties between 1939 and 1951. Bernard
(1967) also considered this species far less numerous
in fall than in spring in Douglas County. *The Passenger
Pigeon* has published few autumn reports, compared
with the number of spring observations. But aggrega-
tions of 1,000 or more have been frequent at a few key
locations—particularly at the refuges at Horicon and
Necedah, at Lake Butte des Morts, and along the Mississippi River. Peaks at these locations have occurred

between 10 October and 5 November. Numbers drop greatly by 15 November, with only a few remaining until the 20 November—15 December freeze-up.

The number that remain to overwinter is very small. One or more have been reported on the CBC every year since 1960, and the largest number in any one year is 12. Mainly, these include individuals mixed with wintering flocks of Mallards in Brown, Winnebago, Dane, Walworth, and Milwaukee counties. There have been isolated CBC individuals in Barron

(1978), St. Croix (1971–1973, 1975), Trempealeau (1978), La Crosse (1969), Marathon (1972), Lincoln (1973), Marinette (1971), and Door (1975, 1977) counties. As many as 52 have been recorded on the annual mid-January waterfowl inventory, but some years this species is missed entirely. Most unusual are the sightings of a bird in Burnett County on 12–13 January 1949 (F. A. Hartmeister), an individual in Bayfield County on 16 January 1984 (A. J. Roy), and one that spent the winter of 1984–1985 at Ashland (R. L. Verch).

Blue-winged Teal (*Anas discors*)

STATUS. Abundant migrant. Common summer resident. Rare winter resident east.

HABITAT. Inland lakes. Ponds. Wooded swamp. Shallow marsh.

MIGRATION DATES. *Spring:* late March to mid-May. *Fall:* mid-August to late October.

BREEDING DATA. Nests with eggs: 30 April to 12 July. Clutch size: usually 8–12 eggs; occasionally 6–15.

WINTER. Occasionally present north to Buffalo, Chippewa, Winnebago, and Brown counties.

PORTRAIT. *Birds of Wisconsin:* Plate 8.

By the time the "crescent-cheeks" arrive—usually around 1–10 April—most of the other surface-feeding ducks have already been present for a week or two. Small wonder. The major wintering grounds for most other "puddlers" is along the Gulf or Atlantic coasts. Banding data show that many of Wisconsin's breeding Blue-wings winter in Central America and northern South America, although some move northwest from Florida and the West Indies. A sizable wintering area has developed in coastal Louisiana as a result of hurricane damage in 1957. Coastal marshes that once had too much timber for wintering teal are now open enough to harbor thousands of wintering Blue-wings. This may explain why first arrivals are found increasingly in the southern counties during the last week of March. Exceptionally early March arrivals have been detected on the 1st (1973, Racine, M. Stoffel), 5th (1929, Dane, H. G. Anderson [1941b]; 1971, Jefferson, R. Sharp), 7th (1941, La Crosse, A. M. Peterson), and 8th (1974, Fond du Lac, R. A. Knuth).

Spring peaks at Horicon Marsh in Dodge County often number over 1,000 birds, usually between 15 April and 5 May. In smaller wetland areas, concentrations are not as large; but because more limited flocks spread out over many shallow lakes and flooded fields, this species is truly abundant for 2–3 weeks. Between 1960 and 1968 I found that the period of peak

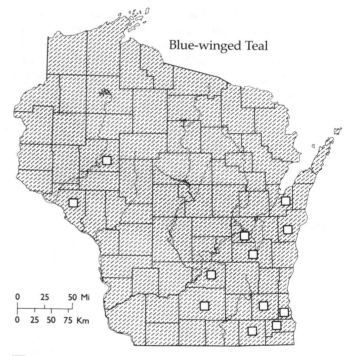

Blue-winged Teal

0   25   50 Mi

0 25 50 75 Km

▨ Summer range
☐ Mid-November to mid-March

Records since 1960

numbers in St. Croix County consistently occurred between 20 April and 10 May. Birds not summering in the state are usually gone by 20 May.

As a nesting species, the Blue-wing is not common in the counties bordering the Mississippi River in the southwest, or in the counties bordering Michigan in the northeast. Elsewhere, the heaviest concentrations occur in the Rock and Fox River valleys in the southeast, and in the prairie pothole region (Burnett, Polk, St. Croix counties) to the northwest. March, Martz, and Hunt (1973) estimated that the annual breeding population between 1965 and 1970 fluctuated between 66,800 and 107,400. These numbers doubled during the 1970s, peaking at 244,000 in 1975.

Most egg-laying occurs between 15 May and 5 June, but probably starts as early as 30 April for birds that arrive by the end of March. Broods of young have been reported as early as 4 June. Birds still incubating eggs between 1 and 10 July are presumably renesting after previous failures. Nest failures are frequent because of early cuttings of hay on the alfalfa fields where Blue-wings often nest. Estimates of the Wisconsin Department of Natural Resources indicated that fewer than 25% of Blue-wing nesting pairs produced young in 1974 and 1975.

By early August considerable flocking has occurred at some locations. In part, this represents a consolidation of local birds dispersed in early summer; in part it also includes some early fall migrants moving in from the west and north. Bellrose (1976) depicts migration corridors passing through Wisconsin in a southeasterly direction, channeling birds from Manitoba, western Ontario, and Minnesota either to Florida or to Louisiana. Concentrations build up through late August and early September to a 20 September–5 October peak that often brings reports of flocks of 1,500–5,000.

Many of the birds depart before the start of the hunting season in early October. A large portion of the kill during the first days of hunting is made up of Blue-wings, and this coincides with a general exodus of survivors. Few remain beyond the end of October. November departure dates include the 18th (1966, Brown, E. O. Paulson), 19th (1955, Grant, H. H. Burgess), 24th (1971, Brown, E. D. Cleary), and 26th (1967, Milwaukee, E. W. Strehlow).

Attempts to survive the winter have occurred in greater frequency in recent years. At Green Bay the CBC reported 10 individuals in 1949, and 20 in 1970. At other locations there have been only one or two birds, but CBC records exist for all but 6 years during the 1963–1984 interval. All have been in southern or eastern counties, except for lone individuals in Chippewa (1969) and Buffalo (1972) counties. At least a few of these make it through winter.

Cinnamon Teal (*Anas cyanoptera*)

STATUS. Rare spring migrant; accidental fall migrant. Accidental summer visitant.
HABITAT. Ponds. Shallow marsh.
MIGRATION DATES. *Spring:* mid-April to late May. *Fall:* early October to late November. *Extremes:* 10 April, 25 May; 9 October, 29 December.
PORTRAIT. *Birds of Wisconsin:* Plate 8.

When A. W. Schorger collected a male Cinnamon Teal at Madison on 7 May 1939, it marked the state's first twentieth-century record of this colorful western dabbler. The bird had been discovered on the previous day by J. S. Main (1940); Schorger donated the specimen to the Milwaukee Public Museum.

Previously, there had been only two definite state records. Thure Kumlien mounted a specimen shot by a hunter at Lake Koshkonong in Jefferson County on 18 October 1879. Another Lake Koshkonong bird was shot on 9 October 1891 and examined by Ludwig Kumlien; but the hunter refused to part with it. The whereabouts of these specimens is not now known. Kumlien and Hollister (1903) wrote, "There are several more or less authentic records among well informed sportsmen in different parts of the state." Does this indefinite statement refer to birds taken in spring or fall? Early fall records are suspect because birds are in eclipse plumage and extremely difficult to separate from the Blue-winged Teal.

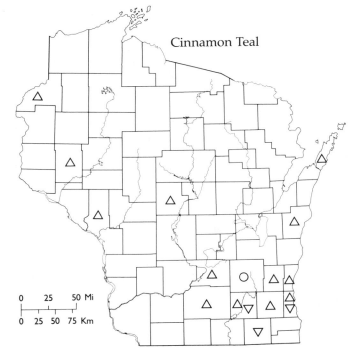

Cinnamon Teal

0   25   50 Mi
0 25 50 75 Km

△   Mid-April to late May
○   19 June
▽   9 October to 29 December

All records

A second twentieth-century record dates to 14 April 1953, when N. R. Stone observed six individuals in Burnett County (Faanes 1981, p. 41). Between 1953 and 1981 there were 22 more April and May sightings. All were bright-plumaged males, in company with Blue-winged Teals. On several occasions birds were associated with females (Cinnamon or Blue-winged?). April records were reported from the 10th to the 14th (1971, Wood, D. G. Follen), and on the 11th (1959, Jefferson, E. Degner), 13th (1974, Milwaukee, J. W. Barnes), 14th (1981, Trempealeau, J. Clapp), 20th (1981, Washington, W. Cowart), 21st (1968, Burnett, R. A. Hunt; 1976, Columbia, D. K. Gustafson), 24th (1973, Door, A. Freitag), and 28th (1973, Waukesha, V. Aune [1974]). In April 1985 wanderers turned up in three counties: the 20th–22nd (Trempealeau, C. L. Wilda), 22nd (Manitowoc, C. R. Sontag), and 28th (Milwaukee, J. H. Idzikowski). A male remained near Menomonie (Dunn County), 14–21 April 1989 (J. L. Polk).

A Cinnamon Teal first observed on 30 April 1961 in Dane County was subsequently collected on 3 May and donated to the Milwaukee Public Museum by R. A. Hunt. Additional May sight observations have been tallied on the 5th (1973, Wood, J. S. Fadness),

from the 6th to the 12th (1980, Dane, A. K. Shea), on the 8th (1964, Ozaukee, M. F. Donald; 1965, Burnett, N. R. Stone), from the 11th to the 16th (1959, Columbia, H. A. Winkler), and on the 13th (1979, Waukesha, H. A. Bauers) and 25th (1978, Milwaukee, M. F. Donald).

Wisconsin's sole summer sighting occurred on 19 June 1981, when Richard Biss spotted a male at Horicon Marsh in Dodge County. It kept company with a female teal (Cinnamon or Blue-winged?).

One fall record has been substantiated by photographs. A male discovered in Milwaukee on 22 November 1968 (M. F. Donald) was observed by many people during the next 2 days. Five weeks later, what was presumed to be the same bird was recorded on the Lake Geneva CBC—40 miles distant in Walworth County—on 29 December (C. O. Palmquist).

All of these observations involved adult males in breeding plumage. One wonders how many times females may have wandered to Wisconsin but remained undetected because of their similarity to the Blue-winged Teal. And one wonders if Cinnamons have wandered here in early fall when eclipse plumage renders them indistinguishable from Blue-wings.

Northern Shoveler (*Anas clypeata*)

STATUS. Common migrant. Uncommon summer resident west and east. Rare winter resident south and east.

HABITAT. Inland lakes. Ponds. Shallow marsh.

MIGRATION DATES. *Spring:* mid-March to early June. *Fall:* early September to late November.

BREEDING DATA. Nests with eggs: 27 May to 28 June. Clutch size: 7–12 eggs.

WINTER. Regularly present in Dane County; occasionally present north to Winnebago, Brown, and Manitowoc counties.

PORTRAIT. *Birds of Wisconsin:* Plate 9.

The average observer making the rounds of lakes, ponds, and flooded fields in April is likely to find a few "spoonbills"— a pair here, a small flock of 10–15 there—particularly in shallow water near mud or grassy edge. Searching my own records of observations in a variety of locations and habitat for 40 years, I find no instance when I tallied more than 45 individuals on a spring field trip. At Necedah (Juneau County), between 1939 and 1973, the highest 1-day total was 75, except for a peak of 350 in 1967. Horicon National Wildlife Refuge in Dodge County sometimes has peaks in excess of 1,000, but those are birds dispersed over many acres of wet-

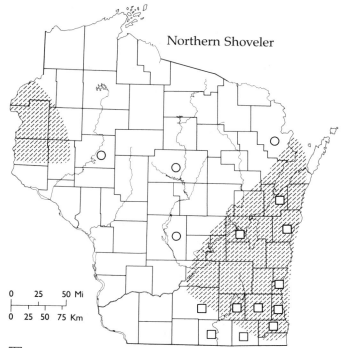

Northern Shoveler

0   25   50 Mi

0   25 50 75 Km

▨ Summer range
○ Mid-June to late August
☐ Early December to early March

Records since 1960

land habitat rather than concentrated in one or two large flocks.

Wisconsin lies east of the chief winter and summer range. Bellrose's (1976) map of migration corridors shows that many of eastern Wisconsin's spring migrants are birds that are moving west-northwest toward breeding grounds in the Dakotas and western Minnesota, coming from Atlantic coastal wintering territory between Delaware and North Carolina. A second flight corridor carries through western Wisconsin some of the birds that have been wintering along the Gulf Coast.

Although early March arrivals have been noted on the 3rd (1974, Grant, W. A. Smith) and 7th (1973, Jefferson, E. J. Stock), usually it is not until the 20th that the first birds appear in the south. Birds can be expected by 1 April in the central areas and 10 April in the northwest. Horicon concentrations of 1,180 on 2 May (1974) and 1,180 on 1 May (1975) indicate the timing of spring peaks. Good numbers can be expected between 20 April and 10 May, with a rapid decline by 15 May. A few late migrants remain through 5 June.

March, Martz, and Hunt (1973) estimated Wisconsin's breeding population at 5,000 per year. Horicon probably has the highest concentration, varying from 60 to 600 birds per year since 1967. North of Burnett, Marathon, and southern Marinette counties I know of no recent summer observations. Although full sets of eggs have not been reported earlier than 27 May, brood observations from 21 May on imply that nesting probably begins by 15 April. Most brood observations occur in late June and July.

Many observers would agree with Bernard (1967), who commented that birds in Douglas County are more common in spring than fall. (*The Passenger Pigeon* has published noticeably fewer reports for autumn than for spring.) A few birds begin to migrate in late August, but these earliest birds are sometimes overlooked because of their resemblance to Mallards. The largest numbers go through Wisconsin between 5 October and 15 November. At Necedah, maximum daily counts sometimes reach 250, sometimes only 30–50, and in some years none at all. The 15–25 November freeze-up dispatches nearly all the "spoonbills" toward their Atlantic and Gulf Coast wintering areas.

Winter records outside Milwaukee and Madison are scarce, with one to four birds noted occasionally on the CBC in Brown, Winnebago, Manitowoc, Jefferson, Waukesha, Rock, and Racine counties. But from 1940 to 1960, Milwaukee had anywhere from 1 to 35 wintering individuals nearly every year. In 1958, birds began to remain in Madison and have consistently wintered there ever since. At first, numbers were small—1–5; then they increased from 27 (1972) to 61 (1975), then to 105 (1979).

As with other waterfowl species, this bird declined somewhat in the latter part of the nineteenth century. However, Kumlien and Hollister (1903) thought that this duck showed less of a decline than did other surface-feeding waterfowl.

Bellrose (1976) pointed to a modest continental increase since the 1950s. J. R. March (pers. comm.) agreed: "In Wisconsin the breeding population has also probably increased or stabilized during that period."

Gadwall (*Anas strepera*)

STATUS. Fairly common migrant. Uncommon summer resident east and northwest. Rare winter resident south.

HABITAT. Inland lakes. Ponds. Shallow marsh.

MIGRATION DATES. *Spring:* mid-March to mid-May. *Fall:* mid-September to late November.

BREEDING DATA. Nests with eggs: 29 May to 8 July. Clutch size: usually 8–11 eggs; occasionally up to 18 in "dump" nests.

WINTER. Often present in Dane County; occasionally present north to St. Croix, Barron, Adams, and Brown counties.

PORTRAIT. *Birds of Wisconsin:* Plate 8.

Kumlien and Hollister (1903) thought the Gadwall was once common, but that its numbers had declined during the latter years of the nineteenth century. Schoenebeck (1902) listed it as common in Oconto County, but Richter (1939a) asserted that it was no longer common. Hoy (1853b) and Barry (1854) both listed it as rare near Racine.

As recently as the 1940s most observers thought the "gray widgeon" to be one of the least numerous of surface-feeding ducks as a migrant, very rare as either a breeder or a winter resident. The Mississippi Flyway population has shown a dramatic increase since 1955, and observers have found birds by the dozens—sometimes by the hundreds—along the Mississippi in both spring and fall. Gadwalls have also more frequently used an east-west flyway between Dakota-Canadian breeding grounds and wintering grounds along the mid-Atlantic Coast. This flyway crosses southern and central Wisconsin.

This species is still rated as uncommon by commentators in the St. Croix Valley (Faanes 1981) and Barron (Faanes 1975a), Chippewa (Kemper 1973a), Fond du Lac (Knuth 1970), and Waukesha (Bielefeldt 1974b) counties. Bernard (1967) listed the bird as rare in Douglas County.

An occasional early migrant shows up between 10 and 20 March, but in an average year birds are first found around the 25th. After a 10–25 April peak, numbers decline. In numerous instances small numbers have appeared around 1–10 May in areas not frequented during April. Some of these birds may be late arrivals from the Atlantic Coast. A few strays remain until 5 June, but most have moved on by 20 May. On 17 May 1974, Horicon (Dodge County) still had an estimated 530 individuals (T. Sanford).

Modest breeding colonies have developed on the islands and marshes around Green Bay since 1947,

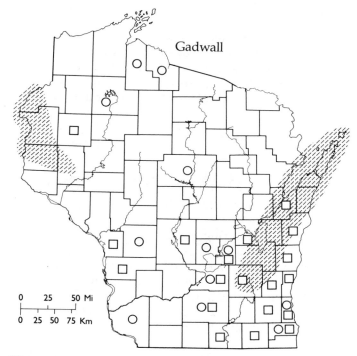

Gadwall

- ▨ Summer range
- ○ Late May to early September
- □ Early December to early March

Records since 1960

and at Horicon National Wildlife Refuge since 1954. Nests and/or broods have also been found since 1960 in areas adjacent to the St. Croix River and the Rock and Fox rivers. In 1973 one Green Bay brood family numbered 18 young in mid-July. Broods usually number 6–12 young per pair.

Quite a period of time elapses between hatching and fall migration. Francis Zirrer (pers. comm. to O. J. Gromme) studied three Sawyer county broods during late summer in 1940 and commented: "About the tenth of August the birds began to assemble in the middle of the pond just a little before dusk and I could count 25–32 birds. . . . Then they started to play: 3, 4, or 5 in a group would turn toward each other, raise their bodies almost vertically out of the water, so that their white bellies would show, and began to leap over one another like frogs."

A few birds begin migration by 15 September, their numbers increasing noticeably after 1 October. Peaks usually occur between 20 October and 10 November, when hundreds can be seen mixed in with Coot and American Wigeon at many points along the Mississippi River. Gadwall peaks also reach into the hundreds at Horicon, listed by Jahn and Hunt (1964) as the major autumn concentration point. Most migrants have left by 25 November.

One conspicuous sign of the increase in Gadwall population is the size of the overwintering flock at Madison. Where there were 10–20 individuals between 1940 and 1970, numbers annually since 1970 have fluctuated between 150 and 550. Although no other locations have had wintering birds consistently, observations have occasionally been made in Walworth, Waukesha, and Milwaukee counties. Exceptional were CBC sightings in St. Croix (1972, 1978), Barron (1977, 1978), La Crosse (1973), Vernon (1965), Adams (1963), Winnebago (1971, 1978, 1980, 1984), Brown (1979, 1984), Manitowoc (1980, 1982), and Sheboygan (1978) counties.

Eurasian Wigeon (*Anas penelope*)
Formerly European Widgeon

STATUS. Rare spring migrant south and east; casual fall migrant.
HABITAT. Inland lakes. Ponds. Shallow marsh.
MIGRATION DATES. *Spring:* late March to mid-May. *Fall:* late October to late November. *Extremes:* 14 March, 12 June; 24 October, 3 December.
PORTRAIT. *Birds of Wisconsin:* Plate 7.

Imagine! Here is a duck that has never been known to nest in North America, yet has been found in Wisconsin on 45 occasions. Several states have even more records of this Old World species. If the North American occurrences were limited to the Pacific and Atlantic coasts, one could believe that the birds had moved from nesting grounds in Siberia and Greenland. But there have been a sizable number of reports from midwestern states.

This is not just a recent phenomenon. Although this wanderer was not mentioned by most nineteenth-century commentators, Kumlien and Hollister (1903) mentioned undated hunter-kills in Dane (1874) and Jefferson (1877, plus one for which no year is listed) counties. And Ludwig Kumlien shot one in Jefferson County in 1875. Kumlien and Hollister commented, "There are other records for the state about which there is no doubt." But no other nineteenth-century records have been dated or documented, and none of the above specimens can be located today.

Deane (1911), listing midwestern records in the nineteenth and early twentieth centuries, credited A. G. Holmes with shooting birds in Brown County on 11 November 1906 and 23 October 1910. "Mr. Holmes writes me that he believes these widgeon to be more numerous than is generally supposed, and are considered hybrids by gunners, as he himself first thought until he learned the characteristic differences between the English and American species from an old

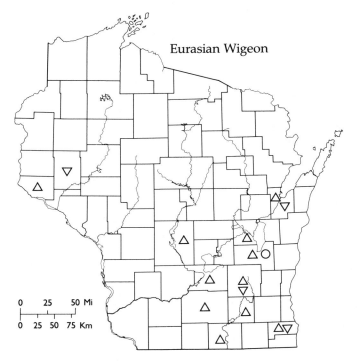

Eurasian Wigeon

0   25   50 Mi
0 25 50 75 Km

△   Late March to mid-May
▽   24 October to 3 December

All records

hunter naturalist who knew the former in the Old World before settling here." The skins were not saved.

In the ensuing 20 years, Dane County furnished four sight observations: 22–26 April 1917 (Schorger 1918), 14 April 1918 (Taylor 1919), 3 April 1927 (Schorger 1928), and 27 April 1930 (J. S. Main 1930a). On 12 June 1934, O. J. Gromme secured a specimen for the Milwaukee Public Museum; it had been discovered 2 days earlier on the edge of Lake Winnebago in Fond du Lac County (G. Breitenstein). Another bird was seen near the same location 2 years later (26 April 1936, W. C. Pelzer; MPM files). And one was found in Jefferson County on 21 April 1937 (A. S. Hawkins; MPM files).

The sole record for the 1940s was a hunter-kill in Brown County on 30 November 1940 (*fide* E. O. Paulson). In contrast there were 18 reports in the 1950s, 11 in the 1960s, 4 in the 1970s, and 5 in the 1980s. Of the 38 sightings since 1950, 35 were found between 14 March (1987, Rock, D. D. Tessen) and 17 May (1959, Brown, E. O. Paulson). Observation dates occur mostly in the 20 April–5 May interval. R. H. Behrens obtained excellent color movies of a male near Hager City (Pierce County), present there between 20 and 30 April 1966.

The Hager City bird is the only one known to have visited the western part of the state in spring. Nearly all spring reports have been close to a line connecting the cities of Madison and Green Bay. Exceptions include birds in Adams (1955, S. D. Robbins), Rock (1958, D. Hammel), and Racine (1964, 1975, E. B. Prins) counties.

The only autumn observations since 1930 involve individuals in Dodge (7 November 1987, B. Harriman), Brown (30 November 1940, E. O. Paulson), Dunn (24 October–13 November 1988, J. L. Polk), and Racine (3 December 1967, L. W. Erickson) counties.

American Wigeon (*Anas americana*)
Formerly Baldpate

STATUS. Common migrant south and central; fairly common migrant north. Rare summer resident. Rare winter resident south and east.

HABITAT. Inland lakes. Ponds. Shallow marsh.

MIGRATION DATES. *Spring:* mid-March to late May. *Fall:* late August to late November.

BREEDING DATA. Nests with eggs: 22 May to 2 July. Clutch size: 5–11 eggs.

WINTER. Occasionally present north to La Crosse, Portage, and Manitowoc counties.

PORTRAIT. *Birds of Wisconsin:* Plate 7.

If one wants to see "Baldpates," a drive along the Mississippi River in late September or October is highly recommended. At many of the numerous vantage points along the Great River Road (Highway 35) from Hager City to Prairie du Chien these attractive ducks can be seen by the hundreds or thousands.

The Mississippi River corridor in western Wisconsin channels migrating birds between wintering grounds along the Atlantic Coast and breeding areas in Minnesota, North Dakota, western Ontario, and Manitoba (Bellrose 1976). Numbers swell in autumn, when adult populations are expanded to include young of the year. But even in spring there are thousands using this corridor in their northwest flight.

Away from the Mississippi River, Baldpates in spring often occur in flocks of from 20 to 50. Numerically, Bielefeldt (1974b) rated this species about equal to the Green-winged Teal during the springs of 1961–1964 in Waukesha County; he also rated the species more common than the Northern Shoveler and Northern Pintail, but less common than the Mallard and

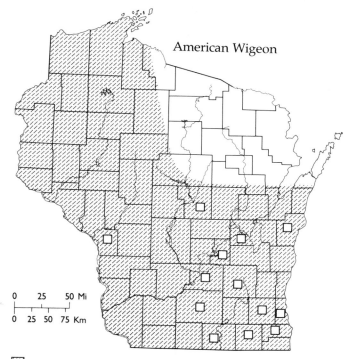

American Wigeon

0   25   50 Mi
0 25 50 75 Km

▨ Summer range
☐ Early December to early March

Records since 1960

Blue-winged Teal. At Necedah (Juneau County), 1961–1973, the peak flocks were larger than those of the Northern Shoveler and Gadwall, but usually smaller than those of other surface-feeding ducks.

Goddard's (1975) figures for St. Croix County, 1968–1971, showed the American Wigeon to be more numerous than the Gadwall and Northern Pintail, but less numerous than the Green-winged Teal, Blue-winged Teal, Mallard, and Northern Shoveler.

The wigeon's spring migration is protracted. Some individuals sighted during the first week of March may be winter residents, but probable migrants have been noted on 3 March (1974, Grant, W. A. Smith) and 5 March (1966, Jefferson, R. Sharp). A more typical arrival date for the southern counties is 20 March, with birds appearing in central counties by 30 March, and by 10 April in the north as water opens. Peaks usually occur between 10 and 25 April in the south and from 20 April to 10 May farther north. Most migrants have moved on by 20 May, but nearly every year a few linger into the first week of June, then disappear.

Wisconsin contributes very little to the continental production of young each year. A few pairs nest frequently in Burnett, Dodge, and Brown counties, and at least occasionally in Rusk, Marathon, Wood, La Crosse, and Racine counties. Between 1951 and 1956 a pair nested nearly every year at a residence along the Lake Michigan shore at Racine—once under the edge of the porch, twice in a window box (Abbott 1957). Families of hatched young have been reported from 18 June on.

Although there have been numerous summer observations, some birds are probably nonbreeders. Bernard (1967) found no evidence of nesting in Douglas County. Faanes and Goddard (1976a) found the same situation in St. Croix and Pierce counties. "Though there are summer residents in the area, we have no evidence of nesting." Northeast of a line between the cities of Ashland and Green Bay records of summer observations are sparse.

The first fall migrants move into the state very early. Jahn and Hunt (1964) have reported influxes into Horicon (Dodge County) in late July, and estimated that 10,000 birds were present there on 15 August 1949. The birds are common by 15 September, peaking between 10 and 31 October. The Upper Mississippi River National Wildlife Refuge personnel estimated that 26,000 birds were present in the La Crosse region on 26 October 1974. At other locations, the size of the peaks is smaller, but the timetable is similar. Considerable fluctuation in peak size has been noted at Necedah (Juneau County), varying from no birds (1949) to 15,000 (1963). Peaks of 4,000–8,000 have typically occurred since 1957. The exodus of flocks begins in early November and is usually complete by the 25th.

American Wigeons appear on two to seven CBCs nearly every year. Usually these are singles or birds in small groups of two to five, and at least a few of them are present through January and February. Rarely, there are CBC flocks of up to 50 (1971, Madison); these disappear in January. Most wigeons occur among flocks of wintering ducks in Winnebago, Dane, Walworth, and Milwaukee counties. In addition to these southeastern occurrences there are two records from La Crosse (1967, 1975) and one from Stevens Point (1970).

Canvasback (*Aythya valisineria*)

STATUS. Common migrant south and central; fairly common migrant north. Rare summer resident west and east. Uncommon winter resident southeast; rare winter resident south and central.

HABITAT. Inland lakes. Ponds. Shallow marsh.

MIGRATION DATES. *Spring:* mid-March to late May. *Fall:* late September to mid-December.

BREEDING DATA. Nests with eggs: late May to early June. Brood observations: 29 June to 6 August.

WINTER. Regularly present in Racine and Milwaukee counties. Occasionally present north to St. Croix, Marathon, Outagamie, Brown, and Door counties.

PORTRAIT. *Birds of Wisconsin:* Plate 10.

Imagine a 1-day tally of 147,000 "Cans"! This was the estimated number of these birds on the Mississippi River near and below La Crosse, in La Crosse and Vernon counties, on 8 November 1975 (K. Butts). Other peak estimates for the same region were 63,000 (1972), 100,000 (1973), and 74,000 (1974). Primarily, these are birds coming from breeding grounds in Saskatchewan, Manitoba, North Dakota, and western Minnesota, pausing before moving on through southern Michigan to the Atlantic Coast for the winter. According to Bellrose (1976), close to half of the continental population makes this northwest-southeast pilgrimage each year.

But Wisconsin is not always on the itinerary. An alternate route angles through western Minnesota and Iowa, then swerves east. When the Cans choose this route, as they did from 1965 to 1970, the peak numbers in Wisconsin are much smaller.

Before 1960, the major autumn stopover spots were the larger lakes in eastern and southeastern Wisconsin: Lakes Poygan and Butte des Morts in Winnebago County, Puckaway and Green Lake in Green Lake County, Mendota in Dane County, and Koshkonong in Jefferson County. The Winnebago County lakes still attracted fall peaks of 28,000 as recently as 1964 (R. A. Hunt), but these numbers have lessened steadily since then. The shift to the Mississippi River locations may be partly due to a decline in the quality of water and food on the eastern lakes, but the existence of the series of pools above the many locks and dams that have so greatly altered the riverine habitat has undoubtedly also had a considerable effect. North of the La Crosse-to-Sheboygan corridor not many Cans are found.

The first fall migrants appear between 1 and 10 October. There are few September records of early transients, the earliest occurring on the 15th (1967, Brown,

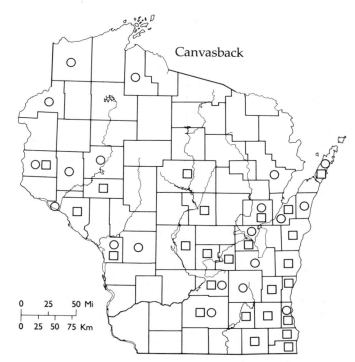

Canvasback

```
0    25    50 Mi
0  25  50  75 Km
```

○ Early June to mid-September
□ Early January to late February

Records since 1960

E. D. Cleary) and 22nd (1957 and 1960, Dane, T. L. Ashman). Jahn and Hunt (1964) stated: "The main flight in October occurs almost every year between 18 and 25 October. Experienced Canvasback hunters in Wisconsin know this well." Numbers decline gradually from 1 to 15 November, then drop more rapidly. Several hundred often move to the larger lakes in Dane and Walworth counties as other lakes freeze over, while most birds head for the Atlantic Coast.

At least a few individuals are found on the CBC every winter. At various times over 100 have been noted in Milwaukee (1953, 1956, 1957), Dane (1956, 1957, 1965, 1974, 1975), Walworth (1956, 1957), and Buffalo (1974) counties; in 1954 there were exceptional numbers: 2,500 (Walworth) and 2,084 (Dane). These large numbers represent late migrants that move on in early January as the last of the lakes freeze.

Scattered individuals and small flocks (10–40) sometimes remain throughout the winter along Lake Michigan, and where open water remains in Dane and Winnebago counties. Unusual central and western winter sightings have been made in St. Croix (1974), Buffalo (1973, 1974), La Crosse (1973), Eau Claire (1980),

Marathon (1970), Adams (1957), and Marquette (1949) counties.

The spring flight is somewhat more diffuse, though there is some concentration at those locations which get the heaviest fall use. On 29 March 1953, an aerial survey revealed the presence of 65,000 on Lakes Poygan and Butte des Morts. Birds spread out to other areas as well. The northern counties, missed almost entirely in the fall, attract modest numbers in April and early May. Comparing Cans with other diving ducks in Waukesha County for the years 1961 to 1964, Bielefeldt (1974b) found their numbers to be much the same as those for the Ruddy Duck, and below those of other regular species. Similarly, in St. Croix County, 1968–1971, Goddard (1975) found numbers to be well below those of other divers.

Early March arrivals are likely in the southern counties if there is mild weather in late February. Otherwise it is 15 March or later when the first southern birds arrive, and 25 March when they find enough open water in the central region. Few birds make it to the Lake Superior region before 10 April. Birds usually peak in the southeast between 25 March and 20 April, and in the northwest between 15 April and 5 May. Most are gone by 15 May, but late stragglers are occasionally seen into early June: the 2nd (1953, Milwaukee, I. N. Balsom; 1954, Bayfield, D. A. Bratley; 1973, Ozaukee, T. Bintz), 3rd (1975, Burnett, J. O. Evrard), 4th (1971, Columbia, S. D. Robbins), 8th (1976, Dunn, S. D. Robbins), and 9th (1966, Polk, S. D. Robbins).

This species has seldom bred in Wisconsin. Kumlien and Hollister (1903) knew of three brood observations, but did not give definite information about date and location. Schoenebeck (1902) procured a set of six eggs (preserved at the University of Wisconsin–Stevens Point) in Oconto County on 28 May 1892. A nest was found at Madison in June 1927, with eight of nine eggs hatching (J. G. Dickson [Schorger 1929b]). Broods of young, mainly in July, have been noted in St. Croix (1976, C. A. Faanes), Brown (1975, D. D. Tessen), Winnebago (1952 and 1953, R. C. Hopkins; 1972 and 1974, D. L. Strohmeyer [1976]), and Dodge (1976, W. E. Wheeler) counties.

Isolated instances apparently involving nonbreeding birds have been recorded between 15 June and 15 August in Douglas (1981), Burnett (1977, 1978), St. Croix (1975, 1981, 1982, 1983), Dunn (1976), Chippewa (1972), Pepin (1976), La Crosse (1981), and Monroe (1983, 1984) counties in the west, and in Oconto (1976), Brown (1970, 1971, 1976), Outagamie (1945), Fond du Lac (1966), Dodge (1957, 1958, 1968, 1975, 1984), Columbia (1959, 1960), Dane (1956, 1957), and Milwaukee (1967) counties in the east and south. Some may represent sick or injured birds, but increasing summer observations since 1970 could signal the beginning of a different trend.

Despite huge flocks seen in fall, this species is apparently declining across the continent. Kumlien and Hollister (1903) called it common, rather than abundant or very common, yet indicated that it had not decreased as much in the latter part of the nineteenth century as had some other duck species. But Bellrose (1976) made the following comment on recent North American population levels: "Of all the extensively distributed game ducks in North America, the Canvasback is the least abundant. . . . Both the breeding ground surveys and January inventories show a downward trend in Canvasback numbers for the 20-year period 1955–1974."

Redhead (*Aythya americana*)

STATUS. Common migrant. Fairly common summer resident east; rare summer resident west. Uncommon winter resident east; rare winter resident south and central.

HABITAT. Inland lakes. Ponds. Shallow marsh.

MIGRATION DATES. *Spring:* mid-March to late May. *Fall:* late September to late November.

BREEDING DATA. Nests with eggs: 10 June to 3 July. Clutch size: usually 7–9 eggs; larger in "dump nests."

WINTER. Regularly present in Milwaukee. Occasionally present north to Dunn, Marathon, Marinette, and Door counties.

PORTRAIT. *Birds of Wisconsin:* Plate 10.

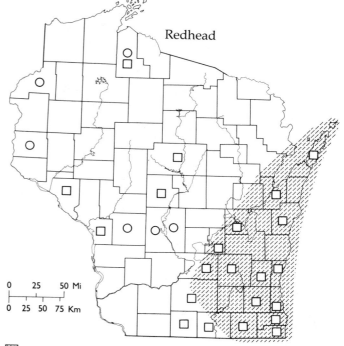

Redhead

0   25   50 Mi
0 25 50 75 Km

▨ Summer range
○ Early June to early September
□ Early December to late February

Records since 1960

Beginning birders sometimes think of the Redhead as a hardy species that appears as soon as ice breaks up in late March and departs northward following receding ice to the Arctic tundra. This is a misconception. Only a few Redheads reach central Canada and Alaska. The major breeding range extends from southern Alberta to southern Manitoba and North Dakota. Birds passing through Wisconsin in April head west-northwest from wintering grounds along the Atlantic Coast. Only a few of Wisconsin's Redheads winter along the Gulf Coast.

In the nineteenth century the Redhead was one of the most common ducks. But reflecting on the bird's decline, Kumlien and Hollister (1903) observed: "It has been greatly reduced in numbers in late years, more so than most ducks. Formerly very abundant, it is disappearing at an alarming rate." Schorger (1931a) also commented on the growing scarcity of the Redhead, with flocks of over 30 rarely seen in Dane County. The drought in the mid-1930s was a factor in reducing the continental population further.

Eventually hunting regulations were revised to offer the Redhead complete protection. This bird has staged a modest comeback since 1940, but with continued precarious fluctuations. Bellrose (1976) cited several studies indicating that Redheads have an unusually high mortality rate—close to 80% for young of the year.

The first spring migrants typically appear between 1 and 15 March in the southeastern counties. Non-wintering individuals have been found as early as 22 February (1964, Racine, E. B. Prins) and 24 February (1967, Winnebago, D. D. Tessen). In the west, arrivals are expected around 25 to 30 March, with 5 to 10 April typical in the north. There are years when flocks of 200–500 are present between 5 and 20 April, with

most birds gone by the end of the month. In other years, numbers gradually build up in April and peak at the end of the month, with a few late migrants lingering through May.

Recently, breeding populations have increased, particularly in the Rock and Fox River valleys. At Horicon (Dodge County) there was a single brood observation in 1942, followed by observations of six broods in 1945. By 1954, Redheads produced an estimated 1,900 young at Horicon. In the late 1960s and 1970s, nesting spread to other Rock and Fox River valley locations (Dodge, Green Lake, Winnebago, Manitowoc, and Brown counties). Aerial estimates of summer populations statewide reached 5,000 in the 1973–1975 period. Away from the Rock and Fox rivers, nest or brood observations have occurred in Kenosha and St. Croix counties. Nesting is suspected also at the Crex Meadows Wildlife Area in Burnett County. Summer observations, for which there is no evidence of breeding, are known for Ashland, Monroe, Juneau, and Adams counties.

Few fall migrants are noted before 25 September.

The earliest records are 15 September (1961, Winnebago, D. D. Tessen) and 20 September (1947, Milwaukee, G. H. Orians). It is between 10 October and 10 November that one can see rafts of birds, usually far out on a large lake with the Lesser Scaup, Canvasback, American Wigeon, and American Coot. Redheads often seem less common in fall than in spring to the average observer. Actually, they are more numerous in fall because adults travel with young of the year, particularly in the Green Bay-to-Horicon area and along the Mississippi River. Most birds have left by 25 November, but a few linger into early December.

Only in 1961 and 1964 was this species missed entirely on the 1946–1985 CBCs. From 1 to 12 individuals have been reported in Milwaukee almost regularly during that interval, and from 1 to 8 birds have fre-

quented Winnebago County each year since 1967. Often, observers report a few from Dane, Dodge, Waukesha, and Walworth counties. Lake Michigan individuals have occurred as far north as Washington Island in Door County (1970).

The mid-January waterfowl inventory has often tallied 200–300 wintering individuals since 1952. Most records come from the southeastern counties, north to Dane and Winnebago counties. Farther north are late-December sightings in Buffalo (1973), Ashland (1974), Marathon (1967), Wood (1979), Brown (1970, 1977), and Door (1965) counties. The most northerly January records are the 24th (1950, Dunn, H. M. Mattison), 28th to 31st (1957, Marinette, W. N. MacBriar), and 29th (1977, Ashland, R. L. Verch).

Ring-necked Duck (*Aythya collaris*)

STATUS. Common migrant. Fairly common summer resident north and central; rare summer resident southeast. Rare winter resident central and south.
HABITAT. Inland lakes. Ponds. Shallow marsh.
MIGRATION DATES. *Spring:* mid-March to early May. *Fall:* mid-September to early November.
BREEDING DATA. Nests with eggs: 28 April to 8 July. Clutch size: 8–11 eggs.
WINTER. Occasionally present north to Dunn, Marathon, and Outagamie counties.
PORTRAIT. *Birds of Wisconsin:* Plate 10.

For the majority of waterfowl species, Wisconsin lies somewhat off the beaten path. The major migration passageways lie farther west, and it is the birds traveling on secondary corridors that visit this state. This is not the case with the Ring-neck. Bellrose (1976) depicted one of three major "duck lanes" passing from northwest to southeast through the state and connecting Mackenzie-Saskatchewan-Manitoba breeding territories and Florida wintering grounds. Significant numbers of Wisconsin birds also winter along the Gulf Coast.

This species does not rival the scaup in abundance; where the latter collects in rafts of hundreds, the former moves in groups of 10–50 birds. The Ring-neck prefers medium-sized lakes and ponds, rather than large lakes and shallow flooded fields. This bird,

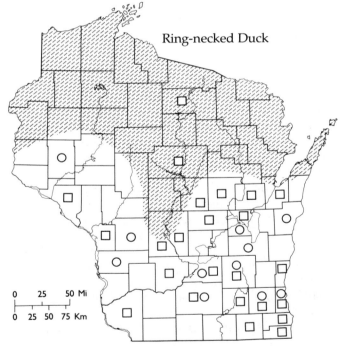

Ring-necked Duck

▨ Summer range
○ Mid-May to early September
□ Late November to late February

Records since 1960

however, often feeds near the shallower portions of ponds where water is 6–10 feet deep. In St. Croix County, 1968–1971, Goddard (1975) observed that scaups and Ring-necks showed a preference for the same ponds, with one exception: a large but shallow water surface that attracted large numbers of Ring-necks.

First arrivals usually show up in the south around 15–20 March. When late February is mild, arrivals may appear between 1 and 10 March. Unusually early birds appeared on 26 February (1953, Crawford, H. H. Burgess) and 27 February (1951, Dodge, R. B. Dryer). Nearly all migrants have departed by 20 May. April is the main month for migration. Peaks occur between the 5th and 25th in the south, and the 15th and 30th in the north, with many birds sometimes lingering until 10 May. The peak number fluctuates considerably. At Necedah (Juneau County), 1939–1972, top numbers varied from fewer than 100 to 2,000 per spring, with an exceptionally large population, estimated at 4,000, in 1954. In St. Croix County, Goddard's season-long count of 4,835 (1968) was nearly double that for each of the subsequent 3 years.

Most breeding pairs have been found north of a line from St. Croix through Taylor, Shawano, and Door counties, plus a projection through central Wisconsin south to Juneau County. Localized breeding has occurred in Dane, Waukesha, Dodge, and Winnebago counties. At Crex Meadows Wildlife Area in Burnett County up to 70 broods have been counted in a season. Statewide breeding populations averaged 6,500 per year for 1965–1970, and 5,600 per year for 1973–1975.

Egg-laying begins around 30 April in some instances. But nesting usually commences about 10 days later. Broods have been observed from 8 June on. Small young seen between 25 July and 8 August are probably the product of renesting when earlier nestings fail. In late summer wild rice beds in northern Wisconsin become important staging areas.

Only the barest trickle of fall migrants is apparent before 15 September. In the last 10 days of the month there is a buildup in the northwest that spreads over the rest of the state through October. An estimated 5,500 birds were seen at Crex Meadows on 2 October 1967. Peaks have reached as high as 6,000 at Necedah (1947), and 19,600 in the Upper Mississippi River National Wildlife Refuge near La Crosse (1975). Other areas of substantial concentrations include Horicon Marsh in Dodge County and the Grand River Marsh Wildlife Area in Green Lake and Marquette counties. Numbers start to diminish in the north by 15 October and in the south 10 days later. Few birds remain after 5 November.

Most Ring-necks reported on late-December CBCs are individuals that have lingered at southern spots such as Madison and Lake Geneva (Walworth County), where the larger lakes have been slow to freeze. These birds depart by early January. But where open water remains, an occasional individual persists. Most northerly reports have come from Dunn (1949), Buffalo (1974), Marathon (1950, 1974), Portage (1964), Waupaca (1965, 1978–1980), and Outagamie (1966) counties. The mid-January waterfowl inventory has listed Ring-necks approximately 1 year in every 3 since 1951.

Greater Scaup (*Aythya marila*)

STATUS. Common migrant east and north; fairly common spring migrant south and west; uncommon fall migrant south and west. Rare summer visitant east and north. Common winter resident east.

HABITAT. Great Lakes. Inland lakes.

MIGRATION DATES. *Spring:* mid-March to late May, rarely to early June. *Fall:* late September to mid-December.

WINTER. Regularly present along Lake Michigan north to Ozaukee County; occasionally present north to Marinette County and inland to Waukesha, Walworth, Dane and Winnebago counties.

PORTRAIT. *Birds of Wisconsin:* Plate 10.

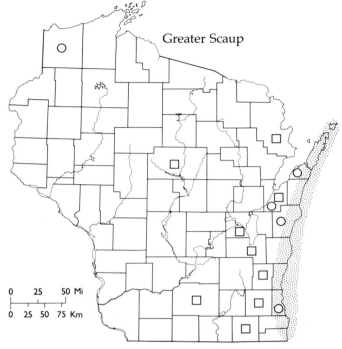

Greater Scaup

0   25   50 Mi
0   25 50 75 Km

▨ Winter range
○ Early June to early September
☐ Late December to late February

Records since 1960

When scaups flood into the state from their Alaskan and Canadian breeding grounds in October and November, it is doubtful if one bird in a thousand is specifically identified as a Greater or Lesser. On inland lakes and streams the hunting season is in full swing when the first "bluebills" arrive. Whether a scaup is Greater or Lesser makes little or no difference to the hunter, and data collected from hunter bags do not differentiate between the two species. Bird-watchers who would like to distinguish one from the other usually find that scaups raft so far out in the water that specific identification is impossible. Similarly, along the shores of Lakes Michigan and Superior the largest flocks are usually too distant to allow specific naming. The familiar nickname "bluebill" applies to both species.

Many observers have long assumed that the birds on Lakes Michigan and Superior were chiefly Greater, while those elsewhere in the state were mainly Lesser. But this assumption lacks corroborative evidence. Kumlien and Hollister (1903) stated of the Greater Scaup: "More common on Lake Michigan. We have seen large numbers of these birds, with a few of *affinis* and *collaris* in the Milwaukee market, all killed on the lake, and we suspect this is the common form which winters on Lake Michigan." Both species are present statewide during spring and fall. Clearer patterns of distribution would emerge if the average observer would carefully report a bird as "Greater," or "Lesser," or "Scaup sp.," instead of assuming it is one species or the other.

Bernard (1967) showed 20 September as an expected fall arrival date for Greater Scaups in Douglas County. It is closer to 5 October when the first migrants reach lower Lake Michigan. Fairly early was a 13 September sighting (1975, Ozaukee, D. D. Tessen); exceptionally early were seven birds on 27 August (1972, Milwaukee, D. D. Tessen). Along Lake Superior, birds are numerous from 10 October to 15 November, with a few lingering into early December some years. Along Lake Michigan there is considerable movement from 20 October into December. Inland records also cluster primarily in late October and November.

Tallies on Milwaukee County CBCs since 1964 have varied from 296 (1978) to 12,870 (1969), averaging about 4,400 per year (these figures based largely on assumptions about species identification, rather than on specific Greater-Lesser differentiation). Elsewhere along Lake Michigan a few are reported on CBCs annually in Ozaukee and Racine counties. In some winters the birds range from Kenosha County to Door County. Rarely have the numbers for any one count exceeded 50. On rare occasions late-December CBC birds have been detected in Marathon, Marinette, Brown, Winnebago, Fond du Lac, Washington, Waukesha, Walworth, and Dane counties. Many of these late December birds move on in early January, leaving only modest numbers at Milwaukee in January and February.

Small numbers return along Lake Michigan around 1 March. They build gradually through 15 March and increase more rapidly through the remainder of the month. April is the peak month, with a general exodus 1–20 May.

Inland, there have been occasional appearances in Waukesha, Winnebago, and Dane counties by 15 March, but usually observers report small numbers at the end of the month. Knuth (1970) listed the bird as common in Fond du Lac County in spring. It is designated uncommon in Chippewa and Eau Claire counties (Kemper 1973a), as well as in Pierce and St. Croix counties (Faanes and Goddard 1976a). I have found this species regularly in various central and western locations from 10 April to 20 May, in numbers from 1 to 20, often sharing the same pond with Lessers but not associating with them. Records for stragglers remaining beyond 25 May are 29 May (1968, Burnett, N. R. Stone), 30 May (1967, Douglas, R. F. Bernard), 1

June (1969, Fond du Lac, R. A. Knuth), and 2 June (1973, Ozaukee, T. Bintz).

Nonbreeders rarely frequent the Great Lakes during the summer. At Milwaukee six were seen intermittently all summer in 1974 (E. L. Basten), one throughout the summer in 1975 (D. K. Gustafson), and one on 12 June 1976 (D. D. Tessen). Observers discovered one nonbreeder in Manitowoc County, 12 June 1979 (S. D. Robbins), one in Door County, 22–24 June 1962 (L. W. Erickson), and another in Brown County on 22 July 1975 (J. Trick). In Douglas County six were identified in company with 36 Lessers on 9 July 1967, and nesting was suspected in 1969 (R. F. Bernard). But there are no confirmed Wisconsin nestings to date. Since this species breeds almost exclusively in the arctic and subarctic regions of Alaska and western Canada, any nesting in Wisconsin would be most exceptional.

Lesser Scaup (*Aythya affinis*)

STATUS. Abundant migrant. Rare summer resident north and east. Uncommon winter resident south and east; rare winter resident west and north.
HABITAT. Great Lakes. Inland lakes. Ponds.
MIGRATION DATES. *Spring:* mid-March to mid-May. *Fall:* mid-September to late December.
BREEDING DATA. Nests with eggs: one record. Brood observations: 4–18 July.
WINTER. Regularly present north to Dane, Outagamie, and Brown counties; occasionally present north to Douglas, Bayfield, Oneida, Marinette, and Door counties.
PORTRAIT. *Birds of Wisconsin:* Plate 10.

Soft breezes blow. Aged ice groans. Finally the balmy breath of spring nudges Old Man Winter into retirement and unlocks the frozen lakes. Soon after, the dingy ice gives way to rippling blue wavelets; the blue in turn becomes dotted with specks of black and white. The "bluebills" are back.

The birds usually return by 25 March in the south, 10 April in the north, and earlier if the first 2 weeks of March are mild. (Small flocks may appear by 5 March in the south or 25 March in the north, before the lakes are completely open.) Observers who tally other species of ducks in the dozens between 5 April and 10 May number scaup in the hundreds. In St. Croix County, 1968–1971 (Goddard 1975), and in Barron County, 1973–1974 (Faanes 1975a), the numbers of scaup exceeded those of all other diving ducks combined. This species also outnumbered the combined total of Mallards and Blue-winged Teal. In Waukesha

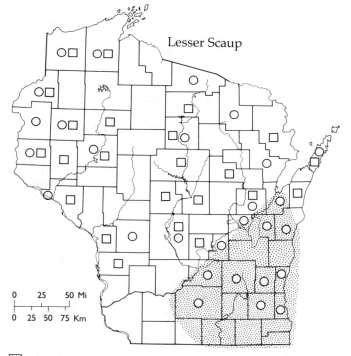

Lesser Scaup

0   25   50 Mi
0   25 50 75 Km

▦ Winter range
○ Early June to early September
□ Late December to late February

Records since 1960

County, 1961–1964, Bielefeldt (1974b) found these bluebills (the familiar nickname is applied to both Lesser and Greater Scaup) far more numerous than any other waterfowl species. At refuges such as Necedah in Juneau County, where marsh habitat is more plentiful than open water, scaups do not predominate. In broad expanses of open water, such as Lake Winnebago and Petenwell Flowage, mid-April peaks may number 5,000 or more. In the south, numbers diminish gradually after 20 April and rapidly after 1 May, with only an occasional straggler after 10 May. Farther north the time schedule is 7–10 days later.

The ratio between Greater and Lesser Scaup in spring has not been calculated. Both are numerous along Lakes Michigan and Winnebago. At other inland sites most scaups are Lesser, but the Greater is present more often than is generally recognized.

In addition to listing the Lesser as an abundant migrant, Kumlien and Hollister (1903) listed it as a breeding species: "To a limited extent a breeding species even in southern Wisconsin, having been known to nest anywhere from the southern counties northward." These observers also mentioned the frequent presence of nonbreeding flocks on Lakes Winnebago, Koshkonong, and Delavan.

Recent nesting has been reported in Polk (1976, C. A. Faanes), Lincoln (1955, 1959, L. R. Jahn), Winnebago (1972, 1976, D. L. Strohmeyer), Dodge (1949, 1952, 1954, L. R. Jahn), and Ozaukee (1952, L. R. Jahn) counties. Late June and July observations of probable nonbreeders have been widespread since 1940 in all regions except the southwest. But except for concentrations of 20–40 at Superior, most sightings involve only one or two birds.

In fall most of the inland scaups are probably Lessers, while both species are common along Lakes Superior and Michigan. Only occasional individuals or small flocks arrive before October. Suspected migrants were reported on 19 August (1922, Sheboygan, O. J. Gromme), 23 August (1961, Juneau, C. E. Pospichal), and 26 August (1956, Columbia, R. G. Wills).

The population builds after 1 October, gradually or rapidly, depending upon how quickly cold weather forces the ducks from their Canadian breeding grounds. The peak period is from 20 October to 10 November, with flocks sometimes in the 5,000–10,000 range. An estimated 36,000 Lessers were present on 8 November 1975 in the Upper Mississippi River National Wildlife Refuge of the La Crosse area.

Fall hunting statistics indicate that Lesser Scaups make up 3–7% of the total duck harvest each year. Because scaups prefer the larger, deeper lakes that are the last to freeze, sizable flocks sometimes remain through November. Few birds remain after 10 December, except on Lake Michigan.

Observers have reported 25 to 300 individuals on CBCs each year since 1964; only a few have come from the Lake Michigan region. Most birds have been found in small flocks at Madison and Neenah, but scattered individuals have come from all parts of the state. Even northwestern counties have had individuals at least through December, sometimes all winter long. It seems probable that Lessers are widely distributed among the wintering Greater Scaups along Lake Michigan, but this has not been adequately determined. Since 1960 there have been observations between 15 December and 28 February from over half of Wisconsin's counties.

Common Eider (*Somateria mollissima*)

STATUS. Accidental. Four records.
HABITAT. Great Lakes. Inland lakes.
MIGRATION DATES. One March record. Three November records.

Doubtless the memorable Armistice Day snow and ice storm of 1940 was responsible for the presence of a female Common Eider in Burnett County, shot that year on 11 November from a flock of seven eiders (N. R. Stone, pers. comm.). Although the specimen was not saved, Stone, recalling the episode in 1977, commented: "Even though it occurred 37 years ago, my memory is quite vivid regarding the plumage and the bill. Several people thought it a Canvasback because of the shape of the bill. . . . Both have relatively straight bills with the top or uppermost part extending quite far into the forehead."

It was 28 years later, almost to the day, that hunter David Johnson shot another bird at the same Burnett County location. J. R. March identified this 10 November 1968 specimen, and he preserved a wing (*Pass. Pigeon* 31:290).

An immature male was discovered at Two Rivers (Manitowoc County) on 24 March 1960 (J. Kraupa) and was seen again on 26 March (B. N. Brouchoud). The bird was observed at close range as it swam in the harbor, giving a good view of the profile of the head (*Pass. Pigeon* 22:189).

Kumlien and Hollister (1903) listed one positive nineteenth-century record as a female shot at Lake Koshkonong in Jefferson County in November 1891. These writers also mentioned three indefinite instances: one bird said to have been recorded by P. R.

Hoy at Racine in the winter of 1875, and two other specimens supposedly located at the Milwaukee Public Museum. All current specimens of this species in the Milwaukee museum were taken in Alaska. I could not locate any Wisconsin specimens.

King Eider (*Somateria spectabilis*)

STATUS. Accidental spring migrant east; casual fall migrant east. Accidental summer visitant. Casual winter visitant east.
HABITAT. Great Lakes. Inland lakes.
MIGRATION DATES. Observed between 21 September and 28 November. One March record.
WINTER. Five December–January records.
PORTRAIT. *Birds of Wisconsin*: Plate 12.

There are eight specimens of King Eiders at the Milwaukee Public Museum. Two bear no date but were collected at Milwaukee presumably before 1880. One may have been referred to by Kumlien and Hollister (1903) as "taken at Milwaukee many years ago." Two were taken in Milwaukee by H. Russell on 25 December 1899 and 7 January 1900. Another Milwaukee specimen was added on 28 November 1903 (*fide* H. L. Ward). A hunting casualty from Muskego Lake in Waukesha County on 8 November 1933 was donated to the MPM by W. Erlach. Two more Milwaukee discoveries followed: one taken on 21 March 1936 (I. J. Perkins) and one found dead on 16 June 1937 (H. Meyer).

Although no other state specimens can now be located, Kumlien and Hollister (1903) did mention a mounted bird thought to have been shot at Madison around 1874. They saw a mounted male in a fisherman's house near Sheboygan in 1880; it had been captured in a fisherman's net the previous winter.

One individual has been photographed: a female at Oshkosh between 22 December 1973 and 7 January 1974. This bird had a noticeably injured wing when first seen, but eventually recovered its flying capabilities (J. L. Kaspar).

There have been three well-documented sight records. Three males and a female were observed on 21 September 1953 at Virmond Park in Ozaukee County, and were carefully studied both in flight and on the water by Richard Gordon and others (*Pass. Pigeon* 16:31–32). A severe storm had passed through James Bay just previous to this date. The birds were seen again in the same area on 30 September (I. N.

King Eider

△   21 March
○   16 June
▽   21 September to 28 November
□   11 December to 7 January

All records

Balsom). On 11 December 1960 Carl and Dorothy Frister got within 100 feet of a female at Port Washington in Ozaukee County (*Pass. Pigeon* 23:95). David Brasser got a close view of a female in Sheboygan County on 25 November 1984 (*Pass. Pigeon* 47:121).

Adrian Freitag detected two male eiders swimming offshore near Sturgeon Bay (Door County) on 27 December 1969 (*Pass. Pigeon* 32:17). While there is every likelihood these were Kings, conditions of observation were not adequate to rule out the remote possibility of another eider species.

Harlequin Duck (*Histrionicus histrionicus*)

STATUS. Rare migrant north and east. Accidental summer visitant. Rare winter resident south and east.
HABITAT. Great Lakes.
MIGRATION DATES. Most records between early November and late March.
WINTER. Occasionally present along Lake Michigan between Racine and Ozaukee counties. Casually present in Dane and Columbia counties.
PORTRAIT. *Birds of Wisconsin:* Plate 11.

Hoy (1853b) mentioned the taking of a Harlequin Duck at Racine on 15 December 1851. According to Kumlien and Hollister (1903), Hoy procured another three birds as well. These writers also alluded to "an old record, specimen not extant, however, for Milwaukee." Not only are dates lacking for three of Hoy's specimens, but the whereabouts of all four skins is also unknown. A group of eight was observed at Milwaukee on 21 December 1921; one remained through 7 January 1922 (C. S. Jung; MPM files). Through 1950, these were the state's only records.

On 25 March 1951 one Harlequin was discovered at Milwaukee (D. L. Larkin) and viewed the following day (A. Kruger). Six months later, 1 October 1951, an individual was collected at Milwaukee for the Milwaukee Public Museum (W. Schultz; MPM files). One month later another Milwaukee bird appeared, seen by several observers between 1 and 8 November. The 1950s produced two additional sight observations, both at the Port Washington harbor (Ozaukee County): 5 February – 14 March 1955 (C. P. Frister) and 1 January – 31 March 1956 (T. K. Soulen).

Since 1961, visits of this diminutive surf-lover have become almost an annual affair. Of 48 observations between 1961 and 1989, 41 have come from the Lake Michigan shore. Wisconsin's first Lake Superior bird (5 November 1976, Douglas, G. J. Niemi) was part of an influx that brought 19 birds to northeastern Minnesota. Additional Douglas County birds were found on 30 May 1978 (D. D. Tessen) and 26 October 1985 (R. J. Johnson). Away from the Great Lakes were individuals on the Mississippi River in Pepin County on 25 November 1979 (R. M. Hoffman), in Dane County (14 December 1980—14 March 1981, many observers), in Iron County (17 April 1981, M. E. Butterbrodt), and in Columbia County (7 November 1987, E. Hansen).

Of the 48 sightings since 1960, 32 have occurred between 1 November and 31 March. Earlier fall observations include a Milwaukee bird present from 22 August to 6 October 1974 (J. H. Idzikowski) and one at Racine from 11 to 27 September 1966 (E. B. Prins). Ob-

Harlequin Duck

△   Early March to early June
○   Mid-June to late August
▽   Early September to late December
□   Early January to late February

All records

servers recorded late spring birds at Milwaukee from 3 to 6 May 1976 (D. K. Gustafson), at Racine from 3 April to 6 May 1963 (L. W. Erickson) and 19 May 1962 (photographed, E. B. Prins), and a pair photographed at Sheboygan on 3 June 1988 (D. and M. Brasser). Most remarkable were the female seen off and on in Milwaukee between 10 June and 2 September 1975 (D. K. Gustafson) and the individual in Milwaukee between 3 August and 1 September 1976 (E. J. Epstein).

While the rash of records since 1950 may represent a change in the habits of this northern species, there is a strong possibility that the Harlequin had been present earlier but had gone unnoticed. Observers scanning the Lake Michigan harbors tend to concentrate on the waterfowl swimming out in the open water. A small duck, half-hidden by breaking waves near pilings and breakwaters, is easily overlooked. More records from Lake Superior, as well as Lake Michigan, are to be expected.

Oldsquaw (*Clangula hyemalis*)

STATUS. Common migrant east; uncommon migrant north; rare migrant west. Common winter resident east.
HABITAT. Great Lakes.
MIGRATION DATES. *Fall:* mid-October to early January. *Spring:* late February to mid-May. *Extremes:* 29 September; 14 June.
WINTER. Regularly present along Lake Michigan from Kenosha to Door counties. Occasionally present along Lake Superior.
PORTRAIT. *Birds of Wisconsin:* Plate 11.

Along the Lake Michigan shore, from Kenosha to Door County, the Oldsquaw is a common species from November through April. The first individuals usually appear by 25 October; occasionally they are seen by the 15th; the earliest sighting, 29 September, occurred in 1971 (Ozaukee, T. Bintz). After a late November buildup hundreds or thousands of these birds will be present until late March. By 15 April most have left, with only small flocks or scattered individuals remaining beyond 10 May. The latest departures include 25 May (1961, Ozaukee, K. Brown; 1962, Manitowoc, H. A. Bauers), 26 May (1963, Sheboygan, H. C. Mueller), and the exceptional 14 June bird (1947, Milwaukee, G. H. Orians).

Numbers on Lake Michigan vary widely. The greatest concentrations are usually in the Milwaukee area, where CBC totals have occasionally reached 15,000. During the 1960s, Milwaukee or Hales Corners led all North America in numbers of CBC Oldsquaws. Birds spread out or concentrate offshore during the winter, depending upon the amount of ice present in different areas. Observers usually report flocks in the hundreds on CBCs from Kenosha to Ephraim.

Lake Superior also attracts a modest winter population. Most are Minnesota and Michigan birds, because nearly all of Wisconsin's part of the lake is frozen during the winter months. Observers in Douglas, Bayfield, and Ashland counties primarily see spring and fall migrants, and then only occasionally in small numbers. The largest reported concentration is an estimated 200 in Bayfield County on 22 April 1943 (W. S. Feeney).

In February 1962 severe cold resulted in a virtually complete ice-lock of Lake Superior, forcing ducks to move elsewhere. At least two Oldsquaws wandered inland into Bayfield County; on 11 March, in separate areas, one was found live and one dead (B. F. Klugow). In a similarly cold February in 1967, an individual with a broken wing was found along a Price

Oldsquaw

```
0      25     50 Mi
├───┼───┼───┤
0   25  50  75 Km
```

▦ Winter range
△ Late February to mid-May
▽ Mid-October to early January
☐ Mid-January to mid-February

Records since 1960

County highway on the 14th (H. DeBriyn), while a second was discovered in eastern Douglas County on the 20th (B. Norman).

Away from the Great Lakes this duck is rare in Wisconsin. As a fall migrant it has been recorded up to three times per year since 1940. These sightings during the 1940–1980 period include a 30 September record (1957, Adams, E. Thomsen), 5 in October, 12 in November, and 12 in December. There have been 5 sightings in January, the latest ones occurring on the 10th (1971, Sauk, P. Ashman) and 14th (1961, Outagamie, A. S. Bradford).

Inland, this white-and-black beauty is even rarer as a spring migrant. Since 1940, published reports include a 23 February date (1962, Dodge, P. Burhans), 6 observations in March, and 10 in April, with one bird that lingered until 5 May (1965, Price, A. C. Vincent). Spring sightings were of 1–4 individuals.

Oldsquaws were common at Racine in the 1850s (Hoy 1853b) and considered "very abundant" on Lake

Michigan by Kumlien and Hollister (1903). Somewhat puzzling is Kumlien and Hollister's assessment of inland records. "Of late years becoming more and more common on the inland waters. Twenty-five years ago it was considered 'quite a find' in the interior, and those found were usually young birds in October and November. Now they are anything but rare on most of the larger lakes, and are sometimes taken in numbers even in spring." It is unfortunate that no further evidence was offered to support this statement. Away from the Great Lakes, they are "anything but common" now, and seemingly have been uncommon for at least the last 50 years. Mid-January federal and state waterfowl inventories suggest a significant decline over the past 20 years. The average annual midwinter count has dropped from 2,450 (1950s) to 1,600 (1960s) to 800 (1970s).

Black Scoter (*Melanitta nigra*)

Formerly American Scoter, Common Scoter

STATUS. Uncommon fall migrant east; rare fall and spring migrant elsewhere. Casual summer resident east. Rare winter resident east.
HABITAT. Great Lakes. Inland lakes.
MIGRATION DATES. *Fall:* early October to early January. *Spring:* mid-March to early June.
BREEDING DATA. One record.
WINTER. Rarely present along Lake Michigan from Milwaukee to Kenosha.
PORTRAIT. *Birds of Wisconsin:* Plate 12.

The pattern for the bird formerly known as the American Scoter is similar to that of the other scoters: it is seen most frequently as an October-November migrant, less often as an April–May transient. Numerically, it is on a par with the Surf, but is less numerous than the White-wing.

The earliest fall arrivals have been noted on 27 September (1976, Douglas, G. J. Niemi), 2 October (1977, Ozaukee, D. D. Tessen), and 7 October (1974 Sheboygan, M. F. Donald). In western and northwestern counties since 1935, there have been 16 reports between 15 October and 10 November, plus four late individuals seen in Juneau County on 27 November 1979 (D. G. Follen); and an exceptionally late bird appeared in St. Croix County west of River Falls on 1 January 1977 (C. A. Faanes). On a line between Madison and Oconto during the 1935–1985 span, 12 sightings fell between 16 October and 1 December. Along Lake Michigan the 48 autumn observations (all sightings at one location in one season treated as one record) were made between 2 October and 30 December, mainly between 15 October and 25 November. Most observations have involved from 2 to 6 individuals, but since 1975 observers have seen flocks of 30–40 birds on several occasions.

The midwinter status is not entirely clear. Kumlien and Hollister's (1903) statement that this is a "rather common winter resident on Lake Michigan" no longer

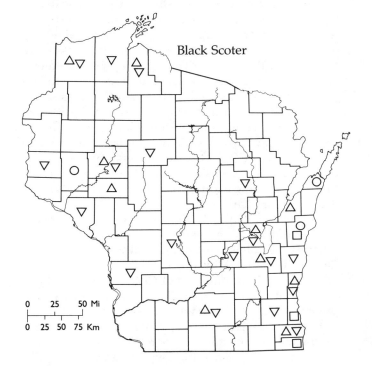

Black Scoter

△ Mid-March to early June
○ Mid-June to early July
▽ Early October to early January
□ Mid-January to early March

Records since 1960

holds. Yet two were seen in Milwaukee on 12 January 1941 (C. N. Mason), with one still present on 28 February (W. J. Mueller), and one appeared in Kenosha on 4 February 1975 (L. W. Erickson), suggesting that on rare occasions an individual may find the wintry waters of Lake Michigan to its liking. A 27 February bird along the Manitowoc County shore (1978, Bro. Columban) could have been a wintering individual or an early spring wanderer. There seems a real possibility that birds wintering somewhere in the Great Lakes may account for Wisconsin's three March detections: the 12th (1955, Ozaukee, G. W. Foster), 17th (1963, Racine, L. W. Erickson), and 24th (1972, Manitowoc, J. Woodcock).

It is between 15 April and 10 May that this dark diver is most apt to be seen in the southeastern counties. Records during this interval have included individuals in Dane, Fond du Lac, and Winnebago counties, as well as a few small flocks along Lake Michigan from Kenosha to Manitowoc. Lake Superior sightings include individuals in Ashland (1983) and Douglas (1967, 1977, 1980) counties, all between 11 May and 9 June.

Until 1981, Wisconsin had no record between early June and late September. So it came as a complete surprise to J. B. Hale to find a female escorting five downy chicks along the Lake Michigan shore in Door County on 6 July, 1981. Equally surprising was the wanderer in Dunn County on 6 and 24 June 1983 (J. L. Polk), possibly the same individual Polk saw on 14 May in Chippewa County. A bird was present in

Manitowoc, 19–24 June 1985 (J. L. Baughman). W. J. Reardon found one in Forest County on 5 July 1986.

Pre-1935 records are few. Although Kumlien and Hollister (1903) implied that birds were numerous on Lake Michigan in winter, and "less common in the interior, occurring principally as a migrant in late fall," they listed no specimens. Hollister added later (1920a, p. 367) that six had been killed at Lake Delavan between 1892 and 1899. This species was included in Willard's list (1885b) of birds for Brown and Outagamie counties, but with no explanatory data. Grundtvig (1895) mentioned it as "shot in Fox River," but gave no further data. Carr (1885a) mentioned having obtained an "American Velvet Scoter" in Madison in the fall of 1885, and described this as "the second record of its occurrence in the interior of the state."

The Milwaukee Public Museum is the repository for specimens taken during the autumn in 1895, 1902, 1922, 1925, and 1940. The University of Wisconsin–Madison collection contains a specimen obtained in Dane County on 2 November 1930 (L. Atkinson; *The Auk* 48:282).

Surf Scoter (*Melanitta perspicillata*)

STATUS. Uncommon fall migrant east; rare spring and fall migrant elsewhere. Accidental summer visitant.

HABITAT. Great Lakes. Inland lakes.

MIGRATION DATES. *Spring:* mid-April to early June. *Fall:* late September to late December. *Extremes:* 5 April, 3 June; 12 September, 30 December.

PORTRAIT. *Birds of Wisconsin:* Plate 12.

Kumlien and Hollister (1903) described the Surf Scoter as "usually found on all the larger inland lakes in late fall . . . not rare on Lake Michigan in winter . . . ," and rare in spring. Yet it was not mentioned at Racine by either Hoy (1853b) or Barry (1854). Grundtvig (1895) mentioned one Brown County bird, shot on 1 October 1883. Schoenebeck (1902) listed a bird shot in Oconto County in November 1897. The Milwaukee Public Museum has three specimens dating from the 1890s, and Hollister collected an additional three at Delavan Lake in Walworth County between 1892 and 1899. But these records hardly qualify the bird for the regular status that Kumlien and Hollister's comments would seem to imply.

Little is known of the status of this species between 1900 and 1940. The MPM acquired four specimens, all taken between 15 and 27 October, donated by hunters. But there are no published data to indicate how

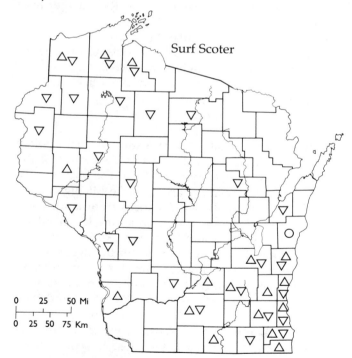

Surf Scoter

△   Mid-April to early June
O   17 to 19 June
▽   Late September to late December

Records since 1960

many other Surf Scoters may have been shot during those decades.

Between 1939 and 1985, *The Passenger Pigeon* published 42 fall records: 4 in the 1940s, 7 in the 1950s, 10 in the 1960s, 17 in the 1970s, and 14 in the 1980s. The lone early September sighting was of four birds on the 12th (1971, Racine, D. D. Tessen). Since 1979, migrants have been noted from 27 September through November, occasionally through 5 December. Late December occurrences include sightings in Dane County on the 18th (1965, G. W. Foster) and 20th (1952, G. W. Foster), Walworth County on the 22nd (1957, C. O. Palmquist), and Racine on the 30th (1967, B. Weber).

Since 1975, sizable flocks have been seen regularly along the Lake Michigan shore in Ozaukee County from mid-October to mid-November, with daily peaks of 40–100 birds (110 on 16 October 1976, D. D. Tessen). Other fall observations, widely scattered throughout the state, were of single individuals or of flocks of three to seven.

Spring observations are fewer in number. Published records, 1939–1985, number only 29: 11 along Lake Michigan from Kenosha to Ozaukee counties, 9 along Lake Superior from Douglas to Ashland counties, and 9 at scattered inland locations. The earliest sighting was of a bird in Ozaukee County on 5 April (1981, D. D. Tessen). The latest was a Douglas County observation on 3 June (1970, H. A. Mathiak). Most of the southeastern records occur between 10 April and 10 May, while western and northern records fall in the 5–30 May interval. Only once has a flock of over a dozen been reported (20 on 3 May 1980, Ozaukee County, D. D. Tessen).

An individual turned up in Manitowoc County on 17 June 1985 (J. L. Baughman), remaining until the 19th (C. R. Sontag). This is Wisconsin's only summer record.

White-winged Scoter (*Melanitta fusca*)

STATUS. Fairly common migrant east; uncommon migrant north; rare migrant elsewhere. Casual summer resident north and east. Rare winter resident east.

HABITAT. Great Lakes. Inland lakes.

MIGRATION DATES. *Fall:* early October to early January. *Spring:* early March to late May.

WINTER. Occasionally present on Lake Michigan from Kenosha to Manitowoc counties.

PORTRAIT. *Birds of Wisconsin:* Plate 12.

Kumlien and Hollister (1903) made two main points when describing the status of this dark diver at the turn of the twentieth century. First, the bird was "at times exceedingly abundant on Lake Michigan, vast flocks being met, at long distances from land." Second, the species was "found on all the larger inland waters from October until the ice makes."

How times have changed! Part of the decline is recent. Bellrose (1976) quoted figures for southern Manitoba showing that a 1957–1961 summer population of 4,700 had plummeted to 1,100 (1962–1966) and then 500 (1967–1971). Part of the decline must have happened earlier than the 1960s. When *The Passenger Pigeon* began publishing field notes, all scoter observations from any part of Wisconsin were deemed worthy of mention.

This bird is a regular fall migrant along Lake Michigan. Birds do not often come into the sheltered har-

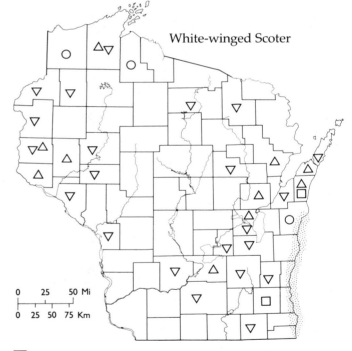

White-winged Scoter

0 25 50 Mi

0 25 50 75 Km

▦ Winter range
△ Early March to late May
○ Early June to early July
▽ Early October to early January
□ Mid-January to late February

Records since 1960

bors; they prefer the open lake. The high bluffs of southern Ozaukee County and Harrington Beach State Park slightly farther north provide two of the best observation points. Here, daily counts of 30–50 birds can sometimes be made in late October and November. The first birds generally appear by 15 October, occasionally by the 5th. The only pre-October dates on record for Lake Michigan are 18 August (1974, Milwaukee, E. W. Peartree), 15 September (1940, Milwaukee, W. J. Mueller), and 30 September (1972, Racine, D. D. Tessen). By early December most birds have moved on, presumably to Atlantic coastal wintering grounds.

A few remain through the winter months nearly every year along the lakeshore from Kenosha to Port Washington, rarely to Manitowoc. Birds are missed entirely on the CBC some years, but from one to eight individuals are counted on the lake in other years. Possibly there are others farther out from shore, but they are rarely found on the federal mid-January waterfowl inventory.

By 1 March, Lake Michigan observers spot a few returning birds. Numbers remain small through March, then build appreciably from 10 April to 5 May, when 20–50 individuals per day are sometimes found. A phenomenal count of 400 was made in Ozaukee County on 3 May 1980 (D. D. Tessen). By 10 May most Milwaukee-area birds are gone, but a few linger through 25 May in Manitowoc, Kewaunee, and Door counties.

Away from the eastern shore, the White-wing is a rare fall and spring migrant. Sightings since 1960 are shown on the map, but in a majority of counties there are only one or two records. Apparently there are now no inland areas where the White-wing can be found regularly in either spring or autumn. La Crosse, Green Bay, Madison, and Lake Geneva (Walworth County) have had the most sightings, from mid-November to late December.

A remarkably early inland migrant was the 12 August 1975 bird in Burnett County (J. O. Evrard). All others were observed between 15 October and 1 January—one or two birds per sighting. The only midwinter observations away from Lake Michigan were one in Waukesha County, early January to 5 March 1966 (E. W. Peartree), and one in Douglas County on 3 February 1968 (M. Baillie). Since 1940, there have been seven spring sightings along Lake Superior and six at inland locations. The earliest: 2 April (1967, Pierce, R. H. Behrens) and 9 April (1958, Bayfield, D. A. Bratley). The latest: 26 May (1975, Douglas, C. A. Faanes).

I know of four summer records: one bird remained in Douglas County from 25 May through 4 July (1967, R. F. Bernard); one was observed in Manitowoc County on 7 July (1963, J. Kraupa); a flock of 14 was noted in Door County, 19–22 June (1960, J. B. Hale); a bird in Ashland County on 15 June (1983, F. Z. Lesher). No summer observations were indicated by any of the commentators in the nineteenth century, when this species was more common.

Common Goldeneye (*Bucephala clangula*)

STATUS. Common migrant. Rare summer resident east and north. Abundant winter resident east; common winter resident south and central; fairly common winter resident north and west.
HABITAT. Great Lakes. Inland lakes.
MIGRATION DATES. *Fall:* mid-October to mid-December. *Spring:* late February to mid-May.
BREEDING DATA. Brood observations: 15 June to 8 July. Clutch size: 6–9 eggs.
WINTER. Regularly present where open water is found.
PORTRAIT. *Birds of Wisconsin:* Plate 11.

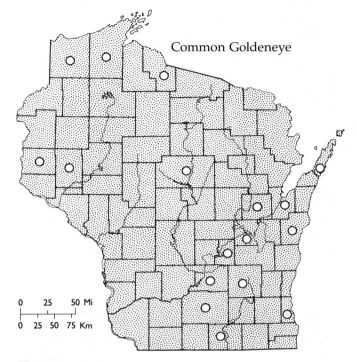

Common Goldeneye

0   25   50 Mi
0   25 50 75 Km

▨ Winter range
○ Late May to late September

Records since 1960

It is only after most teal have departed, and most other ducks have reached or passed their peaks, that the first fall goldeneyes appear. In September isolated individuals have been reported on the 3rd (1949, Marinette, F. Holman King), 10th (1961, Chippewa, C. A. Kemper), 16th (1966, Milwaukee, D. K. Gustafson), and 20th (1973, Trempealeau, S. D. Robbins). These are exceptional sightings and may represent birds that summered in the state. Normally first arrivals are not expected before 10 October. Birds fan out across the state in late October; their numbers peak in mid-November and then diminish as waters freeze in late November and early December. Fall peaks have reached as high as 2,500 at La Crosse (1975); the figure represents the combined total of many small flocks numbering 20–50 birds, rather than a few large rafts.

The "whistler" is best known as a winter resident. Since 1960 it has been recorded on 53% of the CBCs. In the north and west, where open water is limited to small pockets, the birds number in the dozens; at a few central and southern spots, in the hundreds. Along Lake Michigan there are often a thousand or more tabulated in a given circle. The combined Hales Corners and Milwaukee count areas have averaged 4,690 individuals per year since 1960. In 1957, the 13,500 birds at Milwaukee constituted the largest Common Goldeneye tabulation of any North American count that year.

Some of these late December birds depart in early January when more of the open water freezes, but small numbers remain through the winter months in all parts of the state. Early January movements away from frozen-over locations may simply swell the Lake Michigan population. Depending on offshore ice conditions, birds may winter up to half a mile offshore, where they are not visible from land. Mid-January aerial censuses of offshore areas along the entire eastern Wisconsin border recorded an average of 7,300 Common Goldeneyes per year in the 1950s, 10,200 in

the 1960s, dropping to under 3,000 in the 1970s. Annual variations in early winter weather may be important in determining how many of the birds remain in Wisconsin's portion of Lake Michigan waters and how many move to Illinois or Michigan.

Goldeneyes require little open water as they begin spring migration. There is usually some movement by 25 February in the southeastern counties. Birds travel north and west throughout March. The earliest migrants often choose to swim and dive within a few feet of the edge of receding ice. As the 25 March–15 April peak approaches, the males utter their "kee-pah" mating call more frequently and the birds pair off. Most birds leave the southern lakes and streams by 20 April and the northern regions by 30 April. Only a few stragglers remain through 20 May.

A few birds spend the summer each year on Lake Superior in Douglas and Bayfield counties and on Lake Michigan in Door County. Broods were seen in Door County on 16 June 1973 and 6 July 1975 (L. W. Erickson) and on 15 June and 8 July 1976 (J. Trick). Concerning Douglas County birds, Bernard (1967) wrote, "Uncommon in summer; many sight records exist, but without proof of breeding." Kumlien and Hollister (1903) indicated that they had known of nesting in northern Wisconsin, but they were not specific about dates and locations. Nearly every year one or two nonbreeding individuals stay all summer at some Wisconsin location.

Barrow's Goldeneye (*Bucephala islandica*)

STATUS. Rare spring migrant. Rare winter visitant.
HABITAT. Great Lakes. Inland lakes.
MIGRATION DATES. *Fall:* uncertain; not noted before late December. *Spring:* early March to mid-May. *Extremes:* 27 December; 12 May.
WINTER. Occasionally present along Lake Michigan between Manitowoc and Racine counties.
PORTRAIT. *Birds of Wisconsin:* Plate 11.

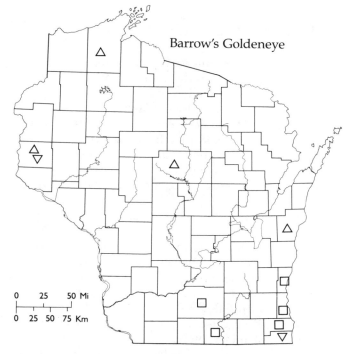

Barrow's Goldeneye

0   25   50 Mi
0   25 50 75 Km

△   Early March to mid-May
▽   Late December to early January
☐   Mid-January to late February

All records

If all the observations that have been published could be relied upon as positive identifications, Wisconsin could claim over 30 records for this wanderer. This, indeed, would be completely out of character for a species that inhabits the coastal East and West, the mountainous West, engages in relatively short migratory journeys, but rarely wanders to the Midwest.

No Wisconsin specimen is extant. A bird thought to be this species, shot in Jefferson County on 14 November 1896 (A. L. Kumlien [Kumlien and Hollister 1903]), proved on reexamination to be a Common Goldeneye. Similarly, specimens taken in Rock County on 4 April 1899, and at Milwaukee on 9 February 1922, proved after careful examination to be *clangula*. Kumlien and Hollister mentioned an 1860 report from Racine (P. R. Hoy) and an 1877 specimen sent to Thure Kumlien after being taken in Rock County. But these specimens no longer exist. In the winter of 1934–1935, E. B. Prins (pers. comm.) secured a specimen at Racine that had been frozen in the harbor ice, but it was inadvertently destroyed.

Four observations of adult males have been substantiated by photographs. One bird, filmed in Ozaukee County on 5 March 1967 (E. B. Prins), had been present since 28 January (E. W. Peartree). Pictures were obtained of a bird noted at Milwaukee between 24 February and 2 March 1969 (D. K. Gustafson). Between 9 March and 1 April 1972 one was present in Manitowoc County, photographed and vividly described by John Woodcock. G. W. Foster discovered a bird on 27 December 1973, and gave me a thorough description over the telephone. Documentation was never published, but between that date and 24 February 1974, many observers saw this rarity, and several people obtained film evidence.

Before the first of these Barrow's was photographed, four others had been well documented after close observation under favorable conditions. A male observed in northeastern Manitowoc County on 29 March 1946 was accompanied on 1 April by a probable female (W. M. Smith). On 12 May 1959 D. A. Bratley found a bird in Chequamegon Bay off Bayfield County. It was on 5 February 1961 that a male, in company with a probable female Barrow's, was seen swimming in the Rock River in northeastern Rock County, close to a group of 100 Common Goldeneyes (M. T. Maxson). Another turned up in Milwaukee on 2 January 1967 (L. A. Johnson).

Additional Ozaukee County individuals were reported in 1969 (15 January–15 February, R. H. Sundell) and 1971 (early January–7 March, T. Bintz). Carefully identified birds were sighted in Milwaukee in 1972 (15 January–29 February, M. F. Donald) and 1980 (1–4 April, M. F. Donald). Good details were submitted (WSO files) for a Kenosha County sighting on 30 December 1978 (R. R. Hoffman).

Outside southeastern Wisconsin there is one winter record: a male near Hudson (St. Croix County) on 1–2 January 1977 by Manley Olson (Faanes 1981). North-

ern and western Wisconsin have three additional spring sightings: 3 May 1966 (Marathon, S. N. Doty), 8 May 1975 (Bayfield, A. J. Roy), and another 8 May 1975 male (St. Croix, C. A. Faanes).

Bufflehead (*Bucephala albeola*)

STATUS. Common migrant. Rare summer resident north and east. Fairly common winter resident east; rare winter resident west and north.
HABITAT. Great Lakes. Inland lakes.
MIGRATION DATES. *Fall:* early October to late December. *Spring:* mid-March to mid-May.
WINTER. Regularly present along Lake Michigan from Kenosha to Ozaukee counties. Occasionally present north to Douglas, Bayfield, Ashland, Portage, and Door counties.
PORTRAIT. *Birds of Wisconsin:* Plate 11.

In fall, Buffleheads follow a time schedule similar to the Common Goldeneye's, usually arriving around 10 October. But exceptionally early arrivals have been noted in August on the 16th (1966 and 1972, Dane, T. L. Ashman), 19th (1980, Eau Claire, J. L. Polk), and 25th (1983, Kewaunee, E. J. Epstein). There are an additional four mid-September arrival dates on record.

Jahn and Hunt (1964) listed only four areas where substantial fall concentrations occur: Green Bay, Lake Geneva in Walworth County, and the Mississippi River in Pierce and La Crosse counties. The La Crosse area had an estimated peak of 2,820 birds on 5 November 1975 (K. Butts). At other points around the state, small groups of 10–50 individuals are the rule. During weekly checks between 1948 and 1956, Jahn and Hunt found a 15 November peak, then a rapid decline after 1 December. The same time schedule still holds.

"Butterballs" are listed on from 3 to 13 CBCs each year. These late December sightings have come from Lake Superior in Douglas, Bayfield, and Ashland counties, the St. Croix–Mississippi River valley north to St. Croix County, the Wisconsin River valley north to Portage County, and the Lake Michigan shore north to Door County. In most instances these birds are lingering fall migrants that are gone by early January. Mid-January waterfowl inventories generally show 300–400 birds in the state. Noteworthy are the flock of 40 still present in Burnett County on 14 January 1949 (F. A. Hartmeister) and the individual that wintered in Douglas County in 1965–1966 (R. F.

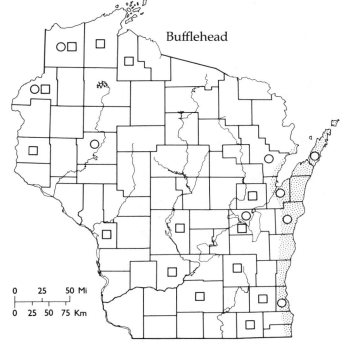

Bufflehead

0   25   50 Mi
0 25 50 75 Km

▓ Winter range
○ Early June to early August
□ Early January to late February

Records since 1960

Bernard). Most January and February observations have been along Lake Michigan.

In spring the Bufflehead's migration timetable is a bit behind the Common Goldeneye's. The Bufflehead is more likely to wait until a lake is nearly free of ice before it puts in an appearance at inland locations. There are a handful of 1–10 March records where birds did not overwinter, and even a 25 February sighting (1949, Dunn, H. M. Mattison). First arrivals are normally expected by 15 March in the south, 25 March in the central regions, and 10 April in the north. Most of Wisconsin's spring migrants are moving northwest from Atlantic coastal wintering grounds to the Canadian prairie provinces. The peak hits the southeastern counties between 5 and 15 April and the northwest between 20 April and 10 May. In most areas a peak means a modest daily total of 20–30 birds. At the major refuges 200–300 birds are present. In 1969, Necedah National Wildlife Refuge personnel in Juneau County counted a phenomenal 1,760 birds on a peak April day.

Most birds have moved on by 15 May in the south and by 20 May in the north. Occasionally, individuals linger until June. Very late wanderers were noted on the 14th (1980, Door, R. J. Lukes), 16th (1964, Douglas, R. F. Bernard; 1984, Winnebago, T. Ziebell), and 17th (1976, Burnett, N. R. Stone). Midsummer records in the twentieth century were unknown until 1970, when a male remained near Cornell (Chippewa County) through 12 July (S. D. Robbins). A female was discovered in Oconto County on 15 July (1974, D. D. Tessen); another female was seen in Brown County

on 16 July (1976, J. Trick). A straggler was present in Milwaukee County from 17 June into August (1977, D. K. Gustafson); another appeared in Manitowoc County on 16 July (1978, R. Korotev).

Kumlien and Hollister (1903) stated, "Immature birds are frequently taken in the larger inland lakes in summer, but are evidently not breeding." The sole record of nesting is credited to B. F. Goss, who once captured flightless young near Pewaukee (Waukesha County) (Schorger 1946). No date was given, but Goss did most of his collecting between 1866 and 1883.

Numbers have undoubtedly decreased since the time of Kumlien and Hollister, and these observers had in fact referred to the species as "greatly diminished in numbers in recent years." At present, the population is relatively stable, but the Bufflehead is not one of our more numerous divers.

Hooded Merganser (*Lophodytes cucullatus*)

STATUS. Fairly common migrant. Fairly common summer resident central and north; uncommon summer resident east. Uncommon winter resident south and east; rare winter resident west and north.

HABITAT. Inland lakes and streams.

MIGRATION DATES. *Spring:* early March to late April. *Fall:* mid-September to late November.

BREEDING DATA. Nests with eggs: 11 April to 18 June. Clutch size: usually 7–10 eggs; occasionally 6–12.

WINTER. Regularly present north to Dane, Walworth, and Milwaukee counties; occasionally present north to Polk, Bayfield, Vilas, and Oneida counties.

PORTRAIT. *Birds of Wisconsin:* Plate 13.

No commentator nowadays describes the Hooded Merganser as abundant. That term was, however, applied to it by Hoy (1853b), Barry (1854), King (1883), Hollister (1893), Kumlien and Hollister (1903), and Cory (1909). Schorger (1929b) aptly summarized its status for Dane County: "The Merganser is still a common migrant, but its numbers have decreased greatly."

One hesitates even to call the species common in the 1980s. As a spring migrant the Hooded Merganser is listed among the least numerous ducks in Waukesha (Bielefeldt 1974b), St. Croix (Goddard 1975), and Barron (Faanes 1975a) counties. It must be pointed out, however, that these three studies were more concerned with lakes and ponds than with rivers and

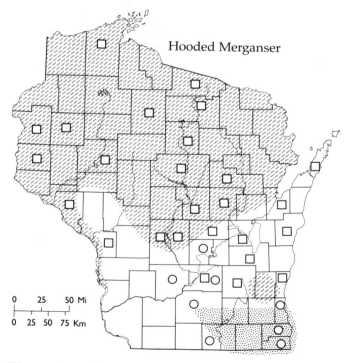

Hooded Merganser

0 25 50 Mi
0 25 50 75 Km

▨ Summer range
▦ Winter range
○ Early May to late August
□ Early December to late February

Records since 1960

swamps, where this merganser is typically found. At Necedah (Juneau County), where spring peaks numbered 200–300 birds in the early 1940s, they now rarely exceed 100.

The first "Hoodies" do not wait for a complete ice breakup. Patches of fast-running river water are enough to bring a few birds to the southern counties during the first 10 days of March. Observers have found migrants in the south as early as 26 February (1944, Dane, A. S. Jackson) and 2 March (1966, La Crosse, F. Z. Lesher), and in the north by 12 March (1966, Burnett, N. R. Stone). The main migration period is from 25 March to 15 April in the south, and from 10 to 30 April in the north. All or most of the individuals present on 15 May are likely to be present for the summer. Most observers find this species in small groups of 2–15 birds; only at the major refuges are there reports of 50–300 birds, usually as collections of small flocks of 5–20 individuals.

This species is an early nester. Egg-laying has been observed as early as 11 April, and broods have been sighted by 21 May. Since broods of small young have been seen as late as 4 and 8 August, it can be presumed that incubation sometimes extends into July. C. H. Richter once found an Oconto County nest in a cavity 45 feet up in an elm. Francis Zirrer (pers. comm. to O. J. Gromme; MPM files) discovered a Sawyer County nest 40 feet up in a butternut tree, which blew down in a storm the following day. Four eggs had broken, but eight remained intact, "protected by a peck of fibrous material, apparently brought in by squirrels at some prior time." At times, this species appropriates Wood Duck nest boxes for its own use; occasionally, both species lay eggs in the same nest.

Theoretically, the bird's summer range should blanket the state. Nesting records are known for nearly all states east of the Mississippi River. Kumlien and Hollister (1903) summarized, "Breeds sparingly, in suitable localities, from the southern tier of counties northward." As the twentieth century has progressed, "suitable localities" have disappeared from most of southern Wisconsin. Since 1960, breeding records have been confined to the northern half of the state, with three exceptions: (1) the Mississippi River region south to Crawford County, (2) the central region drained by the Wisconsin River and tributaries south to Juneau and Adams counties, and (3) a pocket encompassing the Kettle Moraine State Forest area of Dodge, Washington, Ozaukee, and Waukesha counties.

The fall migration is inconspicuous, for this species continues the retiring habits it exhibits strongly throughout late spring and summer. Some influx is noted from 15 September on. Peaks run from 15 October to 10 November; most birds depart by 25 November. Necedah has had peaks of 100–400 birds annually since 1960. Otherwise, no sizable concentrations have been reported. Hoodies probably constitute less than 1% of the ducks harvested every autumn, judging by the number of wings registered by fall hunters.

Since 1960, CBC records show late December birds present at from three to nine locations per year. Ordinarily, this means 1–10 individuals at a given site. Although some late December stragglers disappear in early January as the freeze-up widens, a few remain all winter every year. Some have lingered in open spots along rivers north to Barron (1976), Chippewa (1970, 1976), Price (1971), Vilas (1972), Oneida (1963), and Shawano (1980) counties. Away from the rivers, one was found in Bayfield County on 21 December 1965 (B. F. Klugow); another was seen in Door County on 15 December 1979 (C. M. Lukes).

Common Merganser (*Mergus merganser*)

Formerly American Merganser

STATUS. Common migrant. Uncommon summer resident north. Common winter resident south; fairly common winter resident central; rare winter resident north.

HABITAT. Great Lakes. Inland lakes.

MIGRATION DATES. *Spring:* mid-February to late April. *Fall:* early October to early January.

BREEDING DATA. Nests with eggs: 27 May to 11 June. Clutch size: usually 7–9 eggs; occasionally 5–12.

WINTER. Regularly present north to St. Croix, Chippewa, Portage, Outagamie, Brown, and Door counties; occasionally present north to Douglas, Ashland, and Marinette counties.

PORTRAIT. *Birds of Wisconsin:* Plate 13.

In late December 1955, Milwaukee CBC observers tallied 10,168 Common "Mergs," while a few miles farther south Racine observers counted another 8,104. The following year the respective totals were 12,000 and 3,887. No numbers have come close to matching these figures before or since. During the 1946–1954 era, Milwaukee counts averaged 1,800 individuals. For the 1957–1961 span the average was 315 per year. Since 1961 the annual total has exceeded 100 only once. The larger flocks are now found farther east in Michigan.

Fall migrants often wait until 25 October to put in a first appearance. Observations predating 15 October are rare, but include two exceptional September 1974 dates: the 7th (La Crosse, F. Z. Lesher) and 30th (Ozaukee, D. K. Gustafson). November is the main month for migration, a time when flocks of 10–300 pay at least brief visits to the larger lakes and rivers. Gatherings of 1,000 or more have been observed in Brown, Winnebago, and Green Lake counties. The 15–25 November freeze-up sends most of these migrants on their way to wintering grounds south and east of Wisconsin.

Where open water permits, the fall migration extends through December. The CBC has recorded Common Mergansers north to Douglas and Bayfield counties in the west, to Oneida and Langlade counties in the central region, and to Marinette and Door counties in the east. Many of these birds were lingering fall migrants that moved on by early January. Birds present between 10 January and 10 February are the only ones that can be termed true winter residents. Mid-January aerial surveys by state and federal waterfowl biologists since 1950 show that counts of Common and Red-breasted Mergansers diminish

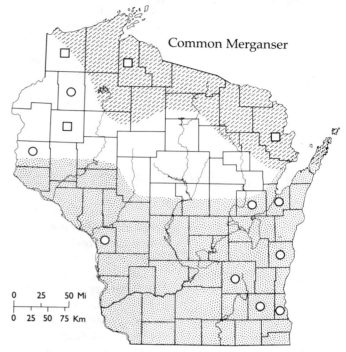

Common Merganser

0   25   50 Mi
0 25 50 75 Km

▨ Summer range
▧ Winter range
○ Mid-May to early September
□ Mid-January to early February

Records since 1960

from CBC totals in early January. In the 1950s the average annual midwinter tally of "large mergansers" was 4,600; this declined to 2,800 in the 1960s and to under 400 in the 1970s. Small numbers winter north to St. Croix, Juneau, Adams, Winnebago, and Door counties, but most of the birds remain on lower Lake Michigan.

Early spring migrants sometimes are noticeable by 15 February, surely by 1 March, in southern and central counties. Birds often make it as far north as Burnett and Douglas counties by 15 March, vying with the Common Goldeneyes for emerging patches of open water. In late March it is fascinating to watch a group of 50 birds swimming rapidly and playfully within a few feet of the edge of receding ice. As soon as the ice is gone, the mergs move on; peak numbers occur in the south between 20 March and 10 April, and in the north between 5 and 20 April. Most birds have left the south by 25 April, the north by 5 May. Late May stragglers have been found on the 24th

(1962, Columbia, K. Brown), 25th (1950, Outagamie, N. M. Rogers), 29th (1976, Winnebago, D. K. Gustafson), and 30th (1964, Racine, B. Weber). A female also lingered at Racine until 5 June (1965, R. E. Fiehweg).

Northern Wisconsin lies barely within the merg's breeding range. Broods have been observed in Sawyer, Rusk, Price, Langlade, Outagamie, and Oconto counties, as well as in the northernmost counties. In early June 1939 and 1940 Carl Richter investigated six nests on islands in Door County. The birds were nesting in cavities in basswood trees. One pair chose an 8-foot stump with an entrance at the top and a drop of 5 feet to the floor of the cavity. Another pair used a tree that had an entrance 30 feet up and a drop of more than 25 feet to the cavity floor. Quite a climb and drop for newly hatched chicks!

Presumed nonbreeders were recorded on 21 June (1961, Sheboygan, H. Koopmann), 22 June (1975, St. Croix, B. A. Moss) through 30 June (1966, injured in Waukesha, J. E. Bielefeldt), and 29 June through 6 July (1967, Milwaukee, D. K. Gustafson).

Red-breasted Merganser (*Mergus serrator*)

STATUS. Common migrant east and west; fairly common migrant elsewhere. Uncommon summer resident north. Fairly common winter resident east; rare winter resident elsewhere.
HABITAT. Great Lakes. Inland lakes.
MIGRATION DATES. *Spring:* late February to mid-May. *Fall:* early October to early January.
BREEDING DATA. Nests with eggs: 6 June to 25 July. Clutch size: usually 8–12 eggs; occasionally 6–17.
WINTER. Regularly present along Lake Michigan from Kenosha to Ozaukee counties; occasionally present north to Buffalo, Wood, and Door counties.
PORTRAIT. *Birds of Wisconsin:* Plate 13.

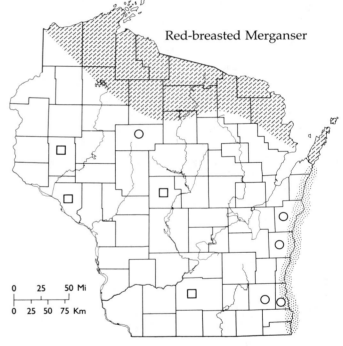

Red-breasted Merganser

▨ Summer range
▦ Winter range
○ Early June to late September
□ Mid-January to mid-February

Records since 1960

The timing of the fall migration of the Red-breast closely parallels that of the Common Merganser. Early arrivals have been noted on 11 September (1966, Dane, T. L. Ashman) and 21 September (1968, Sheboygan, D. K. Gustafson). The first migrants usually are not found until 10 October, with another 10 days elapsing before more birds appear. Most of the birds that choose an inland route hurry through in early November, ahead of the late-November freeze-up. Those birds choosing a Lake Michigan route extend their migration through December; few are left after 5 January except in the Milwaukee-Racine-Kenosha region.

Although Red-breasts are reported in fall from the western and central counties, they gravitate toward Lake Michigan far more than other mergansers do. In biweekly aerial and ground censuses between 1948 and 1956, federal and state waterfowl researchers found this species on only 17 of 200 inland waterfowl areas (Jahn and Hunt 1964). Necedah National Wildlife Refuge personnel in Juneau County recorded only 2 years in the 1938–1973 span when autumn Red-breasts were noted. Rarely have gatherings of more than 50 individuals been reported on inland lakes and streams, except on Mississippi River pools. Larger counts are made along Lake Michigan, where 200–700 are sometimes found—not as a single flock but as a total of several small flocks of 10–20 birds.

In late December, CBC results show that a few individuals sometimes remain along Lake Superior in Douglas, Bayfield, and Ashland counties; along the

St. Croix and Mississippi rivers north to St. Croix and Buffalo counties; along the Wisconsin River north to Juneau and Adams counties; in the northeast in Marinette and Menominee counties; and on Lake Michigan north to Door County. By early January nearly all birds have departed.

In January and early February the Red-breast is regularly present only along the Lake Michigan shore from Ozaukee County south. There have been occasional observations in Dunn (1949), Buffalo (1973), Wood (1972), Dane (1941, 1957, 1975), and Manitowoc (1971) counties.

This species, like the Common Merganser, begins its spring migration about 15 February along the southern Lake Michigan shore. At Racine, numbers build to 500–800 in late February and early March. But there the similarity of these mergansers' migration schedules ceases. Although the Common pushes north and spreads across the state in March as rapidly as melting ice permits, the Red-breast moves only gradually north along Lake Michigan. Few birds move up the Mississippi or appear at other inland locations before 1 April. By 15 April observers in Pierce and St. Croix counties find 300–500 Red-breasts, and small groups of these birds show up on various inland lakes. Late April brings peaks of 1,000–2,000 in Racine and Milwaukee counties, 300–500 in Ozaukee and Sheboygan counties, and modest numbers to Lake Superior. In the south, numbers diminish after 5 May, with only an occasional straggler after the 15th. In the north, birds move out rapidly after a 1–15 May peak, with virtually all birds gone by 25 May.

This bird has long been known to nest on the islands off Door County. Kumlien and Hollister (1903) mentioned records before 1886. Strong (1912) made a detailed study of seven nests there in June 1911. In 1939 and 1940, Carl Richter collected data on nine nests. Nineteen nests were observed in 1975 (T. C. Erdman; C. G. and M. A. Kjos). After spending part of the summer of 1919 in northwestern Wisconsin, H. H. T. Jackson (1943) wrote, "These 'fish ducks' were frequently seen on Lake Superior, more commonly along the shores of the islands, but also in the coves and inlets of the mainland." After censusing the Apostle Islands in Ashland County in 1957 and 1958, Beals (1958) concluded that the Red-breast was the most common summer duck there.

Broods were discovered at several unusual sites in the 1940s: in Racine and Marathon counties in 1948 (E. B. Prins) and in Dunn County in 1949 (Buss and Mattison 1955). Since 1960, however, breeding has been known only in the northern counties, south to Douglas, Sawyer, Lincoln, and Door counties. One wonders if the female which R. J. Lukes observed escorting 36 chicks in Door County in mid-July 1980 was a professional baby-sitter! Apparent nonbreeders have been recorded in June and July in Milwaukee (1961, 1967, 1971, 1977), Waukesha (1975), Sheboygan (1964), and Taylor (1974) counties.

Ruddy Duck (*Oxyura jamaicensis*)

STATUS. Common migrant. Uncommon summer resident south, east, and west. Uncommon winter resident south and east.
HABITAT. Inland lakes. Ponds. Shallow marsh.
MIGRATION DATES. *Spring:* late March to mid-May. *Fall:* early September to late November.
BREEDING DATA. Nests with eggs: 20 May to 9 August. Clutch size: usually 6–10 eggs; rarely 5–15.
WINTER. Occasionally present north to Dane, Winnebago, Brown, and Ozaukee counties.
PORTRAIT. *Birds of Wisconsin:* Plate 11.

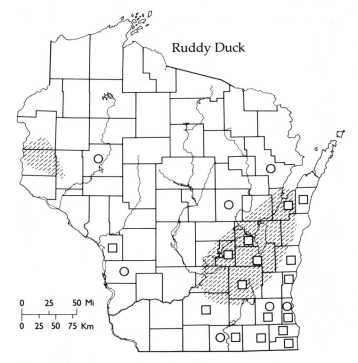

Ruddy Duck

0   25   50 Mi
0 25 50 75 Km

▨   Summer range
○   Late May to late August
☐   Mid-December to early March

Records since 1960

Although this chubby little diver breeds regularly in both western and eastern Wisconsin, winters in small numbers in some Lake Michigan harbors, and is highly migratory, it is not statewide in distribution. Bernard (1967) listed it as a rare transient in Douglas County, with sightings in May and August. I have been unable to locate another record for the northernmost tier of counties. Records from the second and third tiers are also scarce, except for Polk County in the extreme west and Oconto and Marinette counties in the extreme east. North of a line from St. Croix Falls through Wausau to Marinette, the Ruddy is rare at any season.

South of this line, this species is a common migrant—sometimes abundant at one or two concentration points. Spring birds passing through Wisconsin are moving westward from Atlantic coastal wintering grounds (mainly the Chesapeake Bay) to breeding grounds in Saskatchewan, Manitoba, North Dakota, and western Minnesota. They associate closely with shallow ponds in heavily farmed areas; thus, the wetlands of northern Wisconsin are not their preferred habitat. Spring migrants sometimes concentrate at Green Bay (2,500 on 15 April 1975), sometimes on Lake Winnebago (thousands in mid-April 1965), sometimes disperse into many smaller wetlands. A given location can have a large flight one year and a virtual absence the next.

Unusually mild weather in early March 1974 brought birds to Fond du Lac County on the 7th and to Waukesha, Dane, and Winnebago counties on the 9th. Usually, few birds are seen before 20 March in the southeast. At the Necedah National Wildlife Refuge in Juneau County, the earliest arrival date for the 1946–1958 period was 30 March. In Dunn County, 1942–1951, the earliest date was 17 April. In St. Croix County, 1961–1968, I found this bird to be consistently the last of the ducks to arrive—usually between 15 and 20 April. Peak numbers usually occur

between 10 and 25 April in the east, 25 April and 10 May in the west. Individuals present beyond 20 May are likely to remain through the summer.

The size of the state's breeding population fluctuates widely. In 1973, March, Martz, and Hunt (1973) estimated an annual breeding population of 400. Within 2 years it had risen to 3200. Horicon Marsh in Dodge County attracts the largest summer population each year (J. R. March, pers. comm.), with smaller numbers scattered over other prairie marshes between Goose Pond in Columbia County and Green Bay. A second nesting region in western Wisconsin encompasses portions of Dunn, St. Croix, and Polk counties. Broods have been observed between 20 June and early September.

During September local birds and those moving east from the major breeding grounds congregate at a few concentration points, building to a peak from mid-October to early November. A chief concentration point is Lake Winnebago, where 10,000–20,000 birds are not unusual. In 1963 a peak of 50,000 was estimated. On 5 November 1975 W. E. Wheeler estimated 57,388 birds. Green Bay is another heavy concentration point, with smaller numbers on various lakes in Winnebago, Fond du Lac, Green Lake, and Columbia counties. Birds diminish greatly by 5 November in an ordinary year, but in 1974 Green Bay still held 10,000 on 23 November; 80 were still present for the Oshkosh CBC on 14 December.

The number of Ruddies wintering in the state each year is very small. Occasionally there have been groups of 10–20 in the harbors at Port Washington (Ozaukee County) and Milwaukee through January and February. Usually, from one to six birds winter at two or three southeastern locations. CBC observations have been made north to Winnebago and Kewaunee counties; there is also one record for La Crosse (1967).

Ruddies are missed entirely on the mid-January waterfowl inventory in some years; up to 50 birds are found in southeastern counties in other years.

Masked Duck (*Oxyura dominica*)

STATUS. Accidental. One record.
HABITAT. Inland lakes.

It must have been a much-traveled female Masked Duck that appeared in Rock County in November 1870. Thure Kumlien procured this wanderer along the Rock River, and determined that it was not a form of the similarly plumaged Ruddy Duck. At the time it was the second record for the United States. This species has been more at home in South America than in North America, and it was probably a flight greater than 2,000 miles off course that brought this stranger to southern Wisconsin. The AOU *Check-list of North American Birds* mentions accidental wanderings to Maryland, Massachusetts, Vermont, and Tennessee, and assigned a "casual" status to the bird in southern Texas, Louisiana, and Florida.

Even in death, Kumlien's bird traveled widely. For many years the specimen was housed in the collection of the Boston Society of Natural History after Brewer (1872a) had confirmed the identification. Then the specimen was transferred to the University of Michigan. Early in 1950, personnel at the Milwaukee Public Museum negotiated for its exchange and obtained it for that institution.

Family **Cathartidae:** American Vultures

Black Vulture (*Coragyps atratus*)

STATUS. Accidental. Three records.
HABITAT. Old field. Open grassland and cropland.
MIGRATION DATES. Observed between 2 July and early November.
PORTRAIT. *Birds of Wisconsin:* Plate 14.

Janesville High School has a specimen of the Black Vulture, killed on a nearby farm in November 1925. Exact date and collector are unknown, but Naeser (1931d), a student at the time, published an account 6 years later.

On 2 July 1951, a crippled bird was captured at the Kotraba farm on the south side of Milwaukee. After a week in captivity, the bird was checked and photographed by J. L. Diedrich and William Schultz of the Milwaukee Public Museum staff, and then placed in the Milwaukee County Zoo. Diedrich's notes describe the bird as having "dull black plumage, short square tail, folded wings to the end of tail, white shafts of primaries and light under surface of primaries, black head with feathers to occiput on nape, wingspread 58 inches."

A sight record followed in 1980. While trapping hawks at the Woodland Dunes Nature Center in Manitowoc County on 26 October, James Steffen spent 20 minutes observing a Black Vulture flapping and soaring with two adult Red-tailed Hawks. The next day what may have been the same individual was sighted 40 miles to the south at the Cedar Grove Ornithological Station in Sheboygan County by Dan Berger and Chris Whelan. The bird remained in sight for 25 minutes, flew directly over the observers less than 100 feet up, and was photographed by Whelan (*Pass. Pigeon* 43:143–144, 44:125).

Two additional sightings are highly probable. H. L. Stoddard observed a bird near Prairie due Sac (Sauk County) in the spring of 1909. Sight records were looked upon with considerable doubt in that era, so this record went unpublished for many years. Writing to O. J. Gromme in 1952, Stoddard remembered: "It circled right over my head when I was plowing on the old farm. . . . There was no question about identification; had seen thousands in Florida before 1900. It was along in April or early May, and I can see the bird in my mind's eye as clearly as if it was yesterday."

The second sighting involved an injured bird captured in southern Lincoln County by Arthur Chase on 19 September 1943. At first it was thought to be an immature Turkey Vulture. But after examining the bird on 25 September, F. R. Zimmerman (MPM files) wrote: "It appears to me to be a Black Vulture. It lacks the grayish brown fur-like feathers around the head. The head and neck are bare and blackish in color. Feathers of neck extend up back of head in a point." Unfortunately, no one snapped a photograph, and the specimen has now been lost.

Although this species migrates but little, it has wandered sufficiently to neighboring states to suggest that further Wisconsin observations are entirely possible.

Turkey Vulture (*Cathartes aura*)

STATUS. Uncommon migrant. Uncommon summer resident. Casual winter resident.

HABITAT. Upland deciduous forest.

MIGRATION DATES. *Spring:* mid-March to mid-May. *Fall:* early September to late November.

WINTER. Occasionally present in late December and January north to Buffalo, Jackson, Oneida, and Marinette counties.

PORTRAIT. *Birds of Wisconsin:* Plate 14.

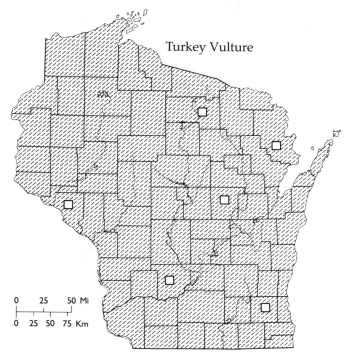

Turkey Vulture

0   25   50 Mi

0   25 50 75 Km

▨ Summer range
☐ Late December to late January

Records since 1960

The scenery is always spectacular along the Mississippi River on the Great River Road between Maiden Rock and Fountain City. It is even more so on a summer afternoon when 15 or more vultures can be seen lazily riding the air currents around and above the high bluffs. With nary a flap of the wing a bird may soar for miles, buoyed up on distinctively tilted wings. It was to the presence of Turkey Vultures in this area that Stoddard (1947) was referring when he described them as common, on a summer 1910 collecting trip. Through 1945 this was the one area in Wisconsin where "buzzards" could be regularly seen in summer. Breeding was sometimes suspected but never proved. Elsewhere in the state, records of migrating or wandering birds were few and far between.

The nineteenth-century observers thought of this species as an uncommon wanderer from southern climes, mainly along Wisconsin's eastern and western margins, during July and August. They knew of isolated records as far north as Manitowoc, Outagamie, Brown, Portage, and Iron counties.

In the late 1940s, significant population increases became noticeable. In 1948, in the Kettle Moraine State Forest region in Waukesha County, observers were aware of flocks of a dozen or more, remaining throughout the summer. Another communal roost was developing simultaneously in Oconto County, producing a count of 22 birds in 1950. It was here that C. H. Richter discovered the first positive nest record for the state: a juvenile not yet feathered-out on 20 July 1947.

During the late 1960s, still larger roosts developed in the Baraboo hills in Sauk County. Extensive studies between 1973 and 1976 revealed the presence of 50–65 birds each year, and the discovery of one or two nests each year (Mossman 1976).

Groups of similar size were reported near Cassville (Grant County) before 1965, but numbers dissipated in succeeding years (R. Bandekow; according to G. J. Knudsen 1976). During the 1970s, summer concentrations of 20 or more individuals were recorded in

Pierce and Clark counties, suggesting that additional roosts may be developing. These roosts are apparently made up largely of nonbreeders. But additional nests have been reported from Pierce (24 July 1955, Manley Olson), Oconto (2 June 1974, T. C. Erdman), and Waukesha (17 June 1980, J. E. Bielefeldt) counties.

It is perhaps a misnomer to speak of a Turkey Vulture "nest." Mossman's (1976) studies show that breeding birds lay one or two eggs in a narrow rocky crevice where the flat rock surface is covered with old leaves. Since the hatching that he recorded occurred between 25 May and 11 June, there is a presumption that egg-laying may start any time after 15 April. Young become capable of flight by early August.

As recently as 1950, there were spring observations in fewer than five counties. In 1978, spring sightings were reported in 28 counties. Spring and summer sightings in the 1980s come from all parts of the state.

When William Smith (pers. comm.) counted raptors 3–4 days a week near Potosi (Grant County) between 29 January and 2 May 1974, he found this bird to be the third most numerous raptor species at that location. The 91 individuals counted between 21

March and 2 May were exceeded only by the numbers for the Bald Eagle and the Red-tailed Hawk.

In the southern counties, spring migrants can be expected any time between 20 March and 30 April, with the 5–20 April period providing a peak. Exceptionally early are records on 26 February (1989, Columbia, M. Korducki), 28 February (1942, Racine, E. Madsen), 4 March (1950, Rock, C. Southwick; 1983, Sauk, K. I. Lange), and 7 March (1977, Walworth, E. Carnes). In northern Wisconsin, migration starts around 5 April, with maximum numbers appearing between 20 April and 10 May. Unusually early is a 6 March individual (1964, Douglas, R. F. Bernard).

First departures come soon after 1 September. Most migrants move between 20 September and 10 November. Exceptionally late November birds have been observed on the 23rd (1948, Burnett, N. R. Stone), 27th (1970, Racine, D. and J. Joslyn), and 30th (1950, Burnett, H. A. Erickson), with even later fall stragglers on 10 December (1977, Dane, S. Thiessen) and 12 December (1973, Douglas, J. Degerman).

Nine remarkable winter records are known: 27 December 1973 (Buffalo, L. Maier), 30 December 1974 (Oneida, P. V. Vanderschaegen), 1 January 1975 (Sauk, CBC), 1 January 1976 (Sauk, CBC), 2 January 1972 (Waukesha, E. W. Peartree), 9 January 1947 (partly decomposed bird estimated to have been killed 3 weeks previously in Jackson, W. Radke), 9 January 1949 (Juneau, H. Skilling), 15 January 1989 (Waupaca, M. Korducki), 26 January 1947 (Dane, W. E. Scott), and 28 January 1976 (Marinette, L. J. Lintereur).

It is not known if most of Wisconsin's summer vultures winter in the southern United States, or if they move on to Mexico and Central America. But there is one banding recovery: an individual banded as a nestling in Sauk County on 2 August 1973 (D. D. Berger) was retaken near San Sebastian, Honduras, on 8 March 1974.

Family **Accipitridae:** Kites, Eagles, Hawks

Osprey (*Pandion haliaetus*)

STATUS. Uncommon migrant. Uncommon summer resident north; rare summer resident central.
HABITAT. Great Lakes. Inland lakes. Wooded swamp.
MIGRATION DATES. *Spring:* early April to mid-May. *Fall:* early August to mid-October. *Extremes:* 7 March; 2 January.
BREEDING DATA. Nests with eggs: probably 5 May to 30 June. Clutch size: 2 or 3 eggs.
PORTRAIT. *Birds of Wisconsin:* Plate 18.

Looking at a map of the Osprey's breeding range, which covers North America from Hudson Bay to the Gulf Coast, one might expect this bird to occur throughout Wisconsin each summer wherever suitable lake and river habitats exist. The nineteenth-century observers found it to be so. Kumlien and Hollister (1903) described the Osprey as a "summer resident in all the suitable localities in the state, but not common anywhere."

They also detected the beginnings of a change. "Summer resorts, with all the attendant features, have driven the fish hawks from many of the smaller lakes where they formerly bred." By 1940, summer birds had deserted most southern and central wetlands. The most recent summer sightings were made in Ozaukee (1941) and Dane (1946) counties. Since 1960, the breeding region has been north of a line from St. Croix Falls through Stevens Point to Marinette, with the exception of a few birds along the Wisconsin River south to Mauston and the Necedah National Wildlife Refuge in Juneau County.

In the 1950s and 1960s, production of young showed an alarming decrease. Berger and Mueller (1969b) detected a noticeable reduction of young per active nest between 1951 and 1965. Sindelar (1971a) reported a further decline in the 1965–1969 period. In 1955 the state's largest concentration was on the Rainbow Flowage, in Oneida County, where up to 25 nesting pairs were present. By 1970 the number of nesting pairs had dwindled to four. Aerial surveys of the U.S. national forests in northern Minnesota, northern Wisconsin, and Upper Michigan conducted by U.S. Forest Service personnel since 1962 have shown that fewer than 60% of the Osprey nests have produced young in most years. Sindelar reported even more drastic production declines: only one-third of 90

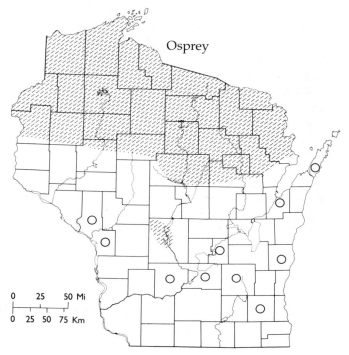

Osprey

0 25 50 Mi
0 25 50 75 Km

▨ Summer range
○ Late May to late July
Records since 1960

known Wisconsin nests produced young in 1969. Small wonder that this species was placed on the Wisconsin endangered species list.

Two recent developments have helped the Osprey stage a comeback. One was the 1969 ban on DDT in Wisconsin, followed by a nationwide prohibition, which resulted from the disclosure that pesticide-induced eggshell thinning cut seriously into the production of young. The second was the successful experiment of constructing artificial nest platforms, providing sturdier and more sheltered nest sites. Results have been particularly encouraging at the Mead Wildlife Area in Marathon County, the Rainbow Flowage in Oneida County, and the Turtle Flambeau Flowage in Iron County. In 1989, the Bureau of Endangered Resources transferred the Osprey from "endangered" to "threatened" status.

Usually observers spot first arrivals between 1 and

10 April, with the main migration occurring from 15 April to 10 May. A remarkably early spring bird was found dead in Iowa County on 7 March 1941 (*fide* A. G. Koppenhaver). Other exceptional March observations have been reported on the 13th (1952, Lafayette, E. Olson), 17th (1959, Waukesha, E. Hoffmann; 1972, Dane, N. Ashman), 22nd (1953, Burnett, H. Barrett), 23rd (1947, Dunn, H. M. Mattison), 24th (1962, Chippewa, C. A. Kemper), and 26th (1974, Grant, W. A. Smith). An occasional migrant may still be seen south of the breeding range as late as 20 May. Migrants observed beyond 5 May are likely to be nonbreeders or Canada-bound individuals, since most Wisconsin breeders have reached nesting territory, repaired old nests, and prepared for egg-laying by that time.

July is banding month. Young are old enough to be ringed but are not yet mature enough to leave the nest. Birds banded in July have been recovered before the end of the ensuing September in Georgia, Florida, Alabama, Arkansas, Kansas, Oklahoma, and Texas. There are late fall or winter recovery records from Haiti, Panama, Colombia, and Ecuador for birds banded in northern Wisconsin nests the previous July.

The fall migration is often under way by 15 August, occasionally as early as 1 August. With only 15–30 birds being counted at any of the hawk observation points in the course of an autumn flight, it is hardly appropriate to speak of a migration peak. But birds are most frequently observed in the 25 August–30 September period, with scattered individuals seen through 15 October nearly every year. Birds occasionally linger through October. There are seven November records: the 6th (1947, Milwaukee, D. L. Larkin), 9th (1968, Marinette, R. J. Flaherty), 10th (1953, Dane, M. A. Walker; 1975, Sheboygan, D. D. Berger), 25th (1945, Dane, A. W. Schorger), 27th (1979, Chippewa, J. L. Polk), and 29th (1959, Columbia, D. Cors). Most remarkable were six even later stragglers, seen in December on the 3rd (1977, Sheboygan, D. D. Berger), 22nd (1983, Outagamie, J. S. Anderson), 27th (1969, Shawano, K. E. Hafemann), 28th (1985, Sauk, K. I. Lange), and 31st (1970, St. Croix, Manley Olson), and one on 2 January (1983, Fond du Lac, W. K. Volkert).

American Swallow-tailed Kite (*Elanoides forficatus*)

STATUS. Accidental. Four modern records.
HABITAT. Wooded swamp. Open grassland.
MIGRATION DATES. Observed between 15 May and 8 June. One September record.
BREEDING DATA. Formerly bred.
PORTRAIT. *Birds of Wisconsin*: Plate 17.

The A. J. Schoenebeck collection, now preserved at the University of Wisconsin–Stevens Point, contains a specimen of an adult female Swallow-tailed Kite and an egg, taken from her nest in Oconto County on 23 July 1906. Five years earlier, on 26 July 1901, another specimen was taken by Richard Blome (Deane 1906a) in Ashland County.

These were the only records known for northern Wisconsin at the time. Indeed, for most of the first half of the twentieth century, they appeared to be the final Wisconsin appearances of this southern raptor. Hoy (1853b) found it nesting near Racine until 1848. Thure Kumlien (L. Kumlien 1891c) observed a nest in Dane County in 1854. Ludwig Kumlien wrote (1891c), "I have several times seen them in the southern part of the state, but never found them nesting." Kumlien and Hollister (1903) mentioned a Milwaukee County male collected on 15 May 1888 and donated to the Milwaukee Public Museum. Barry (1854) referred to the Swallow-tail's presence in southeastern Wisconsin as "at one time quite numerous upon our prairies, and quite annoying to us in grouse shooting; now rarely met with in this vicinity."

The decline that must have become evident by 1850 had become almost complete by 1900. Schorger (1951a) concluded, "It is doubtful if it will again be found in the state."

Yet even as Schorger wrote, a major autumn 1949 storm brought two of these flyers to southern Minnesota and one to western Wisconsin. H. M. Mattison observed this kite on 27 September 1949 perched on a snag on an island at Menomonie (Dunn County). The bird spent two hours devouring a snake or frog (*Pass. Pigeon* 12:52).

On 30 May 1965, G. J. Knudsen and family had a breath-taking view of a soaring bird at Blue Mounds State Park in western Dane County. The 5-minute observation was brief, but sufficient to show off the spectacular antics of this southern species (*Pass. Pigeon* 28:12).

In May and early June 1982, one or more of these

aerial acrobats performed for another 30 observers. Between 15 and 17 May, outside a popular restaurant near Valmy (Door County), several astonished diners joined J. B. Hale in observing the soaring and stooping of a Swallow-tail. By 31 May another, or what may have been the same bird, turned up at Oconomowoc (Waukesha County). Richard Sharp discovered the wanderer and shared subsequent observations on 6 and 8 June with several other birders (*Pass. Pigeon* 45:42–44).

Northward movement has been reported increasingly in the 1970s and 1980s, reaching Vermont, Massachusetts, New Jersey, Pennsylvania, Indiana, and Illinois. The wandering usually occurs in May.

Black-shouldered Kite (*Elanus caeruleus*)
Formerly White-tailed Kite

STATUS. Accidental. Two records.
HABITAT. Open grassland and cropland.

The Black-shouldered Kite is nonmigratory. Its normal range comes no closer to Wisconsin than Louisiana and Texas. Its extralimital wanderings are far less extensive than those of the Mississippi and Swallow-tailed Kites. Despite all these odds, there was one standing on a fence post in western Portage County when Frances Hamerstrom (1965) drove by on 6 June 1964. During the next 3 weeks it was photographed by Joseph Hagar and observed by dozens of appreciative watchers as it perched on fence posts and trees, fed on mice and voles, and displayed the aerial acrobatics that are typical of kites. The most spectacular exhibitions of flying occurred when the wind was gusting to 40 miles per hour.

The bird's movements were carefully monitored. It spent most of its time in sections 26 and 27 (T21N, R7E), where it was seen defending territory against Northern Harriers. Only three times between the first and last sightings, on 6 and 27 June, was the bird observed outside these two sections. One sighting was 4 miles north. Extended efforts to trap the kite were unsuccessful (*Pass. Pigeon* 27:3–7).

A second Black-shouldered Kite appeared in Wood County on 15 May 1987, discovered by Dennis Seevers. The time and place were a happy coincidence, for the annual meeting of the Wisconsin Society for Ornithology was in progress at Marshfield 20 miles away. K. J. Luepke led a caravan of 65 eager birders to the site where D. G. Follen was monitoring the bird on 16 May. The bird disappeared on the 17th (*Pass. Pigeon* 50:85–86).

There may be some correlation between the rapid expansion of the species' population and range in California and Central America in the early 1960s and the bird's appearance in Wisconsin. Eastward wanderings of this species have recently occurred in Florida and South Carolina, and westward sightings north to Oregon have been frequent. The only other Midwest observations are birds in Arkansas and Minnesota in 1976 and in Arkansas and Indiana in 1981.

Black-shouldered Kite, 6 June 1964, Portage County (photo by J. Hager)

Mississippi Kite (*Ictinia mississippiensis*)

STATUS. Casual migrant.

HABITAT. Wooded swamp. Inland lakes and streams.

MIGRATION DATES. *Spring:* mid-May to late June. *Fall:* early September. *Extremes:* 14 May, 25 June; 10 September, 20 September.

September 1970 produced some remarkable raptor observations in the upper Midwest. None were more astonishing than two sight records for this southern wanderer on consecutive days. It was nearly 6 P.M. on 10 September at the end of a hawk-trapping day at the Cedar Grove Ornithological Station in Sheboygan County when D. D. Berger caught sight of what he first took to be a Peregrine Falcon. When the flier did not make the expected response to the lures, Berger took a closer look. The bird's head and body were an unusual harrierlike gray; the body was slimmer and the tail longer than a Peregrine's, with the tail broadening instead of tapering near the tip. The buoyancy of the flight further convinced Berger he was seeing Wisconsin's first Mississippi Kite (*Pass. Pigeon* 33:155).

The following afternoon, 150 miles farther north in Oneida County, Louise and Paul Engberg were boating on Tomahawk Lake when a flock of 20–25 gray falconlike birds flew by not more than 20 feet overhead. Light heads, yellow hooked beaks, and long,

Mississippi Kite

△   14 May to 25 June
▽   10 to 20 September

All records

Mississippi Kite, 21 May 1972, Door County (photo by E. B. Prins)

narrow, slightly notched tails were all clearly visible. The birds appeared to be in adult plumage (*Pass. Pigeon* 33:155–156).

These are Wisconsin's first sight records. Little did anyone realize that the ensuing decade would produce an additional seven sightings. Two of these were substantiated by photographs: one in Door County (21 May 1972, E. B. Prins) and one in Milwaukee County (20 May 1978, H. A. Bauers). Two observations were made on the same day, 14 May 1977: one in Oconto County (D. K. Gustafson), the other 30 miles south and 3 hours later in Brown County (R. Korotev; *Pass. Pigeon* 40:387–388).

The most northerly observation of the species was made at the Crex Meadows Wildlife Area in Burnett County on 27 May 1976 by P. B. Hofslund, G. J. Niemi, and members of an ornithology class (*Pass. Pigeon* 39:204). A Dane County observation on 17 May 1979 (M. Myers; *Pass. Pigeon* 42:51), and an Ozaukee County sighting on 5 June 1980 (M. E. Decker) document 5 consecutive years of Mississippi Kite visits to Wisconsin. But there was a 5-year lapse before the next sighting: 25 June 1985 in Dane County by G. W.

Foster and J. T. Emlen (*Pass. Pigeon* 48:92). In 1987 there were Ozaukee County sightings on 7 June (M. F. Donald) and 20 September (W. A. Cowart).

Writing in *The Wisconsin Naturalist*, Ludwig Kumlien (1891c) listed this species as "a bird of Wisconsin and no doubt used to breed if they do not at the present day. They must be rated among our rarest hawks, however." But since this kite was not listed in

The Birds of Wisconsin (1903), even in the hypothetical list, Kumlien must have realized that his earlier statement was in error.

I. mississippiensis appears to be broadening its range. Illinois had its first nesting records in 1972. First sight records occurred in Minnesota in 1973 and 1975, New England in 1969, and Iowa in 1978. Birds are sighted almost annually in New Jersey.

Bald Eagle (*Haliaeetus leucocephalus*)

STATUS. Fairly common migrant west; uncommon migrant east. Uncommon summer resident north and central; rare summer resident southwest. Fairly common winter resident west; uncommon winter resident north and central.

HABITAT. Inland lakes and streams. Wooded swamp.

MIGRATION DATES. *Spring:* mid-February to late April. *Fall:* late September to early January.

BREEDING DATA. Nests with eggs: probably 15 March to 25 May. Clutch size: 2 or 3 eggs.

WINTER. Regularly present along the Mississippi, Chippewa, and Wisconsin rivers north to St. Croix, Chippewa, and Portage counties; occasionally present throughout the northern counties.

PORTRAIT. *Birds of Wisconsin:* Plate 18.

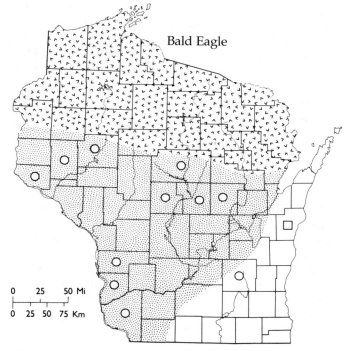

Bald Eagle

```
0    25    50 Mi
0  25  50  75 Km
```

▨ Resident range
▦ Winter range
○ Mid-May to early September
□ Early January to early February

Records since 1960

"The summer resorts about our lakes have gradually driven this species from its former nesting haunts." This sounds like a 1980s commentary on the effects of motorboats and summer resorts on our northern lakes. Actually, it was Kumlien and Hollister's (1903) appraisal of a late nineteenth-century decline from Lake Koshkonong in Jefferson County and other southern lakes. The withdrawal these authors foresaw has continued unabated in the twentieth century.

With two notable exceptions along the Mississippi River in Grant and Crawford counties, breeding birds have long since withdrawn from southern Wisconsin. Pairs ceased nesting along the Lake Michigan shore in the mid-1950s. Sindelar (1985) could find but 10 nesting pairs in the central counties in his statewide survey of 1984. In the north, nesting has diminished on the Apostle Islands in Ashland County, and along the Lake Superior shore. Only along northern Wisconsin lakes and streams where relatively little human disturbance occurs have these impressive raptors come close to holding their own.

Low points in breeding populations were reached in the 1960s. Widespread DDT use resulted in the thinning of egg shells and a serious decline in the

number of young produced in Wisconsin nests. After the DDT ban in 1969, the 1970s and 1980s have seen a gradual increase in nest success and in number of eagle-nesting territories. Since 1973, when this species was added to the Wisconsin endangered species list, eagle nesting has been closely monitored by personnel of the U.S. Forest Service and the Wisconsin Department of Natural Resources. Sindelar (1985) indicated that the number of young produced in Wisconsin nests more than doubled between 1973 and 1984.

The main breeding territory is in the northern third of the state, north of a line from St. Croix Falls through Medford to Oconto. Public interest in these nests has led to an "adopt-an-eagle" program sponsored by the DNR Bureau of Endangered Resources, whereby an individual or organization pledging $100 or more receives pictures and a report of an active nest. By 1989, nesting success had improved enough to warrant a change in status from "endangered" to "threatened."

To many Wisconsinites this species is better known as a winter resident. Wherever water is kept open by dams along the major rivers of central and western Wisconsin, these impressive predators are likely to be present. Concentrations of 20 or more are frequent at Petenwell Dam (maximum of 70 on 30 December 1961), at Alma-Nelson (108 on 1 January 1970), at Prairie du Sac–Mazomanie (52 on 1 January 1965), and at Cassville (Grant County) (302 on 17 December 1983). Smaller numbers, 1–10, winter regularly in other open-water regions along the Mississippi and St. Croix rivers north to Hudson, along the Chippewa north to Chippewa Falls, and along the Wisconsin north to Stevens Point.

Winter records exist for nearly every county north of these points, indicating that individuals occasionally remain throughout the state. In areas where open water and fish are not available, the birds survive on carrion. Sindelar (pers. comm.) reports finding remains of deer, coyote, beaver, raccoon, porcupine, raven, and muskrat in eagle feeding areas. Only along the Lake Michigan shore is there a significant amount of open water and a complete absence of Bald Eagles in winter.

To help preserve suitable wintering territory, the Eagle Valley Foundation, organized in 1970, purchased prime wintering lands in Grant and Sauk counties and helped with the national midwinter population survey. This survey is conducted annually between 10 January and 10 February, the relatively brief period between the end of the fall migration and the start of the return flight.

A few migrants follow the Lake Michigan shore in spring and fall, but it is an unusual season when more than 15 are spotted at any of the eastern Wisconsin hawk-banding stations. The migration is far heavier along the Mississippi.

Migration is prolonged. In fall, sightings have been made at the Cedar Grove Ornithological Station in Sheboygan county as early as 13 September; but most observations have been made between 1 October and 15 November. It is during this same span that individuals are most frequently seen at the main waterfowl refuges. These birds disappear when the water freezes. Along the major rivers of central and western Wisconsin the migration may continue through late December. Some relocation even occurs in early January, if some stretches of open water freeze then.

Immatures travel considerable distances in fall. From the 700 or more eaglets Sindelar has banded in northern Wisconsin since 1964, there have been recoveries in Kentucky, Mississippi, Arkansas, Oklahoma, and Texas. Adults that have established breeding territories in northern Wisconsin probably winter in or near Wisconsin—close enough to return by early March. Northbound migrants are frequently observed in Grant County after 20 February. Birds migrating in late March and April may be nonbreeders.

Northern Harrier (*Circus cyaneus*)
Formerly Marsh Hawk

STATUS. Common migrant. Common summer resident south, east, and central; fairly common summer resident west and north. Uncommon winter resident south.

HABITAT. Open grassland and cropland. Sedge meadow.

MIGRATION DATES. *Spring:* early March to mid-May. *Fall:* mid-August to mid-November.

BREEDING DATA. Nests with eggs: 20 April to 5 August. Clutch size: usually 3–5 eggs; rarely 6–8.

WINTER. Irregularly present north to St. Croix, Chippewa, Marathon, Shawano, Brown, and Manitowoc counties; rarely present north to Burnett, Sawyer, Lincoln, and Kewaunee counties.

PORTRAIT. *Birds of Wisconsin:* Plate 14.

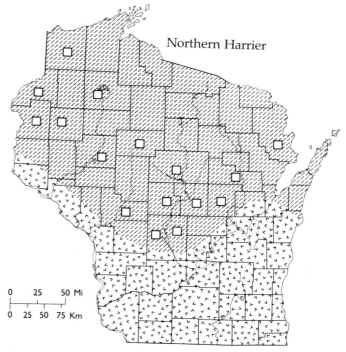

Northern Harrier

0   25   50 Mi

0 25 50 75 Km

▨ Resident range
▨ Summer range
▢ Early December to mid-February

Records since 1960

The Northern Harrier's spring migration is a prolonged one. If bare patches of ground are present, a few arrivals can be expected during the first week of March, or even in late February. N. R. Stone noted remarkably early birds in Burnett County on 17 February 1954 and 28 February 1951. Numbers gradually increase through March, with the main part of the migration occurring between 1 and 20 April. Migrants may still be moving north through 15 May.

At the Cedar Grove Ornithological Station in Sheboygan County there is observed at times a "reverse migration" of southbound birds in April and early May. One such bird, banded on 7 May 1964 (D. D. Berger), was recaptured in southwestern Michigan 4 days later. Possibly birds may drift farther west than they intend, then attempt an eastward correction. Upon striking the Lake Michigan shore, they may circle south rather than fly across the lake.

It is probable that this bird nests in every Wisconsin county, but its abundance is greatly limited by its narrow habitat preferences. The extensive grass meadows and marshes that it favors are numerous only in the southern, eastern, and central portions of the state. In one such area, the Buena Vista Marsh in Portage County, Frederick and Frances Hamerstrom (pers. comm.) have found as many as 27 nesting pairs in a year. Their studies show that the number of nests is highest when the vole population is high. But during the period of widespread use of DDT (1964–1969), harrier populations declined alarmingly and remained low even when vole numbers were high. An encouraging increase has been noted on the Buena Vista Marsh since 1969.

Reporting on seven nests in Oconto and Marinette counties, C. H. Richter observed that all nests were on the ground, usually in a clump of willow brush surrounded by a wet marshy area. The Hamerstroms (pers. comm.) have recorded 1 nest with six young between hatching and fledging, 22 nests with five young, 28 with four, 24 with three, 9 with two, 3 with one, and 12 nests that were entirely unsuccessful. The Hamerstroms' banding data indicate that birds that nest successfully one year usually return the following year, while those that are unsuccessful may not return.

Suitable nest habitat is less abundant in western and northern regions. Observers frequently see harriers in the prairie pothole areas of St. Croix and Polk counties and at the Crex Meadows Wildlife Area in Burnett County. Elsewhere north of Highway 64, there is a significant drop-off in summer populations.

Fall and spring migration are similar: both are diffuse. Migrants (immatures) have been detected moving past the major hawk-observation posts by 10 August but at little more than a trickle. Adults join the flight around mid-September. The main movement takes place between 25 September and 5 November; observers witness a few transients through 20 November.

Although the Northern Harrier can stand Wisconsin cold, the bird will not tolerate the deep snows that make rodents, its principal food, hard to find. In December 1960, after a relatively sparse early winter snowfall, the CBC tallied 75 individuals on 23 of 47 counts. The following year, after heavier snowfall, only 8 were found on 46 counts. The yearly average since 1960 is 28 individuals on 15 of 70 counts. How many of these remain and survive through late winter

is not known. The likelihood is that in the northern half of the state nearly all of them have disappeared by the end of January, except during winters of exceptionally light snow.

Birds that pass through Wisconsin in fall disperse widely across the southern United States in winter. The winter and early spring recoveries for birds banded in Wisconsin the previous summer and fall show that many birds move in a southeasterly direction after leaving the state. One bird traveled from Wisconsin to North Carolina in 21 days; another flew from Wisconsin to South Carolina in 20 days.

Sharp-shinned Hawk (*Accipiter striatus*)

STATUS. Common migrant. Uncommon summer resident north; rare summer resident central. Uncommon winter resident south and east; rare winter resident west and north.

HABITAT. Coniferous forest. Northern maple-hemlock-pine forest. Lake shores (during migration).

MIGRATION DATES. *Spring:* late March to late May. *Fall:* early August to late November.

BREEDING DATA. Nests with eggs: 5 May to 15 June. Clutch size: 4 or 5 eggs.

WINTER. Occasionally present north to Pierce, Eau Claire, Portage, Shawano, and Kewaunee counties; rarely present north to Douglas, Oneida, and Marinette counties.

PORTRAIT. *Birds of Wisconsin:* Plate 15.

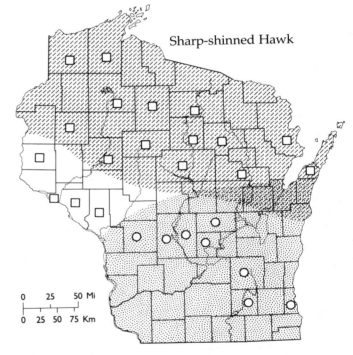

Sharp-shinned Hawk

▨	Summer range
▦	Winter range
○	Early June to late July
□	Early December to early March

Records since 1960

Next to the Broad-winged Hawk, the Sharp-shin is the most numerous raptor passing the major hawk observation posts during autumn. Instead of the "kettles" of 100 or more Broad-wings, the Sharpy migration consists of from one to three individuals at a time. But on a peak day in autumn 200–400 birds can be expected. The all-time high at the Little Suamico Ornithological Station in Oconto County was 550 (26 September, T. C. Erdman). At the Cedar Grove Ornithological Station in Sheboygan County, two spectacular days have been recorded, with over 1,200 birds counted on 15 September 1952 and on 13 October 1955 (H. C. Mueller; D. D. Berger).

Although many birds are concentrated along Lakes Michigan and Superior, many others disperse widely across the state. Given a clear September or October day with a northwest breeze, and an unobstructed vantage point, one is likely to see at least an occasional Sharpy coasting or flapping overhead—particularly during late morning or early afternoon. At

woodland edges in early morning, one sometimes encounters a Sharp-shin hunting small birds or animals for breakfast. The hawk feeds largely on small birds but frequently attacks species as large as Northern Flickers.

A few Sharpies are migrating by 5 August. By

15 August the movement picks up and continues through 20 October before tapering off. There are two peaks: 10–25 September for immatures, 5–15 October for adults. Observers have seen a few late migrants in November, and the Sharpy has been recorded at Cedar Grove as late as 6 December.

Significant numbers of fall migrants have been trapped and banded along the Lake Michigan Flyway. There are over 40 instances of fall birds being recovered before the following summer. One made it to Mississippi in 9 days, one to Alabama in 17, one to Louisiana in 29, and one to Georgia in 34. Banding data also show that some Wisconsin birds winter considerably farther south. Birds banded at Cedar Grove were recovered in Guatemala 3 and 5 years later. Two other Cedar Grove birds were recovered in Mexico 1 and 8 years later.

Although most Sharp-shins move far south for the winter, a few scattered individuals remain in the state. From 2 to 17 individuals have been reported on the CBC every year since 1952. The bird cannot be described as a regular winter resident anywhere in the state. Yet winter records exist for nearly every county north to St. Croix, Dunn, Eau Claire, Marathon, Shawano, Oconto, and Kewaunee. Before 1970, winter observations north of this line were virtually absent. During the 1970s an increasing number of observations occurred in Douglas, Bayfield, Sawyer, Price, Taylor, Oneida, Langlade, and Marinette counties.

Numbers reported for spring migration represent a small fraction of those in fall. Far less time has been spent studying patterns of spring migration for most Wisconsin hawks. It is not clear whether birds sighted before 20 March can be considered true migrants or whether they may be birds that have wintered nearby. By 25 March an occasional bird has been spotted in obvious migratory movement, but the migration does not get under way consistently until 10 April. The principal flight occurs between 20 April and 10 May, with late stragglers sometimes detected until 5 June.

Most of these migrants move on into Canada for the summer; a few remain in the northern counties. Breeding has been reported south to Polk, Portage, and Manitowoc counties. Small numbers may be present regularly north of a line from St. Croix Falls through Stevens Point to Two Rivers. In addition, there have been isolated June and July sightings in Monroe, Juneau, Adams, Waushara, and Marquette counties. The summer of 1959 was exceptional: June and July observations occurred in Dane (W. L. Hilsenhoff), Rock (F. Glenn), and Columbia (D. Cors) counties. The following year there was a 21 June discovery in Jefferson County (T. K. Soulen). Unusual also were the observations in Dodge (19 June 1970, J. F. Fuller; 9 June 1979, D. D. Tessen) and Grant (10 June 1978, R. Korotev) counties.

During the nineteenth century, the Sharp-shin probably nested in small numbers in the southeastern counties. Hoy (1853b) considered the bird a breeding species, and Kumlien and Hollister (1903) mentioned two breeding records for the Milton area in Rock County, but they gave no details.

Cooper's Hawk (*Accipiter cooperii*)

STATUS. Uncommon migrant. Uncommon summer resident. Uncommon winter resident south and central.

HABITAT. Deciduous forest. Northern maple-hemlock-pine forest.

MIGRATION DATES. *Spring:* late March to early May. *Fall:* late August to late November.

BREEDING DATA. Nests with eggs: probably 10 April to 20 June. Clutch size: usually 4 or 5 eggs; occasionally 3 or 6.

WINTER. A few regularly present north to Buffalo, Portage, Outagamie, and Manitowoc counties; irregularly present north to Barron, Shawano, Marinette, and Door counties.

PORTRAIT. *Birds of Wisconsin:* Plate 15.

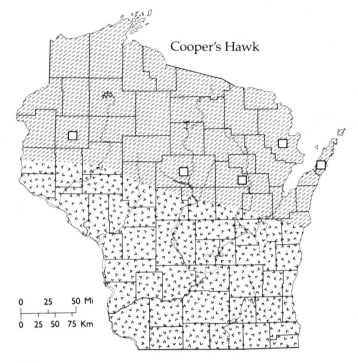

Cooper's Hawk

0   25   50 Mi
0 25 50 75 Km

☐¹ᵞ Resident range
▨ Summer range
☐ Early December to early March

Records since 1960

Virtually every commentator from Hoy (1853b) to Buss and Mattison (1955) considered the Cooper's Hawk a common migrant and summer resident. This audacious species thrived wherever woodlands and developing farmland existed close together, preying especially on flocks of exposed poultry. Schorger (1929b) wrote for Dane County that it "exceeds in numbers all other members of the family."

Poultry flocks are still numerous today, but the Cooper's is not. At the Cedar Grove Ornithological Station in Sheboygan County the total number of migrants per autumn shrank significantly in the 1960s. At Duluth this species is now a rarity. At the Little Suamico Ornithological Station in Oconto County the numbers observed in fall in the early 1970s represented but 0.15% of the total hawks seen. The decline has been so widespread that *American Birds* placed this predator on its Blue List of declining species when the list first appeared in 1971. By universal acclaim from observers in all parts of North America, the Cooper's has remained on this list each succeeding year. In Wisconsin, the Department of Natural Resources noted the "changing status" of the species in 1973 and listed it as "threatened" 6 years later (Les 1979).

Why the decline? The likelihood is that the widespread use of DDT and similarly persistent organochlorines, which had adversely affected the nesting success of the Bald Eagle, Osprey, and Peregrine Falcon, also took its toll on the Cooper's Hawk. With the banning of indiscriminate use of these pesticides in 1969, hopes for recovery increased. Frances Hamerstrom (1972) observed that whereas she knew of no breeding Cooper's in central Wisconsin from 1962 to 1970, she located five pairs in 1971.

Between 1980 and 1983, Rosenfield and Anderson (1983) researched this species under the auspices of the DNR Bureau of Endangered Resources, and noted an encouraging increase. Between 1980 and 1982 these observers studied 83 active nests in 23 counties, with 57 nests producing young of bandable age. In 1989 the Cooper's Hawk was removed from the state's list of threatened species.

Early spring migration may begin by 15 March, although the presence of a few overwintering birds complicates the migration picture. North of the winter range, individuals have been found in Bayfield County on 18 March (1964, J. L. Kozlowski) and in Lincoln County on 25 March (1968, D. J. Hendrick). The 25th is a more typical arrival date for the southern half of the state, with the main migration occurring between 10 and 25 April. The few that move north of Wisconsin for summer residency have left the state by 10 May. Unusually late was a 20 May 1963 migrant in Sheboygan County (H. C. Mueller).

Long before the middle of May most birds are paired and nesting. C. H. Richter estimated that in 17 of 19 nests observed between 1923 and 1957 incubation had begun by 15 May. The earliest evidence of incubation he encountered was on 19 April 1957, where egg-laying may have started a week earlier. Near Marsh-field (Wood County) during the early twentieth century, John Stierle (MPM files) estimated that incubation began between 1 and 15 May for all but 1 of 18 nests; the exception was a 10 June 1910 nest with fresh eggs.

Before the most recent decline, there were summer records from most Wisconsin counties. During the 1960s, however, there was alarmingly little evidence of breeding. There were occasional summer sightings by some observers, but hawk-investigators T. C. Erdman (northeastern Wisconsin) and Frances Hamerstrom (central Wisconsin) could find no nests between 1963 and 1970. A majority of the summer observations since 1960 have come from the central counties. But there are enough records both north and south to consider the summer range to be statewide.

The fall migration extends from late August to early November. Ordinarily, a peak day might have meant 10–20 birds before the decline of the 1960s. An exceptional flight at Cedar Grove produced 50 birds on 13 October 1955 (D. D. Berger). The 1970s saw a slight increase over the small numbers of the 1960s. But it is still inappropriate to speak of a fall "peak" at present. Most birds are reported between 15 September and 20 October; observers have seen late stragglers passing Cedar Grove as late as 24 November (1976, D. D. Berger).

A few Cooper's Hawks are reported every winter. At least four have been listed on the CBC every year since 1950. In the 1960s and 1970s numbers dropped slightly from the 18–20 birds noted in 1958 and 1959, but maintained an average of 11 individuals per year. Nearly all observations have come from the southern and central regions, north to St. Croix, Chippewa, Wood, Portage, Outagamie, and Manitowoc counties.

Northern Goshawk (*Accipiter gentilis*)

STATUS. Uncommon resident north. Uncommon migrant central and south. Rare winter resident central and south, uncommon when irruptions occur.

HABITAT. Deciduous forest. Northern maple-hemlock-pine forest.

MIGRATION DATES. *Fall:* early September to late November. *Spring:* early March to late April.

BREEDING DATA. Incubation dates: probably 10 April to 15 May. Clutch size: probably 2–4 eggs.

WINTER. Regularly present south to Burnett, Portage, and Brown counties; irregularly present throughout the state.

PORTRAIT. *Birds of Wisconsin:* Plate 15.

The Northern Goshawk is a powerful flier best known as a fall migrant or winter visitant during those years when it invades Wisconsin in exceptional numbers. Perhaps once every 8 or 10 years, when Ruffed Grouse and snowshoe hares are in short supply, an invasion occurs that sends birds into all parts of Wisconsin at any time between October and April. Mueller and Berger (1967a) pointed out the magnitude of the fall 1962 flight by comparing the 55 migrating birds they counted with the usual seasonal total of 0–5 birds. Nearly as large a flight occurred the following year. If sustained observations could be made at Superior's Wisconsin Point, even greater counts could be made. Bernard (1967) recorded 40 individuals there in 1 hour

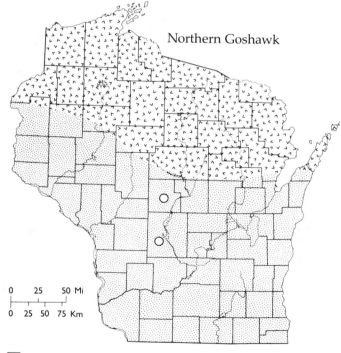

Northern Goshawk

0   25   50 Mi
0 25 50 75 Km

⌄⌄ Resident range
∴∴ Irruptive winter range
○ Early May to mid-August

Records since 1960

on 14 April 1964 and another 44 on 22 March 1965. A spectacular flight of 1,800 hawks on 8 April 1967 was mostly Goshawks.

Even more remarkable was the 1972–1973 invasion that not only blanketed Wisconsin but also sent birds all the way to Louisiana. One-day high counts at the Cedar Grove Ornithological Station in Sheboygan County totaled 206 (14 October, D. D. Berger) and 215 at the Little Suamico Ornithological Station in Oconto County (15 October, T. C. Erdman). Many—if not most—of the 5,100 birds counted at Duluth that fall must have passed into Wisconsin. This flight began earlier than usual (25 August, Wood, D. G. Follen) and extended later than usual into December. Instead of the 5–8 individuals normally recorded on CBCs, the 1972 state total was 39. In 1973 at least three birds remained until summer well south of the usual breeding range (7 July, Chippewa, S. D. Robbins; 11 July, Wood, D. G. Follen; 22 July, Juneau, F. Z. Lesher). In a better-than-average ensuing flight during the fall of 1973, Bernard Brouchoud (pers. comm.) banded 33 birds in Manitowoc County between 15 October and 28 November.

In noninvasion years only a trickle of birds move south of a line from St. Croix Falls through Stevens Point to Green Bay. They can be seen any time from 10 September to 25 April. Movement has been detected at Little Suamico by 12 August, but the main migration period extends from 10 October to 10 November. Occasionally, migration extends into early December.

Spring migration centers around the 10 March–25 April interval. Unusually late were a mid-May 1971 sighting in St. Croix County (C. A. Faanes) and an 8 May 1963 report in Racine County (L. W. Erickson).

In the northern forests a few birds are permanent residents. Schoenebeck (1902) mentioned finding four nests in Oconto County. A set of three eggs, taken from one of these on 19 April 1895, now resides at the University of Wisconsin–Stevens Point. Zirrer (1947) found nests in Rusk County yearly from 1933 to 1940. His accounts of these, as well as Gromme's (1935a) story of photographing the 1934 nest, make fascinating reading. Additional published records include nests in Bayfield (1943, W. S. Feeney), Vilas (1947, D. Q. Thompson), Oconto (1951, C. H. Richter), and Ashland (1958, E. W. Beals [1958]) counties. Unpublished data in the 1970s and 1980s indicate more widespread breeding than had previously been known. T. C. Erdman and associates have located as many as 15 nests per year and have banded numerous juveniles. Four banded young turned up 3–4 months later, 40–100 miles from the nest site. In one instance a pair has used the same nesting area for 11 consecutive years.

This species was noted during all seasons at Racine in the 1850s (Hoy 1853b; Barry 1854), but with adults restricted to the winter season. Kumlien and Hollister (1903) knew of no breeding records and surmised that the Northern Goshawk was becoming rarer in all parts of the state.

Red-shouldered Hawk (*Buteo lineatus*)

STATUS. Uncommon migrant. Uncommon summer resident. Uncommon winter resident south; rare winter resident central.

HABITAT. Southern silver maple–elm forest.

MIGRATION DATES. *Spring:* late February to mid-April. *Fall:* mid-August to mid-December.

BREEDING DATA. Nests with eggs: 10 April to 25 May. Clutch size: usually 3 or 4 eggs; rarely 2 or 5.

WINTER. Regularly present in small numbers north to St. Croix, Adams, Waushara, Outagamie, and Ozaukee counties; occasionally present north to Polk, Sawyer, Taylor, Langlade, and Marinette counties.

PORTRAIT. *Birds of Wisconsin:* Plate 17.

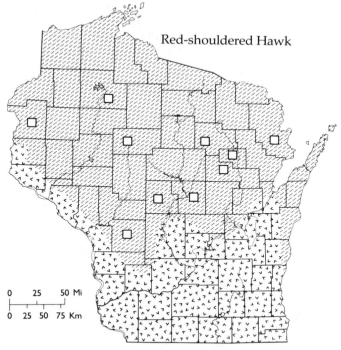

Red-shouldered Hawk

⬛ Resident range
▨ Summer range
☐ Late December to mid-February

Records since 1960

In most sections of the state the Red-shouldered Hawk is decidedly uncommon. But Buss and Mattison (1955) considered it one of the most numerous breeding raptors in Dunn and Eau Claire counties, and T. C. Erdman (1978, pers. comm.) described it as second only to the Broad-winged Hawk in summer numbers in Oconto and Marinette counties. Where heavily wooded bottomlands exist, the bird can be fairly common; but since such habitat is greatly limited, most observers consider this hawk uncommon. Because suitable habitat is dwindling, this bird has been placed on the Department of Natural Resources list of threatened species.

Nonwintering Red-shoulders arrive in southern Wisconsin any time after 25 February and in central Wisconsin between 15 and 25 March, often while deep snow is still present. Migrants trickle in unobtrusively, settling on nesting territories by mid-April. Even those few that reach the northern counties arrive by 30 April.

When Buss and Mattison (1955) discussed studies of 14 nests in Dunn County between 1946 and 1951, they noted that incubation had started by 12 April and hatching by 7 May. The 40 young fledged from these nests represented an average of 2.8 young per nest. The success ratio has been far lower on Erdman's nesting studies in Marinette and Oconto counties during the 1970s; it has varied from 0.75 to 1.50 young fledged per nest.

Summer records exist for nearly every county. Beals (1958) listed it for the Apostle Islands in Ashland County in 1957, and Bernard (1967) included it in his Douglas County listing. But mainly, the Red-shoulder occupies heavily wooded bottomlands along the major rivers: the St. Croix north to St. Croix Falls, the Chippewa to Chippewa Falls, the Wisconsin to Wausau, the Wolf to Shawano, the Green Bay shore and adjacent streams to Marinette.

Itinerant immatures have been spotted at the Little Suamico Ornithological Station in Oconto County by 20 August and at the Cedar Grove Ornithological Station in Sheboygan County by 24 August. But there is no concentration of fall migrants, for few—if any—go beyond Wisconsin's northern border. At Cedar Grove the average number of individuals tallied per autumn season is 17. Adults migrate during October and November. Erdman has recorded migrants in southern Oconto County as late as 20 December.

Several individuals overwinter every year in the southern half of the state. Birds are frequently recorded on CBCs along the Mississippi–St. Croix rivers north to St. Croix County, the Wisconsin River north to Wood and Portage counties, and on the Wolf and Fox rivers north to Outagamie and Brown counties. Occasionally, the Red-shoulder has been counted on CBCs in Polk (1960), Sawyer (1973), Taylor (1978), Langlade (1978), Shawano (1973, 1975), Menominee (1964), and Marinette (1978, 1980) counties.

This species probably was never common in Wisconsin. Hoy (1853b) described it as "extremely numerous," but possible confusion with the Broad-wing is suggested by a subsequent comment: "The great number of hawks, of this and other species, that are often seen soaring in company during fine weather, about the 20th of September . . . is almost incredible." Barry (1854) writing of the same region (Racine), described the bird as only "occasional," but said it was more numerous around marshes. To Kumlien and Hollister (1903) it was "by no means a common bird." And Stoddard (1917) commented, "While this species is far from common, a few pairs breed in the heavy timber along the Wisconsin River and Honey Creek in Sauk County."

Broad-winged Hawk (*Buteo platypterus*)

STATUS. Abundant migrant. Common summer resident north; uncommon summer resident west and central (rare along the Mississippi River).
HABITAT. Deciduous forest.
MIGRATION DATES. *Spring:* late March to mid-May. *Fall:* mid-August to early October. *Extremes:* 6 March; 16 December.
BREEDING DATA. Nests with eggs: 5 May to 30 June. Clutch size: usually 2 or 3 eggs; rarely 4.
PORTRAIT. *Birds of Wisconsin:* Plate 17.

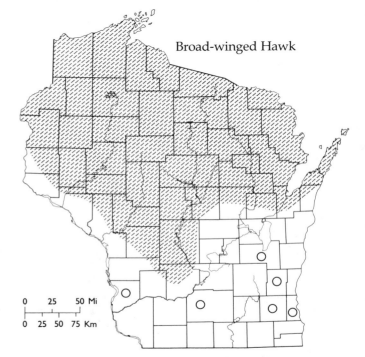

Broad-winged Hawk

▨ Summer range
○ Early June to late July

Records since 1960

For a brief 3-week period, usually 10–30 September, the Broad-winged Hawk is truly an abundant migrant throughout Wisconsin. When weather conditions are favorable—generally clear, cool weather following the passage of a cold front, with north or northwest winds aloft—the sky may be filled with migrating Broad-wings. They may be circling low enough to display their broad black-and-white tail bands; they may be gliding high enough to appear only as microscopic specks against a white cloud. In many locations around the state an observer at a good vantage point might see hundreds in a single day between 10 A.M. and 3 P.M. On peak days, observers at key posts along the Lake Michigan shore count birds in the thousands. At the Cedar Grove Ornithological Station in Sheboygan County, 5,564 were tallied on 18 September 1962; at the Little Suamico Ornithological Station in Oconto County, 13,084 passed by on 21 September 1975. Many of the 15,000–25,000 birds that pass over Duluth on a September peak day undoubtedly move through western Wisconsin, but after rounding the western tip of Lake Superior they fan out over a broad front. A few birds appear by 10–15 August, and scattered individuals or small groups may be observed in late October, but 95% of the migrants are likely to be concentrated in the 10–30 September span. For an entire autumn season, total numbers at a given observation point vary greatly, owing largely to varied weather conditions, but Cedar Grove has had as many as 11,018 in one season (1952), while at Little Suamico one-season totals have gone as high as 17,000 (1979).

In rare instances, sightings have been reported in November and early December, but most are suspect because of possible confusion with Red-shoulders. Sightings beyond question were a bird found dead in Milwaukee County on 12 November 1932 (C. S. Jung; MPM files) and an individual seen at close range in Ozaukee County on 16 December 1978 (J. E.

Grootematt). By 1 December most birds should be in Mexico or Central America. Birds banded in Wisconsin have been recovered in winter in Nicaragua, Costa Rica, Panama, and Colombia.

The spring flight is less spectacular, and has been less widely studied. Nevertheless, observers have reported concentrations in the hundreds in a variety of locations during late April and early May. Driving along a forest road on a drizzly May morning, Frances Hamerstrom (1972) counted seven Broad-wings perched in the trees; when the sun came out and a breeze sprang up, she climbed a tall pine and was able to watch dozens of hawks rise from the forest and form a migratory "kettle." Occasionally, early migrants reach the southern counties by 25 March. In 1971 there were exceptional sightings on 14 March in Dane (T. L. Ashman) and Ozaukee (T. Bintz) counties. More unusual yet was a 6 March find in Walworth County (1976, D. D. Tessen). Usually, first arrivals occur in the 10–20 April span, with a 25 April–15 May peak. Small numbers of subadults are still migrating through 25 May.

Anyone who misses out entirely on the spectacular flights might assume that this bird is an uncommon migrant. Because it is a woodland species, perching on relatively inconspicuous branches, the Broad-wing is far less obvious than the Red-tail, Northern Harrier, or American Kestrel. Even when concealed by the forest, the bird often reveals its presence with its piercing peweelike "kee-ee."

The Broad-wing is unobtrusive throughout the breeding season. But extensive work by John Stierle in Wood County and C. H. Richter in Oconto County attest to its common status in central and northern Wisconsin in summer. Between 1908 and 1932, Stierle (MPM files) located 54 nests in his study area. In all but six instances incubation began, according to his estimates, between 8 and 26 May, with one clutch by 5 May and five by early June. Nests were located exclusively in deciduous trees: elm, birch, maple, and basswood. In Richter's area, from 1924 to 1958, all but 2 of 35 nests were in deciduous trees, poplar and ash predominating. In three nests, incubation began between 1 and 5 May, while in most other nests egg-laying started between 10 and 20 May. Twice, Richter found nests with four eggs; on all other occasions he found two or three eggs per clutch. More recently, T. C. Erdman (pers. comm.) investigated 20 nests in northeastern Wisconsin, 17 of which produced 35 young.

The "common summer resident" status applies to the region north of Polk, Chippewa, Marathon, and Oconto counties. The Broad-winged Hawk is more sparse in the upland wooded areas of western Wisconsin south to Monroe and Sauk counties.

One of the more interesting summer observations occurred on 26 June 1960 when Mueller and Berger saw approximately 300 birds circling over the tip of Washington Island (Mueller and Berger 1965). Nearly all were subadults, presumably nonbreeders, attempting a belated northward migratory flight. Unable to negotiate the 5 miles from Washington Island to St. Martin's Island, the birds made a counterclockwise movement around the Door County peninsula. Perhaps this phenomenon occurs more frequently than observers have noticed.

Swainson's Hawk (*Buteo swainsoni*)

STATUS. Rare migrant. Rare summer visitant.
HABITAT. Open grassland and cropland.
MIGRATION DATES. *Spring:* early April to late May.
 Fall: mid-August to mid-October. *Extremes:* 16
 March; 14 December.
PORTRAIT. *Birds of Wisconsin:* Plate 17.

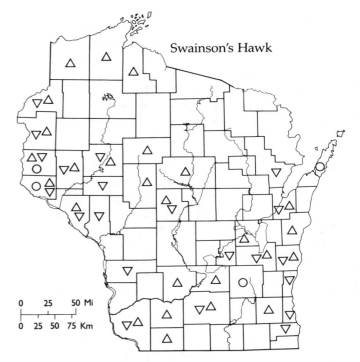

Swainson's Hawk

△   Early April to late May
○   Early June to early August
▽   Mid-August to mid-October

All records

What the status of this visitor from the western plains
was before 1930 is poorly known. Considerable confusion in *Buteo* identification existed in the nineteenth
century. Hoy (1853b) referred to the Swainson's Hawk
as a "not common" winter resident, but it is doubtful that his identification was correct. Kumlien and
Hollister (1903) described the bird as an occasional
visitant in September and October. Thure Kumlien is
said to have collected 12 specimens, and Ludwig
Kumlien another 6. But the only remaining specimen
proved on reexamination to be a Red-tail, so again
identification is suspect. The one nineteenth-century
observation that has been substantiated is a bird killed
in Dunn County in December 1896 by J. N. Clark (Buss
and Mattison 1955). Clark had three additional Dunn
County sight records: 3 and 13 September 1897 and
19 April 1899.

No records are known for the ensuing 30 years. With
the development of hawk-observation and -trapping
at the Cedar Grove Ornithological Station in Sheboygan County in the 1920s, it became apparent that
this species is a rare migrant in both spring and fall.
O. J. Gromme (MPM files) collected one bird there on
16 September 1930, and observed three more 12 days
later. Since then, Cedar Grove personnel have banded
11 individuals and observed 13 others.

When the Mississippi–St. Croix River valleys began to get more systematic coverage in the late 1950s
and early 1960s, records of Swainson's Hawks increased markedly. One or more individuals have been
noted nearly every spring and fall through the 1970s
and 1980s.

With the exception of a remarkably early bird on
16 March (1982, Wood, D. G. Follen), the earliest
spring arrivals are all in western counties: 3 April
(1965, Burnett, N. R. Stone), 4 April (1974, Pierce,
C. A. Faanes; 1978, Chippewa, C. A. Kemper), and
7 April (1972, St. Croix, S. V. Goddard). The latest
spring migrants have been recorded on 29 May (1965,
Sheboygan, D. D. Berger), 31 May (1976, Waukesha,
L. L. Safir), 5 June (1948, Dunn, I. O. Buss), and 7 June
(1973, Chippewa, C. A. Kemper [1973a]). Most observations have been made between 10 April and 20 May.
If a line is drawn between Burnett and Sheboygan

counties, all but four spring sightings have occurred
south and west of that line.

The same line also marks the extremes for fall migrants, with two exceptions. Since 1960, fall observations have equalled those of spring, but have been
spread out over a longer period. Starting with August
records on the 6th (1975, Burnett, J. O. Evrard), 12th
(1971, Fond du Lac, D. D. Tessen), and 17th (1974,
Oconto, T. C. Erdman), the sightings since 1960 include six in August, eight in September, seven in October, and three in November: the 5th (1972, Green
Lake, D. D. Tessen), 13th (1968, Vernon, V. E. Weber),
and 16th (1975, Dane, R. E. Fiehweg). Even later were
the individuals on 19 November (1953, Brown, E. D.
Cleary) and a phenomenal 14 December bird (1961,
Dane, L. W. Erickson).

With nesting taking place recently in western Illinois and southeastern Minnesota, breeding in western Wisconsin is a distinct possibility. In June and
July 1978 two pairs were resident in St. Croix County
and one pair in Pierce County, but no evidence of
nesting could be found (W. Norling). In 1960, an indi-

vidual remained in Dodge County from late May to early August (K. Brown). In the same year an immature was observed at Washington Island in Door County on 26 June (D. D. Berger).

Two of the birds banded at Cedar Grove were re-

captured: one in Arkansas on 24 October 1939, 18 days after banding, and one in South Dakota in July 1966, 13 months after banding. A bird found dead in Trempealeau County in October 1953 had been banded in Saskatchewan the previous July.

Red-tailed Hawk (*Buteo jamaicensis*)

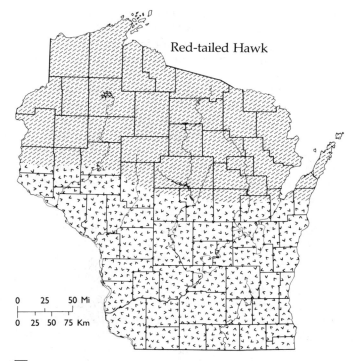

Red-tailed Hawk

0 25 50 Mi
0 25 50 75 Km

▭ Resident range
▨ Summer range

Records since 1960

STATUS. Common migrant. Common summer resident south and central; fairly common summer resident north. Common winter resident south; fairly common winter resident central.

HABITAT. Open grassland and cropland. Deciduous forest.

MIGRATION DATES. *Spring:* late February to early May. *Fall:* early August to mid-December.

BREEDING DATA. Nests with eggs: 7 March to 25 May. Clutch size: 2 or 3 eggs.

WINTER. Regularly present north to St. Croix, Chippewa, Portage, Outagamie, and Brown counties; irregularly present north to Barron, Shawano, and Oconto counties.

PORTRAIT. *Birds of Wisconsin:* Plate 16.

The winter and spring distribution patterns for the Red-tailed Hawk in northern and southern Wisconsin are noticeably different. North of a line from Hudson through Wausau to Kewaunee, winter sightings are scarce. In this region the fall migration is generally completed by the end of November, and few spring migrants appear before 10 March. The exceptions are two observations by W. S. Feeney: 2 March 1942 in Forest County and 19 February 1943 in Bayfield County. The main migration occurs between 15 March and 25 April, with at least a trickle continuing through 10 May. Nests with eggs have most often been reported between 15 April and 25 May; the earliest date is 9 April.

South of the Hudson-Kewaunee line, winter observations are frequent. In fact, southeast of a line from Prairie du Chien to Waupaca, this bird is one of the most common cold-weather hawks, with 30 or more individuals often reported on a single CBC. Most of Wisconsin's wintering Red-tails are adults, usually seen perched on utility poles or on the upper branches of large trees overlooking open areas. Many of these adults have established permanent residence, and begin prenesting activity by the end of January. In their Green County study area, Orians and Kuhlman (1956) reported late January sightings of birds settling on nest sites and gathering nest materials, with incubation usually beginning before 15 March.

Although some southern Wisconsin Red-tails nest throughout the spring months, others are migrating. Migration begins by 25 February, peaks from 20 March to 20 April, and extends to 30 April, sometimes to 10 May. In his Waterloo study area in Dodge and Jefferson counties, Petersen (1979) noted that resident Red-tails frequently rose and circled in defense of nesting territory whenever migrant Red-tails appeared.

In the more heavily farmed areas of southern and eastern Wisconsin the Red-tail is a common nesting species. Orians and Kuhlman (1956) calculated that a 95-square-mile Green County area had a breeding density of 0.41 pairs per square mile in 1954 and 0.29 in 1955. In a 42-square-mile study area near Waupun (Fond du Lac County), Gates (1972) found a density of 0.27 pairs per square mile in the 1962–1964 period. No comparable studies have been conducted in the more heavily wooded regions of central and northern Wisconsin. A few birds undoubtedly breed in virtually every county, but north of a line from St. Croix Falls through Wausau to Marinette sightings are spotty. Half of the 30 BBS transects north of this line have never reported a Red-tail.

Young birds from southern Wisconsin nests fledge in early July. In many instances, they soon move northward. T. C. Erdman (pers. comm.) has trapped several first-year birds in Oconto County in August; these are birds that had been banded in May as nestlings in southern Wisconsin (100 miles distant). Transient immatures have been detected at the Little Suamico Ornithological Station in Oconto County as early as 24 July, with considerable movement occurring through August. These early-fall transients—many of which may have drifted north from southern Wisconsin, Illinois, and Iowa—move leisurely. Observations of banded birds marked with streamers indicate that birds may take up to 10 days to move the 40 miles from Green Bay to Manitowoc.

As the migration proceeds through September and October, immatures and adults from farther north swell the numbers, and birds move more rapidly. The main flight passes through the state in October and November. A good flight may send over 100 birds per day past a strategic Lake Michigan observation point. Less consistent hawk-watching has been done along the Mississippi River. But William Smith's tally of 197 individuals in Grant County on 14 October 1973 implies that major flights occur through western Wisconsin as well as near Lake Michigan. The highest 1-day tally at the Cedar Grove Ornithological Station in Sheboygan County is 563 (5 November 1960, H. C.

Mueller). In years when trapping stations have been manned into December, observers have spotted a few late migrants during the first week of that month.

Hawk-bander T. C. Erdman (pers. comm.) has commented: "I do not believe that our Wisconsin nestlings winter in the state. I have no recoveries of nestlings in Wisconsin in the first winter." First-year birds he has banded have been recovered in Alabama and Missouri. Nestlings banded by Petersen in Dodge and Jefferson counties have been recovered in Alabama and Florida (Petersen 1979). Immatures banded in Oconto County between 28 August and 15 October have been retaken the following winter in Florida, Georgia, Alabama, and Arkansas (Erdman, pers. comm.).

Among the late-fall migrants are some extremely dark individuals, suspected as the western races *calurus* and *harlani* by both nineteenth- and twentieth-century observers. An adult male taken in Brown County (9 January 1974, T. C. Erdman) has given confirmation of *calurus*. Sightings of dark individuals have come from all parts of the state—particularly the western region—in late fall and early winter.

Numerous reports of very light individuals (suspected *krideri*) have come from the Crex Meadows Wildlife Area in Burnett County and other western Wisconsin locales. These birds also are wanderers from farther west, and are most frequently reported between April and June.

The number of individuals reported on the CBC each year since 1960 has varied from 249 (1963) to 1,077 (1987). Most counts south of the Hudson-Kewaunee line report them; most counts north of that line lack them. Occasional CBC records report birds in Douglas, Burnett, Barron, Price, and Marinette counties may refer to lingering fall migrants.

Ferruginous Hawk (*Buteo regalis*)
Formerly Ferruginous Rough-leg

STATUS. Rare migrant. Accidental summer visitant.
HABITAT. Open grassland and cropland.
MIGRATION DATES. *Fall:* late September to early December. *Spring:* one record.
WINTER. Three records.
PORTRAIT. *Birds of Wisconsin:* Plate 14.

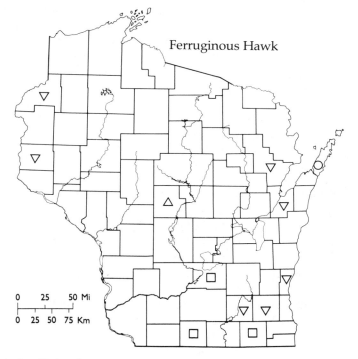

Ferruginous Hawk

△   12 April
○   24 June
▽   Late September to early December
□   2 January to 26 February

All records

Although regular in the Great Plains and occasional in western Minnesota, this bird has wandered to Wisconsin only rarely. Four specimens have been collected: two near Lake Koshkonong in Jefferson County, on 10 November 1893 (A. L. Kumlien [Kumlien and Hollister 1903]), one in Jefferson County, in October 1894 (*fide* A. L. Kumlien), and one near Muskego Lake in Waukesha County, on 11 November 1913 (R. E. Martin; MPM files). Mike Jones trapped and banded an immature in Ozaukee County on 8 October 1988 (D. D. Berger; *Pass. Pigeon* 51:234).

There are seven sight records of light-phase adults that have been well documented for fall and winter: 24 September 1978 (St. Croix, C. A. Faanes), 9 October 1950 (Brown, W. Fisk), 25 October 1974 (Burnett, W. Norling, *fide* Faanes [1981]), 8 December 1951 (Oconto, C. H. Richter), 2 January 1971 (Walworth, C. O. Palmquist), 17 February 1978 (Columbia, R. M. Hoffman), and 26 February 1950 (Green, G. H. Orians).

One sure spring observation of an adult, closely compared with five Rough-legged Hawks, occurred on 12 April 1979 (Wood, D. G. Follen). On 24 June 1965 a wandering bird was seen circling over Washington Island in Door County; it was subsequently sketched and documented by L. W. Erickson. This is Wisconsin's only summer record.

Several additional sightings have been suspected, but have lacked complete enough documentation to be considered valid. It should not be inferred from Wisconsin's December–February records that winter is a plausible time to look for this species. The winter range lies well to the west of us. Recent Minnesota sightings include only spring and fall migrants.

Rough-legged Hawk (*Buteo lagopus*)

STATUS. Fairly common migrant. Casual summer visitant. Fairly common winter resident, sometimes common south and east.
HABITAT. Open grassland and cropland. Savanna.
MIGRATION DATES. *Fall:* mid-September to late December. *Spring:* mid-February to early May.
BREEDING DATA. One record.
WINTER. Regularly present north to St. Croix, Chippewa, Marathon, Outagamie, and Kewaunee counties; occasionally present north to Douglas, Ashland, Oneida, and Marinette counties.
PORTRAIT. *Birds of Wisconsin:* Plate 14.

It is a long flight from their breeding grounds in the Arctic tundra to Wisconsin, so it is not surprising that first fall arrivals of Rough-legged Hawks may not appear until late September or early October after the peak of the Broad-wing flight has passed. The earliest date recorded for this species is 16 August (1975, Outagamie, D. D. Tessen); other unusually early dates are 30 August (1965, Douglas, R. F. Bernard), 1 September (1955, Bayfield, D. A. Bratley), and 4 September (1966, Outagamie, D. D. Tessen; 1966, Waukesha, P. W. Hoffmann; 1974, Burnett, N. R. Stone). Usually, first arrivals reach the northern counties around 20 September, and the southern counties 5 days later. The migration is under way in earnest from 5 October on; it peaks between 25 October and 25 November. Migrants continue to be seen into December at hawk-observation points. The highest seasonal total at the Little Suamico Ornithological Station in Oconto County is 107 (1974), with a 1-day high of 40. At the Cedar Grove Ornithological Station in Sheboygan County up to 35 birds have been recorded in 1 day, with a total seasonal count as high as 86.

The winter of 1974–1975 was exceptional. An unusually large rodent population, combined with less-than-normal snow cover, produced a CBC total of 402 individuals—more than double the tally of any previous year. The Sauk City count listed 56. Far to the north at Ashland, where usually there are none, 20 were counted, with another 38 at Grantsburg (Burnett County). Eugene Jacobs, trapping at two Portage County locations, estimated that over 150 Rough-legs moved through his area that winter. By contrast, the CBC in 1976–1977 had no more than eight individuals on any one count. Numbers again rose spectacularly in 1980–1981, with 61 of 79 counts totaling 382 individuals.

In some years the winter population becomes stable by 15 December. But deepening snow in January

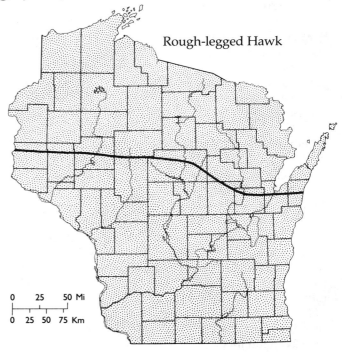

Rough-legged Hawk

0   25   50 Mi
0 25 50 75 Km

▨ Winter range
   South of line: regular
   North of line: occasional

Records since 1960

often sends birds farther south. Only in years of unusually light snowfall will birds winter north of St. Croix, Chippewa, Marathon, Outagamie, and Kewaunee counties. The highest midwinter concentrations are usually south of this line and east of the Wisconsin River.

The northward movement that begins slowly by 20 February becomes pronounced by 10 March. The peak is normally between 1 and 20 April, and by 10 May only a few stragglers remain. These are usually gone by 20 May. After the influx of 1974–1975, several stragglers remained into June, with birds being seen on the 7th (Burnett, C. A. Faanes), 12th (St. Croix, C. A. Faanes), and 13th (Price, M. Hardy). Other exceptionally late departures include 29 May (1978, Marathon, K. J. Luepke), 2 June (1978, Portage, A. Beske), and 10 June (1976, St. Croix, C. A. Faanes).

Ludwig Kumlien documented the only positive instance of breeding (Kumlien and Hollister 1903). He discovered a nest in eastern Dane County in May 1872. The nest was located 8 feet up in a bur oak and contained three eggs. The female was injured, capable of only short flights. Another breeding probably took place in Door County. Murl Deusing (MPM files) observed an adult and two young on 12 August 1945. He witnessed the passing of food from an adult to one of the young in midair. An individual spent

the summer of 1950 north of Milwaukee in southern Ozaukee County, but there was no suspicion of nesting (H. C. Mueller). A 24 June 1961 record in Outagamie County (D. D. Tessen) presumably indicates the presence of a nonbreeding summering individual.

Golden Eagle (*Aquila chrysaetos*)

STATUS. Rare spring migrant; uncommon fall migrant north and west; rare fall migrant south and east. Uncommon winter resident north and west; rare winter resident south and east.
HABITAT. Deciduous forest.
MIGRATION DATES. *Fall:* early October to mid-December. *Spring:* mid-February to late April. *Extremes:* 16 August; 22 May.
BREEDING DATA. One probable record.
WINTER. A few present each winter south to Buffalo, Monroe, Adams, and Shawano counties; rarely present elsewhere.
PORTRAIT. *Birds of Wisconsin:* Plate 18.

Of all the raptors that visit the state every year, this magnificent hunter is one of the rarest. The Golden Eagle is seen most often at the major waterfowl refuges—Crex Meadows Wildlife Area in Burnett County, Necedah and Horicon National Wildlife refuges in Juneau and Dodge counties, respectively—in October and November. Each of these may attract from one to three birds nearly every autumn. As the lakes freeze and the waterfowl move south, most of these eagles disappear. At the hawk observation stations at Little Suamico in Oconto County and Cedar Grove in Sheboygan County, from one to three individuals are seen passing overhead each fall, usually between 10 October and 25 November. Remarkably early is a 16 August sighting (1975, Outagamie, D. D. Tessen). September sightings include one on the 4th (1974, Burnett, N. R. Stone), followed by seven from the 13th on.

A few individuals remain as winter residents each year. Before 1962 the species was recorded only twice on the CBC, but most counts in those years were taken in southern Wisconsin. Between 1962 and 1975, there were 24 CBC records. There have been CBC sightings of 1–5 individuals each year since 1976. With the exception of single records in Brown and Grant counties, all birds were seen north of a line from Alma to Tomah and Adams, and west of a line from Adams to Wausaukee. It is near hills and bluffs that this species is most frequently seen.

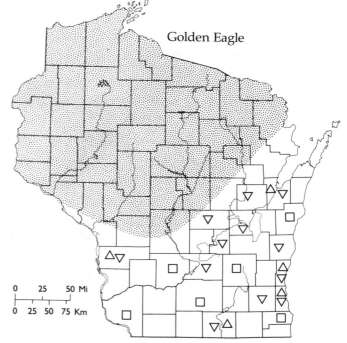

Golden Eagle

0   25   50 Mi
0   25 50 75 Km

▨ Winter range
△ Mid-February to late April
▽ Early October to mid-December
☐ Late December to early February

Records since 1960

On rare occasions a Golden Eagle may join a group of Bald Eagles wintering below the dams of the Wisconsin and Mississippi rivers, but this does not happen often because the Golden prefers mammals to the fish that attract the Bald. Nevertheless, Grant County observations did occur on 18 January 1964 (T. N. Ingram) and 9 January 1972 (W. A. Smith). Smith also recorded migrating birds near Cassville (Grant County) on 20 February 1972, and three times in 1974: 26 and 28 February and 3 March.

Records are too scanty to allow us to speak of a "spring flight." Wintering individuals usually disappear by 10 March. Lone migrants are occasionally spotted between 15 February and 20 April. Unusually late are observations on 29 April (1975, Ozaukee, D. K. Gustafson), 2 May (1975, Burnett, C. A. Faanes), 18 May (1945, Oneida, F. A. Hartmeister), and 22 May (1940, Marinette, W. C. Pelzer).

The presumption that this species once nested in the state rests primarily on secondhand evidence furnished by Stoddard (1917, 1969). On 21 May 1911 he was shown a nest on a sheltered ledge 60 feet up on Ferry Bluff in Sauk County. He commented, "This nest was typical of the Golden Eagle, made principally of juniper limbs, some of which were over an inch and a half in diameter." Previously, Stoddard had acquired two Golden Eagle specimens shot by farmers in the area: a female in February 1908 and a male shot a year later. Another local resident, Bert Laws, described the birds that had been using the

nest for one or two years before 1908 and that had previously had a different nest on a neighboring bluff. Stoddard (1917) concluded, "That this species nested in Sauk County prior to 1908, there can be no doubt." He also mentioned having seen this species twice in the nearby Baraboo hills in early summer, but gave no dates.

Hoy (1853b) took an egg from what he believed to be a Golden's nest in a large oak between Milwaukee and Racine in 1851, but Kumlien and Hollister (1903) questioned his identification after examining the egg years later.

This bird was evidently as rare in the nineteenth century as it is today. Kumlien and Hollister (1903) handled 15 specimens over a 15-year period. After extensive research, Schorger (1945b) was able to annotate another 23 state records.

American Kestrel (*Falco sparverius*)
Formerly Sparrow Hawk

STATUS. Common migrant. Common summer resident. Fairly common winter resident southeast and east; uncommon winter resident south, west, and central.

HABITAT. Open grassland. Savanna. Commercial areas.

MIGRATION DATES. *Spring:* early March to early May. *Fall:* early August to early November.

BREEDING DATA. Nests with eggs: 2 April to 30 June. Clutch size: 4 or 5 eggs.

WINTER. Regularly present in small numbers north to St. Croix, Chippewa, Wood, Outagamie, and Brown counties; occasionally present north to Burnett, Taylor, Shawano, and Marinette counties.

PORTRAIT. *Birds of Wisconsin:* Plate 20.

Reflecting on 35 years' experience around Columbus (Columbia County), George vos Burgh wrote in 1930: "At one time before the timber was butchered off and every hollow post and tree destroyed, it was possible to find this handsome little falcon nesting about here, but today all this has changed." Kumlien and Hollister (1903) also associated the "sparrow hawk" with heavy timber, and observed that where the larger trees had been cut the hawks' numbers had diminished.

But this falcon has adapted well to a changed environment. In the southern urban areas a few are found nesting on the taller buildings and feeding in

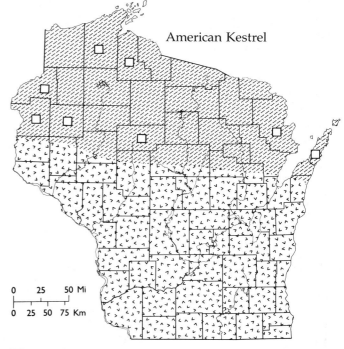

American Kestrel

	Mi
0 25 50	
0 25 50 75 Km	

⌁ Resident range

▨ Summer range

☐ Early December to late February

Records since 1960

open areas near industrial sites. Farther north the birds nest in tree cavities and frequent the utility poles and wires adjacent to open fields and pastures. The birds are particularly conspicuous in August when young are on the wing and grasshoppers are at their peak.

Further successful adaptation has developed wherever people erect nest boxes in suitable habitat. In the Plainfield area in Waushara County, where only three nesting pairs had been found in the previous 20 years, the Hamerstroms erected 50 nest boxes in 1968. Hamerstrom, Hamerstrom, and Hart (1973) reported 8–12 broods fledged each year from 1968 to 1972.

The normal winter range covers the southern half of Wisconsin, north roughly to Highway 29, spanning the state from Prescott to Green Bay. When CBC coverage first became statewide in the late 1950s, these small falcons were recorded on 25–35% of the counts. The composite totals for a given year varied from 30 to 60, and were concentrated mainly around Milwaukee and other urban centers. The next 20 years brought a notable increase. American Kestrels are now found on 60–70% of the state's CBC areas, with composite annual totals of 200–275. The 1981 total was an impressive 549, with birds recorded on 54 of 84 counts.

Some northward movement takes place in early March, or even the last days of February if the weather is relatively mild, but the first migrants in the north usually do not arrive until 25 March. Even during the peak, which occurs in the 5–25 April period, the spring flight is not spectacular at any location. Most of these Kestrels, instead of joining Sharp-shins and Broad-wings in utilizing rising thermals, move steadily along on the strength of their own flapping. They concentrate along leading ridges of landscape, such as lake edges. Spring migration is usually completed by 5 May.

Kestrels breed statewide. Traditionally, this hawk has chosen tree cavities and old buildings for nest sites. For a time it appeared that increased competition with starlings for suitable nest cavities might affect the hawks adversely, but the falcons are holding their own. Where nest boxes are also made available, the Kestrel has further profited. In the Hamerstroms' studies, the fledging rate rose steadily from 3.2 per

successful nest box in 1968 to 4.7 in 1972 (Hamerstrom, Hamerstrom, and Hart 1973).

Researcher John Jacobs (pers. comm.), working in the Green Bay area in 1976–1978, estimated that 10% of the breeding pairs he studied resided in buildings, 10% nested in boxes he had erected, 40% preferred cavities in dead trees, and 40% occupied cavities in live trees. Most eggs were laid in mid-April. A few were laid in early April, and in a few instances eggs were still being laid in mid-June. Jacobs' earliest date for fledged young is 2 June, with most fledging following by mid-June. The time schedule is probably slightly earlier in southern Wisconsin. In northern Wisconsin, where birds are not present until mid-April, nesting commences in early May.

The recent increase in winter population is matched by increases in summer also. During the first 3 years of the Breeding Bird Survey, 1966–1968, the number of individuals per transect per year was approximately 0.50. The 1978–1980 average stood at 0.94. If the BBS transects were run in early August instead of June, numbers might double, for it is in late July and early August that these birds are most readily seen.

Early August also inaugurates the fall migration. Many more migrant Kestrels are detected by banders at the eastern Wisconsin hawk-watch stations than by observers elsewhere. But the migration is widespread throughout the state, with few birds migrating through August and greatest numbers between 10 September and 15 October. Undoubtedly, many late-October and early-November sightings are of late migrants. Beyond mid-November whether one is seeing fall migrants or winter residents is a matter of conjecture.

Banding recoveries of Kestrels show no clearcut patterns. Some Kestrels are banded as nestlings, some are netted as fall migrants, some are road-trapped at any season. Several of T. C. Erdman's (pers. comm.) birds, banded as nestlings, evidently did not migrate and were recovered within 50–100 miles from the point of banding. There have been seven known recoveries of Wisconsin-banded birds the subsequent winter in Texas, one in Mississippi, and one in Oklahoma. A female banded in Brown County on 11 December 1974 (T. C. Erdman) was recovered in Panama 20 months later.

Merlin (*Falco columbarius*)

Formerly Pigeon Hawk

STATUS. Uncommon migrant. Rare summer resident
north. Rare winter visitor south and central.
HABITAT. Coniferous forest. Lakeshores.
MIGRATION DATES. *Spring:* early March to late May.
Fall: late August to late November.
BREEDING DATA. Nest with eggs: 2 June. Nests with
young: 25 June to 5 August. Clutch size: 3 eggs.
WINTER. Occasionally present north to Buffalo, Wood,
Langlade, and Manitowoc counties.
PORTRAIT. *Birds of Wisconsin:* Plate 20.

The Merlin is best known as a fast-flying fall migrant
along the shores of the Great Lakes. In 1919, H. H.
Sheldon and A. J. Poole (Jackson 1943) found numerous Merlins between 7 and 16 September along the
beach on Outer Island in Lake Superior, pursuing
sparrows, warblers, and flickers. The success of the
predators was evident when the stomachs of 10 collected falcons were examined, revealing remains of a
Red-breasted Nuthatch, Cedar Waxwing, Philadelphia Vireo, Black-throated Green Warbler, Gray-
cheeked and Swainson's Thrushes, and Chipping,
Lincoln's, and Song Sparrows.

More recently, at the Cedar Grove Ornithological
Station in Sheboygan County, observers have counted
as many as 75 in one day (10 October 1948) and 164 in
one season (1958). Since 1965, numbers have declined
noticeably, with seasonal totals consistently remaining under 75 at Cedar Grove and even fewer seen
each year at the Little Suamico Ornithological Station
in Oconto County.

Away from the lake shorelines, observations are
few and far between, although they have been made
in all parts of the state. The earliest migrants have
been seen in mid-August: the 17th (1958, Manitowoc,
J. Kraupa), 19th (1953, Lincoln, S. D. Robbins), and
20th (1955, Douglas, A. Sprunt). The principal migration period is from 10 September to 20 October, with a
few scattered migrants being sighted nearly every
year until 5 November. Occasional sightings have
been made through late November and early December, including one found dead on 4 December
1962 (Marinette, H. L. Lindberg).

Once the birds leave Wisconsin, they travel far and
fast. Birds banded along Lake Michigan in fall have
been retaken in Tennessee (7 and 14 days after banding), Alabama (15 days), Virginia (25 days), and South
Carolina (17 days). Others have been retaken during
winter in Mississippi, and in Colombia, Ecuador, and
the Dominican Republic.

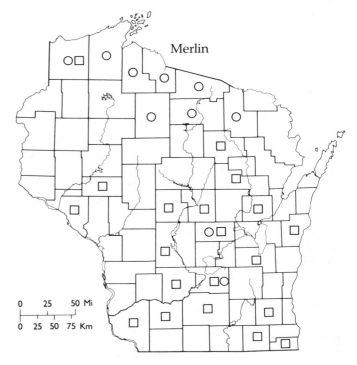

Merlin

○ Early June to early August
□ Early December to late February

Records since 1960

Merlins don't belong in Wisconsin in winter. Yet on
30 occasions since 1960 individuals have been recorded on the CBC. A few of these sightings have not
been adequately documented, and suspicions exist
that some of these birds may have been Sharp-shinned
Hawks misidentified as Merlins. Even so, the Merlin
must be considered an occasional winter visitant. Reliable late-winter sightings include birds on 20 January (1974, Columbia, W. A. Smith), 27 January (1979,
Wood, G. Stout), 3 February (1973, Juneau, D. D.
Tessen), 5 February (1956, Rock, H. G. Liebherr), 14
February (1965, Iowa, L. W. Erickson), and 26 February (1956, Milwaukee, C. P. Frister).

Rarely, a bird has appeared among the first waves
of spring migrants in early March: there have been
sightings on the 2nd (1985, Eau Claire, J. L. Polk), 3rd
(1973, Milwaukee, D. D. Tessen), 4th (1971, Dane,
B. Vogelsang; 1983, Kenosha, J. H. Idzikowski), and
6th (1947, Dane, W. B. Jackson). A more likely time
for a first arrival is 25 March in the south and 5 April
farther north. Most spring sightings occur between 10
April and 15 May. Late-May migrants have been re-

corded on the 28th (1977, St. Croix, C. A. Faanes), 29th (1947, Sauk, H. C. Kruse), and 30th (1954, Sheboygan, G. H. Orians). Numbers in spring are far below those in fall at the hawk-banding locations along Lake Michigan.

Nesting evidence is fragmentary. The first positive nest record is that of Schoenebeck (1902) on 2 June 1897 in Oconto County: a cavity nest 40 feet up in a dead pine stub contained three eggs. Beals (1967) discovered a nest in the Apostle Islands in Ashland County on 5 August 1966, 30 feet up in a black spruce. He did not ascertain nest contents, but the parents reacted vigorously and vociferously in defending the nest, suggesting young were present. It was the behavior of noisy parents that led Charles Sindelar and

Allen Jacobsen to an Oneida County nest with two young on 25 June 1967; the nest sat 20 feet up in a black spruce. The young were subsequently banded by Sindelar and Jacobsen and photographed by T. C. Erdman.

Additional nesting in the northern forests is probable, but unconfirmed. Forest County observations of adults were made on 26 June and 22 July 1975 (C. : A. Faanes; D. D. Tessen); adults were detected in Douglas County on 30 June 1975 and 8 July 1977 (C. A. Faanes). A Price County bird was discovered on 12 July 1977 (M. Hardy). There were two July 1983 sightings: on the 11th (Ashland, S. W. Matteson) and 30th (Oneida, D. D. Tessen).

Peregrine Falcon (*Falco peregrinus*)
Formerly Duck Hawk

STATUS. Uncommon migrant. Rare summer visitant; formerly bred. Rare winter visitant south and central. Recently reintroduced.

HABITAT. Great Lakes. Inland lakes and rivers.

MIGRATION DATES. *Spring:* late February to early June. *Fall:* mid-August to early December.

BREEDING DATA. Former nests with eggs: probably 15 April to 25 May. Clutch size: usually 3 or 4 eggs; rarely 5–7.

WINTER. Occasionally present north to Grant, Sauk, Waukesha, and Milwaukee counties. Rarely present north to Douglas, Clark and Wood counties.

PORTRAIT. *Birds of Wisconsin:* Plate 19.

Gone—for more than 20 years—was the peerless Peregrine as a breeding bird in Wisconsin. Every year, from the late nineteenth century until 1940, one or more pairs maintained summer residence along the Wisconsin River at Ferry and Cactus bluffs west of Sauk City. The aerial acrobatics of these powerful predators awed many an ornithologist during that span. Still vivid is the memory of a summer night in 1937 when I camped on a sand bar beneath the bluffs. Sleep was fitful, constantly interrupted by the eerie screams and squeals emanating from the Peregrine eyrie. At another Sauk County site in 1933, L. Wolfe and E. R. Ford (MPM files) discovered a set of seven eggs (the world's largest known clutch for this species) on 21 April. Human disturbance led to the disappearance of these birds after 1940.

One by one the remaining eyries also disappeared.

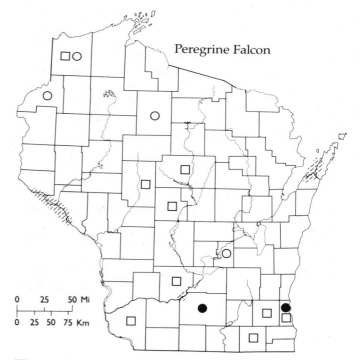

Peregrine Falcon

▨ Pre-1964 breeding locations
● 1988 to 1989 release sites
○ Mid-June to early August
□ Mid-December to mid-February

Records since 1960

The last known nesting along the Wisconsin River occurred in 1957. One year later, nests in Peninsula State Park in Door County were also deserted. Along the Mississippi River bluffs, where an estimated 30 pairs bred as late as 1948, none were reported nesting after 1964. This is part of a worldwide decline that has placed the bird on endangered species lists. Eggshell thinning due to widespread DDT use is a major contributing factor to the decline.

In the pre-1964 era, spring migrants often appeared by mid-April, sometimes as early as 15 March. Nesting activity occupied these birds soon after arrival, with egg-laying reported as early as 13 April (1921, Sauk, Stoddard [1921a]). Unusually early were two individuals noted in Milwaukee on 23 February (1941, M. Deusing).

In general, the spring migration has followed a somewhat later pattern since 1964. Observations, erratic between 20 March and 15 April, increase slightly between 15 and 30 April, with a majority of spring sightings between 1 and 20 May. Migrants have lingered until early June, observed on the 2nd (1962, Waukesha, E. W. Peartree), 3rd (1966, Winnebago, D. D. Tessen), 4th (1983, Waukesha, D. D. Tessen), and 8th (1973, Green Lake, D. D. Tessen).

After the disappearance of breeding birds in the 1960s, Peregrine Falcon observations between 11 June and 10 August were limited to three sightings: 25 June (1983, Green Lake, M. J. Mossman), 21 July (1981, Price, M. Hardy), and 26 July (1969, Douglas, D. D. Tessen). These were one-time observations, with no suggestion of summer residency.

Unusually early fall migrants were found on 11 August (1955, Douglas, A. Sprunt IV) and 14 August (1979, Oneida, P. V. Vanderschaegen). Usually, autumn arrivals can be expected from 25 August on, with most observations occurring between 15 September and 20 October.

Much of the fall migration data has come from the hawk observation and banding posts along Green Bay and Lake Michigan. Of particular interest are two individuals banded at the Little Suamico Ornithological Station in Oconto County (T. C. Erdman). One radio-equipped individual was tracked by Cochran (1975) from its 12 October 1974 banding to its 26 October passage into Mexico. The bird followed a southward path to Louisiana, then drifted southwest. A second individual was retrapped in Georgia on 6 October 1977, only 10 days after being banded at Little Suamico.

Several individuals banded at the Cedar Grove Ornithological Station in Sheboygan County have been known to move hundreds of miles in a few days. Birds banded in eastern Wisconsin in September and October have been retaken in Tennessee (4, 9, 10 days later), Ohio (12, 17 days), Florida (16 days), Texas (21 days), Uruguay (68 days), Cuba (95, 135 days), and off the coast of Colombia (49 days).

Cedar Grove hawk-watchers often observed 30–40 birds per autumn in the 1950s. In the early 1970s there were only a third as many. There has been a modest increase in the early 1980s. A similar trend in the 1970s and 1980s is evident at Woodland Dunes in Manitowoc County and at Little Suamico. Fall observations have been made in all parts of Wisconsin, but only of individuals sighted briefly here and there.

Only rarely does a Peregrine remain beyond 10 November. Late fall records include sightings on 20 November (1955, Barron, J. Butler), 2 December (1945, Dane, A. W. Schorger; 1962, Racine, E. B. Prins), and 4 December (1979, Dane, P. Thiessen).

There are no known records of successful overwintering in Wisconsin, but several attempts have been made. Late December records include birds seen on the 20th (1961, Milwaukee, M. F. Donald), 25th (1940, Sauk, S. D. Robbins), 26th (1953, Walworth, C. O. Palmquist), 27th (1962, Waukesha, J. E. Bielefeldt), and 31st (1966, Grant, T. N. Ingram). Still later were sightings on 2 January (1977, Marathon, E. R. Bierbrauer), 16 January (1988, Douglas, R. J. Johnson), and 7 February (1981, Wood, D. G. Follen).

Efforts to reintroduce the Peregrine in various parts of its pre-1965 eastern North America nesting range began to take shape in the early 1970s. Suitable nesting habitat still exists. The banning of DDT in the United States offers hope. Five individuals were released in western Wisconsin in 1986. Additional releases have followed, including 10 juveniles in downtown Milwaukee in 1987, and 6 juveniles in Madison in 1988. In Milwaukee a pair nested in 1988.

Gyrfalcon (*Falco rusticolus*)

STATUS. Rare migrant. Rare winter visitant.

HABITAT. Open grassland and cropland. Savanna.

MIGRATION DATES. Occasionally observed between late November and early April. *Extremes:* 30 September; 23 April.

WINTER. Occasionally present south to Trempealeau, Sauk, Walworth, and Milwaukee counties.

PORTRAIT. *Birds of Wisconsin:* Plate 19.

North America's most northerly hawk has been visiting Wisconsin with increasing frequency in recent years. No positive nineteenth-century records are known. Between 1900 and 1940 four Gyrfalcon specimens were collected, three of which are preserved at the Milwaukee Public Museum: one shot near Beaver Dam (Dodge County) on 27 November 1904 (*fide* Snyder 1905); one killed in Sauk County on 22 October 1916 (*fide* Stoddard 1923b); and one found injured in Milwaukee County on 26 December 1936 (*fide* Gromme 1938a). A fourth specimen procured in Jefferson County on 10 December 1939 (R. R. Roehl), is

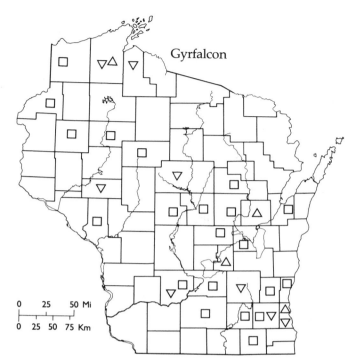

Gyrfalcon, 10 March 1972, Douglas County (photo by S. Meyer)

△   Early March to early April
▽   Late November to late December
☐   Early January to late February

All records

presently on display at the Mackenzie Nature Center at Poynette.

A sight record on 31 December 1938 (Waukesha, H. A. Clapp; MPM files) was followed by another on 9 November 1942 (Milwaukee, O. J. Gromme) and by yet another Milwaukee individual 10 years later (10–17 October 1952, M. F. Donald). After a 14 February 1959 (Sauk, H. C. Kruse) find, the frequency of observations has picked up noticeably, with five well-documented reports during the 1960s.

Then for three consecutive winters between 1971 and 1974, larger than usual numbers showed up all across Canada and the northern United States. *Audubon Field Notes* listed 140 individuals sighted during those winters. The 10 Wisconsin reports during that interval nearly equal the number of previous state records; one involved a gray-phase bird photographed as it perched on a wire in Douglas County (10 March 1972, S. Meyer). The winter of 1974–1975 was the peak year, with an additional six observations. Between 1975 and 1980, known occurrences numbered an additional 11. The presence of one or more individuals somewhere in the state has become almost an annual event.

An unusually early fall observation occurred on 30 September 1980 (Ashland, S. W. Matteson). Most records have occurred between 25 November and 20 March. The following dates suggest a somewhat uniform dispersal: 8 in late November, 17 in December, 8 in January, 8 in February, and 8 in March. At Superior in the early 1980s, individuals stayed for weeks. An adult banded there by D. L. Evans in the winter of 1983–1984 was retrapped the following winter. Nearly all other observations have been of short duration—birds here today and gone tomorrow. An exception was a gray-phase bird in Outagamie and Winnebago counties, noted three times between 13 March and 6 April 1969 (D. D. Tessen). It was the end of the unusual winter of 1971–1972 that produced the state's other two April sightings: the

2nd (Bayfield, A. J. Roy) and 23rd (Milwaukee, M. F. Donald).

The accompanying map also shows a fairly even geographic distribution. The state's 52 observations reflect scattered sightings across 29 counties. Only in the extreme northeastern and southwestern regions has this arctic wanderer escaped detection. This may reflect the paucity of observers more than the absence of birds. Aside from the city of Superior, no one region of the state can be said to have a predominant number of sightings.

In instances where the color phase is known, observers have recorded 16 individuals as white, 21 as gray. The black-phase Gyrfalcon, whose normal range is western Canada, has been recorded in Wisconsin only once: 7–16 January 1984 (Douglas, R. J. Johnson).

Family **Phasianidae:** Partridges, Grouse, Turkeys, Quail

Gray Partridge (*Perdix perdix*)
Formerly Hungarian Partridge

STATUS. Fairly common resident south and east; uncommon resident west-central. Introduced.

HABITAT. Open grassland and cropland.

BREEDING DATA. Nests with eggs: 21 April to 5 August. Hatching peak: 1 July. Clutch size: usually 14–20 eggs; occasionally up to 22.

WINTER. Regularly present north to Grant, Waushara, and Brown counties, and in a small portion of St. Croix County; occasionally present north to Portage and Marinette counties.

PORTRAIT. *Birds of Wisconsin:* Plate 23.

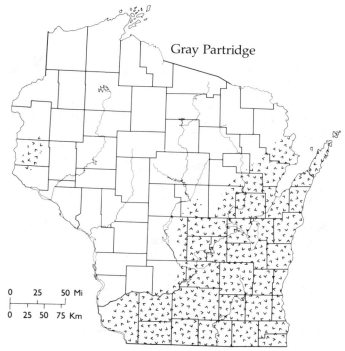

Gray Partridge

0 25 50 Mi

0 25 50 75 Km

⊡ Resident range

Records since 1960

The introduction of this European game bird was largely due to the persistent efforts of one man: Colonel Gustav Pabst of Milwaukee. After an initial release in 1908 that proved unsuccessful, Pabst made four releases in Ottawa Township in Waukesha County in 1910, 1913, 1915, and probably 1918 (Leopold 1931a). Pabst had planned a release for 1914, but all birds died en route. Small supplemental releases followed in 1927 and 1929. Leopold's estimate is that about 5,000 birds were released during this 20-year span.

Private individuals and groups attempted additional introductions in Fond du Lac (1910, 1930), Trempealeau (1914), St. Croix (1923, 1930), Polk (1925–1931), Green Lake (1929), Juneau (1929, 1933), and Columbia (1931) counties.

The gradual spread of this partridge is evident from the accompanying map. The spread has been sporadic, with occasional spurts, some withdrawals, and some consolidations. As numbers increased throughout the 1940s, the heaviest populations were in the easternmost counties. During the severe winter of 1950–1951, concentrations were especially dense along lands adjacent to Lake Michigan; a 100-mile January transect between Milwaukee and Two Rivers tallied 783 individuals.

By 1954 there was a marked trend away from the southeastern counties toward more northerly locations in the Appleton–Green Bay–Manitowoc region. The bird, known at that time as the "Hungarian partridge," also moved gradually westward through much of Columbia, Marquette, and Waushara counties. Between 1955 and 1975 it gradually expanded its range into Grant County in the southwest. A Pierce–St. Croix County pocket has persisted from 1923 and 1930 releases. Another pocket in Clark and Marathon counties developed from 1966 and 1968 releases in the McMillan Wildlife Area near Marshfield, but disappeared in the 1980s. A 1975 survey (Dumke 1977) indicated that the greatest density occurred in Calumet, Manitowoc, and Brown counties, closely followed by Outagamie, Kewaunee, and southern Door counties.

Gates (1973) and Dumke (1977) have shown that the "Huns" prefer alfalfa and other hayfields on small family-sized farms. They avoid the denser cover of marshlands, frequenting instead level cultivated fields, brushy fencelines, and roadsides. In a Dodge–

Fond du Lac–Green Lake County study area, 1960–1965, Gates located 39 nests in hayfields, 15 along roadsides, 12 along fencelines, but none in wetlands. While nest success for roadside locations was 40%, the success rate for fledged young was only 10% in hayfields and 8% along fencelines. Since egg-laying rarely starts before 1 May, and the peak hatching period normally occurs around 1 July, early- and mid-June hay-mowing is frequently disastrous for Hun production. Not only are eggs destroyed but occasionally hens are killed as well, and hens that do survive are often reluctant to renest late in the season.

Weather is also critical for newborn chicks during the first month of life. Gates (1973) noted that brood counts in August were relatively low in 1960–1962 following cool, wet July weather. They were significantly higher in 1963–1965 following a more normal July rainfall and temperature range.

Autumn hunting pressure has apparently not had a significant effect on population levels in recent years. Nor has the amount of snow in winter. Winter habitat is essentially the same as that in other seasons.

Ring-necked Pheasant (*Phasianus colchicus*)

STATUS. Common resident south and east; fairly common resident west and central; uncommon resident northwest. Introduced.

HABITAT. Open grassland. Old field. Sedge meadow.

BREEDING DATA. Nests with eggs: usually 15 April to 15 June; rarely to 20 August. Clutch size: usually 10–12 eggs; rarely up to 20. Main hatching period: 1 June to 15 July.

WINTER. Regularly present north to Pierce, Dunn, Monroe, Portage, Outagamie, Brown, and Kewaunee counties; occasionally present north to Polk, Barron, Marathon, and Marinette counties.

PORTRAIT. *Birds of Wisconsin:* Plate 23.

Between 1895 and 1900, releases of various species of pheasants were attempted independently in Milwaukee, Waukesha, Jefferson, Crawford, La Crosse, Monroe, Wood, Marathon, Waupaca, Brown, Manitowoc, Door, and Bayfield counties (Schorger 1947b). Apparently none of these efforts was successful.

The first successful introduction took place in Waukesha County in 1916. The increase and spread of the birds through the southeastern counties were sufficient to allow limited hunting from 1927 on. In 1928 the state began a propagation program. Promising lands were purchased for public hunting grounds, and thousands of cocks were released in them shortly before and during the fall hunting season. So successfully did this game bird take hold in the southern counties through the 1930s, and so well did the planned stocking program work, that hunters were able to take 800,000 birds in 1942. But there has been a noticeable decline since 1942, with annual hunter kills fluctuating between 300,000 and 500,000 birds.

Contributing to the decline has been the drainage of wetlands that provide the best nesting habitat. Between 1935 and 1955, more than a fourth of the wet-

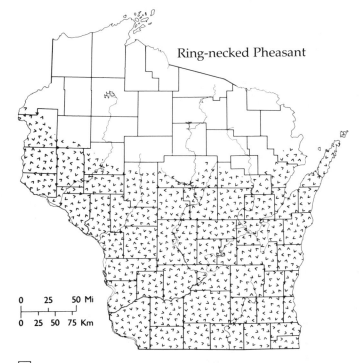

Ring-necked Pheasant

0   25   50 Mi
0 25 50 75 Km

1 ⌐   Resident range

Records since 1960

lands in prime pheasant range were converted to cropland. As a result, more birds were forced to seek nesting cover in hayfields. But hay harvest, formerly begun in late June, now commences in late May. Gates and Hale (1975) estimated that in their study area near Waupun (Dodge County) the average rate of nest success was 3% in pastured hay, 16% in mowed hay, and 63% in undisturbed hay. If the hens survive to renest, the young hatch so late in the season that their chances of fall and winter survival are slim.

Gates and Hale (1975) found that over 92% of all pheasant nesting attempts take place in wetlands, hayfields, and strip cover. Birds nesting in strip cover are highly vulnerable to animal predation. Those nesting in hayfields are interrupted by hay harvest that virtually precludes nesting success. "That pheasants are largely dependent on wetland cover for successful reproduction appears to be a basic principle of Wisconsin pheasant ecology."

In the early 1960s the stocking program was expanded by the release of day-old chicks to cooperating game clubs. Releases at one time or another have taken place across much of the state. When the average birder observes a pheasant in the wild during winter and spring he has no way of knowing whether it is a well-established bird or merely a release from the previous year.

The approximate 1985 Wisconsin pheasant range is shown in the accompanying map. An occasional pheasant may be seen north of the Grantsburg-Wausau-Marinette line, but such birds are not well-established ones. The Monroe-Appleton-Kenosha triangle contains the greatest density. Nesting in this area gets under way in April. First eggs are sometimes laid in the first 2 weeks of April, but more often late in the month or early in May. A second egg-laying peak comes in mid-June if mowing destroys many earlier nests. In a few instances, broods from late-nesting pairs do not appear until early August; their chances of survival are slim.

Spruce Grouse (*Dendragapus canadensis*)

STATUS. Uncommon resident north.
HABITAT. Coniferous forest.
BREEDING DATA. Specific nesting data unknown. Coveys with small young observed between 21 June and 11 August.
WINTER. Regularly present south to Sawyer, Lincoln, and Florence counties.
PORTRAIT. *Birds of Wisconsin:* Plate 21.

Scott (1943) estimated that there was a total state population of 500–800 Spruce Grouse in the early 1940s. In arriving at these figures, he gathered information from local game wardens and others familiar with the northern forests, listed every known sighting between 1935 and 1941, and extrapolated a minimum and maximum estimate for each northern county, based on the amount of favorable Spruce Grouse habitat known to exist. The range he depicted included portions of the northernmost tier of counties from Bayfield to Florence, and second-tier counties Sawyer, Price, Oneida, and Langlade, plus one area in Taylor County (see the accompanying map).

In 1976 Department of Natural Resources personnel indicated that population changes since 1943 had been slight. Observations are scant, but populations remain stable. Clifford Wiita and Jack Moulton (pers. comm.) surmised that Spruce Grouse may have increased slightly in recent years because more acres of favorable coniferous habitat now exist within the range described by Scott. Nearly all recent observations continue to fall within the Scott range. Records published in *The Passenger Pigeon* in Douglas (1969, 1977, 1978, 1985), Burnett (1978, 1981), Barron (1976),

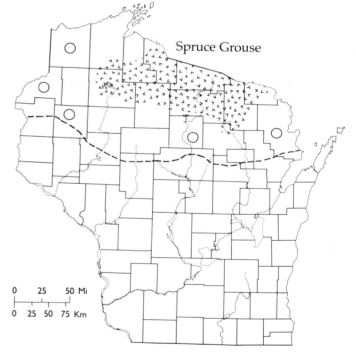

Spruce Grouse

```
0      25      50 Mi
0   25   50   75 Km
```

▱ Resident range in 1943 (after Scott)
--- Southern edge of possible early range (after Scott)
◯ Records since 1960

Rusk (1948), Lincoln (1965, 1966), and Marinette (1972) counties may point to the existence of small populations present in 1943 but not known to Scott.

In the prelogging era this species was probably quite numerous over a much larger portion of the state. The map shows Scott's estimate of the probable range in presettlement days. W. W. Cooke (1888) inferred that this species "in winter occurs as far south as Racine." But since this bird is not known to be migratory and was known to Hoy (1853b) only as a resident of northern Wisconsin, Cooke's inference is questionable.

Ornithologists have thought of the "fool hen" as an endangered species in Wisconsin for much of the twentieth century, as its range has receded. Schorger (1942c) included it in his list of "Extinct and Endangered Mammals and Birds of the Upper Great Lakes Region." When the DNR began tabulating "endangered species" in 1973, this species warranted a place on the list. An effort to restock birds was made in 1952, with the release of 18 birds in Price and Rusk

counties, but it was unsuccessful and has not been repeated.

In Canada the Spruce Grouse is not an endangered bird. Northern Wisconsin lies at the edge of its range, but the bird is subject to cyclic population swings. In favor of its continued survival as a Wisconsin species is its preference for relatively undisturbed spruce-cedar-tamarack swamps, and the gradual increase in favorable habitat in the northern counties. Militating against its survival is the advent of the snowmobile, which makes almost any area accessible and disturbable in winter. Perhaps it will owe its survival most of all to the fact that it is not a tasty bird, and therefore not particularly tempting to hunters—in or out of season.

Willow Ptarmigan (*Lagopus lagopus*)

STATUS. Accidental. One record.
HABITAT. Upland carr.

The one positive record of this arctic resident's visiting Wisconsin dates back to December 1846: Hoy (1853b) examined two individuals trapped near Racine. At the time he suggested that breeding might take place in the evergreen swamps of the northwestern counties.

Although it has since become apparent that nesting activity does not occur in Wisconsin, there is evidence that the ptarmigan has reached the state on at least two other occasions. Kumlien and Hollister (1903) recorded as secondhand information the procuring of a bird by W. F. Bundy in Sauk County in 1876. No details are known and the specimen has never been located, but Professor Bundy was described as "a reliable naturalist."

Another indefinite record reaches back to the 1850s, when Thure Kumlien saw the frozen mutilated remains of a ptarmigan said to have been taken by a land hunter in the northern region of the state. Again, evidence is lacking, and Kumlien and Hollister (1903) listed nothing to prove that either this bird or the Sauk County bird was a Willow Ptarmigan.

An attempt was made to introduce 18 of these birds into Wood County in 1941. On 31 January, Wisconsin Conservation Department personnel banded and released these birds (originally captured 300 miles north of Winnipeg) in Remington Township. Most, if not all, of them evidently moved northward; one bird was recaptured in Bayfield County on 28 April (H. Baldwin), two appeared in Vilas County on 14 May (R. Jacoubek), and a fourth may have been sighted in Price County (date and observer uncertain).

Ruffed Grouse (*Bonasa umbellus*)

STATUS. Common resident north and central; fairly common resident southwest; uncommon resident southeast.

HABITAT. Deciduous forest. Northern maple-hemlock-pine forest.

BREEDING DATA. Nests with eggs: 27 April to 28 June. Clutch size: usually 9–14 eggs; rarely up to 20.

WINTER. Regularly present in all but extreme southeastern counties.

PORTRAIT. *Birds of Wisconsin:* Plate 21.

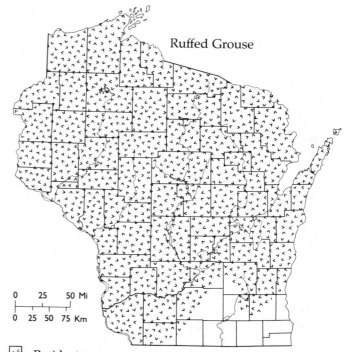

Ruffed Grouse

0   25   50 Mi
0   25 50 75 Km

☐ Resident range

Records since 1960

Although much land that was once forested has yielded to the plow, this woodland drummer can still be found in all but five counties (Kenosha, Racine, Milwaukee, Walworth, and Rock). The Ruffed Grouse has endured the low points of many a 10-year cycle. It has survived prolonged and severe hunting pressure, such as that described by Kumlien and Hollister (1903). "In the sections of northern Wisconsin where the grouse are still abundant, every subterfuge possible is practiced to evade the law in regard to shipments and the number each hunter is allowed to carry on the trains, and great quantities find their way into the city markets despite the strict and careful vigilance of the game wardens." It has survived severe winter weather when drifted and crusted snow has decimated the numbers of other game species. These grouse often spend winter nights by diving into snow banks, but when snow becomes too heavily drifted or encrusted they choose to roost instead in the branches of dense evergreens.

North of a line from Potosi to Manitowoc, wherever suitable woodland exists, this bird is common. South of this line, modest numbers exist in Sheboygan and Ozaukee counties and in the Kettle Moraine State Forest of Fond du Lac, Washington, and Waukesha counties. Only in the extreme southeast is it not found. Birds were last reported on the CBC in Kenosha in 1949, in Racine in 1955, and in Milwaukee in 1951.

Neither the CBC in December nor the BBS in June, however, points to an accurate population index. Males have been known to drum during every month of the year, but drumming is rarest between December and February and between June and August. Population levels and habitat preferences were studied extensively by Grange (1948), Dorney (1959a), and Kubisak, Moulton, and McCaffery (1980). Ruffed Grouse show a preference for stands of 10–25-year-old aspens, with drumming often done from logs near the edge of upland aspens and lowland alders.

After much drumming and courting in April, birds settle down to nest in May and June. Observers have found eggs from 27 April on, and noted broods of young as early as 27 May. Grange (1948) reported on 32 nests in Wood County in 1941; the clutch size varied between 9 and 13 eggs. In 18 instances he found that the eggs were destroyed by snakes, skunks, cows, owls, and crows, or they were abandoned for unknown reasons. Doubtless there is further mortality in June and July from predators, affecting successfully fledged young.

Although the familiar "partridge" is almost exclusively a bird of the forest, a few individuals each autumn have made local headlines after slamming into windows and wandering into garages in residential areas. The 26 October 1887 issue of an Elkhorn (Walworth County) newspaper contained this item: "A Ruffed Grouse in its mad course the other day struck the subscriber's house kerthump! dropped onto the ground, got up, spread its tail, shook its feathers and resumed its flight. Later one went through Mrs. John Meig's pantry window, the misguided bird cutting itself so badly with the broken glass that it was a mercy to kill the poor thing." A neighbor once showed me a dusty windowpane in his house with an imprint of a clearly recognizable wing pattern, indicating precisely where a partridge had struck it that morning.

Greater Prairie-Chicken (*Tympanuchus cupido*)

STATUS. Locally uncommon resident central and northwest.
HABITAT. Open grassland.
BREEDING DATA. Nests with eggs: 15 April to 10 July. Clutch size: usually 10–15 eggs; rarely 5–17; average 12.
WINTER. Regularly present in portions of Adams, Portage, Wood, Clark, Marathon, Taylor, and Burnett counties.
PORTRAIT. *Birds of Wisconsin:* Plate 22.

Vivid in my memory is an April morning in 1954 when S. Paul Jones and I stood on the Leola Marsh in Adams County. Ruffed Grouse were drumming, Common Snipe were winnowing, Sandhill Cranes were trumpeting, and in the distance there was the hollow "tympanuchal thunder" of the dancing Prairie-Chicken. Jones wistfully commented, "We used to hear this in Waukesha County."

Used to! So goes the refrain for the "pinnated grouse" in Wisconsin. Schorger (1942b) estimated that the original breeding range extended north to a line from what is now River Falls east to Green Bay, then south—west of Lake Winnebago—to Milwaukee. In the earlier stages of agricultural development in the southern region, the birds flourished, and between 1845 and 1870 they seemed abundant. During this period their range spread northward as settlement and land-clearing progressed. Hunters had a heyday at that time. It was not unusual for a gunner to bag 50 birds in a day, and it is estimated that tons of birds found their way to eastern markets every year. Scott (1947b) reported: "There are records from 1845 to 1869 showing that farmers burned the prairies in spring just before plowing, and sometimes deliberately to kill birds which would later feed on the grain, so that thousands of scorched eggs could be found in the fields alongside the charred bodies of young birds."

Although this practice undoubtedly took its toll in local areas, it was the disappearance of habitat—as grassland gave way to plowed cropland—that was primarily responsible for the gradual decline of southern populations from 1870 on. This was partly compensated for by an increase in the central region of the state—particularly in the developing meadows in the Wisconsin Rapids–Stevens Point area—and by new invasions into suitable open areas in the northern counties. By 1920 these birds had been observed in virtually every county. Greater Prairie-Chickens have exhibited a modest but little-understood ten-

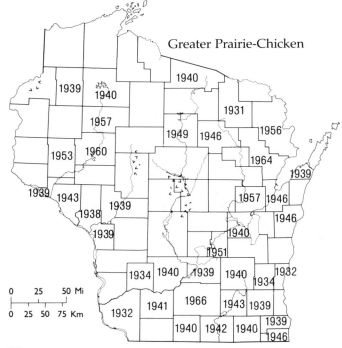

Greater Prairie-Chicken

Resident range

Years of last county records in former range, where known

dency to migrate, which may well have taken them northward.

Suitable habitat, according to W. B. Grange (pers. comm. to O. J. Gromme), requires: (1) relatively open grassland, (2) dense grassland, (3) a plentiful weed supply, (4) berries, (5) cultivated grains, (6) acorns (usually), (7) some shrubbery (usually), and (8) aspen or birch for budding (sometimes). As long as accidental forest and prairie fires occurred, there was a stage between burning and the redevelopment of forest edge that provided suitable habitat. Because the habitat kept changing, there was often a shifting of chickens to other places.

By 1930 methods of controlling accidental forest and grass fires had improved greatly, and the concept of controlled burning for wildlife management had not yet gained wide acceptance. In addition, agriculture was becoming more widespread and more mechanized. As these developments took place, chicken habitat began to dwindle with alarming rapidity. A 1929 survey of chickens by A. O. Gross, A. Leopold, and F. J. W. Schmidt (Gross 1930a) showed birds still present in every county except three along the western border (Crawford, Vernon, Pepin) and three along

Lake Michigan (Racine, Milwaukee, Ozaukee). The statewide population estimate was 54,850, with 4,000 birds or more per county in Green Lake, Shawano, Portage, Wood, and Pierce counties.

From 1930 on the decline was rapid. The accompanying map traces this decline by listing the last year for which observations are known in each county. Also shown is the last stronghold: portions of Adams, Portage, Wood, and Marathon counties, where an estimated 2,500 birds were still present in 1981, and tiny colonies in Clark and Taylor counties.

These, too, might well have disappeared, had it not been for the dedicated efforts of Frederick and Frances Hamerstrom and the supplementary support of a host of determined conservationists. The Hamerstroms lived with the chickens for over 30 years, studied them, and alerted the public to the birds' needs. Together with Oswald Mattson, the Hamerstroms devised a preservation plan that is now being implemented by the Department of Natural Resources. Strong financial support in the form of significant land purchases came from the Society of Tympanuchus Cupido and allied conservation groups. Between 1957 and 1971 over 14,000 acres of prime chicken habitat in Portage and Adams counties were purchased by the DNR, or by concerned individuals and organizations and leased to the DNR, for management. This was intended to provide a substantial grassland base for establishing a stable population, even if land use in adjacent areas changes, as, indeed, is already happening. Lands once used for production of bluegrass seed became increasingly used for cattle grazing, and still more recently, for muck farming. But the chicken population has stabilized on lands managed for their preservation. The "boomer" may yet be forced to retreat from some outlying range, but if the Hamerstrom-Mattson plan can continue, at least a modest population will persist.

In 1974, efforts aimed at restocking birds began at the Crex Meadows Wildlife Area in Burnett County. Plantings subsequently have resulted in the establishment of a few resident wild birds, but more time is needed before the project can be termed successful.

Sharp-tailed Grouse (*Tympanuchus phasianellus*)

STATUS. Uncommon resident north and central.
HABITAT. Young forest saplings. Old field. Open grassland.
BREEDING DATA. Nests with eggs: 15 April to 30 June. Clutch size: 9–17 eggs; average 12.
WINTER. Regularly present north of a line from Burnett through Juneau to Florence counties.
PORTRAIT. *Birds of Wisconsin:* Plate 22.

"Probably doomed to speedy extinction," wrote Kumlien and Hollister (1903). Thure Kumlien had found Sharp-tailed Grouse "extremely abundant"; he considered this bird the common prairie grouse of southern Wisconsin in the 1840s. Hoy (1853b) had already noticed a decrease in the southeast as human settlement advanced. The Kumliens procured their last specimen in the southeast in 1869. They had the word of J. N. Clark that Dunn County populations, which had remained high through 1885, were dwindling in 1902. With a constantly expanding human population, it was no wonder that Kumlien and Hollister believed that the Sharp-tail could be "found in any numbers only in isolated sections of the central and northwestern part." They feared that the bird's days were numbered.

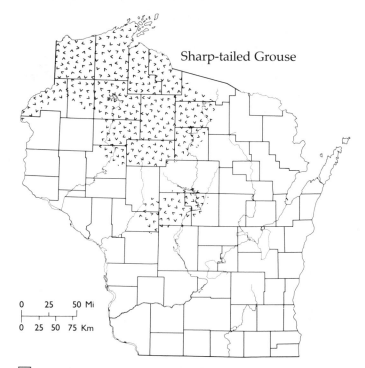

Sharp-tailed Grouse

0   25   50 Mi

0   25   50   75 Km

Resident range in 1989

Yet 80 years later, extirpation has not occurred. Populations have dwindled during the twentieth century, as is evident from the accompanying map. The map compares Hamerstrom and Hamerstrom's (1961) estimate of the range in 1948–1953 with Vanderschaegen's assessment 25 years later. Even though the apparently solid areas probably denote separate pockets, it is clear that a significant reduction in range has occurred. What once included portions of 31 (possibly 35?) counties has shrunk to portions of 23 counties. How many of the small isolated pockets shown here will continue to exist in future years is problematical.

Nesting studies by F. N. Hamerstrom (1939) indicate that the typical grouse pair lays 12 eggs, usually during May. There is only a slight loss from infertility or parental desertion, but because of predation close to half of the nests fail to produce young.

One factor favoring the continued preservation of the Sharp-tail is its predilection for open spruce bogs—one type of habitat that has been relatively undisturbed. W. B. Grange (pers. comm. to O. J. Gromme) stated: "Quite often the sharptail is present in open muskeg types of environment, where Christmas tree spruces dot the bog landscape. Such places are truly open lands, but they are not primarily grasslands."

A second factor favoring survival is periodic forest fire. Grange continued: "The sharptail also occurs almost wherever fires have destroyed the main forest growth; the species exists in this temporary habitat from the time of fire until the forest has again reclaimed the land. . . . Possibly no other species is so closely tied, environmentally, to the occurrence of fire and to the plant succession stages which follow fire but precede reforestation."

A third positive factor is the active concern of aroused conservationists. Under the auspices of the University of Wisconsin, the former Wisconsin Conservation Department, and the present Department of Natural Resources, research and management plans have been developed that offer hope for preserving the species. In the early 1930s the statewide game survey by Leopold (1931a) and the studies of Gross (1930b), Schmidt (1936), and Grange (1940b) provided a database for shaping Sharp-tail management. And since 1935 the work of the Hamerstroms has been instrumental. The publication of "Sharptails into the Shadows?" (Hamerstrom, Hamerstrom, and Mattson 1952) increased public concern, and helped in the development of management areas at various central and northern sites. Here, controlled burning has saved pockets of suitable habitat. As long as this practice continues, and as long as open spruce bogs remain in a relatively undisturbed state, Sharp-tails have a chance of persisting in groups of 10–30 birds. As of 1984, however, a gradual decline in numbers had continued. F. N. Hamerstrom (pers. comm.) commented, "The species is not by any means saved as yet, and won't be unless a more determined effort is made than anything seen so far."

Vanderschaegen (1975) expressed similar reservations. He described six types of suitable habitat: (1) old burns, (2) abandoned farms, (3) frost pockets, (4) off-site aspen, (5) open bogs, and (6) large clearcuts. Much habitat is deteriorating as reforestation progresses and as farming intensifies. Of 16 wildlife areas maintaining some Sharp-tails in 1975, Vanderschaegen named only 5 (Burnett, Douglas, Taylor, Marathon, and Jackson counties) that showed continued promise for maintaining adequate populations.

Wild Turkey (*Meleagris gallopavo*)

STATUS. Formerly common resident south and east-central. Reintroduced; uncommon resident southwest, central, and northeast.

HABITAT. Deciduous forest.

BREEDING DATA. Nests with eggs: 18 April to 1 August. Clutch size: 8–15 eggs.

WINTER. Reintroduced birds regularly present north and east to Pierce, Dunn, Portage, and Manitowoc counties.

PORTRAIT. *Birds of Wisconsin:* Plate 24.

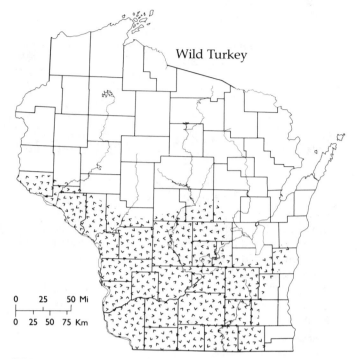

Resident range in 1989, following introductions since 1976

When the first white settlers came to southern Wisconsin, they found these turkeys wild and plentiful. Schorger (1942a) described the early nineteenth-century range as south of "a line running southwest from Green Bay through Green Lake and Sauk Counties, thence due west along the Minnesota-Iowa boundary." Within that range the level of abundance must have been spotty, for in "The Birds of Dane County" (1929b, 1931a) Schorger stated, "I have been unable to obtain an entirely satisfactory record of the Wild Turkey in Dane County." He listed it as common in the southeast and southwest, less common elsewhere. The northern range limit oscillated; hard winters with deep snows hurt this bird.

Perhaps the turkey's demise would have been inevitable as the human population increased and the oak woods decreased. But the species' decline also accelerated when deep crusted snow made food hard to get during the hard winter of 1842–1843. Whole flocks were wiped out in sizable areas. Hoy (1853b) listed 1846 as the last date for turkeys near Racine. Other final dates in Waukesha (1847), Rock (1854), Crawford (1872), and Lafayette (1881) counties help trace the species disappearance across southern Wisconsin. According to Kumlien and Hollister (1903), Grant County residents found a few birds as late as 1894.

Between 1929 and 1939 a vigorous effort was made by the Wisconsin Conservation Department to reintroduce turkeys, with plantings made chiefly in Sauk and Grant counties. The WCD began with a modest flock of 39, building up to a high of 1,258 in 1938, for a total of 2,942 birds in this 11-year period. But the birds seemed to prefer neighborhood farms to the more remote hills and oak woods. Disease, domestication, predation, and hunting took their toll. The last survivors of this experiment probably died in southern Adams County in 1958.

A second major transplant experiment began with the release of 290 birds in the Meadow Valley region of Juneau County in 1954. Yearly additions con-

tinued through 1957, and for several years the outlook seemed promising. In 1963–1964 there were an estimated 750 birds spread over 80 square miles. Two years later there were 2,500 scattered over 300 square miles. Dispersal from the Meadow Valley–Necedah area may well explain sightings in Portage (1966, F. M. Baumgartner), Clark (1968, F. Seiling), and Adams (1972, D. E. Greenman) counties. But in 1967 and 1968 along came heavy rains that caused high brood losses, and in the winter of 1968–1969 there was heavy snow. The rain and snow took a heavy toll, and by 1973 the estimated population had dropped to 70 individuals.

In the early 1970s the Department of Natural Resources transplanted Meadow Valley birds to new locations in Marinette, Pepin, Grant, and Crawford counties. These efforts were followed by additional importations of wild Missouri birds into the hills of western Crawford and Vernon counties, beginning in 1976 (29 birds) and 1977 (16 individuals). Early in 1978, 20 more Missouri imports were released in Buffalo County. The western Wisconsin hills offer plentiful supplies of acorns and waste grain, which this species requires. So successfully has the Wild Turkey taken hold in southwestern Wisconsin, especially between Grant and Buffalo counties, that DNR officials were able to start a controlled spring hunt in 1983 and an autumn season in 1989.

There have been occasional private releases as well. Observers sighted birds in Outagamie County in 1969 following a 1968 planting, and in Fond du Lac County in 1974 following a 1973 release. New releases, DNR and private, continue. Small populations now exist in northern Oconto and Marinette counties. By trapping wild birds in the southwestern counties and releasing them in favorable habitat throughout the southern region, DNR personnel are attempting to establish this species in 34 counties north to Pierce, Dunn, Jackson, Portage, Waupaca, and Manitowoc.

Northern Bobwhite (*Colinus virginianus*)

STATUS. Fairly common resident west and south; uncommon resident central and southeast.
HABITAT. Upland carr.
BREEDING DATA. Nests with eggs: usually 5–31 May; rarely to 20 September. Main hatching period: 15 June to 10 July. Clutch size: usually 10–16 eggs; rarely up to 20.
WINTER. Regularly present north to Dunn, Wood, and Waupaca counties.
PORTRAIT. *Birds of Wisconsin:* Plate 23.

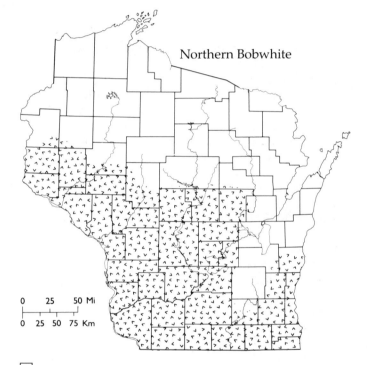

Resident range

Records since 1960

One of Wisconsin's first game laws, enacted in 1852, limited the capture and sale of quail to the period from the first Tuesday in October to 1 February. Large numbers of quail existed in southern Wisconsin at that time, and birds were being shipped by the ton from Milwaukee and Chicago to eastern cities. Even after the law was passed, the traffic remained so heavy that it was estimated that 55,000 birds were shipped from Beloit in the winter of 1854–1855. Barry's (1854) statement that the Northern Bobwhite is "distributed in immense numbers over the entire state," however, must be interpreted in terms of what we now know as the southern and central portions. Grundtvig (1895) and Willard (1885b) found it only sparingly in Outagamie and Brown counties in 1883. I doubt that it ever occurred more than sporadically in the north.

Numbers had dropped significantly by 1870. In 1884 restocking efforts were begun in order to stem the decline. At times there have been rather sudden increases, usually after a succession of mild winters, and these were probably responsible for the occasional records of birds in Douglas, Bayfield, Washburn, Price, Barron, and Langlade counties. A sizable population developed in Polk and Burnett counties following the 1895 Hinckley, Minnesota, fire. These outposts were then completely or nearly wiped out when, inevitably, severe winters once again occurred.

The most stable quail territory lies in the southwestern part of the state, south of a line from Hudson to Stevens Point and Waupaca, and west of a line from Waupaca to Whitewater and Beloit. The bird was common within this region in the 1930s and 1940s, and fairly common farther east almost to Lake Michigan. But changing agricultural practices since the early 1950s have wrought significant declines. Mechanization has led both to the removal of hedgerows and to the disappearance of cornshocks. These were the major providers of food and shelter, and with them a 160-acre farm could adequately support one or two coveys of 20–30 birds each.

Without such sources of sustenance and cover, these cheery whistlers have experienced a marked decline. Since 1931, researchers Leopold (1931a), Errington and Hamerstrom (1939), Errington (1945), Kabat and Thompson (1963), and Dumke (1975) have studied the quail. Dumke's annual totals from road transects run since 1948 dropped precipitously in 1959. State hunting kills showed a drop from 47,400 birds in 1958 to 8,500 in 1960. Populations have leveled off since 1960. Even after a series of closed seasons, 1962–1972, annual hunter kills since 1980 have remained under 8,000.

Within the resident range shown on the accompanying map, the highest quail densities exist in the southwest corner from Grant County northeast to Marquette County. Numbers remain small northwest to St. Croix, Dunn, and Clark counties.

Some wandering north of a St. Croix Falls–Green Bay line has occurred in recent years. Since 1960, observers have sighted birds in Burnett (1964, 1976, 1980), Washburn (1962), Marathon (1969, 1980), Langlade (1964), and Shawano (1978, 1980) counties. But since quail are often reared in private game farms north of their usual range, there is a strong possibility that some of the more northerly records may represent local releases or escapes.

Family **Rallidae:** Rails, Gallinules, Coots

Yellow Rail (*Coturnicops noveboracensis*)

STATUS. Rare migrant. Rare summer resident north and east.

HABITAT. Shallow marsh.

MIGRATION DATES. *Spring:* late April to late May. *Fall:* late August to early October. *Extremes:* 29 March; 18 October.

BREEDING DATA. Nests with eggs: 23 May to 26 June. Clutch size: usually 8 or 9 eggs; rarely 7–11.

PORTRAIT. *Birds of Wisconsin:* Plate 26.

On 13 October 1901, Ned Hollister flushed a Yellow Rail on a marsh near Delavan (Walworth County) and carefully watched where the bird landed. For nearly an hour two men and two bird dogs worked the area thoroughly, but could not flush the bird again (Hollister 1902). It is because of such extremely secretive habits that this bird remains a mystery to most Wisconsin ornithologists.

Much of our present knowledge comes from C. H. Richter, who studied these birds in the Green Bay marshes of Oconto and Marinette counties from 1926 to 1973. He wrote (pers. comm.): "This rail is far more choosy regarding its nesting grounds. If suitable it will sometimes colonize. In 1959 in one Marinette County area there were eight or ten nesting pairs in an area of only a few acres." He found 15 nests, all built up on tussocks well hidden under a thick canopy of old marsh grass. Most nests were discovered between 25 May and 5 June, with full clutches numbering eight or nine eggs.

Away from the Green Bay marshes, no positive nest records are known. Kumlien and Hollister (1903) stated: "We have authentic records from Racine, Milwaukee, Elm Grove, Delavan, Janesville, Milton, etc., and even breeding records as far north as Brown County." But they gave no specific nesting data. Near Superior, a young bird incapable of flight was captured on 6 August 1965; this bird must have come from a Douglas County nest. Breeding is probable at Powell Marsh in Vilas County, where observers have detected birds calling in June and July in 1942, 1973, 1975, 1978, 1980, and 1984. Nesting is also probable at Crex Meadows Wildlife Area in Burnett County. Individuals were heard in late May in 1978, 1979, and 1981, and in June in 1962, 1976, 1977, and 1983. Brown County records for 25 June (1963) and 16 August

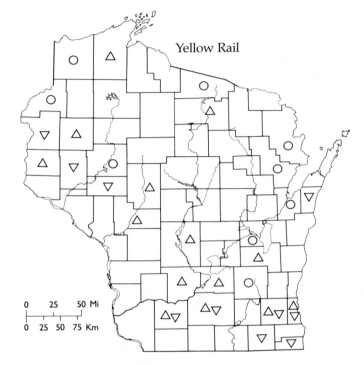

Yellow Rail

0   25   50 Mi
0 25 50 75 Km

△ Late April to late May
○ Early June to mid-August
▽ Late August to early October

Records since 1900

(1970, D. D. Tessen) were only 15–25 miles south of the areas Richter visited. Other isolated summer records include: 21 July (1965, Dodge, R. B. Dryer), 15 July (1975, Winnebago, D. D. Tessen), 18 June (1980, Chippewa, C. A. Kemper), and 24 July (1982, Dodge, J. H. Braastad).

As can be seen from the accompanying map, spring migrants have been recorded sparingly from a variety of locations. Some were individuals seen scurrying across a road; some were spotted flying from one part of a marsh to another; and some were identified by the distinctive "tick-tick" sound these birds utter in the evening or early morning. Of particular interest is the experience of Frederick Hamerstrom and Lawrence Walkinshaw on 7 May 1941. From their blind on the Leola Marsh in northern Adams County they heard a dozen Yellow Rails.

All but one of the spring birds were recorded between 23 April (1908, Sauk, H. L. Stoddard; MPM files) and 28 May (1980, Oneida, C. Schroeder). The exception was a storm-blown bird found dead near Madison on 29 March 1950 (D. H. Pimlott).

Kemper (1973a) listed September towerkills at Eau Claire on the 5th (1961), 22nd (1971) and 25th (1972) and one on 3 October (1962). Other fall migrants have been observed or collected between 20 August (1933, Waukesha, W. E. Scott; MPM files) and 18 October (1908, Waukesha, C. Brandler; MPM files).

It is even more difficult to find these elusive birds in fall than in spring, because then they are virtually silent. Autumn observations published in *The Passenger Pigeon* average but three per decade.

Much more remains to be learned about the presence of this species in Wisconsin, both as migrant and as breeder. Richter's success in finding these birds in Oconto and Marinette counties, plus the increasing frequency with which alert ears are picking up the distinctive call note in Vilas and Burnett counties, lends support to Kumlien and Hollister's (1903) assessment: "This little rail is not nearly so rare as generally supposed, though by no means common." In Schorger's revision (1951a) of Kumlien and Hollister's work, he listed spring specimens taken in 1908, 1911, and 1920 and autumn birds collected in 1901 and 1932, all falling within the same migration schedule as that suggested by recent records.

King Rail (*Rallus elegans*)

STATUS. Uncommon migrant south and east; rare migrant west and north. Uncommon summer resident south and east; rare summer resident west and central.

HABITAT. Shallow marsh.

MIGRATION DATES. *Spring:* late April to mid-May. *Fall:* mid-August to late September. *Extremes:* 2 April; 19 December.

BREEDING DATA. Nests with eggs: 18 May to 7 July. Clutch size: 6–13 eggs.

PORTRAIT. *Birds of Wisconsin:* Plate 26.

To most observers the King Rail is a rare bird. One can spend a long time peering into the edges of an extensive marsh and catch nary a glimpse of this secretive species. Although the largest of Wisconsin rails, Kings remain remarkably well hidden. Oftentimes observers have waited on the edge of promising marshes in early morning and evening, listening for the deep-throated call of *R. elegans*—in vain, for this bird calls less frequently than its smaller cousins. Only rarely—by sheer good fortune—is an observer rewarded with a glimpse of one of these birds scurrying across the road to get from one part of a marsh to another.

Yet sustained observation has shown that in certain areas the bird is more common than is generally supposed. Detailed efforts by O. J. Gromme resulted in the discovery of 14 nests in Adams County between 14 June and 8 July 1930. At the Horicon National Wildlife Refuge in Dodge County managers D. E. Gray and L. F. Gunther estimated summer populations at 100 during the 1950s.

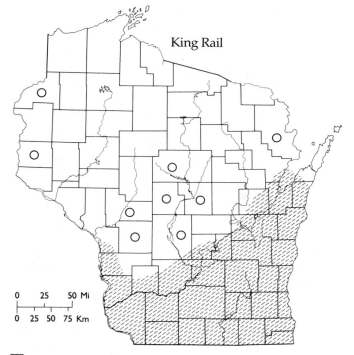

King Rail

◱ Summer range
○ Late May to early August

Records since 1960

Records since 1960 show probable regular summer residence in La Crosse, Waukesha, Milwaukee, Dodge, Brown, and Oconto counties, although records for the entire state published in *The Passenger Pigeon* number but five to eight per year. Concerted efforts probably could produce sightings of individuals in small numbers south of a curved line from La Crosse through Columbia to Oconto counties, wherever extensive marshy habitat exists. The notations north of this line, depicted on the accompanying map, show that the normal range may well be more extensive.

Exceptionally early arrivals have been recorded on 2 April (1963, Dodge, J. Kurtz), 17 April (1930, Jefferson, E. E. Bussewitz; MPM files; 1986, Dodge, J. L. Baughman), and 19 April (1948, Milwaukee, D. L. Larkin). On five occasions observers have reported late April dates, but the more typical arrival dates are 1–15 May.

Reporting on three Oconto County nests in 1938–1939, Carl Richter indicated that the nest in each case was located at the base of marsh vegetation which was surrounded by water. He observed clutches of 13, 13, and 9 eggs and estimated that 15 May was the approximate date when egg-laying began. Broods of young have been seen by the end of June.

Few observations have been reported beyond 20 September. But at Horicon NWR birds have been known to linger into November on four occasions; the latest involved a bird banded on 11 November 1952 (L. F. Gunther). Four still later dates reflect records of collected specimens. The Milwaukee Public Museum has a skin from Green Lake County dated 20 November 1925. Buss and Mattison (1955) recorded a bird killed in Pepin County on 20 November 1939. A bird was found dead on 14 December (1952, Manitowoc, J. Kraupa) and another on 19 December (1906, Dodge, W. E. Snyder [1907]). Two live birds were encountered on a 14 December CBC (1974, Dane, W. L. Hilsenhoff).

Kumlien and Hollister (1903) noted that this bird did much of its late-summer feeding on oats and grasshoppers. Evidently responding favorably to agricultural development in southern Wisconsin, the King Rail was considerably more numerous around 1900 than it had been in the 1870s. If this interest in oats and other cultivated crops still prevails among today's generations of King Rails, it has escaped notice. Recent records all come from wetlands.

Virginia Rail (*Rallus limicola*)

STATUS. Fairly common migrant south and east; uncommon migrant north and west. Fairly common summer resident south and east; uncommon summer resident north and west. Rare winter resident south.

HABITAT. Shallow marsh.

MIGRATION DATES. *Spring:* mid-April to late May. *Fall:* early September to mid-November.

BREEDING DATA. Nests with eggs: 8 May to 30 June. Clutch size: 7–11 eggs.

WINTER. Rarely present north to Dane and Oconto counties.

PORTRAIT. *Birds of Wisconsin:* Plate 26.

If on a cloudy night in early May, you stand outside and listen to the calls of low-flying night migrants, you will have an excellent chance of hearing an occasional "cutta-cutta" along with the usual chips of sparrows and warblers. The first 3 weeks of May mark the main spring migration period for the Virginia Rail. This species is noisier than many others when passing overhead in night migration, and its call is a distinctive one.

The first migrant Virginias usually reach the state between 15 and 20 April. Remarkably early is a 30 March 1986 sighting (Fond du Lac, W. K. Volkert). Ear-

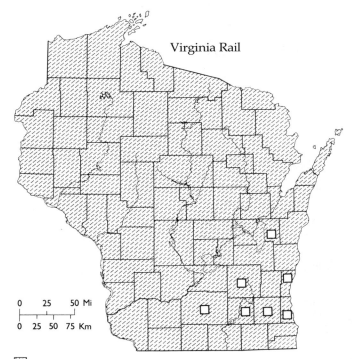

Virginia Rail

▨ Summer range
□ Late November to mid-February

Records since 1960

liest April arrivals include birds on the 3rd (1976, Kenosha, R. R. Hoffman), 4th (1963, Dodge, J. Kurtz; 1971, Dane, N. Ashman; 1980, Kenosha, R. R. Hoffman), 5th (1941, Dane, S. D. Robbins), and 6th (1934, Walworth, E. G. Wright; MPM files). There are records from the northern counties for the 16th (1958, Burnett, N. R. Stone) and 21st (1969, Marinette, H. L. Lindberg). There are no records of sizable concentrations at any one location during the spring, but the larger marshes undoubtedly harbor extensive numbers. The bird is most numerous east of a line from Platteville to Marinette, but nowhere is it as common as the Sora.

The summer range is statewide in scope. As in spring, the greatest numbers of Virginias can be found east of the Platteville-Marinette line, but a few can be expected wherever suitable habitat exists. Faanes (1981) gave this species a "fairly common" rating in Polk and St. Croix counties. It is regular at the Crex Meadows Wildlife Area in Burnett County. Bernard (1967) called it an uncommon summer resident in Douglas County. The BBS has produced records from Polk, Washburn, Taylor, Lincoln, and Langlade counties.

One of the greatest hazards the Virginia faces during the nesting season is high water. Carl Richter (pers. comm.) found a 1967 nest in Marinette County that "showed evidence of having been built up several times, due to fluctuation of water level along the shore of Green Bay." In several other instances he found nests built on tussocks only 2 inches above the level of the surrounding water. For most of the 13 nests he documented, egg-laying took place mainly between 15 and 30 May.

The sighting of a recently fledged young bird in Marathon County on 6 June (1981, S. D. Robbins) suggests that egg-laying sometimes begins before 10 May. It is between 15 July and 15 August that the birds are most in evidence. As parents move around to find food for their young, they often get out into the more exposed portions of a marsh, where they can be seen from nearby roads and dikes. The tossing of a pebble into a moist marshy area often provokes a warning call from a nearby parent.

Eau Claire television tower casualties have been noted between 5 September and 9 October (C. A. Kemper). Presumably, the fall migration is under way by 1 September, with the last fall sighting occurring by 15 October. In mild autumns, however, a few birds remain far beyond that date. At the Horicon National Wildlife Refuge in Dodge County, November dates were recorded in 1947 and 1949 and December dates in 1961 and 1967. During some controlled burning on the marsh on 17 December 1971, at least a dozen rails were flushed—some or all of which were this species (R. G. Personius; Horicon NWR files). CBC observations have been made in Calumet (1980), Ozaukee (1978, 1980), Milwaukee (1977), Jefferson (1980), Waukesha (1956, 1966, 1971, 1980, 1983, 1987), Columbia (1983, 1987), and Dane (1964, 1969, 1972, 1974, 1980, 1983) counties. In Oconto County one of several Virginias was collected on 7 January 1953 (C. H. Richter). Dane County birds have remained into January until the 25th (1981, A. K. Shea) and 28th (1984, W. L. Hilsenhoff). These birds feed along the edges of spring-fed creeks that remain open in early winter. Known survivors into early February include birds sighted on the 2nd (1958, Jefferson, O. L. Compton), 10th (1963, Jefferson, E. Degner), and 15th (1980, Waukesha, S. Stehno). No birds, to my knowledge, have survived an entire winter.

Sora (*Porzana carolina*)

STATUS. Common migrant. Common summer resident south and central; fairly common summer resident north. Rare winter resident south.
HABITAT. Shallow marsh.
MIGRATION DATES. *Spring:* mid-April to late May. *Fall:* late August to early November.
BREEDING DATA. Nests with eggs: 11 May to 15 June. Clutch size: 6–16 eggs.
WINTER. Rarely present to mid-February north to Sauk, Dane, and Brown counties.
PORTRAIT. *Birds of Wisconsin:* Plate 26.

Every commentator—nineteenth and twentieth century—has called the Sora Wisconsin's most common rail. Just how numerous is anyone's guess, because you can only stand at the edge of a marsh in early morning or early evening and count the calls and whinnies emanating from birds skulking in the tall grass. If you hear 5–10 different individuals, you are doing well. But from 8 to 10 May 1954, Alvin Peterson (*Pass. Pigeon* 16:150) observed 150 birds along the shore of Lake Onalaska in La Crosse County. The birds were feeding on windblown masses of old matted vegetation that had accumulated along the water's edge.

It is during the 5–10 May period, probably the spring migration peak, that I have most often heard night-migrating Soras calling as they pass overhead. While these birds are not numerous before 1 May, first arrivals are usually detected in the southern counties between 15 and 20 April and in the north between 25 and 30 April. Besides an exceptional 29 March discovery (1975, Kenosha, R. R. Hoffman), stragglers appeared in early April on the 1st (1972, Rock, E. Brakefield), 4th (1981, Winnebago, T. Ziebell), and 6th (1950, Rock, G. H. Sherman; 1964, Dodge, J. Kurtz; 1964, Burnett, N. R. Stone). By 20 May most birds have arrived on their breeding grounds.

Distribution during the breeding season is statewide, with records known from nearly every county. Because the largest amount of favorable habitat is in the southeastern half of the state, the greatest numbers of birds are found east of a line from La Crosse to Marinette. But this bird does not require large expanses of marshes for nesting. Any slough with a few acres of shallow water overgrown with sedges, cattails, or various kinds of grasses may attract a breeding pair.

Records of 10 Oconto County nests discovered by Carl Richter indicate that Soras usually lay first eggs during the 15–20 May period. In one instance (1927), Carl Richter found a nest containing 11 eggs, suggest-

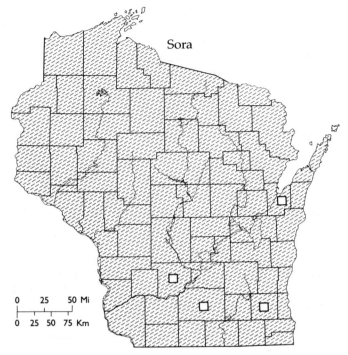

Sora

0   25   50 Mi

0   25 50 75 Km

▨ Summer range
☐ Late November to mid-February

Records since 1960

ing that the first egg was probably deposited around 1 May. Nests were generally in clumps of marsh grass 4–6 inches above the surrounding water. On 2 and 3 June 1950, Roy Gromme (MPM files) investigated eight nests near Milwaukee, with clutch sizes varying from 6 to 13 eggs. Others have reported nests with as many as 15 and 16 eggs. We do not know how often rising water levels wash out nests, but it is highly probable that heavy rains in early June are damaging.

As July progresses the distinctive whinney is heard less and less often. But July is a noisy time anyway, as juvenile birds scurry around peeping, and adults issue sharp alarm notes as self-appointed commanders of the rail expeditionary forces. If an observer waits patiently at a vantage point where openings in the marsh vegetation occur, he will sometimes catch a glimpse of a parent leading a small band of downy black chicks. These youngsters have sometimes been misidentified as Black Rails.

Again, in fall, large numbers must pass through the state, but ordinarily they go unnoticed. An exception occurred on 14 September 1949, when Dixie Larkin estimated that 1,000 individuals flew into the Milwaukee area. At Eau Claire on 6 September 1965,

C. A. Kemper picked up 42 television tower casualties. Tower casualties have been noted as early as 27 August. The presumption is that migration gets under way at least by 25 August, peaks from 20 September to 10 October, and dwindles to a trickle by 20 October. In most years the last state record is noted between 20 October and 5 November.

Mild autumn weather, however, sometimes persuades these marsh dwellers to remain far into November and even December. A late date for central

Wisconsin was established on 5 December 1967 (Wood, D. G. Follen). December stragglers, almost unknown before 1960, have been reported nine times since then, the latest on the 29th (1969, Dane, W. L. Hilsenhoff). Although this species is somewhat less hardy than the Virginia Rail, one Sora managed to survive in Brown County from 28 December 1974 to 2 February 1975 (E. D. Cleary) and another in Dane County until 12 February 1983 (R. M. Hoffman).

Purple Gallinule (*Porphyrula martinica*)

STATUS. Casual spring visitant. Accidental in summer and fall.
HABITAT. Shallow marsh.
MIGRATION DATES. *Spring:* mid-April to mid-May. *Fall:* one record. *Extremes:* 18 April; 24 September.
PORTRAIT. *Birds of Wisconsin:* Plate 89.

April and May 1973 were times of spectacular flooding along the Mississippi and its tributaries south of Wisconsin. Whether displaced by high water or something else, the Purple Gallinule, a colorful bird of southern swamps, made the headlines when it turned up at four Wisconsin locations. One was found dead at Racine on 27 April (M. McGhee); a second was viewed the same day in eastern Waukesha County (B. Spangenberg). On 30 April, O. J. Gromme observed one near his home at Briggsville (Marquette County). On 2 May, Gary Pearson captured an exhausted bird on a small farm pond near Aurora (Florence County). It died the next day, and is now preserved in the Arnold Pearson home as a mounted specimen (Kangas 1974).

Purple Gallinule

△ 18 April to 18 May
○ 15 to 16 June
▽ 24 September

All records

Purple Gallinule, 15 June 1977, Milwaukee County (photo by J. H. Idzikowski)

In just a week's time the number of spring records in this century doubled. First, Watson Beed and Russell Neugebauer spotted two birds in Dodge County on 21 April 1944 (*Pass. Pigeon* 6:76). Twelve years later one was captured at Milwaukee on 5 May 1956, fed and photographed, and turned over to the Milwaukee County zoo on 16 May (*fide* D. L. Larkin). On 18 May 1956, William Hilsenhoff found another bird at Madison (*Pass. Pigeon* 19:31). Another was discovered at Racine on 3 May 1969, remaining until 12 May (Richard Garber).

Since 1973, four additional birds have turned up in southeastern Wisconsin between mid-April and mid-May. On 18 April 1976, an exhausted invididual was picked up on a lawn near Kohler (Sheboygan County), subsequently photographed, banded, and released. It was still present on 5 May (H. Koopmann; J. Brumer). Close to the same April 1976 date, another was discovered in Ozaukee County (C. M. Weise). On 25 April 1981 a Milwaukee County visitor was identified by Eugene Cupertino, and subsequently observed and photographed by numerous other birders through 9 May (*Pass. Pigeon* 44:42). An injured individual found in Milwaukee on 5 May 1983 (J. H. Idzikowski) was captured, rehabilitated, and released on 14 May (*Pass. Pigeon* 46:44).

Outside the mid-April to mid-May period, encompassing all of the above records, Milwaukee had an additional bird on 15–16 June 1977 (D. Hanbury). The only fall sighting known is recorded in the Milwaukee Public Museum files: an adult observed 1 mile south of Platteville (Grant County) on 24 September 1939.

Ben Logan's account was incomplete, but mentioned gallinule size and shape, bright blue plumage, and bright yellow legs.

Kumlien and Hollister (1903) listed this species as occurring in Wisconsin on the basis of three specimens known to them but now lost. One was the specimen P. R. Hoy is said to have procured at Racine sometime after his definitive list of 1853 had been published, but there is no mention of date or of the disposition of the skin. Kumlien and Hollister handled a specimen purported to have been shot north of Milwaukee around 1860. But nothing more is known of either that bird or of an even earlier bird in decomposed condition handled by Thure Kumlien sometime in the 1850s.

There is every reason to suppose that occasional stragglers will continue to wander to Wisconsin. Godfrey (1966) lists over 20 records for Canada. All neighboring states have three or more dates, and birds have wandered to Arizona, Colorado, New York, Massachusetts, and Maine.

Common Moorhen (*Gallinula chloropus*)

Formerly Common Gallinule, Florida Gallinule

STATUS. Fairly common migrant east; uncommon migrant west. Fairly common summer resident east; uncommon summer resident west.
HABITAT. Shallow marsh.
MIGRATION DATES. *Spring:* mid-April to late May. *Fall:* early September to mid-October. *Extremes:* 23 March; 8 November.
BREEDING DATA. Nests with eggs: 23 May to 30 July. Clutch size: usually 7–11 eggs; rarely 13.
WINTER. One January record.
PORTRAIT. *Birds of Wisconsin:* Plate 27.

Residents of western Wisconsin rarely see this marsh-dweller. The Common Moorhen is regularly found only in small numbers north to Buffalo County. Faanes (1981) listed nesting records in St. Croix County for 1976 and 1977. June sightings for Burnett County occurred in 1958 (N. R. Stone) and 1978 (S. D. Robbins). The sole Chippewa Valley listing by Kemper (1973a) was an early June 1971 observation (Eau Claire, P. D. Blanchard).

I have documented three upper Wisconsin River valley wanderings: 26 May–19 June (1960, Adams, S. D. Robbins), 2 October (1961, Juneau, C. E. Pospichal), and 7 June (1980, Marathon, S. D. Robbins). Kumlien and Hollister's (1903) statement that this was "a common summer resident as far as the north central portion of the state, and in less numbers to the

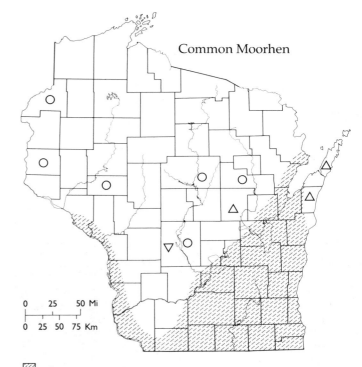

Common Moorhen

0 25 50 Mi
0 25 50 75 Km

▨ Summer range
△ Mid-April to late May
○ Early June to late August
▽ Early September to mid-October

Records since 1960

shore of Lake Superior" lacks supportive evidence—then or now.

It is east of a line from Darlington through Sauk City to Marinette that this bird is to be found in any numbers. There, first arrivals generally appear between 15 and 20 April, often reaching Green Bay by the 25th. Three exceptionally early birds have been recorded at Horicon Marsh in Dodge County: 23 March 1962 (J. Kurtz), 6 April 1968 (H. L. Lindberg), and 8 April 1979 (R. L. Drieslein). The main migration takes place during the 1–15 May period.

The largest concentrations occur at Horicon and Green Bay. Modest numbers exist anywhere in the eastern regions where shallow lakes are rimmed with ample marsh vegetation. "Gallinules" stay out of sight more consistently than do the American Coot and Pied-billed Grebe, which share the same habitat, but varied soft cooing and clacking sounds often reveal the moorhen's presence.

Kumlien and Hollister (1903) listed 10–14 eggs as the usual clutch, with 17 noted on one occasion. More recent studies by Deusing (1941), P. W. Hoffmann (1946; MPM files) and C. H. Richter (1949; MPM files) indicate smaller figures. Reporting on 14 nests near Oconto in 1948 and 1949, Richter found the usual clutch to be 7–11 eggs. Egg-laying as late as 10 July suggests that some pairs engage in renesting. Hoffman has observed that in late July, after the breeding season is over, moorhens sometimes build a series of dummy nests; these are located in more conspicuous open spots; they are clean and lack the sloping runways characteristic of active nests.

There is no migratory buildup in fall. In late August and early September, birds can be seen still feeding young. As September wanes, the birds leave inconspicuously. The last fall bird is usually reported between 10 and 20 October. On four occasions individuals have remained until early November: the 3rd (1950, Dodge, R. S. Dorney), 4th (1967, Waukesha, D. K. Gustafson), 7th (1973, Milwaukee, E. W. Strehlow), and 8th (1970, Milwaukee, D. Juneau). In 1940, one bird spent the month of January with a flock of ducks in an open lagoon in Racine (E. B. Prins).

American Coot (*Fulica americana*)

STATUS. Abundant migrant. Common summer resident west and east central; uncommon summer resident elsewhere. Uncommon winter resident south and central.

HABITAT. Shallow marsh. Ponds. Wooded swamp.

MIGRATION DATES. *Spring:* mid-March to mid-May. *Fall:* late August to mid-December.

BREEDING DATA. Nests with eggs: 1 May to 31 July. Clutch size: usually 7–9 eggs; rarely 10–13.

WINTER. A few regularly present north to Dane and Milwaukee counties. Occasional individuals present north to St. Croix, Eau Claire, Outagamie, and Brown counties.

PORTRAIT. *Birds of Wisconsin:* Plate 27.

An ornithological spectacle awaits the tourist who drives the Great River Road along the western edge of Wisconsin in October. At numerous points between Prairie du Chien and Hager City, Highway 35 winds close to the mighty Mississippi. Wherever shallow water and marsh grass coexist, coots by the hundreds may be seen diving, feeding, or bobbing erratically among the waves. Here 100, there 200, with many another flock out of sight—one wonders how many thousand might be present along this vast expanse during the late October peak. On many other lakes and flowages around the state—usually in relatively

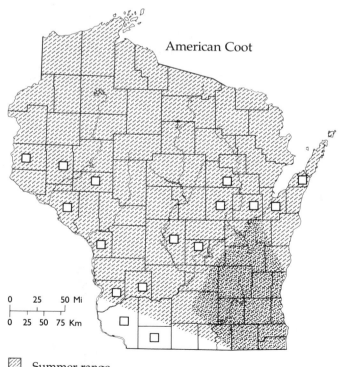

American Coot

0   25   50 Mi

0   25   50   75 Km

▨ Summer range
▦ Winter range
☐ Late December to late February

Records since 1960

sheltered and shallow areas—these birds flock together by the hundreds.

Where do they come from? Recoveries of banded birds show that many of Wisconsin's fall migrants come from breeding grounds in the northern plains states and the prairie provinces of western Canada. There are 80 known instances of birds being recovered in fall in Wisconsin within 4 months of banding in Minnesota, North and South Dakota, Montana, Manitoba, and Saskatchewan.

Many others nest locally, in suitable marsh habitat. The breeding range extends through all but the extreme southwestern portion of the state, but in much of this range birds are few in number. One major nesting territory is a triangular region anchored by Madison, Waukesha, and Marinette. A second smaller area of concentration lies among the prairie ponds of Dunn, St. Croix, and Polk counties.

Nests with eggs have been seen as early as 1 May, and broods are sometimes noticeable by 5 June. More commonly, egg-laying takes place between 20 May and 10 June, and broods are in evidence from 15 June on. In Oconto County, C. H. Richter indicated that he never found a nest containing more than nine eggs; in the Dakotas, however, he had observed nests with 15 and 16 eggs. Many of the nests that Richter observed in Wisconsin were built in the outer rush beds along the Green Bay shore. It was not uncommon for such nests to be destroyed by wave action and high water. Perhaps it is because of the failure of earlier nests that egg-laying continues well into July.

C. A. Kemper's television tower kill at Eau Claire on 4 September 1961 (pers. comm.) probably signifies that fall migration is under way by the first of the month. Large rafts are in evidence from 25 September on, and birds remain until the November freeze-up.

Where do they go then? Some move directly south to the Gulf of Mexico. Six Wisconsin-banded individuals have turned up in Louisiana or Mississippi the following winter (11 birds tagged in Louisiana have been retaken in Wisconsin). Others move in a more easterly direction, wintering in the Atlantic coastal areas. There have been 38 winter recoveries, well distributed from Connecticut to Florida, of birds banded in Wisconsin within the previous 6 months. And 10 individuals banded along the Atlantic Coast have subsequently been found in Wisconsin.

Some coots remain in southern Wisconsin. The late-December CBC regularly records from 300 to 2,500 birds. December 1974 was exceptional, with over 3,500 in Madison, 2,000 at Lake Geneva (Walworth County), and another 500 at scattered points. Although most of these birds depart as more water freezes over in early January, 200 or more remain each winter in Madison, with smaller numbers at other locations in the southeast. Occasional individuals overwinter father north and join groups of semidomesticated Mallards. Records have come from as far north as St. Croix, Dunn, Eau Claire, Adams, Shawano, Brown, and Door counties.

The spring migration begins slowly between 15 and 25 March, then rapidly builds up in early April as lakes open. In the southern counties there is a rapid decline after a 1–10 May peak. In the north the timetable is 5–10 days later. An Eau Claire television tower kill on 28 May 1959 (Kemper 1959) indicates that a few coots may still be migrating at that late date.

Sandhill Crane (*Grus canadensis*)

STATUS. Uncommon migrant. Uncommon summer resident. Rare winter resident southeast.

HABITAT. Shallow marsh. Open grassland and cropland.

MIGRATION DATES. *Spring:* late February to early May. *Fall:* mid-August to mid-December.

BREEDING DATA. Nests with eggs: 22 April to 6 July. Clutch size: usually 2 eggs, rarely 3.

WINTER. Rarely present north to Marquette and Brown counties.

PORTRAIT. *Birds of Wisconsin:* Plate 25.

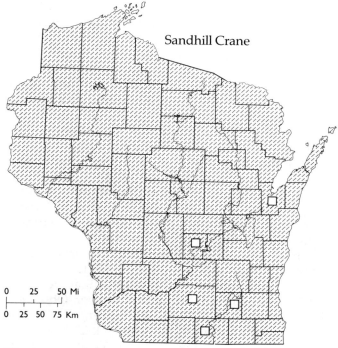

Sandhill Crane

▨ Summer range
☐ Late December to mid-February

Records since 1960

Fifty years ago the outlook was bleak for the survival of this magnificent trumpeter as a breeding species in Wisconsin. Henika (1936) estimated that a total of 25 breeding pairs existed. Most were concentrated in the extensive marshlands of Jackson, Wood, Adams, Marquette, and Green Lake counties; a few were scattered in Burnett and Oconto counties.

This was all that remained of what had constituted large and well-distributed populations in the nineteenth century. Kumlien and Hollister (1903) described the species as an "abundant migrant and common summer resident" in the days of earliest settlement. By the turn of the century they reported, "Still many localities, even in southern Wisconsin, where it occurs regularly in good numbers," although it had retreated from the most populous areas.

The decline since 1900 must have been rapid and extensive, but it has not been well documented. Some commentators have attributed it to heavy hunting, some to human expansion, some to agricultural development, and some to wetland drainage. Hunt, Gluesing, and Nauman (1976) suggested that all these factors contributed to the decline.

Even when the breeding population was at its lowest ebb, migrating flocks of 100–150 birds would pause in early October at various central locations—particularly near Hancock (Waushara County) and Princeton (Green Lake County). When the fall flock grew to 700 in 1949, it became evident that the population decline had been reversed. By 1952, according to estimates by S. G. De Boer, 44 pairs were nesting in Jackson, Juneau, and Monroe counties. Under the encouragement of added protection and preservation of habitat, birds in recent years have responded with what Gluesing (1974) called a "dramatic increase." Conducting a broad census from the air, Gluesing estimated that 850 cranes inhabited the state during the summer of 1973; they occurred in portions of 31 counties. The range extended from Chippewa County east to Marinette County and southeast (west of Lake Winnebago) to Racine County. The major concentrations were located between Black River Falls (Jackson County) and Portage (Columbia County). There was also an isolated population in Burnett County.

Summer range extensions northward and westward continued through the 1980s. Vanderschaegen (1981b) noted successful breeding in Oneida County in 1977. Breeding Bird Survey results include June sightings in Lincoln (1980), Rusk (1980), and Sawyer (1984) counties. The annual spring counts coordinated through the International Crane Foundation showed that by the late 1980s the Sandhill Crane range had become statewide.

Exceptionally early spring dates include 18 February (1938, Wood, W. B. Grange; MPM files), 19 February (1983, Shawano, D. Goers), 23 February (1975, Rock, W. Buchanan), 25 February (1981, Sauk, K. I. Lange), 26 February (1983, Winnebago, T. Ziebell), and 2 March (1973, Milwaukee, M. F. Donald). First arrivals usually appear between 10 and 15 March. During the principal migration period, 20 March–20 April, parts of central Wisconsin see flocks of 25–75 birds, and occasionally the gatherings reach 150. Once in a while a migrating individual or flock may be detected by the distinctive trumpeting call that is uttered by birds flying so high that they can scarcely be detected by the naked eye—the wild call of the crane carries far. Migration is usually over by 25 April. Occasional sightings through 10 May could be wandering nonbreeding individuals.

Birds begin to collect in larger flocks by 10 August, building gradually to the 20 September–10 October peak seen at several central Wisconsin observation points. Gluesing's (1974) figures for 1973 were encouraging: between 25 September and 15 October he tallied 150 in Burnett, 225 in Jackson, 400 in Juneau, and 413 in Green Lake counties. One of the largest staging areas is the White River Marsh in Green Lake County. In 1977 Bennett and Nauman (1978) tallied 1,030 on 20 September and 981 on 30 September. Another major staging area is at the Sandhill Wildlife Demonstration Area in Wood County, where Lisa Hartman counted 1,312 birds on 12 October 1984.

Once the fall waterfowl-hunting season starts, Sandhills depart. Many are gone by 15 October, and by 5 November most have moved out. Scattered individuals often linger through 20 November. Observers have reported exceptionally late sightings on 26 November (1945, Dodge, H. A. Mathiak), 27 November (1963, Bayfield, J. L. Koslowski), 10 December (1939, Milwaukee, W. J. Mueller), and 17 December (1972,

Waukesha, R. R. Adams); a flock of seven was seen on 20 December (1980, Wood, D. G. Follen).

The state's five January records may reflect the presence of injured individuals: birds were seen on the 3rd (1982, Rock, G. Mahlum), 8th (1941, Marquette, S. Paul), 12th (1985, Dane, Sue Martin), 26th (1968, Jefferson, K. Kreger), and throughout the month (1976, Jefferson, T. Bintz). Two birds survived the winter of 1981–1982 in Brown County (E. D. Cleary).

It is doubtful that the state will ever again know the huge flocks that P. R. Hoy and Thure Kumlien found in the 1850s (Kumlien and Hollister 1903). But Gluesing's 1973 summer studies show that the average size of a crane territory is 339 acres. Inasmuch as a similar study in Oregon describes an average territory size of 62 acres, Gluesing concluded that Wisconsin still has range capable of supporting higher populations than those presently maintained. Large cranberry bogs in central Wisconsin offer favorable habitat. The preservation of federal and state-owned wetlands played an important role in the 1950–1980 recovery, and now smaller privately owned wetlands also hold promise for breeding pairs. The spring counts sponsored by the International Crane Foundation and the Wisconsin Wetlands Association point to a broadening range that in 1985 included 56 counties.

Whooping Crane (*Grus americana*)

STATUS. Formerly uncommon migrant south and west. One sight record since 1878.
HABITAT. Shallow marsh. Open grassland and cropland.
PORTRAIT. *Birds of Wisconsin:* Plate 25.

Before 1860 the Whooping Crane's breeding range included parts of Iowa, Minnesota, North Dakota, and western Canada. The winter range extended from Texas to Florida. In migration a few of these birds used to pause in Wisconsin each fall, usually in company with Sandhill Cranes, in the southern and western counties. Hoy (1853b) stated: "A few . . . are occasionally seen in the western part of the state, near the Mississippi, but never approach the lake shores." Much later (1885b) he estimated having seen no more than a dozen in the southeastern counties. Kumlien and Hollister (1903) remarked: "Thirty or forty years ago it was not rare to see a few among the enormous flocks of Sandhill Cranes during the October migrations, and even flocks composed entirely of this species."

Actual dates and places are lacking. Wisconsin's

lone specimen is preserved in the Milwaukee Public Museum, but information about date and location of its collection is incomplete. Hoy (1853b) mentioned no dates. Kumlien and Hollister (1903) gave no definite dates, other than an "October 1878" notation for a Green County specimen brought to Thure Kumlien. Although these authors spoke of Whooping Cranes as "unquestionably breeding to some extent," no positive nesting evidence exists.

Various newspaper accounts in the late nineteenth century made reference to occasional sightings in the 1880s, but the likelihood of mistaken identity is great in most instances, if not all. One such account described a bird that fit the description of a Great Egret perfectly.

The only valid record since 1878 is O. J. Gromme's observation of two birds in Waukesha County on 17 April 1959. Although this is some 500 miles east of the bird's usual migratory route over the Great Plains, in recent years this nearly extinct species has been known to wander occasionally to adjacent states: Missouri (1958), Illinois (1958), and Minnesota (1951, 1974).

Family **Charadriidae**: Plovers

Black-bellied Plover (*Pluvialis squatarola*)

STATUS. Fairly common migrant.
HABITAT. Great Lakes. Inland lakes. Open grassland and cropland.
MIGRATION DATES. *Spring:* early May to early June. *Fall:* late July to mid-November. *Extremes:* 15 April, 27 June; 7 July, 10 December.
PORTRAIT. *Birds of Wisconsin:* Plate 29.

The Black-bellied Plover has been observed in Wisconsin in 9 of the 12 months of the year, with records lacking only for January through March. Typically, it arrives in the south by 1 May, peaks from 15 to 25 May, and has left by 1 June. The timetable is a week later in the north, with a few individuals lingering along the Lake Superior shore through 10 June. The earliest known sighting occurred on 15 April 1976 (St. Croix, C. A. Faanes), and in the 1960s a series of exceptionally early arrivals surprised April observers: the 17th (1963, Chippewa, C. A. Kemper), 22nd (1964, Racine, B. Weber), and 26th (1962, Dane, P. Ashman). Also remarkable was a 28 April bird in Bayfield County (1959, D. A. Bratley). Unusually late June lingerers were seen on the 23rd (1951, Ashland, F. Holman King), 24th (1962, Door, L. W. Erickson), 25th (1975, Brown, T. C. Erdman), 26th (1950, Columbia, W. L. Hilsenhoff), and 27th (1987, Douglas, R. J. Johnson).

In spring most observers are pleased to see small groups of 5–15 birds feeding on exposed mud flats when flooded fields are drying up. Even before one can approach close enough to determine what shorebirds are present, one can often hear the plaintive slurred whistle of the Black-belly. Occasionally birdwatchers have encountered sizable flocks of 100–300 birds in plowed fields far removed from water—feeding by themselves or mixed with Golden Plovers. Flocks of this size have been noted only in the southeastern counties; D. K. Gustafson estimated 500 in a

Racine County flock on 27 May 1969. Black-bellies occur in small numbers in most parts of the state, but they are decidedly more numerous southeast of a line from Madison to Green Bay.

Brief indeed is the interval between late spring stragglers and early fall migrants. Personally, I have never seen a Black-belly in Wisconsin in July. But there are published records for five early or mid-July sightings: the 7th (1973, Marathon, R. M. Hoffman), 9th (1967, Racine, D. K. Gustafson), 11th (1953, Dodge, C. P. Frister), 15th (1978, Winnebago, D. D. Tessen), and 18th (1979, Fond du Lac, D. D. Tessen).

Fall arrival dates become more frequent from 25 July on, with 1–10 August the typical period in most years. Fall flocks cannot compare in size with those of spring, but favored spots like Horicon Marsh in Dodge County may attract 50–100 individuals. At this season birds congregate less often in open fields, but wander more frequently to sandy beaches as well as mud flats.

The fall flight is a prolonged one. Although numbers build up gradually during August, the peak does not occur until the latter half of September. Most birds depart in October, but some seem loath to leave. One remained far north in Bayfield County through 28 October (1957, D. A. Bratley). In the central counties birds have stayed on through mid-November until the 19th (1953, Adams, S. D. Robbins; 1976, Kewaunee, K. J. Luepke) and 21st (1975, Brown, T. C. Erdman). Mild late-fall weather in 1963 resulted in November records on the 9th (Douglas, R. F. Bernard), 10th (Outagamie, D. D. Tessen), 19th (Marinette, H. L. Lindberg), and 21st (Columbia, R. B. Dryer), and a bird that lingered at Racine until 10 December (R. E. Fiehweg). Many other November departure dates have been recorded in the southeastern counties.

Lesser Golden-Plover (*Pluvialis dominica*)

STATUS. Fairly common migrant east; uncommon migrant west.

HABITAT. Open grassland and cropland. Great Lakes. Inland lakes.

MIGRATION DATES. *Spring:* late April to late May. *Fall:* late July to early November. *Extremes:* 19 March, 17 June; 11 July, 27 November.

PORTRAIT. *Birds of Wisconsin:* Plate 29.

The Lesser Golden-Plover was an abundant Wisconsin bird in the 1850s. Hoy (1853b) and Barry (1854) found it plentiful in spring and fall. Barry commented: "Immense bodies of them sometimes gather upon the open prairie, especially upon portions over which fire has run. I have seen hundreds of them thus assembled, and busily engaged in feeding." Kumlien and Hollister (1903) reminisced: "The numbers of these birds that frequented our prairies from 1840 to 1865 seem almost incredible to the younger generation. At that time the birds would scarcely get out of the way of the teams when the farmers were plowing, and followed like chickens in the furrow."

Then came the hunters. As the population of Passenger Pigeons dwindled, gunners turned to the Golden Plovers and slaughtered them by the thousands. Roland Clement, editing Henry M. Hall's *A Gathering of Shore Birds* (1960), commented: "It is on record that in 1890 two Boston wholesalers of game received from the West in one shipment forty barrels of birds. These were crammed with ten thousand Golden Plovers and four thousand Eskimo Curlews, the interstices being stuffed with the bodies of Upland Plovers." How many thousands of Wisconsin's Golden-Plovers ended up in eastern wholesale markets will never be known.

Protective laws in 1918 came none too soon. The sighting of a flock of any size anywhere in the state was deemed noteworthy in the 1920s and 1930s, but since 1940 a gradual comeback has been evident. Today, groups of 10–20 birds are sometimes found in spring along Lakes Superior and Michigan, and flocks of 25–250 are occasionally observed on plowed fields in the southern and eastern counties. The largest numbers occur between 1 and 15 May, although birds are present every year from 25 April to 25 May. Remarkably early migrants have been reported on 19 March (1948, Milwaukee, G. H. Orians), 28 March

(1954, Dane, M. A. Walker; 1954, Columbia, J. L. Kaspar), and 31 March (1956, Milwaukee, C. P. Frister). Rarely, individuals linger beyond 31 May; the latest recorded date is 17 June (1986, Ashland, E. J. Epstein).

In those nineteenth-century years; when this species was an abundant migrant, no evidence of nesting was ever recorded. Kumlien and Hollister (1903) mentioned that there had been sightings in June and July at Lake Koshkonong in Jefferson County, but these birds were apparently vagrants. September and October were the times of fall migration then.

The mid-twentieth-century years have witnessed a gradual extension of the fall migration into August: mid-August by 1960, early August by 1970. Since 1973, July arrivals have been reported on the 11th (1981, Fond du Lac, D. D. Tessen), 16th (1980, Eau Claire, J. L. Polk), 28th (1974, La Crosse, F. Z. Lesher), and 29th (1977, Dodge, D. K. Gustafson). The largest numbers usually occur between 10 September and 15 October. Reminiscent of the days of old were the flocks of 700 in Racine County on 25 September (1970, D. D. Tessen), 600 in Columbia County on 6 October (1980, R. M. Hoffman), 500 in Dane County on 13 October (1958, M. F. Donald), and 500 in Dodge County on 9 October (1972, D. D. Tessen). Flocks of more than 100 are present annually in northern Clark County (S. D. Robbins). Migrants pass through the western counties, but in far fewer numbers.

In mild autumns birds have lingered until late October in Douglas and Langlade counties and through the first week of November in the south. Later November departures include the 15th (1963, Dane, T. L. Ashman), 16th (1959, Milwaukee, E. L. Basten), 19th (1969, Ozaukee, R. H. Sundell; 1976, Milwaukee, E. J. Epstein), 23rd (1940, Racine, E. B. Prins), and 27th (1940, Sheboygan, W. Dettman).

The number of fall sightings varies with the amount of freshly plowed land that is available between mid-August and mid-October. When the weather is sufficiently dry, farmers are plowing larger amounts of land, and plowing earlier in the autumn season. It is during the first week after plowing that the plovers are attracted to particular fields. The organisms in the soil, exposed by plowing, provide favored food for these long-distance travelers. In abnormally wet years, when little fall plowing takes place, few plovers are seen.

Snowy Plover (*Charadrius alexandrinus*)

STATUS. Accidental. Two June records.
HABITAT. Normally Pacific Coast. Inland lakes.

Wisconsin's sole specimen of the Snowy Plover, a male, was collected in Kenosha County on 1 June 1934 by Walter Weber. The bird was subsequently deposited with the Chicago Academy of Sciences, and documented by Ford (1936a); it was determined that the specimen belonged to the southern race *C. a. tenuirostris*. Until 1934 the only specimens known for the Great Lakes region were birds taken at Toronto in 1880 and 1897.

Thirty-three years later a second record was established at the opposite corner of the state. R. F. Bernard and M. Granlund discovered a bird near the mouth of the Bois Brule River in northeastern Douglas County on 4 June 1967. Although the record is not substantiated with specimen or photograph, the bird was seen under favorable conditions at close range by observers thoroughly familiar with the similarly marked Piping Plover (*Pass. Pigeon* 30:94).

Semipalmated Plover (*Charadrius semipalmatus*)

STATUS. Fairly common migrant east; uncommon migrant west.
HABITAT. Great Lakes. Inland lakes. Ponds.
MIGRATION DATES. *Spring:* late April to early June. *Fall:* mid-July to early October. *Extremes:* 18 April, 17 June; 28 June, 14 November.
BREEDING DATA. One record.
PORTRAIT. *Birds of Wisconsin:* Plate 28.

Most spring migrant Semipalmated Plovers pass through the eastern portion of the state between 10 May and 1 June. But even at their peak, in favored shorebird haunts such as the Horicon and Green Bay marshes, it is rare to see groups of more than 15 individuals; however, an exception occurred on 14 May 1980, when 250 were observed in Columbia County (R. M. Hoffman). In the western region one usually sees from one to five birds at a time. Most often on inland mud flats, to a lesser extent along sandy beaches, this small plover is seen in the company of small sandpipers. In the south the number of these plovers peaks between 10 and 25 May, with smaller numbers extending from 25 April to 5 June. Farther north the usual span is from 5 May to 10 June, with a peak from 15 May to 1 June, and lesser numbers from 1 May to 15 June. Earliest April arrivals include individuals on the 18th (1975, St. Croix, C. A. Faanes), 19th (1964, Douglas, R. F. Bernard; 1964, Bayfield, J. L. Kozlowski; 1976, Outagamie, D. D. Tessen), and 20th (1976, St. Croix, C. A. Faanes).
Exceptionally late spring migrants in the south

have been recorded on 16 June (1959 and 1965, Columbia, W. L. Hilsenhoff), a scant 18 days before J. E. Bielefeldt's earliest fall migrant on 4 July (1961, Waukesha). In the north the span is even shorter between a Bayfield County sighting on 17 June (1919, H. H. Sheldon, [Jackson 1943]) and two 28 June observations (1984, Manitowoc, C. L. Sontag; 1985, Ashland, M. J. Mossman).
Few fall migrants arrive before 15 July, however. The main migration period is from 25 July to 15 September, with a 10 August–5 September peak. As in spring, fall flocks are more numerous in the eastern half of the state, but even there rarely number more than 15. The latest departure date for the north is 11 October (1976, Douglas, G. J. Niemi). Only rarely do birds linger beyond 15 October in the south. Exceptions include birds seen on 29 October in Dane (1964, T. L. Ashman) and Columbia (1966, M. Tomlinson) counties, and four November birds, on the 4th (1959, Milwaukee, H. A. Bauers), 7th (1963, Racine, B. Weber), 8th (1947, Milwaukee, G. H. Orians), and 14th (1972, La Crosse, J. R. Rosso).
Kumlien and Hollister thought of this bird as a rare breeder, but gave no definite data. Ludwig Kumlien (1891d) wrote: "I have known this species to nest within Wisconsin (1882, Green Bay)." Kumlien and Hollister (1903) later stated: "We procured the young, still unable to fly, at Lake Koshkonong on one occasion." It is highly unlikely that breeding will occur in Wisconsin again, because the nesting range is now restricted to northern Canada.

Piping Plover (*Charadrius melodus*)

STATUS. Rare migrant. Rare summer resident north.
HABITAT. Great Lakes. Inland lakes. Ponds.
MIGRATION DATES. *Spring:* late April to late May. *Fall:* mid-July to late October. *Extremes:* 21 April; 29 October.
BREEDING DATA. Nests with eggs: 28 May to 10 July. Clutch size: 3 or 4 eggs.
PORTRAIT. *Birds of Wisconsin:* Plate 28.

This light sand-colored beachcomber has almost disappeared as a nesting species in Wisconsin—almost, but not quite. When Harris and Matteson (1975b) conducted an exhaustive search for nesting gulls and terns along the south shore of Lake Superior in 1974, they found four Piping Plovers on the sandy beaches northeast of Ashland on 20 and 21 June, presumably two breeding pairs. Throughout the 1970s one or two pairs nested on Barker's Island at Superior. Invasion of their nesting territory by off-road vehicles led to the plover's disappearance after 1971. I have probed the beaches at Port Wing and Herbster in Bayfield County various times since 1960 and have not found this species there since 1 July 1963. This plover has been on the state's list of endangered species since 1979.

Along the Lake Michigan shore this plover used to nest near Kenosha, Sheboygan, Sturgeon Bay, and Oconto. But numbers were small even in the nineteenth century. Now human encroachment has taken its toll. The last recorded county dates are 1930 for Kenosha, 1932 for Sheboygan, 1940 for Oconto, and 1948 for Door.

If one assumes the birds that breed in northern Minnesota and Manitoba follow a direct path to and from their Gulf Coast wintering grounds, one would expect a few migrants to pass through Wisconsin en route. Published records in *The Passenger Pigeon* show from one to four individuals reported nearly every spring. Geographically these sightings have been well spread out: Lafayette, Crawford, Vernon, and St. Croix counties in the west; Dane, Columbia, and Adams counties in the Wisconsin River valley; Dodge, Winnebago, Outagamie, and Brown counties in the Fox River valley; and along most of the counties bordering Lake Michigan. In most instances migrating birds pause but briefly. But in 1967 a Piping Plover was seen daily from 3 to 15 May in St. Croix County

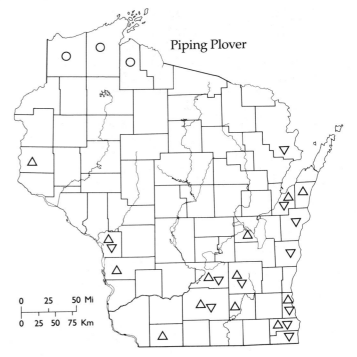

Piping Plover

△   Late April to late May
O   Early June to early July
▽   Mid-July to late October

Records since 1960

(S. D. Robbins), and in 1963 one spent the 11–23 May span at Racine (E. B. Prins). The earliest records are 21 April (1970, Douglas, T. R. Staupe; 1973, Brown, T. C. Erdman) and 22 April (1964, Racine, R. E. Fiehweg). Most observations have occurred between 30 April and 20 May. By 25 May most migrants have departed.

The fall migration begins slowly. In addition to a 12 July bird (1981, Manitowoc, C. R. Sontag) records include other July individuals seen on the 20th (1975, Manitowoc, J. F. Steffen) and 21st (1980, Dane, R. M. Hoffman). Published autumn records number from none to four birds per year; a majority cluster between 15 August and 10 September. Six October dates are known, the latest being the 12th (1970, Columbia, E. H. Werner), 13th (1976, Milwaukee, E. J. Epstein), 14th (1965, Sheboygan, K. Priebe), and 29th (1976, Marinette, D. D. Tessen).

Killdeer (*Charadrius vociferus*)

STATUS. Common migrant. Common summer resident. Rare winter resident south.
HABITAT. Open cropland. Ponds. Great Lakes. Inland lakes.
MIGRATION DATES. *Spring:* early March to mid-April. *Fall:* mid-August to mid-November.
BREEDING DATA. Nests with eggs: 8 April to 7 July. Clutch size: usually 4 eggs; occasionally 3.
WINTER. Occasionally present north to St. Croix, Monroe, Juneau, Adams, Outagamie, Brown, and Manitowoc counties.
PORTRAIT. *Birds of Wisconsin:* Plate 28.

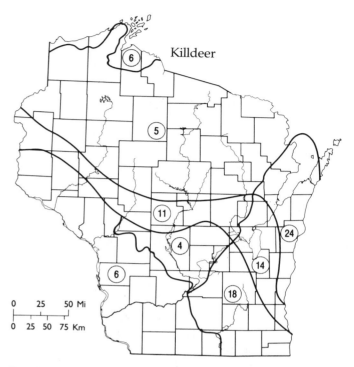

Breeding Bird Survey, averages 1966 to 1980

When A. W. Schorger flushed a Killdeer at Madison on 24 December 1929, he commented that he was unaware of any previous winter record for the state. Unknown to him was an unpublished record of an 11 December 1909 bird (Milwaukee, E. Hauerwas; MPM files). Subsequent December and January sightings in 1930, 1939, and 1949 did not change the status of this bird as a very rare winter resident. Then between 1952 and 1957, seven wintering birds were noted, and since 1965 from 1 to 10 CBC birds have been tallied every year. The most northerly sightings were recorded in St. Croix, Dunn, Outagamie, and Brown counties. How these birds manage to survive—or how many of them survive—is a mystery. While watching a bird circling over a Mauston restaurant in a snowstorm in Juneau County on 25 January 1975, I got the impression that its headquarters were the flat roofs of two nearby gasoline service stations.

The spring migration is prolonged, especially when there is mild February weather in the south. In the south first arrivals usually show up between 1 and 10 March, but birds have been noted occasionally as early as 20 February. Warm temperatures bring a rapid buildup between 15 and 25 March, with most nonbreeding birds moving on by 10 April. Flocks numbering 300–500 birds have been noted during the peak period.

Farther north, where snow and ice linger into April, first arrivals are expected between 20 and 30 March. Exceptionally early stragglers have been noted on 2 March (1961, Burnett, N. R. Stone; 1965, Marinette, H. L. Lindberg), although in some years no birds are recorded until April. The big buildup comes between 1 and 20 April.

The BBS map shows a statewide summer range. Every BBS route has recorded these birds, and though they are common throughout the state, they are especially numerous in the southeast. An analysis of BBS results from 1966 to 1980 (Robbins 1982) shows a sig-

nificant population increase during this period.

Nests with eggs have been found as early as 8 April. Mortality must be high, however, for birds that nest in fields or on roadways traveled by farm machinery. It is surprising how these birds select widely used open areas and survive. George vos Burgh once kept tabs on a nest located less than 5 feet from the rails of a heavily used railroad. Carl Richter reported on a nest that lay between the wagon ruts of a newly constructed road. Alvin Cahn wrote of photographing a nesting pair in a cornfield; the fearless birds alighted on part of his camera equipment.

By early August flocking begins. Congregations of 250 have been reported by 25 August, and 300 by 5 September. It is not unusual to notice 20 birds along the sides of a pond, then discover another 50 in the nearby grass. In the north flocks diminish in late September, with the last migrants leaving by 20 October. Flocks in the central counties dwindle only gradually in October. In most years the central counties lose their last birds between 10 and 20 November, and only occasional birds remain in the south beyond 20 November.

The likelihood is that the Killdeers that nest in Wisconsin winter in the Gulf and South Atlantic states. Two Wisconsin-banded individuals have been recovered in Louisiana and South Carolina.

Family **Recurvirostridae:** Stilts, Avocets

Black-necked Stilt (*Himantopus mexicanus*)

STATUS. Accidental. Four records.
HABITAT. Ponds. Inland lakes.

Sometime in April 1847—the exact date is not known—
Hoy (1853b) "met with a small flock of these singular
birds near Racine." One was collected, and is now
housed in Hoy's collection at the Racine County Historical Museum.

Not until 1951 did this species pay a return visit. On
18 May, R. Mihalek detected one at Horicon Marsh in
Dodge County. The wanderer was subsequently seen
by Laurence Jahn and others, collected by Jahn, and
donated to the University of Wisconsin collection at
Madison (*Pass. Pigeon* 14:102).

Another Black-necked Stilt spent 3 weeks at the
Horicon National Wildlife Refuge between 11 August
and 6 September 1986, with clearly identifiable photographs obtained by Darrell Haugen (*Pass. Pigeon*
49:161).

Eight months later, another of these long-legged
waders appeared in Columbia County. It was first
seen on 24 May 1987 by W. A. Cowart, and subsequently seen by several others before it left on the
25th (*Pass. Pigeon* 50:86–87).

This handsome vagrant engages in a bit of extralimital wandering. Most of it, however, has been
along the Atlantic Coast north to Massachusetts and
the Pacific Coast north to British Columbia. Records
from the Great Lakes region are scarce.

Black-necked Stilt, 11 August 1986, Dodge County (photo
by D. Haugen)

256

American Avocet (*Recurvirostra americana*)

STATUS. Uncommon migrant. Casual summer resident.

HABITAT. Ponds. Great Lakes. Inland lakes.

MIGRATION DATES. *Spring:* late April to late May. *Fall:* early July to late October. *Extremes:* 19 April; 31 October.

BREEDING DATA. One twentieth-century record.

PORTRAIT. *Birds of Wisconsin:* Plate 27.

American Avocet

△ Late April to late May
○ Early to late June
▽ Early July to late October

Records since 1960

When Elsie Sacia discovered an American Avocet by a small pond on her Trempealeau County farm on 10 May 1950, she was looking at the first spring sighting for Wisconsin since the 1870s, and the fourth state record for the twentieth century. The bird was one of several ornithological oddities blown off course by a severe storm a few days earlier.

Although many shorebirds were far more numerous before 1875, this stunning, large wader was not one of them. Hoy (1853b) mentioned only two (Kenosha County?) specimens: a pair on 26 July 1846 "where they had probably nested," and "a small party in May 1847." Thure Kumlien (Kumlien and Hollister 1903) collected a few between 1844 and 1875, including three at Lake Koshkonong in Jefferson County in September 1873. Most if not all of these were fall migrants. In 1879 a pair evidently bred at Green Bay, as Ludwig Kumlien saw specimens of downy young in the possession of a taxidermist there. From then until 1950 only three published records are known. Two are specimens in the Milwaukee Public Museum: one taken on 7 September 1908 (Dodge, L. Crosby) and one on 21 October 1921 (Waupaca, H. J. Nunnemacher). The third is a sight record on 29 August 1936 (Sheboygan, M. Deusing; MPM files).

Hindsight shows that the 1950 straggler was the forerunner of a new trend that brought an additional 7 records in the 1950s, 10 in the 1960s, 33 in the 1970s, and 29 in the 1980s. The sightings have usually been of lone individuals making brief one-day appearances; a few reports have involved flocks of 3–7 individuals. A remarkable flight in 1973 brought flocks of 35 on 21 April (Milwaukee, J. H. Idzikowski) and 15 on 3 May (Dodge, R. G. Personius).

One pair from the 1973 influx remained to nest near Fox Lake (Dodge County). A pair displayed agitation when pursued by a dog along the shoreline of a shallow pond on 9 June (J. R. March); the birds appeared at a nearby pond with three tan-colored chicks 4 days later (J. Beule). On 15 June two adults were again seen, but the young were nowhere in sight (March 1974).

The accompanying map shows the location of the 81 observations between 1960 and 1989, almost equally divided among three regions: western (Mississippi River and tributaries), south central (Madison-Appleton), and eastern (Lake Michigan and Green Bay shore). Nearly all the recent spring records have been concentrated in the 25 April–15 May period. The extremes are 19 April (1982, Brown, M. S. Peterson) and 1 June (1987, Manitowoc, W. A. Cowart).

In addition to the 1973 breeding record, there are June sightings on the 9th (1978, Dodge, Horicon National Wildlife Refuge staff), 17th (1982, Manitowoc, C. R. Sontag), and 19th (1978, Milwaukee, D. K. Gustafson).

Scattered July observations begin with the 3rd (1981, Dodge, D. K. Gustafson) and 8th (1981, Milwaukee, G. S. Casper. The main fall migration period occurs between 15 August and 25 September. In 1982, individuals remained in October until the 14th (Manitowoc, C. R. Sontag) and 31st (Dodge, Horicon NWR staff). In 1984, J. E. Hoefler counted 60 in Burnett County on 20 October. Between then and the 28th, additional birds were sighted in Chippewa, Brown, and Manitowoc counties. The presence of this species has become an annual event, spring and fall.

Family **Scolopacidae:** Sandpipers, Phalaropes, and Allies

Greater Yellowlegs (*Tringa melanoleuca*)

STATUS. Fairly common migrant. Rare summer resident.

HABITAT. Ponds. Flooded fields. Great Lakes. Inland lakes.

MIGRATION DATES. *Spring:* late March to mid-May. *Fall:* early July to early November. *Extremes:* 11 March; 28 November.

PORTRAIT. *Birds of Wisconsin:* Plate 32.

April is the main month for observing this stately prince of the flooded grass meadows. In the south there is usually a scattering of 1–10 April birds and a buildup to a 20–30 April peak, with most birds departing by 10 May. In the north the timetable is about 10 days later. One year out of every three, first arrivals reach the southern region during the last week of March. Exceptionally early March birds have been recorded on the 11th (1956, Walworth, E. B. Prins), 21st (1945, Dodge, H. A. Mathiak), and 22nd (1969, Lafayette, N. R. Barger). Most spring reports involve small groups of 5–20 birds. In a few especially favored localities peak numbers of 75–150 are found. A phenomenal concentration estimated at 700 was noted at Kaukauna (Outagamie County) on 4 May 1963 (D. D. Tessen).

Infrequently, observers have detected late individuals in the 25–31 May period and even into early June, with sightings on the 1st (1972, Taylor, J. O. Evrard), 2nd (1943, Dunn, I. O. Buss), 3rd (1958, Bayfield, D. A. Bratley), and 6th (1966, Chippewa, C. A. Kemper). It is difficult to distinguish between late spring migrants and summer wanderers. The 19 June (1981, Winnebago, T. Ziebell) and 23 June (1980, Eau Claire, J. L. Polk) individuals were presumably summer wanderers. One bird spent the summer in Brown County in 1975 (T. C. Erdman).

Concentrations in the hundreds were probably commonplace in the nineteenth century. Kumlien and Hollister (1903) called the bird common, while Hoy (1853b) and Grundtvig (1895) termed it abundant during migration. Hoy also mentioned that it nested "in all large marshes." Grundtvig surmised: "must undoubtedly breed in Wisconsin, and possibly at Shiocton." Schoenebeck (1902) wrote: "Breeds in the great marshes of the Green Bay shore; I have found it breeding there several times." In 1882 Ludwig Kumlien obtained pre-fledged downy young near Minnesota Junction (Dodge County), and Kumlien and Hollister believed nesting occurred in the Lake Koshkonong marshes in Jefferson County. But corroborative dates and data are missing in every instance. Since the period of heavy indiscriminate shooting of shorebirds ended in the early twentieth century, the nesting range has been restricted to northern Canada. The likelihood that this species will ever again nest in Wisconsin is remote.

Early observers could have mistakenly inferred nesting from the presence of birds in mid-July. The first fall migrants usually appear between 5 and 15 July and on rare occasions even by 30 June. The fall flight is a prolonged one. Small numbers accompany the large flocks of Lesser Yellowlegs in late July and early August, with concentrations of 25–100 birds present in favored localities from 10 August on. After 20 September the peak is past, and some of the haunts are deserted. But smaller numbers remain through October. In 1949 an estimated 500 birds moved south past Cedar Grove Ornithological Station in Sheboygan County on 23 October (H. C. Mueller). A few individuals linger into early November nearly every year. In the central counties there are records for the 11th (1941, Dunn, I. O. Buss), 19th (1953, Adams, S. D. Robbins), and 24th (1972, La Crosse, J. R. Rosso). Birds that linger farther south have been noted on the 23rd (1961, Columbia, A. J. Rusch), 25th (1967, Waukesha, J. E. Bielefeldt), and 28th (1968, Vernon, F. Z. Lesher).

Lesser Yellowlegs (*Tringa flavipes*)

STATUS. Common migrant. Rare summer resident. Formerly bred.

HABITAT. Ponds. Flooded fields. Great Lakes. Inland lakes.

MIGRATION DATES. *Spring:* early April to late May. *Fall:* early July to late October. *Extremes:* 17 March; 28 November.

PORTRAIT. *Birds of Wisconsin:* Plate 32.

After observing Lesser Yellowlegs in the Madison area between 1 July and 21 October 1930 and from 21 March to 28 May 1931, J. S. Main (1932b, p. 82) commented: "The fall migration therefore covered a period of 113 days, and the spring migration 69 days, making 182 days in all, or a full six months. It is doubtful if there is any other shorebird, or indeed any other transient species, that consumes so large a portion of the year in passing through here." Although the 21 March date is exceptionally early, the other dates are more typical for the species. And when one considers that late fall migrants sometimes linger into November, Main's suggestion of a full 6-month migration period is correct.

Warm weather and flooded fields sometimes combine to attract first arrivals by the end of March. Observations have been made on the 17th (1977, La Crosse, J. R. Rosso) and 19th (1978, Ozaukee, M. F. Donald), as well as Main's 21 March sighting. In a typical year, however, arrivals can be expected between 5 and 15 April in the south and between 15 and 25 April farther north. Numbers gradually build through the last days of April and peak between 5 and 15 May at a time when the numbers of Greater Yellowlegs are diminishing. Concentrations of 100–300 birds are sometimes found during this peak period; occasionally, estimates have climbed as high as 700 individuals. A rapid decline occurs after 15 May. In a normal year the latest state departure date will occur by 30 May.

Yet one or more June sightings occur nearly every year. Birds recorded early in June are presumably late spring migrants that soon move on. Rarely, one or two individuals remain throughout the month instead of continuing their migratory journey.

Kumlien and Hollister (1903) stated: "Formerly bred at Lake Koshkonong, Horicon Lake, about Lake Pacana, and presumably in other localities. . . . Young, still unable to fly, are yet obtainable about Lake Koshkonong in July, but of late years not commonly." Schoenebeck (1902) recorded the discovery of a nest with four eggs on 10 June 1896 in Oconto County. In June 1936 Richter (1939a) found a female with three small young near the same Oconto County location.

It is doubtful that nesting was ever common, even before the heavy shorebird hunting of the 1870s. Wisconsin breeding in the twentieth century has occurred rarely. The usual nesting range is far to the north in the Hudson Bay region.

In about 1 year of every 5, early fall migrants appear before the end of June. Normally, fall migrants can be expected any time after 5 July in the north and after 10 July anywhere in the state. Flocks of 100–500 have been observed soon after the 15th, with estimates of 200–1,000 individuals through mid-August in the most favored locations. By mid-September most birds have left the north, and flock size has diminished somewhat in the south, with usually only small numbers remaining into October. The 23 October sighting of 150 birds (1949, H. C. Mueller) passing by Cedar Grove Ornithological Station in Sheboygan County is the latest recorded date for a group of more than 50. In some years all have left the state by 31 October. But approximately every second year late migrants linger into November. Yellowlegs remaining into November are more likely Greater than Lesser, but the latter has been identified as late as the 10th (1964, Dane, T. L. Ashman), 12th (1967, Sauk, K. I. Lange; 1967, Racine, L. W. Erickson), 19th (1963, Columbia, T. L. Ashman), and 28th (1949, Dodge, P. A. Mallow). The exact identity of a Yellowlegs at Cedar Grove on 30 November 1964 was not determined.

Solitary Sandpiper (*Tringa solitaria*)

STATUS. Fairly common migrant.
HABITAT. Ponds. Shallow marsh. Wooded swamp.
MIGRATION DATES. *Spring:* late April to late May. *Fall:* early July to early October. *Extremes:* 6 April, 10 June; 24 June, 24 November.
PORTRAIT. *Birds of Wisconsin:* Plate 32.

Kumlien and Hollister (1903) believed that the Solitary Sandpiper nested in Wisconsin. "There is no Wisconsin bird," they wrote, "of which we have so diligently and systematically sought the eggs, and without success, as this sandpiper. Numbers of times we have found the young just hatched, and judging from the actions of the parents, have often been near the eggs." In the nineteenth century nesting may have been a distinct possibility. In more modern times there have been instances of nesting in northern Minnesota and northern Michigan, but there is no known evidence of breeding in Wisconsin.

Many observers, fooled by early July sightings, assumed they were seeing summer residents. Fall migrants regularly appear by 5 July in the north and by 10 July in the south. The Solitary Sandpiper observed on 24 June 1981 in Chippewa County by J. L. Polk was nearly matched by a 26 June 1980 individual she found in St. Croix County. Since 1960 four more 29–30 June migrants have been seen. From mid-July to mid-September a few individuals can be found along the edges of streams or shallow ponds, where grass and small stretches of grass and mud coexist. Birds are found singly or in small groups, sometimes associated with a nearby Pectoral Sandpiper or Lesser Yellowlegs, but more often leading their own "solitary" life. Although little flocking occurs, it is possible to find 40–50 individuals during the 25 July–10 August peak where favorable habitat abounds. An estimated 100 Solitaries turned up at one Dane County location on 2 August 1977. In the north numbers decline after 1 September, with but a few birds remaining after the 15th; the latest date recorded is 8 October (1966, Douglas, R. F. Bernard). In the south the migrants dwindle after 20 September, with only an occasional bird still present at the end of the month. The last fall migrant is usually spotted around 10 October. Four November dates are known: the 7th (1964, Dane, R. E. Fiehweg), 13th (1939, Kewaunee, J. B. Kendall), 16th (1953, Lafayette, E. Olson), and 24th (1946, Racine, E. B. Prins).

Not until 25 April do spring birds return in numbers. In some years an occasional individual is detected by 15 April. Unusually early are April sightings in southern counties on the 6th (1981, Ozaukee, W. Cowart), 10th (1976, Waukesha, J. E. Bielefeldt), and 11th (1957, Rock, M. T. Maxson); in the central region on the 14th (1972, Portage, A. M. Baumgartner) and 15th (1976, Chippewa, S. D. Robbins); and in the north on the 22nd (1967, Marinette, H. L. Lindberg). During the 5–15 May peak the grassy edge of a small pond or flooded field may harbor from one to five individuals. During this period one can stand outside on a cloudy night when migrating birds are flying low and detect the passage of several Solitaries by recognizing their "pee-twee-tweet." By 25 May virtually all have left the state. It is exceptional when stragglers extend their stay into June, as have birds sighted on the 6th (1981, Dane, S. Thiessen), 7th (1964, Door, L. W. Erickson; 1980, Dane, S. Thiessen), 8th (1940, Jefferson, F. R. Zimmerman), and 10th (1975, Milwaukee, E. L. Basten). The gap between the last spring vagrant and the first fall migrant is indeed short.

Willet (*Catoptrophorus semipalmatus*)

STATUS. Uncommon migrant. Casual summer resident.
HABITAT. Great Lakes. Inland lakes. Ponds.
MIGRATION DATES. *Spring:* late April to early June.
   Fall: mid-July to late September. *Extremes:* 14 April;
   27 October.
PORTRAIT. *Birds of Wisconsin:* Plate 32.

During one brief 5-day span (26–30 April 1974) 30 Willets were seen at scattered locations in Columbia, Dane, Milwaukee, Eau Claire, Portage, and Marinette counties. In nearly every instance the birds were present one day and gone the next. Only three individuals were subsequently reported during the remainder of the spring migration.

This is typical spring behavior for this large, pale shorebird. In the southern two-thirds of the state your best chance to see this wader is to visit a large mud flat during the last few days of April or the first week of May. Don't wait for someone else to tell you where a Willet has been seen—the chances are that the bird will have moved on by the time you get there. Individuals have been known to spend 10–15 days in one spot, but they are the exceptions. Willets occur singly and in small flocks of 5–10, rarely in groups of 15–20; the 37 seen in Milwaukee on 23 April 1981 (J. C. Frank) were exceptional. By 20 May nearly all have left the south.

Along the Lake Superior shore the timetable is somewhat later. Individuals begin to appear by 30 April and are most frequently seen between 10 and 25 May, with birds sometimes lingering several days into early June.

The earliest April sightings have occurred on the 14th (1986, Dunn, J. L. Polk), 16th (1956, Jefferson, E. Degner), 20th (1946, Brown, C. H. Hussong; 1978, Racine, L. W. Erickson), and 21st (1977, Milwaukee, E. J. Epstein). Unusually late spring stragglers have been found on 5 June (1973, Milwaukee, E. L. Basten), 6 June (1981, Marathon, K. J. Luepke), and 10 June (1942, Waukesha, W. J. Aberg).

In 1975 an individual made history by spending the summer in Brown County (T. C. Erdman). The following year, one (possibly two?) also summered there; it seemed agitated, but Erdman doubted that it was nesting. Additional summer wanderers were noted in Manitowoc County, 20–26 June 1980, 23 June 1985, and 26 June 1986 (C. R. Sontag).

Through the 1960s this stately wader was a rare fall migrant: present briefly in one or two locations some years, missing entirely in others. Since 1970 there have been from two to four observations per autumn. As in spring, birds pause briefly—singly or in groups

Willet

△   Late April to early June
○   Mid-June to early July
▽   Mid-July to late September

Records since 1960

of from two to six. Before 1960 there had been but two observations earlier than 25 July: Dane County individuals on 2 July 1925 (J. Gundlach [Schorger 1929b]) and 2 July 1953 (E. Reindahl). More recently, observers have recorded July arrivals on the 7th (1977, Manitowoc, D. D. Tessen), 10th (1978, Marinette, H. L. Lindberg), 12th (1965, Racine, E. B. Prins), and 14th (1964, Marinette, H. L. Lindberg). There is no noticeable pattern for autumn sightings through late July, August, and early September. Beyond 15 September there are only five records: 20 September (1958, Sheboygan, H. C. Mueller), 24 September (1979, Manitowoc, C. R. Sontag), 29 September (1956, Manitowoc, J. Kraupa), 8 October (1939, Brown, C. H. Hussong), and 27 October (1987, Bayfield, R. L. Verch).

Although many of the shorebirds were much more numerous in the nineteenth century, this species does not seem to have ever been common. Kumlien and Hollister (1903) took occasional Willet specimens in May and September, and sometimes found the bird in June, but there was never any indication of nesting. Although they surmised that the Willet might possibly nest in wetlands along the Mississippi, they offered no supportive evidence.

Spotted Sandpiper (*Actitis macularia*)

STATUS. Common migrant. Common summer resident.
HABITAT. Great Lakes. Inland lakes. Ponds.
MIGRATION DATES. *Spring:* mid-April to late May. *Fall:* mid-July to mid-October. *Extremes:* 24 March; 27 November.
BREEDING DATA. Nests with eggs: 18 May to 10 July. Clutch size: usually 4 eggs; rarely 3 or 5.
WINTER. One January record.
PORTRAIT. *Birds of Wisconsin:* Plate 32.

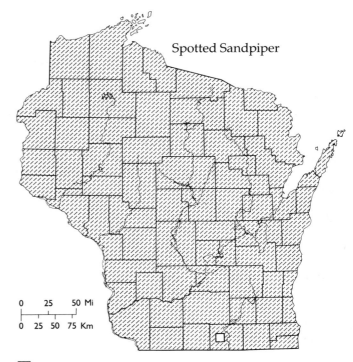

Spotted Sandpiper

▨ Summer range
☐ 1 January

Records since 1960

Anyone restricting shorebird observations to mud flats and flooded fields might conclude that the Spotted is one of the rarer of the sandpipers. Actually it is one of our most common shorebirds. Few are found among the larger concentrations of Pectorals, Leasts, and Yellowlegs. But spread out along sandy beaches, rocky lakeshores, and riverbanks are individuals whose numbers mount up to an impressive total. Populations are greatest along the sandy shores of Lakes Superior and Michigan and at Green Bay, but this species can be found in suitable habitat in all parts of the state.

An occasional migrant may be recorded between 15 and 20 April, but most observers in the south find first arrivals between 25 April and 5 May, while the usual northern arrival dates are 5–10 May. Two birds at Neenah (Winnebago County) on 24 March 1939 (J. H. Evans) were strikingly early. Remarkably warm weather in late March 1953 also brought early stragglers to Winnebago (25 March, W. Urban) and Burnett (2 April, H. Barrett) counties. Other exceptionally early April dates include birds on the 5th (1985, Fond du Lac, W. K. Volkert), 8th (1954, Lafayette, E. Olson), 9th (1964, Douglas, R. F. Bernard), 10th (1954, Kenosha, M. F. Higgins), and 11th (1981, Door, R. J. Lukes).

Some birds still present on 25 May may be migrants destined for Canada, but most are nesters. Kumlien and Hollister (1903) commented that this species "seems to display very little ingenuity in concealing the eggs." C. H. Richter found nests in slight depressions in bare ground, sand, and gravel, and even among wood chips in a lumber yard. Egg-laying occurs mainly in the 20 May–5 June period. Newly hatched young have been observed as early as 7 June, and are numerous by 25 June. The fact that nests with eggs have occasionally been found in the first week of July suggests that some pairs renest, perhaps after earlier nest failures. An enjoyable sight in July and early August is the playful behavior of a family of "spotties" along a lakeshore: teetering, twittering, and making short sorties out over the water with jerky shallow wingbeats.

To most observers the fall migration is inconspicuous, with no noticeable buildup. Some bird-watchers have noted a modest increase in late July and early August; T. C. Erdman (pers. comm.) wrote of often finding 50–60 individuals in Brown County, 1–10 August. A gradual decline sets in by mid-August. By 15 September most individuals have left. A few birds remain through 15 October nearly every year. There have been November records on the 1st (1953, Bayfield, A. A. Axley), 4th (1970, Sauk, K. I. Lange), 8th (1953, Lafayette, E. Olson), 10th (1972, Brown, E. D. Cleary), 11th (1969, Brown, E. D. Cleary), 14th (1973, Racine, L. W. Erickson; 1973, Kenosha, H. L. Lindberg), and 27th (1984, Manitowoc, C. R. Sontag).

Most astonishing was the bird found in Rock County on 1 January 1966 (J. W. Wilde; T. L. Ashman). Its distinctive call note was heard, and the bird itself was seen standing and in flight. Although capable of normal flight, this bird may have had to remain far beyond its usual departure time because of illness or injury.

Upland Sandpiper (*Bartramia longicauda*)
Formerly Upland Plover

STATUS. Fairly common migrant east; uncommon migrant west and central. Fairly common summer resident east; uncommon summer resident west and central.

HABITAT. Open grassland. Old field.

MIGRATION DATES. *Spring:* early April to mid-May. *Fall:* mid-July to mid-September. *Extremes:* 28 March; 13 October.

BREEDING DATA. Nests with eggs: 8 May to 8 July. Clutch size: usually 4 eggs; rarely 3 or 5.

PORTRAIT. *Birds of Wisconsin:* Plate 29.

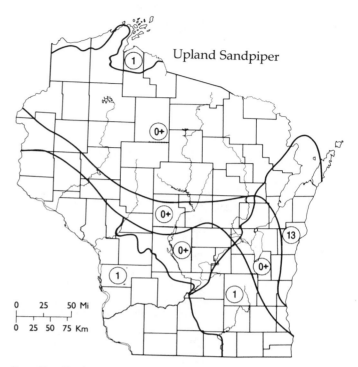

Breeding Bird Survey, averages 1966 to 1980

"Abundant," wrote Hoy (1853b). "Abounds largely upon our prairies in autumn and spring," added Barry (1854). Fifty years later Kumlien and Hollister (1903) recalled the days when the "prairie pigeon" was in its heyday, then warned: "This once abundant species is disappearing at such a rate that, if the decrease in the next twenty years is as great as it has been since 1870, the bird will become extinct. Formerly every meadow, border of marsh, or grassy lake shore contained great numbers of this bird." By 1919 Hollister listed it as having disappeared from the Delavan region in Walworth County. By 1929 Schorger (1929b) referred to the bird as a summer resident in Dane County in very small numbers.

This pasture-loving species has been known by various names (Bartramian Sandpiper, Upland Plover, Upland Sandpiper) and nicknames ("prairie pigeon," "wolf-whistle plover") through the years. The wolf-whistle call is frequently given when the birds first arrive in spring. In the south first arrivals are generally expected between 10 and 15 April, but birds are occasionally found during the first week of April. Unusually early individuals were noted on 28 March (1948, Brown, A. Weber) and 30 March (1973, Wood, D. G. Follen). In the north birds are seldom seen before 25 April. By 20 May migrants have moved farther on, and residents have settled down for nesting.

Current BBS data (see the accompanying map) show a statewide summer range, with small numbers everywhere except in the east. The eastern region, where the bird is more numerous, encompasses a somewhat larger area than the map indicates, for there are a few pockets in Portage, Winnebago, and Brown counties—not covered by BBS transects—where numbers are higher.

In the 1930s Buss and Hawkins (1939) studied one such pocket near Lake Mills (Jefferson County) extensively. Within a 1,600-acre study area, the breeding population rose from 8 pairs in 1935 to 25 in 1938, which represented a strong comeback. Before 1890 these birds were plentiful, but between 1895 and 1920 they nearly disappeared.

Buss and Hawkins (1939) determined that egg-laying began around 10 May for most of the 25 pairs studied in 1938. All observed nests contained four eggs. Full-grown young were evident by 22 June.

In 1974 and 1975 Ailes (1980) conducted intensive studies on a smaller area in the Buena Vista Marsh in Portage County. The 13 nests monitored were all in grasslands undisturbed by grazing at the onset of breeding, with the only loss of eggs occurring subsequently when the grass had grown long enough to make grazing possible. Family groups moved to shorter grass for feeding within 24 hours of hatching. Hatching in some instances was delayed until 8 July.

Ailes (1980) found that young were able to fly 4–5 weeks after hatching and fed mainly in grazed pastures through July. Buss and Hawkins (1939) also noted some flocking in late July and early August (89 on 1 August 1938). Most observers, however, do not find resident birds after mid-July.

Fall migration usually starts by 25 July, and begins

to decline by 20 August. It is in mid-August that I have most often heard the rolling musical twitter that the Upland sometimes utters as it passes overhead. Only occasionally are migrants detected after 10 September. The latest recorded departure dates are 4 October (1953, Lafayette, E. Olson), 6 October (1946, Milwaukee, D. L. Larkin) and 13 October (1963, Racine, B. Weber).

With increasing amounts of pasture lands being converted to corn production since the early 1970s, further declines in Upland Sandpiper populations seem imminent. The productive Jefferson County area studied by Buss and Hawkins has lost its "bartramians" as a result of drainage and cultivation. BBS data suggest a slight decline through 1980 but are not sufficient to tell us more.

Eskimo Curlew (*Numenius borealis*)

STATUS: Formerly casual migrant.
HABITAT: Great Lakes. Inland lakes. Ponds.
PORTRAIT. *Birds of Wisconsin:* Plate 31.

I know of two Wisconsin Eskimo Curlew specimens. Precise data for a bird located in the Racine County Historical Museum are lacking, but J. H. Martin, the donor, wrote in 1940: "The case of birds which my father mounted were probably mounted between the years 1870 and 1876 and were collected in the Township of Yorkville (possibly a few in the Township of Dover) and most of them in the vicinity of his farm" (Racine County Historical Museum files). The probable location was 2 miles north of Union Grove (Racine County).

The second specimen, donated by O. P. Allert and housed at the University of Minnesota, was taken by Delos Hatch on or near Horicon Marsh during the spring of 1903 (Allert 1928). The original label lists the date as 22 March 1903 and describes the location as "on the Horicon Marsh at Leroy, Fond du Lac County, Wis." Allert questioned the exact date, but was satisfied that the bird was shot in the spring of that year.

Some question about the exact location is raised because Leroy is located in Dodge County, as is most of Horicon Marsh.

Unquestionably, collectors found this bird on a few other occasions in the nineteenth century. Hoy (1853b) stated: "Met with . . . in early spring and fall. Rare." Thure Kumlien procured two specimens in 50 years of collecting, but further data are lacking. Kumlien and Hollister (1903) mentioned seeing a specimen shot in Green Bay in the fall of 1879, but apparently no one saved the bird. Schoenebeck (1902) told of a specimen brought to him on 27 April 1899. The bird had been shot near Oconto; its skin was so badly damaged, however, that it could not be saved, and subsequently Ned Hollister (1912, p. 397) questioned the identification on the grounds of inadequate evidence. A Dodge County record originally published under the date of 10 September 1912 (*Auk* 30:269–70; 57:566–567) has had to be discarded because of misidentification.

All evidence suggests that even in early times this wanderer was a rare or casual occurrence in the state.

Whimbrel (*Numenius phaeopus*)
Formerly Hudsonian Curlew

STATUS. Uncommon spring migrant east and north; rare fall migrant east.

HABITAT. Great Lakes. Inland lakes. Ponds.

MIGRATION DATES. *Spring:* mid-May to mid-June. *Fall:* late July to mid-October. *Extremes:* 8 May, 20 June; 20 July, 2 November.

PORTRAIT. *Birds of Wisconsin:* Plate 31.

An astonishing spectacle was seen on the afternoon of 22 May 1980 when an estimated thousand Whimbrels paused to rest and feed at Manitowoc. J. F. Steffen photographed them as they took off, forming large V-shaped flocks reminiscent of migrating geese. Roy and Charlotte Lukes witnessed another 200 of these large shorebirds the same day in Door County. Nothing remotely approaching such numbers has ever been reported in Wisconsin before or since.

Most Whimbrels migrate north along the Atlantic and Pacific coasts in spring. A few move through the Great Lakes region on their way to breeding grounds. If one could be afield daily between 20 and 30 May, either along the Lake Michigan shore between Manitowoc and Sturgeon Bay or along the Lake Superior shore at Superior or Ashland, one would stand a good chance of catching a glimpse of this rarity. It is essential to be at the right place at the right time, for this bird's stopovers are brief.

Observers have recorded from one to seven sightings each May since 1971. The 8 May 1972 individual (Ozaukee, M. F. Donald) is the state's earliest. During the main migration period, 20–30 May, birds are seen individually or in flocks of 15–40. Aside from 3 Mississippi–St. Croix River valley observations and 10 Fox River valley sightings, all spring records since 1960 have come from the shores of Lakes Michigan and Superior. Birds lingering beyond the first 5 days of June have been reported on the 8th (1972, Outagamie, D. D. Tessen), 9th (1972, Columbia, W. Woessner), and 20th (1963, Douglas, R. F. Bernard). One individual remained in Brown County through the summer of 1976 (T. C. Erdman, pers. comm.).

Fall observations are less frequent than those in spring; in most years there will be one or two sightings, or none. With the exception of isolated instances in Douglas, Ashland, and Vernon counties, all autumn occurrences have been along the Green Bay–Lake Michigan shore.

The duration of fall migration, however, encompasses parts of 5 months, compared with 2 in spring.

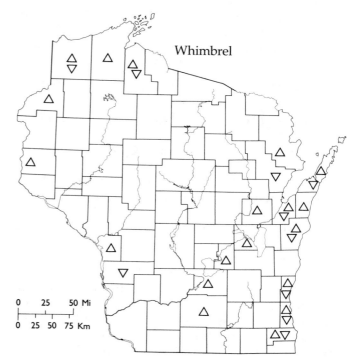

△ Mid-May to mid-June
▽ Late July to mid-October

Records since 1960

Southbound migrants have been noted on 20 July (1939, Sheboygan, E. L. Loyster) and 22 July (1982, Milwaukee, W. A. Cowart). Between 1960 and 1987, eastern Wisconsin observers found this rarity 4 times in late July, 7 in August, and 11 in September. In most instances the birds linger for only a day or two, but there have been two exceptions at Milwaukee: 13–26 September (1978, R. H. Sundell) and 6 September–21 October (1977, J. L. Ingold). Other October sightings have been made on the 1st (1928, Dane, J. Gundlach [Schorger 1929b]), 15th (1952, Milwaukee, C. P. Frister; 1983, Manitowoc, C. R. Sontag), and 26th (1940, Sheboygan, O. J. Gromme). Exceptionally late are two individuals observed on 2 November 1979 (Oconto, T. C. Erdman).

Hoy (1853b) called these birds "common in spring and fall," and mentioned finding a few nesting near Fox Lake (Dodge County) on 15 June 1848. Kumlien and Hollister (1903) described it as rare from 1870 on. No specific nesting data were ever published. Like Hoy, Thure Kumlien mentioned summer observations. If Hoy presumed nesting simply because of the presence of birds in mid-June, the assumption of breeding is unwarranted.

Through the first half of the twentieth century the Whimbrel was considered among the rarest of Wisconsin shorebirds. In 1922, 1929, and 1930, migrants were seen at the Cedar Grove Ornithological Station in Sheboygan County in September by C. S. Jung and others who were engaged in hawk observation work (MPM files). It was during the 1950s that this bird was found with increasing frequency along Lake Michigan. This visitor may well have been present along Lake Superior before 1960, but it was not until the early 1960s that systematic observation began in that region.

Long-billed Curlew (*Numenius americanus*)

STATUS. Casual spring migrant. Casual summer visitant. Formerly bred.
HABITAT. Great Lakes. Inland lakes. Ponds.
MIGRATION DATES. Observed between 15 May and 6 July.
PORTRAIT. *Birds of Wisconsin:* Plate 31.

This striking sickle-billed prairie species has been reliably reported in Wisconsin only seven times in the twentieth century. One was substantiated by photographs: a bird seen in Brown County on 6 July 1975 by T. C. Erdman (*Pass. Pigeon* 38:75). In the Milwaukee Public Museum files there are records of observations in 1911 (15 May, Sauk, H. L. Stoddard), 1936 (14 June, Sheboygan, Fond du Lac, O. J. Gromme and others), and 1952 (17 May, Dodge and Fond du Lac, *fide* O. J. Gromme). Another Sheboygan County sighting occurred on 27 May 1963 (H. C. Mueller; *Pass. Pigeon* 25:156). One appeared in Burnett County on 23 May 1966 (N. R. Stone; *Pass. Pigeon* 29:32). Another appeared in Racine County on 26 May 1969 (Dorothy and Joy Joslyn; *Badger Birder* #75).

In the early settlement years during the midnineteenth century, the Long-billed Curlew was a common breeding species in the southern counties. Hoy (1853b) called it "common on large thinly settled prairies," and mentioned that it nested abundantly in Columbia and Fond du Lac counties. Kumlien and Hollister (1903) were indefinite about exact locations. "During the forties, fifties and sixties it bred in suitable localities in different parts of the state. . . . From 1860 to 1890 it decreased rapidly, and when found at all it was as a migrant only." The last definite date for nesting was May 1859. There are no clues, either in Kumlien and Hollister (1903) or in Hoy (1853b), to indicate how late summer residents remained into the fall.

The major prairie regions in 1850 were pockets extending from Walworth County north to Columbia and west to Grant County. Presumably, this is the region the Long-billed Curlew once occupied. Kumlien

Long-billed Curlew

0   25   50 Mi
0 25 50 75 Km

△   15 to 27 May
○   14 June to 6 July

Records since 1900

and Hollister (1903) attribute the disappearance of the birds to the breakup of the original prairie sod. "The curlew will not stay long on cultivated ground, but leaves with the disappearance of the original prairie sod." The state's lone remaining specimen is located at the Milwaukee Public Museum. Specific data are lacking, but it is believed to be a bird collected at Milwaukee on 17 April 1868 by Albert Busjaeger.

Although this large shorebird may never return to Wisconsin as a breeding species, it should continue to show up rarely as a late May wanderer from the Great Plains.

Hudsonian Godwit (*Limosa haemastica*)

STATUS. Uncommon spring migrant; rare fall migrant.
HABITAT. Great Lakes. Inland lakes. Ponds.
MIGRATION DATES. *Spring:* late April to early June.
Fall: mid-August to late October. *Extremes:* 22
April, 12 June; 3 August, 1 November.
PORTRAIT. *Birds of Wisconsin:* Plate 31.

The world population of this handsome wader has always been small, with its breeding range restricted to
a few colonies on the west shore of James Bay, Hudson Bay, and northern Mackenzie. Small wonder that
it has been classified as rare by all nineteenth-century
commentators as well as more recent observers. Hoy's
(1853b) records at Racine were limited to one bird collected on 1 November 1850. Kumlien and Hollister
(1903) commented: "We have never known this godwit to occur anywhere within the state in any numbers, and of late years it must be considered very
rare." It was regular in small numbers until 1885. One
of Thure Kumlien's specimens, collected at Lake Koshkonong in Jefferson County on 15 May 1885, remains
in the Kenosha County Historical Museum.

From 1885 to 1950 records were few and far between. The Milwaukee Public Museum has five specimens taken during that period: one on 1 June 1910
(Brown, A. J. Schoenebeck), two on 21 May 1931 (Jackson, O. J. Gromme), one on 13 May 1933 (Ozaukee,
C. S. Jung), and one on 12 June 1934 (Fond du Lac,
I. J. Perkins). Schorger (1934c) observed several individuals in Dane County between 12 and 27 May 1934,
collecting one on the 13th. In the 1940s observers recorded three May sightings in Dane and Waukesha
counties.

Starting in 1950, observers covered more favorable
habitat across the state and documented this species
every year. Birds sometimes appear alone, sometimes
in flocks of 15–25, but most often in groups of 5–10.
In recent years birds have been spotted in from 4 to 12
different localities each spring. A majority of the
sightings are concentrated in a brief 10-day interval:
10–20 May. Since 1960 there have been but seven published arrival dates in April, six of them in western or
northwestern locations, including the record-setting
22 April 1977 bird (Ashland, M. E. Butterbrodt). The
few birds that linger beyond 25 May also are mainly in
the northwestern counties. Early June stragglers include individuals on the 9th (1985, Fond du Lac, T. R.
Schultz), 10th (1969, Brown, M. M. Wierzbicki), and
12th (1934, Fond du Lac, O. J. Gromme [1935b]). In

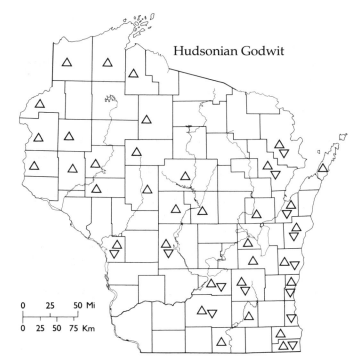

Hudsonian Godwit

△ Late April to early June
▽ Mid-August to late October

Records since 1960

1976 an injured bird spent the summer in Brown
County (T. C. Erdman).

In fall most of these godwits choose a circuitous migratory path that takes them to the Atlantic Coast and
even out to sea. Over a century passed after Hoy's
record of the 1 November 1850 bird in Racine County
before Wisconsin had another fall visitor. But since
1960 the number of autumn observations has increased markedly. There are years when none are
seen, and years with from three to five records. Most
sightings involve lone individuals. Between 1961 and
1987 published records documented 12 sightings in
August, 7 in September, and 13 in October. Early August sightings were made on the 3rd (1972, Brown,
D. D. Tessen) and 9th (1970, Brown, C. H. Hussong).
The latest October records include the 24th (1983,
Manitowoc, C. R. Sontag), 28th (1962, Oconto, C. H.
Richter), and 30th (1985, Manitowoc, Wm. Mueller).
Most autumn birds have been detected along the
shores of Green Bay and Lake Michigan.

Marbled Godwit (*Limosa fedoa*)

STATUS. Uncommon spring migrant; rare fall migrant.
Formerly nested.
HABITAT. Great Lakes. Inland lakes. Ponds.
MIGRATION DATES. *Spring:* mid-April to mid-June.
Fall: mid-July to early November. *Extremes:* 13
April, 24 June; 9 July, 24 November.
PORTRAIT. *Birds of Wisconsin:* Plate 31.

Although not the most colorful of shorebirds, the
Marbled Godwit, a wanderer from the western plains,
is large enough and rare enough to thrill anyone who
finds it in Wisconsin. It is most likely to be seen in
spring, along the muddy or grassy edges of shallow
ponds or flooded fields. From one to five sightings
have been recorded each spring in recent years. Usually only one or two birds are found at any one location, but flocks of 5–10 have been noted on rare
occasions.

When suitable habitat was checked closely in Douglas (1962–1968) and St. Croix (1961–1977) counties,
late April or May observations became almost an annual event. Records have been slightly less frequent
in the region between Madison and Green Bay. Between 1961 and 1987 only 12 spring records were published for the Lake Michigan region.

Approximately a fourth of all spring observations
have occurred in April. This species should be looked
for any time after the 20th, and it has been found as
early as the 13th (1972, Ozaukee, T. Bintz), 15th (1967,
Columbia, R. B. Dryer; 1983, Manitowoc, C. R. Sontag), 16th (1963, St. Croix, S. D. Robbins), 18th (1978,
Bayfield, R. L. Verch), and 19th (1959, Manitowoc,
M. H. Reichwaldt; 1975, St. Croix, C. A. Faanes).
Most birds have been observed between 20 April and
20 May. Birds lingering into June have been reported
six times since 1950, the latest ones on the 11th (1953,
Ozaukee, T. K. Soulen), 16th (1965, Douglas, R. F.
Bernard), and 24th (1985, Dodge, D. Haugen).

Although this large wader is uncommon in spring,
it is even rarer as a fall migrant. The 28 published
records, 1961–1985, have been widely spaced: 9 sightings in July, 12 in August, 2 in September, 2 in October, and 3 in November. The bird's stopovers are
usually brief, but one individual remained from 8 Au-

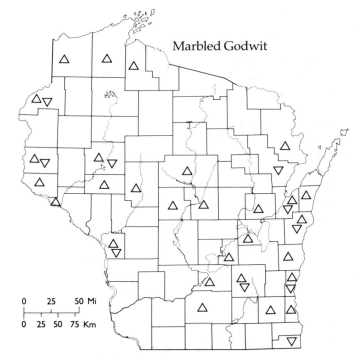

△   Mid-April to mid-June
▽   Mid-July to early November

Records since 1960

gust through 15 September (1979, Dodge, D. K. Gustafson and others). The earliest July dates are the 9th
(1984, Manitowoc, C. R. Sontag) and 16th (1983,
Burnett, J. E. Hoefler). November dates include the
1st (1974, Brown, T. C. Erdman), 8th (1975, injured
bird in Burnett, W. Norling), and 24th (1957, Sheboygan, D. D. Berger).

No evidence exists that the Marbled Godwit was
ever common in Wisconsin. Hoy (1853b) found it near
Racine and mentioned seeing a pair, possibly nesting,
along the Wisconsin River on 15 June 1848. Kumlien
and Hollister (1903) observed birds along Green Bay,
Lake Winnebago, and at Lake Koshkonong. They
commented: "It was not rare from 1870 to 1876, and in
1857–59 it was known to nest in two instances, once
near Stoughton and once at the lake."

Ruddy Turnstone (*Arenaria interpres*)

STATUS. Common spring migrant east; uncommon spring migrant west, central, and north; uncommon fall migrant north and east; rare fall migrant west and central. Rare summer resident east.
HABITAT. Great Lakes. Inland lakes. Ponds.
MIGRATION DATES. *Spring:* late April to mid-June. *Fall:* late July to early November. *Extremes:* 25 April; 9 November.
PORTRAIT. *Birds of Wisconsin:* Plate 28.

For a brief 10-day period, 20–30 May, hundreds of colorful Ruddy Turnstones invade the eastern counties from Kenosha to Marinette. In Racine and Kenosha counties, flocks of 100–500 roam the plowed fields in search of insects. On 30 May 1969 James Hamers estimated that between 3,000 and 4,000 birds occupied fields near Kenosha. At Oshkosh flocks of 200–700 birds move onto the lawns in the residential area along the west shore of Lake Winnebago, just as midges are hatching. An estimated 1,200 were reported on 24 May 1954 (F. Holman King). Sizable flocks occasionally pause briefly at Superior.

Elsewhere, this turnstone is decidedly uncommon in spring, with individuals or flocks of from three to eight scattered wherever suitable shorebird habitat exists. Late April arrivals have been detected on the 25th (1970, Sheboygan, K. H. Kuhn) and 26th (1974, Columbia, E. W. Peartree). In most years first arrivals are spotted between 5 and 10 May. By 5 June the flocks have left the state; the few remaining migrants leave by 15 June.

Rarely, nonbreeding individuals spend the summer here. Small numbers summered in Brown County in 1977 and 1978 (T. C. Erdman, pers. comm.). Kumlien and Hollister (1903) also mentioned having seen birds at Green Bay in late June, with an occasional nonbreeding bird summering at Lake Koshkonong. One hesitates to assign either spring or fall migratory status to the 1 July 1973 individual at Racine (L. W. Erickson) or to the 28 June 1974 bird in Winnebago County (C. Schultz).

The earliest clearly identifiable fall migrant was a 17 July bird (1981, Fond du Lac, D. D. Tessen); later July migrants have been seen on the 24th (1948, Racine, E. B. Prins) and 25th (1973, Brown, M. M.

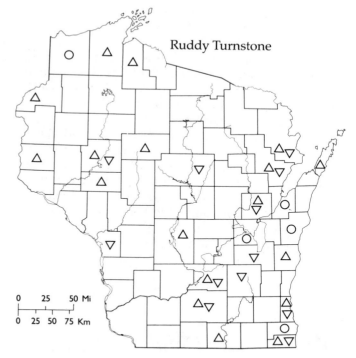

Ruddy Turnstone

△   Late April to mid-June
○   Late June to mid-July
▽   Late July to early November

Records since 1960

Wierzbicki). Missing entirely in fall are large concentrations similar to those in May. Single individuals or small groups of 6–8 birds appear every fall along the shores of Lakes Michigan and Superior and less regularly among fall shorebird concentrations at a few inland locations. The frequency of sightings gradually increases through August, levels off in mid-September, then diminishes. A few birds remain into October nearly every year. A Douglas County bird on 6 October (1968, S. D. Robbins) provides northern Wisconsin's latest recorded date. Farther south, lingering mid-October birds have been sighted on numerous occasions. Four November dates are known: the 4th (1972, Brown, E. D. Cleary), 5th (1986, Ashland, R. L. Verch), 8th (1979, Milwaukee, D. K. Gustafson), and 9th (1980, Manitowoc, C. R. Sontag).

Black Turnstone (*Arenaria melanocephala*)

STATUS. Accidental. One record.
HABITAT. Normally Pacific Coast.

It is hard to imagine a North American species less likely to visit Wisconsin than the Black Turnstone. Its normal range is restricted so exclusively to the Pacific Coast that even records from interior Alaska, Oregon, and California are considered exceptional.

But among a large flock of Dunlins and Ruddy Turnstones at Oshkosh, Robert Pritash discovered an odd dark-breasted bird on 22 May 1971. The birds were feeding on a lawn near Lake Winnebago. Word passed quickly to other ornithologists, and between then and 25 May, some 25 other bird-watchers got good views of the Pacific straggler. Tom Underwood's photographs and Pritash's documentation (*Pass. Pigeon* 34:39) leave no doubt that the visitor was indeed a Black Turnstone.

Black Turnstone, 22 May 1971, Winnebago County (photo by T. J. Underwood)

Red Knot (*Calidris canutus*)

Formerly Knot

STATUS. Uncommon migrant north and east; rare migrant elsewhere.
HABITAT. Great Lakes. Inland lakes. Ponds.
MIGRATION DATES. *Spring:* mid-May to early June. *Fall:* mid-July to mid-November. *Extremes:* 5 May; 17 November.
WINTER. One record.
PORTRAIT. *Birds of Wisconsin:* Plate 33.

The main spring migration route lies east of Wisconsin, and in some years not a single Red Knot is noted in our state in May or June. Southwest of a line from Monroe to Hudson no records are known. At such inland locations as Grantsburg, Roberts, Chippewa Falls, Madison, and Horicon a spring sighting occurs on the average of one or two per year. Most reports come from the Lake Michigan–Green Bay shore from Racine to Marinette and from the Lake Superior shore between Superior and Ashland. Even there the number of spring records is limited to from two to five per year: sometimes single individuals, sometimes small flocks of 6–15 birds.

Kumlien and Hollister (1903) spoke of the Red Knot as a rather common migrant up to 1870, but becoming rare after that time. In recent years most spring observations have been concentrated between 20 and 31 May. The earliest May dates include the 5th (1976,

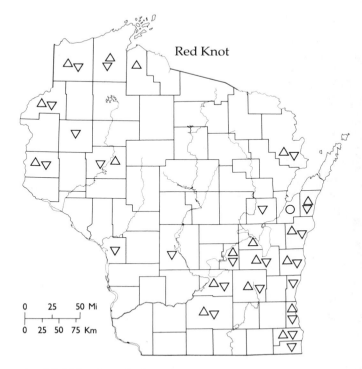

△ Mid-May to early June
○ Mid-June to early July
▽ Mid-July to mid-November

Records since 1960

Dane, W. L. Hilsenhoff), 9th (1950, Dane, S. D. Robbins), 11th (1957, Brown, E. D. Cleary), 12th (1966, St. Croix, S. D. Robbins), and 13th (1975, St. Croix, C. A. Faanes). June departure dates include the 6th (1966, Douglas, R. F. Bernard), 8th (1972, Brown, Bro. Columban), 13th (1968, Burnett, N. R. Stone), and 16th (1975, Milwaukee, M. F. Donald). One bird in Manitowoc County on 14 June (1978, D. D. Tessen) was already in full fall plumage. Wisconsin's only midsummer records concern an individual remaining in Brown County through June and July (1972, T. C. Erdman, pers. comm.) and one in Winnebago County on 28 June (1986, T. Ziebell).

Perhaps this rarity is more apt to be overlooked in fall, once it has lost its gaudy spring plumage; it appears, at any rate, to be just as uncommon in fall as in spring. Two phenomenally early sightings occurred in July 1981, on the 8th (Milwaukee, G. Casper) and 11th (Dodge, D. D. Tessen). With the exception of another straggler on 21 July 1975 (Brown, J. Trick), first fall migrants have appeared in early August. Because

this arctic nester prefers sandy beaches to grass-lined mud flats, inland fall records are few and far between. Ponds temporarily drawn down provide the most favored inland shorebird locations, but only rarely has this species been known to join other migrating shorebirds at these concentration points. Of 72 published fall records in Wisconsin, 52 have been for the shores of Lake Superior, Green Bay, and Lake Michigan. Even along the lakeshores, 3–5 records totaling 5–20 individuals is par for a season.

Although most birds disappear by 25 September, several have been known to linger well into October: until the 12th (1973, Racine, D. D. Tessen), 19th (1952, Brown, E. O. Paulson; 1980, Manitowoc, C. R. Sontag), and 26th (1973, Dodge, L. W. Erickson). Still later are November dates: the 8th (1968, Racine, E. B. Prins) and 17th (1940, Milwaukee, W. J. Mueller). Even more extraordinary is the record of the bird discovered in Milwaukee on 11 December 1948, and seen off and on until it was found dead on 9 January 1949 (H. C. Mueller).

Sanderling (*Calidris alba*)

STATUS. Fairly common migrant along Lakes Superior and Michigan; uncommon migrant elsewhere.
HABITAT. Great Lakes. Inland lakes. Flooded fields.
MIGRATION DATES. *Spring:* late April to mid-June. *Fall:* mid-July to late November. *Extremes:* 20 April, 21 June; 4 July, 12 December.
PORTRAIT. *Birds of Wisconsin:* Plate 35.

The sandy beaches of Lakes Superior and Michigan probably attract 90% or more of all Sanderlings that pass through the state. Small flocks of 10–20 are occasionally found on sandy beaches of inland lakes and on sandbars along the Mississippi, and scattered individuals sometimes wander into mixed flocks of "peeps" on inland mud flats. But it is along the shorelines of the Great Lakes that one looks for the larger concentrations. Bernard estimated 600 individuals at Superior on 29 May 1963. That same fall Mary Donald reported several hundred at Milwaukee on 3 and 4 September. Although concentrations of this magnitude are met with only occasionally, there are many miles of suitable shoreline where smaller flocks (20–60) occur.

Early spring arrivals have appeared at Milwaukee by 20 April (1982, W. A. Cowart), at Racine by 22 April (1939, E. B. Prins; 1964, J. Saetveit), at Kenosha by 27 April (1975, R. R. Hoffman), and at Green Bay

Sanderling

△ Late April to mid-June
▽ Mid-July to late November

Records since 1960

by 29 April (1966, E. D. Cleary). The earliest inland arrival date is 30 April (1974, St. Croix, C. A. Faanes). The earliest Lake Superior date is 7 May (1963, Ashland, J. L. Kozlowski). More typical arrival dates are 5–10 May in the south and 15–20 May in the north. The largest numbers can be expected between 20 and 30 May. Sanderlings frequently linger through 5 June in the north, and have been noted as late as 16 June (1977, Bayfield, R. Korotev) and 21 June (1983, Manitowoc, C. R. Sontag). In the Milwaukee region stragglers have hung on until 19 June (1960, Ozaukee, I. N. Balsom; 1971, Milwaukee, D. K. Gustafson). Possibly these late individuals do not leave the state in summer. T. C. Erdman (pers. comm.) reported occasional sightings of birds that summered on some remote Green Bay islands (Brown, Marinette). No breeding has ever been suspected.

In contrast to a scant 6-week migration span in spring, the fall flight sometimes extends 4 months from mid-July to mid-November. The earliest July observations have come on the 4th (1983, Manitowoc, C. R. Sontag), 7th (1974, Brown, D. D. Tessen), 8th (1980, La Crosse, F. Z. Lesher), and 9th (1977, Oconto, J. C. Frank); only a trickle follows until early August. But flocks of 20 or more Sanderlings can be seen from mid-August to 10 October. By 10 October most have left the Lake Superior beaches. Unusually late was the Douglas County individual seen on 5 November (1976, G. J. Niemi). Most southern migrants have left by 25 October; yet one lingered in Door County through 16 November (1980, R. M. Hoffman). The latest dates have all come from Racine: 27 November (1949, G. Prins; 1963, B. Weber) and 12 December (1964, B. Weber).

Semipalmated Sandpiper (*Calidris pusilla*)

STATUS. Common migrant.
HABITAT. Great Lakes. Inland lakes. Flooded fields.
MIGRATION DATES. *Spring:* early May to mid-June. *Fall:* early July to mid-October. *Extremes:* 28 March; 28 December.
PORTRAIT. *Birds of Wisconsin:* Plate 34.

Bill Weber's 28 March 1964 record at Racine, a stray found dead on top of new snow, was astonishingly early. Most Semipalmated Sandpipers are still south of the United States at that time. The same year brought northern Wisconsin's earliest arrival on record: a 19 April bird (Bayfield, J. L. Kozlowski). Six other records before 20 April are known: the 8th (1954, Columbia, H. A. Winkler), 12th (1969, La Crosse, J. R. Rosso), 16th (1957, Columbia, H. A. Winkler), 17th (1977, Columbia, R. Ake), and 19th (1958, Chippewa, C. A. Kemper; 1970, La Crosse, J. R. Rosso). In 2 of every 3 years, someone spots an early migrant during the last week of April.

First arrivals in the southern half of the state typically come between 1 and 5 May. Northern arrivals usually appear between 10 and 15 May. In the south there is a gradual buildup to a 20–25 May peak, with a few small flocks remaining into early June. In the central and northern regions the largest numbers (flocks of 25–50 in the west, 100–300 in the east) occur between 25 May and 10 June. Banding shorebirds in Brown County in May and June 1976, T. C. Erdman (pers. comm.) found flocks of 500–600 daily in late May. The daily turnover was so great that he re-

trapped very few individuals. One of these birds, banded on 31 May 1976, was retrapped at North Point, James Bay, Ontario, on 20 July 1977. The dropoff after 10 June is so sudden that in most locations no birds are reported after the 15th.

Between 20 June and 10 July Semipals are absent from most areas of the state. But along the Green Bay shore and on the small islands in northeastern Wisconsin, Erdman has seen small groups of nonbreeding summer residents each year since 1965. For most of the 20 records in this 3-week interval published in *The Passenger Pigeon* since 1960, there is little to indicate which birds are late spring migrants, summer residents, or early fall migrants. Since inland locations probably do not harbor summer residents, it seems likely that individuals seen on 2 July (1969, Vernon, J. R. Rosso) and 3 July (1966, Fond du Lac, R. A. Knuth) were harbingers of the fall flight.

The increased frequency of reports after 10 July suggests that the fall flight has started in earnest. Along the Lakes Superior and Michigan shorelines, as well as at suitable inland shorebird concentration spots, numbers gradually build to a 10 August–10 September peak (flocks of 20–50 in the west, 100–500 in the east). Birds must be moving rapidly during this period. In Dane County on 20 August 1978 Randy Korotev observed a color-banded bird that had been tagged in North Dakota 15 days earlier. It had traveled 580 miles in 6 days.

Scattered individuals linger in the north into the first week of October and in the south through 20 October. Birds lingering through 5 November have been reported on five occasions. More remarkable were the reports of a Fond du Lac County bird on 15 November (1966, R. A. Knuth) and three Racine discoveries: on 29 November (1964, E. B. Prins), 10 December (1963, R. E. Fiehweg), and 28 December (1968, L. W. Erickson). The astonishing 28 December record was a report of two birds heard calling, then sighted from a distance of 8 feet.

Western Sandpiper (*Calidris mauri*)

STATUS. Uncommon migrant.
HABITAT. Great Lakes. Inland lakes. Ponds.
MIGRATION DATES. *Spring:* mid-May to early June. *Fall:* mid-July to mid-October. *Extremes:* 2 May, 22 June; 15 July, 7 November.
PORTRAIT. *Birds of Wisconsin:* Plate 34.

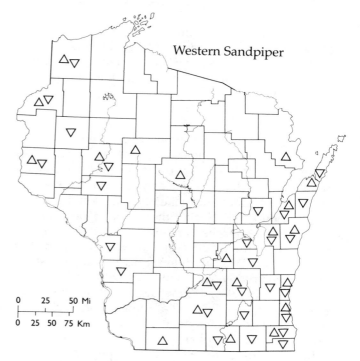

△ Mid-May to early June
▽ Mid-July to mid-October

Records since 1960

Ludwig Kumlien collected two specimens in Jefferson County on 29 May 1896; both are in the Milwaukee Public Museum (Kumlien and Hollister 1903). Kumlien and Hollister never encountered a Western Sandpiper in fall, but considered the species "of regular occurrence in May and often up to the middle of June." Numbers were very small, with all observations limited to Lake Koshkonong in Jefferson County. There is no other record from any other nineteenth- or early twentieth-century observer.

Not until 1930 was this visitor from the West again recorded. Gilbert Raasch's 26 July sight record in Dane County constituted the first autumn record for the state. After another 10-year lapse S. Paul Jones observed two birds in Waukesha County on 18 May 1941. Three additional fall records followed in 1947, 1948, and 1949.

Starting in 1952, sightings have become an annual event. Two additional specimens, collected on 28 and 29 May 1976 (Brown, T. C. Erdman), reside in the C. H. Richter collection at Green Bay. Observers have missed the Western during spring only in 1967, 1970, and 1977; from one to five individuals have been discovered in all other years. The Western is a later migrant than most. Of 34 observations in May published in *The Passenger Pigeon* since 1960, only 9 were earlier than 19 May. The earliest occurred on the 2nd (1975, St. Croix, C. A. Faanes), 3rd (1976, St. Croix, C. A. Faanes), 8th (1954, Columbia, H. A. Winkler), and 9th (1964, Lafayette, N. R. Barger). Nearly half the spring records have come between 25 May and 5 June. The latest: 20 June (1980, Manitowoc, C. R. Sontag) and 22 June (1971, Marinette, S. D. Robbins).

Between 1952 and 1987 from one to eight birds have been reported every autumn except in 1957, 1958, 1963, and 1968. August is the most active month. Of 20 records in July, observers spotted the earliest birds on the 15th (1964, Racine, B. Weber; 1978, Dane, R. Korotev) and 17th (1967, Ozaukee, M. F. Donald). Beyond 5 October there have been four observations: 9 October (1952, Dane, M. A. Walker), 12 October (1974, Burnett, *fide* C. A. Faanes), 18 October (1980, Dane, S. Thiessen), 25 October (1987, Milwaukee, R. M. Hoffman), and 7 November (1959, Milwaukee, H. A. Bauers).

The paucity of records between 1900 and 1950 is probably due more to the difficulty of identification than to the absence of birds. It has long been known that the winter range includes the Atlantic Coast north to North Carolina; this range is now known to extend north to Maryland. A fairly direct migratory route between the Atlantic Coast and the Alaskan breeding grounds should take birds through Wisconsin regularly. This species may be more numerous than has been suspected. But in spring, observers often slacken their fieldwork by the time the Western moves through the state. And in fall the bird's winter plumage is so similar to that of the Semipalmated Sandpiper that most Westerns are indistinguishable in the field.

Least Sandpiper (*Calidris minutilla*)

STATUS. Common migrant.

HABITAT. Great Lakes. Inland lakes. Flooded fields.

MIGRATION DATES. *Spring:* late April to late May. *Fall:* early July to mid-October. *Extremes:* 4 April; 17 November.

PORTRAIT. *Birds of Wisconsin:* Plate 34.

From 1 to 20 May these diminutive "peeps" scamper along the edges of ponds and flooded fields wherever a modest muddy edge appears. In flocks of 5–20—sometimes 50–100—Least Sandpipers run a few feet, stop to probe the mud, take off in unison like a tiny brown cloud, wheel over the water in close formation, and pick another landing spot farther along the same shore. You may see first arrivals during the last week of April in 2 out of every 3 years. Six instances are known of early April arrivals: the 4th (1940, Racine, H. Zell), 8th (1956, Winnebago, C. P. Frister), 12th (1947, Dunn, I. O. Buss; 1958, Outagamie, A. S. Bradford), 13th (1963, Jefferson, E. Degner), and 14th (1956, Sheboygan, R. G. Wills).

In the south numbers build to a peak between 10 and 15 May and drop off noticeably by the 20th; the birds are usually gone by the 25th. Farther north the timetable is 5 days later. Although there is considerable overlap in the migration periods of this species and the similarly plumaged Semipalmated Sandpiper, Leasts peak earlier and are declining while numbers of Semipalmateds are on the rise.

Ordinarily, the Least Sandpiper is absent from the state in June. But approximately every second year northbound birds have lingered into the first week of June, the latest observations being on the 10th (1950, Dane, S. D. Robbins), 11th (1982, Winnebago, T. Ziebell), and 12th (1964, Racine, B. Weber; 1977, Dane, S. Thiessen). By the end of the month early southbound birds are possible (earliest: 28 June 1985, Ashland, M. J. Mossman). A few nonbreeders occasionally linger throughout June in the Green Bay–Marinette region. Wisconsin breeding seems highly unlikely for this tundra-nesting species. But Ludwig Kumlien (1891b, p. 126) wrote: "I have records of two instances of this species nesting within the state, but I believe they nest regularly in the northern part of the state in the extensive swamps and marshes." No further documentation of this suspected nesting is known.

Returning fall migrants often reappear during the first week of July. For the most part, lone birds and very small flocks arrive at this time. Larger flocks of 200 return as early as 8 July. During the autumn peak, from 25 July to 20 August, flocks of 50–500 birds are sometimes seen. A gradual tapering off takes place through 15 September; a more rapid decline continues through the remainder of the month. The last sightings each year usually come between 10 and 20 October. An exception occurred in 1974 when 250 birds were estimated in Dane and Columbia counties on 25 October, with individuals lingering until 17 November (Dane, P. Ashman). Other November observations: the 4th (1972, La Crosse, J. R. Rosso) and 5th (1949, Dodge, F. Holman King; 1969, La Crosse, J. R. Rosso).

White-rumped Sandpiper (*Calidris fuscicollis*)

STATUS. Uncommon migrant.
HABITAT. Great Lakes. Inland lakes. Flooded fields.
MIGRATION DATES. *Spring:* early May to mid-June.
  Fall: mid-July to early October. *Extremes:* 17 April,
  28 June; 8 July, 21 November.
PORTRAIT. *Birds of Wisconsin:* Plate 34.

The best time to see White-rumped Sandpipers is between 25 May and 5 June; this corresponds closely with the spring peak of 20 May to 5 June. Most of the other "peeps" have moved on, leaving only the Semipalmated and this species in a typical year. An errant Western is possible, or an occasional Least or Baird's may linger, but these would be rare. Groups of 5–15 White-rumps are often found mixed with Semipals on exposed mud flats or sandy beaches.

First arrivals appear between 5 and 10 May in a typical year; alert observers are often able to identify scattered individuals that follow during the 10–20 May interval. April 1954 was exceptional, with early stragglers found on the 17th (Winnebago, J. H. Evans) and 22nd (Columbia, H. A. Winkler). There were arrivals on 20 April in 1970 (Dane, T. L. Ashman) and 1974 (St. Croix, C. A. Faanes), and there have been rare sightings on the last 2 days of the month. Ordinarily an April arrival date would seem atypical.

Lingering well into June is more typical. Daryl Tessen estimated that 45 White-rumped Sandpipers were still present at Green Bay on 7 June 1975. Birds remain through the 10th virtually every year, and have been known to linger until the 26th (1977, St. Croix, C. A. Faanes), 27th (1964, Douglas, R. F. Bernard), and 28th (1983, Manitowoc, C. R. Sontag).

The fall flight is much smaller, often consisting of only three to eight reports per year and only an individual or two here and there. Most observations occur between 1 August and 20 September, but records are too scanty to speak of a "peak." Early July arrivals have been spotted by the 8th (1982, Milwaukee, D. D. Tessen), 10th (1956, Washburn, A. Sprunt; 1972, Brown, E. D. Cleary), 13th (1934, Sheboygan, C. S. Jung; MPM files), 14th (1975, St. Croix, C. A. Faanes), and 15th (1973, Brown, D. D. Tessen). A more usual date for first arrivals is 25 July. In the north birds have been reported through 23 September (1965, Douglas, R. F. Bernard), with one exceptionally late straggler on 7 November (1982, Douglas, R. J. Johnson). On four occasions southern birds have remained into November: the 2nd (1961, Columbia, R. B. Dryer), 5th (1978, Dodge, D. D. Tessen), 6th (1948, Milwaukee, G. H. Orians), 10th (1949, Winnebago, N. M. Rogers), and 21st (1987, Douglas, J. L. Baughman).

Baird's Sandpiper (*Calidris bairdii*)

STATUS. Uncommon spring migrant; fairly common fall migrant east; uncommon fall migrant elsewhere.
HABITAT. Great Lakes. Inland lakes. Flooded fields.
MIGRATION DATES. *Spring:* early May to early June.
  Fall: mid-July to mid-October. *Extremes:* 18 April;
  25 November.
PORTRAIT. *Birds of Wisconsin:* Plate 34.

Primarily, the Baird's Sandpiper is a bird of the Great Plains; Wisconsin represents the eastern fringe of the main migratory path for this species. The spring migration is a short one, with most birds passing quickly northward during the last half of May. Published records usually come from 5 to 10 locations per spring. Usually, sightings are of single birds or a flock of 3–10. Daryl Tessen's sighting of an esti-

mated 60 birds in Dodge County on 12 May 1974 was exceptional.

On rare occasions arrivals have been detected well before the end of April, notably on the 18th (1985, Eau Claire, J. L. Polk), 19th (1964, Sheboygan, H. Koopmann), 20th (1974, St. Croix, C. A. Faanes), and 26th (1956, Jefferson, E. Degner; 1979, Ashland, R. L. Verch; 1980, Ozaukee, D. D. Tessen). More frequently, arrivals appear between 5 and 10 May in both southern and western counties, closer to 15 May in the northeast. By 1 June migrants have generally left the south. In central and northern areas a few birds linger through the 5th; some have been noted as late as the 9th and 10th. The 20 June 1979 Dodge County sighting (D. D. Tessen) was unusually late.

In northeastern Wisconsin individuals sometimes remain through the summer. In spring and early summer they associate with Sanderlings along sandy beaches. In late summer and fall they join other small shorebirds on the mud flats. It must have been a summer resident that was spotted in Ozaukee County on 1 July (1973, T. Bintz). Kumlien and Hollister (1903) mentioned that there were summering birds in 1872 and 1873, when water conditions may have persuaded various unusual species to spend the summer months. But no attempted breeding has ever been recorded.

In most instances the fall migration, like the spring, is limited to relatively low numbers: a lone individual here, a flock of 5–15 there. But the migratory period lasts 3 months in fall, compared with only 1 month in spring. First arrivals often appear by 20 July, and have occasionally been reported by the 8th (1975, Outagamie, D. D. Tessen), 10th (1977, Sheboygan, L. W. Erickson), and 13th (1965, Racine, B. Weber). Small numbers (rarely flocks of 50–70) remain through August and most of September, mainly on exposed mud flats. By 20 September nearly all birds have left the north (latest: 6 October 1968, Douglas, S. D. Robbins). In the central and southern parts of the state some linger through October, even as late as 3 November (1982, St. Croix, J. L. Polk) and 10 November (1984, Dane, S. Thiessen). A 25 November 1966 straggler seen by D. K. Gustafson at Racine was most remarkable.

Pectoral Sandpiper (*Calidris melanotos*)

STATUS. Common migrant.
HABITAT. Great Lakes. Inland lakes. Flooded fields.
MIGRATION DATES. *Spring:* early April to late May.
  Fall: early July to early November. *Extremes:* 5 March; 18 December.
PORTRAIT. *Birds of Wisconsin:* Plate 36.

Although their wintering grounds are far to the south, and their breeding range is far to the north, Pectoral Sandpipers frequent Wisconsin haunts for 9 months of almost every year. In 6 years out of every 10, first arrivals can be found in the last 5 days of March, the earliest records coming on the 5th (1986, Dane, S. Thiessen), 12th (1977, Columbia, R. Ake), 13th (1983, Lafayette, J. L. Baughman), and 15th (1968, Milwaukee, M. F. Donald). In more typical years southern counties see first arrivals between 1 and 10 April, with a gradual buildup to a 25 April–10 May peak. In the north earliest migrants show up between 5 and 10 April, followed by a 1–15 May peak. A peak in many areas, where ponds and flooded fields have mixed shorelines of mud and grass, usually means a flock of 10–50 birds. At especially attractive spots—such as in Dane, Columbia, Dodge, Brown, and St. Croix counties—flocks of 100–250 are sometimes seen.

By 20 May the flocks have disappeared, and by 25 May most lingering individuals have also moved on. Occasionally, lone birds remain through 3 June, and even later June birds have been found on the 11th (1965, St. Croix, S. D. Robbins), 12th (1934, Dane, J. S. Main [1935]; 1962, Outagamie, D. D. Tessen), and 13th (1985, Chippewa, J. L. Polk).

Birds lingering into June are probably nonbreeders; those that have occasionally been seen late in the month in Milwaukee (1961, E. W. Strehlow), Columbia (1959, W. L. Hilsenhoff), and Brown (1975, 1976, 1977, J. Trick and T. C. Erdman) counties belong in this category. Kumlien and Hollister (1903) stated: "A few formerly spent the entire summer about the Koshkonong marshes, but there was never any evidence of breeding."

The fall flight is a 5-month-long affair. Because bird-watchers tend to be relatively inactive in early July, they often miss the first fall migrants, which usually reach the northern counties by 10 July and the southern concentration points by 15 July. August is a big month. In some years water levels are too high to provide good habitat, while in others promising shorebird spots are dry. But where shallow water exists with surrounding grass and mud, flocks of 50 or more are not uncommon. If a lake has been temporarily drained for fish-management purposes and there are extensive mud flats in place of water, flocks of 100–300 may be attracted to the spot. Although these conditions may allow the Pectoral to become one of the most common sandpipers, there is testimony from Kumlien and Hollister (1903) that the numbers in 1900 were far below what they were before 1875, when these birds were "exceedingly abudant."

In the northern region large numbers of birds remain through 20 September, then gradually diminish in early October. Flocks of 50 can still be seen well into October in the central and southern regions (300 in Dodge County on 16 October 1979), with numbers rapidly decreasing by 25 October. Individuals and small groups frequently remain into November. In the north birds have lingered through the 9th (1975, Burnett, W. Norling) and 14th (1966, Marinette, H. L. Lindberg), and in the central region late depature dates include the 22nd (1979, Manitowoc, C. R. Sontag) and 24th (1976, La Crosse, F. Z. Lesher). Late southern dates include the 27th (1963, Columbia, T. L. Ashman) and 28th (1973, Vernon, J. R. Rosso). A first state December record was established in 1976 when an individual was discovered on the La Crosse CBC (18 December, F. Z. Lesher).

Purple Sandpiper (*Calidris maritima*)

STATUS. Casual spring migrant; casual late fall and early winter migrant.
HABITAT. Great Lakes.
MIGRATION DATES. *Spring:* observed between 17 May and 7 June. *Fall–Winter:* observed between 14 October and 2 January.
PORTRAIT. *Birds of Wisconsin:* Plate 33.

It must be assumed that Hoy (1853b) was in error when he referred to the Purple Sandpiper as "greatly abundant from 15th of April to 20th of May." In all probability he confused the Purple with the Pectoral Sandpiper, which he did not record at all in spring. It is a wonder that the hardy Purple Sandpiper should ever come to Wisconsin, since it is rare anywhere away from the rockbound Atlantic coastal haunts of New Brunswick, New England, and New York.

Until 1942 the only state record was a specimen located at the Oshkosh Public Museum, said to have been taken at Bay View (Door County) in May 1881. The exact date of collection and name of collector are unknown. On 8 November 1942 George Prins picked up a recently killed female along the gravel beach near Wind Point in Racine County and donated it to the Milwaukee Public Museum.

Wind Point, which probably has habitat as suitable

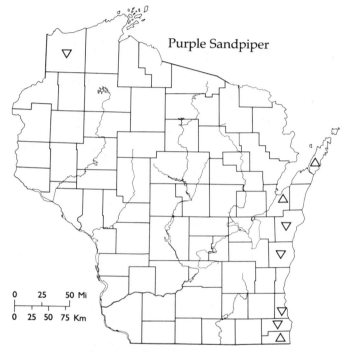

Purple Sandpiper

```
0    25    50 Mi
0  25  50  75 Km
```

△   17 May to 7 June
▽   14 October to 2 January

All records

Purple Sandpiper, November 1964, Racine County (photo by E. B. Prins)

as any spot in Wisconsin for this winter-loving bird, has been the scene of four additional records over an 8-year span: 11–13 November 1963 (photographed by E. B. Prins; *Pass. Pigeon* 26:89), 21 November–13 December 1964 (B. Weber; *Pass. Pigeon* 27:124); 31 December 1965–2 January 1966 (R. E. Fiehweg; *Pass. Pigeon* 28:146), and 31 October 1971 (D. D. Tessen; *Pass. Pigeon* 34:113).

The Milwaukee lakeshore has attracted five individuals: on 9 December 1973 (C. R. Sindelar; *Pass. Pigeon* 36:5), 16 December 1980 (R. M. Smith; *Pass. Pigeon* 43:160–161), 10 November 1984 (D. K. Gustafson; *Pass. Pigeon* 47:124), 17 November–7 December 1985 (J. H. Pratt; *Pass. Pigeon* 48:148), and 1 November 1987 (G. A. De Boer). Additional 1987 sightings include birds at Manitowoc (13 December, C. R. Sontag) and Sheboygan (14 October, 24–25 December (D. Brasser).

Brown County has had visits from four individuals: one in fall on 19 October 1952 (Strehlow et al. 1978), and three in May on the 17th (1970, C. H. Hussong; *Pass. Pigeon* 33:23), 18th (1969, Margaret Olson; *Pass. Pigeon* 32:23), and 19th (1976; Strehlow et al. 1978).

In addition there have been two spring observations along the Lake Michigan shore: one on 29 May 1954 (Kenosha, M. F. Higgins; *Pass. Pigeon* 16:150–151) and one on 7 June 1980 (Door, R. J. Lukes; *Pass. Pigeon* 43:61).

Wisconsin's sole Lake Superior find occurred on 15 October 1986 (Douglas, R. J. Johnson; *Pass. Pigeon* 49:160).

If this eastern visitor continues its rare wanderings to our state, observers will be most apt to find it along rocky shores and outcroppings along Lake Michigan in November and December.

Dunlin (*Calidris alpina*)
Formerly Red-backed Sandpiper

STATUS. Common migrant east; fairly common migrant west. Uncommon summer visitant northeast.
HABITAT. Great Lakes. Inland lakes. Flooded fields.
MIGRATION DATES. *Spring:* mid-April to early June. *Fall:* early August to mid-November. *Extremes:* 2 April; 19 December.
WINTER. One January record.
PORTRAIT. *Birds of Wisconsin:* Plate 35.

In May the Dunlin is numerous east of a line from Madison to Marinette. Flocks of 50–100 are frequent in the easternmost counties, while on suitable flooded fields in the Rock and Fox River valleys flocks of 200–500 birds often appear. On 22 May 1976 an estimated 5,000 birds visited Green Bay (T. C. Erdman). West of the Madison-Marinette line birds can be found in suitable wet areas each May, but in far fewer numbers. Small groups of 5–15 individuals are most likely.

The largest numbers usually turn up between 15 and 30 May. But in some years scattered arrivals are noted by mid-April. The earliest April birds have been seen mostly in the eastern counties: on the 2nd (1954, Columbia, H. A. Winkler; 1978, Milwaukee, M. F. Donald), 6th (1959, Rock, M. T. Maxson), and 10th (1954, Kenosha, M. F. Higgins; 1976, Brown, J. Trick). The earliest April dates in the west are the 6th (1981, Eau Claire, J. L. Polk), 13th (1974, La Crosse, J. R. Rosso), and 14th (1977, Taylor, J. S. Fadness). During the first week of May numbers gradually build in the south, and a few birds begin to appear in the north.

The 15–30 May peak is followed by a rapid decline, with most birds having left by 5 June. A few linger until 15 June nearly every year. In the Green Bay region some nonbreeders can be found all summer long—fewer than a dozen some years, 60–70 other years. Since 1960 in other parts of the state there have been five additional sightings that represented either late spring migrants or summer residents. Away from the Green Bay area, early July observations have been scanty. The presumption is that birds recorded in July on the 1st (1980, Manitowoc, C. R. Sontag), 3rd (1975, Milwaukee, D. K. Gustafson), and 4th (1979, Milwaukee, S. Thiessen) are summer wanderers rather than spring or fall migrants. An 18 July record (1981, Ashland, R. L. Verch) is difficult to classify. Kumlien and Hollister (1903) reported individuals occasionally in summer and suspected the birds were injured. There was never any evidence of breeding.

By the time the first fall Dunlins appear, usually 10–15 August, various other sandpipers have already reached their peak. And by the time Dunlins build to a peak—usually between 25 September and 20 October—most of the other sandpiper species have departed. As in spring, this species concentrates in the eastern counties. Top autumn numbers per day in the west rarely exceed 15; in the east flocks of 200–400 are found. Birds linger into November every year, sometimes in sizable numbers. The latest departure dates for the northern and central regions are 13 November (1971, Outagamie, D. D. Tessen) and 16 November (1963, Douglas, R. F. Bernard). In most years observers sight the last southern bird about 20 November. But mild weather has induced several to remain into the last week of November. December observations have been made on the 2nd (1978, Milwaukee, J. H. Idzikowski), 4th (1962, Racine, L. W. Erickson), 9th (1984, Milwaukee, Wm. Mueller), 10th (1963, Racine, R. E. Fiehweg; 1983, Milwaukee, D. D. Tessen), 12th (1964, Racine, B. Weber), and 19th (1970, Milwaukee, D. K. Gustafson). Many observers shared in the astonishment of seeing a bird that remained in Milwaukee through 25 January 1981.

Curlew Sandpiper (*Calidris ferruginea*)

STATUS. Accidental. Five records.
HABITAT. Inland lakes. Flooded fields.

At least 20 southern Wisconsin observers had excellent views of a gorgeous breeding-plumage Curlew Sandpiper that spent 5 days, 15–19 May 1971, just east of Watertown in northeastern Jefferson County. The discoverer, Philip Mallow (pers. comm.), wrote in his notes for 15 May: "My field notes indicate a general dark chestnut head, back and breast, wings lighter and speckled, and a faint eye line. The decurved bill was also prominent and its size was about the same as some nearby Dunlins." Dennis Gustafson, viewing the bird 2 days later, elaborated: "This beautiful bird was striking with its reddish cinnamon coloration and its decurved bill, unlike the drooping tip of the Dunlin's bill, which was near it for comparison. It was similar in size to the Dunlins, but perhaps slightly taller. Its feet and bill were black, and in flight showed a sharply marked white rump patch, contrasting with its mottled back and dark tipped tail feathers" (*Pass. Pigeon* 34:39). Colored photographs were obtained by Catherine Steuer.

Unfortunately no camera was available to confirm an earlier sight observation of a fall-plumage bird at Green Bay on 15 September 1968. Daryl Tessen's description (*Pass. Pigeon* 31:280) fits this species perfectly in terms of size, decurved bill, and white rump evident when the bird took flight—all noted in comparison with a nearby Dunlin.

On 15 May 1982 Roger Sundell and Mary Donald discovered a bird in partial breeding plumage along the Lake Michigan shore at Milwaukee. From distances as close as 25 feet it was possible to compare this bird with nearby Dunlins. All salient field characteristics were evident when the bird stood or flew. The call note was noticeably different from that of the Dunlin (*Pass. Pigeon* 45:40–41).

A shallow pond in southern Dodge County attracted another bright-colored male briefly on 21 May

Curlew Sandpiper

0   25   50 Mi
0 25 50 75 Km

△   15 to 24 May
▽   15 September

All records

1983. R. M. Hoffman made the discovery and took copious notes. The sandpiper disappeared before other observers arrived (*Pass. Pigeon* 46:43–44).

On 23 May 1987 Darwin Tiede had a splendid view of a bright-hued male in Columbia County, also seen by others then and on the 24th (*Pass. Pigeon* 50:87).

The presence of this species is strictly accidental. Only rarely has it wandered to the Pacific and Atlantic coasts. It has been recorded inland only in Ontario, Michigan, Indiana, Illinois, North Dakota, South Dakota, Kansas, and Alberta.

Stilt Sandpiper (*Calidris himantopus*)

STATUS. Rare spring migrant; uncommon fall migrant.
HABITAT. Great Lakes. Inland lakes. Flooded fields.
MIGRATION DATES. *Spring:* mid-April to late May. *Fall:* late June to late October. *Extremes:* 14 April; 12 November.
PORTRAIT. *Birds of Wisconsin:* Plate 33.

Between 1900 and 1925 there was but one published record of this handsome wader: a bird collected at Cedar Grove (Sheboygan County) on 13 August 1921 (Stoddard 1923a). Between 1926 and 1929 Schorger (1929b) found a few Stilt Sandpipers in Dane County nearly every year, usually in August, and J. S. Main (1930a) found spring migrants there on 18 May 1927 and 20 May 1930. But throughout the 1930s and 1940s observations remained scanty. Between 1939 and 1948 only five sightings were documented in *The Passenger Pigeon*. The first two editions of *Wisconsin Birds— Checklist with Migration Charts* (1942, 1950) listed this species as rare.

A dramatic increase in records began in 1949, with seven August and September reports from Green, Kenosha, Dane, and Winnebago counties. Observers have spotted birds annually since then, frequently in flocks of 5–20, occasionally 40–50. The bird's status was upgraded to uncommon in the 1960 edition of the Wisconsin checklist and by Gromme (1963). The largest numbers are usually found along extensive mud flats at Green Bay and at Horicon Marsh in Dodge County. But the frequency of fall reports from western counties suggests that the Stilt Sandpiper could be fully as numerous in the Mississippi–St. Croix region if comparable habitat existed. Faanes (1981) mentions sightings on islands in the St. Croix River.

The sizable flocks are strictly an autumn phenomenon. Fall migrants usually appear by 15 July; earliest arrivals in the west were recorded in St. Croix County on July 3rd (1963) and 7th (1968, S. D. Robbins) and in the east in Milwaukee County on the 7th (1976, D. K. Gustafson) and 8th (1980, R. P. Gutschow). The wader is most frequently seen between 25 July and 10 September, with highest numbers between 10 and 25 August. Most birds leave the state by 25 September, but scattered individuals remain into early October 2 out of every 3 years. Beyond 20 October three sightings are known: 31 October (1971, Dodge, D. D. Tessen), 2 November (1961, Columbia, R. B. Dryer), and 12 November (1967, Racine, E. B. Prins).

Spring observations occur far less often, usually from one to five per year. Rarely are more than one or two of these sandpipers seen at a time. April arrivals

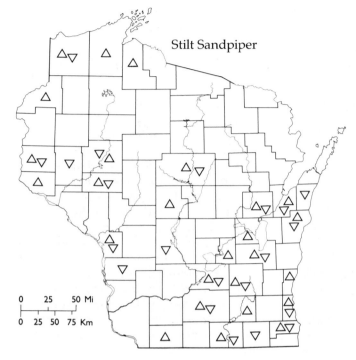

Stilt Sandpiper

△   Mid-April to late May
▽   Late June to late October

Records since 1960

have been detected on the 14th (1956, Dodge, M. F. Higgins), 15th (1954, Columbia, T. K. Soulen), 19th (1975, St. Croix, C. A. Faanes), 20th (1955, Dane, T. K. Soulen), 27th (1950, Waukesha, V. C. Rossman), and 30th (1974, Pierce, C. A. Faanes). Most spring observations cluster around the 10–25 May period. The latest departure records are 30 May (1954, Sheboygan, F. Kuhlman), 31 May (1965, Douglas, R. F. Bernard), and 6 June (1978, Dane, R. Korotev). Defying ready placement as migratory or resident were five late-June birds, seen on the 20th (1987, Manitowoc, C. R. Sontag), 24th (1987, Dane, E. Hansen), 25th (1977, Columbia, D. K. Gustafson), 26th (1975, Brown, T. C. Erdman), and 28th (1986, Chippewa, J. L. Polk).

Before 1900 this species was universally recognized as a rare spring migrant, with opinion about its fall status divided. J. N. Clark encountered it several times in Dunn County and collected at least three specimens in the 1890s. In the Lake Koshkonong region Kumlien and Hollister (1903) described it as "of rather irregular occurrence, sometimes rare and again in such numbers that a dozen might be killed at a single shot." Farther east Hoy (1853b) considered it rare along Lake Michigan. In Oconto County Schoenebeck (1902) considered it rare.

Kumlien and Hollister (1903) suspected nesting near Lake Koshkonong in the 1870s. "We have taken young barely able to fly, readily running them down. These had the head and upper neck still in the natal down." This cannot be accepted as bona fide nesting evidence, and would have been exceptional for a species that normally nests in the Arctic.

Because the usual autumn migration route centers west of the Mississippi and because western Wisconsin received little ornithological coverage in August and September before 1950, one wonders if the dearth of state records between 1900 and 1949 truly reflects the species' status at that time. But even allowing for lack of coverage and the possibility that Stilt Sandpipers may have been overlooked among flocks of Greater and Lesser Yellowlegs, there appears to have been a decided increase in the number of these birds seen in Wisconsin in the past 30 years.

Buff-breasted Sandpiper (*Tryngites subruficollis*)

STATUS. Casual spring migrant; rare fall migrant.
HABITAT. Open grassland. Ponds.
MIGRATION DATES. *Spring:* early to late May. *Fall:* late July to late September. *Extremes:* 8 May, 29 May; 25 July, 25 September.
PORTRAIT. *Birds of Wisconsin:* Plate 34.

What? An estimated 150 Buff-breasted Sandpipers spotted in Wisconsin between 1 August and 25 September 1980? Until 1965 this suggestion would have seemed preposterous. Hoy's comment (1853b) that the bird is "quite common from Sept. 15 to Oct. 15" had never been supported by either corroborative statement or specimen. Kumlien and Hollister (1903) surmised that "this species 'should' pass through the prairie regions of Wisconsin during spring and fall migrations." Yet they called it a rare migrant and listed only three specimens: one from September 1845 (Dane, T. L. Kumlien), one on 10 September 1892 (Rock, A. L. Kumlien), and one shot at Lake Koshkonong (date unknown) by Henry Skavlem.

This species was not recorded again from the time of Kumlien and Hollister until 1948 when Howard and Gordon Orians found one at Milwaukee on 31 July. There followed another Milwaukee bird in 1952 (27 August, M. F. Donald), a Madison bird in 1953 (29 August–3 September, M. A. Walker), Horicon National Wildlife Refuge birds in Dodge County in 1955 (14 August, R. H. Lound) and 1957 (17 August, M. A. Walker), and a Milwaukee individual in 1959 (8 September, E. L. Basten). An additional five discoveries were made in 1960 and 1961; one of these birds was collected and the specimen is now housed at Northern Illinois University (28 August 1960, Washburn, W. E. Southern).

Since 1966 one or more individuals have been located nearly every year. At first the reports told of

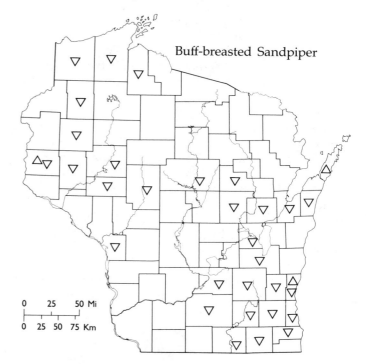

Buff-breasted Sandpiper

△ 8 to 29 May
▽ Late July to late September

All records

lone birds, several in parts of northwestern Wisconsin where observation had previously been neglected. As the practice of fall plowing became increasingly popular, some birds were being spotted near plowed fields. Gradually the word got around among birders that the most favored habitat for the bird was the sod farms of southeastern Wisconsin.

The number of sightings skyrocketed and the size

of groups expanded. The 1980 estimate of 150 individuals was calculated by adding a Dane County peak of 57, a Columbia County high of 47, and counts of scattered individuals and small flocks from nine additional counties. The total far exceeds those of any other recent years. In 1973 there were over 50 individuals in five counties; the 1974 total was 27 birds in five counties.

Most observations have clustered between 20 August and 15 September. The earliest: 25 July (1976, Fond du Lac, R. A. Knuth) and 31 July (1948, Milwaukee, H. L. Orians; 1967, St. Croix, S. D. Robbins). The

latest: 23 September (1978, Walworth, D. D. Tessen) and 25 September (1980, Dane, R. M. Hoffman).

Not until 1973 did Wisconsin record its first spring record: Ozaukee County on 8 May (T. Bintz). One year later another Buff-breast was sighted in St. Croix County on 10 May (C. A. Faanes). A third record was established in Door County on 29 May 1981 (S. Thiessen).

Sod farms are scarce in northeastern and southwestern regions. But it is probably only a question of time before observers fill in some of the blanks now apparent in the accompanying map.

Ruff (*Philomachus pugnax*)

STATUS. Rare spring migrant; casual fall migrant. Accidental in summer.
HABITAT. Great Lakes. Inland lakes. Ponds.
MIGRATION DATES. *Spring:* observed between 8 April and 23 June. *Fall:* observed between 21 July and 14 October.

There was excitement galore among Madison ornithologists when Wisconsin's first Ruff was discovered by five astonished birders. The bird was wading in a shallow flooded field in northern Dane County on 15 May 1959. Between then and 20 May the visitor was photographed by Martha Lound (*Pass. Pigeon* 21:112), documented by S. D. Robbins (*Pass. Pigeon* 21:73–74), and observed by 12 other viewers. At that time there were but five published records from the Great Lakes region.

No one could have guessed that this Eurasian species would stage 22 additional visits to Wisconsin (15

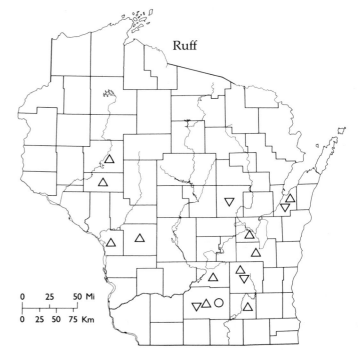

△   Early April to early June
○   22 to 23 June
▽   21 July to 14 October

All records

Ruff, 15 May 1974, La Crosse County (photo by F. Z. Lesher)

in spring, 7 in fall) in the ensuing 30 years. A few individuals have been accommodating enough to remain several days, and have been appreciated by more than one observer.

Four April sightings include: a bird seen from the 8th to the 12th (1969, Winnebago, E. Fisher), one on the 11th (1987, Columbia, P. Ashman), one on the 23rd (1983, Eau Claire, J. L. Polk), and one from the 22nd to the 24th (1983, Fond du Lac, D. Krueger). Seven of the state's 10 May observations occurred between the 14th and the 22nd. F. Z. Lesher photographed one of these at La Crosse on 15 May 1974. A 21 May discovery remained through 2 June (1962, Columbia, W. L. Hilsenhoff). Still later was a Madison bird on 22–23 June (1987, E. Hansen).

Autumn wanderings have not followed so concentrated a time schedule. One of the earliest was a Dane County individual found on 23 July (1983, S. Thiessen). Brown County birds were noted on 21–27 July (1973, D. D. Tessen), 14 August (1976, D. D. Tessen), and mid-August (1968, T. C. Erdman). Tessen also discovered one in Waupaca County on 22–23

August 1971. The state's only September record came on the 9th (1984) when M. F. Donald discovered a female Ruff in Dodge County. Another female at the same Dodge County pond provided the lone October record in 1979; the bird was first found on the 13th by D. D. Tessen and was seen the following day by R. M. Hoffman and T. de Boor. Virtually all these records have been extensively documented in *The Passenger Pigeon*.

Since 1959, Ruffs have also been spotted in Michigan, Illinois, and Minnesota, and at an increasing number of Atlantic and Pacific coast locations. Clearly a change in status is under way. The likelihood of future Wisconsin sightings is great.

Short-billed Dowitcher (*Limnodromus griseus*)
Formerly Dowitcher, Eastern Dowitcher

STATUS. Fairly common migrant. Rare summer resident east.
HABITAT. Great Lakes. Inland lakes. Ponds.
MIGRATION DATES. *Spring:* early May to June. *Fall:* early July to late September. *Extremes:* 26 April; 12 October.
PORTRAIT. *Birds of Wisconsin:* Plate 30.

Previous to 1870, before heavy spring shorebird shooting began, dowitchers could be found in the Rock River valley in huge numbers. Kumlien and Hollister (1903) reminisced: "As to the numbers of dowitchers that frequented Lake Koshkonong thirty to thirty-five years ago . . . we forbear to attempt an estimate, as the younger generation would set it down as fabulous." In other parts of the state, birds must have been far less numerous. Hoy (1853b) found them "sparingly" in spring and fall at Racine.

By the turn of the century a disastrous drop in populations had occurred. Kumlien and Hollister (1903) commented: "At the present time they are known only during migrations and then sparingly. A few appear in May and June, and a very few at that, and again in August and September, but so irregularly that they may pass as rare. We have here a good illustration of what continual spring shooting can accomplish."

In those early years of abundance no effort was made to differentiate between Short-billed and Long-billed forms. Differences of opinion about specific and subspecific status, breeding and migration ranges, and plumage characteristics have clouded subsequent efforts to identify dowitcher species. The matter was

not resolved until 1953 when the AOU *Check-list of North American Birds* accepted Pitelka's classification of the Long-bill as a bird breeding in Siberia and northern Alaska and the Short-bill as breeding widely across Canada, representing three geographic races.

In 1957 Wills (1958) examined 15 Wisconsin dowitcher specimens and applied the Pitelka criteria for bill size, breast-spotting, ventral coloration, and tail-barring. He concluded that seven of the specimens were Short-bills: individuals shot on 12 May (1940, Columbia, A. W. Schorger), 16 May (1915, Dane, A. W. Schorger), 16 July (1939, Dane, J. S. Main), 6 August (1922, Sheboygan, C. S. Jung), 7 August (1886, Jefferson, T. L. Kumlien), 22 August (1879, Jefferson, T. L. Kumlien), and 9 September (1877, Jefferson, T. L. Kumlien).

Further delineation of the dates of Short-bill occurrence has been made possible by keen-eared birders who have learned the distinctive call notes of the two dowitchers. Spring migrants identified by call notes have been detected as early as 26 April (1983, Chippewa, J. L. Polk), 27 April (1986, Ozaukee, R. H. Sundell), 2 May (1969, Ozaukee, D. K. Gustafson), and 3 May (1975, La Crosse, J. R. Rosso), and as late as 6 June (1983, Dodge, S. R. Swengel; 1984, Dane, S. Thiessen) and 11 June (1977, Douglas, C. A. Faanes). Most call-note detections have come in the 10–25 May period, usually with small groups of 3–10 birds but sometimes with sudden mid-May influxes of 30–75 individuals.

In the nineteenth-century years of great abundance, Kumlien and Hollister (1903) mentioned that fewer of these birds were present in July than in spring

(May–June) or fall (August–September). They also commented: "There is positively no question that considerable numbers bred in Wisconsin from 1865 to 1875, and in 1872 and 1873 as far south as Lake Koshkonong." Although there is no assurance that these comments referred to Short-bills, the greater distance from the known present-day breeding range of the Long-bill increases the likelihood that it was primarily the Short-billed Dowitcher that formerly bred in the state.

Nonbreeding individuals sometimes oversummer in the Green Bay region. T. C. Erdman (pers. comm.) found a few birds several times in the 1970s, as well as a summering individual in Manitowoc County in 1976.

Autumn migrants call less often than spring birds. Although the flocks are larger—sometimes numbering 10–20 in the west and 50–100 in the east in late July and August—most of the birds must be listed as

dowitcher sp. Call notes have been heard from returning migrants by 28 June (1977, Milwaukee, D. K. Gustafson), 3 July (1979, Manitowoc, C. R. Sontag), and 4 July (1980, Dane, S. Thiessen). Judging by the sounds that have been identified, I believe that most July and August birds are of this species; few of them remain after 15 September. The latest known dates are 20 September (1967, St. Croix, S. D. Robbins), 21 September (1967, Waukesha, D. A. Bratley), 1 October (1978, Milwaukee, D. K. Gustafson), and 12 October (1983, Manitowoc, C. R. Sontag). It is possible that Short-bills may linger into mid-October among flocks of Long-bills. However, since the two species are rarely separable by plumage characteristics once fall dress has been attained and since fall birds make little sound, it will require the efforts of banders to prove this.

Long-billed Dowitcher (*Limnodromus scolopaceus*)

STATUS. Uncommon spring migrant; fairly common fall migrant.

HABITAT. Great Lakes. Inland lakes. Ponds.

MIGRATION DATES. *Spring:* late April to mid-May. *Fall:* mid-July to late October. *Extremes:* 12 April, 29 May; 6 July, 5 November.

PORTRAIT. *Birds of Wisconsin:* Plate 30.

Much confusion has surrounded the identification of this bird. To some observers, impressed by the length of a dowitcher bill, all dowitchers were Long-billed. Others, aware of distinctions between what used to be called Eastern and Long-billed Dowitcher forms, listed birds as Long-billed Dowitchers, believing this to be the prevailing form in Wisconsin, or as dowitcher sp. Only after William Rowan described the *hendersoni* (midcontinent) race of *griseus* in 1932 and F. A. Pitelka described the *caurinus* (western) race in 1950 did a more definite pattern of dowitcher distribution in Wisconsin emerge.

Wills's (1958) careful examination of museum skins in Madison, Milwaukee, and Chicago showed eight Long-billed Dowitcher specimens taken in Wisconsin. Four had been collected on 1 October 1932 (Jefferson, O. J. Gromme and I. J. Perkins). Others included a May 1888 specimen (Jefferson, T. L. Kumlien, one in September 1896 (Jefferson, T. L. Kumlien), and one on 4 September 1940 (location and collector unknown).

Further insights into the distribution and timing of

Long-bill migration have come from observers who paid careful attention to call notes. In response to my inquiry about this in 1959, Ludlow Griscom (pers. comm.) wrote: "It is perfectly true that the call notes of the two dowitchers are very distinct in the field. . . . To my ear, the [Short-billed] Dowitcher has a very familiar double-syllabled chuckle, which is replaced by a single clear note in the Long-billed." The difference is a striking one. To an observer with a well-trained ear, it is a safer method of dowitcher identification than the study of plumage characteristics, where there is much overlap in bill size and coloration.

Relying partly on identification by sound and partly on coloration of lower abdomen and presence of barring on the flanks, birders have detected spring Long-bills between 12 April (1977, Columbia, D. K. Gustafson) and 29 May (1982, Fond du Lac, T. R. Schultz). The main migration period is between 30 April and 15 May. Rarely are flocks larger than from six to eight birds reported. Flocks of 30–75 dowitchers sometimes found in mid-May may be mixed Long-bills and Short-bills, but the evidence indicates that most are Short-bills.

In fall there is a considerable overlap in migration periods for the two dowitcher species. When a huge concentration (600) appeared in Brown County on 6 July 1975, T. C. Erdman (pers. comm.) estimated 350 Short-bills and 250 Long-bills. Because returning migrants in early July sometimes still sport their spring plumage, coloration can help with identification when birds are carefully scrutinized at close range. In late July and August some Long-bills mix with flocks of Short-bills.

Most records have been obtained between 10 September and 25 October. During this period flocks of 20–120 birds are sometimes found in the region between Madison and Green Bay, with considerably smaller numbers elsewhere. The latest records for call-note identification were 4 November (1984, Dodge, R. M. Hoffman) and 5 November (1983, Dodge, D. D. Tessen). Silent unidentified dowitchers have been re-ported still later in November: the 7th (1953, Brown, E. O. Paulson), 8th (1975, Dodge, D. D. Tessen), and 10th (1940, Oconto, C. H. Richter; 1961, Columbia, R. B. Dryer).

Observers should not presume to distinguish between the species of Wisconsin dowitchers on the basis of date alone. Unless call notes are clearly heard by observers well acquainted with differences in dowitcher sounds, or spring-plumaged birds are seen under very favorable conditions, dowitcher sp. is the best entry in the observer's notebook.

Common Snipe (*Gallinago gallinago*)

STATUS. Common migrant. Fairly common summer resident north and central; rare summer resident southeast. Uncommon winter resident south; rare winter resident central and northwest.

HABITAT. Sedge meadow. Shallow marsh. Lowland carr.

MIGRATION DATES. *Spring:* late March to mid-May. *Fall:* late July to early November.

BREEDING DATA. Nests with eggs: 3 May to 19 June. Clutch size: usually 4 eggs; occasionally 3.

WINTER. Regularly present in small numbers north to La Crosse, Richland, Dane, and Waukesha counties. Occasionally present north to Douglas, Bayfield, Outagamie, and Manitowoc counties.

PORTRAIT. *Birds of Wisconsin:* Plate 30.

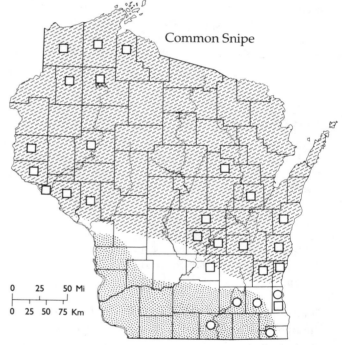

Common Snipe

▨	Summer range
⬚	Winter range
○	Late May to mid-July
☐	Mid-November to early March

Records since 1960

On a warm mid-April evening near a moist meadow anywhere in Wisconsin, you are likely to hear one or more of these birds winnowing as they zoom back and forth in the growing darkness. They are more often heard than seen, both at dusk and during the morning hours. Migrants often reach the southern counties by 25 March, the central counties by 5 April, and the north by 10 April. In atypical springs the timetable may be set back a week. The spring peak spans the last 10 days of April. By 5 May there is a general exodus of Canada-bound birds.

The summer range covers the northern two-thirds of the state. South of a line between La Crosse and Port Washington there are but scattered recent records for the 25 May–10 July interval (Rock, Jefferson, Waukesha, Kenosha counties). North of this line the summer population varies considerably: numerous in extensive marsh areas like Crex Meadows in Burnett County and Horicon in Dodge County, virtually ab-sent in the drier and forested regions. Snipes have been recorded on 46 of the state's 70 BBS routes, most commonly in the northern half of the state.

Of 13 nests found by Carl Richter in Oconto and Marinette counties between 1922 and 1960, the earliest was found on 7 May and the latest on 27 May. He estimated that most egg-laying occurred in the 10–20 May interval. There were four eggs in 10 nests, three in the other 3 nests. A somewhat earlier egg-laying date must have occurred in Juneau County to explain the presence of a family of five young on 23 May (1948, B. Stollberg). A considerably later date for eggs was reported near Marshfield (Wood County) on 9 June (1912, J. W. Stierle; MPM files).

In fall the snipe are more often seen than heard. Much more flocking occurs then than in spring. It is not unusual to catch sight of a bird standing motionless in the mud by a grassy tuft and, if you flush the bird, to have another dozen heretofore unnoticed birds take off with it. During the 10 September–20 October peak, flocks sometimes number 200 or more. Traversing the 1.5-mile federal dike at Horicon on 12 September 1954, Laurence Jahn counted 322 individuals. Horicon National Wildlife Refuge personnel have estimated fall populations to reach as high as 3,000 (1967, R. G. Personius). A few fall migrants show up in nonbreeding areas by 25 July. The main buildup starts in mid-August and drops off at the end of October. Beyond 10 November lingering birds are likely to overwinter.

Kumlien and Hollister (1903) mentioned that a few birds remained through the colder months where suitable spring holes stayed open. The same pattern still exists. From 9 to 37 wintering snipes have been reported on the CBC each December since 1962. One Grant County area produced 13 (1971, T. H. Ingram); a Richland County area annually tallies 3–6; other favored locations are near La Crosse, Madison, and Waukesha. Winter records are frequent north to St. Croix, Waushara, Outagamie, and Manitowoc counties. There have been CBC records in Douglas, Bayfield, Ashland, Washburn, and Sawyer counties, with two known instances of individuals still present in early February.

A century ago the snipe was far more abundant; it was a common breeder in the southeastern counties. After 1875 a decline became noticeable, and the number of breeding pairs in the south diminished. Fifty years ago Schorger (1929b) knew of no recent breeding pairs in Dane County.

American Woodcock (*Scolopax minor*)

STATUS. Fairly common migrant. Fairly common summer resident north and central; uncommon summer resident south.

MIGRATION DATES. *Spring:* mid-March to late April. *Fall:* mid-September to early January.

BREEDING DATA. Nests with eggs: 5 April to 16 June. Clutch size: usually 4 eggs, rarely 3 or 5.

WINTER. One early February date.

PORTRAIT. *Birds of Wisconsin:* Plate 30.

One of the most delightful displays of spring awaits the nature-lover who visits a wooded swamp at dusk on a mild evening in late March or early April. A heavily accented "peent" followed by a musical twitter of wings announces the return of the American Woodcock. There may still be snow on the ground, but the breath of spring is in the air.

The timing of this event varies widely. There are atypical years when southern counties get their first birds after 25 March; northern observers may wait until 10 April. In some years mild weather may induce early migration. Southern arrivals have been detected by 3 March (1972, Dane, B. Vogelsang; 1973, Rock, R. R. Hoffman; 1974, Milwaukee, M. F. Donald), as well as a phenomenal 19 February date (1981, Milwaukee, J. H. Idzikowski). In the north, N. R. Stone

American Woodcock

0   25   50 Mi
0 25 50 75 Km

▨ Summer range
☐ 8 February 1947

Records since 1960

noted Burnett County arrivals on 14 March 1951 and 17 March 1955. The typical pattern has southern birds arriving by 15 March, becoming numerous by the 25th, and declining in numbers by 20 April; northern birds arrive by 25 March and become numerous after 5 April.

Because the wooded swamps it prefers are not plentiful in the southern counties, the American Woodcock is not a common summer resident there. But nests with eggs have been recorded as early as 5 April, and fledged young have appeared by the 24th.

In the northern half of Wisconsin, habitat and birds are more plentiful, particularly in the northwest. In 1940 the U.S. Forest Service estimated a population of 7,600 birds in the Chequamegon National Forest and 1,500 in the Nicolet National Forest (U.S. Fish and Wildlife Service 1940). At the same time Francis Zirrer (MPM files) estimated an average of four pairs per square mile in his home area in Rusk and Sawyer counties. Eggs have been in evidence by 2 May. Most egg-laying and incubation take place in May.

Woodcocks were numerous in southern Wisconsin, too, 120 years ago, but pressure from market hunters increased significantly following the Civil War. Kumlien and Hollister (1903) surmised that populations, which had been increasing in the 1860s, began declining by 1870: "From that time on . . . its numbers have decreased, from too close shooting, settlement of the country, and the draining and drying up of its natural resorts." Few of these birds now remain as summer residents in the southernmost counties, but

the statewide status is suggested by the finding of a nest in Racine County in 1970 (G. Septen).

From July on, the average birder sees and hears little of these birds. But hunters and banders have proved that the woodcock is still a fairly common fall migrant. Through banding activities in Oconto County, T. C. Erdman (pers. comm.) has detected a small amount of movement in mid-August, a small peak around 10 September, a major peak from 25 September through 10 October, and a final late peak between 25 October and 5 November.

Hunting pressure and the onset of freezing conditions undoubtedly affect the exact timing of fall migration throughout the state. Birds lingering through 15 November are not unusual. But it is unusual that 15–20 birds were encountered in Manitowoc on 2 December (1955, J. Kraupa). Other December stragglers have been noted on the 10th (1960, Marinette, H. L. Lindberg), 13th (1947, Milwaukee, H. C. Mueller), and on Christmas Bird Counts in Portage (1971), Dane, (1972, 1984), Waukesha (1981), and Kenosha (1979). R. R. Hoffman found birds in Kenosha County on 2 January 1982 and 3 January 1976. No late-January records are known that might suggest an attempt to overwinter. But an 8 February 1947 (Dane, D. Q. Thompson) sighting could have been a wintering individual.

Birds banded in Wisconsin in summer and fall have been recaptured the following winter in Kentucky (1), Alabama (1), Mississippi (1), Louisiana (5), Arkansas (4), and Oklahoma (1).

Wilson's Phalarope (*Phalaropus tricolor*)

STATUS. Fairly common spring migrant; uncommon fall migrant. Uncommon summer resident west, north, and east.

HABITAT. Ponds. Shallow marsh. Sedge meadow.

MIGRATION DATES. *Spring:* late April to late May. *Fall:* no marked fall flight. *Extremes:* 14 April; 11 November.

BREEDING DATA. Nests with eggs: 19 May to 19 June. Clutch size: usually 4 eggs; rarely 3.

PORTRAIT. *Birds of Wisconsin:* Plate 36.

Wilson's Phalarope

▨ Summer range

Records since 1960

Few ornithological sights are more entertaining than the spectacle of a dozen "willie-dancers" spinning in circles in the shallow waters of a flooded field in early May. The number of these phalaropes that show up in a given place in a given year varies widely. A favorite spot near Roberts in St. Croix County attracts 40 individuals some years, peaks of only 6–10 in other years.

The spring peak usually occurs between 10 and 20 May, after a gradual early-May buildup. First arrivals can be expected around 25 April. They have been detected as early in April as the 14th (1960, Dodge, H. A. Winkler), 15th (1961, Brown, E. D. Cleary), 16th (1960, Columbia, W. L. Hilsenhoff), and 17th (1963, St. Croix, S. D. Robbins; 1970, La Crosse, J. R. Rosso). Observations diminish in the waning days of May.

The decline is due in part to the departure of northwestbound migrants and in part to the start of the nesting season—a time when the birds become much more secretive. Carl Richter's experience with 12 Oconto County nests between 1924 and 1963 indicates that egg-laying begins by 20 May. Most of the nests he observed were placed in slight depressions on or near elevated grass hummocks in the Green Bay marshes. One of the nests contained three eggs; all others had four.

Gromme (1963) depicted the summer range as a triangular region anchored by Kenosha, Columbia, and Oconto counties. Since the bird's main summer range lies west of Wisconsin, the Wisconsin range should be more extensive than seemed apparent in 1963. Recent observations offer confirmation. Faanes (1981) found recently fledged young in St. Croix County in 1978. Kemper (1973a) spoke of the bird as "a fairly regular but not too numerous resident in the summer" in Chippewa and Eau Claire counties. A nest was found in Marathon County on 15 June 1979 (K. J. Luepke). Nesting has been suspected on Powell Marsh in Vilas and Iron counties. I have records beyond mid-June for Douglas, Burnett, Polk, Rusk, Taylor, and Clark counties. Breeding is now suspected

for all but the southwestern quarter of the state.

Even though young are often on the wing by mid-June, they are infrequently seen until mid-July. By mid-July birds are again in evidence. Presumably these are local birds, including full-grown young of the year. Flocks of 15–40 individuals are sometimes found in a few choice locations between 15 July and 15 August, probably including some returning fall migrants. Other than at these concentration points, not many fall individuals are reported.

Few birds remain beyond 10 September. Individuals have been known to linger into October on seven occasions: the 1st (1969, La Crosse, J. R. Rosso; 1984, Brown, E. D. Cleary), 5th (1966, Brown, E. D. Cleary), 14th (1949, Walworth, L. D. McMaster), 20th (1969, Fond du Lac, R. A. Knuth), 29th (1967, Fond du Lac, R. A. Knuth), and 30th (1983, Dane, S. Thiessen). Even more remarkable was the bird carefully observed on 11 November (1939, Dodge, C. T. Black).

Like many other shorebirds, this phalarope was more numerous in the nineteenth century than it is today. Kumlien and Hollister (1903) reported that a Lake Koshkonong colony once numbered over 200 pairs.

Red-necked Phalarope (*Phalaropus lobatus*)

Formerly Northern Phalarope

STATUS. Uncommon migrant.
HABITAT. Great Lakes. Inland lakes. Ponds.
MIGRATION DATES. *Spring:* mid-May to early June.
  Fall: mid-July to early November. *Extremes:* 30 April,
  15 June; 12 July, 15 December.
PORTRAIT. *Birds of Wisconsin:* Plate 36.

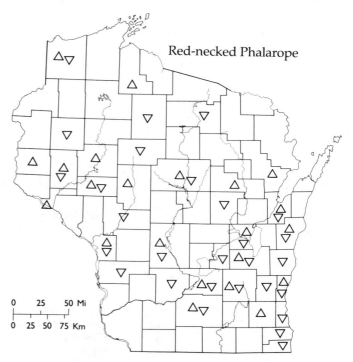

Red-necked Phalarope

△ Mid-May to early June
▽ Mid-July to early November

Records since 1960

This combination swimmer-spinner-wader leads a double life as it moves through Wisconsin in May and early June, and again in September and October. Most Red-necked Phalaropes migrate in flocks so far out on Lakes Michigan and Superior that they are rarely seen from land. Gilbert Raasch (MPM files) found them "abundant several miles off shore" east of Milwaukee in late May 1921. On 28 August 1921, observing along the beach at Cedar Grove (Sheboygan County), Stoddard (1923a, p. 320) caught sight of a flock of 500 birds that "circled and recircled, turned and twisted, some of the flocks finally alighting in some smooth streaks in the water." Determined to get a closer look, Stoddard swam a quarter of a mile out into Lake Michigan, and later wrote: "They were in no way disturbed by my presence . . . swimming high and lightly, with heads and tails well elevated and necks gracefully arched; they spun and twisted as only phalaropes can, while they fed on minute surface animals of some kind."

Between 1964 and 1967 T. C. Erdman (pers. comm.) observed sizable flocks (maximum of 64 on 4 September 1963) feeding offshore at the mouth of the Fox River at Green Bay between mid-August and mid-October. He wrote: "I never saw a Northern with its feet dry. One stormy day in October I went to the river mouth with the idea of finally observing them on land. There in a 25–30 mph wind and four-foot waves bobbed the little flock of marshmallows. They are very hardy birds!"

Just how regular these large flocks are is hard to say. Few ornithologists have traversed the Great Lakes at the appropriate season. Kumlien and Hollister (1903) believed this species to be numerous on Lakes Michigan and Superior in the nineteenth century. Occasionally observers have noted small numbers along the Lake Michigan shore at Milwaukee and Racine.

The "alter ego" of this phalarope shows up in birds that mix with flocks of shorebirds in shallow ponds and flooded fields. At times these individuals wade in shallow water, displaying their distinctive spinning tactics. At times they wade more quietly, behaving much like other feeding sandpipers. The birds observed in such circumstances are lone individuals or small groups of 2–10.

Kumlien and Hollister (1903) labeled this phalarope "a regular spring and fall migrant on Lake Koshkonong, though more often taken in fall than spring." Willard (1885b) recorded the species in Brown County. Snyder (1902) mentioned as his sole Dodge County record five individuals on 4–5 September 1891. Lowe (1915) obtained a Green Lake County specimen on 6 October 1907. Schorger (1929b, 1931a) and others recorded Dane County migrants in 1917, 1923, 1927, 1930, and 1935. The accompanying map shows the location of spring and fall records published in *The Passenger Pigeon* since 1960.

In spring, for nearly every year since 1950, this species has turned up at from one to six locations, mostly as individuals mixing with other shorebirds along the edges of shallow ponds. The usual period for sightings is from 15 May to 5 June. Unusually early were St. Croix County visitors on 30 April 1974 and 1 May 1975 (C. A. Faanes), a storm-blown bird on 6 May (1950, Manitowoc, J. J. Hickey), and a 10–13 May bird

(1962, Dane, T. L. Ashman). June stragglers have been noted on the 11th (1980, Eau Claire, J. L. Polk) and 15th (1973, Ozaukee, T. Bintz).

Autumn records have numbered from one to six nearly every year since 1939. Rarely does this bird appear before 15 August, although there are several early August sightings plus remarkably early stragglers on 12 July (1986, Jackson, T. Risch), 14 July (1972, Brown, D. D. Tessen), 17 July (1981, Fond du Lac, D. D. Tessen), and 23 July (1982, Dunn, J. L. Polk).

The most likely time for finding birds is from 20 August to 10 October. Along the Lake Michigan shore some birds linger considerably later. Late dates include 4 November in Sheboygan County (1966, D. K. Gustafson), 5 November at Milwaukee (1949, A. Simmons), and three December dates at Racine: the 5th (1967, K. Priebe), 6th (1974, L. W. Erickson), and 15th (1962, L. W. Erickson). Away from Lake Michigan the latest record involved a 30 November individual (1969, Fond du Lac, R. A. Knuth).

Red Phalarope (*Phalaropus fulicaria*)

STATUS. Accidental spring migrant; casual fall migrant.
HABITAT. Great Lakes.
MIGRATION DATES. Observed between 3 September and 24 November. One June record.
PORTRAIT. *Birds of Wisconsin:* Plate 36.

For many years it has been suspected that this oceanic species might be found far out on Lakes Superior and Michigan in fall among flocks of Red-necked Phalaropes. Kumlien and Hollister (1903) related seeing "flocks of waders on Lake Superior in October that were no doubt this species, but stormy weather and distance prevented positive identification." Stoddard (1947, pp. 128–129) has related swimming a quarter of a mile out into Lake Michigan, his gun on an accompanying log, hoping to find a Red Phalarope among a flock of Northerns (Red-necked Phalaropes) swimming offshore. Stoddard found only Northerns on his wet venture, and Kumlien and Hollister never procured positive evidence of Reds on Lake Superior. But their theory may well be correct, and is worthy of further investigation.

Wisconsin's sole spring record was a bird collected at Lake Koshkonong in Jefferson County by Thure Kumlien on 4 June 1877 (Kumlien and Hollister 1903). The first autumn record was an individual collected at Racine on 1 November 1847 (Hoy 1853b). Kumlien and Hollister also related taking one adult and three young at Lake Koshkonong on 3 September 1891. An individual collected by N. C. Gilbert at Madison on 18 October 1899 lay misidentified in the University of Wisconsin–Madison collection until reexamined 50 years later (*Pass. Pigeon* 12:88). The Milwaukee Public Museum has specimens taken on 11 October 1902 (Walworth, W. Holland; MPM files) and on 8 October 1921 (Sheboygan, H. L. Stoddard [1923a]). Another

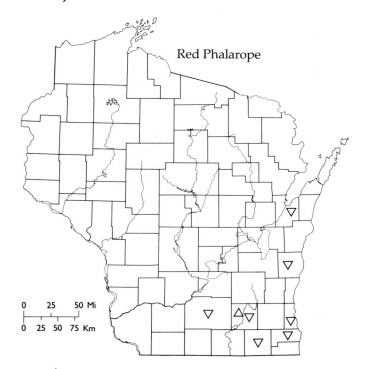

Red Phalarope

0   25   50 Mi

0 25 50 75 Km

△   4 June
▽   3 September to 24 November

All records

Dane County specimen was procured on 22 September 1935 (J. S. Main 1936).

H. L. Orians observed a Red Phalarope at close range in Milwaukee on 21 October 1944 (*Pass. Pigeon* 7:22). Another was photographed at Wind Point in Racine County on 28 October 1949 by G. Prins (*Pass. Pigeon* 12:38). Clara Hussong had Brown County's sole sight observation on 13 September 1953 (Strehlow et al. 1978). Louise Erickson documented three more Racine sight records: 25–28 October 1962 (*Pass. Pigeon* 25:71), 13 November 1972 (*Pass. Pigeon* 35:141), and 5 October 1974 (*Pass. Pigeon* 37:133). On 24 November 1978 a Red Phalarope in Milwaukee was carefully scrutinized by R. C. Glassel (*Pass. Pigeon* 41:136). W. A. Cowart (*Pass. Pigeon* 51:230–231) detected another fall-plumage bird in Milwaukee on 19 November 1988.

None of these birds exhibited spring plumage. Even the 4 June 1877 female had only begun to develop the red plumage characteristic of summer. The prospect of additional spring sightings is slight, as is the likelihood of further records away from the Great Lakes. But more careful scrutiny along the shores of Lakes Superior and Michigan in October—and on boat trips out on the lakes themselves—might well result in additional future discoveries.

Family **Laridae:** Skuas, Gulls, Terns

Pomarine Jaeger (*Stercorarius pomarinus*)

STATUS. Accidental. Five records.
HABITAT. Great Lakes. Inland lakes.
MIGRATION DATES. Observed between 2 July and
22 October.
PORTRAIT. *Birds of Wisconsin:* Plate 37.

The University of Wisconsin-Madison has a Pomarine Jaeger specimen collected in Jefferson County in October 1879 by Thure Kumlien. According to Kumlien and Hollister (1903), this bird was one of three seen at Lake Koshkonong.

The Milwaukee Public Museum also has one Wisconsin specimen. George Curran found the bird dead and partly decomposed at Madison on 2 July 1942. The identification was first confirmed by E. L. Loyster, W. E. Scott, and N. R. Barger in Madison, and subsequently by Herbert Friedman of the U.S. National Museum (*Pass. Pigeon* 4:47).

Two specimens are located in the C. H. Richter collection at the University of Wisconsin-Green Bay. One was picked up injured near Mishicot, Manitowoc County, on 22 October 1983, but C. R. Sontag's efforts to revive the bird were unsuccessful (*Pass. Pigeon* 46:126–127). The second was found near Appleton in Calumet County on 26 July 1984. It too was alive when found by a policeman, but soon died. T. C. Erdman (pers. comm.) determined the bird to be a male coming into adult plumage.

Erdman photographed a dark-phase Pomarine Jaeger at Green Bay on 20 September 1965, as it was being pursued by Herring and Ring-billed Gulls. By the time Erdman and his camera caught up with the bird at the mouth of the Fox River, the jaeger "had every phalarope, gull and tern in the harbor up and flying. The jaeger was slightly smaller than the Herring Gull and much larger than the Ring-bills" (T. C. Erdman, pers. comm.). The photograph, taken of the bird as it circled for altitude, was not in perfect focus, but it showed the massive size of body, head, and bill.

Kumlien and Hollister (1903) related the hour-long sight observation, at Green Bay in early October of 1879, of three birds which flew around fishing boats while nets were being emptied. They commented: "We have positively seen this bird on several occa-

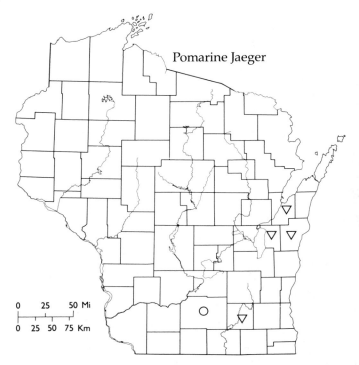

Pomarine Jaeger

0   25   50 Mi
0 25 50 75 Km

○   2 July
▽   26 July to 22 October

All records

sions on Lake Michigan late in the fall." There is no reason to question these as jaeger records, but the presumption that these sight records can be assigned as Pomarines is open to doubt. Kumlien and Hollister listed no records of either the Parasitic or Long-tailed Jaeger. In their day there was imperfect understanding of the different plumages and color phases that make jaeger field identification virtually impossible in many instances, and they did not mention size of bird and heaviness of bill, the only reliable characteristics for Pomarine identification in the field in fall. For the same reason the Milwaukee observations on 19–20 October 1947 (*Pass. Pigeon* 10:35) must remain in doubt.

Of the three species of North American jaegers, this is the one least likely to occur in Wisconsin. But it probably occurs more often than the records indicate.

Parasitic Jaeger (*Stercorarius parasiticus*)

STATUS. Accidental spring migrant; rare fall migrant.
HABITAT. Great Lakes. Inland lakes.
MIGRATION DATES. Observed between 24 and 30 May;
  between 19 July and 1 December.
PORTRAIT. *Birds of Wisconsin:* Plate 37

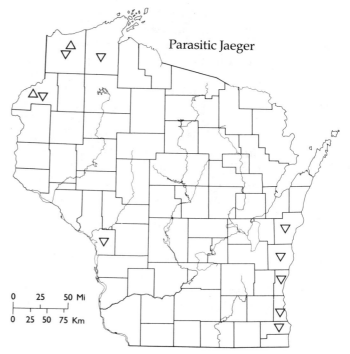

Parasitic Jaeger

△   24 to 30 May
▽   Mid-July to early December

All records

Wisconsin observers have encountered jaegers on over 50 occasions through the years; but in fewer than half of these instances the observers have been successful in determining which jaeger species they were seeing. Occasions when birds were positively identified as Parasitic Jaegers—by specimen, photograph, or thorough documentation—number only 17. The state's first specimen was obtained on 1 December 1933, when G. J. Farmer (MPM files) found a dying bird on a Milwaukee beach. He gave the bird to the Milwaukee Public Museum (W. J. Mueller 1934). This museum has since acquired four additional specimens: one found dead at Racine on 6 November 1937 (E. B. and G. Prins), one shot at Oconto on 26 September 1945 (C. H. Richter), one found dead in Ozaukee County on 3 October 1948 (G. Roux), and one found dead at Milwaukee on 16 September 1978 (T. De Boor).

Two autumn Parasitics have been substantiated by photograph. One was found in Burnett County on 28 August 1957 (A. H. Grewe) and caught on film the next day (N. R. Stone). Four jaegers were present at Lake Onalaska in La Crosse County, 13–23 September 1973. Photographs by F. Z. Lesher and C. A. Kemper showed that three were definitely Parasitics; the fourth was indeterminate.

On 10 additional occasions light-phase adults have been seen under conditions favorable enough to assure positive identification as Parasitics. Three were Wisconsin's only spring sightings: a 28 May 1978 bird flying over Phantom Lake in Burnett County (Tessen 1979a) and Douglas County observations on 30 May 1983 and 24 May 1987 (D. D. Tessen). Positive, well-documented fall sightings include a bird at Milwaukee on 19 July 1982 (W. A. Cowart), one at Racine on 16 October 1948 (E. B. Prins), and five sightings at Superior: on 28 August 1958 (S. D. Robbins), 4 September 1978 (R. M. Hoffman), between 13 September (R. M. Hoffman) and 1 October 1980 (J. L. Polk), on 20 September 1986 (R. J. Johnson), and between 20 September and 29 October 1987 (R. J. Johnson).

With the exception of these records and the few confirmed sightings of Pomarines and Long-taileds, observations have been of jaegers in their virtually indistinguishable dark plumage, or the birds have not been seen well enough or documented well enough to assure positive identification. Aside from the birds in La Crosse, Burnett, and Douglas counties, and single additional Lake Superior records in Douglas and Bayfield counties, the observations have all occurred along the shores of Green Bay and Lake Michigan.

An unusual influx was noted in the fall of 1948, when records were established in Manitowoc, Ozaukee, Milwaukee, and Racine counties. Five or more birds remained in the Racine area from 16 October through 27 November. There are other times when individuals appear to have spent several weeks in one location: 31 October–10 November (1940, Racine), 24 October–6 November (1949, Sheboygan), 15 October–19 November (1950, Milwaukee), 12–27 September (1953, Ozaukee), 13 September–28 November (1953, Milwaukee), 18 October–3 November (1957, Ozaukee), and 9 October–4 November (1972, Ozaukee).

The earliest date for an unidentified jaeger is 18 August (1973, Milwaukee, M. F. Donald). Most observations have been made between 15 September and 5 November. The latest dates for unidentified jaegers are 27 November (1948, Ozaukee, D. L. Larkin) and 28 November (1953, Milwaukee, M. F. Donald).

Long-tailed Jaeger (*Stercorarius longicaudus*)

STATUS. Accidental. Four records.
HABITAT. Great Lakes. Inland lakes.
MIGRATION DATES. Observed on 23 May and between
    1 August and unknown date in October.

Wisconsin's lone specimen of the Long-tailed Jaeger was collected sometime in October (exact date uncertain) 1916 in Walworth County by Francis T. A. Junkin. Writing to F. M. Woodruff (*The Auk* 35:234), Junkin recounted that "it was flying high over the middle of the lake (Como) and seemed to be looking for something. It was so markedly a strange bird that it was taken for my collection." It was a dark, immature bird.

Between 1 and 4 August 1973, an adult Long-tailed Jaeger was present at Fond du Lac, first discovered by Rockne and Kevin Knuth (*Pass. Pigeon* 36:132–133). The bird appeared to be weak at first, and could be seen at distances as close as 5 feet. It was subsequently photographed by Walter Gilles and was seen by numerous other observers. The elongated tail

feathers were unmistakable. At first it did relatively little flying, but rested and fed on lake flies. On 4 August the Willard Browns found it feeding on a road-killed rabbit adjacent to nearby Supple's Marsh, and, when flushed, the apparently rejuvenated bird flew off over Lake Winnebago and was not found again.

Autumn 1981 was a time of frequent jaeger observations in the western Great Lakes region. At Superior an adult Long-tailed Jaeger was studied on 5 September (R. M. Hoffman) and 13 September (R. L. Verch). Minnesota and Michigan observers also detected this species during the same season.

Wisconsin's fourth record was its first spring sighting: on Lake Wissota in Chippewa County on 23 May 1988 (J. L. Polk; *Pass. Pigeon* 50:349).

Since the breeding range includes an extensive area west of Hudson Bay, and since the Chicago area has several records, this species may occur more frequently in Wisconsin than has been supposed. Some of the sightings of unidentified fall jaegers (see Parasitic Jaeger) may well have been birds of this species.

Laughing Gull (*Larus atricilla*)

STATUS. Rare spring and summer visitant east.
HABITAT. Great Lakes.
MIGRATION DATES. Observed between 10 March and
    3 August.

Three visits to Wisconsin by this southern gull have been substantiated by camera. Ornithologists arriving early at the May 1966 Wisconsin Society for Ornithologists convention at Racine had the unusual opportunity of viewing adult Laughing, Franklin's, and Bonaparte's Gulls simultaneously in the field of their telescopes. The Laughing Gull was photographed as it perched along the Lake Michigan shore on 20 May (E. B. Prins).

The previous year one had been photographed in flight at Green Bay on 3 August 1965 (T. C. Erdman). The photo did not show every identifiable feature, but was taken after the bird had been compared with nearby Franklin's Gulls.

A third individual, an adult in winter plumage, was caught on film, both flying and at rest, at Milwaukee on 10 March 1979 (J. H. Idzikowski). This bird was discovered that day by D. K. Gustafson, and was subsequently observed off and on by several observers until 4 April; it constitutes the only state record earlier than mid-May.

Laughing Gull

0   25   50 Mi

0 25 50 75 Km

△   10 March to late May
○   Early June to 3 August

All records

Laughing Gull, 20 May 1966, Racine County (photo by E. B. Prins)

Doubt exists over the one specimen that has been attributed to Wisconsin. Kumlien and Hollister (1903) noted that Thure Kumlien collected a bird at Lake Koshkonong in Jefferson County in July 1860. No information is known of age or plumage, and the specimen cannot be located. When the report on the specimen was published in Baird, Brewer, and Ridgway (1875), it was stated that "Thure Kumlien shot a gull that he thought was this species."

Most of the 40 sight records that were published in *The Passenger Pigeon* between 1939 and 1981 are also open to question. Judging by published documentation, observers of both adult and immature birds were not sufficiently aware of subtle differences in bill size, breast, and tail markings between Laughing and Franklin's Gulls. Observers of adults relied too exclusively on the absence of a white "window" near the wing tip, unaware that an intermediate plumage of the Franklin's is similar.

The earliest of the birds that have been extensively documented was Cutright's 16 May 1978 wanderer near Cleveland (Sheboygan County). His previous experience with Laughing and Franklin's Gulls in other regions helped validate this sighting.

In 1975 T. C. Erdman (pers. comm.) observed individuals between 8 June and 22 July in Brown County. On 19 June he counted four birds: "Two of these were engaged in what appeared to be aerial courtship display. . . . I have most often seen them in association with Ring-billed Gulls rather than Bonaparte's." Erdman also studied one adult in company with Ring-bills in Oconto County on 27 June 1976, and two the same month in Manitowoc that could be closely compared with nearby Franklin's Gulls.

More painstaking observation and documentation have resulted in records of annual sightings along Lake Michigan since 1984. At Manitowoc C. R. Sontag detected individuals every summer from 1984 through 1988. Birds arrived as early as 14 May (1985, 1988) and remained through 9 July (1987). Sheboygan attracted a bird on 14 May 1988 (J. L. Baughman), as did Milwaukee on 19 May 1989 (G. A. De Boer).

While members of the WSO Records Committee found it necessary in 1983 to reject most previously published records because of inadequate documentation, they expressed opinions that several of the reports seemed highly probable. Because the Laughing Gull has wandered northward to neighboring states with increasing frequency in recent years, committee members were unanimous in suggesting that more wandering to Wisconsin can be expected in years to come.

Franklin's Gull (*Larus pipixcan*)

STATUS. Uncommon migrant east and west; rare migrant elsewhere. Rare summer visitant east.
HABITAT. Great Lakes. Inland lakes. Open cropland.
MIGRATION DATES. *Spring:* late March to late May. *Fall:* late July to late November. *Extremes:* 27 March; 30 December.
PORTRAIT. *Birds of Wisconsin:* Plate 38.

Before 1960, spring observations of this wanderer from the West were few and far between. There were but three published records in the 1940s and seven in the 1950s. Before 1940 the Franklin's Gull was even rarer. Kumlien and Hollister (1903) recorded an instance in 1870 when considerable numbers were observed following the plow on a Dane County farm. They commented, "This is the only appearance of the spring birds we have ever noted in eastern or central Wisconsin." In western Wisconsin, J. N. Clark failed to record this species in spring in spite of extensive fieldwork from 1886 through 1901.

Since 1963 this species has become a regular spring visitor, with from one to five observations per year. The number of published records swelled to 14 in the 1960s, to 30 in the 1970s, and to 41 in the 1980s. Roughly a third of the sightings have come from counties adjoining the St. Croix and Mississippi rivers, a third from counties adjoining Lake Michigan, and a third from inland counties. Usually birds have been seen singly or in small flocks of fewer than 10. Rarely have groups of up to 20 been reported. On 7 May 1950, on the heels of a major storm, H. M. Mattison estimated that a flock in Dunn County held 125 birds (Buss and Mattison 1955).

Observations are most frequently made between 20 April and 25 May. The earliest sightings have come on 27 March (1985, Chippewa, J. L. Polk), 30 March (1971, Ozaukee, D. K. Gustafson; 1975, Milwaukee, E. J. Epstein), and 1 April (1978, La Crosse, F. Z. Lesher). Migrants lingering into June have been found on the 3rd (1965, Brown, T. C. Erdman; 1973, Waukesha, J. E. Bielefeldt) and 10th (1981, Pierce, E. J. Epstein).

Until 1945 observers reported this species as infrequently in fall as in spring. Then bird-watchers discovered small numbers mixed in with flocks of Bonaparte's Gulls at some of the major Lake Michigan harbors from Racine to Manitowoc. This has been observed annually since 1953, with the first arrivals being noted in August or September. Most observations have involved isolated individuals or flocks of 10–20.

Franklin's Gull

0   25   50 Mi
0   25   50   75 Km

△   Late March to late May
O   Early June to mid-July
▽   Late July to late November

Records since 1960

During the 1960s hundreds of these dark-headed scavengers staged invasions throughout the month of October—between 25 September and 5 November, but mainly between 5 and 15 October—over a limited portion of western St. Croix County. They frequently mixed with Ring-billed Gulls while foraging in freshly plowed fields. Loose flocks could be seen moving east from Minnesota between 8 and 9 A.M., then returning across the St. Croix River near Hudson between 3 and 4 P.M. On 5 October 1964 I parked my car west of Roberts in midafternoon and observed the passage of an estimated 1,800 Franklin's and 350 Ring-bills in half an hour. Presumably these were birds wandering east from a large nesting colony at the Agassiz National Wildlife Refuge in western Minnesota (50,000 birds in 1971); for when that colony suddenly disappeared in 1972–1973, the western Wisconsin fall invasions also disappeared.

Few Franklin's Gulls linger beyond 10 November anywhere in the state. One remained in Fond du Lac County until 21 November (1968, R. A. Knuth). One was viewed leisurely and sketched in Sauk County on 19 December (1977, J. H. and E. H. Zimmerman).

Late stragglers in Milwaukee were noted on 4 December 1949 and 30 December 1950 (D. L. Larkin).

The bird's summer status is apparently changing. Late June and early July observations were unknown until one bird was discovered on 8 July 1951 (Dane, S. D. Robbins), followed by another on 22 June 1960 (Burnett, W. E. Southern), and four individuals from 17 to 25 June 1964 (Dane, T. K. Soulen). The frequency of summer sightings increased in the 1970s, mainly along Lake Michigan. Since 1978 from 1 to 20 individuals have been found every summer among concentrations of Bonaparte's Gulls in Manitowoc and Milwaukee counties. Nearly all have been nonbreeders in subadult plumage.

Little Gull (*Larus minutus*)

STATUS. Uncommon migrant east. Rare summer resident east.
HABITAT. Great Lakes.
MIGRATION DATES. *Spring:* late April to early June. *Fall:* late July to mid-December.
BREEDING DATA. Nests with eggs: 9 June to 4 July. Clutch size: 3 eggs.
WINTER. One record.

Wisconsin holds the distinction of hosting the first known successful nesting in the United States for this European visitor. Erdman (1976a) first noted nesting attempts at Green Bay in early July 1972. High water washed out the nests of two pairs before egg-laying got under way. At least one pair attempted nesting in another part of Green Bay in 1973, with the same unsuccessful results. A severe hail storm put a sudden end to a nesting attempt in 1974.

Success came in 1975. On 9 June, Erdman (1976a) discovered a colony of six adults and seven immatures in Brown County. Further exploration led to the finding of three nests, each containing three eggs. Two of the nests were eventually lost to predation and high water, while the fate of the third was uncertain. On 21 June 1975 Erdman and J. F. Steffen located

Years of first county records

a nest in Manitowoc County. The two eggs hatched on 4 July with subsequent fledging, making this the first known successful nest recorded in the United States.

Judging by the increased number of Little Gull observations in recent years, I believe it is virtually certain that there has been undetected nesting in this region on other occasions. The first state record of this bird came on 17 November 1938, with a sight observation at Racine by E. B. Prins (*Pass. Pigeon* 17:84). Sixteen years later Prins watched another bird at the same location for a week: 16–23 November 1954. This was preceded by a 22 July 1953 observation in Kenosha County (R. F. Gordon). By this time the bird was turning up in the Chicago area with greater frequency.

Little Gull, August 1985, Milwaukee County (photo by J. H. Idzikowski)

Wisconsin's fourth record was another Racine bird on 5 June 1963 (L. W. Erickson). Since 1965 birds have been seen somewhere along Lake Michigan or Green Bay virtually every year.

The state's earliest spring arrival is a 24 April 1978 find (Milwaukee, E. J. Epstein), closely followed by late April sightings at Manitowoc on the 27th (1981, J. F. Steffen), 28th (1985, C. R. Sontag), and 30th (1984, C. R. Sontag). Most 1 May–15 July birds have been concentrated in the Brown-Manitowoc County region. From 15 July on, individuals wander south along Lake Michigan to Ozaukee, Milwaukee, and Racine counties. Up to 12 birds have been seen at one time (August), suggesting that there may be combinations of recent Wisconsin nesters, nonbreeders, and birds that may have nested in northern Michigan. By 25 August most northeastern birds have departed. In the southeast, observations are frequent through mid-September and intermittent thereafter. Between 1965 and 1985, there have been 12 observations in November, all in Milwaukee and Ozaukee counties. Individuals were found on the Milwaukee CBC on 17 December 1977, 19 December 1981, and 18 December 1982. The 1982 bird subsequently overwintered.

Away from Lake Michigan and Green Bay there have been only four published observations: 24 July 1976 (La Crosse, F. Z. Lesher), 13 May 1979 (Dodge, D. D. Tessen), 21 May 1986 (Ashland, R. L. Verch), and 2 May 1987 (Dodge, J. L. Baughman). It seems only a question of time before there are more sightings around Lake Superior. There have been several recent records from Duluth.

Common Black-headed Gull (*Larus ridibundus*)

STATUS. Accidental. Five records.
HABITAT. Great Lakes.
MIGRATION DATES. Observed between 28 April and 21 December.

When the first American visit of this Eurasian species was recorded in Massachusetts in 1930, exclamations of astonishment echoed in ornithological circles. How did this oddity manage to get on the "wrong" side of the Atlantic?

When a Common Black-headed Gull appeared at Milwaukee on 14 October 1978, independently identified by both Daryl Tessen and Dennis Gustafson, excitement spread throughout Wisconsin. Many observers saw the bird intermittently through 18 November, usually in company with a flock of Bonaparte's Gulls. Although photographs which were taken of the bird were deemed not to be 100% conclusive, there was excellent documentation (*Pass. Pigeon* 41:133–134).

Along with the excitement over these sightings was an underlying "What-took-you-so-long?" feeling. This gull has been regular in New England for 30 years, sometimes in summer as well as winter. Increasingly it has visited the eastern Great Lakes. Birds have appeared in southeastern Michigan annually since 1975. One was photographed near Waukegan, Illinois, in 1976. Surely it was only a question of time before Wisconsin would be on this species' itinerary.

A second record was established in 1983 when C. R. Sontag discovered an individual at Manitowoc on 27 June. The bird remained through 18 July, observed and described by several additional observers (*Pass. Pigeon* 46:93).

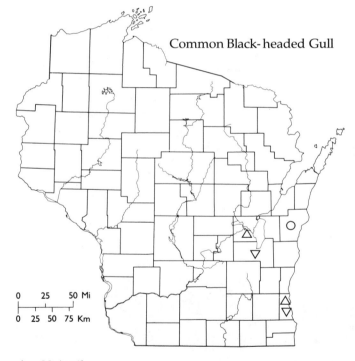

Common Black-headed Gull

0   25   50 Mi
0 25 50 75 Km

△   28 April
○   27 June to 18 July
▽   11 August to 21 December

All records

Two more observations followed in 1984. On 11 August Wendy and Tom Schultz discovered an adult at Lakeside Park in Fond du Lac. Although daylight was fading, the bird was easily distinguished from the 150 Ring-billed Gulls with which the visitor associated.

Both observation and documentation were thorough (*Pass. Pigeon* 47:122).

In Milwaukee on 21 December, John Idzikowski had the kind of gull experience most bird-watchers don't even dream about. Having just observed a Great Black-backed Gull and a Black-legged Kittiwake at Juneau Park, he discovered a Common Black-headed Gull associating with a mixed flock of Bonaparte's and Ring-billed Gulls. His photography produced fair results (*Pass. Pigeon* 47:157–158).

Four months later, Idzikowski had another chance in Milwaukee on 28 April 1985. The Black-head stood tall amid 3,000 surrounding Bonaparte's, some of which offered close comparisons 3 feet away. But before Idzikowski could ready his camera, the entire group took flight (*Pass. Pigeon* 48:41).

With North American nesting verified for the first time in 1977 in Newfoundland, there is every reason to believe that more individuals will wander to Wisconsin in future years.

Bonaparte's Gull (*Larus philadelphia*)

STATUS. Common migrant east and north; uncommon migrant west and south. Common summer resident east; fairly common summer resident north. Rare winter resident east.

HABITAT. Great Lakes. Inland lakes.

MIGRATION DATES. *Spring:* late March to early June. *Fall:* mid-July to late December.

BREEDING DATA. Three records.

WINTER. Rarely present in January along Lake Michigan north to Ozaukee County. Overwintered in 1983.

PORTRAIT. *Birds of Wisconsin:* Plate 38

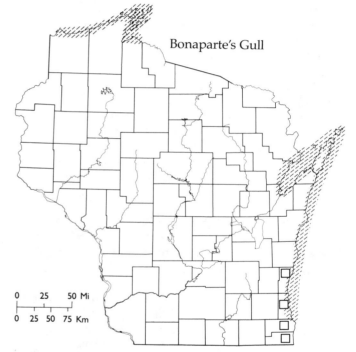

Bonaparte's Gull

0 25 50 Mi
0 25 50 75 Km

▨ Summer range
☐ Early January to mid-March

Records since 1960

Before 1890, the Bonaparte's Gull was an abundant spring migrant at Lake Koshkonong in Jefferson County. Kumlien and Hollister (1903) wrote, "The systematic slaughter of this beautiful gull for millinery purposes has so reduced its numbers that we can no longer claim it as our most abundant species." They proceeded to relate how plume-hunters from Chicago would shoot these birds by the hundreds in southeastern Wisconsin.

By 1900 only small flocks visited the inland lakes. Now, 80 years later, the inland lakes attract small numbers in spring and even smaller numbers in fall. Along Lake Michigan, however, it is not uncommon to see flocks of 300–500 each spring and fall, while on rare occasions flocks have numbered in the thousands. On 13 May 1984 an estimated 12,000 stopped over in Kewaunee County (D. D. Tessen). On 6 April 1965 a congregation of 4,300 was counted at Racine (L. W. Erickson). The size of flocks appearing on Lake Superior in spring has not been reported, but Bernard (1967) listed it as a common spring migrant at Superior.

Occasional late-March arrivals have been reported, including an unusually early Racine bird on 16 March (1985, J. L. Baughman). March 1976 was exceptional, with arrivals on the 20th (Vernon, V. E. Weber), 26th

(Brown, E. D. Cleary), 27th (Walworth, D. D. Tessen), 28th (Dane, W. L. Hilsenhoff), and 31st (Milwaukee, E. J. Epstein). The usual pattern is for southern birds to arrive between 1 and 10 April, peak from 10 to 30 April, then gradually diminish, with the last migrants departing by 25 May. Along Lake Superior birds first come between 15 and 25 April, and numbers peak from 5 to 30 May, with the last migrants pulling out by 15 June.

Small numbers can usually be found throughout the summer along Lake Superior, Green Bay, and the

Lake Michigan shore south to Manitowoc County. In some years Manitowoc has had flocks of 100–200 through June. Most are subadults, and some are as adept at perching on utility wires as on pilings and breakwaters.

Positive nesting evidence is fragmentary. On 7 July 1933 Richter (1937) discovered a nest with three eggs near Oconto. The nest was in the decayed top of a wooden piling at the mouth of the Oconto River, and consisted of twigs, wood chips, grasses, moss, and a few feathers. Richter estimated that the egg-laying began around 20 June. Again in 1934 and 1936, he saw partially constructed nests at the same location, but with no evidence of egg-laying.

On several occasions in the mid-1970s, T. C. Erdman (pers. comm.) found birds acting defensively in Brown and Oconto counties, but he did not succeed in finding the nests that were probably present. A nest (contents unknown) was discovered at Ashland on 2 June 1977, but it was apparently deserted or destroyed by 21 June (D. Pratt, pers. comm.). Also at Ashland, a recently fledged juvenile was observed on 10 July 1981, staunchly protected by a pair of concerned adults. Undoubtedly the pair had nested in the vicinity (S. W. Matteson, pers. comm.).

Ludwig Kumlien (1891a) reported probable nesting on Chamber's Island in Brown County in 1879 and 1880. His evidence was probably secondhand; he gave no specific details.

By 1 August—sometimes 2 weeks earlier—numbers begin to build up, with birds concentrating at the major harbors along Lake Superior, Green Bay, and Lake Michigan. At Manitowoc in 1967, 1,000 had gathered by 1 August. The highest numbers do not usually develop until mid-September in the north, late October in the south. Fall concentrations often number 200–300, occasionally 700–1,000, but they are generally somewhat lower than spring concentrations. This is perhaps because the fall migration is spread out over 4–5 months. Most birds have left the north by 1 November, but there is a record of one remaining in Marinette County through 1 December (1962, H. L. Lindberg), and one in Ashland County on 7 January (1983, R. L. Verch). In some years hundreds remain through December at Milwaukee and Racine, with individuals lingering through 10 January in mild years. The winter of 1953–1954 was exceptional, with CBC counts tallying 125 at Kenosha and 181 at Milwaukee, and stragglers still present on 23 January (Kenosha, M. F. Higgins) and 1 February (Milwaukee, I. N. Balsom). Small flocks overwintered in 1982–1983 in Ozaukee (J. L. Baughman) and Milwaukee (J. H. Idzikowski) counties.

Mew Gull (*Larus canus*)

STATUS. Accidental. Three records.
HABITAT. Great Lakes

Binoculars, telescopes, cameras, telephones, and field guides had a busy time in Milwaukee on 1 March 1986 after Gerald De Boer discovered two Mew Gulls. An adult and a second-year bird performed admirably for him, Lisa and John Idzikowski, and Dennis Gustafson, sometimes from a distance of only 25 feet. The next day gull expert Thomas Schultz observed the birds and wrote a detailed description, while John Idzikowski obtained close-up photographs of both birds. Other observers shared the good fortune through 7 March (*Pass. Pigeon* 49:41–47).

A few individuals of this species have been detected in winter along the Atlantic Coast, and the likelihood is that they have wandered from Europe. Most North American Mew Gulls winter in the Pacific states. One of Idzikowski's photos clearly shows the broken black tail band characteristic of the Pacific *brachyrhynchus* race.

There was no sign of a black band on a Mew Gull closely observed at Manitowoc on 30 October 1986 by

Mew Gull, 2 March 1986, Milwaukee County (photo by J. H. Idzikowski)

J. L. Baughman and C. R. Sontag (*Pass. Pigeon* 49: 158–159). Wisconsin's third record was established at Milwaukee, where R. H. Sundell studied a second-winter bird on 28 February 1988 (*Pass. Pigeon* 50: 264–265).

Ring-billed Gull (*Larus delawarensis*)

STATUS. Common migrant. Common summer resident north and east. Uncommon winter resident east.

HABITAT. Great Lakes. Inland lakes.

MIGRATION DATES. *Spring:* mid-March to mid-May. *Fall:* early August to mid-November.

BREEDING DATA. Nest with eggs: 30 May to 4 July. Clutch size: usually 3 eggs; occasionally 2 or 4.

WINTER. Regularly present along Lake Michigan north to Kewaunee County; occasionally present inland to Brown County.

PORTRAIT. *Birds of Wisconsin:* Plate 38.

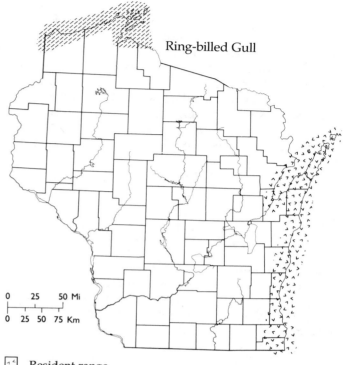

Ring-billed Gull

0   25   50 Mi
0 25 50 75 Km

▨ Resident range
▨ Summer range

Records since 1960

It is a sure sign of spring when one can stand on the bluffs just south of Prescott (Pierce County) on a morning in late March and watch the stream of gulls meandering up the Mississippi. As soon as the ice is out, both Herring and Ring-bills—the latter predominating—move north. There is movement on the other side of the state along Lake Michigan too, but it is less noticeable because the Herring Gull predominates there and because some Ring-bills have been present all winter. Although both species migrate statewide, the Herring is largely a bird of the Great Lakes, while the Ring-bill is equally at home on the Great Lakes and on the rivers and smaller inland lakes.

The main northward push in the southern and central regions lasts from 20 March to 20 April. A majority of the birds move north rapidly, following the breakup of winter ice. A few modest-sized flocks of 10–50 birds linger on the rivers and larger lakes until 15 May. Farther north the first birds reach Lake Superior between 1 and 10 April and are numerous from 15 April to 25 May.

Until recently the Ring-bill was known as a nonbreeding summer resident, mainly along Lakes Michigan and Superior, and only occasionally as a breeder. According to Kumlien and Hollister (1903), birds nested on Spider and Strawberry islands in Green Bay as late as 1882, and Thure Kumlien had found a pair nesting at Lake Koshkonong in Jefferson County in 1860. When A. T. Harris visited Spider Island in 1939 he found only Herrings nesting. But on a small adjacent island he found a nesting Ring-bill colony, which he photographed in 1940 (Harris 1940).

Wisconsin's first Lake Superior nest was found at Superior in 1957. A thorough search of the Wisconsin shore of Lake Superior in 1974 by J. T. Harris and S. W. Matteson led to the discovery of a small colony of 10–20 nesting pairs on Gull Island in Ashland County. Although they found no other breeders

in Wisconsin, a large colony did exist just across the Minnesota line at Duluth (Harris and Matteson 1975a,b).

When T. C. Erdman (pers. comm.) made a similar thorough inventory from Manitowoc to Marinette in 1976, he counted 213 nests in a Brown County colony on 3 June and approximately 60 additional nests in northeastern Wisconsin. One year later numbers had expanded considerably, and a new colony at Kewaunee numbered 1,292 nests. The Brown County area appears to harbor an expanding group that first began using the area in 1969. Erdman's comments support the theory that the Ring-bill is expanding as a breeding species in eastern Wisconsin from flourishing colonies in Michigan, where rapid growth is also occurring (Ludwig 1974). Nesting populations are also expanding on Lake Superior.

When the nesting groups break up in late July, some wandering takes place. Banding recoveries show that some newly fledged young move to the southern tip of Lake Michigan by late August. These may well eventually move on down the Mississippi and winter along the Gulf Coast. Banding recoveries from Mississippi, Louisiana, and Arkansas suggest that some

Wisconsin birds winter in this region. Others disperse eastward to Lake Huron, join the birds that breed there, and eventually make their way to the Carolinas and Florida. If banding recoveries are indicative of population levels, a majority of young Ring-bills raised in Wisconsin winter in Florida.

Adults wander through the Great Lakes region, but banding data are too fragmentary to tell us more about their travels. Starting in early August, a few birds show up on inland lakes and rivers. The real migration takes place between 15 September and the time the lakes and streams freeze over in late November and early December. During peak periods from 25 September to 10 November, flocks are often seen feeding in freshly plowed fields.

Only rarely do individuals attempt to winter on Lake Superior. There are a few instances when CBCs at the cities of Superior, Ashland, and Bayfield have found these birds mingled in flocks of Herrings, but freezing ice in January forces their dispersal. Along Lake Michigan Ring-bills are regular from Algoma to Kenosha and occasional at Green Bay. A few linger by the larger inland lakes at Madison and Lake Geneva (Walworth County) through CBC time. But when open water disappears in early January, the birds move out.

Herring Gull (*Larus argentatus*)

STATUS. Common migrant north and east; fairly common migrant elsewhere. Common summer resident north and east. Common winter resident north, east, and south where open water permits.
HABITAT. Great Lakes. Inland lakes.
MIGRATION DATES. *Spring:* early March to late April. *Fall:* mid-September to early December.
BREEDING DATA. Nests with eggs: 4 May to 19 July. Clutch size: 3 eggs.
WINTER. Present along suitable Lake Superior locations in Douglas, Bayfield, and Ashland counties as long as open water persists; regularly present along Lake Michigan from Marinette to Kenosha counties.
PORTRAIT. *Birds of Wisconsin:* Plate 38.

For many years the Herring Gull nesting colonies off the Door County peninsula have held a strong attraction for people of varied interests. Early in the nineteenth century Indians and early settlers made many trips to them to obtain eggs for food and for sale. Later in the nineteenth century plume-hunters valued the sleek white feathers for millinery use. Early in the twentieth century fruit-growers trying to raise grapes on Strawberry Island attempted to drive off the gulls. Oologists came to collect eggs. Fishermen paid visits to cut down the population of birds that they perceived as a threat to their industry.

Kumlien and Hollister (1903) called this graceful flier a very common bird on Lake Michigan but commented, "Not nearly as numerous as formerly." The gulls needed eloquent spokesmen like J. W. Braun, writing in 1912: "These birds are scavengers of the sea and shore, and are of vast benefit to humanity in ridding places adjacent to the water of dead fish and fish offal. Were it not for these creatures, the sanitary conditions of our fishing towns along the lake shores and coasts would be in a most deplorable condition." Then, as the alewife population increased in the western Great Lakes, so did the Herring Gull (Harris and Matteson 1975b).

In 1923 Harold Wilson (pers. comm.) began banding operations on some of the islands. Largely through his efforts for over 50 years, more than 72,000 Herring Gulls have been banded. Much has been learned about their habits, movements, and longevity. The accompanying map depicts the remarkable travels made by the gulls during their first year of life. From their Door County birthplace, significant numbers wander in late summer to the southern tip of Lake Michigan, continue down the Mississippi River in fall, and follow the Gulf Coast to Texas, Mexico, and occasionally even to Guatemala and Panama. Others move eastward through the eastern Great Lakes and St. Lawrence River to Quebec and on to northern New England. A few move northward as far as Labrador, then southward along the Atlantic Coast, wintering south to Florida. A few banded birds have been recovered in Bermuda, the Bahamas, Cuba, and Jamaica. Banding evidence indicates that considerable wandering also occurs during the gulls' second year of life.

Nearing adult life, birds may return to the land of their birth. They attach themselves to the resident flocks that breed on the Door County islands or related Lake Michigan locations, and they winter in the lower Lake Michigan region from Chicago and Gary north to Algoma (Kewaunee County) and Green Bay.

Substantial numbers of Herrings also breed on Lake Superior islands. When J. T. Harris and S. W. Matteson made an extensive inventory of Wisconsin's Lake Superior shore in 1974, they counted approximately 1,000 nesting pairs, concentrated mainly in the Apostle Islands in Ashland County (Harris and Matteson 1975a). Banding data are lacking for these birds, but presumably they follow patterns similar to Lake Michigan birds, except in winter, when most of Lake Superior freezes over. Several hundred often spend the early winter in Superior and Bayfield harbors as long as open water remains.

Spring migration along Lake Michigan occurs mainly between 10 March and 15 April. In other regions it is slightly later, governed chiefly by the opening of ice-locked lakes and streams. Breeding birds are generally on territory ready to nest by 25 April. Nonbreeders may linger later in spring, but few are seen south of their summer territory after 30 April.

By 1 August adults as well as young disperse. Along Lake Michigan the main southward movement is in October, November, and early December. Around the rest of the state fall migrants move during the same period, but numbers are usually quite limited except below dams on the Mississippi River.

Sites where birds were recovered within 12 months of banding in Door County, Wisconsin. (Based on data from the U.S. Fish and Wildlife Service Bird Banding Laboratory.)

Thayer's Gull (*Larus thayeri*)

STATUS. Rare migrant north and east. Rare winter resident north and east.

HABITAT. Great Lakes. Inland lakes.

MIGRATION DATES. Observed between 9 September and 17 May.

WINTER. Rarely present along Lake Michigan north to Manitowoc.

Few species have given taxonomists more difficulty than the Thayer's Gull. It has alternately been listed as a subspecies of the Herring Gull, a subspecies of the Iceland Gull, and as a separate species. When the American Ornithologists' Union listed this bird as a distinct species in 1972, gull experts advised observers to check 8–10 different points of identification. No one or two plumage features would suffice. Observers, in turn, have asked: What field marks must be observed on immatures, subadults, and adults? How can one approach a suspected Thayer's Gull close enough to appraise all pertinent field marks? Can photographs be trusted for certain identification?

Individuals suspected to be *thayeri* were observed and documented five times between 1974 and 1980, but members of the Wisconsin Society for Ornithology Records Committee deemed the evidence insufficient. The committee granted hypothetical status to birds observed in Douglas County on 9 September and 5 November 1980 by J. L. Polk (*Pass. Pigeon* 43: 140–141), to an individual found in Milwaukee on 5 January 1981 by Robert and Roger Sundell (*Pass. Pigeon* 43:153–154), and to another Milwaukee bird observed on 22 January 1982 by D. K. Gustafson (*Pass. Pigeon* 44:168–169).

Unknown, through all these considerations, was a

Thayer's Gull

△ Early March to mid-May
▽ Early September to late November
□ Early December to late February

All records

Thayer's Gull, 15 December 1984, Milwaukee County (photo by J. H. Idzikowski)

specimen of a Thayer's Gull which had been residing peacefully in the University of Wisconsin Zoological Museum collection at Madison since 1891. O. B. Zimmerman had collected it at Milwaukee on 31 January 1891, and the identifying label had tagged it as an immature female Herring Gull. When E. J. Epstein examined this specimen in 1985, he noted a size difference and arranged to have the skin reexamined. Gull experts Joseph Jehl and Guy McCaskie confirmed the identity as a Thayer's Gull (pers. comm. to E. J. Epstein).

Increasing scrutiny of Milwaukee's wintering gulls has led to new discoveries. Between 15 December 1984 and 8 January 1985 J. H. Idzikowski identified three adults, seen by many other birders, painstakingly described and photographed by T. R. Schultz and J. L. Baughman (*Pass. Pigeon* 47:151–153). On 8 December 1985 Baughman again found an adult in Milwaukee, got within 20 feet of the gull, and obtained photographs. Numerous observers shared sightings of this wanderer through 9 March 1986

(*Pass. Pigeon* 48:174–175). On 17 May 1986 Baughman and Schultz scrutinized another individual at Manitowoc (*Pass. Pigeon* 49:29). Another seven observations in 1987 were accepted by the WSO Records Committee between 17 January and 20 April, and between 31 October and 19 December. One was an 8 November bird at Ashland seen by A. J. Knue; the others were noted at Manitowoc and Milwaukee (*Pass. Pigeon* 49:193, 50:237).

When the methods of identification of this species in its varied plumages can be refined and mastered by competent observers and photographers, the Wisconsin status may well need redefinition. The Thayer's Gull nests in the Arctic, has been found in winter in neighboring states, and could prove to be a regular winter resident along Wisconsin's Great Lakes shores.

Iceland Gull (*Larus glaucoides*)

STATUS. Rare migrant north and east. Rare winter visitant north and east.

HABITAT. Great Lakes. Inland lakes.

MIGRATION DATES. *Fall:* late September to late December, with some shifting of birds in January and February. *Spring:* early March to late April. *Extremes:* 24 August; 14 May.

WINTER. Occasionally present along Lake Superior and along Lake Michigan from Manitowoc to Kenosha counties.

Through 1950 this pale gull's place among Wisconsin's avifauna rested on Kumlien and Hollister's (1903) brief statement: "A regular winter visitant on Lake Michigan, by no means common, although occurring more frequently than [the Glaucous Gull]." There were no specimens and no dates of observations. Since there was no corroborative evidence from other

Iceland Gull

△ Early March to late April
▽ Late September to late December
□ Early January to late February

All records

Iceland Gull, 24 January 1981, Milwaukee County (photo by J. H. Idzikowski)

sources, recent writers included the Iceland Gull on a hypothetical list.

Credit is due R. F. Gordon for the detection of gulls the size of Herring Gulls but with light-colored wings at Kenosha in 1951 (7 April), 1952 (30 March–21 April), and 1953 (2 January). Three additional sightings in Milwaukee and Ozaukee counties followed in 1953 and 1955. After a 10-year lapse, from one to four observations have occurred each year, producing a total of 48 records between 1951 and 1989.

When the Thayer's Gull was accepted as a separate species in 1972, rather than a Herring-Iceland hybrid, it brought front and center a question that had previously lurked in the background: How many of the state's "Iceland" records might be attributable to *thayeri*?

Documentation for 11 of Wisconsin's 48 post-1950 sightings is virtually worthless. There are no specimens. Of the 37 records with some supportive evidence for Icelands in Wisconsin, 2 are supported by photographs and 10 by reasonably complete descriptions. The other 25 include some documentation—enough on size and bill to rule out the Glaucous but not enough to differentiate between *glaucoides* and *thayeri*.

One photograph taken in Bayfield County on 3 January 1971 (D. A. Bratley) is indeterminate. The second, taken at Kenosha in January 1975 (E. B. Prins) is clearly an Iceland. This bird remained from 28 December 1974 to 28 March 1975 and was seen by many people. Well-documented *glaucoides* sightings were recorded at Racine from 10 February to 9 March 1966 by L. W. Erickson, at Port Washington (Ozaukee County) on 18 February 1967 by D. D. Tessen, at Milwaukee on 5 January 1975 by L. W. Erickson, again at Milwaukee on 25 February 1977 by E. J. Epstein, at Manitowoc on 12 April 1986 and between 18 March and 20 April 1987 (C. R. Sontag), and at Superior between 18 November (R. J. Johnson) and 28 December (L. Semo) 1987.

Icelands have been seen along Lake Superior on four occasions: 29 December–3 January (1970–1971, Bayfield, B. F. Klugow), 1 February–15 March (1975, Douglas, C. A. Faanes), and 11–15 April (1966, Douglas, R. F. Bernard). Inland observations have occurred five times: 23 November–late December (1971, Waukesha, J. E. Bielefeldt), 4 December (1978, Dane, R. M. Hoffman), 31 January (1973, Waukesha, M. F. Donald), 27 March (1978, Dane, G. W. Foster), and 7 May (1983, Fond du Lac, T. R. Schultz).

All other sightings have been along the Lake Michigan–Green Bay shore, with one to three nearly every winter since 1965. No discernible pattern of first arrival dates has emerged. It might be expected that the largest numbers would be recorded in late December when CBC activity is at its height. But birds seem to turn up any time in January, February, or March with just as much regularity. The earliest fall sightings include 24 August (1971, Brown, E. D. Cleary), 28 August (1953, Milwaukee, D. L. Larkin), and 23 September (1973, Brown, E. D. Cleary). There have been three additional October arrival dates and one in November. All of these early fall records have constituted 1-day sightings of birds that did not linger. Later in the winter an individual is more likely to settle down in one area for several weeks.

Most birds disappear before the end of March. Lingerers in April have been observed on the 21st (1977, Racine, L. W. Erickson), 25th (1965, Ozaukee, M. F. Donald), and 30th (1978, Milwaukee, L. W. Erickson). Exceptionally late was an individual lingering through 14 May (1982, Manitowoc, C. R. Sontag).

Lesser Black-Backed Gull (*Larus fuscus*)

STATUS. Casual spring and fall migrant.

HABITAT. Great Lakes. Inland lakes.

MIGRATION DATES. Observed between 12 October and 30 December, and between 3 March and 4 June.

Among several hundred gulls standing on a Milwaukee breakwater on 12 October 1980, John and Lisa Idzikowski discovered a dark-mantled gull that proved to be an adult *L. fuscus* when closely examined through binoculars and telescope. These experienced gull-watchers had excellent opportunity for close comparison with nearby Herring, Ring-billed, and Franklin's Gulls. They carefully observed and noted size, mantle coloration, and eye and leg coloration (*Pass. Pigeon* 43:140). Several observers, poised with cameras, scanned the area the following day, but to no avail.

In the fifth edition of the AOU *Check-list of North American Birds* (1957), this European species was listed as "accidental in Greenland, New York and Maryland." It began to appear regularly in New York in 1954 and gradually spread along the Atlantic Coast during the next 20 years. By 1975 individuals were appearing in the eastern Great Lakes region. First state records in Ohio (1977), Michigan (1979), Illinois (1980), and Missouri (1980), synchronize well with Wisconsin's first sighting.

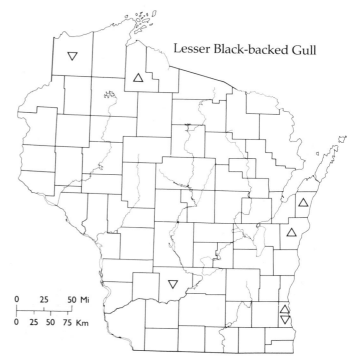

Lesser Black-backed Gull

0   25   50 Mi
0   25   50   75 Km

△   3 March to 4 June
▽   12 October to 30 December

All records

Lesser Black-backed Gull, 19 October 1984, Douglas County (photo by D. Bolduc)

The state's second record was added in March 1984, with D. D. Tessen's discovery of an adult in Kewaunee County on the 29th, observed the following day in Manitowoc County by R. H. Sundell (*Pass. Pigeon* 47:39). On 20 October 1984 R. J. Johnson found a bird at Superior—presumably the same bird that had provided Minnesota's first state record at nearby Duluth a few days earlier (*Pass. Pigeon* 47:121–122). Gerald De Boer and William Cowart had a splendid view of yet another adult at Milwaukee on 3 March 1985 (*Pass. Pigeon* 48:44).

Additional sightings in 1988 include a bird in Ashland County on 4 June (R. L. Verch; *Pass. Pigeon* 51:121–122) and one in Sauk County between 14 and 30 December (K. F. Legler; *Pass. Pigeon* 51:301–302).

Glaucous Gull (*Larus hyperboreus*)

STATUS. Uncommon migrant north and east; rare migrant elsewhere. Rare summer resident east. Uncommon winter resident north and east; rare winter resident elsewhere.

HABITAT. Great Lakes. Inland lakes.

MIGRATION DATES. *Fall:* early November to late December, rarely starting by mid-August. *Spring:* mid-February to early May, rarely extending to early June.

WINTER. Regularly present along Lake Superior, and along Lake Michigan from Manitowoc to Kenosha counties.

PORTRAIT. *Birds of Wisconsin:* Plate 37.

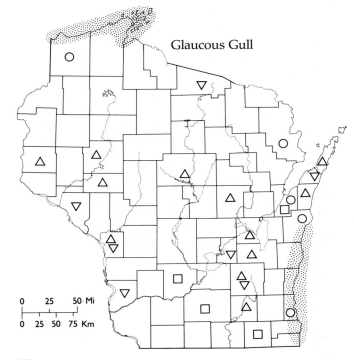

Glaucous Gull

0   25   50 Mi

0   25 50 75 Km

▨   Winter range
△   Mid-February to late May
○   Early June to early August
▽   Mid-August to late December
□   Early January to early February

Records since 1960

When the *Wisconsin Birds—a Preliminary Checklist with Migration Charts* (Barger et al.) was first published in 1942, this large light gull was listed as "rare on Lake Michigan." The presence of the species from late December to early March was based mainly on three Milwaukee specimens taken on 8, 12, and 14 January 1895, comments by Hoy, Cory, Schoenebeck, and Kumlien and Hollister that this species occasionally occurs along Lake Michigan in severe winters, and sightings at Oconto in February 1939 (Richter 1939a) and at Milwaukee in February 1941 (L. P. Steven). Unknown to the checklist authors at that time was the specimen collected at Cedar Grove (Sheboygan County) on 18 May 1930 (Jung 1930a) and additional Sheboygan County sight records on 27 July 1926 and 30 April 1940.

Since 1942, observations have become an annual event. Wherever concentrations of large gulls occur from mid-November through April along Green Bay or Lake Michigan—Marinette, Green Bay, Manitowoc, Port Washington, Milwaukee, Racine, and Kenosha—the presence of a Glaucous is a distinct possibility. From two to seven sightings per winter are now recorded along Lake Michigan, especially at Manitowoc and Milwaukee.

Observations have also been frequent along Lake Superior. One or more birds have been listed on the Bayfield CBC nearly every winter. There and at Superior a few individuals are present in early winter, moving out if that region freezes over completely in January. Frequently at least one individual returns to the Superior harbor from March through May when open water is again available.

Since 1965 the presence of wanderers away from Lakes Superior and Michigan has been detected with increasing frequency. Individuals overwintered in

Dane (1979–1980, 1980–1981) and Sauk (1982–1983) counties. Fall vagrants made brief appearances in Crawford (1986), Buffalo (1980), La Crosse (1967, 1971), Vilas (1975), and Dodge (1974) counties between 5 October and 13 December. Between 1 March and 10 April 1-day spring observations have been made in La Crosse (1981, 1983), Eau Claire (1982), Chippewa (1986), Jefferson (1976), Dodge (1977), Fond du Lac (1966), and Winnebago (1971) counties. Late spring dates include 30 April (1978, Dane, T. De Boor) and 16 May (1972, Waupaca, W. L. Hilsenhoff).

Between mid-May and early November, all Wisconsin sightings have been limited to the Great Lakes and Green Bay. Twice birds prolonged spring migration to 10 June (1973, Douglas, J. L. Kaspar; 1976, Marinette, T. C. Erdman).

Two subadults were present in midsummer 1981 in Milwaukee (23 June, R. Biss) and Manitowoc (28

June–18 July, C. R. Sontag). In 1982 a nonbreeder spent the summer in Manitowoc (C. R. Sontag), and another was observed in Milwaukee on 30 July (D. K. Gustafson).

T. C. Erdman (pers. comm.) commented: "I've observed subadults in June and July on Green Bay. Carl Richter suspected a pair were nesting on Green Isle in the late 1930s. He could not find the exact nest the birds were staying near."

The seven instances of Lake Michigan sightings between 16 and 31 August may indicate either summer wanderings or fall migration. But there is no significant increase in numbers until early November.

Great Black-backed Gull (*Larus marinus*)

STATUS. Rare migrant north and east. Casual summer visitant east. Rare winter visitant north and east.
HABITAT. Great Lakes. Inland lakes.
MIGRATION DATES. *Spring:* early March to late April. *Fall:* late August to late November. Casual wandering in May, June, and July.
WINTER. Occasionally present between Ozaukee and Kenosha counties. Three Lake Superior records.
PORTRAIT. *Birds of Wisconsin:* Plate 37.

Between 1939 and 1968 this imposing gull wandered to Wisconsin on 13 known occasions. With the exception of Douglas County observations on 23 November 1948 (photo, W. J. Breckinridge) and 29 April 1941 (K. W. Kahmann), all Great Black-backed Gull records came between 25 December and 10 April. Six of the intervening sightings involved birds that spent brief periods in the harbor at Kenosha between 1949 and 1956. One was a most unusual inland observation near Lake Mills (Jefferson County) on 31 March 1939 (H. G. Anderson 1939).

In the 1960s, as this species extended its range south along the Atlantic Coast and west through the eastern Great Lakes, Wisconsin observers anticipated that there might come a change of pattern—both in terms of frequency and the timing of wandering to the Lake Michigan shore. A new pattern did emerge, starting in 1969.

Thirty-two visits have been documented between 1969 and 1987, including records every year except 1976, 1977, and 1981. Seven sightings occurred in autumn: 26 August (1974, Milwaukee, M. F. Donald) to 27 November (1972, Kenosha, R. R. Hoffman); 19 occurred between early December and mid-April. Three have been midsummer detections of immatures: 8 June (1974, Brown, D. D. Tessen), 13 June (1974, Racine, L. W. Erickson), and 13 July (1978, Manitowoc, D. D. Tessen). An adult was present at Manitowoc between 14 May (J. Johnson) and 10 July

Great Black-backed Gull

0 25 50 Mi
0 25 50 75 Km

△ Early March to late April
○ Early May to early July
▽ Late August to late November
□ Early December to late February

Records since 1939

(M. Bontly) 1982. Another remained at Oshkosh from 12 May to 8 June 1983 (C. Schultz). D. D. Tessen discovered an adult at Superior on 25 May 1987.

As would be expected, most observations have been made along the shores of Lake Michigan and Green Bay. One exceptional wanderer appeared in Pierce County on 2 April 1974 (C. A. Faanes). Another turned up on a CBC in Winnebago County on 1 January 1972 (D. D. Tessen).

The occasional presence of this species in the nineteenth century is attested to by Kumlien and Hollister (1903), who mentioned a sight observation at a Milwaukee lighthouse in the winter of 1880–1881 and two additional sightings offshore (no dates given), but they thought this a rare winter visitant. Barry (1854) listed it as common at Racine, but this seems unlikely, since it was not mentioned by Hoy (1853b), living in the same area at the same time. Kumlien and Hollister made mention of a specimen located at the Oshkosh Normal School and labeled "Lake Michigan." No date, no collector, no exact location was listed, and now the specimen cannot be located. No other specimens are known for Wisconsin.

Early twentieth-century information is fragmentary. Cahn (1913) listed it in Waukesha County, but gave no indication of specific records. Clarence Jung's notes mentioned a bird seen on 2 November 1919, but failed to give location.

W. J. Breckinridge provided Wisconsin's first photographic evidence on 23 November 1948, when he took colored motion pictures of an adult just east of Duluth and Superior—a bird that qualified for both Wisconsin and Minnesota records. If the present range extension trend continues, there are sure to be more records and more photographs.

Black-legged Kittiwake (*Rissa tridactyla*)

STATUS. Casual spring migrant; rare fall migrant.
HABITAT. Great Lakes.
MIGRATION DATES. *Spring:* mid-March to late April. *Fall:* mid-October to mid-December. *Extremes:* 17 March, 27 April; 19 October, 29 December.
WINTER. One February record.

Since 1967 this oceanic wanderer has appeared 19 times in Wisconsin. On eight of these occasions Black-legged Kittiwakes were detected along Lake Michigan in Ozaukee County: 19 October (1974, immature, D. D. Tessen), 26 October (1980, adult, M. F. Donald), 27 October (1973, adult, D. D. Tessen), 2–5 November (1971, age-class unknown, M. F. Donald), 6 November (1970, immature, D. K. Gustafson), 11 November (1972, adult, D. D. Tessen), 17 November (1973, immature, D. D. Tessen), and 29 December (1984, J. H. Idzikowski). Barely north of the Ozaukee County line was an immature found dead on the beach at Cedar Grove (Sheboygan County), on 26 November 1967, by R. Weinke (MPM files). Just to the south in Milwaukee, John Idzikowski found an adult on 21 December 1984 and an immature on 28 December 1984. These 11 records within an 18-year span strongly suggest that small numbers of these birds may occur along Lake Michigan every year. If this is true, the birds generally must stay well offshore, coming close enough to be seen from land only rarely. Until recently, Lake Michigan observations had been considered accidental or casual in nature. But the frequency of detections in southeastern Wisconsin and northeastern Illinois in recent years suggests that changes may be in the making.

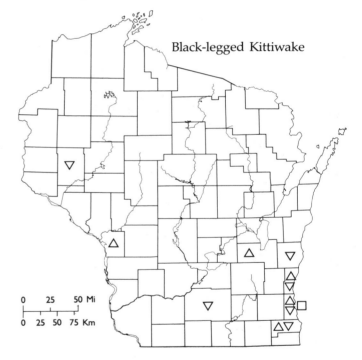

Black-legged Kittiwake

0   25   50 Mi
0 25 50 75 Km

△   17 March to 27 April
▽   Mid-October to mid-December
□   4 February

All records

Three additional late autumn sightings have come from Madison: one bird seen from 4 to 17 December 1978 (R. M. Hoffman), another in December 1974, noted on the 13th (G. W. Foster) and 14th (J. T. Harris), and one discovered on the Christmas Bird Count on

15 December 1984. J. L. Polk found one at Menomonie (Dunn County) on 15 November 1988.

Since 1967, observers have found spring migrants on four occasions: 14 April (1968, La Crosse, F. Z. Lesher—later taken for the University of Wisconsin–La Crosse collection by H. F. Young), 21 April (1974, Milwaukee, M. F. Donald), 26 April (1976, Fond du Lac, R. A. Knuth), and 27 April (1972, Ozaukee, R. H. Sundell).

Before 1967 only five state records existed. P. R. Hoy documented three nineteenth-century sight records at Racine. Although he never got close enough to collect any of the birds, he was satisfied with sightings in November 1853 (Hoy 1853b), December 1870 (E. W. Nelson 1876), and 17 March 1884 (W. W. Cooke 1884–1885). The fourth record—the state's first speci-

men—was procured in Milwaukee on 4 February 1938 (W. P. Dettman) after John Schaeffer discovered the bird on 1 February (Deusing 1938). The fifth record was an 8 December 1957 observation at Milwaukee by C. P. and D. E. Frister.

The closest thing to a Lake Superior record for the Black-legged Kittiwake comes from Kumlien and Hollister (1903). They once examined an immature bird mounted at Ashland, supposedly shot by a Canadian among the Apostle Islands. But since the collector had recently come from the St. Lawrence River country, where he might have obtained the bird, Kumlien and Hollister listed no date and considered this record "of no value." Minnesota has had several Lake Superior observations, however, so it seems likely that Wisconsin's turn will come.

Sabine's Gull (*Xema sabini*)

STATUS. Accidental. Four records.
HABITAT. Great Lakes. Inland lakes.
MIGRATION DATES. Observed between 22 September and 30 October.

Wisconsin's only specimen of the Sabine's Gull was procured on 7 October 1900 by H. P. Hare in Walworth County: a young male shot on Lake Delavan, whose skin was subsequently preserved in the Ned Hollister collection (Hollister 1901b).

Not until 1968 was this arctic and coastal species known to wander to Wisconsin again. Two individu-

Sabine's Gull, 22 September 1968, Dane County (photo by D. W. Anderson)

als appeared on Lake Mendota in Madison on 22 September, were clearly seen by several observers, and photographed by G. W. Foster (*Pass. Pigeon* 31:294).

On 6 October 1978 one bird was leisurely observed at a Dodge County pond in company with Bonaparte's Gulls by R. M. Hoffman (*Pass. Pigeon* 41:138). The bird obligingly remained for several days, and was appreciated by many observers before departing on 12 October.

One appeared at Superior in late October 1987, seen at close range and photographed by Robbye Johnson on the 28th. The bird remained through the 30th, observed by eight other birders (*Pass. Pigeon* 50:267–268).

Kumlien and Hollister (1903) mentioned two additional possible records, which lack sufficient documentation to be considered positive. They quoted P. R. Hoy as having observed a bird at Racine in November 1853, but documentation for this sight observation is lacking. And sometime in April 1897 they examined two fresh wings, the remains of a bird killed near Janesville; they identified them as belonging to this species, but the feathers ended up on a woman's hat instead of in a scientist's collection.

Although the Sabine's migratory range is limited mainly to the Pacific Coast and to a lesser extent to the Atlantic Coast, many of the states west of the Mississippi have records of occasional interior wanderings. In extralimital meanderings, individuals are as likely to visit small shallow ponds as larger deepwater lakes.

Ivory Gull (*Pagophila eburnea*)

STATUS. Accidental. Four records.
HABITAT. Great Lakes. Inland lakes.
MIGRATION DATES. Observed between 7 March and
6 April.
WINTER. One January record.

Late in the afternoon on 7 March 1947, fisherman Lyle Follett observed a small white gull east of Oconto. The information was relayed to Carl Richter, and on the following day the two men investigated further. They found the bird in the ice fields of Green Bay 7 miles out from Oconto, and they collected what proved to be an adult female Ivory Gull. The specimen was donated to the Milwaukee Public Museum.

Later on the afternoon of 8 March 1947, 60 miles away, a second individual appeared along the breakwater in Two Rivers (Manitowoc County). LeRoy Lintereur observed the bird's white plumage in flight and its black webbed feet as it stood on the breakwater scarcely 30 feet from him (*Pass. Pigeon* 9:120).

On 3 April 1959, N. R. Stone discovered three white "pigeon-like gulls" at Crex Meadows in Burnett County. The distinctive flight, white plumage, and black legs were clearly seen as the birds flew about and landed 40 yards away. The birds were observed again on 5 and 6 April (*Pass. Pigeon* 21:149).

At each of these locations there was the combination of ice and open water, which this gull prefers in its arctic haunts. But there was no ice within hundreds of miles when Daryl Tessen saw and heard what he believed to be a bird of this species at Horicon Marsh in Dodge County on 24 July 1972. With no

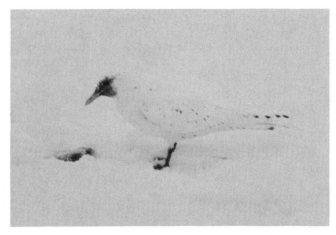

Ivory Gull, 10 January 1989, St. Croix County (photo by J. Smith)

other summer record for any of the lower 48 United States known, a casual reader could be forgiven for substituting "preposterous" for "hypothetical" to describe such an occurrence. How an individual could stray so far from its usual haunts at this most unlikely time of year staggers the imagination, but how the bird Tessen described (*Pass. Pigeon* 35:100) could belong to any species other than the Ivory Gull is equally incredible.

One wandered to St. Croix County at a more likely time: 7–10 January 1989; it was well described and photographed by Ted Schmidt (*Pass. Pigeon* 51:299–300) and by Jerry Smith.

Caspian Tern (*Sterna caspia*)

STATUS. Fairly common migrant north and east; uncommon migrant west; rare migrant central. Uncommon summer resident east; rare summer visitant northwest.

HABITAT. Great Lakes. Inland lakes.

MIGRATION DATES. *Spring:* mid-April to early June. *Fall:* mid-July to mid-October. *Extremes:* 26 March; 1 December.

BREEDING DATA. Nests with eggs: 30 May to 4 July. Clutch size: usually 3 eggs; occasionally 2.

PORTRAIT. *Birds of Wisconsin:* Plate 39.

To understand the patterns of movement of the Caspian Tern, largest of Wisconsin's terns, it is helpful to remember that this species nests in a series of isolated regions rather than across one continuous range. In his *Birds of Canada,* Godfrey (1966) shows one nesting pocket in Alberta and Mackenzie, another in Saskatchewan and Manitoba, a third in southeastern Ontario, and a fourth in Newfoundland. The major nesting colonies in Michigan are contiguous to the Ontario pocket.

Wisconsin appears to have two spring migratory tracks. Along Lake Michigan first arrivals appear between 15 and 20 April anywhere from Kenosha to Kewaunee counties. Unusually early were April sightings on the 9th (1978, Ozaukee, R. Korotev) and 11th (1981, Ozaukee, J. L. Polk). One bird reached Marinette County by the 17th (1962, H. L. Lindberg).

A second track follows the Mississippi and St. Croix rivers, with similar arrival dates, including an early bird on 8 April (1961, Burnett, N. R. Stone). Spring birds are occasionally found on the larger lakes in late April and May. A 26 March 1979 record-breaker was discovered by A. A. Carpenter on Lake Winnebago. Some years no inland spring migrants are reported.

Although there are no banding recoveries to prove it, it is possible that birds along the rivers move north through the western Lake Superior region in May and eventually join the breeding colony in Manitoba. Groups of 5–15 birds frequently turn up in La Crosse, Pepin, St. Croix, and Burnett counties in May; and in Douglas, Bayfield, and Ashland counties from 10 May to 5 June.

Those birds that move into the region from Green Bay to Marinette may move northward from Lake Michigan or westward from Lake Huron. According to banding recovery data, birds ringed in summer on the Wisconsin side of Lake Michigan have been retaken the following fall or winter in Maryland, North Carolina, and Florida, as well as in Indiana and Loui-

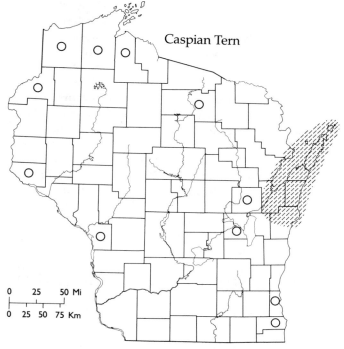

Caspian Tern

0 25   50 Mi

0 25 50 75 Km

▨ Summer range
○ Mid-June to early July

Records since 1960

siana. During May, observations have come from all parts of Lake Michigan, with Brown County concentrations sometimes numbering 75–150 birds.

A few Caspian Terns are seen all summer from Brown and Manitowoc counties north. Some are nonbreeders; some wander from nesting colonies in Michigan's Grand Traverse Islands. Breeding in northeastern Wisconsin has been intermittent. Kumlien and Hollister (1903) recorded breeding Caspians on islands in Green Bay between 1874 and 1893. H. L. Ward visited a nesting group on Gravel Island in Door County in 1905 (Ward 1906). In 1939 and 1940 visits by A. T. Harris to Barker's Reef off the Door County peninsula revealed the presence of a Caspian Tern colony adjacent to a Ring-billed Gull colony. His vivid account (Harris 1940, pp. 19–21) portrayed how the terns—as well as gulls—often attacked juveniles from neighboring nests: "They fought with each other, trying to spear their opponent with their formidable bills. Should a neighbor's chick wander from its own ground to another's territory, the adult tern would throw itself in a frenzy upon the shrilly complaining chick and peck viciously at it." T. C. Erdman photographed young incapable of sustained flight in Brown County in 1966, but could find no Wisconsin nests during his extensive Lake Michigan–Green Bay studies in 1976. Confirmed nesting in Wisconsin was not certain again until 1984, when S. W. Matteson discovered nests on Kidney Island in Brown County. The fragile hold this tern has as a nesting species led to its inclusion on the state's list of endangered species in 1989.

Some wandering to inland locations occurs as early as 1 July (1947, Clark, S. D. Robbins; 1949, Dane, A. Keitt). Soon after mid-July observers have spotted returning birds along the St. Croix and Mississippi rivers. Perhaps the best place to see these handsome birds in fall is along the Fox River below the Kimberly dam where concentrations of 75–150 individuals have occurred in August and early September. Similar-sized groups often appear at Manitowoc, Kewaunee, Green Bay, and Marinette.

By mid-September most Caspians have departed, but some linger into early October. The latest date for Lake Superior is 8 October (1966, Douglas, R. F. Bernard). In the eastern counties birds have been noted as late as 23 October (1973, Milwaukee, M. F. Donald) and 25 October (1953, Winnebago, E. Fisher). Exceptionally late were individuals on 28 November (1953, Brown, E. O. Paulson) and 1 December (1938, Milwaukee, C. L. Strelitzer).

Kumlien and Hollister (1903) mentioned that this bird is "frequently found on Lake Michigan in winter." Schoenebeck (1902) and Cory (1909) made similar claims, but neither provided any supporting data.

Royal Tern (*Sterna maxima*)

STATUS. Accidental. Four records.
HABITAT. Normally oceanic.

It was fortunate that Thomas Schultz and Jeffrey Baughman were armed with camera and telescope when they visited the Manitowoc harbor on 18 June 1985. There, they discovered a flock of Caspian Terns, and with the flock a smaller tern with shorter legs and a thinner orange-yellow bill. A Royal Tern! The bird remained in the area through 15 July, when last seen by C. R. Sontag. Baughman's photo (*Am. Birds* 40:117)

Royal Tern, 18 June 1988, Manitowoc County (photo by J. L. Baughman)

and the observers' written accounts offer valuable documentation (*Pass. Pigeon* 48:89–91).

Imagine Sontag's surprise on 6 July 1986 at the same Manitowoc location when he found another Royal Tern within the resident flock of Caspian Terns. The straggler from the Gulf states could not be found on succeeding days, but flew within 20 feet of Sontag on the day of observation (*Pass. Pigeon* 49:113–114).

Paul Sunby discovered an individual on 2 August 1988, associating with Common and Caspian Terns and Ring-billed Gulls in Milwaukee. The bird disappeared the next day, after being admired by several other observers (*Pass. Pigeon* 51:231–233).

Nearly 23 years earlier, on 5 September 1965 at Kimberly (Outagamie County), D. D. Tessen spent almost an hour studying a bird that showed all the characteristics of this species. The bird perched on a rock by the Fox River and could be compared with four Caspian Terns resting nearby (*Pass. Pigeon* 28:110). Because the bird could not be seen in flight and was not photographed, the record was treated as hypothetical.

Late-summer hurricanes occasionally blow individuals north along the Atlantic Coast to New York and New England. The 1965 individual could have been a storm-blown vagrant. No ready explanation exists for the 1985 and 1986 wanderers, arriving before the start of the hurricane season and remaining for 4 weeks. I know of no other Upper Midwest records for this species, which normally selects only saltwater habitat.

Common Tern (*Sterna hirundo*)

STATUS. Common migrant north and east; fairly common migrant south and west. Uncommon summer resident north and east.

HABITAT. Great Lakes. Inland lakes.

MIGRATION DATES. *Spring:* mid-April to mid-June. *Fall:* early August to mid-October. *Extremes:* 1 April; 28 November.

BREEDING DATA. Nests with eggs: 27 May to 6 August. Clutch size: usually 3 eggs; occasionally 2.

PORTRAIT. *Birds of Wisconsin:* Plate 39.

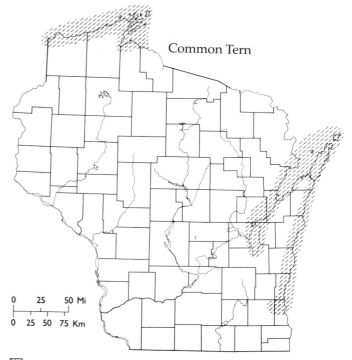

Common Tern

0   25   50 Mi

0   25 50 75 Km

░░ Summer range

Records since 1960

Typically, it is the Lake Michigan and Green Bay observers who see the first spring migrant Common Terns. This generally happens between 10 and 20 April, with first arrivals at inland locations appearing between 20 and 30 April. Birds usually return to Lake Superior between 1 and 5 May. I know of three unusually early April sightings: two on the 1st (1956, Jefferson, E. Degner; 1967, Outagamie, A. S. Bradford) and one on the 5th (1967, Fond du Lac, R. A. Knuth).

But in April observers find only small numbers. And most April records of white terns refer to Forster's Terns. Along Lake Michigan migrating flocks of Commons build up rapidly in early May, peaking (sometimes up to 15,000) between 10 and 20 May. By contrast, flocks at most inland locations, including the Mississippi River, rarely exceed 15 birds. Migrants remain through 5 June east and west and through 15 June along Lake Superior.

It is not easy for the casual observer to differentiate between migrants and nesting birds in June. Until recently relatively small numbers nested in Wisconsin. Kumlien and Hollister (1903) used to find a few pairs breeding in Jefferson County, and B. F. Goss (1887) collected eggs in Waukesha County. In the late 1940s, J. L. Kaspar recorded the nesting of 60 pairs in Fond du Lac County. Common Terns formerly nested in considerable numbers on the Door County islands.

But by the early 1970s it was clear that breeding numbers were declining, and in 1979 the bird was added to the state's endangered species list. In a thorough search of the Lake Superior shoreline in 1974, J. T. Harris and S. W. Matteson (1975a,b) could find but three small Wisconsin colonies totaling 56 nests. Nearly all resulted in failure, presumably because of the combined effects of dense vegetation and human disturbance; this species is highly susceptible to changes in water level. In a similar 1976 search in northeastern Wisconsin from Manitowoc north (including the Door County islands), T. C. Erdman (pers. comm.) located only 110 nests. Expanding Ring-billed

Gull nesting populations also pose a threat to the nesting success of Common Terns.

In 1979 the only known Wisconsin Common Tern nesting location along Lake Superior was a small colony in Chequamegon Bay at Ashland (called the Ashland Pier), although there were other nesting pairs just across the state line at Duluth (Matteson 1979). In 1984 at least 134 Common Tern pairs nested at the Ashland Pier, up 235% since 1979. Across the bay at Washburn (Bayfield County), Commons began to recolonize a former site; here, six pairs nested in 1984. And in Superior about 13 pairs attempted nesting on Wisconsin Point (Matteson 1984). Elsewhere in Wisconsin during 1984, Matteson reported that 35 pairs nested at a small island in western Lake Winnebago and about 55 pairs nested on a dredge spoil island in Green Bay. Experiments with artificial nest platforms are showing encouraging results.

Most egg-laying takes place between 1 and 15 June, with young on the wing in early July. But studies by Matteson (1982) have shown a significant amount of incubation through 20 July, followed by fledging in early August. It is uncertain whether the later nestings are by younger adults or by birds whose first nests have failed. In both northwestern and northeastern Wisconsin, nonbreeding individuals augment summer populations.

Autumn flocks along Lake Michigan do not approximate the size of spring concentrations. One explanation for this is the length of the migratory season. Whereas in spring the period lasts but 6 weeks, with a concentrated 2-week span, the fall flight extends over a 12-week period from 1 August to 20 October, with a broad 10 September–10 October peak.

Along Lake Superior there is a gradual reduction after 15 September and a general pull-out by 5 October. At Green Bay last sightings occur between 15 and 20 October; it is 5 days later in the southeast. Individuals lingering into November have been recorded on the 6th (1958, Brown, E. D. Cleary), 10th (1948, Milwaukee, G. H. Orians), and 28th (1953, Brown, E. O. Paulson).

Even more remarkable than the 28 November straggler was a bird observed at Racine on 29 December 1966 (R. E. Fiehweg). It was reported as a Common Tern (*Pass. Pigeon* 29:138), but the description does not rule out the possibility of its being a Forster's Tern.

Arctic Tern (*Sterna paradisaea*)

STATUS. Rare spring migrant; accidental fall migrant.
HABITAT. Great Lakes.
MIGRATION DATES. *Spring:* late April to mid-June. *Fall:* mid-July to early August. *Extremes:* 24 April, 22 June; 16 July, 13 August.
PORTRAIT. *Birds of Wisconsin:* Plate 39.

Kumlien and Hollister (1903) listed this species as "a somewhat irregular migrant, at times fairly common, and again quite the opposite." Four nesting records were mentioned: at Lake Koshkonong in Jefferson County in 1871 and 1872, at Green Bay in 1879, and again at Lake Koshkonong in June 1891. Two Arctic Tern specimens were documented: one parent collected at the Lake Koshkonong nesting site in June 1891 and one partly destroyed specimen discovered

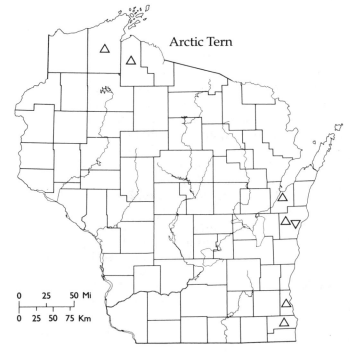

Arctic Tern

0   25   50 Mi
0 25 50 75 Km

△   Late April to mid-June
▽   16 July to 13 August

Records since 1960

Arctic Tern, 25 April 1965, Brown County (photo by T. C. Erdman)

near Milton (Rock County) by H. H. T. Jackson on 27 May 1899. Kumlien and Hollister thought of this species as "readily distinguished from either of these [Forster's and Common] by its smaller, redder bill and much darker underparts." Schoenebeck (1902) also mentioned a specimen from Oconto on 21 September 1897.

Unfortunately no one can locate any of the specimens. In the 1940s, tern investigations indicated that the bill color was unreliable for field identification purposes. This led Schorger, in his 1951 commentary on Kumlien and Hollister, to stipulate, "This bird must be removed from the list as there is no specimen for the state."

But it now appears that Kumlien and Hollister were correct. While reexamining in 1975 some tern photographs taken in Green Bay 10 years earlier, on 25 April 1965, T. C. Erdman discovered two birds that showed a darker breast, a more pronounced white area on the side of the face below the black cap, and decidedly shorter legs. George Watson of the Smithsonian Institution eventually confirmed Erdman's suspicions: the photographs proved the presence of two Arctic Terns (Erdman 1976b).

Erdman carefully scrutinized two birds at Green Bay on 8 May 1976 and identified them as Arctic Terns. These were among a flock of 150 Common Terns, which afforded excellent comparisons. Additional documented records include two birds sighted at Madison on 15 May 1922 by Warner Taylor (1923)

and an exceptionally well-documented bird at Racine on 22 June 1974 sighted by L. W. Erickson (*Pass. Pigeon* 37:27).

I suspect that this species has passed through Wisconsin frequently—unnoticed—in May and early June. With more attention being given to the white terns congregating on the beaches between Manitowoc and Two Rivers, observers spotted individuals in May and early June in 1979, 1980, 1981, 1983, 1987, and, in 1988, on 24–26 April. Additional 1980 observations took place in Milwaukee on 7 May (D. K. Gustafson) and 10 June (D. D. Tessen) and in Bayfield County on 15 May (S. D. Robbins). I detected another in Ashland County on 24 May 1984.

The frequency of these sightings in the past decade, combined with several recent Minnesota sightings, suggests that more records will be forthcoming from Lakes Michigan and Superior between 25 April and 20 June. Beyond 22 June Wisconsin's only recent records concern an individual sighted between 6 and 13 August (1980, Manitowoc, C. R. Sontag) and one on 16 July (1988, Manitowoc, W. Mueller).

Forster's Tern (*Sterna forsteri*)

STATUS. Uncommon migrant. Uncommon summer resident east, north, and west.
HABITAT. Great Lakes. Inland lakes. Ponds.
MIGRATION DATES. *Spring:* mid-April to early June. *Fall:* early August to mid-October. *Extremes:* 5 April; 8 November.
BREEDING DATA. Nests with eggs: 28 May to 20 July. Clutch size: usually 3 eggs; occasionally 2.
WINTER. One January record.
PORTRAIT. *Birds of Wisconsin:* Plate 39.

The Forster's Tern has had a checkered history in Wisconsin. Kumlien and Hollister (1903) referred to it as a common migrant, with modest numbers breeding at numerous inland locations. By 1919 Hollister noted that the birds had disappeared from the haunts in Delavan (Walworth County) where he had previously found them regularly. Its status through the 1920s and 1930s was poorly documented, but the first edition of the Wisconsin Society for Ornithology's *Wisconsin Birds* checklist (Barger et al. 1942) listed the Forster's as a "fairly common transient visitor; rare summer resident."

By 1961 a sizable nesting colony had developed at Horicon Marsh in Dodge County, and by 1964 birds were known to be nesting in the Green Bay region. The Green Bay colony expanded to an estimated high of 700 pairs in 1969, then dropped to under 200 pairs

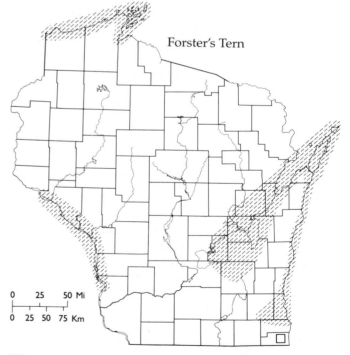

Forster's Tern

0   25   50 Mi

0 25 50 75 Km

▨ Summer range
▢ 2 January

Records since 1960

by 1978 because of high water and destruction of marsh habitat (T. C. Erdman, pers. comm.).

Smaller nesting colonies in eastern Wisconsin have been active during the 1970s in Winnebago, Marquette, Green Lake, Dodge, Jefferson, and Waukesha counties, but these have also shown relatively poor nesting success. In 1977 an intensive summer survey of the Mississippi River region revealed three small colonies totaling 34 nests in Crawford, Vernon, and Buffalo counties (D. H. Thompson, pers. comm.). The poor reproductive success and subsequent population decline led the Department of Natural Resources to place this species on the endangered species list in 1979.

The location of nesting colonies has shifted from year to year, depending upon water levels and availability of suitable habitat, rendering difficult an annual census of population levels. But since 1978, extensive studies by Harris and Trick (1979) and Mossman (1981) all point to very poor reproductive success. Sizable numbers apparently do not attempt to nest, and many pairs that do lose out to storms, changing water levels, and human disturbance.

Although breeders are concentrated in the marshes and estuaries of the eastern counties and along the Mississippi River, spring migrants are widely distributed around the state where extensive shallow-water areas exist. A few migrants may appear by 15 April, with exceptional early-April birds noted on the 5th (1972, La Crosse, J. R. Rosso), 9th (1981, Fond du Lac, T. R. Schultz), and 10th (1969, Washington, D. K. Gustafson). Most areas receive their first arrivals about 25 April. Nonbreeders move on by 5 June.

As nesting colonies disband in early August, birds spread out to some extent in the eastern region of the state. But there is no marked flight. Observers spot birds in small numbers through August and September and during the first half of October. Most sightings come from the eastern half of the state. But more careful coverage since 1973 has resulted in 10 observations in Pierce, St. Croix, and Barron counties between 28 August and 25 September.

The latest dates on record are November sightings on the 1st (1980, Sheboygan, D. D. Tessen), 2nd (1980, Manitowoc, C. R. Sontag), and 8th (1946, Milwaukee, G. H. Orians). Beyond that there is one phenomenal winter record: a single bird recorded at Kenosha on 2 January 1971 (L. W. Erickson).

Least Tern (*Sterna antillarum*)

STATUS. Casual migrant. Casual summer visitant.
HABITAT. Great Lakes. Inland lakes.
MIGRATION DATES. Observed between 28 May and 20 August.
PORTRAIT. *Birds of Wisconsin:* Plate 39.

Only one of six Least Tern specimens reported to have been collected has ever received proper documentation: an immature female taken east of Cedar Grove (Sheboygan County) on 19 August 1934 by Jung (1935a), now in the collection of the Milwaukee Public Museum. A specimen taken by I. N. Mitchell in Green Lake County is located in the Oshkosh Public Museum, but bears no date. Kumlien and Hollister (1903) mentioned three full-plumaged birds shot at Lake Koshkonong in Jefferson County by Ludwig Kumlien in June 1893; but they provided no exact date, and the whereabouts of the specimens are unknown. Also lost is a bird Kumlien and Hollister saw mounted in a Janesville store and believed to have been collected near that city. No date is known.

Three wanderers have been photographed. On 3 and 4 June 1969, R. A. Knuth found a bird near the south end of Lake Winnebago at Fond du Lac, stalked and photographed it, and showed it to numerous other observers (*Pass. Pigeon* 32:65). On 29 May 1980 a

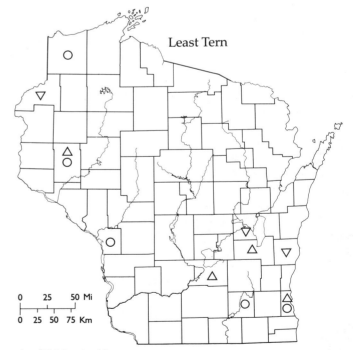

Least Tern

0   25   50 Mi
0 25 50 75 Km

△   28 May to 4 June
○   14 June to 2 August
▽   17 to 20 August

All records

Least Tern, 14 June 1984, La Crosse County (photo by F. Z. Lesher)

Milwaukee bird was photographed by J. H. Idzikowski after R. P. Gutschow had discovered it (*Pass. Pigeon* 43:32–33). F. Z. Lesher photographed an adult that lingered at La Crosse from 14 June to 2 August 1984 (*Pass. Pigeon* 47:82).

I know of six additional sight records. On 20 August 1936, F. S. Dayton observed a bird at Oshkosh "scolding me right over my head amidst a great concourse of terns and gulls" (pers. comm.; MPM files). Another bird put on a fine display at the Crex Meadows Wildlife Area in Burnett County on 17 August 1971, witnessed by more than 50 observers during a Wisconsin Audubon camp field trip. The bird flew within 25 feet of the birders as they watched and as R. A. Knuth took notes (*Pass. Pigeon* 34:78).

Winnie Woodmansee detected another Milwaukee visitor on 8 and 9 July 1982 (*Pass. Pigeon* 45:68–69). Janine Polk discovered one in Dunn County on 14 June 1983, and watched it for an hour in comparison with nearby Black and Forster's Terns (*Pass. Pigeon* 46:94). Four years later, on 28 May 1987, Polk found another Least Tern at the same Dunn County location (*Pass. Pigeon* 50:88). Between 28 and 30 May 1987, Allen and Susan Shea et al. documented the presence of yet another in Columbia County (*Pass. Pigeon* 50:88–89). The northernmost record is of a bird in Douglas County seen by Jane Stephan on 19 June 1986 (*Pass. Pigeon* 49:114).

Sooty Tern (*Sterna fuscata*)

STATUS. Accidental. One record.
HABITAT. Normally oceanic.

A freshly road-killed specimen caught the eye of Peter McCormick along a Columbia County highway on 10 September 1984. He recognized the bird as something unusual, and took it to R. A. Hunt, one of Wisconsin's waterfowl specialists. Hunt identified the specimen as a Sooty Tern, and forwarded it to the Milwaukee Public Museum for permanent preservation (*Pass. Pigeon* 50:268–269).

This vagrant is much more at home on islands in the Caribbean Sea than in the Great Lakes. But individuals are often caught in Atlantic hurricanes in late summer and blown far off course. In 1979 Hurricane David carried nearly 200 Sooty Terns to New York and New England. Undoubtedly it was Hurricane Diana in early September 1984 that brought this oceanic species to Wisconsin.

White-winged Tern (*Chlidonias leucopterus*)
Formerly White-winged Black Tern

STATUS. Accidental. One record.
HABITAT. Inland lakes.

A female White-winged Tern in breeding condition was shot at Lake Koshkonong in Jefferson County on 5 July 1873 by A. L. Kumlien (Brewer 1874). It was in the company of a large colony of Black Terns and showed a vivid contrast to the others. Kumlien and Hollister (1903) later commented, "The partially denuded abdomen and well formed ova prove that it would have bred—whether with its own kind or with the common species we know not, as no others were seen at the time nor since." T. M. Brewer studied the skin, then placed it in the U.S. National Museum, since at that time it constituted the only North American record for a species that normally ranges through Europe, Asia, and Africa.

It remained the only North American sighting for 90 years. Not until 1963 was a second record established, this time in Virginia. There have been additional sightings since 1970 in Virginia, Delaware, New Jersey, Georgia, Indiana, and New Brunswick.

Black Tern (*Chlidonias niger*)

STATUS. Common migrant. Common summer resident south and east; fairly common summer resident west and north.
HABITAT. Great Lakes. Inland lakes. Ponds.
MIGRATION DATES. *Spring:* late April to late May. *Fall:* late July to late September. *Extremes:* 1 April; 24 October.
BREEDING DATA. Nests with eggs: 23 May to 8 July. Clutch size: usually 3 eggs; occasionally 2 or 4.
PORTRAIT. *Birds of Wisconsin:* Plate 39.

When a Black Tern banded in Waukesha County on 6 July 1952 (R. R. Adams) was recovered in Ecuador on 13 January 1958, the record proved a vivid reminder that these bouncy little terns make a round trip of over 8,000 miles each year. The long northward journey ends in late April or early May in southern Wisconsin. Extremely early migrants have turned up in April on the 1st (1956, Rock, M. T. Maxson), 17th (1963, Jefferson, E. Degner), and 19th (1976, Langlade, B. Pickering). A more typical arrival date is 25 April; numbers build to a 10–20 May peak. The timetable is roughly a week later in the central counties and 2 weeks later in the northern areas. By 30 May, birds are well distributed throughout the state.

Although well represented as a breeding species over the state as a whole, the Black Tern is noticeably more numerous east of a line from La Crosse to Marinette. Northwest of that line favorable marsh habitat is less plentiful, and in some of the most heavily forested counties this tern is found only as an occasional wanderer. But its presence along the Missis-

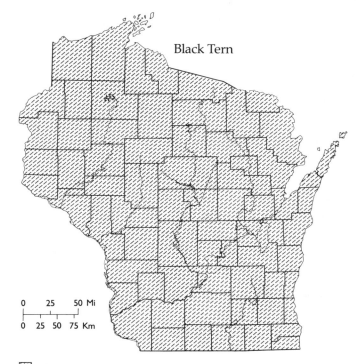

Black Tern

0   25   50 Mi
0 25 50 75 Km

▨ Summer range

Records since 1960

sippi River, in the prairie potholes in St. Croix, Polk, and Burnett counties, and along the Lake Superior marshes, warrants statewide designation as "common" or "fairly common."

The tameness of this noisy little tern on its nesting

grounds has delighted many an observer. I have fond memories of swimming in Madison's Lake Mendota, with terns hovering so closely overhead that I could almost reach up and touch them. When Paul Hoffmann studied the Muskego Lake nesting colony in Waukesha County, birds would alight on his boat and even on his head (E. Hoffmann 1954).

Both Hoffmann and Carl Richter in Oconto County determined that most egg-laying occurred during the last week of May and the first week of June. Richter's nests almost always contained three eggs; Hoffmann's (1954) varied from two to four but usually contained three. Young were usually on the wing in early July.

It is difficult to pinpoint the start of fall migration. Adults lose their breeding plumage in late July. In August birds from farther north begin to migrate, and presumably numbers gradually increase until they reach a peak from 15 to 25 August; by the end of the month an exodus is noticeable. No conspicuous flights of fall migrants have been reported. By 5 September most Lake Superior birds have departed; by the 15th most have gone from the central regions. Only stragglers remain in the south beyond 30 September. The latest dates on record are October birds: the 12th (1940, Dane, W. E. Scott), 13th (1963, Brown, E. O.

Paulson), 15th (1965, Outagamie, A. S. Bradford), and 24th (1972, La Crosse, J. R. Rosso).

Although the BBS may not accurately gauge population changes of marsh-dwelling species, there have been indications that a significant drop in numbers has occurred since that project began in 1966. In 1968 a total of 101 individuals was tallied on 10 transects. In 1975 this species was again found on 10 transects but with a combined total of only 29 individuals. Faanes (1979) monitored six wetland areas in St. Croix and Polk counties in 1975, 1976, and 1977 and determined that the number of breeding pairs dropped from 42 to 18 during those 3 years.

This apparent decline led to a statewide survey sponsored by the Department of Natural Resources in 1979 with over 75 volunteers participating. Fluctuations in water level and changes in vegetation make year-to-year comparisons difficult. But results described by project leader Tilghman (1980) indicated breeding birds present in at least 48 Wisconsin counties. Mossman (1980b) subsequently reported on 127 nests, with an average clutch size of 2.65 but a poor fledging rate. He estimated that for every four eggs laid, only one young fledged. Continued decline is occurring for reasons unknown.

Family **Alcidae:** Alcids

Dovekie (*Alle alle*)

STATUS. Accidental. Two records.
HABITAT. Normally oceanic.

On 11 January 1908 some boys hunting along the Lake Michigan shore at Port Washington (Ozaukee County) shot a Dovekie, a small Atlantic alcid. Dr. C. W. Beemer of that city identified the strange bird, had it mounted, then donated the specimen to the Milwaukee Public Museum. Ward (1908a,b) confirmed and documented the record.

Forty-one years later a second state record was procured when Joe Rice found a dead bird underneath some power lines 10 miles north of Tomah (Monroe County) on 3 March 1949. The bird was taken to

Dorothy Mead of Tomah for tentative identification. She then forwarded the specimen to the University of Wisconsin–Madison for confirmation and preservation. John Emlen examined the specimen, photographed it, and determined that the stomach contained nothing but a single piece of quartz (*Pass. Pigeon* 11:95–97).

It is well known that this species is apt to be blown off course during severe Atlantic storms in winter. But this usually means it is blown inland to New York and New England or south along the Atlantic Coast. There are known occurrences in Manitoba, Minnesota, and Michigan, but they are extremely rare.

Ancient Murrelet (*Synthliboramphus antiquus*)

STATUS. Accidental. Five records.
HABITAT. Inland lakes.
MIGRATION DATES. Observed on 2 April and between an unknown date in October and 9 December.

Could there possibly be a small breeding population of Ancient Murrelets in northern Canada that has so far escaped attention? Such a question arises naturally from the realization that there are five records for Wisconsin, six for Minnesota, six for central and eastern Canada, as well as single records for Colorado, Nebraska, and Ohio. A remarkable wandering record for a bird thought to be limited to the Pacific Coast!

Wisconsin's first specimen was procured in October 1882 at Lake Koshkonong in Jefferson County by G. E Gordon. Sennett (1884) examined it, and Kumlien and Hollister (1903) sketched it, but it remained in Mr. Gordon's possession. The present whereabouts of the specimen are unknown.

A second record was established at Lodi (Columbia County) on 9 December 1941 when three small boys captured an exhausted bird swimming in Spring Creek on the edge of town. When the bird was taken to H. L. Van Ness for identification, he made sketches and a written description before releasing it. Subsequent efforts by others to find the wanderer the next

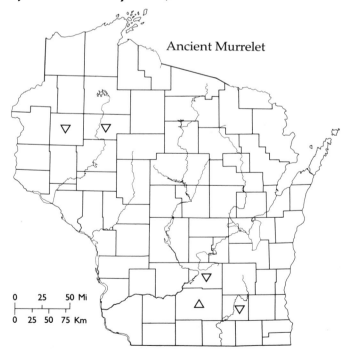

Ancient Murrelet

0   25   50 Mi
0 25 50 75 Km

△   2 April
▽   Late October to 9 December

All records

day were unsuccessful. When the sketch and description were sent to the Smithsonian Institution for positive identification, the verdict was—an immature Ancient Murrelet (*Pass. Pigeon* 3:102).

Another live, though exhausted, bird was found on a lawn near Tony (Rusk County) on 10 November 1964 by Alvin Christman. Warden Lester Tiews cared for the bird until its death on 12 November, then forwarded the specimen to the University of Wisconsin–Madison collection. When a photograph and story first appeared in print (*Pass. Pigeon* 27:146–147), the bird was erroneously listed as a Dovekie; subsequent examination, however, led to a corrected identification as an adult female Ancient Murrelet.

On 2 April 1967 Nicki Russos rescued a bird floating live on Lake Monona in Madison, but it was too emaciated to survive. James Hale confirmed the identification and gave the specimen to the University of Wisconsin–Madison (*Pass. Pigeon* 30:99).

Jerry Perkins found a dead bird 5 miles west of Barron on 12 November 1975. Craig Faanes confirmed the identification, then added the specimen to the collection of the University of Wisconsin–River Falls (*Pass. Pigeon* 38:127).

Why have Ancient Murrelets turned up in Wisconsin? No evidence of an arctic breeding ground or a Great Lakes winter area has been found. A more widely held theory is that autumn storms in the Pacific may catch an occasional migrant and blow it far off course. Most of the extralimital wanderings have been noted in late October and November, and the condition of exhaustion suggests that the birds have traveled far on little food.

Family **Columbidae**: Pigeons, Doves

Rock Dove (*Columba livia*)

STATUS. Common resident south and central; fairly common resident north. Introduced.
HABITAT. City parks. Farmsteads. Open cropland.
BREEDING DATA. Nests with eggs: probably April through August. Clutch size: 2 eggs.

This species did not appear on any published regional or statewide bird roster until 1942 when it made the first edition of *Wisconsin Birds: A Preliminary Checklist with Migration Charts* (Barger et al. 1942) as a "common permanent resident; introduced." Doubtless it had been present in the state for many previous years, but it was looked upon strictly as a domesticated bird, raised and kept by pigeon-fanciers for sport, research, or simply a household pet. Records of the Milwaukee Public Museum show that the institution's first specimens were obtained in 1905. Leon Cole began using pigeons for his famous genetics studies soon after coming to Madison in 1910. How long before that the first introductions occurred in Wisconsin is not known.

Off and on some observers reported Rock Doves on the CBC between 1942 and 1954. Other observers declined to list them, noting that pigeons in city parks were so tame they could virtually be fed in the hand. The counting was discontinued in 1955 but was resumed in 1974 as part of a new continental policy. Although we do not know that all pigeons are truly wild birds, this species has been expanding and developing independently.

CBC figures point to a rapid increase within the past 30 years. In 1953 Rock Doves appeared on 18 of 44 counts. The highest total for an individual count area was 93, and the composite total of doves was 505. In 1976 doves were found on 61 of 65 counts, with a composite total of 14,013. The tally was over 1,000 on 2 counts, over 100 on 33 more.

When the BBS began in 1966, observers were asked to count this species along with all others. Pigeons have been recorded on 58 of the state's 70 routes, being missed mainly on forest-dominated transects in northern Wisconsin. Since few of the 70 routes happen to pass through urban areas, BBS sightings reflect mainly rural populations—birds often perched atop barns and silos or feeding in grain fields. It is clear from the accompanying map that while the Rock

Rock Dove

Breeding Bird Survey, averages 1966 to 1980

Dove is present in all parts of the state in summer as well as winter, numbers are far more concentrated in the southeast.

Population increases have been most evident in the cities. Birds nest and roost on tall buildings and often congregate in flocks of 100 or more. Droppings on buildings and city sidewalks are considered a nuisance by urban residents. Extermination or control programs were undertaken in numerous cities in southern and central Wisconsin in recent years.

Appreciate or eliminate? Witness the conflict among officers of a church in central Wisconsin when pigeons gathered in the cupola and cooed loud enough to distract Sunday worshippers. Two officers climbed to the cupola and blocked it off with wire mesh, forcing the birds to roost elsewhere. Two days later another church officer was seen descending from the same tower, metal shears in hand; he had just cut an opening in the wire mesh and sprinkled corn for the displaced doves.

Mourning Dove (*Zenaida macroura*)

STATUS. Common migrant south and central; uncommon migrant north. Common summer resident south and central; uncommon summer resident north. Uncommon winter resident south and central; rare winter resident north.

HABITAT. Farmsteads. Residential areas. Conifer plantations.

MIGRATION DATES. *Spring:* mid-March to late April. *Fall:* late August to mid-October.

BREEDING DATA. Nests with eggs: 14 April to 13 September. Clutch size: 2 eggs.

WINTER. Regularly present north to St. Croix, Barron, Chippewa, Lincoln, Langlade, and Marinette counties; occasionally present north to Douglas and Ashland counties.

PORTRAIT. *Birds of Wisconsin:* Plate 40.

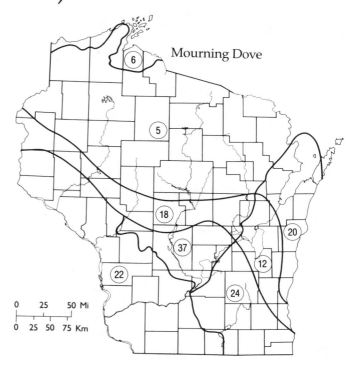

Breeding Bird Survey, averages 1966 to 1980

At first glance it would appear that there has been little change in the status of this delightful bird since 1850. Hoy (1853b) called the Mourning Dove "common," and his contemporary Barry (1854) preferred the term "abundant." It was "common" to Kumlien and Hollister (1903) as well, and "abundant" to Lowe (1915). There are years when "abundant" might be substituted for "common" today in the central and west-central counties during late summer.

But the likelihood is that these reporters wrote about their local areas in the southeast and did not represent the state as a whole. The Mourning Dove is not common in the northern regions now, and it is doubtful that it ever has been. But as agriculture has spread north, so has the range of the dove.

The accompanying BBS summer distribution map shows the breeding range to be statewide, with wide variations in abundance. These doves are decidedly more numerous south of the tension zone, and in the central sand area they are twice as numerous as anywhere else in the state.

Although they are not the very first spring migrants to appear, the vanguard of Mourning Doves usually reaches the southern and central counties between 20 and 30 March. The bird often takes another 10 days to reach the northernmost counties. By 15 April the distribution is quite complete in the southern and central portions, and by 25 April the northern birds also are ready to nest.

In the south nesting is usually under way by 25 April, occasionally by the 15th. Cold and snow are a real threat to mid-April attempts. Adults have been known to perish on the nest while trying to protect eggs from spring snow. Even in the north, where

nesting starts in early May, pairs complete three nestings in a year. Mathiak (1953) kept data on 110 nests in Dodge County in 1950, showing nest sites to vary in height from 4 to 40 feet, averaging 13 feet. Preferences shown for various trees included willows (42), spruce (26), red cedar (13) and box elder (7). Five pairs chose to nest in rain gutters.

Considerable flocking takes place by early August as young of earlier nests mature. By early September flocks may number 100–200. The autumn exodus is under way by that time and continues apace throughout September. By the 25th, withdrawal from the north is virtually complete. The sizable flocks still present in southern and central Wisconsin through October may either be late migrants or birds that will overwinter.

The most striking change in status concerning this species involves its winter status. The nineteenth-century writers mentioned occasional wintering. Throughout the first half of the twentieth century, wintering flocks were few and far between, deserving of special mention. CBC records show that, as recently as 1955, the 37 counts—representative of most sections of the state—produced a total of 211 doves, an average of 6 birds per count. The per-count average then rose to 21 (1960), 30 (1966), 62 (1970), and 89 (1975). The figure for 1973, 102 per count, was perhaps inflated by the huge total of 1,601 at Beloit that year. Some of these CBC birds undoubtedly succumb as the winter wears on, and others probably survive with frozen feet.

Those birds that migrate to warmer climates fall into two groups. Commenting on winter banding recoveries, F. H. Wagner (1956, p. 15) showed that one group winters in Georgia and Florida, with an occa-sional individual reaching Cuba. A second group winters in Louisiana, Texas, and Mexico. It would be oversimplification to assume that all southeastern individuals belong to the eastern race *carolinensis* and that all southwestern birds represent the western race *marginella*. But examination of specimens in the Milwaukee Public Museum has proved that both subspecies come to Wisconsin. The two forms are indistinguishable in the field.

Passenger Pigeon (*Ectopistes migratorius*)

STATUS. Extinct. Formerly abundant migrant; abundant summer resident; rare winter visitant.
PORTRAIT. *Birds of Wisconsin:* Plate 40.

The story of the abundance of the Passenger Pigeon, the prodigious nesting season of 1871, and the bird's subsequent extirpation in 1899 has been told in far greater detail (Schorger 1937b, 1951b,c, 1955; Scott 1947a) than I can relate here. In 1950, in the early stages of the preparation for this volume, A. W. Schorger prepared a manuscript for O. J. Gromme, portions of which I quote here.

"The Passenger Pigeon was a wanderer in its search for food, but its migration in spring was as regular as that of the waterfowl and contemporaneous with it. It arrived in the state as soon as the ground showed areas bare of snow, sometimes in February, but usually in'March.

"Several hundred dates on the spring migration in Wisconsin have been collected, covering a period of forty-six years. There were only six years in which the Passenger Pigeon arrived in February: 1848 (February 9, Janesville), 1873 (February 18, Janesville), 1874 (February 21, Appleton), 1877 (February 20, Two Rivers), 1880 (February 26, Mineral Point), and 1882 (February 7, Racine and Baraboo). The spring arrival, during twenty-seven years, ranged from March 2 to 28, the average being March 16. During the twelve years of April arrivals, the dates ranged from the 2nd to the 14th, the average being the 7th. There was but one year, 1857, when it arrived as late as May.

"The fall migration was influenced only slightly by the weather, and by far the largest number of the pigeons moved southward in September. It is difficult to give exact dates on the initiation of migration, since numerous flocks roamed the northern portion of the state throughout the summer. This held also for the southern portion during the middle of the nineteenth century. Small flocks usually reached the southern counties early in August, but the numbers did not become impressive until September. As a rule the bulk of the population passed southward during the first two weeks of September. In some years, e.g., 1881, the large flights took place the last week in the month. Straggling flocks remained into October. On October 21, 1869, pigeons were reported numerous at Janesville, and on October 21, 1886, a few were still present at Florence.

"A few birds may have attempted to winter in Wisconsin, but not a single reference to this effect was found. On rare occasions, during mild weather, a flock became sufficiently bold to make a brief intrusion. Pigeons were reported flying in all directions at Madison on December 13, 1875. Two flocks were seen at Watertown on January 3, 1876. During the mild winter of 1881–82, a large flock and two small ones were seen at Platteville on December 24, 1881.

"There were two well defined migration routes in Wisconsin: the valley of the Mississippi and the western shore of Lake Michigan. Flocks frequently left the Mississippi in southwestern Wisconsin and traveled northeast. Those arriving at the foot of Lake Michigan either turned northwest or went directly northward along the shore of the lake.

"Passenger Pigeons were drowned in large numbers in Lake Michigan on a few occasions. Mr. Frank Kaufman has written me that he can remember a morning at Two Rivers when dead pigeons were piled three and four feet high along the beach. A fog was much more disastrous than a storm, for the birds became completely helpless in it. In an effort to find a place to alight until the fog lifted, they flew around until exhausted. Pigeons moving along the shore of the lake could become bewildered in a fog of long duration and drown.

"It was characteristic of this species to nest in compact colonies, usually of large size. There were always, however, nestings ranging from single pairs up to several hundreds. These nestings usually took place in late May and June, an indication of delayed sexual maturity. The pigeons arriving in the state in some years were merely migrants. They would not remain to nest unless mast was abundant, but a large supply of food was no assurance that nesting would take place. Michigan drew the pigeons after a good crop of beechnuts, the preferred food. The range of the beech in Wisconsin was limited to a narrow strip along the Lake Michigan shore. Oaks of various species were the predominant forest trees in the southern half of the state, and in some years the crop of acorns was immense.

"Nesting took place in April with considerable regularity in those years in which the birds chose to concentrate in Wisconsin. There were major nestings somewhere in the state approximately once in every two years. The largest nesting ever described took place here in 1871. It was approximately 100 miles long, extending from Grand (Wisconsin) Rapids south to Kilbourn (Wisconsin Dells), then northwest to Black River Falls. The nesting population was estimated at 136,000,000.

"The year 1882 was the last in which the Passenger Pigeon appeared in numbers approaching former years. The decline was then quite rapid until total extinction was reached. During the last decade of the nineteenth century, birds were reported every year.

"It is unnecessary to seek a mysterious cause for the disappearance of this species. The economy of the bird was dependent on vast numbers. It flew by millions, roosted by millions, and nested by millions. There is no denying that its mode of life was enormously successful prior to the arrival of Europeans; nor was there any sound reason to accuse the bird of stupidity because it failed to meet the new conditions.

"The persecution began with the landing of Cartier in 1534, and continued with increasing momentum. As transportation improved, there was an increasing market in the large cities. The pigeon shunned civilization for nesting, but by 1870 scarcely a suitable

nesting area remained that was not adequately close to a railroad. The telegraph kept the professional trappers in touch with the birds' movements so that they had no rest throughout most of the year."

Schorger's summary, the manuscript of which is now in the files of the Milwaukee Public Museum, was the result of extensive research, and one outgrowth of his investigations was the publication in 1955 of a 438-page book, *The Passenger Pigeon: Its Natural History and Extinction*. Schorger delved into hundreds of nineteenth-century newspapers from all parts of the state, interviewed men who had shot and trapped pigeons, and corresponded with ornithologists in Wisconsin and elsewhere. His commentary on the fate of the species was penned with half a century of perspective following the last few Wisconsin records.

Kumlien and Hollister did not have the advantage of this historical perspective when they commented on the state's last few observations. It must have seemed inconceivable to them that the pigeons were gone from Wisconsin—irrevocably—when *The Birds of Wisconsin* was published in 1903. After mentioning 1879–1883 as the last period of abundance, and enumerating six sightings by J. N. Clark in Dunn County between 1886 and 1898, Kumlien and Hollister commented: "Small flocks, pairs and solitary individuals have been reported from various parts of the state nearly every year since this time, however, and it is highly probable that a very few still nest in isolated pairs within its limits."

Members of the Wisconsin Society for Ornithology erected a monument in the pigeons' memory at Wyalusing State Park in 1947. Their wish was that a more enlightened citizenry might learn from the disastrous experiences with the Passenger Pigeon and practice a more far-sighted brand of conservation toward other species of plants and animals. The monument bears the inscription: "Dedicated to the last Wisconsin Passenger Pigeon, shot at Babcock, Sept. 1899. This species became extinct through the avarice and thoughtlessness of man."

Common Ground-Dove (*Columbina passerina*)

STATUS. Accidental. Two records.
HABITAT. Residential areas.

The state's only specimen of the Common Ground-Dove was obtained on 15 October 1973 when a bird was killed flying against a window at Mary Decker's home in Milwaukee. The skin, that of an adult female, has been preserved at the Milwaukee Public Museum (*Pass. Pigeon* 36:126).

Previously, there had been one sight record, on 22 May 1966. Walking along a cinder lane close to her home near West Bend (Washington County), Ann Maurin discovered two sparrow-sized doves just ahead of her. As they walked 25 feet ahead of her, she could see the dovelike head-bobbing behavior. When the birds flew to a nearby tree, she could see stubby tails and rust color on the wings (*Pass. Pigeon* 29:33–34). While there is no conclusive proof that these were not escaped birds, there was nothing in either plumage or behavior to suggest previous captivity.

Although essentially nonmigratory, this southern species has engaged in considerable extralimital wandering—especially in autumn. Within the past 15 years observations have been reported from Illinois, Indiana, Colorado, Missouri, Tennessee, and along the Atlantic Coast north to Maryland and Delaware.

Family **Psittacidae:** Parrots

Carolina Parakeet (*Conuropsis carolinensis*)

STATUS. Extinct. Formerly accidental. One record.

The Milwaukee Public Museum houses a Carolina Parakeet specimen taken by Thure Kumlien in Waukesha County in 1844 (exact date and location not recorded). In connection with this, Kumlien and Hollister (1903) wrote: "Thure Kumlien saw a considerable flock near Lake Koshkonong in 1844 or 1845. One specimen which he secured at this place at an early day was sent to John G. Bell of New York." Nothing further is known of this second specimen.

Wisconsin lay somewhat north of the former range of this gaudy southern bird. Hoy (1853b) stated, "Formerly Parakeets were common on the Mississippi within this state, latterly they are seldom met with." But Schorger (1951a), investigating early Wisconsin historical data, could find nothing to substantiate this claim, raising the possibility that Hoy was relying on hearsay evidence.

The last record of a bird in any midwestern state occurred in 1912; ornithologists have considered the species extinct since 1920.

Family **Cuculidae**: Cuckoos, Anis

Black-billed Cuckoo (*Coccyzus erythropthalmus*)

STATUS. Fairly common migrant. Fairly common summer resident.

HABITAT. Deciduous forest. Upland carr.

MIGRATION DATES. *Spring:* early May to early June. *Fall:* mid-August to late September. *Extremes:* 22 April; 31 October.

BREEDING DATA. Nests with eggs: 22 May to 23 August. Clutch size: usually 3 eggs; occasionally 2–5.

PORTRAIT. *Birds of Wisconsin:* Plate 41.

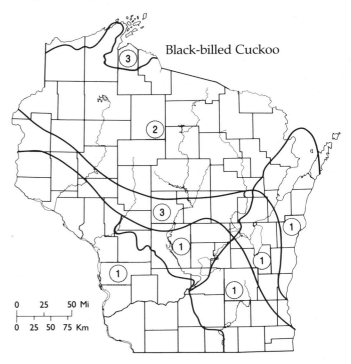

Black-billed Cuckoo

Breeding Bird Survey, averages 1966 to 1980

Considering the state as a whole, BBS figures show the Black-billed Cuckoo outnumbering the Yellow-bill better than 3 to 1. The Black-bill shows an even distribution over the entire state, being equal with *americanus* in the south but much more numerous and widespread in the north. At Chippewa Falls C. A. Kemper banded 41 "Blacks" and only 2 "Yellows" over a 10-year span.

Cuckoos are much more often heard than seen. With training, one learns to distinguish the two species by the quality of voice: soft and dovelike for the Black, harsh and coughlike for the Yellow. More often than not, my first Black-bill in spring is a night migrant, giving its three-syllable call as it passes overhead on a late-May evening.

Usually, 20–30 May is the main migration period for the better part of the state. Finding individuals before 10 May is unusual in the south, although there have been April sightings on the 22nd (1959, Rock, R. E. Ohm), 25th (1974, St. Croix, P. A. Tweet), 26th (1960, Vernon, V. E. Weber), 28th (1957, Marinette, W. N. MacBriar), and 29th (1976, Taylor, J. S. Fadness). The arrival pattern is irregular. In some years arrivals are extensive by 20 May, with most birds on territory by 31 May. In some years very few birds appear until 25 May, prolonging the migration period until 10 June.

The irregularity also carries over into the size of the summer population. A BBS transect containing 3 individuals one year may have 15 the next. Any year in which there is a large infestation of caterpillars is likely to attract higher populations of cuckoos.

Much has been written about the flimsy construction of cuckoo nests. Those seen in Wisconsin are no exception. The birds usually build nests in brushy areas. Of nine nests reported by Grundtvig (1895) in

Outagamie County, three were 5–8 feet up in young trees, three were in bushes 1–3 feet up, and three were in brush. Vos Burgh (1928a) found five nests in Columbia County, all in willow thickets. Three of C. H. Richter's five Oconto County nests were in bushes, and two were in trees 6–14 feet up. Concerning the way the nests were built, Richter related: "I have seen some nests about completely washed away after a severe storm, because of the flat construction. Eggs and sometimes young are lost by simply falling off the nests." It may be because of earlier nesting failures that the nesting season sometimes extends well into August. J. W. Stierle (MPM files) found a nest with three eggs in Wood County on 23 August 1918, a remarkably late date.

The fall migration is an inconspicuous affair with no pronounced buildup of numbers. Some movement is detected from 20 August on, with most fall sightings coming in the 1–15 September period. The birds are rarely seen in the north after 15 September, and in some years birds vanish from the entire state by the end of the month. Usually, however, a few birds linger through 15 October. The state's latest records include two Vernon County birds seen by V. E. Weber (29 October 1960; 31 October 1962), a transient in Sauk County (27 October 1974, P. Ashman), and one in Winnebago County (26 October 1953, E. Fisher).

Yellow-billed Cuckoo (*Coccyzus americanus*)

STATUS. Fairly common migrant south; uncommon migrant central; rare migrant north. Fairly common summer resident south; uncommon summer resident central; rare summer resident north.

HABITAT. Deciduous forest. Upland carr.

MIGRATION DATES. *Spring:* early May to early June. *Fall:* mid-August to late September. *Extremes:* 22 April; 19 November.

BREEDING DATA. Nests with eggs: 18 May to 5 August. Clutch size: usually 3 eggs; rarely 2–5.

PORTRAIT. *Birds of Wisconsin:* Plate 41.

The Yellow-billed is our southern cuckoo, encountered most frequently in the wooded bottomlands of the southern and western counties. It is regularly seen along the Mississippi north to Hager City, along the Chippewa to Eau Claire, along the Wisconsin to Necedah, and along the Rock to Horicon. Suitable woodlands in between these river bottoms harbor a few birds each year. Birds are frequently—but less regularly—found north to Polk, Chippewa, Portage, Outagamie, and Door counties. As can be seen in BBS figures on the accompanying map, the bird's distribution is not widespread in any of these areas.

Seventy years ago this bird appeared to be extending its range. Kumlien and Hollister (1903) stated that "it appears to be more numerous than 35 years ago." Hollister commented on further gains when he revisited his Delavan haunts in Walworth County in 1919. There have been no appreciable gains numerically since then, but there have been more frequent occasional sightings in the northern counties. Careful documentation of summer observations has brought records from Douglas (26 June 1941; collected by O. J. Gromme), Bayfield (15 June 1971; S. D. Robbins), Price (21 June 1965; W. L. Hilsenhoff), Vilas (24 June 1964; S. D. Robbins), Forest (23 June 1967 and 16 June 1972; M. F. Donald), and Florence (8 June 1966; F. Z. Lesher) counties.

The spring arrival pattern is somewhat erratic. Most often, first birds are sighted between 10 and 15 May, the main movement occurring between 20 and 30 May. There are years when scarcely a bird is noted before June. During other years several sightings are made in the 1–10 May period. On four occa-

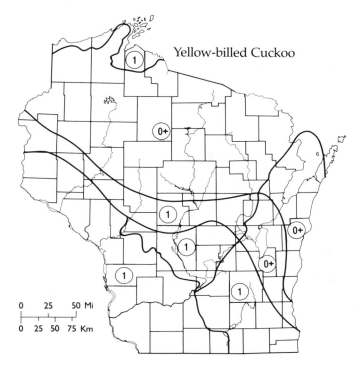

Breeding Bird Survey, averages 1966 to 1980

sions birds have appeared in April: the 22nd (1942, Sawyer, K. W. Kahmann), the 24th (1960, Vernon, V. E. Weber), the 27th (1942, Dunn, I. O. Buss), and the 30th (1964, Vernon, V. E. Weber). The erratic pattern was certainly evident in 1941 when N. R. Barger found a nest with eggs on 18 May, well ahead of what would constitute the typical arrival date in many years.

In some of the backward years nesting has been observed well into August. During other years the majority of birds begin their southward migration in August. Observers have not recorded any noticeable fall flights. Birds are silent from mid-July on, and when migration time comes, the "rain crow" silently disappears. A few remain nearly every year until 10 October, rarely to the 25th. Remarkably late November departures have been recorded on the 5th (1965, Racine, D. Kuehnl), 6th (1961, Vernon, V. E. Weber), 12th (1963, Dane, W. L. Hilsenhoff), and 19th (1970, Milwaukee, M. F. Donald).

Groove-billed Ani (*Crotophaga sulcirostris*)

STATUS. Casual fall visitant.
HABITAT. Upland carr.
MIGRATION DATES. Observed between 24 August and
18 November.

For many years most Wisconsin ornithologists were
unaware that the Groove-billed Ani had ever visited
the state. W. L. Gantenbein collected one at Diamond
Bluff (Pierce County) on 12 October 1913. He mounted
the bird and donated it to the James Ford Bell Museum of Natural History at the University of Minnesota. Having been brought to the museum by a
Winona, Minnesota, resident, the specimen received
a "Winona, Minn." label. It is probably the bird the
AOU *Check-list of North American Birds* mentions as a
Minnesota record. When I visited with Mr. Gantenbein in 1963, I found that both his memory and his
journal clearly indicated that he had collected the bird
on the Wisconsin side of the Mississippi River (Robbins 1964b).

A second state sighting occurred near Stoughton
(Dane County) on 27 October 1949, when Enoch
Reindahl (pers. comm.) spotted a gracklelike bird
with a peculiar bill on a brush pile in his back yard.
The bird was seen also by Mr. Reindahl's brother and
neighbor, and all agreed that "the flight seemed weak
and the tail seemed to trail as though insecurely
fastened."

A third ani, like the first, was long unknown to
Wisconsin ornithology. It was a bird killed at the
Simon Vanderploeg mink ranch near Arpin (Wood
County) in the latter half of September 1953. Don
Follen (pers. comm.) salvaged the bird; remembering
it 28 years later, he wrote, "It looked like a grackle
with an abnormally large parrot-like beak, and it
did have the grooves." He tried to preserve the specimen in a freezer, which unfortunately became dis-
connected, "and the whole smelly mess had to be
discarded."

A fourth ani was accidentally killed in Milwaukee
on 8 November 1968; its skin has been preserved at
the Milwaukee Public Museum.

The Milwaukee Public Museum is also the repository for the fifth state record: a bird that died shortly
after it had been captured near Portage (Columbia
County) on 31 October 1969 by Mr. and Mrs. John
Slepicka and their sons. This bird had been heard and
seen feeding in a brushy area, but much of its tail had
been lost, making flight difficult (*Pass. Pigeon* 32:184).

The state's next sighting occurred in 1973, when a
male was collected in Iowa County on 7 October

Groove-billed Ani

0   25   50 Mi
|—|—|—|
0 25 50 75 Km

▽   24 August to 18 November

All records

(R. S. Ellarson). Odd calls had drawn attention to the
wanderer. The skin has been preserved in the University of Wisconsin–Madison collection.

Green Bay had its turn 2 years later. Amy Kienitz
found a recent roadkill in Brown County on 8 October 1975; she donated the specimen to the University of Wisconsin–Green Bay collection. This bird
was an adult female that had subsisted on grasshoppers (*Pass. Pigeon* 38:128).

The University of Wisconsin–Green Bay collection
received an additional specimen when a bird was
found dead in Manitowoc County on 18 November
1979 (L. Hoffman). A second individual was observed
live on the same date (*Pass. Pigeon* 43:109–110).

Autumn 1981 brought two additional stragglers
to Wisconsin: one observed in Columbia County on
17 October by W. A. Smith, and one found dead in
Marathon County on 23 October by James Bragg and
donated to the University of Wisconsin–Stevens
Point. Anis were also observed at close range at two
Ashland County locations in autumn 1981: one on
Outer Island (26 September, C. Loewecke) and one in
Ashland (21 October, R. L. Verch). But doubt remains
whether these were Groove-billed or Smooth-billed,

or whether they were the same or different individuals (*Pass. Pigeon* 45:84).

Yet another appeared in Buffalo County in 1982, first discovered on 24 August by F. N. Freese. The visitor remained through 11 September, viewed by several other bird-watchers (*Pass. Pigeon* 45:106).

Five years elapsed before the next ani visit. H. W. Kuhn found one on his farm near Elkhart Lake in Sheboygan County on 19 October 1987, but was unable to determine which ani species he was observing (*Pass. Pigeon* 50:269).

Although the Groove-billed Ani is mainly a bird of Mexico and Central America whose range extends only into parts of Texas and Louisiana, its status is listed here as "casual" instead of "accidental" because it appears to be extending its range and may well pay additional visits to the state. Since 1965 the species has appeared in Florida, Tennessee, Ohio, Michigan, Minnesota, South Dakota, Missouri, Arkansas, Oklahoma, New Mexico, and Arizona. In every case these have been fall sightings between late August and early December. Observers should check flocks of Common Grackles in brushy areas carefully for possible future discoveries in Wisconsin.

Family **Tytonidae:** Barn Owls

Barn Owl (*Tyto alba*)
Formerly Common Barn-Owl

STATUS. Rare summer resident south and central. Rare winter resident south and central.

HABITAT. Farmsteads. City parks.

MIGRATION DATES. Uncertain. *Spring:* probably mid-March to late April. *Fall:* probably October–November.

BREEDING DATA. Nests with eggs: 20 April to 20 August. Nests with young: to 17 November. Clutch size: 3–6 eggs.

WINTER. Rarely present north to Polk, Clark, Vilas, and Marinette counties.

PORTRAIT. *Birds of Wisconsin:* Plate 42.

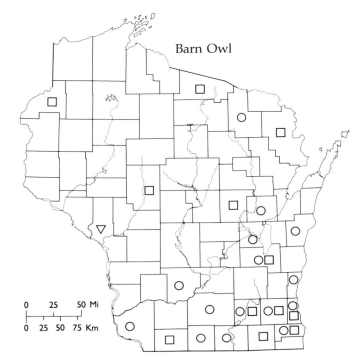

Barn Owl

△ Mid-March to late April
○ Late April to late September
▽ Early October to late November
□ Early December to mid-March

Records since 1960

Apparently the Barn Owl has always been an uncommon species in any part of Wisconsin at any season. Reports from nineteenth-century observers are sparse. Schorger (1951a), commenting on Kumlien and Hollister's (1903) appraisal, wrote, "This species remains uncommon as it is unable to cope with a severe winter." He listed only six nesting records between 1924 and 1950.

Sightings published in *The Passenger Pigeon* for any season totaled 24 in the 1940s, 16 in the 1950s, 23 in the 1960s, 10 in the 1970s, and 9 in the 1980s. Since 1966, published records have numbered no more than two in any year, and, as a result, Department of Natural Resources personnel undertook an investigation into the status of the bird. LeRoy Petersen's extensive efforts, by means of questionnaires, media publicity, and rewards, to uncover sightings between 1973 and 1979 turned up only seven reports he deemed "likely" (Petersen 1980). In 1979 this bird was placed on Wisconsin's endangered species list.

Most observations have come from the southeastern counties, south of a line from Platteville to Port Washington. Before 1950, occasional reports came from as far north as La Crosse, Adams, Waupaca, and Brown counties. Since 1960 the only birds noted north of the Grant-Ozaukee County line have been a small cluster of individuals in the Lake Winnebago region, lone birds in Sauk (22 June 1971, D. K. Gustafson), Polk (21 December 1985, H. Jorgenson), Trempealeau (11 November 1978, K. Roll), Clark (1–20 December 1983, D. G. Follen), Waupaca (12 January 1985, M. S. Peter-

son), and Forest (10–13 August 1987, S. Burns) counties, and individuals found dead or dying in Vilas (early December 1988, T. C. Erdman) and Marinette (6 February 1989, T. C. Erdman) counties.

Wisconsin has few April records, but when birds are seen during that month, they may already be nesting. D. D. Berger found a nest with six eggs in Fond du Lac on 20 April 1961 (*Pass. Pigeon* 23:145). In April 1899, H. H. T. Jackson found a nest with three eggs in Green County (Kumlien and Hollister 1903).

Since 1940 the number of May records published in *The Passenger Pigeon* is four times the number of April sightings, implying that there is a modest migratory movement in late April and May. But the data are too fragmentary to suggest the precise migratory period.

Most nest discoveries occur in June, July, or early August when adults are feeding young. Old silos, unused barn lofts, and vacant structures are most frequently selected for nesting purposes. In 1961 one pair used a cupola atop a Fond du Lac fire station. In 1980 a church steeple in Ozaukee County played host to an owl family. Tree cavities are occasionally used. In 1984 a pair nested in a silver maple cavity in Dane County (S. W. Matteson, pers. comm.). Nest boxes have been used successfully in other states, but there are no records of such use in Wisconsin.

Wisconsin has no proven record of a pair nesting more than once in a season, although double-brooding is known in other states. The possibility that a pair may raise a second family is suggested by the discovery of nests with young well into the fall: September observations in 1950 (Ozaukee, C. P. Frister), 1966 (Milwaukee, D. D. Berger), 1974 (Green, L. R. Petersen [Petersen and Petersen 1975]), and 1980 (Ozaukee, R. Wolf) and November sightings in 1954 (Winnebago, F. Holman King) and 1973 (Jefferson, L. R. Petersen [Petersen and Petersen 1975]).

Aside from these observations of autumn breeding-related activities, Barn Owl sightings after August are rare. A bird spotted in October or November might still be engaged in raising young, migrating, or preparing to spend the winter. The irregular movement patterns are illustrated by banding recoveries made of six nestlings from Milwaukee (D. D. Berger, pers. comm. 1953). One owlet was recaptured in Dane County the following October, a second was taken in Florida in November, and a third was discovered in Florida the following June. Other individuals banded by Berger in subsequent years have been recovered in Kentucky, Ohio, and Louisiana. Yet another recapture came in Milwaukee on 20 December 1953, 18 months after banding. In Waupaca County on 12 January 1985, M. S. Peterson discovered a dead bird that had been banded in Iowa in 1984.

A few birds do not migrate. It is probable that those few individuals that overwinter in Wisconsin have a difficult time. For sustenance they are heavily dependent on small rodents, hard to find when snow deepens. Three instances of emaciated birds found dead in early February attest to this problem. An individual trapped near Chili (Clark County) on 1 December 1985 had been feeding on Rock Doves and appeared to be healthy. But it died on 23 December, following a series of nights with subzero temperatures (Follen 1986b). However, three mid-March sightings suggest that wintering hangers-on sometimes survive. The individuals found nesting in April are likely to be birds that overwintered successfully.

Family **Strigidae:** Typical Owls

Eastern Screech-Owl (*Otus asio*)

STATUS. Fairly common resident south; uncommon resident central; rare resident north.
HABITAT. Residential areas. Deciduous forest. Farmsteads.
BREEDING DATA. Nests with eggs: 31 March to 31 May. Clutch size: usually 3–5 eggs; occasionally 6.
WINTER. Regularly present north to Polk, Marathon, and Oconto counties.
PORTRAIT. *Birds of Wisconsin:* Plate 43.

If one were to rely on CBC data, one might draw a line from St. Croix Falls through Wausau to Marinette and presume that the Eastern Screech-Owl is absent north of that line, present in small numbers throughout the central counties, and more numerous in the southern regions. The one exception to the rule would be an individual recorded in Douglas County in December 1974 (B. F. Klugow).

Late December, however, is not the most propitious time to appraise the population status of this species. The owl does little calling until February and March, and it is strictly nocturnal in its habits. Nonetheless, this is indeed a rare species in the northern quarter of the state. I know of two additional Douglas County records: a roadkill at Superior on 1 November 1967 (A. Nelson), and an individual noted on 13 September 1980 (R. M. Hoffman). Another bird was found dead in Oneida County on 14 March 1979 (P. V. Vanderschaegen). Wintering individuals were noted in Washburn (1963, B. A. Bailey) and Langlade (1980, L. J. Schimmels) counties.

When Gromme (1963) depicted a statewide range, it was shortly after members of his museum staff had encountered northern birds in Price (1940) and Iron (1946) counties. Birds have not been recorded in these counties since, and there are suspicions that the northern range limit is receding. Richter (1939a) had already detected a decline in Oconto County; he found numerous nests in the 1920s, but none after 1934. In my years of residence in St. Croix County (1960–1968) and Chippewa County (1968–1978) I witnessed a noticeable decline.

These birds prefer large, old deciduous trees near the outskirts of residential areas. They need trees with large cavities which provide suitable roosting and nesting areas. Apple orchards used to provide

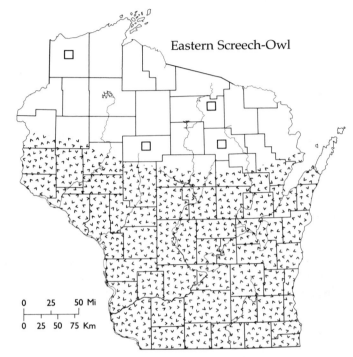

Eastern Screech-Owl

0   25   50 Mi
0   25 50 75 Km

☑ Resident range
☐ Mid-November to late March

Records since 1960

favorable habitat, but since fruit-growers have become meticulous in removing dead wood, trees with cavities are no longer found there. In some areas these owls have taken over artificial nest boxes intended for Wood Ducks. Out of 10 nests found in the Columbus area, 9 occupied oak cavities and 1 an elm (vos Burgh 1913a). Five of eight Oconto County nests were in ash trees, 25–30 feet up, the others 8–15 feet up in oaks. In several instances cavities were used that had originally been dug by Northern Flickers. Eggs are often laid on a bed of dead leaves, but in a few instances the rotted wood lining the bottom of a cavity has sufficed.

Most foraging is done after dark. Francis Dayton (pers. comm. to O. J. Gromme) described the owls' habit of feeding on roosting House Sparrows: "These little owls in fall and winter grab the roosting sparrows out of their nests and out of the holes and crevices. I have seen [the owls] at night come up under the eaves of the porches and take the sparrows out from under the eaves."

Some birders have had success in eliciting a response from an owl by imitating its distinctive whinny. On a few occasions I have whistled this call in broad daylight, hoping to attract the attention of migrating chickadees and warblers, and have been surprised by a whinnied response from a Screech-Owl I did not know was present.

The observers who have the best success in locating

these mysterious little featherballs are those who play tape-recorded calls in wooded residential neighborhoods, city parks, or college campuses during early evening or early morning hours. When CBC participants adopted this practice in the early 1970s in southern counties, they began producing tallies of 10–15 birds per count. Kenosha had 21 Screech-Owls in 1973. Madison's count rose to 23 in 1982 and soared to 75 in 1984, 81 in 1985, and 106 in 1987 as the numbers of counters increased.

Great Horned Owl (*Bubo virginianus*)

STATUS. Common resident.
HABITAT. Deciduous forest. Northern maple-hemlock-pine forest.
BREEDING DATA. Nests with eggs: 20 January to 8 April. Clutch size: 2 or 3 eggs.
PORTRAIT. *Birds of Wisconsin:* Plate 44.

During the Adams County CBC on 2 January 1956, observers in three parties drove carefully planned routes before dawn, and tallied 41 Great Horned Owls, the highest total for any North American CBC that year. Conditions did not favor repeating the routes in succeeding years, but smaller samplings indicated observers in another year would have been fortunate to achieve half that total. That 1956 CBC tally was not exceeded until 1986 when listeners at Newburg (Ozaukee County) found 45 birds. The 1987 CBC counts were exceptional at Madison (45), Sauk City (48), and Newburg (54).

Clearly, occasional winters bring significant influxes, presumably from farther north. Zirrer (1956) indicated that the winter of 1932–1933 brought a population explosion. After describing an abundance of available food and cover, and severe conditions of cold and snow, he reminisced: "From late afternoon throughout the night their terrifying screams, piercing shrieks, booming hoots, and maniacal guffaws reverberated through the silent winter woods. Although we have listened to these owls almost nightly for many years, we have never heard anything like it before or since." Several owls, seen in broad daylight, had the very light plumage associated with the Canadian race *wapacutho*, which has been reported in the state on five other occasions.

Further evidence of migratory movement some years has been furnished by banding recoveries. A

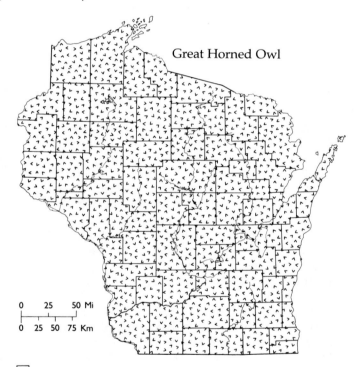

Great Horned Owl

0   25   50 Mi
0   25 50 75 Km

Resident range

Records since 1960

bird banded at Waukesha on 20 December 1964 (E. W. Peartree) showed up near Chicago, Illinois, 3 months later. One banded near Green Bay on 18 January 1970 (R. A. Hasterlik) was captured near Iron Mountain, Michigan, the following May. Between November 1960 and the ensuing July a bird moved from Waushara County (F. Hamerstrom) to western Minnesota. Another, banded at the Cedar Grove Ornithological Station in Sheboygan County on 31 March 1961 (H. C.

Mueller) was recovered 16 months later west of Duluth, Minnesota.

Most Great Horned Owls do not migrate. Their "woo hoo-hoo, hoo-hoo, hoo" is heard increasingly in January, leading into the nesting season that is usually under way by mid-February. Three reports of the laying of first eggs before the end of January are known. Rarely if ever does the Great Horn build its own nest. Of 48 nests studied in Green County, 1953–1955, Orians and Kuhlman (1956) determined that 31 had previously been used by Red-tailed Hawks, 4 by Cooper's Hawks, 3 by Crows, 2 by fox squirrels, and 1 by a Great Blue Heron, while 7 were of unknown origin. Errington (1932c) reported that 13 of 29 southern and central Wisconsin Great Horn nests had previously been occupied by Red-tailed Hawks, 8 by Crows, and 1 by a fox squirrel; 3 were in hollow trees, 2 on rock faces, and 2 were unidentified stick nests.

Reporting on 28 Oconto County nests, C. H. Richter identified 16 former Crow nests, 5 Great Blue Heron structures, 5 nests previously used by hawks, 1 nest in a tree cavity, and 1 unidentified. Not always are dense woods used. Buss and Mattison (1955) described a Dunn County nest in an isolated jack pine 600 yards away from the closest tree and 3 miles removed from the nearest farm woodlot. Nests are sometimes found over water amid heron rookeries.

Records for all seasons come from all parts of the state. If significant differences in numbers occur in different sections of the state, they are not apparent. Frances Hamerstrom (1972) described this species' statewide abundance: "Unless you live deep in the city, there is probably at least one horned owl within 2 miles of your home." Although this may seem like a modest exaggeration to some, it speaks eloquently of the widespread status of this predator.

Snowy Owl (*Nyctea scandiaca*)

STATUS. Uncommon winter resident north, central, and southeast; rare winter resident southwest.
HABITAT. Open grassland. Inland lakes.
MIGRATION DATES. *Fall:* late October to mid-December. *Spring:* early March to late April.
WINTER. Regularly present from Douglas to Ashland counties and from Brown to Winnebago counties, often south to St. Croix, Clark, Dane, and Milwaukee counties; and irregularly present throughout the state.
PORTRAIT. *Birds of Wisconsin:* Plate 44.

The mystery of the source of Wisconsin's Snowy Owl population was partly solved in 1961. Three birds banded in the Green Bay region between 22 January and 12 February (F. Hamerstrom, H. C. Mueller, D. D. Berger) were subsequently recovered in Upper Michigan (14 May) and northeast Ontario (14 May and mid-August). Subsequently, there have been additional recoveries in eastern Ontario and northwest Quebec, both east and west of James Bay. Since the recaptured birds were still migrants at the time, their recovery does not indicate breeding location, but at least it shows the direction from which most of our birds come.

Birds tend to concentrate in the more densely populated cities close to large areas of ice or water. Coming from the northeast, they seem to find Green Bay an attractive area. A few congregate near the bay shore

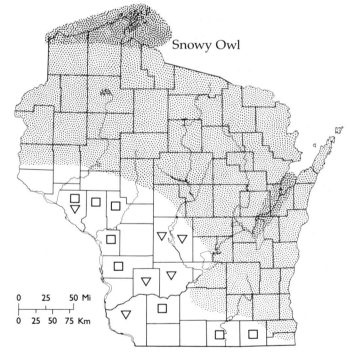

Snowy Owl

0   25   50 Mi
0 25 50 75 Km

▨   Winter range (every winter)
▢   Winter range (most winters)
▽   Late October to mid-December
▢   Late December to late February

Records since 1960

and the Fox River marshes every winter. A few appear every winter south to Oshkosh and west along the Lake Superior shore to Ashland and Superior—even in the leanest years, such as the winters of 1972–1973 and 1979–1980, when CBC totals numbered five or less. Banding results show that individuals often return to the same wintering locations in succeeding autumns.

In average winters CBC figures total 12–15 individuals in 8–10 areas. In the western region this may include birds south to St. Croix and Chippewa counties. In the central region birds frequently wander to the level farm lands of Clark, Wood, and Marathon counties. From the Fox River valley, Snowies often range to Columbia and Dane counties, while Lake Michigan birds often reach Milwaukee.

Larger flights occur occasionally. In 1964, 1967, 1977, and 1981 the CBC totaled 20–25 individuals—numbers that probably represent only a small fraction of the birds that actually reach the state in a peak year. By late December some November arrivals have already fallen victim to misguided gunners. Some wanderers do not reach us until January. Some escape notice, even though these are ordinarily very conspicuous birds. It is in these "flight years" that individuals may reach almost any part of Wisconsin that has extensive open areas. The state has had at least one observation from every county except Florence, Menominee, Pepin, and Monroe.

Having examined banding data extensively and studied the stable Green Bay populations for years, T. C. Erdman (pers. comm.) has commented: "Generally the peak lasts two years. The first is made up of mostly immatures, and the second year is largely adults. Then few birds are recorded for two years."

Fall arrival dates depend upon the size of the winter flight. In noninvasion years few birds are spotted before 20 November. Heavy flights often bring individuals to our borders by early November or even the last week of October. Earliest known arrivals are 10 October birds at Superior (1964 and 1965, R. F. Bernard).

A majority move northward again in March, with a few individuals remaining through mid-April nearly every year. Since 1960 stragglers have lingered into early May in 1968, 1969, 1972, 1977, 1978, and 1979. In 1964, 1973, 1975, 1976, and 1981 birds were still present in June. Although some of these birds have seemed capable of sustained flight, there is proof in some instances—suspicion in most others—that these were sick or injured individuals. On 15 May 1973 Erdman (pers. comm.) received a bird that had just been shot, and discovered that it also showed signs of earlier wing injuries that might have prevented migration at the usual time. Another bird, trapped on 23 April 1968, had lost its upper mandible to gunshot. One suspects that the straggler seen on 17 August 1963 (Vilas, A. S. Bradford) may have summered nearby, rather than migrated very early.

Perhaps the main reason so many Snowy Owls are shot during their sojourn in Wisconsin is that they offer a large, inviting target. They perch on trees, fence posts, snow banks, ice floes, utility poles, barn roofs, and even television aerials in residential areas. Occasionally one is shot because it attacks a wintering duck. But pellet examination has proved over and over again that the staple Snowy Owl food in Wisconsin is the meadow vole rather than waterfowl.

Northern Hawk Owl (*Surnia ulula*)

STATUS. Accidental summer resident. Rare winter
visitant.
HABITAT. Coniferous forest. Northern maple-hemlock-pine forest and adjacent fields.
MIGRATION DATES. *Fall:* late October to late November. *Spring:* early March to early April. *Extremes:*
27 October; unknown date in early April (except
breeding birds).
BREEDING DATA. Two records.
WINTER. Occasionally present in Douglas County;
rarely wanders south to Rock and Milwaukee
counties.
PORTRAIT. *Birds of Wisconsin:* Plate 43.

In the winter of 1962–1963 a remarkable invasion took
place that brought over 100 Northern Hawk Owls to
Minnesota and unprecedented numbers to southern
Ontario. The edge of this irruption touched Douglas
County, where eight birds were recorded: a 25 November observation at Superior (R. F. Bernard), two
sightings near Dairyland in early March and 20 March
(T. Jelich), a specimen found near Solon Springs on
17 March (T. Jelich), and four present in Cloverland
Township north of Brule from late November on (Roy
Johnson). It was my privilege to see three of the
Cloverland birds on 22 March, and to watch one of
them, perched 15 feet up in a pine tree, while I leaned
on the tree's trunk and listened to the distinctive "er-
r-rick."

A week later Bernard Klugow observed copulation
among these birds; by 7 April he had discovered two
nests. Both were in cavities: one 20 feet up in a pine
stump, the other 25 feet up in a black ash. He did not
determine timing of first egg-laying but noticed advanced incubation by 1 May. By 23 May two young
fledged from one nest, but five eggs in the second
nest were destroyed, presumably by raccoons. One
bird was still present in the nesting area on 1 August
(Bernard and Klugow 1963). These, the lone breeding
records for Wisconsin, are among the few known instances of nesting anywhere in North America south
of the Canadian border.

Even in early days when forests were more extensive, this species was a rarity. Hoy (1853b) asserted
that "a few visit us every winter" but offered no specific data. Thure Kumlien recorded a specimen from
Racine in the winter of 1869 and mentioned taking
several near Lake Koshkonong in Jefferson County
"at an early day." Kumlien and Hollister (1903) recorded a Milwaukee specimen collected on 27 October 1892 (R. P. Hanson) and three Bayfield County

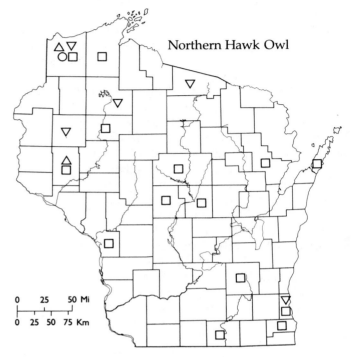

Northern Hawk Owl

△ Early March to early April
○ 7 April to 1 August
▽ Late October to late November
□ Early December to late February

All records

specimens procured by hunters later that year. Buss
and Mattison (1955) noted that J. N. Clark collected
Dunn County birds in April 1885, on 10 December
1898, and in December 1900. A bird taken in Oconto
County on 10 January 1899 (C. Schoenebeck) is the
sole nineteenth-century record from that region.

The following 60 years produced but six records:
16 November 1925 (collected in Vilas, O. LaChance;
MPM files), February 1933 (Rusk, F. Zirrer; MPM files);
16 November 1935 (collected in Douglas, W. B. Grange;
MPM files), 2 January 1944 (Dodge, H. A. Mathiak),
4 February 1945 (Bayfield, A. A. Axley), and 24 February 1951 (Milwaukee, D. L. Larkin).

Within 4 years of the 1962–1963 invasion, an additional three records were added: one bird observed in Marathon County (20–27 December 1964,
L. Mattern), one in La Crosse County (28 February
1965, H. F. Young), and one in Wood County (present
18 December 1965–14 January 1966, banded by D. G.
Follen).

Seven additional visits have been noted since 1966:

1–4 January 1970 (Rock, E. Brakefield), late January–early March 1972 (Portage, *fide* F. M. Baumgartner), 20–21 January 1976 (Door, N. Schutz),12–20 November 1976 (Barron, C. A. Faanes), 21 November 1979 (Douglas, B. F. Klugow), 15 March 1980 (Douglas, R. R. Perala), 6 November 1982 (Sawyer, D. G. Follen and K. J. Luepke), and 23 December 1985 (Douglas, B. F. Klugow).

Most sightings have been of birds in trees adjacent to open fields. Sometimes the perch is at the top of a tree, similar to a shrike's. Sometimes the perch is in a less conspicuous spot in the tree, but still at a point where the bird has a good view of the surrounding territory. The bird that Follen trapped successfully in 1965 was perched on a fence post.

Burrowing Owl (*Athene cunicularia*)

STATUS. Casual migrant.
HABITAT. Open grassland and cropland.
MIGRATION DATES. Observed between 23 March and 28 May; and between 5 September and 8 November.

Although this western species regularly reaches western Iowa and Minnesota, the Burrowing Owl has been recorded in Wisconsin with certainty only nine times. Two birds have been collected. Elder (1939) discovered and collected the state's first Burrowing Owl

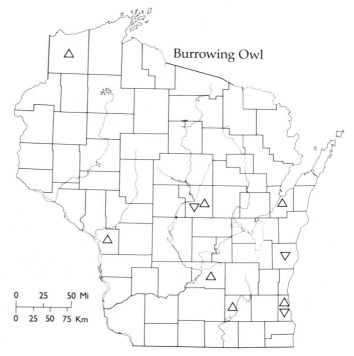

Burrowing Owl

△ 23 March to 28 May
▽ 5 September to 8 November

All records

Burrowing Owl, 25 April 1988, Columbia County (photo by G. A. De Boer)

at Faville Grove (Jefferson County) on 9 April 1939. The specimen is now in the University of Wisconsin–Madison collection. Walter Pelzer collected a second bird for the Milwaukee Public Museum at Cedar Grove (Sheboygan County) on 8 October 1941.

Three Burrowing Owls have been photographed. One, possibly blown off course by a mid-March storm, appeared at Milwaukee on 23 March 1948; it was found and photographed by Howard and Gordon Orians, and viewed by other birders through 29 March (*Pass. Pigeon* 10:127–128). At Green Bay on 6 April 1971

John and Eugene Jacobs trapped a bird that was first observed hovering Kestrel-style, then photographed it (*Pass. Pigeon* 34:1). T. C. Erdman banded the bird and released it the following day. In Douglas County on 16 May 1983, Ronald and Julie Perala discovered one of these owls being attacked by Eastern Kingbirds, and obtained photographs the next day (*Pass. Pigeon* 46:44–45).

Four sightings have been well documented. Frank Renn made the first near Bancroft (Portage County) on 19 May 1967. The bird was standing on a mound near a burrow when first seen, and was resting near another clump of grass later in the day when Frances Hamerstrom saw it and confirmed the identification. The bird did not linger, and subsequent efforts to trap and band it were unsuccessful (*Pass. Pigeon* 30:27).

A year later Frederick Lesher flushed a bird from short grass at the La Crosse airport on 28 May 1968. Although he wrote it up as a "probable" record, his documentation is so complete that it deserves recognition as an authentic sight record. The small size, hovering flight, and vertical descent "in helicopter fashion" were accurately described, and a subsequent search revealed the presence of a few pellets near a burrow. Additional efforts to find the visitor on subsequent days were futile (*Pass. Pigeon* 31:223).

On 8 November 1975 another bird turned up at Milwaukee, first discovered by Eric Epstein, subsequently viewed by others (*Pass. Pigeon* 38:126). The next observation occurred 6 years later, when Jonathan Wilde and five companions discovered a wanderer on 5 September 1981. This was in Portage County, only 4 miles from the 1967 point of observation (*Pass. Pigeon* 43:110–111).

Ronald Hull discovered a Burrowing Owl near his Columbia County home on 24 April 1988. During the next 3 days two photographers got close-ups from within 20 feet (*Pass. Pigeon* 50:364–365).

There have been two additional probable sightings, heretofore unpublished and lacking the necessary on-the-spot documentation. Corresponding with the Milwaukee Public Museum in 1953, Henry Huber of Colfax described from memory what he believed was the raising of two young Burrowing Owls during the summer of 1943 on his farm in Tainter Township (Dunn County). The nest was in an abandoned badger hole. "It was very amusing to watch them. They would stare at us in the same manner that other owls do until we got too close; then they would go into the hole. They would do it so quickly that it appeared as though they fell over backwards."

Bernard Klugow has vivid memories of three birds discovered along Highway 14, probably between Lone Rock and Spring Green, on the morning of 9 October 1946. While waiting for a flat tire to be fixed, Klugow and his wife, Joyce, had close views of three birds standing near each other on a small sandy mound. Reminiscing 29 years later, Klugow (pers. comm.) wrote: "They were sandy brown in color, with lighter colored legs and throat. They made only body movements and did not walk or run. They appeared to look comical, and we both laughed because of the actions of the birds. They were no more than 30 feet from the fence next to the highway."

It is unfortunate that these probable sightings were not documented until years after the time of observation. But they support the theory that this species may appear rarely in dry open country in western Wisconsin.

Barred Owl (*Strix varia*)

STATUS. Fairly common resident.
HABITAT. Deciduous forest. Northern maple-hem-
  lock-pine forest.
BREEDING DATA. Nests with eggs: 6 March to 8 May.
  Clutch size: usually 2 or 3 eggs; occasionally 4.
PORTRAIT. *Birds of Wisconsin:* Plate 44.

Buss and Mattison (1955) and Kemper (1973a) suggest
that the Barred Owl outnumbers the Great Horned
Owl in their Dunn and Chippewa county areas. Perhaps this was true in past years in the heavily wooded
river bottoms along major streams. But today, taking
the state as a whole, the numbers of Barred Owls are
quite modest. The highest number ever recorded on
a single Wisconsin CBC—13—is a far cry from the 41
Great Horned Owls recorded in Adams County in
1956, or the 25 or more Barreds sometimes recorded
on Texas and Louisiana counts.

Compared with the Great Horn, the Barred has
more selective habitat requirements. In the south and
central regions it frequents the mature forests close to
the moist river bottoms. Farther north, in addition
to wooded bottomlands, this owl frequents dense
stands of maple-beech hardwoods far removed from
human disturbance. Occasionally a stray bird comes
into a residential neighborhood, perhaps attracted by
a garden rabbit, but it soon retreats to more secluded
terrain.

This species generally nests several weeks later
than the Great Horn. A nest with three eggs on
16 March (1930, Dane, A. W. Schorger) is exceptionally
early. Carl Richter found 16 nests in Oconto County: 1
in late March, 12 in April, and 3 in early May. Most
nests occupied cavities in large maple, beech, and aspen trees, from 18 to 50 feet up. One pair took over an
old crow nest 45 feet up in the crotch of a cottonwood.

Most people know the "eight-hooter" better by
sound than by sight. Its eerie calls can be heard in almost any season and at any hour of the night. Francis
Zirrer (pers. comm. to O. J. Gromme) once commented: "The concerts of these owls, especially in
winter and when several birds congregate in one
place, are worth coming long distances to hear. It
sounds as if the woods were full of maniacs or devils,
and except for a few intervals, lasts all night." The

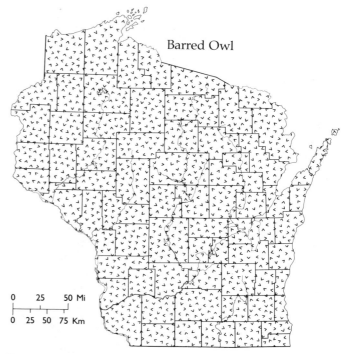

Barred Owl

0   25   50 Mi

0 25 50 75 Km

⬛ Resident range

Records since 1960

hooting becomes more frequent in March and April
as nesting advances, and in May one sometimes hears
it in broad daylight. The birds become quieter in July
and early August, then become noisier again. Zirrer
added, "In late summer and fall they produce a series
of shrieks that sound very much like young wolves;
and if it were not for the hoo-hoo that follows, one
would take it for such."

Suitable habitat is sparse in the Milwaukee-Kenosha
area, but elsewhere throughout the state distribution
is widespread. Records are known for every Wisconsin county.

Little is known about movement of Barred Owls
from one area to another. Two individuals banded in
southern Wisconsin have been recovered in Illinois:
one moved 40 miles in 6 months, and one traveled
200 miles in 4 years.

Great Gray Owl (*Strix nebulosa*)

STATUS. Rare migrant north and central. Rare summer resident north. Rare winter resident north and central.

HABITAT. Coniferous forest. Northern maple-hemlock-pine forest.

MIGRATION DATES. *Spring:* early March to early May. *Fall:* late September to late November.

BREEDING DATA. Nested in 1988. One additional record of recently fledged young.

WINTER. Irregularly present south to Burnett, Taylor and Forest counties. Rarely present south to Buffalo, Wood, and Marathon counties.

PORTRAIT. *Birds of Wisconsin:* Plate 44.

The Great Gray Owl made ornithological headlines in the winter of 1968–1969 when an unprecedented influx brought 7 birds to Wisconsin and over 50 to Minnesota. Late in 1968 one was shot in Waupaca County (*fide* B. Parfitt). Early in 1969, six records occurred between 21 January and mid-April, including specimens from Chippewa and Washburn counties and a bird photographed in Sauk County. The mid-April record, previously unpublished, was a Clark County bird substantiated by photograph (I. Kaufman).

Before 1968, Wisconsin ornithologists thought of this owl as a casual winter visitant restricted primarily to the northernmost counties, although Hoy (1853b, 1885b) had collected specimens in Racine County in 1848, 1858, and 1860. Kumlien and Hollister (1903) reported two specimens brought to them by Bayfield County hunters in November 1891. These authors mentioned that Thure Kumlien had obtained two birds shot in Jefferson County sometime before 1860, and that he had received at least six specimens from northern Wisconsin hunters in subsequent years. Schoenebeck (1902) mentioned knowledge of two specimens for Oconto County, but gave no further details. The lone nineteenth-century record with a specific date is for an individual shot in Jackson County on 9 March 1893 (E. E. Voss), now preserved at the Milwaukee Public Museum.

A dearth of records follows. Both Schorger (1951a) and Gromme (1963) indicated no knowledge of any twentieth-century birds. Unknown to them was a specimen taken near Sullivan (Jefferson County) on 2 November 1934 (*fide* W. E. Scott, pers. comm.) and a specimen collected near Merrill (Lincoln County) during the winter of 1947–1948 (*fide* D. G. Follen, pers. comm.).

It was small wonder that Bernard and Klugow (1966)

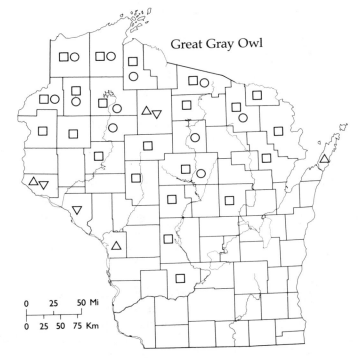

Great Gray Owl

```
0    25    50 Mi
|----|----|
0  25  50  75 Km
```

△   Early March to early May
○   Mid-May to mid-September
▽   Late September to late November
□   Early December to late February

Records since 1960

surprised many Wisconsin ornithologists with news of two Douglas County sightings: one bird found dead near Brule on 1 November 1965 by George Gillette, one photographed at Superior on 14 March 1966 by John Ward. Minnesota had an influx of Great Gray Owls that winter. A sighting in Wood County on 15 December 1965 by D. G. Follen (pers. comm.), along with the Douglas County finds, may have been related to the Minnesota influx.

Then came the spectacular invasion of 1968–1969 and a remarkable increase in sightings ever since. Between 1969 and 1978, observers related 11 sightings. Most were November and December birds in Douglas, Bayfield, Sawyer, and Taylor counties. Two were February visitors in Vilas and Oconto counties.

Most intriguing was the 31 May 1975 sighting in Vilas County by Mr. and Mrs. James Albrecht. Perhaps this species is not just a winter visitant. Suspicions of nesting were further aroused by a Douglas County report on 17 July 1978 (A. Clarke). Follen

(1979a) followed up on 18 August, and found two adults and three young—probably 6–8 weeks old—1 mile north of Moose Junction (Douglas County).

Follen then embarked on a 5-year project designed to determine more precisely the status of this large mouser in Wisconsin. He distributed posters depicting the bird and calling for reports of known or suspected sightings throughout the northern and central regions. Some accounts had to be rejected as misidentifications, but Follen's list of reliable observations totaled 17 in 1979 (Follen 1980), 26 in 1980 (pers. comm.), 11 in 1981 (Follen 1982b), 29 in 1982, and 22 in 1983 (Follen 1985). These include additional suspected nesting activity in 1979 and 1980 in Forest County, plus three summer 1981 observations in Rusk, Lincoln, and Forest counties. These also include the first Wisconsin banding of this species.

Between 1979 and 1986 Follen and his associates in the Wisconsin Foundation for Wildlife Research erected 72 nest platforms in promising northern Wisconsin forest habitat. These efforts brought results in 1988 when K. J. Merkel discovered an active nest near Clam Lake in Ashland County, on 2 April. By 14 May four owlets fledged successfully (Merkel 1989).

Some of the birds reported to Follen may have been duplicate sightings. Little is known about how widely these birds may travel in a few weeks. But it is clear that we must now revise the pre-1968 assumptions that this is a very rare winter wanderer to the northernmost counties.

Great Gray Owl, 2 December 1981, Marathon County (photo by J. Rankl)

Long-eared Owl (*Asio otus*)

STATUS. Uncommon resident central. Uncommon migrant. Uncommon summer resident north. Uncommon winter resident south.

HABITAT. Conifer plantations. Deciduous forest.

MIGRATION DATES. *Spring:* early March to mid-April. *Fall:* mid-September to mid-November.

BREEDING DATA. Nests with eggs: 22 March to 19 May. Clutch size: usually 4 or 5 eggs; occasionally 3 or 6.

WINTER. Regularly present to La Crosse, Wood, Adams, Outagamie, and Brown counties; occasionally present north to St. Croix, Barron, Taylor, and Marathon counties.

PORTRAIT. *Birds of Wisconsin:* Plate 42.

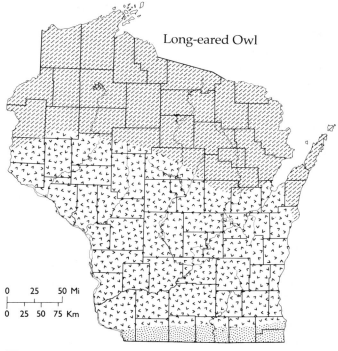

Long-eared Owl

0   25   50 Mi

0 25 50 75 Km

⌐ ˙ ⌐ Resident range
▨ Summer range
⠿ Winter range

Records since 1960

The Long-eared Owl is best known as a winter resident in southeastern Wisconsin. When Christmas bird counters have searched diligently in dense pine groves near major cities, they have often flushed flocks of 15 or more birds. The birds perch inconspicuously on the inner branches of the trees and cannot be detected easily by an approaching observer. But when one bird is roused to flight, the entire flock quickly follows suit. It is not enough to stop the car and look at a pine grove from a distance. You must walk right up to the edge of the trees to find the owls. Since 1950 concentrations have been reported at Kenosha, Racine, Milwaukee, Waukesha, Madison, and Green Bay. On occasion similar concentrations have been noted in areas of birch, aspen, and alder. During the winter of 1969–1970 Don Follen estimated that 50 birds occupied two roosting sites in a Wood County alder swamp.

In an average year 12–15 birds turn up on six to eight CBCs. The 25 individuals recorded on 14 CBCs during 1977–1978 constitute the highest totals in recent years. Most of these are birds heard or seen singly in areas north to St. Croix and Barron counties in the west, to Wood and Marathon counties in the central region, and to Outagamie and Brown counties in the east.

Little effort has been made to determine what happens to the city-oriented concentrations at other seasons. Presumably they disperse by early March, with some of the birds migrating northward. I have heard more Long-ears calling in early evening between 20 March and 15 April than in any other season; they are probably migrants that pause for a day or two en route. If more listeners spent more evening time near hardwood swamps or pine groves during this season, the scope of the spring migration might become more apparent. The earliest dates for birds north of the

usual wintering region are 28 March (1975, Burnett, J. O. Evrard), 3 April (1941, Sawyer, F. Zirrer), and 8 April (1969, Douglas, R. F. Bernard). Carl Richter has found them nesting in Oconto County by 19 April.

Some birds that occupy winter roosts probably remain to nest nearby. Summer records anywhere in the state are scanty, but since 1950 there have been summer reports as far south as Grant, Rock, Dane, Waukesha, and Milwaukee counties. In the Wood County area, where Follen (1971) found large roosts of 50 birds in January 1970, he discovered five nests between 21 April and 11 May. He commented: "The thing that strikes me as the most fascinating about the Long-eared Owl is its ability to hide itself. This bird has the ability to compress its body until it looks much like a snag or branch. Once while observing a nest, I spotted one adult next to the trunk of the tree on a dead limb. I would swear that this bird was not over 1½ inches in diameter."

A typical Long-ear nest is an abandoned crow nest, composed largely of sticks. Follen's five nests stood 20–30 feet up in deciduous trees: poplar, birch, and maple. Of four nests reported by Carl Richter in Oconto County, two were in poplars and two in white pines. Of the four, three were old crow nests, while the fourth was a made-over Broad-winged Hawk nest.

Banders are helping to determine the duration of the fall migration. From 1965 to 1973 Bernard Brouchoud (pers. comm.) banded 15 birds in Manitowoc County between 3 October and 5 November. In southern Oconto County T. C. Erdman (pers. comm.) has trapped migrants between 6 September and 26 November, finding that there usually is an early November peak. One of the Oconto County birds, banded on 7 November 1971, was retaken near Joliet, Illinois, on 24 January 1972. Two other birds trapped at the Cedar Grove Ornithological Station in Sheboygan County had moved to north-central Illinois within a month's time. A bird banded as a nestling near Madison on 15 May 1939 was recaptured in Texas on 5 December 1943. One bird found dead near La Crosse in January 1969 had been banded the previous spring near Sault Ste Marie, Michigan.

Short-eared Owl (*Asio flammeus*)

STATUS. Uncommon migrant. Rare summer resident north and central. Uncommon winter resident south and central.

HABITAT. Open grassland. Sedge meadow. Old field.

MIGRATION DATES. *Spring:* early March to early May. *Fall:* early October to late November.

BREEDING DATA. Nests with eggs: 25 April to 10 May. Nests with young: to 15 June. Clutch size: 5–10 eggs.

WINTER. Frequently present north to St. Croix, Sauk, and Manitowoc counties; rarely present to Burnett, Douglas, Langlade, and Oconto counties.

PORTRAIT. *Birds of Wisconsin:* Plate 42.

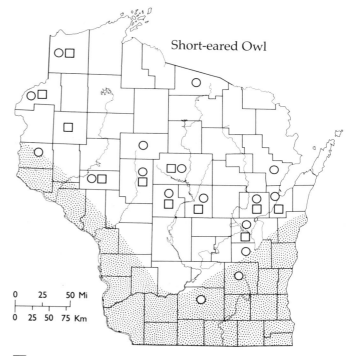

Short-eared Owl

▨ Winter range
○ Mid-May to late September
□ Early December to late February

Records since 1960

You can drive slowly by some open grass meadows in midmorning or midafternoon on a sunny day from October through April and find no hint that Short-ears are present. But you can pause along the same fields at dawn or near sundown and glimpse 10 or more of these owls, flapping low over the grass or perched on nearby fence posts. No other Wisconsin owl "flocks" as consistently as this species. "Flock" is actually a misnomer: the birds come together to share an area where meadow mice abound.

Groups of 15 or more are sometimes encountered in winter. Since 1950, observers have reported such flocks on CBCs from Beloit, Lake Geneva, Kenosha, Racine, Milwaukee, and Waukesha. But the birds do not appear consistently. A spot that held several one year may have none the next.

A large portion of each year's observations cluster around late December, not because these owls are more numerous at that time, but because CBC observers are afield at the times of day when one must be abroad to see this mouse-hunter. I have encountered the owls at dawn when it was barely light enough to see, and I have found them, too, at sunset, but rarely during the intervening daylight hours. The only winter records known for the northern counties are sightings in Douglas (7–21 February 1968, M. Granlund), Burnett (4 January 1978 and 15 February 1981, J. O. Evrard), Vilas (18 January 1956, R. C. Hopkins), Langlade (7 February 1941, C. J. Miersch), and Oconto (6 January 1941, C. H. Richter) counties. Winter records occur more frequently south of a line from New Richmond to Green Bay, with the larger numbers concentrating in the southeast.

A wide fluctuation is the rule for summer as well.

Sometimes there may be a stretch of 3 or 4 years in which there is a complete absence of summer records (1951–1954, 1965–1968). Then, alternating periods of 3–5 years ensue when there is at least one summer observation per year (1948–1950, 1960–1964, 1969–1971). Most remarkable was the summer of 1970 when 17 pairs fledged an estimated 70 young on the Buena Vista Marsh in Portage County (Beske and Champion 1971) during a year of exceptionally high vole populations. A similar set of circumstances may explain Francis Zirrer's report (pers. comm. to O. J. Gromme) of 50 birds in Rusk County on 2 May 1937, followed by the discovery of a nest with four nearly grown young. The summer of 1978 brought high numbers in Clark, Wood, and Marathon counties; Ken and Jan Luepke and Don Follen found 13 pairs feeding young between 28 May and mid-July (pers. comm.). Unusual numbers were present 3 years later, with summer observations in Eau Claire, Clark, Taylor, Marathon, and Brown counties. Since 1960 additional summer observations have occurred in Douglas, Oconto, Winnebago, Fond du Lac, Dodge, and Dane counties, suggesting that nesting may be possible in any part of the state where suitable habitat exists.

You most often find this owl in extensive marshes or in other undisturbed grass meadowlands during migration. Between 10 March and 5 May birds may be seen singly or in groups of 10–15 at dusk or dawn. Observers occasionally report birds in late May, but these are probably summer residents.

Early September observations also probably represent wanderers. Fall migration concentrates in October and November. In the extensive Horicon marshes in Dodge County fall peaks sometimes reach 50 birds. Managers W. E. Beed and J. G. Bell estimated phenomenal peaks of 1,000 at the Horicon National Wildlife Refuge on 24 October 1944 and 24 November 1945 (Horicon NWR files).

I know of one interstate banding recovery: an individual trapped in Waukesha County on 22 February 1966 (E. W. Peartree) was retaken in southern Indiana on 26 January 1967.

Boreal Owl (*Aegolius funereus*)
Formerly Richardson's Owl

STATUS. Rare migrant. Accidental summer visitant. Rare winter visitant north and east.
HABITAT. Coniferous forest.
MIGRATION DATES. *Fall:* late October to late November. *Spring:* early March to mid-April. *Extremes:* 24 October; 3 May.
WINTER. Occasionally present south to Burnett, Marathon, and Oconto counties.
PORTRAIT. *Birds of Wisconsin:* Plate 43.

Definite dates are known for 37 visits of this hardy Canadian owl. Of these, 17 were collected or found dead, 8 were trapped and/or banded, and 12 were sight observations. The Boreal Owl is remarkably tame, allowing extremely close approach. Fell (1952) photographed his bird from a distance of 3 feet. J. N. Clark captured his specimen by hand as it perched on a strawstack on his farm (Buss and Mattison 1955).

The earliest fall records are two late October birds: one observed on the 24th (1937, Sheboygan, O. J. Gromme) and one banded and photographed on the 28th (1978, Oconto, T. C. Erdman [1979a]). Another was banded and photographed on 3 November (1962, Sheboygan, H. C. Mueller; *Pass. Pigeon* 25:83).

Most observations have been scattered between 25 November and the end of March: 7 in December, 5 in January, 7 in February, and 10 in March. Four of the March observations fell between the 27th and 30th,

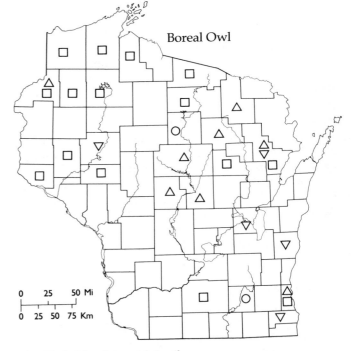

Boreal Owl

△ Early March to mid-April
○ 11 August
▽ Late October to late November
□ Early December to late February

All records

Boreal Owl, 26 January 1988, Oneida County (photo by C. Vig)

suggesting that this might be a migratory period for those few years when birds reach Wisconsin. Beyond 31 March I know of only three spring migration dates: 13 April (1975, Burnett, W. Norling), 20 April (1890,

Milwaukee, C. E. Akeley; MPM files), and 3 May (1897, Oconto, A. J. Schoenebeck [1902]).

An individual was photographed in Chippewa County in the late fall of 1950 by Gordon Peterson, but the exact date is unknown. Also lacking specific dates are another specimen at the Milwaukee Public Museum, and some nineteenth-century references by Kumlien and Hollister (1903): "Thure Kumlien procured three or four specimens in Dane and Jefferson Counties during nearly fifty years' residence in these parts. L. Kumlien has taken two: one in Dane County, 1869, and one at Fort Atkinson, August, 1872."

What does one make of this August 1872 record and the specimen picked up on the Lincoln-Marathon county line on 11 August 1978 by Follen (1982a)? Preposterous? No indeed. The irruption into the northern United States in the winter of 1977–1978 was the greatest on record, resulting in the banding of 23 birds in northern Michigan between 24 April and 7 May and the detection of 15 calling individuals in northern Minnesota during the same period (*Am. Birds* 32:1010–11). Minnesota's first breeding record came in June 1978. Follen's bird was probably a holdover from that spectacular influx.

Winter irruptions will continue to occur from time to time. Persons engaged in the nocturnal trapping of Saw-whet Owls are likely to net *funereus* on rare occasions. More listeners (knowing what sound to listen for) afield in northern Wisconsin during late March and April may discover that this species is not as rare as the records might indicate.

Northern Saw-whet Owl (*Aegolius acadicus*)

STATUS. Uncommon resident central. Fairly common migrant east; uncommon migrant west and central. Uncommon summer resident north. Uncommon winter resident south; rare winter resident north.

HABITAT. Coniferous forest. Northern maple-hemlock-pine forest.

MIGRATION DATES. *Spring:* early March to late April. *Fall:* early September to mid-November.

BREEDING DATA. Nests with eggs: 18 March to 26 April. Nests with young: to 24 June. Clutch size: 4 or 5 eggs.

WINTER. Regularly present east of a line between La Crosse and Rhinelander; occasionally present in Douglas, Sawyer, Barron, Rusk, Taylor, and Buffalo counties.

PORTRAIT. *Birds of Wisconsin:* Plate 43.

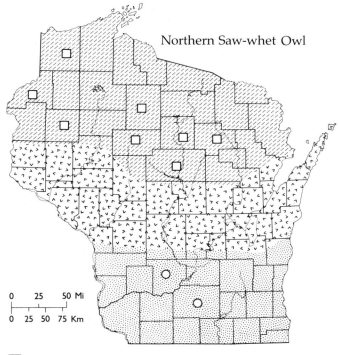

Northern Saw-whet Owl

0   25   50 Mi
0 25 50 75 Km

◫ Resident range
▨ Summer range
▦ Winter range
○ Early May to late August
□ Late November to late February

Records since 1960

To the casual backyard or roadside bird-watcher, the Northern Saw-whet Owl is a rarity. Two or three times a year someone accidentally comes upon a roadkill somewhere in the state. In December an enterprising CBC observer sometimes flushes a bird from a grove of dense young evergreens. On a warm April evening an alert listener may occasionally hear the soft, monotonous, bell-like tones of a migrant calling from the edge of a conifer swamp. But because the bird is so nocturnal in its habits, and its favorite haunts so seldom visited by birders in the evening hours, such encounters are but rarely reported.

It is the banders who have revealed how common this bird is, particularly as a fall migrant. Banders have trapped hundreds since 1960 near the Lake Michigan shore in Sheboygan (Mueller and Berger 1967c), Manitowoc (B. N. Brouchoud), Brown (M. M. Wierzbicki), and Oconto (T. C. Erdman) counties. During the autumn of 1987, Erdman banded 526 Saw-whets in Oconto County. Brouchoud trapped 30 individuals on 24 October 1968, part of a total of 136 that autumn. One of Brouchoud's birds, banded on 4 September 1972, was an exceptionally early arrival. The usual pattern is for the owls to appear around 25 September, with the flight building to a 15–25 October peak before diminishing sharply in early November. It is not known how many of these birds winter south of Wisconsin's borders. One bird was retrapped in northern Illinois on 10 February 1967, 3 months after banding in Manitowoc County (B. N. Brouchoud). One banded at the Cedar Grove Ornithological Station in Sheboygan County on 14 October 1969 (D. D. Berger) had reached Arkansas 2 months later.

I know of no similar spring flights, but they probably do occur. Catling (1971) has witnessed pronounced flights in the Toronto region, with an almost daily turnover between 23 March and 25 April. Whitefish Point in northern Michigan also attracts significant numbers in late April. Most Wisconsin spring records fall within the same span. On the evening of 23 March 1956 I made frequent listening stops along a 25-mile drive from Nekoosa to Friendship, and heard Saw-whets calling at six locations.

Efforts by Follen (1981b, 1982c) to list Wisconsin nesting records and birds recorded during the breeding period are deceptively fragmentary. The implications of some findings in Price (L. E. Gregg, pers. comm.) and Oneida (Vanderschaegen 1981a) counties are that this secretive species may well nest in considerable numbers throughout forested northern Wisconsin. Follen's summary points to confirmed nesting (since 1960) south to Buffalo, Monroe, Juneau, Adams, Marquette, and Fond du Lac counties. Additional summer observations have come from Sauk and Dane counties. Previous summer records, dating back to 1935, include Columbia, Dodge, Waukesha, and Milwaukee counties.

Migration and nesting periods overlap extensively, making it difficult to delineate the bird's breeding range. Follen (1981a) observed a nest with eggs on 18 March (1981, Wood). Young have been observed as early as 24 April (1966, Marquette, O. J. Gromme). Banders trap migrants as late as 10 May in northern Michigan. Birds found between 15 April and 15 May may be either migrants or nesting birds. Zirrer (1944b) provided a fascinating account of a nest in Sawyer County. He first detected owls on 26 January and frequently heard them in the same locality through mid-March, when he observed mating behavior. Frequent searches for a nest proved futile until 2 May when he found the nest a quarter of a mile from the courtship area. The nest occupied a cavity 25 feet up in a half-dead cedar. By 27 May three young had fledged. Most other nests reported for the state have been found in deciduous tree (maple, basswood, cottonwood, aspen) cavities 25–50 feet up. A 1981 nest, however, was discovered in a Wood Duck nest box (Follen 1981a).

Family **Caprimulgidae**: Goatsuckers

Common Nighthawk (*Chordeiles minor*)

STATUS. Common spring migrant; abundant fall migrant. Fairly common summer resident.
HABITAT. Commercial areas. Sand and gravel. Shallow marsh.
MIGRATION DATES. *Spring:* early May to early June. *Fall:* early August to mid-October. *Extremes:* 15 April; 7 November.
BREEDING DATA. Nests with eggs: 21 May to 16 July. Clutch size: 2 eggs.
PORTRAIT. *Birds of Wisconsin:* Plate 45.

The late-August flights staged by this aerial acrobat are nothing short of spectacular. A flight day may occur any time from 15 August to 5 September in the north, 20 August to 15 September in the south. Between 3 P.M. and dusk, if you are situated in an open area not far from water, you may witness flights of Common Nighthawks in the hundreds or even thousands. Birds come in loose flocks, unhurriedly zigging this way and that as they flap and sail, seemingly in an endless stream. After witnessing one such flight, Hoy (1853b) wrote: "For two hours before dark, these birds formed one continuous flock moving south. They reminded me, by their vast numbers, of Passenger Pigeons."

Kumlien and Hollister (1903) remarked, "The immense autumnal flights, formerly a regular feature of the fall migrations, are becoming less regular, and although still locally common, are a mere fraction of what they once were." Partly responsible for the suspected decline was the widespread use of these birds for target practice.

If there has been a significant decline, the nineteenth-century populations must indeed have been prodigious. Flights today are large enough to defy careful estimation. I well remember the late-August afternoon when I rode the train from Milwaukee to Chicago while a flight was in progress. Ten or more nighthawks were in view every moment from Milwaukee to well across the Illinois border south of Kenosha. An estimated 18,000 migrated past the Cedar Grove Ornithological Station in Sheboygan County on 31 August 1958, following a movement of 6,000 the previous day. On 20 August 1963 Norman Stone pegged the flight of birds over the Crex Meadows Wildlife Area in Burnett County at 10,000. Most

Common Nighthawk

0   25   50 Mi
0   25 50 75 Km

▨ Summer range

Records since 1960

witnesses have been content to record "thousands" or "heavy migration" instead of estimating numbers.

Although the largest flights end by 10 September, modest numbers may still be sighted in the southern counties through 25 September, with scattered detections occurring through 15 October. Most October sightings report single birds; exceptional were the 300 birds recorded in Dane County on the 8th (1949, E. A. Nott) and the 30 in Rock County on the 17th (1953, J. W. Wilde). Most notable among the latest departure dates are 29 October (1946, Milwaukee, D. L. Larkin), 30 October (1975, Milwaukee, E. L. Basten), 2 November (1940, Waukesha, C. A. Anthes), and 7 November (1929, Oconto, collected by J. Chylinski, now part of the A. J. Schoenebeck collection at the University of Wisconsin–Stevens Point).

In spring this species is among the latest migrants. Flocks are much in evidence between 20 May and 5 June but number only in the dozens rather than the thousands. In the south first arrivals appear around 5 May. Numbers do not build until 15 May. Farther north few are recorded before 15 May. Most nesting birds are on territory by 25 May, with some migration still detectable through 5 June.

A few observers have reported hearing the emphatic "hak" of this species in mid-April, even in late March. Such records are dubious because of possible confusion with the similar-sounding American Woodcock. More reliable April sightings have been noted on the 15th (1978, Winnebago, T. Ziebell), 24th (1979, Brown, Bro. Columban), and 25th (1974, St. Croix, C. A. Faanes).

As a summer resident this bird concentrates in urban areas where it nests on warm gravel on flat rooftops. It is also found in dry, sandy, rural areas. Sometimes nighthawks lay their eggs on sand dunes, piles of gravel, out-of-the-way blacktop areas, and in piles of chips and sawdust around lumber yards and sawmills. The bird's distribution covers the entire state; there are records for every Wisconsin county.

One adult banded in Grant County on 31 May 1962 (T. N. Ingram) was recaptured 3½ months later in West Virginia.

Chuck-will's-widow (*Caprimulgus carolinensis*)

STATUS. Casual migrant. Casual summer resident west and south.
HABITAT. Southern oak-hickory forest. Conifer plantations.
MIGRATION DATES. Observed between 8 May and 8 September.

Wisconsin's first record of a Chuck-will's-widow occurred near Lone Rock (Richland County) on the night of 28–29 May 1969. Warren Scott was camping overnight, tape recorder at hand, hoping to record Whip-poor-wills. In the darkness of early morning he was awakened by the call of a strange bird he did not recognize. He recorded the song at distances ranging from 300 down to 50 yards. When Mary Donald heard the tape later, she recognized the song instantly as that of the Chuck-will's-widow. It was my privilege to hear this tape weeks later and to talk extensively with Mr. Scott. Scott taped his narration, accompanying the bird's call, and donated copies of the tape to the State Historical Society of Wisconsin and to the Milwaukee Public Museum.

Four years later a similar scene was reenacted at Jamieson Park near Poynette (Columbia County). On the evenings of 18, 19, 25, 26, and 27 May 1973 a singing bird put on a command performance for Mr. and Mrs. Albert Bentley, Mr. and Mrs. William Smith, and Steven Krings. The Smiths and Krings had become familiar with the bird in Florida. On the 19th they succeeded in recording the song. They also saw the bird in dim light when it perched on a fence at the edge of a wooded area with dense undergrowth. The view was sufficient to enable them to determine size and light edges on the tail, but insufficient for all field marks. The recording of the song is definitive (*Pass. Pigeon* 35:150–151).

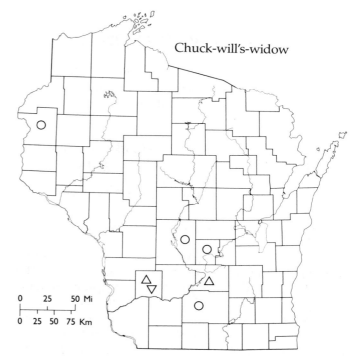

Chuck-will's-widow

△   8 May to early June
○   Early June to mid-August
▽   16 August to 8 September

All records

In between these occasions the R. J. Flahertys reported another bird heard near Montello (Marquette County) on 16 August 1970. They did not record this bird, but there is no reason to doubt the occurrence.

One Chuck-will's-widow spent several weeks at the George MacLean farm near Blue Mounds (Dane County) during the summer of 1976. Precise dates were not recorded, and this observation did not come to light until an individual turned up at the same location the following year. Its identification was confirmed on 29 May 1977; it was last heard on 7 July. This bird's song was heard by numerous other observers and subsequently taped (*Pass. Pigeon* 40:387).

Not until 1983 could these auditory identifications be supplemented by positive visual evidence. On 8 September, Brad Grover stopped to investigate a roadkill along Highway 60 in Richland County, and was surprised to discover that it was a Chuck-will's-widow. The specimen was beyond salvaging, but tail feathers were saved (*Pass. Pigeon* 46:125).

One of these birds (possibly more) was heard repeatedly in Adams County in May and June 1984, 1985, and 1986 by Joan Humphrey (*Pass. Pigeon* 48: 96–97). She did not record precise dates in 1984. In 1985 she and many others heard the singer from early May to 6 September. The 1986 bird was present from 8 May to 2 July (*Pass. Pigeon* 48:93).

On 10 May 1986 Joseph Schraufenbuel heard this southerner near his home at Dresser, Polk County (*Pass. Pigeon* 49:49). The bird remained well into June. The same individual (or another?) returned in 1987 (22 May into June), 1988 (15 May to 28 June), and 1989 (17 May to 7 June).

Other casual extralimital records have been established in the neighboring states of Michigan, Indiana, Illinois, Iowa, and Minnesota, as well as in Ontario, Nova Scotia, and most of the New England states. Most of these wanderings have been recorded since 1970, suggesting a gradual range extension northward.

Whip-poor-will (*Caprimulgus vociferus*)

STATUS. Fairly common migrant. Fairly common summer resident north, central, and west; uncommon summer resident south and east.
HABITAT. Deciduous forest. Northern maple-hemlock-pine forest.
MIGRATION DATES. *Spring:* mid-April to late May. *Fall:* mid-August to early October. *Extremes:* 9 April; 20 October.
BREEDING DATA. Nests with eggs: 7 May to 19 July. Clutch size: 2 eggs.
PORTRAIT. *Birds of Wisconsin:* Plate 45.

No woods, no "Whips." Because this bird shuns heavily populated areas, it is no longer found in the southeastern counties except as a passing migrant. And because the Whip-poor-will has never had an affinity for coniferous forests, it is absent from considerable portions of the northern counties as well. Yet there are enough favorable woodlands—particularly oak forests—to attract summer residents to all parts of the state except the southeastern urbanized areas.

Although in some years first arrivals may not appear before 1 May, a more usual date for the southern counties is around 20 April. K. I. Lange's 9 April 1981 record in Trempealeau County was exceptionally early, but several others have been detected in the 13–18 April period. Farther north the earliest arrivals include birds on 13 April (1944, Oconto, C. H. Richter), 16 April (1977, Price, M. Hardy), and 18 April (1972, Oconto, J. Woodcock). Not until early May does calling become regular in most parts of the state. The discovery of an individual killed at an Eau Claire tele-

Whip-poor-will

0   25   50 Mi
0 25 50 75 Km

▨ Summer range

Records since 1960

vision tower on 22 May (1960, C. A. Kemper) indicates that migration is still continuing beyond 20 May.

Oaks provide favored nesting habitat. One can hardly speak of "nest construction," for a nest simply consists of a level spot of ground. But wherever specific vegetation has been mentioned in descriptions of nests, oak leaves invariably have provided the carpet on which the female lays her two eggs. There is some evidence that parents will actually move their eggs from one location to another after predator disturbances. Francis Zirrer (MPM files) found a parent with two eggs at 2 o'clock one morning, marked the site, and returned to the site 7 hours later. He could find no trace of birds, eggs, or predator tracks. As the female has been known to fly, carrying young between rigidly held thighs, so Zirrer believed that the eggs may have been moved in this manner.

Persons who live in Whip-poor-will territory can listen to a lively serenade every evening from early May through mid-July, and, if awake in the predawn hours, can hear a second song period. Beyond mid-July singing becomes much less regular, but may be heard occasionally until mid-September.

With birds largely silent in August, the start of autumn migration remains a mystery. Birds heard in mid-September could be either summer residents or transients. The suggestion that birds are migrating by 20 August is based more on plausible guesswork than on documented evidence.

Although rarely heard after mid-September, this bird shows up in banders' mist nets frequently enough to prove that migration often extends into early October. Beyond the 10th, I know of five October records: 13th (1964, Waukesha, P. W. Hoffmann), 16th (1971, Sauk, E. W. Peartree), 17th (1966, Manitowoc, B. N. Brouchoud), 19th (1966, Oconto, C. H. Richter), and 20th (1980, Ozaukee, J. H. Idzikowski).

Family **Apodidae**: Swifts

Chimney Swift (*Chaetura pelagica*)

STATUS. Common migrant. Common summer resident south and central; fairly common summer resident north.
HABITAT. Residential areas. Commercial areas.
MIGRATION DATES. *Spring:* mid-April to late May. *Fall:* early August to early October. *Extremes:* 1 April; 11 November.
BREEDING DATA. Nests with eggs: 11 May to 17 July. Clutch size: 4 or 5 eggs.
PORTRAIT. *Birds of Wisconsin:* Plate 45.

From time to time an occasional migrant Chimney Swift rides a balmy southern breeze and shows up in Wisconsin in early April. The state has isolated records on the 1st (1882, Brown, S. W. Willard [1885b]), 5th (1952, Wood, E. A. Becker), 7th (1959, Kenosha, M. F. Higgins), 8th (1948, Sheboygan, E. A. Becker), and 10th (1950, Dane, G. A. Hall). These birds usually disappear quickly, and no more are recorded until the normal time around 25 April. Although a few make it to the state's borders by 20 April each year, it is at the end of the month that the arrival becomes widespread. First arrivals cover the state with surprising rapidity, sometimes reaching the northern counties within a week of the appearance of the first southern birds.

By 20 May there is not only a general dispersal into virtually every city and village, but also a buildup of strong migratory concentrations at a few locations. Howard Winkler described a scene he had witnessed several times in mid-May at Prairie du Chien (Crawford County) near the elongated chimney of a deserted factory: "At dusk we have noticed increased activity and agitated flying of the swifts. They gather together and fly in ever-smaller concentric circles, but continue to add to their numbers. This continues for perhaps 20 minutes when the entire flock must number in the tens of thousands. As if at a predetermined signal, some of the swifts leave the major group and drop—as if mortally shot—into the chimney. These are followed rapidly by the remainder of the swifts and the entire process lasts nearly an hour" (*Pass. Pigeon* 22:31).

By 5 June nonbreeding birds have moved northward and summer residents have begun nest con-

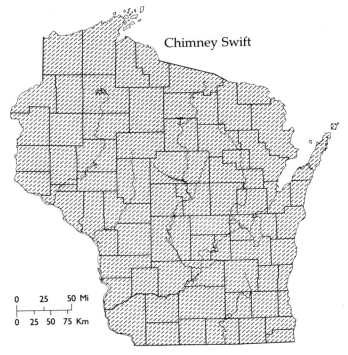

Chimney Swift

0   25   50 Mi

0   25 50 75 Km

Summer range

Records since 1960

struction. Most birds use the insides of chimneys. What a remarkable bit of engineering goes into a swift's nest! Birds break off twigs as they skim by treetops, then cement them firmly to a smooth brick surface with the saliva they secrete. Some swifts—particularly in the northern forested areas—continue to nest in dead tree stumps or on the walls of little-used barns and shacks. During the summer Carl Richter used to visit Chambers Island in Green Bay, where he would rap on hollow basswood trees and watch parent swifts flush out.

Because these "flying cigars" use natural cavities, even when chimneys are available, the birds have appeared on every BBS transect. Most people associate this species with urban industrial areas where tall chimneys abound. Undoubtedly a high percentage of the state's swifts frequent such habitat. But the pres-

356

ence of a few birds flying over openings in the northern forests—especially openings near small forest streams—allows for statewide distribution throughout the summer.

Although some young are on the wing by early July, nesting continues late for some birds. A. W. Schorger witnessed parents gathering new nesting material on 12 July 1931. On 29 September 1939 Francis Zirrer (pers. comm. to O. J. Gromme) saw a brood of young leave their nest for the first time.

Ordinarily most birds depart well before the end of September. In the north the fall migration is under way by 10 August and peaks from 20 August to 5 September, with all but stragglers gone by 15 September.

In many southern communities swifts also depart by the 15th, but in a few concentration areas groups may remain for another month. Beyond 25 October I know of 10 dates, including November stragglers on the 1st (1968, Fond du Lac, R. A. Knuth), 4th (1922, Dane, A. W. Schorger [1929b]), 7th (1882, Outagamie, F. L. Grundtvig [1895]), and 11th (1974, Sheboygan, D. D. Berger; Ozaukee, L. W. Erickson).

Banding recoveries indicate that birds leaving Wisconsin move due south or slightly farther east. Fall birds banded in Tennessee have been recaptured in Wisconsin the following spring or summer on 35 occasions. An additional six recoveries have come from Illinois, three from Louisiana, and one from Georgia.

Family **Trochilidae:** Hummingbirds

Ruby-throated Hummingbird (*Archilochus colubris*)

STATUS. Fairly common migrant. Fairly common summer resident.
HABITAT. Deciduous forest. Residential areas.
MIGRATION DATES. *Spring:* early May to early June. *Fall:* early August to late September. *Extremes:* 15 April; 19 December.
BREEDING DATA. Nests with eggs: 24 May to 5 August. Clutch size: 2 eggs.
PORTRAIT. *Birds of Wisconsin:* Plate 46.

The people who see this tiny jewel most often in spring and summer are those who live in residential areas with bright showy flowers and who have placed sugar-and-water feeders in their yards. In less populated areas in the north, the Ruby-throated Hummingbird is also at home around woodland edges, not far removed from beds of blossoming wild flowers. Rarely is it discovered in perching position. It is seen first hovering at blossoms or flying from one area to another. If the observer then follows the path of flight, a subsequent perch can be discovered. An exception occurs when utility wires pass close to a favored feeding area; birds then perch on these wires and use them as a departure point for their distinctive pendulum-swing maneuver.

Ordinarily this bird is not expected until 5 May in the south, 15 May in the north. It has been reported occasionally from 25 April on, and on four earlier April dates: the 15th (1977, Brown, Bro. Columban), 17th (1976, Ozaukee, D. K. Gustafson), 18th (1967, Sauk, H. C. Kruse), and 22nd (1975, Milwaukee, M. Wolver). The peak of spring migration, 20–30 May, is more evident from the frequency of observations than from the numbers of birds seen, for rarely does an observer encounter more than three or four on a spring field trip.

In the fall the picture is different. When a field of jewelweed is in blossom in late August or September, "hummers" may concentrate, as did the 50 birds Mrs. Walter Peirce encountered near her Racine home on 20 September 1941. In the northern and central regions, fall observations are most numerous in the 10 August–10 September period, with most birds gone by 20 September. A similar pattern, 10 days later, exists for the south, with a few late birds remaining through 20 October. There were two remarkably late birds in Madison in 1939 (23 October, L. Koehler;

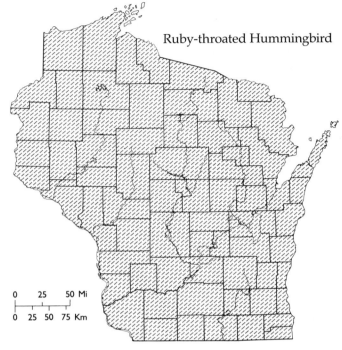

Ruby-throated Hummingbird

0   25   50 Mi

0 25 50 75 Km

Summer range

Records since 1960

2 November, S. D. Robbins), and two 1954 stragglers (24 October, Milwaukee, M. E. Decker; 30 October, Rock, H. G. Liebherr). More astonishing was a bird that was seen in Buffalo County several times in late November 1971 before it died on the 28th (M. and L. Maier). Even this late date was exceeded by 3 weeks in 1980 when an individual was a daily visitor into December at the Nelson and Olson feeders in Jacksonport (Door County). It survived snowstorms and subzero cold before it disappeared on 19 December (Lukes 1980).

Summer distribution is general throughout the state, with records known from all 72 counties. Vos Burgh (1928a) has had more success than most other observers in finding nests. The six nests he described were all saddled on oak branches, with height above ground varying from 6 to 40 feet. One wonders how the parents are able to gather the fuzzy fibers from the undersurface of oak leaves and the lichens that are essential nesting materials. John Stierle (pers. comm. to O. J. Gromme) once found a nest built against the bark on the main trunk of a tree, 5 feet above ground level. The tendency to use soft downy material in the nest may be a factor in inducing some later nesting dates at the time when dandelion and milkweed fluff becomes available. One of vos Burgh's

nests contained fresh eggs on 2 August; one of Schorger's (1929b) nests had eggs on 5 August. In Rusk County, Francis Zirrer (pers. comm. to O. J. Gromme) noted young just fledging on 29 August 1936, at the end of what had been an unusually dry summer. All documented Wisconsin nests have contained the typical clutch of two eggs per nest.

Anna's Hummingbird (*Calypte anna*)

STATUS. Accidental. One record.
HABITAT. Residential areas.

Between late August and 3 December 1990, a bright-plumaged male made daily visits to a feeder in the backyard of David and Susan Schmidt near Wales (Waukesha County). Although facial features suggested the possibility of an out-of-range Anna's Hummingbird, it was not until 28 November that R. R. Adams made positive identification and Lee Kranich obtained photographs. During the next 4 days another 55 birders observed this tiny jewel from the Pacific Coast. On 3 December, in the midst of a blizzard, the bird was trapped and moved to the tropical dome of Milwaukee's Mitchell Park Conservatory.

Anna's Hummingbird, 28 November 1990, Waukesha County (photo by L. Kranich)

Rufous Hummingbird (*Selasphorus rufus*)

STATUS. Accidental. Three records.
HABITAT. Residential areas.

Imagine a hummingbird feeder just outside your parlor window, frequently visited by Ruby-throats. Imagine that one day the Ruby-throats are frightened away by a strange hummingbird with a reddish-brown back. This was the experience of Linda and Vincent Vogt at their Cedarburg (Ozaukee County) home on 13 June 1986. The Vogts had close-up views of this male Rufous Hummingbird on the 13th and 14th, sometimes only 2 feet from the bird, and took splendid photographs. The stranger from the West acted aggressively, not only toward the Ruby-throated Hummingbirds, but also toward birds that attempted to visit nearby seed and suet feeders (*Pass. Pigeon* 49:114–115).

Two sight records preceded this observation. Wis-

consin's first sight observation involved a male at Racine in mid-September 1976. It was first seen on the 14th by Norma Struckhoff as it alternately perched on a tree and fed on insects in a patch of jewelweed. Subsequent observations were made on the 15th and 16th by Richard Kinch (*Am. Birds* 31:181).

On 31 August 1980 Randy Hoffman got within 6 feet of a male feeding among a group of Ruby-throats near Waunakee (Dane County). Realizing the rarity of the bird, the observer spent a half-hour with this group of "hummers," making careful comparisons and taking copious notes of the one individual whose back was rufous rather than green (*Pass. Pigeon* 43:139).

There has been a rash of extralimital sightings in summer and fall since 1973, with observations in New Hampshire, Vermont, Virginia, Georgia, Ohio, Minnesota, Iowa, and Missouri.

Family **Alcedinidae:** Kingfishers

Belted Kingfisher (*Ceryle alcyon*)

STATUS. Fairly common migrant. Fairly common summer resident. Uncommon winter resident south and central; rare winter resident north.

HABITAT. Ponds and streams. Inland lakes. Sand and gravel.

MIGRATION DATES. *Spring:* late March to late April. *Fall:* mid-September to early November.

BREEDING DATA. Nests with eggs: 26 April to 11 June. Nests with young: through 28 August. Clutch size: usually 5–7 eggs; rarely 4–9.

WINTER. Regularly present along main waterways north to St. Croix, Adams, Outagamie, and Manitowoc counties; occasionally present north to Douglas, Ashland, Vilas, Marinette, and Door counties.

PORTRAIT. *Birds of Wisconsin:* Plate 41.

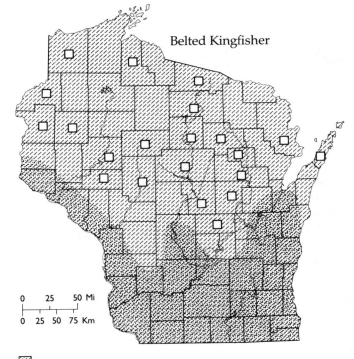

Belted Kingfisher

0   25   50 Mi

0   25 50 75 Km

     Summer range
     Winter range
☐   Mid-November to mid-March

Records since 1960

If kingfishers could have been trained to stay away from fish hatcheries, they might be considerably more numerous today. Aldo Leopold once heard a fish warden boast of having shot over 500 of these birds at one hatchery in one year.

If the kingfisher were as numerous as the Red-winged Blackbird, anglers might have just cause for looking askance at this avian custodian of the streams. They might better appreciate the kingfishers by learning from them where the fish are to be found. Although this bird is distributed evenly over all parts of the state, its numbers are not large anywhere. From one to four individuals are found on one-third of the BBS transects each year.

One need not be at a lake or stream to see a Belted Kingfisher. These birds nest in gravel pits that are sometimes 1½–2 miles away from water, and their sturdy rattle may be heard at any time as they fly over towns, fields, or woods between gravel pit nests and feeding grounds. Persons who have examined these birds' nesting sites have been impressed with the large burrows they dig. E. E. Davison (pers. comm. to O. J. Gromme) measured three tunnels 4–5 feet long; three of Carl Richter's nests measured over 6½ feet. More often than not, a layer of fish bones make up the nest surface near the end of the nest cavity. Francis Zirrer (pers. comm. to O. J. Gromme) related the sad tale of baby birds coming to the mouth of their nest cavity searching for cool air during the height of the 1934 drought; they toppled one by one down an embankment to their deaths because they were in such weakened condition.

Spring and fall migration are not conspicuous. There are no visual evidences of diurnal flocking or migratory movement; there are no reports of birds calling in overhead nocturnal migration. But some time in April there will suddenly be birds where there were none the previous day; and birds that were in evidence one day in September or early October will be gone the next. Most spring arrivals occur during the first half of April in the south, and from 10 to 25 April in the north. In the fall, observers note few birds in the north after 25 September; in the south most birds are gone by 15 October.

360

Extreme dates are impossible to fix because a few birds remain through the winter each year. There were few references to wintering birds before 1940, but the number of records has increased noticeably since then. The damming of rivers and creeks has in-creased; below each dam there is fast-running water which may remain open all winter and attract a king-fisher. Winter records have come from 56 counties, the most northerly being Douglas, Ashland, Vilas, Marinette, and Door counties.

Family **Picidae:** Woodpeckers

Lewis' Woodpecker (*Melanerpes lewis*)

STATUS. Accidental. One record.
HABITAT. Deciduous forest.

On a farm 10 miles from Peshtigo (Marinette County) a wandering Lewis' Woodpecker turned up on 1 January 1969. Commented Harold Lindberg: "The bird was in typical habitat (large trees in the open). It had the dark red cheeks, light neck band, reddish belly, dark greenish plumage, and was larger than a Hairy. When he flew he had the crow-like flight." Lindberg and Marvin Balwit photographed the bird and kept close track of it throughout the winter. By the time it finally disappeared on 10 April dozens of appreciative ornithologists had observed the bird (*Pass. Pigeon* 31:182).

Unlike some other western species, this bird is not known for its extralimital wanderings. It has been recorded in Massachusetts, Rhode Island, Missouri, Minnesota, Iowa, and Arkansas. An accidental record is as likely to occur in winter as in any other season. Sooner or later some sharp-eyed observer will discover a second Wisconsin bird.

Lewis' Woodpecker, 1 January 1964, Marinette County (photo by H. L. Lindberg)

Red-headed Woodpecker (*Melanerpes erythrocephalus*)

STATUS. Common migrant south and central; fairly common migrant north. Common summer resident south and central; fairly common summer resident north. Uncommon winter resident south and central.

HABITAT. Deciduous forest. Savanna. Residential areas.

MIGRATION DATES. *Spring:* late April to late May. *Fall:* early September to early October.

BREEDING DATA. Nests with eggs: 12 May to 19 June. Clutch size: usually 4 or 5; occasionally 3 or 6.

WINTER. Regularly present north to La Crosse, Waushara, and Brown counties; irregularly present north to Burnett, Washburn, Price, Oneida, Marinette, and Door counties.

PORTRAIT. *Birds of Wisconsin:* Plate 47.

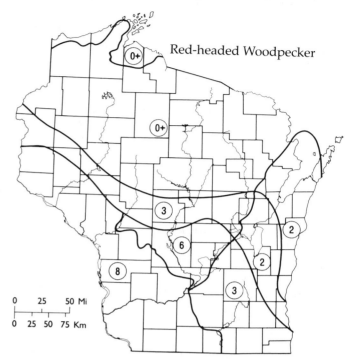

Breeding Bird Survey, averages 1966 to 1980

During the 1969 CBC, 65 counts tallied 473 of these colorful birds, with 30 or more on each of 5 counts. The following year only 85 Red-headed Woodpeckers were recorded on 61 counts; no area produced more than 10. Such is the wide fluctuation this bird exhibits as a winter resident. Whenever there is an abundant crop of acorns, significant numbers of Red-heads do not migrate. With great diligence they store hundreds of acorns during the autumn months. In the worst of the winter weather the birds remain sheltered in tree cavities; but in less severe weather they can often be seen and heard moving about in mature oak woodlots. No one knows how many of these overwintering birds survive, but many do. Individuals observed before 20 April are almost certainly birds that have wintered nearby. Those detected between 20 and 30 April could be either winter residents or migrants.

The main spring migration occurs between 1 and 15 May in the south, and 5 and 20 May in the central area. Birds reaching the northern counties are few, usually appearing between the 10th and 20th. But in the southern two-thirds of the state, when that first warm May day arrives, the population of Red-heads seems to explode. Along secondary roads where there were no birds one day, there seems to be one on every utility pole the next.

In spring and summer, as well as during winter, birds prefer mature oak woodlots. Since this habitat is most prevalent in the southwestern and central regions, it is not surprising that BBS results show the greatest summer populations in these areas. Farther north, as oaks become less numerous, this species chooses other deciduous trees for nesting sites. Six nests in Oconto County were located in willows,

poplars, and ash. Observers have found nest cavities as low as 3 feet above ground in fence posts, and as high as 60 feet, with a majority of locations between 20 and 30 feet.

The breeding season is a critical time for these woodpeckers. In July and August, as parents search for food for developing young, Red-heads are attracted to the insects that congregate close to paved roads. Being unusually slow in flight, these woodpeckers often fall victim to speeding cars. In an 18-year study of roadkills in southern Wisconsin, Schorger (1954a) found more dead specimens of this bird than of any other species except the House Sparrow.

Red-heads sometimes act aggressively toward other species. They have been known to pull baby Tree Swallows from their nesting boxes and to throw baby Northern Orioles from their nests. Strong (1891) observed a Red-head destroying an Eastern Kingbird nest after a vigorous battle. In another instance eggs were removed from a Northern Flicker nest.

Generally, birds depart from the northern counties by 10 September. In the central and southern regions the fall migration peaks between 5 and 20 September, with a gradual tapering off through 10 October. Individuals remaining beyond 20 October are likely to stay for the winter.

Populations have fluctuated considerably in the past 100 years. Whereas Hoy (1853b) described the species as common, Kumlien and Hollister (1903) called it very common and commented, "Few birds have so modified their habits in the past forty years as this species." In part they were referring to an increasing incidence of overwintering, but Hollister reiterated that these birds were becoming more abundant in 1919. Since 1930 a significant decline has occurred. Schorger's roadkill summary depicted a drop from 47 specimens per year in 1932 and 1935 to a low of 6 per year in 1948 and 1949. Highway casualties themselves would contribute to a decline; for the death of a parent in June and July might result in the starvation of orphan nestlings. Kemper (1973a) suggested that the decline might also be attributable to competition from starlings for suitable nesting cavities.

BBS figures show only minor fluctuations from 1966 through 1976 (usually 2.02–3.25 birds per transect per year), but show a 1977–1980 upswing (3.90–4.56) (Robbins 1977, 1982).

Red-bellied Woodpecker (*Melanerpes carolinus*)

STATUS. Fairly common resident west and south; uncommon resident north and east.
HABITAT. Deciduous forest. Southern silver maple–elm forest. Farmsteads.
BREEDING DATA. Nests with eggs: 28 April to 4 June.
    Clutch size: usually 3 eggs; occasionally 4.
PORTRAIT. *Birds of Wisconsin*: Plate 47.

Nineteenth-century ornithologists described this southern species as an uncommon resident in the eastern section of the state. The Red-bellied Woodpecker was known in Racine County by 1852 (Hoy 1853b), in Milwaukee and Jefferson counties by 1869 (T. L. Kumlien [Schorger 1944c]), in Brown County by 1877 (Willard 1885b), and in Outagamie County by 1882 (Grundtvig 1895). By the time of Kumlien and Hollister's writings (1903), there were records from Waukesha, Rock, Dane, Columbia, Dodge, and Oconto counties in the east and along the Mississippi in the west. Minnesota's first record came in 1893 just across the river from La Crosse. In 1894 a Red-bellied Woodpecker reached southern Dunn County (J. N. Clark [Buss and Mattison 1955]). The accompanying map shows the probable range extension by 1910.

During the ensuing 30 years no further advance occurred in the northeast. In fact, Richter's (1939b) comment that he had seen but one of these birds in Oconto County during the 1930s suggests that the birds' territories had diminished there. But a modest increase took place along the major river bottoms farther west; penetrations into the Wisconsin River area to Adams County occurred by 1929 (Gromme 1930c) and into the St. Croix River region north to Polk County by 1940 (S. P. Owen). Since 1940 a modest spread has continued in the western and central areas, mainly along the rivers. A. J. Petersen (1951) and Hamerstrom and Hamerstrom (1963) believed the tension zone imposed a northern range limit.

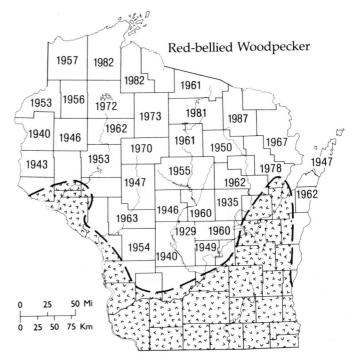

Red-bellied Woodpecker

▢ Resident range in 1910

Years of first county records

Through 1960 this was true. But further perusal of the range map shows that some penetration north of the tension zone has been in progress since 1960. Although there have been sporadic sightings north of the Grantsburg-Wausau-Marinette line, the bird is not yet established as a resident in the northernmost areas.

Evidence of advancing range has been most apparent in late fall and winter. CBC data show that in addition to expanding range limits in the northwest, the Red-belly has been increasing in numbers in the south. From Ellsworth (Pierce County) south and east to Sauk City, the Red-belly now outnumbers all other woodpeckers except the Downy. As many as 75 individuals have been recorded on a single count (Mazomanie [Dane County] 1975). In addition to populating the river-bottom woodlands, the "zebra-back" frequents suet feeders and corn cribs around neighboring farms.

Once established, the birds become permanent residents. Spring and summer sightings are noticeably less numerous than those in fall and winter, but this does not mean birds withdraw from an extensive winter range to a more limited summer area. In spring the birds retreat from the conspicuous corn cribs and concentrate in the heavier deciduous woodlands. As they enter the breeding cycle, they become characteristically quieter, and thus escape notice.

Precise breeding data are scanty. According to Kumlien and Hollister (1903) "the eggs have been taken several times in Jefferson County, where the nesting sites were always in large dead trees over-

hanging water, and generally at a considerable height, and very hard to reach." In Dane County on 1 June 1911, Stoddard (1917) found a nest hole on an elm limb suspended at a 45-degree angle over water. Observers have discovered other nests in oak, birch, maple, apple, and butternut trees, with nest cavities 12–40 feet up. No definite reports of nests containing eggs beyond 4 June exist; but it is likely that egg-care extends beyond the 15th, because nests with noisy young have been noted through 14 July. Various observers who maintain year-round feeders have found family groups—parents with two or three young—coming to the feeders in July and August.

If this species is still extending its range, the spread is gradual indeed. CBC participants habitually look upon open corn cribs as "gigantic winter feeders" where Red-bellies can often be found. Open corn cribs are uncommon north of the 1980 range limit; without them, Red-bellies may find winter survival difficult.

Yellow-bellied Sapsucker (*Sphyrapicus varius*)

STATUS. Fairly common migrant. Fairly common summer resident north; uncommon summer resident central and southwest. Uncommon winter resident south; rare winter resident central.

HABITAT. Deciduous forest. Northern maple-hemlock-pine forest.

MIGRATION DATES. *Spring:* late March to mid-May. *Fall:* early September to late October.

BREEDING DATA. Nests with eggs: 4 May to 11 June. Clutch size: usually 4 or 5 eggs; occasionally 3 or 6.

WINTER. Regularly present north to Dane and Ozaukee counties; occasionally present north to Buffalo, Jackson, Waushara, Outagamie, and Manitowoc counties; rarely present north to Barron, Sawyer, Ashland, Langlade, and Door counties.

PORTRAIT. *Birds of Wisconsin:* Plate 49.

On a quiet morning drive from Ladysmith to Park Falls on 29 April 1973, I was amazed by the number of Yellow-bellied Sapsuckers that I could hear from the highway. The distinctive "ta-ta, ta, ta, ta" rhythm could be heard from one to three directions at almost every stop. If this was not the most common bird in the northwoods that day, it was certainly the noisiest. Small wonder that some writers (notably, Kumlien and Hollister [1903]) have called it abundant.

But that day in the northwoods was probably "general arrival day" when migrants joined local residents.

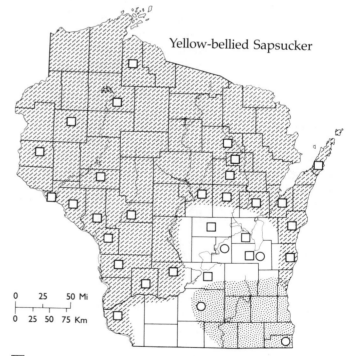

Yellow-bellied Sapsucker

0   25   50 Mi
0   25 50 75 Km

▨ Summer range
▦ Winter range
○ Late May to late August
□ Early November to late February

Records since 1960

At no other time does one get such an impression of abundance. Urban and suburban dwellers experience these sapsuckers in quite a different way. One or two birds may spend a few April days in a certain neighborhood sampling the sap of several maple or spruce trees, but their pecking is so delicate and their movements so unobtrusive that they often escape notice. An observer can easily go through a spring migration and see no more than five individuals.

Most Wisconsin sapsuckers migrate in April. In the south the main flight occurs between 10 and 25 April; a few span the 30 March–10 May period. In the north a few may appear by 5 April, with the main push coming between 20 April and 15 May. Grundtvig's (1895) comments on spring habits of this bird still hold true: "Early in the spring it feeds a great deal on the sap of the sugar maple. . . . It makes small holes in the trees. Usually a band of such holes . . . reach only half way round the trunk and are then found mostly on the south side where the sap runs most freely."

For nesting sites birds prefer deciduous trees with a somewhat thin bark. The three nests reported by C. H. Richter near Oconto were all in aspen cavities 8–20 feet up. In the Marshfield (Wood County) area J. W. Stierle (pers. comm. to O. J. Gromme) found three nests, 20–34 feet up, two in birch trees and one in a basswood. Parents have been observed feeding young in the nests as late as 17 July.

In the nineteenth century the summer range encompassed the entire state. The bird was an uncommon breeder in the south and became progressively more common farther north. A curious range now exists, as depicted in the accompanying map. North of a line from St. Croix Falls through Medford, Shawano, and Sturgeon Bay this sapsucker is a fairly common breeder. It is regular in small numbers through much of the western region south along the Mississippi to the Illinois border, and along the Wisconsin to the Baraboo hills and Prairie du Chien. Also, it regularly occurs in a narrow band of the eastern region south to Cedarburg Bog in Ozaukee County. Only three modern summer records from the southeastern region exist: 4–25 June (1948, Rock, M. T. Maxson), 27 June (1980, Green Lake, S. D. Robbins), and 1 July (1970, Kenosha, W. O. Moye).

BBS figures are deceptively low, since June is a relatively quiet month in the life of this species. On only 5 of the state's 70 June transects is an average of five individuals per year maintained. The Grandview route (Bayfield County) leads with nine birds.

The fall migration occurs in a remarkably unobtrusive fashion. My personal records show no more than six individuals found on a single day. Similarly, other observers have reported small numbers. Television-tower casualties have been few. There should be a larger number of migrants in fall than in spring; one can only conclude that many birds pass through unnoticed because they are quiet. In the central region migrants appear by 10 September, with numbers peaking from 20 September to 5 October; they are gone by 15 October. Farther south the migration is 5–10 days later. Birds present after 25 October are likely to remain for the winter. Francis Zirrer (pers. comm. to O. J. Gromme) aptly observed that in fall this species shows a preference for tamarack and spruce bogs.

Although Wisconsin is north of the regular winter range, at least 2 birds—sometimes as many as 15—are found every winter. Most are immatures attracted to feeders where suet is available. They generally seek shelter in spruce trees, where they sometimes spend long periods huddled motionless on the trunk. Most wintering observations have come from Madison, Cedarburg, and Milwaukee. As the accompanying map shows, recent winter sightings have occurred in virtually every county in the west, north to Buffalo County, and in the central and eastern regions north to Portage, Shawano, and Brown counties. Still farther north there have been exceptional records from St. Croix, Barron, Sawyer, Ashland, Langlade, Menominee, and Door counties.

Downy Woodpecker (*Picoides pubescens*)

STATUS. Common resident.
HABITAT. All forests. Residential areas.
BREEDING DATA. Nests with eggs: 11 May to 18 June.
  Clutch size: usually 4–6 eggs; occasionally 7.
PORTRAIT. *Birds of Wisconsin:* Plate 49.

It is perhaps an exaggeration to state that anyone who maintains a fresh supply of suet can expect one or two Downy Woodpeckers at his feeder all winter anywhere in Wisconsin. But it is a fact that winter distribution of this bird blankets the state. Out of 1,579 CBC surveys conducted between 1960 and 1987, 1,526 have recorded Downies, with an average of 20 per count. The well-organized counts in the major metropolitan areas—Milwaukee, Madison, Beloit, Waukesha, Appleton—often record over 50 per count, mainly at feeding stations. Comparable numbers are also found on counts near Wautoma (Waushara County) and Sauk City where feeders are less numerous but deciduous woods are plentiful. In 1978, Newburg (Ozaukee County) CBC observers tallied a phenomenal 271 individuals.

Young's (1961a) projection of 1939–1959 CBC data, indicating greatest abundance in the southwest and smallest numbers in the northwest, is substantiated by more recent figures. Data since 1971 show an average of 0.9–1.0 Downies per party-hour in the southwestern, western, and central regions, 0.6–0.8 in the south and east, and 0.4–0.5 in the north. Recent figures also support Young's thesis that the Downy outnumbers the Hairy throughout the state; a 10:9 ratio in the northwest increases to a 3:1 difference in the southeast. The 10:9 margin holds north of a line from New Richmond through Barron, Shawano, and Sturgeon Bay. The 3:1 comparison exists south of a line linking Blanchardville, Madison, Oshkosh, and Manitowoc.

Do our Downies migrate? The fact that northern range limits in Canada are virtually the same in winter and summer might imply little, if any, migratory movement. Yet there is some evidence of modest migration of some Wisconsin birds. On the basis of the frequency with which he saw birds, Francis Dayton (pers. comm. to O. J. Gromme) of New London (Waupaca County) believed there was a northward movement in March and some southward traveling in October. In the revision of Kumlien and Hollister (1903) Schorger (1951a) suggested that a few birds of the *nelsoni* race might move south and winter in Wisconsin. Data are lacking. But on 4 October 1956 a tower-kill was reported in Milwaukee (C. S. Jung). A bird banded at Milton (Rock County) on 13 January 1948

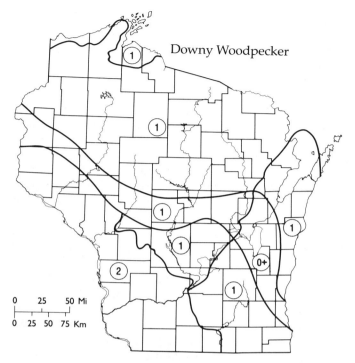

Downy Woodpecker

Breeding Bird Survey, averages 1966 to 1980

(Maxson 1949) was recovered a year later at Clintonville (Waupaca County). Two banded Illinois birds and one from Iowa have been caught in Wisconsin, while birds ringed in Wisconsin have been found in Minnesota, Michigan, and Illinois.

BBS data in June depict a summer range covering the entire state. This species has been recorded on 69 of the state's 70 transects. Yet BBS results are probably deceptive when applied to population levels. BBS densities of one bird per transect per year suggest uniform density in most areas of the state. But since June is a quiet time of year for these diminutive woodpeckers, population levels are undoubtedly higher than these data show.

June is a month for raising young. Nest sites typically are excavations 10–30 feet up in the trunks of deciduous trees. A few nests have been located as high up as 40–55 feet. Kumlien and Hollister (1903) mentioned one nest scarcely 2 feet off the ground. Angie Main (pers. comm. to O. J. Gromme) described one in a wooden clothes post. Observers have detected nests with noisy nestlings as early as 22 May, but usually it is in June that parents are kept busiest satisfying juvenile appetites. People who maintain suet feeders in summer often see family groups through July as baby birds are gradually learning to be self-sufficient.

Hairy Woodpecker (*Picoides villosus*)

STATUS. Common resident.
HABITAT. All forest. Residential areas.
BREEDING DATA. Nests with eggs: 1 May to 11 June.
  Clutch size: usually 4 eggs; occasionally 3.
PORTRAIT. *Birds of Wisconsin:* Plate 49.

During winter the Hairy Woodpecker is widely distributed throughout the state. CBC data between 1960 and 1985 show birds recorded on 1,617 of 1,834 counts, with an average of 8–18 individuals per count per year. In an analysis of CBC data from 1939 to 1959, Young (1961a) surmised that this woodpecker was more numerous in the southwest, less numerous in the east, with reports from the north too fragmentary for evaluation. With more complete coverage since 1960, it now appears that the bird is most plentiful in the central, western, and northwestern regions (0.5–0.7 birds per party-hour), moderate in the southwest (0.4–0.5), and least numerous in the east and southeast (0.2–0.3). The smaller numbers in the southeast are dictated by the habitat. In suitable wooded territory, such as near Lake Geneva (Walworth County) and Cedarburg (Ozaukee County), the population is strong.

They are readily attracted to winter feeders wherever suet is provided. Living in a cabin in the Hayward area in Sawyer County, Francis Zirrer (pers. comm. to O. J. Gromme) found the birds to be very tame, "taking a morsel off one's knife or picking one's hand through the porch screen. If no food is on the table, they come to the roof and pound until food is given."

In early spring Zirrer saw birds feeding on maples in a manner similar to the Yellow-bellied Sapsucker. Zirrer commented: "Sometimes when a tree is leaning to one side, frozen sap in the form of an icicle several feet long hangs from it. Later in the day when it warms up, the icicle falls off." Hairies feed on these "sapsicles."

By late April preparation for nesting is under way. Of nine Oconto County nests reported by C. H. Richter, six held eggs during the first week of May. With the exception of one nest cavity 6 feet up in a popple stub, all nests were 20–48 feet up in trunks of deciduous trees: birch, aspen, and poplar. Nests with noisy young are often encountered between 20 May and 20 June.

At BBS time in June these birds have become largely

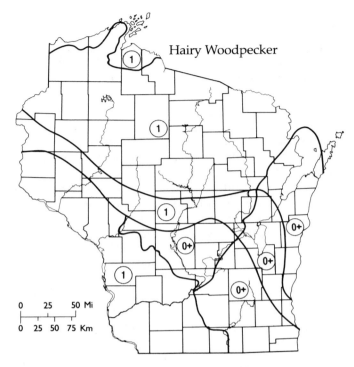

Hairy Woodpecker

Breeding Bird Survey, averages 1966 to 1980

quiet. If one were to rely on the BBS as a sole measure of this bird's abundance in summer, one would conclude that the Hairy Woodpecker is an uncommon species. Only 10 of 70 routes have averaged more than one individual per transect per year since the project's inception in 1966. On the transects south of Green Bay close to Lake Michigan, the bird has been recorded but once. In reality it is not that scarce.

Although the BBS figures are far below those of winter, it cannot be assumed that there is a significant migratory exit in spring. Most if not all winter birds probably remain in the vicinity. But they retreat to more remote areas for breeding and are less likely to be seen or heard on roadside transects.

Some observers have suggested that there is some northward migration in March and a southward movement in October. But positive evidence is lacking. There are no verified banding recoveries, no towerkills, no published reports of visible migration. Continent-wide, there is no significant northerly extension of breeding range beyond the species' winter range.

Three-toed Woodpecker (*Picoides tridactylus*)

Formerly Northern Three-toed Woodpecker, American Three-toed Woodpecker

STATUS. Rare migrant north. Casual summer visitant north. Rare winter resident north.
HABITAT. Coniferous forest.
MIGRATION DATES. *Spring:* mid-February to mid-April. *Fall:* late September to mid-November.
WINTER. Rarely present south to Polk, Rusk, Taylor, and Oconto counties.
PORTRAIT. *Birds of Wisconsin:* Plate 50.

Although the Three-toed Woodpecker had been considered mainly a winter resident, the only observations between 1900 and 1925 were in late summer. This species was probably never anything other than a rarity in Wisconsin. Kumlien and Hollister (1903) described it as a rare winter visitant on the basis of an estimated 12 specimens collected during winter in the Jefferson County tamarack bogs in the 1860s (T. L. and A. L. Kumlien) and on specimens taken on 23 and 30 September 1898 in Iron County (H. V. Ogden, E. Copeland). One additional nineteenth-century bird, collected in Dunn County by J. N. Clark (Buss and Mattison 1955), bears no date.

When H. H. T. Jackson (1943) collected a pair in Sawyer County on 9 August 1919, he speculated that they may have been a breeding pair. Two additional summer sightings followed when Jung (1927) saw in-

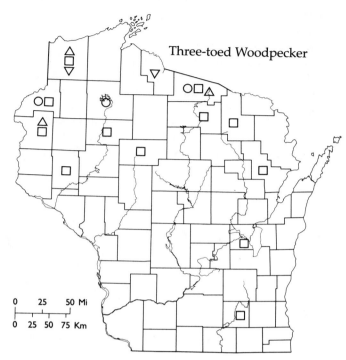

Three-toed Woodpecker

△ Mid-February to mid-April
○ 5 July to 26 August
▽ Late September to mid-November
□ Late November to early February

All records

Three-toed Woodpecker, 8 February 1986, Taylor County (photo by J. H. Idzikowski)

dividuals near Phelps (Vilas County) on 26 August 1920 and from 28 to 31 July 1921.

The only record at any season in the 1930s is of a bird seen on 9 February 1930 (Forest, O. J. Gromme; MPM files). The 1940s added six observations: 21 February 1941 (Vilas, E. B. Miles), 24 March 1944 (Douglas, W. Berner), 30 March 1945 (Vilas, E. B. Miles), 30 October 1945 (Douglas, F. A. Hartmeister), 6 December 1945 (Douglas, W. C. Pelzer), and 11 January 1946 (Rusk, B. Stollberg).

When Thiel (1978a) listed published notes and records gleaned from Department of Natural Resources personnel for this species, he noted only two observations between 1946 and 1966. Talbati (MPM files) observed individuals in Winnebago County on 6 February and 7–8 March 1956. The late 1960s produced four sightings: 24 December 1966 (Forest, T. K. Soulen), 10 March 1968 (Douglas, M. Granlund), 21 December 1968 (Douglas, B. F. Klugow), and 30 November 1969 (Oneida, L. E. Compton).

Four more wanderers were detected in the 1970s: 10 February 1972 (Taylor, J. O. Evrard), 7 February 1973 (Oconto, T. C. Erdman), 8 March 1975 (Polk, K. H. Dueholm, photographed by C. A. Faanes [1975b] on 14 March), and 11 April 1976 (Polk, B. F. Klugow).

Three additional sightings were made in the northwestern counties in 1982: 5 July (Burnett, P. Fuller), 23 November (Polk, C. Jorgenson), and 30 November (Douglas, J. L. Polk). Fuller continued to see her bird off and on through February 1983.

In 1984 Robert Spahn discovered another summer vagrant in Vilas County on 4 August. When Leonard Risch found one in Taylor County on 19 September 1985, it marked the fourth consecutive year of the presence of this Canadian visitor in northern Wisconsin. It also marked the beginning of an unprecedented influx that brought at least five individuals to Taylor County by 30 December, with some remaining until 15 March 1986 (Robbins 1986).

I know of no records between 11 April and 5 July; but taking into consideration the inaccessibility of the tamarack-spruce bog habitat the "ladder-back" prefers, one can easily imagine that this species may be more numerous than these records indicate. There may possibly be a few pairs in the remote northern areas in summer. The answers may come from observations yet to be made.

Black-backed Woodpecker (*Picoides arcticus*)

Formerly Black-backed Three-toed Woodpecker, Arctic Three-toed Woodpecker

STATUS. Uncommon resident north. Rare winter resident east and central.

HABITAT. Coniferous forest.

MIGRATION DATES. *Spring:* mid-February to late April. *Fall:* mid-September to late November.

BREEDING DATA. Nests with eggs: 8 May to 30 June. Clutch size: 3–5 eggs.

WINTER. Regularly present south to Sawyer, Oneida, Marinette, and Door counties; occasionally present south to Polk, Taylor, Waupaca, and Manitowoc counties; accidental elsewhere.

PORTRAIT. *Birds of Wisconsin:* Plate 50.

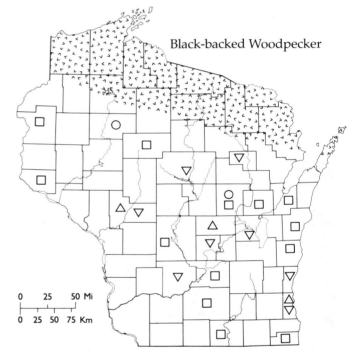

Black-backed Woodpecker

0   25   50 Mi
0 25 50 75 Km

⌐ᴧ⌐┐ Resident range
△ Mid-February to late April
○ Early May to early September
▽ Mid-September to late November
□ Early December to early February

Records since 1960

It is hard for present-day ornithologists to realize that the Black-backed Woodpecker was once a common winter resident in the southeastern part of the state. In the 1860s such concentrations existed in the Jefferson County tamarack swamps that Kumlien and Hollister (1903) spoke of these birds as abundant in winter. But as the heavy timber was cut this species receded, and by the turn of the century the bird was scarce. In western Wisconsin no such southern range was known. There are no records south of Dunn County, where J. N. Clark (Buss and Mattison 1955) took four winter specimens between 1889 and 1899, a time of intensive logging. As the logging proceeded, the birds retreated northward.

The current range of the permanent residents is confined to the northernmost counties. North of a line from Danbury through Phillips, Rhinelander, Marinette, and Sturgeon Bay, birds can be found in

Black-backed Woodpecker, July 1981, Ashland County (photo by L. E. Gregg)

are not nearly as noisy as other woodpeckers. Flying from one tree to another, they occasionally emit a faint 'eek-eek-eek'; but most of the time they fly—or rather sneak—away without a sound." This silence is particularly true during summer when woodpeckers in general are relatively quiet. The birds' tendency to avoid conspicuous perches also makes locating them difficult. According to Zirrer, "in searching for food, most of their work is done low, not much over ten feet above ground. Usually they land with a very faint 'zick-zick' about eight feet up, investigate a little, then move backward down to about two feet above the ground, and from there fly with another faint 'zick-zick' to the next tree. One must be very near to hear the call."

Few people have observed actual nests. In June 1940 J. L. Diedrich examined a Price County nest in a cavity 12 feet up in a white cedar. Diedrich found two young Black-backs and two cowbird eggs. In June 1968 a Douglas County pair nested 12 feet up in a spruce and fledged five young (R. F. Bernard). Several observers watched a pair feeding young at the same site in mid-June 1977. From the 11 nest records listed by Thiel, including 6 pre-1920 observations, egg-laying presumably starts around 5–15 May, with parents feeding nestlings through 20 June.

Rarely, a few individuals wander south in the eastern portion of the state for the winter months. Occasionally they turn up at winter feeders; more often they are attracted to parks or woodlots. Observers have noted extralimital movement by 11 September (1965, Langlade, T. K. Soulen) and 15 September (1973, Jackson, R. Auler). October 1965 produced added sightings on the 20th (Winnebago, E. A. Natzke), 26th (Rock, M. T. Maxson), 27th (Manitowoc, R. J. Rensink), and 31st (Milwaukee, W. Seifert). The accompanying map shows where other October-April wanderers have been recorded since 1960. Few birds remain beyond mid-April. Notable exceptions include one through 23 May (1973, Dane, W. L. Hilsenhoff), one between 28 May and 1 June (1957, Waukesha, N. F. Smith), and one on 30 May (1983, Jackson, D. D. Tessen).

a few selected locations. The only positive nesting records since 1940 have come from Douglas, Price, Iron, and Waupaca counties. When Thiel (1978a) published a list of sightings by Wisconsin Conservation Department personnel in northern Wisconsin, 1941–1947, he listed summer observations in Sawyer, Forest, and Florence counties. Since 1960 summer observations have come from the same areas, plus Bayfield, Ashland, Oneida, Vilas, and Door counties. Regular breeding is probable in all these counties, except Waupaca.

Finding these birds is a challenge. They prefer two types of habitat: tamarack bogs and recently burned-over jack pine stands. If one finds trees from which portions of bark have recently been removed, there is a good chance that Black-backs are in the area. Then it is often a matter of patient observation from a good vantage point, plus luck. Francis Zirrer's (pers. comm. to O. J. Gromme) comments are typical: "They

Northern Flicker (*Colaptes auratus*)

Formerly Yellow-shafted Flicker, Common Flicker

STATUS. Common migrant. Common summer resident. Uncommon winter resident south; rare winter resident central.

HABITAT. Deciduous forest. Savanna. Residential areas.

MIGRATION DATES. *Spring:* late March to early May. *Fall:* early September to late October.

BREEDING DATA. Nests with eggs: 3 May to 11 June. Clutch size: usually 6 or 7 eggs; occasionally 4–9.

WINTER. Small numbers are regularly present north to St. Croix, La Crosse, Waupaca, and Manitowoc counties: occasionally present north to Burnett, Ashland, Shawano, and Marinette counties.

PORTRAIT. *Birds of Wisconsin:* Plate 47.

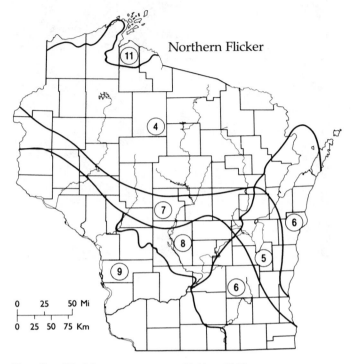

Breeding Bird Survey, averages 1966 to 1980

April is "flicker month." During the first half Northern Flickers reach all sections of the state; during the second half the main flight occurs, seemingly placing a pair in every residential backyard that has a sizable tree. When weather conditions are favorable in April, it is delightful to watch migrating "yellow-hammers" move along their main migration paths. In an hour's observation time at the ridge at Cedar Grove, along the shore of the Petenwell Flowage, atop the Mississippi bluffs below Prescott, or along Wisconsin Point at Superior, one can see 50 or more birds loping by in their characteristic undulating flight—one, two, or three at a time. More than many other species, this bird does much of its migrating by day.

By early May, when breeding activity starts, a reasonably general distribution pattern throughout the state has occurred. As one might expect of a bird that prefers deciduous trees to conifers, the Northern Flicker is most numerous in the heavily wooded southwestern region and least plentiful in the north-central part of the state. But a glance at the BBS map shows that there is representation in all sectors. Birds have been recorded on all of the state's 70 BBS transects.

Strictly a cavity-nester, this bird has been reported using holes at heights ranging from 5 feet (fence post) to 40 (mature poplar). The presence of nests of other species nearby in the same tree is no deterrent to these birds. I once watched a pair of Northern Flickers excavate a nest hole 10 feet up in a decaying white ash; an active American Robin nest stood barely 3 feet below, in a rotted depression in the same tree trunk. The shower of chips and sawdust filtering down through the decaying trunk, as a result of the flick-

er's drilling, eventually blanketed the robin nest completely.

The Northern Flicker's propensity for laying six or seven eggs per clutch was vividly illustrated by oologist E. A. Davison (pers. comm. to O. J. Gromme) in 1932. He discovered a nest with three eggs on 5 May, removed two, and found new eggs on each succeeding day. Although he removed 17 eggs over a 15-day period, persistent egg-laying eventually resulted in the birds' raising a family of seven young.

Although flickers remain in the vicinity of their breeding sites through July and August, they apparently do not raise second broods. Most young are on the wing by 10 July. Frequently in late summer family groups are seen on the ground feeding around anthills.

A modest migratory movement gets under way by 1 September, with the main push spanning the 10 September–15 October period. This flicker may travel long distances in a few short weeks. Melva Maxson banded one in Rock County on 16 August 1950; the bird was recovered in Mississippi on 20 October 1950. Few birds remain beyond 15 October in the north, 25 October in the south.

Individuals still present on 15 November are likely to overwinter. Every winter observers see and hear birds in the lower Wisconsin River bottomlands, in tamarack bogs in Jefferson County, and at Cedarburg Bog in Ozaukee County. The winter of 1969–1970 was exceptional, with CBC sightings of 25 at Oconomowoc (Waukesha County), 20 at Lake Geneva (Walworth County), 13 at Sauk City, and scattered individuals north to St. Croix, Barron, Chippewa, and Outagamie counties, totaling 138 individuals on 29 counts. A more usual pattern at that time would have been 35–40 birds on 10–15 counts. Since 1978 the number of individuals observed on the CBCs has consistently exceeded 100, suggesting that this species is gradually increasing as a winter resident in the southern half of the state. Kumlien and Hollister (1903) made no mention of the bird as a wintering species.

At the same time the BBS indicates that summer populations may be decreasing. After averaging 7.69 individuals per transect per year in the 1966–1969 interval, 4-year averages dropped steadily, reaching 4.76 in the 1978–1980 span but holding their own since 1980.

Birds banded in Wisconsin in summer or early fall have been recovered the following winter in Tennessee (1), Mississippi (3), Louisiana (3), and Missouri (1), implying that our birds mainly winter due south of us. But the possibility that Wisconsin gets a few individuals from farther west is suggested by rare visits of birds exhibiting traces of the red-shafted race *cafer*. Five such birds were collected near Milton (Rock County), one on 10 May 1892 (Kumlien and Hollister 1903). One was taken at Milwaukee on 28 May 1937 (J. L. Diedrich; MPM files). One frequented the Joann Klink (1970a) feeder at Eau Claire from 31 December 1968 to 3 March 1969, and again on 19 November 1969. One was observed in Iron County on 7 July 1978 (M. E. Butterbrodt).

Pileated Woodpecker (*Dryocopus pileatus*)

STATUS. Uncommon resident north, central, and southwest; rare resident southeast.
HABITAT. Deciduous forest. Northern maple-hemlock-pine forest.
BREEDING DATA. Nests with eggs: 27 April to 25 May. Clutch size: usually 4 eggs; occasionally 3–6.
WINTER. Regularly present south to Grant, Dane, and Ozaukee counties; occasionally present elsewhere.
PORTRAIT: *Birds of Wisconsin*: Plate 48.

When G. C. Becker (1942) wrote his definitive "Notes on the Pileated Woodpecker in Wisconsin," he described a range covering all of northwestern Wisconsin bounded roughly by the Mississippi River south into northern Illinois, the Wisconsin River bottomlands from Prairie du Chien to Stevens Point, and an erratic line from Stevens Point through Peshtigo and Sturgeon Bay (see the accompanying map). Ninety years earlier, this bird could have been found anywhere in the state where there was mature timber. Hoy (1853b) found it in suitable habitat near Racine. Kumlien and Hollister (1903) recorded it breeding in Jefferson County through 1872, with last sightings there in 1877, and in Walworth County in 1899.

Not only was the bird pushed back from one-third of the state by the advancing plow, but also its numbers were reduced in much of the other two-thirds by the intensive logging that decimated much of the virgin forest. Reminiscing about boyhood days in the

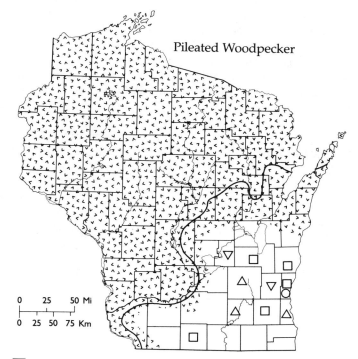

Pileated Woodpecker

0   25   50 Mi
0 25 50 75 Km

⊡ Resident range (— edge of Becker line, 1942)
△ Mid-March to mid-May
○ Late May to late August
▽ Early September to late November
☐ Early December to early March

Records since 1960

Baraboo hills, Stoddard (1947) wrote: "As early as 1900 pileated woodpeckers had apparently been 'shot out' of both the Baraboo bluffs and the Wisconsin River bottoms. . . . The birds had disappeared while their forest range was still in pretty good condition. Then they staged a spectacular comeback on more or less devastated range." Stoddard believed that the decline was due more to shooting by woodsmen and fur trappers than to habitat deterioration.

For many years birders from the Milwaukee region have had to journey north and west to meet up with "pilly." Their favorite trip has taken them to the Wisconsin River bottomlands near Mazomanie and Sauk City. Such trips have produced sightings of birds in every season. Invariably, observers find these birds on the Christmas count there; numbers climbed to 22 in 1966. The sorties into the river bottoms have been particularly successful in April and May when the birds are noisiest. The wild flickerlike "wuk-wuk-wuk" call has thrilled many an expectant listener. The distinctive drumming—starting loudly, then diminishing in intensity—excites the imagination of anyone who has ever gazed at the huge holes that the birds gouge out of dead or dying tree trunks. "Wow!" exclaimed a youngster once at a summer camp when we viewed a recent Pileated excavation along a path to his cabin, "and to think that I walked right by this tree this morning and didn't notice it!" When told that the hole had not been there that morning and had been dug within a 10-minute span during the afternoon, the boy responded with an even louder "Wow!"

Spring visits have sometimes included opportunities to witness nesting activities. Nests reported in Wisconsin have all been found in deciduous trees: some live, some dead. Some nests are no more than 14 feet from the ground, but usually the cavities are from 25 to 50 feet up. The observation of copulation on 26 March (1941, K. W. Kahmann) suggests that some egg-laying may begin by early April. But the earliest known date for eggs is 27 April. Carl Richter, reporting on 14 nests, estimated the probable date for first egg deposition at 2 May. Most observations of parents feeding young in the nest have occurred between 20 May and 10 June.

Every now and then individuals engage in considerable wandering. Birds took up brief residence in the University of Wisconsin Arboretum at Madison in December 1966 and 1967, but did not become established. Birds have also been seen briefly in Jefferson, Dodge, Waukesha, and Ozaukee counties, usually in winter or spring.

It may be because of similar wanderings that this species is gradually reestablishing itself in some of its former range. Buss and Mattison (1955) cited Lawrence Johnson's long-term observations in Dunn County to show how the bird's status has changed; in the early 1900s it was rare, but there was at least a moderate increase in numbers by 1949. G. C. Becker (1942) also detected signs of increased numbers and expressed the hope that "the Forest Crop Law perhaps will be instrumental in bringing the bird back to the now unoccupied counties in southern and eastern Wisconsin." The accompanying map shows a modest fulfillment of this hope, with gains primarily in the eastern region.

Increasing numbers have appeared on CBCs since 1973. Annual averages, 1962–1966, showed 46 individuals on 23 of the 67 counts taken per year. There was little change from 1967 to 1971, with an annual average of 45 birds on 20 of 64 counts. From 1972 to 1976, averages increased to 65 birds on 29 of 65 counts. The average was 115 birds on 44 of 77 counts (1977–1981), and 123 birds on 43 of 83 counts (1982–1986). Part of the increase could reflect improved coverage, but a real population gain is also likely. Slight but definite increases have also been apparent in the June BBS as well.

Family **Tyrannidae:** Tyrant Flycatchers

Olive-sided Flycatcher (*Contopus borealis*)

STATUS. Uncommon migrant. Uncommon summer resident north.

HABITAT. Conifer swamp.

MIGRATION DATES. *Spring:* mid-May to mid-June. *Fall:* early August to mid-September. *Extremes:* 1 May; 25 October.

BREEDING DATA. Nests with eggs: 17–24 June. Clutch size: probably 3 eggs.

PORTRAIT. *Birds of Wisconsin:* Plate 51.

On a late-July 1955 tour through northwestern Wisconsin, I counted Olive-sided Flycatchers singing or calling in six areas in Burnett, Douglas, Sawyer, and Taylor counties. Because this was one of my first trips through this region, and many birds were in a quiet period, I was led to believe that this species was a fairly common summer resident throughout the northwoods wherever suitable spruce-tamarack swamps existed. Subsequent sorties indicated that I was exceptionally lucky on the 1955 trip, for two to four birds per tour is all that my more recent explorations have produced. I know of no data that suggest this species has ever been a common summer resident south of its current range: north of a line from Grantsburg through Shawano to Sturgeon Bay.

To see an Olive-sided Flycatcher in summer one must look for an extensive spruce-tamarack bog with underlying sphagnum moss. The bog should be relatively open, with a few trees—preferably one or more dead trees, too—offering suitable perches. The males sing their distinctive three-syllable "whip-three-beers" from the conspicuous uppermost perches, sally forth in quest of insects, and usually return to the same treetop. The females, incubating eggs or caring for young, are far more difficult to spot, for the nest is generally located in thick foliage on lateral spruce branches. The state's only positive nesting records consist of Schoenebeck's (1902) 17 June 1899 discovery of a nest with two eggs in Oneida County, and J. L. Diedrich and O. J. Gromme's finding of two nests in Price County on 24 June 1940 (Gromme 1941a).

This flycatcher is one of the latest spring migrants, one of very few for which there is no well-documented April record. Arrivals on 1 May (1942, Waukesha, H. A. Clapp), 2 May (1965, Rock, M. T. Maxson),

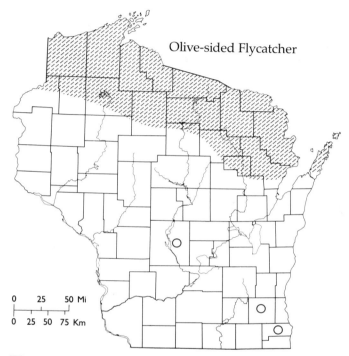

Olive-sided Flycatcher

0   25   50 Mi
0 25 50 75 Km

▨ Summer range
○ Mid-June to late July

Records since 1960

3 May (1970, Milwaukee, M. F. Donald), and 4 May (1949, Milwaukee, G. H. Orians) were unusually early. Most sightings are made from 15 to 30 May in the south, 20 May to 5 June in the north. Migrants lingering into early June are not unusual, the latest coming on the 11th (1967, Rock, M. K. Stocking), 12th (1968, Monroe, D. K. Gustafson), 13th (1955, Chippewa, C. A. Kemper), and 15th (1974, Winnebago, C. Schultz). Midsummer observations far south of the species' known nesting range have taken place on 24 June (1973, Adams, D. D. Tessen), 2 July (1976, Waukesha, J. E. Bielefeldt), and 16 July (1967, Racine, L. W. Erickson).

It is not clear whether all of these birds observed in early August in the north are summer residents, or whether some might be early fall migrants. The earliest sure migrants are birds on 29 July (1979, Milwaukee, J. H. Idzikowski), 2 August (1972, Marathon, R. R. Hoffman), 9 August (1955, Dane, A. E. Eynon), 12 August (1972, Rock, T. R. Ellis), and 13 August (1964, towerkill at Eau Claire, C. A. Kemper). Observers have noted small numbers from 15 August through 20 September, mainly in the 25 August–10 September span. Beyond 25 September there are but four September dates and the following dates for late stragglers in October: the 3rd (1953, Sheboygan, G. H. Orians), 8th (1966, La Crosse, F. Z. Lesher; 1969, Wood, E. Hebard), 11th (1979, Oconto, T. C. Erdman), 20th (1971, Dodge, E. W. Peartree), 23rd (1966, Milwaukee, C. P. Frister), and 25th (1962, Vernon, V. E. Weber).

In migration these birds are usually spotted on conspicuous treetop perches. But rather than being confined to wet bogs, as in summer, these perches may be in almost any kind of woodland. More often than not, the abrupt three-syllable "kip-kip-kip" call has directed my attention to spring migrants, but it is seldom heard in fall. Unless an observer is afield looking for fall migrants well before Labor Day, he may miss the species entirely.

Eastern Wood-Pewee (*Contopus virens*)

STATUS. Common migrant. Common summer resident.
HABITAT. Deciduous forest. Savanna.
MIGRATION DATES. *Spring:* early May to early June. *Fall:* mid-August to late September. *Extremes:* 12 April; 30 October.
BREEDING DATA. Nests with eggs: 6 June to 25 July. Clutch size: usually 3 eggs; occasionally 2.
PORTRAIT. *Birds of Wisconsin:* Plate 52.

One must beware of suspected April sightings of this species. Rarely, a migrant Eastern Wood-Pewee may be blown off course and show up on an outlandish date, as did Dennis Gustafson's well-documented 12 April 1968 bird at Milwaukee. But I suspect that most other April reports may be misidentifications. Even Kumlien and Hollister's (1903) 28 April–5 May date of general arrivals raises eyebrows now. Although two or three individuals may be detected during that week, most observers must wait until 10 May to spot first arrivals in the south, 15 May farther north. It is from 20 May to 5 June that birds disperse over the state in numbers.

To the eye this species is inconspicuous, not only because it lacks striking plumage, but also because it shows a preference for trees in the interior of forests and woodlots rather than at the edge. Much of the flycatchers' behavior takes place within and beneath the canopy of the taller forest trees. To the ear this species is one of the most attractive and distinctive. In the morning the plaintive "pee-a-wee" stands out in marked contrast to the warbles and chatters uttered by other woodland inhabitants. In the evening the soft intervening phrases added to the morning song make for a delightful twilight concert all summer long.

This distinctive song has been noted on all 70 June

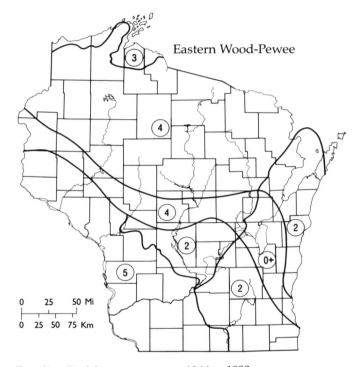

Eastern Wood-Pewee

Breeding Bird Survey, averages 1966 to 1980

BBS transects, attesting to a statewide summer range. But suspicions arose that during the early 1970s a modest decline took place. In 1970 the average number of birds per transect per year was 5.01; this declined steadily to 2.85 in 1976, recovering only to 3.72 in 1980. But since 1984 a 4.50 average has been maintained.

Although the bird is generally common throughout the state in summer, its abundance shows considerable variation. With the exception of heavily wooded Washington Island in Door County, it is most numerous in the west, where the favored oaks abound.

Doubtless it used to be more numerous throughout the southern counties when that region was more heavily wooded. It can still be considered common locally in the south wherever suitable oak woodlots exist. In the northern forests there are far fewer Wood-Pewees per acre than Least Flycatchers. Pewees avoid coniferous trees for the most part and show only a moderate interest in maples. Yet they are found often enough in other upland deciduous woodlands to be considered common in the north as well.

The willingness of this bird to reside in various kinds of deciduous trees is illustrated by C. H. Richter's report of four nests in Oconto County: one each in an oak, maple, elm, and aspen. In each case the nest saddled a horizontal limb 10–15 feet above the ground. Some birds choose to nest at higher levels, 30–35 feet up, but always in deciduous trees. Six of

seven nests reported in Sauk County, 1976–1978, were in oaks (Mossman and Lange 1982). Nesting activities continue through July. Parents have been observed bringing food to their nests as late as 9 August and feeding fledged young as late as 2 September.

A modest amount of fall migration is under way by 20 August, as indicated by towerkills at Eau Claire from 23 August on. This builds gradually to a 5–15 September peak in the north, with nearly all birds gone by the 20th. In the south the fall flight is mainly a 10–20 September event, with a gradual tapering off through the 30th. A few birds linger until 10 October nearly every year. Remarkably late are four 25 October records (1962, 1963, 1964, and 1971), and the record-breaking bird in my backyard at Cadott (Chippewa County) on 30 October 1971.

Yellow-bellied Flycatcher (*Empidonax flaviventris*)

STATUS. Fairly common migrant. Uncommon summer resident north.

HABITAT. Coniferous forest. Northern maple-hemlock-pine forest.

MIGRATION DATES. *Spring:* mid-May to early June. *Fall:* late July to early September. *Extremes:* 1 April; 6 October.

BREEDING DATA. Nests with eggs: 7 June to 12 July. Clutch size: 4 eggs.

PORTRAIT. *Birds of Wisconsin:* Plate 52.

An observer relying on sight alone would rate the Yellow-bellied Flycatcher a rarity. Because it avoids outer branches, migrates late in spring and early in fall when foliage is thick, and is quiet and unobtrusive in its movements, it escapes the detection of all but the most persistent viewer who knows just where and when to look. One who recognizes the short soft song—the "per-wee" that has been likened to the call of the Semipalmated Plover, or an abbreviated hushed version of the Eastern Wood-Pewee—has slightly better success in spring; yet this bird seldom sings when transient. An observer does well to detect as many as 3 birds per day, or 10 throughout its entire spring passage.

Usually this bird does not reach the southern tip of the United States in spring until late April. So it was astonishing—to say the least—when Dennis Gustafson found a bird in Milwaukee on 1 April 1967, one of many exotic birds pushed north by a sudden burst of unseasonably hot air. The next earliest arrival of which there is a record was a bird banded on 2 May

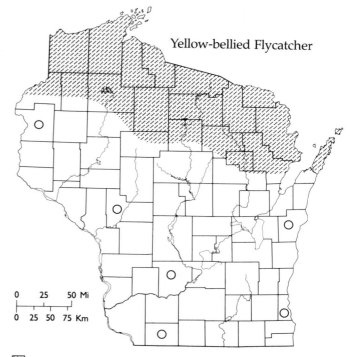

Yellow-bellied Flycatcher

▨ Summer range
○ Mid-June to late July

Records since 1960

(1959, Rock, M. K. Stocking), remarkable in its own right. A handful of other arrival records cluster around 10 May, but these birds are regular in the south only from the 15th on and in the north after the 20th.

A few migrants linger into June every year, the

latest being on the 10th (1980, Milwaukee, W. Wood-mansee), 11th (1945, Dane, S. D. Robbins), and 18th (1978, Sauk, R. M. Hoffman).

The only known breeding records for the state consist of a nest with four eggs on 12 July (1941, Douglas, J. L. Diedrich), and two early-day records in the south: 7 June (1860, Jefferson, T. L. Kumlien [Kumlien and Hollister 1903]) and 25 June (1891, Dane, A. L. Kumlien [Kumlien and Hollister 1903]). As a breeding bird the Yellow-belly has long since been gone from southern Wisconsin, but recent summer records exist for Burnett, Washburn, Sawyer, Taylor, Price, Oneida, Lincoln, Langlade, Menominee, and Door counties, in addition to the northernmost counties. The southern limit of the summer range is a line from Grantsburg through Merrill, Shawano, and Sturgeon Bay. South of that line there are numerous spruce-tamarack bogs that have received little attention where this species might persist as a summer resident. Such a bog in Manitowoc County had a singing male on 20 June 1964 (F. Alyea). Additional singing males were found in Sauk County on 18 June 1978 (R. M. Hoffman) and Jackson County on 23 June 1985 (M. J. Mossman).

Late in spring, early in fall—that is the story of this species. Were it not for banders, it would be difficult to fix the dates of fall migration with precision. Birds are usually silent, as unobtrusive as in spring, and difficult to distinguish from other small flycatchers. Most field sightings fall within the 20 August–10 September span. This is probably the peak of a considerably longer migration period. Banders have trapped birds as early as 19 July (1940, Outagamie, N. M. Rogers), 22 July (1974, Chippewa, C. A. Kemper), 30 July (1940, Racine, E. L. Loyster), and 1 August (1962, Rock, M. K. Stocking). Late departures of banded birds include 28 September (1963, Chippewa, C. A. Kemper), 2 October (1965, La Crosse, F. Z. Lesher), and 6 October (1958, Sheboygan, H. C. Mueller).

It is the banders who have made clear that this bird is fairly numerous as a migrant, particularly in late August and early September. The 499 fall migrants banded at the Cedar Grove Ornithological Station in Sheboygan County, 1958–1963 (Mueller and Berger 1967e), average out to over 80 individuals per season. Kemper (1973a) showed lower totals because of a more limited operation, but indicated that at least one-tenth of the *Empidonax* flycatchers trapped at Chippewa Falls or killed at the Eau Claire television tower were *flaviventris*.

Acadian Flycatcher (*Empidonax virescens*)

STATUS. Uncommon summer resident southwest and southeast.

HABITAT. Deciduous forest.

MIGRATION DATES. *Spring:* early to late May. *Fall:* probably early August to early September. *Extremes:* 2 May; 20 September.

BREEDING DATA. Nests with eggs: 28 May to 25 July. Clutch size: 3 or 4 eggs.

PORTRAIT. *Birds of Wisconsin.* Plate 52.

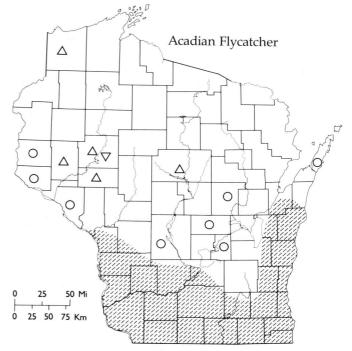

Acadian Flycatcher

0 25 50 Mi
0 25 50 75 Km

▨ Summer range
△ Early to late May
○ Early June to late July
▽ Early August to early September

Records since 1960

In his *Birds of the New York City Region* Griscom (1923) wrote: "Collecting has proved that in spite of the greatest care, it is impossible to be absolutely certain in separating the Acadian, Alder and Least Flycatchers by color characteristics even in the spring. In the fall plumage it is out of the question." The confusion over small flycatchers has been so great that the Acadian Flycatcher bears the name of a region which is totally outside its range! Wisconsin has not escaped the results of this confusion. It was Hoy's (1853b) opinion that this was "the most numerous of the flycatchers in Wisconsin."

To Kumlien and Hollister (1903), and to nearly all the twentieth-century commentators, the Acadian is one of the least numerous flycatchers. To be certain of its identification one must be a bander, capable of measuring wing and tail feathers in the hand, or be thoroughly acquainted with the songs and call notes of all the state's small flycatchers. To the trained ear the explosive "pit-eet" song is distinctive. Late one May, C. A. Kemper (pers. comm.) let his tape recorder run in his woodlot near Chippewa Falls for 30 minutes. When he and I heard the tape that evening, we were able to pick out the song of an Acadian whose presence he had not detected. Sure enough, his banding nets held two the following morning.

Observers note first spring arrivals generally between 10 and 15 May. Birds have dispersed to their breeding range by 25 May. Early arrivals have occasionally appeared during the first week of May: the 2nd (1981, Rock, D. D. Tessen), 5th (1954, Columbia, H. A. Winkler), and 6th (1962, Rock, M. K. Stocking). It is during the last week of May that "overshooting" individuals have been detected north of the usual summer range. Instances include birds in Pierce (1956, M. E. Olson), St. Croix (1973, 1974, C. A. Faanes), Eau Claire (1978, C. A. Kemper), Chippewa (1967, 1973, C. A. Kemper), Clark (1947, S. D. Robbins), Marathon (1978, K. J. Luepke), and Waushara (1971, I. Chipman) counties. Most exceptional was a storm-blown bird in Douglas County on 29 May (1978, D. D. Tessen).

The most recent resident records have occurred south of a line from Galesville through Wisconsin Dells to Green Bay, with concentrations in four areas: Wyalusing State Park (Grant), Baraboo hills (Sauk), Kettle Moraine State Forest (Fond du Lac), and the Golden Lake Woods (Jefferson-Waukesha). If more fieldwork took place in the coulee region of southwestern Wisconsin, the records from Crawford, Vernon, La Crosse, and Monroe counties might well reveal another major area. Two or three pairs find their way to the Green Bay and Manitowoc areas nearly every year. Habitat requirements are dense deciduous woods where both a canopy and understory occur. If the woods are on a steep slope bordering a small stream, so much the better.

Such habitat is extensive in the Baraboo hills. It was here that Stoddard (1922a) established Wisconsin's first nesting record in 1921. And it was here that Mossman and Lange (1982) and associates gathered data on 90 nests between 1976 and 1980. Nest construction occupies the birds during the last week of

May, often in sugar maples, sometimes in basswoods and hemlocks, sometimes in witch hazel. In this region the Acadian is a common species, heard readily through June and July as nesting activities progress.

Populations at other locations are not nearly as numerous. The BBS routes bypass almost completely the few areas frequented by the bird. What takes place after mid-June is difficult to determine. Three times (1973–1975) Louise Erickson heard birds on Washington Island in Door County in late June; apparently the birds were not present earlier. Through the song and the distinctive call note I was able to detect the presence of wandering birds in a wooded ra-

vine near Hudson (St. Croix County) on 21 June and 5 July 1963, and on 22 July 1965. Is this postbreeding wandering?

Song diminishes markedly in August, and without song there is no sure differentiation between this and other *Empidonax* flycatchers. Voice identification established records on 5 September (1969, Sauk, K. I. Lange) and 8 September (1967, Waukesha, J. E. Bielefeldt). Banders have proved that at least a few birds remain into September as far north as Manitowoc (1 September 1966, B. N. Brouchoud) and Chippewa (15 and 20 September 1968, C. A. Kemper) counties.

Alder Flycatcher (*Empidonax alnorum*)
Formerly Traill's Flycatcher

STATUS. Common migrant. Fairly common summer resident north and central; uncommon summer resident east.
HABITAT. Lowland carr. Shallow marsh. Wooded swamp.
MIGRATION DATES. *Spring:* early May to early June. *Fall:* mid-August to mid-September. *Extremes:* 28 April; 17 September.
BREEDING DATA. Nests with eggs: 15 June to 26 July. Clutch size: 3 or 4 eggs.
PORTRAIT. *Birds of Wisconsin:* Plate 52.

Throughout northern Wisconsin—in alder thickets bordering creeks and small rivers—this drab but cheerful singer is widely distributed during summer. The Alder Flycatcher is particularly numerous in the Lake Superior marshes near Ashland and Superior and can be found regularly in suitable habitat south to a line from Hudson southeast to Necedah, northeast to Stevens Point, and southeast to Port Washington. In addition, a few breeding pairs frequent isolated bogs at several southern Wisconsin locations, as shown on the accompanying map. It seems likely (but is unproven) that this species formerly inhabited southern conifer-alder swamps. As humans drained swamps and cut brush, the Willow Flycatcher invaded; only a few pockets exist where Alder Flycatchers remain.

Until 1973 the Alder and Willow Flycatchers were lumped together as one species, *Empidonax traillii,* known since 1957 as "Traill's Flycatcher" and previous to 1957 as "Alder Flycatcher." Two subspecies had been described before 1900: *traillii* ("Traill's") and *alnorum* ("Alder"). Kumlien and Hollister (1903) be-

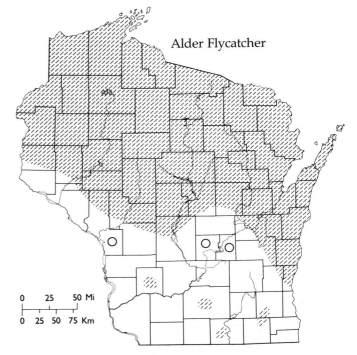

Alder Flycatcher

0   25   50 Mi
0   25 50 75 Km

▨ Summer range
○ Mid-June to early August

Records since 1960

lieved both occurred in Wisconsin, one sparsely, one fairly commonly. But since the differences used for identification purposes then do not match perfectly those now used to separate the newly described Willow and Alder Flycatchers, Kumlien and Hollister's comments do not easily apply.

Although the breeding range is largely restricted to the northern half of the state, the Alder can be expected as a spring migrant anywhere in the state. It is infrequently recorded in the southwest, since segments of suitable habitat there are few and far between. But I have personal records of birds singing their distinctive "wee-bee-o" in May in Pierce, Pepin, Buffalo, La Crosse, Grant, and Iowa counties. This bird is a late migrant, occasionally appearing by 10 May, found most frequently between 20 May and 5 June. Exceptionally early is the individual found near Ashland on 28 April 1975 (R. L. Verch).

The nesting phenology is poorly known. Carl Richter assembled data on 10 nests of "Traill's Flycatchers" in Oconto and Marinette counties between 1922 and 1966. Seven nests contained four eggs and three had three eggs. Eight nests were found between 15 June and 2 July, with one on 8 June and one on 11 July. But Richter's territory, while predominantly used by *alnorum,* contained a few *traillii,* and it is not possible to distinguish with certainty which species used which nest. According to Stein (1963), Alder nests are almost always located no more than 2½ feet from the ground, while Willow nests are usually between 2 and 6 feet up. Richter's nests were located between 1½ and 3 feet up, except for one 5 feet up in an ash sapling.

On the June BBS transects, this bird has been noted on 47 of the 70 routes, including virtually all routes north of a line between Hudson and Green Bay. In the counties adjoining Lake Superior, routes average three individuals per year. The average drops to two birds per route in the remainder of the northern forested region, and to one per route in the counties adjoining Lake Michigan.

During summer there is an area of overlap in the ranges of Alder and Willow Flycatchers, narrow in the west, extensive in the central and eastern counties (Robbins 1974b). At times both species can be found in the same swamp, Alders showing a preference for alder shrubbery, Willows preferring young willows. It is song and nest structure, rather than habitat, that makes identification positive.

Once the song period ends (10 August), differentiation between *alnorum* and *traillii* becomes impossible for all but banders and collectors. Observers have been advised to refer to both species as "Traill's Flycatchers." In fact, similarity with Least, Yellow-bellied, and Acadian Flycatchers is such that "*Empidonax* sp." is the safest designation. The latest dates for singing birds have been 8 September (1979, Waukesha, D. D. Tessen) and 13 September (1976, Douglas, G. J. Niemi). A 17 September individual was banded and measured (1982, Chippewa, C. A. Kemper).

Kemper (1973a), reported that nearly half (705) of 1,483 flycatchers banded at Chippewa Falls between 1953 and 1972 were Traill's. At Eau Claire, television-tower casualties between 1960 and 1972 numbered 300 Traill's compared with 234 of all other species of *Empidonax* combined. Although measurements have not been made to determine probable percentages of *traillii* and *alnorum,* the geographical location, so close to the northern limit of the Willow's range, makes it certain that nearly all of Kemper's birds were Alders. The autumn migration in the Eau Claire region is mainly between 20 August and 20 September, with a few stragglers appearing through the first week of October. "Traill's Flycatchers" undetermined as to species have been detected through 10 October (1948, Sheboygan, G. H. Orians).

Willow Flycatcher (*Empidonax traillii*)

Formerly Traill's Flycatcher, Alder Flycatcher

STATUS. Fairly common migrant south and central.
Fairly common summer resident south and central;
uncommon summer resident northeast.
HABITAT. Upland and lowland carr. Shallow marsh.
MIGRATION DATES. *Spring:* early May to early June.
Fall: mid-August to mid-September. *Extremes:* 3
May; 15 September.
BREEDING DATA. Nests with eggs: 7 June to 9 July.
Clutch size: 3 or 4 eggs.
PORTRAIT. *Birds in Wisconsin:* Plate 52.

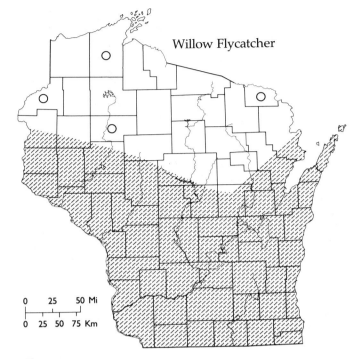

Willow Flycatcher

0   25   50 Mi

0   25 50 75 Km

▨ Summer range
○ Mid-June to early August

Records since 1960

To the majority of Wisconsin birders, this is the familiar "Alder" or "Traill's" Flycatcher that inhabits the
willow thickets bordering swamps and streams in
the southern counties from late May through mid-
August. Its nasal, sneezy, two-syllable "fitz-bew" is
heard most often in early morning and—to a lesser
extent—in early evening.

Much remains to be learned about the Willow Flycatcher and the similar-appearing Alder Flycatcher:
arrival and departure dates, nesting phenology, habitat preference, and relative abundance in areas of
overlapping range. Records previous to 1974 were almost always listed as "Traill's" Flycatchers (1957–
1973) or "Alder" Flycatchers (pre-1957). The one exception consists of my personal records (1937–1977),
in which birds were listed separately by song whenever possible.

On the basis of the limited information available
it appears that the regular summer range extends
north to a line from St. Croix Falls east-southeast to
Waupaca, then northeast to Marinette and Washington Island. North of this line occasional summer records have come from Burnett (1977), Bayfield (1968,
1973), Rusk (1977), and Florence (1973) counties. South
of this line the Willow is present in suitable habitat,
being locally common south of La Crosse, Columbia,
and Sauk counties.

This is one of the later spring migrants. Although
arrivals have appeared in the southern counties by
3 May (1979, Dane, L. A. Erickson) and 5 May (1985,
Fond du Lac, W. K. Volkert), the 15th is a more usual
first date. The main influx comes between 20 May and
5 June. By 10 June nearly all birds are inhabiting their
nesting territory.

True to its name, this species is particularly attracted to willows—low-growing willow shrubs interspersed with tall grasses in damp regions. The
marshes at Horicon (Dodge County) and along the

shore of Madison's Lake Wingra are favorite spots. A
few birds inhabit drier regions where lightly traveled
country roads pass extensive patches of sumac. The
distinctive "pip" can be heard from this species at
any time of day. But to hear the "fitz-bew" song, you
should be in the birds' territory before or soon after
dawn, or near sunset. The birds sing infrequently at
other hours.

Nesting begins in early June. Schorger's (1931a)
Dane County records, referring quite certainly to
traillii, show 14 June as the earliest date for a full
clutch of eggs, 20 June as the average date for a
full complement of three or four eggs, and 12 July
as the time when young fledge. Schorger described
the nest as "deep and compact, resembling that of the
yellow warbler, placed three to eight feet from the
ground."

On the June BBS transects this species is usually
found on about half of the 70 routes, all in the southern half of the state. The highest composite total of

individuals for any one year is 70, suggesting that suitable habitat is spotty and localized.

The timing of fall migration must remain a matter of guesswork until banders can furnish precise data for August and September. Singing ceases by 10 Au-gust, rendering field identification virtually impossible after that date. Although 15 September is the latest sure date (1978, Dane, S. Thiessen), it is highly probable that the Willow remains in Wisconsin through September.

Least Flycatcher (*Empidonax minimus*)

STATUS. Common migrant. Common summer resident north; fairly common summer resident central; uncommon summer resident south.
HABITAT. Northern sugar maple forest. Northern
   aspen-birch forest.
MIGRATION DATES. *Spring:* early to late May. *Fall:*
   mid-August to early October. *Extremes:* 22 April;
   17 October.
BREEDING DATA. Nests with eggs: 30 May to 10 July.
   Clutch size: usually 4 eggs; occasionally 3 or 5.
PORTRAIT. *Birds of Wisconsin:* Plate 52.

Common throughout the state as a summer resident in the nineteenth century, the Least Flycatcher has been forced progressively farther north as mature forest has disappeared in the southern half of the state. The BBS data show vivid contrasts: presence in only a few limited areas in the southernmost counties, numbers gradually building up in the central region, with high populations north of a line from St. Croix Falls through Wausau, Shawano, and Crivitz. North of this line observers have found the bird on every BBS transect since 1966.

Living north of this line, Francis Zirrer (pers. comm. to O. J. Gromme) commented that the Least prefers mature maple-dominated forest to poplar and other small growth. The familiar "che-bec" of this species is frequently heard; in concert with the songs of the Red-eyed Vireo and the Ovenbird, it is one of the most conspicuous sounds of the deciduous upland woods. The Least is especially dominant at the crack of dawn. A male may sing every 2 seconds or so, almost as if trying to make up for time lost during the previous night's sleep.

Singing persists through June but diminishes noticeably in early July. In areas where I have found 15–40 individuals on a June morning, I have found only 1–5 birds in July and early August. Observers have reported active nests mainly in June. Reporting on seven nests near Marshfield (Wood County), J. W. Stierle (pers. comm. to O. J. Gromme) noted five located 9–15 feet up in maples, and two 6–10 feet up

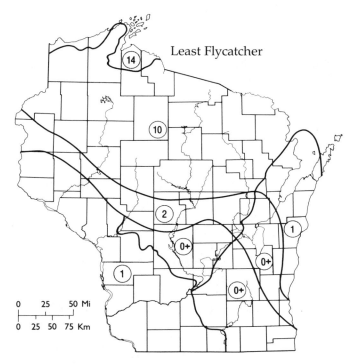

Breeding Bird Survey, averages 1966 to 1980

in alders. C. H. Richter's three Oconto County nests were 12–20 feet up in alders. In Outagamie County Grundtvig (1895) found five nests at heights varying from 12 to 50 feet up in birch and ash. In Sauk county's Baraboo hills, one of few remaining southern Wisconsin sites where this species is numerous, Mossman and Lange (1982) found that 23 of 30 nests were located in sugar maples. Nests with eggs have been observed through 8 July.

In most years first spring arrivals coincide with the first warm spell in May. But if migration conditions are favorable in the last three days of April, an occasional bird may appear not only in the south but even as far north as Lincoln (28 April 1965, D. J. Hendrick) and Sawyer (2 May 1961, K. Fuller) counties. The earliest dates on record are 22 April (1939, Brown, E. W.

Strehlow) and 24 April (1969, Winnebago, T. J. Underwood). Even when early May is cool, birds populate all parts of the state by 15 May.

For the pattern of fall migration we must rely on towerkills and banding data. Birds are usually silent, and are so similar to other *Empidonaces* in plumage as to defy positive identification. Unless a field observer hears a recognizable song or call note, he is well advised to list his fall eye-ringed flycatchers as "*Empidonax* sp." C. A. Kemper's Eau Claire towerkill figures show that migration extends at least from 23 August to 10 October, with a 5–25 September peak. The total represents 30% of the entire *Empidonax* population—below the combined Alder-Willow total but outnumbering the Yellow-bellied Flycatcher two to one. Kemper's banding data span similar dates, with a 40% total.

At the Cedar Grove Ornithological Station (Sheboygan County) the fall peaks have occurred between 30 August and 25 September, with a final date of 11 October. Over the 1958–1963 period, the 557 birds banded represent 28% of the transient *Empidonax* population, outnumbering the Yellow-bellied Flycatcher six to five but falling short of the Alder-Willow combination by three to two (Mueller and Berger 1967e). Late dates for small eye-ringed flycatchers thought to be this species include 15 October (1968, Manitowoc, M. Albrecht; 1972, Kenosha, R. R. Hoffman) and 17 October (1941, Dunn, I. O. Buss). Beyond these dates there is one remarkable record: an *Empidonax* believed to be *minimus* (although silent) put in brief appearances at Tom Ashman's feeder in Madison on 13 November and 2 December 1962.

Eastern Phoebe (*Sayornis phoebe*)

STATUS. Fairly common migrant. Fairly common summer resident.

HABITAT. Streams. Upland carr. Residential areas.

MIGRATION DATES. *Spring:* late March to late April. *Fall:* early September to late October. *Extremes:* 28 February; 28 November.

BREEDING DATA. Nests with eggs: 14 April to 13 July. Clutch size: usually 4 or 5 eggs; occasionally 3; rarely 6.

WINTER. Three December records; one January record.

PORTRAIT: *Birds of Wisconsin:* Plate 52.

Prolonged cold in the southeastern United States in January and February 1958 was extremely hard on wintering insect-eating species. In the following spring and for years to come, the Eastern Phoebe was referred to as a "disaster species." For the previous 100 years this had been an abundant bird in Wisconsin: "met with everywhere" (Hoy 1853b), "abundant" (Barry 1854), "hardly a lake cottage which does not have its Phoebe" (Kumlien and Hollister 1903), "well distributed . . . very common" in 1919 (Jackson 1943), "abundant" (Schorger 1931a). The abundance was such that Clarence Jung estimated that 500–750 fall migrants passed through the Cedar Grove Ornithological Station (Sheboygan County) on 23–24 September 1922.

Since the 1958 disaster, numbers have been but a small percentage of former levels. Even at the height

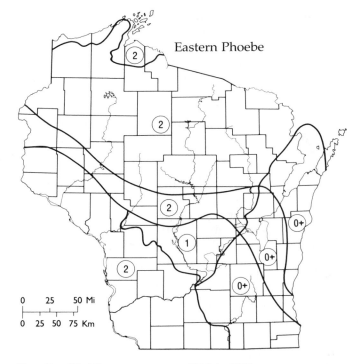

Eastern Phoebe

Breeding Bird Survey, averages 1966 to 1980

of spring or fall migration, an observer is fortunate to see 10 individuals in a day. Spring migration is tied to the emergence of the earliest insects. As thawing temperatures occur, the first birds generally arrive between 15 and 25 March in the south, and between

30 March and 10 April in the north. Observers have reported earlier migrants: 28 February in the south (1965, Racine, B. L. von Jarchow), 12 March in the central area (1945, Door, H. C. Wilson), and 25 March in the north (1941, Sawyer, K. W. Kahmann). Doubtless there are times when early March arrivals perish because of prolonged cold conditions. Most of the migration takes place between 10 and 25 April when warmer weather makes for a more reliable supply of insects.

Nest construction sometimes begins in early April, with the depositing of eggs coming as early as the 14th, but the more usual time for egg-laying is early May. A second egg-laying period follows in mid-June, leading to fledging in early and mid-July. Nests with young have been observed as late as 3 August.

Phoebes are found on two of every three BBS transects each year. Every route, with the exception of one in Dodge County, has recorded the species at least once. But on only 5 of 69 routes is an average of four individuals per transect per year maintained. One wonders how this might have compared with pre-1958 figures, had the BBS been in existence at that time.

The population decline cannot be attributed to disappearing habitat. The few pairs that prefer to build on rocky ledges as their ancestors did can still do so. Those that choose to nest under rustic bridges on side roads still do. And many potential sites exist around summer cottages and hunting shacks.

Fall migration occurs mainly in September. Some movement away from the nesting areas occurs in early August, but nearly all migrating flycatchers observed in late August are other species. As the *Empidonax* population declines in mid-September, this phoebe becomes more noticeable. By 5 October all but a few stragglers have left the northern counties. Few birds are left in the south beyond 20 October, but lingering birds occasionally remain into the first week of November. Exceptionally late are birds recorded on 17 November in 1946 (Milwaukee, G. W. Treichel) and 1971 (Portage, J. Bickford). In 1947 one appeared in Milwaukee on 28 November (G. H. Orians), followed by another in Kenosha on 26 December (G. W. Treichel). On 21 December 1975 one was reported on the Waukesha CBC. The Fort Atkinson (Jefferson County) CBC listed one on 31 December 1988. Even more remarkable was the straggler at Green Bay that visited the E. O. Paulson feeder between 17 December 1966 and 6 January 1967. This species can adjust its diet from insects to seeds and fruit, but it is doubtful that an individual could survive a Wisconsin winter.

Say's Phoebe (*Sayornis saya*)

STATUS. Accidental. One record.
HABITAT. Open grassland. Upland carr.

Hoy (1853b) discovered this western counterpart to the Eastern Phoebe at Racine on 10 May 1848. In his *Notes on the Ornithology of Wisconsin* he relates collecting two specimens. Although the specimens have disappeared, John Cassin of the Academy of Natural Sciences of Philadelphia confirmed the identification (Baird, Brewer, and Ridgway 1875). History has not supported Hoy's additional comment: "Probably not very rare." The Great Plains form a barrier that this bird has rarely traversed.

The only other suspected Wisconsin sighting came on 2 September 1963, when Edith Brakefield saw two birds at her home near Evansville (Rock County). The birds perched first on the clothesline, then on a nearby fence. Their size, shape, long tails, pink breasts, and upright posture all pointed to their being members of this species. But the light was poor and the observation brief, and documentation was too sketchy for a positive record (*Pass. Pigeon* 26:90). It is, however, a matter of record that Iowa had had a severe storm the previous day, and that another Say's Phoebe turned up in southeastern Minnesota the following day.

Extralimital wandering is frequent, both in spring and fall. In recent years individuals have been detected in Nova Scotia, Quebec, Ontario, New York, Pennsylvania, Virginia, Illinois, and Florida.

Great Crested Flycatcher (*Myiarchus crinitus*)

STATUS. Common migrant. Common summer resident north and central; fairly common summer resident south.
HABITAT. Deciduous forest.
MIGRATION DATES. *Spring:* late April to late May. *Fall:* mid-August to late September. *Extremes:* 2 April; 5 November.
BREEDING DATA. Nests with eggs: 22 May to 25 June. Clutch size: usually 4–6 eggs; occasionally 3–7.
PORTRAIT. *Birds of Wisconsin:* Plate 51.

The Great Crested Flycatcher has extended its range noticeably since the end of the nineteenth century. Commenting on a return visit to Delavan after a 20-year absence, Hollister (1919b) wrote: "In my collecting days at Delavan I had to go to certain unfrequented woods to find the great-crest, but now it is much more common; I saw it often in places it never used to inhabit, and it has actually become a town bird." Similarly Schoenebeck (1902) did not list the bird in his *Birds of Oconto County.* But Richter called it common in his 1939 addition to Schoenebeck's list.

In fact, BBS results plotted on the accompanying map now show higher populations in the northeastern sector than for any other portion of the state. The Crested's raucous call makes it one of the more conspicuous birds along the edge of deciduous forests, sometimes mixed with jack pine. The bird does not frequent dense timber but prefers areas with at least a few openings and with enough dead wood to offer suitable feeding perches and nesting cavities.

Records exist for every county. This species has been found on all 70 BBS transects. A nesting pair is possible wherever a sizable stand of deciduous woods exists. Of eight nests reported by Carl Richter, one was in a fence post, one was 5 feet up in a black ash stub, one was 6 feet up in a natural poplar cavity, one was 8 feet up in a willow stub, and four were in old woodpecker cavities 8–18 feet above ground. Mary Nelson observed this bird nesting in bluebird houses with enlarged openings, 4–8 feet above ground. Subsequent study of one nest revealed these contents: coarse plant stems, pieces of dried corn stalks, grapevine stems, grasses, oak leaves, roots, a little shredded bark of red cedar, cedar needles, two white opossum whiskers, a piece of cellophane, a piece of fur, and a great many reddish brown chicken feathers that billowed up and around the young birds. Perhaps the piece of cellophane substituted for dried snake skin that frequently occurs among the nesting materials of this species.

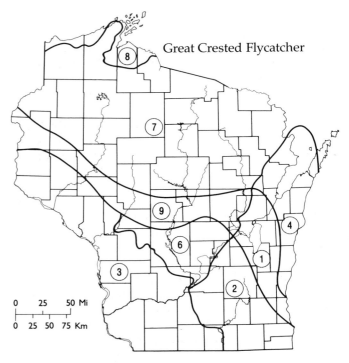

Great Crested Flycatcher

Breeding Bird Survey, averages 1966 to 1980

The Great Crested Flycatcher has a reputation as a vigorous defender of its nesting territory. I once watched a pair feeding young in a natural cavity 15 feet up in a black oak, with a dead stub located above and 10 feet away from the nest hole. As one parent foraged, the other performed sentry duty on the dead stub. Only when a feeding was completed would the parents exchange places; one always remained on guard. Eventually the potential enemy appeared: a gray squirrel that had jumped to the upper canopy of the nest tree from a neighboring oak. As soon as the squirrel began its descent, it was vigorously and noisily attacked, first by one parent and then by both, until it beat a hasty and unceremonious retreat.

Southern Wisconsin observers look for first arrivals among the first waves of early May migrants. Occasionally, mild weather brings a late-April sneak preview for some lucky observer. Earliest April records have occurred on the 12th (1984, Milwaukee, J. H. Idzikowski), 20th (1970, Barron, A. Goff; 1970, Price, M. Hardy), 21st (1948, Milwaukee, H. L. Orians; 1957, Lafayette, E. Olson), 22nd (1964, Racine, J. Saetveit), and 23rd (1960, Marinette, H. L. Lindberg). Most astonishing was the storm-blown bird which A. L. Hehn observed in Milwaukee on 2 April

1967. By 10 May spring arrivals are well scattered throughout the south, and have been penetrating the northern counties. By 25 May most birds are on territory, ready to begin nesting.

Following breeding, birds quiet down in July but remain at least through mid-August. The principal migration period is from 20 August to 10 September in the north, and from 30 August to 20 September in the south. Beyond 15 October five records are known: October 16th (1978, Manitowoc, C. R. Sontag), 25th (1975, Brown, E. D. Cleary), 28th (1971, Marinette, H. L. Lindberg), and 30th (1950, Sheboygan, H. C. Mueller), and 5 November (1987, Sheboygan, D. D. Berger).

Western Kingbird (*Tyrannus verticalis*)

Formerly Arkansas Kingbird

STATUS. Rare spring migrant; casual fall migrant. Rare summer resident west and south.

HABITAT. Farmsteads.

MIGRATION DATES. *Spring:* early May to early June. *Fall:* mid-August to mid-October. *Extremes:* 12 April; 20 October.

BREEDING DATA. Nests with eggs: 11–20 June; nests with young: 3–17 July. Clutch size: 3–5 eggs.

PORTRAIT. *Birds of Wisconsin:* Plate 51.

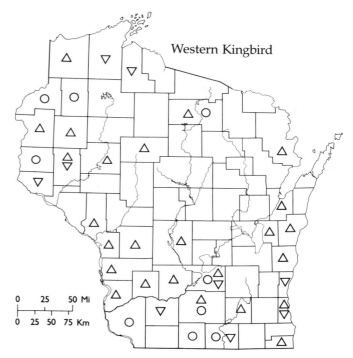

Western Kingbird

△ Early May to early June
○ Mid-June to early August
▽ Mid-August to mid-October

All records

In the late 1930s, Bent suggested in his *Life Histories* that the Western Kingbird might be extending its range eastward through the Great Lakes region. Previous to that time, Wisconsin had only one nineteenth-century record (11 June 1877, Dane, collected by T. L. Kumlien [Kumlien and Hollister 1903]) and four twentieth-century specimens: 2 June 1935 (Kenosha, pair collected and now in the Chicago Museum of Natural History, E. G. Wright), 31 May 1931 (Dane, A. W. Schorger [1931c]), 31 July and 1 August 1927 (Dane, G. E. French and W. E. Griffee [1927]). But instances of breeding in Minnesota, Michigan, and Ohio, plus frequent fall wanderings to the Atlantic Coast, have lent credibility to his theory.

Further encouragement came from southern and eastern counties during the 1940s and 1950s. Discoveries of May migrants were made on the 5th (1956, Brown, E. D. Cleary), 6th (1950, Manitowoc, H. Dietrich), 14th (1958, Columbia, R. B. Dryer), 18th (1940, Brown, E. D. Cleary; 1947, Columbia, G. A. Hall), 22nd (1940, Sauk, G. O. Raasch), 24th (1956, Adams, S. D. Robbins), and 31st (1954, Sheboygan, G. H. Orians).

One pair of Westerns nested in the J. Studnicka farmyard in Rock County every year through the 1930s (Gromme 1940). Repeat visits continued at least through 1942, and two other pairs nested in the Beloit-Janesville area in 1949 and 1950 (P. Boynton). In 1942 a pair produced at least one young in Columbia County (F. M. Kozlik). Far north in Oneida County one bird was spotted on 9 June 1943 (W. S. Feeney).

But events since 1955 have presented a different picture. Bent's hope for further range extension has not materialized, and Wisconsin must still be considered east of the bird's regular breeding range. The only subsequent spring migrants in the eastern region have been Milwaukee birds on 19 May 1970

(D. K. Gustafson) and 10 May 1973 (N. Fadel), a Sauk County record on 3 June 1971 (M. F. Donald), an exceptionally early wanderer in Brown County from 12–14 April 1974 (T. Baumann), a Calumet County individual on 1 June 1974 (B. Parfitt), one in Marinette County on 27 May 1978 (H. L. Lindberg), and one in Jefferson County on 9 May 1983 (R. M. Hoffman).

In the western region, however, sightings have become more frequent in both spring and summer. It started with a Burnett County individual on 27 July 1953 (N. R. Stone), and another in the same county in 1956 (11 July–15 August, A. Sprunt). Manley Olson found one in St. Croix County on 25 June 1958.

Just east of the bridge over the St. Croix River at Hudson (St. Croix County), I discovered a nesting pair in a farmyard on 17 July 1961. Here, three young fledged. In each succeeding year through 1971 a pair nested in the same group of trees even though some trees were removed in 1964 and a drive-in restaurant built where they had stood. The proprietors missed a promotional opportunity: they might have advertised "Enjoy Kingbirds with your Kingburgers!" The nesting tradition, unfortunately, came to an untimely end in 1971 when some youngsters who were better marksmen than conservationists shot the entire family of recently fledged young. Additional summer observations in the Hudson area in 1964, 1966, 1967, and 1968 indicated that there was probably at least one additional nesting pair during those years. But no birds have been found at the Hudson site since the 1971 shooting.

A nest with young was observed in a farmyard near Sarona (Washburn County) on 16 July 1971 (R. A. Knuth). Since 1975 from one to three individuals have been found somewhere in western Wisconsin in May or June nearly every year, but with no further indication of nesting.

Summer records come mainly from farmyards where tall trees surround a house and there is considerable open expanse nearby. The birds at Hudson rarely perched on wires or on conspicuous treetops as their Eastern counterparts did. They chose instead to perch in the upper canopy of elms, and could best be seen when they were coming or going. Their presence was most often detected by their distinctive "chatter" call. It is quite possible that several pairs might nest in the northwestern counties every year; observers might do well to concentrate on the many farms in that region.

Summer residents probably stay on location from mid-May to mid-August. A 9 August bird (1958, Oneida, R. F. Gordon) was an early fall wanderer. Manley Olson's finds on 15 August (1963, Dunn) and 18 August (1956, Pierce) could have been summer residents or fall migrants. Beyond 15 August only these fall records are known: 18–26 August (1976, St. Croix, C. A. Faanes), 27 August (1960, Milwaukee, W. N. MacBriar), 31 August (1962, Columbia, R. B. Dryer), 1 September (1975, St. Croix, C. A. Faanes), 12 September (1962, Columbia, A. J. Rusch), 11–25 September (1955, Rock, J. W. Wilde), 22 September (1980, Ashland, R. L. Verch), 5 October (1980, Milwaukee, M. F. Donald), 6 October (1974, Ozaukee, M. F. Donald), and 20 October (1979, Iowa, A. K. Shea). Strangely enough, during September and October this species is more apt to turn up along the Atlantic Coast than in Wisconsin.

Eastern Kingbird (*Tyrannus tyrannus*)

STATUS. Common migrant. Common summer resident.

HABITAT. Farmsteads. Wooded swamp. All carr.

MIGRATION DATES. *Spring:* late April to early June. *Fall:* early August to late September. *Extremes:* 25 March; 17 October.

BREEDING DATA. Nests with eggs: 29 May to 25 July. Clutch size: usually 3 or 4 eggs; occasionally 2 or 5.

PORTRAIT. *Birds of Wisconsin:* Plate 51.

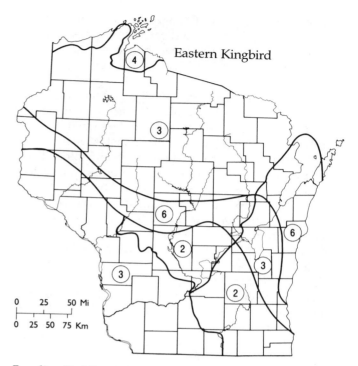

Breeding Bird Survey, averages 1966 to 1980

The files used to prepare this book included 3 sight records for March and an additional 28 for the 1–20 April period. Accepting each record without question, I should conclude that the Eastern Kingbird occurred almost regularly by 15 April, and sometimes by 25 March. But this is utterly out of step with the usual pattern that finds the bird barely reaching Texas and Louisiana in late March, southern Illinois in mid-April, and the northern tier of states in early May.

Any kingbird appearing in the state before 15 April probably arrived here wind-blown by a southern storm. Such was the case of the 25 March 1939 bird in Waukesha County, for which C. E. Nelson stated, "Definitely identified at close range, with temperature near 80°." Corroborating details are absent in 12 other 25 March–15 April reports; some of these were surely misidentifications.

Any kingbird seen between 15 and 25 April is exceptionally early. Well-documented observations have occurred on the 17th in four different years: 1964 (Sheboygan, H. C. Mueller), 1976 (Wood, D. G. Follen), 1977 (Dane, R. Ake), and 1978 (Door, C. M. Lukes). Close behind was an individual seen on the 18th (1965, Dodge, W. D. Carter). Most southern observers find first arrivals during the first week of May, but with only a modest buildup of numbers until a 15–20 May peak. Farther north observers see few birds until 10 May; there is a gradual increase to a 25–30 May peak. In some years migration is still in progress as late as 5 June.

During summer a fairly even distribution is maintained throughout the state. Observers have recorded this bird on all 70 of the BBS transects, with no pronounced concentrations in any one section.

Wherever wooded swamps are available, this voracious insect-eater gravitates to them for nesting. A. W. Schorger, investigating by boat some stumps left from logging operations and the subsequent flooding of new flowages in northern Wisconsin, often found nests 100–200 feet out from shore, and sometimes only 1½ feet above water. Carl Richter reported a variety of nesting sites: the crotch of an apple tree, a horizontal limb of a scrub oak, a jack pine, a black ash sapling, an alder bush, as well as an overhanging willow crotch. Several nests stood far from water, showing the bird's adaptiveness to open or brushy fields as well. In late July and August, when many passerines have stopped using fences and utility wires for perches, families of clean white-breasted kingbirds have these wires all to themselves.

But not for long. This is one of the earlier fall migrants. Counts of 150 (13 August 1977, Bayfield, R. Korotev) and 135 (24 August 1979, Oconto, T. C. Erdman) testify to the timing of the peak fall migration. In many years the final sighting anywhere in the state has occurred by 15 September. More commonly a few lingering migrants can be spotted in the south through the 20th, but anything beyond the 25th is unusual. Nine October dates are known, with the latest on the 11th (1970, Ozaukee, J. L. Jarboe; 1977, Ozaukee, N. J. Cutright) and 17th (1964, Marquette, R. E. Fiehweg). Usually by mid-October these birds have left the entire continental United States on the long trek to South America.

Scissor-tailed Flycatcher (*Tyrannus forficatus*)

STATUS. Rare migrant. Casual summer visitant.
HABITAT. Old field. Upland carr. Open grassland.
MIGRATION DATES. Observed between 17 April and
24 October.

Wisconsin's lone specimen of the Scissor-tailed Flycatcher, now in the Milwaukee Public Museum, bears
the date 1 October 1895. It was a cold windy day when
Ludwig Kumlien (Kumlien and Hollister 1903) discovered this bird on a roadside fence near Milton (Rock
County). The bird proved to be an adult "in perfect
condition, being very fat."

Not until 1956 did this spectacular visitor from the
southern plains appear again. The bird, viewed for
over an hour in Ozaukee County on 12 May, perched
first on a telephone wire, then later displayed its re-
splendent tail and plumage as it alternated between
the wire and a nearby field (E. L. Basten).

Three years later Winnifred Mayer spotted one
perched on a roadside fence near Two Rivers (Manitowoc County) on 3 July 1959. Her first view was distant and unsatisfactory, but on a return visit to the
scene 2 hours later, she found the visitor again and
had a close view of the bird—including its striking tail.

The fourth bird spent several days in the New
Lisbon (Juneau County) area in late April 1964. Exact
dates were not recorded, but in a 3 May letter to O. J.
Gromme, Theodora Starnes described a bird she had
seen in an open field at the edge of a school forest. It
"resembled the [Eastern] Kingbird in size . . . largely
white or grayish white, long forked tail, roseate coloring under wing. It had a strange erratic pattern of
flight and a peculiar cry or call." She estimated that
the bird had been present 4 or 5 days, but she did not
see it after 3 May.

Between 1973 and 1980, state records more than
doubled. Two records concerned individuals that remained for weeks in Rock County. One of these, first
noted at Janesville on 19 July 1977 (M. Sayre), was
seen periodically in August and September, and was
eventually photographed on 20 October (M. T. Maxson, pers. comm.) shortly before it disappeared. In
1980 two birds—adult and immature—spent much of
September and October west of Beloit. Gyda Mahlum
observed them on 28 September and 24 October and,
from conversation with the farmer on whose land the
birds resided, learned that the visitors had been present since late August.

Far to the north in Washburn County, Bernard
Kinnel (pers. comm.) discovered a bird near Sarona

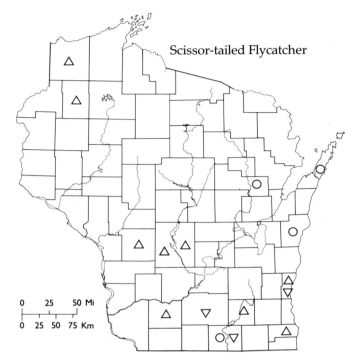

Scissor-tailed Flycatcher

△ Mid-April to early June
O Mid-June to early August
▽ Mid-August to late October

All records

on 5 June 1980. It was perched 50 feet away on an
electric fence wire, from which it dropped to the
ground for insects several times. "It was a smallish
gray bird with an unusually long tail, bright salmon-
pink sides and under-surface of wings."

Widely scattered, both in terms of distance and sea-
son, are four additional observations: 17 April (1974,
Juneau, R. Peterson; *Am. Birds* 28:804), 8 June (1973,
Iowa, A. J. Rusch), 20–22 June (1975, Shawano, K. E.
Hafemann; *Am. Birds* 29:977), and 28 June (1978,
Door, C. M. Lukes).

Eight additional 1-day sightings have occurred
since 1980. On 7 June 1982, D. A. Ross watched an
adult foraging in an Adams County sandpit for 5
minutes before being attacked and driven away by an
Eastern Kingbird. A manure pile was the attraction
for an adult that made a brief visit to a Racine County
farm on 27 April 1983. David Kosterman approached
to within 15 feet of the bird. In May 1985 two birds
were seen 2 days apart: one on the 5th (Monroe, E. J.
Epstein) and one on the 7th (Jefferson, D. Fallow).
Near Cross Plains (Dane County) Greg and Debbie

Geller photographed another of these distinctive fly-catchers on 17 August 1985. J. L. Baughman photographed an immature Scissor-tail in Ozaukee County on 17 October 1987. In 1988 two birds were found: on 7 May (Ozaukee, K. Wegman) and 20–22 May (Douglas, R. J. Johnson).

Although the Scissor-tail has a limited breeding range in the southern plains, it has a reputation for wandering. Since 1965, extralimital records have come from British Columbia, Saskatchewan, Ontario, New Brunswick, Minnesota, Michigan, West Virginia, and almost every Atlantic state from Virginia to Maine.

Fork-tailed Flycatcher (*Tyrannus savana*)

STATUS. Accidental. Two records.
HABITAT. Lowland carr.

On three occasions between 13 and 16 November 1978, Frank Freese observed this South American wanderer near Doylestown (Columbia County). At times the bird was no more than 20 feet away. Conditions for photography left much to be desired, but among 20 snapshots that were taken there were several that clearly showed one elongated tail feather and the broken stub of a second. This Fork-tailed Flycatcher showed a preference for willow shrubs in a marshy area, from which it made numerous fly-catching sorties. Occasionally it dropped to the ground, presumably in search of food. A thorough written description was accepted by the WSO Records Committee, then published (*Pass. Pigeon* 41: 41–42). The observer had had previous experience with both Fork-tailed and Scissor-tailed Flycatchers.

Since 1970 this distinctive species has developed quite a reputation for wandering. One or two are found somewhere in the eastern United States or the maritime provinces every year. Nearly all sightings have come between mid-September and mid-November. Nearly all have been in coastal regions, the exceptions provided by birds seen in Ontario, Michigan, and Kentucky.

Not conforming to this pattern was an individual that wandered to Douglas County on 24 June 1988. The bird disappeared after a 5-minute observation period, but not before R. J. Johnson and W. Penning had photographed it and taken copious notes (*Pass. Pigeon* 51:122–123).

Fork-tailed Flycatcher, 13 November 1978, Columbia County (photo by F. N. Freese)

Family **Alaudidae:** Larks

Horned Lark (*Eremophila alpestris*)

STATUS. Common migrant. Common summer resident south and central; fairly common summer resident north. Fairly common winter resident south; uncommon winter resident central.

HABITAT. Open cropland.

MIGRATION DATES. *Spring:* early February to mid-April. *Fall:* mid-September to early December.

BREEDING DATA. Nests with eggs: 27 March to 17 July. Clutch size: usually 3 or 4 eggs; occasionally 2 or 5.

WINTER. Regularly present north to La Crosse, Sauk, Fond du Lac, and Sheboygan counties; irregularly present north to St. Croix, Chippewa, Marathon, and Brown counties.

PORTRAIT. *Birds of Wisconsin:* Plate 53.

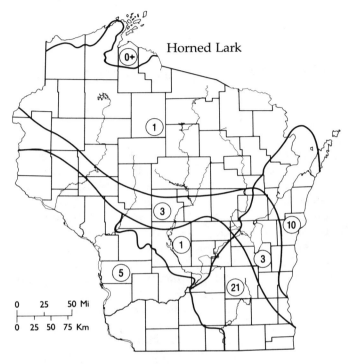

Breeding Bird Survey, averages 1966 to 1980

Early in February—sometimes late in January—the Horned Lark begins its northward movement. It was unusually early in 1965 when birds reached Washburn County on 30 January (B. Bailey), Marinette County on 1 February (C. H. Richter), and Burnett County on 2 February (N. R. Stone). Movement is noticeable by mid-February nearly every year. Birds are most conspicuous in late February and March, when fresh snow blankets the fields. After plows clear the roads, larks congregate on the shoulders individually or in small flocks of from 5–10 birds; occasionally they gather in large flocks of 25–50. When fields are snow covered, it is not unusual to find 100 or more larks on a mile-long stretch of a secondary road. When bare spots reappear in the fields, birds move to these for feeding purposes and are less conspicuous. Numbers dwindle in early April. Birds still present on 20 April will probably be summer residents.

Numerous instances are known of nesting being under way before that date. Francis Dayton (pers. comm. to O. J. Gromme) related that several times he found parents incubating eggs in nests surrounded by snow. On 2 April 1892 Hollister (1892a) found four newly hatched young from eggs that must have been laid in mid-March. Early nestings are fraught with danger, not only from March and April cold and snow, but also from farm machinery. The lark insists on bare ground for nest sites, and since considerable plowing is done in fall, much favorable habitat is available in early spring. But much of this land is subsequently disked in late April and May, inevitably

disrupting many nesting larks. If first nests are unsuccessful, there is time for second and third attempts. Carl Richter has observed eggs as late as 17 July, a likely date for a third nesting attempt.

From BBS numbers it is clear that June populations are concentrated in the south and east. Larks are not as scarce in the northernmost counties as the map indicates, but suitable agricultural areas are few and far between in the areas dominated by forest. There are 14 BBS transects in the northern counties that have never listed the Horned Lark.

Few observers have commented on late-summer activities. Birds move around to take advantage of various patches of bare ground as they become available. Wherever crops are harvested from a field, the resulting open soil is sure to attract any nearby larks.

It is late September when noticeable migration takes place. From then until 10 November individuals or small groups of two to six birds may be heard flying overhead—over city or forest, far from favored habitat—giving their plaintive two-syllable call. Large flocks are rarely seen in fall, but as winter snows come, birds that have chosen to remain may gather in groups of 20–50.

CBC data show wide variation in winter populations. In 1963 observers noted larks on 23 of 68 counts, totaling 1,504 birds; the following year only 248 individuals were recorded on 14 of the 61 counts. Snow depth is probably the key factor in determining the size and extent of the wintering population. An absence of bare ground does not necessarily mean an absence of larks; they are fond of freshly spread manure on snow-covered fields.

Family **Hirundinidae:** Swallows

Purple Martin (*Progne subis*)

STATUS. Abundant migrant. Common summer resident.
HABITAT. Residential areas. Great Lakes. Inland lakes.
MIGRATION DATES. *Spring:* early April to early May. *Fall:* mid-July to mid-September. *Extremes:* 13 March; 21 October.
BREEDING DATA. Nests with eggs: 9 May to 29 June. Clutch size: usually 4 or 5 eggs; occasionally 3–7.
PORTRAIT. *Birds of Wisconsin:* Plate 55.

As many as 8 weeks may elapse between the spotting of the first spring arrival and the laying of the first egg. In approximately 1 of every 5 years, an early Purple Martin is spotted in southern Wisconsin by 25 March. Exceptionally early was a bird on 13 March 1936 (Dane, N. R. Barger, pers. comm.). Occasional sightings of single males in the last week of March have led to the theory that scouts move in advance of the main flocks of migrants, rejoin their companions, and lead them northward when suitable weather conditions prevail. The more probable explanation is that these early stragglers move northward when mild late-March weather brings about the emergence of some insects; then when cold weather returns and insects cannot be found, the earliest martins are hard put to survive. It simply is not "safe" for these birds to invade Wisconsin until mid-April, and usually this is when most first arrivals are detected. Although occasional sightings have been recorded in the northern region in late March (Lincoln, 30 March 1945, D. J. Hendrick) and early April (Oneida, 1 April 1950, R. G. Dery; Oconto, 2 April 1942, C. H. Richter; Sawyer, 4 April 1942, G. Ruegger), most of these sleek flyers wait until early May to spread throughout the state.

Even in areas where birds are well established in late April, nesting activities progress slowly. Few birds have taken to man-made nest boxes as readily and as completely as this species. Deusing (1942) reported that the sample of southern Wisconsin birdwatchers he questioned believed that martins were using nest boxes almost exclusively (96% of the time), while in the north observers felt that nest boxes were used 60%, and rocky cliffs and holes in trees 40%, of the time. Martins have evidently been reluctant to nest as isolated pairs, preferring to move in en masse where a multiapartment house is available. Although

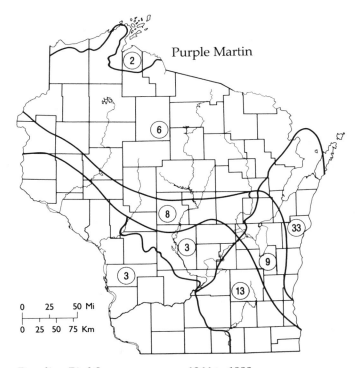

Breeding Bird Survey, averages 1966 to 1980

breeding colonies by the hundreds have been observed from all parts of the state, surprisingly little data have been compiled about egg dates, clutch size, and nesting success in Wisconsin. Deusing's summary showed 9 May as the earliest egg-laying date and late May and early June for the main egg-deposition period, with young fledging from 20 June through July.

Although summer distribution is statewide, it is clear from the BBS results that this species is far more numerous in eastern and southeastern Wisconsin than in other regions. The fact that these birds have been located on 68 of 70 BBS routes is testimony to widespread human effort to erect martin houses. While there is evidence that a few Chimney Swifts continue to use natural cavities in the northern forests, such evidence is lacking for the Purple Martin.

Great activity centers around a nesting colony in June and July when there are young to be fed. Anyone who is awake at 4 A.M. can hear parent birds al-

394

ready flying about collecting insects. Almost any time during the 16 hours of daylight there are goings and comings around a martin house. Some idea of what a baby bird consumes is evident from Mrs. Frank Reich's diary (*Milwaukee Journal*, 10 November 1939). Raising by hand two nestlings that had been orphaned near Lake Tomahawk (Oneida County), she first found it necessary to feed them every half-hour from 5 A.M. to 7 P.M. "By the time the birds were two weeks old they ate less frequently, only once every hour. One day's feeding for a bird was 60 to 100 young grasshoppers, 30 dragon flies, eight pellets of hard boiled egg yolk with cod liver oil, ten moths and three meal worms."

Several observers have commented on a high ratio of desertions causing considerable loss of life in martin colonies. Some attribute this to competition from European Starlings and House Sparrows, some to prolonged inclement weather, and some to the fall flocking and migratory urge that comes to this bird. Dernehl (1900) commented: "From the four or six eggs which the martin lays, but three are hatched and reared successfully, on an average. . . . I have always

found when lowering my martin boxes that the parents left behind them either eggs or more frequently one or two of their young."

Fall flocking begins in late July and builds up in many local areas through 15 August. A concentration of 10,000 was reported in Oconto County on 10 August 1972 (T. C. Erdman). The disappearance from many of these locations is sudden; wires that are laden with 200 martins one day will be empty the next. But in a few spots near water around the major cities, huge concentrations build up in late August. I estimated 1,500 birds at Superior and Duluth on 28 August 1964, and suspect that a more thorough search might have produced five times that figure. By 10 September these flocks disappear, leaving only a few late stragglers remaining until 5 October. Latest dates for the north are: 27 September (1946, Oconto, C. H. Richter) and 30 September (1980, Brown, E. D. Cleary); for the south they are: 15 October (1972, Kenosha, R. R. Hoffman), 17 October (1948, Milwaukee, I. N. Balsom), and 21 October (1954, Kenosha, M. F. Higgins).

Tree Swallow (*Tachycineta bicolor*)

STATUS. Abundant migrant. Common summer resident north and central; fairly common summer resident south.
HABITAT. Inland lakes. Great Lakes. Open grassland. Residential areas.
MIGRATION DATES. *Spring:* late March to early May. *Fall:* early August to late October. *Extremes:* 2 March; 7 December.
BREEDING DATA. Nests with eggs: 8 May to 7 July. Clutch size: usually 4–6 eggs; occasionally 3–9.
PORTRAIT. *Birds of Wisconsin:* Plate 54.

"Where do they all come from?" I wondered, as I stood at the edge of the Green Bay marshes on 29 August 1971, gazing at the thousands of swallows congregated on the wires or skimming over the grass. I wrote down 20,000 in my notes, but the number might have been 30,000 or 40,000. Most of them were Tree Swallows. Many must have been local birds amassing for fall migration. Some were doubtless birds from farther north already started on their southward journey. Such gatherings are not unusual at that location. On 27 August 1977 the birds numbered about 50,000 (D. K. Gustafson).

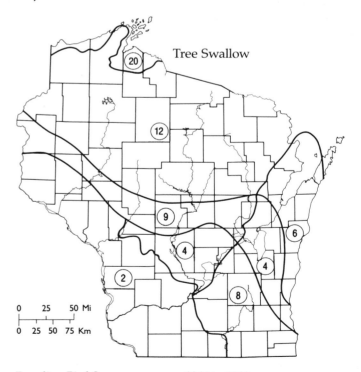

Breeding Bird Survey, averages 1966 to 1980

Fall departure dates are often misleading. Some observers note that their summer resident birds are gone before 31 July. Others find them regularly until mid-October. Apparently the birds that are widely dispersed through the nesting season in June and July move into a few areas of concentration in August. The concentrations wane in September as the migrating urge sends the birds southward, but some concentrations remain in southern and central areas through 15 October. By the end of October even late lingerers have departed. Stragglers found after 10 November include: 11 November (1947, Dane, W. E. Scott), 16 November (1984, Dane, R. M. Hoffman), 18 November (1972, Door, A. Freitag), 21 November (1987, Oconto, W. Mueller), 27 November (1948, Sheboygan, H. C. Mueller), and 7 December (1968, Racine, J. Greenberg).

When winter hangs on through March, first spring arrivals do not appear until the first week of April. Otherwise, a few harbingers reach the southern counties by 25 March, and can be expected in the north from 10 April on. March 1973 was exceptional, with birds sighted on the 2nd (Milwaukee, M. F. Donald), 9th (Kenosha, J. Hamers), 14th (La Crosse, J. R. Rosso), and 15th (Monroe, S. D. Robbins). The previous early state record had been the 16th. Numbers build up strongly after 15 April, sometimes with disastrous results. Snowstorms in late April and early May are not uncommon, and if they are followed by prolonged cold, the flying insect population may be reduced to zero. The Tree Swallow, more than any other species, has suffered from starvation as a result.

As a whole, however, this species has maintained its numbers very well. It has learned to make good use of man-made houses as well as the natural cavities in dead or dying trees that are always to be found around lakes and streams. Nests have been reported in cavities as high as 20 feet above ground, but most are less than 10 feet up. I once found a nest at ground level within a hollow, 1-foot stump. H. L. Stoddard (Wisconsin State Historical Society files) located a nest within a fallen hollow log 34 inches from the end of the log.

These birds show no great haste in starting breeding operations. Rarely has nest construction been observed before 1 May, or egg-laying before 15 May. Most young have fledged by early July. In a few instances nestlings have been observed through 20 July.

BBS results depict a statewide distribution, but the bird is decidedly more numerous in the north, where it competes with the Barn and the Cliff for high population honors among swallows. In the south the Tree is outnumbered by the Purple Martin and Bank and Barn Swallows.

Although large numbers have been banded, the number of recoveries is small. They indicate that birds on the Wisconsin side of Lake Michigan one year may locate on the Michigan side the next. One remarkable recovery involved a nestling banded at Marinette on 19 June 1957 (W. N. MacBriar) and recaptured at Canaan, New Hampshire, on 29 April 1964.

Northern Rough-winged Swallow (*Stelgidopteryx serripennis*)

Status. Fairly common migrant. Fairly common summer resident south and central; uncommon summer resident north.

Habitat. Inland lakes and streams.

Migration Dates. *Spring:* mid-April to mid-May. *Fall:* early July to mid-September. *Extremes:* 3 April; 29 October.

Breeding Data. Nests with eggs: 15 May to 25 June. Clutch size: usually 4 or 5 eggs; occasionally 6.

Portrait. *Birds of Wisconsin:* Plate 54.

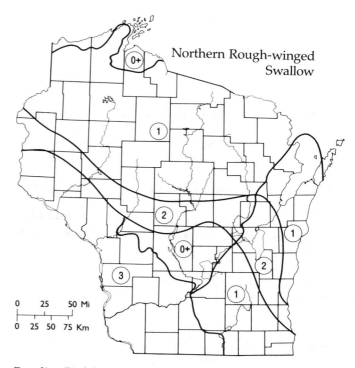

Breeding Bird Survey, averages 1966 to 1980

Within a block of the busy downtown area of Eau Claire and Chippewa Falls these brown-backed swallows can be seen from late April through July flitting over small streams leading into the Chippewa River. The Rough-wing is partial to small streams wherever rocks or steep exposed banks provide adequate nesting space. Such habitat is plentiful among the streams that feed into the St. Croix, Chippewa, and Mississippi rivers of western Wisconsin, and doubtless influenced Buss and Mattison (1955) to describe this species as "probably the most common swallow in the Lower Chippewa River area." Goddard (1972) also found this to be the most numerous of the swallows in the Kinnickinnic River valley west of River Falls (Pierce County). Kumlien and Hollister (1903) thought this bird to be more common than the Bank, and suspected that misidentification had caused other writers to refer to the Rough-wing as rare.

Taking the state as a whole, this bird can be considered neither common nor rare. Its habitat requirements are strictly limited, and suitable habitat is not plentiful. BBS figures show that it is found on only one-third of the state's transects each year, while all other swallows are noted on over half the routes. In terms of total numbers, each of the other swallows outnumbers the Rough-wing by at least five to one. The BBS distribution shows that very few birds reach the northern counties. My personal records and those from the Wisconsin Society for Ornithology files show that this bird has been found in every county but is decidedly uncommon north of a line from Grantsburg to Oconto.

Earliest arrivals are usually spied in the south around 15 April. Exceptional are E. W. Peartree's record sighting on 3 April (1960, Waukesha), a bird on 5 April (1913, Dane, A. W. Schorger [1931a]), individuals on 6 April (1976, Kewaunee, J. Trick; 1976, Milwaukee, E. J. Epstein), and one on 7 April (1972, St.

Croix, S. V. Goddard). Between 20 April and 10 May, birds disperse in the southern and central regions and penetrate the north in small numbers. At this time they often join mixed flocks. On several occasions, particularly on cool raw mornings when insects are concentrated close to the surface of a lake or stream, I have detected all six species of Wisconsin swallows skimming back and forth close to the water in search of food. By 15 May Rough-wings have moved to their breeding haunts and are beginning nesting activities.

Once birds leave their breeding environs in early July, their movements are difficult to follow. With brown-backed immature Tree Swallows also on the wing, confusion is easy. It helps when a well-trained ear can pick out the distinctive "grunt" call of the Rough-wing, but the birds make less and less noise as the summer progresses. Most Rough-wings appear to join the mixed flocks of swallows that build up in late July and August. An estimated group of 300 in Dane County on 20 August 1980 (R. M. Hoffman) is one of few sizable flocks reported beyond 15 August. Numbers diminish greatly by 25 August, but those few that remain sometimes linger through 25 September or even into October. The year 1969 was phenomenal not only for R. A. Knuth's 29 October record-breaker (Fond du Lac), but also for the flock of 15 birds that remained at La Crosse through 18 October (F. Z. Lesher). Observers have noted other October strag-

glers on the 8th (1964, Racine, L. W. Erickson), 9th (1977, Ozaukee, D. D. Tessen), 10th (1929, Dane, H. G. Anderson, pers. comm. to A. W. Schorger), 15th (1978, La Crosse, F. Z. Lesher), 21st (1984, Ozaukee, W. A. Cowart), and 25th (1987, Outagamie, D. D. Tessen).

Bank Swallow (*Riparia riparia*)

STATUS. Common migrant. Common summer resident south and central; fairly common summer resident north.
HABITAT. Sand and gravel banks. Inland lakes. Great Lakes.
MIGRATION DATES. *Spring:* mid-April to mid-May. *Fall:* early July to mid-September. *Extremes:* 2 April; 19 October.
BREEDING DATA. Nests with eggs: 17 May to 16 June. Clutch size: usually 5 or 6 eggs; occasionally 4 or 7.
PORTRAIT. *Birds of Wisconsin:* Plate 54.

Some people believe that the Bank Swallow is the state's most abundant swallow. Others judge it to be one of the least numerous. The reason for this feast-or-famine status lies in the bird's colonizing tendencies. A person living close to the Petenwell Flowage in Adams and Juneau counties, for instance, will find this bird outnumbering every other bird from May through July. An observer residing among suburban woods and gardens will be "Bank-less." People inhabiting an open field area with a gravel pit nearby will see swarms of these small brown-necklaced fliers. Those dwelling in forested regions will see none.

Rarely if ever does one find an isolated nesting pair. In his 1959–1962 nesting studies, MacBriar (1972) worked with 33 colonies in the Milwaukee-Washington-Waukesha county region, each located in a gravel pit. He estimated populations as high as 500 pairs in a colony, an average of 100 pairs, and never fewer than three pairs. It is not hard to spot a nesting colony. Any sizable exposed bank, either by a gravel pit or the edge of a lake or stream, should be scanned for a series of holes close to the top with swallows flying in and out. The holes look simple from a distance. But those who have examined them in detail have been amazed at the lengthy intricate tunnels the birds have excavated, leading to their nests. Vos Burgh (1923b) commented: "I examined the nests, or rather burrows, and was greatly surprised to find they run way in, so I procured a long root and thrust it in each bur-

Breeding Bird Survey, averages 1966 to 1980

row and found them to vary from three feet to over six feet, and average three or four inches across. . . . They started straight back, maybe came to a stone or very hard place, swerved to right or left, down or up, and then turned again a little further in as far as I could reach, so the back end must have been three feet below the entrance."

The BBS picture portrays a statewide range that is somewhat sparse in the north. It is not reliable in assessing accurate population densities in the central and southern regions. On the Pierce-Pepin county transect, for instance, the total of 91 birds reported in 1966 dropped to 9 in 1967 simply because discontinued use of a gravel pit caused the relocation of a colony.

First spring arrivals have been remarkably constant in recent years. With the exception of the 2 April 1960 sighting (Brown, E. D. Cleary) and 1973 sightings on the 6th (Manitowoc, R. Hallisy) and 7th (Columbia, W. A. Smith), all first dates since 1960 have fallen within the 8–22 April span. By 1 May arrivals are general, and by 15 May birds are generally dispersed throughout the state. Not many birds go farther north into Canada, but the likelihood is that most of those who do have left by 20 May.

Although most migrant species that appear in the state by mid-April make their southward trek in late September and October, this swallow is remarkable in timing its departure for July and early August. Most young are on the wing by 5 July. Premigration flocking takes place from 15 July on, and by 15 August the bulk of these flocks are gone. My personal notes for 40 years show only eight records beyond 5 September. Scattered individuals are found through 20 September somewhere in the state nearly every year, but there are only two known records beyond 8 October: 18 October (1968, La Crosse, F. Z. Lesher) and 19 October (1931, Dane, H. G. Anderson, pers. comm. to A. W. Schorger).

Cliff Swallow (*Hirundo pyrrhonota*)

STATUS. Common migrant. Common summer resident north; fairly common summer resident south and central.

HABITAT. Farmsteads. Open grassland. Inland lakes. Great Lakes.

MIGRATION DATES. *Spring:* late April to mid-May. *Fall:* early August to early October. *Extremes:* 30 March; 18 October.

BREEDING DATA. Nests with eggs: 17 May to 1 August. Clutch size: usually 4 eggs; occasionally 3–6.

PORTRAIT. *Birds of Wisconsin:* Plate 55.

Now and then this bird has been called "Eave Swallow" rather than "Cliff Swallow." In Wisconsin the former term seems more appropriate; for while there are instances of colonies breeding on steep rocky cliffs, there are far more records of groups nesting on the sides of barns just below the eaves. In the 1940s great publicity was given to a gigantic colony of 2,000 pairs that nested for years on the Cory Bodeman barn in eastern Dane County. Mr. Bodeman encouraged this colony by erecting strips of wood under the eaves to help the birds anchor their nests. Jokingly, swallow-watchers used to wonder how many times parent birds wandered into the wrong apartment by mistake only to be "thrown out" by furious neighbors. But the birds showed an uncanny sense in finding their way around in this huge apartment complex.

In an ambitious attempt to determine the size and location of as many Cliff Swallow colonies as possible, in 1957 and 1958 Aumann and Emlen (1959) mapped 455 colonies containing over 11,000 nests. Colonies were found in nearly every county, but their distribution was decidedly spotty. Many small colonies were scattered throughout the north, plus that

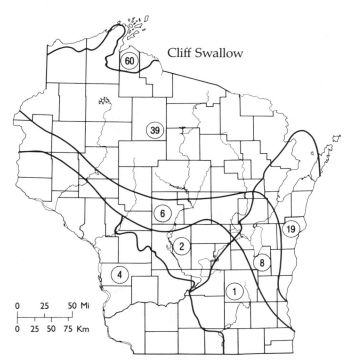

Cliff Swallow

Breeding Bird Survey, averages 1966 to 1980

portion of the central area drained by the Wisconsin River. A few larger colonies concentrated birds in the south-central region. Only a few were reported in the western coulee region and near Lake Winnebago.

Numbers gleaned from BBS data also indicate a wide and predominant distribution in the northern third of the state. North of a line from Prescott to Green Bay this bird has been recorded on 79% of the transects, with an average of 35 birds per transect;

south of this line, the bird has shown up on 44% of the transects, with an average of 5 individuals. Overall, the Cliff outnumbers all other species of swallows.

Aumann and Emlen's (1959) study shows that habitat requirements include (1) a structure (cliff or barn) with a protective overhang, (2) meadows, marshes, water, or a similar open area for feeding, and (3) a supply of mud suitable for use in constructing cohesive nests. Some nesting efforts have met with disastrous results when the dried mud proved to be too crumbly. To the list of structures suitable for nest colonies must be added bridges. On 27 May 1980 the underside of the main bridge over the Wisconsin River at Stevens Point (Portage County) was closely censused, with 1,590 active nests counted by H. H. Halvorsen.

In spring this bird is the last of the swallows to arrive. Although there are April records for the 10th (1980), 11th (1963), and 12th (1947), as well as a 30 March 1981 straggler (Eau Claire, J. L. Polk), the usual arrival time is 25 April in the south and 5 May in the north. In early May birds often join mixed flocks of migrating swallows and may be seen perched on wires or darting low over water surfaces in search of insects. After 15 May birds tend to concentrate more around the cliffs and barns that provide suitable nesting habitat.

The fall migration is more drawn out. By 1 August some birds are leaving their breeding areas, and flocking is sometimes reported in nonbreeding areas by the 10th. But usually there is no huge buildup comparable to that for the Purple Martin and Tree Swallow. An exception occurred on 7 September when flocks estimated at 6,000 were viewed in Eau Claire County (J. L. Polk). The main exodus occurs between 20 August and 10 September. By 15 September nearly all the Cliff Swallows have left the northern counties, and all but late stragglers have left the south by the 25th. Beyond 4 October the only records known are for individuals on 11 October (1963, Racine, L. W. Erickson) and 18 October (1980, Oconto, T. C. Erdman).

Barn Swallow (*Hirundo rustica*)

Status. Common migrant. Common summer resident.

Habitat. Farmsteads. Open grassland. Inland lakes. Great Lakes.

Migration Dates. *Spring:* mid-April to mid-May. *Fall:* early August to early October. *Extremes:* 23 March; 15 December.

Breeding Data. Nests with eggs: 15 May to 9 August. Clutch size: usually 4–6 eggs; occasionally 3–8.

Portrait. *Birds of Wisconsin:* Plate 55.

Schorger (1931a) wrote of the Barn Swallow, "It is more widely distributed during the breeding season than any of our other swallows, but numerically it ranks low." Concerning part one of this comment, there can be no doubt. This bird has been recorded on 95% of the 935 BBS transects run between 1966 and 1980, compared with 37–78% for the other swallows. The accompanying map shows a relatively even distribution from one end of the state to the other.

With the second part of Schorger's comment, however, some observers will take issue. In certain areas of northern Wisconsin the "fork-tailed swallow" ranks low in comparison with the Tree and the Cliff. In parts of southern Wisconsin, numbers seem low in

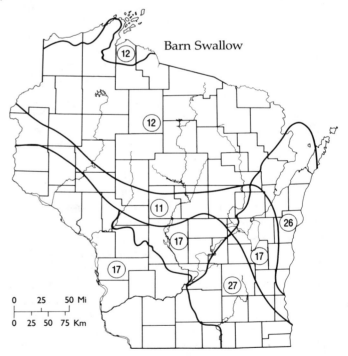

Barn Swallow

Breeding Bird Survey, averages 1966 to 1980

comparison with those for the Bank and the Purple Martin. Yet on 35 of the 70 BBS transects the Barn shows up as the most numerous swallow, and composite 70-transect totals show this species ranking second, outnumbered only by the Cliff.

In spring and fall, when summer residents are augmented by migrants, Trees and Purple Martins also outnumber the Barns. Wisconsin lies close to the northern limit of the Barn's range, so there is no vast buildup of flocks in fall, as there is for species that invade more northern climes.

Observers in the southern counties look for spring arrivals by 15 April. Sometimes the birds are delayed until the 20th, sometimes they make it by the 10th; on rare occasions early scouts have been sighted during the first week: the 1st (1981, Milwaukee, W. A. Cowart), 2nd (1962, Racine, L. W. Erickson), 3rd (1976, Kenosha, R. R. Hoffman), and 4th (1940, Milwaukee, G. O. Raasch). Exceptionally early was a 23 March sighting (1987, Monroe, E. J. Epstein). Northern observers may wait until the end of April for first arrivals, but by 10 May distribution is general throughout the state.

From mid-May to mid-August nesting activities dominate the fork-tail's life. I have never counted the number of trips a pair of birds will make when carrying mud for a nest they are building. The trips must number in the hundreds, and nest construction often requires 2 weeks or more. Mary Nelson's (1965) diary describing 1964 breeding behavior tells a typical story: 7 May, nest construction started; 24 May, five eggs laid; 24 June, four well-feathered young in nest; 26 June, first fledging; 28 June, last use of nest by fledglings. For a second pair, whose first brood had probably fledged a week earlier, the schedule included: 2–6 July, nest construction; 7 July, incubation starts for first egg; 11 July, fifth egg laid; 23 July, first hatching; 8 August, first fledging; 14 August, final fledging; 20 August, final use of nest by fledglings.

Birds usually remain in the nesting area in August, rather than combining into large concentrations elsewhere, as do other swallows. By the end of August numbers are noticeably declining, and migration is under way. By 10 September most Barn Swallows have left the north, and by the 20th all but a few are gone from the south. The date for the state's last sighting usually falls between 10 and 20 October. Observers have sighted unusually late stragglers on 31 October (1950, Outagamie, N. M. Rogers), 2 November (1969, Fond du Lac, R. A. Knuth), 12 November (1969, Milwaukee, O. R. Lemke), 20 November (1971, Ozaukee T. and C. Bintz), and 26 November (1980, Manitowoc, C. R. Sontag). A remarkable discovery involved a straggler present in Dane County between 9 and 15 December (1984, S. Thiessen).

Family **Corvidae:** Jays, Magpies, Crows

Gray Jay (*Perisoreus canadensis*)
Formerly Canada Jay

STATUS. Uncommon resident north. Rare winter visitant central.
HABITAT. Coniferous forest.
BREEDING DATA. Nests with eggs: 20 March to 15 April. Clutch size: 3 or 4 eggs.
WINTER. Regularly present south to Burnett, Sawyer, Price, Lincoln, Langlade, and Marinette counties. Occasionally wanders south to Pierce, Dunn, Jackson, Sauk, Columbia, and Washington counties.
PORTRAIT. *Birds of Wisconsin:* Plate 56.

Through the nineteenth century the Gray Jay was a common winter resident in the virgin timber of the northern counties. Only sporadic winter sightings were made in the south, and the breeding status in the north was uncertain. To the men who worked at lumber camps in winter, this was the "Camp Marauder" or "Whiskey Jack" that would come boldly into camp and feed on every available meat scrap.

Those days are gone. With the drastic reduction of virgin forests and changes in lumbering practices, the bird has become an uncommon species. To find it one must spend time in the coniferous forests of the northernmost two tiers of counties. Stands of white cedar offer particularly promising sites. On several occasions I have paused to "squeak" in such habitat and watched as from one to three birds sailed in, alighted on conspicuous treetops, and looked me over with a curiosity equal to my own. This can happen wherever suitable habitat exists north of a line from Grantsburg east through Ladysmith to Shawano and northeast to Wausaukee. This species is regular in small numbers, winter and summer, in the few cedar swamps that exist in this boreal region. Less commonly, the birds are found in balsam and spruce. I have rarely seen them in pine or in deciduous woodlands. They are more numerous from Ashland and Price counties eastward than in the northwestern counties.

Nesting activities, though not well understood, begin remarkably early. In Sawyer County, John Cole (Schorger 1937a) found a pair building a nest 7 feet up in a balsam in late February 1935, with the birds incubating four eggs on 20 March. On 28 March 1898 a nest with eggs was discovered 15 feet up in a

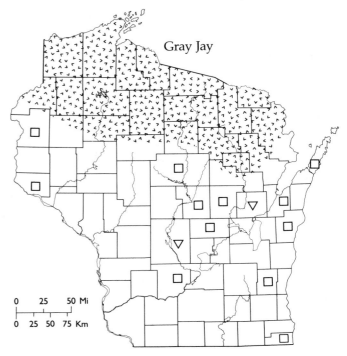

Gray Jay

0	25 50 Mi
0	25 50 75 Km

⊡ Resident range
▽ Mid-October to late November
☐ Early December to late February

Records since 1940

cedar in Octonto County (Schoenebeck 1902). On 30 March 1941 three eggs hatched in a Price County nest (W. Woodruff). On numerous occasions parents have been observed feeding fledged young in May.

It is in late summer that Gray Jays are least frequently seen, probably because they—like most other resident birds—are notably quiet at that time. Some migratory movement apparently takes place from mid-September through October. No records of visible migration have been reported, but a buildup in numbers has been noted within the birds' regular range. In Oneida County 21 were counted on 11–12 September 1956 (R. G. Wills).

It is in October and November that wandering individuals are most likely to turn up outside their usual range. Of the 30 extralimital sightings reported since 1939, all but 6 have occurred between late October and January. Such wanderings have probably been going on for many years, but before the advent of published field notes in *The Passenger Pigeon* they were not widely reported. Hoy (1853b) mentioned an occasional wanderer at Racine before 1852. Kumlien

and Hollister (1903) mentioned early records near Jefferson and Janesville but gave no precise dates. What happens to extralimital visitors is not known. In the winters of 1963–1964 and 1964–1965 an individual spent several weeks at a Stevens Point (Portage County) feeder. Most observations, however, have involved brief 1- or 2-day stands.

Blue Jay (*Cyanocitta cristata*)

STATUS. Abundant migrant. Common summer resident. Common winter resident.
HABITAT. Deciduous forest. Coniferous forest. Residential areas.
MIGRATION DATES. *Spring:* mid-April to late May. *Fall:* early September to late October.
BREEDING DATA. Nests with eggs: 27 April to 8 July. Clutch size: usually 4 or 5 eggs; occasionally 3 or 6.
PORTRAIT. *Birds of Wisconsin:* Plate 56.

Most writers have referred to the Blue Jay as a common or abundant permanent resident because these birds are widely present in every season. But it is not known how many individuals remain in a given area throughout the year. Since many observers have witnessed migratory flights of hundreds of birds passing overhead in May and September, and since banding has provided abundant proof of large-scale migration, the designations "summer resident" and "winter resident" seem more appropriate.

A study of CBC data makes clear how common and widespread the bird is as a winter resident. From Brule to Kenosha, from Hiles to Cornelia, this species shows up on 99% of the counts taken every year. In some locations it is eclipsed in numbers by the starling and House Sparrow, in others by the goldfinch and the redpoll, in others by the junco and the Tree Sparrow, in others by the crow and the chickadee. But on most Christmas counts the bird is one of the 10 most numerous species year after year.

The Blue Jay's abundance shows up less conspicuously in BBS data. Many additional species are present in June, so that overall 70-transect totals show the Blue Jay to be outnumbered by more than 15 other species, although it has been recorded on 98% of the transects. The jay, preoccupied with nesting in June, is quieter than usual, and thus is probably more numerous than BBS numbers indicate. The accompanying map shows a statewide distribution, with the bird most numerous in the central sand area where oaks abound, least numerous in the heavily cropped southeast.

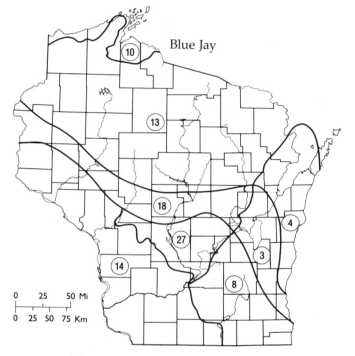

Breeding Bird Survey, averages 1966 to 1980

Whatever the season, this noisy resident is at home in a variety of wooded habitats. It is found in tall timber or shrubbery, in coniferous or deciduous trees. Oak woodlots are particular favorites. Nest sites also show the same kind of variety. Nests have been found as little as 3 feet up in barberry hedges, and as much as 50 feet up in yellow birches. Spruce, maple, apple, pine, oak, willow—all have harbored nests.

Periods of greatest abundance occur in spring from 20 April to 20 May in the south, 10 days later farther north. In fall the bird migrates from 5 September to 15 October in the north, 10 days later farther south.

Migratory flights in spring consist mostly of small, loose flocks flying just above treetop level. Watching them only briefly, one might assume this to be nothing more than random movement of local birds. But sustained watching on a flight day may produce counts in the hundreds. An estimated 2,500 birds passed Cedar Grove (Sheboygan County) on 16 May 1954. In 3 hours of counting in Sauk County on 4 May 1982, R. M. Hoffman (1982) saw 1,800.

In September one sometimes espies a flock of 100 or more steadily flapping birds and determines them to be high-flying Blue Jays. Near Green Bay on 1 October 1970 Richard Hasterlik counted 1,100 birds in a 5-hour period. Near Adams on 24 September 1952 three flocks totaling 750 birds passed over within an hour's time.

Banding recoveries further substantiate the bird's migratory habits. A bird banded at Milton (Rock County) on 2 September 1941 (M. T. Maxson) turned up in Arkansas 13 months later. One banded at Madison on 11 September 1956 (M. B. Hickey, pers. comm.) appeared in Missouri in November. Another of Mrs. Hickey's birds, trapped during the summers of 1955, 1956, and 1958, was caught in Arkansas in January 1959. Other recoveries of Wisconsin-banded jays have occurred in Illinois, Louisiana, and Georgia. Between 1950 and 1959 Mrs. Hickey banded 199 immature jays in summer; she found that only 4 were known to re-main the following winter, but 54 returned the following spring.

While some Blue Jays are migrating overhead, others are busy preparing for the winter by storing acorns for later use. C. P. Fox (pers. comm. to O. J. Gromme) took these notes on 24 September 1955: "Jay landed in grass, regurgitated four acorns from gullet, then picked up one and re-swallowed it. Flew off fifty feet, poked around in grass for two or three minutes until he found a suitable spot. Coughed up acorn and poked it into a hole he had made in a tuft of grass, then with beak pulled dry grass over acorn. Hopped a foot away, picked up dry grass and returned to acorn and covered it carefully. Even brought over a piece of bark and put it on the grass. Bird constantly worked grass with beak until all evidence of the acorn was gone."

Whenever there is a bumper crop of acorns, winter jay populations will be high; when acorns are few, the number of wintering jays will be below average. The average number of jays per Christmas count has varied from 125 in 1976 and 182 in 1985 to 35 in 1963 and 41 in 1967.

Clark's Nutcracker (*Nucifraga columbiana*)

STATUS. Accidental. Five records.
HABITAT. Savanna. Residential areas.
MIGRATION DATES. Observed between 19 October and 13 January.
WINTER. Two records.

Fire caused the loss of the only specimen of the Clark's Nutcracker known for the state. It had been shot at Milwaukee by a Mr. Hawley, then preserved in the collection of Dr. G. W. Peckham. A late-nineteenth-century fire destroyed this collection, including the recording of the exact observation date. Dr. Peckham remembered it as being in the late fall of 1875.

For 85 years this remained the lone state record. On 6 November 1961 a second bird made a brief visit to the backyard of Fred Babcock at Land O'Lakes in Vilas County (*Pass. Pigeon* 24:45).

In 1964 two birds were recorded. One, discovered at Rhinelander (Oneida County) on 1 January, was seen frequently through 10 January (C. Vig; *Pass. Pigeon* 26:152). The other was carefully observed on 19 October as it fed among a mixed flock of blackbirds near Evansville in Rock County (J. W. Wilde; *Pass. Pigeon* 27:125).

The state's fifth record was established on 13 January 1973, when Darwin Tiede observed a bird at Point Beach State Park near Two Rivers (Manitowoc

Clark's Nutcracker

0   25   50 Mi
0 25 50 75 Km

▽   19 October to mid-November
☐   1 to 13 January

All records

County). For 5 minutes he watched the bird move from ground to tree and from limb to limb along the edge of a pine grove. Then it was gone (*Pass. Pigeon* 35:169–170). In the previous October and November three of these birds had been observed in Ontario and three in Missouri.

Occasionally, this bird moves out of its normal

Rocky Mountain range in late fall. Records are also extant for Nebraska, Minnesota, Iowa, Illinois, Arkansas, Louisiana, Michigan, and Pennsylvania. But since this species is essentially nonmigratory, instances of extralimital wanderings probably will remain infrequent.

Black-billed Magpie (*Pica pica*)
Formerly American Magpie

STATUS. Rare migrant. Accidental in summer. Casual winter visitor.
HABITAT. Savanna. Upland carr.
MIGRATION DATES. *Spring:* early April to mid-May. *Fall:* early October to late November.
WINTER. Occasionally wanders east to Ashland, Oneida, and Marathon counties; very rarely to Milwaukee and Racine counties.
PORTRAIT. *Birds of Wisconsin:* Plate 57.

The probability of escapes, combined with fragmentary data, make the assessment of 35 state observations difficult. Wisconsin is east of the normal range of the Black-billed Magpie, but the recent field guides all mention the species' tendency to wander south and east in fall and winter.

In Minnesota this wanderer is regular in fall and winter in the northwest, roaming occasionally to the northeast. It is probably wandering from this region that explains one cluster of Wisconsin records. Several of these are nineteenth-century sightings, with tantalizingly vague dates. Kumlien and Hollister (1903) attributed two Dunn County observations to J. N. Clark: one bird trapped sometime in 1870 and one observed at close range in February 1884. They also mentioned a specimen collected in Ashland County in 1880 and a hunter who said he had seen a half dozen in all his experience of many years in northern Wisconsin.

More recent northwestern observations include birds on 25 November (1921, St. Croix, C. G. Stratton [Schorger 1951a], 11 January (1963, Marathon, P. Macht), 23 November (1969, Vilas, W. Nicewander), December (1972, Oneida, B. Kohn), early February (1973, trapped in Price, *fide* B. F. Klugow), 25 October (1973, Polk, K. H. Dueholm), 8 October (1980, Eau Claire, T. Balding), and most of January (1982, Douglas, *fide* K. R. Eckert). These individuals followed a set pattern: appearing in late fall or winter, then disappearing.

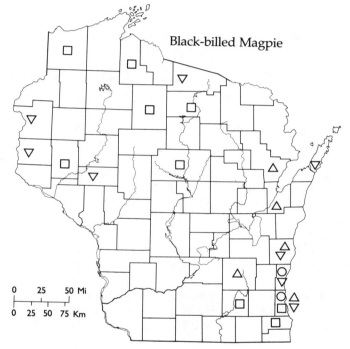

Black-billed Magpie

△ Early April to mid-May
○ Early June to mid-August
▽ Early October to late November
□ Mid-December to early February

All records

A second cluster of sightings centers in eastern Wisconsin, including the Lake Michigan shore and the Fox River valley. Nineteenth-century records include two birds shot in Racine County in December 1848 (Hoy 1853b), one obtained in Door County on 15 November 1849 (*fide* P. R. Hoy), and one observed several times in Jefferson County during the winter of 1859–1860 by T. L. Kumlien (Kumlien and Hollister 1903).

Not until 5 November 1944 did this region produce

another record (Milwaukee, W. J. Mueller). Then between 1947 and 1959 came nine sightings, including these five in Milwaukee: 8 June 1947 (O. J. Gromme), 2 October 1949 (C. P. Frister), approximately 10 April 1952 (E. Hunter), 7 October 1954 (R. Schoonmaker), and 21 October 1959 (K. Egger). One bird spent 2 days at Cedar Grove (Sheboygan County) after a tornado: 3–4 April 1956 (H. C. Mueller). Another turned up in Ozaukee County on an indefinite date in the fall of 1956 (E. Schluter). Brown County attracted a bird on 19 May 1957 (E. O. Paulson). One was present at Horicon (Dodge County) between 29 April (H. A. Mathiak) and 11 May 1959 (R. A. Hunt). There is little pattern to these dates.

There is even less pattern to another five observations between 1967 and 1974: 7 May 1967 (Milwaukee, F. A. Marks), 28 December 1968 (Racine, *fide* E. B. Prins), 25 April 1970 (Oconto, C. H. Richter), mid-August 1970 (Ozaukee, J. L. Jarboe), mid-December 1973–6 January 1974 (Milwaukee, M. F. Donald), and 13 April–22 May 1974 (Milwaukee, E. Judziewicz).

An individual appeared briefly on 8 October 1980 (Eau Claire, T. L. Balding). Two observations occurred in 1982. A bird visited a Douglas County neighborhood frequently in January (K. R. Eckert). On 3 October one flew over the Cedar Grove Ornithological Station in Sheboygan County (H. C. Mueller and others).

American Crow (*Corvus brachyrhynchos*)
Formerly Common Crow

STATUS. Abundant resident south and central. Common summer resident north. Fairly common winter resident north.
HABITAT. Deciduous forest. Northern maple-hemlock-pine forest. Open cropland.
MIGRATION DATES. *Spring:* mid-February to late April. *Fall:* early October to late November.
BREEDING DATA. Nests with eggs: 31 March to 28 May. Clutch size: usually 4 or 5 eggs; occasionally 3–7.
PORTRAIT. *Birds of Wisconsin:* Plate 57.

After witnessing gigantic winter roosts of over 10,000 American Crows, one is hard put to realize that this was a scarce bird in Wisconsin in 1850. Hoy (1853b) thought it absent from the area around Racine in his day and present only rarely elsewhere. Appraising early references to this species, Schorger (1941b) concluded, " . . . the Crow was distributed sparsely in the state prior to 1855, became common in the southern portion by 1875, and abundant by 1890." By 1938 crows had become such pests that residents in Rock County dynamited a huge roost, killing over 5,000 birds.

In spite of dynamiting, extensive shooting, and other abortive attempts to control an enlarging population, numbers continue to swell. Christmas bird-counters have sometimes stationed themselves at various observation points surrounding a woodland roost area in midafternoon, to tally the number of crows as they congregate, coming from miles around in every direction. Winter roosts of 200 are commonly found in southern and central locations; flocks of

Breeding Bird Survey, averages 1966 to 1980

1,000–5,000 have been counted near Madison, Poynette (Columbia County), Waukesha, and Janesville (Rock County). At Milwaukee's Whitnall Park there is a gathering that sometimes exceeds 15,000.

It is only since 1975 that crows have been found on every Wisconsin CBC. For many years this species migrated from northern regions in October and November, returning as one of the first spring migrants in late February and March. CBC figures trace the slow but steady expansion of the bird's northern winter range. Through 1954 few birds were recorded north of Highway 29 and none north of Highway 64. Then came firsts for Polk (1955), Langlade (1956), Marinette (1961), Douglas (1963), Oneida (1964), Price (1964), Forest (1964), Sawyer (1966), Lincoln (1968), and Bayfield (1968) counties.

The spring migration pattern continues. By 20 February, birds at the southern roosts begin to disperse, and migrants begin to appear in the north. Birders note sizable loose flights of migratory birds frequently through March and early April and again throughout October. H. L. Stoddard's (pers. comm.) report of a roost of 300–500 birds in Sauk County on 23 April 1921 suggests that migration sometimes extends into late April.

But by that date considerable nesting activity has begun, with nest construction under way by 19 March. Nests with eggs have been located by 31 March. Observers have detected hatched young by 27 April. With eggs still being reported as late as 28 May and young in the nest as late as 11 and 25 July, second nestings appear probable in many instances.

From BBS results one might conclude that this is one of the state's six most abundant species in summer. The average annual statewide total of 2,288 individuals on the state's 70 transects is exceeded only by the Red-winged Blackbird, European Starling, House Sparrow, Common Grackle, and American Robin. Perhaps this species merits that rank. But it must be remembered that the American Crow is a conspicuous bird, flying over open areas where it is visible from great distances and feeding in plain sight on open fields and meadows and along roadsides, with the calls of both adults and young frequently heard on June mornings. The accompanying map shows populations to be high and well distributed throughout the state.

Even in late summer when most passerines become relatively quiet, crows abound. Sizable roosts have already developed by late June; soaring hawks and ravens often stir up a swarm of agitated crows in July and August. On sultry August afternoons I have accompanied C. A. Kemper as he played amplified crow calls in open country, and marveled at how many crows would suddenly appear out of "nowhere."

Hawk-watchers sometimes observe migrating crows in late September, for this species is a diurnal traveler. But the main fall flight occurs between 1 October and 15 November.

Some of the bird's feeding habits are well known. The crow has developed a negative image because it destroys eggs of other birds in early summer and because it feeds on agricultural crops in summer and fall. On the positive side, the bird feeds on roadkilled animals at all seasons.

In winter, crows are often seen on ice at the edge of open water along the major rivers where they feed on fish remains. H. H. T. Jackson (1943), A. W. Schorger, and others have commented on the bird's ability to skim close to the surface of open water and pick up edible tidbits with its beak. C. L. Strelitzer reported a 3 October 1940 observation in Milwaukee where birds jumped from the ground to the low branches of a maple, fastened their beaks to developing seeds, and swung upside down, chickadee-fashion, until the seeds came loose.

Common Raven (*Corvus corax*)

STATUS. Fairly common resident north; uncommon resident central. Rare fall migrant west and east.

HABITAT. Northern forest.

MIGRATION DATES. No spring flight. *Fall:* late September to late November.

BREEDING DATA. Nests with eggs: 16 February to 18 April. Clutch size: usually 5 eggs; occasionally 3–6.

WINTER. Regularly present south to Polk, Jackson, Wood, Shawano, and Brown counties; occasionally present south to Juneau and Manitowoc counties.

PORTRAIT. *Birds of Wisconsin:* Plate 57.

Common Raven

	Resident range
△	Early March to early April
▽	Late September to late November
□	Early December to late February

Records since 1960

The earliest settlers found Common Ravens present throughout most of the state, wherever forests prevailed. Hoy (1853b) recorded them at Racine, where they sometimes outnumbered crows. Schorger (1941b), investigating early references, concluded that the species was once widespread over much of southern Wisconsin. By 1900 Kumlien and Hollister (1903) recorded that the bird was restricted to the northern and central regions, with southern observations confined mostly to the Lake Michigan area. Prevailing sentiment in the 1940s had the bird regular in the northern third of the state—uncommon in winter and a rare summer breeder—with occasional late fall wanderings into the less populated central region.

Present indications are that this species is more numerous in winter in the northern counties than had previously been supposed. Of the 322 Christmas counts conducted north of a line from St. Croix Falls to Oconto between 1960 and 1980, the Common Raven has been recorded on 274 (85%). Numbers are especially high in the northwestern counties. The 476 ravens recorded at Brule (Douglas County) on 21 December 1963 was the highest figure for North America that year. South of this line, CBC birds are now found regularly in Chippewa, Eau Claire, Clark, Wood, and Jackson counties, and occasionally in Monroe, Juneau, and Marathon counties.

In summer this bird also persists farther south than had been suspected. Observations in Clark (12 July 1945, F. A. Hartmeister), Taylor (29 June 1948, S. D. Robbins), and Jackson (30 July 1950, W. B. Grange) counties seemed exceptional at the time. But since 1969 I have regularly found a few birds in the forested areas of Chippewa, Eau Claire, Clark, and Jackson counties.

Noticeable summer increases have shown up during the June BBS. The Exeland-Bruce run (Sawyer-Rusk counties) is typical: no ravens through 1973, 5 in 1974, and 11–17 each year since 1977. Composite BBS figures show that the average total number of individuals per year, 1966–1970, was 56 (on 23 of the 70 state transects); for the 1971–1975 interval the average increased to 79 individuals per year (on 26 transects); and for 1976–1980 the per-year average was 139 (on 33 transects).

The few nesting studies available indicate that this raven is an unusually early breeder. Because the bird builds large bulky nests, sometimes starts nesting as early as late February, and chooses sites 50 or more feet up in the tallest trees, one might think that nests are readily detected. But the raven builds nests in relatively inaccessible areas at times when the snow is at its deepest, and few people engage in the kind of snowshoeing or skiing that would take them into the most promising nesting habitat. Evron Davison (Gromme 1942b) snowshoed 1½ miles and climbed a 60-foot hemlock to obtain the nest he procured for the Milwaukee Public Museum in 1942. And Richard Gysendorfer walked 12 miles on 31 March 1957 to observe raven nests located on two railroad trestles in Iron County.

No extensive search for Wisconsin nests has been undertaken. But I have heard sounds of recently fledged young in early May in Eau Claire, Chippewa, and Clark counties.

There is evidence of a modest southward movement in October and November. A bird banded as a nestling by Gysendorfer near Marquette, Michigan, on 7 April 1957 was recovered near Phillips (Price County), 150 miles southwest, on the following 19 October. In fall, not only does the number of ravens increase in the northern sector, but there are also oc-

casional sightings in some southern counties. Hawk-watchers at Cedar Grove (Sheboygan County) have encountered ravens frequently since 1939. Recent records have also been obtained in Ozaukee (1972), Dane (1953, 1954), Iowa (1972), Monroe (1980), and Vernon (1976) counties, all between 26 September and 23 November. What happens to these autumn vagrants remains a mystery. Few if any are reported farther south. They do not remain long enough for inclusion in the December Christmas bird counts. No northward movement has been detected, either in late fall or early spring.

Family **Paridae:** Titmice

Black-capped Chickadee (*Parus atricapillus*)

STATUS. Abundant migrant. Common summer resident. Abundant winter resident.
HABITAT. All forest. All shrubs. Residential areas.
MIGRATION DATES. *Spring:* early March to mid-April.
Fall: mid-September to mid-November.
BREEDING DATA. Nests with eggs: 2 May to 8 July.
Clutch size: usually 7 eggs; occasionally 4–9.
PORTRAIT. *Birds of Wisconsin:* Plate 58.

In the sense that it is present in every season of the year, the Black-capped Chickadee can be said to be a permanent resident. But this term belies the fact that the species is at least partly migratory. Several individuals banded in Wisconsin between October and January have been recovered the following spring in Illinois, Michigan, and Minnesota.

It is during winter that the "dee-bird" endears itself most to humans. So tame is it that it will often wait scarcely more than an arm's-length away while I place sunflower seeds in the feeder on a subzero snowy morning. Such a morning never seems quite so frigid whenever I watch these well-insulated balls of fluffy feathers go about their daily feeding chores. Chickadees are widely present in winter. No matter whether one sets up a bird feeder in the country, in a suburb, or close to the downtown section of a major city, it is likely to attract at least a couple of Black-caps, as long as there are a few trees or shrubs nearby. On 1,381 CBCs conducted in all parts of Wisconsin during the 1960–1980 period, observers recorded Black-capped chickadees on 1,366 (99%). On occasion a single party has tallied over 300 individuals on a 1-day count.

With the coming of spring, Black-caps are seen less frequently. Some migrate, but there is no sudden increase in one area or dearth in another, allowing observers to pinpoint times of movement. Birds choosing to move northward probably do so in March and early April. Others move away from human dwellings, seeking more secluded nest sites. The preferred nest site is a hole in a fence post or a small dead tree. Nest construction has been observed as early as 15 April, but usually the first eggs are not laid until May. The major part of the egg-laying comes between 20 May and 10 June, and the presence of eggs in early July suggests that some pairs may nest twice. Family groups can often be seen foraging in July.

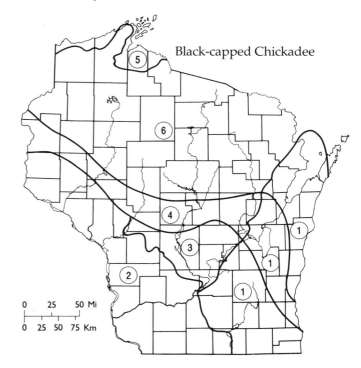

Breeding Bird Survey, averages 1966 to 1980

This species breeds in all sections of the state. In contrast to the 99% distribution figure for the CBC, there was only a 70% representation on the 1966–1980 BBS, birds being found on 659 of 942 transects. Each of the 70 BBS transect areas has had this species at least once, but as the accompanying map indicates, "chicks" are decidedly more numerous in the northern half of the state.

Some uncertainty surrounds the start of fall migration. Birds are more in evidence from mid-August on. Single birds are occasionally found, but the birds generally move in groups of 5–10. Usually they are mixed with migrant warblers, vireos, kinglets, and flycatchers. Because chicks are noisier and more responsive to "squeaking," the presence of the Black-caps is often a valuable clue to the presence of the mixed migrating flocks. Many a time have I paused at the edge of a wooded area in fall, heard nothing but the single call note of a chick, and been led to a mixed flock of 10 or more birds of different species. It is uncertain

410

whether these early fall birds should be considered true fall migrants or merely summer residents exhibiting greater mobility.

On 7 September 1956 I watched a flock moving from tree to tree following the shore of the Petenwell Flowage in northern Adams County. I counted 33 Black-caps, almost certainly migrants. Other observers have reported sizable flocks passing along Hawk Ridge at Duluth, Minnesota, by mid-September. But the main migration period is in October. Records at the Cedar Grove Ornithological Station in Sheboygan County show 102 banded on a single day (13 October 1959) and 216 banded over a 3-day span (23–25 October 1961), suggesting the timing of the fall migratory peak for that area.

Although there are year-to-year fluctuations in population levels, there has been no discernible change in the bird's status through the years. Kumlien and Hollister (1903) described the bird as abundant; we use the same term today.

Boreal Chickadee (*Parus hudsonicus*)

Formerly Brown-capped Chickadee, Hudsonian Chickadee

STATUS. Uncommon resident north; rare resident northwest. Casual fall and winter visitant central and south.

HABITAT. Upland spruce-fir forest.

BREEDING DATA. Nest with young: 20 June.

WINTER. Regularly present south to Sawyer and Langlade counties.

PORTRAIT. *Birds of Wisconsin*: Plate 58.

Once every 3–5 years this Canadian species stages a mild winter irruption. When this happens, from one to five Boreal Chickadees venture into central and southern Wisconsin and spend some weeks in favorable coniferous habitat, occasionally visiting well-stocked feeders.

This explains Hoy's (1853b) January 1952 record in Racine and Thure Kumlien's (Kumlien and Hollister 1903) specimen that same winter in Jefferson County. It accounts for the bird that visited Madison from 24 December 1946 to 18 March 1947 (N. R. Barger and others) and the bird that was photographed at Oconomowoc (Waukesha County) on 2 February 1947 (C. P. Fox). Another bird wintered in Dane County from 4 December 1954 to 26 March 1955. Birds reached Dane and Brown counties in December 1959. In the fall and winter of 1966–1967 birds reached Barron, St. Croix, Chippewa, and Shawano counties. There were winter observations, 1975–1976, in Burnett, Marathon, and Milwaukee counties. In the autumn of 1978, individuals were attracted to feeders in St. Croix, Vernon, and Racine counties.

Although these occurrences are highly irregular, this nasal-voiced "chick" is regular as a year-round resident in suitable spruce-cedar-tamarack bogs scattered across northern Wisconsin. During the 1950s and 1960s most observations came from the northeastern region (Iron and Price counties eastward).

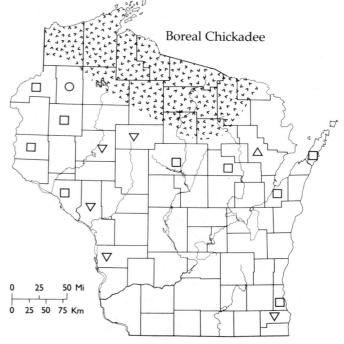

Boreal Chickadee

⊡	Resident range
△	Early April
○	Early May to late August
▽	Early September to late November
☐	Early December to mid-March

Records since 1960

Virtually all CBC records were from Forest, Oneida, Langlade, and Price counties. Most summer sightings also emanated from this region, as did the meager nesting data available. On 20 June 1959 Martha and Roy Lound found a nest in Forest County. Young birds could be heard "cheeping" as parents brought food to a hole 10 feet up in a dead birch stump. Recently fledged young have been noted on three other occasions: on 12 July 1926, Klotz (1927) collected an adult and young from a small flock at Mamie Lake in Vilas County; on 14 July 1971 C. H. Richter met a parent and five young in Forest County; on 9 August 1966 T. K. Soulen watched a parent feeding three young in Oneida County.

Through the 1970s reports from the northeast became less frequent, while those from the northwest expanded. There are suspicions that this reflected changes in coverage by birders rather than shifts in the bird population. CBC records since 1975 have been evenly divided between the two regions. The southern limit of the range—both winter and summer—is a line extending southeast from Gordon to Antigo, then northeast through Florence.

Now, as in the nineteenth century, the Boreal Chickadee remains a decidedly uncommon species in Wisconsin. Even where the "brown-cap" appears most frequently, it is greatly outnumbered by the Black-cap: On visits to brown-cap territory over the past 20 years, I have missed the bird far more often than I have found it.

Tufted Titmouse (*Parus bicolor*)

STATUS. Uncommon resident south and central; rare resident northwest.
HABITAT. Southern oak-hickory forest. Residential areas.
BREEDING DATA. Nests with young: 26 and 29 May.
WINTER. Regularly present north to St. Croix, Chippewa, Marquette and Waukesha counties.
PORTRAIT. *Birds of Wisconsin*: Plate 58.

The presence of this southern species is strictly a twentieth-century phenomenon. The Tufted Titmouse was unknown in Wisconsin until 1900 when N. C. Gilbert (Kumlien and Hollister 1903) collected one near Madison on 15 December. This was followed by two 1912 sightings (Mitchell and Mitchell 1913), both in Walworth County, one at Lake Geneva on 12 March (E. Peaks), and one at Whitewater from 12 December to the following 15 March (I. N. Mitchell and others). During the 1920s, however, a major push took place that carried birds north to Racine and Milwaukee counties in the east, to Sauk and Winnebago counties in the central region, and along the Mississippi River at least to Buffalo County. Wisconsin lacked observers in the west at that time, but in 1923 Minnesota had records for Redwing and St. Paul.

The spread of the Tufted Titmouse has often been compared with the northward range extension of the Red-bellied Woodpecker and the Northern Cardinal. Although the same time span is involved, the titmouse spread has been far more limited in numbers. Its presence has been noted during winter more than in any other season. Yet the largest numbers on Wisconsin Christmas counts for any one year were the 179 recorded in 25 count areas in 1968. Usually, num-

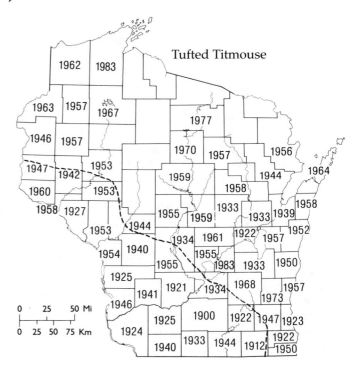

Years of first county records; not yet established north of dashed line

bers have been under 100, with the bird recorded on 12–15 counts.

A glance at the accompanying map might suggest that birds are now well established over the southern two-thirds of the state and are found in at least a few localities over much of the north. Not so. In many counties appearances were brief, with no stable populations developing. Only four CBC areas have sustained populations of 5–10 individuals for as much as 10 years. One of these, Beloit (Rock County), tallied high numbers in the 1950s, building to a peak of 49 in 1962. Numbers dwindled to four in 1970 and have varied from none to four ever since. Wide fluctuations have also occurred at Madison and on the Grant County counts at Cornelia and Beetown. The other stronghold is much farther north at Chippewa Falls, where the "tits" find the combination of suet feeders and oak woods near the south shore of Lake Wissota much to their liking.

The years of first sightings in the southwestern counties are suspect. There were few reports until the Wisconsin Society for Ornithology began collecting field notes statewide in 1940. If one surmises that the first titmice may have reached all Mississippi River counties north to Pierce County by 1930, it appears that the 1950s and early 1960s were a time of considerable expansion. Since 1964 there have probably been more losses than gains.

Analyzing CBC records from 1939 through 1964, Young (1967) determined that titmice had been recorded on 46% of the counts south of the tension zone, on 28% of the counts within the zone, and on 6% of counts north of this zone. Data have not been analyzed thoroughly enough to determine whether this trend continues today or whether population fluctuations correlate to weather conditions. Are Wisconsin winters proving too hard for some of our titmice?

At other seasons birds are more dispersed. They spend time largely in river bottoms or on nearby hillsides where oaks abound; they are less frequently seen in summer than in winter. Nesting occupies their attention during May, June, and early July.

Despite the probability that the titmouse nests sparsely across at least half of Wisconsin's counties, published records of positive nesting are scanty. On 28 June 1925, Schorger (1927a) collected one of five recently fledged young in Dane County. In 1957 nest construction was observed in Rock County (J. W. Wilde); nests with young were found in Barron County on 26 May (E. Butler) and in Adams County on 29 May (F. N. and F. Hamerstrom). Nesting was suspected in Dane and Grant counties in May 1947, but positive evidence is lacking. The appearance of two adults and four young at a feeder near Appleton on 14 July (1957, N. M. Rogers) indicates probable breeding in that area.

Family **Sittidae:** Nuthatches

Red-breasted Nuthatch (*Sitta canadensis*)

STATUS. Fairly common migrant. Fairly common summer resident north; rare summer resident central. Fairly common (sometimes common) winter resident.
HABITAT. Coniferous forest. Northern maple-hemlock-pine forest. Residential areas.
MIGRATION DATES. *Spring:* mid-April to late May. *Fall:* late July to mid-November.
BREEDING DATA. Nest (eggs?): 5 June; nest with young: 4 July.
PORTRAIT. *Birds of Wisconsin:* Plate 58.

A southern Wisconsin observer who finds a Red-breasted Nuthatch in July or August may well surmise that this is the beginning of a heavy fall flight, a larger-than-usual winter population, and a strong flight the following spring. Within the past 30 years incursions have taken place in the fall of 1954, 1957, 1961, 1963, 1965, 1968, 1969, 1971, 1974, 1977, 1980, and 1982. They can be expected every 2–4 years, timed with a coniferous cone shortage in the northern forests.

In flight years, a few individuals do not wait until August to begin. A Milwaukee observation on 16 July 1945, a Rock County banding on 10 July 1961, and a sighting on 7 July 1971 in Ozaukee County were probably early harbingers of major fall flights that were to follow. When an invasion occurs, the buildup is gradual but noticeable in July and August. A strong peak occurs from late September to mid-October. During the 1954 flight, 323 individuals were counted in 1½ hours' migration past the Cedar Grove Ornithological Station in Sheboygan County on 17 October. On 12 October 1969, C. A. Kemper counted 82 individuals killed at the Eau Claire television tower. On 12 September 1977 in residential Milwaukee, 84 appeared in one backyard in an hour's time (W. Woodmansee). In a nonflight year an occasional individual may be spotted, but birds will be few and far between.

A similar contrast can be seen in CBC figures. In a "low" year observers report these birds on about half of the state's count areas, with all parts of the state represented—but mainly by two individuals here, three there, with no sizable concentrations. Typical of a "down" winter was 1973, when there were birds recorded on 31 of 60 counts, totaling 109 individuals.

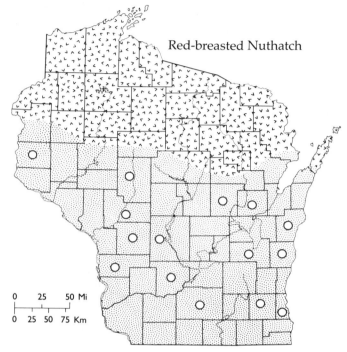

Red-breasted Nuthatch

0   25   50 Mi
0 25 50 75 Km

▱ Resident range
▦ Winter range
○ Early June to mid-July

Records since 1960

In an "up" winter this bird is found on 70% or more of the counts, with 100 or more individuals sometimes concentrated in a single count area. The winter of 1969–1970 was a banner season, with 112 "nutsies" recorded at Rhinelander (Oneida County), 25 or more at each of eight other locations, and birds spotted on 51 of 65 count areas, making a grand total of 664 individuals. Even more spectacular was the 1977–1978 flight. Red-breasts were found on 58 of 72 counts, totaling 914 individuals: 261 at Brule (Douglas County), 109 at Rice Lake (Barron County).

The year-to-year winter fluctuations are dramatic and not easily explained. Some years birds desert northern Wisconsin and invade farther south; some years the north gets an invasion from Canada that does not extend to the south; some years the population is high in all parts of the state.

The spring flight is far less spectacular than the fall

influx during an invasion year. Come March, many of the birds that favored winter feeders disperse, and yet little northward migration is evident. Migration is apparent mainly between 20 April and 20 May, and then only following winters of a high population. One needs a combination of sharp eyes, keen ears, and a bit of luck to find a spring migrant after a winter when the population has been low.

The main part of the nesting range in Wisconsin lies north of a line from St. Croix Falls through Shawano to Sturgeon Bay. Here the bird is regular in small numbers wherever pines are plentiful. Tall red pines are

particularly favored. South of this line there are pockets where the bird is probably a regular summer resident: in Jackson, Juneau, Waupaca, and Sauk counties. Nesting in the Baraboo hills in Sauk County became established on 5 June 1970, when Kenneth Lange (pers. comm.) observed parents entering a nest cavity. Three days later Winnie Woodmansee watched a pair with two recently fledged young at her feeder in suburban Milwaukee. Other recent June records have come from St. Croix, Clark, Vernon, Outagamie, Waukesha, and Dane counties.

White-breasted Nuthatch (*Sitta carolinensis*)

STATUS. Common resident.
HABITAT. Deciduous forest. Northern maple-hemlock-pine forest. Residential areas.
BREEDING DATA. Nests with eggs: 10 April to 27 May.
    Clutch size: usually 7 or 8 eggs; occasionally 4–9.
PORTRAIT. *Birds of Wisconsin*: Plate 58.

Most observers know the White-breasted Nuthatch best as a common visitor to winter feeders. It does not flock, as do most other feeder visitors; but comes alone or in pairs. But when a large CBC includes many feeders, a day's total can run to well over 100 individuals. Madison counters experienced spectacular results on 22 December 1962, tallying 324 "upside-down birds." This is one of relatively few species that is truly statewide in winter. It has been recorded on 1,405 of 1,465 (96%) Christmas counts since 1960. Numbers from the northern counties are generally lower than those from the south and central regions, because the White-breast has a strong preference for deciduous trees. In the hardwoods of northern Wisconsin it is common; in the coniferous forests it is absent.

Although numbers seem to diminish in most areas as spring advances, there is no evidence of significant migration. No reports of visible diurnal migration are known, nor are there any known instances of banded birds being recovered out of state. Any time from early April on, the nuthatch prepares for nesting, sometimes dispersing to nearby woodlands, sometimes remaining in its winter neighborhood.

Nesting procedure begins with the search for suitable nest cavities. Hollowed knots in large deciduous trees are especially favored: sometimes 10–15 feet up, sometimes as high as 50 feet. Nest sites 2–3 feet above ground are known, but these are exceptional. The next step involves cleaning the nest hole and ar-

White-breasted Nuthatch

Breeding Bird Survey, averages 1966 to 1980

ranging wood chips to form the outer part of the nest. Soft material is then added as an inner lining. George vos Burgh (pers. comm. to O. J. Gromme), reporting on seven nests in the Columbus area in the 1890s, noted that birds used some kind of hair or fur—rabbit, horse, cow, mouse—to line every nest. All this is in preparation for eggs that are often laid by the end of April or first week in May. A clutch of nine eggs discovered by vos Burgh on 5 May 1895 was unusual, but clutches of seven and eight are common.

Because White-breasted Nuthatches are relatively

silent during and beyond the nesting season, BBS numbers in June do not compare with those of the Christmas count. Nevertheless, the species maintains a fairly general distribution around the state (see the accompanying map). Of the 935 BBS transects that were run from 1966 to 1980, 528 (56%) recorded this species—sometimes 1 or 2 individuals, sometimes 18–20.

This bird becomes more noticeable again in July when family groups are abroad. As summer turns toward autumn, the White-breast joins the mixed flocks of congregating chickadees and migrating warblers. Sometimes five or six nuthatches will be seen together; rather than being a migrating flock, the birds probably constitute a family group that has not yet separated. By October the family groups have dispersed; the parent birds often return to their wintering grounds of the previous year. C. A. Kemper (pers. comm.) has records of four birds, originally banded in November, that left during the spring but returned the following two winters. Other banders have had similar experiences.

Brown-headed Nuthatch (*Sitta pusilla*)

STATUS. Accidental. One record.
HABITAT. Coniferous forest. Residential areas.

Mountains, rivers, and 750 miles separate Milwaukee from the regular range of this tree-climber. But somehow a Brown-headed Nuthatch negotiated these barriers and appeared at Laurie Otto's feeder in October 1971. During November and December it became a daily visitor, sharing suet feeders with several Red-breasted Nuthatches. By the time it had disappeared in January 1972, the Brown-headed Nuthatch had been seen by numerous other Milwaukee ornithologists and had been photographed by Harold Liebherr. It was my privilege to see this bird on 29 December. From Mrs. Otto's porch we could hear scolding notes, resembling somewhat the call of the Western Kingbird, as the nuthatch vied with its red-breasted cousins for a turn at the suet. We could also see vividly the rich chocolate brown color on the head (*Pass. Pigeon* 34:43).

Checking the coloration of the top of the head is of paramount importance in identifying this species. Twice before, small nuthatches of this type had been reported: at Milton (Rock County) on 1 May 1964 (M. T. Maxson; *Pass. Pigeon* 27:11) and at Madison on 14 May 1970 (D. G. Baker, pers. comm.). But written descriptions did not give sufficient attention to the head coloration that distinguishes this species from the Pygmy Nuthatch of the West.

Outside the bird's regular range in the southeastern states, south of Maryland and Tennessee, additional sightings have occurred only as far away as New York. Unless this species undergoes some major changes in its habits, it should be considered strictly accidental in Wisconsin.

Family **Certhiidae:** Creepers

Brown Creeper (*Certhia americana*)

STATUS. Fairly common migrant. Uncommon summer resident north, east, and west, and southwest along major rivers; rare summer resident central. Fairly common winter resident south; uncommon winter resident north and central.

HABITAT. Northern maple-hemlock-pine forest. Southern silver maple–elm forest. Residential areas.

MIGRATION DATES. *Spring:* mid-March to early May. *Fall:* early September to early November.

BREEDING DATA. Nests with eggs: 4–31 May. Clutch size: usually 6 eggs; occasionally 5 or 7.

WINTER. Regularly present in numbers north to La Crosse, Sauk, Outagamie, and Brown counties; occasional scattered individuals present throughout the north.

PORTRAIT. *Birds of Wisconsin:* Plate 58.

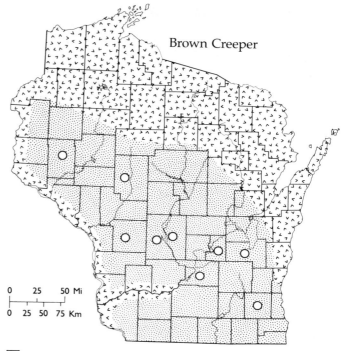

Brown Creeper

```
0    25    50 Mi
0  25  50  75 Km
```

⌐⌐ Resident range
    Winter range
○   Late May to late August

Records since 1960

The status of the Brown Creeper is difficult to determine. There are few banding records. Few television tower casualties have been reported. The song is rarely heard except on breeding grounds. The call note uttered in winter and in migration is unobtrusive and easily missed, especially by those whose ears cannot pick up high-pitched sounds. The plumage matches the bark of the birds' favorite trees so perfectly that it presents one of the most effective camouflages known to ornithologists. When threatened by a migrating hawk or some other enemy, the creeper can flatten itself against a tree trunk and remain motionless for minutes, seemingly "disappearing" into the trunk.

The creeper is best known as a winter resident. On the well-organized Christmas counts at Madison and Appleton, from 15 to 30 birds are usually tallied each year, with Madison scoring a high of 74 in 1987. In the northern counties this bird is decidedly uncommon in winter. But recent winter records exist for nearly every county in northern Wisconsin. Few people have had success in attracting Brown Creepers to their feeders. The bird's preference is for the trunks of large deciduous trees in residential areas or in bottomlands. When foraging, it begins at the bottom of a tree, works its way up the trunk, drops down to the base of the next tree, and then repeats the performance.

The Brown Creeper is less well known as a migrant. The start of migratory movement in the south is difficult to distinguish from the end of winter residency, but probably is under way by 20 March. It is more noticeable by 1 April in south and central regions, and by 10 April in the north. April may be a "peak period," except that the peak is never large. Rarely have I encountered more than six birds on an April morning field trip. A count of 34 on 14 April (1975, Rock, T. R. Ellis) was exceptional. The creeper's unobtrusive habits seem all the more pronounced in spring when other birds are becoming noisier. The call note can be heard quite frequently, but the song hardly ever. Most creepers have left the south by 10 May and the central area by the 15th. Unusually late were a Columbia county bird on 22 May (1963, N. R. Barger) and a Monroe County bird on 23 May (1970, E. Hebard).

The creeper is even less well known as a breeder.

Carl Richter regularly found it nesting in the Oconto area. Invariably the nests were located behind loose strips of bark, usually —but not always—in deciduous trees in low wet woods, 4–8 feet above ground. Most eggs are laid in May.

Few observers besides Richter have discovered nests, but June records suggest regular breeding in small numbers all across northern Wisconsin north of a line from Grantsburg through Shawano to Sturgeon Bay. In western Wisconsin, breeding is probable in suitable bottomland forest along the Mississippi River south through Grant County (1984, M. J. Mossman), and east along the Wisconsin River to Sauk City (Mossman and Lange 1982). In the eastern region, summer residency is regular in swamp forests east of Lake Winnebago, south to the Cedarburg Bog in Ozaukee County. Additional summer sightings have occurred in Columbia (1966, M. Tomlinson), Green Lake (1983, M. J. Mossman), and Waukesha (1962, M. F. Donald) counties.

Any time after 10 September fall migrants can be looked for in northern and central areas, with birds typically reaching the southern region by the 20th. The heaviest part of the fall flight comes between 25 September and 25 October, dates that correspond precisely to towerkills at Eau Claire. Casualty figures have been small: seven or fewer per year. Banding results at the Cedar Grove Ornithological Station in Sheboygan County have been decidedly greater: 630 birds trapped during the 1958–1963 period. Most observers would consider themselves fortunate to see more than five individuals on a 2-hour field trip in September or October. Exceptional was a count of 40 on 20 October (1979, Ozaukee, D. D. Tessen).

Family **Troglodytidae**: Wrens

Carolina Wren (*Thryothorus ludovicianus*)

STATUS. Rare visitant at any season, south and central; casual visitant north.
HABITAT. Southern silver maple–elm forest. Upland carr. Residential areas.
MIGRATION DATES. Nonmigratory. Observed in all seasons. No definite pattern governs arrivals or departures.
BREEDING DATA. Young recently fledged: 2–25 July.
WINTER. Occasionally present north to Polk, Chippewa, Adams, and Outagamie counties.
PORTRAIT. *Birds of Wisconsin:* Plate 59.

Wisconsin lies just north of the Carolina Wren's regular range, but close enough to make ornithologists wonder if this southern songster is actually extending its range into the state. Every few years a rash of sightings occurs, lifting the hopes of bird-watchers; but then a dearth of records follows. Such was the situation in 1953 and 1954 when Milwaukee had at least four birds, with additional birds in Outagamie, Calumet, Adams, Sauk, Sheboygan, and Ozaukee counties. In 1955 there was but one wintering bird in Madison, and one outlandish wanderer in the Amnicon River ravine 10 miles southeast of Superior (1 August, S. D. Robbins).

Perhaps winter weather offers a clue. It is well known that this bird is as apt to turn up in late fall as at any other season. But it is fiercely independent. The bird will come to a suet feeder but does not depend solely on feeders. It searches out its own alternate sources of food and shelter, and when heavy snow comes the Carolina Wren is in trouble. Far north in Osceola (Polk County) a Carolina Wren showed up at the Walter Gantenbein feeder in December 1965 and disappeared after 13 January 1966. A year later another appeared, only to vanish after 14 January 1967. Ralph Christofferson hosted a bird at his Chippewa Falls feeder through December 1971, but the bird vanished after a heavy snowfall on 4 January 1972. The fate of most of the birds recorded on CBCs is not known, but individuals have been known to survive the winter in Dane, Racine, Milwaukee, Ozaukee, Calumet and Door counties.

A second promising time for new occurrences is in April or early May. Wisconsin has had 38 such records between 1938 and 1989, reaching as far north

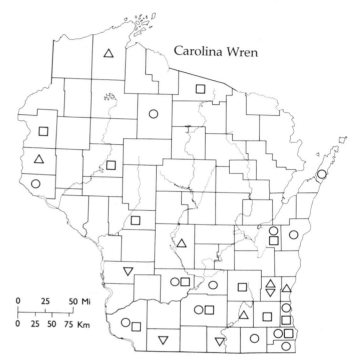

Carolina Wren

△ Late March to mid-May
○ Late May to late August
▽ Early September to mid-November
□ Late November to mid-March

Records since 1960

as Polk (1938), St. Croix (1965), Chippewa (1979), Bayfield (1978), Outagamie (1954), Calumet (1961), Brown (1946), and Door (1971) counties. It is possible that some of these birds wintered nearby undetected and became more conspicuous as the spring song period developed. It is also possible that some first-year birds, not able to establish breeding territories in areas where they fledged, had to wander. The species is essentially nonmigratory, but territorial requirements sometimes trigger a modest amount of movement that usually occurs at the advent of the breeding season.

If spring nomads succeed in finding mates, breeding results; in a few cases this is known to have happened. The 1938 Polk County record involved a pair in St. Croix Falls on 15 April that remained through

4 September. Mrs. Stella Owen (pers. comm. to O. J. Gromme) searched unsuccessfully for their nest, but on 2 and 3 July she saw the two adults and four fully grown young. A pair that appeared in La Crosse in mid-April 1946 also nested (P. C. Gatterdam). Nesting also followed the arrival of a pair in Columbia County on 4 May (1959, H. A. Winkler). A sighting in Kenosha County on 25 July (1970, W. O. Moye) also concerned young birds recently fledged. In 1975 a pair raised four young in Milwaukee (L. Otto).

A third time of year for appearances by this species is in July and August. I shall not soon forget the bird that appeared in my yard in Adams on 21 July 1953. It sang lustily for 15 minutes, then disappeared as suddenly as it had appeared. Where did it come from? Where was it headed? Similar July and August surprises have been recorded 24 times between 1940 and 1989, as far north as Douglas (1955), Price (1976), Winnebago (1947), and Manitowoc (1954) counties.

In its normal range this species sometimes raises three broods. Possibly some of the late-summer sightings involve full-grown young from a first brood; some may involve nonbreeding birds. The simplest way to summarize the status of this denizen of ravines and thick shrubbery is to list it as rare at all times, but apt to turn up anywhere in Wisconsin in any season of the year.

Bewick's Wren (*Thryomanes bewickii*)

STATUS. Rare migrant south. Rare summer resident southwest.
HABITAT. Upland carr. Residential areas.
MIGRATION DATES. *Spring:* late March to late May. *Fall:* present until late October.
BREEDING DATA. Nest with eggs: probably 25 April to 15 June. Recently fledged young: 1 July, 18 July, and 5 August. Clutch size: 7 or 8 eggs.
WINTER. Two records.
PORTRAIT. *Birds of Wisconsin:* Plate 59.

During my 1951–1960 sojourn in Adams, the Bewick's Wren was a delightful backyard companion. From mid-April to mid-June it sang frequently in the early morning hours. Singing from treetop perches, it would drop down to nearby bushes, chattering or scolding, then move to another treetop. By 9 A.M. the vocalizing would cease, and no trace of the bird would be evident until the following morning. By mid-June the early morning song routine had largely ceased, and the birds were hard to find even though they undoubtedly nested in the area. Several searches for nests were unsuccessful. But in 1953, from 5 to 11 August, I frequently saw parents feeding four recently fledged young. Late-summer glimpses during the 1950s were sporadic, but I sometimes found the birds until late September. In 1954 and 1955 singing males inhabited five areas in the vicinity of Adams; before and after those years I knew of only two areas.

Seen in perspective, these Adams County observations represent the northeasternmost limit of an expanding range. Wisconsin had no sight record until 1916, when Warner Taylor (1922b) saw a bird near Madison on 15 April. Five years later two pairs turned up near Prairie du Sac (Sauk County) and were seen

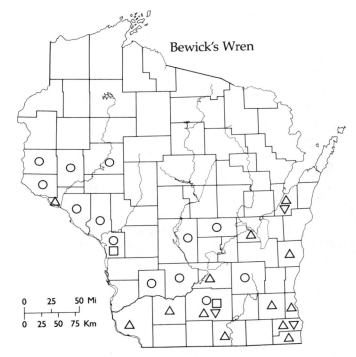

△ Late March to late May
○ Early June to late August
▽ Early September to late October
□ 10 October to 23 January

All records

by H. L. Stoddard, W. Taylor, and S. P. Jones. Breeding occurred here in 1922 (Taylor 1922b), and the first specimen was collected on 30 April 1923 near Madison (Taylor 1926b).

No widespread diffusion has ever developed after

this beginning. Birds apparently retired from the Prairie du Sac area after 1929, but by the early 1940s they had appeared in new areas in Rock, Dane, Sauk, Richland, and La Crosse counties. At Reedsburg (Sauk County) Ethel Nott found them yearly from 1945 through 1950, with a mid-April nest containing three eggs in 1945. At La Crosse, J. J. Hickey and A. M. Peterson noted them intermittently from 1942 to 1960. Near Mazomanie (Dane County) many observers shared spring and summer observations from 1942 to 1960 but never found a nest.

During the 1950s observers noted some northward movement near the Mississippi River. In Pierce County parents were seen carrying food to a nest near Maiden Rock on 7 July 1955 (Manley Olson, pers. comm.). In the same location in 1956 a pair was constructing a nest on 13 June and feeding recently fledged young on 24 July (Manley Olson, pers. comm.). June sightings were made in Buffalo County in 1960, 1961, 1962, 1964, and 1976; a June sighting was also made in Dunn County in 1963 (nested at Elk Mound, Manley Olson, pers. comm.).

After moving to St. Croix County in 1960, I found a singing male near Hudson each summer, 1961–1965, which subsequently disappeared. Other counties with possible summer residency in late May and June include Waushara (1952), Chippewa (1962), Dodge (1966), Sauk (1972), and Trempealeau (1975). Although these observations hint at continued range expansion, the number of observations statewide has dropped noticeably since 1966.

In addition to the summer records in the south-west, spring migrants sometimes have appeared in a few eastern areas. The bird seen on 25 March in Sauk County (1948, E. A. Nott) was exceptionally early. Spring movement is most likely to occur in April and the first half of May. I know of sporadic sightings during this period for Kenosha (1969, 1977), Racine (1961, 1963), Milwaukee (1947, 1950, 1982), Waukesha (1949), Sheboygan (1969), Winnebago (1953), and Brown (1959) counties.

Even rarer are the wanderings in late fall and early winter, following the usual 25 September departure date. At Green Bay one bird was present from 16 September to 3 October (1971, E. D. Cleary and Bro. Columban). At Madison one turned up on 7 October (1955, R. G. Wills). Racine had a visitor on 21 October (1939, E. B. and G. Prins). La Crosse attracted a lingerer from 9 November to 7 December (1954, A. M. Peterson [1955]). And at Madison a wintering bird survived from 10 October to 23 January (1959–1960, W. L. Hilsenhoff).

There is no ready explanation for the decline since 1966. No Bewick's Wrens have been reported from the familiar Adams County haunts since 1970. Since 1972, with the exception of a 31 July 1975 bird (Trempealeau, C. A. Faanes), I know of no summer or autumn observations recorded anywhere in Wisconsin. The four observations since 1976 have all been of birds appearing briefly in spring, then quickly disappearing.

Wisconsin's sole record since 1979 is a Milwaukee bird on 18 May 1982 (W. Woodmansee). This species was added to the state's endangered species list in 1989.

House Wren (*Troglodytes aedon*)

STATUS. Common migrant. Common summer resident.

HABITAT. Residential areas. Southern silver maple–elm forest. Upland carr.

MIGRATION DATES. *Spring:* mid-April to mid-May. *Fall:* late August to mid-October. *Extremes:* 31 March; 15 November.

BREEDING DATA. Nests with eggs: 3 May to 8 August. Clutch size: usually 6 or 7 eggs; occasionally 4–9.

WINTER. One December record.

PORTRAIT. *Birds of Wisconsin:* Plate 59.

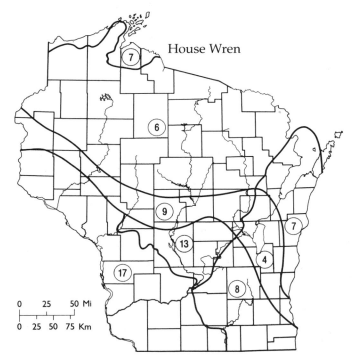

House Wren

Breeding Bird Survey, averages 1966 to 1980

Commenting on a return visit to Wisconsin after a 17-year absence, Hollister (1919b), was particularly impressed with the increase in House Wrens. Previously he had known the bird primarily as a migrant. In 1919 he found it moving into residential areas as a common nester. Actually it was a common nester in much of the state before Hollister's day, but even now it continues to become still more common. Along the floodplain of the Mississippi the bird is abundant. Near the confluence of the Wisconsin and Mississippi rivers there are myriads of tiny islands, each with a full complement of House Wrens.

Southern Wisconsin observers sometimes detect early arrivals by 15 April, and on rare occasions even earlier. Extremely early were the birds on 31 March 1967 at Racine (M. Stoffel) and in April on the 2nd (1953, Dane, M. A. Walker), 3rd (1976, Milwaukee, D. K. Gustafson), 4th (1900, Columbia, G. vos Burgh, pers. comm. to O. J. Gromme), and 5th (1970, banded in Brown, R. A. Hasterlik). The 25th is a more typical first date. By 5 May large numbers appear, including the early vanguard in the more northern areas. First arrivals are conspicuous not only because the males immediately burst forth with their rich bubbling song, but also because they have adapted themselves to backyard suburban living. We do not need to look for the House Wren; this wren comes looking for us. Perhaps it is an exaggeration to say that every residential neighborhood in every Wisconsin town and village has its pair of House Wrens; but this must be close to the truth. Before the state became widely settled, the species was primarily a resident of wooded swamps. Today, in addition to populating residential areas, the bird continues to be common in the wooded swamps bordering major rivers in the south and central areas.

The June BBS shows the highest summer concentrations in the southwest, with distribution general throughout the state. Each of the 70 transects has recorded this diminutive chatterer at least half the time.

Of the 933 routes completed, 1966–1980, the wren was noted on 866 (93%).

Volumes could be written about this wren's nesting activities. This bird has endeared itself to many people by building in the nest boxes they erected. In the woods almost any kind of small cavity in a stump or fence post will do. House Wrens have taken over nests previously used by robins and phoebes. Pairs have been found nesting in old hanging automobile tires, in overalls and pants left hanging beside deserted buildings, over doorways, and in empty pipes. Cahn (1913) tells of a pair that took over an unused street lamp in Oconomowoc (Waukesha County), brought in sticks to fill the chimney, and raised a family. Nesting begins in early May and continues well into August with second broods. Nests with young have been reported as late as 26 August.

Come September, the wrens disappear from the towns and villages. But fall migrants can be seen commonly in brushy areas and along woodland edges all through the month. Singing has ceased, but the scolding note is frequently uttered. At this season the bird usually associates with mixed flocks of other passerines. But while warblers and vireos may often move in the middle or higher tree branches, the House Wren tends to stay in the lowest vegetation.

By 25 September these wrens have left the north; most have left the south by 10 October. Observers have recorded this bird in Barron County as late as 10 October (1969, A. Goff), in Buffalo County through 25 October (1975, C. A. Faanes), in Dane County on 12 November (1978, R. M. Hoffman), and in Milwaukee on 15 November (1979, D. K. Gustafson). The only record beyond mid-November involved the re-markable sighting at Racine on 23 December 1939 (G. Prins).

Although many of these birds have been banded, the number of returns and recoveries is small. Melva Maxson (pers. comm.) once commented that in 20 years of banding, 1937–1956, she had only three returns.

Winter Wren (*Troglodytes troglodytes*)

STATUS. Uncommon migrant. Uncommon summer resident north; rare summer resident central. Rare winter resident south and central.

HABITAT. Conifer swamp. Streams.

MIGRATION DATES. *Spring:* early April to early May. *Fall:* mid-September to late October.

BREEDING DATA. Nests with eggs: 6 May to 19 June. Clutch size: 4 or 5 eggs.

WINTER. Occasionally present north to St. Croix, Pierce, Adams, and Brown counties.

PORTRAIT. *Birds of Wisconsin:* Plate 59.

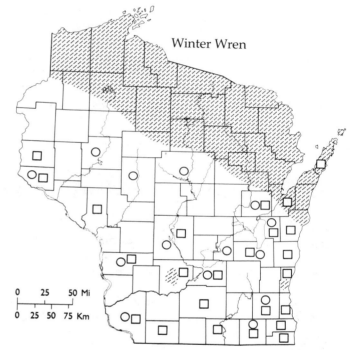

Winter Wren

▨ Summer range
○ Early June to late August
☐ Late November to early March

Records since 1960

Everyone has a favorite bird. The Winter Wren is mine. It is sheer bliss for me to drift down the Bois Brule River on a June morning and listen to the endless rollicking trills of this coloratura soprano. The length of a single song, 7–8 seconds, is two or three times the length of the song of most other birds. And in the brief intervals between songs, one can—with but a modest amount of poetic license—imagine that the bird is still trilling in pitches too high to be audible to the human ear.

To hear this "troglodytian concert" one must visit the breeding areas between mid-May and mid-July. For the most part, this means northern Wisconsin's heavily wooded bottomlands bisected by brooks and streams. The Winter Wren is regularly present, and in some places it is numerous, in the two northernmost tiers of counties north of a line from Grantsburg through Medford, Shawano, and Two Rivers. In addition there are pockets considerably farther south where this sweet singer spends the summer: as far south as Grant (Wyalusing State Park), Sauk (Baraboo hills), and Ozaukee (Cedarburg Bog) counties. It is uncertain how regularly individuals may be present at other southern locations shown on the accompanying map.

Most of the nesting evidence has come from the Oconto area where Carl Richter each year donned his boots, waded the wooded swamps, and examined the upturned root systems of fallen trees. Here on several occasions he found well-concealed nests, which most often contained five eggs, usually laid by 15 May. A much later nest, reported in Sauk County in 1976, still had nestlings on 21 August (Mossman and Lange 1982). It remains to be proved, but it is entirely possible that this reticent species nests in at least half of Wisconsin's counties each year.

Formerly, when wood was widely used for heating

and cooking purposes, and backyard wood piles were common, the sighting of a migratory Winter Wren was almost to be expected in April. On occasion, southern observers have found birds from 25 March on. The spring of 1952 was a phenomenally early one, with birds reaching Chippewa County by 19 March and Winnebago county by the 20th. A 10 March 1974 bird (Milwaukee, J. H. Idzikowski) was exceptional. Most spring records fall between 10 April and 5 May. Late stragglers have turned up as late as 22 May (1965, Racine, R. E. Fiehweg) and 28 May (1961, Milwaukee, H. A. Bauers).

In fall the principal migratory month is October. First arrivals are often found by 20 September, and have been detected as early as the 3rd (1949, Dane, S. D. Robbins) and 5th (1956, Pierce, Manley Olson). Although most birds have left the northern region by 20 October and the south by the end of the month, numerous instances of lingering into November are known. A particularly late migrant was reported from Marinette County on 18 November (1962, H. L. Lindberg). Farther south there are still later November

dates, but these may well represent wintering birds.

Virtually every winter from one to five individuals attempt to overwinter. Wherever small streams remain open and brushy undergrowth is heavy, birders should look or listen for this tiny brown mouselike creature. Only twice since 1952 have observers missed it entirely on the CBC. Most often it has appeared at Madison, Milwaukee, Beloit (Rock County), and Lake Geneva (Walworth County), but since 1960 it has turned up also in St. Croix, Pierce, Vernon, Adams, Outagamie, Brown, Calumet, Manitowoc, and Sheboygan counties. December 1974 was exceptional, with 10 CBC areas reporting 15 wintering individuals. The success these birds have in surviving Wisconsin winters is not known, but it is probably low. Beyond early January individuals have been detected on 24 January (1954, Rock, H. G. and H. Liebherr), 1 February (1948, Racine, B. L. von Jarchow), 10 February (1966, Sheboygan, K. Heidel), and 11 February (1954, Milwaukee, I. N. Balsom). Successful overwintering in Manitowoc County was reported in 1982–1983 and 1983–1984 (C. R. Sontag).

Sedge Wren (*Cistothorus platensis*)

Formerly Short-billed Marsh Wren

STATUS. Common migrant. Common summer resident.

HABITAT. Sedge meadow. Shallow marsh. Open grassland.

MIGRATION DATES. *Spring:* early May to early June. *Fall:* early September to mid-October. *Extremes:* 21 March; 10 November.

BREEDING DATA. Nests with eggs: 21 May to 15 July. Clutch size: usually 6 or 7 eggs; occasionally 8.

WINTER. One December record.

PORTRAIT. *Birds of Wisconsin:* Plate 59.

Writing of ornithological changes that had occurred in southeastern Wisconsin, 1855–1885, Hoy (1885b) commented that in earlier years the Sedge Wren could be heard in every low prairie covered with fine *Carex* sedges. "The nests were so abundant that I collected some twenty for exchange. I have seen or heard scarcely a bird of this kind for fifteen or twenty years. Their song has been silenced by the click of the mower. The hay harvest comes before the young are fledged, hence the mower is fatal to this wren's best interests." Vos Burgh (1911a) of Columbus had similar thoughts, based on his early experiences of making marsh hay

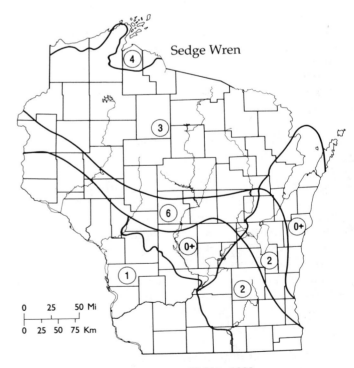

Sedge Wren

Breeding Bird Survey, averages 1966 to 1980

and seeing "hundreds of eggs" destroyed by the machinery around the turn of this century.

The use of machinery for cutting, baling, and gathering hay has increased enormously since then and doubtless destroys many nests. Yet somehow the bird has survived in sufficient numbers to be considered common all over the state where upland or lowland meadows exist. Observers have reported the bird on 64 of the state's 70 BBS transects. One Taylor County route averages over 20 individuals per year. The accompanying map shows this bird to be decidedly more numerous in the north and west than in the south and east.

Observers spot first arrivals somewhere in the state during the last week of April, the birds becoming more general by mid-May. April arrivals are not necessarily limited to the southernmost areas. Notable early sightings have occurred on the 15th (1938, Dane, J. T. Curtis, pers. comm. to O. J. Gromme), 18th (1948, Sheboygan, C. S. Jung), 20th (1952, Brown, E. O. Paulson), 21st (1965, Wood, D. G. Follen), 27th (1970, Waupaca, K. D. Rill), and 29th (1965, Burnett, N. R. Stone). By far the earliest of all was the straggler that Grundtvig (1895) collected in Outagamie County on 21 March 1882—a record that has stood for 100 years. In some years only a few birds have put in an appearance by the end of May, with the main migration delayed until early June.

Nesting usually begins the last week of May, when meadow grass is already fairly tall. In wet low meadows the harvest of hay is often delayed; this can mean undisturbed nesting success, with from four to eight young fledging. In the drier upland meadows, harvests are likely to interrupt nesting attempts. But if June nestings are disturbed, the birds still have time to relocate and try again. There are numerous records of nests with eggs between 25 June and 15 July that appear to be attempts at renesting. In 1883, Grundtvig (1895) noted a pair building a new nest on 2 July. Later mowings, however, endanger later nest attempts.

The song period does not end in early July as it does for most passerines. It continues strongly through July, and then tails off in early August, with only occasional repetitions of the distinctive "chit-chit-chur-r-r-r" heard after 15 August. Migration is probably greatest from 10 September to mid-October. Birds are not often seen during this period, as they stay hidden in long grass. But if one tramps through the grass and stops occasionally to "squeak," it is often possible either to catch a glimpse of "little stub-tail" or to hear its extremely low-pitched call note.

By 30 September most birds have left the northern counties. An unusually late bird appeared on 19 October (1976, Douglas, G. J. Niemi). Beyond 15 October only stragglers remain in the south. November records include the 2nd (1969, Sauk, K. I. Lange), 3rd (1945, Dane, H. G. Anderson), and 10th (1968, Kenosha, J. Hamers).

Working the Yahara River marshes on the Madison CBC on 21 December 1957, I was astonished to hear the call note of this species. Clearly it was not the medium-pitched call of the Marsh Wren, which is known to linger through December occasionally; it was the low-pitched call of the Sedge Wren, confirmed by sight moments later. This remains Wisconsin's only winter record.

Marsh Wren (*Cistothorus palustris*)

Formerly Long-billed Marsh Wren

STATUS. Common migrant. Common summer resi-
dent. Casual winter resident south.
HABITAT. Shallow marsh.
MIGRATION DATES. *Spring:* late April to late May. *Fall:*
early September to early November.
BREEDING DATA. Nests with eggs: 26 May to 6 July.
Clutch size: usually 4–6 eggs; occasionally 7.
WINTER. Occasionally present in December north to
Adams, Dodge, and Brown counties. Three Janu-
ary records.
PORTRAIT. *Birds of Wisconsin:* Plate 59.

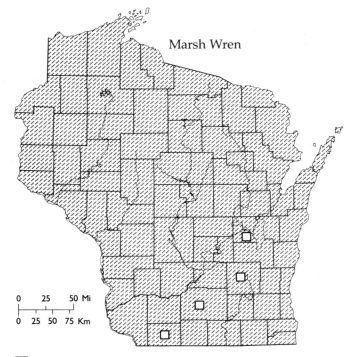

Marsh Wren

0   25   50 Mi
0 25 50 75 Km

▨ Summer range
☐ Late November to mid-January

Records since 1960

This acrobat of the cattails is greatly limited in its
habitat preferences, but wherever suitable marshes
exist in the state the Marsh Wren is likely to be present
in summer. There is a pocket in the north-central region including Iron, Price, Oneida, Lincoln, Forest,
Florence, Langlade, Menominee, and Shawano counties where it has not been recorded, but since it is
found on Powell Marsh in Vilas County, it might reasonably be expected in neighboring counties if suitable cattail marshes were present. In other sections of
the state records exist for every county except Richland, Waushara, and Washington. Although understandably scarce in some regions, the bird is abundant in places like Horicon Marsh in Dodge County
and the western shore of Green Bay north to Peshtigo
(Marinette County), where hundreds of acres of preferred vegetation exist.

Most spring migration takes place in May. In the
south numbers build up during the first 2 weeks,
with marshes holding their full breeding complement
by the 20th. Farther north first arrivals rarely occur
before the 10th, with more birds showing up between
the 20th and 30th. In roughly 2 out of every 3 years,
however, some early birds arrive in the last 10 days of
April. Notably early were an exhausted bird picked
up and banded in Milwaukee on 8 April (1929, F. L.
Hook, pers. comm. to O. J. Gromme), another Milwaukee bird on the 10th (1949, I. N. Balsom), a Winnebago County visitor on the 13th (1977, T. Ziebell),
and a straggler found in Rusk County on the 16th
(1938, F. Zirrer, pers. comm. to O. J. Gromme). Twice,
Schorger (1931a) discovered birds in Madison in March.
His 5 March 1922 bird almost certainly was a bird that
survived a Wisconsin winter; his 25 March 1928 record (1931d) also may have overwintered.

In summer this is a "fun bird" to see and hear. You
can stand near a cattail marsh before dawn, after
dusk, or even in the middle of the night, and hear the

delightful rattle of the "long-bill." Once it is light, you
can see considerable activity as the nervous birds
move around. Sometimes the Marsh Wren sings from
hidden perches, sometimes from the tip of a cattail,
sometimes as it clings precariously to the side of a
stalk, and sometimes in flight as it moves from one
perch to another.

Much nervous energy goes into the making of many
more nests than the birds will use. On 3 June 1883
Grundtvig (1895) investigated an Outagamie County
colony and found that only 5 of 28 nests contained
eggs. Cahn (1913) found as many as seven nests belonging to one pair. In June 1971 David Bratley and
Harold Mathiak (pers. comm.) found birds in 4 of 17
nests in the Lake Superior marshes at Superior and
Ashland.

As the summer wanes, so do song and activity. Observations are still made in most parts of the state
through September but in far fewer numbers than in
June and July. I know of no published records for the
northern counties beyond September, but late birds
frequently remain in the southern and central areas

through 15 October. Unusually late is the 17 November sighting in Chippewa County (1979, C. A. Kemper). If extensive cattail areas were thoroughly searched, even later dates might be established. At Horicon Marsh in 1953 (20 November) and 1955 (12 November), F. Holman King found Marsh Wrens to be still fairly numerous.

How often individuals attempt to overwinter is not known. Eight December records are known, from Adams (1955), Winnebago (1967), Dodge (1943, 1971), Waukesha (1954), Lafayette (1975), and Dane (1928,

1957) counties. In addition, there are three recorded dates for birds that survived into January: the 3rd (1931, Dane, A. W. Schorger [1931d]), 12th (1948, Dodge, H. A. Mathiak), and 19th (1980, Dane, A. K. Shea). These 11 winter records are enough to suggest that wintering attempts occur more often than is generally supposed, but the bird's sluggish activity in dense cattail marshes makes it very difficult to find. How this insect-eating bird manages to survive even part of a Wisconsin winter is a mystery. I know of no records between 19 January and 5 March.

Family **Muscicapidae:** Kinglets, Thrushes, Gnatcatchers

Golden-crowned Kinglet (*Regulus satrapa*)

STATUS. Fairly common migrant. Uncommon summer resident north. Fairly common winter resident south and central; rare (sometimes uncommon) winter resident north.

HABITAT. Coniferous forest.

MIGRATION DATES. *Spring:* mid-March to early May. *Fall:* mid-September to mid-November.

BREEDING DATA. Positive nesting evidence lacking.

WINTER. Occasionally present in north and regularly present in varying numbers in south and central in December, decreasing in January and February.

PORTRAIT. *Birds of Wisconsin:* Plate 63.

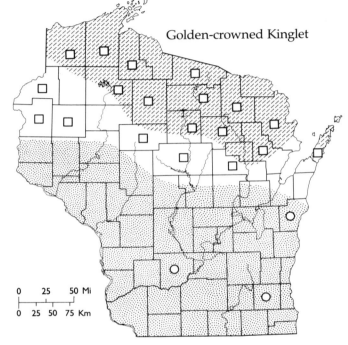

Golden-crowned Kinglet

0   25   50 Mi
0 25 50 75 Km

▨ Summer range
▦ Winter range
○ Late May to late August
☐ Early December to early March

Records since 1960

My first Christmas count in Adams County in 1952 was made exciting by the Golden-crowned Kinglet. The pine trees were plentiful, the kinglets were plentiful in the pines, and by day's end my solo count of 63 individuals was far more than any 1-day tally I had previously experienced. It started me thinking that this bird must be more abundant in winter, in suitable coniferous habitat, than most people realized. I was mistaken. That winter of 1952–1953 proved to be an exceptional one that has not been duplicated.

This diminutive conifer-lover is at the northern limit of its range when it winters within our borders. Christmas count records show that populations fluctuate widely in December. There are years, such as 1962, 1969, 1974, 1979, and 1982, when these birds show up on half of the CBCs. There are other years, such as 1963, 1964, 1972, 1983, and 1985 when scarcely 20% of the CBCs record this species and when the statewide total of individuals falls short of 40. In all but the leanest years, CBC birds are regularly noted north to St. Croix, Chippewa, Portage, Outagamie, and Manitowoc counties. December observations have come from virtually all the northern counties, but invariably the numbers have been very small.

Even when birds are numerous in December, they are scarce in January and February. This is partly because of the much more limited amount of fieldwork done during those months. And this species is not one to frequent feeding stations. It is found in residential areas only where extensive groves of evergreens exist. Mostly, one must visit coniferous forests to find this species, and few birders make such sojourns in midwinter. How many December birds migrate in January or succumb to severe midwinter weather is not known.

Spring migrants begin to appear in southern Wisconsin around 20 March, and another 10-day interval brings early arrivals to the more northern areas. Flocks of more than 10 birds are rarely met, but in suitable conifer habitat small flocks are frequently seen during most of April. In the southern region nearly all have departed by the end of April, except for an occasional late straggler. A 29 May 1969 sighting in Ozaukee County by Dennis Gustafson is phenomenal. In the central sector a few are still present until 10 May. Edwin Cleary's 28 May 1959 record at Green Bay is exceptional.

In the northernmost counties a few birds remain all summer. Although I know of no nesting, I suspect that breeding is regular in small numbers all across northern Wisconsin. Jackson (1943) found recently fledged young being fed by parents on the Apostle Islands in Ashland County on 4 July 1919. Walter and Gertrude Scott observed similar behavior in Vilas County on 25 July 1942, as did Roy and Martha Lound in Bayfield County on 5 July 1957. In the A. J. Schoenebeck collection there is a set of two eggs, but there is no identifying information to confirm the probability that these eggs were collected in northeastern Wisconsin. Additional summer sightings have oc-

curred north of a line from Gordon southeast through Medford and Shawano and northeast through Sturgeon Bay.

Fall migrants reach the northern counties by 15 September; they can be seen in southern areas any time after 25 September. Exceptionally early were two 30 August finds in Dane County in 1975 (D. D. Tessen) and 1978 (T. De Boor). October is the principal migration month. On 12 October 1969, C. A. Kemper found 128 individuals killed at an Eau Claire television tower. Ron Hoffman estimated that 1,000 individuals migrated through Kenosha on 30–31 October 1972. Most birds still present beyond mid-November remain through December.

Ruby-crowned Kinglet (*Regulus calendula*)

STATUS. Common migrant. Uncommon summer resident north; casual summer resident central. Rare winter resident south and central.

HABITAT. Coniferous forest (during summer). All forest; all carr (during migration).

MIGRATION DATES. *Spring:* early April to late May. *Fall:* early September to early November.

BREEDING DATA. Nests with young: 26 June to 4 July.

WINTER. Occasionally present through early January north to St. Croix, Eau Claire, Portage, and Brown counties.

PORTRAIT. *Birds of Wisconsin:* Plate 63.

For a few short weeks in spring and fall Ruby-crowned Kinglets jitterbug their way through the state in considerable numbers. Occasionally, the start of the spring migration is detected in the last week of March, with exceptionally early individuals having been observed on the 20th (1974, Brown, Bro. Columban) and 24th (1963, Iowa, R. S. Ellarson). But in most years few birds are seen before 10 April. In the southern region the numbers build to a 20–30 April peak, and quickly taper off, so that most birds are gone by 15 May, with only a rare straggler remaining beyond the 20th. Farther north the timetable is delayed only slightly. First arrivals can be expected any time after 15 April, with a peak from 25 April to 10 May. Late spring migrants lingering into June have been found on the 1st (1963, banded in Sheboygan, H. C. Mueller), 3rd (1961, Dane, J. H. Zimmerman), 8th (1978, Clark, R. M. Hoffman), and 10th (1963, St. Croix, S. D. Robbins; 1972, Chippewa, D. Folczyk).

The Ruby-crown is not particularly fussy about habitat in migration. Any kind of small trees or shrubs

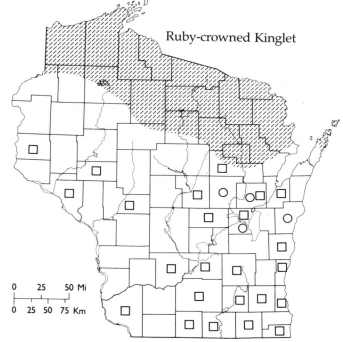

Ruby-crowned Kinglet

0 25 50 Mi
0 25 50 75 Km

▨ Summer range
○ Mid-June to mid-August
□ Late November to late January

Records since 1960

will do—oaks, lilacs, spruce, alder, willow—this kinglet likes them all. All that matters is that there be another branch close to any branch the bird perches on, for this bird rarely stays in one spot more than a few seconds.

At the height of the spring flight it is not unusual for a field trip to produce sightings of 30–50 Ruby-crowns. Some are singing their distinctive rollicking song; some are giving their peculiar little staccato call note; some are silent, but ever on the move looking for tiny insects among the developing foliage.

Most Ruby-crowns move on into Canada to breed. Before 1940 no records of summer residency existed; but during the 1940s observers discovered June or July birds in Sawyer, Vilas, Iron, Oneida, and Brown counties. Positive nesting evidence was obtained in 1964 when Tom Soulen discovered a nest and nestlings in Oneida County on 26 June. Additional nests have been found in Winnebago and Outagamie counties, but these are south of what appears to be the bird's regular summer range.

Northern Wisconsin, receiving much improved coverage by birders since 1965, now is seen to be a regular part of this species' breeding range. Bernard (1967) called the Ruby-crown rare in Douglas County in summer. Vanderschaegen (1981b) used "uncommon" to designate summer status in Vilas, Oneida, and Forest counties. North of Minong, Medford, Merrill, Shawano, Marinette, and Sturgeon Bay, regular summer residency in small numbers in suitable habitat is probable.

Suitable habitat means tamarack and black spruce bogs. I have personally met with these birds at least 20 times in the northern counties in the past 10 summers, and on each occasion the birds were either in spruce and tamaracks in bogs, or in pines at the edge of bogs.

Returning fall migrants have been sighted as early as 19 and 23 August, but this is 3 weeks earlier than the usual arrival time. It is not until 15 September that fall migrants become conspicuous throughout the state, with an early-October peak in the northern counties followed by a mid-October peak farther south. C. A. Kemper found 80 of these birds at the foot of an Eau Claire television tower on 11 October 1961, after a night of heavy migration. Comparable towerkills in late September have included far fewer Ruby-crowns. By 20 October nearly all have left the northern counties, while only a few stragglers remain in the southern region after 10 November.

Because this bird feeds so largely on insects, it is surprising that any Ruby-crowns stay in Wisconsin beyond early November. Yet 2 years out of every 3, at least one individual is reported somewhere in Wisconsin in late November or December. Generally these stragglers are found in the southern counties, but records have come from St. Croix, Eau Claire, Waushara, Outagamie, and Brown counties. This species cannot be considered regular in winter anywhere in Wisconsin, but it has been reported on as many as nine CBCs (1974) in a single year.

No Ruby-crown has been known to survive a Wisconsin winter. Beyond CBC-time, January sightings have taken place on the 9th (1955, Pierce, Manley Olson), 11th (1966, Outagamie, D. D. Tessen), 15th (1972, Columbia, W. A. Smith), and 26th (1972, Brown, E. D. Cleary).

Blue-gray Gnatcatcher (*Polioptila caerulea*)

STATUS. Uncommon spring migrant; rare fall migrant. Uncommon summer resident south and central.

HABITAT. Southern silver maple–elm forest.

MIGRATION DATES. *Spring:* mid-April to late May. *Fall:* late August to mid-September. *Extremes:* 5 April; 18 November.

BREEDING DATA. Nests with young: late June to 25 July. No definite egg dates.

PORTRAIT. *Birds of Wisconsin:* Plate 63.

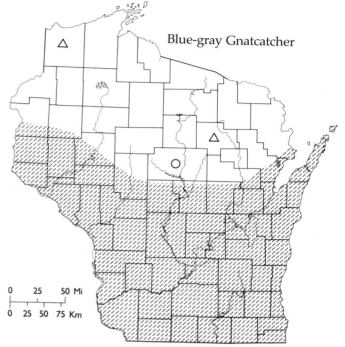

Blue-gray Gnatcatcher

0   25   50 Mi
0   25   50   75 Km

▨   Summer range
△   Mid-April to late May
○   Early June to late August

Records since 1960

In the southern states where the Blue-gray Gnatcatcher is more common, it is sometimes found in low shrubbery. In Wisconsin a birder can develop a stiff neck peering high up in the taller oaks to watch the antics of these nervous little tail-twitchers. When in its proper habitat, this bird is easily overlooked, partly because of its preference for high foliage and partly because its soft insectlike sounds have little carrying power.

But even making allowance for birds that may be overlooked, this species is at best an uncommon visitor on the northern fringe of its range. In the nineteenth century the northern range limit was southern Wisconsin. Kumlien and Hollister (1903) found small numbers yearly in the Fort Atkinson area in Jefferson County, but J. N. Clark (Buss and Mattison 1955) did not find it in the Menomonie region in Dunn County, nor did Schoenebeck (1902) near Oconto.

The spread northward probably took place during the late 1920s and 1930s. Southeastern Minnesota sightings were recorded in 1926, with a 1932 nesting across the Mississippi River from Pepin County. In western Wisconsin, observers noted individuals in Richland County in 1916 (Sugden 1943), Chippewa County in 1943 (C. Toppe), and St. Croix County in 1944 (S. P. Owen). Farther east birds were found in Wood County by 1942 (H. A. Mathiak) and in Outagamie County in 1944 (N. M. Rogers). Had Wisconsin had a network of well-distributed observers in the 1930s, the extension of the gnatcatcher's range might well have been delineated with greater precision.

In western and central Wisconsin the summer range has extended throughout most of the heavily wooded river bottomlands. The bird is regular along the Mississippi River throughout its course in Wisconsin. Along the St. Croix River it is regular north to St. Croix Falls, along the Rush River to Spring Valley, the Red Cedar to Menomonie, the Chippewa north to Eau Claire and Chippewa Falls, the Black north to Neillsville, and the Wisconsin as far north as Wisconsin Rapids. In eastern Wisconsin observations have

not been limited to river bottoms; they have occurred at various locations along Lake Michigan or inland in the vicinity of heavily wooded swamps. The bird is regular in summer north to Peshtigo (Marinette County) and Sturgeon Bay (Door County).

In the southernmost counties first arrivals are noted any time from 20 April to 1 May. Unusually early were April sightings on the 5th (1986, Dane, P. Ashman), 8th (1981, Washington, R. Cleek), 9th (1956, Jefferson, E. Degner), 10th (1941, Waukesha, S. P. Jones), and 11th (1977, Dane, R. M. Hoffman). It is generally during the second week in May that birds arrive in the central counties at the limit of the species' range. Individuals overshooting the regular range appeared in late May 1972 in Douglas (P. B. Hofslund) and Langlade (B. Pickering) counties.

Much remains to be learned about nesting activities. Nest construction has occurred on various occasions in the last half of May, even as early as 30 April, but egg-laying does not necessarily follow. Schorger (1931a) tells of climbing trees where nests were located, only to find the parent bird sitting on an empty nest. The possibility that egg-laying may be delayed until well into June is suggested by sightings of parents feeding young in the nest on such July dates as the 11th (1953, Oconto), 13th (1948, Clark), 16th (1947, Adams), and 25th (1959, Dane). If there is a published record of a Blue-gray Gnatcatcher nest with eggs in Wisconsin, it has escaped my notice. Most of the nests that have been reported were located in oaks (one in a jack pine) at altitudes of 7–55 feet (Faanes 1981).

No fall migration buildups have been reported from any part of the state. Summer residents simply disappear any time from early August to early September, with most birds gone by 15 September. October lingerers include birds on the 14th (1940, Dane, S. D. Robbins), 15th (1982, Milwaukee, M. Bontly), 19th (1968, Monroe, E. Hebard), and 26th (1973, La Crosse, F. Z. Lesher). November stragglers have been detected on the 6th (1949, Milwaukee, D. L. Larkin) and 18th (1975, Dane, J. J. Hickey).

Eastern Bluebird (*Sialia sialis*)

STATUS. Fairly common migrant. Fairly common summer resident north and west; uncommon summer resident south and east. Rare winter resident south.
HABITAT. Savanna. Farmsteads. Upland carr.
MIGRATION DATES. *Spring:* mid-March to late April. *Fall:* mid-September to early November.
BREEDING DATA. Nests with eggs: 7 April to 1 August. Clutch size: usually 4 or 5 eggs; occasionally 3–7.
WINTER. Occasionally present in December and January north to Buffalo, Columbia, and Brown counties.
PORTRAIT. *Birds of Wisconsin:* Plate 61.

In the spring and summer of 1959, observers in Wisconsin and other northern states detected a sharp decline of Eastern Bluebirds. It was even more pronounced in 1960. Some blamed the prolonged cold spells that had been prevalent in much of the winter range. Some blamed the widespread use of powerful insecticides that were being sprayed on millions of acres of southern United States cropland. Some blamed the loss of natural nesting sites in the breeding range, as farmers increasingly replaced wooden fence posts with metal ones. Whatever the cause, various commentators described the decline as a "disaster."

Reacting to this, Mr. and Mrs. Paul Romig, Vincent Bauldry, and other members of the Green Bay Bird Club began an extensive program of erecting bird houses to improve breeding conditions in 1960. This effort expanded to become a statewide program of the Wisconsin Society for Ornithology in 1962. The publication of a "Bluebird Trail Guide" has led to the placement of many more houses in other parts of the state. Observers have detected a modest comeback through the 1960s and 1970s in areas well populated with nest boxes. In 1969 the Green Bay project re-

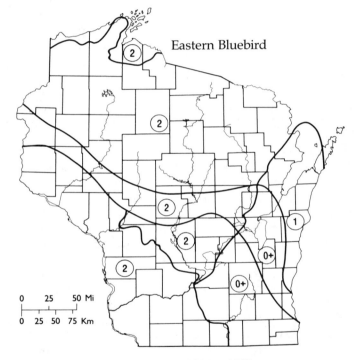

Eastern Bluebird

Breeding Bird Survey, averages 1966 to 1980

sulted in the nesting of 46 pairs and the banding of 242 bluebirds.

But the overall summer population, as evidenced by the June BBS, continued to decline. From 1966 through 1972 annual totals for all routes ranged from 108 (1969) to 165 (1972); from 1973 through 1977, annual totals fluctuated from 91 (1977) to 121 (1974). Totals plummeted to 50 in 1978 and 22 in 1979.

This is not the first crisis the Eastern Bluebird has faced. Kumlien and Hollister (1903) recorded a dearth of bluebirds in 1895 and 1896, attributing this to a hard winter freeze throughout the southern states.

Again in 1912 numbers dropped significantly after a hard winter in many of the eastern states (Cooke 1913). Although these setbacks have been temporary, more persistent difficulties have developed from changing agricultural practices since 1950. Formerly, apple orchards provided the most favored habitat, with cavities in aging trees offering attractive nest sites. As the practice of removing aging trees developed and heavy spraying to control insect pests became widespread, bluebirds were almost completely forced out of the orchards they had once frequented. Moreover, the metal fence posts now in general use on pastureland have deprived the birds of a favorite nesting site. And throughout the twentieth century this bird has also suffered from nest-site competition with the ever-increasing House Sparrow and European Starling.

Human efforts to help the Eastern Bluebird deal with this competition are showing encouraging results. Thousands of bluebird houses have been erected. Public interest led to the formation of the Bluebird Restoration Association of Wisconsin in 1986. June BBS figures rose to 113 (1985), 175 (1986), 205 (1987), and 262 (1989).

When the bluebird was more abundant, the earliest spring arrivals appeared during the first week of March, or even in late February if the weather was mild. In recent years observers have detected few birds before 15 March in the south and 25 March in the north. Sizable patches of bare ground are a necessity for foraging, and many are the years when the northern region must wait until late March for suffi-cient thawing. The main migratory push comes in April. Birds arrive not in large flocks but as individuals and pairs exploring for suitable nesting territory.

The BBS map shows that the summer range is state-wide, with populations particularly sparse in the southernmost counties. Nests with eggs have been found as early as 7 April and more frequently by the end of the month. Not only are second broods the norm but instances are known where fledged young from a first brood have assisted with the feeding of a second family. Nests with young have been reported as late as 23 August.

Fall migration begins in mid-September, gathers momentum in late September, and peaks around 10 October in the north and 20 October in the south. Only rarely are flocks of 15–20 seen; formerly flocks often numbered over 100. By 5 November nearly all birds have left the state. Banding records indicate a migratory path that is almost due south, with winter recoveries in Alabama, Mississippi, Louisiana, and Tennessee.

Nearly every year an individual or small group appears in late December or early January. Most of these show up in the far southwest (Grant and Dane counties). A few attempts at overwintering have been successful, but the likelihood is that most birds have disappeared by mid-January. The most northerly January records have come from Buffalo (1927, 1970, 1973, 1979), Trempealeau (1970), Brown (1947), and Washington (1976) counties. Most unusual was the 7–8 February 1948 sighting in Polk County by W. D. Barnard.

Mountain Bluebird (*Sialia currucoides*)

STATUS. Casual spring and winter visitant.
HABITAT. Savanna. Upland carr. Residential areas.
MIGRATION DATES. Observed between 17 October and 20 May.
WINTER. Occasionally present in Douglas County; accidental elsewhere.

Little did they realize it at the time, but when Mr. and Mrs. Carl Peterson drove into the newly developed Wisconsin Audubon Camp near Sarona (Washburn County) on 17 October 1954, they observed a species previously unrecorded for Wisconsin. There on the ground they saw a Mountain Bluebird feeding in a casual, unconcerned manner. The bird exhibited a beautiful blue and gray plumage.

The account of this sighting did not come to light until 2 months later when several additional sightings were made at Superior. Between 16 and 19 December, Mary Hayes observed one bird feeding on mountain ash berries, Mrs. W. J. Bohn saw two feeding on mountain ash berries and highbush cranberries, and Mrs. Henry Flemming found four around hopa crab trees. The birds then disappeared, but two reappeared briefly in Mrs. Flemming's yard on 8 March 1955 (*Pass. Pigeon* 17:59).

The first and only specimen was secured accidentally 2 years later, when a bird struck Henry Anderson's car near Ellison Bay (Door County) in early January 1957. Harold Wilson forwarded the specimen to the Milwaukee Public Museum, where the identification was confirmed.

Ten years passed before another sighting occurred. On 27 March 1967 at the Spooner airport in Washburn County, W. S. Feeney watched a bird leisurely as it alternately fed between snowbanks and bare ground patches in company with two Horned Larks (*Pass. Pigeon* 30:28). Two days previously, another Mountain Bluebird turned up at Moorhead, Minnesota, also north and east of the regular winter range.

It was Door County's turn again in 1974 when a bird appeared near Gills Rock on 21 December and was seen by R. J. Lukes (*Am. Birds* 29:695).

A fleeting but unmistakable glimpse of an individual near Arpin (Wood County) on 10 May 1979 gave Wisconsin its only late-spring sighting. Don Follen's mountain ash tree attracted the bird momentarily, but the bird disappeared before photographic equipment could be assembled (*Pass. Pigeon* 42:49).

Eight months later Douglas County entertained another visitor. On 19 January 1980, A. C. Clarke observed one for 15 minutes on Wisconsin Point, Supe-

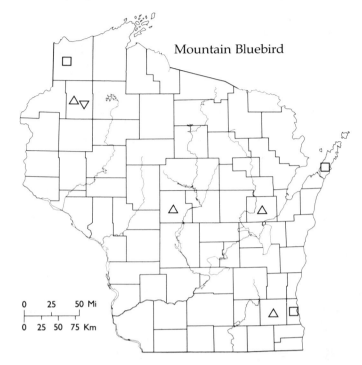

Mountain Bluebird

0   25   50 Mi

0 25 50 75 Km

△   27 March to 20 May
▽   17 October
☐   16 December to 8 March

All records

rior, as it foraged on an exposed spot beside the road. The length of time the bird spent in the area is not known (*Pass. Pigeon* 42:146).

A male wandered to the Bubholz Nature Center near Appleton on 19 April 1983. It was discovered by B. N. Brouchoud, later photographed by M. Brandel and observed by others, but could not be found the following day (*Pass. Pigeon* 46:45).

Another male turned up in Milwaukee on 20 December 1987 (J. H. Idzikowski). Many other area birders enjoyed this western visitor through 1 January 1988 (*Pass. Pigeon* 50:271–272). Wisconsin's latest spring record is provided by the individual D. D. Tessen found in Waukesha County on 20 May 1989 (*Pass. Pigeon* 51:413–414).

This colorful westerner was not noted for its extralimital wandering before 1970. The fifth edition of the AOU *Check-list of North American Birds* (1957) mentions no sightings east of the Mississippi River. The sixth edition (1983) lists records in Pennsylvania, New York, Mississippi, and Ontario. Most involved winter or early spring observations.

Townsend's Solitaire (*Myadestes townsendi*)

STATUS. Casual spring visitant; rare fall visitant; rare winter resident.

HABITAT. Parks. Upland carr.

MIGRATION DATES. Observed between 9 October and 14 May.

WINTER. Rarely wanders east to Lake Michigan between Manitowoc and Milwaukee counties.

PORTRAIT. *Birds of Wisconsin:* Plate 60.

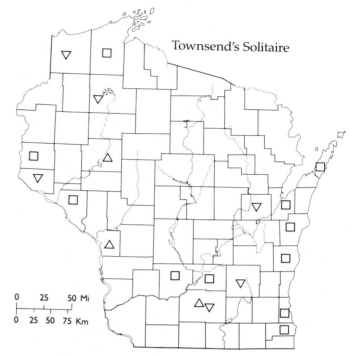

Townsend's Solitaire

△ Mid-March to mid-May
▽ Early October to early December
☐ Mid-December to early March

All records

Three specimens exist. Albert Gastrow collected a Townsend's Solitaire in Columbia County east of Prairie du Sac on or about 20 February 1910. A second, purportedly one bird out of a small flock, was struck by a car in Sawyer County south of Hayward on 9 October 1961 (K. W. Kahmann). Both specimens now reside at the Milwaukee Public Museum. A third, collected by A. J. Rusch in Dodge County on 6 December 1952 is in the collection at the University of Wisconsin–Madison.

When Lange (1988) summarized the Wisconsin records through the spring of 1987, he listed two October birds: the 1961 Sawyer County specimen and a bird seen on the 9th (1978, Douglas, C. A. Faanes). Other brief fall sightings included three in November and three in early December. One straggler made a brief midwinter appearance from 11 to 14 January (1985, Bayfield, R. L. Verch). Four more sightings concerned one-time observations of late winter or spring wanderers: 1 March (1953, Brown, E. D. Cleary), 10 April (1963, Chippewa, C. A. Kemper), 3 May (1979, Dane, R. M. Hoffman), and 14 May (1975, La Crosse, F. Z. Lesher).

Most sightings, however, have involved birds with extended stays of several weeks. Favored habitat includes the steep cedar slopes in Sauk (notably Devil's Lake State Park), western Columbia, and northern Dane counties. One or more of these berry-eaters have overwintered in this region nearly every year since 1979.

There have also been lengthy stays in St. Croix (1942–1943), Buffalo (1987), Door (1985–1986), Brown (1976), Manitowoc (1981), Sheboygan (1955–1956), and Milwaukee (1973) counties. All fall within the period from 26 October to 9 April.

The route followed by these vagrants from the western mountains appears to follow closely that of the Varied Thrush. The accompanying map shows that all observations cluster fairly close to a line extending southeast from Grantsburg to Sheboygan. This solitaire has been recorded in extralimital wanderings far less frequently than the Varied Thrush. But the solitaire has been known to reach Quebec, Nova Scotia, New Hampshire, Massachusetts, Rhode Island, and New Jersey, suggesting that a few birds wander eastward north of the Great Lakes. Adventurers have also appeared in Minnesota, Michigan, Illinois, and Ohio. The wandering trend seems to be increasing. Half of Wisconsin's sightings have occurred since 1978.

Veery (*Catharus fuscescens*)
Formerly Wilson's Thrush, Willow Thrush

STATUS. Common migrant. Common summer resident north; fairly common summer resident central; uncommon summer resident south.
HABITAT. Deciduous forest. Northern maple-
hemlock-pine forest. Wooded swamp.
MIGRATION DATES. *Spring:* late April to late May. *Fall:*
mid-August to late September. *Extremes:* 17 April;
27 October.
BREEDING DATA. Nests with eggs: 26 May to 5 July.
Clutch size: usually 3 or 4 eggs; occasionally 2 or 5.
PORTRAIT. *Birds of Wisconsin:* Plate 62.

When the first arrivals appear, generally in the first
week of May, they are nearing the end of a long migration journey. Veeries winter in South America.
A few end their northward trek just south of Wisconsin. Many pass through the state and continue on to
southern Canada. But large numbers settle here for
the summer. In migration this species is outnumbered by the Swainson's, Gray-cheeked, and Hermit
Thrushes. As a summer resident the Veery outnumbers all thrushes except the American Robin in all but
the southernmost counties, where the Wood Thrush
is somewhat more numerous.

Only a few early arrivals reach the state in April,
but several of these have turned up surprisingly far
north. Close behind two Milwaukee birds on the 17th
and 18th (1941, 1944, W. J. Mueller) are birds on the
21st (1943, Bayfield, W. S. Feeney; 1961, Manitowoc,
M. Albrecht), 23rd (1965, Brown, T. C. Erdman), and
25th (1957, Marinette, R. A. Stefanski).

A more typical time for first arrivals to move
through the state is between 1 and 10 May. Numbers
build to a 10–20 May peak in the south and a 15–25
May peak farther north. By the end of May most migrants have left the state. A few migrants accompany
Swainson's and Gray-cheeked Thrushes as they explore the shrubbery in city parks and residential areas.
They are usually quiet until they reach the breeding
grounds, when singing begins. The heavily wooded
swamps preferred by this species are few and far between in the southernmost counties, so the "tawny
thrush" moves quickly to the central and northern
regions.

The 1966–1980 BBS shows how this bird changes
from a decidedly uncommon summer resident in the
south to a common bird in the north—not numerous
along the Mississippi River or the Lake Michigan
shore, yet almost abundant in the far northwest. In
the southernmost two tiers of counties there have
been recent summer records only in Grant, Dane,

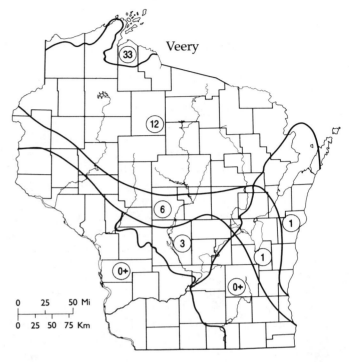

Veery

Breeding Bird Survey, averages 1966 to 1980

Rock, Jefferson, and Walworth counties, mainly in
the remnants of formerly widespread tamarack bogs.
Although it was not a common southern breeder in
Kumlien and Hollister's (1903) day, it was more numerous then than now.

As nesting territory, the bird prefers damp dark
woodland areas. Reporting on nine Oconto County
nests, C. A. Richter observed that all were either on
the ground or a few inches above it. Most nests were
in mossy or grassy depressions well concealed by varied surrounding foliage: some tamarack, ash, willow,
alder, cedar, and birch. All but one nest contained
four eggs, and one had two additional cowbird eggs.
A. W. Schorger once found a nest containing two
Veery eggs and five cowbird eggs.

As summer advances, these birds become progressively more quiet. By mid-July song is restricted to
brief periods at the beginning and end of the day. By
early August even this song ceases, and there is but
an occasional call note to reveal a bird's presence.

Continued silence makes the Veery seem decidedly
uncommon as a fall migrant. I have gone through
a September seeing as few as six birds in 30 hours
afield. But modest numbers can be detected as night
migrants when cloud banks force birds to fly low. The

banding of 432 during the 1958–1963 span at the Cedar Grove Ornithological Station in Sheboygan County and of another 213 in 15 years at Chippewa Falls suggests that this is at least a fairly common fall migrant. Among Eau Claire television tower casualties, 30% of the thrush specimens are Veeries.

Little migration has been detected before 20 August. The main movement in north and central regions, judging by banding and towerkill data, is between 30 August and 10 September. Numbers diminish through 20 September, with virtually all birds gone by 1 October. Farther south a 5–25 September peak is normal, with last departures noted by 15 October. Unusually late were October departures from the north on the 6th (1972, Bayfield, A. J. Roy), the central area on the 19th (1966, Manitowoc, B. N. Brouchoud) and 27th (1980, Brown, Bro. Columban), and the south on the 24th (1937, Dane, J. T. Curtis, pers. comm. to A. W. Schorger).

Gray-cheeked Thrush (*Catharus minimus*)

STATUS. Fairly common migrant.
HABITAT. Deciduous forest. Northern maple-hemlock-pine forest. Residential areas.
MIGRATION DATES. *Spring:* early May to early June. *Fall:* late August to mid-October. *Extremes:* 19 April, 9 June; 28 July, 4 December.
BREEDING DATA. No records.
WINTER. Two records.
PORTRAIT. *Birds of Wisconsin:* Plate 62.

Much of what has been written about the migratory patterns and habits of the Swainson's Thrush applies equally well to the Gray-cheeked Thrush. Its nasal, sneezy-sounding call note can be detected as night migrants fly low on cloudy May and September nights. I have attempted no precise counts, but I would estimate that for every Gray-cheek there are 30–40 Swainson's when the night flights are in full swing.

The similarity between the species extends to daytime habitat preferences. In May or September both species are frequently found feeding together on the ground near park and suburban shrubbery or perched together on the low branches of the same woodland edges. In fall they show a particular fondness for berry-producing shrubs.

The similarity further extends to the timing of migration periods. Although there have been published reports of birds arriving as early as 11 April, no adequate documentation is known for anything before the 19th (1964, Brown, T. C. Erdman). Usually the bird does not reach even the southernmost states before the 20th. Late-April arrivals are occasional at best. It is in the first warm spell in May that birds make their first appearance in southern Wisconsin. During the 10–20 May period the peak numbers move quickly through the state, slowing to a trickle by 25 May in the south and 30 May in the north. Late departures occasionally linger into the first week of June, the latest dates being on the 7th (1945, Dane, S. D. Robbins) and 9th (1948, Brown, G. Church).

There are no breeding records for this species. Indeed, none should be expected, for the normal breeding range lies far to the north near Hudson Bay. In most years it is 25 August or later when the first southbound migrants appear. I know of five exceptions: a bird in Iron County on 28 July 1948 (H. Sell); individuals in Outagamie County on 30 July (1968), 2 August (1962), and 11 August (1971, D. D. Tessen); and a visitor trapped in Fond du Lac County on 17 August (1955, G. Henseler).

The main fall flight coincides with that of the Swainson's in September and early October. Eau Claire towerkills have been heaviest in the 10–20 September period. At Manitowoc and the Cedar Grove Ornithological Station in Sheboyan County, banding captures have been most numerous between 10 and 25 September. At Manitowoc 470 were banded on 21 September 1967 (B. N. Brouchoud). Between 1958 and 1963 Cedar Grove banders netted 1,553 birds, roughly one Gray-cheek for every five Swainson's. Eau Claire banding and towerkill ratios have been 1:4.

In the north, numbers drop off rapidly after 25 September; and rarely is a Gray-cheek found beyond 5 October. In the south, the last migrant may remain until the last week in October. On five occasions birds have lingered into the first 5 days of November. Remarkably late was an individual on 21 November (1972, La Crosse, J. R. Rosso) and one viewed daily 1–4 December (1961, Outagamie, D. D. Tessen).

One must presume that only sickness or injury would detain a bird that normally winters in Central or South America. Two such overwintering attempts are known. On 30 December 1965 a Gray-cheek appeared at the Reinhold Link feeder at Keshena (Menominee County), sampling off and on a mixture of raisins, currants, and mush; it was not seen again. And one was reported in Door County on 24–25 March 1951 by Fred Zimmerman, who learned from local residents that it had been present in the area for a considerable period.

Swainson's Thrush (*Catharus ustulatus*)

Formerly Olive-backed Thrush

STATUS. Abundant migrant. Uncommon summer resident north.

HABITAT. Deciduous forest. Residential areas. Coniferous forest (during breeding).

MIGRATION DATES. *Spring:* early May to early June. *Fall:* early August to late October. *Extremes:* 9 April; 5 December.

BREEDING DATA. Nests with eggs: 17 June to 17 July. Clutch size: 4 eggs (one record).

WINTER. One January record.

PORTRAIT. *Birds of Wisconsin:* Plate 62.

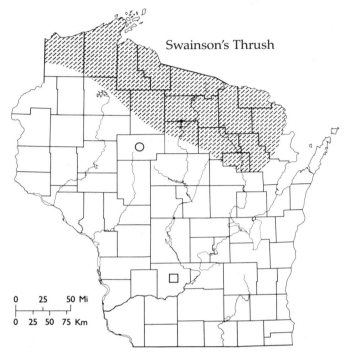

Swainson's Thrush

```
0    25    50 Mi
|----|----|
0  25  50  75 Km
```

▨ Summer range
○ Mid-June to late July
□ 1 January

Records since 1960

Long before the advent of radio and television transmitter towers, Kumlien and Hollister (1903) commented, "This is one of the birds that one most frequently finds dead beneath the ever increasing network of electric wires that annually cause the death of thousands of individuals of the low-flying night migrating species." Could they have anticipated the casualties that would result when giant metal fingers reached 2,000 feet up into low-level clouds? Seventy years later C. A. Kemper reported 822 Swainson's Thrush casualties in 18 years of tower-kill tabulations at Eau Claire.

Large as that number seems, it represents only a small percentage of the number of birds that pass by a given point during a given fall migration season. To grasp the magnitude of the fall thrush migration, one should spend an hour outdoors in a quiet location on a night in early September when the cloud ceiling is low, and listen to the call notes emanating from low-flying migrants. Many of these migrants are thrushes, and the Swainson's is one of the few species that can be identified by a trained ear. I have heard upwards of 500 Swainson's on a single night. The peak of such flights occurs any time from 1 to 20 September in the northern and central regions, 5 to 25 September in the south.

The fall migration actually begins much earlier. It is probable that a few birds move into the central and southern counties by 1 August nearly every year, but little fieldwork is being done in suitable woodland habitat at that time, and few ears are alert to the distinctive soft musical call note which often provides the clue to this bird's presence. Ten 23–31 July arrival dates are known. Most remarkable was an immature bird banded on 19 July 1960 at Milton (Rock County) (M. T. Maxson). Until 25 August the migration is a mere trickle; thereafter the buildup is rapid. In the north the fall migration subsides by 25 September and is over by 10 October. In the south most migrants are gone by 15 October, with the 25th the usual date for a last sighting. Late lingering birds have been recorded on 15 November (1979, Brown, E. D. Cleary), 1 December (1946, Milwaukee, M. F. Donald), 2 December (1972, Dane, P. Ashman), and 5 December (1953, Milwaukee, C. P. Frister).

Only once has a Swainson's Thrush been known to attempt overwintering in this state. Six Christmas bird-counters found one near Sauk City on 1 January 1972 (Barger 1972). The weather had been unusually mild during the previous 2 months.

The return spring flight is relatively late, with a strong 2-week peak from 10 to 25 May in the south and 15 to 30 May farther north. During this time birds can be found on the low branches of trees near the edges of forests and woodlots, from which they sometimes forage along the edge of neighboring plowed fields. They like to skulk in backyard and park shrubbery, and anyone who is abroad just at dawn near the height of the spring migration may find these birds roaming the sidewalks and streets in residential areas. From what observers are able to find during the rest of the day, one would not guess the true abundance of this bird. Yet listening to low-flying night migrants on cloudy nights in mid-May will provide convincing evidence that this is indeed an abundant species.

In the southern part of the state an occasional bird is detected between 20 and 30 April. Several earlier dates have been published, but most are undocumented and suspect. Adequate documentation supported the unusual sighting of a 9 April bird (1954, Rock, C. A. Skelly) and three birds that turned up on 16 April 1964 in Brown (T. C. Erdman), Dane (P. Krombholz), and Racine (M. Stoffel) counties. Equally unusual: a bird found dead in Lincoln County on 22 April 1962 (D. J. Hendrick). It is not exceptional for migrants to linger south of the breeding range through 5 June. Later June dates include the 13th (1960, Outagamie, D. D. Tessen), 14th (1962, Dane, J. H. Zimmerman), 16th (1980, Milwaukee, J. Frank), 17th (1965, Racine, R. E. Fiehweg), 19th (1980, Eau Claire, J. L. Polk), and 21st (1954, Kenosha, M. F. Higgins).

It is a real treat to hear this songster on its northern forest breeding grounds, partly because of the rich melodic quality of the song, and partly because of the rarity of the bird. The Swainson's is far less numerous than the Veery or the Hermit Thrush, and is restricted to the mixed spruce and maple forests of the northern counties. There are published reports of only three nestings: one nest photographed in Price County on 19 June 1912 (*fide* T. S. Roberts [1932]), one with four eggs in Oconto County on 17 June 1894 (Schoenebeck 1902), and one in Oneida County in early July 1945 (D. L. Larkin). The nests were 3–4 feet up in spruce and maples. These records, plus other 15 June–15 July observations, suggest that this species nests sparingly every year north of a line extending southeast from Solon Springs through Hayward and Shawano, then northeast to Wausaukee.

Distances traveled by these birds after they leave Wisconsin are remarkable—especially these five banded at the Cedar Grove Ornithological Station in Sheboygan County (H. C. Mueller): one banded on 17 September 1964, recaptured 12 days later in South Carolina; a bird netted on 25 September 1962, found in Colombia the following January; one caught on 11 September 1961, rediscovered in British Columbia 2 years later; a bird ringed on 9 September 1955 that reappeared 2 years later in Alabama; and one trapped at Cedar Grove on 14 September 1957, retaken on 21 May 1959 in Manitoba.

Hermit Thrush (*Catharus guttatus*)

STATUS. Fairly common migrant. Fairly common summer resident north; uncommon summer resident central. Rare winter resident southeast.

HABITAT. Conifer swamp. Northern maple-hemlock-pine forest. Oak–jack pine forest.

MIGRATION DATES. *Spring:* late March to early May. *Fall:* mid-September to early November.

BREEDING DATA. Nests with eggs: 22 May to 12 July. Clutch size: usually 4 eggs; occasionally 3 or 5.

WINTER. From 1 to 3 birds present nearly every year north to Crawford, Portage, Outagamie, and Manitowoc counties.

PORTRAIT. *Birds of Wisconsin:* Plate 62.

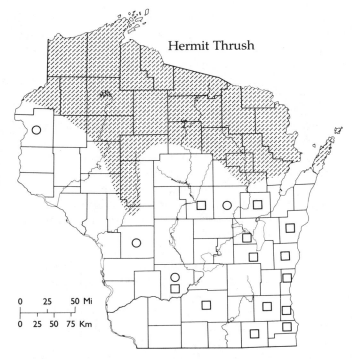

Hermit Thrush

0   25   50 Mi

0   25 50 75 Km

▨ Summer range
○ Late May to late August
□ Mid-November to late February

Records since 1960

To most Wisconsin observers the Hermit Thrush is an uncommon migrant. Stealthy in its movements on the ground or in the lowest branches of trees and shrubs at the edge of a woodland, silent except for an occasional barely audible "shuck," it steals northward in April and southward in October so unobtrusively that one can easily miss it entirely during a migration season.

Actually it is not that uncommon. An observer who watches carefully along the edges of either deciduous or coniferous woods in April, and who is not too distracted by the conspicuous outer branches of the trees and bushes at the forest edge, may often glimpse a Hermie on one of the less conspicuous inner branches of vegetation at the edge.

Again in late September and October this visitor prefers the same forest edge habitat and the same sparrow companions and maintains the same retiring habits. Banding data reveal that this bird is a fairly common migrant. At her house in Milton (Rock County), Melva Maxson (pers. comm. to O. J. Gromme) banded 309 birds between 1948 and 1955. At the Cedar Grove Ornithological Station in Sheboygan County, 142 were netted on a single day (7 October 1963), part of a total of 1,701 for the 1958–1963 period.

In parts of northern Wisconsin the Hermit Thrush is also fairly common as a summer resident. North of a line from Grantsburg through Medford, Shawano, and Sturgeon Bay, summering birds are present in every county and are fairly numerous in selected spots. Observers have noted birds on 24 of the state's 70 BBS transects. On four of these transects there is an average of over 10 individuals per transect per year.

South of this line a few summer residents have been detected in the extensive state and county forest lands of Chippewa, Eau Claire, Clark, and Jackson counties (see the accompanying map). In 1979, singing birds were found in two Sauk County locations

(K. I. Lange), and in 1983 and 1984 a summering bird was detected in Monroe County (E. J. Epstein). In summer Hermies are sometimes found along the edges of spruce-tamarack bogs. I have encountered them most frequently in the drier upland jack pine regions. It is a great aesthetic treat to visit such a stand soon after dawn or near dusk on a June day and be serenaded by this prima donna of the ornithological chorus.

Detailed nesting evidence is scanty. All reported nests have been located on the ground, with from three to five eggs per nest. Throne (1941) witnessed an unusual feeding experience in Florence County in 1939 when a parent brought a freshly killed 8-inch snake to the nest. Two nestlings began to devour the food, starting from opposite ends. A half hour later, with only 2 inches of the prey still showing and the bills of the competing nestlings nearly touching, the parent finally succeeded in yanking free the tail of the snake. The nestlings had sucked on the snake body, but had not swallowed it.

The start of spring migration is sometimes difficult to identify. Dates for five early-March birds are known: the 3rd (1972, Dane), 5th (1968, Kenosha),

11th (1964, Waukesha), 12th (1960, Dane), and 14th (1964, Racine). One or all could have been birds that wintered nearby, but birds sighted from 20 March on are quite certainly migrants. While early arrivals have been known to reach La Crosse, Waupaca, Outagamie, and Brown counties by 30 March, the usual pattern is for arrivals to reach the southern region by 1 April and the northern region 10 days later—often while patches of old snow still remain. After a 10–30 April peak, numbers drop off sharply in early May, with only stragglers remaining after 10 May. Remarkably late are individuals banded on 23 May (1958, Chippewa, C. A. Kemper) and 3 June (1953, Fond du Lac, G. Henseler) and the sighting on 31 May (1971, Milwaukee, M. F. Donald).

Remarkably early as fall migrants were the bird banded on 19 August (1952, Dane, M. B. Hickey) and

the one observed on 29 August (1967, St. Croix, S. D. Robbins). Ordinarily migrants are not detected until 15 September in the central counties and 20 September in the south. After a 25 September–20 October peak most birds move rapidly on. Birds remaining beyond 10 November are potentially overwintering individuals.

Through 1987 there had been 54 sightings recorded on CBCs. Most often birds appear in the southeastern counties, where there is considerable low coniferous cover and a supply of edible berries. The northernmost December records come from Portage (1969), Outagamie (1968, 1971, 1973, 1979), and Manitowoc (1950, 1955, 1966, 1977, 1982, 1983) counties. Clarence Paulson's 26 December 1955 record in Crawford County is the only instance of a bird wintering west of Madison.

Wood Thrush (*Hylocichla mustelina*)

STATUS. Uncommon summer resident.
HABITAT. Deciduous forest.
MIGRATION DATES. *Spring:* late April to late May. *Fall:* mid-August to early October. *Extremes:* 17 April; 18 November.
BREEDING DATA. Nests with eggs: 19 May to 23 July. Clutch size: 3 or 4 eggs.
PORTRAIT. *Birds of Wisconsin:* Plate 62.

According to Hoy (1853b) and Kumlien and Hollister (1903), the Wood Thrush was a common species in southern and central regions of the state, but was much scarcer in the north. Whether the bird actually was scarce in the north is open to question because very little fieldwork had been done in the north during the nineteenth century and because Schoenebeck (1902) thought it common in his Oconto County area. But undoubtedly birds were more numerous in the southern half of the state.

The situation now is reversed. Populations in the south have dwindled as deciduous forests have given way to the plow. Numbers have increased modestly in the north as the bird's range has expanded to include every northern county. Thus, although the major part of the summer range lies south of Wisconsin, the areas of greatest density within Wisconsin lie to the north. This is borne out by the June BBS showing densities north of the tension zone four times that of regions farther south.

The Wood Thrush has a statewide summer range. Only 3 of the 70 BBS routes have failed to record it.

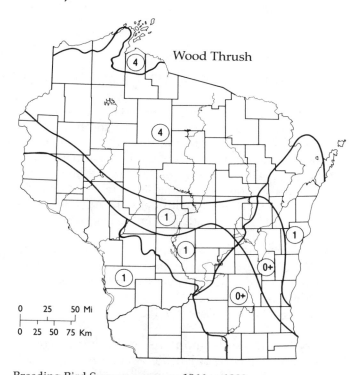

Breeding Bird Survey, averages 1966 to 1980

I have personal observations from all of the state's 72 counties. But no one calls this species common any more in any section of the state. "Uncommon" is the term used for Douglas County (Bernard 1967), for the Vilas-Oneida-Forest County region (Vanderschaegen 1981b), and for the St. Croix River valley (Faanes 1981).

Because northern Wisconsin constitutes part of the northern limit of the range, there are no well-defined migration peaks, as there are for other species of this family that move on into Canada in summer. Although one or two early arrivals are spotted each year during the last week of April, this is otherwise exclusively a May migrant. The bird disperses widely over southern areas between 1 and 15 May and into the north between 10 and 25 May. The earliest known April arrivals include birds on the 17th (1915, Milwaukee, W. J. Mueller, pers. comm. to O. J. Gromme; 1959, Outagamie, A. S. Bradford), 19th (1964, Vernon, V. E. Weber), and 20th (1971, Dane, B. Vogelsang).

The fall migration pattern is more difficult to discern, for the birds are silent and secretive. In 18 years of monitoring Eau Claire towerkills, C. A. Kemper recorded only 25 specimens. Banding studies at Milwaukee, the Cedar Grove Ornithological Station in Sheyboygan County, and Chippewa Falls indicate that less than 1% of trapped thrushes are of this species. The greatest period of movement is from 20 August to 20 September. Nearly every year a few birds remain until 10 October, with an occasional migrant lingering until the 25th. Three November stragglers are known: birds recorded on the 2nd (1974, Racine, L. W. Erickson), 6th (1927, Dane, A. W. Schorger [1931a]), and 18th (1962, Dane, L. B. Hunt).

May and June are the best months to see and hear this melodic maestro of the maples. Few bird songs can match the rich caroling phrase of the male, but to hear it one had best be listening during the first 2 hours of daylight. Wisconsin BBS studies show that 60% of the Wood Thrushes found on state transects are recorded on the first 20 stops, usually completed 1½ hours after sunrise. Conspicuously less song occurs thereafter, except for a modest "twilight concert" at the end of the day.

For song, nesting, and all other purposes, this bird restricts itself to dense woodlands. In the southern regions the bird prefers the maple woodlands; Schorger (1931a) also found several nests in bur oaks. In the northern forests habitat preferences are more varied. C. H. Richter has found nests in dogwood, black cherry, black ash, and balsam fir. Hemlock, spruce, cedars, and maples have also been used. Nests are generally located on horizontal limbs 5–10 feet above ground level, occasionally as low as 3 or as high as 15 feet.

American Robin (*Turdus migratorius*)

STATUS. Abundant migrant. Abundant summer resident. Uncommon winter resident south and central; rare winter resident north.

HABITAT. Residential areas. All forest. Farmsteads.

MIGRATION DATES. *Spring:* early March to mid-April. *Fall:* early September to mid-November.

BREEDING DATA. Nests with eggs: 12 April to 7 August. Clutch size: usually 3 or 4 eggs; occasionally 2 or 5.

WINTER. Regularly present in small numbers north to Grant, Sauk, Outagamie, and Manitowoc counties; has been recorded in every county except Vilas, Forest, and Florence.

PORTRAIT. *Birds of Wisconsin:* Plate 61.

Every BBS transect run in Wisconsin since its inception in 1966 has recorded the American Robin each year. The BBS figures show not only that this bird is present in all parts of the state, but also that it is one of the most numerous birds present. It ranks behind only the Red-winged Blackbird, the European Starling, the House Sparrow, and the Common Grackle as one of Wisconsin's five most abundant summer residents, and thus richly deserves its recognition as the state bird.

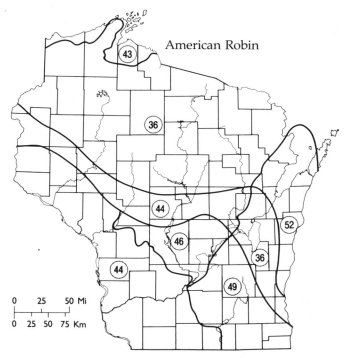

American Robin

0   25   50 Mi

0   25 50 75 Km

Breeding Bird Survey, averages 1966 to 1980

It is not without difficulty that the robin has maintained its position of eminence. Fifty to a hundred years ago some people considered it sport to invade a nocturnal roost area and club robins to death by the hundreds with sticks and clubs. In the 1950s and 1960s the robin population in some of the Midwest's major cities, including Milwaukee and Madison, was seriously affected by DDT when it was being widely used in an attempt to stop the spread of Dutch elm disease. But once substitutes for DDT were developed and its use banned, the birds made a strong recovery.

It is amusing to read newspaper accounts in January or February of someone sighting "the first robin of spring." These are not spring migrants but over-wintering birds that may be moving about in search of berries. A few robins winter every year. They winter by the scores among the ornamental plantings of the residential areas around Madison and Milwaukee. They winter by the dozens in clumps of cedars when the berry crop is good. Even in winters of below-par berry crops this bird is reported on 25% of the Christmas counts; in some years the figure is closer to 50%. The winter of 1969–1970 was a particularly remarkable one, with 676 birds present on 33 counts, including records north to Bayfield and Oneida counties. The same two northern counties were included in the 1983–1984 CBC when 762 robins were tallied in 35 count circles.

Also it is misleading to call the robin the first spring bird. There are years when central and northern observers have to wait until the last 5 days of March to see their first arrivals. Farther south, where observers may sight first arrivals any time from 1 to 20 March, the robins are generally preceded by migrating Kill-deers, Canada Geese, and Red-winged Blackbirds. As warm weather moves across the state during the 1–20 April period, flocks of robins in the hundreds are often seen. The flocks do not linger long in one location. Birds pass rapidly through the state and disperse into every town and hamlet.

Few species have used as wide a variety of nesting sites as the robin. Most robins' nests are in trees, but this bird seems equally at home building 30 feet up in an elm, 3 feet up in a willow thicket, 20 feet up in a spruce, or 6 feet up in arbor vitae (white cedar). Pairs have often chosen nesting sites on a residential porch or a door ledge in spite of heavy human traffic; they have taken over rural mailboxes, grape trellises, and tractor seats.

The pattern of breeding behavior was carefully studied in Madison, 1947–1949, by Young (1949, 1951, 1955). He found first eggs as early as 12 April; first young from 11 May on. Pairs had two or three nestings per season. Young observed eggs until 5 August, but 90% of the young from 99 nests had fledged by 20 July.

The effect of severe dry weather during the nesting season in 1934 was vividly revealed by G. W. Burdick's (MPM files) observations. He noted that one pair had its first two nests destroyed by moderate winds, and he suspected that lack of mud had contributed to weakened construction. After he provided a mud puddle, the birds built a third nest that proved successful. But when the young fledged, the parents could not find earthworms in the parched earth. He then provided suet, which was avidly devoured.

Some flocking begins in late June as males and recently fledged young gather at nocturnal roosts. These roosts get progressively larger through July and early August. In late August many of these birds disappear, and for a 2-week period in early September only a few robins are evident. From 15 September on there is an influx of migrants from the north, many of which are noticeably lighter in plumage. After a 1–15 October peak, most birds depart for winter homes, leaving only the wintering stragglers present after 10 November.

Varied Thrush (*Ixoreus naevius*)

STATUS. Rare winter resident north, central, and southeast.

HABITAT. Residential areas. Northern maple-hemlock-pine forest.

MIGRATION DATES. *Fall:* early November to mid-December. *Spring:* mid-March to early April. *Extremes:* 22 October; 24 April.

WINTER. From 3 to 12 birds present every year, north and east of a line from Vernon to Green County.

It is 1,200 miles from western Montana to northwestern Wisconsin, but the number of wandering Varied Thrushes known to have made this long trip between October 1944 and April 1987 stands at 136—far more than any other species usually restricted to the Pacific states.

The first bird known to make this trek turned up in the H. R. English yard in Madison on 26 October 1944, then disappeared. Subsequent records indicate that this occurrence was somewhat atypical for two reasons. First, the date is earlier than most. Wisconsin's earliest arrival was a 22 October bird (1980, Dane, E. H. Zimmerman). Additional late October arrivals were logged in 1964 (Door, T. Jessen), 1978 (Clark, K. S. Hansen), and 1984 (Sheboygan, D. D. Berger). Another 19 birds were first sighted in November.

Second, most birds have established residence at a winter feeding station, remaining for weeks at the same location. Exact arrival and departure dates are unknown for a majority of Wisconsin's visitors. But only 28 are single-day records; 69 of the birds visited

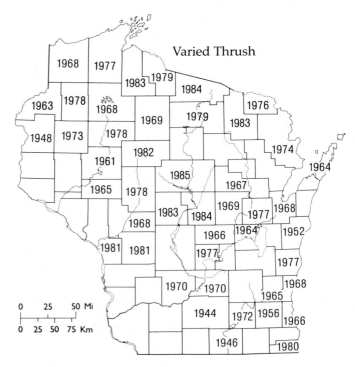

Varied Thrush

Years of first county records

Varied Thrush, 16 February 1982, Door County (photo by R. J. Lukes)

for from 1 week to 3 months; 24 remained at their chosen winter locations for 4 months or more.

During this period birds depend heavily on feeding stations, especially those located close to oak woodlots. At one such feeder I once watched a male move in from the neighboring woods and take his turn feeding on cracked corn. Although he showed the typical unobtrusive movements of the thrush family, he was not intimidated by competing squirrels and jays. When through feeding, the thrush moved to the edge of a neighboring oak woodlot, and for the next 30 minutes sat virtually motionless sunning himself before returning to the feeding area.

As snow disappears in March, birds become less dependent on feeders and are seen less frequently. Observers have noted the latest departures on the following April dates: the 6th (1968, Sawyer, R. Perkins), 12th (1970, Waupaca, C. W. Lewis), 13th (1969, Brown, R. Schulde), 19th (1978, Brown, R. Hibbard), 21st (1949, Polk, O. T. Simmons), and 24th (1968, Douglas, B. F. Klugow).

How many of these wanderers make it back to their normal Pacific Coast breeding range? Because numbers of these birds have wandered to eastern Canada, New England, and other North Atlantic states, it is presumed that autumn birds moving east near the

Canadian border probably divide when they reach the Lake Superior region: some proceed north of the Great Lakes and continue eastward, some select a more southeasterly route into and through Wisconsin. If one were to draw a diagonal line from Grantsburg to Port Washington, one would discover that most Wisconsin records fall within 60 miles of that line. Through 1975 no Varied Thrushes were found in northeastern and southwestern Wisconsin. Several northeastern sightings were made in the early 1980s, but there are no records southwest of a La Crosse–Green county line.

The one Florence County bird (22–23 March 1976) and one in Douglas County (24 April 1968) involved 1- or 2-day observations of birds that may have been retracing their autumn route. One individual that did not have the chance to return was the bird found dead in a snow-covered driveway near Chippewa Falls on 28 November 1977 (F. Hillery). The specimen is now preserved at the Milwaukee Public Museum.

The map also shows how recently the tendency of this bird to wander to Wisconsin has developed. There were only three records in the 1940s and four more in the 1950s. Beginning in 1963, one or more birds have turned up every winter. The 24 observations in the 1960s were followed by 48 in the 1970s. There seems to be no reason why this trend should not continue.

Family **Mimidae:** Mimic Thrushes

Gray Catbird (*Dumetella carolinensis*)

STATUS. Common migrant. Common summer resident. Rare winter resident south and central.

HABITAT. Residential areas. All carr. Southern silver maple–elm forest.

MIGRATION DATES. *Spring:* late April to late May. *Fall:* late August to mid-October.

BREEDING DATA. Nests with eggs: 3 May to 31 July. Clutch size: usually 3 or 4 eggs; occasionally 5 or 6.

WINTER. Occasionally present north to Dane, Outagamie, and Brown counties; casually present to Polk, Ashland, and Langlade counties.

PORTRAIT. *Birds of Wisconsin:* Plate 60.

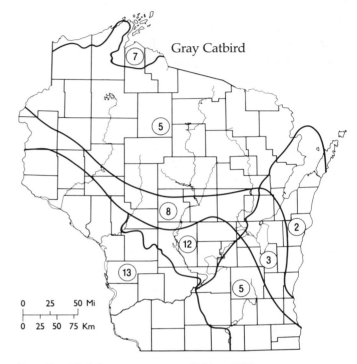

Gray Catbird

Breeding Bird Survey, averages 1966 to 1980

The Gray Catbird is one of Wisconsin's best-known summer birds. Because the bird takes readily to shrubbery in residential areas all over the state and is not overly secretive in the selection of its nest site, it is a favorite even among those whose ornithological knowledge is minimal. Bird-watchers of all types appreciate its comical sounds: the plaintive "mew" that emanates from a hidden perch in the shrubbery, and the wide variety of mimicry that is produced by a male conspicuously perched high in a medium-sized tree. What the singer lacks in melody it makes up in buffoonery.

It is not possible to list an extreme early arrival date for the catbird because of the likelihood of occasional overwintering. Two February sightings on the 21st (1976, Jefferson, J. Burbach) and 26th (1973, Kenosha, L. W. Erickson) and two March observations on the 9th (1948, St. Croix, G. Riegel) and 26th (1978, Door, C. M. Lukes) must have been birds that wintered nearby. Another seven observations between 1 and 15 April also seem too early for true migrants. Early migrants are often sighted in the south by 25 April, but May is the usual migration month. The southern counties usually have a strong 1–10 May buildup, a 10–20 May peak, with nonbreeders gone by the 25th. The schedule for the northern areas is 5–10 days later.

Banding results show that this species often finds its way back to the same backyard it used the previous year. Paul and Emma Hoffmann, reporting from Milwaukee and Waukesha counties from 1940 to 1954, retrapped 12 individuals that had returned in successive years, 4 of which were 3-year sojourners.

Three of the catbirds that Margarette Morse (1960) banded at her Vernon County home between 1950 and 1953 returned for 2 successive years.

Nesting begins soon after arrival, with nest construction often under way by 20 May and first eggs laid during the last week of the month. A remarkably early nest was discovered near Beloit (Rock County) on 3 May (1968, T. R. Ellis). By the 10th two of the five eggs it contained had hatched, with two more hatching on the 11th. Had the nest not met with an untimely end on the 17th, young might have fledged before most other catbirds had laid their first eggs. At the other extreme, incubating eggs have been found as late as 31 July and nests with young as late as 5 August. A great majority of nests are located 2–8 feet up, either in residential shrubbery or in small trees bordering streams. Willow and alder thickets, lilac, and berry bushes are favorites. Occasionally a pair will desert the undergrowth and build a nest 30–40 feet up in a deciduous tree.

As a summer resident, this species is well represented in all regions. Of the 935 BBS routes run, 1966–1980, observers recorded this mimic on 873 (93%) routes, including each of the 70 transects. Although populations are significantly greater in the western half of the state than in the eastern half, the term "common" fits in all sections.

September encompasses the main migratory period in fall. Birds are not often found in backyards at this time. Instead, they frequent hedgerows and woodland edges. An observer who stops in such habitat in late August and September and tries some "squeaking" will often find from one to four catbirds. The size of the fall migration is evident in the 1,544 birds banded at the Cedar Grove Ornithological Station in Sheboygan County over a 6-year span, 1958–1963.

One does not generally associate this species with east-west migration, but a Cedar Grove individual banded on 2 September 1964 (H. C. Mueller) was recaptured in New Jersey just 26 days later.

Most migrants have left the north by 30 September, the central region by 10 October, and the south by 20 October. Beyond these dates there are numerous instances of late stragglers. Of those birds lingering into but not beyond November, the most northerly was a Price County individual on the 3rd (1971, M. Hardy), and a Door County individual on the 12th (1976, R. M. Evanson). Over 35 instances of birds remaining into December have come to light. Fourteen of these birds survived into January. Seven of the 14 were still present in February, in Dunn (1954), Ashland (1964), Door (1940), Waukesha (1956), Dane (1981), and Milwaukee (1960, 1973) counties.

Northern Mockingbird (*Mimus polyglottos*)

STATUS. Uncommon spring migrant south; rare spring migrant central and north; casual fall migrant. Rare summer resident. Rare winter resident south and east.

HABITAT. Residential areas. Upland carr. Savanna.

MIGRATION DATES. *Spring:* early April to late May. *Fall:* no discernible period.

BREEDING DATA. Nests with eggs: 16 May to 11 June. Clutch size: 3–5 eggs.

WINTER. Occasionally present north to Vernon, Columbia, Outagamie, and Brown counties.

PORTRAIT. *Birds of Wisconsin:* Plate 60.

If a Northern Mockingbird were to wander north from its usual range and take up residence in your neighborhood, you would know it right away. This bird has an affinity for residential areas and is not at all secretive in habits. It perches readily on conspicuous branches of trees and bushes, on utility wires, and even on television aerials. And if by some strange combination of circumstances you missed sighting the visitor, you would surely hear it. At any hour of day—or night—this ventriloquist is apt to give forth a series of varied sounds—original or plagiarized from other birds—that would make up the most astonishing repertoire you have ever heard.

Not many Wisconsin bird enthusiasts have had this thrill, for the northern edge of the normal range lies through northern and central Illinois. But wanderings into Wisconsin occur moderately often, with an

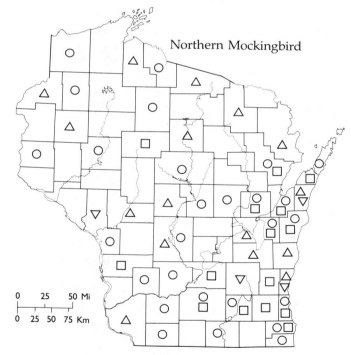

Northern Mockingbird

△ Early April to late May
○ Early June to late August
▽ Early September to late November
□ Early December to late March

Records since 1960

average of eight published records per year since 1960. Records are more numerous in the Milwaukee-Racine-Kenosha area, as one might expect. But this wanderer is known to have visited at least 45 counties.

Birds are as apt to appear in early winter as at any other time of year. But December-to-March sightings have been restricted almost entirely to the eastern counties. With the exception of individuals in Pierce (16 November 1920–25 March 1921, F. Gable; MPM files), Buffalo (11–12 December 1927, M. Lees [Roberts 1938]), Vernon (1 October 1970–5 January 1971, V. E. Weber), and Taylor (28 November–21 December 1983, S. D. Robbins) counties, the westernmost winter sightings have been in Dane, Columbia, Waupaca, Oconto, and Marinette counties.

A second period of frequent arrivals extends from 10 April to 25 May. Nearly all records from the northwestern counties are for May. Many of the sightings involve wandering birds that are present one day and gone the next. They may well be unmated first-year birds that could not establish a breeding territory. Spring vagrants have wandered as far north as south Outer Island, Ashland (1976, 1977), Iron (1976, 1977, 1982), Douglas (1965, 1967, 1970, 1984), Washburn (1962, 1967, 1968), and Burnett (1958, 1964, 1980, 1984) counties. The Northern Mockingbird was not mentioned for northeastern Wisconsin by Vanderschaegen (1981). A Vilas County observation on 13 May (W. J. Reardon) is the only known record from the region between Price and Marinette counties.

But some birds remain and breed. When Ralph Morse found fledged young near Beloit (Rock County) on 13 July 1958, this was erroneously publicized as a first state breeding record. Hoy (1885b) mentioned six nests at Racine before 1856, but listed no exact dates. Kumlien and Hollister (1903) also listed nests in Jefferson County in 1879 and 1880 and near Milwaukee in 1897, again lacking specific dates. The 1958 record was the first for the twentieth century and the forerunner of several subsequent nestings. In 1959 there were three nesting pairs in Rock County (D. Hammel), with another in 1960 (F. Glenn; B. Andrews). On 26 May 1959 a nest was found in Columbia County, but its contents and success are not known (H. A. Winkler). In Portage County nesting was discovered in July 1960, with the subsequent fledgling of five young on 1 August (F. Peterson). One of the juveniles was subsequently found dead, and the specimen was forwarded to the Milwaukee Public Museum. On 22 July 1966 three young were banded and photographed in a Portage County nest (Sindelar 1968). Nesting has also taken place in La Crosse (1968), Marathon (1964), Door (1973), Calumet (1974), and Milwaukee (1974) counties, and has probably occurred at several of the other summer locations noted on the accompanying map.

Fall wanderings in the north have occurred only casually. One bird was collected on Outer Island in Ashland County on 9 September (1919, H. H. Sheldon [Jackson 1943]). Another was detected in Douglas County on 19 November (1962, E. Fisher).

Sage Thrasher (*Oreoscoptes montanus*)

STATUS. Accidental. Three records.
HABITAT. Upland carr.

It was an astonished John Fitzpatrick who found himself staring at this western visitor during the Madison CBC on 15 December 1979. The encounter occurred on the embankment of a railroad trestle surrounded by deciduous brush, cattails, and berry-laden nightshade plants. "Squeaking" brought the Sage Thrasher within 15 feet while the observer alternately watched, sketched, and took notes. Soon count partner David Willard shared the observation. This bird remained in the Dane County area into early February 1980. During this interval the wanderer was viewed by dozens of observers, and photographed by Stephen Lang (*Pass. Pigeon* 42:44–45).

The sole previous Wisconsin observation for this westerner took place in Waukesha County on 10 May

Sage Thrasher, 19 December 1979, Dane County (photo by S. J. Lang)

1972. John Bielefeldt's slow drive past fencerow-lined fields was interrupted when he flushed a grayish bird that displayed white tips on outer tail feathers. Parking and pursuing the stranger, Bielefeldt "was surprised to find a thrasher-like bird scratching in the leaves beneath a small bush. . . . The bird obligingly hopped—not walked—directly in front of the car and into a plowed field, using its wings and tail like stabilizers, in typical thrasher behavior, during these quick hops." The bird could not be found when Bielefeldt and other observers returned to the scene later that day (*Pass. Pigeon* 35:35–36).

On 14 May 1988 Kevin Glueckert had the good fortune to spot one of these westerners on his front lawn near Ellison Bay in Door County—only 5 yards away (*Pass. Pigeon* 50:366).

The presence of this bird from the arid West is not readily explained. There were no exceptional storms at either time that might have carried a westerner far off course. Since 1966, individuals have turned up in South Dakota, Ontario, Illinois, New York, Maryland, North Carolina, Florida, and Louisiana. Most of these birds have been autumn vagrants.

Brown Thrasher (*Toxostoma rufum*)

STATUS. Common migrant. Common summer resident south and central; fairly common summer resident north. Rare winter resident south and central; casual winter resident north.

HABITAT. Upland carr. Old field. Farmsteads.

MIGRATION DATES. *Spring:* mid-April to mid-May. *Fall:* early September to early October.

BREEDING DATA. Nests with eggs: 5 May to 21 July. Clutch size: usually 3 or 4 eggs; occasionally 2–6.

WINTER. From 1 to 20 birds present every winter, north to Chippewa, Marathon, Langlade, Oneida, Marinette, and Door counties.

PORTRAIT. *Birds of Wisconsin:* Plate 60.

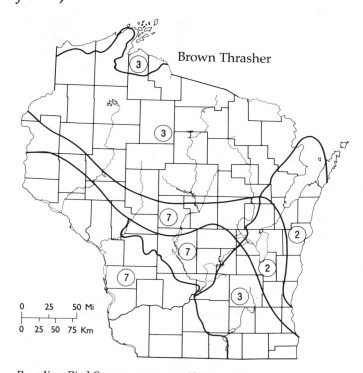

Breeding Bird Survey, averages 1966 to 1980

"Formerly an abundant summer resident." This was Kumlien and Hollister's (1903) appraisal of the status of the "brown thrush" in 1903. They felt that the Brown Thrasher's decline had occurred within the previous 15 years: "Until now it is scarcely common in many localities, and really rare in some, where it once bred in good numbers." Following a return visit to Wisconsin in 1919, Hollister (1919b) wrote of a further noticeable decline at Delavan (Walworth County).

The 1966–1980 BBS points to a stable population but not an overly large one. The BBS has recorded birds in all 70 transect areas and on 855 of the 935 routes run during these 15 years (91%), showing a statewide distribution. But the map shows that the population density in the central, western, and southern regions is twice that of the northern and eastern sectors. No significant increases or decreases are apparent for this 15-year interval.

Most observers encounter their first spring "loud-mouths" between 15 April and 5 May. In the south there have been frequent 1–10 April sightings, but

one can never be sure whether these are true migrants or birds that have overwintered. Mid-April arrivals build to a 1–10 May peak.

In the north birds are rarely seen before 25 April; exceptions include a 12 April individual (1969, Lincoln, D. J. Hendrick) and one on the 13th (1963, Douglas, R. F. Bernard). After a 10–20 May migration peak, nesting begins in earnest. Dry upland brushy habitat is preferred during both spring and summer. The male often picks the tallest tree as a singing perch, voicing a varied repertoire of repeated phrases that can be obnoxiously loud and continuous when one is trying to listen to other birds. Overheard on a mid-May field trip was the comment of a frustrated observer: "Oh shut up, loud-mouth! Give the other birds a chance to sing!"

Nesting occupies most of the 15 May–31 July period. Most thrasher nests are located 1–3 feet up in brush piles or thick shrubbery. But a few nests have been built on the ground, and a few have been found 5–7 feet up.

In late summer the thrasher becomes surprisingly inconspicuous. No noticeable buildup of numbers occurs during fall migration, but by searching the hedgerows and brushy hillsides one can find a few birds through 20 September in the north, 30 September in the central region, and 10 October in the south. Nonwintering birds occasionally linger through 5 November.

Fall migration carries Wisconsin birds to wintering grounds across a broad span of Gulf Coast states. One banded at the Cedar Grove Ornithological Station in Sheboygan County on 28 August 1964 was recovered 2½ months later in Florida. Four other birds banded in Wisconsin have turned up the following winters in Louisiana, with additional recoveries reported from Mississippi, Alabama, and Georgia.

An increasing number of thrashers remain in Wisconsin to winter. This appears to be a relatively recent phenomenon. There was no mention of the bird's wintering here by any of the nineteenth-century writers. The first known winter record was established on 25 January 1913 (Dane, A. W. Schorger [1931a]). In the 1930s there were occasional overwintering birds, but from 1940 on, observers have reported one or more birds nearly every year. Since 1968, CBC birds have numbered between 7 and 13 individuals each December. Most winter records come from the southern counties, with occasional central records from Pierce, Chippewa, Marathon, Waupaca, Outagamie, Brown, Kewaunee, and Door counties. Most remarkable are records from Bayfield (1980), Vilas (1944), Oneida (1966), Price (1976), Lincoln (1980), Langlade (1966), and Marinette (1969) counties. No one knows how many of these birds live through the winter. Some manage to find enough berries to survive, but most disappear in January.

Curve-billed Thrasher (*Toxostoma curvirostre*)

STATUS. Accidental. Two records.
HABITAT. Residential areas. Old field.
BREEDING DATA. Nests with eggs (infertile): 8 May to 15 August.

Most rarities that wander accidentally to Wisconsin vanish within an hour, a day, or at most a few days after sighting. After "Curvi" appeared at the Merton Maier feeder in Buffalo City in early October 1971, it remained in the neighborhood for 4 years. During that interval the Maiers opened their home to more than 300 appreciative birders. Few if any of them failed to see the Curve-billed Thrasher. They viewed and photographed this southern visitor comfortably through a large picture window that overlooks one of the finest bird-feeding stations in western Wisconsin (*Pass. Pigeon* 34:47–49).

Although the bird first appeared in early October 1971, Merton and Lorena Maier had for several weeks been hearing a strange call note: two, three, or four sharply whistled notes all on the same pitch. The Maiers recognized later that these sounds came from this individual.

Possibly no other Curve-bill has ever experienced the −30°F temperatures which Curvi survived that winter. An abundance of cedars and shrubbery offered good cover, and the Maiers kept an abundant supply of ground suet, cracked corn, cracked sunflower seeds, and nutmeats available.

On 3 May 1972 the bird was observed gathering sticks and fashioning them into a nest 16 feet up in a

Curve-billed Thrasher, January 1987, Marathon County (photo by A. Gauger)

nearby spruce. She was incubating three eggs by 17 May, and she continued to do so until the eggs were broken on 6 June—well past the normal incubation period for this species. The eggs were undoubtedly infertile. By 23 June she was incubating one egg in a second nest 18 feet up in another spruce. This egg did not hatch. A third nest was started by 16 July, but the eggs in this nest were soon lost to predation (Maier and Maier 1973).

Much the same sequence of events occurred again in 1973, 1974, and 1975. Curvi did her best to attract a male Brown Thrasher as a mate, but she was consistently rejected. Yet she carried through two or three nesting attempts each summer. The eggs were either destroyed by Common Grackles or abandoned after 3 weeks of fruitless incubation. The third of the 1973 nests was built as an upper level of the second of that year's nests.

In the summer of 1974 the bird developed a defect in her beak. "The top mandible was at least twice as long as the bottom and very, very curved, so that she had to eat and drink by tipping her head to one side or other and scooping things in." Two days after being photographed in this condition, she appeared with her bill back again at normal length (Maier and Maier; *Pass. Pigeon* 36:90). She was last seen on 15 November 1975 by C. A. Kemper and P. D. Blanchard, after the Maiers had left to go south for the winter.

A second bird spent much of the winter of 1986–1987 at the Gary Hendrickson feeder near Spencer (Clark County). It was first seen by Hendrickson on 24 November, photographed in December (K. Merkel), banded in December (D. G. Follen), and viewed by many others through 10 February (*Pass. Pigeon* 49:17–19).

Although this species is not migratory in its normal Texas-Arizona-Mexico range, nor noted for much extralimital wandering, individuals turned up during the 1967–1969 interval in Colorado, Oklahoma, Kansas, Nebraska, and South Dakota. Minnesota had its first record in the fall of 1976. One bird wintered in Iowa, 1980–1981.

Family **Motacillidae:** Wagtails, Pipits

American Pipit (*Anthus rubescens*)
Formerly Water Pipit

STATUS. Uncommon migrant.
HABITAT. Open cropland. Ponds.
MIGRATION DATES. *Spring:* late April to late May. *Fall:* mid-September to early November. *Extremes:* 20 March, 3 June; 24 August, 24 December.
BREEDING DATA. No positive records.
WINTER. One January record.
PORTRAIT. *Birds of Wisconsin:* Plate 53.

Going over my personal records for the past 40 years, representing six areas of Wisconsin residence, I find a remarkably consistent pattern: approximately three pipit observations each spring and five each fall. This is a far cry from the "abundant" status described by Hoy (1853b), or the "common" pattern suggested by Kumlien and Hollister (1903); it adheres much more closely to the "uncommon" status described by Gromme (1963).

This bird is most often observed in areas of exposed soil: freshly plowed fields, muddy edges of shallow ponds, fields where small grains have been recently planted (spring), and plots near barns where cattle have worn extensive areas bare. Most often, birds travel in small flocks of 10 or fewer, but observers have reported groups of up to 100. Birds may be feeding in a plowed field and their movements be so unobtrusive that the entire flock escapes notice.

Frequently, birds are encountered only in overhead flight; identification is made by the bird's call note. Passing overhead, American Pipits often utter a distinctive staccato two-syllable "tsik-tsik" call. I would hazard the guess that between a third and a half of my personal encounters with this species would never have been made, had it not been for the recognition of this call note.

Most spring birds are found in the first 3 weeks of May. There are a few records scattered throughout April, with six late-March dates, the earliest on the 20th (1975, Racine, L. W. Erickson) and 21st (1976, Milwaukee, L. W. Erikson). I know of seven 25–31

May observations, plus A. L. Kumlien's (Kumlien and Hollister 1903) 3 June 1879 specimen in Jefferson County. But the bulk of the spring observations, from any part of the state, falls in the 1–20 May period.

The autumn migration period is more prolonged. Early arrivals can be expected any time after 15 September. Unusually early were a Douglas County discovery on 7 September (1966, S. D. Robbins) and Oneida County viewings on 24 August (1973, E. L. Basten) and 4 September (1979, R. G. Spahn). Although the main migration period lasts from 25 September through October, sightings through 10 November are not unusual. Four times birds have been found in late November, and on another five occasions individuals have lingered into December, with observations on the 5th (1975, Dane, T. L. Ashman), 7th (1983, Waukesha, J. E. Bielefeldt), 9th (1964, Racine, L. W. Erickson), 23rd (1952, Manitowoc, J. Kraupa), and 24th (1948, Milwaukee, G. W. Treichel).

Two additional state records fall completely outside the normal pattern. One involves a 28 January 1942 sighting at Horicon Marsh in Dodge County by Earl Mitchell. If the bird had been sick or injured at the usual migration time, that might have explained why it was present; but how it could survive that long in a Wisconsin winter remains a mystery.

The other inexplicable sighting is a midsummer observation on Washington Island in Door County. On 19 July 1917, H. H. T. Jackson (1927) found six birds in a field in company with Vesper and Savannah Sparrows. He collected a male that proved to have testes in postbreeding condition. This is such an extraordinarily early date for a fall migrant from the normal Hudson Bay breeding range that the possibility of local nesting must be considered. But there was no indication that any of the six pipits were recently fledged young of the year, and the likelihood that breeding occurred this far south is equally fantastic. It must remain a mystery.

Family **Bombycillidae:** Waxwings

Bohemian Waxwing (*Bombycilla garrulus*)

STATUS. Rare winter visitant. Irregular.

HABITAT. Residential area trees and shrubs.

MIGRATION DATES. *Fall:* early November to mid-December. *Spring:* present until early April. *Extremes:* 19 September; 13 May.

WINTER. Major influxes occur on an average of 1 in every 6 years; occasional sightings occur on an average of 9 in every 10 years.

PORTRAIT. *Birds of Wisconsin:* Plate 64.

The Bohemian Waxwing has to rank as one of the most irregular, unpredictable birds to visit our state. There are winters like that of 1958–1959, when flocks of 100 or more arrive by mid-October, blanket most of the state all winter long, and remain until April. There are winters like that of 1967–1968, when nary a bird is reported. There are winters like that of 1963–1964, when birds show up in fair numbers in early winter but disappear in January. There are winters like that of 1966–1967, when birds begin to appear in late December or January and are numerous until early April.

Some species that are popularly characterized as irregular in winter, such as the Common Redpoll, are so nearly cyclic that one can almost predict the years when high populations will occur. Not so the Bohemian. There was a period between 1961 and 1967 when fair numbers were present in four out of six winters. In the previous decade, however, numbers per winter were very small until the major flight of 1958–1959 occurred. Data are fragmentary for the years before 1939, when *The Passenger Pigeon* began publication of current field notes. But by piecing together fragments of information from various sources, I have surmised that major incursions occurred during the winters of 1879–1880, 1883–1884, 1897–1898, 1908–1909, 1921–1922, 1931–1932, 1942–1943, 1947–1948, 1958–1959, 1961–1962, 1966–1967, 1972–1973, 1980–1981, 1983–1984, 1986–1987, and 1987–1988.

Major flights used to be as much as 10 years apart. In the 1980s incursions have become more frequent. Even in noninvasion years, a few individuals appear somewhere in the state nearly every winter. Since 1939 there has been at least one published record every winter except 1943–1944, 1950–1951, and 1967–1968. In the years when Bohemians do occur, whether

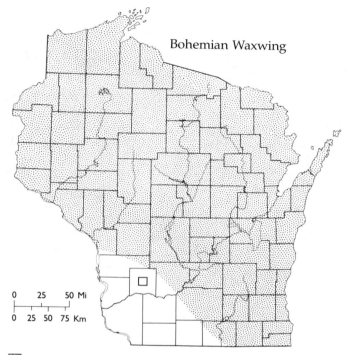

Bohemian Waxwing

```
0     25     50 Mi
0  25  50  75 Km
```

▨ Winter range in invasion years
☐ Mid-December to early April

Records since 1960

in major flights or in rare sporadic instances, they may show up almost anywhere in the state. But there appears to be a concentration of records from the northwest to the southeast, with a scarcity in the extreme southwest. In the southwest, no records are known for Crawford, Richland, Grant, Iowa, Lafayette, and Green counties, and observations south of a line connecting La Crosse and Beloit are scanty. The inference is that this western species enters the state from northeastern Minnesota and follows a southeasterly band centered along a line from Superior to Sheboygan.

In invasion years birds roam around in flocks of up to 200 birds. In noninvasion years flocks are usually much smaller, and at times only a single bird appears—either alone or in company with some Cedar Waxwings. These birds are strictly fruit-eaters in winter. The berries of mountain ash trees are particular favorites. During the 1961–1962 invasion observers also mentioned apples, highbush cranberries, multiflora rose, bittersweet, sumac, buckthorn, and black locust as favored food.

Remarkably early are three September arrival dates: the 19th (1986, Ashland, R. L. Verch), 24th (1980, Ashland, R. L. Verch), and 26th (1954, Sheboygan, T. K.

Soulen). Birds have occasionally been noted between 15 and 31 October, but early November is a more typical arrival period. Few birds remain beyond 31 March except in invasion years. Beyond 15 April, there have been reports from Ashland County on 26 April 1978 and 13 May 1977 (R. L. Verch).

Cedar Waxwing (*Bombycilla cedrorum*)

STATUS. Common migrant. Common summer resident. Uncommon winter resident south and central; rare winter resident north.

HABITAT. Residential areas. All carr. Ponds and streams.

MIGRATION DATES. *Spring:* mid-May to mid-June. *Fall:* early September to mid-October.

BREEDING DATA. Nests with eggs: 9 June to 12 September. Clutch size: usually 4 or 5 eggs; occasionally 3–7.

WINTER. A few present every winter north to La Crosse, Dane, Outagamie, and Door counties; occasional wanderers present to the northernmost counties.

PORTRAIT. *Birds of Wisconsin:* Plate 64.

The Cedar Waxwing's year can be divided into two 6-month segments. From May through October it follows a regular and predictable schedule of migration and breeding. From November through April it follows an erratic, unpredictable pattern of residency, wandering, or disappearance.

In early May usually a few individuals appear, generally concentrated in the southern and eastern counties. In mid-May, when avid birders sometimes spend all day afield striving for lists of 130–160 species at the peak of the spring migration, the Cedar Waxwing may be missed entirely. It is one of the latest of the spring migrants, usually not appearing in large numbers until the last 10 days of May. As many as 900 have been reported during a morning field trip at this time. The birds are not found in one huge flock, but in numerous small flocks that may suddenly flood a particular area. In early and mid-June, when most other species are engaged in nesting, small flocks of migrant waxwings can be found in residential areas and along the edges of almost any kind of woodland. Spring migrants show a particular fondness for flowering shrubs and fruit trees but also are often seen in elms, oaks, and maples.

Breeding Bird Survey, averages 1966 to 1980

Undoubtedly the BBS results include migratory individuals as well as summer residents, since the resident population does not stabilize until late June. But the following pattern is an accurate picture of summer distribution: present in small numbers in the south, noticeably more numerous in the north.

By late June, birds have largely settled down for nesting activities that keep them occupied through July, August, and early September. Nest sites are sometimes in thick shrubbery, both deciduous and evergreen, 4–6 feet above ground. More often, the birds build nests 8–15 feet up in trees, and in a few instances at heights of 25–35 feet. Whenever cedars are widely present, these are likely to be chosen as nesting locations. But when cedars are not available, "cedarbirds" have been known to build in maples, elms, willows, oaks, and hawthorns. One nest with eggs was reported in Manitowoc on 12 September 1969, but ordinarily most young are on the wing by the end of August, and are being fed by parents throughout much of September.

Some fall migration occurs in early September in the northern counties. By late September considerable flocking has taken place throughout the state, with the peak of the southward migration coming between 1 and 15 October. Usually the northern counties have only a few birds left by 15 October, while a general exodus from the southern counties takes place during the remainder of the month.

The months from November through April certainly constitute a period of great irregularity, both unpredictable and mysterious in terms of our present fragmentary information. The varied patterns of winter residency include the following: (1) birds may be virtually absent from the entire state, except in the Madison–Milwaukee region; (2) they may be frequently seen in the south and central regions of the state but are absent north of a line from New Richmond to Green Bay; (3) scattered flocks may be found in all parts of the state; and (4) flocks may be numerous in the eastern region from Kenosha to Green Bay but absent from the western counties. There have been winters, such as 1958–1959 and 1968–1969, when most birds present in November and December disappear in January. There have been other winters, such as 1964–1965 and 1980–1981, when a sudden influx occurs in February and March and dissipates before the usual late-May migration period. In some winters the heaviest concentration of wintering waxwings in North America is recorded in the Florida region; in other winters the Louisiana-Texas area is most favored; in yet other winters the largest numbers occur still farther west. Some evidence of the varied fall movements of this species is provided by recoveries of two birds banded at Chippewa Falls by C. A. Kemper: one ringed on 28 July 1965 was killed at Worthington, Ohio, the following October; one banded on 2 August 1963 was killed at San Antonio, Texas, the following January. Who will unravel the mysterious winter movements of this species?

Family **Laniidae:** Shrikes

Northern Shrike (*Lanius excubitor*)

STATUS. Uncommon migrant. Uncommon winter resident.
HABITAT. Open grassland. Savanna. Residential areas.
MIGRATION DATES. *Fall:* mid-October to mid-December. *Spring:* late February to early April. *Extremes:* 6 September; 20 May.
WINTER. Present throughout the state in most years.
PORTRAIT. *Birds of Wisconsin:* Plate 64.

Northern Shrike

0   25   50 Mi
0 25 50 75 Km

☐ Winter range

Records since 1960

Ornithologists have long looked upon this hardy winter visitor with mixed feelings. On a typical winter field trip, when the variety of birds that can be found is severely limited, excitement abounds when a dark spot at the tip of a distant bare tree is transformed by binoculars or telescope into a live Northern Shrike. Probably there are dozens of Wisconsin Christmas bird counters who have reached the midafternoon hours feeling they have virtually exhausted the possibilities for adding a new species to the day's list, only to be surprised by the unexpected appearance of one of these boreal wanderers.

Those who operate feeding and banding stations, on the other hand, shudder when the sudden vanishing of small birds from the feeding areas announces the arrival of a "butcherbird" on the scene—though few tears are shed when the target is a House Sparrow. But this predator is not really choosy; it is as likely to pursue a chickadee or a junco. If the shrike takes a liking to a neighborhood and remains for several weeks, as occasionally happens, an entire winter feeding program may be affected.

It is mainly in January and February that shrikes are attracted to the birds congregating at feeders. The first fall arrivals generally appear in the northern counties between 10 and 20 October. The only northern arrival before 8 October that has been reported is one on 17 September (1966, Douglas, R. F. Bernard). Even earlier was the 6 September 1891 individual shot in Jefferson County (Kumlien and Hollister 1903). A few others have reached the southern counties by 25 October, but the 1–10 November period holds greater promise. One can scarcely think of a buildup following the first arrival dates, because the bird never becomes numerous. But sightings are more frequent as November and December progress. Observations are most likely in open fields and meadows where an occasional deciduous tree is present. The birds perch in treetops where they have a wide view in all directions, allowing them to spot the mice and small birds that will provide the next meal. Only rarely does this bird substitute a utility wire or pole for a treetop perch. I have sometimes watched a shrike fly fully half a mile to move from one tree to another, shunning utility poles that were much closer.

There has been a steady increase in CBC numbers since 1965. During the 1961–1965 interval this species appeared on nearly one-fourth of the December counts; rarely were more than three individuals recorded on any one count, nor did the cumulative shrike total for any one year exceed 30. By 1970, observers recorded birds on half the counts, and cumulative totals reached 60. By 1975 two-thirds of the counts listed the species, with sometimes as many as eight per count and cumulative totals approaching

456

100 per year. There are annual fluctuations, of course, but cumulative totals have risen as high as 162 (1976), 171 (1978), 193 (1981), and 278 (1985).

Little can be said about numbers in late winter, because comparatively little bird-watching takes place between early January and March. But the limited data do suggest that populations of late December remain stable through February. It is during March that most of the wintering birds move out of the state. Occasionally a March vagrant will be found uttering a few song fragments: an odd variety of chirps and warbles that follow no set pattern. This is the only time of year that one is likely to hear any vocalizations within Wisconsin's borders. The detection of spring departures becomes difficult because the similar Loggerhead Shrike arrives in early April. But reports are numerous through 10 April and occasional through the 20th. Exceptionally late were a sight record on 24 April (1978, Oneida, P. V. Vanderschaegen), a specimen collected on 29 April (1955, Waukesha, C. P. Fox), and a close sighting of a bird on 20 May (1967, Brown, T. C. Erdman).

Loggerhead Shrike (*Lanius ludovicianus*)
Formerly Migrant Shrike

STATUS. Uncommon migrant. Uncommon summer resident. Casual winter visitant south and central.
HABITAT. Savanna. Upland carr.
MIGRATION DATES. *Spring:* early April to mid-May. *Fall:* no noticeable flight; birds usually depart by 10 October.
BREEDING DATA. Nests with eggs: 21 April to 5 July. Clutch size: 4–6 eggs.
WINTER. Occasionally present north to St. Croix and Chippewa counties.
PORTRAIT. *Birds of Wisconsin:* Plate 64.

Since 1955, Wisconsin's summer shrike has been experiencing an alarming decline. The first edition of *Wisconsin Birds—Checklist with Migration Charts* (Barger et al. 1942) described the Loggerhead Shrike as common, continuing the designation previously given by Kumlien and Hollister (1903) and other early writers. When the 1942 *Wisconsin Birds* checklist was revised in 1960, the designation was changed to uncommon. During the 1947–1948 period Buss and Mattison (1955) located seven nests in the southern half of Dunn County alone. In 1967 and 1968 only seven nesting sites per year were reported in a cooperative survey, coordinated by Erdman (1970), which encompassed the entire state. So serious has the decline become that the Loggerhead Shrike was added to the Wisconsin Department of Natural Resources list of threatened species (Les 1979).

The reason for the decline is not clear. There have been no noticeable changes in the bird's habits or its preferred habitat. Now, as in earlier years, this predator shows a fondness for hedgerows and small trees that border flat cultivated fields. It is possible that roadside spraying by utility companies has affected the species, but much suitable habitat remains. There

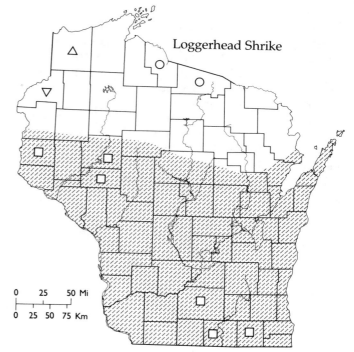

Loggerhead Shrike

0   25   50 Mi
0 25 50 75 Km

▨ Summer range
△ Early April to mid-May
○ Late May to mid-August
▽ Late August to late November
□ Early December to mid-February

Records since 1960

has been no marked change in the population of small mammals, birds, and insects that constitute the food supply for this species.

Before the decline set in, observers generally noted spring arrivals in the southern counties during the last week of March. Birds would appear during a warm spell on or soon after 25 March and promptly stake out a territory for subsequent nesting. The earliest arrival date—17 March—was recorded in Winnebago County in 1957 (N. M. Rogers). Wisconsin has had only two confirmed March arrival dates since 1963. Earliest sightings since then have usually come between 5 and 15 April. Since birds are sometimes found as late as 29 May in areas without a certain breeding pair, migration may still be in progress through May.

Well before then nesting has started for established pairs. Schorger (1931a) gave 26 April and 10 May as extreme dates for sets of fresh eggs in Dane County. C. H. Richter observed incubation starting between 21 April and 16 May for the seven nests he found in Oconto County (1925–1962). With young fledging in late May or early June, there is plenty of time for second nestings, but I know of no positive evidence of second broods.

All of Richter's nests were situated in hawthorn trees. Of eight Dunn County nests located in 1947–1948, Buss and Mattison (1955) found six in plum thickets, one in hawthorn, and one in poplar. Most nests are 4–8 feet above ground.

The accompanying map shows the location of recent summer records, mainly since the 1955–1965 decline, but also shows some modest gains since 1982. Although the map shows the summer range restricted to the southern two-thirds of the state (with the exception of records from Iron and Vilas counties), the summer range may be statewide in suitable habitat. The nesting range extends into Canada both east and west of Wisconsin. Migrant birds have been reported from Douglas and Burnett counties.

This species is fairly conspicuous when parents are feeding recently fledged young in June and early July. The birds become less noticeable in late July and August. By 15 September nearly all have left the state.

Birders who assume that any shrike seen after 15 October is bound to be a Northern may be right 99% of the time. But carefully observed Loggerheads have been noted on 26 October (1971, Oconto, T. C. Erdman), 29 October (1955, Pierce, Manley Olson; 1970, La Crosse, C. P. Frister), 2 November (1972, Burnett, W. L. Hilsenhoff), and 8 November (1914, Dane, N. D. Betts [Schorger 1931a]).

Still later were three December sightings: the 8th (1954, banded in Rock, M. T. Maxson), 20th (1971, Eau Claire, S. D. Robbins), and 21st (1977, Chippewa, S. D. Robbins). In Dane County a bird was observed intermittently from late November 1970 through 13 January 1971 (N. Ashman). The state's only other winter record came on 15 February 1978 when a Loggerhead visited a feeder in St. Croix County (R. E. Faanes). This species is regularly recorded, however, on the CBC in Iowa and central Illinois.

Observers need to exercise great care in shrike identification both in winter and during the periods in April and October when migration of Northerns and Loggerheads overlaps.

Family **Sturnidae:** Starlings

European Starling (*Sturnus vulgaris*)

STATUS. Abundant resident south and central; common resident north. Introduced.

HABITAT. Commercial areas. Farmsteads. Savanna.

MIGRATION DATES. *Spring:* late February to late April. *Fall:* early September to early November.

BREEDING DATA. Nests with eggs: 27 April to 19 June. Clutch size: usually 4 or 5 eggs; occasionally 3 or 6.

PORTRAIT. *Birds of Wisconsin:* Plate 78.

Introduced into New York in 1890, the European Starling gradually expanded westward, crossed the Appalachians and the Rockies, and began appearing in the Pacific states in 1940. Wisconsin's first sightings came in Milwaukee in 1923: emaciated specimens that succumbed to severe snow and cold on 17 February (Stoddard 1923c) and 12 March (G. W. Paine [Scott 1939d]). The first breeding record occurred 3 years later with the discovery of two nests near Waukesha on 13 and 28 June 1926 (S. P. Jones 1927). From that time on, the spread throughout the state was rapid. Birds reached Dane and Dunn counties in 1928, Brown and Oconto in 1929, Waupaca in 1930, Grant in 1931, Marathon by 1935, and Ashland and Barron by 1936.

Some idea of the rapid buildup in numbers can be seen from CBC figures. In the 1940s most counts were limited to the southern and eastern counties. By 1942, 100 or more birds per count were being recorded in Milwaukee, Racine, Jefferson, Dane, and Brown counties. With expanded coverage in the early 1950s, similar numbers were obtained in Green County in 1951; Winnebago in 1952; Iowa, Adams, and Marathon in 1953; Outagamie, La Crosse, and Trempealeau in 1954; and Chippewa in 1955. By 1955 Madison and Milwaukee counts numbered starlings in the thousands. The Milwaukee winter roost exceeded 50,000 in 1969 and subsequently zoomed to 150,000 (1976) and 200,000 (1981). Even without the benefit of the Milwaukee roost, this species would rank as one of the most numerous on Christmas counts, since it occurs on virtually every count in the state.

In summer, too, the starling now ranks as one of the state's most numerous species. BBS results show that only in heavily forested areas is this bird anything but abundant. Farms, villages, and other openings have attracted enough starlings to make them common in the north even though they avoid forests. By the time

European Starling

Breeding Bird Survey, averages 1966 to 1980

the BBS began in 1966, this stubby-tailed blackbird already outnumbered such abundant native species as the American Crow, American Robin, and Common Grackle. It was third in abundance behind the Red-winged Blackbird and House Sparrow.

One reason for the bird's rapid increase is its aggressive behavior toward other species, especially during the nesting season. By early April starlings seem to examine every old woodpecker hole that can be found in city, village, or farmyard. If another species has designs on the same nest site, it usually loses out to the starling. Although equipped with a sturdy beak, this bird does little or nothing to create its own nest cavities. But it will linger nearby while a Common Flicker or Red-headed Woodpecker makes an excavation, then drive out the would-be nester and take over the newly constructed site, and it may even remove eggs or young from a tree cavity. In downtown city areas, nests occur in crevices on tall buildings. In a 1941–1942 study of 70 Milwaukee nesting sites, Donald Bierman found 46 on city buildings, 16 occupying tree hollows in city parks, and 8 in bird houses.

Young birds are much in evidence from mid-June on. As the breeding season ends in rural areas, large flocks congregate in grainfields by day and in marshes at night—alone or in company with flocking Red-winged Blackbirds, Common Grackles, and Brown-headed Cowbirds. To the farmer the birds are a mixed blessing. On the one hand starlings are responsible for some grain damage in late summer and fall, while on the other hand they feed heavily on grasshoppers and other insect pests.

By late October the rural flocks dissipate. Some birds simply move to nearby urban centers and help build up huge winter roosts. Others migrate out of state. Recoveries of Wisconsin-banded birds have occurred as far away as Wichita, Kansas.

No conspicuous concentrations of early spring arrivals, have been noted, but numbers do start increasing in late February, and seem to build steadily through March and early April.

Family **Vireonidae**: Vireos

White-eyed Vireo (*Vireo griseus*)

STATUS. Uncommon spring migrant south; rare spring migrant central. Rare summer resident south.
HABITAT. Upland carr.
MIGRATION DATES. *Spring:* late April to early June. *Fall:* present until early September. *Extremes:* 17 April; 25 October.
BREEDING DATA. One probable breeding record.
WINTER. One December record.
PORTRAIT. *Birds of Wisconsin:* Plate 65.

Most Wisconsin sightings have been of spring migrants overshooting their regular Illinois range limit in May and early June. Through the 1960s, White-eyed Vireo observations came mainly from the Lake Michigan area between Kenosha and Sheboygan and in the Beloit-Madison region. North and west of these areas there were only single sightings in Grant, Vernon, Outagamie, and Manitowoc counties. The 1940s produced only one spring record, while an additional 10 occurred in the 1950s.

The banding of eight individuals and the sighting of two others during May of 1962, 1963, and 1964 at the Cedar Grove Ornithological Station in Sheboygan County hinted that this species might wander to southeastern Wisconsin more frequently than previously supposed. These bandings and sightings in the 1960s helped lift the number of spring records to 27.

An additional 54 spring reports came between 1970 and 1987, including wanderers in Eau Claire (1980, J. L. Polk), Buffalo (1975, T. C. Roskos; 1978, D. D. Tessen), La Crosse (1981, F. Z. Lesher) and Calumet (1975 and 1976, D. Tiede) counties. Most northerly was a singing male in Taylor County on 14 May 1982 (S. D. Robbins). Exceptionally early were April individuals on the 17th (1977, Milwaukee, J. H. Idzikowski), 19th (1976, Milwaukee, R. H. Sundell), 22nd (1976, Rock, M. Stabb), 23rd (1960, Rock, J. W. Wilde; 1965, Rock, M. K. Stocking), and 25th (1971, Racine, E. B. Prins).

Through 1966 all April and May birds appeared to be strictly transients that disappeared by 5 June. In 1967 one bird remained in Milwaukee through 14 June (M. F. Donald), and a pair remained near Mazomanie (Dane County) through 29 July 1972 (S. G. Martin). Four times in late June these Dane County birds were

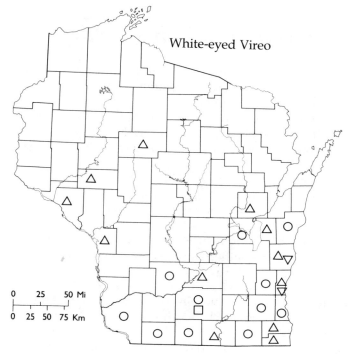

White-eyed Vireo

```
0      25      50 Mi
|———————|———————|
0   25  50  75 Km
```

△ Late April to early June
○ Mid-June to mid-August
▽ Late August to late October
□ 15 December

Records since 1960

observed carrying food, but no nest was found. Summering individuals were subsequently detected in 1971 (Sauk), 1976 (Manitowoc), 1978 (Grant, Lafayette), and 1979 (Walworth, Sauk, Dane, and Washington). A gradual range extension is clearly evident. Kumlien and Hollister (1903) thought of this bird as rare at best, penetrating no farther north than Jefferson County.

The origin of Wisconsin's eight autumn sightings is unknown. Some birds could have been within our borders undetected all summer; some could have wandered north in late summer. August observations occurred on the 20th (1980, Manitowoc, C. R. Sontag), 21st (1943, Dane, S. D. Robbins), 27th (1962, banded in Sheboygan, H. C. Mueller), and 31st (1946,

Milwaukee, G. H. Orians). Later finds turned up on 5 September (1980, Milwaukee, W. Woodmansee), 6 September (1980, Dane, R. M. Hoffman), 5 October (1962, banded in Sheboygan, H. C. Mueller), 21 October (1923, collected in Dane, A. W. Schorger [1924b]), and 25 October (1987, Ozaukee, R. M. Hoffman). Most astonishing was the 15 December 1979 individual found on the Madison CBC (W. L. Hilsenhoff).

Bell's Vireo (*Vireo bellii*)

STATUS. Uncommon migrant southwest; rare migrant southeast. Uncommon summer resident southwest.

HABITAT. Upland carr.

MIGRATION DATES. *Spring:* early May to early June. *Fall:* present until late September. *Extremes:* 1 May; 4 October.

BREEDING DATA. Nests with eggs: 28 May to 14 July. Clutch size: 3 or 4 eggs.

PORTRAIT. *Birds of Wisconsin:* Plate 65.

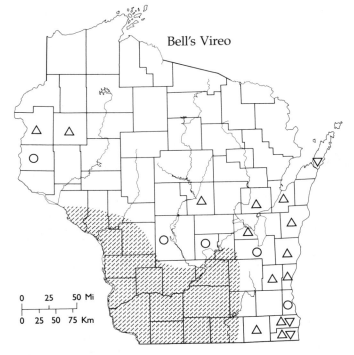

Bell's Vireo

⬚ Summer range
△ Early May to early June
○ Mid-June to early August
▽ Mid-August to late September

Records since 1960

When S. G. Martin (1972) reviewed Wisconsin records of this southern species, he reported clusters of observations at various points south and west of a line from Galesville through Madison to Beloit, and recommended a "locally common" designation for that region. Some clusters had persevered there for 30 or more years.

The Bell's Vireo did not appear among lists of nineteenth-century Wisconsin ornithologists. The state's first record involved a specimen taken in Dane County on 3 July 1914 by A. W. Schorger (Betts 1914). A nest with one egg was discovered by Warner Taylor (1922b) in the same area on 9 June 1922. Schorger (1931a) found several nesting pairs south of Boscobel (Grant County) between 1925 and 1928, and described the birds as locally common there.

My preference for the "uncommon" designation stems from the fact that areas of known summer colonies are few and far between. One area, encompassing French Island and the airport in La Crosse County, has attracted up to five nesting pairs off and on since 1942. Two colonies near Mazomanie (Dane County) have had nesting pairs frequently since 1949. The Madison region where the first bird was recorded in 1914 continues to have one or two pairs nearly every year.

The state's largest colony through the 1960s was in southwestern Trempealeau County. Singing males were present each year from 1960 to 1976. Although no complete census was ever taken, Kenneth Krumm and I counted 13 singers on 17 June 1970 and esti-

mated a probable 20 nesting pairs. A 1930 record at nearby Winona, Minnesota, suggests that this cluster may have existed for many years. The colony disappeared when a prairie restoration project resulted in the destruction of the large grove of black locust trees that provided a home base for these soft-voiced singers.

Outside of these colonies, the Bell's Vireo is known primarily as a rare breeder in the southwestern counties. Since 1950, there have been June and July observations in Buffalo, Jackson, Monroe, Vernon, Crawford, Sauk, Iowa, Lafayette, Green, Rock, Columbia,

Green Lake, and Dodge counties. Exceptional summer sightings involved birds in St. Croix (17 June 1977, C. A. Faanes; 3 July 1963, S. D. Robbins), Juneau (24 June 1978, R. M. Hoffman), and Milwaukee (7 July 1977, D. E. Frister) counties.

Most spring migrants arrive on territory between 10 and 20 May, with the earliest noted on the 1st (1944, Dane, G. Koehler) and 6th (1970, La Crosse, J. R. Rosso). It is during the same period that an occasional vagrant appears outside the breeding range. Observers have noted overshooting spring migrants as far north as Polk, Barron, Portage, Outagamie, and Brown counties. In most instances the bird's presence is detected by its song: a varied warble suggestive of the Warbling Vireo but with a more abrupt ending. Often the Bell's gives two phrases in close succession, alternating a different inflection at the end of each. With a bit of poetic license one might imagine that the songster is first posing a question and then providing the answer.

In addition to its favorite black locusts, the Bell's Vireo is also fond of other types of low-growing vegetation. In Madison it has been found in hawthorn and lilac clumps, at Mazomanie in alder thickets, and near Boscobel in hazel brush. Most nests have been located from 2 to 5 feet up, well concealed in thick foliage, but there are exceptions. One nest was located at a height of 16 feet, and, at the other extreme, I once nearly stepped on a well-hidden nest scarcely 1 foot above ground. Nesting occupies most of July as well as June, with young in the nest reported as late as 24 July.

Birds apparently remain in the nesting territory throughout August and early September. Unlike many birds whose song periods end by early July, this vireo often sings well into August. Song fragments have also led to most of the September records, usually concentrated in the first 10 days of the month.

Fall wanderers in 1974 were noted by Louise Erickson north and east to Door (3 September), Racine (28 September), and Kenosha (3 October) counties. These dates and a 4 October 1973 individual she observed in Kenosha County constitute Wisconsin's latest records.

Gray Vireo (*Vireo vicinior*)

STATUS. Accidental. One record.
HABITAT. Upland carr.

This straggler from the far Southwest was trapped at the Cedar Grove Ornithological Station in Sheboygan County on 3 October 1964 by H. C. Mueller and D. D. Berger (1966). They collected the specimen, determined that it was an immature female, and donated it to the collection of the Zoological Museum of the University of Wisconsin. No known reason can be offered for the appearance of this exotic so far from its normal range. The AOU *Check-list of North American Birds* (1983) lists Oklahoma and Utah as the points nearest to Wisconsin for even a casual observation. This is over 1,000 miles from Cedar Grove!

Solitary Vireo (*Vireo solitarius*)

STATUS. Uncommon migrant. Uncommon summer resident north.

HABITAT. Northern maple-hemlock-pine forest. Coniferous forest.

MIGRATION DATES. *Spring:* late April to late May. *Fall:* late August to mid-October. *Extremes:* 17 April; 9 December.

BREEDING DATA. Nests with eggs: 6–21 June. Clutch size: 4 eggs.

PORTRAIT. *Birds of Wisconsin:* Plate 65.

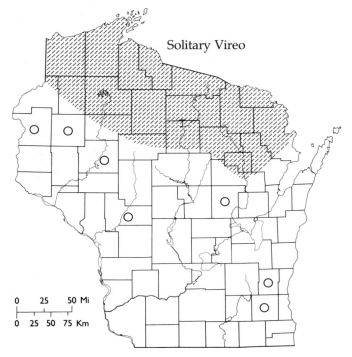

Solitary Vireo

▨ Summer range
○ Early June to early August

Records since 1960

The Solitary Vireo rivals the Warbling Vireo for the honor of being the first vireo to arrive in late April. A few are seen from the 28th on nearly every year, with early stragglers noted on the 17th (1950, Dane, P. H. Greeley; 1974, La Crosse, J. R. Rosso), 20th (1980, Milwaukee, J. H. Idzikowski), and 23rd (1969, Dane, D. D. Tessen). The Solitary Vireo has appeared as far north as St. Croix and Manitowoc counties by 1 May, but usually it is not until 10 May that first arrivals make it to the northern counties. Spring migrants rarely travel alone; they are usually found one or two at a time in company with flocks of the earlier-arriving warblers (Yellow-rumped, Black-and-white, Nashville) and Ruby-crowned Kinglets. By the time the later-arriving warblers put in their appearance in mid-May, the majority of Solitaries have moved on. Yet an occasional migrant may linger south of the breeding range until the last week of May. This bird shows no narrow habitat preferences during migration; it is sometimes found well up in the taller trees, sometimes in low, dense shrubbery, and it is equally at home in deciduous and coniferous vegetation.

During the breeding season the bird typically prefers mixed woods: spruce or hemlock mixed with maple and birch. I know of only a handful of nests in recent years, and these have been located in white birches, 10–20 feet up.

The Solitary has been detected on 17 of the state's 70 BBS transects from Douglas and northern Polk counties east to Langlade and Forest counties. But the numbers are consistently small. Unlike the ubiquitous Red-eyed Vireo, which can be found in numbers of 50–100 on a morning field trip in the north woods, the Solitaries can usually be counted on the fingers of one hand.

Numbers remain similarly small throughout a rather prolonged fall migration. First arrivals south of the breeding range are occasionally noted in the last week of August and have been known as early as 13 August (1953, Adams, S. D. Robbins). The more usual time is from 5 September on. Although not numerous at any time, the bird is seen most frequently in northern Wisconsin from 1 September through 10 October and in the southern counties from 15 September through 20 October. During this period the birds move freely with mixed flocks of other migrating vireos and warblers; they can be found in almost any kind of shrub or tree. The Solitary is often the last of the vireos to depart, out-lingering most of the fall warblers, except the Yellow-rumped. The Solitary has remained in the north as late as 21 October (1966, Douglas, M. Granlund) and in the central region until 17 November (1974, Sheboygan, H. Koopmann). In the south, Dane County has hosted three very late individuals: 9 November (1959, T. L. Ashman), 12 November (1966, J. T. Emlen), and one that was singing on 9 December (1973, G. W. Foster).

Ornithologists in the nineteenth century occasionally found this species during summer in the southeastern counties. Now, nearly all June and July sightings occur only in the northern forest region. But I detected June singing males near Black River Falls (Jackson County) in 1972 and 1978, and Bielefeldt (1981) noted five singers in Waukesha County in 1979 and 1980, with an unsuccessful nesting recorded in 1980.

Yellow-throated Vireo (*Vireo flavifrons*)

STATUS. Fairly common migrant. Fairly common summer resident south and central; uncommon summer resident north.
HABITAT. Deciduous forest. Residential areas.
MIGRATION DATES. *Spring:* early to late May. *Fall:* late August to late September. *Extremes:* 23 April; 13 October.
BREEDING DATA. Nests with eggs: 19 May to 4 July. Clutch size: 3 or 4 eggs.
PORTRAIT. *Birds of Wisconsin:* Plate 65.

A glance at the accompanying BBS map shows a wide distribution for the Yellow-throated Vireo throughout nearly all parts of the state. Records exist for every county. Some confusion exists about its presence in the northern areas in earlier years. Kumlien and Hollister (1903) listed this bird for "all parts of the state" but gave no specific northern records. Jackson (1943) did not find the bird during his studies in the northwest in 1919. Gromme (1963) knew of but a handful of records north of a line from Grantsburg through Wisconsin Rapids to Oconto. Most of the northern observations have come since 1955, with a first nesting record for Douglas County in 1963 (Bernard 1964). But since fieldwork in the north was only sporadic before that time, one cannot be sure that these birds are of only recent occurrence there.

The BBS map also indicates that the bird is not common anywhere in the state. The largest number recorded on any one BBS transect is 9, while the largest tally for all 70 transects in any one year is 68.

The Yellow-throated Vireo shows a strong preference for mature deciduous woods during the nesting season. Maples are acceptable, but oaks are preferred. In the northern counties large maple stands offer what should be suitable habitat, but the few birds that have been found in the north have been in oaks.

This vireo spends much time in the middle or upper elevations of the higher trees. Here feeding takes place, and here the male perches as he utters the brief hoarse, drawling phrases that make up his song. Because nests are located high up in the leafy canopy— at heights of 10–38 feet—few have been observed.

The spring migration period is short. The first warm spell at the beginning of May brings the first migrants to southern areas, and within 2 weeks— sometimes only 10 days—the northern counties get

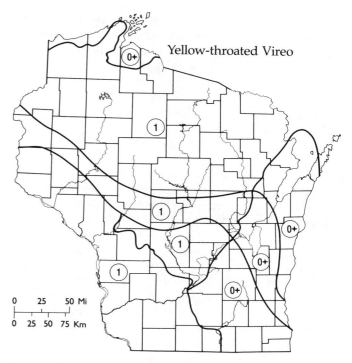

Yellow-throated Vireo

Breeding Bird Survey, averages 1966 to 1980

their first arrivals. Only nine times since 1960 has an individual been detected in April and then only in the last 7 days of the month. The earliest report for the state is a 23 April bird seen in Sauk County in 1986 (K. I. Lange). By the time the more abundant Red-eyed Vireo arrives in numbers, around 20 May, the Yellow-throated Vireo has virtually completed its migration. Nest construction has been reported as early as 17 May, with eggs being laid and incubated by the end of the month.

Few observers have detected enough of a buildup to speak of a pronounced fall migration. But residents usually disappear from the northern counties between 25 August and 5 September, while in the southern counties there may be a slight buildup during the first 10 days of September. Only a few birds have been seen after the 20th. Several early October observations in the southern counties, supported by a few television tower casualties, prove that at least a little fall migration persists through 10 October in some years. A late date for central Wisconsin was 10 October (1961, Chippewa, C. A. Kemper) and for the south 13 October (1954, Milwaukee, H. A. Bauers).

Warbling Vireo (*Vireo gilvus*)

STATUS. Common summer resident west and central; fairly common summer resident east and north.
HABITAT. Residential areas. Farmsteads. Savanna.
MIGRATION DATES. *Spring:* early to late May. *Fall:* mid-August to mid-September. *Extremes:* 19 April; 14 November.
BREEDING DATA. Nests with eggs: 27 May to 20 June. Clutch size: 3 or 4 eggs.
PORTRAIT. *Birds of Wisconsin:* Plate 65.

Virtually all previous Wisconsin writers have referred to the Warbling Vireo as a common or abundant species. How long it remains common depends on how these birds adjust to the loss of elms from Dutch elm disease.

Indeed, a modest decline is evident from a comparison of BBS results for 1966–1969 with those for 1978–1980. All 70 BBS routes have listed this species, but while the average number of birds per transect per year was 4.08 for the 1966–1969 interval, and 4.14 for 1970–1973, the figure dropped to 3.14 for the 1974–1977 span, 2.93 for 1978–1981, and 2.75 for 1982–1985.

The BBS shows a statewide population, with the strongest concentration in the west-central area. Among the taller trees in city parks and residential areas, and often in shade trees surrounding farm dwellings, this inconspicuously marked bird announces its presence with its lazy warbling song. Were it not for the song, this would appear to be a rather uncommon species, for it is relatively inactive in movement and is easily concealed among the leaves.

Most Warbling Vireos spend scarcely 4 months in the state: from 10 May to 10 September. With remarkable consistency the first state arrival each year since 1955 has appeared between 26 April and 7 May; the only exception is E. O. Paulson's record-breaking 19 April 1957 bird at Green Bay. General arrivals disperse rapidly across the state in the 5–15 May period. By 20 May in the south and 25 May in the north, birds are ready to begin nesting.

Nests are more often found in late May and June, 10–35 feet up in elms, but maples, willows, and poplars have also been reported as nesting sites. Oologist J. N. Clark (1897b) once collected seven sets of eggs in one 2-day period (28–29 May 1896) and found that all seven pairs were incubating second clutches within 11 days.

Warbling Vireo

Breeding Bird Survey, averages 1966 to 1980

Although no positive nesting activity has been recorded beyond early July, an occasional song reminds us of the bird's continued presence through July and August. The fall flight is a very inconspicuous one, occurring mostly in the latter half of August. If the first few days in September are mild, these birds remain in modest numbers through that period. But once the first cool snap occurs in September, they disappear. Banders report very few birds after 10 September. Towerkills have also been few; the fact that only 23 Warblings have been found among over 50,000 vireo and warbler casualties at Eau Claire in the 1960–1971 period indicates further that most of the fall migration has ended before September. Yet nearly every year one or more late stragglers remain into October, with two recorded instances at La Crosse through the 18th (1968, F. Z. Lesher; 1970, J. R. Rosso). Most remarkable, however, is the bird banded at the Cedar Grove Ornithological Station in Sheboygan County on 14 November 1962 (H. C. Mueller). Birds are normally gone from the entire United States before the end of October.

Philadelphia Vireo (*Vireo philadelphicus*)

STATUS. Uncommon spring migrant; fairly common fall migrant.

HABITAT. Deciduous forest. Upland carr.

MIGRATION DATES. *Spring:* early May to early June. *Fall:* late August to early October. *Extremes:* 29 April, 7 June; 4 August, 12 November.

PORTRAIT. *Birds of Wisconsin:* Plate 65.

Of the five species of vireos that visit all parts of Wisconsin, the Philadelphia Vireo is the least common as a spring migrant. Published sight records in *The Passenger Pigeon* usually number fewer than 10 per spring. Few birds are banded. Only 20 of the 2,000 spring warblers and vireos killed at the Eau Claire television tower between 1960 and 1972 belonged to this species.

The Philadelphia is one of the later spring migrants. April arrivals have been detected on the 29th (1962, Columbia, R. B. Dryer; 1970, Dane, T. L. Ashman) and 30th (1967, Dane, C. R. Sontag), but first arrivals usually occur between 1 and 10 May. Observations fall mainly in the 15–25 May period, coinciding with the heavy migration of the similarly marked Red-eyed Vireo. Banding and towerkill data show that a few late migrants are present during the first week of June. The latest record is an individual banded on 7 June (1963, Sheboygan, H. C. Mueller).

It is not inconceivable that a few pairs might remain in northern Wisconsin to breed, for the known breeding range touches northern Minnesota and Upper Michigan. Among the thousands of Red-eyed Vireos that fill the northern Wisconsin maple forests with their incessant songs in June, there could be a Philadelphia, whose vocal offering is so similar to the Red-eye's that the average listener would never detect the difference. No positive state record exists between 7 June and 4 August.

Early August arrivals include birds on the 4th (1954, Chippewa, C. A. Kemper), 12th (1940, Price, J. L. Diedrich; 1961, Washburn, W. E. Southern), 14th (1960, Washburn, W. E. Southern), and 18th (1929, Oneida, A. W. Schorger). The more typical first arrival period is 25–31 August in the north and central areas, and 1–5 September in the south. Then, for a brief 3-week period, 10–30 September, this bird migrates through in numbers far greater than one would expect on the basis of the spring flight. Most vivid evidence is the total of 2,457 Eau Claire tower casualties during the 1960–1971 period (4.8% of 50,000 warbler and vireo specimens). Banding records show a significant increase in fall. My personal observations over the past 35 years indicate four times as many birds seen in fall as in spring, although I spent approximately the same number of hours afield.

As the mixed flocks of flycatchers, thrushes, warblers, and vireos build toward a peak around 15 September in the north and a week later in the south, the chance of finding the Philadelphia Vireo increases. It is found in mixed groups of passerines but is often overlooked because it may be less active than some of the warblers. One looks for this bird not high in the canopy but among the lower tree branches and in the bushes.

Most birds are gone from the northern and central counties by 1 October and from the south by 10 October. Beyond the 25th are three November records: one bird banded on the 3rd (1956, Marinette, W. N. MacBriar), one banded on the 6th (1965, Waushara, I. Chipman), and one seen on the 12th (1969, Milwaukee, O. R. Lemke). Although extreme dates encompass a 3-month span, from 4 August to 12 November, the probability is that 95% or more of the fall migrants pass through the state in the 1-month interval between 5 September and 5 October.

The comparative paucity of spring records is not easy to explain. No banding recovery data exist to provide clues to the origin of breeding birds that pass through in the fall. The migration path extends modestly west of the state, but nowhere are numbers of spring Philadelphias known to be significantly greater than in Wisconsin. Since the song resembles that of the Red-eye so closely, and the migration period coincides with that of this more abundant relative, it is entirely possible that Philadelphias pass through unnoticed in spring—missed entirely if the birds are silent, passed off as Red-eyes if they are singing.

Red-eyed Vireo (*Vireo olivaceus*)

STATUS. Abundant migrant. Abundant summer resident north; common summer resident south and central.
HABITAT. Deciduous forest. Northern maple-hemlock-pine forest. Upland carr.
MIGRATION DATES. *Spring:* early May to early June. *Fall:* mid-August to mid-October. *Extremes:* 19 April; 17 November.
BREEDING DATA. Nests with eggs: 20 May to 14 July. Clutch size: 3 or 4 eggs.
PORTRAIT. *Birds of Wisconsin:* Plate 65.

The Red-eyed Vireo has been recorded only seven times in April: the 19th (1957, Brown, E. O. Paulson), 25th (1987, Sauk, K. I. Lange), 26th (1985, Polk, P. Fuller), 27th (1986, Milwaukee, R. P. Gutschow), 28th (1976, La Crosse, J. R. Rosso; 1984, Milwaukee, R. P. Gutschow), 29th (1970, Milwaukee, D. K. Gustafson), and 30th (1941, Marinette, C. H. Richter; 1942, Vilas, W. S. Feeney). The 19 April date is exceptional. Birds must travel 5,000 miles from their wintering grounds to reach Wisconsin; usually they reach only the southern states by mid-April.

A few early arrivals reach the southern counties between 1 and 10 May each year, but most first sightings occur between the 10th and 15th. Warm weather occasionally brings early stragglers to the northern counties by the 10th, but a more usual time is between the 15th and 20th. During the final 10 days a veritable flood blankets the state. This species dominates the last of the major passerine waves in spring, and can be found in almost any grove of deciduous trees. Late migrants are often still passing through between 1 and 5 June.

As a nester this is the most common bird of the north woods, being particularly abundant in the poplars, birches, and maples. The BBS shows it as far less numerous in the more open spaces of southern Wisconsin; but enough farm woodlots exist to provide birds on all of the state's 70 transects. Throughout the northern forests the bird is present in large numbers (88 on one 4-hour BBS transect in 1980). Wherever suitable woodlands exist, this is a conspicuous nester because of its vigorous, incessant song that can be heard at any time of day. Even in late morning and early afternoon, when most other birds are silent, the short vigorous phrases of the "preacher bird" keep ringing from the leafy canopy.

Nesting activities sometimes begin by 25 May. Nests are usually located 10–25 feet up in deciduous trees, but they have also been found in pines and spruces.

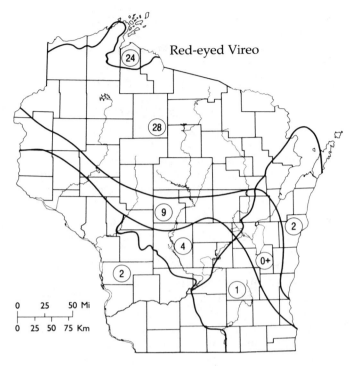

Breeding Bird Survey, averages 1966 to 1980

A few have been noted as low as 5 feet and as high up as 35 feet. One has been found in a small shrub only 2 feet from the ground. The usual clutch of three or four eggs is often augmented by one or two Brown-headed Cowbird eggs. One nest was reported to include two vireo and four cowbird eggs. Nests with eggs have been found frequently in early July, with young still present in the nest as late as 29 July. Although song gradually decreases during the last half of the month, the call note is evident: a distinctive whinelike note rapidly descending in pitch. When sounds of baby birds calling for food are heard in the poplars, birches, oaks, and maples in late summer, more often than not they come from members of a Red-eyed Vireo family. Young are still being fed in mid-August as migration-time approaches.

Fall migration gets under way by 20 August. In 1961 the list of television tower casualties at Eau Claire included 21 Red-eyed Vireos on 25 August and another 318 just 4 days later. Fall migration is heavy in the northern counties through 15 September, tapering to just a trickle by the 25th. In the southern counties the peak occurs between the 10th and the 25th. Heavy towerkills of over 100 Red-eyed Vireos per night have been recorded at Eau Claire 14 times since 1957, all between 28 August and 23 September. A few birds remain in the central counties through the first week of October, and in the south as late as the 15th nearly every year.

It is highly unusual for individuals to linger into November, but I know of five such records: the 1st (1968, Dane, J. T. Emlen), 3rd (1970, Outagamie, D. D. Tessen), 5th (1952, Milwaukee, I. N. Balsom), 15th (1971, Milwaukee, E. L. Basten), and 17th (1971, Rock, G. Mahlum). Early November is considered late even for Louisiana!

Family **Emberizidae:** Wood-Warblers, Tanagers, Buntings, Sparrows, Blackbirds, and Allies

Blue-winged Warbler (*Vermivora pinus*)

STATUS. Uncommon migrant south and central. Uncommon summer resident south and west-central; rare summer resident east.
HABITAT. Southern silver maple–elm forest. Upland and lowland carr.
MIGRATION DATES. *Spring:* early to late May. *Fall:* present until 15 September. *Extremes:* 23 April; 10 November.
BREEDING DATA. Nests with eggs: 17 May to 24 June. Clutch size: 4–6 eggs.
PORTRAIT. *Birds of Wisconsin:* Plate 66.

When I first heard the nasal two-buzz song of the Blue-winged Warbler, I was reminded of the uncomplimentary sound emitted by a teenage schoolboy who reacted to teacher discipline (out of earshot, of course) by sticking out his tongue and seemingly saying "Aw, fudge." Aside from this unmusical offering, however, all connotations with this brilliant yellow bird are entirely favorable.

The Blue-wing is one of our rarest regularly appearing spring warblers. Even in the southwestern corner, where it is most frequently found, this bird is by no means numerous.

Summer observations have occurred frequently in suitable habitat as far north as St. Croix, Dunn, Trempealeau, Juneau, Adams, Marquette, Fond du Lac, and Manitowoc counties. In addition, there have been isolated summer sightings in Washburn (1956, A. Sprunt), Sawyer (1985, J. L. Polk), Clark (1981, S. D. Robbins), Langlade (1970, L. J. Schimmels), Shawano (1984, M. S. Peterson), and Door (1980, R. P. Gutschow) counties. And May records have come from Burnett, Rusk, Chippewa, Ashland, Portage, Winnebago, Outagamie, and Brown counties. Some of these records may involve birds temporarily overshooting the regular range; some may represent established populations that have escaped previous discovery; some may represent new range extensions only now taking place.

This species has extended its range markedly over the past 50 years. P. R. Hoy never found one at Racine in the 1850s. Thure Kumlien (Kumlien and Hollister 1903) procured the first state specimen in 1867 in Jefferson County. An 1885 specimen collected by C. H.

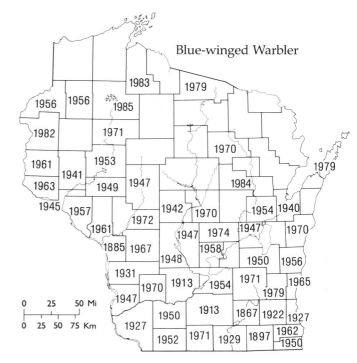

Blue-winged Warbler

Years of first county records

Stoddard at La Crosse was the second (Grundtvig 1895). Not until 1897 did Hollister (1901a) start finding the Blue-winged Warbler regularly near Delavan (Walworth County). The bird was unknown to J. N. Clark in Dunn County at that time. So little investigation took place in the southwestern corner of the state in those years that no one can say when the birds first became well established there. Stoddard (1917) found them in Dane and Sauk counties from 1913 on. In 1923, A. W. Schorger and Warner Taylor (1926b) found them numerous in the Wisconsin and Mississippi river bottoms and presumed they had been well established for years. By 1941 Irven Buss (Buss and Mattison 1955) was finding them in Dunn County. I have found a few regularly in Adams County from 1952 on. By 1955 a population had become well established in eastern Fond du Lac County (J. Vogelsang).

When Taylor and Schorger began finding significant numbers in the 1920s, they found the birds in the wooded river bottomlands. This is still favored habitat, but the Blue-wing has now spread to the wooded hillsides of the western coulees. A third type of habitat, as yet used sparingly in Wisconsin, consists of relatively small deciduous trees on the edge of fairly open pasture. It is in this habitat, as well as in some of the bottomland, that this bird is most apt to encounter the Golden-winged Warbler with which interbreeding sometimes takes place.

Arrival dates for the southern counties vary from 28 April to 7 May, the 23 April individual (1973, Waukesha, R. H. Sundell) being exceptionally early. In the central counties arrivals are generally a week later. Numbers are too small to designate migration peaks, but if an observer is going to find a bird outside its usual breeding haunts, it will probably happen during the 10–25 May period. Supportive evidence is given by Eau Claire television tower casualties on 13 May 1972, 23 May 1963, and 25 May 1961 (C. A. Kemper).

Little is known about nesting activities. The few nests that have been discovered have all been located on the ground, in grassy tufts concealed by shrubbery. In 1899 Hollister (1901a) found nest construction under way on 14 May, with a first egg laid on the 17th and a full clutch of six eggs present on the 22nd. In Sauk County a nest with five eggs was discovered on 25 May 1977 (M. J. Mossman), and a nest with six young was located on 16 June 1979 (P. Urbanski). Apparently the nesting schedule is slightly ahead of that for most other warblers.

Once song ceases in early July, this bird is rarely seen. But it is found occasionally on its breeding grounds through August. Scattered migrants are found nearly every year until 15 September. Later September sightings include birds on the 20th (1957, Chippewa, C. A. Kemper), 24th (1967, Milwaukee, M. F. Donald), and 29th (1971, La Crosse, J. R. Rosso). October lingerers are known for the 1st (1972, Vernon, V. E. Weber), 9th (1954, Sheboygan, H. C. Mueller), and 31st (1964, Sheboygan, H. C. Mueller). Philip Ashman's straggler seen in Dane County on 10 November 1978 was feeding on goldenrod stalks and on the ground, in company with a Dark-eyed Junco.

Golden-winged Warbler (*Vermivora chrysoptera*)

STATUS. Fairly common migrant. Fairly common summer resident central and north; rare summer resident south.

HABITAT. Southern silver maple–elm forest. Upland and lowland carr.

MIGRATION DATES. *Spring:* early to late May. *Fall:* early August to mid-September. *Extremes:* 26 April; 17 October.

BREEDING DATA. Nests with eggs: 27 May to 28 June. Clutch size: usually 4 or 5 eggs; occasionally 3.

PORTRAIT. *Birds of Wisconsin:* Plate 66.

Previous writers have designated the Golden-winged Warbler's breeding range as statewide. Formerly, this was so, and possibly an occasional summer record may still come from the southernmost tier of counties. But people living along the Mississippi and lower St. Croix rivers find very few of these birds either as migrants or summer residents. Those living close to Lake Michigan find them only in small numbers during migration, and as summer residents only in an occasional pocket such as the Cedarburg Bog in Ozaukee County. In Dane and Rock counties Goldenwings are known only as spring and fall migrants. But from Sauk County north, both to the northwest and the northeast, this bird is a fairly common summer resident. Small isolated pockets also exist in east-

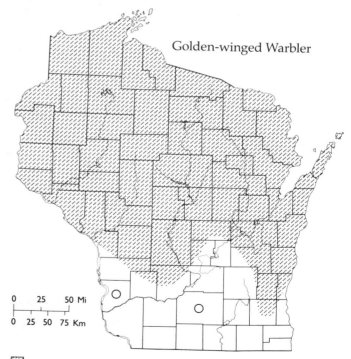

Golden-winged Warbler

0   25   50 Mi

0   25 50 75 Km

▨ Summer range
○ Early June to late July

Records since 1960

ern Wisconsin, south through the Kettle Moraine State Forest.

The most favored habitat is the dense deciduous brushy area that borders small creeks and swamps. Such habitat abounds in the bed of the ancient Glacial Lake Wisconsin in Jackson, Juneau, Wood, Adams, and Waushara counties. The BBS transects show the species to be most numerous along a band from this region northwest to Douglas County. Small numbers can be found throughout northern Wisconsin where suitable brushy, swampy habitat exists. Birds are sometimes found along the edges of tamarack-spruce bogs, but otherwise usually avoid conifers. The Golden-wing has been listed on 49 of the state's 70 BBS routes but is consistently found on only 17 routes.

First arrivals almost always appear around 2 May. Eleven times in the 1951–1985 period the first state migrant was sighted on that date, and only five times did the first arrival date vary more than 4 days from that day. The spread throughout the state is rapid, so that by 10 May migrants have often reached the northern counties. Peak periods are 10–20 May in the south, 5 days later farther north. Migrants rarely remain after the 25th.

The songs of the Golden-wing vary. Field guides generally describe two song types: a series of three or four distinctly separate buzzes on two different levels of pitch, and a series of four to six notes run together rapidly, succeeded by two slower notes and a final sustained buzz. I have heard Wisconsin birds give at least seven different songs. Three of these are variations of the first type, in which there may be as few as two notes, or the pitch may remain constant. The others are variations in length, rhythm, or pitch of the second type. One is led to wonder how many of these variations come from birds who have both Golden-wing and Blue-wing ancestry. In June 1960 T. K. Soulen found a male Golden-wing singing a typical Blue-wing song in Menominee County. The bird sings frequently during the early morning hours through June, sometimes from a conspicuous high perch, more often from the underbrush; but it is not often heard after the first few days of July.

While the male is singing, the female is engrossed in nesting activity. Carl Richter has described six nests in Oconto County. All were located on the ground, well concealed by grass, nettles, or jewelweed.

Birders who wait until September to observe the fall warbler migration see few of these birds, because much of the migration takes place in August. Occasional observations of migrants have been made during the first week of August, with sightings becoming frequent by the 20th. By 10 September nearly all Golden-wings have left the northern region; after another 10 days only a few stragglers remain in the south. On six occasions these stragglers have remained into October; the latest being Sheboygan County birds on the 15th (1964, H. C. Mueller) and 17th (1962, H. C. Mueller).

Vermivora Warbler Hybrids:
Brewster's Warbler, Lawrence's Warbler

STATUS. Rare migrant south and central. Rare summer resident south and west-central.

HABITAT. Southern silver maple–elm forest. Lowland carr.

MIGRATION DATES. *Spring:* late April to late May. *Fall:* present until early September. *Extremes:* 26 April; 4 September.

BREEDING DATA. Nests with young: 12 July.

With the spread of the Blue-winged Warbler into the state, there has come an accompanying vivid spread of hybrids between Golden-wings and Blue-wings. One hybrid, the Brewster's Warbler, was unknown in the state until the late 1930s. One of the first issues of *The Passenger Pigeon* (1939:49) made an indefinite reference to a sight observation in Madison, but listed no date, observer, or substantiating details. During the next decade observers sighted birds on 16 May 1943 (Dane, L. Koehler), 20 and 30 May 1947 (Clark, S. D. Robbins), 20 May 1948 (Milwaukee, M. F. Donald), and 31 May 1949 (Eau Claire, L. Almon).

By 1950 one or more were being found every year. The 1950s produced records of at least 23 birds, some of which involved summer residents in Dane and Adams counties. Another 28 records have been published for the 1960s; of these, six were banded birds, and two were specimens: one collected in Washburn County on 23 August 1961 (Southern 1962b), the other picked up dead at the Eau Claire television tower on 4 September 1961 (C. A. Kemper; donated to the University of Minnesota collection).

Among another 22 published accounts in the 1970s was a nesting record in Washington County in 1979. On 12 and 13 July, Judy Haseleu observed two parent Brewster's Warblers bringing food to young in a well-concealed ground nest. Two areas where this hybrid has been found nearly every year through the 1970s are the Baraboo hills in Sauk County and the Kettle Moraine State Forest in Waukesha County. In the latter area, J. E. Bielefeldt located singing males at five spots in June 1978. The counties in which observers have found birds since 1939 are shown in the accompanying map. The range approximates closely that of the Blue-winged Warbler.

The Lawrence's Warbler hybrid was first found on 15 May 1947 (Winnebago, E. Fisher) and 11 June 1947 (Sauk, H. C. Kruse). One sighting in the 1950s (2 June 1954, Waukesha, E. W. Peartree) was followed by three in the 1960s: 25 August 1966 (banded at Manitowoc, B. N. Brouchoud), 26 April 1969 (Waukesha,

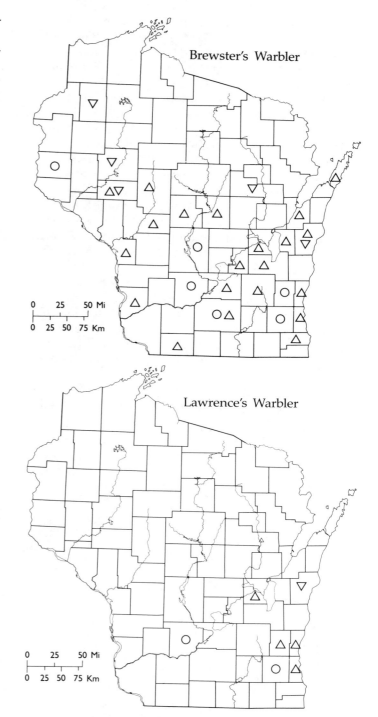

Brewster's Warbler

Lawrence's Warbler

△ Late April to late May
O Early June to late July
▽ Early August to early September

All records

O. L. Compton), and from late May through 10 June 1969 (Sauk, T. L. Ashman). One was photographed on 13 May 1973 (Milwaukee, O. R. Lemke), and another noted between 15 and 18 May 1973 (Waukesha, E. M. Leppla). The Waukesha County area has continued to be productive, with observations on 5 June 1978, 8 May 1979, and 10 May 1980 (J. E. Bielefeldt). The state's 12th, 13th, and 14th records were established on 10 May 1980 (Milwaukee, H. A. Bauers), 16 May 1981 (Ozaukee, J. T. Harris), and 25 May 1987 (Sauk, R. M. Hoffman). A 15th followed on 14 May 1988 (Washington, N. Zehner).

Most unusual of all the *Vermivora* hybrid records is that described by Hollister in May 1899 in Walworth County (Kumlien and Hollister 1903). On the 14th a female Blue-wing was discovered building a nest in a tuft of grass, and by the 17th it had laid one egg. By the 22nd the nest contained six eggs. Since this was the first known nesting record for this species in the state, Hollister collected the female as it flushed from the nest. Half an hour later the male appeared, showed the expected parental anxiety, and was then collected. But when Hollister examined the specimen, he discovered it was a male Nashville Warbler, with enormously developed testes. Wrote Hollister, "There is not a shadow of a doubt that this bird was the male parent of the clutch of eggs; no one could question that for a moment who had seen his actions at the nest."

No other instance of cross-mating of the Nashville and the Blue-wing is known. It is unfortunate that the true identity of the nesting pair was not known before the birds were collected. As Hollister expressed it: "Possibly in our haste to positively identify this rare Wisconsin take, more interesting hybrids between the Blue-winged and allied species were destroyed in embryo; as had we known the true state of affairs, the eggs would have been allowed to hatch unmolested in the hope of further developments."

The birds identified as Lawrence's all showed the typical plumage: yellow crown and breast, black throat and ear patch, white wing bars. Among the Brewster's some unusual variations have been noted. Although most of those whose plumage has been documented displayed the typical white throat, yellow wing bars, and wash on the upper breast, several have been reported with a clear white breast. One bird was described as having a white throat, with a light gray wash at the bottom of the throat area. Another had much yellow underneath and no black in the throat area, and might have passed as a Blue-wing except for noticeably yellow wing bars.

For those hybrid males whose songs have been reported, most have sung like Golden-wings. Two instances of typical Blue-wing songs revealed that one song had the quality of the Blue-wing, but the second drawn-out buzz was consistently interrupted two or three times, making a succession of notes reminiscent of the typical Golden-wing.

Observers would do well to check visually any bird singing a Golden-wing or Blue-wing song, particularly if it contains any sort of atypical variation.

Tennessee Warbler (*Vermivora peregrina*)

STATUS. Abundant migrant. Rare summer resident north.

HABITAT. Deciduous forest; residential areas (during spring). All forest; all carr; residential areas (during fall).

MIGRATION DATES. *Spring:* early May to early June. *Fall:* late July to mid-October. *Extremes:* 20 April; 24 November.

PORTRAIT. *Birds of Wisconsin:* Plate 66.

For a brief period, usually less than a week, the ringing staccato song of the Tennessee Warbler issues from the top of nearly every deciduous tree in the residential areas of Wisconsin cities and towns. One would not guess the true abundance of this bird on the basis of sight observations alone, for this is a tree-top species easily concealed among the developing leaves. The Tennessee Warbler chorus usually occurs around 15 May in the southern counties and 5–8 days later in the north. This brief period marks the peak of the spring warbler-vireo flight. Once the Tennessee chorus subsides, many observers might assume that the spring migration has ended. It has almost—but not quite.

Late April sightings are occasionally recorded in southern and central counties. The earliest include sightings on the 20th (1980, Dane, L. A. Erickson), 21st (1948, Dunn, I. O. Buss), 23rd (1977, Milwaukee, E. W. Strehlow), 24th (1975, Walworth, E. Carnes), and 25th (1948, Polk, L. Heinsohn). The more usual pattern is for first arrivals to advance from 5 to 15 May south to north. The buildup to the peak is a gradual 10–14–day process in the south and a more rapid 7–10–day period farther north. Once the peak has passed, the flight subsides with surprising suddenness. Twenty singing males may be heard in the treetops one day and nary a one on the next day. There are years when no Tennessees are reported anywhere in the state after the end of May, but usually a few stragglers—mainly nonsinging females—remain into the first week of June. Rarely is spring weather so retarded that the timing of the entire migration is delayed, but in 1947 the spring peak did not come until 1 June in the central and northern counties, and migrants remained until the 14th (Polk, L. Heinsohn). One of the 1 June birds found at Neillsville (Clark County) was a partial albino with a completely white head and a body otherwise in typical male plumage.

In fall the Tennessee Warbler is abundant for a more extended period. From 20 August to 20 September this is usually the most abundant of the warblers,

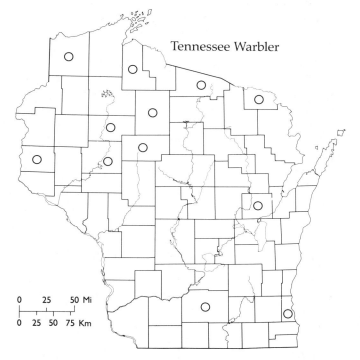

Tennessee Warbler

0   25   50 Mi
0 25 50 75 Km

O   Mid-June to mid-July

Records since 1960

dominating the early part of the fall flight much as the Yellow-rump dominates the later part in late September and October. Evidence from my own observations, from banding, and from television tower casualties all indicate that the Tennessee constitutes more than 10% of the entire fall warbler-vireo population. The figure is much higher in early fall before the Yellow-rump flight begins; as many as 972 have struck the Eau Claire tower on a single night. Birds can be found in almost any kind of vegetation in fall: trees high or low, coniferous or deciduous, bushes, and even cornfields.

In addition to the 1-month peak period, the migration period includes a full month on either side of the peak. It was not until the 1960s that banders and alert observers became aware that fall migrants arrive in late July, but it is now apparent that first arrivals can be regularly expected any time after 20 July. Birds are usually gone from the northern counties by 5 October, and from the south by 20 October. I know of six November dates: the 2nd (1974, La Crosse, F. Z. Lesher), 3rd (1959, Outagamie, D. D. Tessen; 1957, Vernon, M. E. Morse), 6th (1957, Dane, T. L. Ashman), 16th (1963, Rock, M. T. Maxson), and 24th (1975,

Milwaukee, E. J. Epstein). The latter two dates would be considered late anywhere in the United States.

The summer of 1980 produced several exceptional sightings: singing males on 27 June (Milwaukee, R. :P. Gutschow), 4 July (two separate locations in Taylor, T. K. Soulen and S. D. Robbins), and 14 July (Taylor, S. D. Robbins), plus a bird banded on 13 July (Chippewa, C. A. Kemper). Are singing males to be considered possible breeders, nonbreeding wanderers, or early fall migrants? Similar out-of-season singers were encountered on 25 June 1971 (Dane, J. J. Hickey), 4 July 1979 (Dane, W. L. Hilsenhoff), and 8 July 1963 (St. Croix, S. D. Robbins).

One of the most likely spots for possible breeding is in the Apostle Islands in Ashland County. Jackson (1943) heard one singing on Outer Island on 9 July 1919, and Beals (1958) found several on Oak and Stockton islands in June and July 1957 and 1958. On 21 June 1977 S. A. Temple (pers. comm.) discovered an active nest on Oak Island. Other breeding instances are possible but unproven. I heard a singing male while canoeing on the Bois Brule River in Douglas County on 29 June 1961. Robert Spahn noted one in Vilas County between 6 and 15 July 1978. On 10 July 1972 Tom Ellis trapped a female near Weyerhauser (Rusk County) and noted a well-developed brood patch; there were two singing males nearby.

Orange-crowned Warbler (*Vermivora celata*)

STATUS. Uncommon spring migrant; fairly common fall migrant.

HABITAT. All carr. Wooded swamp.

MIGRATION DATES. *Spring:* late April to mid-May. *Fall:* mid-September to late October. *Extremes:* 15 April, 18 June; 9 August, 1 January.

PORTRAIT. *Birds of Wisconsin:* Plate 67.

Kumlien and Hollister (1903) thought of the Orange-crowned Warbler as a probable breeder in some parts of the state for three reasons: they had taken specimens in Manitowoc County in July; Thure Kumlien had collected two birds in Jefferson County on 16 June 1860; and P. R. Hoy "was positive it bred in the state." According to present patterns of behavior, it is doubtful that the bird now nests within 300 miles of Wisconsin. There is only one June record in Wisconsin for the twentieth century. It is unfortunate that the specimens Kumlien and Hollister obtained cannot be located.

Kumlien and Hollister (1903) further expressed the belief that this bird was more common in the western than the eastern part of the state. Present evidence supports this view. My records show that the number of birds seen in 8 years of fieldwork in St. Croix County (1960–1968) equaled or outnumbered the combined totals from 20 years of observations in other parts of the state (mainly Dane, Adams, and Chippewa counties, 1949–1959, 1969–1977): 134 to 134 in spring, and 181 to 161 in fall. This is to be expected, considering the normal summer and winter ranges. The race that passes through Wisconsin winters along the Gulf Coast from Georgia to Mexico and summers from northern Ontario westward. The northwest-southeast migratory path would cover the southwestern part of Wisconsin more than the northeastern.

The Orange-crown is one of the few warblers that habitually reach the state in April. The earliest recorded sighting is 15 April (1954, Kenosha, M. F. Higgins). Observations from the 20th on are frequent in the southern counties, with birds reaching the northern counties by the end of the month. A modest peak spreads quickly through the state from 1 to 10 May; by the time most of the other warbler species are reaching a peak, Orange-crown numbers are declining. One's best chance to find this bird is to go afield during the first week in May, look closely in thickets and shrubbery, and listen for a very sharp "chip." Rarely does the Orange-crown sing during migration, but its sharp chip contrasts dramatically with the soft calls of the Yellow-rumps and Palms most likely to be present at the same time. Few Orange-crowns remain after 20 May. Observers have spotted migrants in the south as late as the 26th (1976, Milwaukee, E. J. Epstein) and in the north through 3 June (1983, Oneida, P. R. Engberg) and 4 June (1985, Ashland, S. W. Matteson). The only other June sighting, in addition to T. Kumlien's 1860 specimens, involved an individual carefully studied on 18 June 1974 (Winnebago, C. Schultz).

In fall, the bird is conspicuously late. In most years first arrivals are not noted until mid-September. August 1961 was most unusual, with arrivals on the 13th (Washburn, W. E. Southern), 19th (St. Croix, S. D. Robbins), 28th (Dane, J. J. Hickey), and 29th (Sheboygan, H. C. Mueller); but there are only eight other records of arrivals before 28 August. The most exceptional of these involved a northern Wisconsin bird on the 9th (1986, Douglas, R. J. Johnson) and a southern Wisconsin bird on the 17th (1977, Racine, L. W. Erickson). It is after the peak of many other warbler species has passed that the Orange-crown comes into its own. It is most common in the north from 20 September to 10 October and in the south from 1 to 20 October. I have seen as many as 30 on a 2-hour field trip at the height of this season by looking in alders and other shrubs and small trees. Often Orange-crowns associate with Tennessees, and considerable care is required to distinguish the two species in fall plumage. The last migrants usually depart by the end of October; occasionally a few linger until 12 November. Beyond that date three Dane County records exist: 1 December (1979, R. M. Smith), 3 December (1965, T. L. Ashman), and a bird collected on 10 December (1925, W. Taylor [1926b]). In Manitowoc County a very late straggler remained until 1 January (1985, C. R. Sontag).

Nashville Warbler (*Vermivora ruficapilla*)

STATUS. Common migrant. Common summer resident north; uncommon summer resident central.

HABITAT. Coniferous forest. Deciduous forest (during migration).

MIGRATION DATES. *Spring:* late April to late May. *Fall:* mid-August to mid-October. *Extremes:* 18 April; 11 December.

BREEDING DATA. Nests with eggs: 21 May to 5 June; nests with young to 1 July. Clutch size: 3 or 4 eggs.

PORTRAIT. *Birds of Wisconsin:* Plate 67.

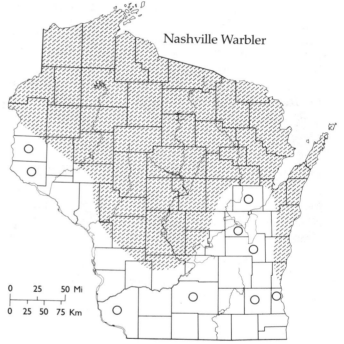

Nashville Warbler

▨ Summer range
○ Early June to late July

Records since 1960

More often than not, my first annual sighting of a Nashville Warbler has been of an individual probing a budding apple tree during the first week in May. If favorable mild weather occurs in late April, a few early birds reach the southern counties during the last week of the month. Exceptionally early individuals turned up on 18 April 1972 in Milwaukee (M. F. Donald) and Brown (M. M. Wierzbicki) counties.

It is in the first half of May, with plum and apple trees bursting into full bloom, that sizable numbers of these birds move northward through the state. Nashvilles frequent other types of vegetation, deciduous and coniferous, during migration, but their preference for fruit blossoms is particularly noticeable. Although the migration spans most of May, this species occurs more often during the early May flight than later. Numbers in the southern counties are already diminishing by the 15th. By the 25th birds are nearly gone from the south and are established on breeding territories in the central and northern counties.

No longer does the Nashville Warbler breed in the southernmost counties as it did in the nineteenth century. Faanes (1981) described this species as common north of St. Croix Falls (Polk County) but absent as a breeding species elsewhere in the St. Croix River valley. The bird apparently shuns the Mississippi River region in summer; it is found in modest numbers throughout the jack pine regions of Monroe, Sauk, Juneau, Adams, and Marquette counties. It is regular in small numbers in tamarack bogs in the Lake Michigan area south to Ozaukee County and is at least occasional in pockets in the Kettle Moraine State Forest in Fond du Lac and Waukesha counties.

In the northern counties, however, this bird becomes common as a summer resident. Virtually every black spruce and tamarack bog has one or more pairs; the more mature jack pine areas attract many pairs; and to some extent these birds are found in the deciduous hardwoods as well. In the coniferous forests as a whole, this is one of the commonest warblers in the northernmost counties. In this region I have on several occasions counted 75–80 singing males on a June morning. On the BBS, on those routes north of the tension zone, an average of five Nashvilles per transect per year is maintained. South of the tension zone, BBS routes rarely record a single bird.

Nesting data are surprisingly scarce for such a common bird. Milwaukee Public Museum files mention 13 reported nests, but information is incomplete in each instance. One can conclude only that nests are laid on or near the ground in moss or grass; the usual clutch of three or four eggs is sometimes complicated by cowbird parasitism; and nesting begins promptly after spring arrival. Sets of eggs have been reported by 21 and 25 May, slightly earlier than for most other warblers. By early July young have fledged.

In fall the Nashville is not particularly associated with either the early-fall warbler flight (dominated by the Tennessee) or the late flight (dominated by the Yellow-rump). Its migration is fairly evenly spread out from late August through early October; and when one includes the earliest stragglers that some-times show up at the beginning of August and the occasional late migrant that lingers through October, the flight may encompass a full 3-month period. A 2-month spread is more typical. First fall arrivals usually begin to appear south of the breeding range during mid-August, with numbers building up through the last week of August into the first week of September. Numbers then remain quite constant through the month. During the first week of October most birds leave the north and their numbers diminish in the central and southern regions, with only a few remaining anywhere after the 15th. Eau Claire television tower kill figures illustrate the pattern well. During the tragic fall of 1965, 603 dead birds were found from 28 August to 20 October, including 84 on 6 September, 26 on 20 September, 139 on 24 September, and 180 on 1 October.

Banders have on rare occasions trapped tardy migrants through 5 November. Observers recorded even later sightings on 11 November (1967, Ozaukee, D. K. Gustafson), 19 November (1974, Milwaukee, L. W. Erickson), 2 December (1979, Dane, A. K. Shea), and 4–11 December (1969, Brown, E. D. Cleary).

Northern Parula (*Parula americana*)

STATUS. Uncommon migrant. Uncommon summer resident north; rare summer resident southwest.
HABITAT. Coniferous forest. Deciduous forest (during migration).
MIGRATION DATES. *Spring:* early to late May. *Fall:* mid-August to late September. *Extremes:* 18 March; 25 November.
BREEDING DATA. Nests with eggs: 23 June to 9 July.
PORTRAIT. *Birds of Wisconsin:* Plate 67.

Several nineteenth-century commentators (Hoy [1853b], Grundtvig [1895], Schoenebeck [1902], Kumlien and Hollister [1903]) described the Northern Parula as a fairly numerous breeding species throughout the state. Times have changed. The average observer in southern and central Wisconsin is fortunate nowadays to see three individuals on any given day of migration and 10 individuals during any migration season—spring or fall. Among 50,000 warblers and vireos killed at the Eau Claire television tower, 1960–1969, only 60 were parulas. The only location in Wisconsin where I have found this species to be common is along the Bois Brule River in Douglas County. On 27 June 1966, while on a canoe trip, I counted 55 singing males.

The habitat preferences of the Northern Parula are

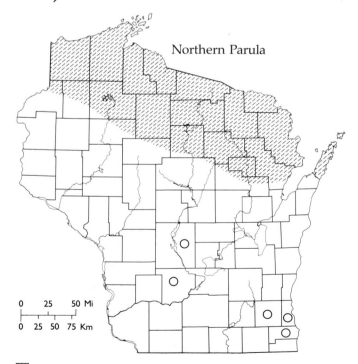

Northern Parula

0   25   50 Mi
0 25 50 75 Km

▨ Summer range
○ Early June to late July

Records since 1960

more restricted than those of many other warblers. For breeding purposes the bird prefers swampy land where tall conifers (spruce, hemlock, cedar, tamarack) are present and where *Usnea* lichen abounds. The parula constructs nests largely of *Usnea* high in one of the taller trees. Murl Deusing (MPM files) found two nests on 1 July 1945: one, containing four eggs, 40 feet up in a live spruce, the other 30 feet up in a dead spruce (contents unknown). Hoy (1853b) mentioned a nest 50 feet up in an *Usnea*-covered oak. Most of the other nests reported in the state have been at similar altitudes, and little effort has gone into determining nest contents.

A century ago considerable suitable habitat existed in southeastern Wisconsin; most of it has now disappeared. The remnant tamarack swamps are small, and lack the large timber they once had. Most of Wisconsin's remaining nesting habitat lies in the swampy riverine areas north of a line running southeast from Danbury to Shawano, then east to Sturgeon Bay. The sizable population along the Bois Brule may well be matched by numbers along some of the other wild rivers of the north; but such areas are more readily reached by boat than by car or by foot, and thus are difficult for observers to penetrate.

The last recorded nest south of this line was found in Green Lake County on 18 June 1908 (Lowe 1915). Additional summer sightings include one bird in Eau Claire County on 13 June 1951 (L. Almon), two noted in Racine County on 18 June 1974 (L. W. Erickson), one in Waukesha County on 27 June 1982 (W. A. Cowart), one in Milwaukee County on 25 June 1983 (J. Bronson), and birds I found in Adams County on 25 July 1960, in Dane County on 17 and 28 July 1951, and in Sauk County on 9 July 1976. These records,

plus the continued presence of the Northern Parula in suitable habitat in Illinois, suggest that summer records in the southwestern and south-central portions of Wisconsin are rare but still possible.

During spring and fall migration the parula's habitat preferences are less restricted. Birds travel in mixed flocks of warblers and vireos, and may be found in any kind of tree or shrub. In spring the parula is sometimes encountered during the last days of April. Exceptionally early were birds reported on 11 April (1976, Marinette, H. L. Lindberg; 1981, Milwaukee, D. K. Gustafson), and 18 April (1977, Dane, R. E. Fiehweg). Most astonishing was the individual found dead at Milwaukee on 18 March 1942 (M. Allen). First arrivals usually wait until the first week in May to appear in the southern counties, and a week later farther north. The migration lasts but 3 weeks; only in delayed spring migrations are birds likely to be seen south of the normal breeding range after 25 May. In 1978 one bird remained in Milwaukee through 6 June (D. K. Gustafson).

Fall migrants may be encountered south of the breeding range in early August on rare occasions, but the more usual time to see the first returning birds is 20–25 August. The flight is not extensive enough to designate a peak, but September is clearly the chief migration month. Again, birds migrate in mixed flocks and are found in any type of vegetation. By 25 September birds have left the north, and in the south there are few records beyond 5 October. Unusually late was a lone individual sighted on 14 October (1967, Dane, J. T. Emlen). The only record beyond that date is a phenomenal sighting of one bird at a feeder on 25 November (1972, Iowa, R. S. Ellarson).

Yellow Warbler (*Dendroica petechia*)

STATUS. Common migrant. Common summer resident.

HABITAT. Deciduous forest. All carr. Shallow marsh.

MIGRATION DATES. *Spring:* late April to late May. *Fall:* mid-July to late August. *Extremes:* 16 April; 20 October.

BREEDING DATA. Nests with eggs: 21 May to 16 July. Clutch size: 4 or 5 eggs.

PORTRAIT. *Birds of Wisconsin:* Plate 67.

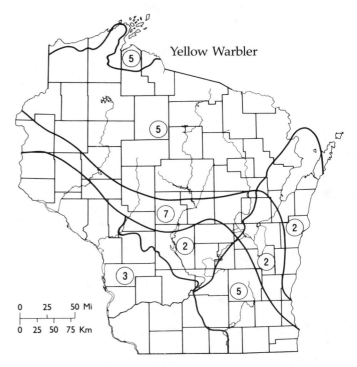

Yellow Warbler

Breeding Bird Survey, averages 1966 to 1980

In the northern forests, where many of the breeding warblers abound, the Yellow Warbler is one of the scarcer species. But in city parks, and along the edges of lakes and streams, it is one of the most common. In the morning—early or late—and again as dusk is approaching, the clear sweet song of this lovely bird can be heard from early May through early July.

BBS figures may be surprising to some observers who have thought of this species as particularly characteristic of the southern half of the state. It is characteristic of the southern area, in the sense that most other warblers are not present there, except in a relatively few woodland pockets. This leaves the Common Yellowthroat and the Yellow as the most widely distributed warbler species. But the BBS figures show the Yellow to be most numerous in the west-central area, where favorable habitat is more plentiful. Earlier writers invariably described this species as abundant. But as woodland and savanna have given way more and more to the plow, Yellow Warbler habitat has diminished.

Much can be learned about habitat preferences by studying nesting data. Reporting on 14 nests in Oconto and Marinette counties, Carl Richter mentioned that all 14 were near water: one along a river bank, six near the shore of Green Bay, and seven along the edges of swamps. The highest was 8 feet up in a dogwood bush; the lowest 18 inches up in a raspberry clump; other nests were located in willow, meadow-rue, and lilac bushes. In similar observations of 16 nests in Outagamie County, Grundtvig (1895) observed that although only one was actually erected over water, all were located in bushes with water nearby. Willow and hazelnut bushes were preferred; and with the exception of one 8 footer, all nests occurred between 1½ and 5 feet above the ground.

Brown-headed Cowbird parasitism is frequent. One report documents the existence of four cowbird eggs in a single Yellow Warbler nest. In Wisconsin, as elsewhere, parent warblers have often reacted to parasitism by covering the eggs with new nesting mate-

rial and building up the sides of the nest, thus creating a second-story nest, or even a third level if necessary. Richter once watched a pair add to its nest by gradually dismantling a nearby American Redstart nest that was in active use.

If there is favorable warm weather in the last week of April, the first migrants make their appearance at that time. Unusually early are migrants on the 16th (1898, Dunn, J. N. Clark [Buss and Mattison 1955]) and 20th (1952, Lafayette, E. Olson). In 1942 late-April arrivals occurred as far north as Polk, Wood, and Oconto counties. The usual pattern, however, is for birds to spread over the southern counties during the first week of May and over the northern counties 7–10 days later. Most birds remaining in the south through the 20th will nest there, while the last migrants will have left the north before the end of the month.

Early July finds a few pairs still nesting, but for others the fall migration is about to begin. On various occasions around 15 July I have heard nocturnal migrants which I believe to be this species. The fact that birds often appear in mid-July in territories not occupied earlier offers further evidence of a very early start to the southward flight. Most of the migration is completed in August, with only a slight spillover into early September. Yet an occasional migrant is detected in late September or early October. Eau Claire television tower kills have been reported as late as 20 September (1963), 21 September (1964, 1968), 27 September (1965), 3 October (1962), and 12 October (1969). Even later was the straggler on 20 October (1927, Dane, H. G. Anderson [H. G. Anderson et al. 1942]).

Chestnut-sided Warbler (*Dendroica pensylvanica*)

STATUS. Common migrant. Common summer resident north; fairly common summer resident central; rare summer resident south.

HABITAT. Deciduous forest. Lowland carr.

MIGRATION DATES. *Spring:* early to late May. *Fall:* mid-August to early October. *Extremes:* 23 April; 25 October.

BREEDING DATA. Nests with eggs: 27 May to 6 July. Clutch size: 3 or 4 eggs.

PORTRAIT. *Birds of Wisconsin:* Plate 69.

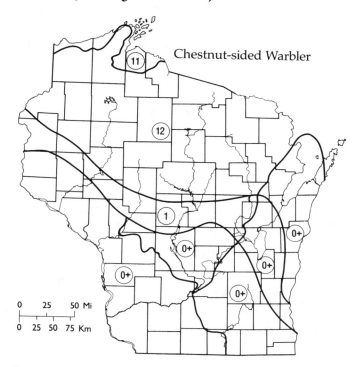

Breeding Bird Survey, averages 1966 to 1980

With uncanny consistency first arrivals reach southern Wisconsin between 1 and 4 May nearly every year. I know of only seven April arrivals, the earliest being on the 23rd (1956, Lafayette, E. Olson), 24th (1929, Winnebago, M. J. Overton), and 25th (1934, Winnebago, M. J. Overton). In the southern counties Chestnut-sided Warblers are most numerous during the 10–20 May period, showing a preference for shrubs and small trees adjacent to patches of deciduous woods. An occasional migrant may remain until the end of May, but most birds are gone by the 25th. Farther north, they are numerous from 15 May on. The presence of five casualties at the Eau Claire television tower on 1 June 1968 suggests that a few birds are still migrating in early June in some years.

The accompanying map shows that this bird becomes progressively more common as a summer resident as one moves northward. It is rarely found in conifers and usually avoids the tallest, most mature stands of oaks and maples. But it abounds in the cutover brush where Hill's oak, poplars, birches, and raspberry thickets offer plentiful understory. In such habitat in the northern counties, south to Polk, Chippewa, Marathon, Shawano, and Oconto counties, this is one of the most common summer warblers. On most BBS routes in the northern third of the state, it is outnumbered among the warblers only by the Ovenbird and the Common Yellowthroat.

According to Hoy (1853b) and Kumlien and Hollister (1903), the Chestnut-side was common in the southern counties as well through the nineteenth century. The clearing of land for agriculture has brought a virtual disappearance of this species from most of the southern third of the state, and has severely limited numbers in much of central Wisconsin. A few pairs are found each summer in Hill's oak areas in western counties south to Monroe, Sauk, and Adams counties. Farther east, some birds frequent the Kettle Moraine State Forest south to Waukesha and Ozaukee counties. There have been recent isolated summer occurrences in La Crosse, Vernon, Grant, and Walworth counties.

Nests with eggs have been noted from 27 May to 6 July. C. H. Richter's discovery of a 5 July 1945 nest containing three fresh eggs suggests the likelihood that it may be close to 15 July when the last young hatch. Presumably, a pair produces one brood a season, with the late-season nestings made necessary because of extensive Brown-headed Cowbird parasitism. Nests are relatively easy to find, both by cowbirds and by humans, usually being located in thickets from 1 to 4 feet above ground level. Out of 13 nests located in Green Lake County, Lowe (1915) observed that 8 were in huckleberry bushes. In Oconto County, Richter found nests in raspberry bushes. Francis Zirrer's (pers. comm. to O. J. Gromme) discovery of a nest in a small spruce in Washburn County is the only instance I know of where a pair nested in a conifer.

South of the regular breeding range, first fall migrants appear during the 15–20 August period. Television tower casualties at Eau Claire have often been reported by the 25th. Figures from the heavy towerkill autumn of 1965 indicate the typical progression of the fall flight through the state: 24 August (first casualties), 6 September (312), 16 September (242), 20 September (210), 24 September (106), and 1 October (68 and last). Casualties at Eau Claire have been reported as late as 12 October, but usually birds have left the northern counties by 25 September and the central area by 5 October. In the south the peak comes during the last half of September, with only stragglers seen after 10 October. The latest state records include October sightings on the 17th (1963, Sheboygan, H. C. Mueller), 23rd (1986, Eau Claire, C. A. Kemper), 24th (1975, Brown, M. M. Wierzbicki), and 25th (1939, Brown, J. B. Kendall).

Data from banding stations and field observations point to the bird as a moderately common fall migrant, compared with other warblers with which it associates in mixed flocks. The species is by no means as numerous as the Yellow-rump, Tennessee, Magnolia, and American Redstart; yet it outnumbers many other warbler species. Its preference for low shrubbery and small trees makes it relatively easy to find; its white underparts and conspicuous wing bars make it quite easy to identify.

Magnolia Warbler (*Dendroica magnolia*)

STATUS. Common migrant east; fairly common migrant west. Uncommon summer resident north.
HABITAT. Coniferous forest (during breeding). All forest; all carr (during migration).
MIGRATION DATES. *Spring:* early May to early June. *Fall:* mid-August to early October. *Extremes:* 18 April; 11 November.
BREEDING DATA. Nest with young: 9 July.
PORTRAIT. *Birds of Wisconsin:* Plate 68.

After picking up 1,346 Magnolia Warbler specimens at the Eau Claire television tower following the exceptionally heavy kills of 18–20 September 1963, C. A. Kemper commented, "[There were] more, I dare say, than most field ornithologists will see in a lifetime." Although this bird is a common migrant in all parts of the state, the average observer along Lake Michigan would have to look long and hard for years to match that total, and the average observer in the western half of the state would have to work twice as hard and long. Those observers most likely to sight comparable figures would be the eastern Wisconsin banders.

Weise (1971a) determined that 815 of 9,541 fall warblers and vireos (8.5%) netted at trapping stations in Milwaukee and Cedar Grove (Sheboygan County) between 1958 and 1970 were Magnolias. He recommended a status classification of "abundant," be-

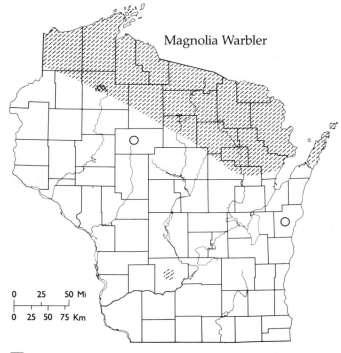

Magnolia Warbler

0   25   50 Mi
0 25 50 75 Km

▨ Summer range
○ Mid-June to late July

Records since 1960

cause this figure nearly matched the 8.8% figure for the Tennessee Warbler. My personal sight observations during fall in Adams County in the 1950s indicate a drop to 3.8% (342 of 9,011), with further drops to 2.7% (128 of 4,654) in Chippewa County during the 1970s and 1.8% (116 of 6,448) in St. Croix County during the 1960s. Banding figures are apt to be consistently higher than sight observations because of the species' preference for small trees and shrubbery where nets are usually located; even so, there is a noticeable drop-off in population figures as one moves westward.

The spring flight is concentrated in May, with a few exceptions. I know of 11 documented April arrivals: 8 during the 25–30 April period, and 3 very early dates: the 18th (1956, Jefferson, E. Degner), 19th (1946, Milwaukee, G. W. Treichel), and 22nd (1949, Milwaukee, A. Kruger). Late migrants are occasionally spotted during the first week of June. J. T. Emlen noted an exceptionally late migrant in Dane County on 15 June 1981. The more usual pattern, however, is for first arrivals to reach the southern counties during the 1–5 May period, with numbers building to a peak around 15–20 May, and the birds departing by the 25th. Farther north the expected schedule is generally a week later.

Positive evidence of nesting is scanty. On 10 July 1894, Schoenebeck (1902) found a nest 4 feet up in a small spruce in Oconto County, but he did not mention the contents in his published notes. On a Milwaukee Public Museum excursion in Forest County in 1940, W. C. Pelzer and L. P. Steven watched a pair of Magnolia Warblers carrying food on 5 July and saw the male feeding newly fledged young 2 days later (MPM files). Near Trout Lake in Vilas County, Schorger (1951a) found a nest with two young 4 feet up in a small black spruce on 9 July 1945. Three days later in Waupaca County, J. L. Kaspar observed parents feeding two recently fledged young.

Without doubt this bird is a regular breeder in small numbers in suitable spruce and hemlock areas in the northern counties. In the northwest, summer records have come mainly from Douglas, Bayfield, and Ashland counties, with occasional observations in northern Washburn and Sawyer counties. In the northeast the range is more extensive, including parts of Lincoln, Shawano, and Door counties. Late-June observations in Taylor (1980, S. D. Robbins) and Manitowoc (1976, J. Woodcock) counties suggest a slightly more extensive summer range on occasion. Farther south in hemlock groves of the Baraboo hills in Sauk County, Mossman and Lange (1982) have found from one to five singing males nearly every summer since 1970. Breeding there is probable but not proved.

Early-August sightings do not necessarily imply nearby nesting, for the fall migration sometimes begins during the first few days of the month. The more usual pattern is for the first migrants to reach the central region around the 20th and the southern sector around the 25th. Numbers build up strongly in early September, peak around the 15th to 20th in the northern and central regions, and a week later in the south. Occasionally, substantial numbers remain through the first 5 days in October, but the decline is usually rapid once September wanes. The timing of the fall migration is illustrated by the Eau Claire television tower casualty figures for the fall of 1965, when on five occasions major disasters were recorded: 28 August (first casualties), 6 September (295), 20 September (175), 24 September (135), and 1 October (132).

The last migrant is usually spotted between 10 and 20 October. Beyond the 25th only four November records are known: the 1st (1974, Milwaukee, D. K. Gustafson), 6th (1975, Milwaukee, D. K. Gustafson), 7th (1962, Sheboygan, H. C. Mueller), and 11th (1957, Winnebago, E. Fisher).

Cape May Warbler (*Dendroica tigrina*)

STATUS. Fairly common spring migrant; uncommon fall migrant. Uncommon summer resident north.
HABITAT. Coniferous forest.
MIGRATION DATES. *Spring:* early to late May. *Fall:* early August to mid-October. *Extremes:* 23 April; 23 December.
BREEDING DATA. Nest with 3 eggs: 11 June 1899.
PORTRAIT. *Birds of Wisconsin:* Plate 68.

Unlike a majority of the warblers that migrate northward into or through Wisconsin during spring after wintering in Central or South America, the Cape May Warbler winters in the West Indies and travels northwest from Florida to reach our state. Perhaps that is why there are no records of phenomenally early April stragglers. The earliest records on file are late-April visitors on the 23rd (1985, Dane, W. L. Hilsenhoff), 28th (1929, Winnebago, M. J. Overton; 1974, Dane, W. L. Hilsenhoff) and 30th (1970, Ozaukee, T. Bintz; 1972, Waukesha, J. E. Bielefeldt).

The spring migration period is brief. In the southern counties few birds are seen before 5 May or after 20 May. Farther north the time schedule is 5–7 days later. The peak is sudden, scarcely lasting 3 days. I have seen up to 10 individuals in a single tree—sometimes in spruces, sometimes in blossoming fruit trees—on one of those peak days, a "wave" day between 10 and 15 May. On those occasions when Memorial Day birders have discovered late waves of grounded migrants along the Lake Superior shore, a few Cape Mays have been among them. A late-spring record for the southern sector occurred on 1 June 1974 (Racine, L. W. Erickson).

Schoenebeck (1902) established the only positive nesting record on 11 June 1899. Among thick clumps of spruce and cedar he found a nest containing three eggs 2 feet up in a spruce. The eggs are now in the A. J. Schoenebeck collection located at the University of Wisconsin–Stevens Point. Kumlien and Hollister (1903) mentioned June records in Kewaunee and Door counties and a July record near Ashland, but offered no specific data. In 1919 Harry Sheldon collected a female in breeding condition in Bayfield County on 8 June, and H. H. T. Jackson saw recently fledged young on Madeline Island in Ashland County on 21 July (Jackson 1943). Other summer sightings, before or since, have been so scarce that until the 1960s the Cape May was not recognized as a regular summer resident anywhere in the state.

On 26 June 1962, Roy and Martha Lound found a pair in Forest County, and for 3 days they observed

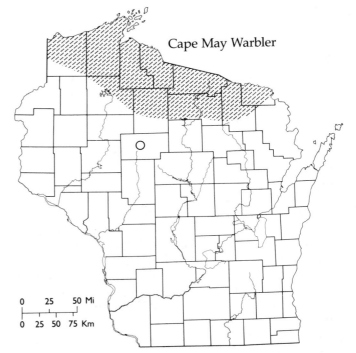

Cape May Warbler

0   25   50 Mi
0   25 50 75 Km

▨ Summer range
○ Early June to late July

Records since 1960

food being brought to a spot near the top of a 45-foot tall balsam. Although they could not see the nest, there is little doubt that an active nest was present. Recent nesting is also suspected in Douglas County. In the balsam-spruce-tamarack headwaters of the Bois Brule River north of Solon Springs, I found 3 singing males on 11 June 1969, 11 males and a female on 10 June 1970, 10 males on 15 June 1971, and 3 males on 27 June 1972. Cape May Warblers frequent the upper branches of the taller black spruce, often singing from concealed perches close to the trunk. In such a colony nesting is highly probable, but has not yet been proved (Robbins 1973).

Since 1970 singing males have also been detected in Bayfield, Ashland, Sawyer, Price, Iron, Vilas, Oneida, Florence, and Taylor counties between mid-June and mid-July. It now appears likely that this species has bred for many years in small numbers north of a line from Gordon through Phillips, Pelican Lake, and Aurora. The Cape May's presence is difficult to detect, not only because the bird tends to keep out of sight near the tops of the spruces, but also because its song is extremely high in pitch and similar to that of other warblers. I have heard three distinct songs in summer; these are so similar to song variations of the Black-and-white, Blackburnian, and Bay-breasted Warblers and the American Redstart that establishing identification requires the utmost care.

Observers have often gone through an entire fall season without seeing a single Cape May, and thereby have concluded it is one of the rarer warblers. Eau Claire television tower casualties disprove this notion. Five times during the 1960–1969 period, over 50 of these birds were killed there in a single night.

Fall arrivals have reached the central counties as early as 1 August and the southern counties by 17 August. The heaviest towerkills have occurred during the 5–20 September period, indicating a probable peak in the central counties at that time, with the

peak passing through the southern counties a week later. Frequently, observers note the last migrants during the first week of October, but on occasion a stray may linger longer. Late-October dates are known for the 22nd (1948, Milwaukee, G. H. Orians) and 29th (1959, Vernon, V. E. Weber; 1968, Dane, T. L. Ashman). Phenomenally late sightings include birds banded in Portage County on 7 November 1972 and 25 November 1971 (A. M. Baumgartner) and observations on 8 November (1979, Winnebago, G. S. Peterson), 23 November (1967, Milwaukee, D. K. Gustafson), 27 November (1962, Outagamie, D. D. Tessen), and 6 December (1979, Milwaukee, J. H. Idzikowski). More remarkable was the bird that fed daily at Thomas Hunter's suet feeder in Trampealeau County until 23 December 1984.

Black-throated Blue Warbler (*Dendroica caerulescens*)

STATUS. Uncommon migrant east; rare migrant central and west. Uncommon summer resident north.
HABITAT. Coniferous forest. Northern maple-hemlock-pine forest.
MIGRATION DATES. *Spring:* early to late May. *Fall:* mid-August to early October. *Extremes:* 24 April; 6 November.
BREEDING DATA. Nest with 3 eggs: 15 June 1895.
PORTRAIT. *Birds of Wisconsin:* Plate 68.

Wisconsin lies on the western edge of the Black-throated Blue Warbler's range. Its rarity in the western regions of the state has been demonstrated by several indicators. In 8 years of observation in St. Croix County, 1960–1968, I observed this bird but once in spring and five times in fall. In 15 years of viewing in Dunn County, 1886–1901, J. N. Clark recorded it three times (Buss and Mattison 1955). At the Eau Claire television tower only 28 specimens were discovered among nearly 40,000 fall warbler casualties in the 1960–1969 period. It has been described as rare in Douglas County (Bernard 1967), rare in the St. Croix River valley (Faanes 1981), and very uncommon in Chippewa and Eau Claire counties (Kemper 1973b).

Migrants are somewhat more numerous in the eastern regions. They are regular along the Lake Michigan shore each spring and fall, but ornithologists in that area consider themselves lucky if they find as many as 10 individuals during a season. Both at Milwaukee and at the Cedar Grove Ornithological Station in Sheboygan County, where extensive banding

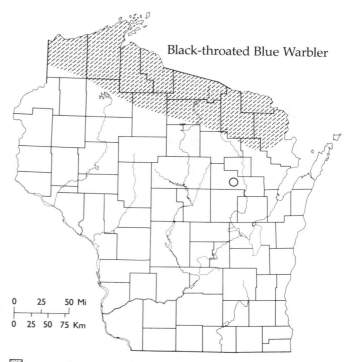

Black-throated Blue Warbler

0   25   50 Mi
0 25 50 75 Km

▨ Summer range
○ Early June to late July

Records since 1960

operations have been carried on since 1958, this species has proved to be one of the least numerous of the regular migrant warblers.

In spring southern Wisconsin observers find this bird most frequently between 10 and 20 May. First arrivals often appear during the first week of May, and there are two 30 April dates (1948, Milwaukee, I. N. Balsom; 1949, Manitowoc, W. M. Smith) in addition to a 28 April (1942, Milwaukee, M. Deusing) record and a 24 April arrival (1984, Milwaukee, J. H. Idzikowski). A 5 June 1967 sighting in Racine (L. W. Erickson) and a 10 June 1980 straggler in Milwaukee (D. K. Gustafson) were remarkably late. Usually, birds have departed from southern Wisconsin by 25 May. In northern Wisconsin this species is rarely seen before 15 May.

In the north, however, a few pairs remain to breed. Schoenebeck (1902) found several nests in Oconto County. A set of three eggs collected there on 15 June 1895 remains in the A. J. Schoenebeck collection at the University of Wisconsin–Stevens Point. O. J. Gromme (MPM files) found a nest in Iron County on 29 June 1946. Doubtless, the bird nests sparingly across the northernmost tier of counties. Appraising the birds of Forest, Oneida, and Vilas counties, Vanderschaegen (1981b) listed northern Forest and eastern Vilas counties as the area where most of these warblers are found. In the nineteenth century, nesting may have occurred south to Outagamie and Sheboygan counties, but this can no longer be considered summer range.

In fall, as in spring, migrants favor the eastern half of the state. A few migrants have turned up in Douglas, Polk, and St. Croix counties in the northwest; no recent records exist for the southwest. The bird is regular in the southeast, but even there numbers are consistently small. At the Cedar Grove Ornithological Station during the 1958–1963 period, only 16 of 6,311 warblers trapped in fall were of this species (Mueller and Berger 1967e).

Observers have noted migrants in central counties as early as 15 August. An even earlier start farther north is suggested by sightings on the 1st (1955, Douglas, S. D. Robbins), 3rd (1970, Shawano, J. A. Ready), and the 9th (1961, Bayfield, S. D. Robbins); all of these birds behaved more like migrants than residents. Most sightings have been scattered throughout September and early October. The last sighting in the northern and central regions is usually around 30 September. Unusually late are October sightings on the 10th (1978, Price, M. Hardy), 20th (1980, Eau Claire towerkill, C. A. Kemper), and 21st (1961, Polk, M. Pedersen). In the southern region 10 October is the expected departure date. One bird lingered at Milwaukee through 21 October (1963, M. F. Donald) and another in Sheboygan County until 6 November (1927, C. S. Jung; MPM files).

It is easy to miss the Black-throated Blue Warbler in fall. The adult male is indeed vivid in plumage, but inexperienced observers may mistake females and young for fall Tennessee Warblers or vireos. A clue to the bird's presence is its soft call note, strikingly similar to the note of the Dark-eyed Junco. The Black-throated Blue Warbler prefers low, dense vegetation, where it often hides. In summer its preferred habitat is hemlock, spruce, or maple or birch tangles dense with fallen logs. In spring and fall, the denser the understory, the better this bird seems to like it. No Black-throated Blue Warbler is going to suffer from sunburn!

Yellow-rumped Warbler (*Dendroica coronata*)
Formerly Myrtle Warbler

STATUS. Abundant migrant. Fairly common summer resident north and central. Rare winter resident south and central.

HABITAT. Coniferous forest (during breeding). All forest; all carr (during migration).

MIGRATION DATES. *Spring:* late March to late May. *Fall:* early September to mid-November.

BREEDING DATA. Nests with young: 19 June to 2 July.

WINTER. Occasionally present through early January; seven records of successful overwintering.

PORTRAIT. *Birds of Wisconsin:* Plate 68.

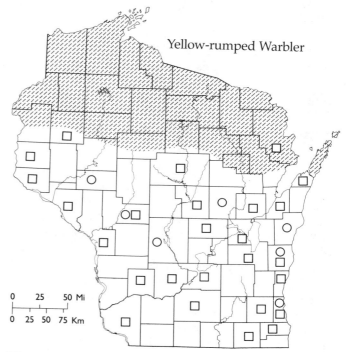

Yellow-rumped Warbler

▨ Summer range
○ Early June to mid-August
□ Late November to early March

Records since 1960

More casual Wisconsin bird-watchers have become acquainted with the Yellow-rumped Warbler than with any other member of this large family. They should. It is the most abundant warbler. The birds are present when there are few leaves to hinder vision, and they are easily attracted to conspicuous perches in trees and shrubs of any size or kind. Francis Zirrer (pers. comm. to O. J. Gromme) found he could attract them to his feeder by offering mashed potato!

Every third or fourth year, the first spring arrivals are detected in late March. One can never be sure whether such arrivals represent a slight displacement from a nearby wintering location or a real northward migration; but such sightings have occurred as early as 16 March (1980, Kenosha, R. R. Hoffman). In most years arrivals reach southern counties during the first week of April, with their numbers experiencing a mild buildup during the following 2 weeks, then exploding into large flocks from late April until 10 May. By that time other warblers are migrating strongly, and numbers of Yellow-rumps decline sharply. Few birds remain after 20 May in a typical year. In the central and northern sectors the peak is expected during the 1–20 May period, with an occasional migrant lingering until 30 May.

The spring migration peak is sometimes spectacular. Ordinarily, on a short field trip during the peak period one can find 50–75 "myrtles" without much trouble. But occasionally weather conditions trigger much larger flights. Such a day occurred on 7 May 1950, when Wallace Grange estimated 1,000 birds near his Babcock (Wood County) home. My notes show a conservative estimate of 500 birds moving through the Crex Meadows Wildlife Area in Burnett County on 8 May 1966, with the conjecture that numbers would have reached the thousands had I been able to cover the territory more adequately. Chipman (1968) described 2 May 1967 as a tremendous day; she mist-

netted 130 at her Wautoma (Waushara County) home and saw many more.

Much remains to be learned about nesting patterns. Nests with young were found on 19 June (1923, Bayfield, A. W. Schorger [1925a]) and 2 July (1945, Vilas, A. W. Schorger). Recently fledged young were found on 21 July (1919, Ashland, H. H. T. Jackson [1943]). Adults carrying food were noted on 12 June (1972, Chippewa, S. D. Robbins) and 3 July (1945, Door, M. Deusing). Yet I can find no record of anyone having observed eggs.

Concerted efforts in the northern forests would certainly substantiate the presumption that this soft-chip warbler nests regularly throughout the northern two tiers of counties each year. Its preference is for mature white pines. On the BBS it has been recorded on 26 of the state's 70 transects. In June this species has been detected frequently south to Polk, Taylor, Lincoln, Menominee, Oconto, and Door counties, and occasionally south to Eau Claire, Jackson, Juneau, Sheboygan, and Milwaukee counties.

Ordinarily, fall migrants are not noticeable until 5 September or later. Yet twice in recent years something apparently triggered an early-August movement into the central area: in 1956 I found birds on the 6th in Monroe County and the 14th in Adams County; in 1972 I found birds in eight locations in Chippewa and Clark counties on the 12th and 13th. Fall movement generally begins to build in the northern and central regions during the 10–20 September period, followed by a strong peak from the 20th to 10 October. By 25 October most birds have left. The timetable for the southern counties runs a week later, with a few migrants lingering until 15 November nearly every year.

One would never guess the magnitude of the fall flight by studying television tower kill data. At Eau Claire the total 1960–1969 casualty figure of 740 represents only 1.9% of the total number of 40,000 warblers killed. Even allowing for the fact that close to half of the major towerkills occur before the beginning of the usual myrtle migration, this is still a far cry from the 20–30% figure that has been tallied at various banding stations and other observation points. In fall, as in spring, flocks of 30–50 are commonplace, and a morning's field trip in early October can sometimes produce numbers in the hundreds. The birds are conspicuous as they move among bushes and trees of any size and sometimes dart for flying insects in the open.

Unlike most other warblers, this species can adapt its diet to include berries as well as insects, and thus can remain into the winter months. The first CBC sighting occurred in 1957; between then and 1971, from one to nine birds have been recorded in 35 count areas as far north as St. Croix, Marathon, and Door counties. Additional late-December reports have come from Barron (1976) and Brown (1967) counties. Most often, the birds have been found in tamarack or cedar habitat, where thick cover and plentiful berries exist. It is probable that most of these birds perish during January. Yet individuals did make it into March in St. Croix (1961, C. A. Pemble), Portage (1974, A. M. Baumgartner), Outagamie (1976, J. Shillinglaw), and Walworth (1961, C. O. Palmquist) counties. Most northerly was a bird observed in Marinette County between 6 and 8 February (1980, banded by H. L. Lindberg).

The yellow-throated western race *auduboni* has been identified on four occasions: 3 May 1943 (Sawyer, F. Zirrer), 3 May 1947 (Juneau, W. B. Jackson), 18 April 1975 (banded and photographed in Brown, M. M. Wierzbicki), and 12–13 June 1984 (Outagamie, D. Minkebige).

Black-throated Gray Warbler (*Dendroica nigrescens*)

STATUS. Accidental. One record.
HABITAT. Deciduous forest. Upland carr.

The bird that Charles Lloyd found dead on the doorstep of his Madison home on 5 December 1968 constitutes the only state record of the Black-throated Gray Warbler. It was identified as a female by George Knudsen and A. W. Schorger; the skin now resides in the University of Wisconsin–Madison collection. Presumably strong west winds blew the bird off course (Schorger 1969).

Within the normal range, in the mountains of the Pacific states and the Southwest, most birds have left the United States for their Mexican wintering grounds by the end of October. Yet a majority of the accidental occurrences that have been noted (Ontario, North Dakota, Ohio, Massachusetts, Connecticut, New York, New Jersey, South Carolina, Florida, Alabama, Louisiana) have come in November and December. Future occurrences in Wisconsin might be possible but would be strictly accidental.

Hermit Warbler (*Dendroica occidentalis*)

STATUS. Accidental. One record.
HABITAT. Coniferous forest.

On 27 April 1982 Dan and Paula Minkebige spent 45 delightful minutes with this western visitor in their yard at Kaukauna (Outagamie County). From distances as close as 5 feet they watched the typical flitting warbler behavior and observed all the distinctive field markings that made the identification unmistakable. Photographs and extensive documentation confirmed the only known instance of the Hermit Warbler's presence in Wisconsin. The visitor took a liking to a row of Scotch pines and punctuated its feeding with occasional call notes. It could not be found the next day (*Pass. Pigeon* 45:41–42).

Occasional extralimital wanderings have occurred in Louisiana, Colorado, Missouri, Minnesota, Ontario, Connecticut, and Nova Scotia. Nearly all have involved adult males making brief appearances in late April and early May.

Black-throated Green Warbler (*Dendroica virens*)

STATUS. Fairly common migrant. Fairly common summer resident north; rare summer resident south.
HABITAT. Northern maple-hemlock-pine forest. Coniferous forest.
MIGRATION DATES. *Spring:* early to late May. *Fall:* mid-August to mid-October. *Extremes:* 10 April; 27 November.
BREEDING DATA. Nests with eggs: 8–26 June.
PORTRAIT. *Birds of Wisconsin:* Plate 68.

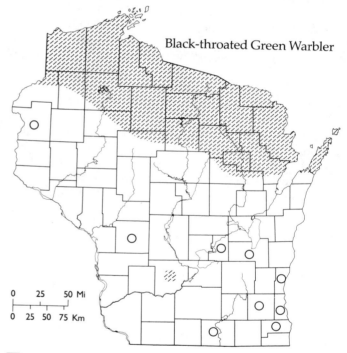

Black-throated Green Warbler

▨ Summer range
○ Mid-June to late July

Records since 1960

In the nineteenth century the Black-throated Green Warbler's summer range included suitable forest habitat throughout the state. Hoy (1853b) found these birds near Racine. Kumlien and Hollister (1903) had summer records from Jefferson, Dane, and Rock counties. Most of the southern forest has long since disappeared, and the current summer range of this species normally embraces only the northern two tiers of counties. But a few of these wheezy singers continue to spend the summer in one southern pocket: in the Baraboo hills in Sauk County, where Mossman and Lange (1982) have found from one to six birds almost annually since 1966. The possibility of summer residents in the Lima Bog in Rock County was raised in 1972 when T. R. Ellis discovered four singing males on 25 June. But this area has not been revisited often enough to know the true summer status there. Singing birds on 19 June (1978, Milwaukee, D. K. Gustafson) and 27 June (1963, Racine, L. W. Erickson) were presumably nonbreeding wanderers.

Abundance within the regular summer range is spotty. Beals (1958) thought this one of the most numerous species in the Apostle Islands in Ashland County during his 1957–1958 surveys. On the Land O' Lakes and Eagle River BBS transects in Vilas County, this is one of the most numerous warblers. I have visited other spots in Sawyer, Oneida, and Menominee counties where this bird outnumbered most other warblers. In most of the northern forest area, however, populations are relatively small. It is in stands of white pine that one is most apt to find this species. Mature stands of sugar maples and yellow birches also attract some birds; few are found in the forests that are predominantly spruce, balsam, or tamarack.

Nests are located well up in the trees. In an extensive area of cedars in Door County in June 1945, Murl Deusing (MPM files) found five nests located 8–25 feet above ground; one contained three eggs, which hatched on 26 June, with young fledgling on 5 July. This bird is generally known as one of the "high tree warblers," descending to the lower branches only occasionally.

Anyone who depends on eyesight alone will find few birds, but someone who has learned to detect the soft call note and the wheezy song will find this bird frequently in summer north of a line from Danbury through Medford, Shawano, and Sturgeon Bay. This species continues to sing later in the summer months than most other warblers. On 20 July 1972 along a 4-mile stretch of Menominee County forest where a variety of warblers was undoubtedly present, I heard songs from 20 "greens" but nary a song from another warbler species.

Passing through the southern and central counties in spring migration, this bird appears regularly but in relatively small numbers. In the 1961–1968 period I never recorded more than six individuals on any given day in St. Croix County; and in the 1952–1960 era in Adams County my maximum daily count was 15. Nearly every year a first arrival is spotted during the last week of April. Exceptionally early were "BTGs" on the 10th (1981, Sauk, K. I. Lange), 19th (1948, Milwaukee, I. N. Balsom), and 20th (1976, Brown, M. M. Wierzbicki). But the general arrival in the south usually takes place closer to 10 May, with a drop-off after 20 May. In the central counties the peak may come 3–5 days later. In the north the main influx is 20–30 May. Occasionally a late migrant remains in the south until 5 June, but usually birds have departed by 25 May.

Few fall migrants have been reported before 20 August (central) or 25 August (south). September is the principal migration month, but numbers are never great. It is not surprising that banding totals (less than 1% of warblers trapped at Cedar Grove [Sheboygan County] and Milwaukee) are small, since the bird maintains its preferences for the higher tree branches. But since figures for fall casualties at television towers at Eau Claire and Milwaukee are also below 1%, this bird cannot be considered common at this season.

The migration continues well into October most years. The latest northern date is 16 October (1943, Vilas, A. W. Schorger). Five times in the 1960–1969 period towerkills were evident at Eau Claire during the first 2 weeks of October. The latest dates for central counties are October 20th (1971, Outagamie, D. D. Tessen) and 29th (1970, Manitowoc, M. Albrecht). In the southern counties five November dates are known: the 1st (1925, Dane, W. Taylor [Schorger, 1931a]), 4th (1978, Kenosha, R. R. Hoffman), 5th (1955, Rock, M. T. Maxson), 15th (1952, banded in Rock, M. T. Maxson), and 27th (1972, Dane, G. W. Foster).

Blackburnian Warbler (*Dendroica fusca*)

STATUS. Fairly common migrant. Fairly common summer resident north; casual summer resident central.

HABITAT. Coniferous forest. Northern maple-hemlock-pine forest.

MIGRATION DATES. *Spring:* early May to early June. *Fall:* early August to early October. *Extremes:* 25 April; 14 October.

BREEDING DATA. Nests with eggs: 6 June to 6 July.

PORTRAIT. *Birds of Wisconsin:* Plate 69.

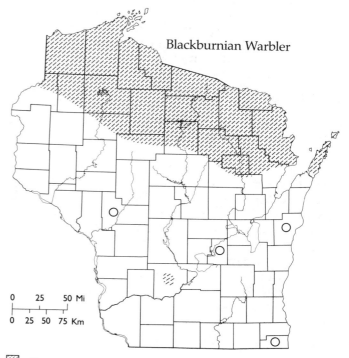

Blackburnian Warbler

0   25   50 Mi
0 25 50 75 Km

▨ Summer range
○ Mid-June to late July

Records since 1960

There are occasional years when warm southerly winds at the beginning of May not only usher the first migrant Blackburnian Warblers into the southern counties but also induce some individuals to penetrate more northern realms. Southern Wisconsin's earliest arrival is 25 April (1987, Rock, T. R. Schultz), but central and northern records exist for 27 April (1983, Langlade, B. Pickering), 30 April (1942, Wood, C. A. Searles), 2 May (1957, Manitowoc, M. H. Reichwaldt; 1959, Adams, S. D. Robbins), and 3 May (1970, Price, S. D. Robbins). Usually first arrivals in the south appear around 5 May, with numbers building to a 10–20 May peak, then rapidly dwindling so that nearly all the birds are gone by the 25th. In the north the schedule may be 7–10 days later.

Several early and mid-June records exist for central and southern areas. Birds in Madison as late as the 10th (1947) and 11th (1957) and in Milwaukee until the 12th (1973) and 13th (1977) presumably represented late-spring migrants, as did a 16 June 1956 songster in Adams County. But a singing male in Green Lake County, heard daily 18–24 June (1961, S. D. Robbins), and one in Kenosha County, 2–26 July (1972, R. R. Hoffman), may have been resident.

Kumlien and Hollister (1903) mentioned late-nineteenth-century nesting in the Jefferson County tamarack swamps, and presumably there were a few other southern breeding locations. Most of these have long since disappeared. With one exception, the regular summer range is now north of a line from Danbury through Medford, Shawano, and Sturgeon Bay. The exception is in the Baraboo hills in Sauk County, where 5–10 pairs are found nearly every summer (Mossman and Lange 1982).

During summer this bird lives in the high branches of the more mature evergreens. In hemlocks, balsam, spruce, or white pine, the birds are well concealed, but their thin high-pitched song can be heard frequently through June and early July. The few nests observed in the state have been located high in evergreens. Harold Lindberg (pers. comm.) found a nest

30–35 feet up in a pine in Marinette County on 26 May 1961. A 7 June 1897 nest in Oconto County was reported to be 16 feet up in a pine; the nest contained four eggs (Schoenebeck 1902).

In migration, spring and fall, the birds continue to prefer high branches, but now they often make use of deciduous trees. The fall migration gets under way early in August (earliest recorded date, 1 August 1980, Ozaukee, J. H. Idzikowski). Eau Claire television tower kills have been reported by the 13th. Tower casualty figures show that the migration already flourishes in the central counties by 25 August, peaks by 10 September (171 Blackburnians killed on 6 September 1965), and dwindles by the 20th, with scattered individuals until 5 October. In southern areas, too, the Blackburnian is regarded as one of the earlier fall warblers, with numbers peaking in mid-September and only late stragglers remaining into October. The latest October dates are the 11th (1970, Eau Claire, C. A. Kemper; 1970, Ozaukee, H. G. Liebherr), 12th (1960, Waukesha, E. Hoffmann), and 14th (1957, Outagamie, N. M. Rogers; 1984, Ozaukee, R. M. Hoffman).

Yellow-throated Warbler (*Dendroica dominica*)

Formerly Sycamore Warbler

STATUS. Rare spring migrant south; accidental fall migrant south. Rare summer resident south.
HABITAT. Southern silver maple–elm forest. Conifer plantations.
MIGRATION DATES. *Spring:* late April to late May. *Fall:* One September record. *Extremes:* 23 April; 9 September.
PORTRAIT. *Birds of Wisconsin:* Plate 69.

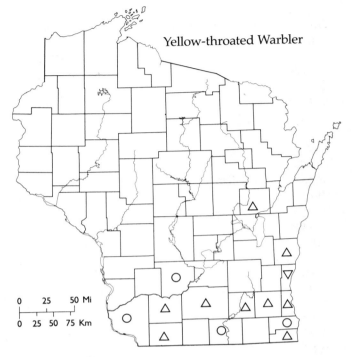

Yellow-throated Warbler

△   Late April to late May
○   Early June to early August
▽   9 September

All records

Although the normal range of the Yellow-throated Warbler extends north to northern Indiana and Illinois, within 50 miles of the Wisconsin border, this bird was found in our state only three times in the nineteenth century. One bird was collected by Hoy (1853b) at Racine on 20 June 1848. Kumlien and Hollister (1903) mentioned two individuals collected by Thure Kumlien: one in Jefferson County in 1877, one at an unrecorded location some time before 1850. At the Hoard Museum at Fort Atkinson (Jefferson County) there is an unlabeled specimen of this species which may well be the pre-1850 bird collected by Kumlien.

Only three sight records were added between 1900 and 1950. Two were males I found in Madison: one on 6 May 1940, silent, flitting in a small spruce an arm's length away; one on 8 May 1942, singing in a cemetery. F. M. Kozlik found one in Jefferson County on 3 May 1942. Continued rarity persisted through 1970, with three more sightings of overshooting spring migrants: 10 May 1958 in Lafayette County (J. A. Simpson), 4 May 1959 in Outagamie County (D. D. Tessen), and 2–6 May 1963 in Dane County (J. T. Emlen).

Contrasting sharply with the pre-1970 pattern of no more than two observations per decade, the 1970s produced 7 records, with an added 12 sightings between 1980 and 1987. Of these 19 most recent finds, 5 were detected in late April (earliest recorded date, 23 April 1975, Milwaukee, D. K. Gustafson), and 7 were noted between 1 and 21 May. This appears to be the period in which overshooting migrants are most likely to be found.

Two observations were made in Wyalusing State Park in Grant County, on 26 May 1984 (D. D. Tessen) and 16 June 1981 (J. L. Polk). If this species were to establish itself as a summer resident in Wisconsin, the tall deciduous trees among the backwaters of the Wisconsin and Mississippi rivers would provide ideal habitat. A singing male on 21 June 1983 near Devil's

Lake in Sauk County (S. R. Swengel) also took to tall trees in habitat similar to the haunts favored by these birds in their normal range.

In 1985 Wisconsin observers learned that Yellow-throated Warblers had spent the last three summers along the Sugar River bottoms just south of the Illinois state line. On 2 June 1985 R. M. Hoffman found a singing bird north of the state line in southern Rock County. Subsequent observations in 1986 and 1987 suggest that this species may now be a regular summer resident there. Proven breeding there led the Bureau of Endangered Resources to add this species to the state's list of endangered species in 1989.

I know of one record beyond 2 August. Wisconsin's lone autumn observation came on 9 September 1978 near Cedarburg (Ozaukee County), when Roger Sundell spent 30 minutes studying a bird that mixed with a varied flock of fall warblers.

With the exception of the 1959 sighting in Outagamie County, all records have come from the southern counties, south of a line from Prairie du Chien through Baraboo to Sheboygan. Within this range, the status has changed from "accidental" to "casual," and from "casual" to "rare." Perhaps the future will see yet another change.

Pine Warbler (*Dendroica pinus*)

STATUS. Uncommon migrant. Fairly common summer resident north; uncommon summer resident central.

HABITAT. Coniferous forest.

MIGRATION DATES. *Spring:* mid-April to late May. *Fall:* late August to early October. *Extremes:* 9 April; 8 November.

BREEDING DATA. Primary nesting data lacking. Recently fledged young: 5 July to 15 August.

WINTER. Four records.

PORTRAIT. *Birds of Wisconsin:* Plate 70.

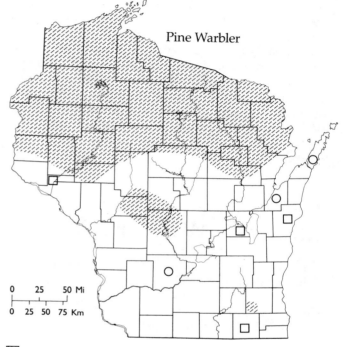

Pine Warbler

0   25   50 Mi

0   25 50 75 Km

⬚ (hatched) Summer range
○ Early June to mid-August
□ Mid-December to early February

Records since 1960

Southern Wisconsin observers find it difficult to realize that the Pine Warbler is fairly numerous in parts of some northern counties. Some call it downright rare as a spring and fall migrant; they often go through a season without spotting a single one. Seldom do banders succeed in trapping these birds. Numbers of television tower casualties are also remarkably low. At the Eau Claire tower during the 1960–1969 period, only one specimen turned up in spring and four (out of a total of 40,000 towerkills) in fall.

But the northern counties have many areas where small, loose stands of tall white pines can be found. Often, these stands are near lakes where summer cottages abound. It may well be that hundreds of summer vacationers have Pine Warblers nesting overhead but are unaware of them because they are not familiar with the bird's trill-y song.

The earliest spring arrivals are as apt to turn up in the central region as in the southernmost counties. The earliest April arrivals include the 9th (1985, Shawano, M. S. Peterson), 11th (1977, Jackson, D. Harmer), 16th (1955, Fond du Lac, G. Henseler; 1976, Chippewa, C. A. Kemper), and 18th (1967, Wood, S. D. Robbins) in the central region. Northern arrivals have appeared by the 25th (1942, Sawyer, K. W. Kahmann; 1948, Oneida, L. Almon). The main migration occurs between 25 April and 15 May. The latest spring date for the southern area is 25 May (1961, Milwaukee, D. L. Larkin).

The summer range is a spotty one. Although this species is described as being a summer resident far to the south of Wisconsin, it occurs nowhere in southern Wisconsin except for a small colony in Waukesha County (J. E. Bielefeldt). In the central region small numbers are present all summer long in suitable habitat between Adams and Black River Falls (Jackson County), but no comparable area is known in the eastern counties. It is in the northern half of the state that the distribution becomes more widespread, with the greatest numbers in the northwest. The Pine Warbler has been found on 27 of the state's 70 BBS transects, with six the largest number recorded on any one route.

In spite of all these summer occurrences, I can find no recorded instance where any observer has actually looked into an active Wisconsin nest. Schorger (1931a) watched three fledged young being fed by a female on 15 August (1929, Oneida). In Vilas County, 5 July 1962, Martha and Roy Lound watched a pair feeding four recently fledged young. On 22 June 1965 in the same county I watched two pairs making frequent trips into thick vegetation in a grove of white pines, one pair frequenting a spot 30 feet up, the other pair 35 feet up in a different tree. But I did not see either nest. Nests are characteristically built high up in mature pines. Although specific information is scanty, the likelihood is that this species nests in at least 30 counties in Wisconsin every year.

Once singing stops in mid-July, birds are hard to find. But occasional song fragments and chipping suggest that birds often remain on breeding grounds well into August. During fall migration birds move out of the tall pines to join mixed warbler flocks in deciduous trees, and may be seen any time from 25 August to 5 October. But records are scanty. My personal sightings average two to three per fall. Few other birders have had more success. The paucity of field observations, banding records, and tower casualties suggests that most of the summer residents leave as they come: nonstop.

Unusually late were birds noted on 20 October (1974, Manitowoc, M. Albrecht), 29 October (1963, Racine, L. W. Erickson), and 8 November (1914, Dane, N. D. Betts [Schorger 1931a]). Even more remarkable are three CBC records. One bird was found near Durand (Pepin County) on 14 December 1974 (S. D. Robbins); one was in a tamarack bog in company with Yellow-rumped Warblers in Walworth County on 26 December 1960 (C. O. Palmquist); and one appeared in Manitowoc County on 27 December 1980, remaining through 6 January 1981 (C. R. Sontag). Later yet, one was observed at close range in a cemetery at Oshkosh on 1 February 1975 (R. A. Knuth).

Kirtland's Warbler (*Dendroica kirtlandii*)

STATUS. Casual spring migrant. Casual summer resident north and central.
HABITAT. Young coniferous forest.
MIGRATION DATES. *Spring:* observed between 18 and 26 May. Present in summer until 24 July.

Just as fishermen have had their favorite stories about "the big one that got away," so have Kumlien and Hollister (1903) related how a specimen of this great rarity escaped from their hands in Jefferson County on 24 May 1893. After watching the bird carefully from a distance of 10 feet, the observers wounded the warbler as they were trying to collect it, and then finally captured it after a mad scramble. But in their zeal to handle the specimen with the greatest of care, they lost control of the bird, which promptly disappeared into an impenetrable thicket. Before that time, the only state report of any kind was a brief sight record in Racine by Hoy (1853b) on 20 May 1853.

As the narrow habitat requirements of this bird became better known, various observers began searching appropriate habitat in central Wisconsin in hopes of finding more individuals. The latitude of the central Michigan range parallels that portion of Wisconsin between Adams and Wausau. Much jack pine, preferred by the Kirtland's, occurs in this central Wis-

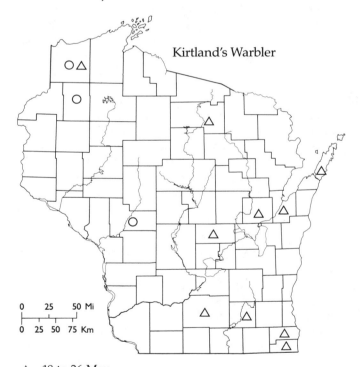

Kirtland's Warbler

△ 18 to 26 May
○ 9 June to 24 July

All records

Kirtland's Warbler, 10 June 1978, Jackson County (photo by N. G. Tilghman)

consin region, west of Wautoma and east of Black River Falls.

Until 1978 all such efforts were fruitless. Then in May 1978, spurred by the discovery of an extralimital wanderer in southern Ontario, a project sponsored by the Wisconsin Department of Natural Resources began, with 13 teams of observers covering possible jack pine areas. One of these teams was successful. On 10 June project leader Nancy Tilghman and Randy Rogers found two singing males east of Black River Falls (Jackson County). One was trapped and photographed; it proved to be an individual banded 6 years previously near Grayling, Michigan, by L. H. Walkinshaw. One of these birds was still present on 24 July. Thirty-five miles farther east in northern Juneau County another individual apparently responded to a tape-recorded song on 9 June 1978, but all attempts to obtain visual confirmation proved unsuccessful (*Pass. Pigeon* 41:16–24).

In early June 1979 DNR personnel checked 38 jack pine sites in central Wisconsin. A singing male responded to a taped song on 15 June, a mile from the 1978 Jackson County site (E. Kohlmeyer, T. Valen). Although the singer was not seen on that occasion, it was probably the same individual, observed subsequently on 7 July by D. G. Follen (*Pass. Pigeon* 42:86). Although DNR personnel searching in 1980 found no Kirtland's Warblers, Daryl Tessen saw and heard one on 14 June in the same Jackson County region (*Pass. Pigeon* 43:64). All subsequent efforts have failed to yield results.

Between the time of Kumlien and Hollister's near-record and 1978, these additional sight records have occurred: 19 May 1917 (Dane, W. Taylor [1917]); 18 May 1941 (Outagamie, N. M. Rogers; *Pass. Pigeon* 3:59); 23 May 1942 (Kenosha, J. L. Diedrich); 23 May 1946 (Oneida, L. Almon; *Pass. Pigeon* 9:52); 20 May 1956 (Door, C. H. Hussong; *Pass. Pigeon* 18:122–123); 25–26 May 1967 (Brown, Bro. Columban; *Pass. Pigeon* 30:29); and 21 May 1971 (Waushara, D. E. Greenman; *Pass. Pigeon* 34:40). Most of these birds have been seen under ideal conditions at close range. Taylor, for instance, watched the Madison bird for 45 minutes, sometimes so close that he could almost capture it by hand. The Hussongs were able to show their Door County bird to numerous additional observers over a period of several hours. But rainy weather prevented photography.

In 1988 the Bureau of Endangered Resources staff renewed the search for Kirtland's Warblers in the jack pine regions of western and northwestern Wisconsin. Between 9 and 18 June J. L. Polk noted four singing males in Jackson County (*Pass. Pigeon* 51:124–125). R. J. Johnson found another on 20 June in Douglas County (*Pass. Pigeon* 51:123). Yet another sighting was made in Washburn County. All were singing males. Similar efforts in 1989 were less successful, but Larry Semo found a singing male in Douglas County on 21–22 May (*Pass. Pigeon* 51:414). Should a female appear, with breeding following, this species would qualify for the state's endangered species list.

Prairie Warbler (*Dendroica discolor*)

STATUS. Rare spring migrant; casual fall migrant. Rare summer resident south.

HABITAT. Upland deciduous forest. Upland carr.

MIGRATION DATES. *Spring:* early to late May. *Fall:* early September to early October. *Extremes:* 25 April; 8 October.

PORTRAIT. *Birds of Wisconsin:* Plate 70.

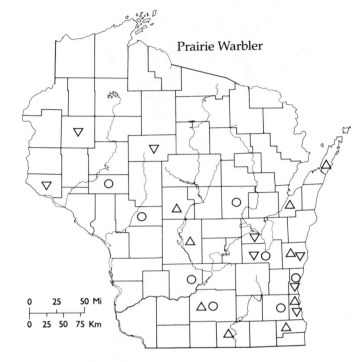

Prairie Warbler

```
0     25    50 Mi
0  25  50  75 Km
```

△   Early to late May
○   Early June to early August
▽   4 September to 8 October

All records

Before 1947 the Prairie Warbler was considered one of Wisconsin's rarest warblers. What few records exist for that time are indefinite both in terms of dates and locations. The Racine County Historical Society lists an adult male in the P. R. Hoy collection. Presumably the bird was taken after 1853, because it was not mentioned in Hoy's list of that year (1853b). In that publication Hoy stated only that "a few are occasionally seen about the middle of May."

Kumlien and Hollister (1903) were equally indefinite. They mentioned the Hoy specimen, and another collected by Thure Kumlien in Jefferson County before 1860. They mentioned sight observations "by amateurs," but rejected the sightings as unreliable. Anonymous reference was made in 1940 to three sight observations in Milwaukee in 1933, 1934, and 1935 (*Pass. Pigeon* 2:29), but with no dates, observers, or corroborative data given. It seems strange that an eastern species whose range extends to northeastern Illinois should have been found so rarely in southeastern Wisconsin.

A sudden change began in 1947. Within a 4-day span in May, birds were reported on the 16th and 17th (Dane, H. F. Young) along with two others on the 19th (Milwaukee, M. F. Donald; Sheboygan, H. Koopmann). The following autumn the state's first fall record was established on 8 October (Milwaukee, D. L. Larkin). Spring observations followed in 1948, 1949, and 1950. Since 1952, observers have identified from one to four individuals each year, with only six exceptions.

Most of these birds were "overshooting" May migrants. The 25 April 1949 sighting (Dane, S. D. Robbins) is the state's earliest record, followed by a 30 April discovery (1985, Door, G. Yeomans). The earliest May dates include the 1st (1980, Milwaukee, J. H. Idzikowski), 3rd (1979, Dane, R. M. Hoffman), 5th (1977, Dane, R. Korotev), and 6th (1964, Brown, T. C. Erdman). Through 1973 these overshoots occurred mainly between 10 and 25 May south and east of a line from Dodgeville to Green Bay, and lingered only a day or two. The latest and most distant spring wanderers were singing males seen on 28 May (1954,

Adams, S. D. Robbins), 1 June (1953, Wood, S. D. Robbins), and 26 May–12 June (1985, Eau Claire, J. L. Polk).

Summer residency, first suspected in 1974 (12 June, Waukesha, J. E. Bielefeldt), was confirmed in 1976 when Waukesha County had two summering individuals, one present from 11 May to 22 June (J. E. Bielefeldt), another observed on 6 July (D. K. Gustafson). Another singing male was present near Millston (Jackson County) concurrently (11 June–2 July, S. D. Robbins). June 1978 brought visitors to Dane (R. M. Hoffman) and Sauk (K. I. Lange) counties. In 1981 an individual was present in Fond du Lac County between 9 May (T. R. Schultz) and 13 June (D. D. Tessen). Summer residency has occurred annually, 1985–1989, in Ozaukee County. No suspicions of nesting accompanied any of these June-July observations.

Of nine known late summer and autumn sightings, five occurred in the eastern counties, where a majority of spring records have been made: 6 September (1983, Fond du Lac, W. K. Volkert), 20 September–6 October (1971, Sheboygan, E. Kuhn), 30 September (1968, Winnebago, E. Fisher), 1 October (1965, Ozaukee, M. F. Donald), and Larkin's 8 October 1947 bird at Milwaukee. The other four represented remarkable wandering: 23 July (1987, Waupaca, R. M. Hoffman), 4 September (1956, Pierce, Manley Olson), 10 September (1981, Taylor, S. D. Robbins), and 4 October (1956, Barron, E. Butler).

No definite habitat preference has been noted for those birds that have wandered to Wisconsin. Within its regular range the Prairie shows a preference for partly open land interspersed with Hill's oak and pine. Two of the six Wisconsin birds I have encountered were singing in oaks, two were in sparse jack pine stands, one was in an apple tree in a residential area, and one in an alder thicket. But all were less than 12 feet up. And all spring and summer birds were singing their distinctive song—a rapid series of buzzes gradually ascending in pitch. One's best chance to meet up with this bird is first to learn the song thoroughly from the fine recordings now available and then go afield in mid-May and listen.

Palm Warbler (*Dendroica palmarum*)

STATUS. Common migrant. Uncommon summer resident north.

HABITAT. Conifer swamp (during breeding). Deciduous forest; all carr (during migration).

MIGRATION DATES. *Spring:* mid-April to late May. *Fall:* late August to late October. *Extremes:* 24 March; 16 November.

BREEDING DATA. Nest with 3 eggs: 20 May. Nest with young: 29 June.

PORTRAIT. *Birds of Wisconsin:* Plate 70.

It is hard to make numerical comparisons between the Palm and other warbler species. If one bander sets his nets in a wooded region, he may trap good numbers of a large variety of warbler species, but he will take few Palms. If an observer spends most of his time afield in sparsely overgrown pasture, he may find Palms by the dozen but draw a blank on most other warbler species. But there is general agreement that this is one of the more common warblers for at least a short period each spring and fall, and on occasion it seems almost abundant.

Not having as far to travel in migration as most other warblers, it is one of the earliest to arrive. In favorable springs it spreads across the state from 20 to 30 April, while in backward years arrivals may appear as much as 10 days later. An exceptionally early arrival was present in Walworth County between 24 and 27 March 1968 (J. Lustyk). Early-April sightings have occurred on the 5th (1976, Manitowoc, M. Albrecht), 6th (1948, Milwaukee, M. H. Doll), and 10th (1977, Brown, E. D. Cleary). By the time the numbers of most other warblers are reaching a peak, around 15–20 May, the Palms are declining in number. An occasional bird has been recorded in the southern counties as late as 30 May, but the 20th is the more usual departure date.

Palm Warbler

0	25 50 Mi
0	25 50 75 Km

▨ Summer range
○ Early June to early August

Records since 1960

Fall migrants have been recorded as early as 20 August (1963, Milwaukee, M. F. Donald) and 21 August (1980, Brown, E. D. Cleary). Normally, first birds are not seen before 30 August, then they progress through the state during the 1–10 September interval. Between 1960 and 1969, Eau Claire television tower kills were noted between 4 September and 12 October. Kills of 100 or more birds occurred on 19 September 1963, 26 September 1965, 1 October 1965, and

12 October 1969. This represents fairly well the peak period for most of the state. Numbers drop off rapidly after 15 October. November lingerers have been noted on the 10th (1972, Oconto, T. C. Erdman; 1980, Waupaca, J. S. Anderson), 11th (1973, Milwaukee, M. F. Donald), 12th (1955, Dane, M. A. Walker), and 16th (1974, La Crosse, F. Z. Lesher). In fall, as in spring, the Palm avoids the woodlands. In sparsely wooded edges, along hedgerows, and even along the shoulders of the less-traveled country roads this warbler can often be found in fall in company with migrating sparrows.

Between spring and fall a few individuals remain in suitable habitat to nest in the northern counties. "Suitable habitat" has sometimes been described as a spruce-tamarack swamp. But no ordinary bog will do. It must be one in which there is an abundance of grass and sphagnum moss and a minimum of woody vegetation. There is a favored bog a mile south of Three Lakes (Oneida County) where this bird has been recorded frequently since 1962; observations have included watching agitated parents carrying food, but no positive nest was found until 1978 (nest with young, 29 June, R. Spahn). The only other observer known to have viewed a Wisconsin nest is Francis Zirrer. In Sawyer County he found a nest with three eggs on 20 May 1949. The nest was sunk in a moss depression under the overhanging boughs of a small black spruce. Zirrer recorded this bird on numerous other occasions in Rusk and Sawyer counties during the 1930s and 1940s, and believed it to be a regular nester in that area. Concerning the habitat requirements, Zirrer wrote (pers. comm. to O. J. Gromme): It "does not breed in or even frequent, bogs where conifers—especially tamarack and black spruce—shade the sphagnum in close formation; or where the bog is overgrown densely with bog shrubbery with few or no trees. It prefers situations where trees—tamarack, black spruce, balsam and cedar, large and small, in groups and singly, alternate with sphagnum and scattered bog shrubbery."

Grange (1924a) observed probable nesting in Rusk County in 1923. Additional summer records have come from Douglas, Sawyer, Price, Ashland, Iron, Vilas, and Forest counties, each representing probable but unconfirmed breeding.

Bay-breasted Warbler (*Dendroica castanea*)

STATUS. Fairly common spring migrant; common fall migrant. Rare summer resident north.
HABITAT. Deciduous forest. Savanna.
MIGRATION DATES. *Spring:* early to late May. *Fall:* mid-August to early October. *Extremes:* 20 April; 12 November.
PORTRAIT. *Birds of Wisconsin:* Plate 69.

The Bay-breasted Warbler's passage through the state in spring is rapid, often with only 2 weeks separating arrival and departure dates at any one locality. For the southern counties the main migration occurs between 10 and 25 May; for the north the schedule is 5–7 days later. The 2 weeks extend to 3 when a few of the earlier vanguard accompany earlier waves of migrants between 1 and 10 May. Only three April arrivals have been discovered: the remarkable 20 April bird (1953, Waushara, F. H. Wagner), one on the 26th (1984, Milwaukee, J. H. Idzikowski), and one on the 30th (1974, Dane, T. L. Ashman). The 3 weeks extend to 4 on those rare occasions when stragglers remain until early June. Late dates for the southern counties include the 6th (1947, Milwaukee, I. N. Balsom) and 10th (year uncertain; collected in Jefferson, Kumlien and Hollister [1903]).

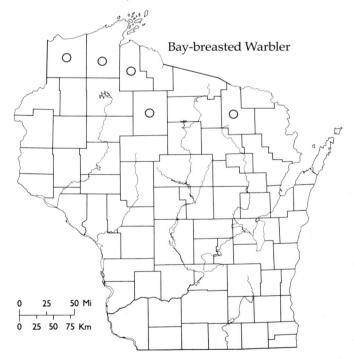

Bay-breasted Warbler

0   25   50 Mi

0   25   50   75 Km

○   Mid-June to early August

Records since 1960

The Bay-breast is not numerous in spring. But if one walks the streets of a residential area during some of the later "wave" days in May, searches the upper branches of the taller elms, and listens for a short, high-pitched, wavy song, one is likely to find a few. And an observer who walks along the edge of an oak woodlot as the tiny new leaves are just emerging may find several Bay-breasts. During spring migration this species shows a pronounced preference for oak woods.

I know of no positive evidence either for breeding or for sustained summer residency in the northern Wisconsin forests. But since the Bay-breast is known to breed in northern Minnesota and Upper Michigan, it should be looked for as a possible summer resident in northern Wisconsin. In addition to June observations on the 16th (1941, Price, W. Woodruff) and 21st (1976, Douglas, C. A. Faanes), there have been four July reports on dates that seem too early for fall migration: the 6th (1960, Bayfield, R. H. Lound), 9th (1919, female collected in Ashland, H. H. Sheldon [Jackson, 1943]), 15th (1933, Forest, W. E. Scott, pers. comm.), and 21st (1970, Forest, D. K. Gustafson).

The fall migration pattern differs markedly from the spring flight. Replacing the typical 2 week spring passage period is a 4–6–week period nearly every autumn. In the northern counties this is from 20 August to 25 September, with scattered sightings between 1 August and 30 September. In the south it is from 30 August to 15 October, with occasional records between 14 August and 25 October. Exceptionally late were two November finds on the 6th (1971, Racine, M. Stoffel) and 12th (1974, Chippewa, C. A. Kemper). Central Wisconsin patterns are typified by Eau Claire television tower casualty figures for the 1960–1969 period, occurring from 23 August to 12 October, with one very late bird on 20 October 1968. During that span 100 or more individuals per night were found on 10 occasions, 8 of which were between 16 and 26 September.

Were it not for tower casualty figures, one would not guess the real fall abundance of this species. Mistnet trapping figures are low because this species usually remains in the higher branches during migration. Field observation figures are low because many individuals are not seen well enough for positive identification. Close views under ideal conditions are needed to distinguish this species from the similarly plumaged Blackpoll Warbler. Of the 40,000 fall warbler casualties at Eau Claire, 1960–1969, 4,424 were Baybreasts; only the Tennessee and the Ovenbird exceeded this number. Even when allowance is made for the disproportionately small numbers of Yellowrumps and Palms striking the towers, the conclusion is inescapable that the Bay-breast is among the most common of fall warblers.

Blackpoll Warbler (*Dendroica striata*)

STATUS. Common migrant. Casual summer visitant.
HABITAT. Deciduous forest. Savanna.
MIGRATION DATES. *Spring:* early May to early June.
  Fall: mid-August to early October. *Extremes:* 25
  April; 31 October.
PORTRAIT. *Birds of Wisconsin:* Plate 69.

To someone who cannot hear high-pitched sounds,
the Blackpoll Warbler must seem decidedly uncommon as a spring migrant. The bird prefers the higher
branches of the tallest deciduous trees and lacks the
conspicuous coloration of many of its close relatives.
Its song, though uttered frequently, is pitched so
high that many observers miss it entirely.

Those who can detect the high, piercing song find
this to be a common May migrant, with a slightly
later pattern than that of most other warblers. Only
five late-April arrival dates have been recorded in the
state, the earliest being the 25th (1957, Waukesha,
O. L. Compton). Most southern Wisconsin observers
have to wait until 10 May for the first appearance of
this warbler. Normally, the southern peak falls between 15 and 25 May, and stragglers into the first
week of June are frequent. Farther north the peak is
from 20 to 30 May. The regular period lies between 15
May and 5 June, while stragglers are noted from 10
May to 10 June. Extremely late birds have been recorded on 13 June (1925, Dane, A. W. Schorger
[1931a]), 16 June (1968, Sauk, K. I. Lange), and 23 June
(1981, Douglas, R. J. Johnson).

There is no indication that a mid-June songster has
intentions of nesting. Kumlien and Hollister (1903)
mentioned June and July records for the northern
counties and surmised that "no doubt a few breed
within our borders." But they gave no specific July
dates; nor should any be expected for a species whose
normal nesting range lies north of central Ontario. I
have spent many hours afield in the northern counties during late June and July without finding a trace
of this bird. I have looked in vain in both the deciduous
forests and the black spruce swamps that provide favored habitat within the normal breeding range. Only
four July records for Wisconsin in the twentieth century are known: one bird spending 4 days between
the 4th and 7th (1977, Winnebago, C. Schultz), one
seen on the 15th (1979, Vernon, V. E. Weber), one on
the 20th (1941, Shawano, E. W. Strehlow), and one on
the 21st (1977, Ashland, S. A. Temple).

August arrivals have been noted as early as the 6th
(1952, banded in Fond du Lac, G. Henseler), 9th

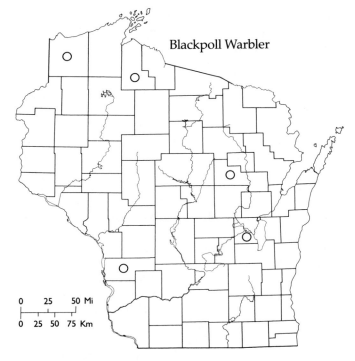

Blackpoll Warbler

○   Mid-June to late July

Records since 1960

(1975, Door, L. W. Erickson), and 10th (1922, Ashland,
H. H. T. Jackson [1943]; 1962, Douglas, S. D. Robbins)
in the northern and central regions, and in the south
by the 14th (1977, Racine, L. W. Erickson).

Usually it is not until 25 August that returning fall
migrants become noticeable. Migrants can be found
anywhere in the state any time during September,
but appear to be less numerous along the western
edge. Schorger (1931a) considered them scarce in
Dane County. My St. Croix County records (1960–
1967) showed fewer than 1% of the identifiable warblers to be Blackpolls, compared with 2% during a
comparable stretch in Adams County (1951–1959). Yet
television tower casualties at Eau Claire numbered
2,259 (5.7%) during the 1960–1969 span, indicating
that this is a common migrant. Heavy towerkills at
Milwaukee have also been recorded. Wisconsin apparently catches just the fringe of the huge flight that
passes eastward through Canada and New England
before taking an oceanic route to the South American
wintering grounds.

In most years the fall flight has ended by 30 September in the north, 5 October in the central region,

and 10 October in the south. But tower casualties at Eau Claire have occurred as late as the 12th, and birds have been sighted at the Cedar Grove Ornithological Station in Sheboygan County as late as the 19th. The latest dates on record are the 21st (1973, Milwaukee, E. L. Basten), 25th (1968, Outagamie, D. D. Tessen), 27th (1961, Rock, M. K. Stocking), and 31st (1982, Winnebago, T. Ziebell).

Cerulean Warbler (*Dendroica cerulea*)

STATUS. Uncommon migrant south and central; rare migrant north. Uncommon summer resident south and central; rare summer resident north.

HABITAT. Deciduous forest.

MIGRATION DATES. *Spring:* late April to late May. *Fall:* no discernible flight, but present until 25 August. *Extremes:* 23 April; 12 October.

BREEDING DATA. Nest with eggs: 17 June. Nests with young: 23 June to 1 July. Clutch size: 4 eggs.

PORTRAIT. *Birds of Wisconsin:* Plate 69.

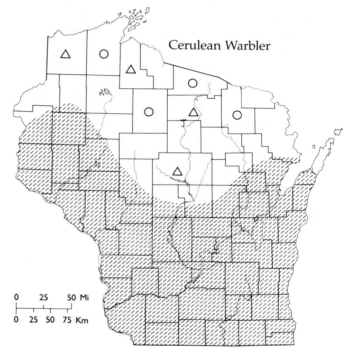

Cerulean Warbler

⬚ Summer range
△ Late April to late May
○ Early June to late July

Records since 1960

Writing of the only Cerulean Warbler he had ever seen in 20 years of birding in Oshkosh (11 May 1950), J. H. Evans (pers. comm. to O. J. Gromme) recounted, "It practically sat on my nose, and I had a thrilling look at it as it fed." This is most atypical behavior. This bird, more than almost any other warbler, is usually found far up in the canopy of tall oaks and maples. Few observers have a chance to fully appreciate the lovely blue plumage of this southern visitor, for the sunlight that might accentuate the color rarely penetrates the canopy where the bird resides.

But observers can appreciate the delicate, distinctive song of a bird that is more often heard than seen. The song has a buzzy quality. With a bit of poetic license, one might imagine that the bird is giving off a sneeze after several introductory gasps: "ah, ch-ch-ch-ch-cheez." The song has little carrying power; ordinarily one must be within 100 yards of the bird to hear it at all.

The Cerulean is strictly a bird of the deciduous woodland. Although the bird was known as a rarity in southeastern Wisconsin in the nineteenth century, it remained for H. L. Stoddard and A. W. Schorger to determine that there were localities in the southwest where this species was fairly common. In 1913 Stoddard (1917) collected 10 specimens in the Baraboo Bluffs in Sauk County and across the Wisconsin River in the Mazomanie region in Dane County. These birds inhabited the maple-basswood-oak moist lowlands between the bluffs. Schorger thought it abundant in the Potosi area in Grant County, and found it to be common in Grant, Green, Dane, and Sauk counties in the 1920s. He found the birds not only in the bottomlands but also along the densely wooded hillsides. He collected one specimen in a thin stand of oaks atop a rocky bluff.

This oak- and maple-dweller has gradually extended its range northward. Gromme (1963) described the northern range limit as a line stretching from La Crosse through Adams, Fond du Lac, and Cleveland. A few pioneers had already penetrated north of that line, as indicated by first county records in Pierce (1942), Wood (1942), Waupaca (1946), Clark (1947), Winnebago (1947), Manitowoc (1947), Marathon (1954), Brown (1956), and Door (1957). By 1968 summering birds had been discovered in Polk, Barron, Washburn, Chippewa, Menominee, and Marinette counties. Little extension has occurred since 1968. Summer observations in Bayfield (27 June 1972, S. D. Robbins), Price (27 June 1979, M. Hardy), and Forest (12 June 1988, S. D. Robbins) counties were not repeated in succeeding years. May 1977 brought overshooting May migrants to Douglas, Ashland, and Vilas counties. Since 1970 the summer range has been thought of as the southern half of the state, with a bulge in the west, north to St. Croix Falls and Sarona, and one in the east, north to Keshena, Peshtigo, and Sturgeon Bay.

There are no exceptionally early spring migration records. Only in the more backward springs have first arrivals not been noticed by 10 May. Usually an observer spots one by 5 May. The earliest birds have been recorded in April, on the 23rd (1975, Waukesha, J. E. Bielefeldt; 1975, Milwaukee, M. F. Donald), 24th (1977, Sheboygan, H. Koopmann), and 25th (1979, Dane, R. M. Hoffman). In the central counties most spring dates fall between 15 and 25 May, with the earliest being a television tower casualty at Eau Claire on 4 May 1960 (C. A. Kemper).

Kumlien and Hollister (1903) mentioned a nesting record in the Lake Koshkonong area in Jefferson County on 14 June 1872 but gave no details. Adults feeding fledged young have been reported in Waukesha County on 6 August 1922 (Jones 1923) and 24 July 1943 (W. B. Jackson). Positive nesting evidence came on 17 June 1960, when W. E. Southern (1962a) and N. L. Cuthbert found a nest with four eggs in Washburn County. Three young fledged by 26 June from this nest, which was 15 feet up in a white oak on a wooded hilltop. Near the same site, the following June, Southern found and photographed another nest, 35 feet up in a different oak. There can be no doubt that this bird nests every year in small numbers in various parts of Wisconsin.

Because this is a bird of the treetops, it is hard to find once the summer song period ends. Observers agree that the song period generally ceases by 10 July, but instances exist of occasional song fragments being heard through July and August. Kenneth Lange detected song from a Sauk County bird on 29 September 1968. No birds have turned up during the extensive fall trapping ventures at Milwaukee and Cedar Grove (Sheboygan County), and none have been identified among the 40,000 fall warbler casualties at Eau Claire. In addition to Lange's late songster, the only records beyond 15 September are 16 September 1967 (Waukesha, D. A. Bratley), 20 September 1942 (Dane, S. D. Robbins), and 12 October 1967 (Waukesha, E. Hoffmann).

Black-and-white Warbler (*Mniotilta varia*)

STATUS. Common migrant. Common summer resident north; fairly common summer resident central; rare summer resident west and southwest.

HABITAT. Northern maple-hemlock-pine forest. Coniferous forest.

MIGRATION DATES. *Spring:* late April to late May. *Fall:* mid-August to early October. *Extremes:* 4 April; 8 December.

BREEDING DATA. Nests with eggs: 28 May to 15 June. Clutch size: 4 or 5 eggs.

PORTRAIT. *Birds of Wisconsin:* Plate 66.

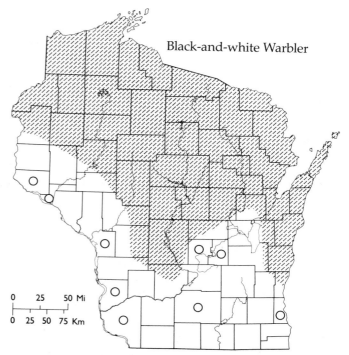

Black-and-white Warbler

0   25   50 Mi
0 25 50 75 Km

▨ Summer range
○ Early June to late July

Records since 1960

Glancing at a range map in any of the popular field guides showing the summer range to extend south nearly to the Gulf of Mexico but north only moderately into Canada, one might assume that the Black-and-white Warbler would be more common in southern Wisconsin than in the northern section. Just the opposite is true. In the southern counties it is common as a spring and fall migrant, but few birds remain to breed.

Feeding on insects associated with bark rather than with leaves, Black-and-white Warblers have a spring migratory pattern slightly in advance of most other warblers except the Yellow-rumped, the Pine, and the Palm. First sightings in the southern counties usually occur around 25 April, sometimes closer to the 15th. Exceptionally early were April birds on the 4th (1974, Milwaukee, J. H. Idzikowski), 5th (1939, Milwaukee, A. L. Throne), 6th (1975, Jefferson, C. Steuer), 8th (1980, Door, T. De Boor), and 12th (1973, Racine, M. Stoffel). The peak period in the south is 5–15 May. First arrivals in the north are expected around 5–10 May, and have been detected by 29 April (1955, Barron, J. Butler) and 30 April (1942, Vilas, E. T. Mitchell). A 15–25 May peak follows.

By 25 May the migration is usually over. In the nineteenth century this meant the start of nesting throughout the state. By 1930 Schorger (1931a) thought of this bird as strictly a migrant in the Madison area. By that year it had probably ceased to be a breeding bird in the two southernmost tiers of counties, with the possible exception of Grant and Crawford counties. Summer observations along the Mississippi and lower St. Croix river valleys are too sporadic to indicate regular residence there. But in the forested regions of central Wisconsin a few birds are regularly found in June and July south to the Baraboo hills in Sauk County. In eastern Wisconsin small breeding populations exist in the northern Kettle Moraine region in Fond du Lac County and in the Cedarburg

Bog region in Ozaukee County. Since 1965 the Black-and-white Warbler has been recorded on 44 of the state's 70 BBS routes, but it is regular on only 26. This species is common in summer only north of a line from St. Croix Falls through Wausau to Sturgeon Bay.

Of seven reported nests, six have been on the ground, the seventh 2 feet up in a shrub. Black-and-whites frequently conceal nests under fallen logs. Most egg-laying occurs between 1 and 15 June, but incubation undoubtedly continues into early July, for parents have been reported feeding recently fledged young as late as 22 July.

Early August ushers in the beginning of fall migration. Eau Claire television tower casualties have occurred as early as the 13th, and fall arrivals have been detected in Milwaukee on the 4th and in Racine on the 10th. Migration becomes much stronger by the 25th and continues through most of September, with only a few birds left in early October. Substantial numbers of migrants appear in both the eastern and western parts of the state during that interval.

Neither in migration nor in the breeding season does the "black-and-white creeper" display a narrow habitat preference. In the northern forests the bird prefers mixed coniferous-deciduous woods, but it is frequently seen in swamp conifers as well. During migration it mixes with other passerines in a variety of woodland habitats. It is most often found in the understory, less than 15 feet above ground, and frequently responds to "squeaking."

The latest departure date for the northern counties is 8 October (1966, Marinette, H. L. Lindberg). In the central counties a bird remained until 22 October (1950, Sheboygan, G. H. Orians). Late individuals in the south have been sighted on 25 October (1977, Racine, L. W. Erickson), 30 October (1972, Kenosha, R. R. Hoffman), and 4 November (1978, Kenosha, R. R. Hoffman). It was an astonished G. W. Foster who encountered a very late straggler in Dane County on 8 December 1973.

American Redstart (*Setophaga ruticilla*)

STATUS. Abundant migrant. Common summer resident north and central; fairly common summer resident south.

HABITAT. Deciduous forest. Northern maple-hemlock-pine forest. Lowland carr.

MIGRATION DATES. *Spring:* early to late May. *Fall:* mid-August to mid-October. *Extremes:* 20 March; 26 November.

BREEDING DATA. Nests with eggs: 20 May to 13 July. Clutch size: usually 4 eggs; occasionally 3 or 5.

PORTRAIT. *Birds of Wisconsin:* Plate 72.

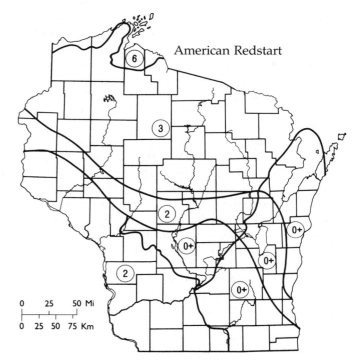

Breeding Bird Survey, averages 1966 to 1980

W. W. Cooke (Cooke and Widmann 1883) estimated 200–300 American Redstarts while birding in Jefferson County on 19 May 1883, finding them "as numerous as all the other warblers together." Various other observers—including Kumlien and Hollister (1903), Schorger (1931a), Buss and Mattison (1955), and Gromme (1963)—have referred to this bird as abundant, while others have been content to call it common.

Without question the redstart is one of the most conspicuous warblers. The coloration is vivid. The song is loud, clear, and incessant. The bird frequents low and medium-height vegetation, and it moves among the more visible perches rather than hiding stealthily behind the thickest foliage. It responds to "squeaking" far more readily than do most other warblers.

In certain types of habitat this flashy singer is indeed abundant both as a summer resident and as a migrant. It is fond of deciduous woods near swamps, lakes, and streams. Any kind of leafy woods will do, but maples are particularly attractive. Less favored but acceptable in summer are densely wooded hillsides, especially in the southern and central areas such as the Kettle Moraine State Forest in Fond du Lac County, the Baraboo hills in Sauk County, and the coulee region of western Wisconsin. In the northern forests many thousands of acres of suitable habitat lack redstarts. In those forests these birds show a still greater tendency to concentrate near water, but even there the population is spotty. If one canoes along the lower stretches of the Flambeau in Rusk County, one can hear them by the dozen; along the Bois Brule in Douglas County, one hears only a few.

The BBS data show that redstarts are common in the north, but less numerous than several other warbler species; present in the southern and central regions, but suitable habitat is sparse; and abundant on

Washington Island in Door County, where favored habitat is plentiful.

The earliest arrivals on record were discovered on 20 March (1946, Milwaukee, L. P. Steven) and 7 April (1950, Dodge, R. Pillmore); these probably represent birds blown far off course by violent storms. Unusually early also were birds observed on 12 April (1977, Door, R. J. Lukes) and 15 April (1973, Grant, C. Ruttman; 1987, Vilas, J. E. Baughman). Another 12 records exist for the 23–30 April period, with most southern Wisconsin first arrivals appearing in the 1–5 May span. This is followed by a 10–20 May peak—sometimes modest, sometimes spectacular—during which birds disperse over a wide variety of deciduous woodlands and residential habitats. At this time a rapid departure of nonbreeding birds occurs. Farther north birds are few in number before the 10th, but are common between the 15th and 25th. Eau Claire television tower casualty data show that some migration is still in progress at the end of May.

Well before the last nonbreeders have departed, some breeders have paired off and begun nest construction. Nest-building has been reported by 10 May, and complete sets of eggs have been discovered as early as the 20th. Most nesting activity occurs between the 30th and 5 July, with a small amount continuing through July. Margarette Morse once observed nest construction still in progress on 30 June. Nests with eggs have been reported through 13 July. Significant information about a variety of nest sites was obtained by Grundtvig (1895), who studied 38 nests in Outagamie County in 1882. Over half (23) were placed over water. One was 32 feet up, with all others at heights of 2–15 feet. All were in deciduous trees: maple (10), elm (7), ash (6), oak (5), willow (4), alder (2), and other (4). Reporting on eight nests in

Oconto County more recently (1946–1964), C. H. Richter also found all nests at fairly low elevations (3–12 feet), mostly in alders. A nest he saw in a white cedar is the only recorded instance of one in a conifer. All were near water.

Birds banded on 8 August (1938, Waukesha, V. C. Rossman) and 10 August (1944, Rock, M. T. Maxson) indicate that fall migrants are sometimes moving south well before the 15th. Heavy towerkills at Eau Claire (100 or more per night) occurred six times during the 1960–1969 period, all between 4 and 20 September. This suggests a 1–20 September peak for the northern and central areas, with a presumed southern peak a week later. A few Eau Claire tower specimens have been picked up as late as 12 October, but usually only stragglers remain in northern and central counties after 30 September. In the south there is a rapid tapering off in early October, with most birds gone by the 20th. Occasional lingerers have been noted as late as the 30th (1955, Dane, G. H. Orians) and 31st (1949, Winnebago, E. Fisher; 1954, Vernon, M. E. Morse). A phenomenally late bird was briefly sighted in Milwaukee on 26 November 1966 (D. K. Gustafson) at a time when it normally should have been in Mexico or Central America.

Banding operations, as well as television tower casualty figures, show the fall migration to be very heavy in some years. At the Cedar Grove Ornithological Station in Sheboygan County 422 birds were banded during the fall of 1960. A bird banded there on 19 May 1962 (H. C. Mueller) was recaptured in Honduras on 8 January 1963. Another, banded at Manitowoc on 5 September 1966 (B. N. Brouchoud), was found in northeastern Ohio on 22 September, having traveled some 400 miles in 17 days.

Prothonotary Warbler (*Protonotaria citrea*)

STATUS. Fairly common migrant and summer resident along the Mississippi and lower St. Croix rivers; uncommon migrant and summer resident along the lower Wisconsin River; rare spring migrant and summer resident elsewhere south and central.

HABITAT. Southern silver maple–elm forest.

MIGRATION DATES. *Spring:* late April to late May. *Fall:* no discernible flight, but present until early September. *Extremes:* 16 April; 22 September.

BREEDING DATA. Nests with eggs: 31 May to 16 June. Clutch size: 3–5 eggs.

PORTRAIT. *Birds of Wisconsin:* Plate 66.

For the Wisconsin observer who glimpses this gorgeous bird, it is hard to decide which provided the greater thrill: the bird's vivid plumage or its rarity. It would indeed be a nonchalant bystander who could gaze at this tiny burst of golden sunshine and not feel a tinge of extra excitement.

For most Wisconsinites the Prothonotary Warbler is certainly rare. Nearly every year two or three strays turn up during spring migration outside the regular breeding range, usually in city parks in Madison, Milwaukee, Appleton, and Green Bay. These birds show themselves briefly in the shrubbery near streams or lagoons and are quickly gone.

The largest numbers are found along the Mississippi River and are best seen by boat. On 18 June 1969 Kenneth Krumm and I spent an hour boating on the Mississippi-Wisconsin River channels in Wyalusing State Park in Grant County. We counted 18 singing males. The next day, 100 miles farther north in Buffalo County, in another hour's boating we tallied 15 more males. The numbers both days could have been doubled or trebled had we had more time.

As a regular summer resident, the Prothonotary is found along the Mississippi and St. Croix rivers north to Osceola, and along the Wisconsin River north to Stevens Point. A small nesting colony east of New London, active in the 1930s, still exists where the Wolf River meanders through wooded bottomlands in western Outagamie County. Canoeists find them in the Sugar River bottoms in Green County. A few pairs continue to nest in the Rock River valley between Beloit and Fort Atkinson, a remnant of the sizable population Kumlien and Hollister (1903) knew in the 1890s around Lake Koshkonong in Jefferson County.

The most northerly sightings of spring transients have been in Douglas (1970), Dunn (1979), Chippewa (1953), Waupaca (1961), and Door (1978) counties.

Prothonotary Warbler

0 25 50 Mi
0 25 50 75 Km

▨ Summer range
△ Late April to late May
○ Early June to early August
▽ Mid-August to late September

Records since 1960

These northern "overshoots" occur between 10 and 20 May at the height of the spring migration. But on a few occasions this bird has arrived in the southern counties during April. Such discoveries have occurred on the 16th (1963, Dane, J. J. Hickey; 1977, Dane, R. M. Hoffman), 20th (1957, Dane, R. G. Wills), and 23rd (1985, Milwaukee, W. A. Cowart).

Nesting activities extend from late May to early July. Stoddard (1917) located five nests on 9 and 11 June 1913, one of which already contained newly hatched young. Schorger (1931a) observed nests with eggs between 31 May and 16 June, with young on the wing by 28 June. I have seen recently fledged young on 4 July. M. J. Mossman found parents feeding young on 26 July. Both Schorger and Stoddard reported that most nests they had seen were located in decayed tree stubs over water, usually 6–10 feet up; one of Schorger's, however, was 35 feet up. The bird sometimes uses nest boxes. On 27 June 1972 three nestlings were banded in a box beside a paper mill shed in Portage County (A. M. Baumgartner).

North of the regular summer range, summer sightings have come from Barron (5 July 1975, C. A. Faanes), Marathon (13 June 1978, S. H. Krings), and Manitowoc (18 June 1981, D. D. Tessen) counties. Much more fieldwork is needed to determine what happens after early July, when young are on the wing and singing stops. Observations in Jackson (7 July 1948, N. M. Roberts) and Dunn (8 July 1943, I. O. Buss)

counties, in areas where the bird had not previously been known, suggest that some postbreeding wandering may take place. In a few instances birds have been noted on their breeding grounds into early September, the latest dates being the 10th (1974, Pierce, C. A. Faanes; 1975, St. Croix, C. A. Faanes), 16th (1949, Dane, S. D. Robbins), 18th (1972, La Crosse, J. R. Rosso), and 22nd (1985, Dane, D. Cederstrom).

Worm-eating Warbler (*Helmitheros vermivorus*)

STATUS. Rare spring migrant south and east; accidental fall migrant. Rare summer resident southwest.
HABITAT. Deciduous forest.
MIGRATION DATES. *Spring:* late April to early June. *Fall:* rarely present until late September. *Extremes:* 3 April; 2 October.
BREEDING DATA. Nest construction: 20 May; fledged young: 7 June.
PORTRAIT. *Birds of Wisconsin:* Plate 66.

Nearly every year from one to five Worm-eating Warblers overshoot the northern edge of their normal Illinois range in spring migration and enter southern Wisconsin. Between 1939 and 1987 *The Passenger Pigeon* published 93 spring records, most of them April and May sightings southeast of a line from Madison to Sheboygan. Exceptional were observations in St. Croix (18 May 1962, S. D. Robbins), Door (12 May 1974, A. Freitag), Brown (17 May 1941 and 13 May 1944, C. H. Hussong), Outagamie (9 May 1981, D. D. Tessen), and Winnebago (13 May 1972, M. Faust) counties.

This species often arrives on its Illinois and Indiana breeding territories in the latter half of April. Thus, it is not surprising that 12 of Wisconsin's records have come during the latter half of April, including birds banded on the 17th (1964, Sheboygan, H. C. Mueller) and 23rd (1962, Waukesha, E. W. Peartree). It is surprising that a bird should have turned up in Milwaukee on 3 April 1976 (J. Jansen); it was seen twice more during the next 8 days (D. K. Gustafson, D. D. Tessen).

Most appearances have been brief: here today, gone tomorrow. On three occasions birds remained at Racine for periods of 1 week; and one bird remained at Cedar Grove (Sheboygan County) for 2 weeks. Most May observations have occurred before 20 May, but two 30 May dates (1968, Milwaukee, M. E. Decker; 1971, Ozaukee, T. Bintz) and a 5–8 June period (1978, Vernon, E. J. Epstein) suggest occasional lingering.

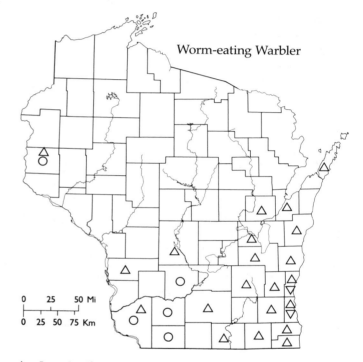

Worm-eating Warbler

0   25   50 Mi
0 25 50 75 Km

△ Late April to early June
○ Mid-June to mid-July
▽ 26 September to 2 October

All records

It is in Wyalusing State Park in Grant County that the possibility of nesting first arose. Late in June 1934, C. S. Robbins saw and heard this bird. Four May sightings followed in 1941, 1956, 1960, and 1961. On 8 June 1963, N. R. and C. L. Barger and R. H. and M. Lound noted a singing male; and on 18 June 1970, K. H. Krumm and I observed another male. To date, no one familiar with the bird has spent sufficient time in this wild area to determine whether it may nest. The steep wooded hillsides of the park provide ideal habitat for it.

A second area where summer residency is probable is in the Baraboo hills in Sauk County. Birds were first discovered there in May 1968, and have been encountered annually since 1976. June observations have taken place regularly at three locations. At Hemlock Draw in 1981 "several observers saw a pair carrying nest material and food, but a nest was never found" (Mossman and Lange, 1982). One or two singing males have been found there every year since I found an individual on 10 July 1976. And one or two singing males have been found in Baxter's Hollow every year since 1977 (M. J. Mossman, pers. comm.). Positive breeding was finally established on 7 June 1984 when M. S. Peterson discovered an active nest.

Wisconsin's only other summer record involved an individual located east of Hazel Green (Lafayette County) on 28 June 1969 (T. R. Ellis). This area has not been adequately checked for possible additional observations. Only twice have birders found Worm-eaters in autumn: 26 September 1920 (Milwaukee,

W. J. Mueller; MPM files) and 2 October 1971 (Ozaukee, T. Bintz).

This species was evidently just as rare a century ago, if not more so. Hoy (1853b) mentioned this species for Racine County, but listed no specimens. There are no specimens in the remnants of his collection now housed at the Racine County Historical Museum. Yet Kumlien and Hollister (1903) recalled three specimens collected by Hoy, as well as individuals procured by Thure Kumlien in Jefferson County in May 1873 and May 1877. In 1910 I. N. Mitchell (MPM files) found individuals on 8 May (Walworth) and 10 May (Dane). *The Passenger Pigeon* published five spring records for the 1940s and another five between 1950 and 1958. Beginning in 1959, spring reports have occurred every year except 1965 and 1973.

This species, nesting only sparingly in southern Wisconsin, was added to the state's list of endangered species in 1989.

Ovenbird (*Seiurus aurocapillus*)

STATUS. Common migrant. Abundant summer resident north; fairly common summer resident central; uncommon summer resident south.
HABITAT. Deciduous forest. Northern maple-hemlock-pine forest.
MIGRATION DATES. *Spring:* early to late May. *Fall:* late August to mid-October. *Extremes:* 31 March; 15 November.
BREEDING DATA. Nests with eggs: 20 May to 7 July. Clutch size: 4 or 5 eggs.
WINTER. Three records.
PORTRAIT. *Birds of Wisconsin:* Plate 70.

State records for the Ovenbird exist for every month except February. This is largely due to five astonishing sightings. One was the bird that spent 2 days eating cracked corn at the Roy Lound feeder in Madison near the end of an unusually mild period (25–26 December 1965). The second was a CBC find in Waukesha County on 17 December 1978. The third was a daily visitor at Paul Blanchard's Eau Claire feeder from 23 November 1982 to 14 January 1983. These three birds should have been some 800 miles farther south by then; but near the Atlantic Coast, individuals have been known to survive December and January as far north as Massachusetts. The fourth and fifth exotics turned up in Madison on 31 March 1950 (R. W. Nero) and 1 April 1943 (I. O. Buss). Cyclonic disturbances occurring just before those dates proba-

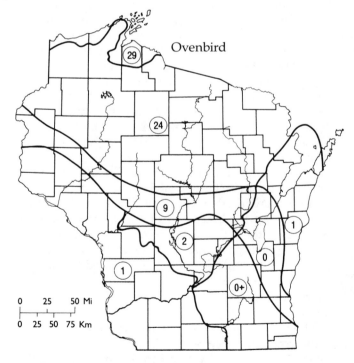

Breeding Bird Survey, averages 1966 to 1980

bly caught these birds near the Gulf states and swept them far off course, so that they reached Wisconsin at a time when they would normally be arriving in the southernmost tier of states.

The usual time for the appearance of first migrants is from 25 April to 5 May. April birds have been found as early as the 8th (1974, Milwaukee, J. H. Idzikowski) and 16th (1977, Racine, J. Rohan) in the south, the 22nd (1980, Brown, M. M. Wierzbicki) in the central counties, and the 30th (1942, Vilas, W. S. Feeney) in the north. There is a modest buildup to a 10–20 May peak. Although usually restricted to deciduous woods, this bird is sometimes found in city parks and residential areas amidst dense shrubbery at the height of the migration. Television tower kills at Eau Claire on 29 May and 1 June 1968 suggest that a small number of migrants may still be passing through at the end of May.

It is hard for southern Wisconsin observers to appreciate how common this bird can be. During spring migration it is moderately common, but no more so than many other transient warblers. In summer it is frequently heard where dense woods exist, but the extensive tracts of deciduous woods preferred by this species are found only in a few locations. In the vast stands of hardwoods in the northern forests, however, the air fairly echoes with its loud emphatic calls of "teacher, teacher" on a typical June morning.

Equally entertaining is the twilight concert on a June evening when the male Ovenbirds offer the novel variations of their flight song. The BBS map shows vividly how this bird's status changes from "uncommon" as a summer resident in the south to "abundant" in the northernmost counties. As many as 81 individuals have been recorded on a single 4-hour transect.

Carl Richter described the typical clutch as four or five eggs, but he noted that it was often depleted by invading Brown-headed Cowbirds. One nest he found contained two host eggs and four of the intruder. Another nest near Marshfield (Wood Country) had three Ovenbird eggs plus four cowbird eggs. All nests reported for the state have been of the kind typical for this bird, with a dome and a side entrance, and have been located on the ground among grass tufts underneath overhanging vegetation. Nesting may take place in deciduous woods or in mixed stands, but rarely does the Ovenbird resort to strictly coniferous areas.

Most nesting takes place in June, with young able to fend for themselves by late July. Singing ends in early July, but one frequently catches sight of these birds by investigating soft call notes heard along the forest edge. Birds are generally on the ground or on low branches; often they respond to "squeaking."

The fall migration is a study in contrasts. Relying on sight observations alone, one would appraise this species as one of the less common fall warblers. My own observations in St. Croix and Chippewa counties have shown that less than 2% of the warblers identified were Ovenbirds; in Adams County the figure was 2.5%. Many observers have gone through an entire fall without seeing a single migrating "teacherbird." Relying on tower casualty data, however, one finds numbers that are more typical for such a common summer bird. Of the 40,000 warblers killed at the Eau Claire television tower, 1960–1969, over 6,500 (16%) were Ovenbirds. More limited towerkill data at Milwaukee place the figure even higher: 24%. The wide discrepancy between sight reports and towerkill records appears to be due to the bird's secretive habits. It rarely joins in the mixed flocks that command an observer's attention, preferring the lower vegetation levels of the forest.

Eau Claire tower figures show fall migrants moving from 20 August through 10 October, with the heaviest flight between 5 and 25 September. When 327 birds were killed there on 1 October 1965, this represented an unusually late date for a heavy kill. The southern migration peak may be a week later; but even there, few birds are seen after 15 October. Birds lingering into November were noted on the 1st (1962, Racine, B. Weber; 1980, Manitowoc, J. L. Polk), 4th (1978, Kenosha, R. R. Hoffman), and 15th (1971, Brown, E. D. Cleary).

Northern Waterthrush (*Seiurus noveboracensis*)

Formerly included Grinnell's Waterthrush

STATUS. Fairly common migrant. Uncommon summer resident north and east.

HABITAT. Wooded swamp. Lowland carr.

MIGRATION DATES. *Spring:* late April to late May. *Fall:* early August to early October. *Extremes:* 9 April; 9 November.

BREEDING DATA. Nests with eggs: 16 May to 23 June. Clutch size: 4 or 5 eggs.

WINTER. One record.

PORTRAIT. *Birds of Wisconsin:* Plate 70.

Northern Waterthrush

0   25   50 Mi

0   25 50 75 Km

▨ Summer range
○ Early June to late July
□ 29 January to early March

Records since 1960

It is not enough to say that the Northern Waterthrush is attracted to water, as its name implies. As a summer resident or a migrant, this thrush-colored bird has a strong preference for quiet water: stagnant pools in swamps, and the brushy banks of small slow-moving streams. During spring and fall migration the pattern varies only when an occasional wanderer turns up in a residential backyard, where it wanders among the more secluded shrubbery. The bird spends much of its time on the ground and does most of its singing from the lower tree branches.

A bit of confusion surrounds some of the historical references to the waterthrushes. Attempts to differentiate between the Northern and the Louisiana were hampered by inadequate descriptions in the major field guides. Too much emphasis used to be placed on the coloration of throat and eye stripe, and too little attention was given to bill size and to the width of the light stripe behind the eye. In addition, observers sometimes tried to differentiate between two geographic races: *noveboracensis* ("Northern") and *notabilis* ("Grinnell's"). It has been established that both have been collected in the state (Schorger 1931a). For the species as a whole, 25 April is the approximate arrival date for the earliest migrants. Because the Louisiana typically arrives a week or more earlier, great care must be used in identifying waterthrushes appearing before the 25th. Exceptionally early Northerns have been identified on the 9th (1981, Door, R. J. Lukes), 16th (1972, Waushara, R. Sharp; 1972, Ozaukee, T. Bintz), and 18th (1964, Dane, W. L. Hilsenhoff; 1975, Brown, T. C. Erdman).

In the south a 25 April beginning gradually builds to a 10–20 May peak, followed by a gradual diminution until 30 May. A bird banded at Beloit (Rock County) on 3 June 1961 (M. K. Stocking) was unusually late. In the central region, records exist for Dunn County between 18 April (1946, I. O. Buss) and 1 June (1947, A. M. Wallner). In the north, birds may be ex-

pected around 5 May; the earliest on record is a 2 May 1965 bird in Bayfield County (J. L. Kozlowski). Maximum numbers are most likely between the 15th and 25th, with small numbers remaining to nest while the rest move on to Canada.

Well before the last spring migrants have departed, resident birds have started nesting. In 1951 Carl Richter observed nest construction under way in Oconto County on 12 May, with eggs laid 4 days later. Richter reported on nine nests in his area; all had eggs before the end of May. Brown-headed Cowbird parasitism was indicated in four instances. Eight of the nests were located in the root systems of fallen trees less than a foot above pools of water. The ninth nest was in a crevice of a fallen cedar log, again only inches above water. Eggs have been reported as late as 23 June, while the possibility of still later nesting is raised by Jackson's (1943) observation of a juvenile barely able to fly near Mercer (Iron County) on 26 August 1919.

The line marking the southern limit of the breeding range follows closely the edge of Curtis' (1959) tension zone. If suitable bog habitat were more plentiful in central Wisconsin, this species might be much more numerous; for in the Cedarburg Bog in Ozaukee County—at the southern extremity of its range—the waterthrush is one of the more numerous nesting warblers. But suitable habitat is not plentiful, even in the northern counties. Areas where this teeterer abounds are few and far between. It has been recorded on 23 of Wisconsin's 70 BBS routes; only on five has this bird occurred regularly.

Several instances are known of fall migrants reaching the southern counties between 25 and 31 July. Usually, 1 August is a typical arrival time; a gradual increase through August leads to a 1–20 September peak. Records of casualties at the Eau Claire television tower, 1960–1969, show all the heaviest kills occurring between 4 and 19 September; on 6 September 1965 there was a major disaster, when 517 water-thrushes perished. Occasional collisions have occurred through 12 October, an unusually late date for migrants in northern and central areas. Lingering in the south beyond 20 October have been six late-October stragglers, plus three individuals seen on 4 November (1978, Kenosha, R. R. Hoffman) and one on 9 November (1969, Racine, L. W. Erickson). Fall migrants rarely travel in mixed warbler flocks; they inhabit low shrubbery in swamps near the edges of ponds and streams or in parks and suburban areas.

It was along an open stream that William Hilsenhoff flushed an individual in Dane County on 29 January 1983. Subsequent observations in February and early March by other observers point to successful overwintering. One wonders what kind of food frigid Madison offered that substituted for the insects this bird would have favored in its usual Middle American winter haunts.

Louisiana Waterthrush (*Seiurus motacilla*)

Status. Uncommon spring migrant south and central; rare fall migrant south. Uncommon summer resident west and central.

Habitat. Along streams in deciduous forest. Wooded swamp.

Migration Dates. *Spring:* mid-April to late May. *Fall:* mid-August to early October. *Extremes:* 4 April; 20 October.

Breeding Data. Nests with eggs: 5 May to 27 June. Clutch size: usually 4 or 5 eggs; occasionally 6.

Portrait. *Birds of Wisconsin:* Plate 70.

Since Wisconsin lies at the northwestern range limit for this hillside brook-lover, one might expect that the southeastern counties would get the greatest numbers of birds. But the southeastern portions of the state have little suitable nesting habitat. There is no evidence that the Louisiana Waterthrush was ever anything but a rarity in the Beloit-Kenosha-Milwaukee region. Kumlien and Hollister (1903) listed seven records—all spring migrants—with no specific summer records, even though they surmised that it "doubtless breeds." Gordon (1958) found a pair nesting in Kenosha County in June 1948, but this is the only sure nesting record for that portion of the state.

As a summer resident the bird is much better known in southwestern Wisconsin. It has been recorded along the St. Croix River as far north as North Hudson, along the Red Cedar to Menomonie, along the

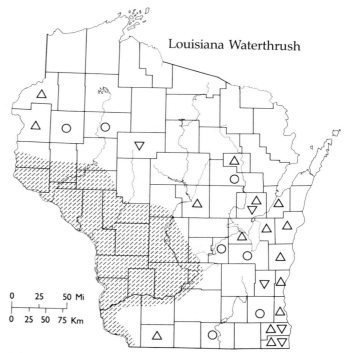

Louisiana Waterthrush

0   25   50 Mi

0   25 50 75 Km

▨ Summer range
△ Mid-April to late May
○ Early June to early August
▽ Mid-August to early October

Records since 1960

Chippewa to Chippewa Falls, along the Black to Hatfield, and along the Wisconsin to Port Edwards.

The birds prefer the steep ravines along the small brooks that feed into the larger rivers, and especially those portions of the feeder streams where the current is rapid and where rocks and low vegetation abound. Usually it is only during migration that Louisianas show the same liking for stagnant swampland that Northern Waterthrushes show. In spring and early summer one's best chance to meet up with this species is to visit favored territory in the first hour of daylight. The song period begins and ends earlier in the day than it does for most other passerines. Song is only occasional after the first hour of daylight, but it provides the easiest means for separating the two waterthrush species. The ringing metallic call note is another helpful clue to the presence of waterthrushes, but by itself it is not a reliable means of specific identification.

Ideal habitat exists in the Baraboo hills in Sauk County. Mossman and Lange (1982) estimated a probable breeding population of 50 pairs per year and found nests with eggs between 5 May and 27 June. No such concentrations have occurred in any other region, but nests have been found north to St. Croix (1975, C. A. Faanes) and Dunn (1886, J. N. Clark [Buss and Mattison 1955]) counties. Birds were located in Barron and Rusk counties on 26 July 1981 (K. I. Lange), and I heard a singing male near Bruce (Rusk County) on 7 June 1969. Faanes (1981) mentioned a summer observation in Polk County.

Eastern Wisconsin attracts a few migrants nearly every spring. Most northerly observations have oc-curred in Menominee (1968, 1971, J. H. Zimmerman), Outagamie (1975, D. D. Tessen), and Brown (banded on 26 April 1969, M. M. Wierzbicki) counties. The rarity of these eastern Wisconsin wanderings is evident from Helmut Mueller's comment, after banding a bird on 27 April 1964, that although he had trapped more than 900 Northerns, this was his first Louisiana.

Most years it is a toss-up whether the Louisiana or the Pine will be the second warbler species to arrive in spring. The Yellow-rump comes first. Often the Louisiana is present by 15 April. Exceptionally early April migrants have appeared on the 4th (1948, Milwaukee, G. H. Orians), 7th (1947, Milwaukee, G. H. Orians), and 9th (1981, Milwaukee, D. K. Gustafson). Farther north one turned up on 15 April (1976, Chippewa, S. D. Robbins). Migrants are then in evidence until 25 May.

It may well be that some of the summer population has left by early August. But in Adams County, where I have found summer birds in seven separate areas, I have heard song fragments as late as 8 September. Three birds were banded at Oconomowoc (Waukesha County) between 28 August and 18 September 1960 (E. W. Peartree). Among Eau Claire television tower casualties on 20 September 1957 were four Louisianas, proving that these birds do wander quite far north. Also far north were individuals in Taylor (30 August 1980, S. D. Robbins) and Outagamie (25 August 1973, D. D. Tessen) counties. Kenneth Lange has records from the Sauk County breeding grounds for 30 September 1969 and 14 October 1970. The Madison bird Harry Anderson saw on 20 October 1934 is exceptional (H. G. Anderson et al. 1942).

Kentucky Warbler (*Oporornis formosus*)

STATUS. Uncommon migrant southwest; rare migrant southeast. Uncommon summer resident southwest.

HABITAT. Southern silver maple–elm forest.

MIGRATION DATES. *Spring:* early to late May. *Fall:* mid-August to mid-September. *Extremes:* 2 May; 7 October.

BREEDING DATA. Nests with eggs: 11–18 June. Clutch size: 4–6 eggs.

PORTRAIT. *Birds of Wisconsin:* Plate 71.

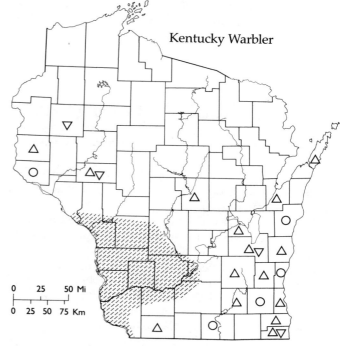

Kentucky Warbler

▨	Summer range
△	Early to late May
○	Early June to early August
▽	Mid-August to mid-September

Records since 1960

When Schorger (1927a) discovered two nests at Potosi on 16 and 18 June 1924 and determined that the Kentucky Warbler was fairly numerous in Grant County, he was pioneering in an area that had not been previously examined. Perhaps he discovered something that had been going on for many years. Grant County remains today the main stronghold for the Kentucky. It is frequently found in early summer in parts of Wyalusing State Park, particularly in the heavily wooded bottomlands close to the base of the surrounding bluffs, where Eric Moir and O. J. Gromme discovered two nests on 11 and 13 June 1941 (Gromme 1941a). Without doubt it is a regular breeder in this area.

From Grant County the summer range extends east along the Wisconsin River to Portage and Necedah, then north along the Mississippi River to Fountain City. Birds are found not only in the wooded bottomlands of the major rivers but also in ravines and hillsides of smaller streams that feed into these rivers. Kentucky Warblers are recorded regularly in the Baraboo hills in Sauk County, where an empty nest was found in 1980 (Mossman and Lange 1982). A 7 July 1981 record in Pierce County (E. J. Epstein) suggests that the summer range may be extending gradually northward.

No nesting has been reported from the eastern counties. June records are known for Manitowoc (1968, M. Albrecht), Ozaukee (1977, D. K. Gustafson), Waukesha (1978, 1979, J. E. Bielefeldt), and Rock (1968, M. T. Maxson) counties, but these observations were of nonresident wanderers.

The arrival dates for summer residents in the southwestern sector have not been well documented but probably fall in the 5–15 May period. The temporary wanderers in the east show up between 5 and 25 May. The earliest were noted on 2 May (1959, Dane, W. L. Hilsenhoff; 1974, Dane, P. Ashman) and 3–6 May (1967, banded in Brown, M. M. Wierzbicki).

From one to four sightings are made in eastern

Wisconsin nearly every spring. A majority of these have taken place southeast of a Madison-Sheboygan line, but instances are known north to Portage, Winnebago, Brown, and Door counties. In the west an "overshoot" migrant appeared in St. Croix County on 28 May 1963 (S. D. Robbins).

Once the rich "turdle, turdle" song ceases in early July, records become even scarcer. In the nesting area near Mazomanie (Dane County) birds have been found as late as 22 September (1930, G. O. Raasch; MPM files). Not enough fieldwork has been done in Grant County during fall to determine when birds leave their breeding grounds there. Northwestern wanderers were identified in Eau Claire (24 September 1982, J. L. Polk; 17 September 1948, L. Almon), Trempealeau (28 August 1980, R. L. Drieslein), and Barron (18 September 1971, A. Goff) counties. In the southeast, migrants have been detected on 31 August (1969, Kenosha, J. Hamers), 3 September (1962, Rock, G. Mahlum), 9 September (1962, Columbia, R. B.

Dryer), 26 September (1953, banded in Rock, M. T. Maxson), and 7 October (1961, Rock, G. Mahlum).

Evidently this species was equally rare in the nineteenth century. Hoy's (1853b) sole record for the Racine area was a bird noted on 10 May 1851. Kumlien

and Hollister (1903) could recall but six instances when either they or Thure Kumlien had found this southerner in the Lake Koshkonong region in Jefferson County.

Connecticut Warbler (*Oporornis agilis*)

STATUS. Uncommon migrant. Uncommon summer resident north.

HABITAT. Oak–jack pine forest; conifer swamp (during breeding). Upland carr; residential area shrubs (during migration).

MIGRATION DATES. *Spring:* early May to early June. *Fall:* mid-August to early October. *Extremes:* 25 April; 26 October.

BREEDING DATA. Nest with eggs: 8 June. Nest with young: 7 July. Clutch size: probably 4 eggs.

PORTRAIT. *Birds of Wisconsin:* Plate 71.

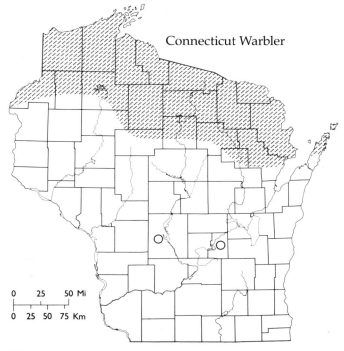

Connecticut Warbler

0   25   50 Mi
0 25 50 75 Km

▨ Summer range
○ Mid-June to early August

Records since 1960

Commentators through the years have been in general agreement that the Connecticut Warbler is an uncommon spring migrant. Few observers have recorded more than 5 individuals during a spring season, and often the total number of individual birds seen by all Wisconsin observers combined has been fewer than 15. An occasional early migrant appears by 5 May. Two phenomenally early stragglers have been reported: one collected in Milwaukee on 25 April 1897 (H. Russell; MPM files), and one seen in Vilas County on 1 May 1942 (E. T. Mitchell). But these warblers are most likely to be discovered in the south from 15 to 25 May and in the north from 20 May on.

In spring this bird is most often found in dense low vegetation, such as lilac bushes in city parks. It is hard to spot because it moves stealthily and remains well hidden among the leaves, because it does not respond readily to "squeaking," and because it chips and sings only occasionally.

The presence of probable late spring migrants in mid-June complicates the appraisal of summer status and the delineation of the bird's breeding range. In southern and central counties, birds beyond 10 June have been detected on the 11th (1949, Dane, M. A. Walker; 1977, Milwaukee, D. K. Gustafson; 1977, Juneau, F. Z. Lesher), 14th (1976, Milwaukee, D. K. Gustafson; 1980, Jackson, D. D. Tessen), and 16th (1947, Winnebago, M. J. Overton; 1970, Juneau, S. D. Robbins). No late-June or early-July follow-up in the jack pine region in Jackson and Juneau counties has

been undertaken to see if summer residency is possible. A wanderer was observed in Green Lake County on 1 July 1984 (T. R. Schultz).

Historically, there has been confusion about the bird's summer status. Kumlien and Hollister (1903) believed that it nested in the dense tamarack swamps in Jefferson County; but since they failed to recognize the existence of the similarly plumaged Mourning Warbler as a summer resident in that region, their records for the Connecticut have been questioned by more recent commentators.

Positive nesting evidence finally came on 7 July 1941 with the discovery of a nest with four young (Douglas, O. J. Gromme [1942a]). A nest with two eggs was discovered on 8 June 1945 (Sawyer, F. Zirrer). Recently fledged young were also sighted from 25 to 27 July 1942 in Vilas and Oneida counties (W. E. Scott) and from 6 to 15 July 1977 in Vilas County (R. G. Spahn).

It is in the jack pine barrens extending from the southwestern corner of Burnett County to southern Bayfield County that the Connecticut can be found in considerable numbers in late June and July. In 2 hours of stop-and-go driving east of Solon Springs (Douglas County) on 27 June 1973, I counted 41 singing males. Another 30 males were detected a year later in southwestern Bayfield County (Robbins, 1974a). On 22 June 1977 I tallied 12 near Grantsburg (Burnett County). In this jack pine habitat birds are not found in young 15-foot trees or in taller trees that have been cleanly trimmed; instead they prefer the more mature trees that have considerable underbrush.

Away from the extensive jack pine stands, smaller numbers are scattered in other parts of northern Wisconsin. It is mainly along the edges of tamarack bogs that an occasional pair is encountered throughout the forests south to a line connecting Grantsburg, Ladysmith, Merrill, Shawano, Oconto, and Sturgeon Bay.

There has also been disagreement about the magnitude of the fall migration. Bird-watchers who rely on field observations have found the Connecticut one of the most uncommon of fall warblers. My personal records, covering over 45 years in various parts of the state, show a grand total of only 30 Connecticuts identified between 15 August and 10 October.

Yet banding records at Cedar Grove (Sheboygan County) and Milwaukee show that 1% of all fall warblers trapped are Connecticuts. Towerkills at Milwaukee and Eau Claire report the figure for this species as 2% of all warblers killed. As many as 300 have been killed in a single season at Eau Claire, and as many as 140 in a single night.

At Eau Claire, tower strikes have occurred between 23 August and 12 October. This spans the fall migration period for the state quite well. Unusually early were August sightings on the 14th (1932, Sheboygan, C. S. Jung; MPM files) and 15th (1953, Rock, M. T. Maxson). Most sightings have come during the 10–25 September period, with a gradual tapering off through 10 October. Beyond the 12th, three October records are known, on the 22nd (1984, Chippewa, C. A. Kemper), 25th (1963, Racine, L. W. Erickson), and 26th (1936, Dane, H. G. Anderson [H. G. Anderson et al. 1942]).

Mourning Warbler (*Oporornis philadelphia*)

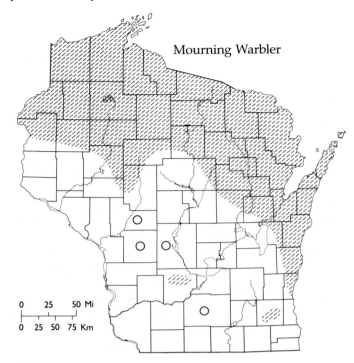

Mourning Warbler

▨ Summer range
○ Late June to late July

Records since 1960

STATUS. Fairly common migrant. Fairly common summer resident north; uncommon summer resident east and central.

HABITAT. Northern aspen-birch forest. Young forest saplings.

MIGRATION DATES. *Spring:* early May to early June. *Fall:* early August to late September. *Extremes:* 3 May; 14 October.

BREEDING DATA. Nests with eggs: 22 May to 1 July. Clutch size: 4 or 5 eggs.

PORTRAIT. *Birds of Wisconsin:* Plate 71.

The first Mourning Warbler I encountered during my youth was a male that sang repeatedly from a large dense clump of forsythia. Time and again I encircled the clump, "squeaking," trying to entice the songster to a visible perch. After an hour of frustration I ran back to my home, pored rapidly through song descriptions in field guides, then returned to the clump. It was only after a second hour that the bird showed itself briefly and flew off to another clump. Such are this bird's secretive habits that make it appear less common than it really is. During the last 10 days of May it often frequents lilac clumps or other types of dense shrubbery in city parks, residential areas, or near the edges of swampy areas. A Mourning Warbler will often reveal its presence by its distinctive song or call note; but if it is silent, it is easily overlooked.

To my knowledge, no one has detected this species in Wisconsin in April. Several observers have come close. Joseph Hudick found one in Polk County on 1 May 1984. H. G. Anderson's (H. G. Anderson et al. 1942) arrival date of 3 May (1928, Dane) was equaled in 1974 (Milwaukee) and 1980 (Kenosha), and closely followed by a 4 May record in 1964 (Dane), 1968 (Winnebago), and 1969 (Milwaukee); but 10 May is a more typical arrival date for southern Wisconsin. Farther north the bird is rarely seen before the 15th. The largest numbers arrive between the 20th and the 30th. It is difficult to pinpoint the end of spring migration, because breeding territory is extensive. Migrants are found outside the breeding range every year through 5 June, often through the 10th. A male was banded in Rock County on the 21st (1971, M. T. Maxson). Other sightings of late migrants beyond the 15th include individuals on the 20th (1981, Milwaukee, J. Frank) and 21st (1961, Vernon, V. E. Weber).

During summer this is a fairly common resident in the two northernmost tiers of counties. Almost every BBS transect in these areas has these birds every year, often with 10 or more individuals per transect. The Mourning Warbler inhabits those parts of the forest where there is much deciduous understory, particularly in damp lowlands. Such habitat becomes much scarcer along the Lake Michigan shore, but wherever suitable pockets exist, the Mourning can be found south to the Cedarburg Bog in Ozaukee County, just north of Milwaukee. Beimborn (1970) correctly observed that the edge of the breeding range follows closely the tension zone (Curtis 1959) that runs roughly southeast from Polk to Milwaukee counties.

There are a few pockets south and west of the tension zone, where this thicket-lover is found in midsummer. One is in Sauk County, where K. I. Lange and M. C. Brittingham located a nest on 17 June 1980. Mossman and Lange (1982) estimate about 25 nests per year in the Baraboo hills. A few are found frequently in the Kettle Moraine State Forest in Waukesha County. Occasional summer residency has been noted in the tamarack swamps of eastern Dane and Jefferson counties in recent years, but the Mourning's regularity there has not been documented. It now seems likely that in that region summer residents which Kumlien and Hollister (1903) took to be Connecticut Warblers were probably Mournings.

Reporting on 11 nests found in the Oconto area, C. H. Richter observed that all nests were either on the ground, or no more than 6 inches from it. They were hidden in clumps of nettle or jewelweed, either in tamarack bogs or in low deciduous woods. Only one nest had been victimized by a Brown-headed Cowbird; all others contained four or five warbler eggs. All nests were discovered between 31 May and 18 June.

Fall migration data can be gleaned from television tower casualty figures at Eau Claire. During the 1960–1969 period, the 361 specimens of this species represented slightly less than 1% of the total warbler kill, placing the Mourning Warbler among the less common warbler species. Yet it is by no means rare. Earliest casualties usually came during the last week of August, and the heaviest kills were recorded between 6 and 20 September. The extremes were 23 August (1964) and 1 October (1965).

Banders at Cedar Grove (Sheboygan County) and Milwaukee also found that Mournings represented slightly less than 1% of the total warbler catch. But the average field observer finds decidedly fewer. Even an active field observer can easily go through a fall migration and miss this bird entirely. If he is lucky he may see three to five birds. Not only does the Mourning maintain its spring habit of hiding in dense low vegetation, but it also is largely silent, almost never giving forth song fragments or uttering its distinctive call note. In most years the last migrants are spotted between 20 and 25 September. The latest state records have come from Milwaukee on 12 October 1961 (W. N. MacBriar) and 14 October 1950 (C. P. Frister).

Common Yellowthroat (*Geothlypis trichas*)

STATUS. Common migrant. Common summer resident. Casual winter resident.

HABITAT. Shrub carr. Wooded swamp. Deciduous forest.

MIGRATION DATES. *Spring:* early to late May. *Fall:* late August to mid-October.

BREEDING DATA. Nests with eggs: 26 May to 7 July. Clutch size: 4 or 5 eggs.

WINTER. Casual in December; three January records.

PORTRAIT. *Birds of Wisconsin:* Plate 71.

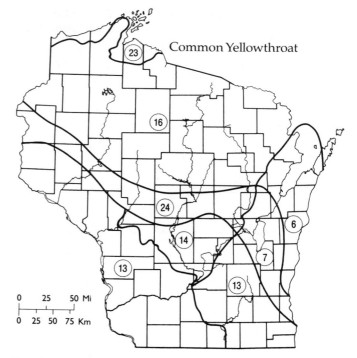

Breeding Bird Survey, averages 1966 to 1980

More than any other summer resident warbler, the Common Yellowthroat shows an even distribution south and north. On a few northern BBS transects it is outnumbered by the Ovenbird and the Chestnut-side, but on 49 of the state's 70 routes the yellowthroat is the most abundant warbler. This and the Yellow are the only warblers that have been recorded on all 70 routes. Almost any moist area—swamp, marsh, edge of stream or pond—attracts one or more pairs in the adjacent low vegetation each nesting season.

The nests reported for Wisconsin have always been located on the ground or within inches of it. Typically, the bird builds a nest in a clump of long grass next to such brushy undergrowth as nettles or berry bushes. It seems surprising that this bird escapes Brown-headed Cowbird parasitism as much as it does. Reporting on nine nests in Oconto and Marinette counties, Carl Richter observed only one instance where three cowbird eggs were found in a yellowthroat nest.

Most observers think of the yellowthroat as strictly a May migrant. Yet nearly every year someone manages a late April sighting. When a bird-watcher with sharp eyes spots a small yellowish bird with a black face mask, or when keen ears pick up the familiar multiple-pitch sneezy call note, the identification is unmistakable. The earliest April dates on record are the 18th (1951, Milwaukee, E. K. Urban), 20th (1970, La Crosse, J. R. Rosso; 1981, Manitowoc, C. R. Sontag), and an astonishingly early straggler on the 9th (1953, Dodge, T. K. Soulen). Most southern Wisconsin observers find first arrivals during the 5–10 May period, with birds common from the 15th on. Farther north only scattered individuals can be expected by the 10th, with the main migration between the 15th and 25th.

June and July are nesting months. In most cases young have fledged by early July, but nests with eggs have occasionally been reported through the first week of July. Through July and early August, even though song has ceased, it is easy to find yellowthroat families by going to the habitat they prefer and "squeaking." These birds—old and young—are especially responsive and curious.

It is not easy to distinguish between early fall migrants and summer residents. But data from television tower kills show that the migration is under way by 25 August. The heaviest kills for this species at Eau Claire have been surprisingly low, representing only 2.1% of the total warbler kill. Banding records from Cedar Grove (Sheboygan County) and Mil-

waukee, plus my personal observation notes, indicate the number of yellowthroats to be closer to 7%.

In northern and central counties most yellowthroats have departed by the end of September. An occasional bird may linger into October, but the only records beyond the 15th involved a bird that struck the Eau Claire television tower on the 20th (1968, C. A. Kemper) and one detected in Barron County on the 28th (1975, C. A. Faanes). In the southern counties small numbers usually linger through mid-October.

On occasion individuals have been found in marshy regions around Milwaukee, Waukesha, and Madison through November and into December. One lingered at Ashland through 20 December (1987, R. L. Verch). Madison CBC observers have detected individuals in mid-December in 1920, 1941, 1973, 1975, 1979, 1983, 1984, and 1987. Additional CBC discoveries were made in Lafayette (1979) and Jefferson (1981, 1986) counties. One wintering bird visited a feeder daily through 4 January (1982, Sauk, K. I. Lange). Still later was a 19 January 1920 record (Dane, C. S. Jung, pers. comm.), a 30 January 1983 sighting (Dane, A. K. Shea), and a 20 February 1987 survivor (Waukesha, J. E. Bielefeldt).

Hooded Warbler (*Wilsonia citrina*)

STATUS. Rare spring migrant south and east; casual spring migrant central; casual fall migrant south. Rare summer resident south and east.

HABITAT. Southern silver maple–elm forest. Southern sugar maple–basswood forest.

MIGRATION DATES. *Spring:* late April to early June. *Fall:* mid-August to late September. *Extremes:* 27 March; 4 October.

BREEDING DATA. Nests with eggs: 6–21 June. Clutch size: 3 eggs.

PORTRAIT. *Birds of Wisconsin:* Plate 72.

From 1 to 10 Hooded Warblers have been identified almost every year since *The Passenger Pigeon* began publishing field notes in 1939. In a few instances these southern visitors have remained in a given area from 2 to 3 weeks from mid-May to early June. Most, however, have been birds that were present momentarily, then quickly disappeared. These were males that had attracted attention by their loud distinctive song or by their tameness. Several observers have been able to come within 6 feet of these birds. Howard Van Ness (pers. comm. to O. J. Gromme) tells of a male that alighted on his fishing pole! Most of these 1-day stands occurred between 5 and 25 May.

Through 1974, Wisconsin records were concentrated in the southeast, mainly near Madison and Milwaukee and to a much lesser extent north to Green Bay. Five sightings involve late-April arrivals (earliest recorded date, 21 April 1973, Racine, W. H. Pugh). Eight birds wandered far north of the more expected Madison–Green Bay line: to Marathon (4 May 1981, V. A. Heig), Shawano (mid-May 1984, M. S. Peterson), Langlade (23 May 1950, S. G. Spurgeon), St. Croix (29 May 1963, S. D. Robbins), Chippewa (28 May 1976, C. A. Kemper), Eau Claire (5 May 1982, J. L. Polk), Crawford (26 May 1984, D. D. Tessen), and Douglas (23 May 1987, R. J. Johnson).

Most remarkable were four wanderers that turned up in 1950 between 27 March and 8 April. A cyclonic disturbance apparently caught a few of these birds as they were passing over Texas or Mexico and swept them all the way to Ontario, Ohio, Illinois, and Wisconsin. One Wisconsin bird was present from 27 to 31 March in Madison (J. H. Zimmerman), one from 27 to 29 March in Milwaukee (M. F. Donald, D. L. Larkin), one was found dead on 29 March at Two Rivers in Manitowoc County (J. Kraupa), and another was found dead on 8 April near Oostburg in Sheboygan County (A. P. Maul). No such phenomenon has occurred before—or since.

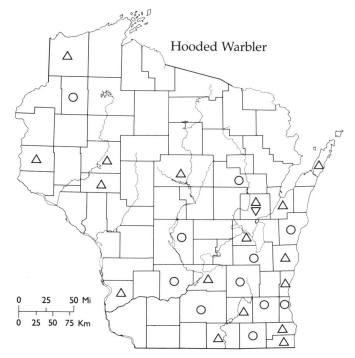

Hooded Warbler

△ Late April to early June
○ Mid-June to early August
▽ Mid-August to late September

Records since 1960

The first modern midsummer observations came in 1974: an individual noted on 24 June (Waukesha, J. E. Bielefeldt), and one whose song was taped between 18 and 24 July (Washburn, R. Palmer). The state's first known nesting occurred in 1975, with a pair seen repeatedly, 20 June–1 September, in Manitowoc County. The birds were photographed and banded, and their nest was found after they left (B. N. Brouchoud).

In 1976 Hooded Warblers established summer residency in Sauk and Waukesha counties. A pair also returned to the 1975 nesting area in Manitowoc County. In the following 3 years, summer observations occurred in Walworth, Dane, Milwaukee, and Adams counties. Concerted efforts in the Baraboo hills in Sauk County led to the discovery of 12 singing males and four nests (Brittingham and Temple 1980; Mossman and Lange 1982) in June 1980. These birds preferred shrub-dominated openings in mature deciduous forest. The nests were in shrubs and saplings, from 1 to 5 feet above ground.

Only rarely has this colorful southerner been recorded after mid-August. Singing males have been encountered on 23 August (1954, Adams, S. D. Robbins) and 7 September (1973, Waukesha, J. E. Bielefeldt). An immature was found dead on 15 September (1973, Milwaukee, M. F. Donald). Individuals in fall plumage have been detected on 21 August (1968, Dane, T. K. Soulen), 25 August (1973, Outagamie, D. D. Tessen), 12 September (1949, Dane, S. D. Robbins), 20 September (1970, Milwaukee, E. Sheridan), 23 September (1986, Milwaukee, B. Frank), 26 September (1975, Milwaukee, M. F. Donald), and 4 October (1979, Waukesha, J. E. Bielefeldt).

History has little changed the status of this species. Kumlien and Hollister (1903) encountered the Hooded Warbler mainly as a spring migrant in the Milwaukee area and recorded it in Manitowoc County in July, but had no positive nesting records.

Wilson's Warbler (*Wilsonia pusilla*)

STATUS. Fairly common migrant. Casual summer resident.
HABITAT. Deciduous forest. All carr.
MIGRATION DATES. *Spring:* early to late May. *Fall:* mid-August to late September. *Extremes:* 20 April; 23 November.
BREEDING DATA. Adults feeding young: 27 July.
PORTRAIT. *Birds of Wisconsin:* Plate 72.

On 26 July 1977, when S. A. Temple and associates were mapping bird populations on Devil's Island in Ashland County, they discovered a pair of Wilson's Warblers feeding recently fledged young (Temple and Harris 1985). Not only was this the first state record of breeding, but also it marked the first time this species had ever been seen in Wisconsin in July. It is mainly transient for 3–4 weeks in spring and for another 4–5 weeks in fall. For much of this time, the bird frequents garden shrubbery and other forms of dense low vegetation. Occasionally in spring it moves up to more conspicuous perches 10–15 feet high in deciduous trees to sing its brief chatterlike song, but these are momentary departures from the usual pattern.

Favorable weather brings the first migrants to southern Wisconsin during the first week of May. The only published arrival dates for April are records on the 20th (1977, Milwaukee, D. K. Gustafson), 21st (1985, Sauk, R. Whitemarsh), and 30th (1964, Dane, T. L. Ashman). It takes a second warm spell around the 10th to 15th to bring a general influx. The movement through the state is rapid, with birds reaching the northern counties between the 15th and 20th. At the height of the migration most observers do well to find 5–10 birds on a day's field trip, but on 10 May 1964 the observers who covered the Racine area for their May peak-day count tallied a surprising 63 birds. By 30 May nearly all Wilson's have left even the northern areas, but birds lingering through 5 June are not uncommon.

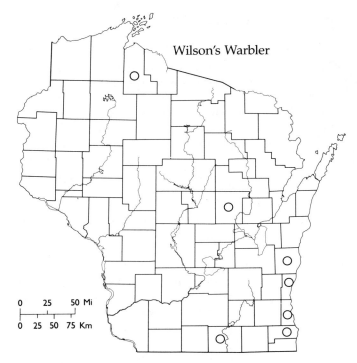

Wilson's Warbler

○ Mid-June to early August

Records since 1960

Beyond 10 June, observers have recorded stragglers on the 15th (1971, Ozaukee, T. Bintz), 17th (1965, Racine, R. E. Fiehweg), 21st (1981, Milwaukee, J. Frank), and 25th (1963, banded in Rock, M. T. Maxson; 1972, Waupaca, J. L. Kaspar). None gave any indication of breeding or residency.

The birds that depart in late May cannot be expected to return for another 3 months. Sightings after 20 August are frequent, but earlier August dates include only birds on the 6th (1977, Door, L. W. Erickson), 8th (1976, Price, M. Hardy), 12th (1967, Milwaukee, D. K. Gustafson; 1972, Outagamie, A. S.

Bradford), and 16th (1964, Eau Claire specimen, C. A. Kemper). Again, passage through the state is rapid. The peak generally occurs in the north before 10 September, and if an observer has not seen these birds in the southern region by the 15th, the chances are diminishing. By the 25th most birds have gone; but when the weather in late September is balmy, a few remain through 5 October. The latest October records are a towerkill on the 9th (1961, Eau Claire, C. A. Kemper) and sightings on the 15th (1949, Rock, M. T. Maxson) and 17th (1959, Vernon, V. E. Weber; 1973, La Crosse, J. R. Rosso). One extremely late bird remained in La Crosse until 23 November 1972 (F. Z. Lesher).

Even during the peak 25 August–20 September period numbers are not large. The largest number killed at the Eau Claire television tower on any night is 34, well below the record for most other regular warblers. Banding and observation data indicate that scarcely 1% of the fall warblers are Wilson's Warblers. Observers searching for Wilson's in fall must keep a sharp eye on the dense shrubbery. Sharp ears will not help much, for call notes and song fragments are rarely uttered.

Canada Warbler (*Wilsonia canadensis*)

STATUS. Fairly common migrant. Fairly common summer resident north; uncommon summer resident east and central.

HABITAT. Coniferous forest. Northern maple-hemlock-pine forest.

MIGRATION DATES. *Spring:* early May to early June. *Fall:* early August to mid-September. *Extremes:* 30 April; 12 October.

BREEDING DATA. Nests with eggs: 8 June to 3 July. Clutch size: 4 or 5 eggs.

PORTRAIT. *Birds of Wisconsin:* Plate 72.

The Canada is one of the last warblers to arrive in spring, and one of the first to depart in fall. Of those that nest in Wisconsin, few stay as long as 4 months of the year, and some may stay only 3 months.

In the south first arrivals can be expected by 10 May, followed by a 15–25 May peak, with departure by 5 June. A 30 April bird in Sauk County (1970, K. I. Lange) was exceptionally early. So were the more northerly surprises observed on 30 April (1981, Eau Claire, J. L. Polk), 1 May (1942, Vilas, E. T. Mitchell), and 2 May (1959, Brown, E. D. Cleary). The main spring migration occurs between 20 May and 5 June.

Beyond 10 June it is difficult to distinguish between summer residents and late migrants. The likelihood is that birds observed at Milwaukee on the 17th (1984), 18th (1983), 19th (1985), and 24th (1982) were transients, since in recent years July records there are unknown. A. W. Schorger thought his 9 June 1925 bird in Grant County was a resident; but since there is no other summer record from that part of the state, it seems more probable that the bird was a late migrant.

Confusion between residents and migrants is as great in early August as in early June. Since definite fall migration has been noted in nonbreeding loca-

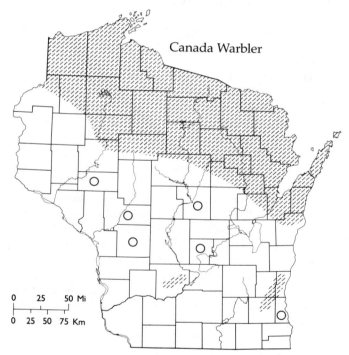

Canada Warbler

0   25   50 Mi
0 25 50 75 Km

▨ Summer range
○ Mid-June to late July

Records since 1960

tions on the 12th (St. Croix), 13th (Rock), 14th (Outagamie), and 15th (Adams, Dane), it is presumed that some of the birds seen farther north in the first week of August are also migrants. Nearly all television tower casualties at Eau Claire occur between 25 August and 20 September. These dates appear to span the main migratory period for the entire state. Field observations, banding data, and tower casualty figures all indicate that the Canada is one of the less common of the regular migrant warblers, representing less than 1% of the total warbler population. Records beyond 20 September are scanty, the latest being 10 October (1943, Milwaukee, I. N. Balsom) and 12 October (1961, Brown, E. D. Cleary).

Between 15 June and 31 July the Canada is restricted largely to the northern three tiers of counties. It is regular in small numbers south to Grantsburg, Cornell, Wausau, Shawano, and Manitowoc. Additional pockets exist much farther south. One is in the Baraboo hills in Sauk County, where Mossman and Lange (1982) found an active nest and estimated the presence of 20 breeding pairs. A second pocket includes the

Cedarburg Bog in Ozaukee County and a portion of the Kettle Moraine State Forest in Waukesha County. The Bear Bluff swamps in eastern Jackson County may well be a third. But south of the northern forests favorable habitat is scarce.

For the Canada, favorable habitat consists of a dense forest canopy, some dense undergrowth, and moist ground. Spruce, balsam, and hemlock are most favored. Maple forests are sometimes chosen. Carl Richter discovered a nest under the roots of a leaning white birch at the side of a mossy hummock in a dense tamarack swamp in Oconto County. Lynn Schimmels also found this species to be a ground-nester in Langlande County bogs in 1965 and 1969.

Yellow-breasted Chat (*Icteria virens*)

STATUS. Uncommon migrant south and west; rare migrant east and central. Uncommon summer resident south and west.
HABITAT. Upland carr. Deciduous forest.
MIGRATION DATES. *Spring:* early May to early June. *Fall:* mid-August to early October. *Extremes:* 29 April; 12 November.
BREEDING DATA. Nests with eggs: 9 and 11 June. Nest with young: 26 July.
PORTRAIT. *Birds of Wisconsin:* Plate 71.

The Yellow-breasted Chat is not as common a summer resident as it was in Kumlien and Hollister's day. They recorded (1903) that they commonly found this oversized warbler in "hazel brush and dogwood" openings near the edge of deciduous woods. But so many of these areas have now been cleared for agricultural and residential use that favorable nesting habitat has been greatly reduced.

The bird's range has not changed perceptibly. Summer residency is confined to the westernmost counties adjacent to the Mississippi River, from Pierce County south to the two southernmost tiers of counties. People who are fortunate enough to live near a resident pair are sometimes treated to a "circus" of sound and activity. Angie Kumlien Main (1925) described meeting with a bird while she was picking blackberries: "After working for some time . . . I felt that I was being laughed at and barked at by a boy and his dog. I heard the bark and chuckle, now here and now there. . . . After some searching and much listening, I found the actor in this strange vocal performance to be his clownship the Yellow-breasted Chat. I was filled with amusement and delight that a

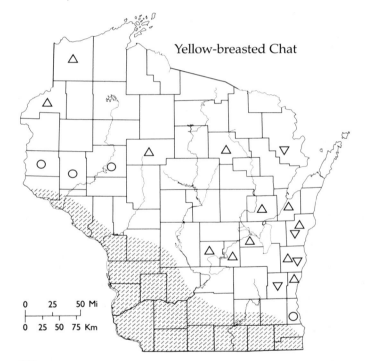

Yellow-breasted Chat

▨ Summer range
△ Early May to early June
○ Mid-June to early August
▽ Mid-August to early October

Records since 1960

bird could assume the role of a human ventriloquist, and could even bark like a dog."

No longer can this be called a common species in any part of its Wisconsin range. In the past 25 years published reports have recorded only five or fewer summer resident pairs per year. If birders surveyed the dry brushy hillsides of western Wisconsin more thoroughly, they would surely find a few additional pairs, north to Pierce, Buffalo, Monroe, and Juneau counties. The only BBS detections have been in Monroe, Juneau, Grant, Green, and Dane counties. I found a singing male near Hudson (St. Croix County) every June from 1961 to 1964, but failed to find any thereafter. One was banded in Chippewa County on 30 July 1963 (C. A. Kemper). One was discovered in Dunn County on 12 June 1976 (D. Tiller).

Little is known of nesting habits in the state. Although Kumlien and Hollister (1903) found several nests, they provided no precise data. They did describe how readily the parents would desert a nest after human disturbance. Presumably, birds may desert readily after any kind of predation, which may explain the lateness of the 26 July 1958 date on which S. Paul Jones found a nest with two young, 7 feet up in a clump of prickly ash in Waukesha County. More typical dates have been provided by Schorger (1931a), who found a nest in Grant County on 9 June 1925, containing one egg plus a cowbird egg, and another nest in Dane County on 11 June 1927, with four eggs plus a cowbird egg. This nest was 4 feet up in a clump of blackberry bushes.

In spring nonterritorial migrants show up, particularly in the eastern counties. Both in 1963 and 1964, when passerine banding operations were going strong at the Cedar Grove Ornithological Station in Sheboygan County, eight birds were banded each May. Eleven times since 1950 spring vagrants have been found in the Fox River valley in Brown, Outagamie, or Winnebago counties. Nearly every May there are sightings of temporary transients in Milwaukee, Racine, and Kenosha counties. Exceptionally far north were the individuals seen in Langlade County on 13 May 1972 (B. Pickering) and in Douglas County on 13 May 1987 (R. J. Johnson) and 18 May 1987 (J. E. Hoefler). The earliest recorded arrival is a 29 April 1975 bird (Milwaukee, E. L. Basten), and there have been observations on 3 May in 1964 (Outagamie, D. D. Tessen), 1965 (Milwaukee, E. W. Strehlow), 1969 (Milwaukee, M. F. Donald), and 1980 (Ozaukee, D. Hanbury). Most migrants appear between 10 and 25 May.

Fall sightings are less numerous than those in spring, but curious chat wanderings have been noted. After 15 August, birds are seldom seen on their summer territories. But by the end of the month they sometimes turn up at other locations, some of which are well to the north of the summer range. Among 14 published September observations are birds on the 18th (1970, Washington, N. Schmidt), 20th (1964, Marinette, H. L. Lindberg), and 22nd through 29th (1948, Polk, L. Heinsohn). Most northerly of six October records is one in Manitowoc County on the 10th (1953, W. Mayer). Observers have detected especially late stragglers on 1 November (1951, Winnebago, S. Wellso) and 12 November (1961, Sheboygan, H. C. Mueller).

Summer Tanager (*Piranga rubra*)

STATUS. Rare spring migrant. Casual summer and fall visitant.
HABITAT. Deciduous forest. Savanna.
MIGRATION DATES. *Spring:* late April to late May. *Fall:* late August to mid-October. *Extremes:* 20 April; 3 November.
BREEDING DATA. Bred in 1862.
PORTRAIT. *Birds of Wisconsin:* Plate 79.

Although the northern limit of the Summer Tanager's breeding range lies south of Wisconsin, observers have spotted from one to four spring "overshooters" in the Madison-Milwaukee region nearly every year. Since *The Passenger Pigeon* began publishing field notes in 1939, published records numbered 3 in the 1940s, 6 in the 1950s, 7 in the 1960s, 17 in the 1970s, and 16 in the 1980s. Most observations occurred between 27 April and 28 May. A bird banded on 20 April 1974 (Rock, M. K. Stocking) was unusually early.

A 3-week interval in 1956 was remarkable, with a male found dead in Manitowoc (30 April, J. Kraupa), a female closely observed in Adams (11 May, S. D. Robbins), and males seen in Milwaukee (13 May, D. L. Larkin) and Polk (18 May, M. Pedersen) counties. North of a line from Madison to Sheboygan, the only other spring wanderers have been noted in Monroe (1984), Fond du Lac (1984), Winnebago (1972, 1974), Outagamie (1960), Door (1984), and Douglas (1981) counties.

A century ago this species nested sparingly in the southern regions. On 10 June 1862 P. R. Hoy collected sets of two eggs from each of two nests near Racine. Kumlien and Hollister (1903) mentioned the Summer Tanager as a rare but regular summer resident in the Johnstown woods near Milton in Jefferson County. A reminiscing Angie Kumlien Main wrote (1925): "It is a day long to be remembered when the beautiful rosy-red Summer Tanager is seen in Wisconsin, where he is a rare but regular summer visitor in certain sections of the southern part of the state from May on into September." I know of no summer records for this species since the turn of the twentieth century, except an 8 July 1975 bird in Milwaukee County (E. L. Basten), and a 7 August 1956 bird in Pierce County (Manley Olson).

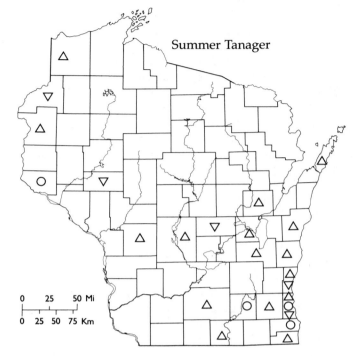

Summer Tanager

0   25   50 Mi
0 25 50 75 Km

△   Late April to late May
○   Early June to mid-August
▽   Late August to mid-October

All records

No published fall record was known until 29 September 1967, when Helen Caldwell spotted a red male in the unlikely region of Grantsburg (Burnett County). A second record followed a year later with a male in Milwaukee on 3 November 1968 (D. R. Bierman). In 1969 another Milwaukee bird, a female, was carefully observed on 16 October (E. Sheridan), and yet another bird was banded in Waushara County on 1 October 1969 (I. Chipman). Edith Sheridan identified another in her Milwaukee yard on 4 October 1970. Just why a species should go unrecorded in fall for so many years, and then suddenly put in five appearances within 4 years, defies ready explanation. The only autumn records after 1970 were a bird observed on 14 October 1978 (Ozaukee, D. D. Tessen) and one on 22 August 1984 (Eau Claire, J. L. Polk).

Scarlet Tanager (*Piranga olivacea*)

STATUS. Fairly common migrant. Fairly common summer resident.

HABITAT. Deciduous forest. Northern maple-hemlock-pine forest.

MIGRATION DATES. *Spring:* early to late May. *Fall:* mid-August to early October. *Extremes:* 13 April; 22 November.

BREEDING DATA. Nests with eggs: 28 May to 4 July. Clutch size: 3 or 4 eggs.

PORTRAIT. *Birds of Wisconsin:* Plate 79.

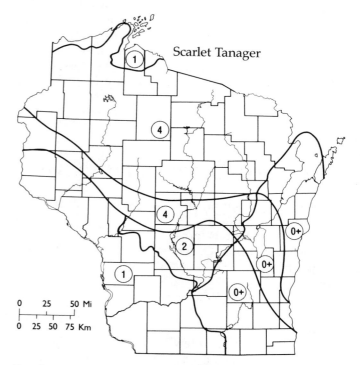

Breeding Bird Survey, averages 1966 to 1980

Most nineteenth century writers referred to the Scarlet Tanager as a common species in the parts of the state they knew. Barry (1854) even described its status as abundant. The current status may be described more accurately as fairly common. Perhaps the change reflects a drop in numbers occasioned by the gradual change of the southern Wisconsin landscape from woodland to open farmland; perhaps the earlier writers happened to live near unusually good tanager habitat; perhaps different meanings have been attached to the terms used to describe relative abundance. My preference for the "fairly common" designation stems from (1) figures in the BBS showing but one to four birds per transect per year in any of the state's biogeographic regions, (2) my personal records showing no more than 20 individuals ever encountered on a single field trip even at the height of the spring migration, and (3) my observations that, even in the most favorable habitat, the numbers of Scarlet Tanagers are far exceeded by such species as the Eastern Wood-Pewee, Great Crested Flycatcher, Red-eyed Vireo, Ovenbird, Rose-breasted Grosbeak, and Indigo Bunting.

Personally I have never seen this oak-dweller in Wisconsin during April. Few people have. In addition to a remarkable 13 April 1974 observation (Waushara, I. Chipman), unusually early sightings have occurred on the 22nd (1985, Rock, G. Mahlum), 23rd (1973, Milwaukee, E. J. Epstein; 1975, Milwaukee, E. Sheridan), 26th (1964, Rock, M. T. Maxson), and 27th (1979, Ozaukee, R. H. Sundell). First arrivals generally appear around 5 May in the south and 10 May farther north. The main movement is from 10 to 25 May in the south and from 15 to 30 May in the north. During this interval the males are conspicuous, with the brilliant red plumage standing out among the slowly developing oak leaves, and the throaty song being rendered frequently during the early morning hours.

Nesting activity begins within a few days of arrival. Most nests reported in the state have been found in oaks, well out on branches 8–15 feet up. Sometimes maples and elms are chosen. Although nests with eggs have been noted only between 28 May and 4 July, young in the nest have been seen as late as 17 July, suggesting that incubation continues further into July than the records indicate.

Although the breeding range is statewide, suitable woodlots are infrequent in southern and eastern counties. All 70 BBS transects have recorded the "black-winged redbird," but on routes in the southeastern counties, the bird is missed more often than it is found. Yet on three transect routes where oaks are plentiful (Burnett, Jackson, Juneau counties), 10 or more tanagers are recorded each year.

Following cessation of song early in July, birds become more difficult to find. They normally feed quietly with a minimum of movement at any season, and in late summer the male stays especially quiet and unobtrusive as he molts. On those rare occasions when a molting male is seen, his odd conglomeration of red-black and yellowish-green patches is noticeable.

A few fall migrants are on the move from 20 August on. September is the main fall migration period, but the bird is by no means common. Even an active field observer can easily go through an entire fall migration period without seeing a single tanager. The species is not that rare, of course, but the birds remain well hidden in the foliage, and rarely reveal their presence by the soft "chip-burr" note that is heard in early summer. By 20 September nearly all these tanagers have left the northern counties. Exceptionally late is an Outagamie County individual on 20 October (1971, D. D. Tessen). In the south, birds rarely linger beyond 10 October. Exceptions include one bird on 28 October (1974, Racine, L. W. Erickson) and November stragglers on the 1st (1975, Racine, L. W. Erickson), 5th (1955, Dane, M. A. Walker), 10th (1975, Milwaukee, E. L. Basten), 18th (1987, Sheboygan, D. D. Berger), and 22nd (1979, Milwaukee, W. Woodmansee).

Western Tanager (*Piranga ludoviciana*)

STATUS. Rare spring migrant. Accidental summer visitant.
HABITAT. Deciduous forest.
MIGRATION DATES. Observed between 1 and 19 May; and between 29 July and 8 August.
BREEDING DATA. Bred in 1877.
PORTRAIT. *Birds of Wisconsin:* Plate 79.

Few ornithologists have ever seen the Western Tanager in Wisconsin, and few are likely to see it in years to come. The regular range extends eastward only to the Black Hills; and although the bird has been known to wander to Quebec, New York, and New England, these meanderings are rare indeed.

Only once has this species been known to breed east of the Black Hills: in the summer of 1877 in Jeffer-

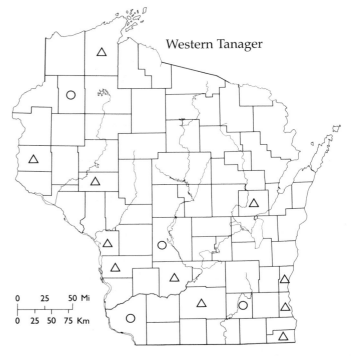

Western Tanager

△ 1 to 19 May
○ 29 July to 8 August

All records

Western Tanager, 17 May 1980, Ozaukee County (photo by M. E. Decker)

son County, Wisconsin (Kumlien and Hollister 1903). Thure Kumlien discovered a pair near his home late in May and subsequently found their nest in a white oak. The collected specimens—parents, nest, and eggs—now reside in the University of Wisconsin–Madison collection. Although Thure Kumlien collected a male in the same location in June 1878, and Ludwig Kumlien collected yet another male in July 1891, they recognized the unusual nature of these records and never thought of this species as anything other than an accidental visitant.

Not until 1955 was another Wisconsin visit recorded. A male was spotted in Madison on 8 (R. H. Lound) and 12 (J. Ela) May. Additional May sightings include 1-day glimpses on the 4th (1966, Sauk, K. I. Lange), and 6th (1959, Kenosha, W. Forbes). Spring wanderers have been almost an annual event since a 14 May 1978 observation in La Crosse County. Birds were found on 12 May 1979 (Vernon, W. E. Wheeler), 8–19 May 1980 (Ozaukee, L. A. Smith), 10 May 1982 (Eau Claire, J. L. Polk), 18 May 1983 (Milwaukee, W. Woodmansee), 6 May 1984 (Outagamie, P. R. Wydeven), 9 May 1984 (Bayfield, R. L. Verch), 19 May 1985 (Eau Claire, J. L. Polk), and 1–3 May 1986 (St. Croix, M. K. Ward).

On 29 July 1961 Roy Ivens (pers. comm. to O. J. Gromme) had the good fortune to find a male near the Wisconsin Audubon Camp at Sarona (Washburn County). Nearby were three female tanagers, but their specific identification was never certain. Ivens observed the male for half an hour and concluded, "There can be no doubt about the male as a Western Tanager because of his extremely distinctive coloring."

Dennis (1969) discovered another male on a small island in the Mississippi River channel in Grant County on 8 August 1969. Wisconsin's only other modern late-summer observation was made by R. F. Boehmer in the Necedah National Wildlife Refuge in Juneau County on 1 August 1984: a female feeding along the shoulder of a road, in company with two American Robins.

Northern Cardinal (*Cardinalis cardinalis*)

STATUS. Common resident west and south; fairly common resident east; uncommon resident north.
HABITAT. Residential areas. Farmsteads. Deciduous forest.
BREEDING DATA. Nests with eggs: 14 April to 14 September. Clutch size: 3 or 4 eggs.
PORTRAIT. *Birds of Wisconsin:* Plate 80.

At the beginning of the twentieth century Kumlien and Hollister (1903) listed the Northern Cardinal as rare and limited to Wisconsin's southern border. In 1980 the totals from the state's December CBC showed 3,049 birds in 67 of 79 count areas. Few species, except for the introduced House Sparrow and European Starling, can show as extensive an increase in numbers and distribution as this bird. Yet the increase has not been dramatic. Young, Stollberg, and Deusing (1941) described the growth as a series of limited invasions, beginning around 1900, following the major waterways, and then gradually fanning out into neighboring areas.

Young (1946) listed the years of first sightings for each Wisconsin county as he knew them. This information has been expanded in the accompanying map, with lines added to indicate those portions of the state where this species had become established by 1920, 1940, and 1960. It is evident that individuals have occasionally wandered north briefly (Forest, 1910; Lincoln, 1911; Iron, 1912; Burnett, 1920; Sawyer, 1928; Taylor, 1934; Washburn, 1935; Price, 1937; and Douglas, 1938) long before continuing populations

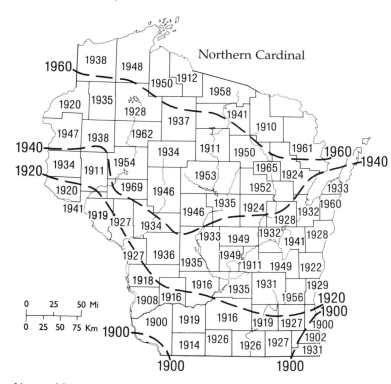

Northern Cardinal

Years of first county records

became established. The increase in Wisconsin is part of a growth pattern throughout the northeastern United States, where a comparable range extension into northern New York and New England has taken place during the same time interval.

North of a line running through New Richmond, Wausau, and Green Bay, this bird still occurs in only small numbers. Records from the two most northerly tiers of counties are still scant and irregular. But observations have come from every county in the state except Florence County.

It is in the winter that this brilliantly colored whistler is most conspicuous. That is the time when these birds congregate near the corn cribs and hedgerows of southern and western Wisconsin farms, often in flocks of 15–30. They are frequent visitors at winter feeding stations, often waiting their turn in the nearby bushes while the more aggressive Blue Jays and House Sparrows take first pick, but coming forward when the other birds have had their fill. In late January and February, weeks before other species are ready to engage in spring singing, a cardinal may react to a warm sunny morning by breaking out into a burst of spring whistling. In winter, too, more than in any other season, this bird tends to wander into new areas. Many of the first sightings, representing the gradual extension of this bird's range, have come in December and January.

During the other seasons of the year, this gaudy red bird is less conspicuous. By early April preparations for nesting may be under way. Although some pairs may choose a nesting site in the shrubbery close to the homes where they have found winter food, the majority move away from human dwellings, picking nest sites in the low vegetation bordering wooded areas. The loose flocks of winter disperse into nesting pairs, who set up territories which are vigorously defended. Frequently a male remaining in residential areas will spot his mirrored reflection in a window pane and spend considerable time pecking on the window to defend against his imagined rival.

The nesting season is a prolonged one. Nests with eggs have been observed as early as 14 April, with young leaving the nest before the middle of May. Nests have been reported in late August. In 1974 a late nest at La Crosse hatched three eggs on 15 September, with two youngsters fledging on the 24th (H. F. Young). Three nestings in a season are common. The

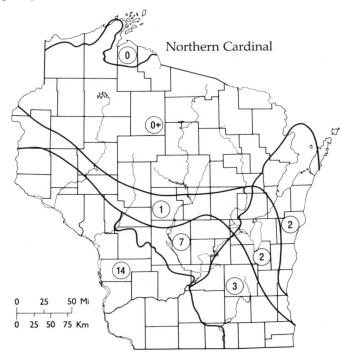

Breeding Bird Survey, averages 1966 to 1980

male continues to sing periodically, and the distinctive call note can be heard frequently by an attentive observer who happens to be in a nesting area. But during the late spring and summer period, when song and activity of other birds is at a peak, the cardinal is relatively inconspicuous.

Although this species has been reported from nearly every Wisconsin county, and can be considered common south of the New Richmond–Wausau–Green Bay line, it is decidedly more numerous in the western counties than in the eastern ones. This species has been found on 50 of the state's 70 BBS routes; the 20 cardinal-less routes are all north of the New Richmond–Wausau–Green Bay line. The bird is most numerous in the western counties, in the valleys drained by the St. Croix, Mississippi, Chippewa, and Wisconsin rivers. Wherever riverbanks are lined with stands of red cedars, cardinals abound.

Rose-breasted Grosbeak (*Pheucticus ludovicianus*)

STATUS. Common migrant. Common summer resident north and west; fairly common summer resident south and east. Casual winter resident.

HABITAT. Deciduous forest. Northern maple-hemlock-pine forest. Residential areas.

MIGRATION DATES. *Spring:* early to late May. *Fall:* mid-August to late September.

BREEDING DATA. Nests with eggs: 23 May to 1 August. Clutch size: 3 or 4 eggs.

WINTER. Six records, with one bird surviving into March.

PORTRAIT. *Birds of Wisconsin:* Plate 80.

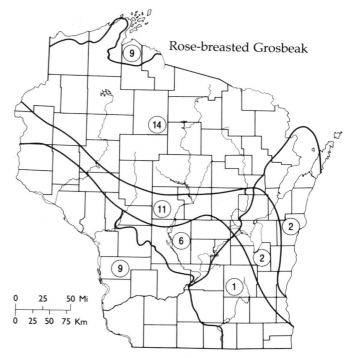

Breeding Bird Survey, averages 1966 to 1980

The spring arrival of the Rose-breasted Grosbeak is not difficult to detect. Unlike some species that trickle in unobtrusively, and may be present for days before beginning to sing, the male Rose-breast flies in during one of the first warm nights in early May and promptly announces his presence with a robinlike warble the next morning. The songster is likely to be well up in a tree, high enough to make a full appraisal of plumage difficult to the unaided eye; but because first arrivals come before the trees are fully leafed out, the bird's rosy breast stands out conspicuously. When the bird flies, the vivid black-and-white wing markings are unmistakable.

The spring migration proceeds rapidly. The southern counties usually have their first arrivals between 1 and 5 May. One bird that visited a Milwaukee feeder, 2–29 March 1976 (M. F. Donald), and a female found in Kenosha County on 28 March 1975 (J. Hamers) may well have wintered far north of usual winter haunts. The only known April arrival dates earlier than the 25th involve individuals on the 14th (1953, Chippewa, C. A. Kemper) and 20th (1977, Milwaukee, D. K. Gustafson). By 10 May birds have spread widely over the southern counties and have arrived at a few northern locations. Between 10 and 20 May the peak spreads northward; by 25 May it has come and gone, and birds are well distributed over the entire state, wherever there are suitable deciduous woods: farm woodlots, parks, cemeteries, and residential areas. Ordinarily one is unaware of the magnitude of this species' migration at its peak, but occasionally it becomes vivid. After a drenching rain, birds may flock to the ground to bathe in the remaining puddles, and this brightly plumaged bird will be among the most conspicuous and most numerous. Francis Zirrer (MPM files) once reported an estimated 80 birds near his Rusk County home late one afternoon (14 May 1935); they were gone by the following morning.

Nest building has been observed as early as 13 May. Usually it gets under way by 25 May and occupies the birds throughout June and July. Nests have been found as low as 3 feet up in bushes; Carl Richter once located a nest 58 feet up in an elm. Usually birds prefer a small deciduous tree as a nesting site, with the nest located from 7 to 12 feet up. The nest, loosely made, often suffers from summer rain and wind. Nott (1923) related an experience of discovering two nestlings that had fallen from a nest during a severe thunderstorm near her Reedsburg home. She placed the young in a hastily devised container, a strawberry box lined with cloth, and suspended it from a grape vine with safety pins. The young eventually fledged successfully.

The male continues to sing until early July. The Rose-breast's widespread presence throughout the state is indicated by its showing in the June BBS. On 66 of 70 BBS routes birds are encountered every year. On only four routes in the southeastern counties has this attractive singer sometimes been missed. Two northern routes average over 35 individuals per transect per year.

Although song ceases in early July, birds remain in their nesting areas through much of August while the young gradually attain full size and full independence. The males begin to change to a brown-and-white fall plumage. Birds are not conspicuous in this stage, but when observers do spot them—perhaps feeding on maple or sumac seeds—it can be seen that some birds display an odd mixture of gray and brown, as well as splotches of red on the upper breast.

The fall migration gets under way during the last half of August and is at its peak in mid-September. As in spring, the migration coincides with the main flight of warblers, vireos, and flycatchers. This grosbeak often associates with these birds, and stands out—even in drab plumage—by its larger size. Only rarely is this species recorded after the first week in October. Exceptions include lingering birds on 24 October (1971, Rock, G. Mahlum), 26 October (1955, Waukesha, E. Hoffmann), 4 November (1978, Kenosha, R. R. Hoffman), 15 November (1983, Brown, E. D. Cleary), and a bird that spent 2 weeks in Racine County, 17–29 November (1972, L. W. Erickson).

Since the regular winter range lies south of the United States, one would hardly expect this species ever to occur in Wisconsin in winter. But it has happened three times. Tom Ashman found a Rose-breast on a CBC in Dane County on 21 December 1957; it was not seen thereafter, and its fate is not known. On 30 December 1968 an immature male began coming to the Joan Krager feeder in Madison. The bird remained until 15 March 1969, feeding on millet and sunflower seeds; it presumably survived the winter. Between 28 January and 15 February a young male frequented the Karl Baltus feeder in Wood County. In December 1985 the number of winter records doubled within a 2-week span when Christmas bird counters found stragglers on the 20th (Kenosha), 21st (Wood), and 30th (Taylor). The Taylor County bird was a male in spring plumage, a daily visitor at a Gilman feeder until succumbing on 15 January 1986 (K. J. Luepke).

Black-headed Grosbeak (*Pheucticus melanocephalus*)

STATUS. Casual migrant. Accidental summer visitant. Casual winter resident.
HABITAT. Deciduous forest. Residential areas.
MIGRATION DATES. Observed between 23 September and 29 May.
WINTER. Six records.

Why is it that the Black-headed Grosbeak never visits Wisconsin? This question was occasionally asked by Wisconsin birders in the 1940s and 1950s, especially when these birds were known to wander to Minnesota, Connecticut, and Massachusetts. At the time Wisconsin had no specimen or even a sight record. The question may well have been raised by the nineteenth-century writers, too, for no mention of this species appears in their works.

But on 11 November 1969 an immature male showed up at the Doris Baker feeder in Madison. The bird remained a frequent visitor through 25 February 1970. It was seen by many additional observers, photographed by Peter Connors, and documented (*Pass. Pigeon* 32:52–53).

At the time this was thought to be Wisconsin's first record. Subsequently it was learned that a bird had been observed and photographed in southwestern Crawford County on 8 July 1969 by Ronald Morrein (photo in Upper Mississippi River National Wildlife Refuge files in Winona, Minn.).

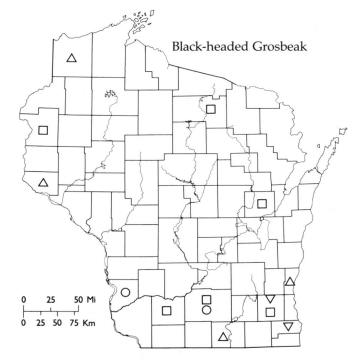

Black-headed Grosbeak

△   23 March to 29 May
○   8 July to 8 August
▽   23 September to 5 October
□   10 November to 13 April

All records

Black-headed Grosbeak, 25 April 1974, Ozaukee County (photo by H. G. Liebherr)

Three additional sight records followed in rapid succession during 1971: an adult male in Dane County on 8 August (M. Lound), one in Racine County on 5 October (D. Joslyn), and a young male at a feeder in Appleton on 10 and 11 November (M. Bowker).

Two birds wandered to the state in the spring of 1974. One was a young male sighted at the Martin Stabb feeder in Janesville (Rock County) from 23 March to 25 April, substantiated by documentation and a photograph (*Pass. Pigeon* 37:84–85). The other was an adult male that appeared briefly at an Ozaukee County feeder on 25 and 26 April (H. G. Liebherr). In 1975 another adult male was a daily visitor at the Charles Lloyd feeder in Iowa County from 3 March to 13 April; it was photographed, and was seen and enjoyed by other observers (*Pass. Pigeon* 37:163).

The remarkable experiences of that decade were rounded out with the photographing of a female on 14 May 1978 (Ozaukee, R. H. Sundell; *Pass. Pigeon* 41:38), the viewing of a singing male on 24 May 1979 (Pierce, C. A. Faanes; *Pass. Pigeon* 42:50), and the close viewing of a female at the Robert Thompson feeder at Rhinelander (Oneida County) between 29 December 1979 and 3 January 1980 (*Pass. Pigeon* 42:46).

The 1980s have produced four records. On 29 May 1983 a male joined a group of Evening and Rose-breasted Grosbeaks at the Fred Hennessy feeder near Gordon (Douglas County) for a brief 15-minute period (*Pass. Pigeon* 46:48). Between 25 December 1985 and 30 March 1986 Loretta Hernday entertained an individual daily at her Waukesha County home (*Pass. Pigeon* 48:177). At the opposite corner of the state, R. W. Diers observed a male at his Balsam Lake (Polk County) home on 22 January 1986 (*Pass. Pigeon* 48:173). Then it was Waukesha County's turn again: V. D. Aune observed an immature on 23 September 1987 (*Pass. Pigeon* 50:273).

No specimen exists for Wisconsin. But the four photographs that exist are all definitive. No clear pattern emerges to indicate at which seasons this species is most apt to occur in Wisconsin. Perhaps if the trend which began in the 1970s continues in years to come, a pattern may appear.

Blue Grosbeak (*Guiraca caerulea*)

STATUS. Rare spring migrant south. Casual summer
   visitant south.
HABITAT. Upland deciduous forest. Savanna.
MIGRATION DATES. Observed between 4 May and
   23 August.
BREEDING DATA. Nested in 1970.
PORTRAIT. *Birds of Wisconsin:* Plate 83.

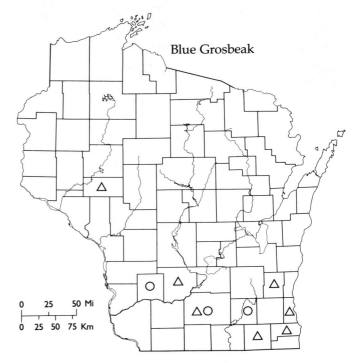

Blue Grosbeak

△   Early May to early June
○   Mid-June to late August

All records

When fire destroyed the bird collection at the Oshkosh Public Museum in 1916, it claimed Wisconsin's
only extant specimens of this southern straggler.
Records are incomplete, but these may have been the
two birds captured by Thure Kumlien in Jefferson
County in June 1860 (Kumlien and Hollister 1903).
These authors also mentioned a Milwaukee specimen
and one taken by P. R. Hoy at Racine, but nothing
further is known of these records.

No twentieth-century specimens exist. No photographs are known. For 19 purported sight observations between 1914 and 1981, documentation is either
nonexistent or too fragmentary to assure positive
identification. Since some Indigo Buntings coming
into first nuptial plumage still show brown wing
feathers, observers must be careful to note wing bars
and size when dealing with bluish birds in May.

For 11 other sight records, written details are more
complete. The first involves a bird in a wooded ravine
near Williams Bay (Walworth County) on 23 May 1950
(H. Morgan). Mrs. Morgan's notes described a "blue
bird with brown wings; thick bill, lightish. . . . The
blue was bright, though not as light or the same kind
of blue as an Indigo Bunting" (pers. comm. to O. J.
Gromme).

Between 1956 and 1961 three well-substantiated observations occurred. One involves an astonishing
flock of about 40 birds—males and females equally
represented—feeding on dandelion seeds on the
ground in Whitnall Park, Milwaukee, on 23 May 1956
(L. P. Smith). On 14 May 1957 a female and singing
male were discovered in Vilas Park, Madison (J. J.
Brenner). It was on 14 May 1961 on a golf course at
Racine that R. J. Barndt approached to within 10 feet
of another pair as they fed on the ground. Five of the
imperfectly documented sight records also fell within
the 1956–1961 interval.

After an 8-year lapse, Blue Grosbeaks reappeared
in 1970. On 10 May a male was observed hopping on a
pile of logs near West Bend (Washington County) by
Ann Maurin. On 16 August at her farm home in
northern Richland County, Janice Jensen discovered a

nest with two ready-to-fledge young. She had heard a
strange song and answering call note, and discovered
a male and a female bird near her garden. After carefully checking the birds' identity, she looked further
for a possible nest. The female led her to a nest half-
way up a 6-foot evening primrose stem. The nest contained two large nestlings. A week later the male was
still present, but the female and the young could not
be found (*Pass. Pigeon* 33:98).

Two males were discovered near Mazomanie (Dane
County) on 11 June 1978 (R. M. Hoffman), with one
still present on 13 June (T. De Boor), in brushy habitat. Hoffman found another in the same area on
9 May 1979.

Central Wisconsin's only record occurred on 10 May
1982. Mrs. J. G. Larson found two males at her Eau
Claire County feeder on the same warm day that
brought a wandering Western Tanager to Eau Claire.

Three individuals turned up during a 17-day period
in 1983: a female in Milwaukee (4–9 May, W. Woodmansee), a male in Milwaukee (8 May, J. H. Idzikowski), and a male in Dane County (21 May, R. M. Hoff-

man). A male reached Sauk County on 15 May 1985 (W. K. Volkert).

It is a pity that inadequate documentation rules out an additional 19 observations that seem probable.

These would confirm the pattern set by the verified records: mainly an "overshooting" of May migrants and an occasional June straggler.

Lazuli Bunting (*Passerina amoena*)

STATUS. Accidental. Four records.
HABITAT. Young forest saplings. Upland carr.
MIGRATION DATES. Observed between 5 May and 3 June.

A severe cyclonic disturbance on 5 and 6 May 1950, which brought to Wisconsin a spetactular migration including several outstanding rarities, is believed responsible for a singing male Lazuli Bunting that turned up at Milton (Rock County). First discovered on 6 May by Mattie Anderson, the bird was subsequently studied on the 7th at distances as close as 20 feet by Melva Maxson and Mabel West, as it moved from Maxson's lawn to a lilac bush, then to an elm. The song matched perfectly Mrs. Maxson's recordings. The blue back, cinnamon breast band, and white wing bars were unmistakable (*Pass. Pigeon* 13:36).

Another male appeared at Brule (Douglas County) on 19 May 1967. Mark Baillie discovered it at his backyard feeder, and spread the word among fellow birders. Bernard (1967) confirmed the identification. An 18 May storm that brought to the western Lake Superior region two Western Tanagers (Minnesota) and a

Lark Sparrow (Ontario) was probably responsible for blowing the Lazuli Bunting eastward from its normal range west of the Great Plains.

A third sight observation occurred on 3 June 1980 in the Mead Wildlife Area in Marathon County. Harry Tiebout detected an unusual song emanating from a sparrow-sized bird atop a 30-foot dead tree. The song, size, and shape bore resemblance to the Indigo Bunting. But close observation revealed that the blue of the back and head gave way to a rust-colored breast and white under tail coverts (*Pass. Pigeon* 43:62).

Kay Ogren eventually obtained a photograph—needed to lift this species off the state's hypothetical list. She observed the visitor on 6 May 1984 at her Spooner (Washburn County) home, as it and an Indigo Bunting fed together on cracked corn that the Ogrens had scattered on the lawn. The Lazuli Bunting was a daily visitor for the next 10 days (*Pass. Pigeon* 47:34).

While this attractive bunting is not known for its extralimital wandering, it may well stage future visits—particularly following gale-force westerly winds in May.

Indigo Bunting (*Passerina cyanea*)

STATUS. Common migrant. Common summer resident.

HABITAT. Deciduous forest. Savanna. Upland carr.

MIGRATION DATES. *Spring:* early May to early June. *Fall:* mid-August to mid-October. *Extremes:* 22 April; 23 October.

BREEDING DATA. Nests with eggs: 2 June to 5 August. Clutch size: 3 or 4 eggs.

WINTER. One record.

PORTRAIT. *Birds of Wisconsin:* Plate 81.

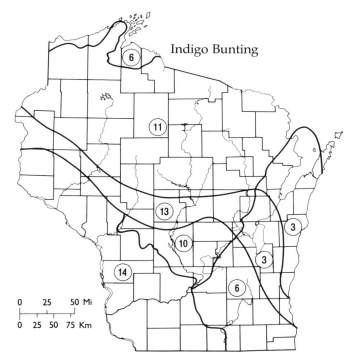

Breeding Bird Survey, averages 1966 to 1980

From late May to early August the Indigo Bunting is one of Wisconsin's most conspicuous birds. The earliest arrivals usually reach the southern counties during the first week of May or even the last few days of April. Unusually early were birds discovered on 22 April (1957, Lafayette, E. Olson; 1985, Brown, E. D. Cleary), followed by individuals on the 26th (1970, Vernon, V. E. Weber; 1974, Milwaukee, E. W. Strehlow) and 27th (1964, Dane, S. G. Curtis; 1980, Vernon, V. E. Weber). In the north first arrivals are usually detected between 5 and 10 May. Buntings are well distributed throughout the southern regions between the 15th and 20th and in the north between the 20th and 25th. In some years the migration spills over into the first week of June.

After a prolonged nesting season, the birds show a bit of fall movement by 20 August, but September is the main migration month. A few birds linger into October each year, even in the central region. Eau Claire television tower casualties have been reported as late as 12 October (1969, C. A. Kemper). Indigos were banded on 18 October (1980, Oconto, T. C. Erdman) and 19 October (1984, Chippewa, C. A. Kemper). The latest October dates in the southern counties have been the 17th (1979, Columbia, R. M. Hoffman), 18th (1972, La Crosse, J. R. Rosso), and 23rd (1961, Dane, M. B. Hickey).

Between late May and mid-August this species is an ideal attraction for the beginning ornithologist who desires to go afield to make the acquaintance of birds not usually found in the backyard. The bird is conspicuous for several reasons.

First, this is a bird of the "edge." Rather than living in either deep woods or open meadows, the bird prefers the brushy vegetation at the edge of woodlands, where the female has thick brush available for nesting and the male has a high perch on a tree or a utility wire from which to sing. Such habitat generally occurs along roadsides; a drive along a few miles of less-traveled roads should reveal several of these songsters in season.

Second, the bird is easily recognized when seen in good light. The solid blue color of the male is of a different hue from that of the Eastern Bluebird, Blue Jay, or any other bluish-colored bird. When seen against the sun, the bird seems dark and nondescript; when light conditions are favorable, there is a vivid blue color that has excited admiration in many a nature-lover. Even the brownish-hued female can be distinguished from the similarly plumaged sparrows because of the unstreaked brownish wash on the breast.

Third, the bird's song is loud, clear, and distinctive. Usually given from an open perch, the song has a carrying power that often helps it stand out even when birds of other species are singing simultaneously. Even the call note is unusually strong and distinctive to the trained ear.

While the male is devoting much time to singing, the female is busy with housekeeping duties. Nesting activities often occupy these birds for much of August, as well as June and July, and it is not unusual to see juveniles being fed by parents in mid-September, long after the migration of many other passerines has begun. Nests are generally constructed in thick tangles and shrubbery, 2–4 feet above ground; some nests have been reported only inches off the ground, while others have been found at heights up to 12 feet. June nests are heavily parasitized by the Brown-headed Cowbird. Second nests in July and early August are often more successful.

Although its northern range limit is not far north of Wisconsin's borders, in northern Minnesota and western Ontario, the Indigo Bunting is a common bird throughout Wisconsin. It has been reported on all of the state's 70 BBS transects. Even in the north-ern counties, transects often show 10 or more singing birds per 25-mile route. Greatest numbers of these buntings are reported from the hills and valleys of the western counties, where the preferred habitat is most abundant.

The usual winter range includes Mexico and Central America. So it was with astonishment that Carol Rudy and her CBC companions discovered a winter-plumage bird near Stockbridge (Calumet County) on 20 December 1986. The bird survived the winter, starting in March to develop blue feathering (*Pass. Pigeon* 49:195–196).

Painted Bunting (*Passerina ciris*)

STATUS. Casual spring migrant; accidental fall migrant.
HABITAT. Deciduous forest. Residential area shrubs.
MIGRATION DATES. Observed between 23 April and 20 May, and between 24 August and 27 November.

The spring of 1972 was remarkable in the history of the Painted Bunting. Not only were there extra-limital wanderings to Virginia, Maryland, Pennsylvania, and Rhode Island, but, in addition, two males wandered to Wisconsin. One was killed when it flew into a house at Point Beach State Forest near Two Rivers (Manitowoc County). Its identity was confirmed by Larry Ketchbaw and subsequently by Mary Donald (pers. comm.). The exact date in late April is not known; efforts to save the specimen were unsuccessful.

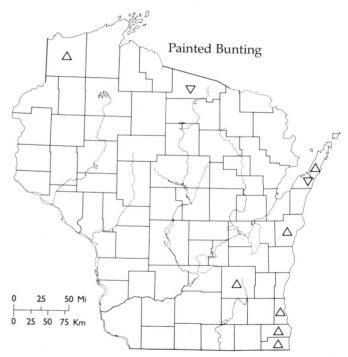

Painted Bunting

△ 23 April to 20 May
▽ 24 August to 27 November

All records

Painted Bunting, 16 May 1972, Kenosha County (photo by E. B. Prins)

The other bird struck a dwelling in Kenosha on 16 May (*Am. Birds* 26:814). It was picked up, nursed back to health by Louise Erickson and Edward Prins, photographed by Prins, and released on 17 May. It was seen during the next 3 days, then disappeared.

On four other occasions males have been known

to wander north along the Lake Michigan shore in spring. The first was a 23 April 1942 sighting in Milwaukee. An entry in O. J. Gromme's field notebook states: "Mrs. Thomas E. Bell and five other people (including her husband) saw a bird at close range which answered the description of a painted bunting perfectly. The lady worked with Dr. Ogden and seems to know her birds better than the average person." No further documentation exists.

The second and third were found the same day—12 May 1984—at feeders in different parts of Racine. Edward Prins photographed one and reported on the other. Neither bird could be found on subsequent days (*Pass. Pigeon* 47:35). On 10 May 1985 Evelyn McNamara photographed a male in Door County.

Two exceptional wanderings occurred in 1983. Far removed from Lake Michigan was the male that fed daily at a Douglas County feeder, 12–16 May (L. L. Erickson; *Pass Pigeon* 46:46). Far removed from spring was a female or immature that fluttered into Roy and Charlotte Lukes' garage in Door County on 27 November. Roy captured the stranger, and Charlotte

photographed it. The bird was not seen again after its release (*Pass. Pigeon* 46:126).

Wisconsin's only other record of a Painted Bunting in greenish plumage was a female that Dixie Larkin and I encountered near Lowell (Dodge County) on 17 May 1957. The bird was so tame that it was nearly struck by passing cars. As I stood by the front door of my car, the bunting hopped onto the car bumper 6 feet away (*Pass. Pigeon* 19:112–113). The tameness of this individual suggested that it may have been a recent escape.

The same possibility exists for a male observed at close range on 24 August 1966 in Vilas County (G. Orr; *Pass. Pigeon* 29:93). Although there is no doubt about the identity, the likelihood that the bird would reach this northern location at this season under its own power seems remote.

This species has been wandering with increasing frequency north to New York and New England, nearly always in spring. If this trend continues, occasional wandering to Wisconsin should continue.

Dickcissel (*Spiza americana*)

STATUS. Common migrant south and west; fairly common to uncommon migrant east and central. Common summer resident south and west; fairly common to uncommon summer resident east and central; rare summer resident north.

HABITAT. Open grassland and cropland.

MIGRATION DATES. *Spring:* mid-May to early June. *Fall:* early to late August. *Extremes:* 30 March; 31 October.

BREEDING DATA. Nests with eggs: 28 May to 3 August. Clutch size: 3–5 eggs.

WINTER. Two December records. Two January records.

PORTRAIT. *Birds of Wisconsin:* Plate 73.

As agriculture has gradually advanced northward in the state during the past 100 years, so has the range of this grassland species. In the mid-nineteenth century, when most of Wisconsin was still forested, the Dickcissel was reported only from the southern tier of counties. By the end of that century Kumlien and Hollister (1903) had noted a conspicuous increase in numbers and enlargement of range through southern Wisconsin, and J. N. Clark (Buss and Mattison 1955)

Breeding Bird Survey, averages 1966 to 1980

had recorded several birds as far north as Dunn County in western Wisconsin. By 1940 birds had sometimes been noted as far north as Wood, Waupaca, and Brown counties, with occasional sightings during periods of unusual abundance as far north as Rusk, Oneida, and Forest counties. By 1970 the species was being found at least occasionally north to Douglas, Bayfield, Oneida, Marinette, and Door counties.

The population swings have been more pronounced for this species than for any other Wisconsin summer passerine. Kumlien and Hollister (1903) referred to this as a very erratic species. In Walworth County, where it had once been rare, these writers found that "in the season of 1901 it was one of the most common of roadside birds, a male sitting every few rods along favorite highways." Stoddard (1922a) described similar abundance in 1921. Taber (1947) identified years of peak abundance as 1922, 1928, 1934, 1940, and 1946. Minor amendment to a predictable 6-year cycle was offered by Emlen and Wiens (1965), pinpointing high populations in 1950, 1956, and 1959. Then came an astonishing invasion in 1964, causing Emlen and Wiens to estimate a Wisconsin summer population of a million individuals. They commented, "The increase over 1963 was of the order of 50-fold in the south central counties." The expected drastic decline occurred in 1965, but populations were high again in 1967 and 1968.

But between 1968 and 1986 there were no "highs"— only a steady and serious decline. BBS figures told an ominous tale. On the 54 transects on which the "miniature meadowlark" has been recorded, there was an average of 20.29 birds per transect in 1968. This dwindled to 6.72 in 1972, 3.24 in 1976, 1.50 in 1980, and 0.30 in 1986. Dickcissels finally recovered slightly in 1987, reaching a high of 5.17 birds per transect in 1988.

Most Dickcissel activity in Wisconsin is limited to June and July. In addition to a phenomenal 30 March 1973 bird (Brown, T. C. Erdman), exceptionally early arrivals have been detected on 24 April (1975, Rock, T. R. Ellis) and 26 April (1970, Green, W. Rohde).

Rarely do the first migrants arrive in the southern counties before 10 May. Birds are still arriving on location in early June, setting up territories in their preferred habitat: open pastures and fields of clover and alfalfa. Fields of corn and oats are generally avoided. Areas bordering woodlots are likewise avoided, but the male wants at least a few tall weeds and fences or utility lines as prominent perches from which to sing. His throaty song can be heard at any time of day, even in early afternoon when most other birds are quiet. He continues to sing all through July; this is in contrast to most of his field-bird counterparts that stop singing by mid-July.

The female is as inconspicuous as her mate is conspicuous. She plunges into housekeeping duties shortly after arrival and is occupied with nesting until early August. Nests in hayfields are sometimes found on the ground, but more commonly are located a few inches above ground.

By mid-August this species has virtually vanished from the state. In more southern states Dickcissels are reported to concentrate in roosts of 50–300 birds in August, preparatory to migration. No such roost has been reported in Wisconsin. Once the song period ends at the beginning of August, this bird is rarely reported. But scattered observations, plus a few casualties at television towers, indicate that migration goes on through August and sparingly through much of September. October observations include birds on the 1st (1971, La Crosse, J. R. Rosso), 16th (1972, Milwaukee, R. G. Treder), 29th (1971, Ozaukee, T. Bintz; 1972, Washington, N. Andrich), and 31st (1966, Milwaukee, M. F. Donald).

It has been theorized that some Dickcissels, instead of migrating south, wander eastward. Winter records for New England and the Middle Atlantic states have been numerous in the past 30 years. But winter records in Wisconsin have been very rare. Individuals have been noted at feeders on 1 December (1972, Buffalo, M. Maier), 23–26 December (1961, Rock, M. K. Stocking), 1 January (1966, Waukesha, D. A. Beimborn), and 21 January (1969, Dane, J. J. Hickey).

Green-tailed Towhee (*Pipilo chlorurus*)

STATUS. Casual winter resident.
HABITAT. Residential area shrubs. Upland carr.
MIGRATION DATES. Observed between early November and 10 May.

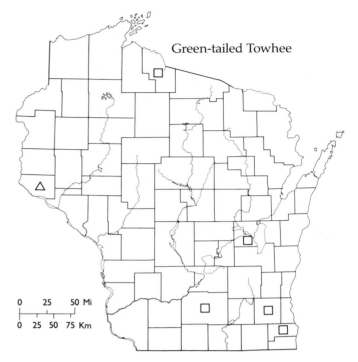

Green-tailed Towhee

△ 10 May
☐ Early November to 15 April

All records

Ornithological history was made on 14 December 1952 when a Green-tailed Towhee appeared at the Lynn Cooper feeder at Neenah (Winnebago County). It frequented both the feeder and the nearby evergreens daily for 2 weeks, but not until it was collected on 29 December was the identification confirmed beyond doubt by N. M. Rogers (*Pass. Pigeon* 15:120–121). The specimen is now in the Milwaukee Public Museum. Some unknown circumstance caused an unprecedented irruption that winter, bringing other stragglers to Kansas, Louisiana, Mississippi, Tennessee, Illinois, Virginia, and Massachusetts.

Other accidental wanderings of this bird of the arid West have occurred from time to time in other central and eastern states, usually in winter. Such was the case with Wisconsin's second record. A bird was discovered foraging in a disposal area on the University of Wisconsin campus in Madison on 23 December 1956 and collected by R. A. McCabe. The specimen is in the university collection (*Pass. Pigeon* 19:92).

Accidental winter stragglers give few clues to the habitat and behavior that could be associated with this species within its normal range. But an inkling of what that might be came to Robert Garber when he discovered and photographed a bird at Prescott (Pierce County) on 10 May 1964 (*Pass. Pigeon* 27:12–13). The hillside pasture overgrown with scrub oak, where the bird was seen, is similar to this species' preferred habitat in the West. The bird was observed scratching around dead oak leaves in typical towhee behavior. It kept company with some migrating Rufous-sided Towhees; this also is typical, for in the West both towhee species are often found on the same brushy hillsides. The Prescott bird was evidently an off-course migrant making a momentary stop. Several subsequent efforts to find the bird were made the same afternoon and on succeeding days, all to no avail. Garber's experience is exceptional. It is one of only a few instances when an errant spring migrant has been recorded so far from the species' regular range. Wisconsin's fourth record was an individual trapped in Waukesha County on 25 February 1968 (D. Stoner; MPM files).

The following year Richard Garber played host to a vagrant at his Racine feeders from 17 February to 4 April 1969. This bird was tame and cooperative, allowing itself to be photographed and viewed by dozens of ornithologists during this 6-week sojourn (*Pass. Pigeon* 31:183).

The longest period of residency was established by the bird that appeared at the Harvey Beach feeder in Iron County in early November 1979. It was a daily visitor through the winter, remaining through 15 April 1980, and was seen and photographed by numerous observers (*Pass. Pigeon* 42:148; 43:36).

Because the Green-tailed Towhee is given to occasional eastern meanderings, it can be expected to visit Wisconsin occasionally. But these occasions will not be frequent.

Rufous-sided Towhee (*Pipilo erythrophthalmus*)

Formerly Red-eyed Towhee

STATUS. Fairly common migrant. Fairly common summer resident. Rare winter resident south.

HABITAT. Upland deciduous forest. Upland carr.

MIGRATION DATES. *Spring:* early April to mid-May. *Fall:* early September to late October.

BREEDING DATA. Nests with eggs: 19 May to 21 July. Clutch size: usually 4 or 5 eggs; occasionally 3.

WINTER. Occasionally present north to Sauk, Outagamie, and Manitowoc counties; rarely present to Barron, Price, Oneida, Marinette, and Door counties.

PORTRAIT. *Birds of Wisconsin:* Plate 80.

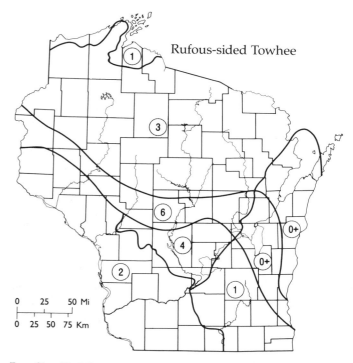

Breeding Bird Survey, averages 1966 to 1980

Kumlien and Hollister (1903) considered the Rufous-sided Towhee abundant in summer. In a few areas of favored habitat it might still be called abundant; but these areas are limited "islands," and considering the state as a whole, the designation of fairly common seems more apt. This picture stands out boldly in BBS results. The statewide character of the summer range is indicated by the recording of the bird on 69 of the state's 70 transects. Six of these routes, widely scattered in Douglas, Bayfield, Burnett, Oconto, Jackson, and Juneau counties, run through favorable towhee country and produce a combined average of over 17 birds per transect per year. The other 63 routes show an average of only two birds per transect per year.

Ths six favored transects run through areas where the undergrowth is heavy. Mixed Hill's oak and jack pine are popular with this bird, and if there is a small swampy area nearby, the "chewinks" like the undergrowth near the edge. This is a relatively conspicuous bird. Its song carries well, and is often uttered from a perch atop one of the taller trees in the area. It is larger than most birds inhabiting the same territory. It shows prominent white tail spots in flight. Even while feeding on the ground it attracts attention by the vigorous way it scratches through the fallen oak leaves in search of insects, larvae, and seeds,

Spring arrival in the central and northern counties comes around 1 May. But in the southern counties the first arrivals are often widely dispersed. A handful may appear during a warm spell in late March, with a few others arriving on succeeding warm periods in early April. But not until late April is the arrival general.

Migration leads quickly into the nesting season. Nests with eggs are commonly found from 20 May on. Two broods per summer are sometimes raised,

stretching the nesting season well into August. Nests with young have been found as late as 1 September. Nests are usually placed on the ground or in dense shrubbery at heights of less than 3 feet. Although the Brown-headed Cowbird usually restricts egg-laying to the nests of birds smaller than itself, it often parasitizes the larger Rufous-sided Towhee. On 19 May 1922, S. P. Jones discovered a nest with one towhee egg, one broken towhee egg, and three fresh cowbird eggs.

Autumn migration begins around 1 September. In the north there is no fall buildup, just a disappearance of resident birds in the first half of September. In the central and southern counties the birds gradually build to a peak in late September and early October, tapering off by the end of October. Even during a migration peak there is little tendency toward flocking; the family groups of the summer have dispersed, and only rarely does one see more than two or three together in fall.

If a bird is still present in mid-November, the chances are that it will attempt to overwinter. From one to eight birds have been known to stay in Wisconsin for at least the early part of the winter nearly every year. Because it is essentially a ground-feeding bird, this species' success in wintering depends largely upon well-kept feeding stations. Probably only a few of those that attempt to overwinter survive. No part of Wisconsin can be considered normal winter range for this species. But since 1960, December and/or January observations have occurred in 24 counties. Most northerly sightings were in Barron (1978), Chippewa (1973, 1984), Price (1974, 1977), Lincoln (1984), Langlade (1987), Oneida (1977, 1980), Marinette (1980), and Door (1977, 1980) counties.

American Tree Sparrow (*Spizella arborea*)

STATUS. Abundant migrant. Common winter resident south and central; uncommon winter resident north.
HABITAT. Old field. All carr. Residential areas.
MIGRATION DATES. *Fall:* early October to mid-December. *Spring:* mid-March to early May. *Extremes:* 8 August; 25 May.
PORTRAIT. *Birds of Wisconsin:* Plate 85.

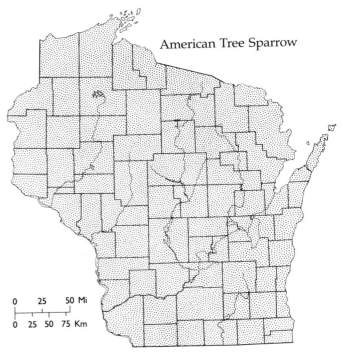

American Tree Sparrow

0   25   50 Mi

0   25   50   75 Km

▨ Winter range

Records since 1960

The American Tree Sparrow is Wisconsin's winter sparrow. By the time first arrivals come to the northern counties in the first week of October and spread to central and southern counties during the second and third weeks, most of the other migrating sparrows are just leaving for the south. First arrivals are often mixed in with Song, Swamp, Savannah, and Lincoln's Sparrows, and sometimes with Fields and White-throats. But within a few days the other species will have moved on, and by the end of October the Tree Sparrow will have become the dominant brownish sparrow. Occasionally first arrivals have been detected in the last 10 days of September. Two phenomenally early birds were detected on 8 August 1982 (Ashland, R. L. Verch) and 12 August 1963 (Marinette, H. L. Lindberg). No other records before 21 September are known.

Juncos and Tree Sparrows often flock together as they migrate in large numbers through the state in November, with mixed flocks often numbering in the hundreds. As the snow depth increases in the northern counties in late November and December, most Tree Sparrows move farther south. By late December a line approximating Highway 64 from New Richmond through Medford, Peshtigo, and Sturgeon Bay seems to form the northern limit for the early winter range. On CBCs taken north of this line since 1957, only 28% have recorded this species; south of this line this bird has been represented on 88% of the counts.

Wide variations in populations have been reported on the CBC in the last 10 years: as few as 7,087 statewide (1978), as many as 22,835 (1975). By late December, 70–80% of the CBC birds are found in the southern third of the state (south of Highway 33) every year.

Even the few birds remaining in the north in December are driven south in January. Numbers also decrease in the central counties in late December and January in winters of considerable snowfall. The birds feed largely on weed seeds, and when the weeds in open fields become covered with snow the birds must move elsewhere. A few may linger at feeding stations, but most move south. In the southern counties the early winter populations may remain relatively constant through the winter, may increase as new birds move in from the north, or may decrease if heavy snow in the southern counties covers their natural food.

By mid-March the northward movement begins, with northbound migrants reaching the northern counties near 1 April. The average first arrival date in Sawyer and Rusk counties (1929–1940) was 7 April. In Iron County the average first arrival date (1946–1955) was 13 April. As the birds move northward in April they disperse into smaller groups. Instead of the flocks of 100 or more observed in winter, one sees flocks of 10–20 in spring. It is unusual to see a Tree Sparrow in the southern counties after 30 April, in the central counties after 10 May, in the north after 15 May. The state's lone record beyond 20 May is a 25 May 1970 record at Superior (R. F. Bernard).

Chipping Sparrow (*Spizella passerina*)

STATUS. Common migrant. Common summer resident. Casual winter resident south.
HABITAT. Residential areas. Savanna. Young forest saplings.
MIGRATION DATES. *Spring:* early April to mid-May. *Fall:* early September to late October.
BREEDING DATA. Nests with eggs: 3 May to 1 August. Clutch size: 3 or 4 eggs.
WINTER. Rarely present in early winter north to Grant, Waushara, and Marinette counties. Two February records.
PORTRAIT. *Birds of Wisconsin:* Plate 85.

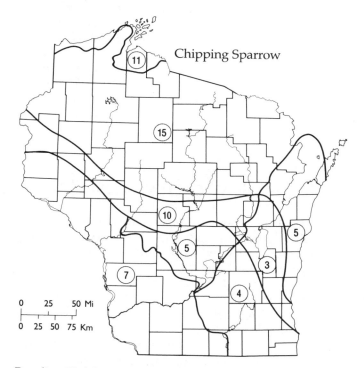

Breeding Bird Survey, averages 1966 to 1980

From mid-April to mid-October the Chipping Sparrow is one of Wisconsin's most familiar and best-loved birds. Its plumage is not unusually brilliant, nor is its song strikingly melodious; its popularity arises from its friendly cohabitation with people. In city parks it inhabits the lawns and shrubs close to the busy parking lots. Near houses in residential areas it is often seen feeding on the ground outside the living room, and its nest is often found in shrubbery within a few feet of the house. When one visits a cottage or campground in the north, the "chippy" is as likely as not to be the first bird spotted, flying up from the driveway as the car approaches. In the northern counties, even when there are no buildings close by, these birds are often found along the roadsides wherever there is a substantial cleared area between the road and the edge of the woods.

On rare occasions an early arrival has been reported on warm days in late March. A more usual date for a first arrival is 10 April. These average arrival dates have been reported over extended periods of observation in different counties: 14 April (Grant), 17 April (Dane), 19 April (Sheboygan), 22 April (Wood), 25 April (Washburn), 27 April (Oconto), and 2 May (Iron). By adding 2–3 weeks to these dates it is possible to estimate the spring migration peaks.

Before the last northbound migrants have departed, nesting activity for resident birds has begun. Nest locations are varied. Some nests are placed in low shrubbery scarcely 2 feet off the ground. Some are located in pine trees 8–10 feet up; a few are even higher. Jackson (1943) once reported a nest 40 feet up in a white pine. Mossman and Lange (1982) mentioned a pair completing three successful nestings in one summer. Recently fledged young are often seen in late August, which suggests that many pairs attempt two or more nestings in one summer.

BBS figures clearly show the summer range to be statewide. Each year the bird is recorded on over 90% of the survey routes. It is only in the routes in the southeastern sector that the species is sometimes missed. It is most numerous in the north-central areas.

Flocks of 30–40 are not unusual in late August and early September, especially in the northern counties, but it is difficult to tell whether these flocks include migrants moving in from farther north, or simply represent the flocking of locally breeding birds. By mid-September migration is much in evidence. Song is rarely heard during migration, but the birds frequently move around and "chip" quite a bit. By the end of September they have become quiet, and many have left for the south. But small numbers linger well into October, even though they are quiet and less noticeable. The end of October finds birds entirely gone from the northern counties; only stragglers remain in the central and southern counties. By 10 November even the stragglers are gone.

Winter records are few. A banded bird remained in Marinette County through 7 December (1970, H. L. Lindberg). Another bird was present at a Milwaukee feeder from 15 December through 5 January (1972–

1973, M. F. Donald). Additional CBC reports have come from Grant (1980), Wood (1980), Waushara (1981), Outagamie (1967, 1973), Walworth (1981), and Milwaukee (1971, 1974) counties. Most exceptional were an individual surviving from 10 January into March (1981, Marinette, H. L. Lindberg) and a bird discovered on 8 February (1975, Kenosha, D. D. Tessen).

Kumlien and Hollister (1903) described this diminutive sparrow as abundant in towns and cities before the introduction and spread of the House Sparrow, but commented: "Now all is changed, and in most towns it is a rare occurrence for a pair to settle for the summer where it was formerly common. It is still plenty [sic], however, in the country." Although House Sparrows have spread far and wide since 1903, the Chipping Sparrow has held its own. BBS figures point to a modest increase statewide; the 6.42 average per transect per year in 1966 (when the BBS was instituted) rose steadily during the next 15 years and had nearly doubled (12.43) by 1980.

Clay-colored Sparrow (*Spizella pallida*)

STATUS. Fairly common migrant west and north; uncommon migrant east and south. Fairly common summer resident west and north; rare summer resident south and east.
HABITAT. Old field. All carr. Young conifer plantation.
MIGRATION DATES. *Spring:* late April to late May. *Fall:* mid-August to mid-October. *Extremes:* 29 March; 8 November.
BREEDING DATA. Nests with eggs: 30 May to 10 July. Clutch size: usually 3 or 4 eggs; occasionally 5.
PORTRAIT. *Birds of Wisconsin:* Plate 85.

To many a southern Wisconsinite it has come as quite a surprise to find out how common a bird the Clay-colored Sparrow is throughout much of central and northern Wisconsin, because it appears to be so scarce in the southern counties during migration. Although the summer distribution is somewhat spotty and localized, north of a V-shaped line from Hudson to Adams to Green Bay, many pockets exist where the bird is fairly common. The number of birds detected migrating through the southern counties in spring and fall is but a fraction of the more northerly summer population.

It is not surely known why this is so. Some ornithologists have conjectured that most Clay-colors fly

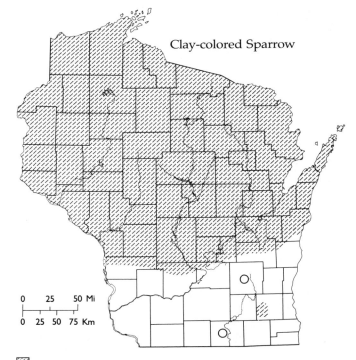

Clay-colored Sparrow

▨ Summer range
○ Early June to early August

Records since 1960

northward over the southern counties nonstop on the final leg of their spring migratory journey. But Illinois observers see little of this bird. Part of the answer may lie in the historical changes in summer range that have taken place during the past century. Formerly this species bred in Indiana, Illinois, and southern Wisconsin, but as most of this land was developed for agriculture and urbanization, the Clay-color withdrew. In Wisconsin it bred in Madison through 1920, but has been known only as a migrant since. The last breeding colony around Milwaukee disappeared about 1950. The bird has been found in recent summers in Sauk, Columbia, Dodge, and Waukesha counties, but only sparingly. On the other hand, it is found in much of northern Michigan. Because the main range lies west of the Mississippi River, a southwest-northeast migratory path across most of Wisconsin is suggested.

Occasionally the earliest spring migrants arrive around 20 April. Exceptionally early (storm-blown?) birds were found on 29 March (1949, Dane, M. A. Walker) and 3 April (1981, Door, R. J. Lukes). But 30 April is a more typical arrival date. In about 1 year in every 5, no Clay-colors are detected in the state until early May. Once the first birds arrive, they seem to irrupt throughout their range almost simultaneously. In 1955, for instance, first arrivals were observed in Adams County on 29 April, in Milwaukee and Marathon counties on 30 April, and in Bayfield County on 3 May. In 1964 an early bird in Rock County on 22 April was followed swiftly by a 23 April debut in Brown County and a 24 April sighting in St. Croix County. No sizable spring peaks have been reported. The birds move quickly onto their breeding grounds, with the migration usually completed by 25 May. Migrants may make brief stops in parks, cemeteries, or residential areas, but most of the birds prefer dry brushy areas, hedgerows bordering fallow pasture lands, or, especially, acreages with young pine or spruce plantings. I have found them along little-used town roads far more frequently than along main highways.

Nests are usually under construction during the last week of May. Rarely if ever are nests built on the ground, but they are often constructed in tufts of old grass only inches off the ground or in small trees and shrubs no more than 2–3 feet up. While the female is occupied incubating eggs, the male is perched near the top of a nearby shrub seemingly working hard to make as musical a song as possible. Yet try as he may, the effort produces nothing melodious—merely a series of harsh, drawn-out, monotonous buzzes. An inexperienced observer could easily mistake a Clay-color for a Chipping or Field Sparrow on sight; but there is no mistaking this song.

In June, Clay-colors are found regularly on 24 of the state's 70 BBS transects, and with somewhat less regularity on another 29 routes. In the northernmost counties the average number of individuals per transect per year is seven. In the remainder of the forest-dominated area north of the tension zone, the average is four. South of the tension zone the average is less than one. The full scope of the summer range is shown in the accompanying map. Numbers are very small in the counties adjoining the Mississippi River, the Lake Michigan region, and the Waukesha County "island."

Flocks of 25–30 birds often occur in late August as birds gather for fall migration. The fact that a bird was trapped at Milton (Rock County) on 15 August 1953 suggests that fall migration may start by mid-August. These sparrows disappear gradually from their breeding grounds in September and early October; there are no pronounced migration peaks. Birds are generally gone from the northern areas by 20 October and from the southern areas a week later. There is but one November record (for the 8th, 1957, Vernon, V. E. Weber), and none at all for the winter months.

Field Sparrow (*Spizella pusilla*)

STATUS. Common migrant south and central; uncommon migrant north. Common summer resident west and central; fairly common summer resident east; uncommon summer resident north. Rare winter resident south and central.

HABITAT. Old field. Upland carr. Young forest saplings.

MIGRATION DATES. *Spring:* late March to early May. *Fall:* early September to late October.

BREEDING DATA. Nests with eggs: 10 May to 16 August. Clutch size: 3 or 4 eggs.

WINTER. Occasionally present north to St. Croix, Marathon, Outagamie, and Manitowoc counties.

PORTRAIT. *Birds of Wisconsin:* Plate 85.

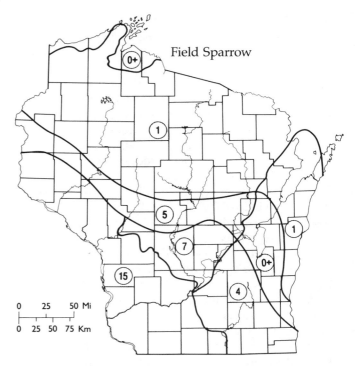

Breeding Bird Survey, averages 1966 to 1980

If one thinks of fields in terms of cultivated land planted to corn, oats, soy beans, or other grains, one would conclude that the Field Sparrow was poorly named; it is not often found on plowed land. But if one thinks of fields in terms of overgrown and unused pasture, perhaps formerly under cultivation but now interspersed with brush and small shrubs, this species seems admirably named. The Field Sparrow is neither a bird of the open prairie nor one of the heavy timber; it is rather a bird of the edge, where substantial areas of brushy hillsides and uncultivated margins separate trees from cornstalks.

The summer range is a curious one. Because it is primarily a bird of the eastern United States, this species might be expected to be more prevalent in the eastern section of Wisconsin than in the western. The BBS results reveal a very different pattern. It is in the southern and western counties that this bird is common, with numbers sharply reduced northward and eastward. The bird has been found sparingly in Douglas, Bayfield, Ashland, Vilas, Oneida, and Forest counties but not at all in Iron and Florence counties.

First spring arrivals often reach the southernmost counties in late March, but nearly all migration is concentrated in April and early May. Average county arrival dates include: 30 March (Dane), 3 April (Waukesha, La Crosse), 9 April (Milwaukee), 14 April (Fond du Lac), 15 April (St. Croix), 16 April (Wood), and 20 April (Waupaca).

With breeding birds on their territories during the first week of May, nesting activity proceeds through the summer months. The discovery of nests with eggs as late as mid-August suggests the possibility of multiple broods. The nests are often placed low down in shrubs or bushes or even fragile weed clumps, in areas easily accessible to people and predators and subject to other disturbing influences.

Because Wisconsin is on the northern extremity of its range, the Field Sparrow exhibits no sizable buildup of numbers in fall migration. Birds are on the move by mid-September, with the general pullout completed by 20 October. Average late departure dates for counties are: 7 October (St. Croix), 8 October (Waupaca), 10 October (Adams), 13 October (Dane), and 17 October (Waukesha). Late migrants occasionally linger into November.

Through the first half of the twentieth century this bird was almost unknown in winter. In 1952 it turned up on four separate Christmas counts, and ever since—with the exception of 1955 and 1970—it has been found on one or more of the state's counts each December. These winter reports have come from 18 counties, as far north as St. Croix, Barron, Clark, Marathon, Outagamie, and Manitowoc counties. These birds are usually discovered by sharp-eared birders who, in examining a flock of feeding Tree Sparrows, detect the distinctive soft lisping call of the Field. No one knows how many of these CBC birds survive the winter, but some have managed to do so.

Vesper Sparrow (*Pooecetes gramineus*)

STATUS. Common summer resident. Rare winter resident south.

HABITAT. Open grassland and cropland. Old field.

MIGRATION DATES. *Spring:* late March to early May. *Fall:* early September to late October.

BREEDING DATA. Nests with eggs: 29 April to 10 July. Clutch size: usually 3 or 4 eggs; occasionally 5.

WINTER. Rarely present north to Crawford, Sauk, Jefferson, and Washington counties.

PORTRAIT. *Birds of Wisconsin:* Plate 84.

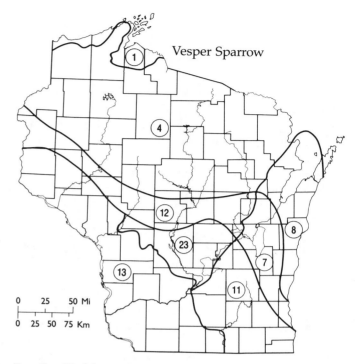

Breeding Bird Survey, averages 1966 to 1980

Throughout much of the state the Vesper Sparrow is recognized as one of the most typical early April arrivals. Sometimes the southernmost counties have a few scattered individuals during the last week of March, and sometimes the most northern areas do not have first arrivals until the beginning of May. But for most areas the first 2 weeks of April usher in the first arrivals, with birds fanning out over the entire state during the remainder of the month.

From April through July the Vesper is the most conspicuous of the grassland sparrows that come to Wisconsin. Only in those parts of the state that feature a light sandy soil does the Vesper outnumber the Savannah. But the Vesper is more apt to be noticed. It takes to utility wires, fence posts, and other conspicuous perches more readily than other species of sparrows. From its prominent perch the bird sings a melody that is stronger, more sustained, and with greater carrying power, than the song of other field and meadow sparrows.

This species reaches all parts of the state, but in the northern tier of counties the numbers are significantly smaller. The birds are not plentiful either along the Lake Michigan shoreline or the Mississippi and St. Croix rivers. But the Vesper is common throughout the rest of southern and central Wisconsin, as far north as Polk and Burnett counties in the west. It has been found on 67 of the 70 BBS transects, missing only on forest-dominated routes in Taylor, Ashland, and Forest counties.

A modest population decline appears to have set in since the beginning of the BBS in 1966. On the 67 counts that have recorded this species, from 10 to 13 individuals per route were found each year through 1972. In 1973 the average dropped below 8. The 1980 average (6.78) was but half that of 1966 (13.54), with a slight decline continuing through the 1980s.

The trend toward an earlier schedule of hay-cutting (the first crop in early June instead of late June) may be partly responsible for this decrease. But some Ves-

per Sparrow egg-laying occurs in the last few days of April and the first week of May, with young likely to fledge by the time the hay harvest starts. It is not known whether eggs being incubated as late as early July represent second nestings or renestings following earlier failures.

In late summer, as young of the year learn to exist on their own, both young and old display an affinity for the dusty shoulders of the less-traveled town roads. They take "dust baths" on or near the edge of the road, and when flushed, fly ahead or behind a short distance and resume their roadside dusting behavior. Although Vespers remain primarily a grassland species, it is not unusual to find these birds flying to trees along the edge of neighboring woodlots, particularly in areas where jack pines are present.

A modest amount of flocking takes place in September, with the bird remaining common in most parts of the state until early October. Most Vespers depart by mid-October, but individuals have been reported in the north as late as 31 October (Iron) and in the central region until 17 November (Manitowoc) and 21 November (Adams).

In the southernmost counties a bird occasionally attempts to overwinter. There are 27 CBC records since 1948, another 8 in January. Three February dates plus birds on 3 and 4 March—3 weeks early for migrants—suggest that in rare instances the attempts to overwinter succeed.

Lark Sparrow (*Chondestes grammacus*)

STATUS. Uncommon spring migrant south, west, and central; rare fall migrant south. Uncommon summer resident west and central.

HABITAT. Sand and gravel. Old field. Upland carr.

MIGRATION DATES. *Spring:* late April to late May. *Fall:* mid-August to mid-September. *Extremes:* 15 April; 29 October.

BREEDING DATA. Nests with eggs: 5 May to 7 July. Clutch size: usually 4 eggs; occasionally 3.

WINTER. One December record.

PORTRAIT. *Birds of Wisconsin:* Plate 84.

Hoy (1853b) referred to the Lark Sparrow as a common bird in the unbroken prairie areas around Racine. In the immediately succeeding years it was also found commonly around Milwaukee and other parts of southeastern Wisconsin. But as more of the land there came under the plow, the range of this species began to recede. Kumlien and Hollister (1903) stated, "Formerly quite common about Lake Koshkonong, but of late years has greatly decreased in numbers."

The Lark Sparrow is no longer found in the southeastern corner of the state, except as a rare migrant (seven published records in the past 35 years). Birders from Milwaukee now journey to the Arena–Spring Green–Lone Rock region in Iowa and Sauk counties to see this boldly marked sparrow and listen to its rich trilly song. Nor is it found today around Green Bay and New London (Waupaca County), where it was occasionally seen 40–50 years ago; one must travel to Stevens Point (Portage County) and Plainfield (Waushara County) to find the bird regularly.

The decline is due to agricultural development. Schorger (1931a) commented, "This fine sparrow, accustomed from time immemorial to the unbroken prairie, has adapted itself reluctantly, when at all, to cultivated ground." Hence its range in Wisconsin is now restricted to those regions where the soil is too sandy for agriculture, where grass is short and sparse and interspersed with Hill's oak and jack pine. The present summer range is a series of colonies, clustered mainly near the major rivers, in the shaded area shown in the accompanying map.

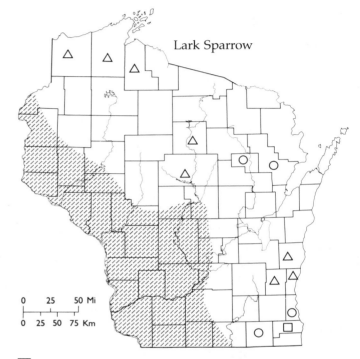

Lark Sparrow

```
0    25    50 Mi
0  25  50  75 Km
```

▨ Summer range
△ Late April to late May
○ Early June to early August
▽ Mid-August to mid-September
☐ 19 December

Records since 1960

In certain pockets within this region, the bird can be found in some numbers. One such spot is near Spring Green (Sauk County), where 16 birds were counted on 18 July 1964 (J. Saetveit). Another is in the northern half of Adams County; there in 1954 I found singing males, probably representing breeding pairs, in 15 locations. The northernmost colony, near Grantsburg (Burnett County), contains up to six pairs.

Spring migration normally begins around 25 April; the bird seen on 15 April 1958 in Lafayette County (E. Olson) was unusually early. In nine consecutive years of observation in Adams County in the 1950s, I recorded first arrivals on dates varying from 21 April to 5 May. By 15 May birds are present throughout their limited range. Rarely, wanderers have shown up in eastern and northern counties. Exceptional were a bird in Douglas County on 18 May (1971, P. B. Hofslund), one on Outer Island in Ashland County on 14 May (1976, J. T. Harris), and one in Bayfield County on 16 May (1985, S. R. Swengel).

The regular summer range lies west of a line from Grantsburg to Beloit, with a bulge in central Wisconsin extending east to Stevens Point and Westfield (Marquette County). Since 1960 the only June sightings east of that line have been on the 9th (1972, Oconto, D. D. Tessen), 18th (1974, Oconto, D. D. Tessen), and 29th (1971, Milwaukee, D. K. Gustafson).

Sometimes nests are built directly on the ground in slight depressions surrounded with some grass cover. At times nests are built in low shrubbery. Nesting activities take place primarily from mid-May through June. A Pierce County nest with four eggs on 7 July 1981 (E. J. Epstein) seems unusually late. Occasional instances of parasitism by the Brown-headed Cowbird have been reported.

Through June the male remains quite conspicuous. He sings from utility wires or exposed perches in the trees that form the edge of the bird's sandy haunts. When the male is not singing, he may be feeding on the ground—often close to the roadside. Rarely have I found this bird on the gravel shoulder where it could be seen from inside the car, but often I have got out of the car and flushed birds from the sparse grass only a few feet away from the shoulder.

Nesting, feeding, and caring for the young continue into July and August; but when singing stops in early July, birds are less frequently detected. Although observations in July and August are far less numerous than in May and June, this species remains on territory at least through mid-August. Records thereafter are scarce, but there are a few through 25 September, plus reports of two October stragglers in Milwaukee, on the 4th (1965, K. Priebe) and 29th (1979, D. K. Gustafson). Most remarkable is the presence of a Lark Sparrow seen among a flock of Tree Sparrows on the Racine CBC on 19 December 1987.

Black-throated Sparrow (*Amphispiza bilineata*)

STATUS. Accidental. Five records.
HABITAT. Residential areas. Open grassland.
MIGRATION DATES. Observed between 30 October and an unknown date in early May.
WINTER. Four records.

There was a touch of longing—almost of apology—when Ralph Morse reported to Wisconsin ornithologists the sighting of a Black-throated Sparrow near Beloit (Rock County) on 3–4 May 1959. It was not that Morse had difficulty identifying the bird with

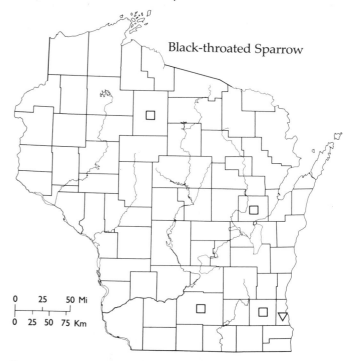

Black-throated Sparrow

▽ 30 October to 10 November
☐ 21 November to early May

All records

Black-throated Sparrow, December 1982, Price County (photo by R. L. Verch)

certainty, for he obtained clear photographs. The "trouble" was that the bird was a few hundred yards across the state line in Illinois, and no efforts to entice it to cross the state line succeeded. When, if ever again, would Wisconsin have another chance to add this resident of the arid Southwest to its avifauna?

The answer came surprisingly soon. Seven months later, on 23 December 1959, another Black-throated Sparrow took up residence at the Earl Fetterer feeder in Madison. For a full 4 months, through 22 April 1960, this wanderer frequently visited the Fetterer residence: on the ground, in the nearby shrubbery, and at the window feeder scarcely an arm's length away from a succession of appreciative viewers. Observers came from far and near for a sight of this bird. The Fetterers were cordial hosts. The bird was tame and cooperative; several photographers recorded it on film. The triangular black bib provided a vivid plumage feature that made it striking and memorable. For most observers this bird was a "lifer" (*Pass. Pigeon* 22:32–33).

No less surprising was the appearance of another Black-throated Sparrow at the Gordon Krenn home in Brookfield (Waukesha County) in 1976. Exact dates of arrival and departure were not recorded, but many Milwaukee-area birders observed this individual between mid-February and early May (*Am. Birds* 30:723).

Milwaukee was the scene of a third state record when Gary Casper discovered a vividly marked wanderer on 30 October 1979. It was photographed the following day (J. H. Idzikowski; *Am. Birds* 34:165) and observed frequently by other birders through 10 November (*Pass. Pigeon* 42:122).

Late autumn 1982 brought two more strangers who must have decided to desert the desert. One can scarcely imagine a bird of the arid Southwest taking up residence at a feeder on the snowy wooded banks of the Flambeau River in northern Wisconsin. But that is what happened at the William Gralow home near Fifield (Price County) on 30 November. The bird was photographed (L. E. Gregg) and observed at close range by numerous other observers before it disappeared on 3 January 1983 (*Pass. Pigeon* 45: 108–109).

Preceding this wanderer by only a few days was another Black-throated Sparrow seen near Hortonville (Outagamie County) on 21 November 1982 (M. Jurack). It was a daily visitor until 5 February 1983, and was photographed by M. S. Peterson; its presence was enjoyed by many other observers (*Pass. Pigeon* 45:109).

This species' tendency to wander beyond the normal range, especially in November, has increased since the 1950s. Individuals have been detected north to Nebraska, Montana, Alberta, and Minnesota and east to Michigan, Ohio, New Jersey, and Massachusetts.

Lark Bunting (*Calamospiza melanocorys*)

STATUS. Rare spring migrant; accidental fall migrant. Accidental in summer. Accidental in winter.
HABITAT. Open grassland and cropland. Residential areas.
MIGRATION DATES. Observed between 4 April and 30 May; and between 5 and 29 September.
WINTER. One record.

On 17 December 1963 a heavily streaked, brown, sparrowlike bird appeared at the E. M. Rumpf feeder near Milton (Rock County). The bird's identity was puzzling at first. Although it resembled a female Purple Finch, it fed on the ground more like nearby House Sparrows, and showed buff wing patches and a buffy eyering. The stranger kept coming throughout the winter. By April a distinctive black plumage was replacing brown feathers and clearly revealed the identity of a male Lark Bunting. The bird, which was subsequently photographed and banded, remained in the area until 20 May 1964. This was the first fully substantiated Wisconsin record for the species.

Previous to this record, six other sight records had been reported, but no supporting specimen or photograph was ever produced. A male was observed singing from a utility-wire perch near Milwaukee on 16 May 1922 by Gilbert Raasch (pers. comm. to O. J. Gromme). Two birds were noted east of La Crosse on 24 June 1953 (O. L. Compton). In both cases observers were familiar with the bird in its normal range, and wrote substantiating details. Additional sightings

△ 4 April to 30 May
○ 13 June to 15 July
▽ 5 to 29 September
□ 17 December to 20 May

All records

Lark Bunting, 26 May 1989, Ashland County (photo by J. L. Baughman)

have been noted in Brown County on 25 April 1941 (O. Langosch), and in Douglas County on 4 May 1932 (T. J. McCarthy [Bernard 1967]), 4 May 1933 (T. J. McCarthy [Bernard 1967]), and 11 May 1961 (B. F. Klugow), but published details are lacking.

Within 4 years after the winter occurrence at Milton, three more birds were identified and documented: one in Wood County near Arpin on 15 July 1965 (D. G. Follen), one at Ashland on 13 June 1966 (C. H. Snyder), and one at Milwaukee on 13–15 May 1967 (R. G. Treder).

Between 1971 and 1987 birds put in brief appearances on another 14 occasions, 12 during spring. The earliest were on 4 April (1982, Dane, R. M. Hoffman), 12 April (1979, Dane, C. F. Barnett), when four males were observed the day after a severe storm, and 18 April (1987, Fond du Lac, K. Pruski). May sightings occurred on the 3rd (1979, Dodge, M. F. Donald), 4th (1982, St. Croix, J. O. Evrard), from the 12th to the 23rd (1982, Ashland, R. L. Verch), 16th (1981, Iron, U. Schramm), 20th (1971, Ozaukee, T. Bintz; 1980,

Manitowoc, J. F. Steffen), 26th (1984, Bayfield, T. R. Schultz), 28th (1987, Ashland, R. L. Verch), and 30th (1972, Milwaukee, M. L. Hallett). The other two birds were September discoveries on the 5th (1975, Milwaukee, E. J. Epstein) and 29th (1978, Columbia, R. M. Hoffman).

These recent sightings indicate that we can expect the Lark Bunting to continue to visit the state occasionally. In recent years it has also wandered to northeastern Minnesota, Ontario, Nova Scotia, New Brunswick, and most of the Atlantic coastal states. But it cannot be assumed that this species is gradually extending its normal range closer to Wisconsin's borders. It is a bird of the open prairies, and as the prairies have gradually given way to the plow the range of this species has gradually receded. The Lark Bunting was more common in western Minnesota and Iowa 50 years ago than it is today.

Savannah Sparrow (*Passerculus sandwichensis*)

STATUS. Abundant migrant. Abundant summer resident east; common summer resident north and west. Rare winter resident southeast.
HABITAT. Open grassland. Sedge meadow. Old field.
MIGRATION DATES. *Spring:* early April to mid-May. *Fall:* early September to mid-November.
BREEDING DATA. Nests with eggs: 16 May to 19 July. Clutch size: usually 4 or 5 eggs; occasionally 3–7.
WINTER. Rarely present north to Dane, Waukesha, and Milwaukee counties through 10 January.
PORTRAIT. *Birds of Wisconsin:* Plate 84.

Perhaps it is an exaggeration to assert that every grass meadow of 20 acres or more in Wisconsin will have at least one pair of breeding Savannah Sparrows. But from late April to early October this is certainly one of the most typical species found on farms throughout the state. In some of the extensive farmland in eastern Wisconsin it is abundant. There are BBS transects in Winnebago, Dodge, Sheboygan, and Ozaukee counties that tally over 100 individuals per 50-stop route each year. In northern Wisconsin, forests are far more dominant than farmlands; yet wherever farm clearings are found, Savannahs are present. In western Wisconsin numbers do not match those of the eastern counties, but the species still rates as common. This sparrow tends to avoid cornfields, but it inhabits fields of other grains, alfalfa, timothy hay, and open pasture that is free of shrubbery. It may visit hedgerows for brief periods, but it usually remains out in fields or perched on fences and wires that border these fields.

Anyone starting to learn the open field sparrows of Wisconsin would do well to begin with the Savannah. Not only is it the most common of the meadow sparrows, but it is also one of the most easily observed. While some species sing from hidden perches within the long grass, the Savannah generally gives its thin lisping musical song from an exposed perch. The

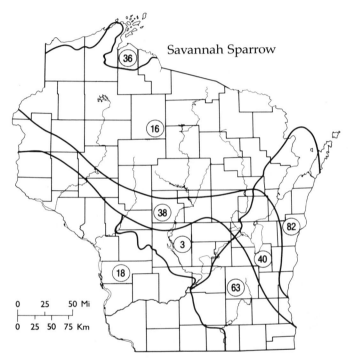

Breeding Bird Survey, averages 1966 to 1980

"savvy" can also be secretive at times, scuttling along the ground between grass tufts while hidden by an overhanging grass canopy, especially when near its nest. But the singing males spend much time on conspicuous perches and often allow close human approach.

Several instances of March arrivals have been reported, the earliest being the 11th (1977, Waukesha, J. E. Bielefeldt), 19th (1964, Brown, T. C. Erdman), 20th (1973, Portage, S. H. Krings), 21st (1957, Rock, D. Hammel), and 22nd (1981, Brown, M. M. Wierzbicki). But few birds normally arrive before 10 April in the southern region and 20 April in the central and northern regions. The migration is heavy in late April and early May, and by mid-May most of the summer population is on territory. Grass is short when the birds first arrive, then grows rapidly in May, affording suitable nesting habitat by mid-May.

Although the earliest recorded nest with eggs is 16 May, the likelihood is that some nesting begins a bit earlier. I. O. Buss recorded a nest with four large young in Waukesha County on 26 May, which would point to a probable starting date close to the 5th. Nests are made in depressions next to clumps of grass, and often contain one or two eggs of the Brown-headed Cowbird. There is no way of knowing how many nests are lost in summer to farm machinery; but with hay-harvesting often underway by early June, the loss must be considerable. It is not known whether mid-July nests represent normal second broods or renesting attempts by pairs whose first nests have failed or been destroyed.

By late July singing has become sporadic. In August some of the birds are attracted to ponds and may be seen feeding close to the water's edge along with fall migrant sandpipers. From mid-September to mid-October almost any field overgrown with uncut weeds has its share of migrating Savannahs. Often in early October I have found small flocks totaling 50 or more birds in a mile of stop-and-go driving.

By 1 November nearly all have departed. Unusually late were November sightings on the 21st (1976, Barron, C. A. Faanes), 23rd (1973, Dodge, M. F. Donald), 25th (1979, Manitowoc, C. R. Sontag), and 30th (1979, Barron, J. M. Humphrey). There are nine December records of CBC finds in Rock, Dane, Dodge, Fond du Lac, Sheboygan, Outagamie, and Brown counties. The chances of these birds surviving a Wisconsin winter are not good. However, there have been January lingerers on the 5th (1967, Milwaukee, M. F. Donald), 11th (1948, Milwaukee, G. W. Treichel), 14th (1963, Rock, M. K. Stocking), 16th (1966, Milwaukee, M. F. Donald), and 22nd (1960, Milwaukee, M. F. Donald), plus still later birds on 6 February (1960, Waukesha, J. E. Bielefeldt) and 21 February (1971, Waukesha, D. K. Gustafson).

Baird's Sparrow (*Ammodramus bairdii*)

STATUS. Casual spring and summer visitant.
HABITAT. Open grassland. Old field.
MIGRATION DATES. Observed between 29 April and 26 June.

After a series of six hypothetical sightings, 1949–1980, a firm record for the Baird's Sparrow was established when Bernard Brouchoud discovered a singing male in Manitowoc County on 16 June 1982. The distinctive song, uttered repeatedly from a conspicuous weed-tip perch, impressed the discoverer and another dozen or more observers during the next 10 days as a melody not previously known to them. The bird was subsequently photographed (J. H. Idzikowski), trapped, and banded (*Pass. Pigeon* 45:66–68).

Six probable sight observations had been reported previously in *The Passenger Pigeon*: a singing individual in Ozaukee County on 26 May 1949 (I. N. Balsom and others; 11:180), a singing bird in Burnett County on 12 May 1957 (N. R. Stone and others; 19:124–125), another Burnett County find on 2 May 1975 (S. V. Goddard; 38:52), one in Door County on 17 May 1975 (E. B. Prins; 38:52–53), a singer in Waushara County on 29 April 1979 (R. M. Hoffman; 42:48), and a vocal individual in Burnett County on 25 May 1980 (C. Schroeder; 43:34). The three Burnett County birds

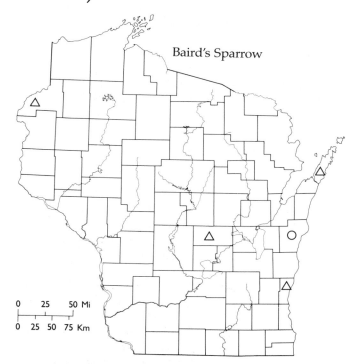

Baird's Sparrow

0   25   50 Mi
0 25 50 75 Km

△   29 April to 26 May
○   16 to 26 June

All records

Baird's Sparrow, 17 June 1982, Manitowoc County (photo by J. H. Idzikowski)

were found in prairie habitat similar to that on the bird's normal range in the Dakotas and the prairie provinces. The three central and eastern Wisconsin wanderers were seen in open grassy fields. In each instance it was a song unlike any previously heard that drew the attention of the observers to the birds.

Although this species is rarely found east of the western edge of Minnesota, there are records from Ohio and Maryland. An occasional wandering bird in Wisconsin is a definite possibility.

Grasshopper Sparrow (*Ammodramus savannarum*)

STATUS. Fairly common migrant west and central; uncommon migrant east and north. Fairly common summer resident west and central; uncommon summer resident east and north.

HABITAT. Open grassland.

MIGRATION DATES. *Spring:* late April to late May. *Fall:* mid-August to early October. *Extremes:* 13 April; 28 October.

BREEDING DATA. Nests with eggs: 20 May to 14 July. Clutch size: 3–5 eggs.

PORTRAIT. *Birds of Wisconsin:* Plate 84.

The annual sojourn of this grassland species is relatively short in Wisconsin. Because Grasshopper Sparrows prefer long grass habitat, it is at least late April before even the southern counties can offer suitable habitat. Nevertheless, observers have sighted mid-April birds as early as the 13th (1930, Sheboygan, C. S. Jung; 1966, Chippewa, C. A. Kemper), 17th (1972, Dane, N. Ashman), and 19th (1972, St. Croix, S. V. Goddard; 1981, Ozaukee, N. J. Cutright). The movement through the central counties is rapid in early May, and by 20 May the bird is usually present in all areas where it is likely to be found in summer.

Rarely is this species encountered after singing

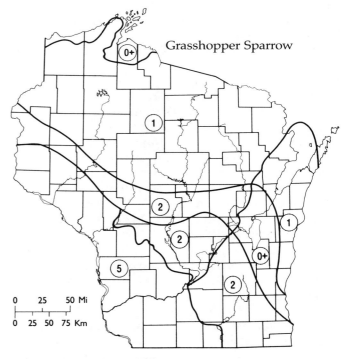

Breeding Bird Survey, averages 1966 to 1980

stops around the beginning of August. The likelihood is, however, that the bird remains at least into September in much of its breeding territory. But the bird is so secretive in its behavior, and birdwatchers are so inattentive toward grass and grain fields in August, that these sparrows usually escape notice. The observations that are made in September and early October usually occur away from the cut hay and grain fields, in the undisturbed fallow ground overgrown with uncut weeds. The 28 October 1970 record (C. A. Kemper) involved a bird found dead at the Eau Claire television tower. Other October lingerers were recorded on the 11th (1976, Waukesha, J. E. Bielefeldt) and 13th (1977, Brown, E. D. Cleary).

In the intervening mid-May to late July period, the insectlike song of this bird is often heard in extensive hayfields and grainfields. Ornithologists visiting suitable habitat in central and western Wisconsin find this species fairly common, provided that their ears can pick up the bird's extremely high-pitched song, and that they can distinguish the bird's song from the similar sound of the insect for which the sparrow is named. In eastern Wisconsin, where equally suitable habitat exists, the Grasshopper Sparrow is decidedly less numerous. The more abundant the Savannah Sparrow, the less common is the Grasshopper.

During the breeding season the female is very secretive. She is busy incubating the eggs she has laid in a nest concealed at the base of a tuft of grass; she usually stays well out of sight. The male is not so secretive when he sings. Only occasionally does he visit a utility wire or a hedgerow near the roadside, as the more common Savannahs and Vespers do. But he often sings from atop one of the tallest stalks in the field. If one looks carefully through binoculars over a grassy field from which the song of the Grasshopper Sparrow emanates, one can usually spot the songster.

Some uncertainty exists concerning the northern limit of this species' summer range. In the 1960s there were sightings in Douglas, Bayfield, Price, Oneida, and Forest counties, and Gromme (1963) indicated a range encompassing the state. However, BBS figures have shown a gradual but steady decline since 1968. Of the 70 BBS transects, 56 have recorded this diminutive sparrow. In 1968, tallies on these 56 routes averaged 4.05 birds per count; the average dropped steadily to 2.04 (1973), 1.05 (1978), and 0.85 (1983). There have been no records in the northernmost tier of counties since 1977.

The northern range limit in 1983 was a line from Grantsburg through Ladysmith, Merrill, and Marinette. If numbers continue to decline, the northern limit may recede still farther. No sure reason for the decline has been identified. But with land use changing from an emphasis on pasture and small grains to corn production, and with the timing of the first hay harvests moving from late June to early June, birds are experiencing mounting difficulties in producing adequate numbers of young.

Henslow's Sparrow (*Ammodramus henslowii*)

STATUS. Uncommon migrant south and central; rare
migrant north. Uncommon summer resident south
and central; rare summer resident north.

HABITAT. Old field. Open grassland.

MIGRATION DATES. *Spring:* mid-April to late May. *Fall:*
departure by 20 October. *Extremes:* 30 March; 29
November.

BREEDING DATA. Nests with eggs: 22 May to 11 July.
Clutch size: 4 or 5 eggs.

WINTER. One December record.

PORTRAIT. *Birds of Wisconsin:* Plate 84.

Henslow's Sparrow

▨ Summer range
○ Early June to early August

Records since 1960

A person who wants to make the acquaintance of the
Henslow's Sparrow in Wisconsin might well stop his
car alongside a wet grass meadow between 10 and
12 P.M., or 2 and 4 A.M., and listen for a "song" that is
little more than a hiccup. During the day this song is
nearly drowned out by the Bobolinks, Sedge Wrens,
and Savannah Sparrows. But the Henslow's often
sings at night, and without the competing songs of
other species, this unobtrusive little vocal effort can
be distinctly heard and catalogued in the ornithologist's mind.

The birder needs to learn this song to detect the
presence of this species. It inhabits undisturbed pastures and meadows. A few Henslow's are also found
in timothy hay fields and in fallow land grown up to
tall weeds. Sometimes an observer is fortunate enough
to see the songster atop one of these weeds; but as
often as not, the bird sings from a hidden perch.
This species is somewhat colonial. It is not unusual to
hear three or four males singing in one field, while a
neighboring field with equally promising habitat will
have none.

There are years when none of these unobtrusive
sparrows have been detected before 1 May. But frequently a few singing males are present by 20 April,
and in some instances 10 April arrivals have been detected. Exceptionally early were a 30 March 1986 arrival (Richland, B. F. Duerksen) and 3 April sightings
in 1949 (Dane, G. A. Hall) and 1981 (Ozaukee, N. J.
Cutright). Most migration occurs between 1 and 20
May. Singers have been detected in Bayfield (31 May
1965, J. L. Koslowski) and Forest (25 April 1935, W. H.
Elder, pers. comm.) counties. But these are north of
the usual range limit and represent "overshooting"
spring migrants.

The normal summer range covers about four-fifths
of the state, north to a line from Grantsburg through
Phillips, Antigo, Marinette, and Sturgeon Bay. But

nowhere in the state can the bird be called common,
or even fairly common. It has been found on 41 of 70
BBS transects, but on none are birds found every
year. Rarely have more than three individuals appeared on any one transect in a given year.

Singing often persists through 5 August, suggesting that nesting may continue late into the season. Although most reported nests have contained eggs by
early June, Carl Richter found eggs as late as 11 July.
Kumlien and Hollister (1903) mentioned observations
of nestlings in early September.

Most Henslow's quiet down by 10 August. In some
years the bird goes completely unreported once song
ceases. But it has been seen on enough occasions in
September and October to indicate that it usually remains at least through September, often until 20 October. The discovery of a fresh roadkill at Racine on
29 November 1954 (J. A. Simpson) must be considered
exceptional. Even more remarkable was a bird carefully studied in Dodge County on 20 December 1942
(E. T. Mitchell)—Wisconsin's only winter record.

Le Conte's Sparrow (*Ammodramus leconteii*)

STATUS. Uncommon migrant. Uncommon summer resident north and central.

HABITAT. Open grassland. Sedge meadow. Shallow marsh.

MIGRATION DATES. *Spring:* mid-April to late May. *Fall:* mid-September to mid-October. *Extremes:* 29 March; 5 November.

BREEDING DATA. Nests with eggs: 6 May to 5 July. Clutch size: 3–5 eggs.

PORTRAIT: *Birds of Wisconsin:* Plate 84.

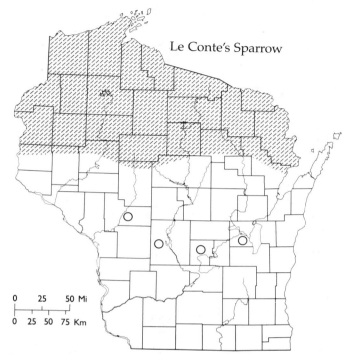

Le Conte's Sparrow

0   25   50 Mi

0 25 50 75 Km

▨ Summer range
○ Early June to mid-August

Records since 1960

Many Wisconsin ornithologists have never seen the Le Conte's Sparrow, yet it is a regular breeder in suitable habitat in the northern third of the state, and passes through the remainder of the state in migration. Ever since the time of the earliest ornithological work in Wisconsin, the Le Conte's has been considered one of the rarest of the state's sparrows. But recent findings, triggered by the advent of the BBS in 1966, prove that this sparrow is not as rare as it was previously thought to be. It has now been found on 8 of the 27 transects in the northern third of the state.

One reason why this bird has rarely been seen is that its habitat preferences were misunderstood. Most observers associated it strictly with "hip-boot habitat"—vast acreages of almost impenetrable grasses growing in wet marshes—and few birders have ventured into such territory on foot. It is now known that the Le Conte's also favors extensive plantings of timothy hay and other dry upland grasslands during the breeding season. The preferred areas are large, level, and relatively undisturbed.

A second reason for the apparent scarcity lies in the bird's secretive habits. It spends most of its time in the long grass, deserting this shelter for the more exposed roadside only rarely. Seldom does the bird climb to the top of an exposed stalk to sing. Usually the song is uttered from a perch hidden within the grassy expanse. One rarely gets a satisfactory look at the songster by stalking him; the bird is likely to desert his hidden perch, fly in "jerky" fashion low over the grass meadow, then drop into an equally well-hidden location. Continued stalking will only cause the bird to move around on the ground, hidden from view. During the summers of 1969 and 1970 I found singing males on 86 occasions but got identifiable views of only eight birds (Robbins 1969).

A third reason for the bird's apparent rarity relates to its song. By all odds the best way to detect the presence of this species in spring and summer is to hear the song. But the song is weak, thin, and high-pitched, with little carrying power. At a distance it can easily be mistaken for a portion of an imperfectly heard song of the Savannah Sparrow—a bird that often inhabits the same fields and meadows. The Le Conte's generally confines its singing to periods at dawn and dusk. If an observer goes looking for these birds after a leisurely 8 o'clock breakfast, the chances of hearing one are virtually nil.

This bird has been known to nest in Oconto and Marinette counties almost every year since 1927. By careful searching Carl Richter found numerous nests, most of which contained three to five heavily spotted grayish-white eggs. The nests were carefully concealed in or next to tufts of grass in a meadow or hayfield (Richter 1969).

This bird has also been known as a summer resident at the Crex Meadows Wildlife Area in Burnett County since 1959. Recent summer records have been reported from nearly every county south to St. Croix, Chippewa, Marathon, and Oconto. South of this line singing birds have been detected between 11 June and

31 July in Clark (1972, 1981), Jackson (1969, 1973, 1976), Juneau (1978), and Winnebago (1981) counties. More fieldwork is needed to determine the normal southern limit of this species' breeding range.

South of its breeding range, the Le Conte's is known only as a rare migrant. Between 1939 and 1970 *The Passenger Pigeon* listed but 12 spring dates and 18 fall dates south of Highway 29, from Prescott to Kewaunee. Since 1970, observations in the southern half of the state have averaged two per season, spring and fall. The same behavior patterns that make the bird difficult to find in summer also make the bird hard to locate during migration. The absence of song accentuates the difficulty in fall. The chances are good that this bird is decidedly more numerous during migration than the records show, but observers have spent insufficient time looking in suitable grass habitat in late April and early May, and in September and Oc-

tober. Frequent visits to an extensive grass marsh east of Arena in Iowa County from late September to early November, 1949–1955, resulted in 12 observations of over 30 birds. With comparable effort, observers could perhaps duplicate this record at many other southern Wisconsin locations.

Most spring observations have occurred between 20 April and 25 May. Exceptionally early are sightings on 29 March (1981, Milwaukee, W. A. Cowart), 3 April (1942, Dunn, I. O. Buss), and 14 April (1941, Waukesha, W. P. Dettman). Spring migrants have lingered in southern counties until 5 June (1975, Waukesha, J. E. Bielefeldt) and 10 June (1979, Columbia, R. M. Hoffman).

In autumn, birds show up south of the breeding range around 15 September; they remain through mid-October. The latest occurrence: G. W. Foster's 5 November 1955 bird near Arena (Iowa County).

Sharp-tailed Sparrow (*Ammodramus caudacutus*)

STATUS. Rare spring migrant; uncommon fall migrant. Rare summer resident north; casual summer resident south-central.

HABITAT. Shallow marsh. Sedge meadow.

MIGRATION DATES. *Spring:* late April to late May. *Fall:* late August to mid-October. *Extremes:* 28 April; 20 October.

PORTRAIT. *Birds of Wisconsin:* Plate 84.

If one were to draw lines from the western Canada breeding grounds of the *nelsoni* race of the Sharp-tailed Sparrow to the main wintering grounds along the Gulf Coast, one would notice that a direct migration route skirts just west and south of Wisconsin. However, a few of the *nelsoni* birds winter along the coast of Georgia and South Carolina, and a direct migration route would carry them over southern and western Wisconsin. Proof that at least a few migrate through western Wisconsin is provided by television tower casualties. Four birds were killed flying into the tower at Galesville (Trempealeau County) on 3 October 1965. At the Eau Claire tower, specimens were discovered twice in spring (28 April 1967, 4 May 1960), and on seven occasions between 20 September and 9 October.

There is universal agreement in the past and present literature that this bird is rare in Wisconsin in spring. Only 30 published records of spring observa-

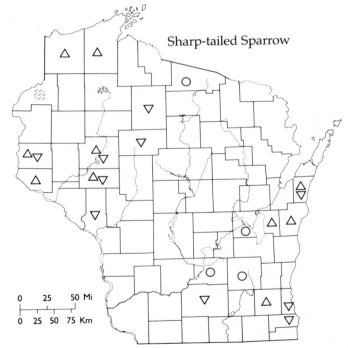

Sharp-tailed Sparrow

△ Late April to late May
○ Early June to mid-August
▽ Late August to mid-October

Records since 1960

tions are known between 1900 and 1985. Kumlien and Hollister (1903) failed to find it in spring, and knew of no spring records for the nineteenth century. The only known April sightings are the Eau Claire tower casualty on the 28th (1967, C. A. Kemper), a bird observed on the 29th (1937, Sawyer, F. Zirrer; MPM files), and one on the 30th (1987, Manitowoc, C. R. Sontag). Most May records have occurred between the 5th and 25th.

There is less general agreement about the bird's status as a fall migrant. Kumlien and Hollister (1903) described the Sharp-tail as exceedingly abundant at Lake Koshkonong in Jefferson County in the 1890s, but expressed surprise that Thure Kumlien covered the same haunts in the 1870s without a single record. Schorger (1931a) found it near Mazomanie (Dane County) regularly from 1926 to 1929, with a sighting of as many as 20 birds on 24 September 1927. But prior to those years he found Sharp-tails only rarely. Near the same Mazomanie marshes in late September 1951 I frequently found as many as six birds, but with comparable efforts failed to find them in the same area between 1948 and 1950. It may be that in some years the fall migration stays west of our borders, while in other years the migration route moves eastward just enough to include parts of our state.

As suggested by the Eau Claire tower casualties, the main fall migration comes between 15 September and 15 October. Exceptionally early was the 18 August 1977 bird (St. Croix, C. A. Faanes). The 12 specimens collected in western Dane County by A. W. Schorger and W. Taylor during the 1920s (Schorger 1931a) were all taken within this time span. The state's latest dates are 17 October (1964, Racine, L. W. Erickson) and 20 October (1980, Milwaukee, M. F. Donald).

There was no indication of summer residency until 1969, when Dennis Gustafson heard in Burnett County on 21 and 22 July the same insectlike trill he had learned in North Dakota earlier that summer (*Pass. Pigeon* 32:67). He detected the same song in the same Crex Meadows location on 31 July and 1 August 1970. In the same location, additional summer observations were made in 1975 (T. C. Baptist), 1977 (C. A. Faanes), 1983 (F. Z. Lesher), and 1984 (J. L. Polk), raising the strong possibility that breeding occurs there.

Gustafson also detected the distinctive song at Horicon Marsh in Dodge County in late June 1971. In Winnebago County three singing males were present from 28 May to 21 July 1980 (A. A. Carpenter). Summer residents were detected in Powell Marsh in Vilas County in 1980 (R. G. Spahn), 1983 (J. E. Baughman), and 1984 (R. M. Hoffman). Additional June sightings have been reported from Bayfield (1983, R. Maercklein) and Columbia (1980, W. L. Hilsenhoff) counties.

None of the current field guides include Wisconsin within the known limits of the Sharp-tail's nesting range. Perhaps changes are in the making.

Fox Sparrow (*Passerella iliaca*)

STATUS. Common migrant. Accidental summer visitant. Uncommon winter resident south; rare winter resident central and north.

HABITAT. Upland and lowland carr. Residential areas. Conifer plantations.

MIGRATION DATES. *Spring:* mid-March to early May. *Fall:* mid-September to early November. *Extremes:* 28 May; 28 August.

WINTER. Occasionally present north to St. Croix, Marathon, and Door counties; rarely present north to Douglas, Bayfield, Ashland, and Vilas counties.

PORTRAIT. *Birds of Wisconsin:* Plate 87.

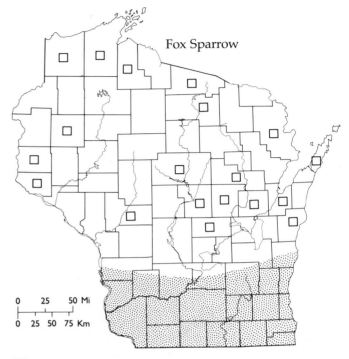

Fox Sparrow

▨ Winter range
☐ Late November to late February

Records since 1960

There is no need for all the winter snow to melt before the Fox Sparrow begins its migratory journey to its far-north breeding grounds. The bird needs only a few patches of bare ground and a couple of mild March nights. It arrives not with the earliest vanguard of Robins, Red-winged Blackbirds, Killdeers, and Meadowlarks, but generally accompanies a second wave consisting of the general arrivals of these earliest migrants plus the first Eastern Bluebirds, Brown-headed Cowbirds, and Song Sparrows.

Southern Wisconsin observers usually detect the first spring migrants between 15 and 20 March. If mild weather ensues in the last week of March, a considerable buildup in the south may occur. A deeper snow blanket usually prevents the first migrants from reaching the northern counties before 5 April. The heaviest migration occurs between 5 and 20 April, with nearly all birds gone from the southern counties by the 25th. In the north a few birds remain through 5 May nearly every year. Occasionally a late-departing individual is reported on a "big day count" around the 15th. Exceptionally late May stragglers have been noted on the 23rd (1980, Ashland, R. L. Verch), 25th (1970, Douglas, R. F. Bernard), and 28th (1975, Bayfield, V. D. Aune).

Only once has this arctic nester been recorded in Wisconsin in summer. Vernon Rossman (MPM files) trapped and banded an adult in Vilas County on 25 June 1935. The bird was not recorded again, and any explanation of its presence at such an unlikely time would be pure guesswork. Wisconsin has no other records for June and none for July or early August.

The Fox is one of the latest of the migrating sparrows in fall, with only the Tree following a still later pattern. First fall migrants generally appear around 15 September in the northern portion and a week later in the south. Unusually early were individuals on 28 August (1956, Washburn, A. Sprunt), 1 September (1980, Brown, E. D. Cleary), and 6 September (1977, Price, M. Hardy). In fall as in spring, this bird prefers brushy thickets along woodland edges. It is often found with White-throats but is less frequently seen in backyard residential areas. October is the main month for fall migration. The bird is numerous throughout the state during the first half of the month, with numbers diminishing in the north after the 15th. In the south birds are still numerous at the end of the month, but numbers drop off sharply during the first days of November. Most fall flocks number 5–15 birds, but sometimes larger concentrations are found. On 15–16 October 1965 Edward Peartree banded 250 individuals in Sauk County. An occasional migrant lingers until late November before departing, and any bird still present in December is likely to try to spend the winter.

The AOU *Check-list of North American Birds* lists southern Wisconsin as the northern limit of the winter range. It is indeed barely on the fringe. Data from

CBCs show from 1 to 10 individuals wintering in the state each year since 1958, and similar numbers irregularly before then. Two-thirds of the wintering birds have been found south of a line from Viroqua to Sheboygan. The rest are widely scattered throughout the rest of the state.

Song Sparrow (*Melospiza melodia*)

STATUS. Abundant migrant. Abundant summer resident. Uncommon winter resident south and central; rare winter resident north.

HABITAT. All carr. Wooded swamp. Residential areas.

MIGRATION DATES. *Spring:* mid-March to late April. *Fall:* early September to early November.

BREEDING DATA. Nests with eggs: 1 May to 2 August. Clutch size: 4 or 5 eggs.

WINTER. Regularly present north to La Crosse, Portage, and Brown counties; rarely present throughout the state.

PORTRAIT. *Birds of Wisconsin:* Plate 87.

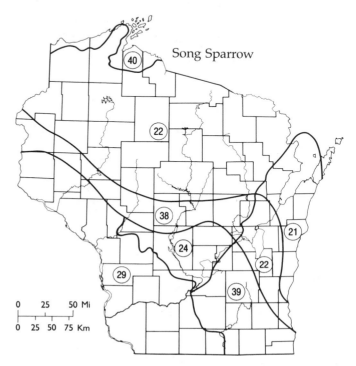

Breeding Bird Survey, averages 1966 to 1980

In 1883 Franklin H. King wrote of the Song Sparrow: "No finch in Wisconsin is as abundant, and none of the summer residents arrive as early or tarry as late as this species. The borders of cultivated fields and the fringing shrubbery of woodlands, groves and banks of streams are its favorite haunts." A century later the same statement still holds. The Song Sparrow is truly a bird of the "edge." It avoids deep woods, but frequents the small trees and shrubs that form the edges of forests and farm woodlots. It stays away from the middle of grainfields and open prairie, but frequents the surrounding hedgerows. If anything, it has prospered with the spread of people everywhere except in the heavily urbanized regions. It has taken to residential shrubbery and to the additional edges created by roads, fire lanes, and power lines cutting through forests. If one habitat preference stands out above all others, it is the long grass and bushes that form the edges of ponds and streams; but one of the strong characteristics of this species is its adaptability to many types of environment.

Into this varied terrain the Song begins its northward journey on some of the milder March days, once melting snows have left some bare patches of earth. Often this occurs by 10–15 March in the southern counties and between 25 March and 5 April farther north. The first bird to arrive is a singing male; his arrival invariably quickens the ornithologist's excitement over the advent of a new spring migration. Soon after the first arrivals appear, there is likely to be

a return to colder weather that will delay the northward movement temporarily, but the first half of April is normally a time when these birds move abundantly throughout the entire state. By the end of April, breeding birds have paired off on territory, and the last migrants are leaving for the north.

This bird is primarily occupied with nesting from early May through mid-August. A typical nest in May and early June is concealed on the ground within a tuft of grass on the bank of a small stream, and is likely to contain one or two cowbird eggs along with four or five sparrow eggs. The stream bank is not a necessity. This species nests in many locations far from water, but the nests are usually on or near the ground.

This sparrow blankets the state in summer as do few other species. Only once in the 935 repetitions of

Wisconsin's 70 BBS transects, 1966–1980, was *M. melodia* missed. Breeding populations are fairly evenly divided in all parts of the state. This is one of only 11 species that maintain an average of over 20 individuals per transect every year.

In fall migration, as well as in spring and summer, not much flocking is evident. Banding records and observations of increased numbers indicate that the main fall migration lasts from 15 September to 31 October in the northern regions and from 25 September to 10 November farther south. Birds remaining through mid-November are likely to overwinter.

As one might expect for a bird on the fringe of its winter range, southern Wisconsin shows a sizable fluctuation in the size of the wintering population. Totals found on state CBCs since 1960 have varied from a low of 27 (1961) to a high of 223 (1973). Between 1960 and 1985, 87% of the CBC birds were found south of a line connecting La Crosse and Sheboygan. Only 1% were north of a line between Hudson and Green Bay. CBC individuals have been recorded north to Ashland (1974, 1984), Burnett (1978, 1980), Sawyer (1972), Price (1973, 1983), Vilas (1972), and Marinette (1971) counties.

Lincoln's Sparrow (*Melospiza lincolnii*)

STATUS. Uncommon spring migrant; fairly common fall migrant. Uncommon summer resident north. Casual winter resident south.

HABITAT. Conifer swamp. All carr.

MIGRATION DATES. *Spring:* late April to late May. *Fall:* early September to late November.

BREEDING DATA. Nests with eggs: 20 May to 5 June. Clutch size: 4 eggs.

WINTER. Occasionally present north to Buffalo and Kewaunee counties.

PORTRAIT. *Birds of Wisconsin:* Plate 87.

The Lincoln's Sparrow is best known as a fall migrant. In marshes and swamps, in farm hedgerows and overgrown pastures, this inconspicuous bird can often be found by persistent searching from early September to mid-October. It helps to know the bird's soft chip, which resembles that of a junco. Many a time this has led to the discovery of birds whose presence would otherwise have been overlooked. It helps to "squeak" when in suitable habitat; the Lincoln's is one of the most responsive of brush-loving species in fall. Seldom does one find more than 3 or 4 individuals at a time, but one can often find 10–15 in a 2-hour field trip. In a single fall season Charles Kemper has banded as many as 83 birds.

South of the breeding range, first arrivals usually make their appearance in the northern and central counties in the first week of September, gradually building to a peak in late September. By 10 October numbers begin to diminish, and by 20 October most birds have departed. In the southern counties first arrivals show up around 10–15 September, increase to an early October peak, with most departures between 15 and 25 October. November lingerers have been

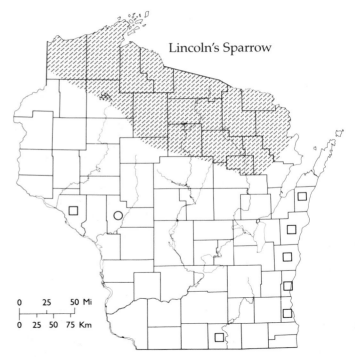

Lincoln's Sparrow

```
0    25    50 Mi
0  25  50  75 Km
```

▨ Summer range
○ Early June to mid-August
□ Early December to late March

Records since 1960

noted through the 23rd (1960, Milwaukee, D. K. Gustafson) and 24th (1976, Milwaukee, E. J. Epstein).

The spring migration is but a fraction of the fall flight. My records from 1950 to 1980 show an average of only one-sixth as many migrants in spring as in fall. This species is one of the least conspicuous of spring sparrows, partly because it rarely sings until it arrives at its breeding grounds, and partly because it moves slowly and deliberately in dense shrubbery, making little movement that would attract attention. Those that are heard and seen generally are found between 25 April and 25 May. A southern Wisconsin observer has the best chance of finding the Lincoln's between 5 and 20 May; farther north the 10–25 May period is most promising. A 5 April bird (1981, Milwaukee, D. D. Tessen) appeared after a severe storm. Other unusually early April arrivals were detected on the 7th (1959, Rock, M. T. Maxson), 9th (1971, Brown, E. D. Cleary), 10th (1945, Sheboygan, C. L. Strelitzer), 12th (1965, Rock, banded by M. K. Stocking), and 15th (1975, Buffalo, T. C. Roskos). One lingering individual was banded on 3 June (1963, Sheboygan, H. C. Mueller). Another remained until 8 June (1983, Manitowoc, C. R. Sontag).

Positive nesting evidence includes two nineteenth-century records: a 20 May 1889 nest with eggs in Waukesha County (in the B. F. Goss collection, Milwaukee Public Museum) and a 5 June 1852 nest with three eggs at Racine (collected by P. R. Hoy; in the U.S. National Museum, Washington, D.C.). No longer can breeding be expected to occur in southern areas. Most birds move to Canada for the summer, but nesting is probable in selected northern Wisconsin locations. On at least 15 occasions I have detected agitated birds in open bogs in Douglas, Taylor, Lincoln, Oneida, and Forest counties. Singing males have turned up on six BBS routes in the northern counties. The one positive nesting record in recent years was established on 28 May 1972 (Forest, C. H. Richter). The most open parts of spruce bogs, where trees and shrubs are sparse and grass is moderately long, are preferred as nesting sites. The footing is soft, wet, and treacherous for human investigation, but some persistent observer will surely prove eventually that the Lincoln's Sparrow is a regular breeder in most of the northern counties. Summer records have come most frequently from Oneida, Forest, Langlade, and Lincoln counties. Unusually far south was a bird seen in Jackson County on 23 June 1985 by M. J. Mossman.

Only on eight occasions has the Lincoln's been recorded in winter. One was discovered in Kewaunee County on 29 December (1963, R. J. Lukes). Birds appeared on the Milton CBC on 1 January (1969, Rock, M. T. Maxson) and the Newburg CBC on 17 December (1988, Ozaukee). Another individual turned up in Rock County on 26 January (1970, E. Brakefield). Birds were present at feeders until early February in Buffalo (1973, L. Maier), Milwaukee (1981, D. Hanbury), and Manitowoc (1989, C. R. Sontag) counties. One in Sheboygan County on 27 February (1971, H. Koopman) must have overwintered in the area. A more typical winter location is indicated by the January 1963 recovery at Gonzales, Texas, of a bird banded by C. A. Kemper at Chippewa Falls on 28 September 1962.

Swamp Sparrow (*Melospiza georgiana*)

STATUS. Common migrant. Common summer resident south and central; fairly common summer
resident north. Uncommon winter resident south;
rare winter resident central.

HABITAT. Shallow marsh. All carr. Wooded swamp.

MIGRATION DATES. *Spring:* early April to mid-May.
Fall: early September to late October.

BREEDING DATA. Nests with eggs: 2 May to 2 July.
Clutch size: usually 4 or 5 eggs; occasionally 3.

WINTER. Regularly present north to Crawford, Dodge,
and Sheboygan counties; rarely present north to
Polk, Adams, and Brown counties.

PORTRAIT. *Birds of Wisconsin:* Plate 87.

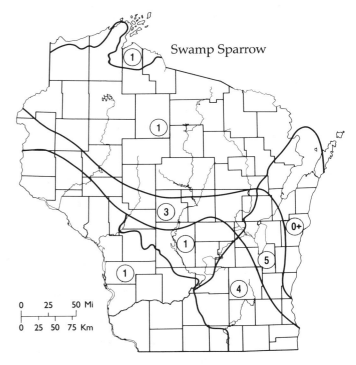

Breeding Bird Survey, averages 1966 to 1980

The breeding habitat of the Swamp Sparrow is more
narrowly limited than that of most sparrows. As the
species' name implies, it must be a swamp or marsh,
but the bird is quite selective as to the kind of marsh it
will inhabit. A too-small moist area will not do. The
bird will reject a swamp overgrown with numerous
trees and shrubs, and will avoid an open area that
dries up as the season progresses. But wherever extensive areas of open sedges and cattails thrive together with a good supply of standing or running
water, the Swamp Sparrow is a common bird. Because in Wisconsin the favored habitat is located most
prominently in the environs of the Rock and Fox
rivers and along Madison lakes, this species is most
numerous in the southern and eastern portions of the
state. However, the BBS map clearly shows a range
that includes all parts of the state. This species has
been recorded on 59 of the state's 70 BBS routes. But
since the wetlands where this bird abounds are often
at the end of dead-end roads, avoided by BBS transects, the Swamp is assuredly more numerous than
BBS figures would indicate. And since the summer
range is much more extensive north of Wisconsin
than to the south, one assumes that the bird would
prove to be as common in northern Wisconsin as in
the south if there were more favorable habitat in the
north.

Although nesting sites lie in wet swamps not easily
accessible by foot, the bird is fairly easy to locate and
see. The Swamp often offers a distinctive chatter from
a conspicuous perch; and even when birds are hidden in the long grass, they may reveal their presence
by a distinctive call note that resembles the note of
the White-throated Sparrow. The bird responds readily to human "squeaking."

But to find a nest an observer needs hip boots or a
boat. The nest is generally low down in a grass clump
a few inches above the ground, and sometimes only

inches away from water. All 13 nests reported by
Richter in Oconto and Marinette counties, 1926–1965,
were located in the tussocks of old dead grass. Several instances of cowbird parasitism have occurred
when a nest is located close to the bushes on the edge
of a swampy area; no instances of parasitism have
been reported when nests are in the shrub-free grassy
areas.

During fall migration this species disperses into
more varied habitat. It still shows a preference for tall
grass, but scatters to dry upland areas as well as the
wetter marshes. The Swamp is often found in company with Song and Lincoln's Sparrows. At times it
moves to farm hedgerows and even to residential
shrubbery; but its habits are so retiring that it easily
escapes detection.

September and October are the principal fall migration months. The start of the migration is difficult to
determine because of the presence of summer residents and the lack of song. In the northern counties
some migrants are noted during the first week of September; there is then a gradual buildup to a 20–30
September peak, with most birds gone by 20 October.
Migrants are noticeable in the southern counties from
mid-September on, with a peak from 25 September to
10 October. Migration out of the state depends on the

severity of the late October weather. Some years nearly all the birds are gone by 25 October; in other years several remain until 10 November.

In a few favored southern and eastern Wisconsin marshes some individuals remain throughout the winter. Observers have recorded the species on one or more CBCs every year since 1951. Between 1970 and 1980 birds have turned up on 100 of 683 counts (15%), with the total number of individuals per year varying from 15 (1972) to 85 (1976). Of these individuals, 85% were located south of a line from Prairie du Chien to Sheboygan. Occasional winter birds have been found as far north as Polk, Jackson, Adams, Waupaca, Outagamie, and Brown counties.

In southern Wisconsin spring migrants return during the first week of April or sometimes in the waning days of March. Arrival is generally around 15–20 April, with the first birds concentrating in marshy breeding areas. During the 20 April–10 May period, migration peaks and the birds spread out temporarily into more varied habitat that is less damp, even including residential backyard shrubbery. By 15 May most migrants have left for the north. In northern Wisconsin arrivals are general during the last week of April, followed by a 5–20 May peak.

Once the migration is over, the Swamp helps make up the fascinating evening chorus that emanates from marshes in May and June. Along with rails, bitterns, and Marsh Wrens this species competes with the frogs long after sunset. One wonders when the Swamp Sparrow sleeps, for it is sometimes heard singing even in the middle of the night.

White-throated Sparrow (*Zonotrichia albicollis*)

STATUS. Abundant migrant. Fairly common summer resident north; uncommon summer resident central and east. Uncommon winter resident south and east; rare winter resident west and north.

HABITAT. Conifer swamp. Young forest saplings. Residential areas (during migration).

MIGRATION DATES. *Spring:* mid-April to late May. *Fall:* late August to early November.

BREEDING DATA. Nests with eggs: 5 May to 4 July. Clutch size: usually 4 or 5 eggs; occasionally 6.

WINTER. Regularly present north to Grant, Brown, and Door counties; rarely present throughout the state.

PORTRAIT. *Birds of Wisconsin:* Plate 86.

The White-throated Sparrow is one of the most characteristic species of the spruce bogs in northern Wisconsin in summer. It is also found frequently in the partly open slashings where lumbering operations have been carried on. In June and early July the White-throat's presence is easily detected by the clear whistling song heard early and late in the day, and often even in the normally quiet midday period. While the male is engaged in singing and defending territory, the female may be busy incubating eggs—often one or two of the Brown-headed Cowbird as well as her own. Most nests found in Wisconsin have been located on the ground, close to bushes or small trees, well concealed by overhanging grass.

The BBS data indicate a summer range of fairly common abundance only in the northernmost counties: south to Douglas, Sawyer, Price, Langlade, and Marinette. The bird becomes progressively rarer farther south, but can be found in small numbers in

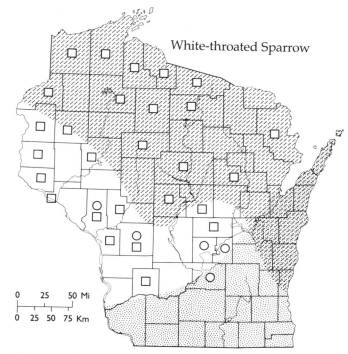

White-throated Sparrow

0   25   50 Mi
0   25 50 75 Km

▨ Summer range
▥ Winter range
○ Early June to early August
□ Early December to late March

Records since 1960

pockets as far south as Polk, Chippewa, Jackson, Wood, Portage, Fond du Lac, and Ozaukee counties, where a few suitable bogs exist. Formerly a few birds remained to nest in some southern counties, but these populations have now disappeared. Madison had a summering (breeding?) bird in 1970 (W. L. Hilsenhoff), but this was the first summer record there since 1939.

Each winter a few individuals remain in suburban areas in the southern and central counties. As many as 25 have been recorded on a single CBC, but the more usual pattern consists of one or two birds that are attracted to well-stocked feeders adjacent to some brushy woodland edges. South of a line from Prairie du Chien to Green Bay, small numbers are found every winter. Occasional winter records have come from as far north as Douglas, Bayfield, Iron, Vilas, Marinette, and Door counties. Two-thirds (48) of Wisconsin's 72 counties have had winter records since 1960.

But it is as a spring and fall migrant that the White-throat is best known. Migration begins with birds moving into the southern region around 15 April, builds up to a veritable flood from 25 April to 10 May, and tapers off so quickly that only occasional stragglers remain after 20 May. The pattern is similar in the northern region, but occurs about a week later. All but summer residents usually depart before the end of May. During the peak period a brushy area on the edge of a wood may play host to a flock of 30–50 individuals, and one may encounter several such flocks on a field trip. When a migrating flock moves into a residential yard during this peak period, the ground and nearby shrubbery seem to be alive with these brown-and-white foragers. The birds become quite noisy at times. Not often do they sing the full whistled song heard on the breeding grounds; but they offer whistled song fragments, and excited "chipping" often accompanies the competition between two rivals for the same favored feeding spot. The White-throat's call note is sufficiently distinct to make detection possible in flocks of night migrants passing low overhead on overcast nights in early May.

The fall flight is equally strong. It may not seem so to an observer on fall field trips who spends his time on fields and hedgerows where most other migrating sparrows are to be found. But the observer who checks along the edges of wooded areas will find many White-throats and very few other sparrows. As in spring, White-throats cluster in flocks of up to 50 birds, and make the fallen leaves in a particular feeding area come alive. Fall migrants usually begin to show up in the central counties south of the breeding range around 25 August, gradually build to a 20 September–5 October peak, and depart by 25 October. The southern Wisconsin schedule is 10–15 days later: early arrivals appear around 10 September, and numbers build to a 5–20 October peak, then gradually diminish until 5 November. Only stragglers remain after that time.

Golden-crowned Sparrow (*Zonotrichia atricapilla*)

STATUS. Accidental in spring and fall. Four records.
HABITAT. Northern lowland carr.

The precise data documenting Golden-crowned Sparrow occurrences are lost with the passing of 130 years. The exact dates when P. R. Hoy collected birds near his Racine home are not known. One specimen resides in the Hoy Museum at Racine, but locations of the others are not known. There is even confusion over the number of specimens Hoy secured. Hoy's personal journal mentions wanderers taken in the fall of 1853 and 1854 and the spring of 1856. E. W. Nelson (1876) published a further record, having examined a specimen supposedly collected by Hoy in April 1858 and confirmed by Cassin. The occurrence of even one of these Pacific stragglers is remarkable. The presence of three or four birds so far from their normal range seems inexplicable.

Over a century later, during the period 1963–1965, inconclusive but strong evidence pointed to a recurrence of this species, this time during spring in the Ashland area. On 5 May 1963 Janet Kozlowski, who had lived in southeastern Alaska where Golden-crowns are common migrants, heard a bird she believed to be of this species in eastern Bayfield County 4 miles west of Ashland, in the brushy tangles through which Fish Creek meanders as it nears Lake Superior. The bird remained in this area until 5 June, and was heard many times during the month-long period singing the distinctive typical melody the Kozlowskis had associated with the "oh-dear-me bird"—the Golden-crowned Sparrow. The monumental frustration for the observers was that they never saw the bird. Consistently the bird remained on the far side of the stream from the observers' vantage point in an area that could not be successfully approached from any side. It sang from perches that could not be spotted. I made a trip to the area with Mrs. Kozlowski on 14 May 1963, but the morning proved to be disappointingly cloudy and windy, and there was virtually no bird song of any kind. No amount of whistling, imitating, or squeaking brought a response from the elusive feathered visitor. Mrs. Kozlowski's whistled imitation certainly sounded like no variation of any Wisconsin bird I have ever heard, however (*Pass. Pigeon* 25:158–159). In 1964 the same song was again heard in the same area from 15 May to 2 June by Mrs. Kozlowski and three other observers; but again, all attempts to get a glimpse of the songster failed. Again in 1965, the same song emanated from the same area from 10 to 17 May; but the frustration of the bird's defying visual observation was as great as before.

The plausibility of Golden-crowned Sparrows inhabiting northern Wisconsin during the early 1960s is greatly enhanced in relation to some homing experiments being carried on at that time with Golden-crowns and other sparrows. Dr. L. Richard Mewaldt of San Jose State College, endeavoring to detect homing instinct in sparrows that normally winter in California, released several Golden-crowned Sparrows in Louisiana during the winter of 1961–1962 and in Maryland during the winter of 1962–1963. Not only did some of these released birds find their way back to the Pacific Coast, but also one of the Maryland birds was trapped in Ontario on 13 May 1963 en route. Although not a proven fact, it is a fascinating supposition that one of Dr. Mewaldt's transplanted birds may have made Ashland, Wisconsin, a stopping place on the route between its winter release in Maryland and its summer home in western Canada or Alaska.

On other occasions this species has been known to wander all the way to Alabama, Pennsylvania, New Jersey, and Massachusetts. But today, just as in Dr. Hoy's time, the occurrence of this bird in Wisconsin is strictly accidental.

White-crowned Sparrow (*Zonotrichia leucophrys*)

STATUS. Fairly common migrant. Accidental summer resident. Rare winter resident south and east.

HABITAT. Upland carr. Old field. Farmsteads.

MIGRATION DATES. *Spring:* late April to late May. *Fall:* mid-September to early November.

BREEDING DATA. One nest with eggs in early June; young barely able to fly, 16 July.

WINTER. Occasionally present north to La Crosse, Shawano, and Outagamie counties.

PORTRAIT. *Birds of Wisconsin:* Plate 86.

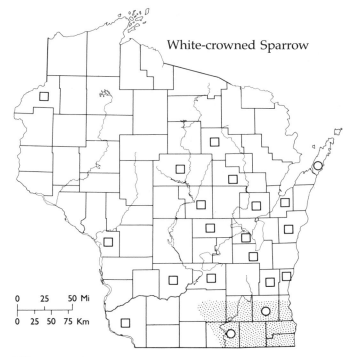

White-crowned Sparrow

0   25   50 Mi

0 25 50 75 Km

▨ Winter range
○ Early June to late August
□ Late November to early April

Records since 1960

The same farm hedgerows that harbor Harris' Sparrows also provide the favorite habitat for the White-crown. Reference has sometimes been made in the literature to an association between the White-crowned and the White-throated Sparrows. Although the two are sometimes found in close proximity, it is more typical in Wisconsin for the White-crown to occupy the hedgerows bordering open fields and orchards, while the White-throat shows a preference for the edges of woodlots and forests.

May and October are the principal months for White-crowns. First spring migrants arrive during late April on the average of 2 years in every 3, but usually these birds represent only an advance guard. The few records that exist for March and early April presumably are sightings of birds that overwintered nearby. The bulk of the migration comes in the first 3 weeks of May. The size of the spring flight varies considerably. Some years it is unusual to see more than two or three birds at a time, even during the usual peak period around 10 May. In other years one can find 10–15 birds on a short field trip. On 5 May 1964 William Hilsenhoff counted 40 White-crowns in Madison. Some years migrants tend to concentrate in the eastern counties near Lake Michigan; other years the numbers are greater in the western counties. Nearly every spring alert observers are able to identify a few individuals of the *gambeli* race. Since birds of this race winter only as far east as the southern Great Plains, and since birds of the nominate *leucophrys* race also winter in the same region, it is likely that many if not most of Wisconsin's spring birds have moved northeastward from this wintering area. The usual date of departure for the last spring migrant is 25 May. Early June lingerers were noted on the 6th (1953, Burnett, N. R. Stone) and 12th (1943, Door, M. Deusing).

One looks for returning fall migrants from 15 September on in northern and central areas, 20 September on in the south. Exceptionally early are August sightings on the 18th (1938, Vilas, W. N. MacBriar; MPM files), 24th (1977, Door, L. W. Erickson), and

26th (1964, Brown, T. C. Erdman), and a 5 September bird (1974, Dane, D. D. Tessen). But only in the last week of September do birds spread over the state. During the first half of October a field trip in suitable habitat may produce 10–15 birds, and occasionally one may encounter enough small flocks to total as many as 50 birds in a day. By the end of October only a few birds remain, and nearly all the remnant have left by mid-November.

Until 1947 Wisconsin had no winter record. Little did Milwaukee observers realize that a significant new trend was starting when they found an individual on their 1947 CBC, with another three found on their 1948 count. Birds then appeared on counts in various communities in 1949, 1952, 1953, 1954, and 1957, and from 1960 on there has been at least one late December record each year. One favored Kenosha County spot has attracted from 4 to 14 individuals each winter. The fate of most of the early winter birds is uncertain. But a few birds have survived the winter at feeding stations as far north as La Crosse, Shawano, and Outagamie counties.

According to Schoenebeck (1902) and Kumlien and

Hollister (1903), a few early nesting records exist. Writing about an Oconto County record, Schoenebeck stated: "On July 16, 1899 I found four young birds of this species which had just left the nest. By watching them a while I saw the parent bird approaching with food for them. I have since then found a nest containing five nearly fresh eggs. Begins laying the first of June." Kumlien and Hollister mentioned collecting two recently fledged young in Ozaukee County in June 1882, a nesting in Madison in 1873 (no specific dates), and a report that P. R. Hoy had discovered a few birds nesting near Racine.

No further nesting evidence is known, and in view of the 500 miles separating Wisconsin from the regular Canadian nesting range, present-day nesting in the state must be considered unlikely. But it is not impossible. Even if it is assumed that observations through 12 June are lingering spring migrants, and that records from 18 August on are early fall visitors, there are four additional midsummer records: 30 June 1968 (Rock, G. Mahlum), 2 July 1964 (Door, L. W. Erickson), 11 July 1964 (Waukesha, E. Hoffmann), and a bird that spent the entire summer in Door County in 1945 (H. C. Wilson).

Harris' Sparrow (*Zonotrichia querula*)

STATUS. Uncommon migrant. Rare winter resident south and central.
HABITAT. Upland carr. Old field. Farmsteads.
MIGRATION DATES. *Spring:* early to late May. *Fall:* mid-September to early November. *Extremes:* 2 June; 15 September.
WINTER. Occasionally present north to Douglas, Shawano, and Brown counties.
PORTRAIT. *Birds of Wisconsin:* Plate 86.

Few spring migrants make as rapid a passage through the state as does the Harris' Sparrow. Over the past 35 years the average arrival date for the first spring migrant anywhere in the state is 4 May, while the average date for the departure of the last migrant is 20 May. Thus, within the short span of 16 days this distinctive large sparrow completes its entire migratory swing through Wisconsin. This swing encompasses nearly the entire state; birds have been noted frequently from the counties along Lake Michigan, as well as those along the Mississippi and St. Croix rivers, missing only the extreme northeastern corner. But where observers see only one or two birds on a spring day in the east, they may see as many as 10–15 in a day along the western edge from Pierce County north to Douglas County.

The spring flight is also remarkable for its consistency. In 3 of every 4 years throughout the past 35 years, the first spring arrival date has varied no more than 3 days from the average 4 May date, and the last spring departure has varied no more than 4 days from the average 20 May date. Thus, a southern Wisconsin observer who hopes to see one of these gaudy birds in spring had better keep a sharp lookout between 1 and 15 May. An observer in northern Wisconsin needs to be on the alert between 9 and 24 May. Exceptions to this pattern are provided by published

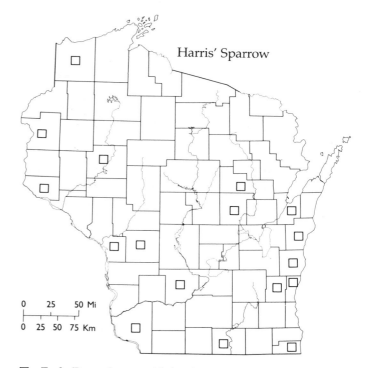

Harris' Sparrow

☐ Early December to mid-April

Records since 1960

records of three mid-April observations on the 8th (1967), 10th (1967), and 14th (1963), and a 23 March bird. But in view of the otherwise consistent pattern of this species, it seems most likely that these individuals may have overwintered nearby. The sole instance of a spring migrant lingering beyond 25 May occurred in 1968 when a bird remained in Price County until 2 June (M. Hardy).

The fall migration pattern differs from the spring flight in several aspects. Considerably more birds are present in fall. In the eastern counties one continues to see only a bird or two at a time, as in spring; but birds are usually reported in more locations. In the north and west the increase in numbers is especially conspicuous. A remarkable instance occurred on Outer Island in Ashland County on 16 September 1919, when Harry Sheldon estimated a flock of 200 following the passage of a severe storm the previous day (Jackson 1943). Although there is no record of another flight of this magnitude, I have on several occasions found 25–30 birds in St. Croix County around 1 October, and I believe I could have counted up to 100 each time had I spent the whole day in the field.

Birds in fall also show greater variation in plumage. Some still have the full black face and bib of spring plumage. Other adults lose the black face but retain black in the throat area. Then there are immatures showing the white throat and black blotch on the upper breast. There are no systematic studies to show the percentage of Wisconsin birds that appear in these different plumages, but I suspect that it is largely the presence of immature birds that accounts for the greater numbers each fall.

Another contrast with spring is found in the length of the migration period. With average fall arrival and departure dates of 23 September and 30 October, the migration period extends over a 5–6–week period. Thus, observers in the northern counties could expect these birds any time from 20 September to 25 October. In the southern counties the most promising period is from 25 September to 5 November. Unusually late were sightings on 27 November (1932, Sheboygan, C. S. Jung) and 3 December (1977, Pepin, R. M. Hoffman).

Hedgerows bordering fields and the less-traveled roads provide this species' favorite habitat, spring and fall. A thick clump of bushes surrounded by relatively open land is promising. An observer who pauses in such an area and spots a White-crowned Sparrow should search diligently for a Harris'. The species often travel together. Frequently their presence is first detected by the unusually musical call note that is similar for both species but quite unlike that of other sparrows.

Since the regular winter range extends northward well into Iowa, it is not surprising that Wisconsin should have an occasional wintering bird. Some have been known to overwinter successfully: in 1953–1954 (Green, H. L. Orians), 1964–1965 (Shawano, L. H. Schultz), 1969–1970 (Waupaca, M. Steinbach), 1972–1973 (Kenosha, R. R. Hoffman), 1973–1974 (La Crosse, F. Z. Lesher), and 1977–1978 (Washington, J. Haseleu). Additional late December observations have been reported from Douglas (1988), Pierce (1971), Manitowoc (1974), Sheboygan (1978), Ozaukee (1973), Sauk (1982), Monroe (1968), Grant (1966), and Rock (1958) counties. Brief January records have come from Manitowoc (1954), Polk (1963), Brown (1974), and Rock (1972) counties.

Buss and Mattison (1955) mentioned that J. N. Clark sighted a pair in Dunn County on 4 July 1902. These authors also detailed a series of observations, highly suggestive of nesting, made by Mrs. Leon Snyder near Colfax (Dunn County) in the summer of 1924. But the likelihood that the bird nested in Wisconsin 800 miles south of its nearest known nesting range is extremely remote.

Dark-eyed Junco (*Junco hyemalis*)
Formerly Slate-colored Junco, Northern Junco

STATUS. Abundant migrant. Uncommon summer resident north. Common winter resident south and central; uncommon winter resident north.

HABITAT. All carr. Residential areas. Conifer plantation (during nesting).

MIGRATION DATES. *Spring:* mid-March to early May. *Fall:* mid-September to mid-November.

BREEDING DATA. Nests with eggs: 16 May to 24 June. Clutch size: 4 or 5 eggs.

PORTRAIT. *Birds of Wisconsin:* Plate 85.

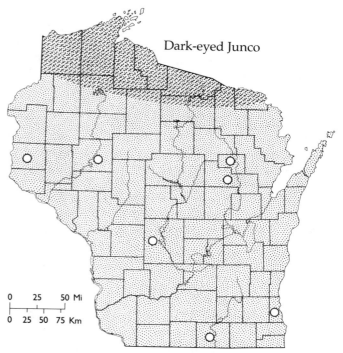

Dark-eyed Junco

0   25   50 Mi

0 25 50 75 Km

▨ Summer range
▦ Winter range
○ Late May to late August

Records since 1960

Birds know nothing of political boundaries. Yet across much of North America the boundary between Canada and the United States approximates the boundary of both the summer and winter ranges of the Dark-eyed Junco. Generally, with the exception of the eastern states, this bird resides north of the border in summer and south of the border in winter.

In Wisconsin the edge of the summer and winter ranges lies a little south of the border, along a line that runs east from Grantsburg to Park Falls, southeast to Shawano and east to Sturgeon Bay. North of this line juncos are found in small numbers during summer, sometimes at the edge of spruce bogs but more often in arid upland areas where extensive plantings of young pines exist. It takes a finely tuned and trained ear to distinguish the monotonous "trilly" song of this species from the similar song of the Chipping Sparrow, which is usually common wherever the junco is found. But meticulous effort will show the junco to be present in small numbers throughout most of the northern counties. In June it has been found on eight northern BBS transects, but not with regularity.

Little effort has been made to study the bird's nesting habits in Wisconsin. Apparently typical, however, is H. H. T. Jackson's experience in Vilas County in June 1918. "A nest containing five eggs was located in a shallow excavation, somewhat overgrown with moss, in the side of a steep bank along the road near Mamie Lake June 8" (Jackson 1923, p. 478). A few other nests have been found in similar terrain (Kumlien and Hollister 1903; Young and Bernard 1978).

Only rarely has this bird been recorded south of the Grantsburg–Park Falls–Sturgeon Bay line in summer during recent years. June individuals were banded in Chippewa County (1963, 1966, C. A. Kemper) and in Rock County (1971, M. T. Maxson). Other June observations include finds in St. Croix (1976, C. A. Faanes), Clark (1947, S. D. Robbins), and Juneau (1975, S. D.

Robbins) counties. One seen in Milwaukee on 25 July (1957, D. L. Larkin) seemed out of place. None of these showed evidence of nesting.

In winter the northern limit of the regular range follows an almost identical line. Occasional individuals have wintered in the northernmost counties at well-stocked feeders, so in a sense the winter range may be said to be statewide. But only from the Grantsburg-Shawano line south is it regular. Statewide totals on late December CBCs during the 1970s ranged from 12,000 to 18,000. On well-organized counts in Sauk, Dane, and Waukesha counties numbers annually exceed 1,000. Throughout the central counties numbers were in the hundreds. Counts in the north had few if any juncos. This species is still migrating in late December. Were CBCs to be repeated in late January, central Wisconsin populations would be lower.

It is during spring and fall migration that this species becomes truly abundant. Fall migrants begin to show up in the northern counties around 10 September and reach the southern counties 2 weeks later.

The average arrival date in Sawyer and Rusk counties (1929–1939) was 13 September; in Adams County (1952–1959) it was 21 September; in Dane County (1939–1951) it was 26 September. In early October one can drive across much of northern Wisconsin and find flocks of 100 or more every half mile wherever there is brushy habitat along the roadsides. By late October this influx has reached the southern counties. Only gradually does this taper off; by mid-November, however, there are but a few scattered individuals remaining in the northern counties.

The return flight in spring hits the central areas during the first warm days in March and spreads to the northern counties by 25 March. In Sawyer and Rusk counties the average arrival date (1929–1940) was 25 March. April is a heavy junco month throughout the state, with flocks of these feathered travelers scattered over the countryside wherever there are weeds to be found. At feeders these juncos are welcome scavengers, cleaning up the mess of sunflower seed hulls left by wintering Evening Grosbeaks. In southern Wisconsin only scattered individuals remain after 30 April, and generally even these have departed by 10 May. By 20 May the last migrants have left the northern regions, leaving behind the relatively small remnant of a breeding population.

Confusing to some observers have been the names attached to this species. At various times printed references have been made to "slate-colored," "Oregon," "northern," "pink-sided," "Montana," "Shufeldt's," and "gray-headed." Before 1950, taxonomists tried various methods of describing and naming geographic races, primarily in the western states. Since 1973 all *hyemalis* juncos have been combined under the name Dark-eyed Junco. Unquestionably, Wisconsin plays host to a few visitors of one or more western races every winter.

Lapland Longspur (*Calcarius lapponicus*)

STATUS. Common migrant south and central; fairly common migrant north. Accidental summer visitant. Uncommon winter resident south and central.

HABITAT. Open grassland and cropland.

MIGRATION DATES. *Fall:* late September to late December. *Spring:* mid-February to mid-May. *Extremes:* 3 August; 29 May.

WINTER. Regularly present north to St. Croix, Clark, Outagamie, and Kewaunee counties; occasionally present north to Douglas, Price, Langlade, and Door counties.

PORTRAIT. *Birds of Wisconsin:* Plate 88.

Because Lapland Longspurs have occasionally been recorded on up to one-third of the state's CBCs in late December, sometimes with hundreds of birds detected, some commentators have assumed that this is a common winter species. Strictly speaking, that is not true, for in late December the tail end of the fall migration may still be in progress. On 23 December 1968 Joel Greenberg reported hearing hundreds of night migrants passing overhead in central Wisconsin. On at least four other occasions in Adams and St. Croix counties, I too have heard major movements of migrant Lapland Longspurs overhead on calm nights in late December.

The typical CBC pattern consists of flocks of 100 or more at two or three locations and scattered individu-

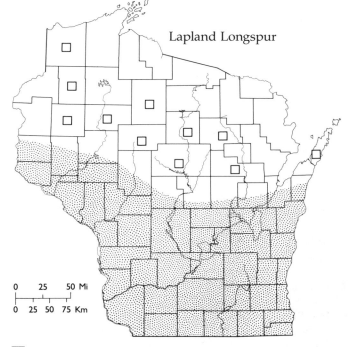

Lapland Longspur

0   25   50 Mi

0 25 50 75 Km

▨ Winter range
☐ Early January to early February

Records since 1960

als at three or four more sites. These late-December observations have occurred frequently north to St. Croix, Chippewa, Wood, Outagamie, and Kewaunee counties and rarely north to Douglas, Washburn, Price, Lincoln, Langlade, and Door counties. Most midwinter records have come from south of a line between La Crosse and Sheboygan.

When the main movement of Horned Larks gets under way in the latter half of February (in southern areas) and early March (in central and northern areas), these longspurs are not far behind. The Lapland rarely appears along the gravel shoulders of roads in singles and pairs, as does the lark. But both species are often found together in open fields where snow cover is occasionally interspersed with patches of bare ground or freshly spread manure.

As long as the fields are mostly snow-covered, Snow Buntings may also be found in mixed flocks. As the snow recedes in March, the Snow Buntings move northward, the Horned Larks pair off and prepare to breed, while the Lapland Longspurs build up in favored spots until flocks number hundreds or even thousands of birds. Through all of April longspur-searchers will experience either feast or famine as they scan the broad expanses of fields which this species favors. An observer may scan field after field without success, then suddenly spot a huge swarm of birds circling a field that looks no different from the other barren spots. When a flock lands, birds sometimes perch on fences and hedgerows and sing fragments of the sweet musical songs that reach full development only on the far-north breeding grounds. More often, however, these longspurs land in plowed fields and conceal themselves as they feed in the furrows.

Habitat requirements during migration necessarily limit the portions of the state where this bird appears. Most favored are the heavily farmed parts of Columbia, Dodge, and Winnebago counties; these are the principal territories where flocks of up to 9,000 have most often been reported. Smaller numbers occur almost anywhere in southern and central Wisconsin, wherever broad expanses of flat open farmland prevail. Modest numbers have also been reported in many of the northern counties, wherever promising habitat is found.

The main exodus to northern breeding areas takes place between 25 April and 10 May, with only scattered individuals remaining beyond 15 May. Late-May stragglers have been sighted on the 27th (1955, Columbia, G. W. Foster), 28th (1976, Ashland, J. T. Harris), and 29th (1978, Douglas, D. D. Tessen).

Exceptional also is the only summer record: a flock of 30–40 found near Madison on 17 July 1937 by John Main (1937b). This sighting almost defies logical explanation, since this species should still be on its Canadian tundra breeding grounds at that time.

Equally astonishing was the sighting of a Lapland on 3 August 1982 (Dodge, D. K. Gustafson), a month earlier than any other fall migrant longspurs. Unusual also are early September arrival sightings on the 6th (1979, Burnett, J. L. Polk), 7th (1966, Douglas, S. D. Robbins), and 9th (1976, Milwaukee, E. J. Epstein). Normally fall arrivals are first detected around 25 September, with numbers building up in October and November. Habitat preferences in fall are essentially the same as in spring—especially since the practice of fall plowing has become widespread.

Smith's Longspur (*Calcarius pictus*)

STATUS. Casual migrant south.
HABITAT. Open grassland.
MIGRATION DATES. Observed between 19 March and 28 April; and between 29 September and 26 November.
PORTRAIT. *Birds of Wisconsin:* Plate 88.

Both Hoy (1853b) and Kumlien and Hollister (1903) mentioned rare and irregular sightings of Smith's Longspurs on southern Wisconsin prairies. If they succeeded in collecting any specimens, these are now lost; but a sight record appears on A. L. Kumlien's list for 19 March 1869 (Schorger 1944c). The state's only known specimens consist of three birds collected by Stoddard (1922a) from a flock of 20–30 birds in Sauk County on 27 and 28 April 1921. These specimens are now in the collection of the Milwaukee Public Museum.

There are but four additional spring sight records for the twentieth century. Warner Taylor (1923) made another Sauk County observation on 17 April 1922. In the MPM files there are notes relating to a bird near Oconomowoc (Waukesha County) on 12 April 1938 (H. A. Clapp) and one at Mineral Point (Iowa County) on 5 April 1940 (G. O. Raasch). It was again on 12 April that R. M. Hoffman found three individuals in Columbia County in 1984 (*Pass. Pigeon* 47:34).

Autumn sight records are also three in number. The MPM files list a bird seen near New London (Waupaca County) on 19 November 1912 (F. S. Dayton). A sighting in Racine County on 26 November 1964 (J. A. Simpson) was accompanied by an excellent description (*Pass. Pigeon* 27:127) which is now lost. The most recent record—Randy Hoffman's sighting of a bird in a flock of Lapland Longspurs in Columbia County on 29 September 1978—is well documented (*Pass. Pigeon* 41:135–136).

In recent years, various observers, believing that this species should be found more frequently than the records indicate, have made occasional special

Smith's Longspur

△   19 March to 28 April
▽   29 September to 26 November

All records

efforts to find it in southwestern Wisconsin during April. Investigators have reasoned that: (1) the regular migratory range lies only slightly to the west of Wisconsin; (2) in some years the eastward movement of fall birds has carried them to Chicago, to Indiana, and even to western Ohio; (3) if Smith's are present, they may so conceal themselves in short grass that they are easily passed over; and (4) plumages between winter and summer are difficult to identify unless seen at close range. Sorties to locate birds have produced only negative results to date. But they should be continued.

Chestnut-collared Longspur (*Calcarius ornatus*)

STATUS. Accidental. Three records.
HABITAT. Open grassland.

On 6 June 1978 Noel Cutright encountered a Chestnut-collared Longspur in a field of young oats in Sheboygan County near Lake Michigan. The visitor, an adult male, was observed intermittently for over 2 hours, then photographed by Cutright and John Brumer (*Pass. Pigeon* 41:90–92). This is Wisconsin's only record substantiated by photograph. There are no specimens.

Two years earlier, 27 May 1976, James Harris observed another adult male under favorable conditions on Outer Island in Ashland County. Careful notes were taken on the spot, but by the time a camera was obtained, the bird had disappeared (*Pass. Pigeon* 39:202).

Within a flock of Lapland Longspurs in southern Polk County on 20 March 1976, Keith Dueholm picked out at least three—possibly up to six—Chestnut-collars. Black extending far down on the belly was clearly seen, and a song noticeably different from that of the Laplands was distinctly heard. He revisited the area with camera 3 days later, but the birds could not be found (pers. comm.).

There is a strong likelihood that several individuals were mixed in with several hundred Lapland Longspurs on the Glen Fisher farm in Winnebago County between 15 and 25 March 1948. Eunice Fisher hiked across her fields several times to view the flocks during that interval, describing song as well as plumage characteristics that fit this species. Unfortunately, the equipment needed to photograph the birds was not available (*Pass. Pigeon* 10:115; 11:70).

Another tantalizing indefinite record was obtained in June 1893 in northwestern Rock County. B. F. Goss and Ned Hollister came upon one nest with four eggs and a second nest under construction. Reflecting on this 19 years later, Hollister (1912) wrote: "We were not careful enough about the identification. I shot the female bird and Mr. Goss as well as myself found it a true longspur, and on account of the black wing-coverts we called it the chestnut-collared. We did not save the bird." He concluded, "I think we may safely refuse to accept the determination of this bird, so far out of the known breeding range of the supposed species, by even so accomplished an ornithologist as Captain Goss." True. Yet Hollister failed to mention that southern Wisconsin would be equally far removed from the normal breeding range of any other species of longspur.

Snow Bunting (*Plectrophenax nivalis*)

STATUS. Common winter resident north and central; fairly common winter resident south.
HABITAT. Open grassland and cropland.
MIGRATION DATES. *Fall:* early October to early January. *Spring:* mid-February to late April. *Extremes:* 16 September; 19 May.
PORTRAIT. *Birds of Wisconsin:* Plate 88.

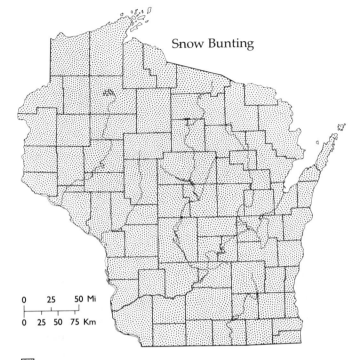

Snow Bunting

☐ Winter range

Records since 1960

The Snow Bunting is one of the last passerine migrants to arrive in fall. Long after most fall warblers have come and gone, after the peak of the sparrow flight has passed, the first Snow Buntings begin to arrive. On three occasions first arrivals have been detected in September: the 16th (1983, Bayfield, A. J. Roy), 22nd (1965, Marinette, H. L. Lindberg), and 23rd (1948, Iowa, S. D. Robbins). Birds were noted on 1 October in 1968 (Door, H. C. Wilson) and 1971 (Oneida, L. J. Schimmels). Usually first arrivals are spotted around 10 October in the north, 20 October in the south. By the end of October flocks may be present anywhere in the state.

Some years, the flocks are largest in November, tapering gradually so that relatively few birds are noted in January and February. Other years, flocks numbering up to 2,000 continue to be found any time during the winter. These large flocks are sometimes reported from the southern counties, but in most winters the largest flocks are confined to the central and northern counties.

The main northward migration takes place in March. It is almost as if the birds cannot stand the sight of bare ground, for as snow-melting progresses, the buntings disappear. An April bird in the southern counties is unusual, but one was photographed on 23 April (1964, Washington, N. Schmidt) and one was observed on 5 May (1929, Sheboygan, C. S. Jung). Farther north the main exodus is completed by 20 April, with stragglers occasionally lingering until 5 May. Exceptionally late are May observations on the 14th (1970, Brown, E. D. Cleary), 16th (1954, Outagamie, N. M. Rogers), 17th (1964, Brown, T. C. Erdman), and 19th (1983, Ashland, R. L. Verch).

There are winters when only a few birds reach the southern counties. In other winters some of the larg-est flocks are seen in the south. In an average winter, buntings are found on 40–50% of the CBCs, with combined annual totals of 2,500–3,000 individuals. Birds were unusually numerous in 1975 (5,134), 1981 (6,870), and 1987 (8,862).

The Snow Bunting is a gregarious bird, rarely found singly or in pairs. Finding winter flocks is often a matter of chance. Sometimes the flocks frequent a roadway, where they can scarcely be overlooked. Sometimes they congregate on snow-covered plowed fields where fresh manure has been spread. Most often they occur on large expanses of fallow fields where the snow depth still leaves exposed weed tips for bunting food. Occasionally these birds mix with flocks of Lapland Longspurs and Horned Larks in late fall and early spring.

Bobolink (*Dolichonyx oryzivorus*)

STATUS. Common migrant. Common summer resident.

HABITAT. Open grassland. Sedge meadow. Old field.

MIGRATION DATES. *Spring:* late April to late May. *Fall:* late July to early October. *Extremes:* 12 April; 27 October.

BREEDING DATA. Nests with eggs: 20 May to 13 July. Clutch size: usually 5 or 6 eggs; occasionally 4 or 7.

PORTRAIT. *Birds of Wisconsin:* Plate 74.

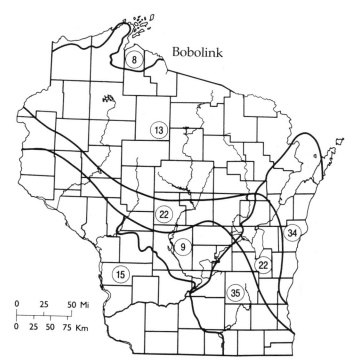

Breeding Bird Survey, averages 1966 to 1980

Although it is a member in good standing in the blackbird family, the Bobolink differs from most other blackbirds in several respects. Most blackbirds arrive in March or early April; this species migrates mainly in May. Most blackbirds are represented in winter by at least a few birds; this bird is unheard of in Wisconsin from November through March. Most black members of the family have squeaky, rather unmelodic songs; this songster can bring an entire meadow to life with its lilting, rollicking melody. Most blackbird males experience only minor plumage changes between spring and fall; this species undergoes drastic plumage changes. Most birds in this family have adapted themselves to a variety of habitats; this representative shows a particular liking for wild rice, timothy hay, and related forms of grass meadows, but is rarely found in any other type of habitat.

The only Bobolinks that normally reach Wisconsin before May are a handful of early males that manage to get to the southern and central counties during the last week in April. Gertrude Pedersen's bird near Luck (Polk County) on 12 April 1960 is exceptional, for birds are usually only reaching the southern states in early April. No others have been recorded in the state until the 17th. My first spring "rice bird," more often than not, has not been a bird that has already arrived in its typical habitat; rather it has been a migrant passing overhead giving forth with his full song as he flies along. This song must surely be one of the most distinctive vocal utterings of any North American species. Once learned, it can scarcely be mistaken for that of any other bird.

It is only after the first week of May that the bird becomes numerous and widespread. First arrivals reach the northern counties around 10 May and are well established on nesting territories by the 25th. The females are much less conspicuous than the males; little sound is heard from the females, and they tend to perch on or near the ground in inconspicuous spots. By contrast the male perches atop a tall weed, on a fence wire, or even on the gravel shoulder of the road; he frequently flies back and forth over the meadow in full song.

The male continues this eye-catching behavior through June. BBS results show that this bird is present in all sections of the state, but is found in considerably smaller numbers in the northernmost counties. It is found on transects in Douglas, Bayfield, and Forest counties, but it is absent on routes in Ashland, Iron, and Vilas counties. There are transects in Polk, St. Croix, Clark, La Crosse, Winnebago, Dodge, and Racine counties that sometimes produce over 50 Bobolinks per transect.

While the males are displaying, the females are occupied with nesting. Nests are built on the ground, well concealed in tall grass. There are increasing possibilities that nesting success may be lessening in hayfields. Farmers who used to harvest their first crop of hay in early July are now mowing in late May and early June, well before young Bobolinks fledge. The BBS average of 21–23 Bobolinks per transect per year (1970–1972) has dropped to 13–14 (1978–1980) and to 11–13 (1983–1985).

By early July the singing stops. The males stay out of sight while they molt. The females and fledged young feed inconspicuously in hay and grain fields.

Often I have paused in suitable habitat in July, detecting no Bobolinks; yet a "sh-psh-psh" sound has agitated a flock of 20–50 birds, all in brown plumage. As the birds move nervously about, they utter their distinctive "pink" call that is especially characteristic during fall migration. From July into October alert observers may detect, by means of this call note, the presence of "rice birds" that they would otherwise miss.

The fall migration gets under way by late July, judging from the occasional "pinks" of night migrants that can be heard from that time on, and from the fall arrival dates in nearby states where this species does not breed. Flocks become larger as August progresses, often numbering in the hundreds. On 5 September 1915 A. W. Schorger estimated 3,000–4,000 birds present at one Dodge County location. Flocks are rarely met after 10 September, but scattered small groups and individuals are occasionally found in the southern counties until 5 October. Exceptionally late are October sightings on the 15th (1971, Rock, E. Brakefield) and 27th (1940, Brown, D. F. Liebmann).

Red-winged Blackbird (*Agelaius phoeniceus*)

STATUS. Abundant migrant. Abundant summer resident. Uncommon winter resident south and central; rare winter resident north.

HABITAT. Shallow marsh. Wooded swamp. Open cropland.

MIGRATION DATES. *Spring:* early March to mid-May. *Fall:* mid-September to mid-November.

BREEDING DATA. Nests with eggs: 1 May to 15 July. Clutch size: usually 3 or 4 eggs; occasionally 2 or 5.

WINTER. Frequently present north to Pierce, Marathon, and Brown counties; rarely present to Douglas, Bayfield, Vilas, and Marinette counties.

PORTRAIT. *Birds of Wisconsin:* Plate 75.

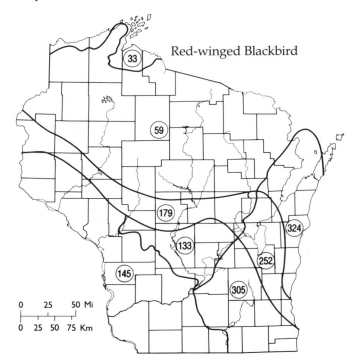

Red-winged Blackbird

Breeding Bird Survey, averages 1966 to 1980

W. E. Snyder of Beaver Dam (Dodge County) recorded: "On November 9, 1924, there occurred here, about 4 P.M., a flight of blackbirds, the like of which no local resident ever saw before. The procession, passing from due north to due south, was of such length that those in the lead as well as those in the rear, faded out into mere specks. . . . The flight lasted for a full half hour. The flight was at a great height, a solid column, unbroken by any bunched formation" (Snyder 1925). Presumably all or most of this vast horde were Red-winged Blackbirds.

Katherine Rill had a similar experience driving between Oshkosh and Fond du Lac on 17 October 1965, witnessing what she called an unbroken "ribbon of birds" at least 5 miles long (*Pass. Pigeon* 28:112). No estimates have been recorded on the number of birds in such a tremendous flock, but Wisconsin obviously makes a significant contribution to wintering flocks that reach into the millions in the southern states.

The annual spring buildup begins modestly shortly before or after 1 March when the first migrant males reach the southernmost counties. Mild weather any time after 15 February may coax a few early migrants to move northward. By mid-March the trickle reaches the central areas, and the trickle becomes a flood as waves of males pour into the southern sections. Northward progress is sometimes held up by March blizzards and lingering snow in the north, but most areas have their first males by 1 April. Females follow in April, with wave after wave progressing throughout the month. Helmut Mueller's observations of spring migrants still passing by Cedar Grove (Sheboygan County) on 19 May 1964 gives some indication of the length of the spring migration.

By the time nesting starts, these birds will have staked out territories in every marsh and spilled over into pastures and fallow fields in great abundance. The accompanying BBS map shows how numerous this bird has become. It is by all odds the most common bird in Wisconsin in summer. The map also shows how the density decreases as the birds move northward into the more heavily forested regions. South of a line from Hudson to Marinette this is the most numerous species on 30 of 40 transects and second only to the House Sparrow on 5 others. North of this line it is outnumbered by some of the forest birds, but is still common enough to be the most numerous species on 9 of the remaining 30 transects.

Information on nesting habits can be gleaned from a study of the 358 nests reported to the North American nest-card project from 1965 to 1970. Most (196) nests were located in marshes, usually in marsh grass or low down in small shrubs. Another 41 nests were constructed in swamps or along the shore of a river or lake. There were 57 nests in fields, compared with 8 in woodland. In all, 308 nests were no more than 3 feet off the ground; the 50 that were higher up in trees and shrubs included one 25 feet up in a dead tree. Of the 316 active nests reported, there were 19 with five eggs or young, 146 with four, 82 with three, 34 with two, and 35 with one.

Since a given marsh may have 100 or more nesting pairs to begin with, a sizable amount of flocking takes place as the nesting season nears its end. Adults and young from adjacent areas join those flocks for daytime feeding and night-time roosting. These birds are a particular nuisance to farmers in August and September, partly because some flocks already number in the thousands, and partly because these birds are fond of corn in the soft milk stage. In former years farmers were encouraged to use strychnine to poison blackbirds as a means of improving crop production.

By late September the exodus of fall migrants begins. Birds leave the smaller marshes and either depart for the south or congregate in still larger flocks in the larger marshes. It is from these larger marshes that the huge "ribbons" of birds emanate in October and November.

Not all Red-wings leave Wisconsin in winter. Scattered individuals have been found in December and January even in some of the most northerly counties. Some rely on feeders, others forage around city and village dumps, but few of those individuals survive in the north. In the southern counties small flocks remain in marshes where open water is found and where nearby farms offer food. The survival rate of these flocks is higher. From 1955 to 1958 Madison had sizable wintering flocks consisting of 3,000–20,000 birds. On the CBC since 1960, flocks of 1,000 or more have been noted in Pierce, La Crosse, Dane, and Kenosha counties.

Eastern Meadowlark (*Sturnella magna*)

STATUS. Abundant migrant south and east; common migrant west and north. Common summer resident south and central; fairly common summer resident north. Uncommon winter resident south and central.
HABITAT. Open grassland and cropland.
MIGRATION DATES. *Spring:* early March to mid-April. *Fall:* mid-September to early November.
BREEDING DATA. Nests with eggs: 1 May to 16 July. Clutch size: 4–6 eggs.
WINTER. Occasionally present north to Pierce, Outagamie, and Marinette counties.
PORTRAIT. *Birds of Wisconsin:* Plate 74.

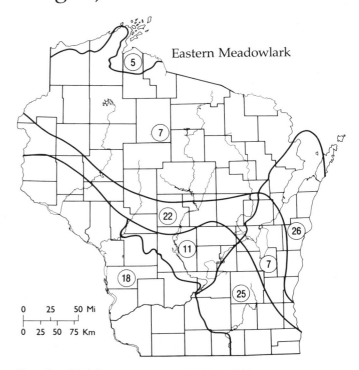

Breeding Bird Survey, averages 1966 to 1980

Eastern Meadowlarks are among the first migrants to arrive each spring. Originally, when most of Wisconsin was forested, this species was common only in the open grasslands in the south but was present in other portions of the state wherever suitable openings existed. In the latter half of the nineteenth century, as open areas replaced forest, this bird spread widely throughout the entire state. In the northern counties where forests still predominate, numbers have remained moderately low; but almost any grassland opening of 20 or more acres is likely to have its pair of these colorful whistlers each summer.

In the western and southern counties this bird has been overshadowed by the invasion of the Western Meadowlark during the past 60 years; yet, even though the Western outnumbers the Eastern south of a line from St. Croix Falls to Wausau to Sheboygan, the Eastern remains common in most areas. North of this line and south of the northern forests, the Eastern continues to outnumber its prairie-oriented relative.

The first nonwintering males are occasionally detected in late February, but they usually arrive by 10 March in the southern counties, with general arrivals a week later. They gradually work their way northward as melting snows permit, reaching the northern areas soon after 1 April.

Confusion between Eastern and Western Meadowlarks, frequent when the birds are silent, is usually dispelled quickly when the song or call note is heard. With the exception of a few rare instances when birds have been known to utter an "intermediate" song, the vocal quality and tonal pattern of the Eastern and Western songs are clearly discernible. Equally separable are the call notes: the "dzeep" of the Eastern and the "chupp" of the Western.

Nesting activity starts in late April with nest construction in pastures and meadows. Nests are built on the ground where old grass is dense enough to provide substantial covering for the nest structure. The accompanying BBS map clearly shows the summer distribution to be statewide. Yet in parts of the northern counties there are extensive areas where suitable habitat is lacking. There are BBS transects in Burnett, Ashland, Iron, and Vilas counties that have never recorded this species.

Throughout late July and all of August one would never dream that this is a common species unless one were afield in the earliest daylight hours. No longer do the birds frequent the road shoulders; no longer do the males sing from the fence posts and utility wires. A bit of song may be heard near dawn, but the birds remain largely silent and out of sight. Some flocking takes place during this period, but the flocks are rarely visible to the roadside birder.

It is mid-September when the birds are again lively as migration gets under way. Migration is not as pronounced in fall as in spring, but a peak is generally reached around 1–10 October in the northern counties and 15–25 October in the south. A few birds remain in the north through the 25th, while in the south the last migrants leave by 5 November. Francis Zirrer (MPM files), writing about his home area in Rusk and

Sawyer counties, stated: "During the blizzard of October 21–22, 1936, when about two feet of snow fell, an enormous number of meadowlarks perished. A farmer from Barron County told me that in one field of about two acres he plowed under more than 30 meadowlarks." Both species of meadowlark were probably affected.

Small numbers remain on farms in the southern counties throughout the winter, usually relying on fresh manure spreadings for food when snow covers the fields. The relative numbers of wintering Easterns and Westerns is not known. Observers generally report simply "meadowlark sp.?" Since the birds are usually silent and their plumage characteristics are similar, sure identification is rarely possible. A bird that survives the winter will often reveal its specific identity with call notes or song fragments on warm days in February before spring migrants arrive. Ob-

servers have reported wintering Easterns as far north as Pierce, Outagamie, and Marinette counties. Unidentified meadowlarks have also been noted as far north as Ashland, Langlade, and Door counties, and the probabilities are high that most of these are Easterns.

The statewide numbers of "meadowlark sp." appearing on the CBC have been as high as 287 (1974) and 155 (1975). This has decreased significantly to 4 (1979), 11 (1980), and 4 (1981). Likewise, BBS figures show a pronounced decline since 1976. Between 1966 and 1976 the number of Easterns varied between 13 and 18 individuals per transect per year. Figures slumped to 10–11 during the period 1977–1980. Prolonged deep snow south of Wisconsin in the winter of 1976–1977 is one suspected cause for the decline. The 1981–1983 average rose to 13–14.

Western Meadowlark (*Sturnella neglecta*)

STATUS. Abundant migrant south and west; common migrant east and north. Abundant summer resident south and west; common summer resident east; fairly common summer resident north. Uncommon winter resident south and central.

HABITAT. Open grassland and cropland.

MIGRATION DATES. *Spring:* early March to mid-April. *Fall:* mid-September to early November.

BREEDING DATA. Nests with eggs: 28 April to 16 July. Clutch size: 4–6 eggs.

WINTER. Occasionally present north to St. Croix, Chippewa, and Winnebago counties.

PORTRAIT. *Birds of Wisconsin:* Plate 74.

From a virtually unknown stranger to one of the 10 most abundant breeding birds in Wisconsin: this is the dramatic story of the Western Meadowlark during the last 100 years. It was known as a breeder in St. Croix County by 1883 (Franklin H. King 1883) and in Dunn County by 1889 (J. N. Clark [Buss and Matteson 1955]), but Kumlien and Hollister (1903) spoke of it only as a fall migrant in the southeastern part of the state. The progressive spread of this bird during the next 50 years has been well told by Lanyon (1953a, b). At that time he delineated the edge of this bird's common-and-regular occurrence as a line from St. Croix Falls southeast to Waupaca, northeast to Oconto, and south just west of the Lake Michigan shore. Numerous instances of less common occurrence had been recorded north and east of that line,

Breeding Bird Survey, averages 1966 to 1980

but 11 northern counties still had had no reports.

Now, 30 years later, this species has established itself in suitable habitat in the Superior-Ashland areas. The line of common and regular occurrence may be drawn from Ashland southeast to Antigo, then east to include Washington Island and the Lake Michigan shore. Records exist for every county except Florence.

Along with its spread across the state, this songster built up tremendous populations in the heavily cropped farmlands. The BBS through 1976 included 14 transects that regularly produced over 40 individuals per transect each year. These transects pass through heavily cropped farmland, highly favored by this bird. Whereas the Eastern Meadowlark shows a preference for untilled pasture, particularly lowlands where soil moisture is higher, the Western tends to concentrate on drier upland cultivated lands—particularly grainfields. The exceptions to this general rule are numerous, and there are many vantage points from which it is possible to hear both species simultaneously. But the increase in agricultural development throughout the state is undoubtedly a key factor in the phenomenal spread of the Western.

Some observers have suggested that the Western is gradually replacing the Eastern throughout the state. Insofar as more and more grassland has given way to the plow, this may be partly true. In St. Croix County, where the Western probably gained its first foothold in Wisconsin, I estimate that the Western outnumbers the Eastern at least 50:1. According to BBS figures, the Western now outnumbers the Eastern south of a line from Grantsburg to Sheboygan. Yet the Eastern remains a common species throughout most of the state; and as long as the dairy industry continues to require extensive unplowed pasture, the Western is not likely to replace its counterpart entirely.

BBS results also point to a dramatic decline in summer populations, especially since 1976. Statewide, average numbers of individuals per transect per year were stable at between 28 and 31 through 1973, then experienced a mild drop to 25 or 26 for the next 3 years. Averages then sagged to 15–18 (1977–1978), 11 or 12 (1981–1982), and 5 or 6 (1984–1989). Suspected factors contributing to the decline include heavy, prolonged snow and cold in the wintering range during the winter of 1976–1977, and the conversion of considerable pasture and small-grain land to corn production. If this trend continues, the Western Meadowlark will soon lose its position as one of the 10 most numerous summer species and its "abundant" classification.

The two meadowlarks follow a similar timetable throughout the year. First arrivals generally reach the state by 10 March; but whereas the Eastern is moving nearly due northward from its wintering grounds, the Western is moving in a northeasterly direction from its wintering grounds in the Southwest. During years when the west-central counties have little snow remaining in early March, first arrival dates for the Western may match those of the southernmost counties; in years when snow cover remains far into March, arrivals are delayed.

Nesting patterns for the two meadowlarks are similar. Dates for earliest and latest nestings are nearly identical. Nest sites and construction show no significant variation. The eggs are indistinguishable, the size of the usual clutch is the same, and both species experience considerable cowbird predation.

The fall migration period (15 September–5 November) is similar. The early October peak usually subsides before the first snowfall in the northern sections, while in the south and west numbers drop off sharply during the last week of October.

The winter status is not well known because most meadowlarks are not seen clearly enough to make specific identification possible. But wintering meadowlarks have been found in the southern counties every winter, and frequently in some of the central counties as well. Birds positively identified as Western have been noted as far north as St. Croix, Chippewa, and Winnebago counties. The suspicion is that unidentified wintering birds in Polk, Burnett, and Barron counties were also Westerns. Much research needs to be carried out to determine the winter range of our meadowlarks.

Yellow-headed Blackbird (*Xanthocephalus xanthocephalus*)

STATUS. Fairly common migrant. Fairly common summer resident south and central; uncommon summer resident north. Rare winter resident south and east.

HABITAT. Shallow marsh. Open cropland.

MIGRATION DATES. *Spring:* mid-April to late May. *Fall:* early August to mid-October.

BREEDING DATA. Nests with eggs: 14 May to 5 July. Clutch size: usually 4 eggs; occasionally 2–5.

WINTER. Rarely present in December and January north to La Crosse, Outagamie, and Brown counties. Three February records.

PORTRAIT. *Birds of Wisconsin:* Plate 75.

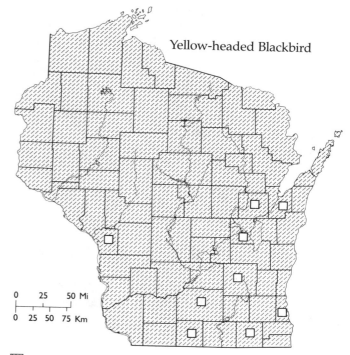

Yellow-headed Blackbird

⬚ Summer range
☐ Early December to late February

Records since 1960

Kumlien and Hollister (1903) wrote, "In some sections of the state the yellow-head seems to be totally absent, while on certain lakes it breeds abundantly." This statement is equally true 85 years later.

That is not to say that populations have not fluctuated significantly during the twentieth century. Kumlien and Hollister (1903) described the bird as "becoming more common in localities where it was once almost unknown." Ellarson (1950) gathered information suggesting that populations expanded until 1920, then decreased—especially during the drought-stricken 1930s. The 1940s brought some recovery.

The Yellow-head colonies known to Ellarson in 1950 were concentrated mostly east of a line from Madison to Oconto. Beyond this line there were nesting groups along the Mississippi River marshes between La Crosse and Alma and at isolated spots in Dunn, Burnett, Oneida, Vilas, and Forest counties. Unknown to Ellarson, nesting had begun on the prairie ponds in St. Croix County by 1936 (L. Hope; MPM files).

There has been considerable expansion since 1950. With the summer range pattern the accompanying map shows those regions where nesting colonies persist each year. With breeding symbols it also points to other counties where colonies have appeared from time to time, but have not established themselves over a lengthy period of years. Only in the southwest and in portions of the north-central region have Yellow-heads been absent.

Rarely is an isolated individual or pair reported. At one extreme, observers have noted a few colonies of 100 or more pairs in such widely separated areas as St. Croix, Dodge, Waukesha, Winnebago, and Brown counties; at the other extreme, a few colonies have numbered only three or four pairs. Historically speaking, colonies have shown considerable fluctuation in size. The drainage of a marsh has sometimes led to the disappearance of a colony altogether. The erection of dams along the Mississippi and Wisconsin rivers, creating extensive flowages with occasional marshy edges, has offered new habitat attracting incipient colonies. Sometimes the increase or decrease of a colony has had no discernible explanation.

Ornithologists who have studied the nesting habits of the Yellow-head have had to do so with hip boots or boat. The nests are usually built 1–3 feet above open water, firmly attached to sturdy cattails. Extensive studies of 242 nests by H. A. Mathiak in 1969 (pers. comm.) showed 12 with five eggs, 149 with four, 46 with three, 29 with two, and 6 nests with one egg each. Eggs are generally brown-spotted, grayish white, and laid in rather deep nests, which are apparently free of cowbird parasitism.

Most birds arrive on the nesting grounds during the first 3 weeks of May, but a few males turn up by 15 April. Exceptionally early were individuals on 28 March (1985, Dodge, W. K. Volkert), 29 March (1980, Dodge, J. H. Idzikowski) and 30 March (1963, Sheboygan, H. C. Mueller), and April birds on the 3rd (1976, Columbia, D. D. Tessen) and 5th (1972, Brown, E. D. Cleary; 1978, Columbia, R. M. Hoffman; 1981, Manitowoc, J. F. Steffen).

Once nesting is completed in early July, birds leave

the nesting marshes and join mixed flocks of black-birds feeding in corn- and grainfields in the vicinity. The gaudy yellow head feathers of the males are replaced with an attractive but much less conspicuous winter plumage. They also give up their ludicrous tin-ny "songs" and restrict their vocal efforts to a single call note.

The birds become progressively inconspicuous in August as residents molt and then depart. Few birds are seen in September, but have been noted in early October to indicate that 15 October can be roughly taken as a terminal date for fall migrants. Later October sightings have been recorded on the 20th (1979, Iowa, A. K. Shea), 22nd (1921, Sheboygan, C. S. Jung), and 24th (1941, Winnebago, N. M. Rogers).

Considering how far removed Wisconsin is from the bird's normal wintering range, it seems unlikely that this species would occur here during the cold, snowy winter months. For many years none were found between October and April. But one was spotted in Green County on 15 February 1948 (S. H. Richards). In 1952 one was found in Oshkosh three times between 12 January and 22 February and is presumed to have survived the winter (S. Wellso). Another survived the 1968–1969 winter at the Earl Fetterer feeder at Madison. The CBCs have recorded additional late December birds in La Crosse (1966), Outagamie (1979), Winnebago (1965), Brown (1972), Dodge (1961, 1969, 1979, 1981, 1983, 1987), Walworth (1969, 1979, 1981), and Milwaukee (1980) counties.

Rusty Blackbird (*Euphagus carolinus*)

STATUS. Common migrant. Casual summer resident. Uncommon winter resident southeast; rare winter resident elsewhere.

HABITAT. Wooded swamp. Open grassland and cropland.

MIGRATION DATES. *Spring:* mid-March to early May. *Fall:* mid-September to early November. *Extremes:* 26 May; 29 August.

BREEDING DATA. Three records: 11 May into June.

WINTER. Present every year north to Dane, Dodge, and Waukesha counties; rarely to Polk, Barron, Chippewa, Waushara, Outagamie, and Brown counties.

PORTRAIT. *Birds of Wisconsin:* Plate 77.

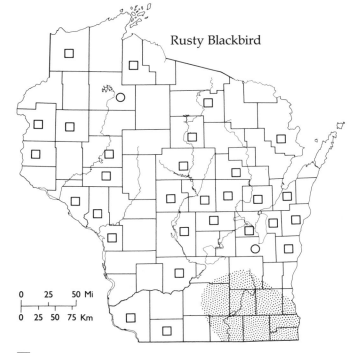

Rusty Blackbird

0   25   50 Mi
0 25 50 75 Km

▨ Winter range
○ 11 May to 16 June
□ Early December to mid-February

Records since 1960

Late in March, shortly after the general arrival of Red-winged Blackbirds and Common Grackles, flocks of Rusties begin to appear in the southern counties. There, first arrivals around 20 March are followed by general arrivals a week later. Numbers are greatest from 1 to 20 April, with birds tapering off so rapidly that few are noticeable after 25 April. In the northern areas the pattern is similar, but is delayed about 10 days; few individuals are seen before 30 March or after 5 May. Suspicions have arisen that several mid-May reports may involve cases of mistaken identity because of confusion with the similarly plumaged Brewer's Blackbird. Reliable observations occurred in Ashland County, however, on the 19th (1977, R. L. Verch) and 26th (1976, R. L. Verch).

Spring migrants usually travel in flocks of 10–150. Birds often frequent the edges of moist areas where they can alternate between trees and the ground. They sometimes feed and drink standing in or next to

shallow water. Occasionally observers have noted huge flocks of 500–1,000 in mid-April. But no longer is the species considered abundant, as it was by Kumlien and Hollister (1903) and Schorger (1931a).

The nesting evidence is perplexing because of possible confusion with the Brewer's. Currently the normal breeding range of the Rusty is entirely to the north of Wisconsin, while that of the Brewer's covers most of the state. But up until 1930 the Rusty was apparently more numerous than it is today, and may have nested within the state's borders more frequently.

According to available evidence, the Rusty must be considered a very rare breeder. Kumlien and Hollister (1903) recorded a set of eggs collected at Milton (Rock County) in June 1861 by Thure Kumlien. On 11 May 1961 George Henseler located two nests 8 feet up in black spruces in Fond du Lac County, one with three eggs and one with four downy young (MPM files). On 16 June 1961 Kate Fuller found a pair in a spruce swamp in Sawyer County but found no evidence of nesting. In each case the observer was well aware of the possibility of confusion with the Brewer's.

By the time these northerners reappear as fall migrants in late September, flocks of resident blackbirds are already large. The first fall visitors appear in the northern counties around 15 September, are most numerous from 1 to 20 October, and are largely gone by the end of October. In the southern counties the time-

table is 10 days later, except that when early November is unusually warm, sizable flocks may remain until cold weather hits later in the month. As in spring, this bird travels almost exclusively in flocks. Sometimes these flocks mix with flocks of Red-winged Blackbirds, Common Grackles, and Brown-headed Cowbirds. More often the flocks remain by themselves, numbering up to 1,000 or more, and concentrate more on the edges of swamps than in grainfields. Exceptionally early were appearances on 29 August (1976, Oconto, D. D. Tessen), 4 September (1973, Outagamie, A. S. Bradford), and 6 September (1977, Oneida, P. R. Engberg).

A few remain for the winter months—some mixed with larger flocks of Red-winged Blackbirds in the southern counties, some as scattered individuals where streams provide open water. Occasional individuals have been found in flocks of House Sparrows near farm buildings. CBC records since 1960 have averaged 61 individuals on seven counts per year. Observations have occurred frequently north to La Crosse, Outagamie, and Manitowoc counties, but rarely north to Douglas, Ashland, Oneida, and Marinette counties.

Brewer's Blackbird (*Euphagus cyanocephalus*)

STATUS. Fairly common migrant. Fairly common summer resident central and north; rare summer resident south. Rare winter resident south and central.
HABITAT. Open grassland and cropland. Old field.
MIGRATION DATES. *Spring:* early April to mid-May. *Fall:* late August to early October, occasionally to early November.
BREEDING DATA. Nests with eggs: 12 May to 2 July. Clutch size: usually 4 or 5 eggs; occasionally 3 or 6.
WINTER. Occasionally present north to Douglas, Ashland, Marinette, and Door counties.
PORTRAIT. *Birds of Wisconsin:* Plate 77.

The range of the Brewer's Blackbird has undergone drastic changes over the past 100 years. Kumlien and Hollister (1903) knew it only as a rarity, with one breeding record and two additional specimens. Franklin H. King (1883) collected a specimen in Green Lake County in 1883. These authors conjectured that it might occur more frequently near the Minnesota border, but J. N. Clark failed to record it in Dunn County during the 1886–1902 period.

It was not until 1926 that observers began to report this species in numbers. That year, Earl Wright col-

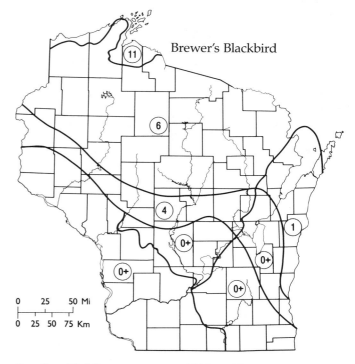

Breeding Bird Survey, averages 1966 to 1980

lected a male in Walworth County on 29 May, and John Main found a nest at Madison (Main 1926). Within the next 5 years considerable numbers turned up in the Wood-Adams-Portage county area and farther north in Polk and Sawyer counties. By 1933 the Brewer's had reached Waukesha (S. P. Jones), by 1935 Kenosha (E. G. Wright) and Price (L. W. Wing) counties, and in 1937 it had begun nesting at Oconto (C. H. Richter; MPM files).

Although it would appear that the Brewer's had swept across the state in the short span of 11 years, the range expansion probably took somewhat longer. Roberts (1932) gives 1919 as the first date for the Minneapolis region, but the bird was well established in other parts of Minnesota during prior years. Small colonies could easily have started in both the Wood-Adams-Portage county region and the Polk-Sawyer-Washburn county region by 1920 or before, and have escaped notice because Wisconsin had virtually no ornithologists visiting those areas at the time. Since the bird was already rather common near Hayward (Sawyer County) in 1927 and had an estimated population of 500 in the Wisconsin Rapids (Wood County) region by 1931, the likelihood is that these colonies were established well before the 1926 date of first recording.

An examination of June BBS figures shows three significant features. First, the Brewer's is now well distributed all across the northern half of the state. Second, two of the three regions where the birds had established themselves by 1930, near Wisconsin Rapids and Hayward, remain in the species' most heavily populated territory. And finally, the third region established by 1930, in the southeastern counties, has not maintained its population. The bird was reported in Dane and Waukesha counties in small numbers each year until 1960, but has been reported in summer only on rare and irregular occasions in any of the southeastern counties since then. South of a line from La Crosse to Portage to Sheboygan the Brewer's is now no more than a rare summer resident.

It is in the southern counties, however, that first spring migrants are noted on or about 5 April. By 15 April birds are well spread out in the central counties, with the northern counties being populated by the 25th. Migration is heaviest from 15 April to 10 May. Although the migration period overlaps that of the similarly plumaged Rusty Blackbird, the Brewer's is marked by a strong preference for open pasture and plowed fields. Flocks of up to 50 birds have been reported, but spring flocks quickly break up once birds reach their nesting grounds.

In some of the western states this species nests in trees, but in Wisconsin it is known strictly as a ground nester. The nest may be placed at the base of a shrub or simply in a slight depression in the ground with minimal cover from nearby grass clumps. Cowbird parasitism is frequent.

Following nesting, the blackbirds wander about and gradually gather in migrating flocks. Flocks of up to 300 birds have been noted, mostly between 25 August and 15 September. D. D. Tessen observed a flock of 1,000 in Outagamie County on 5 September 1965. By the time the Rusty Blackbirds arrive at the end of September, virtually all the Brewer's have departed.

Wisconsin had no winter records until 1939 and only six before 1960. But since 1960 there have been over 60 CBC observations, plus several in January and February. Most of these have been sightings of single birds mixed in with small groups of other wintering blackbirds. Since 1962 Brewer's Blackbirds have been found on from one to seven CBCs annually except in 1973. There is no one portion of the state where the winter observations have clustered. In the northwest, observers have sighted birds in Douglas, Bayfield, Ashland, and Sawyer counties; in the northeast, birds have been found in Marinette, Brown, Outagamie, and Manitowoc counties. In the southwest, CBC observers have noted birds in La Crosse, Grant, Dane, and Rock counties; in the southeast, stragglers have been sighted in Dodge, Washington, Waukesha, and Walworth counties.

Common Grackle (*Quiscalus quiscula*)

STATUS. Abundant migrant. Abundant summer resident south and central; common summer resident north. Uncommon winter resident south; rare winter resident central and north.

HABITAT. Residential areas. Open cropland. Wooded swamp.

MIGRATION DATES. *Spring:* early March to late April. *Fall:* early September to early November.

BREEDING DATA. Nests with eggs: 15 April to 25 June. Clutch size: usually 4 or 5 eggs; occasionally 3–7.

WINTER. A few birds present every year north to St. Croix, Chippewa, Portage, and Brown counties; occasionally present north to Douglas, Bayfield, Ashland, Oneida, Marinette, and Door counties.

PORTRAIT. *Birds of Wisconsin:* Plate 78.

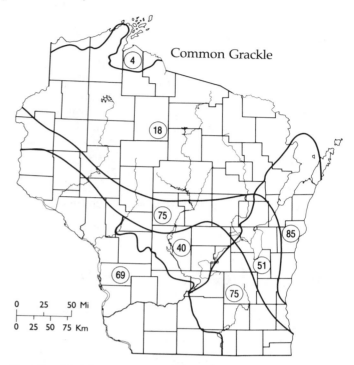

Common Grackle

Breeding Bird Survey, averages 1966 to 1980

For people living in heavily populated urban and suburban areas, the Common Grackle is often the first spring arrival to be noted. The first spring grackle may be preceded by the first Red-winged Blackbird and Killdeer, but these prefer a rural setting. The first grackles go immediately to the residential spruces and pines that have provided good nesting habitat in previous years.

Banding evidence indicates that the migrants coming to Wisconsin have wintered in the southern states due south or slightly to the west of us. Banders Rossman, Hoffmann, and MacBriar have reported a series of recoveries in which six of their birds turned up the following winter in Mississippi, three in Louisiana, three in Arkansas, and one in Oklahoma.

Arrivals in March spread across the state as rapidly as receding winter weather permits. By early April first arrivals have reached most parts of the state, and large numbers have dispersed over the southern counties. By late April the spring migration is not only completed, but nesting activity has begun.

Most Wisconsinites know this species as a colony nester in clumps of evergreens in city parks and residential areas. Such nests are common, with a particular grove of trees harboring 25 or more nests in one colony. The nests may be as low as 6 feet or as high as 40. Less well known is the variety of other types of nesting sites that have been recorded. Some grackles choose to live near the edges of rivers, ponds, and wooded swamps. Nests have been found atop river pilings or in holes in trees. C. H. Richter reported as many as 15 nests on the supporting beams of a single bridge. Birds sometimes choose to nest on buildings. In cities some have built nests high up on public buildings—pigeon-style—and on farms some have nested in barns where close company is kept with Barn Swallows. John Stierle (MPM files) once reported a nest 30 feet up atop a pile of lumber.

Petersen and Young (1950), studying nesting activity in a Madison park area, 1947–1949, determined that first eggs were laid between 15 and 21 April, with fledging following between 12 May and 12 June. Of 62 nests monitored, 34 (55%) produced at least one surviving fledgling.

The summer range is statewide, with birds found on all 70 BBS transects. But there is wide variation in abundance between the agricultural and forested regions. In the southern and central regions this is the fourth most numerous summer resident, exceeded in numbers only by the Red-winged Blackbird, European Starling, and House Sparrow. Although not nearly as numerous in the northernmost counties, and sometimes missed on certain forest-dominated BBS routes, the "crow blackbird" is a common species throughout most of northern Wisconsin.

Common Grackles exhibit varied habits of feeding as well as nesting, some of which are not exactly appreciated by humans. Farmers are not happy when they see their crops swarmed upon, and have often retaliated with the shotgun. Bird-lovers react adversely when they see Common Grackles invade the nests of other birds, break the eggs, dismember the nests, and occasionally destroy the parent birds. On the whole, however, the grackles feed so largely on such animal pests as cutworms, beetles, spiders, crickets, and various insects that the species is quite beneficial to agriculture. Occasionally these birds are seen beside streams, where they catch and eat minnows. As summer wanes, birds by the hundreds can be seen flying toward night roosts in swamps and marshes shortly before sunset. The sounds emanating from wetlands where these birds mix with Red-winged Blackbirds for the night is almost deafening.

Sizable flocks begin moving south in mid-September, with a very prolonged migration period lasting into early November. A flock of several thousand may descend upon a given area with much screeching, but be gone again within an hour. Or a flock may settle in a particular area for several weeks before moving on.

The remnant left behind to overwinter is never large. Only when mixed with occasional larger flocks of wintering Red-wings have flocks of 50–100 wintering grackles been recorded. But individuals have surprised many people by showing up in winter at such far-north locations as Superior, Ashland, Fifield, Tomahawk, Rhinelander, and Minocqua. Wintering individuals are usually found at feeders, around feed mills, in farmyards where loose grain may be available, or around landfills where birds evidently manage to scavenge successfully enough to keep themselves alive.

Brown-headed Cowbird (*Molothrus ater*)

STATUS. Common migrant. Common summer resident. Uncommon winter resident south.
HABITAT. All forest edge. All carr. Residential areas.
MIGRATION DATES. *Spring:* late March to mid-May. *Fall:* late July to mid-October.
BREEDING DATA. Eggs observed: 27 April to 18 July.
WINTER. Regularly present north to La Crosse, Dane, Dodge, and Waukesha counties; occasionally present north to St. Croix, Chippewa, Lincoln, Langlade, and Door counties.
PORTRAIT. *Birds of Wisconsin:* Plate 77.

Disgustingly common! This is the opinion which some birders have of the Brown-headed Cowbird. The "common" designation applies to all parts of the state and to a variety of habitats: fields and farms, forest edges, and residential regions. As a summer resident this bird has been recorded on all 70 BBS transects and shows a more even June distribution than almost any other species.

The "disgust" stems from its parasitic habit of laying eggs in the nests of other birds, often to the detriment of the host species. Sometimes the cowbird is content to add her egg to those already laid. At other times she removes the existent eggs and replaces them with her own. Kraus (1910) told of finding a Black-billed Cuckoo nest containing two cuckoo and two cowbird eggs. He removed the latter. Two days later when he revisited the nest, the two cuckoo eggs were on the ground broken, while the nest contained two fresh cowbird eggs.

Wisconsin has had no definitive studies to measure

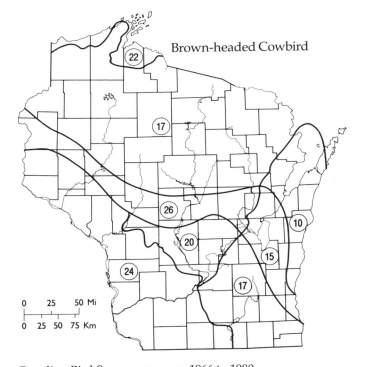

Breeding Bird Survey, averages 1966 to 1980

the success ratio of fledged young of host species after cowbird parasitism, but the suspicions are that the success level is very low. Schorger (1931a) mentioned observing an Indigo Bunting incubating three cowbird eggs and none of its own. He also found a Veery nest with two host eggs and five of the cowbird. Even when only one cowbird egg is added to the clutch of a host warbler or sparrow, it is usually the cowbird—alone—that fledges.

N. C. Otto (MPM files) related a typical experience involving a Yellow Warbler family. On 30 June two warbler eggs and one cowbird egg hatched. On 2 July one of the warbler infants died, apparently from lack of nourishment. On 4 July the young cowbird was moving about restlessly in the nest, causing serious overcrowding. On 5 July the tiny warbler was pushed out of the cup of the nest and barely managed to hold on to the outside edge. Later that day Mr. Otto placed a second empty nest just below the original nest and transferred the nestling cowbird to the second nest while leaving the warbler in the first nest. On 6 July the parent visited both nests and fed both babies, but the young cowbird protested so vigorously when the parent stopped to feed the young warbler that the parent tended more and more to care primarily for the cowbird. By 7 July the baby cowbird was getting all the attention and the young warbler died.

It is only in April, May, and June that the cowbird is common. Its first appearance in spring in the southern counties is usually during the last week of March. Sizable flocks of males are seen in early April, but generally it is in the last half of April that males and females blanket the state. Some cowbird migration still is in progress during mid-May.

As July progresses these birds are less and less in evidence. Some of the later hatching young are still being fed by foster parents, while earlier hatching young have joined flocks of mature males and females. Those birds are usually silent and are often overlooked in larger flocks of other blackbirds. Some birds begin their fall migration in July, for there are many July fall arrival dates in states south of the regular breeding range. Yet flocks continue to be seen in Wisconsin off and on through August, September, and early October. The fall flight is leisurely, prolonged, and inconspicuous.

The number of birds that linger to overwinter was very small until 1965. Since then, Horicon Marsh in Dodge County has had a sizable wintering flock each year, with an exceptional count of 2,000 in 1967–1968. Flocks of 25 or more have also been frequent at Madison, Milton (Rock County), and Milwaukee. Each December, Brown-headed Cowbirds are found on 10–17 CBCs. Only in the southeastern counties are birds recorded every year. Scattered CBC records have come from counties north to St. Croix, Eau Claire, Portage, Waupaca, Outagamie, and Manitowoc—on rare occasions, even farther north. Most northerly are observations in Douglas (1974), Ashland (1977), Sawyer (1966), Lincoln (1975), Langlade (1971), and Door (1966, 1974) counties.

Orchard Oriole (*Icterus spurius*)

STATUS. Uncommon spring migrant south and central; rare spring migrant north; rare fall migrant south and west. Uncommon summer resident west, south, and east.

HABITAT. Southern silver maple–elm forest. Farmsteads. Savanna.

MIGRATION DATES. *Spring:* late April to early June. Rarely seen after 15 August. *Extremes:* 26 April; 14 October.

BREEDING DATA. Nests with eggs: 23 May to 23 June. Clutch size: 4 or 5 eggs.

PORTRAIT. *Birds of Wisconsin:* Plate 76.

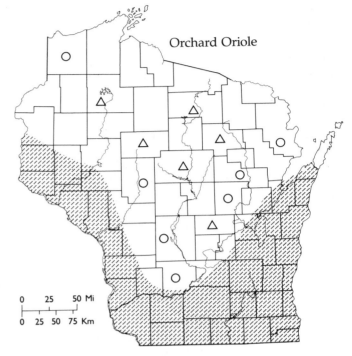

Orchard Oriole

0   25   50 Mi

0   25 50 75 Km

▨ Summer range
△ Late April to early June
○ Mid-June to mid-August
▽ Late August to late September

Records since 1960

Since 1960, June or July observations of Orchard Orioles have occurred in over half of Wisconsin's counties. But in no part of the state can this bird be considered common—or even fairly common. Some June records are of wanderers that are present one day and gone the next. Some birds maintain summer residency (probably breeding) in a given area one year but do not return in subsequent years. It is in the counties adjoining the Mississippi and lower St. Croix rivers that this melodious singer is found most consistently, year in and year out. To a lesser extent, scattered individuals or pairs frequent isolated spots in the southernmost tier of counties. A few summer residents are found nearly every year in the Fox River valley or along the eastern shore north to Marinette and Door counties, but the species is decidedly rare in central and northern Wisconsin.

This is similar to the pattern described in earlier Wisconsin literature, but according to Hoy (1853b), Kumlien and Hollister (1903), Cory (1909), and Cahn (1913), the Orchard Oriole was once apparently more common in southern counties than it is today. Kumlien and Hollister surmised that this species was increasing and extending its range northward toward Lake Superior. This prediction has not materialized, although the bird reaches a comparable latitude in parts of Minnesota, and there have been three Douglas County records in 1966 and 1969.

If the residents of every well-shaded farm dwelling recognized the rich warbling song of the Orchard Oriole, significantly more records might exist. Now that orchards are heavily sprayed, the orioles no longer find a sufficient supply of insect life for food there. Instead, they have taken to the tall shade trees around farm dwellings and in the outskirts of residential areas. The song is a prolonged warble, suggestive of the song of the Purple Finch. Song recognition is helpful, for the songster—either an adult male or a male still in immature plumage—is often concealed in the foliage.

The song is most likely to be heard from 10 May to 5 June. Only three April arrival dates are known: the 26th (1975, Kenosha, R. R. Hoffman), 27th (1969, Milwaukee, M. F. Donald), and 30th (1986, Ozaukee, R. H. Sundell). Arrivals in the main nesting range usually occur between 10 and 15 May. It is between 15 May and 5 June that occasional wanderers to northern locales have been recorded: Sawyer (1979), Taylor (1980), Marathon (1980), Langlade (1972), and Oneida (1978) counties.

Recent nesting data are sparse. Because the basketlike structures lie far out on the higher branches, it is not easy to determine their contents. Two recent nests have contained four eggs apiece, and this is probably the usual clutch. Cowbird parasitism is frequent.

Few of these birds are seen beyond 15 August. Observers within the wintering range have noted that the Orchard Oriole may be present on the wintering grounds 8 months of the year. Hence, the handful of September records in Wisconsin must be considered exceptional. Early September sightings have been made on the 1st (1967, Racine, N. Barkley), 2nd (1984, Waukesha, F. Broerman), and 7th (1933, Waukesha,

W. E. Scott; MPM files). Late September records have come on the 23rd (1973, Rock, E. Brakefield) and 27th (1963, Dane, T. L. Ashman; 1972, La Crosse, J. R. Rosso). Most remarkable was Murl Deusing's 14 October 1943 find in Milwaukee.

Northern Oriole (*Icterus galbula*)

Formerly Baltimore Oriole

STATUS. Common migrant. Common summer resident. Rare winter resident south.
HABITAT. Residential areas. Farmsteads. Deciduous forest.
MIGRATION DATES. *Spring:* early to late May. *Fall:* early August to mid-September.
BREEDING DATA. Nests with eggs: 24 May to 28 June. Clutch size: usually 4 eggs; occasionally 3.
WINTER. Rarely present in early winter north to Chippewa, Calumet, and Door counties.
PORTRAIT. *Birds of Wisconsin:* Plate 76.

For a brief 6-week period the Northern Oriole is one of the most conspicuous birds in residential areas throughout the state. In the southern counties this occurs from 1 May to 15 June; in the northern regions the period lasts from 15 May to 30 June. Unusually early or late springs rarely cause more than a week's deviation from these dates. But exceptionally early April sightings have occurred on the 2nd (1976, Brown, E. D. Cleary) and 10th (1954, Milwaukee, F. L. Hook).

The males arrive in a splash of color and a chorus of fluting that dominate the bird scene. Many other spring migrants arrive at the same time, but few catch the eye and ear of the casual observer as do these orioles. The bulk of the males follow close upon the first arrivals, and the females also put in an almost immediate appearance. So rapidly does pairing take place that nest-building has sometimes been observed by 15 May. Banding studies show that individuals often return to exactly the same spot year after year.

The breeding range is statewide. Vanderschaegen (1981b) described this species in Forest, Vilas, and Oneida counties as a "fairly common summer resident of spotty distribution." Commentators for other portions of the state—past and present—have been unanimous in calling the species common. It occurs on all 70 BBS transects in June and is most numerous in the western and west-central regions.

Several observers expressed concern that Northern Oriole populations might suffer when elms fell prey

Northern Oriole

Breeding Bird Survey, averages 1966 to 1980

to Dutch elm disease, spreading across the state since the early 1950s. Previous to this time, the species' preference for elms had been clearly indicated. Alvin Peterson (1947a), censusing oriole nests in trees in La Crosse County one winter in the early 1940s, determined that 60 of 104 Northern Oriole nests (57%) had been constructed in American elms, with another 29 in silver maples and cottonwoods. Buss and Mattison (1955) conducted studies of oriole nests in Dunn County in 1942 and 1947. They calculated that 369 of 425 nests (87%) were located in American elms, with another 46 in silver maples and cottonwoods. Although no concerted studies were made in the late 1970s, when large numbers of elms succumbed to the disease, many individuals have pointed to the bird's successful adaptation to other shade trees. Results from the 70 BBS transects scattered throughout the state indicate that populations continue to remain stable.

The usual complement of four young make for a full, well-laden nest. It is between the first and second weeks of life that the baby orioles are particularly noisy, making noticeable a nest that hitherto had been well concealed in the foliage. A few nests have been reported as low as 3–6 feet above the ground. But most are 15–30 feet up, and three nests have been reported an estimated 60 feet up in tall elms.

Once the young fledge and learn to care for themselves, the birds are no longer conspicuous. The Northern Oriole is one of the first birds to diminish its singing in June. By the time the young fledge during the latter half of June, little parental song remains, and the birds' movements are largely concealed in the canopy of nearby shade trees.

Although the birds are relatively quiet in July, they remain in the area and become a bit more active in August. The first migrants are on the move before mid-August. Migration is strongest during the last 2 weeks of August; by 10 September all but a few late stragglers have departed. Late television tower casualties were noted at Eau Claire on 21 September 1963 and 1 October 1965 (C. A. Kemper).

Before 1950, records beyond early October were unknown in Wisconsin. Then in 1952 Mary Donald spotted an oriole in Milwaukee on 7 November. MPM personnel collected the bird on the 11th (*Pass. Pigeon* 15:39). This proved to be a bird of the western race *bullockii*, the only individual of this race to have been identified in Wisconsin.

Late November and December sightings have come with increasing frequency: seven in the 1960s, nine in the 1970s, five in the 1980s. Presumably these birds have all succumbed to cold and snow after the CBC period in late December. One remarkable individual came frequently to Irene Jack's feeder at Cassville (Grant County) between 7 January and 14 February 1958 before falling victim to cold and snow (pers. comm. to O. J. Gromme).

Family **Fringillidae:** Finches

Rosy Finch (*Leucosticte arctoa*)
Formerly Gray-crowned Rosy Finch

STATUS. Accidental. One record.
HABITAT. Normally mountain meadows (summer), residential areas (winter).

This vividly marked visitor from the Rocky Mountains appeared among a flock of Evening Grosbeaks at the John Russell feeder 5 miles north of Menomonie (Dunn County) on 19 February 1981. For 20 minutes it fed on the ground while Russell (pers. comm.) took copious notes and made a sketch of the stranger. "It had a distinctive gray crown with a black spot on its forehead. Its body—including chin, throat, breast, back and sides—was a rosy tan in color. The belly, especially around the leg area, appeared to be a brighter pink. The bird was slightly smaller and slimmer than the grosbeaks. It was larger than a Purple Finch, a frequent visitor but not in company with the bird in question."

The Rosy Finch was not seen the following day but was present off and on for 2 hours on 21 February, at which time Russell took stills and motion pictures. Then after a 4-week absence, it reappeared on 17 March. The following day it was observed by Janine Polk and myself, and photographed by Polk and Richard Robbins (*Pass. Pigeon* 44:44).

An individual of this species had previously been present in Minneapolis, Minnesota, in mid-January 1981. Only rarely has the species engaged in extralimital wandering, and records east of the Mississippi River are known only from Michigan, Ohio, and Maine.

Pine Grosbeak (*Pinicola enucleator*)

STATUS. Uncommon migrant north; rare migrant south. Casual summer visitant north. Uncommon winter resident north; rare winter resident south. Irregular.

HABITAT. Deciduous forest. Upland carr. Residential areas.

MIGRATION DATES. *Fall:* early November to mid-December. *Spring:* mid-February to late March.

BREEDING DATA. Two records.

WINTER. Irregularly present south to Buffalo, Jackson, Sauk, Dane, Rock, and Kenosha counties.

PORTRAIT. *Birds of Wisconsin:* Plate 73.

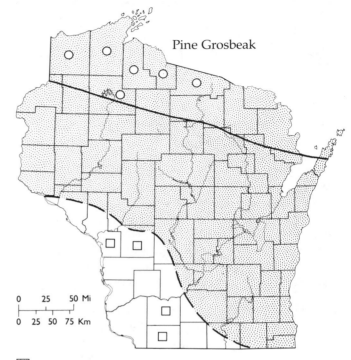

Pine Grosbeak

□ Winter range
  North of line: regular
  South of line: irruptive
○ Early July to late August
□ Late December to early February

Records since 1960

One wonders how often the presence of the Pine Grosbeak has been overlooked. The rosy plumage of the male would seem to stand out vividly against a white blanket of winter snow, but most of the birds that come to Wisconsin are in the duller plumage of the female and the immature. The birds are fully as large as the conspicuous Evening Grosbeak, but they feed in the sumac shrubbery and mountain ash trees with remarkably little movement. Here, they are concealed by their coloration, which is similar to that of the vegetation. Their plaintive three-note whistle is distinctive but so softly uttered that it can be heard for only a short distance. How many people are familiar with this call and can remember it over a span of several winters between one visit and the next?

Even allowing for the probability that many individuals escape notice, this species ranks among the rarer winter finches. In the northern forested areas a few birds can be seen almost every winter. They arrive in mid-November and rove the countryside in search of food. A few have been detected in October, the earliest on the 5th (1974, Price, M. Hardy), 12th (1957, Milwaukee, M. F. Donald), and 13th (1957, Brown, E. O. Paulson).

An arrival in late October or early November generally anticipates a larger influx than usual. Approximately one year in every two, some birds will move on into central Wisconsin, where they are observed in December, January, and February. Only rarely are such incursions extensive enough to encompass southern Wisconsin as well. But such was the case during the winter of 1977–1978, with CBC results showing this species present on 55 of 72 counts. The 1946 individuals recorded on those counts far exceeded the totals from any other year. More modest incursions occurred in 1961–1962, 1965–1966, 1968–1969, 1980–1981, and 1985–1986.

The rarity of this species in comparison with other winter finches is underscored by the number of birds counted per CBC for the entire state. At no time during the past 25 years have numbers of this species equaled numbers of Evening Grosbeaks, Common Redpolls, or American Goldfinches. Only in the flight years of 1961, 1965, 1968, 1977, and 1985 did Pine Grosbeaks outnumber Pine Siskins. The Pine Grosbeak population exceeds only that of the Red and White-winged Crossbills.

Birds usually travel in small flocks of 3–15. Flocks of 40–50 have been reported but are rare. Northern Wisconsin observers sometimes find the birds in young pine plantings, but more often this species prefers deciduous trees: maples, birches, and ashes, whose seeds prove attractive. In central and southern areas the preference for deciduous trees is even more pronounced. Birds show a particular fondness for sumac and mountain ash shrubbery wherever they are available. It is delightful to hear birds softly twittering when feeding; but more often than not, these birds feed in silence.

Most "pine-beaks" leave in late February or early

March, a few perhaps lingering until early April. Departures delayed into May have been reported eight times, the latest on the 15th (1955, Sheboygan, C. P. Frister; 1977, Ashland, R. L. Verch), 19th (1963, Brown, E. D. Cleary), 26th (1951, Washburn, F. Holman King), and 29th (1982, Douglas, R. J. Johnson).

Any summer records in Wisconsin must be treated as exceptional. Two records indicate breeding. On 5 May 1890 Schoenebeck (1902) found a nest in Bayfield County, but unfortunately details are lacking. On 3 August 1940 near Hayward (Sawyer County), Francis Zirrer (MPM files) made a careful study of a female

and four juveniles that appeared to be a family group. Not until 16 November that year did he see migrant Pine Grosbeaks from the north.

July observations include a pair on the 2nd (1981, Vilas, R. G. Spahn), a male on the 7th (1958, Ashland, R. B. Dryer), and a flock on the 25th (1963, Vilas, H. F. Young). One bird was observed on 1 August (1980, Iron, M. E. Butterbrodt) and one on 28 August (1964, Douglas, R. F. Bernard). During the summer of 1977, Temple and Harris (1985) noted birds on Devil's Island in Ashland County.

Purple Finch (*Carpodacus purpureus*)

STATUS. Common migrant. Fairly common summer resident north and central. Fairly common winter resident south and central; uncommon winter resident north.
HABITAT. Conifer swamp. Northern maple-hemlock-pine forest. Residential areas.
MIGRATION DATES. *Spring:* early April to mid-May. *Fall:* mid-September to mid-November.
BREEDING DATA. Nests with eggs: 24 May to 10 July. Clutch size: 3 or 4 eggs.
PORTRAIT. *Birds of Wisconsin:* Plate 82.

The presence of Purple Finches follows a more definite pattern than that of most finches. People who live in southern Wisconsin often have at least a few of these birds patronizing feeding stations in winter. Numbers begin to build around 1 April as migrants arrive from the south; the peak comes in late April, and birds move northward rapidly in early May. It is rare to see a Purple Finch between 15 May and 1 September. Migrants move south in earnest in late September, build to a mid-October peak, and move on out of the state in November, leaving behind a modest winter population.

Wisconsinites living in the northern region usually see no Purple Finches until 10 April. As the birds build to an early-May peak, their rich melodious songs are a joy to residents who have experienced a long snowy winter. Nesting activities and care of the young take up most of June and July. Some wandering takes place in August, but no sizable migration is expected until 15 September. The main push occurs from then until 25 October. In some years none are found after 15 November.

Although this is the usual pattern, there are significant departures from it. The most frequent exception occurs in winter when birds remain farther north

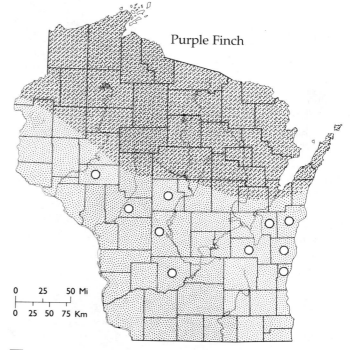

Purple Finch

0 25 50 Mi	
0 25 50 75 Km	

▨ Summer range
▣ Winter range
○ Early June to mid-August

Records since 1960

than usual. A study of CBC results for the past 25 years shows that birds were present in northern Wisconsin in significant numbers in 1958, 1960, 1962, 1964, 1971, 1978, and 1983. Numbers wintering in the southern counties also vary greatly from year to year. Since 1959 the average number of birds per CBC for the entire state has ranged from 29.8 in 1961 to a mere 3.6 in 1967. In 1958 the entire state experienced a tremendous influx, resulting in a CBC figure of 57 birds per count.

Deviations from the pattern in summer are also known. Observations on the June BBS have all taken place north of a line from Grantsburg southeast to Greenwood and east through Mosinee and Green Bay to Algoma. Nearly all nesting records are north of this line. But occasional summer observations have occurred in Polk, Eau Claire, Juneau, Fond du Lac, and Ozaukee counties. Late summer wanderings occasionally bring individuals to the southern counties in early August. Exceptional is the discovery of one in Dane County on 31 July (1949, S. D. Robbins).

The varied wanderings of this melodious finch have resulted in recoveries of Wisconsin-banded birds coast to coast. Individuals ringed in winter have been recovered within 6 months in Manitoba (6), Saskatchewan (1), and British Columbia (1). Fliers tagged in spring turned up the following winter in Arkansas (3), Kansas (1), Oklahoma (2), and Texas (1). Four others, banded in spring, were retaken the following spring in New Jersey, Pennsylvania, Connecticut, and Maine. A bird banded in New Hampshire on 23 August 1960 was retrapped in Chippewa County 7 months later (C. A. Kemper).

House Finch (*Carpodacus mexicanus*)

STATUS. Uncommon resident south and east.
HABITAT. Residential areas.
WINTER. Present north to Trempealeau, Marathon, Shawano, and Brown counties.

The westward spread of the House Finch, following its release in New York around 1940, rivals the spread of the House Sparrow in the 1870s and the European Starling in the 1910s. Cutright (1985) listed first state records for neighboring states as 1971 (Illinois), 1972 (Ohio), 1976 (Indiana, Michigan), 1978 (Kentucky, Missouri), 1980 (Minnesota), and 1982 (Iowa).

This colorful relative of the Purple Finch was added to the Wisconsin bird list in 1983, when an adult male visited the R. H. Sundell feeder near Cedarburg (Ozaukee County) on 27 and 28 March. It fed on sunflower seeds, scarcely 7 feet away from the observer,

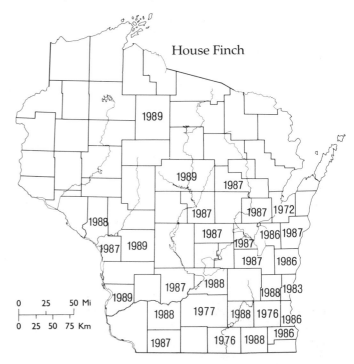

House Finch

Years of first county records

House Finch, 22 July 1989, Dane County (photo by S. J. Lang)

for 15 minutes on the 27th. It spent most of the following day in the same yard, serenading several observers with what Sundell described as "a distinctive rolling warble." Thorough documentation and a photograph validated this sighting.

The 1983 record was preceded by four sight observations that lacked the photographic evidence needed for first state records. On 20–21 January 1972 a male and female joined a flock of 100 Purple Finches at the

Francis Snyder feeder in Green Bay. After watching the birds on the 21st, Edwin Cleary wrote a complete description of the birds, including an account of the manner in which they were constantly harassed by the Purple Finches. How long the birds remained in the area is not known.

On 8 May 1976 a female appeared at Linda Safir's feeder in Brookfield (Waukesha County). Mrs. Safir's previous experience with this species in California and New Jersey helped clinch the identification. The bird was observed by means of binoculars at 15 feet for 5 minutes but was not seen thereafter.

There was an additional 1976 observation in Rock County (5 and 9 November, M. Stabb), followed by two records in 1977 in Dane County: a female on 19 February (R. Korotev) and a male on 15 April (T. De Boor). But observation periods were brief and the documentation was sketchy in each instance.

The first nesting records occurred in 1986. On 20 May F. N. Freese discovered a nest in Madison. Between 27 and 30 August, C. L. Strelitzer banded six recently fledged young in Milwaukee. Additional 1986 observations came from Racine, Sheboygan, and Calumet counties. In 1987 first sightings occurred in another 10 counties. These occurrences apparently come, not through any predictable migratory pattern, but from wandering at any season.

It is only a question of time before this handsome finch spreads through much of Wisconsin as both a wintering and a breeding species.

Red Crossbill (*Loxia curvirostra*)

STATUS. Uncommon migrant. Rare summer resident. Uncommon winter resident north; rare winter resident south. Irregular.

HABITAT. Oak–jack pine forest. Residential areas.

MIGRATION DATES. Observed most frequently between mid-October and mid-May. May be present at any season.

BREEDING DATA. Nests with eggs: 17 April to 9 June. Clutch size: 4 eggs.

PORTRAIT. *Birds of Wisconsin:* Plate 83.

Driving through Solon Springs (Douglas County) one June day, I noticed an area of pines with the nearby ground covered by fresh fallen cones. Thinking this might signify the presence of Red Crossbills, I stopped. Soon I heard the "kip, kip" call, and a group of four Red Crossbills took flight. Two weeks later, 150 miles farther east at Three Lakes, I again spotted cones beneath a pine tree, and subsequent investigation led to the sighting of two more birds.

Efforts to find crossbills are not always that successful. Other factors can explain fallen cones. Even if crossbills were responsible for the fallen cones, the birds could have stripped the cones in 15 minutes and long since left the area. Flocks of crossbills have often been known to invade a particular conifer in a residential area, strip the cones of seeds in a matter of minutes, then fly off and never return.

It is difficult to predict when Red Crossbills may show up in a given area. Most often they appear in late October and November, but this is no guarantee they will persist through the winter months. CBC records show wide variation in late-December popula-

Red Crossbill

0 25   50 Mi
0 25 50 75 Km

Irruptive summer range
Irruptive winter range

Records since 1960

tions. A heavy flight in 1960–1961 was followed by a complete absence on CBCs in 1961–1962. A strong influx in 1968–1969 was followed by a dearth in 1969–1970. The better-than-average totals of 1973–1974 were followed by only scant records the following year. When birds are present in winter in northern Wisconsin, they are likely to reach the central part of the state as well, but not necessarily the southern counties. Since 1968, observers have detected Red Crossbills on 20% of the northern counts, 21% of those in the central areas (between Highways 64 and 33), and 10% in the southern region.

Irruptions can occur at other seasons. In 1969 an incursion began in July, remaining noticeable through November before petering out. The most notable flight in recent years occurred in 1960–1961. Unusually large numbers began appearing in October, and the statewide CBC tally in December nearly doubled the highest number reported in any other Christmas period before or since. Large numbers were sustained through March and April, finally diminishing in early May, with a last straggler on 2 June. During that spring these birds spread out from their preferred conifers and were often found feeding on the ground beneath maple trees. Because many of these spring birds seemed unusually small, specimens were collected in Minnesota and Wisconsin. Some of these Red Crossbills proved to be of the *sitkensis* race normally resident in Alaska.

Little is known of the present-day breeding habits and density in Wisconsin. In other states and provinces this species has nested any time from January through August. In Wisconsin I know of only two instances of nests with eggs; 17 April and 9 June. But in 1980 a pair was observed carrying nest material on 13–15 March, with juveniles out of the nest observed in early May (Waukesha, J. E. Bielefeldt). Fledglings were found on 10 May 1978 (Portage, S. H. Krings). Kumlien and Hollister's (1903) mention of recently fledged young in April points to a very early spring nesting.

On 16 of the state's 70 BBS transects this bird has been recorded one or more years in June, but it is not found regularly on any transect. All routes on which the species has been located have been in the northern and west-central counties. There are occasional summer observations farther south, including vagrants in Dane (1 August 1975, N. R. Barger), Dodge (4 August 1973, H. A. Mathiak), and Milwaukee (22 July 1981, D. K. Gustafson) counties. The Red Crossbill may not nest in the state every year, but it is certainly a more widespread breeder than published records would indicate.

White-winged Crossbill (*Loxia leucoptera*)

STATUS. Uncommon migrant. Rare summer resident north. Uncommon winter resident north; rare winter resident south.

HABITAT. Conifer swamp. Upland spruce-fir forest. Residential areas.

MIGRATION DATES. Observed most frequently between early November and mid-February; observed occasionally between mid-August and mid-May, rarely in June and July.

BREEDING DATA. One record.

WINTER. Irregularly present south to Buffalo, Sauk, and Kenosha counties.

PORTRAIT. *Birds of Wisconsin:* Plate 83.

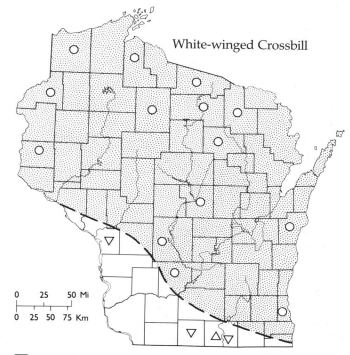

White-winged Crossbill

0   25   50 Mi
0 25 50 75 Km

▦ Irruptive winter range
△ Early March to late May
○ Early June to mid-August
▽ Late August to late November

Records since 1960

Anyone who does not recognize the call note is bound to find the White-winged Crossbill rare. Birds may fly over, but the observer will not be able to identify them. An observer may pass by spruce trees whose branches contain a flock of these feeding crossbills and fail to notice them because the birds feed with very little bodily movement. Even the person who recognizes the call note finds this to be one of the least numerous of winter finches.

From the time *The Passenger Pigeon* began publishing quarterly field notes in 1939 until 1954, this bird's status was indeed one of rarity. There were but 23 records in that 15-year span, only one of which came from south of the Clark-Wood-Juneau county region. Coverage in the northern counties was sparse during that period but in the south it was sufficient to warrant the conclusion that no major flight reached the central or southern counties.

A major flight developed in the autumn of 1954, beginning with October observations in Fond du Lac, Waupaca, Wood, and Vernon counties, then spreading in November and December south to Rock and Waukesha counties. The flight ended with a sighting in Dane County on 19 March 1955. Another major influx occurred in 1971–1972, again bringing birds to the southernmost counties.

The largest flight of all was the incursion that started with a 14 October 1977 observation and rapidly developed into a spectacular November flight that included flocks of 200 or more in Bayfield, Ashland, Barron, Columbia, and Ozaukee counties. Observers noted birds on half of the state's 72 CBCs that year, including phenomenal totals of 592 (Wausau) and 484 (Manitowoc). Although numbers dwindled thereafter, birds were still being seen through March. Numbers were not as great in a heavy flight in 1981–1982, but birds lingered into May in Waukesha, Sheboygan, and

Winnebago counties, and until 9 June in Milwaukee (M. Bontly).

The winters between invasions may be bleak. From 1968 through 1970 no White-winged Crossbills were recorded on any Wisconsin CBC. But nearly every autumn—usually in November—a few are found. They are fond of spruce and tamarack, and if they find sufficient food they linger through mid-March. With the exception of the phenomenal 1982 influx, observations beyond 15 April have occasional at best.

Only one positive nesting record exists. Schoenebeck (1902) procured three eggs from a nest 24 feet up in a spruce in Oconto County on 6 April 1894. The set now resides in the Carl Richter collection at the University of Wisconsin–Green Bay. Francis Dayton (MPM files) reported this species nesting in Ashland County but is indefinite about date and details. Although a few summer birds were noted in Bayfield County in 1919 and 1922, and in Iron County in 1947, these sightings were unusual. Between 1958 and 1968, however, this bird was recorded in the northernmost counties on 14 occasions. The summer of 1969 brought an additional six records, including flocks of 75 and 200 birds. June 1974 was exceptional, with individuals detected on the 7th (Juneau, S. D. Robbins) and 8th (Sauk G. W. Foster). Undoubtedly the White-winged Crossbill nests more frequently in the state than the records indicate, but because the nesting habits of this bird are very irregular, presence in summer is no sure indication of nesting.

Common Redpoll (*Carduelis flammea*)

STATUS. Common migrant. Accidental summer visitant. Common winter resident north and central; fairly common winter resident south. Irregular.
HABITAT. Deciduous forest. Old field. Residential areas.
MIGRATION DATES. Observed between early November and mid-April. *Extremes:* 26 August; 31 May.
PORTRAIT. *Birds of Wisconsin:* Plate 82.

There are winters, like those of 1969–1970 and 1977–1978, when the Common Redpoll outnumbers every other passerine on the Wisconsin CBC except the House Sparrow, European Starling, American Crow, Dark-eyed Junco, and American Tree Sparrow. There are other winters, like those of 1956–1957 and 1964–1965, when it is completely absent except for a mere trickle in the north. The favorite term for describing the status of the Common Redpoll is "irregular."

In some flight years birds congregate in huge swarms of 1,000 to 2,000 birds; they descend upon the snow-covered fields wherever weeds appear above the snow, play their version of "leapfrog" as they move from one patch of weeds to another, and defy anyone to make an accurate count of the numbers in a flock. In other flight years large flocks are rarely seen; but small groups of 10–30 birds will be present everywhere—woods, fields, even at residential feeders. In some flight years Common Redpolls are abundant in the northern counties but absent in the south. In others birds are equally numerous south and north.

In an invasion year the birds are likely to arrive in the north in late October or early November and blanket the entire state within a month. Exceptionally early are September sightings on the 22nd (1985, Taylor, S. D. Robbins), 23rd (1961, Eau Claire, S. D. Robbins), 25th (1968, Douglas, R. F. Bernard), and 28th (1957, Bayfield, D. A. Bratley), and August sightings on the 26th (1920, Vilas, C. S. Jung) and 30th (1981, Ashland, R. Maercklein).

Fields and pastures that have plenty of uncut weeds provide these birds with their favorite food. It is in such fields that the largest flocks are seen. Mixed with these flocks there are sometimes American Goldfinches, Dark-eyed Juncos, and American Tree

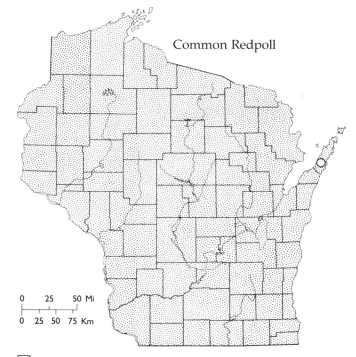

Common Redpoll

☐ Irruptive winter range
○ 27 June

Records since 1960

Sparrows; but often the flocks consist entirely of Common Redpolls. When snow becomes deep enough to cover the weeds, the redpolls may move farther south, or they may remain and rely upon tree seeds for food. Birches and tamaracks are particularly attractive to them.

The frequency of invasion years can be gauged by the number of Common Redpolls per location on the December CBC each year. Starting with 1955–1956, the first winter of statewide CBC coverage, the figures show:

1955–1956	133	1971–1972	128
1956–1957	0	1972–1973	6
1957–1958	78	1973–1974	35
1958–1959	7	1974–1975	7
1959–1960	73	1975–1976	102

1960–1961	1	1976–1977	7
1961–1962	60	1977–1978	118
1962–1963	5	1978–1979	3
1963–1964	19	1979–1980	1
1964–1965	3	1980–1981	40
1965–1966	161	1981–1982	97
1966–1967	2	1982–1983	3
1967–1968	1	1983–1984	12
1968–1969	111	1984–1985	2
1969–1970	134	1985–1986	60
1970–1971	3	1986–1987	73

These numbers suggest that this species may follow an every-other-year cycle. It is not apparent why this 2-year cycle would exist, or what causes a digression from the cycle such as the delay until 1968–1969 of the flight that would have been expected in 1967–1968, or until 1980–1981 of the 1979–1980 flight.

In noninvasion years birds rarely appear before 15 December or after 15 March, but—according to CBC results—they are almost as likely to be found in southern or central regions as in the north. Birds in small numbers have been found on one or more southern counts each year since 1970.

During invasion years large flocks head north between 10 and 31 March, with stragglers remaining through 15 April. Late-May departures have been detected on the 21st (1956, Brown, E. D. Cleary), 26th (1976, Ashland, R. L. Verch), 27th (1982, Taylor, S. D. Robbins), and 31st (1959, Oneida, W. L. Hilsenhoff; 1970, Sauk, D. D. Tessen). One astonishing summer record was established on 27 June (1973, Door, L. W. Erickson).

Hoary Redpoll (*Carduelis hornemanni*)

STATUS. Rare migrant. Rare winter resident.
HABITAT. Deciduous forest. Old field. Residential areas.
MIGRATION DATES. Observed between early November and mid-April. *Extremes*: 3 November; 26 April.
PORTRAIT. *Birds of Wisconsin*: Plate 82.

References to the presence of the Hoary Redpoll in Wisconsin before the 1940s are scant. The collecting of 30 specimens of this species from large flocks of Common Redpolls in Dunn County in the winter of 1895–1896 by J. N. Clark (1896b) has been widely cited. But existing literature shows only two additional state records in the nineteenth century and two more in the early part of the twentieth century. Three observations in the 1940s were followed by 14 in the 1950s, 30 in the 1960s, and 78 in the 1970s.

Increasing abundance? Not necessarily. Before 1950 attention focused on the identification of subspecies as well as species. With four races of *C. flammea* and two of *C. hornemanni* to identify, observers made little effort at identification without the specimen at hand. Only since 1940 have Wisconsin ornithologists developed a cautious confidence that the two recognized species can be separated in the field under favorable conditions. The increased number of records in the 1960s and 1970s probably reflects this growth in confidence rather than a growth in the Hoary Redpoll population.

Perhaps the confidence has now extended to the opposite extreme, with observers too ready to assume that any frosty-backed redpoll must be this species. Nine times out of 10, birds cannot be seen well

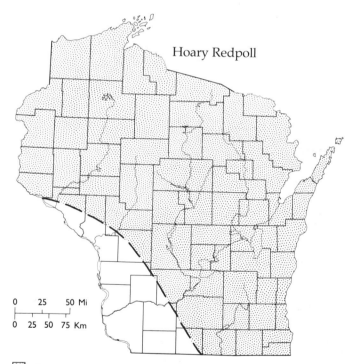

Hoary Redpoll

▨ Irruptive winter range

Records since 1960

enough to allow positive distinctions to be made between Common and Hoary Redpolls. Most of Wisconsin's records have come from observers' picking out single Hoaries in flocks of 100 or more Common Redpolls. On rare occasions as many as five Hoaries have been found within a single flock of Commons.

Most of the pre-1940 records involved collected specimens. Individuals were banded on 11 November 1968 (Manitowoc, B. N. Brouchoud), 8 April 1970 (Brown, M. M. Wierzbicki), 5 April 1972 (Portage, A. M. Baumgartner), and 15 February and 8 March 1978 (St. Croix, C. A. Faanes). Sight records have been infrequent before 15 December, but November dates include the 3rd (1968, Burnett, R. F. Bernard) and 20th (1955, Milwaukee, I. N. Balsom).

Records are widely distributed in all parts of the state from December through March but are most frequent in the northern and central counties. In the 1970s the number of observations varied from 9 to 23 per winter in the years of high Common Redpoll populations. Hoaries are scarcely ever observed in years of low Common Redpoll presence. Individuals have lingered into April through the 8th (1972, Outagamie, D. D. Tessen), 11th (1978, Price, M. Hardy), 14th (1972, Oconto, J. Woodcock), and 26th (1982, Ashland, R. L. Verch).

Pine Siskin (*Carduelis pinus*)

STATUS. Fairly common migrant. Uncommon summer resident north; rare summer resident central and south. Uncommon to fairly common winter resident. Irregular.

HABITAT. Conifer swamp. Upland spruce-fir forest. Residential areas.

MIGRATION DATES. *Spring:* mid-April to late May. *Fall:* mid-September to early November.

BREEDING DATA. Nests with eggs: 13 April to 30 May; nests with young to 21 June. Clutch size: 3 or 4 eggs.

PORTRAIT. *Birds of Wisconsin:* Plate 81.

The most spectacular flight ever recorded for the unpredictable Pine Siskin in Wisconsin occurred on 21 October 1969, when D. D. Berger estimated that over 50,000 small finches passed by the Cedar Grove Ornithological Station in Sheboygan County. There were some Common Redpolls, American Goldfinches, and Purple Finches among them, but most of the birds were Pine Siskins. Flocks in the hundreds were noted at many other Wisconsin locations. The previous summer had seen a phenomenal increase in June and July populations all across the northern third of the state. Numbers remaining for Wisconsin CBCs in late December were normal, because the huge flocks moved on, some penetrating to Florida and Texas.

More typically to be expected, however, are smaller groups, of fewer than 50 birds, first putting in an appearance in the northern counties by mid-September and in southern areas by the end of the month. Their presence is usually detected by the sound of their dainty wheezing call note and the sight of a couple of goldfinch-sized birds in flight. An observer who resides in spruce habitat may then be favored by a stopover of a flock of these brown-streaked visitors in the treetops. Peak numbers normally appear in October, with populations dwindling in early November.

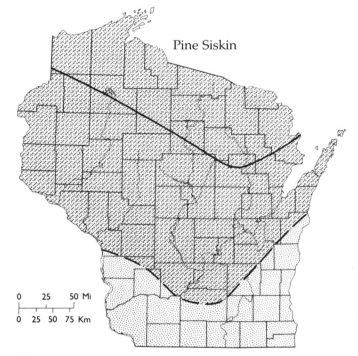

Pine Siskin

0   25   50 Mi

0 25 50 75 Km

▨ Summer range
    North of solid line: regular
    North of dashed line: irruptive
▧ Winter range

Records since 1960

Even in winters when most of the fall migrant Pine Siskins pass on to more southern climes, at least a few remain scattered here and there throughout much of the state. Since 1960 at least a few have appeared on central Wisconsin CBCs every year. On northern December counts they were missed only in 1970–1971 and 1972–1973. The winter of 1967–1968 was unusual, with birds abundant in the north, absent in the south.

CBC results show well the wide fluctuations of winter populations which are characteristic of this species. Between 1966 and 1975, individuals per count per year were down (between 1 and 8) one year, up (between 14 and 25) the next. But just when it appeared that a 2-year cycle could be predicted, 1977–1978 witnessed a huge increase; Pine Siskins were observed on 60 of 72 CBCs, with an average of 68 individuals per count. An even more massive flight developed 3 years later, with an average of 100 individuals per count.

The advent of backyard thistle-seed feeders has undoubtedly served to make siskins more conspicuous, if not more plentiful. Flocks of these little creatures that might have escaped notice in spruce trees frequent thistle-seed feeders in droves during the winter months.

If there has been no sizable influx of fall migrants, no return flight of consequence can be expected in spring. But a sizable flight in fall usually means a noticeable northward movement in late April and May, though not nearly with the numbers of the previous fall. Spruces again afford the favorite food, and since seeds are dropping rapidly at this season, flocks of siskins are likely to be found feeding on the ground as well as in the trees. Most of these birds move on northward in mid-May, but it is not unusual for strays to remain until the end of May or early June.

The extent to which the species breeds in the state is not known. Breeding in the northern counties was suspected by the late-nineteenth-century writers. Various summer observations supported the probability during the first half of the twentieth century. Observers recorded instances of adults carrying nesting material in early June and feeding juveniles in July and August. The first known active nest containing young was found in Iron County on 21 June 1948 (H. Sell).

Not until 1960 was it known that a few of these birds could be found nearly every summer in the northernmost counties. Confirmed breeding has taken place on several occasions well south of the northern region. Between 14 May and 11 June 1963 the family life of a nesting pair at Appleton, from nest construction to the fledging of four young, was photographed and documented (Henseler 1963). Nesting was attempted unsuccessfully in La Crosse in 1974 and in Madison in 1978. In 1979 nest construction was observed in La Crosse County by 29 March (H. F. Young), in Dane County by 13 April (C. Luetkens), in Sauk County by 23 April (K. I. Lange), and in Winnegabo County by 26 April (T. Ziebell).

Presumably, much more nesting takes place in the northern forests, but specific evidence is lacking. The summer of 1969 must have been exceptional, with mid-June to July observations from 18 counties, south to Pierce, Chippewa, Juneau, Columbia, and Manitowoc counties.

American Goldfinch (*Carduelis tristis*)

STATUS. Common migrant. Common summer resi-
dent. Common winter resident south and central;
fairly common winter resident north.
HABITAT. All carr. Old field. Residential areas.
MIGRATION DATES. *Spring:* late April to early June.
Fall: late September to mid-November.
BREEDING DATA. Nests with eggs: 26 June to 30 Au-
gust. Clutch size: usually 5 or 6 eggs; occasion-
ally 4.
PORTRAIT. *Birds of Wisconsin:* Plate 81.

Of the 214 species reported on the BBS from 1966 to
1980, the American Goldfinch ranked 22nd in abundance, being reported on all 70 transects virtually
every year. This comes as no surprise to most observers, for the bird has long been regarded as one of the
most conspicuous as well as most beautiful of summer birds. In June, when most species are busy with
nesting duties, the "per-chic-o-ree" birds are cavort-
ing around residential areas, pastures, and the edges
of wooded areas, often in flocks of 8–10, and only
gradually pairing off for family duties that will occupy them through July, August, and much of September. The BBS map shows a remarkably even distribution throughout the state.

Less well known is the fact that during the same 15-
year period the goldfinch ranked 14th among the 188
species reported on Wisconsin CBCs. It is recorded
by the dozens, if not the hundreds, on most counts in
the southern two-thirds of the state, with smaller
numbers on about half of the northern counts every
year. The number of goldfinches visiting winter feeders has increased with the spreading popularity of
thistle-seed feeders.

Although winter populations of this species are
more regular than those of other winter finches, there
have been years when CBC figures averaged out to
only 15 individuals per count per year (1966–1967),
and there have been other years when the per-count
averages exceeded 100 (1970–1971, 1976–1977, 1978–
1979, 1983–1984). It frequently happens that high
goldfinch numbers coincide with low redpoll counts,
and low populations of goldfinches accompany strong
redpoll showings.

When the northward migration gets under way in
late April, the males are sporting their gaudy summer
plumage. As the spring flight builds to a peak in mid-
May, this bird becomes one of the most conspicuous
in residential areas. The colorful plumage, the frequent musical chattering, and the constant movement during tree-feeding operations make the "wild

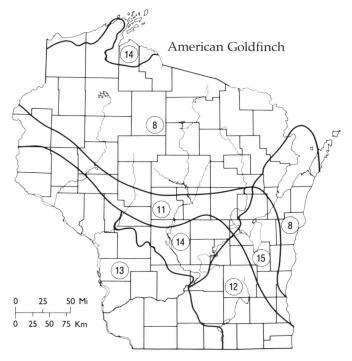

American Goldfinch

Breeding Bird Survey, averages 1966 to 1980

canary" one of nature's showpieces. Perhaps the only
people who do not appreciate this visitor in spring
are the birders who are concentrating on searching
for the less active vireos, warblers, and flycatchers,
and whose attention is often distracted by the movements of the more active American Goldfinches.

Nest construction has been reported by 22 June,
but usually it is not until mid-July that eggs have been
observed. This species has sometimes been known as
the "thistle-bird" because of its use of thistle-down
to line the nest. Nests are sometimes built in sturdy
thistle plants, sometimes in nearby bushes and trees
along the rim of pasture land. The care of the young
occupies the parents through August and early September. Because of the lateness of the nesting timetable, parasitism by the Brown-headed Cowbird is
rare. Goldfinches show special partiality toward sunflowers at this time of year, and look like tiny acrobats
as they perch almost upside down on nodding sunflower heads, extracting seeds.

Flocking and fall migration start in late September.
As long as the land remains snow-free, the flocks remain small and loose. On certain days in late October
and early November, when the finch migration is
near its peak, thousands pass by such flyway obser-

vation points as the Cedar Grove Ornithological Station in Sheboygan County. An estimated 23,000 were tallied there on 10 November 1971 (D. D. Berger). Usually only small numbers remain in the northern counties after 15 November.

Evening Grosbeak (*Coccothraustes vespertinus*)

STATUS. Common migrant north; fairly common migrant central and south. Uncommon summer resident north. Common winter resident north; fairly common winter resident central and south.

HABITAT. Upland spruce-fir forest (during nesting). Sugar maple forest. Residential areas.

MIGRATION DATES. *Spring:* early March to mid-May. *Fall:* mid-October to late December.

BREEDING DATA. Nests with young: 6–13 June.

WINTER. Regularly present south to Polk, Chippewa, Shawano, and Door counties; irregularly present throughout the state.

PORTRAIT. *Birds of Wisconsin:* Plate 73.

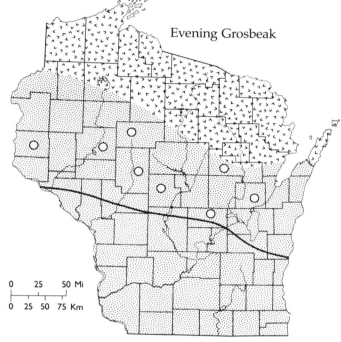

Evening Grosbeak

```
0    25    50 Mi
0   25  50  75 Km
```

▨ Summer range
☐ Winter range
    North of line: regular
    South of line: irruptive
○ Early June to late August

Records since 1960

The Evening Grosbeak is one of the state's most glamorous and exciting winter birds. The glamor stems not only from the gaudy yellow plumage of the male but also from the domineering manner in which a flock suddenly moves in and takes over a feeding station. Whether the flock consists of 4 or 40 birds, it tends to "take over" wherever it finds a supply of sunflower seeds. The fluttering and chattering that accompanies the grosbeaks' jockeying for position on the feeders, the speed and efficiency with which the birds devour the seeds, the boldness with which they cling to the feeders in the face of alarms that frighten even the House Sparrows—all of this is fascinating to watch.

As with all other winter finches, Evening Grosbeak population levels vary greatly from one year to the next and sometimes vary considerably within a given year. Northern Wisconsin attracts a few occasional vagrants in September and early October, but usually the winter influx starts after 20 October. Some years the influx remains relatively small and is limited to the northern counties. Some years the influx builds up strongly in the north but spreads only to the central counties in December and January, leaving the southern areas almost grosbeak-less. Some years the grosbeak influx is so great that it blankets the entire state with large flocks. Some years the numbers in November and early December decline in midwinter, building up again in late March and April.

A study of CBC results, 1958–1984, indicates that on most northern Wisconsin counts these birds are numbered in the hundreds nearly every winter. Only in 1960 were Evening Grosbeaks nearly absent. In central Wisconsin Evening Grosbeaks were absent in 1960 and 1976, and were present in very small numbers in 1962, 1964, 1966, 1967, 1982, and 1984. In the south this species went unrecorded on counts in 1960, 1962, 1964, 1966, 1967, 1976, 1979, 1982, and 1984. There is no discernible pattern of frequency for high and low years.

The major exodus of wintering birds occurs in April. Small flocks often remain through 10 May in the central and northern counties, but by the 15th nearly all have left. Exceptionally late was a 6 June 1973 straggler (Waushara, I. Chipman).

Little is known of the bird's nesting habits in northern Wisconsin. There have been sporadic reports since 1918 describing the feeding of young out of the nest in July and August. Not until 1964 was a nest actually located at Neopit (Menominee County). Exact dates were not listed, but Reinhold Link noted successful fledging. John Juda observed parent birds feeding recently fledged young in Bayfield County in early August 1964. Also in 1964, Bernard Klugow observed recently fledged young near Brule (Douglas County). He subsequently found nests there containing two and four young in 1965. Summer observations in the northern counties now occur frequently every year. The likelihood is that this bird is a regular breeder in the spruce forests south of Lake Superior and near the Upper Michigan border, where it feeds largely on maple and box elder seeds and spruce budworms. A small movement must have taken place in late July and early August 1972, when individuals were noted in St. Croix, Chippewa, Waushara, and Outagamie counties.

The increase in summer records points to a continuing change in range and distribution. The nesting range was limited to the western parts of Canada and the United States through most of the nineteenth century. It gradually spread eastward, reaching New England around 1890. Only recently has this species become a well-established breeder throughout Quebec and northern New England and extended its winter range south to Georgia and Alabama. Banding records show a strong east-west movement. In the invasion of 1961–1962 alone, Wisconsin banders trapped over 20 birds that had been banded in New York, New England, or Quebec.

Family **Passeridae**: Old World Sparrows

House Sparrow (*Passer domesticus*)
Formerly English Sparrow

STATUS. Abundant resident south and central; common resident north. Introduced.
HABITAT. Residential areas. Farmsteads. Commercial areas.
BREEDING DATA. Nests with eggs: 20 April to 27 July. Clutch size: usually 4 or 5 eggs; occasionally 2–6.
PORTRAIT. *Birds of Wisconsin:* Plate 73.

From a virtual unknown to one of the three most numerous Wisconsin species: this is the history of this Eurasian species between 1875 and 1975. The first attempt to introduce the House Sparrow to America occurred in 1850 and was followed by many additional transplants during the next 25 years in New England, New York, Pennsylvania, Ohio, Texas, Utah, California, and doubtless other states.

Although 1875 has usually been mentioned as the date of the first Wisconsin releases at Sheboygan and Fort Howard (Green Bay), mention is made in the 24 March 1869 issue of the *Walworth Independent* that R. C. Tate of Racine had recently received a shipment of these birds from England. Numerous other releases in various southern and eastern Wisconsin locations followed, and many colonies sprang up rapidly. The dispersal was so rapid that Kumlien and Hollister (1903) indicated that the bird's statewide distribution was nearly complete by the start of the twentieth century.

The spread and multiplication have occurred primarily in the populated areas of the state. Birds thrive in the cities wherever homes and public buildings are surrounded by even moderate-sized lawns. A vine-covered brick building will harbor a whole roost of these sparrows in winter and provide a haven for numerous nests in summer. Birds thrive equally well around farms and feed mills. Driving along a country road on a CBC, one has only to stop in front of a farmyard and "squeak"; anywhere from 20 to 200 House Sparrows may respond.

Throughout the northern forests this species is understandably less numerous. Woodlands have little appeal for this seed-eater. Three of the state's 70 BBS routes (Ashland, Iron, Marinette counties) have yet to record their first House Sparrows. Yet wherever urban and agricultural land exists in the north, this bird will be found.

Breeding Bird Survey, averages 1966 to 1980

Of the 214 species recorded in the first 15 years of the BBS, the House Sparrow ranked as the second most numerous over the entire state. A perusal of the CBC data also shows this bird ranking first or second consistently, year after year.

One reason for its rapid spread was the aggressive behavior of the newcomer. Anyone who has operated a winter feeding station has seen the eagerness with which a flock of these birds will fly in and take over a feeding tray. They can be frightened away momentarily but are quick to return. Nothing short of a shotgun seems to discourage them.

They are equally dominant in the selection of nesting sites. Many are content to nest in cornices or cracks in buildings, high enough up to be free of human disturbance. Many others are attracted to houses that were erected for Eastern Bluebirds, Tree Swallows, Purple Martins, and House Wrens. Many a pitched battle has taken place for possession of these houses; but the sparrow usually wins out, even if it means destroying the eggs and dismantling the nest of the previous owner. The House Sparrow has also flourished because it has an unusually long nesting season. It is not unusual for eggs to be laid by 1 May, or for second-family eggs to be found early in July. Schorger (1931a) once observed nest construction in progress in late February when there was a foot of snow on the ground.

Because of its aggressive behavior, nobody likes this bird. But evidently it is here to stay.

Eurasian Tree Sparrow (*Passer montanus*)

Formerly European Tree Sparrow

STATUS. Accidental. Two records.
HABITAT. Residential areas. Farmsteads.

Eurasian Tree Sparrow, 29 March 1966, Waukesha County (photo by J. F. Fuller)

When Donald Beimborn returned to his Oconomowoc (Waukesha County) home after a day at work on 29 March 1966, he was surprised to find an odd bird in one of his banding traps. All winter he had been banding House Sparrows, and at first this looked like an unusually small one. A close look at the head pattern, especially the chestnut cap, convinced him that the stranger was a Eurasian Tree Sparrow. Photographs by J. F. Fuller and E. W. Peartree substantiated the identification. The bird was then taken to the Milwaukee County Zoo, where many visitors subsequently enjoyed watching it (*Pass. Pigeon* 29:34–35).

Not until 1988 did another Eurasian Tree Sparrow appear in Wisconsin. David Lindsley detected one among 200 House Sparrows at his Pierce County feeder on 5 January 1988. I enjoyed watching it on 17 January 1989. The stranger was still present the following summer (*Pass. Pigeon* 51:297).

This species is not known for its wandering. It was introduced in St. Louis, Missouri, in 1870. The House Sparrow was also introduced at the same time, and it forced the Eurasian Tree Sparrow away from the most favored territory in the city. Since then, the Eurasian has taken hold strongly in a six-county area around St. Louis but has not expanded its range farther. No other attempts at introduction in the United States are known.

Species of Hypothetical Status

Clark's Grebe (*Aechmophorus clarkii*)

STATUS. Hypothetical.
HABITAT. Great Lakes. Inland lakes.

When the 35th supplement to the AOU *Check-list of North American Birds* gave formal recognition to the Clark's Grebe as a separate species, members of the WSO Records Committee reviewed the published records of Western Grebes in Wisconsin. But they found no evidence that would point surely to the presence of the newly described species. Previously published records of the similar-appearing Western Grebe were incomplete on those portions of facial plumage that separate the two species.

Then on 7 May 1987 Robbye Johnson (*Pass. Pigeon* 50:83–84) discovered five Western Grebes swimming in the Duluth-Superior harbor—sometimes on the Minnesota side, sometimes on the Wisconsin side. One of the five was slightly smaller, and showed a whiter face and brighter bill. But conditions for photography were not good, and when others looked for the same bird the next day, no grebes were to be found.

Time and patience seem likely to lead to a fully valid state record in the not-too-distant future.

White Ibis (*Eudocimus albus*)

STATUS. Hypothetical.
HABITAT. Wooded swamp.

At the Mead Wildlife Area in southern Marathon County on 31 May 1978, among the black cormorants and the dark herons that inhabited a rookery, one bird stood out as vividly white. An egret? No. Observers James Hoefler and Todd Eisele immediately noticed its long curved bill and realized they were watching a White Ibis. As the bird preened, perched on the limb of a dead tree on the Eau Pleine Flowage, its reddish face and bill were clearly evident. When the bird flew to another perch, it displayed dark wing tips. The observers returned later in the day with cameras, but the straggler from the Deep South could not be located. Dozens of observers combed the area off and on during the next 2 weeks, but the bird had evidently disappeared as mysteriously as it had come (*Pass. Pigeon* 41:43).

The 1970s witnessed considerable wandering of this species. The normal range in the East has extended from South Carolina to Virginia, with nomadic individuals reaching Nova Scotia and Newfoundland. In the West there have been recent sightings in California, Idaho, Wyoming, Kansas, and Missouri.

Prairie Falcon (*Falco mexicanus*)

STATUS. Hypothetical.
HABITAT. Open grassland.

On 23 September 1957 a Prairie Falcon made a sudden appearance at the Cedar Grove Ornithological Station in Sheboygan County. This large western flier came in low over the trapping area, missed one of the lure pigeons, and landed momentarily on the ground 40 yards away from the observers: D. D. Berger, H. C. Mueller, and F. Kuhlman. After a minute the bird rose, circled briefly, and disappeared. The large size, sandy color, and black axillary areas "were extremely conspicuous" (*Pass. Pigeon* 20:28).

Mueller, Berger, and George Allez (1983) experienced a repeat performance 25 years later when a similarly plumaged falcon visited the station on 15

October 1982. The fast-flying visitor made a pass at the bait but eluded the banding nets, passing within 75 feet of the observers.

Greater success in trapping was experienced by W. A. Smith near Genoa (Vernon County) on 31 October 1976. An immature female got tangled in one of Smith's nets. The bird was closely scrutinized, weighed and measured, and banded and photographed, before being released (*Pass. Pigeon* 39:297).

The sole reason for the reluctance of evaluators to accord this record full acceptance was the possibility of its being a recently released falconer's bird.

The same possibility clouds the observation of the large light-colored falcon seen and heard by Janelle Humphrey at Wisconsin Point, Superior, on 16 September 1979. She observed all salient field marks (*Pass. Pigeon* 42:122). Falconers' birds, however, are known to be flying near the Wisconsin-Minnesota border.

Black Rail (*Laterallus jamaicensis*)

STATUS. Hypothetical.
HABITAT. Shallow marsh.

Although only slightly north of the Black Rail's normal range, Wisconsin has no specimen or photograph of this diminutive marsh-dweller, and there are but three sight records sufficiently well documented to eliminate all reasonable possibility of misidentification.

On 13 May 1967, 5 miles southwest of Oshkosh, Eunice Fisher and Mrs. Charles Foote glimpsed a bird that was of the right size, shape, and general coloration to belong to this species. When Mrs. Fisher returned to the spot that evening, she again caught a glimpse of the bird 15–20 feet away. The view was again brief, as the bird darted for cover in the marsh grass. But the bird showed the distinctive white dorsal spots, and it uttered a high-pitched "keeek" as it disappeared (*Pass. Pigeon* 30:28). Subsequently other ornithologists made several attempts to observe the bird but were unsuccessful. It is presumed that the bird was a spring migrant that overshot its mark.

Alvin and Mae Peterson shared a similar experience in La Crosse County in 1956. On 12 May they found themselves only 10 feet away from a small blackish rail as it scampered between clumps of marsh grass. Mrs. Peterson caught another glimpse of the bird the next day and again was satisfied that it was much smaller than nearby Virginias and Soras (*Pass. Pigeon* 18:116–117).

A third brief appearance of a tiny blackish rail took place along the main dike at the Horicon National Wildlife Refuge in Dodge County on 9 May 1972. F. N. MacMillan (pers. comm.) and Ruby Bere stood 25 feet away as this sparrow-sized rail scampered across the road and back. Again, the observation time was too brief to permit detection of every essential field mark.

Buss and Mattison (1955) listed hypothetical sightings in Dunn County: 10 September 1939 (H. B. Apel, J. Gisness, I. O. Buss), 5–6 October 1939 (I. O. Buss, H. M Mattison), and 5 and 17 October 1941 (F. M. Kozlik, H. M. Mattison, I. O. and A. H. Buss). The plausibility of these sightings is enhanced by previous experiences observers have had with other rails, and the proximity of the sightings to eastern Minnesota, where six Black Rail sight observations have occurred since 1934.

But summer and fall sightings are necessarily suspect because of possible confusion with juvenile Soras and Virginia Rails—particularly when only the briefest of glimpses are afforded. It was this consideration that led Hollister (1912) to doubt Schoenebeck's (1902) 9 June 1899 record in Oconto County. Some doubt attaches to G. E. Lindsay's Iron County observations in October 1971 (*Pass. Pigeon* 34:159–160) for the same reason. In the Milwaukee Public Museum files there is a 1956 letter from H. L. Van Ness describing how—in the fall of 1931 or 1932—he held in his hand a small dark rail "speckled with tiny whitish dots on the upper side" while afield near Lodi (Columbia County). But the specimen was not preserved, and written details were incomplete.

Details were also incomplete for the small dark rail being devoured by a Northern Harrier when the latter was shot by Frithiof Kumlien on 20 August (1877 or 1879). Kumlien and Hollister commented on the Black Rail: (1903) "We are quite sure of having seen it on one occasion." But they gave no date or substantiation.

Until there is a specimen or definitive photograph, this species must be considered hypothetical. But with so many probable occurrences to date, it seems only a question of time before a fully substantiated record occurs. Perhaps it will come from some enterprising observer, armed with flashlight and tape recorder, standing at the edge of a southeastern Wisconsin marsh at midnight on a late May evening, looking and listening for responses to taped Black Rail calls.

Spotted Redshank (*Tringa erythropus*)

STATUS. Hypothetical.
HABITAT. Shallow marsh.

Peg and Howard Winkler were glassing a flock of Greater and Lesser Yellowlegs at Horicon Marsh in Dodge County on 28 April 1960, when they were astonished to discover a large black shore bird with "brilliant orange legs . . . and an equally brilliant orange red bill which darkened at the tip." The bird was larger and chunkier than the yellowlegs and showed jet black on the chest and upper belly. After examining the bird through binoculars and telescope for 20 minutes, the Winklers flushed the bird, notic-

ing a large white patch on the rump and lower back and the absence of a wing stripe. Dr. Winkler had previously been acquainted with this species in Europe (*Pass. Pigeon* 22:190). Subsequent efforts to find the straggler the following day were unsuccessful.

Previous to this record, North America—outside of Alaska—had but one other sight record: in Rhode Island in 1955 (Hall 1960, p. 232). Since 1969 additional observations have been made in Newfoundland, Massachusetts, Connecticut, New Jersey, Pennsylvania, Ohio, Ontario, British Columbia, California, Oregon, and Nevada.

Roseate Tern (*Sterna dougallii*)

STATUS. Hypothetical.
HABITAT. Normally oceanic coasts.

Following a major storm that moved out of the Southwest across Wisconsin on 5 and 6 May 1950, several rarities far outside their regular range appeared in the state. One was a Roseate Tern discovered by W. E. Scott, N. R. Barger, and S. D. Robbins near the shore of Lake Wingra in Madison on 11 May. They observed the bird both flying and perched on an almost-submerged stump, in company with a Forster's Tern, and they carefully studied it for 20 minutes at a distance of 40 yards under ideal light conditions (*Pass. Pigeon* 12:153).

A second sight observation is listed in the observation files of the Upper Mississippi River National Wildlife Refuge at Winona, Minnesota: a bird observed on 10 May 1961 at Gernot Lake south of Prairie du Chien (Grant County) by refuge assistant Victor Hall. This record has not been previously published, and the supportive written notes of "black bill and very long tail feathers" are somewhat sketchy.

This state is far removed from the Roseate Tern's usual migration route along the Gulf and Atlantic coasts. Other inland records have turned up in Indiana and western New York, but this coastal species is not known for its extralimital wandering.

Western Wood-Pewee (*Contopus sordidulus*)

STATUS. Hypothetical.
HABITAT. Aspen-birch forest.

Near Port Wing (Bayfield County) Laura Erickson heard the song of this westerner on 7 June 1981. She had become familiar with the Western Wood-Pewee's song 2 years earlier in Colorado, Wyoming, and Washington, and could readily distinguish it from the song of some nearby Alder Flycatchers. Soon, she spotted the singer putting on a display of fly-catching behavior; it exhibited the size, wing bars, and lack of white eye ring characteristic of the Eastern and Western

Wood-Pewees (*Pass. Pigeon* 44:84). But it was the bird's distinctive song that persuaded the Wisconsin Society for Ornithology Records Committee to accept this as a hypothetical record.

Kumlien and Hollister (1903) listed this species as a "rare, straggling summer resident." They provided no dates but stated that several specimens were collected at Lake Koshkonong, in Jefferson County. "One pair, with nest and eggs, were identified by Dr. Coues as unquestionably of this species." In Bent's *Life Histories of North American Flycatchers, Larks, Swallows, and Their Allies* (1942), allusion is made to a specimen collected on 31 July 1890 at Alden (Polk County), identified by Dr. A. K. Fisher. The locations of these specimens are now unknown, and there is no indication of the bases of these identifications. Positive identification, even in the hand, is now considered difficult when the bird does not vocalize. Schorger's (1951a) comment was: "All the records should be considered doubtful."

The possibility that Western Wood-Pewees might wander to Wisconsin is real. Several recent Minnesota observations exist, including breeding records. But it will take a bird-song expert to make the necessary distinction. Wandering in fall is most likely, and has been suspected on several occasions. Unfortunately, birds are silent at that season.

Vermilion Flycatcher (*Pyrocephalus rubinus*)

STATUS. Hypothetical.
HABITAT. Upland carr.

A male and a female Vermilion Flycatcher—presumably blown off course by a severe storm on 5–6 May 1950 which carried winds in excess of 60 miles per hour—were carefully studied in Milwaukee on 9 May. Mr. and Mrs. W. F. Jackson found the pair in their yard along the Milwaukee River, observed the typical fly-catching behavior, the small size, the bright red plumage of the male, and the darkish tan color of the female. The birds were but a few feet away. The Jacksons did not need binoculars to see the dark wings of the male, the breast streaks and pinkish cast on the belly of the female, the short bill and the dark line through the eye of both birds. The visitors must have

flown over 1,000 miles from their normal range. They did not linger long enough to be photographed or seen by other observers (*Pass. Pigeon* 12 : 152–153).

Not until 1982 did a second sight record occur. The lucky observers were C. L. Gilmore, H. Koopman, and R. Triebensee, birding in Harrington Beach State Park in Ozaukee County on 3 October. The 5-minute observation was too brief to allow photography or viewing by other observers, but it was long enough to afford close views of the red-feathered male as it moved from bush to bush (*Pass. Pigeon* 45 : 106–107).

Extralimital wanderings have been infrequent. Nesting has been reported in Colorado, with observations in Nebraska, Minnesota, Illinois, Ohio, West Virginia, Kentucky, Tennessee, and Georgia.

Cassin's Kingbird (*Tyrannus vociferans*)

STATUS. Hypothetical.
HABITAT. Upland carr. Deciduous forest savanna.

At first Louise Erickson thought she had come upon a Western Kingbird as she ran a BBS transect in southern Racine County on 17 June 1969. The yellow breast and belly, the dark brownish gray back and wings and tail, and dark gray head all seemed to fit, as the bird darted forth on repeated insect-catching forays from a fence post 30 feet away. But there was a distinct grayish band separating the white throat and the yellow breast. The tail lacked white outer tail feathers but had a light fringe on the tips of the tail feathers which were noticeably notched. Only on consulting field guides after completing the transect and com-

paring pictures in them with notes she had written down at the time of observation was she certain of the bird's identification. Efforts to find the visitor again proved futile (*Pass. Pigeon* 32 : 68).

Among huge numbers of grounded migrants, including dozens of Eastern Kingbirds, on Wisconsin Point at Superior on 29 May 1978, Daryl Tessen got within 10 feet of two of these stragglers from the Southwest. He carefully noted and documented the birds' head, back, throat, breast, and tail markings (*Pass. Pigeon* 41 : 48–49). One individual was still present the following morning.

Occasional extralimital wanderings have taken this species to Louisiana, Arkansas, Montana, South Dakota, and Ontario.

Northern Wheatear (*Oenanthe oenanthe*)

STATUS. Hypothetical.
HABITAT. Open grassland and cropland.

Among a mixed gathering of 500 Lapland Longspurs, American Pipits, and Snow Buntings feeding in a Kenosha County manure pile on 26 October 1952 was a brownish bird with rusty head and breast, a black eye stripe, and a large white rump and tail area terminating in a black "T." The bluebirdlike fidgety flight and the sharp bill helped convince observer Richard Gordon he was viewing a Northern Wheatear in winter plumage. The bird remained in the area through the 28th (*Pass. Pigeon* 15:40).

Only rarely has this Old World species deviated from its autumn migration route from northeastern Canada to Europe and Africa. But since 1950 extralimital wandering has increased. In the East, wanderers have been reported from most New England states, New York, New Jersey, Pennsylvania, Maryland, Virginia, and Florida. Elsewhere, stragglers have been known to visit Michigan, western and southern Ontario, Manitoba, Oregon, and California. Some day Wisconsin will again host this visitor.

Sprague's Pipit (*Anthus spragueii*)

STATUS. Hypothetical.
HABITAT. Open grassland.

After observing four pipitlike birds in Dane County on 6 April 1930, A. W. Schorger wrote in his field journal: "Looked too light for pipits, and did not wag their tails. Heartily wish that I had collected one." With characteristic caution he declined to list this observation as even a hypothetical record in either "The Birds of Dane County" (1931a) or his 1951 revision of Kumlien and Hollister's *Birds of Wisconsin* (1903). But the comments from an observer of Schorger's caliber and experience indicate a strong probability of the presence of the Sprague's Pipit.

On 30 March 1967 near the Racine coast guard station, Louise Erickson discovered a bird that looked and acted like a member of this species. From distances as close as 30 feet, she could see the light brown streaking of head, back, and breast, thin pointed bill, flesh-colored legs, and white outer tail feathers (*Pass. Pigeon* 30:28–29).

Erickson found a similar bird at almost the same Racine location on 29 September 1974. This individual displayed the same distinctive markings as it meandered through the grass on a golf course. "This bird, when golfers came by, walked or ran hurriedly over to shelter. . . . The bird did not teeter its tail and walked and ran but did not hop. It was observed for fifteen minutes up to 300 feet with 10× binoculars" (*Pass. Pigeon* 37:132–133).

A line from the eastern edges of the breeding range in northwestern Minnesota and the wintering range in Mississippi does not lie far west of Wisconsin. Since migration records exist for Illinois, along with extralimital reports from Michigan, Ohio, Maine, Virginia, and North Carolina, there is every reason to believe that an occasional bird may wander to Wisconsin. If such a happening can be recorded on film, this sweet singer will earn a proper spot on the state list.

Painted Redstart (*Myioborus pictus*)

STATUS. Hypothetical.
HABITAT. Southern silver maple–elm forest.

It was an astonished Mrs. Robert Sutherland who, with three teen-age children, witnessed a 10-minute performance by this southern visitor in the University of Wisconsin Arboretum at Madison on 22 April 1965. Size, actions, and body contour identified it as a warbler, and the brilliant red breast, white belly, white wing patch, and tail feathers were vividly clear as the observers stood enthralled 15–20 feet away. "The bird moved quickly through the branches, down swiftly into the underbrush, back up into the tree tops." It then moved off, and subsequent efforts by Mrs. Sutherland and others during the next 2 days failed to locate the visitor again (*Pass. Pigeon* 28:14–15).

Although not noted for extralimital wandering, this warbler has been recorded in Colorado, Louisiana, Alabama, Ohio, New York, Ontario, and Massachusetts. It is unfortunate that this Wisconsin sight record could not be confirmed by photograph.

Lesser Goldfinch (*Carduelis psaltria*)

STATUS. Hypothetical.
HABITAT. Old field. Upland carr. Residential areas.

On 11 November 1984 Jane Stephan discovered a bright yellow and black individual among the dull winter-plumaged American Goldfinches at her feeder in Superior. The stranger showed the same size and shape as the other goldfinches, with a full black crown that differed from the black forehead one would expect on an American Goldfinch still in summer plumage. The back was olive-green and streaked, suggesting that the bird was more likely of Pacific states origin than of Colorado range, where males have blackish backs.

The bird made repeat visits on the 12th and 13th, feeding on the sunflower seeds within 5 feet of the observer. Colder weather followed on the 14th, and the flock of American Goldfinches, together with the Lesser Goldfinch, disappeared before pictures could be taken (*Pass. Pigeon* 47:119–120).

Only rarely has the Lesser Goldfinch been found east of the Rocky Mountains. It is far more likely to be seen in Mexico than in Wisconsin.

Possible Escapes

Barnacle Goose (*Branta leucopsis*). One observed on Collins Marsh in Manitowoc County, 23 October 1977 by D. F. Brinker. The observer was thoroughly familiar with geese, having been engaged in a goose-trapping project. Efforts to find the bird the following day failed, suggesting that the bird was free-flying with accompanying Canadas. Another Barnacle Goose appeared briefly in Dodge County on 26 October 1985. Because this species is widely kept in captivity, it is assumed that most United States sightings involve escapes.

Harris' Hawk (*Parabuteo unicinctus*). Two were observed near Arlington (Columbia County), 1 September 1969 by H. L. Van Ness. For over an hour the birds were seen flying back and forth over a meadow or perched on fence posts (*Pass. Pigeon* 32:183). Although there were no signs that the birds had ever been kept in captivity, it seems inconceivable that a pair of these southerners—nonmigratory in their normal Mexican range—would have negotiated the thousand or more miles to Wisconsin under their own power.

Ringed Turtle-Dove (*Streptopelia risoria*). Since the first sighting in Oconto County in 1962, observers have encountered this bird in the wild in Kenosha, Racine, Milwaukee, Dane, Dodge, Washington, Manitowoc, Brown, Taylor, and Chippewa counties. Since this species is nonmigratory and has been a popular caged bird in many areas, it is presumed that most of these sightings have involved previously confined individuals. But breeding in the wild was strongly suspected in Milwaukee in 1970 (E. Sheridan).

Gray-breasted Jay (*Aphelocoma ultramarina*). Formerly called Mexican Jay, this is a bird of Mexico and the southwestern United States. One visited a feeder near Menomonee Falls (Waukesha County) between 11 December 1981 and 8 January 1982. There was no question about the bird's identity. The visitor showed normal jay behavior to the many appreciative observers who glimpsed the bird during the 4-week interval. But because this species does not normally wander from its regular range, and has never been reported north and east of Kansas, human assistance in reaching Wisconsin is presumed (*Am. Birds* 36:297).

Red-crested Cardinal (*Paroaria coronata*). One appeared at the Lloyd Jacobson feeder in Rice Lake (Barron County) on or near 5 September 1974. C. A. Kemper photographed the bird on 12 October. Numerous other persons observed this cardinal through the following April (*Pass. Pigeon* 36:179). Another brightly colored individual spent several weeks in the fall of 1980 at the Wayne Hammond (pers. comm.) feeder in Hartland (Washington County). Although these individuals appeared wild and healthy, no one has seriously suggested that these birds traveled here from South American haunts on their own. Escapes/releases have turned up in several other states.

European Goldfinch (*Carduelis carduelis*). One was collected in Milwaukee on 12 May 1935 by C. S. Jung (1936), after having been discovered on the previous day by John Patek. The specimen is in the Milwaukee Public Museum. Another was photographed near Thiensville (Ozaukee County) on 5 May 1956 (S. Moulson; *Pass. Pigeon* 18:139). Although these birds were described and reported as wild birds at that time, historical perspective lends strong credence to the probability that they were escapes. At the few points where the birds have been introduced, they have neither spread nor proliferated to any significant extent. Additional sightings were made in Langlade County (15 April 1988, B. Fox) and in Waupaca County (1–28 February 1989, G. Miller). Presumably these birds were also escapes.

Habitat Preferences
James Hall Zimmerman

Which birds can you expect to find in a given place in a given season? Like most wild species, birds have a high fidelity to habitat, with the exception of accidents of geography, history, and tradition, as noted in "The Landscape and the Birds" in Part I. Thus, we should be able to predict with reasonable accuracy what species to expect in a place by knowing the types of habitat found there. This chapter lists in Table 1 and briefly describes in the subsequent text 29 kinds of sites which are representative of the Wisconsin landscape and to which birds seem to be able to respond in choosing habitats. The habitat preferences of Wisconsin's breeding birds are shown in Table 2, which matches the individual species to these 29 landscape types. The habitat preferences of Wisconsin's wintering birds and migratory birds are shown, respectively, in Tables 3 and 4. The habitat categories shown in these latter two tables are simplifications of those listed in Table 1.

Since vegetation is important to bird habitat and since John Curtis (1959) so thoroughly documented the vegetation of Wisconsin, his text was used as a basis for the habitat descriptions. For correlating common plant names with the scientific ones, Fassett (1976) and Fernald (1950) may be used for further reference. (There will always be some discrepancies, for plant names have not been standardized to the extent that bird names have.)

Habitat Descriptions

Southern Wisconsin Deciduous Forests
The broad-leaved or hardwood forests that occur south of Curtis' tension zone (see "The Landscape and the Birds") generally lack coniferous trees. Because of intensive farming, these forest types occur chiefly in woodlots 20–100 acres in

Table 1. Habitat Types

The habitats in each landscape group (indicated by bold type) share the same general aspect, but they sometimes vary widely because of plant species and life-form.

Southern Wisconsin Deciduous Forests
Southern Wisconsin Dry Forest (oak, hickory)
Southern Wisconsin Mesic Forest (sugar maple, basswood)
Southern Wisconsin Lowland or Floodplain Forest (silver maple, elm)

Northern Wisconsin Forests
Northern Wisconsin Mesic Deciduous Forest (sugar maple)
Northern Wisconsin Pioneer Deciduous Forest (aspen, birch)
Northern Wisconsin Mesic Conifer-Hardwood Forest (sugar maple, hemlock, pine)
Dry Sandy Forest (Hill's oak, jack pine)
Upland Mesic Boreal Forest (spruce, fir)
Conifer Swamps (spruce, tamarack, white cedar)
Conifer Plantations (usually pine or spruce)

Savannas and Shrub Communities—Transition to Open Lands
Deciduous Forest Savanna (mature trees scattered over grass)
Southern Wisconsin Upland Carr (mixed shrubs and/or saplings)
Southern Wisconsin Lowland Carr (red dogwood, pussywillow)
Northern Wisconsin Lowland Carr (alder swamp)
Natural Reforestation Lands (mixed or monotypic saplings)

Open Grasslands and Barrens
Annual Crops (maize, small grains, soybeans, sunflowers)
Perennial Forage and Pasture (alfalfa, grasses)
Old Field (unharvested goldenrod and pasture grasses, north and south)
Sedge Meadow (peatland grasses and sedges, north and south)
Sand and Gravel (barrens, dunes, gravel pits, hilltops)

Waterscapes
Shallow Marsh (cattails, bulrushes)
Wooded Swamp (wooded wetlands, including islands) (red maple, etc.)
Ponds and Streams (narrow or small open waters and shores)
Inland Lakes and Flowages (larger deep waters and their shores)
The Great Lakes (including shores and islands)

Settled Areas
Farmsteads
Residential Areas with Mature Trees
Residential Areas with Few Mature Trees
Commercial and Industrial Areas

---

size, with abrupt edges on roads or fields. They are divided by Curtis (1959) into three intergrading categories primarily on the basis of moisture, which determines tree composition directly or through historical factors such as occurrence of fire. At the wet or lowland extreme, the trees tolerate flooding, at least in spring. The term *mesic* means intermediate between dry and wet, with constantly moist soil and air yet well-drained soil. Dry, or xeric, forest trees, conserving what water they have and being only moderately shady, tend to allow the environment to dry out in sun and wind. The mesic and wet forest types tend to keep a moist site humid by blocking wind and by recycling an abundance of water into the air. So uniform are most deciduous trees in aspect that many forest birds range over two or even all three types at all seasons. Many warblers, however, prefer the moister forests for both migrating and breeding. Forest fragmentation may prevent successful breeding in the smaller tracts.

Southern Wisconsin Dry Forest (Oak, Hickory)

The dominant trees in the dry forests of southern Wisconsin are black and white oaks, usually accompanied by some bur and red oaks, shagbark and yellowbud hickories, black cherry, and aspens. Since considerable light penetrates the canopy, the shrub layer is often dense. It includes gray dogwood, choke-cherry, American hazelnut, and species of *Viburnum*, *Rubus*, and *Ribes*. This is a pioneer forest, unable to reproduce in its own shade. Invading saplings of mesic forest may be present because of more than a century of fire protection. Thorns, burrs, and vines are common. Invasions of a dozen Eurasian ornamental shrubs and trees escaping from gardens are often in progress. Chief among these are the hybrid bella honeysuckle and the common, or cathartic, buckthorn.

The most characteristic sites are in hilly or rolling terrain—especially on south- or west-facing slopes and hilltops and on sandy or gravelly soils. The brush, especially in openings, explains the presence of the birds of carrs, while the hilltop or cliff sites required by species like the Turkey Vulture account for its listing under oak forest. The abundant nuts and berries attract many mammals and birds. The oaks provide many insects for migrating woodland birds and abundant den sites for woodpeckers, chickadees, nuthatches, and titmice, while their acorns feed many birds including Blue Jays, Red-headed Woodpeckers, Wood Ducks, fall-flocking Common Grackles, and wintering Wild Turkeys. Ruffed Grouse prefer large tracts containing their favorite winter food, the buds of aspens, and so may increase in number where state and private recreation lands grow up to pioneer forest. Cherries attract many growing families of songbirds in August, as do Russian mulberries throughout summer where they invade.

Southern Wisconsin Mesic Forest (Sugar Maple, Basswood)

Trees characteristic of the mesic forests in southern Wisconsin are sugar maple and basswood (linden), often accompanied by white ash, slippery, American, and rock elms, ironwood, red oak, yellowbud hickory, and sometimes hackberry, black walnut, and butternut. The generally very shady canopy excludes most shrubs, but maple and ash saplings may be abundant. Conspicuous carpets of ephemeral spring wild flowers and the brilliant autumn coloration of the maples are characteristic. This is a climax forest, able to maintain all its species when windthrow or selective logging locally opens up the canopy.

The characteristic sites are on fertile fine-textured soils, usually near limestone. They were protected from hot winds and presettlement fires, occurring in places such as north- or east-facing slopes, deep valleys, and islands or points isolated by waters and wetlands. Ovenbirds are favored by the lack of underbrush, while maple or ironwood saplings provide low nest sites for the Wood Thrush, Rose-breasted Grosbeak, and Acadian Flycatcher. The Red-eyed Vireo, Great Crested Flycatcher, and Eastern Wood-Pewee may be the chief breeding canopy birds away from the edges and openings needed by the Indigo Bunting, American Redstart, Northern Oriole, and most others.

Southern Wisconsin Lowland or Floodplain Forest (Silver Maple, Elm)

Silver maples and elms and their associates are unusual in being able to tolerate brief floods of up to about 1 week's duration during the growing season, in addition to the usual prolonged early spring inundation. In Wisconsin they can usually be found in the wider floodplains of our major rivers such as the Mississippi, Black, "Big" Fox, Wisconsin, and Rock. Outside of river valleys they also appear in low swampy areas, especially near Lakes Superior and Michigan and Green Bay. Other characteristic trees include the green ash and swamp white oak. In sandy soils of the Mississippi and Wisconsin systems, river birch is also common. Now that most of the large elms have surrendered to disease, some of their lowland associates like hackberry may increase. Upland species sometimes found on the floodplains include basswood and hickory. Newly exposed banks and islands are often first colonized by pioneering cottonwoods and black willows. Although favored by alluvium, this forest type as defined here may occur some distance from open or standing water. (See the Waterscapes section for swamps with water visible among the trees much of the time.)

Even without intervening muddy sloughs and backwaters, this floodplain forest is difficult to penetrate for economic or recreation purposes because of the many uprooted trees, rank tangled vegetation—including the frequently climbing poison ivy and both nettles (*Urtica* and *Laportea*)—and aggressive mosquitoes. Its foliage-height diversity, enhanced by flood-killed and windthrown trees, favors a wide diversity of birds, as does the wild character of its more or less continuous corridors. Here the Barred Owl and Red-shouldered Hawk replace their upland counterparts, the Great Horned Owl and Red-tailed Hawk, among the permanent residents. Some species of southern distribution (see "The Landscape and the Birds") invade Wisconsin along the rivers and turn up most abundantly in or near the floodplain (e.g., the Red-bellied Woodpecker and Blue-gray Gnatcatcher). Two primarily northern birds breed in southern Wisconsin along the major rivers: the Brown Creeper and Yellow-bellied Sapsucker. The Wood Duck is most likely to be found here, although it can nest in any upland forest where water is near.

Northern Wisconsin Forests

In northern and eastern Wisconsin, the climate is more favorable for trees, causing faster forest regeneration, taller trees, and higher tree densities. As a part of the Great Lakes mixed-forest complex, these forests contain many combinations of elements of the generally northern coniferous (cone-bearing, needle-leaved, softwood) region, such as pine and hemlock, and the generally eastern deciduous (flowering, broad-leaved, hardwood) region, such as red oak. Among the latter species, however, a few are primarily of northern distribution, namely the poplars or aspens (quaking, large-toothed, and balsam) and the white and yellow birches. The northern element is well represented by many shrubs and herbs, notably mountain maple, thimbleberry, red elderberry, beaked hazel, many members of the blueberry family, and six species of club moss. Ferns abound in the generally cool, moist, mossy environment north of the tension zone. A mixture of southern and northern wild flowers and birds occurs in this generally forested landscape where the soils as well as climate are seldom amenable to agriculture. The great disparity in aspect of evergreen conifers and deciduous hardwoods counteracts the uniformity of forest cover; so forest birds are both diverse and abundant.

The forest vegetation is far more complex in northern Wisconsin than it is farther south; in a short distance, you may pass through several types, walking from "room" to "room" dominated by successively different trees, because the soils and moisture conditions change and the accidents of history provide different tree mixtures or ages. In general, on coarser soils the conifers, birches, and aspens predominate, while on the finer and more fertile soils the unburned forest may be very much like the southern mesic sugar maple forest. However, the latter may contain "rooms" of white pine, hemlock, yellow birch, or (in the eastern counties) beech. Large burned areas, regardless of soil type, are usually dominated by pioneering aspens and white birch, which frequent logging may perpetuate. Poor soils, especially when waterlogged, favor red maple, which provides the earliest and brightest fall color. Windthrow, local fires, and possibly temporary pasturing favor hemlock and yellow birch regeneration along with white birch, white pine, and red oak.

Four wholly coniferous landscapes occur naturally in our northern counties: (1) fertile cold sites favor white spruce and balsam fir; (2) acid moss peats are exclusively invaded by the two bog conifers, black spruce and tamarack, in either dense or scattered stands; (3) fertile (limy) peaty seepages and shores favor white cedars; (4) former openings caused by local fire or windthrow may produce upland or lowland stands of dense "young" hemlock (100–200 years old) or young white pines (30–100 years old), which are the gloomiest forests of all, apparently suiting few birds. Later (at 100–300 years), accidents open up these uniform groves to provide bird and plant habitats.

A fifth forest type may or may not be exclusively coniferous. On very poor, very dry sandy soils of old lake beds or dunes, you find dense scrubby stands of pioneering jack pines, either alone or mixed with small scrubby mixtures of black oak and Hill's oak. Sometimes the oaks occur without any pines, and sometimes these areas are later invaded by red or white pines and red maples. Rocky hilltops may sport only red oak in scrubby form. Steep sandy or rocky soils on shores, points, and cliffs tend to have the larger pines, either red (Norway) pine or white pine, or both. Near water, where protected from logging or fires, they have reached a size sufficient to harbor owls and support the nests of Bald Eagles and Ospreys. Away from water and major roads, much of the forest is intensively logged, hence is younger and less diverse, whether on public or private lands.

One conifer, the American yew, is not considered here because of its rarity today, although it may have prevailed in several forest types on limy soils before the growing postsettlement population of white-tailed deer eliminated it; its value to birds is not known. Studies are needed where it persists in the Apostle Islands and in Menominee and Door counties.

Only seven of the many forest combinations of the northern Wisconsin forest can be recognized here. It is important to understand that, because many forest types are dovetailed as in a checkerboard, some birds may range through habitats that, individually, could not support them the year-round. For example, a permanent resident, the Ruffed Grouse, might not be abundant in sugar maples or in pines unless aspens occur nearby to provide winter food. (Note: In order to emphasize tree aspect and life-form of importance to birds, we are breaking up Curtis' four northern forest categories into six and keeping plantations separate as a seventh.)

Northern Wisconsin Mesic Deciduous Forest (Sugar Maple)
Generally lacking all conifers, mesic deciduous climax forests tend to have the same plants and birds found in their southern counterparts, including most of the wild flowers as well as the dominant sugar maple, basswood, ironwood, and white ash. However, many northern species are added. These include some northern shrubs and wild flowers. The birds of strictly southern distribution are

replaced by some northern warblers and hawks. Larger birds like the Pileated Woodpecker, Ruffed Grouse, and the raptors and some smaller ones like the Ovenbird and Ruby-throated Hummingbird are more abundant here than they are in the isolated small, less varied, southern woodlots. The typical site for the "sugar bush" in the north is different from the typical site farther south. The northern maples are on hilltops or their upper slopes, where the best soils are, rather than in protected valleys, as explained in "The Landscape and the Birds."

Northern Wisconsin Pioneer Deciduous Forest (Aspen, Birch)

The second type of northern forest that lacks conifers corresponds to the southern oak forest only in its pioneer nature and its light-admitting canopy, for it is composed of species of a very different aspect—white birch and quaking and large-toothed aspens—trees with light-colored bark. These three species often form very extensive stands where big fires eliminated all trees incapable of long-distance dispersal. Some red maple and red oak may be present, and so may any other species of northern-forest tree, often in an understory eventually able to replace the pioneer birch and aspen. Despite the light, airy aspect of the canopy, this forest is relatively moist in comparison with the southern oak forest. The northern climate is damp and cool in summer, and has more snow in winter. The understory includes bracken fern, blueberries, and many northern wild flowers and ground-cover plants.

Isolation from other tree species, frequent logging for paper pulp, and possibly also browsing of the understory by abundant deer are factors that can keep these areas in aspen and birch for many years. Male aspen buds support grouse in winter, and the soft rotting boles of aspen and birch are favorite den sites for woodpeckers and Black-capped Chickadees. Where the stands are young, nesting hawks and owls and Pileated Woodpeckers may be lacking. Note that European Starlings, which require close association with settled areas for food supplies, nest more often in northern than in southern forests, since only in the north are wild forests and settled areas commonly closely associated. In the southern counties they breed on farmsteads and in cities. The brushiness of aspen-birch forest accounts for the frequent occurrence of several breeding species of warblers, including the Mourning and Connecticut.

Northern Wisconsin Mesic Conifer-Hardwood Forest
(Sugar Maple, Hemlock, Pine)

The mesic conifer-hardwood forest is the typical climax shady forest on variable and intermediate soil types in the Great Lakes region, dominated by the temperate forest region's most shady and shade-tolerant trees: sugar maples, hemlocks, and sometimes beeches. Intermediate trees—chiefly the red oak, yellow birch, and red maple—are frequent also, along with relic pioneer trees. The pioneers include aspen, white birch, and red and white pines, all reaching back to the last fire or violent downburst which opened the canopy as much as two centuries before. The relic pines are a unique and conspicuous feature of this forest type, standing out as emergent trees up to 100 feet taller than the dense canopy of mature sugar maples, hemlocks, and other dominant climax species. Seldom censused, these tall pines probably harbor a significant variety of warblers and finches. Their broken tops still provide a few abodes for the Chimney Swift and possibly the Purple Martin.

From the air a mosaic can be seen in autumn, with the major patches of dark hemlocks and pines contrasting with the flaming maples and oaks. The coniferous patches indicate local special conditions that have enabled coniferous seed sources and seedling sites to prevail. Such places include poorer soils, rocky outcrops, or local fires or windthrows near a seed tree spared from destruction.

The birds, in turn, are distributed according to their preference for conifers or for deciduous trees. In the conifers you are apt to find the Red-breasted Nuthatch, Blackburnian Warbler, Sharp-shinned Hawk, and Purple Finch; in the deciduous trees, look for the Eastern Wood-Pewee, White-breasted Nuthatch, Red-eyed Vireo, and Rose-breasted Grosbeak. Sometimes, as a result of logging, you may find an even-aged mixture of pioneer and climax trees including aspen, birch, maple, oak, and fir. However, bird diversity seems to depend on varied foliage height and spacing as much as on varied tree-species composition. So, you would expect the best bird lists in old-growth forest with natural openings and near lake, bog, and river shores where logging is likewise minimal.

Dry Sandy Forest (Hill's Oak, Jack Pine)

The distinctive biotic community composed of sandy pine-oak barrens is the north country's only truly dry forest, occurring on the driest, poorest silica sand soils and frequently kept partly open or in the young stage by recurrent fires even today. Often these areas are called barrens. In the openings, you find prairie grasses such as little bluestem and poverty grass and low shrubs such as sweet fern, blueberry, and bearberry. If bare sand is exposed and trees are few, birds listed under Sand and Gravel habitats may be present. The trees are jack pine and/or black and Hill's oaks, with little understory other than a carpet of Pennsylvania sedge. Older, protected stands can be invaded by red and white pines and red maple as soil moisture builds up. The two largest areas of these sandy pine-oak barrens are in central and northwestern Wisconsin; small examples occur elsewhere across the north, such as in eastern Menominee County, north of Green Bay in Brown County, and near Stevens Point in Portage County.

Dense stands of even-aged jack pines may be quite barren of birds, but the savannalike openings and oak mixtures diversify the fauna. The Clay-colored Sparrow may be present, breeding in small conifers about 4–10 feet tall, while the Chipping Sparrow breeds in all sizes of pines or spruces, and the Pine Warbler prefers large pines. Just as in the previous type, a diversity of trees enables both southern and northern species to breed in these "barrens." Northern species include the Hermit Thrush, Nashville, Yellow-rumped, and Connecticut Warblers, Red Crossbill, and Dark-eyed Junco. Those not tied to the north include the Eastern Bluebird, Mourning Dove, Scarlet Tanager, Northern Oriole, Rufous-sided Towhee, and Indigo Bunting.

Upland Mesic Boreal Forest (Spruce, Fir)

Dominated by white spruce and balsam fir with associated white birch, aspen, balsam poplar, and white pine, boreal forest covers a very large area across Canada and Alaska. Wisconsin has only a few tiny southern relic outliers of this forest in microclimates having damp cold summers and snowy winters. These spots are along the east coast of Door County and in parts of Vilas and Oneida counties. Balsam firs alone may also dominate certain selectively logged areas and often characterize the lower slopes of conifer-hardwood forests as transitions to the wet spruce bogs and white cedar swamps. Because they are unpalatable to deer, firs and spruces, when their seed is available, may even invade the cedar swamps as well as any current aspen-birch forests.

The dark spirelike spruces and firs are home for a group of northern birds that breed nowhere else: permanent residents such as the Spruce Grouse, Gray Jay, Black-backed Woodpecker, and Boreal Chickadee, and summer residents including the Merlin, Swainson's Thrush, Golden-crowned and Ruby-crowned Kinglets, and several warblers.

Conifer Swamps (Spruce, Tamarack, White Cedar)

Most of the northern conifer swamps are acid sphagnum bogs dominated in the older, drier parts of the peat body by black spruce and tamarack. But we are also including here the white cedar swamps on fertile peats and shores, partly because they may intergrade with bogs and partly because they are difficult to travel in and so are little known. None of these three lowland conifer species seems to harbor much birdlife alone; but when you include the scattered, dwarfed trees in muskegs, and the shrubby, mossy, and sedgy openings, edges, and floating mats, the birdlife is distinctive if sparse. For one thing, insect life may be limited, and, for another, we are south of the breeding range of a number of boreal birds such as the Orange-crowned and Tennessee Warblers. We do, however, find Olive-sided Flycatchers and, near mossy open bogs, Palm Warblers breeding there.

Furthermore, many of the bird species characteristic of upland spruce and fir also occur in the conifer swamps—in fact, are numerous there—since the somber skyline is similar and more extensive. We have more acreage of lowland black spruce, tamarack, and white cedar than we have of upland boreal forest, and the solitude of the swamps favors these wilder species. Although absent from the northern swamps, the Rufous-sided Towhee is included, because in southern Wisconsin it sometimes replaces the boreal species in the small relic tamarack bogs, where the only vestige of boreal birdlife is an occasional White-throated Sparrow or Nashville Warbler. The damp upland white cedar groves in eastern Door County need further study.

Conifer Plantations (Usually Pine or Spruce)

Both north and south, plantings of conifers may be recognized by their even spacing, even age, and monotypic composition. Their age ranges from 1 to nearly 100 years. The trees usually planted in our state are white pine, red (Norway) pine, white spruce, and two Eurasian species: Scotch pine and Norway spruce. When repeatedly thinned, these plantings can attain mature size and after a century may develop an understory of deciduous species and an irregular canopy conducive to many nesting birds.

South of the tension zone, most plantings are small in area and usually confined to poor or steep soils. Sometimes white cedars are planted along trout streams. In the north, extensive plantings are part of the commercial paper operations. Statewide, many school forests and state forest and wildlife lands have conifer plantations. Although relatively barren of all other plant life, these dense young plantings vary the landscape and provide roosts for migrant songbirds, food for winter finches, and refuges for owls and crows. Heavy itinerant songbird use is evidenced by the abundance of berry-bearing shrubs and trees (including poison ivy!) that spring up around the plantations. The Clay-colored Sparrow often nests in young plantations with trees under 10 feet tall.

Savannas and Shrub Communities—Transition to Open Lands

Because of fires, storms, droughts, high or fluctuating water tables, farming, and logging, we frequently find considerable acreages dominated by scattered trees (savannas), shrubs (carrs), or saplings (reforestation). Such places abound with deer, rabbits, woodchucks, pheasants, quail, and many songbirds. This richness suggests not only solar access for high productivity of food plants and insect life but also a high frequency of fires and other disturbances during the millions of years in which our modern forms of life developed their adaptations and habitat requirements. Many of our game and songbird species are characteristic "edge" dwellers, depending on the shifting interface between forests, fields, and wetlands. Here they have the best of all worlds within their home ranges—using one or another landscape to meet their requirements for food, shelter, courtship, and rest. Many edge songbirds nest in shrubs or trees but feed in the open, in the air, or on the ground; others nest on the ground but feed higher up. A good example is the Northern Oriole, which uses both milkweed fibers (from open fields) and grapevine fibers in its tree-hung nest.

Note: This landscape group may overlap other groups discussed in this chapter, in particular, the young conifer plantation, the edges of the conifer swamps, pine-oak barrens, the water's edge, and the residential areas. These groups are not treated again here.

Deciduous Forest Savanna (Mature Trees Scattered over Grass)

Primarily in southern and western Wisconsin, fires and possibly the American bison and elk (before settlement) often allowed only scattered oaks (oak openings) and other trees to mature and survive over a relatively extensive low grassland understory. Similar savannas result today in unimproved pastures and abandoned farmland. The tree density is 10–20 per acre. (Trees planted along roadsides or allowed to come up in fencerows qualify for this habitat type, but see the general discussion of lawns and parks under the Settled Areas landscape group.) Birds that nest in trees and feed in trees, grass, or air can thrive in the deciduous forest savanna; but the shrub-nesters of forests and carrs are excluded. Most of today's rural savannas are pastures and have the same birds whether they are dry (oak), mesic (maple), or wet (river floodplain). (Note that bushy old fields and fencerows are treated as upland carrs or reforestation.) In northern Wisconsin, the savanna is covered under the Dry Sandy Forest heading.

Southern Wisconsin Upland Carr (Mixed Shrubs and/or Saplings)

Carrs are plant communities dominated by shrubs. Most references to carrs in this country are to lowland shrubs, which are slower to change into forest than are upland carrs. However, upland carrs are actually not uncommon. The frequent abandonment of crop and pasture land for second homes, public recreational areas, and speculation lands and the abundance of utility rights-of-way and abandoned rail lines produce a constant supply of shrubby areas that are fast invaded by trees. A small supportive movement (e.g., some experiments in Columbia County by the Wisconsin Department of Natural Resources) is under way to restore the old postsettlement brushy fencerow as a replacement for the frequently mowed roadside, since the former is so productive of quail and other wildlife. This trend can only gain momentum from the continuing decline in the ratios of game to hunter and benefit to cost of roadside mowing.

The upland carrs contain a diversity of woody species such as gray dogwood, American hazelnut, cherries, plums, wild crabs, hawthorns, viburnums, blackberries, raspberries, bittersweet, grape, woodbine, sumacs, poison ivy, roses, and of course the invading saplings of oak, hickory, apple, mulberry, red cedar, and many other trees. These shrubs and small saplings may form a dense tangle here and only scattered patches there, gradating to forest or savanna where allowed to do so. In an old field, the first woody invaders, whether trees or shrubs, tend to come in only sporadically, probably on old woodchuck dens and abandoned anthills. These invaders form colonizing sites for other species as they kill the grass by shading, and they attract berry-eating birds to seed new species of fruit.

Birds which breed in fields and roadsides with a few shrubs or saplings (e.g., the Field Sparrow, Ring-necked Pheasant, and American Goldfinch) as well as birds of forest openings (e.g., the Indigo Bunting) and edges (e.g., the Brown Thrasher) may occur together. Occasional stumps or snags and old fence posts harbor the nests of Eastern Bluebirds, American Kestrels, and Tree Swallows. Grapevines, hawthorns, and red cedars are especially good nest sites for many birds. Brushy old fields and pastures have the highest breeding density and diversity of songbirds in any region, and include a large share of our most familiar bird species such as the Song Sparrow, Common Yellowthroat, and Gray Catbird.

Southern Wisconsin Lowland Carr (Red Dogwood, Pussywillow)
Like the upland carr, the lowland carr shows a transition in space (between forest and either sedge meadow or open water) and in time (between meadow and forest); but here high water tables form soggy peat soils which slow down the succession. Perhaps the intense competition offered by shrubs and the sods of waning sedges and grasses also serve to exclude or retard forest invasion. Fire, summer frost, and consumers (deer, mice, rabbits, insects, and fungi) seem to set the shrubs and the saplings back periodically in these peaty lowlands. Although Curtis (1959) ascribed lowland carrs to a cessation of fires and then to a cessation of hay-mowing, they did not develop anywhere immediately following settlement as did the upland brushy fencerows and oak forests. Instead, they became widespread only in the 1940s when a rash of large federally financed drainage projects lowered water tables generally. Many carrs appear to have originated in limy groundwater-fed fen peats after drainage of nearby lands for muck farming. Usually, you can find the ditch not far away, marked by a row of willows or cottonwoods on the spoils. In undisturbed nature, the shrubs of lowland carrs typically grow on stream banks and shores, and only as scattered individuals in undrained fens. The extensive wet, densely shrubby carrs we see today probably resemble the temporary holdovers of dry climatic periods in the past, which periodically succumbed to peat fires and the return of high water. Wood and charcoal layers in peat deposits tell us this story.

The wet carr shrubs include red osier dogwood, silky dogwood, several pussywillows (*Salix discolor, S. bebbiana, S. petiolaris,* and others), bog birch, red raspberry, black currant, common (black) elderberry, and several viburnums, including possible hybrids between the native *V. trilobum* and European *V. opulus.* Some of the drier peaty carrs are heavily invaded by three Eurasian pests: bella honeysuckle, common, or cathartic, buckthorn, and alder, or fen, buckthorn.

Today the carrs are often impenetrable around streams and wetlands; but many of their birds are conspicuous and are often the same as those of upland carrs. To see or hear the Veery, Mourning and Blue-winged Warblers, and Bell's Vireo, however, you must spend some time "bushwhacking" and then sitting quietly! Woodcock-watching is now a traditional sunset carr activity in spring. Woodcocks need open grassy spots for launching into their sky dances; but the nearby nest is usually at the edge of carr or forest. Southern lowland carrs frequently occur around partly drained relic tamarack bogs today. These are particularly difficult to penetrate because the subsiding peat makes footing unstable and because poison sumac grows luxuriantly there. Where drainage, fire, and siltation have brought in monotypic stands of reed canary grass, tall ragweeds, or nettles, there may be little or no birdlife for much of the year.

Northern Wisconsin Lowland Carr (Alder Swamp)

In the north (and more rarely in southern Wisconsin), trout streams are bordered by tall thickets of alder, sometimes together with pussywillows, dogwoods, viburnums, winterberry, and other shrubs. Flowages created by beaver or humans may cause similar carrs to occupy extensive areas intermediate in wetness between swamp forest and sedge meadow or shallow marsh. Logged swamps, roadside ditches, and peatlands that dry up when roadbeds intercept their flow may also become wet carrs. High water tables seem to exclude trees and so make the alder thicket a stable edge community. The alders share many bird species with the southern wet carrs and the northern areas undergoing reforestation, as well as attracting swamp species like the Northern Waterthrush.

Note: The true bog shrubs (called ericads or heaths, in the blueberry family) are covered in the Conifer Swamps section under the Northern Wisconsin Forests heading. But as usual, you will find transitional areas where bog shrubs occur alone or gradate into willows, dogwoods, and alders. Bog shrubs alone are often too low and dense to favor either shrub- or ground-nesters; but Mallards do nest in them.

Natural Reforestation Lands (Mixed or Monotypic Saplings)

In the north, only a few small upland sites fail to grow up to trees naturally immediately following fire, logging, or temporary flooding. They are the sandy barrens and the sod-bound frost pockets. Since many of these are planted to conifers, upland carrs are rare in the north. What is common instead is a dense irregular expanse of very young saplings of aspens, maples, pines, birches, oaks, and so on, usually in mixtures. While they are small (2–10 feet tall), they form a sort of open brushy landscape that is too tall for most grassland birds, yet too low for most forest species. A miscellany of forest-edge and northern-forest birds occurs in such places. Since taller forests usually occur nearby, looming on the horizon today, we no longer have the wide open landscapes following the big fires that brought temporary invasions of Greater Prairie-Chickens and Sharp-tailed Grouse to the north country.

Open Grasslands and Barrens

Large prairie-plains landscapes are wholly or largely devoid of shrubs and trees. In Wisconsin's present climate, which favors forests, open landscapes have two major origins: localized droughty soils (prairies and sand barrens) and land use (agriculture and sometimes mining). There is a sharp break between the birds of forests and carrs and the species of open skylines. Not all of the open-skyline species are covered here; for many require open water and thus are covered under the Shallow Marsh heading. The rest, covered here, seem to range widely over dry to wet sites. Since our relic prairie vegetation is so rare and usually confined to very small areas, we still know little of its bird preferences. Therefore, birds of native (and planted) dry and wet prairies are by implication covered under one or more of the following five subtypes of open landscape.

Annual Crops (Maize, Small Grains, Soybeans, Sunflowers)

As dairying gives way to cash cropping, the already considerable acreage of maize, small grains, soybeans, and now sunflowers is increasing further at the expense of forage, pasture, and even woodland. Short-lived crops, planted and harvested in the same year in relatively large, uniform acreages, are unsuitable for nesting, even if not cultivated or poisoned. However, they provide food for a number of birds and maintain open landscapes, which may make nearby hay crops, grassy rights-of-way, rocky outcrops, and even fencerows attractive for nesting by certain prairie birds. Among these are the Gray Partridge and Horned Lark. The latter, in fact, often nests so early that it can rear its first broods in the plowed fields and unplowed stubble before spring planting. Incomplete or delayed harvests help maintain American Crows, Ring-necked Pheasants, Blue Jays, Northern Cardinals, wintering fringillids, larks, and meadowlarks through the cold season, and the inevitable weedy field edges may well be essential in summer, as well, for nourishing the growing young of many birds attributed to other habitats.

Perennial Forage and Pasture (Alfalfa, Grasses)

The landscape type characterized as perennial forage and pasture includes large flat or hilly areas of (1) moderately grazed unimproved pasture—usually bluegrass, occasionally little bluestem—on steep, sandy, or rocky soils; and (2) mowed perennial forage or hay crops—especially alfalfa or legume-grass mixtures. The perennial hay is usually harvested two or three times each year. Excluded from this grassland type are low meadows, tallgrass prairie, bracken grassland, and tall silage like sudan grass and green corn. Also excluded are the usually smaller isolated acreages of unharvested grass or forage, which are called old field (discussed in the following section). Pastures for dairy cattle have been disappearing as feedlot farming has seemed to be a more efficient use of forage. But beef-feeder operators now often let steers roam for exercise, giving us a taste of the western prairie rangelands. Because of Wisconsin's dairy tradition, we have a much larger proportion of the landscape in extensive, perennial, short herbaceous cover than any adjacent state.

This extensive grassland habitat in all sectors of our state is the last one to which most of our prairie birds are adapted. Where the acreages are ample and grazing or mowing is not too early or frequent, these species take their chances with the machines and livestock just as their ancestors did with fires, bison, elk, and antelope, taking some reproductive losses but surviving often enough to endure. Agricultural reserve programs become important, as alfalfa harvest schedules accelerate and exclude nesting. Today, airports do their part also, providing nest sites for upland birds of the prairie contingent in the large, occasionally mowed acreages needed for aircraft clearance.

Old Field (Unharvested Goldenrod and Pasture Grasses, North and South)

In old-field habitats, the main types of land use are passive; for these are abandoned or nonintensive farmlands. The mostly Old World grasses and common weeds persisting in former fields and pastures and orchards include bluegrass, redtop, quackgrass, timothy, smooth brome, orchard grass, common goldenrod, asters, thistles, wild parsnip, common milkweed, and clovers. Primarily in the north, especially on poor soils, the native bracken fern (*Pteridium aquilinum*) is prominent, along with cool-season Eurasian forbs such as knapweed, Queen Anne's lace, daisy, and hawkweeds. "Bracken grassland" is often the description applied to expanses of cold, treeless northern landscapes persisting on poor soils following the era of big logging, fires, and unsuccessful farming attempts.

This old-field category excludes older fields now growing up to shrubs or trees (see Southern Wisconsin Upland Carr and Natural Reforestation Lands), but it includes northern forest clearings and dry kettles ("sags") in which summer frosts and dense grass sod exclude tree and shrub invasion. The old field used to be much more common than it is today north of the tension zone where temporarily widespread farming was not intensive; now forests again dominate the skyline. Southward in Wisconsin, a spectacular rise in numbers of second homes, recreation properties, part-time farms, and speculation lands within 100 miles or more of every urban center, along with the abandonment of orchards and small hill-country farms and the state purchase of recreation lands, is providing this habitat, but only very temporarily, before tree invasion or planting and lawn mowing begin. A mixture of forest edge and prairie birds uses the old fields. It is not clear whether the expanses of grass along freeways and in interchanges will be used by these birds if and when mowing becomes less intensive and widespread.

Sedge Meadow (Peatland Grasses and Sedges, North and South)

Sedge meadow is really a wetland, for it depends on waterlogging to form its peaty soil and to exclude shrubs and trees. This level grassy landscape may be temporarily flooded, especially in late winter or spring. However, the term *dry marsh* aptly describes the summer condition in which sedges and grasses resemble (and even include) upland prairie plants and permit entry of mowing equipment. Despite species differences north and south and soil differences, the vegetation is very uniform in aspect throughout the state. Extensive sedge meadows have become rare in agricultural regions. Regional drainage and pasturing are suspected of being more important than cessation of marsh hay harvest in converting the remaining unplowed sedge meadows to lowland carrs, for wild fires still occur but seem ineffective in excluding shrubs today. Small scattered areas escaping much drainage, impoundment, or planting to reed canary grass include low prairies, fens, tussock meadows, and sedge–bluejoint grass mixtures near lakes and marshes in the south. In the north, the sedge meadows remain in some stream valleys, upper flowages, and wet kettles; and some extensive burned or logged swamps now have sedge and grass.

In acid wet sands, especially in central and northwestern Wisconsin, the dominants are three sedges: bog wiregrass (*Carex lasiocarpa*), wool grass (*Scirpus cyperinus*), and softwater beaked sedge (*C. rostrata*). These monotypic types of cover gradate through the mossy bog heaths of leatherleaf into the conifer bogs. Elsewhere (e.g., on fertile seepages) these sedges may be joined or replaced by a richer assemblage of grasses and forbs, or there may be monotypes of the fine-leaved tussock sedge (*C. stricta*), which forms the characteristic hummocks, or of one of the coarser sedges that tolerate more flooding (*C. atherodes, C. aquatilis, C. trichocarpa,* and *C. lacustris*). Meadow and prairie grasses found near or with the sedges include bluejoint (*Calamagrostis*), sloughgrass, or cord grass (*Spartina pectinata*), and big bluestem (*Andropogon gerardi*).

When floating, northern moss-sedge mats provide nest sites for Black Terns. Otherwise the sedge meadow avifauna is essentially one of prairie with a few additions like the American Bittern and Sharp-tailed and LeConte's Sparrows. When water levels stay up in summer, the sedge meadow becomes part of the shallow marsh (or lake) and will have an abundance of rails and snipe. When planted to reed canary grass (*Phalaris arundinacea*), the meadows have little wildlife. Native stands of giant reed grass (*Phragmites communis*), an invader of disturbed peatland in our region, seem to be barren of birdlife unless flooded, while monotypes of purple loosestrife apparently are always barren of birds.

Sand and Gravel (Barrens, Dunes, Gravel Pits, Hilltops)

Natural and man-made exposures of dry coarse materials provide grit, food, and special nest sites for a diverse collection of birds. Open gravelly hilltops, dunes, sandy river islands and terraces, and wide sand or gravel beaches are natural nest sites for the Common Nighthawk, Horned Lark, Killdeer, and Spotted Sandpiper. Mourning Doves, Eastern Bluebirds, American Kestrels, and Lark and Vesper Sparrows frequent abandoned farms in the sandy country of central and northwestern Wisconsin, along the sandy terraces of our major rivers such as the Wisconsin and Mississippi, and exposed parts of gravelly glacial moraines. The Sharp-tailed Grouse needs a mixture of sandy barrens, sedge meadows, and small brushy or boggy areas typical of its major range northwest of us. Gravel pits, road cuts, and quarries simulate natural barrens and, in addition, may expose vertical surfaces of rock or of clay or silt overburdens that are fully as suitable as stream banks for the nest cavities of Bank and Northern Rough-winged Swallows and the Belted Kingfisher.

Note: Cliffs, banks, and beaches close to water are covered again under Ponds and Streams and under Lakes and Flowages, while quarries that hold water are included under the Shallow Marsh heading. While some plants are characteristic of sands and gravels, the important feature for habitat recognition is the exposure (i.e., incomplete vegetative cover) of the coarse soils.

Waterscapes

In waterscapes, surface water dominates part or all of the scene most of each year and maintains its dominance by depth, wave and ice action, and the forces of flow, flotation, and flooding. Again—as there was between forest and grassland—there is a break in birdlife from all previous categories. As a group, water birds are highly specialized for travel and feeding, if not nesting, in or on the water or close to it. This landscape group includes quiet waters, flowing waters, and larger open bodies with strong wave action. Other wetlands, which may exist without surface waters, have already been covered: the southern lowland forest, the sphagnum-spruce bogs and cedar swamps, the lowland carrs, and the sedge meadows. All these, and even sand and gravel, may grade into the wetter wetlands discussed below and be used by their birds when flooded.

Note: *Swamp* is frequently used loosely for all wetlands, including the open marshes. In view of the strict habitat preference of birds, I have followed Curtis' (1959) precise clarification of terms and use *swamp* only for wooded wetlands.

Shallow Marsh (Cattails, Bulrushes)

Also called wet or deepwater marsh, the shallow marsh is a place where water is shallow enough for the growth of emergent aquatic plants whose presence and density are closely tied to seasonal water-level fluctuations. This habitat varies little across the state but is rare in the southwestern and northeastern sectors except near the Mississippi River and the Great Lakes. Near the shore you typically find a transition to sedge meadow or wet carr, while in the deeper areas (i.e., in ponds, lake bays, or rivers) is a zone of water lilies.

Much of the cover, bird-nest support, and muskrat food are provided by cattails and bulrushes. Their associates, all too weak to support bird nests, include arrowhead, wapato, pickerelweed, and bur-reeds. When not overabundant, submerged waterweeds, floating duckweeds, and microscopic algae are likewise typical and important food sources. Dense masses of these, however, may signify overfertile (eutrophic) water and consequent lower bird diversity. Monotypic shrubby invasions by alien purple loosestrife and the native water willow—triggered by water level alteration and eutrophication, respectively—may likewise exclude most water birds.

Assuming high water quality (clear, not too fertile), the frequent recycling of nutrient minerals with natural swings from high to low water and back regenerates all the plants of different depths and provides an array of niches for a remarkably high biomass and diversity of animals, including birds. Shallow marshes can support up to four broods per acre, eight times the average density of birds in grassland and forest. Moreover, many water birds are much larger than most land birds. Marsh birds are somewhat nomadic, especially the Black Tern, Least Bittern, and Yellow-headed Blackbird, so that they may find suitable habitat as dry and wet years shift the balance between vegetation and water in each place. Therefore, like the upland edge habitats (savannas and carrs), shallow marsh is most productive when in a state of flux. Many marshes are impoverished of birdlife today simply because of enforced stability. Waters kept too high become open lakes with no nest sites, while waters kept too low become dense dry cattail thickets prone to raccoon predation, attracting only the Red-winged Blackbird and Marsh Wren. A special case of the relation of cyclic changes to bird use is the use of small floating "boggy" islands of debris or peat by Black Terns for much of their nesting. The float-ups, probably caused by changes in water depth, must be new to be suitable, because older ones become too thickly vegetated to suit the terns.

Shallow marshes have been hurt in other ways. Filling or dredging of shores (lagooning) eliminates the shallows where small plants and animals can live and be fed on by rails, herons, and ducks. Abrupt shorelines also erode and bring in shrubs and trees, which many waterfowl dislike, since they are really prairie-plains and tundra species responding to open horizons. The wild rice, once so important to waterfowl, cannot be restored to our marshes in agricultural regions until we can eliminate siltation, eutrophication, and the carp.

The intermittent gradual drying of gently sloping shores of natural marshes and small ponds provides the major feeding sites for itinerant and breeding shorebirds as well as ducks and geese. Ponds that go dry too often for emergent aquatic plants to survive the dry summer or cold winter perform a special service to waterfowl if located near marshes and flyways. Lacking fish and dragonflies, their food chain ends in an unusual abundance of shrimp, snails, tadpoles, and seeds that are an important protein source for migratory water birds just before the breeding season. Thus, another principle for good marsh habitat is a diversity of depths and basin sizes in each natural area or complex of such areas. Aside from the "smorgasbord" value, there is opportunity for marsh birds' temporary use of adjacent meadows and carrs if water levels rise too high. (These incursions are not indicated in Table 2.) An example is the Green Bay wetlands, of which the isolated remnants are vulnerable to drastic natural changes in water levels in Lake Michigan. Many of our marshes at present may not produce all the birds we expect them to, because the principles of good marsh habitat have been violated by human impact (see "The Landscape and the Birds"). Management for shorebirds will need to be different from waterfowl production formulas, too.

Wooded Swamp (Wooded Wetlands, Including Islands) (Red Maple, etc.)

The wooded swamp is a wetter habitat than the southern Wisconsin lowland forest but likewise includes dry islands. In the northern and eastern parts of Wisconsin, cool temperatures and high humidity tend to cause every low spot to collect water. Since the water levels don't fluctuate much, every emergent stump and fallen log stays wet enough, but not too wet, to enable tree seedlings to establish on top of them. Thus, over time most wet spots not burned off or flooded by the beaver support tangles of trees existing just over the water. Many conifer swamps (see this habitat description under the Northern Wisconsin Forests heading) have formed enough peat to fill in the water; but deciduous trees like elms, ashes, red maples, aspens, birches—or mixtures of them with pines, hemlocks, firs, tamaracks, white cedars, and spruces—may be found next to or over water in many places. Our major swamps are near Lakes Superior and Michigan, Green Bay, along the Wisconsin and Mississippi rivers, and in central Wisconsin. The rookeries at Horicon Marsh, Lake Koshkonong, and along the Mississippi River are the reason for listing egrets and many other herons in this category, although the trees used may actually be on upland islands rather than directly in the swamps. Trees that are inaccessible to humans and natural enemies and reasonably close to water are the essential item for these birds, whether it is in a northern red maple swamp or a southern silver maple floodplain forest.

Ponds and Streams (Narrow or Small Open Waters and Shores)

Smaller permanent open waters, such as ponds and streams, and their shores, constitute another kind of water habitat. Streams include springs and small brooks, as well as river channels in the larger valleys, statewide. They may meander through a nearly flat, marshy or forested floodplain, or they may cascade past cliffs and steep ravines. Kettle ponds and river sloughs, likewise, may occur in forest, carr, or grassland landscapes. Therefore, many habitats are included, especially as both shore and water are covered. Spotted Sandpipers and Green-backed Herons occur throughout all this diversity, while other birds, like the Hooded Merganser, nest sparingly only in the northern and central areas of Wisconsin. The other two mergansers are found mainly on larger waters in the northern part of the state.

Here, also, we include natural banks and cliffs and the man-made bridges and buildings used by swallows, Eastern Phoebes, and Belted Kingfishers for nest sites. Since many birds of adjacent forest, grassland, or wetland will use small areas of open water on occasion, the streams, sloughs, and meanders are among the best places to observe birds, especially from a quiet canoe. The American

Redstart and Northern Oriole, in particular, like to nest near water, and the Prothonotary Warbler almost always can see its reflection. The Louisiana Waterthrush nests under wooded stream banks whether along a tiny brook or a river.

Inland Lakes and Flowages (Larger Deep Waters and Their Shores)
Inland lakes and flowages—the larger permanent water bodies, excluding the Great Lakes—constitute a distinctive habitat type. Flowages (caused by beaver or humans) may contain dead trees important for nest sites of Double-crested Cormorants and Ospreys, and they tend to isolate points or islands where live trees become attractive locations for nesting Bald Eagles and Great Blue Herons. However, unstable steep shores exclude wetland birdlife from many flowages. For nesting, Common Mergansers and Common Loons need undisturbed boggy shores on the larger lakes, while the Spotted Sandpiper uses their rocky or gravelly shores. Since all the raptors and waterfowl are so vulnerable to disturbance by recreational beach and boating use, most species no longer occur on our southern lakes and are now lacking from many northern ones as well. Frequent human intrusion may make our lakes sterile of birds and other wildlife, posing perhaps a greater threat than acid rain.

The Great Lakes (Including Shores and Islands)
Wisconsin has large frontages on Lakes Superior and Michigan, where large-scale wind, ice, and wave power have created broad coastal zones of dunes and gravel bars. These in turn have often trapped small lakes and sloughs. Although this habitat still supports a variety of bird species, bird habitat has diminished in recent years. Some of the wetlands on Lake Superior and in Door County are still unpolluted and undisturbed, and some islands among the Apostle Islands and on both sides of Door County have been made federal refuges. Most of the coast, however, has lost much of its special birdlife to development and recreation, even though the water quality often remains very good. Destruction of the eggs of island-nesting gulls, terns, herons, and cormorants by certain commercial fishermen has abated somewhat, but the problem of keeping cormorants from preying on fish in trap nets has to be solved. Another conflict between humans and wildlife centers on Common Terns, which now have few nesting sites not usurped by the increasing population of dump-feeding Ring-billed and Herring Gulls. The "Big" Fox River has been relieved of some of the paper mill waste but not from toxic mud, or from continuing pollution from farms. The few remaining unpolluted and protected Green Bay marshes are not always large enough to accommodate cycles of lake levels that move the birds' habitat to and fro. Our Caspian Terns appear to be breeding only on islands close to the Michigan state line.

Cliff Swallows are particularly abundant where exposed clay soil and cliffs or buildings and loading docks are available. They and Chimney Swifts may use lighthouses—another case of harmony between human and wildlife use.

Settled Areas
Many birds are preadapted for lawns, parks, street trees, gardens, and even gravel roofs and farm buildings. Others may someday adapt to human disturbances and constructions if we can maintain them in the wild for several more centuries. (Could herons and eagles come to nest on our chimneys as the European Storks do? The Peregrine Falcon once took to city skyscrapers and is begin-

ning to do so again, feeding on the abundant city pigeons.) At present we can note a lessening of bird diversity with increased alteration of the landscape as we progress from the rural farmstead and small town to the sterile steel and concrete of the inner city.

Farmsteads

The farmhouse, usually surrounded by a lawn and garden with trees, as well as the farm buildings, feedlot, and nearby fields, are all considered to be part of the farmstead. The adjacent landscape, of course, has much influence on a farmstead's bird diversity. A metal shed surrounded only by a mint farm or soybean or corn fields is like the commercial zone in a city. But if fencerows, wetland, water, forest, and forage crops occur nearby, birds of these habitats will be seen at the farmstead too, and we can add such species as the meadowlarks, Mourning Dove, American Kestrel, Killdeer, Warbling Vireo, and Song Sparrow.

Residential Areas with Mature Trees

Mature trees in urban areas are most common in small towns and older sections of cities that have large lot sizes with space and time for trees to grow up. Parks, campuses, and older cemeteries are the best urban places of all for birds, including the Eastern Screech-Owl. As in the savanna, canopy birds predominate, for species that nest or feed on the ground or in low shrubs and saplings are diminished by pets, human disturbance, and cleanup of brush. For example, the Wood Thrush, Brown Thrasher, Rufous-sided Towhee, and Rose-breasted Grosbeak will persist in new woodland developments only until all of the small lots are sold and landscaped. Crows may move into urban trees to nest and may become nuisances as they prey on songbird nestlings. Lagooning of parkland streams and marshes usually eliminates all water birds except tame Mallards. However, near waterways the trees will abound with migrating warblers and other forest birds each fall and spring. A new arrival, the House Finch, is settling in.

Residential Areas with Few Mature Trees

Newer urban areas lose most of their trees (if they had any) during development, because ranch-style houses occupy most of the small lot. Newly planted trees are not yet large enough to count. Older settled areas that had a preponderance of American elms now lost to disease qualify here as well. Shrub borders, hedges, and foundation plantings provide the chief cover. Certain birds, such as the Chipping Sparrow and Common Grackle, have done very well in conifer plantings. Rock Doves may choose to use private houses as well as larger buildings and may become a nuisance along with the grackles. Some former farmlands retain their European Starling population as a further suburban nuisance. Very new developments that still have their forest or prairie birds (e.g., the American Goldfinch) are excluded from this category, since these species will not persist. A year-round supply of food and cover may explain the incidence of Northern Cardinals and Northern Mockingbirds in these urban areas. Of course, if the residences are near the edge of a small town, they will have additional birds just as the farmstead does—for example, the Yellow Warbler and Song Sparrow. Birdhouses, of course, account for some of the birds in all residential areas and farmsteads.

Commercial and Industrial Areas

Included in commercial and industrial areas are the downtown stores and government buildings, the urban freeways, parking lots and ramps, the manufacturing district, and the strip developments along entering highways. Nearly all the ground is paved. The birds use buildings and overpasses for nests or roosts and feed elsewhere. Our three European imports may also glean food from the streets or be fed by people in parks. A frequent spectacle at dusk is the gathering of thousands of European Starlings to their roost on a public building. Like the Rock Doves, restored Peregrine Falcons are more likely to be found on buildings today than on their original cliff habitat. When water is near enough to attract flying insects, Common Nighthawks and Chimney Swifts may be abundant. Sometimes Barn and Cliff Swallows and Purple Martins are added if there is appropriate housing. Like the Barn Owl and American Kestrel, these birds need no vegetation directly. An occasional pair of American Robins may find a tiny patch of lawn to "worm" in and a building ledge to nest on. Tame Mallards often frequent park lagoons and attempt to nest on roofs. Landscaped commercial areas such as industrial parks may have extensive park or forest land and fall under other habitats of settled areas, namely, residential areas with trees or even parks and farmsteads. Gaggles of Canada Geese are becoming common near urban waters, too.

Breeding Bird Habitats

The birds listed in the breeding bird habitat table (Table 2) remain in Wisconsin through the summer months. In most cases confirmed or presumed breeding records exist for them since 1960. Several additional species are occasionally present in summer as nonbreeders: the American White Pelican, Little Blue Heron, Tricolored Heron, Laughing Gull, Franklin's Gull, Least Tern, Scissor-tailed Flycatcher, Blackpoll Warbler, and Kirtland's Warbler. These are listed as migrants in Table 4, as are arctic-nesting shorebirds that are often present in Wisconsin in June and July.

Table 2 includes all 29 habitats described above for Wisconsin and covers nesting and feeding sites even when these are not the same. Examples of separate feeding and nesting habitats include those of swallows, terns, herons, and kingfishers, which may commute to and from marshes and lakes several miles from their unfledged young. Mallards, Blue-winged Teal, and Wood Ducks may nest in uplands and then herd their chicks to waters as much as half a mile away. In these and similar cases, both habitats are marked for the species.

For some species, you'll see that only one or a few columns are marked, while other birds seem to be very broad in their habitat requirements. To some extent, then, Table 2 explains the relative prevalence of certain birds, like the Redwinged Blackbird, in contrast to the less readily met species, like the Marsh Wren, which require special conditions available in very limited areas. Sometimes, of course, habitat destruction has further limited the available habitat. For the Piping Plover, to take the most extreme case, suitable habitat is now limited in Wisconsin to one remaining undisturbed beach, with room for only 1–3 pairs of birds.

However, some of the apparent width of tolerance of the birds is due to the

Table 2. Habitat Preferences of Wisconsin Breeding Birds

Landscape Group	Southern Forest			Northern Forest							Savanna-Shrub					Open Grassland					Water-scapes					Settled Areas			
Vegetation Type →	Dry Deciduous	Mesic Deciduous	Lowland Deciduous	Mesic Deciduous	Pioneer Deciduous	Mesic Conifer-Hardwood	Dry Sandy	Upland Mesic Boreal	Conifer Swamp	Conifer Plantation	Deciduous Forest Savanna	Southern Upland Carr	Southern Lowland Carr	Northern Lowland Carr	Reforestation Lands	Annual Crops	Perennial Forage	Old Field	Sedge Meadow	Sand, Gravel	Shallow Marsh	Wooded Swamp	Ponds, Streams	Inland Lakes, Flowages	Great Lakes	Farmsteads	Residential (Trees)	Residential (Shrubs)	Commercial
Indicator Plants →	Oak, Hickory, Shrubs	Sugar Maple, Basswood, White Ash	Silver Maple, Elm, Green Ash	Sugar Maple, Basswood, White Ash	Aspen, White Birch	Sugar Maple, Hemlock, Pine	Hill's Oak, Jack Pine	White Spruce, Balsam Fir	Black Spruce, Tamarack, White Cedar	Pine, Spruce	Oak, Maple, Grass (Pasture)	Hazelnut, Cherry, Grape	Red Dogwood, Pussywillow	Alder, Willow	Shrubs, Bracken, Saplings	Maize, Grain, Soybeans, Sunflowers	Alfalfa, Hay Pasture	Goldenrod, Grass, Thistles	Peatland, Grass, Sedge	Barrens, Dunes, Gravel	Cattails, Bulrushes	Red Maple, Ash, Islands	Water, Shores	Water, Shores	Water, Shores, Islands	Yards, Barns, Farm Gardens	Shade Trees, Lawns	Ornamental Shrubs, Lawns	Brick, Concrete, Grass
Common Loon																								•	•				
Pied-billed Grebe																					•		•	•	•				
Horned Grebe																					•			•	•				
Red-necked Grebe																					•			•	•				
Double-crested Cormorant																						•	•	•	•				
American Bittern																			•		•	•							
Least Bittern																					•								
Great Blue Heron	•																				•	•	•	•	•				
Great Egret																					•	•	•	•					
Snowy Egret																					•	•	•						
Cattle Egret																	•				•	•	•						
Green-backed Heron	•																				•	•	•	•					
Black-crowned Night-Heron																					•	•	•		•				
Yellow-crowned Night-Heron	•																					•	•						
Mute Swan																					•			•	•				
Canada Goose																					•		•	•					
Wood Duck	•																				•	•	•						
Green-winged Teal																					•	•	•	•					
American Black Duck																					•	•	•	•					
Mallard																•	•		•		•	•	•	•	•				

Table 2. Habitat Preferences of Wisconsin Breeding Birds, continued

Landscape Group →	Southern Forest			Northern Forest							Savanna-Shrub					Open Grassland					Waterscapes					Settled Areas			
Vegetation Type	Dry Deciduous	Mesic Deciduous	Lowland Deciduous	Mesic Deciduous	Pioneer Deciduous	Mesic Conifer-Hardwood	Dry Sandy	Upland Mesic Boreal	Conifer Swamp	Conifer Plantation	Deciduous Forest Savanna	Southern Upland Carr	Southern Lowland Carr	Northern Lowland Carr	Reforestation Lands	Annual Crops	Perennial Forage	Old Field	Sedge Meadow	Sand, Gravel	Shallow Marsh	Wooded Swamp	Ponds, Streams	Inland Lakes, Flowages	Great Lakes	Farmsteads	Residential (Trees)	Residential (Shrubs)	Commercial
Indicator Plants / Landscape Feature	Oak, Hickory, Shrubs	Sugar Maple, Basswood, White Ash	Silver Maple, Elm, Green Ash	Sugar Maple, Basswood, White Ash	Aspen, White Birch	Sugar Maple, Hemlock, Pine	Hill's Oak, Jack Pine	White Spruce, Balsam Fir	Black Spruce, Tamarack, White Cedar	Pine, Spruce	Oak, Maple, Grass (Pasture)	Hazelnut, Cherry, Grape	Red Dogwood, Pussywillow	Alder, Willow	Shrubs, Bracken, Saplings	Maize, Grain, Soybeans, Sunflowers	Alfalfa, Hay Pasture	Goldenrod, Grass, Thistles	Peatland, Grass, Sedge	Barrens, Dunes, Gravel	Cattails, Bulrushes	Red Maple, Ash, Islands	Water, Shores	Water, Shores	Water, Shores, Islands	Yards, Barns, Farm Gardens	Shade Trees, Lawns	Ornamental Shrubs, Lawns	Brick, Concrete, Grass
Northern Pintail																					•		•						
Blue-winged Teal																	•		•		•	•	•	•	•				
Northern Shoveler																					•		•						
Gadwall																					•		•						
American Wigeon																					•		•						
Redhead																					•			•					
Ring-necked Duck																					•	•		•					
Lesser Scaup																								•	•				
Common Goldeneye																								•	•				
Hooded Merganser																						•	•						
Common Merganser																							•	•	•				
Red-breasted Merganser																							•	•	•				
Ruddy Duck																					•		•	•					
Turkey Vulture	•																			•									
Osprey																						•	•	•					
Bald Eagle						•															•	•	•	•					
Northern Harrier													•	•		•	•	•	•										
Sharp-shinned Hawk					•		•																						
Cooper's Hawk	•	•		•	•																								
Northern Goshawk				•	•																								

Continued on following pages

Table 2. Habitat Preferences of Wisconsin Breeding Birds, continued

Landscape Group → Vegetation Type (Indicator Plants/Landscape Feature)	Southern Forest: Dry Deciduous (Oak, Hickory, Shrubs)	Southern Forest: Mesic Deciduous (Sugar Maple, Basswood, White Ash)	Southern Forest: Lowland Deciduous (Silver Maple, Elm, Green Ash)	Northern Forest: Mesic Deciduous (Sugar Maple, Basswood, White Ash)	Northern Forest: Pioneer Deciduous (Aspen, White Birch)	Northern Forest: Mesic Conifer-Hardwood (Sugar Maple, Hemlock, Pine)	Northern Forest: Dry Sandy (Hill's Oak, Jack Pine)	Northern Forest: Upland Mesic Boreal (White Spruce, Balsam Fir)	Northern Forest: Conifer Swamp (Black Spruce, Tamarack, White Cedar)	Northern Forest: Conifer Plantation (Pine, Spruce)	Savanna-Shrub: Deciduous Forest Savanna (Oak, Maple, Grass (Pasture))	Savanna-Shrub: Southern Upland Carr (Hazelnut, Cherry, Grape)	Savanna-Shrub: Southern Lowland Carr (Red Dogwood, Pussywillow)	Savanna-Shrub: Northern Lowland Carr (Alder, Willow)	Savanna-Shrub: Reforestation Lands (Shrubs, Bracken, Saplings)	Open Grassland: Annual Crops (Maize, Grain, Soybeans, Sunflowers)	Open Grassland: Perennial Forage (Alfalfa, Hay Pasture)	Open Grassland: Old Field (Goldenrod, Grass, Thistles)	Open Grassland: Sedge Meadow (Peatland, Grass, Sedge)	Open Grassland: Sand, Gravel (Barrens, Dunes, Gravel)	Waterscapes: Shallow Marsh (Cattails, Bulrushes)	Waterscapes: Wooded Swamp (Red Maple, Ash, Islands)	Waterscapes: Ponds, Streams (Water, Shores)	Waterscapes: Inland Lakes, Flowages (Water, Shores)	Waterscapes: Great Lakes (Water, Shores, Islands)	Settled Areas: Farmsteads (Yards, Barns, Farm Gardens)	Settled Areas: Residential (Trees) (Shade Trees, Lawns)	Settled Areas: Residential (Shrubs) (Ornamental Shrubs, Lawns)	Settled Areas: Commercial (Brick, Concrete, Grass)
Red-shouldered Hawk		•	•	•																									
Broad-winged Hawk		•		•	•	•																							
Red-tailed Hawk	•	•		•	•											•	•	•											
American Kestrel											•	•			•		•	•		•						•			
Merlin								•																					
Peregrine Falcon																								•	•				•
Gray Partridge																•	•												
Ring-necked Pheasant												•	•			•	•	•	•										
Spruce Grouse								•	•																				
Ruffed Grouse	•	•		•	•	•																							
Greater Prairie-Chicken																	•												
Sharp-tailed Grouse															•		•		•										
Wild Turkey	•																												
Northern Bobwhite												•				•													
Yellow Rail																					•								
King Rail																					•								
Virginia Rail																					•								
Sora																					•								
Common Moorhen																					•	•							
American Coot																					•		•						

636

Table 2. Habitat Preferences of Wisconsin Breeding Birds, continued

Landscape Group →	Southern Forest			Northern Forest							Savanna-Shrub					Open Grassland					Waterscapes					Settled Areas			
Vegetation Type →	Dry Deciduous	Mesic Deciduous	Lowland Deciduous	Mesic Deciduous	Pioneer Deciduous	Mesic Conifer-Hardwood	Dry Sandy	Upland Mesic Boreal	Conifer Swamp	Conifer Plantation	Deciduous Forest Savanna	Southern Upland Carr	Southern Lowland Carr	Northern Lowland Carr	Reforestation Lands	Annual Crops	Perennial Forage	Old Field	Sedge Meadow	Sand, Gravel	Shallow Marsh	Wooded Swamp	Ponds, Streams	Inland Lakes, Flowages	Great Lakes	Farmsteads	Residential (Trees)	Residential (Shrubs)	Commercial
Indicator Plants / Landscape Feature →	Oak, Hickory, Shrubs	Sugar Maple, Basswood, White Ash	Silver Maple, Elm, Green Ash	Sugar Maple, Basswood, White Ash	Aspen, White Birch	Sugar Maple, Hemlock, Pine	Hill's Oak, Jack Pine	White Spruce, Balsam Fir	Black Spruce, Tamarack, White Cedar	Pine, Spruce	Oak, Maple, Grass (Pasture)	Hazelnut, Cherry, Grape	Red Dogwood, Pussywillow	Alder, Willow	Shrubs, Bracken, Saplings	Maize, Grain, Soybeans, Sunflowers	Alfalfa, Hay Pasture	Goldenrod, Grass, Thistles	Peatland, Grass, Sedge	Barrens, Dunes, Gravel	Cattails, Bulrushes	Red Maple, Ash, Islands	Water, Shores	Water, Shores	Water, Shores, Islands	Yards, Barns, Farm Gardens	Shade Trees, Lawns	Ornamental Shrubs, Lawns	Brick, Concrete, Grass
Sandhill Crane																•	•	•	•		•								
Piping Plover																									•				
Killdeer																•	•	•		•			•	•					
Spotted Sandpiper																							•	•					
Upland Sandpiper																	•	•											
Common Snipe													•	•		•			•		•								
American Woodcock		•									•		•	•	•							•							
Wilson's Phalarope																			•		•								
Little Gull																									•				
Bonaparte's Gull																									•				
Ring-billed Gull																								•	•				
Herring Gull																								•	•				
Caspian Tern																									•				
Common Tern																									•				
Forster's Tern																					•		•	•	•				
Black Tern																			•		•	•	•	•	•				
Rock Dove																•							•	•		•			•
Mourning Dove							•				•					•	•	•		•						•	•		
Black-billed Cuckoo	•	•	•	•	•						•																		

Continued on following pages

637

Table 2. Habitat Preferences of Wisconsin Breeding Birds, continued

Landscape Group	Southern Forest			Northern Forest							Savanna-Shrub					Open Grassland					Water-scapes					Settled Areas			
Vegetation Type → Indicator Plants/Landscape Feature	Dry Deciduous (Oak, Hickory, Shrubs)	Mesic Deciduous (Sugar Maple, Basswood, White Ash)	Lowland Deciduous (Silver Maple, Elm, Green Ash)	Mesic Deciduous (Sugar Maple, Basswood, White Ash)	Pioneer Deciduous (Aspen, White Birch)	Mesic Conifer-Hardwood (Sugar Maple, Hemlock, Pine)	Dry Sandy (Hill's Oak, Jack Pine)	Upland Mesic Boreal (White Spruce, Balsam Fir)	Conifer Swamp (Black Spruce, Tamarack, White Cedar)	Conifer Plantation (Pine, Spruce)	Deciduous Forest Savanna (Oak, Maple, Grass (Pasture))	Southern Upland Carr (Hazelnut, Cherry, Grape)	Southern Lowland Carr (Red Dogwood, Pussywillow)	Northern Lowland Carr (Alder, Willow)	Reforestation Lands (Shrubs, Bracken, Saplings)	Annual Crops (Maize, Grain, Soybeans, Sunflowers)	Perennial Forage (Alfalfa, Hay Pasture)	Old Field (Goldenrod, Grass, Thistles)	Sedge Meadow (Peatland, Grass, Sedge)	Sand, Gravel (Barrens, Dunes, Gravel)	Shallow Marsh (Cattails, Bulrushes)	Wooded Swamp (Red Maple, Ash, Islands)	Ponds, Streams (Water, Shores)	Inland Lakes, Flowages (Water, Shores)	Great Lakes (Water, Shores, Islands)	Farmsteads (Yards, Barns, Farm Gardens)	Residential (Trees) (Shade Trees, Lawns)	Residential (Shrubs) (Ornamental Shrubs, Lawns)	Commercial (Brick, Concrete, Grass)
Yellow-billed Cuckoo	•	•										•																	
Barn Owl																										•			•
Eastern Screech-Owl	•	•	•								•															•	•		
Great Horned Owl	•	•		•	•	•																•							
Barred Owl		•	•	•	•	•																•							
Great Gray Owl				•		•																							
Long-eared Owl		•				•				•																			
Short-eared Owl															•		•	•	•										
Northern Saw-whet Owl						•			•	•																			
Common Nighthawk																				•	•						•	•	•
Chuck-will's-widow	•																												
Whip-poor-will	•	•		•																									
Chimney Swift				•		•																				•	•		•
Ruby-throated Hummingbird	•	•	•	•	•	•					•															•	•		
Belted Kingfisher																					•		•	•					
Red-headed Woodpecker	•	•	•	•	•						•															•	•		
Red-bellied Woodpecker		•	•								•															•			
Yellow-bellied Sapsucker			•	•	•	•																							
Downy Woodpecker	•	•	•	•	•	•			•		•	•	•													•	•		
Hairy Woodpecker	•	•	•	•	•	•	•	•	•	•	•	•	•	•												•	•		

Table 2. Habitat Preferences of Wisconsin Breeding Birds, continued

Landscape Group	Southern Forest			Northern Forest							Savanna-Shrub					Open Grassland					Water-scapes					Settled Areas			
Vegetation Type	Dry Deciduous	Mesic Deciduous	Lowland Deciduous	Mesic Deciduous	Pioneer Deciduous	Mesic Conifer-Hardwood	Dry Sandy	Upland Mesic Boreal	Conifer Swamp	Conifer Plantation	Deciduous Forest Savanna	Southern Upland Carr	Southern Lowland Carr	Northern Lowland Carr	Reforestation Lands	Annual Crops	Perennial Forage	Old Field	Sedge Meadow	Sand, Gravel	Shallow Marsh	Wooded Swamp	Ponds, Streams	Inland Lakes, Flowages	Great Lakes	Farmsteads	Residential (Trees)	Residential (Shrubs)	Commercial
Indicator Plants/ Landscape Feature	Oak, Hickory, Shrubs	Sugar Maple, Basswood, White Ash	Silver Maple, Elm, Green Ash	Sugar Maple, Basswood, White Ash	Aspen, White Birch	Sugar Maple, Hemlock, Pine	Hill's Oak, Jack Pine	White Spruce, Balsam Fir	Black Spruce, Tamarack, White Cedar	Pine, Spruce	Oak, Maple, Grass (Pasture)	Hazelnut, Cherry, Grape	Red Dogwood, Pussywillow	Alder, Willow	Shrubs, Bracken, Saplings	Maize, Grain, Soybeans, Sunflowers	Alfalfa, Hay Pasture	Goldenrod, Grass, Thistles	Peatland, Grass, Sedge	Barrens, Dunes, Gravel	Cattails, Bulrushes	Red Maple, Ash, Islands	Water, Shores	Water, Shores	Water, Shores, Islands	Yards, Barns, Farm Gardens	Shade Trees, Lawns	Ornamental Shrubs, Lawns	Brick, Concrete, Grass
Black-backed Woodpecker								●	●																				
Northern Flicker	●	●	●	●	●	●					●	●			●			●								●	●		
Pileated Woodpecker	●	●	●	●	●	●		●														●							
Olive-sided Flycatcher									●						●														
Eastern Wood-Pewee	●	●		●	●						●															●	●		
Yellow-bellied Flycatcher				●		●	●																						
Acadian Flycatcher		●																											
Alder Flycatcher														●							●								
Willow Flycatcher												●	●								●								
Least Flycatcher		●		●	●	●					●																		
Eastern Phoebe	●	●		●	●								●									●	●			●	●		
Great Crested Flycatcher	●	●	●	●	●	●																							
Western Kingbird																										●			
Eastern Kingbird							●				●	●	●			●	●		●		●	●	●	●		●			
Horned Lark																●													
Purple Martin																						●	●	●	●	●	●		●
Tree Swallow											●	●				●	●		●		●	●	●	●	●	●			
Northern Rough-winged Swallow																				●	●		●	●	●				
Bank Swallow																				●	●		●	●	●				
Cliff Swallow																●	●	●			●	●	●	●	●	●			

Continued on following pages

Table 2. Habitat Preferences of Wisconsin Breeding Birds, continued

Species \ Landscape Group	Southern Forest: Dry Deciduous	Southern Forest: Mesic Deciduous	Southern Forest: Lowland Deciduous	Northern Forest: Mesic Deciduous	Northern Forest: Pioneer Deciduous	Northern Forest: Mesic Conifer-Hardwood	Northern Forest: Dry Sandy	Northern Forest: Upland Mesic Boreal	Northern Forest: Conifer Swamp	Northern Forest: Conifer Plantation	Savanna-Shrub: Deciduous Forest Savanna	Savanna-Shrub: Southern Upland Carr	Savanna-Shrub: Southern Lowland Carr	Savanna-Shrub: Northern Lowland Carr	Savanna-Shrub: Reforestation Lands	Open Grassland: Annual Crops	Open Grassland: Perennial Forage	Open Grassland: Old Field	Open Grassland: Sedge Meadow	Open Grassland: Sand, Gravel	Waterscapes: Shallow Marsh	Waterscapes: Wooded Swamp	Waterscapes: Ponds, Streams	Waterscapes: Inland Lakes, Flowages	Waterscapes: Great Lakes	Settled Areas: Farmsteads	Settled Areas: Residential (Trees)	Settled Areas: Residential (Shrubs)	Settled Areas: Commercial
Indicator Plants / Landscape Feature	Oak, Hickory, Shrubs	Sugar Maple, Basswood, White Ash	Silver Maple, Elm, Green Ash	Sugar Maple, Basswood, White Ash	Aspen, White Birch	Sugar Maple, Hemlock, Pine	Hill's Oak, Jack Pine	White Spruce, Balsam Fir	Black Spruce, Tamarack, White Cedar	Pine, Spruce	Oak, Maple, Grass (Pasture)	Hazelnut, Cherry, Grape	Red Dogwood, Pussywillow	Alder, Willow	Shrubs, Bracken, Saplings	Maize, Grain, Soybeans, Sunflowers	Alfalfa, Hay Pasture	Goldenrod, Grass, Thistles	Peatland, Grass, Sedge	Barrens, Dunes, Gravel	Cattails, Bulrushes	Red Maple, Ash, Islands	Water, Shores	Water, Shores	Water, Shores, Islands	Yards, Barns, Farm Gardens	Shade Trees, Lawns	Ornamental Shrubs, Lawns	Brick, Concrete, Grass
Barn Swallow													•	•	•		•	•	•		•	•	•	•	•	•			
Gray Jay								•	•																				
Blue Jay	•	•	•	•	•	•	•	•		•		•		•	•											•	•		
American Crow	•	•	•	•	•	•				•	•					•	•												
Common Raven				•	•	•		•																					
Black-capped Chickadee	•	•	•	•	•	•	•	•				•	•		•														
Boreal Chickadee								•	•																				
Tufted Titmouse	•																										•		
Red-breasted Nuthatch						•		•	•	•																			
White-breasted Nuthatch	•	•	•	•	•	•																				•	•		
Brown Creeper		•				•		•																					
Carolina Wren		•	•									•																	
Bewick's Wren																										•	•		
House Wren			•		•		•				•	•														•	•	•	
Winter Wren								•	•														•						
Sedge Wren													•	•			•	•	•		•								
Marsh Wren																					•								
Golden-crowned Kinglet								•	•	•																			
Ruby-crowned Kinglet								•	•																				
Blue-gray Gnatcatcher	•	•																											

Table 2. Habitat Preferences of Wisconsin Breeding Birds, continued

Landscape Group	Southern Forest			Northern Forest							Savanna-Shrub					Open Grassland					Water-scapes					Settled Areas			
Vegetation Type	Dry Deciduous	Mesic Deciduous	Lowland Deciduous	Mesic Deciduous	Pioneer Deciduous	Mesic Conifer-Hardwood	Dry Sandy	Upland Mesic Boreal	Conifer Swamp	Conifer Plantation	Deciduous Forest Savanna	Southern Upland Carr	Southern Lowland Carr	Northern Lowland Carr	Reforestation Lands	Annual Crops	Perennial Forage	Old Field	Sedge Meadow	Sand, Gravel	Shallow Marsh	Wooded Swamp	Ponds, Streams	Inland Lakes, Flowages	Great Lakes	Farmsteads	Residential (Trees)	Residential (Shrubs)	Commercial
Indicator Plants / Landscape Feature	Oak, Hickory, Shrubs	Sugar Maple, Basswood, White Ash	Silver Maple, Elm, Green Ash	Sugar Maple, Basswood, White Ash	Aspen, White Birch	Sugar Maple, Hemlock, Pine	Hill's Oak, Jack Pine	White Spruce, Balsam Fir	Black Spruce, Tamarack, White Cedar	Pine, Spruce	Oak, Maple, Grass (Pasture)	Hazelnut, Cherry, Grape	Red Dogwood, Pussywillow	Alder, Willow	Shrubs, Bracken, Saplings	Maize, Grain, Soybeans, Sunflowers	Alfalfa, Hay Pasture	Goldenrod, Grass, Thistles	Peatland, Grass, Sedge	Barrens, Dunes, Gravel	Cattails, Bulrushes	Red Maple, Ash, Islands	Water, Shores	Water, Shores	Water, Shores, Islands	Yards, Barns, Farm Gardens	Shade Trees, Lawns	Ornamental Shrubs, Lawns	Brick, Concrete, Grass
Eastern Bluebird							•				•	•			•		•	•								•			
Veery		•		•	•	•			•				•	•								•							
Swainson's Thrush								•	•																				
Hermit Thrush						•	•	•	•																				
Wood Thrush		•		•																									
American Robin	•	•	•	•	•	•	•			•	•	•	•	•	•		•	•					•			•	•	•	
Gray Catbird		•		•							•	•	•	•												•	•	•	
Northern Mockingbird												•														•	•	•	
Brown Thrasher	•			•							•	•						•								•	•		
Cedar Waxwing						•	•		•		•	•	•	•								•	•			•	•		
Loggerhead Shrike											•	•																	
European Starling	•		•	•							•			•		•	•	•					•			•	•	•	•
White-eyed Vireo												•																	
Bell's Vireo												•	•																
Solitary Vireo				•	•	•				•																			
Yellow-throated Vireo	•	•	•	•							•															•			
Warbling Vireo		•	•	•							•												•			•	•		
Red-eyed Vireo	•	•	•	•	•	•					•																		
Blue-winged Warbler		•	•									•	•																
Golden-winged Warbler		•	•	•									•	•															

Continued on following pages

641

Table 2. Habitat Preferences of Wisconsin Breeding Birds, continued

Landscape Group →	Southern Forest			Northern Forest							Savanna-Shrub					Open Grassland					Waterscapes					Settled Areas			
Vegetation Type →	Dry Deciduous	Mesic Deciduous	Lowland Deciduous	Mesic Deciduous	Pioneer Deciduous	Mesic Conifer-Hardwood	Dry Sandy	Upland Mesic Boreal	Conifer Swamp	Conifer Plantation	Deciduous Forest Savanna	Southern Upland Carr	Southern Lowland Carr	Northern Lowland Carr	Reforestation Lands	Annual Crops	Perennial Forage	Old Field	Sedge Meadow	Sand, Gravel	Shallow Marsh	Wooded Swamp	Ponds, Streams	Inland Lakes, Flowages	Great Lakes	Farmsteads	Residential (Trees)	Residential (Shrubs)	Commercial
Tennessee Warbler					●																								
Nashville Warbler								●	●	●																			
Northern Parula								●	●																				
Yellow Warbler		●	●									●	●	●							●					●	●		
Chestnut-sided Warbler	●				●		●							●	●														
Magnolia Warbler								●	●																				
Cape May Warbler								●	●																				
Black-throated Blue Warbler								●	●																				
Yellow-rumped Warbler							●	●	●	●																			
Black-throated Green Warbler				●		●		●																					
Blackburnian Warbler						●		●																					
Yellow-throated Warbler		●	●																										
Pine Warbler								●		●																			
Prairie Warbler	●											●																	
Palm Warbler									●																				
Cerulean Warbler	●	●	●	●																									
Black-and-White Warbler				●		●		●	●																				
American Redstart	●	●	●	●	●	●							●	●	●							●	●	●					
Prothonotary Warbler			●																			●	●						
Worm-eating Warbler		●																											
Ovenbird		●		●	●	●	●																						
Northern Waterthrush									●					●								●							
Louisiana Waterthrush		●	●																				●						
Kentucky Warbler		●	●																										
Connecticut Warbler							●		●						●														

642

Table 2. Habitat Preferences of Wisconsin Breeding Birds, continued

Column key (Landscape Group → Vegetation Type → Indicator Plants/Landscape Feature):

Southern Forest
1. Dry Deciduous — Oak, Hickory, Shrubs
2. Mesic Deciduous — Sugar Maple, Basswood, White Ash
3. Lowland Deciduous — Silver Maple, Elm, Green Ash

Northern Forest
4. Mesic Deciduous — Sugar Maple, Basswood, White Ash
5. Pioneer Deciduous — Aspen, White Birch
6. Mesic Conifer-Hardwood — Sugar Maple, Hemlock, Pine
7. Dry Sandy — Hill's Oak, Jack Pine
8. Upland Mesic Boreal — White Spruce, Balsam Fir
9. Conifer Swamp — Black Spruce, Tamarack, White Cedar
10. Conifer Plantation — Pine, Spruce

Savanna-Shrub
11. Deciduous Forest Savanna — Oak, Maple, Grass (Pasture)
12. Southern Upland Carr — Hazelnut, Cherry, Grape
13. Southern Lowland Carr — Red Dogwood, Pussywillow
14. Northern Lowland Carr — Alder, Willow
15. Reforestation Lands — Shrubs, Bracken, Saplings

Open Grassland
16. Annual Crops — Maize, Grain, Soybeans, Sunflowers
17. Perennial Forage — Alfalfa, Hay Pasture
18. Old Field — Goldenrod, Grass, Thistles
19. Sedge Meadow — Peatland, Grass, Sedge
20. Sand, Gravel — Barrens, Dunes, Gravel

Waterscapes
21. Shallow Marsh — Cattails, Bulrushes
22. Wooded Swamp — Red Maple, Ash, Islands
23. Ponds, Streams — Water, Shores
24. Inland Lakes, Flowages — Water, Shores
25. Great Lakes — Water, Shores, Islands

Settled Areas
26. Farmsteads — Yards, Barns, Farm Gardens
27. Residential (Trees) — Shade Trees, Lawns
28. Residential (Shrubs) — Ornamental Shrubs, Lawns
29. Commercial — Brick, Concrete, Grass

Species	1	2	3	4	5	6	7	8	9	10	11	12	13	14	15	16	17	18	19	20	21	22	23	24	25	26	27	28	29
Mourning Warbler		•		•	•							•	•		•														
Common Yellowthroat			•	•	•	•	•					•	•	•	•						•	•	•						
Hooded Warbler		•																											
Canada Warbler						•		•	•																				
Yellow-breasted Chat		•										•	•																
Scarlet Tanager	•	•	•	•			•																						
Northern Cardinal																										•	•	•	
Rose-breasted Grosbeak	•	•	•	•	•																					•	•		
Blue Grosbeak											•	•																	
Indigo Bunting	•	•	•	•	•	•	•				•	•			•														
Dickcissel																•	•												
Rufous-sided Towhee	•			•			•				•	•			•														
Chipping Sparrow	•	•	•	•		•	•			•	•	•			•			•								•	•	•	
Clay-colored Sparrow							•			•	•	•		•	•			•									•		
Field Sparrow							•				•	•			•			•											
Vesper Sparrow												•				•	•			•									
Lark Sparrow																•	•	•		•									
Savannah Sparrow																	•	•	•										
Grasshopper Sparrow																	•	•											
Henslow's Sparrow																	•	•											
LeConte's Sparrow																	•		•		•								
Sharp-tailed Sparrow																					•								
Song Sparrow											•	•	•		•				•		•	•	•	•		•	•	•	
Lincoln's Sparrow													•	•															
Swamp Sparrow												•	•	•					•		•	•							

643

Continued on following page

Table 2. Habitat Preferences of Wisconsin Breeding Birds, continued

Landscape Groups and their Vegetation Types / Indicator Plants–Landscape Features:

Southern Forest
- Dry Deciduous — Oak, Hickory, Shrubs
- Mesic Deciduous — Sugar Maple, Basswood, White Ash
- Lowland Deciduous — Silver Maple, Elm, Green Ash

Northern Forest
- Mesic Deciduous — Sugar Maple, Basswood, White Ash
- Pioneer Deciduous — Aspen, White Birch
- Mesic Conifer-Hardwood — Sugar Maple, Hemlock, Pine
- Dry Sandy — Hill's Oak, Jack Pine
- Upland Mesic Boreal — White Spruce, Balsam Fir
- Conifer Swamp — Black Spruce, Tamarack, White Cedar
- Conifer Plantation — Pine, Spruce

Savanna-Shrub
- Deciduous Forest Savanna — Oak, Maple, Grass (Pasture)
- Southern Upland Carr — Hazelnut, Cherry, Grape
- Southern Lowland Carr — Red Dogwood, Pussywillow
- Northern Lowland Carr — Alder, Willow
- Reforestation Lands — Shrubs, Bracken, Saplings

Open Grassland
- Annual Crops — Maize, Grain, Soybeans, Sunflowers
- Perennial Forage — Alfalfa, Hay Pasture
- Old Field — Goldenrod, Grass, Thistles
- Sedge Meadow — Peatland, Grass, Sedge
- Sand, Gravel — Barrens, Dunes, Gravel

Waterscapes
- Shallow Marsh — Cattails, Bulrushes
- Wooded Swamp — Red Maple, Ash, Islands
- Ponds, Streams — Water, Shores
- Inland Lakes, Flowages — Water, Shores
- Great Lakes — Water, Shores, Islands

Settled Areas
- Farmsteads — Yards, Barns, Farm Gardens
- Residential (Trees) — Shade Trees, Lawns
- Residential (Shrubs) — Ornamental Shrubs, Lawns
- Commercial — Brick, Concrete, Grass

Species	Dry Dec.	Mesic Dec.	Lowland Dec.	Mesic Dec.	Pioneer Dec.	Mesic Con-Hwd	Dry Sandy	Upland Mesic Boreal	Conifer Swamp	Conifer Plant.	Dec. Forest Savanna	S. Upland Carr	S. Lowland Carr	N. Lowland Carr	Reforest. Lands	Annual Crops	Perennial Forage	Old Field	Sedge Meadow	Sand, Gravel	Shallow Marsh	Wooded Swamp	Ponds, Streams	Inland Lakes	Great Lakes	Farmsteads	Resid. (Trees)	Resid. (Shrubs)	Commercial
White-throated Sparrow						●		●	●					●	●														
Dark-eyed Junco							●			●																			
Bobolink												●	●	●			●	●	●										
Red-winged Blackbird											●					●	●	●	●		●	●	●	●		●			
Eastern Meadowlark												●				●	●	●											
Western Meadowlark																●	●	●											
Yellow-headed Blackbird																●					●								
Brewer's Blackbird														●		●	●		●										
Common Grackle										●	●	●	●			●	●	●			●	●		●		●	●		
Brown-headed Cowbird	●	●	●	●	●	●	●				●	●			●	●		●											
Orchard Oriole			●								●															●			
Northern Oriole	●	●	●	●	●		●				●												●	●		●	●		
Purple Finch						●		●	●																				
House Finch												●															●	●	
Red Crossbill							●			●																			
White-winged Crossbill								●	●																				
Pine Siskin								●	●																				
American Goldfinch											●	●	●	●	●			●								●	●		
Evening Grosbeak								●																					
House Sparrow																●	●									●	●	●	●

arbitrary designation of habitats according to the human viewpoint. For example, many birds respectively of forest, shrubs in the open, or grassland do not care if the terrain is dry or wet, since their landscape requirement does not involve particular plant species or moisture; the life-form of the vegetation and a given size range of insect life are perhaps the only important factors. Likewise, many water birds require open water, but the area or flow rate of the water may not always matter; only the depth may be important for some.

The apparent width of range of bird habitat in Table 2 is also misleading because, in reality, landscapes are a continuum in which the preferred sites of individual bird species may successively overlap. Our arbitrary categories (sectors of the continuum from, say, forest grading to shrubs then grass) may cause bird occurrence to be noted twice for some species (e.g., the Gray Catbird) but only once for others (e.g., the Common Yellowthroat). Together with insufficient knowledge, these imperfections in this system leave plenty of room for surprise and discovery to spice each bird-watching trip! Suggestions for improvement will always be welcome. Success in managing habitat to favor desired bird species (or to discourage pest species) will be the ultimate test of these habitat characterizations. As human pressures move more wild species toward "threatened" status, the needed research may receive higher priority.

Wintering Bird Habitats

Wisconsin's wintering birds are either permanent residents on the breeding grounds or species wintering south of their breeding ranges. For the winter habitats shown in Table 3, the 29 habitat types from Table 1 have been simplified to 10. The winter habitat of a permanent resident is usually similar to that of its breeding site. Therefore, the information of special interest to the bird-watcher is for those northern birds that we do not see in southern Wisconsin (or do not see in Wisconsin at all) in the summer, and may not find every winter. Examples of these birds which we see primarily in the winter include the Oldsquaw, Snowy Owl, Northern Shrike, Common Redpoll, Bohemian Waxwing, Pine Grosbeak, Evening Grosbeak, White-winged Crossbill, Red Crossbill, Lapland Longspur, and Snow Bunting.

Some noteworthy changes in habitat from summer to winter include the types of water sought by waterfowl and the influence of winter bird feeding on the distribution of upland species. In winter, ducks and geese seek larger bodies of water to escape ice cover. They go only as far south as necessary and remain in the state much more abundantly in mild winters. Some, like the Common Goldeneye and Common Merganser, like to stay right on the edge of the ice; so they return as soon as open water appears. Canada Geese frequent waters kept open by springs such as those in Walworth and Rock counties. Warm waters kept open by power-plant heat dissipation attract many ducks, but some water birds nevertheless go much farther south or east for the winter (e.g., the Blue-winged Teal and Common Loon). Many of the Mallards seen in parks have domesticated blood in them and are easily tamed by winter feeding by the public. The Great Lakes attract some of the maritime species in winter, especially the Oldsquaw.

Bald Eagles, too, move only so far as necessary to find fish in open water, and they congregate around dams and power plants such as those at Prairie du Sac

Table 3. Habitat Preferences of Wisconsin Wintering Birds

Species	Southern Forest	Northern Deciduous Forest	Northern Coniferous Forest	Savanna	Deciduous Shrub	Open Crop/Grassland	Residential/Farmyard	Urban	Inland Lakes/Streams	Great Lakes
Pied-billed Grebe									•	
Horned Grebe									•	•
Great Blue Heron									•	•
Tundra Swan									•	
Mute Swan									•	
Snow Goose									•	•
Canada Goose									•	•
Wood Duck									•	•
Green-winged Teal									•	•
American Black Duck									•	•
Mallard									•	•
Northern Pintail									•	•
Northern Shoveler									•	•
Gadwall									•	•
American Wigeon									•	•
Canvasback									•	•
Redhead									•	•
Ring-necked Duck									•	•
Greater Scaup									•	•
Lesser Scaup									•	•
Harlequin Duck										•
Oldsquaw										•
White-winged Scoter										•
Common Goldeneye									•	•
Barrow's Goldeneye										•
Bufflehead									•	•
Common Merganser									•	•
Red-breasted Merganser									•	•
Ruddy Duck									•	•
Bald Eagle									•	
Northern Harrier						•				
Sharp-shinned Hawk	•						•			
Cooper's Hawk	•						•			
Northern Goshawk		•								
Red-shouldered Hawk	•									
Red-tailed Hawk	•			•		•				
Rough-legged Hawk				•		•				
Golden Eagle	•	•								
American Kestrel				•				•		
Merlin							•			
Gyrfalcon				•		•				
Gray Partridge						•				
Ring-necked Pheasant					•	•	•			
Spruce Grouse			•							
Ruffed Grouse	•	•								
Greater Prairie-Chicken						•				
Sharp-tailed Grouse				•	•					
Wild Turkey	•									
Northern Bobwhite				•						
American Coot									•	•
Killdeer						•				
Common Snipe									•	
Ring-billed Gull									•	•
Herring Gull									•	•
Thayer's Gull										•
Iceland Gull										•
Glaucous Gull										•
Great Black-backed Gull										•
Ivory Gull									•	•
Rock Dove							•	•		
Mourning Dove					•		•			
Barn Owl							•			
Eastern Screech-Owl	•						•			
Great Horned Owl	•	•								
Snowy Owl						•			•	
Northern Hawk Owl		•	•							
Barred Owl	•	•	•							
Great Gray Owl		•	•							
Long-eared Owl	•									
Short-eared Owl						•				

646

Table 3. Habitat Preferences of Wisconsin Wintering Birds, continued

Species	Southern Forest	Northern Deciduous Forest	Northern Coniferous Forest	Savanna	Deciduous Shrub	Open Crop/Grassland	Residential/Farmyard	Urban	Inland Lakes/Streams	Great Lakes
Boreal Owl			•							
Northern Saw-whet Owl	•		•							
Belted Kingfisher									•	
Red-headed Woodpecker	•				•					
Red-bellied Woodpecker	•						•			
Yellow-bellied Sapsucker							•			
Downy Woodpecker	•	•	•	•			•			
Hairy Woodpecker	•	•	•	•			•			
Three-toed Woodpecker			•							
Black-backed Woodpecker			•							
Northern Flicker	•						•			
Pileated Woodpecker	•	•	•							
Horned Lark						•				
Gray Jay			•							
Blue Jay	•	•	•	•						
American Crow	•	•		•		•	•			
Common Raven		•	•	•						
Black-capped Chickadee	•	•	•	•	•		•			
Boreal Chickadee			•							
Tufted Titmouse	•						•			
Red-breasted Nuthatch	•		•				•			
White-breasted Nuthatch	•	•	•	•			•			
Brown Creeper	•	•					•			
Carolina Wren					•		•			
Winter Wren	•								•	
Golden-crowned Kinglet	•		•				•			
Ruby-crowned Kinglet							•			
Eastern Bluebird					•	•				
Townsend's Solitaire	•				•					
Hermit Thrush							•			
American Robin	•				•		•			
Varied Thrush	•	•	•							
Gray Catbird					•		•			
Northern Mockingbird					•		•			
Brown Thrasher					•		•			

Species	Southern Forest	Northern Deciduous Forest	Northern Coniferous Forest	Savanna	Deciduous Shrub	Open Crop/Grassland	Residential/Farmyard	Urban	Inland Lakes/Streams	Great Lakes
Bohemian Waxwing					•		•			
Cedar Waxwing					•		•			
Northern Shrike				•	•	•	•			
European Starling				•	•	•	•	•		
Yellow-rumped Warbler	•						•			
Northern Cardinal					•		•			
Black-headed Grosbeak							•			
Green-tailed Towhee					•					
Rufous-sided Towhee					•					
American Tree Sparrow				•	•					
Field Sparrow					•					
Fox Sparrow					•		•			
Song Sparrow					•		•			
Swamp Sparrow					•					
White-throated Sparrow					•		•			
White-crowned Sparrow					•		•			
Harris' Sparrow					•		•			
Dark-eyed Junco				•	•		•			
Lapland Longspur						•				
Snow Bunting						•				
Red-winged Blackbird					•	•	•			
Eastern Meadowlark						•	•			
Western Meadowlark						•	•			
Yellow-headed Blackbird							•			
Rusty Blackbird					•	•	•			
Brewer's Blackbird					•	•	•			
Common Grackle					•	•	•			
Brown-headed Cowbird					•	•	•			
Pine Grosbeak	•	•	•							
Purple Finch	•	•	•				•			
House Finch					•		•			
Red Crossbill	•		•				•			
White-winged Crossbill	•		•				•			
Common Redpoll	•	•	•			•	•			
Hoary Redpoll	•	•	•			•	•			
Pine Siskin	•	•	•				•			
American Goldfinch	•	•	•		•		•			
Evening Grosbeak	•	•	•				•			
House Sparrow					•		•	•	•	

(Sauk County) and Cassville (Grant County) in winters which freeze much of the river surface. Ring-necked Pheasants move into wetlands for cover and farm-yards for food. Northern Bobwhites seek dense hedgerow shrub cover to survive the deep snow and cold, while the hardy Gray Partridge endure the windswept open fields. Wintering Common Snipe, American Robins, and occasional rails move to small springs to obtain the invertebrate food they need. When Pine Grosbeaks visit southern Wisconsin, they eat berries such as highbush cranberry and the buds of ash trees. Usually by winter the popular mountain ash berries have been stripped by migrating robins, Cedar Waxwings, and other birds. Like the highbush, however, the berries of sumac seem to be of lower palatability or else ripen slowly, and remain for spring migrating Hermit Thrushes and others to feed on during April snowstorms.

Pine plantations and ornamental urban conifer plantings of appropriate size in southern Wisconsin are attractive to many birds, including several owls, for roosting. Their seeds may bring in crossbills, finches, and siskins, while their bark may be scoured by Golden-crowned Kinglets and Red-breasted Nuthatches. The reason that redpolls come for the tiny "thistle" seeds provided at bird feeders is that their normal winter fare is birch and alder, whose seeds are extremely small. When attracting an array of winter birds from the northern forest, it is useful to simulate its landscape with plantings of birches, hemlocks, spruces, and pines. No doubt the huge amounts of winter food made available at urban and even rural bird feeders today has made life easier for, and helped boost populations of, northern birds such as Dark-eyed Juncos and American Tree Sparrows, which we presume found neither as much food nor a familiar "north-ern" landscape in the presettlement prairies and oak groves. Winter feeding and conifer plantings may be bringing more of these northern species into urban areas for better viewing by more people.

Migrating Bird Habitats

For birds of passage, Table 4 indicates five categories of habitat (simplified fur-ther from those listed in Table 3). Since migrating birds range widely and don't stay long in one place, a simplified classification of habitats will suffice for the bird-watcher, who must become a gypsy like the birds he or she seeks! The birds in this table are those which neither winter nor summer in our state. The list includes frequent migrants such as the American Pipit, Gray-cheeked Thrush, and many shorebirds. It also includes a number of rarities—those documented for Wisconsin on at least five different occasions during spring or fall migration. Beyond these 79 common or rare migrants in Wisconsin, the breeding and win-tering birds in Tables 2 and 3 are assumed to be found in similar habitats during spring and fall; so they are not repeated in Table 4. However, we do see a large number of conifer-forest breeders such as the Purple Finch, Red-breasted Nut-hatch, and several thrushes and warblers feeding during migration in deciduous trees such as elms, oaks, and maples, while Palm and Yellow-rumped Warblers range into marshes and cornfields. Also, many waterfowl seek small ponds and flooded fields for feeding on seeds and invertebrates—and even dry cornfields in the case of geese—while commuting daily to larger bodies of water for safe roosting and resting during the spring and fall migration periods. Fall hunting tends to move waterfowl into public parks, wildlife refuges, and inaccessible

Table 4. Habitat Preferences of Birds Found in Wisconsin Only during Migration

Woodland: Includes dry and wet deciduous forest, coniferous forest, savanna.
Shrub: Includes farm hedgerows, carr, park shrubbery.
Open Country: Includes grassland, cropland, sedge meadow, gravel pits.
Wetland: Includes shallow marsh, wet wooded swamp.
Lakes and Streams: Includes Great Lakes and shores, inland lakes and shores, major rivers, ponds, flooded fields.

	Woodland	Shrub	Open Country	Wetland	Lakes and Streams		Woodland	Shrub	Open Country	Wetland	Lakes and Streams
Red-throated Loon					•	Hudsonian Godwit					•
Pacific Loon					•	Marbled Godwit					•
Eared Grebe					•	Ruddy Turnstone					•
Western Grebe					•	Red Knot					•
American White Pelican					•	Sanderling					•
Anhinga				•	•	Semipalmated Sandpiper					•
Little Blue Heron				•	•	Western Sandpiper					•
Tricolored Heron				•	•	Least Sandpiper					•
Glossy Ibis				•		White-rumped Sandpiper					•
Greater White-fronted Goose					•	Baird's Sandpiper					•
Brant					•	Pectoral Sandpiper					•
Cinnamon Teal					•	Purple Sandpiper					•
Eurasian Wigeon					•	Dunlin					•
King Eider					•	Curlew Sandpiper					•
Black Scoter					•	Stilt Sandpiper					•
Surf Scoter					•	Buff-breasted Sandpiper			•		
Mississippi Kite			•			Ruff					•
Swainson's Hawk			•			Short-billed Dowitcher					•
Ferruginous Hawk			•			Long-billed Dowitcher					•
Purple Gallinule				•		Red-necked Phalarope					•
Black-bellied Plover			•		•	Red Phalarope					•
Lesser Golden-Plover			•		•	Parasitic Jaeger					•
Semipalmated Plover					•	Laughing Gull					•
American Avocet					•	Franklin's Gull			•		•
Greater Yellowlegs				•	•	Common Black-headed Gull					•
Lesser Yellowlegs				•	•	Lesser Black-backed Gull					•
Solitary Sandpiper				•	•	Black-legged Kittiwake					•
Willet					•	Arctic Tern					•
Whimbrel					•	Least Tern					•
Long-billed Curlew					•	Ancient Murrelet					•

Continued on following page

Table 4. Habitat Preferences of Birds Found in Wisconsin Only during Migration, continued

	Woodland	Shrub	Open Country	Wetland	Lakes and Streams		Woodland	Shrub	Open Country	Wetland	Lakes and Streams
Groove-billed Ani		•				Bay-breasted Warbler	•	•			
Burrowing Owl			•			Blackpoll Warbler	•	•			
Scissor-tailed Flycatcher		•				Wilson's Warbler	•	•			
Black-billed Magpie		•				Summer Tanager	•				
Mountain Bluebird		•				Western Tanager	•				
Gray-cheeked Thrush	•	•				Painted Bunting	•	•			
American Pitpit			•			Lark Bunting		•	•		
Philadelphia Vireo	•	•				Baird's Sparrow			•		
Orange-crowned Warbler	•	•				Smith's Longspur			•		
Kirtland's Warbler	•										

centers of large lakes. Running the fall hunting gauntlet makes these birds very edgy even in spring, requiring stealthy stalking by the bird-watcher with a telescope lest they flush to sites beyond identification range.

And it must be stressed that, since night migrants may come down almost anywhere and since storms may injure birds or strand them in unusual places, on rare occasions one may encounter almost any migrating species anywhere. For example, one spring an American Bittern rested all day in my neighbor's oak tree, far from water; and on a busy May migration day in another year a freshly dead, unmolested Cattle Egret was found on the ground in one of the oak forests of the University of Wisconsin–Madison Arboretum. High winds often ground exhausted upland migrants of many species on the shores of the Great Lakes, placing them temporarily in atypical habitats. Finally, as with wintering birds, some migrants—for example, the White-throated Sparrow—may be attracted to your bird feeder or garden in habitats different from those in which they may breed or winter.

Bibliography

List of Observers

Index of Species

Bibliography
Walter E. Scott and Gertrude M. Scott

This bibliography covers well over 100 years of bird records in Wisconsin, from accounts by early explorers to publications through 1986. It was constructed to be as complete as possible—leaving out only several hundred minor citations of least importance. Special effort was made to include "fugitive" reference sources of significance which commonly are overlooked. Most items have been double-checked against the publication itself.

Acknowledgment is made of help from Helen Northup, who prepared a card file on all articles in *The Passenger Pigeon,* and University of Wisconsin Professor Emeritus Sieghardt M. Riegel, who assisted by interpreting German language articles. Several others who were helpful in various ways include Frank and Charlotte King, Nils P. Dahlstrand, F. R. Zimmerman, and Ruth Hine. Invaluable assistance was given by many who supplied copies of their own bibliographies and double-checked our rough drafts.

Most biographical references as well as articles about organizational business meetings and field trips have been omitted. Titles and locations of unpublished theses related to Wisconsin birds and also the location of unpublished manuscripts and bird collections were included in an effort to widen usefulness of this bibliography.

Abbot, C. A. 1923. Waterfowl near Madison, Wisconsin. Wilson Bull. 35(3):155–57.

Abbot, G. A. 1908. Around the Flambeau. Oologist 25(11):165–67.

Abbott, D. 1957. Widgeons in a window box. Pass. Pigeon 19(3):107–8.

Abraham, H. 1906. Bird list for 1905—Appleton, Wis. By the Wayside 8(8):64.

Abrahamson, Mrs. E. J. 1949. Bird notes from Clearwater Lake, Wisconsin. Pass. Pigeon 11(1):29–30.

Ailes, I. W. 1980. Breeding biology and habitat use of the Upland Sandpiper in central Wisconsin. Pass. Pigeon 42(2):53–63.

Aliesch, F. 1940. Three White Pelicans on Lake Pepin. Pass. Pigeon 2(10):118.

Allen, C. J. 1893. In 1932, deposited in manuscript collections of State Historical Society of Wisconsin the record books of Caw Caw Hunting Club on Horicon Marsh (1865–1929), with records of birds shot in the early days. (Includes MS history of the Diana Shooting Club of Horicon, Wis., 1893.) Milw. Mss. AG.

Allen, D. L. 1968. Dove of no peace [Passenger Pigeon]. Audubon Mag. 70(5):54–57.

Allen, J. A. 1889. Biography of Thure Kumlien. Auk 6:204–5.

Allert, O. P. 1928. An unpublished record of the Eskimo Curlew for Wisconsin. Auk 45(1):95.

Alphonsus, Brother, C.S.C. 1923. Birds of Watertown, Wisconsin. Am. Midl. Nat. 8(7):172–74.

Amadon, D. 1963. A footnote on the last Passenger Pigeon. Pass. Pigeon 25(4):140–41.

Ambuel, B., and S. A. Temple. 1983. Area-dependent changes in bird communities and vegetation of southern Wisconsin forests. Ecology 64:1057–68.

American Ornithologists' Union. 1957. Check-list of North American Birds. 5th edition. Am. Ornith. Union. 691 pp.

American Ornithologists' Union. 1983. Check-list of North American Birds. 6th edition. Am. Ornith. Union. 877 pp.

Anderson, D. W., and F. Hamerstrom. 1967. The recent status of Wisconsin cormorants. Pass. Pigeon 29(1):3–15.

Anderson, D. W., and J. J. Hickey. 1972. Eggshell changes in certain North American birds. Pp. 514–40 *in* Symp. Chemical Pollution, Proc. 15th Ornithol. Congr., Leiden, Netherlands.

Anderson, D. W., and J. J. Hickey. 1976. Dynamics of organochlorine pollutants in Herring Gulls. Environ. Pollut. 10:183–200.

Anderson, D. W., H. G. Lumsden, and J. J. Hickey. 1970. Geographical variation in the eggshells of Common Loons. Can. Field Nat. 84(4):351–56.

Anderson, D. W., J. J. Hickey, R. W. Risebrough, D. F. Hughes, and R. E. Christensen. 1969. Significance of chlorinated hydrocarbon residues to breeding pelicans and cormorants. Can. Field Nat. 83(2):91–112.

Anderson, H. G. 1936. Avifauna of the Arboretum of the University of Wisconsin. BA thesis, Univ. Wis.–Madison, 166 pp.

Anderson, H. G. 1939. Faville Grove area [Lake Mills]. Pass. Pigeon 1(4):61

Anderson, H. G. 1941a. Permanent and winter bird residents of Dane County, Wisconsin. Pass. Pigeon 3(1):6–7.

Anderson, H. G. 1941b. Spring arrivals in February and March for Dane County. Pass. Pigeon 3(2):16–17.

Anderson, H. G. 1941c. Spring arrivals in April and May for Dane County and vicinity. Pass. Pigeon 3(3):24–27.

Anderson, H. G., W. S. Feeney, T. M. Sperry, and J. Catenhusen. 1942. Birds of the University of Wisconsin Arboretum. Trans. Wis. Acad. Sci., Arts, Lett. 34:5–22.

Anderson, J. R., D. O. Trainer, and G. R. DeFoliart. 1962. Natural and experimental transmission of the waterfowl parasite, *Leucocytozoon simondi* M. & L., in Wisconsin. Zoonoses Res. 1(9):155–64.

Anderson, M. L. 1976. Causes of decreased migrant waterfowl use in part of the Upper Mississippi River National Wildlife Refuge. MS thesis, Univ. Wis.–Stevens Point, 63 pp.

Anderson, R. K. 1965. Mating behavior of the Greater Prairie Chicken in Wisconsin. P. 8 *in* Proc. 6th Prairie Grouse Tech. Counc., Sept. 14–16, Warroad, Minn.

Anderson, R. K. 1969a. Mating and interspecific behavior of Greater Prairie Chicken. PhD diss., Univ. Wis.–Madison, 118 pp.

Anderson, R. K. 1969b. Prairie Chicken responses on changing booming-ground cover type and height. J. Wildl. Manage. 33(4):636–43.

Anderson, R. K. 1971. Orientation in Prairie Chickens. Auk 88(2):286–90.

Anderson, R. K. 1977. Crex Meadows Prairie Chicken transplant update. Boom! 16(1):4, 6.

Anderson, R. K., D. K. Jansen, and T. L. Cogger. 1980. Fall and spring migration route, and behavior of eastern Greater Sandhill Cranes: 1978–1979. Rep. submitted to U.S. Fish and Wildl. Serv., Twin Cities, Minn., mimeo., 21 pp.

Andrews, O. V. 1915. An ecological survey of the Lake Butte des Morts Bog, Oshkosh, Wisconsin. Bull. Wis. Nat. Hist. Soc. 13:196–211.

Anonymous. 1828. Birds of the Mississippi Valley. West. Mon. Rev. 1(9):519–23. (Conducted by Timothy Flint, Cincinnati.)

Anonymous. 1851. Chapter 380—An act to permit the killing of game in certain seasons of the year. P. 404 *in* Acts and resolves, Legislature of Wisconsin, 1851. C. Latham Sholes, Kenosha, Wis.

Anonymous. 1875. The pigeons in Pierce County, Wisconsin, from Hudson Star and Times. Rod and Gun 6(10):156.

Anonymous. 1880. Yellow-headed Blackbird shot at Remington, Wis. For. and Stream 12(17):329.

Anonymous. 1897. Pelicans taken at Green Bay. Wis. Nat. 1(4):56.

Anonymous. 1907. Preserve the game: Wisconsin should take no step backward—spring shooting inhumane. Milwaukee Free Press, May 5.

Anonymous. 1908. The value of some birds of prey. By the Wayside 10(9):65–66.

Anonymous. 1920. Crane electrocuted between Minnesota City and Fountain City [Wisconsin] over Mississippi River. Wis. Conserv. 2(5):24.

Anonymous. 1929. Pheasants to be common. Wis. Conserv. Dep. Mon. Surv. 1929(July):13.

Anonymous. 1930a. Hungarian Partridge. Wis. Conserv. Dep. Mon. Surv. 1930(Feb.):10.

Anonymous. 1930b. Prairie Chicken investigation. Wis. Conserv. Dep. Mon. Surv. 1930(May):13.

Anonymous. 1931. Dr. Ogden's gift of 640 [bird] skins to Milwaukee Downer. The Kodak 36(4):30. (Milwaukee Downer College alumnae bulletin.)

Anonymous. 1937. Dane County bird list of the Madison Bird Club. Madison, Wis.

Anonymous. 1938a. The story of Sheboygan Marsh—a great achievement in review. Wis. Sportsman 2(9):8.

Anonymous. 1938b. More game birds for state. Wis. Conserv. Bull. 3(10):3–5.

Anonymous. 1941. Willow Ptarmigan travel over 100 miles after stocking. Pass. Pigeon 3(6):61.

Anonymous. 1944. The Chukar Partridge in Wisconsin. Pass. Pigeon 6(2):41–42. (Historical summary contributed by various members of the Wis. Conserv. Dep.)

Anonymous. 1949. Capercaillie and Black Grouse research. Wis. Conserv. Bull. 14(10):35.

Anonymous. 1957a. Abstracts of Bobwhite quail management papers. Wis. Conserv. Dep., Madison, mimeo., 17 pp.

Anonymous. 1957b. Abstracts of Hungarian Partridge management papers. Wis. Conserv. Dep., Madison, mimeo., 16 pp.

Anonymous. 1966. The Summerton Bog story. Wis. Chap. Nat. Conserv. Newslett. 6(1):1–4.

Anonymous. 1970. Birds of Upper Mississippi River National Wildlife Refuge. Refuge Leaflet 142-R-4. U.S. Dep. Inter. Fish and Wildl. Serv., Winona, Minn.

Anonymous. 1973. Endangered species handbook. Wis. Dep. Nat. Resour., Madison, 71 pp.

Anonymous. 1976a. Wisconsin game and fur harvests, 1930–1975 [statistics]. Wis. Dep. Nat. Resour., Madison, 25 pp.

Anonymous. 1976b. Wisconsin stories—Passenger Pigeons. Wis. Mag. Hist. 59:259–81; reprinted in 1976 as separate booklet, State Hist. Soc. Wis., 23 pp.

Anonymous. 1978a. Horicon Marsh: People and geese in conflict. Wisconservation 5(12):13.

Anonymous. 1978b. Osprey nesting sites increased. Badger Sportsman 35(10):3.

Anonymous. 1978c. More growth seen at Great Blue Heron rookery. Badger Sportsman 36(1):3.

Anonymous. 1979a. Mississippi Valley population of Canada Geese. U.S. Fish and Wildl. Serv., leaflet + map, 8 pp.

Anonymous. 1979b. Canada Goose management plan goes into effect [Mississippi Flyway states]. Wisconservation 6(10):14.

Anonymous. 1980a. Laser beam used in Mississippi River study. Badger Sportsman 37(4):12.

Anonymous. 1980b. Ospreys increasing in northern Wisconsin. Badger Sportsman 37(10):5.

Apel, K. 1975. Auditory predator recognition and mobbing behavior in the Black-capped Chickadee. MS thesis, Univ. Wis.–Milwaukee, 179 pp.

Apel, K. 1978. Predator recognition through audition in the Black-capped Chickadee (*Parus stricapillus*). Univ. Wis.–Milwaukee Field Stn. Bull. 11(2):7–14.

Archibald, G. W. 1974. Misty morning in crane country. Anim. Kingdom 77(2):19–24.

Archibald, G. W. 1975. The evolutionary and taxonomic relationships of cranes as revealed by their unison calls. PhD diss., Cornell Univ., Ithaca, N.Y., 152 pp.

Archibald, G. W. 1978. Winter feeding programs for cranes. Pp. 141–48 in Endangered birds, ed. S. A. Temple. Univ. Wis. Press, Madison.

Artmann, J. W. 1977. Woodcock status report, 1976. U.S. Dep. Inter. Fish and Wildl. Serv., Spec. Sci. Rep. Wildl. No. 209, Washington, D.C., 21 pp.

Atwood, E. L., and F. Wells, Jr. 1961. Waterfowl harvest in the Mississippi Flyway states during the 1960–1961 hunting season. U.S. Dep. Inter. Fish and Wildl. Serv., Spec. Sci. Rep. Wildl. 56, Laurel, Md., 49 pp.

Atwood, W. H. 1948. Contributions of Ludwig Kumlien to the Milwaukee State Teachers bird collection. Pass. Pigeon 10(2):85–87.

Aumann, G., and J. T. Emlen, Jr. 1959. The distribution of Cliff Swallow nesting colonies in Wisconsin. Pass. Pigeon 21(3):95–100.

Ausloos, B. J. and R. Lien. 1988. The 1988 Peregrine Falcon Release at Madison, Wisconsin. Pass. Pigeon 50:305–9.

Babington, R. S. 1949. I remember the Passenger Pigeon. Wis. Conserv. Bull. 14(9):20.

Bacon, B. R., and S. Moore. 1985. Common Goldeneyes nesting in Wisconsin. Pass. Pigeon 47:89–90.

Bagg, A. M., W. W. H. Gunn, D. S. Miller, J. T. Nichols, W. Smith, and F. P. Wolfarth. 1950. Barometric pressure patterns and spring bird migration. Wilson Bull. 62(1):5–19.

Baird, S. F. 1858. U.S. Pacific Railroad surveys, Vol. 9, Part 2—Birds. Pac. Railroad Rep. 9, Washington, D.C., 1,005 pp. (Includes Wisconsin specimens from P. R. Hoy, Thure Kumlien, and Robert Kennicot.)

Baird, S. F., T. M. Brewer, and R. Ridgway. 1875. A history of North American birds. 3 vols., Little, Brown and Co., Boston.

Baker, D. G. 1970. A pair of amateur birders encounter a new bird. Pass. Pigeon 32(2):52–53.

Baldassarre, G. A. 1978. Factors affecting waterfowl production in central Wisconsin. MS thesis, Univ. Wis.–Stevens Point, 124 pp.

Baldwin, J. H. 1977. A comparative study of Sandhill Crane subspecies. PhD diss., Univ. Wis.–Madison, 105 pp.

Barber, W. E. 1916. Division of wild life conservation. Pp. 43–68 in Bien. Rep. State Conserv. Comm., fiscal years 1915 and 1916. Cantwell Print. Co., Madison, Wis.

Barber, W. E. 1918. Wild life conservation. Pp. 15–36 in Bien. Rep. State Conserv. Comm., fiscal years 1917 and 1918. Democrat Print. Co., Madison, Wis.

Barber, W. E. 1922. Partridge and quail suffer from heavy sleet storm. Wis. Conserv. 4(1):5.

Barger, N. R. 1941. Quest of the Worm-eating Warbler in Wisconsin. Pass. Pigeon 3(8):75.

Barger, N. R. 1944a. Ten years of May-day counts as conducted by the Kumlien Club. Pass. Pigeon 6(3):61.

Barger, N. R. 1944b. Feeding songbirds in winter often brings surprises. Wis. Conserv. Bull. 9(11):16.

Barger, N. R. 1945. Some conclusions about the raven. Pass. Pigeon 7(3):69.

Barger, N. R. 1952–1974. Series of 145 popular articles on individual Wisconsin species. Wis. Conserv. Bull. 17(9)–39(4).

Barger, N. R. 1959. A late winter bird count. Pass. Pigeon 21(1):14–17.

Barger, N. R. 1963. Bald Eagles hatched in captivity. Pass. Pigeon 25(1):24–25.

Barger, N. R. 1964. Wisconsin bird lore. Wis. Conserv. Bull. 29(3):11–14.

Barger, N. R. 1972. Footnote for Swainson's Thrush observation on Sauk City census. Pass. Pigeon 34(1):42.

Barger, N. R., R. H. Lound, and S. D. Robbins. 1960. Wisconsin birds—checklist with migration graphs. Wis. Soc. Ornithol., Madison, 32 pp.

Barger, N. R., R. H. Lound, and S. D. Robbins, Jr. 1975. Wisconsin birds—a checklist with migration graphs. 4th rev. ed., Wis. Soc. Ornithol., Madison, 32 pp.

Barger, N. R., E. E. Bussewitz, E. L. Loyster, S. D. Robbins, and W. E. Scott. 1942. Wisconsin birds—a preliminary checklist with migration charts. Wis. Soc. Ornithol., Madison, 32 pp.; 1st rev. ed. 1950.

Barker, J. 1967. Study of a breeding bird population in relation to an arbovirus study. MS thesis, Univ. Wis.–Milwaukee, 126 pp.

Barry, A. C. 1854. Ornithological fauna of Wisconsin. Proc. Boston Soc. Nat. Hist. 5:1–13.

Bartel, K. E. 1975a. Illinois Black-crowned Night Herons go to Wisconsin. Pass. Pigeon 37(2):92–93.

Bartel, K. E. 1975b. Amazing number of bird species recorded in 24 years during Christmas bird count period. Pass. Pigeon 37(4):177–79.

Bartelt, G. A. 1977. Aspects of the population ecology of the American Coot in Wisconsin. MS thesis, Univ. Wis.–Madison, 138 pp.

Bartonek, J. C., and R. K. Anderson. 1966. Duck hunter's diary. Wis. Conserv. Bull. 31(5):20–21.

Bartonek, J. C., J. J. Hickey, and L. B. Keith. 1964. An evaluation of waterfowl regulations and local harvests in Wisconsin. Trans. Wis. Acad. Sci., Arts, Lett. 53:83–107. (Analysis of a Wisconsin hunting journal, 1907–1939.)

Bauldry, V. M. 1971. Bluebird trails report, 1969. Pass. Pigeon 33(1):49–54.

Baumgartner, A. M. 1972. Prairie Warbler in Door County. Pass. Pigeon 34(1):41.

Baumgartner, A. M. 1973. Across the foot bridge: Report of a back yard bird bander. Pass. Pigeon 35(4):194–97.

Beals, E. W. 1958. Notes on the summer birds of the Apostle Islands. Pass. Pigeon 20(4):151–60.

Beals, E. W. 1960. Forest bird communities in the Apostle Islands of Wisconsin. Wilson Bull. 72(2):156–81.

Beals, E. W. 1967. Notes on the summer birds of the Apostle Islands II. Pass. Pigeon 29(1):17–18.

Becker, E. A. 1938. Sheboygan Marsh survey. Wis. Conserv. Bull. 2(9):39–40.

Becker, G. C. 1942. Notes on the Pileated Woodpecker in Wisconsin. Pass. Pigeon 4(4–6):29–34.

Bedford, B. L., E. H. Zimmerman, and J. H. Zimmerman. 1974. The wetlands of Dane County, Wisconsin. Dane Co. Reg. Plann. Comm. and Wis. Dep. Nat. Resour., Madison, 581 pp.

Beebe, R. 1933. Influence of the Great Lakes on the migration of birds. Wilson Bull. 45(3):118–21.

Beer, J. R., and B. L. Dahlberg. 1965. Notes on the winter birds of the Apostle Islands. Pass. Pigeon 27(4):141–43.

Beer, J. R., and D. Tibbets. 1950. Nesting behavior of the Red-wing Blackbird. Flicker 22(3):61–77.

Behrens, R. 1966. European Widgeon near Redwing, Minnesota. Loon 38(2):70–71.

Beimborn, D. 1970. Bird species and the tension zone. Pass. Pigeon 32(2):49–51.

Bell, J. G. 1952. Horicon Marsh: A decade of management. Wis. Conserv. Bull. 17(10):7–10.

Bellrose, F. C. 1950. Mississippi Flyway problems, projects and prospects. Trans. North Am. Wildl. Conf. 15:123–32.

Bellrose, F. C. 1957. A spectacular waterfowl migration through central North America. Ill. Nat. Hist. Surv. Biol. Notes 36, 24 pp.

Bellrose, F. C. 1976. Ducks, geese and swans of North America. Stackpole Books, Harrisburg, Pa., 543 pp.

Bennett, A. J. 1977. Present status and future of Sandhill Cranes in southeastern Wisconsin. Pp. 86–93 in Proc. of the Sandhill Crane Symp., Ind. Wildl. Soc., 24–26 Oct., Michigan City, Ind.

Bennett, A. J. 1978a. Auditory censusing of Greater Sandhill Cranes. Auk 95(2):411–13.

Bennett, A. J. 1978b. Ecology and status of Greater Sandhill Cranes in southeastern Wisconsin. MS thesis, Univ. Wis.–Stevens Point, 116 pp.

Bennett, A. J., and L. E. Nauman. 1978. Summer populations of Sandhill Cranes in southeastern Wisconsin, 1976–1977. Pass. Pigeon 40(1):349–57.

Bennett, J. 1980. The magic of Eagle Valley. Clearwater J. 1(5):4–9.

Bennetts, W. J. 1900a. On the occurrence of the Mockingbird in Milwaukee County. Bull. Wis. Nat. Hist. Soc. 1(1):61–62.

Bennetts, W. J. 1900b. On the occurrence of the Evening Grosbeak and Canada Jay in Milwaukee in the winter of 1899–1900. Bull. Wis. Nat. Hist. Soc. 1(2):129–33.

Bent, A. C. 1942. Life histories of North American flycatchers, larks, swallows, and their allies. U.S. Natl. Mus. Bull. 179, 555 pp.

Berger, D. D. 1954a. Hawk migration at Cedar Grove. Pass. Pigeon 16(1):24–27.

Berger, D. D. 1954b. Hawk banding at Cedar Grove. Pass. Pigeon 16(3):97–100.

Berger, D. D., and H. C. Mueller. 1969a. Nesting Peregrine Falcons in Wisconsin and adjacent areas. Pp. 115–22 in Peregrine Falcon populations: Their biology and decline, ed. J. J. Hickey. Univ. Wis. Press, Madison.

Berger, D. D., and H. C. Mueller. 1969b. Ospreys in northern Wisconsin. Pp. 340–41 in Peregrine Falcon populations: Their biology and decline, ed. J. J. Hickey. Univ. Wis. Press, Madison.

Berger, D. D., F. Hamerstrom, and F. N. Hamerstrom. 1963. The effect of raptors on Prairie Chickens on booming grounds. J. Wildl. Manage. 27:778–91.

Bernard, R. F. 1964. Vireo and woodpecker nests observed. Pass. Pigeon 26(4):175–76.

Bernard, R. F. 1965. A specimen of the Glaucous Gull from Douglas County. Pass. Pigeon 27(2):71–72.

Bernard, R. F. 1966. A Yellow Rail in Douglas County. Pass. Pigeon 28(4):148.

Bernard, R. F. 1967. The birds of Douglas County, Wisconsin. Pass. Pigeon 29(2):3–36.

Bernard, R. F., and B. F. Klugow. 1963. Hawk Owls invade Wisconsin. Pass. Pigeon 25(2):47–50.

Bernard, R. F., and B. F. Klugow. 1966. A new record of the Great Gray Owl in Wisconsin. Pass. Pigeon 28(1):19–20.

Berquist, J. R. 1972. Waterfowl productivity of constructed water areas on the Crex Meadows Wildlife Area. Wis. Dep. Nat. Resour. Final Rep. P-R Proj. W-141-R-7, Madison, 73 pp.

Berquist, J. R. 1973. A study of constructed ponds in relation to waterfowl production in northwestern Wisconsin. MS thesis, Univ. Minn.–St. Paul, 111 pp.

Bertrand, G., J. Lang, and J. Ross. 1976. The Green Bay watershed—past, present, future. Tech. Rep. No. 229, Univ. Wis. Sea Grant Program, Inst. Environ. Stud., Madison, pp. 80–83. (Section on waterfowl and endangered species.)

Besadny, C. D. 1954a. 1953 in review. Pass. Pigeon 16(2):47–52.

Besadny, C. D. 1954b. Disaster strikes. Pass. Pigeon 16(3):102–4.

Besadny, C. D. 1963. Huns on the move. Wis. Conserv. Bull. 30(6):21–23.

Besadny, C. D. 1966. Farm programs—and wildlife. Wis. Conserv. Bull. 31(2):16–18.

Besadny, C. D. 1967. Fateful three weeks. Wis. Conserv. Bull. 32(3):20–22.

Besadny, C. D., and F. H. Wagner. 1963. An evaluation of pheasant stocking through the day-old chick program in Wisconsin. Tech. Bull. 28, Wis. Conserv. Dep., Madison, 81 pp.

Beske, A., and J. Champion. 1971. Prolific nesting of Short-eared Owls on Buena Vista Marsh. Pass. Pigeon 33(2):99–103.

Betts, N. de W. 1914. Bell's Vireo in Wisconsin. Auk 31(4):542–43.

Betts, N. de W. 1915. Notes from Wisconsin. Auk 32(2):237–38.

Betts, N. de W. 1916. Notes from Wisconsin. Auk 33(4):438–39.

Beule, J. 1938. The Hungarian Partridge in Dodge County, Wisconsin. Wis. Sportsman 2(8):8.

Bielefeldt, J. 1974a. Patterns of Blue Jay abundance on Wisconsin Christmas counts, 1954–1972. Pass. Pigeon 36(3):98–109.

Bielefeldt, J. 1974b. Waterfowl in Waukesha County: Spring [loons, grebes, ducks, American Coot]. Pass. Pigeon 36(4):162–69.

Bielefeldt, J. E. 1981. Attempted nesting by the Solitary Vireo in Waukesha County, Wisconsin. Pass. Pigeon 43:1–3.

Black, C. T. 1930–1940. Reports as manager of the Faville Grove Wildlife Area. Pass. Pigeon 1(10):146; 1(11):157; 1(12):167; 2(1):12; 2(2):22; 2(3):41.

Black, C. T. 1935a. Mockingbird in Wisconsin. Auk 52(1):90.

Black, C. T. 1935b. Richardson's Owl in Wisconsin. Auk 52(4):451–52.

Black, C. T. 1941. Gyrfalcon in Wisconsin. Auk 58(2):254.

Bleed, A. S. 1974. Territorial composition and the tactics of the male Red-winged Blackbird (*Agelaius phoeniceus*). PhD diss., Univ. Wis.–Madison, 84 pp.

Bond, R. R. 1957. Ecological distribution of breeding birds in the upland forests of southern Wisconsin. Ecol. Monogr. 27:251–84.

Bookhout, T. A. 1979. Waterfowl and wetlands—an integrated review. Proc. Symp.—39th Midwest Wildl. Conf., 5 Dec. 1977, Madison, Wis., North Central Sect., Wildl. Soc. La Crosse Print. Co., La Crosse, Wis., 147 pp.

Bowers, E. F., and F. W. Martin. 1975. Managing Wood Ducks by population units. Trans. North Am. Wildl. and Nat. Resour. Conf. 40:300–324.

Bradford, A. S. 1946. One November day on Lake Poygan. Pass. Pigeon 8(3):76–78.

Bradley, N. L. 1977. Gray Jay seen at Leopold Shack in Sauk County. Pass. Pigeon 39(4):343–44.

Bradshaw, J. E., and D. O. Trainer. 1966. Some infectious diseases of water fowl in the Mississippi Flyway. J. Wildl. Manage. 30(3):571–77.

Brakhage, G. K., H. M. Reeves, and R. A. Hunt. 1971. The Canada Goose tagging program in Wisconsin. Trans. North Am. Wildl. and Nat. Resour. Conf. 36:275–95.

Brandon, J. A. 1900. Notes on some migratory birds. Wis. Nat. Hist. Soc. Bull. 1(3):191–94.

Braun, J. W. 1912. Our friends the sea gulls (Bailey's Harbor). By the Wayside 13(5):35.

Brewer, T. M. 1854. On the cranes found in southern Wisconsin. Proc. Boston Soc. Nat. Hist. 4:307.

Brewer, T. M. 1859. On Swallow-tailed Kites in Wisconsin during nesting season. P. 39 in North American oology, Part 1, Raptores. Smithsonian contributions to knowledge, Vol. 11. Smithsonian Inst., Washington, D.C.

Brewer, T. M. 1872a. On the occurrence of a Masked Duck at Rock River, Wisconsin. Proc. Boston Soc. Nat. Hist. 14:205.

Brewer, T. M. 1872b. Occurrence of *Empidonax pusillus* in Wisconsin. Proc. Boston Soc. Nat. Hist. 14:303–4.

Brewer, T. M. 1873. Abundance of Bay-breasted Warblers in Wisconsin. Proc. Boston Soc. Nat. Hist. 15:192–93.

Brewer, T. M. 1874. European White-winged Black Tern from Lake Koshkonong. Am. Nat. 8(3):188–89.

Brittingham, M. C., and S. A. Temple. 1980. Hooded Warblers nesting in the Baraboo hills, Sauk County, Wisconsin. Pass. Pigeon 42:128–30.

Brooks, W. S. 1960. Songbird communities of two marsh habitats. Pass. Pigeon 22(3):111–25.

Brooks, W. S. 1971. Songbird communities—comparison of sedge-forb meadow and willow shrub areas. Pass. Pigeon 33(1):39–45.

Brouchoud, B. N. 1966. 1965 annual banding report. IBBA News 38(3):46–49.

Brouchoud, B. N. 1969a. Operation bluebird: Manitowoc County spring cleaning. Pass. Pigeon 31(2):236–38.

Brouchoud, B. N. 1969b. Unusual movements of fall migrants. IBBA News 41(2):78–79.

Brown, C. E. 1921. The bird mounds of Wisconsin. Wis. Conserv. 3(2):8.

Brown, C. E. 1943. Indian bird mounds in Wisconsin. Pass. Pigeon 5(1):5–8.

Brown, C. E. 1980. Photo of a Wild Turkey in Vilas Park, Madison, taken in 1905 on Henry Vilas Parkway. Hist. Madison J. 5:2.

Brown, E. L. 1885. From Wisconsin. Young Oologist 2(1):17–18; 2(2):38–39. (Regarding spring migration at Durand.)

Brown, H. J. 1954. Bandits of the pine barrens. Pass. Pigeon 16(3):87–96; reprinted from Flicker 25:90–98, and Minn. Nat. 3:33–38.

Brown, H. M. 1972. Report of the 1971 bird survey of the Fox River Sanctuary, Waukesha, Wisconsin. Pass. Pigeon 34(2):62–64.

Bruhin, T. A. 1866. Schnabelmissbildungen. Zool. Garten 7:150–52.

Bruhin, T. A. 1869. Einige ältere Angaben über hahnfedrige Hennen. Zool. Garten 10:63–64.

Bruhin, T. A. 1870. Die Iris der Vögel, in besondere der Raub, Sumpf- und Schwimmvögel der deutschen Fauna, als unterscheidendes Merkmal der Arten, des Alters und Geschlechtes. Zool. Garten 11:290–95.

Bruhin, T. A. 1871. Ankunft und Brutezeit einiger Vögel Milwaukee's. [The arrival and breeding of various birds in the vicinity of Milwaukee.] Zool. Garten 12:10–18.

Bruhin, T. A. 1872. Unsere gefiederten Wintergäste. Zool. Garten 13:157–58. (Remarks on about 20 species of winter birds in Milwaukee vicinity.)

Bruhin, T. A. 1875. Die Vögel von New Coeln im Staate Wisconsin. Zool. Garten 16(11):414–17; summarized by W. L. McAtee under the title An obscure Wisconsin bird list, Pass. Pigeon 5:58–59.

Bruhin, T. A. 1877. Zer Fauna Nordamerikas. Zool. Garten 18:394–96. (Letter from Centerville, Manitowoc County, includes dates migrants arrived in spring, 1877.)

Bruhin, T. A. 1878. Frühlingsboten. Zool. Garten 19:125–26. (Correspondence from Potosi, Wis., telling about birds seen in the southwestern part of state.)

Bruhin, T. A. 1880. Phaenologisches. Zool. Garten 21:220. (Correspondence from Potosi giving arrival of migrants in spring 1879 and 1880.)

Brumer, J. 1976. Watching the winter birds. Pass. Pigeon 38(4):165–66.

Brynildson, I. 1979a. Pray for a bird of prey. Wis. Nat. Resour. 3(2):29–31.

Brynildson, I. 1979b. Wisconsin's endangered birds and mammals. Wis. Nat. Resour. 3(5), Spec. Suppl., Life Tracks, 16 pp.

Brynildson, I. 1979c. Boaters threaten loons in north. Badger Sportsman 37(1):12.

Bryson, R. A., and T. J. Murray. 1977. Climate of hunger. Univ. Wis. Press, Madison, 188 pp.

Buech, R. R. 1977. Observations of nesting avifauna under gamma-radiation exposure. Pp. 181–84 in The Enterprise, Wisconsin, radiation forest. Radioecological studies, ed. J. Zavitkovski. Div. Biomed. and Environ. Res. U.S.A.E.C., Oak Ridge, Tenn.

Buengener, A. 1913. Birds that winter in this county and latitude. Pp. 346–49 in History of Brown County, Vol. 1, ed. D. B. Martin. S. J. Clarke Publ. Co., Chicago.

Bunting, H. 1930. Tufted Titmouse and towhee at Madison, Wisconsin, in winter. Auk 47(2):262–63.

Burdick, G. M. 1898. Notes from Wisconsin. Wilson Bull. 19(1):24–25.

Burger, G. V. 1959. Pheasant hunting and management on Wiscon-

sin licensed shooting preserves. PhD diss., Univ. Wis.–Madison, 106 pp.

Burger, G. V. 1962. Licensed shooting preserves in Wisconsin. Tech. Bull. 24, Wis. Conserv. Dep., Madison, 37 pp.

Burns, F. L. 1895. The American Crow (Corvus americanus). Wilson Bull. 5:5–41.

Burns, F. L. 1911. A monograph of the Broad-winged Hawk. (Buteo platypterus). Wilson Bull. 23(2):141–320.

Burrill, A. C. 1909a. Swallow migration, 1909. Nat. Hist. Soc. Wis. Bull. 7(3–4):131–32.

Burrill, A. C. 1909b. Migrations of the swallows and other birds. By the Wayside 11(6):41–42.

Burrill, A. C. 1912. A plea for the Herring Gull. By the Wayside 13(6):41–43.

Burrill, A. C. 1913a. Progress of bird conservation in Wisconsin. Wis. Arbor and Bird Day Annu. 1913:43–45.

Burrill, A. C. 1913b. Letter on Wisconsin's first bird refuges. Wilson Bull. 25(2):99–100.

Burrill, A. C. 1915. Wisconsin establishes 24 refuges containing 30,000 acres. Bull. Am. Game Protection Assoc. 3(2):24.

Burton, J. H. 1958. Some population mechanics of the American Coot (Fulica americana). MS thesis, Univ. Wis.–Madison, 54 pp.

Buss, I. O. 1942. A managed Cliff Swallow colony in southern Wisconsin. Wilson Bull. 54(3):153–61.

Buss, I. O. 1943a. The Upland Plover at Faville Grove, Wisconsin. MS thesis, Univ. Wis.–Madison, 101 pp.

Buss, I. O. 1943b. Population studies in Wisconsin pheasants. PhD diss., Univ. Wis.–Madison, 88 pp.

Buss, I. O. 1946a. Bird detection by radar. Auk 63(3):315–18.

Buss, I. O. 1946b. Pheasants, fox and quail. Wis. Conserv. Bull. 11(4):8–15.

Buss, I. O. 1946c. Wisconsin pheasant populations: Progress report of pheasant investigations conducted from 1936–1943. Wis. Conserv. Dep. Bull. No. 326, Madison, 184 pp.

Buss, I. O. 1955. The biography of a pheasant "flock," northwestern Wisconsin. Wis. Acad. Rev. 2(2):10–14.

Buss, I. O., and A. S. Hawkins. 1939. The Upland Plover at Faville Grove, Wisconsin. Wilson Bull. 51(4):202–20.

Buss, I. O., and H. M. Mattison. 1955. A half century of change in bird populations of the lower Chippewa River, Wisconsin. Milwaukee Public Mus. Publ. in Ornithol. No. 1, 319 pp.

Buss, I. O., H. M. Mattison, and F. M. Kozlik. 1947. The Bobwhite quail in Dunn County, Wisconsin. Wis. Conserv. Bull. 12(7):6–13.

Buss, I. O., C. V. Swanson, and D. H. Woodside. 1952. The significance of adult pheasant mortalities in spring to fall populations. Trans. North Am. Wildl. Conf. 17:269–84.

Bussewitz, E. E. 1939. Field notes from Faville Grove Wildlife Area. Pass. Pigeon 1(9):135.

Butler, A. W. 1892. Notes on the range and habits of the Carolina Parakeet. Auk 9(1):49–56.

Cabot, J. Elliot. 1850. Report of the birds collected and observed at Lake Superior. Pp. 384–85 in Lake Superior: Its physical character, vegetation, and animals, ed. Louis Agassiz. Gould, Kendall and Lincoln, Boston.

Cahn, A. R. 1913. The birds of Waukesha County. Bull. Wis. Nat. Hist. Soc. 11(4):113–49.

Cahn, A. R. 1915a. The status of Harris's Sparrow in Wisconsin and neighboring states. Bull. Wis. Nat. Hist. Soc. 13(2):102–8.

Cahn, A. R., Comp. 1915b. Observations on Wisconsin winter birds, and migration record, 1913 [four charts]. Wis. Arbor and Bird Day Manual, Wis. Dep. Public Instruction, Madison, 115 pp.

Cahn, A. R. 1916a. An ecological survey of the Wingra Springs region, near Madison, Wisconsin, with special reference to its ornithology. Bull. Wis. Nat. Hist. Soc. 13(3):123–77. (Text of Cahn's Univ. Wis.–Madison MS thesis.)

Cahn, A. R. 1916b. LeConte's Sparrow in Wisconsin. Auk 32(4):497.

Cahn, A. R. 1927. Summer birds in the vicinity of Plum Lake, Vilas County, Wisconsin. Wilson Bull. 39(1):23–34.

Calhoun, W. T. 1939. Wisconsin birds. Wis. Conserv. Bull. 7(4):32–42; reprinted as Wisconsin wildlife—birds, 1947, Publ. 607, Wis. Conserv. Dep., Madison, 28 pp.

Campbell, M. 1957. Adventures at the Wisconsin Audubon Camp. Pass. Pigeon 19(1):8–15.

Canfield, W. H. 1873. Catalogue of birds that inhabit or visit Sauk County. Pp. 1–4, Sect. 4 in Guidebook to the wild and romantic scenery of Sauk County, Wisconsin, comp. W. H. Canfield; revised and improved from his list of birds published in the Baraboo Republic, 1866.

Cantwell, G. C. 1890. Notes from Lake Mills, Wisconsin. Ornithol. and Oologist 15(4):63.

Carlton, E. P. 1890. Notes on *Ardea herodias*. Oologist 7(11):227–28.

Carlton, E. P. 1891a. Flycatcher notes. Oologist 8(2):27–29.

Carlton, E. P. 1891b. The extinction of our birds. Oologist 8(3):65–68.

Carpenter, A. W. 1892. Nesting of the American Long-eared Owl in Milwaukee County. Wilson Q. 4(1):13.

Carr, C. F. 1884. Some data on migrants. For. and Stream 22(11):203.

Carr, C. F. 1885a. American Velvet Scoter in Wisconsin. Ornithol. and Oologist 10(12):183.

Carr, C. F. 1885b. The Rose-breasted Grosbeak. Ornithol. and Oologist 10(12):189.

Carr, C. F. 1890a. Passenger Pigeon (*Ectopistes migratorius*) nesting in Wisconsin. Wis. Nat. 1(1):9–10; reprinted in Pass. Pigeon 38(3):134.

Carr, C. F. 1890b. Black Terns abandoning their nesting haunts. Wis. Nat. 1(1):10.

Carr, C. F. 1890–1891. A list of the birds known to nest within the boundaries of Wisconsin, with a few notes thereon. Wis. Nat. 1(2–6):28–30, 45–47, 62–63, 77–79, 94.

Carr, C. F. 1911. Yellow-headed Blackbirds extend range. Oologist 28(7):123.

Carroll, J. M. 1977. Birds of Necedah National Wildlife Refuge. U.S. Dep. Inter. Fish and Wildl. Serv., Necedah, Wis.

Carson, G. 1979. The glorious bird (Old Abe). Nat. Hist. 88(6):33–36.

Carver, J. 1779. Travels through the interior parts of North America, in the years 1766, 1767 and 1768. 2d ed., W. Richardson, London. (Section on Wisconsin birds, pp. 434–44.)

Cassoday, D. 1941. Stalking a Ruffed Grouse. Wis. Conserv. Bull. 6(6):25–30.

Cassoday, D. 1942. Spring chickens. Wis. Conserv. Bull. 7(5):19–22; reprinted in Modern Game Breeding 12(10):4–5, 13.

Catling, P. M. 1971. Spring migration of Saw-whet Owls at Toronto, Ontario. Bird Banding 42(2):110–14.

Cherrie, G. K. 1896. *Ardetta neoxena* from Wisconsin. Auk 13(1):79.

Chipman, I. 1968. A day to remember. Pass. Pigeon 30(1):32–33.

Cholwek, G. 1979. Loon Watch Report—1978 Wisconsin project. Sigurd Olson Inst. Environ. Stud., Northland College, Ashland, Wis., 31 pp.

Church, K. E. 1980. Gray Partridge, *Perdix perdix* L., nesting success and brood survival in east central Wisconsin. MS thesis, Univ. Wis.–Green Bay, 86 pp.

Cialdini, R., and G. Orians. 1944. Nesting studies of the Spotted Sandpiper. Pass. Pigeon 6(4):79–81.

Clark, H. E. 1955. A bee apiary supplies more than honey. Pass. Pigeon 17(2):84.

Clark, J. N. 1896a. Rare winter birds at Meridean, Wisconsin. Wilson Bull. 8(7):4.

Clark, J. N. 1896b. Some notes on the redpolls of Dunn County, Wisconsin. Wilson Bull. 8(8):1–2.

Clark, J. N. 1897a. Notes on some winter birds of Meridean, Dunn County, Wisconsin. Wilson Bull. 9(14):29–30.

Clark, J. N. 1897b. Warbling Vireo (*Vireo gilvus*). Wilson Bull. 9(14):30–31.

Clark, J. N. 1899a. Winter visitants and residents—Meridean, Dunn County, Wisconsin. Wilson Bull. 11(24):6–7.

Clark, J. N. 1899b. June census. Wilson Bull. 11(27):58–59.

Cleasby, E. A. 1912. Birds of value to farmers. Pp. 191–202 in A handbook of agriculture. Wis. Farmers' Inst. Bull. 12.

Cleasby, E. A. 1913. Practical nature study. By the Wayside 14(10):73–74.

Cleaves, H. H. 1913. What the American Bird Banding Association has accomplished during 1912. Auk 30(2):248–55.

Coale, A. K. 1884. *Zonotrichia querula* taken at Trempealeau, Wisconsin. Auk 1(1):106.

Coale, H. K. 1911. Notes on some birds rare or new to Wisconsin. Auk 28(2):275–76.

Coale, H. K. 1915. The present status of the Trumpeter Swan (*Olor buccinator*). Auk 32(1):82–91.

Coale, H. K. 1921. Passenger Pigeon in Wisconsin. Auk 38(3):456.

Cochran, W. W. 1975. Following a migrating Peregrine from Wisconsin to Mexico. Hawk Chalk 14(2):28–37.

Cole, L. J. 1910. The tagging of wild birds: Report of progress in 1909. Auk 27(2):153–68.

Cole, L. J. 1922. The early history of bird banding in America. Wilson Bull. 34(2):108–15.

Cole, L. J. 1932. The egg-laying cycle of the Mourning Dove. Wilson Bull. 44(1):55.

Cole, L. J. 1933. The relation of light periodicity to the reproductive cycle, migration and distribution of the Mourning Dove (*Zenaidura macroura carolinensis*). Auk 50(3):284–96.

Coleman, Mrs. T. E. 1930. The thrills of a bird lover. Wis. Arbor and Bird Day Annu. 1930:22–23.

Collias, N. E. 1952. The development of social behavior in birds. Auk 69(2):127–59.

Collias, N. E., and L. R. Jahn. 1959. Social behavior and breeding success in Canada Geese (*Branta canadensis*) confined under semi-wild conditions. Auk 76(4):478–509.

Collias, N. E., and R. D. Taber, 1951. A field study of some grouping and dominance relations in Ring-necked Pheasants. Condor 53(6):265–75.

Conover, F. L. 1912. Franklin's Gull in Wisconsin. Auk 29(3):388.

Conway, R. C. 1938. Wisconsin and the pheasant. Wis. Conserv. Bull. 3(3):21–25.

Conway, R. C. 1948. Passenger Pigeon monuments. Natl. Humane Rev. 36(8):18–20.

Cook, R. W., Jr. 1960. The big swamp [Peshtigo Brook Marsh]. Wis. Conserv. Bull. 25(4):28–30.

Cooke, M. T. 1923. Report on bird censuses in the United States, 1916 to 1920. U.S. Dep. Agric. Bull. 1165, Washington, D.C., 36 pp.

Cooke, M. T. 1938. Returns of banded birds: Recoveries of banded marsh birds. Bird Banding 9(2):80–87.

Cooke, M. T. 1941a. Returns from banded birds: Recoveries of some banded birds of prey. Bird Banding 12(4):150–60.

Cooke, M. T. 1941b. Banded birds recovered in El Salvador. Auk 58(4):589–90. (Includes Peregrine Falcon banded at Cedar Grove.)

Cooke, W. W. 1884a. Bird nomenclature of Chippewa Indians. Auk 1(3):242–50.

Cooke, W. W. 1884b. Distribution and migration of *Zonotrichia querula* [Harris' Finch]. Auk 1(4):332–37.

Cooke, W. W. 1884–1885. Migration in the Mississippi Valley. Ornithol. and Oologist 15(8, 9, and 10).

Cooke, W. W. 1885. Notes on the occurrence of certain birds in the Mississippi Valley. Auk 2(1):31–33.

Cooke, W. W. 1888. Report on bird migration in the Mississippi Valley in the years 1884 and 1885. U.S. Dep. Agric., Div. Econ. Ornithol., Bull. 2, Washington, D.C., 313 pp.

Cooke, W. W. 1913. The relation of bird migration to the weather. Auk 30(2):205–21.

Cooke, W. W. 1915. Bird migration. U.S. Dep. Agric., Biol. Surv., Bull. 185, Washington, D.C.

Cooke, W. W., and O. Widmann. 1882–1883. Bird migration in the Mississippi Valley. For. and Stream 18(9 Nov. 1882):284; 18(16 Nov. 1882):306; 19(9 Nov. and 14 Dec. 1883):283–84, 306, 384; also published in Am. Field, Vols. 20 and 21.

Cooke, W. W., and O. Widmann. 1883. Bird migration in the Mississippi Valley. Ridgway Ornithol. Club, Bull. No. 1, Chicago, 37 pp.; reprinted in part in Wis. Acad. Rev. 10(2):66–69.

Copeland, D. C. 1980. Hawk sightings in western Great Lakes. Hawk Migration Assoc. of North Am. Newslett. 5(1):14–15.

Correspondent. 1882. A Wisconsin pigeon roost. For. and Stream 19(1):8.

Cory, C. B. 1909. The birds of Illinois and Wisconsin. Public Field Mus. Nat. Hist. (Zool. Ser.) 9:1–764.

Cottam, C. 1939. Food habits of North American diving ducks. Bur. Biol. Surv. Tech. Bull. 643, Washington, D.C., 140 pp.

Cottam, C. 1956. History of waterfowl management in America. Pp. 49–67 in Proc. of Managing Our Fish and Wildlife Resources Conf., Jan. 19–20, Univ. Minn. Cent. for Continuation Study, Minneapolis.

Coues, E. 1874. Birds of the northwest. U.S. Dep. Inter. Geol. Surv. of the Territories. Misc. Publ. No. 3, Washington, D.C., 791 pp.

Coues, E. 1895. The expeditions of Zebulon Montgomery Pike, to headwaters of the Mississippi River, through Louisiana Territory and in New Spain, during the years 1805–6–7. 3 vols. F. P. Harper, New York.

Cox, W. T. 1926. The Upper Mississippi Fish and Wild Life Refuge. Pp. 57–62 in Rep. 4th Annu. Convention Wis. Div. Isaak Walton League of Am., 9–10 Sept., Stevens Point, Wis.

Cranston, D. M. 1919a. Bird migration. Wis. Conserv. 1(2):15.

Cranston, D. M. 1919b. Birds wage war on insects. Wis. Conserv. 1(3):11.

Craven, S. R. 1976. History and ecology of the Canada Geese wintering near Rock Prairie, Wisconsin. MS thesis, Univ. Wis.–Madison, 43 pp.

Craven, S. R. 1978. Distribution and migration of Canada Geese associated with Horicon Marsh, Wisconsin. PhD diss., Univ. Wis.–Madison, 135 pp.

Craven, S. R. 1980. Mad City ducks. Wis. Nat. Resour. 4(1):4–5.

Craven, S. R., and T. S. Smith. 1978. Rock Prairie's giant geese. Wis. Nat. Resour. 2(2):18–19.

Craven, S. R., G. A. Bartelt, D. H. Rusch, and R. E. Trost. 1985. Distribution and movement of Canada Geese in response to management changes in east-central Wisconsin. Wis. Dept. Nat. Resour., Tech. Bull. 158, Madison, 36 pp.

Creed, W. A., and F. Stearns. 1967. Wildlife resources. Pp. 102–6 in Soil resources and forest ecology of Menominee County, Wisconsin, ed. C. J. Milfred, G. W. Olson, and F. D. Hole. Univ. Wis. Geol. and Nat. Hist. Surv. Bull. 85, Soil Ser. 60, 203 pp.

Crete, R. A., and J. E. Toepfer. 1978. Migration of radio-tagged eastern Greater Sandhill Cranes. Rep. submitted to U.S. Fish and Wildl. Serv., Twin Cities, Minn, 42 pp.

Curran, G. A. 1960. The woodcock: Game bird par excellence. Wis. Conserv. Bull. 25(8):20–22.

Currie, D. 1888. Two days field work in Waukesha County. Oologist 5(8–9):122–23.

Currie, D. 1890. A collecting trip at Pewaukee, Wisconsin. Oologist 7(7):45–46.

Curtis, F. W. 1889. The Great Blue Heron. Ornithol. and Oologists (Semi-Annual) 1(2):27–28.

Curtis, J. T. 1933. Brewer's Blackbirds in Waukesha County, Wisconsin. Wilson Bull. 45(3):142.

Curtis, J. T. 1954. Scientific areas in Wisconsin. Wis. Conserv. Bull. 19(1):13–16.

Curtis, J. T. 1959. The vegetation of Wisconsin. Univ. Wis. Press, Madison, 657 pp.

Curtis, S. G. 1969a. Spring migration and weather at Madison, Wisconsin. Wilson Bull. 81(3):235–45.

Curtis, S. G. 1969b. Weather patterns and spring migration. Pass. Pigeon 31(4):151–59.

Cutright, N. J. 1985. House Finch in Wisconsin: What does the future hold? Pass. Pigeon 47:63–66.

Cutright, N. J. 1989. It takes many: Contributions by Wisconsin's other ornithological organizations. Pass. Pigeon 51:19–24.

Daggett, F. S. 1894. A Wisconsin heronry. For. and Stream 43(10):202.

Dahlberg, B. L. 1954. Prospects for Prairie Grouse management—game area 1. Wis. Conserv. Bull. 19(1):18–22.

Dahlberg, E. M. 1939. Conservation of renewable resources. C. C. Nelson, Appleton, Wis., 208 pp.

Dahlberg, E. M. 1944. Random notes from a Flambeau River diary. Pass. Pigeon 6(1):19–21; 6(2):50.

Dahlberg, E. M. 1947. Some interesting bird "shots." Pass. Pigeon 9(3):103–5.

Dahlen, J. H., and D. R. Thompson. 1955. Wisconsin wetlands and their importance. Wis. Conserv. Bull. 20(1):9–12.

Dahlstrand, N. P. 1960. An unruffled grouse. Pass. Pigeon 22(4):181–83.

Damaske, N. E. 1952. Greenwood refuge—home of honkers. Wis. Conserv. Bull. 17(4):3–6.

Danielson, D. 1967. Woodcock on nest, spring 1966, Washington County. Pass. Pigeon 29(2):50.

Dayton, F. S. 1941a. A New London [Wisconsin] starling roost. Pass. Pigeon 3(9):81–82.

Dayton, F. S. 1941b. Sandhill Cranes breed at New London. Pass. Pigeon 3(10):91.

Deane, R. 1880. Destruction of birds by drowning. Bull. Nuttall Ornithol. Club 5(3):192.

Deane, R. 1888. Destruction in migration. For. and Stream 31(20):385; reprinted in Pass. Pigeon 40(4):516–18.

Deane, R. 1896. Additional records of the Passenger Pigeon (Ectopistes migratorius) in Wisconsin and Illinois. Auk 13(1):81.

Deane, R. 1898. The Passenger Pigeon (Ectopistes migratorius) in Wisconsin and Nebraska. Auk 15(2):184–85.

Deane, R. 1906a. A northern record for the Swallow-tailed Kite (Elanoides forficatus) in Wisconsin. Auk 23(1):100.

Deane, R. 1906b. Unusual abundance of the Snowy Owl (Nyctea nyctea). Auk 23(3):283–98.

Deane, R. 1909. The Passenger Pigeon—only one pair left. Auk 26(4):429.

Deane, R. 1911. Additional records of the European Widgeon (Mareca penelope). Auk 28(3):254–55.

DeBoer, S. G. 1962. What's been going on since '50?—And where are we headed? Wis. Conserv. Dep., Madison, 21 pp.

DeGroot, D. 1915. The loon (Gavia immer) on Plum Lake, Wisconsin. Oologist 33(7):112.

DeJong, M. J. 1976. The distribution of breeding birds in relation to vegetation in lowland forests of southern Wisconsin. MS thesis, Univ. Wis.–Madison, 99 pp.

Dennis, C. J. 1969. Western Tanager in Grant County. Pass. Pigeon 31(3):284.

Dennis, C. J. 1971. Great Blue Heron observations on the Mississippi River near Bagley, Wisconsin. Pass. Pigeon 33(2):104–9.

Derleth, A. 1945–1947 and 1949. Sac Prairie winter, spring, summer, and autumn; series of 16 articles. Pass. Pigeon, Vols. 7–11.

Derleth, A. 1952–1953. Country calendar [the four seasons]. Pass. Pigeon, Vols. 14–15.

Derleth, A. 1961. Walden west. Duell Sloan and Pearce, New York, 262 pp.; originally printed in part in Pass. Pigeon, Vols. 12–13, 1950–1951.

Dernehl, P. H. 1900. The Purple Martin. Bull. Wis. Nat. Hist. Soc. 1(3):190–91.

De Stefano, S. 1982. Harvest and distribution of Ruffed Grouse in northeastern Wisconsin. MS thesis, Univ. Wis.–Madison, 107 pp.

Deusing, M. 1938. Atlantic Kittiwake in Wisconsin. Auk 55(3):529.

Deusing, M. 1939a. The Herring Gulls of Hat Island, Wisconsin. Wilson Bull. 51(3):170–75.

Deusing, M. 1939b. Nesting habits of the Pied-billed Grebe. Auk 56(4):367–73.

Deusing, M. 1940. Bald Eagle range and population study [Wisconsin]. Pass. Pigeon 2(9):103–6.

Deusing, M. 1941. Notes on the nesting of the Florida Gallinule. Pass. Pigeon 3(9):79–81.

Deusing, M. 1942. A range and population study of the Purple Martin in Wisconsin. Pass. Pigeon 4(3):17–21.

Deusing, M. 1943. A review of 1943 field notes for southern Wisconsin. Pass. Pigeon 6(1):18–19.

DeWitt, C. B. 1980. Values of Wisconsin's vanishing wetlands. Wis. Nat. Resour. 4(1):28–31.

DeWitt, C. B., and E. Soloway. 1979. Wetlands ecology, values and impacts. Proc. Conf. Wetlands, 2–5 June 1977, Madison. Inst. Environ. Stud. Univ. Wis.–Madison, 388 pp.

Diedrich, J. L. 1949. Snowy Egret in Wisconsin. Auk 66(2):195–96.

Dietrich, E. J. 1906. Letter to editor on egg collecting at Perkinstown, Taylor County. Oologist 23(1):7–8.

Dill, H. H., and F. B. Lee, Eds. 1970. Home grown honkers. U.S. Dep. Inter. Fish and Wildl. Serv., Washington, D.C., 154 pp.

Dillon, S. T. 1956–1957. A nine-year study of fall waterfowl migration on University Bay, Madison, Wisconsin. Part 1. Trans. Wis. Acad. Sci., Arts, Lett. 45:31–57; Part 2. Trans. Wis. Acad. Sci., Arts, Lett. 46:1–30.

Dlutkowski, L. A. 1986. Changes in breeding bird abundance in Dunn's Marsh, Wisconsin. MS thesis, Univ. Wis.–Madison, 88 pp.

Doll, A. D. 1953. Sharptails on the Chequamegon. Wis. Conserv. Bull. 8(9):17–19.

Dorney, R. S. 1954. Wisconsin Ruffed Grouse, 1949 to 1953. Wis. Conserv. Bull. 19(4):23–24.

Dorney, R. S. 1959a. Relationship of Ruffed Grouse to forest cover types in Wisconsin. Tech. Bull. No. 18, Wis. Conserv. Dep., Madison, 31 pp.

Dorney, R. S. 1959b. Relation of hunting, weather and parasitic disease to Wisconsin Ruffed Grouse populations. PhD diss. Univ. Wis.–Madison, 94 pp.

Dorney, R. S. 1963. Sex and age structure of Wisconsin Ruffed Grouse populations. J. Wildl. Manage. 27(4):599–603.

Dorney, R. S., and C. Kabat. 1960. Relation of weather, parasitic disease and hunting to Wisconsin Ruffed Grouse populations. Tech. Bull. 20, Wis. Conserv. Dep., Madison, 62 pp.

Doty, J. D. 1908. Northern Wisconsin in 1820 [letter from Detroit to Lewis Cass dated 27 Sept. 1820]. Pp. 195–206 in State Hist. Soc. Wis. Collections, Vol. 7, Madison, 492 pp.; original issued in 1876; reprinted in March 1938, Wis. Conserv. Bull. 3(3):26–35.

Dudley, W. A. 1856. A new crane in Wisconsin—called *Grus hoyanus* in honor of Dr. Hoy. Proc. Acad. Nat. Sci., Philadelphia 7:64.

Dudley, W. A. 1868. Colored plate of this crane [immature whooping crane]. Trans. Chicago Acad. Sci. 1:129, Plate 19.

Dumke, R. T. 1975. Inventory of Bobwhite quail distribution relative abundance and range quality. Study No. 105, final report, Wis. Dep. Nat. Resour., mimeo., 22 pp.

Dumke, R. T. 1977. Gray Partridge distribution and relative abundance. Rep. 93, Wis. Dep. Nat. Resour., 8 pp.

Dumke, R. T. 1982. Habitat development for Bobwhite quail on private lands in Wisconsin. Tech. Bull. 128, Wis. Dep. Nat. Resour., 46 pp.

Dumke, R. T. and C. M. Pils. 1970. Mortality and life-history studies of pheasants. Pittman-Robertson Proj. W-141-R6, Federal Aid to Wildlife Restoration Act, Wis. Dep. Nat. Resour., Madison, ms, 23 pp.

Dumke, R. T., and C. M. Pils. 1973. Mortality of radio-tagged pheasants on the Waterloo wildlife area. Tech. Bull. 72, Wis. Dep. Nat. Resour., 52 pp.

Dumke, R. T., and C. M. Pils. 1979. Renesting and dynamics of nest site selection by Wisconsin pheasants. J. Wildl. Manage. 43(3):705–16.

Dümling, H. 1879. Illustrirtes Thienleben—die Vögel. Verlag von Geo. Brumder, Milwaukee, 270 pp.

Dunn, J. O. 1895. The Passenger Pigeon in the upper Mississippi Valley. Auk 12(4):389.

Dunwiddie, P. 1980. How many eagles? Clearwater J. 1(5):20–22.

Eagle Valley Environmentalists. 1980. Mid-winter count pinpoints eagles. Eagle 9(2):7.

Eaton, R. J. 1934. The migratory movements of certain colonies of Herring Gulls in eastern North America. Bird Banding 5(2):70–84.

Eckstein, R. G. 1983. Nesting Black-backed Three-toed Woodpeckers in Forest County. Pass. Pigeon 45:16–17.

Eckstein, R. G., P. V. Vanderschaegen, and F. L. Johnson. 1979. Osprey nesting platforms in north central Wisconsin. Pass. Pigeon 41(4):145–48.

Edsall, M. 1965. The freedom-loving, majestic but often misunderstood Bald Eagle is approaching extinction. Wis. Tales and Trails 6(2):12–14.

Edwards, E. P., and A. Sprunt, IV. 1955. Wisconsin Audubon camp birds. Pass. Pigeon 17(4):148–51.

Eickhorst, B. A. 1985. Status of the Red-necked Grebe on Rush Lake, Winnebago County, Wisconsin. Pass. Pigeon 47:60–62.

Eifrig, C. W. G. 1928. On the status of Harlan's Hawk. Wilson Bull. 40(4):216–18.

Elder, W. H. 1935. Early nesting of the Great Horned Owl. Auk 52(1):309–10.

Elder, W. H. 1939. Rare straggler taken in Wisconsin. Pass. Pigeon 1(4):62.

Elkins, Mrs. W. A. 1971. Brown Thrasher wintering at Trempealeau, Wis. Pass. Pigeon 33(3):154.

Ellarson, R. S. 1950. The Yellow-headed Blackbird in Wisconsin. Pass. Pigeon 12(3):99–109.

Ellarson, R. S. 1956a. A study of the Old-squaw Duck on Lake Michigan. PhD diss., Univ. Wis.–Madison, 231 pp.

Ellarson, R. S. 1956b. The Old-squaw Duck on Lake Michigan. Wis. Acad. Rev. 3(2):60–62.

Ellis, M. 1963. Notes from Little Lakes. Milwaukee J. 224 pp.

Ellis, M. 1969. The hunting hawks. Wis. Tales and Trails 10(1):31–33.

Ellis, M. 1970. The glory days of duck hunting. Wis. Tales and Trails 11(3):33–36.

Ellis, M. 1975. Sermons in stone. Holt, Rinehart & Winston, New York, 102 pp.

Emlen, J. T., Jr. 1948. Report on banding activities at the University of Wisconsin. IBBA News 20(2):10.

Emlen, J. T., Jr. 1949. Banding cormorants. IBBA News 21(6):15.

Emlen, J. T., Jr. 1950. Report on banding activities at the University of Wisconsin, Madison (May 1, 1949–April 30, 1950). IBBA News 22(6):30–31.

Emlen, J. T., Jr. 1971a. The centers of learning—the University of Wisconsin. Am. Birds 25(5):820, 908.

Emlen, J. T., Jr. 1971b. Population densities of birds derived from transect counts. Auk 88(2):323–41.

Emlen, J. T., Jr. 1977. Estimating breeding bird populations from transect counts. Auk 94(3):455–68.

Emlen, J. T., Jr. 1989. Fifty years of ornithology at the University of Wisconsin. Pass. Pigeon 51:25–43.

Emlen, J. T., Jr., and J. A. Wiens. 1965. The Dickcissel invasion of 1964 in southern Wisconsin. Pass. Pigeon 27(2):51–59.

Engel, M. S., and A. W. Hopkins. 1956. The prairie and its people. Univ. Wis. Agric. Exp. Stn. Bull. 520, Madison, 37 pp. (Reference to birds found on Goose Pond, Columbia County.)

Epple, A. C. 1962. The Evening Grosbeak invasion of 1961–1962. Pass. Pigeon 14(4):110–24.

Epple, A. C. 1972. WSO's part in the North American nest record card program. Pass. Pigeon 34(3):96–99.

Erbe, L. 1939. Winter birds on Lake Michigan. Field Ornithol. 1(11):9–10.

Erdman, T. C. 1970. Current migrant shrike status in Wisconsin. Pass. Pigeon 32(4):144–50.

Erdman, T. C. 1976a. The first documented nesting of Little Gulls in U.S.A. Pass. Pigeon 38(2):86–87.

Erdman, T. C. 1976b. Arctic Terns in Wisconsin. Pass. Pigeon 38(3):129–31.

Erdman, T. C. 1979a. Boreal Owl in N.E. Wisconsin. Pass. Pigeon 41(2):58–59.

Erdman, T. C. 1979b. Birds' eggs. Wis. Nat. Resour. 3(3):8–12.

Erdman, T. C., and R. S. Cook. 1975. Groove-billed Ani at Green Bay. Pass. Pigeon 37(4):182.

Errington, P. L. 1930a. What can the Wisconsin farm boy do to encourage quail? Wis. Arbor and Bird Day Annu. 1930:45–49.

Errington, P. L. 1930b. Predatory animals of southern Wisconsin and their value to the farmer. Wis. Arbor and Bird Day Annu. 1930:78–85.

Errington, P. L. 1930c. The pellet analysis method of raptor food habits study. Condor 32(6):292–96.

Errington, P. L. 1930d. Wisconsin quail investigation findings. Trans. Am. Game Conf. 17:252–53.

Errington, P. L. 1930e. Territorial disputes of three pairs of nesting Marsh Hawks. Wilson Bull. 42(4):237–39.

Errington, P. L. 1930f. Corn on cob saves wintering quail. Am. Game 19:9–12.

Errington, P. L. 1931a. Winter killing of Barn Owls in Wisconsin. Wilson Bull. 43(1):60.

Errington, P. L. 1931b. The Bob-white's winter food. Am. Game 20:75–78.

Errington, P. L. 1931c. The Bob-white's winter cover. Am. Game 20:90–93.

Errington, P. L. 1931d. Second winter. Am. Game 20:56, 60–61.

Errington, P. L. 1932a. Food habits of southern Wisconsin raptors. Part 1, Owls. Condor 34(4):176–86.

Errington, P. L. 1932b. Great Horned Owls dying in the wild from diseases. Wilson Bull. 44(3):180.

Errington, P. L. 1932c. Studies on the behavior of the Great Horned Owl. Wilson Bull. 44(4):212–20.

Errington, P. L. 1932d. The Northern Bob-white; environmental factors influencing its status. PhD diss., Univ. Wis.–Madison, 120 pp.

Errington, P. L. 1932e. The wintering of the Wisconsin Bob-white. Trans. Wis. Acad. Sci., Arts, Lett. 28:1–35.

Errington, P. L. 1932f. Mobility of the Northern Bob-white as indicated by banding returns. Bird Banding 4(1):1–7.

Errington, P. L. 1933a. The nesting and the life equation of the Wisconsin Bob-white. Wilson Bull. 45(3):122–32.

Errington, P. L. 1933b. Food habits of southern Wisconsin raptors. Part 2, Hawks. Condor 35(1):19–29.

Errington, P. L. 1934. Vulnerability of Bob-white populations to predation. Ecology 15(2):110–27.

Errington, P. L. 1935a. What counts in Northern Bob-white management. Trans. Am. Game Conf., New York, 21:370–76.

Errington, P. L. 1935b. Predators and the Northern Bob-white. Am. For. 41:7–10, 46.

Errington, P. L. 1936. Sex and resistance of Bob-whites and Ring-necked Pheasants to starvation. Auk 53(1):78–79.

Errington, P. L. 1937. Emergency values of some winter pheasant foods. Trans. Wis. Acad. Sci., Arts, Lett. 30:57–68.

Errington, P. L. 1938. The Great Horned Owl as an indicator of vulnerability in prey populations. J. Wildl. Manage. 2(4):190–205.

Errington, P. L. 1939a. The comparative ability of the Bob-white and the Ring-necked Pheasant to withstand cold and hunger. Wilson Bull. 51(1):22–37.

Errington, P. L. 1939b. Foods of Bob-white in Wisconsin. Auk 56(2):170–73.

Errington, P. L. 1945. Some contributions of a fifteen-year local study of the Northern Bob-white to a knowledge of population phenomena. Ecol. Monogr. 15(1):1–34.

Errington, P. L. 1954. The "big boss" of the woods. Audubon Mag. 56(3):124–27.

Errington, P. L. 1957. Of population cycles and unknowns. Cold Spring Harbor Symp. on Quantitative Biol. 22:287–300.

Errington, P. L., and W. J. Breckinridge. 1936. Food habits of Marsh Hawks in the glaciated prairie region of north-central United States. Am. Midl. Nat. 17(5):831–48.

Errington, P. L., and F. N. Hamerstrom, Jr. 1939. The Northern Bob-white's winter territory. Iowa Agric. Exp. Stn. Res. Bull. 201:301–443.

Errington, P. L., F. Hamerstrom, and F. N. Hamerstrom. 1940. The Great Horned Owl and its prey in north-central United States. Iowa Agric. Exp. Stn. Res. Bull. 277:757–850.

Evans, J. H. 1940. Birds and eggs in the Oshkosh Public Museum. Pass. Pigeon 2(2):21.

Evans, J. H., and M. H. Nelson. 1960. The Cattle Egret comes to Wisconsin. Pass. Pigeon 22(4):185–88.

Evrard, J. O. 1971. A winter population of Goldeneyes. Pass. Pigeon 33(4):163–66.

Evrard, J. O. 1975a. Nesting Great Egrets in Burnett County. Pass. Pigeon 37(4):151–52.

Evrard, J. O. 1975b. Waterfowl use of dug ponds in northwestern Wisconsin. Wildl. Soc. Bull. 3(1):13–18.

Evrard, J. O. 1984. Oldsquaw duck in Polk County. Pass. Pigeon 46:79–80.

Evrard, J. O. 1988. Nesting Red-necked Grebes in St. Croix County, Wisconsin. Pass. Pigeon 50:291–95.

Evrard, J. O. and B. Bacon. 1987. Common Loon breeding in St. Croix County. Pass. Pigeon 49:98–100.

Evrard, J. O., E. A. Lombard, and K. H. Larsen. 1978. Response to drought by a breeding population of Common Loons. Pass. Pigeon 40(2):418.

Faanes, C. A. 1974. Great Black-backed Gull and Peregrine Falcon in upper Mississippi River area. Pass. Pigeon 36(2):85.

Faanes, C. A. 1975a. A comparison of spring waterfowl populations in Barron County, Wisconsin. Pass. Pigeon 37(2):63–66.

Faanes, C. A. 1975b. A northern Three-toed Woodpecker in Polk County. Pass. Pigeon 37(3):135–36.

Faanes, C. A. 1976. Winter ecology of Bald Eagles in southeastern Minnesota [includes Wisconsin]. Loon 48(2):61–69.

Faanes, C. A. 1978. Weather grounded migrants in Douglas County. Pass. Pigeon 40(1):386–87.

Faanes, C. A. 1979. Status of the Black Tern in western Wisconsin. Pass. Pigeon 41(3):124–28.

Faanes, C. A. 1980. Breeding biology of Eastern Phoebes in northern Wisconsin. Wilson Bull. 92(1):107–10.

Faanes, C. A. 1981. Birds of the St. Croix River valley: Minnesota and Wisconsin. U.S. Dep. Inter. North Am. Fauna No. 73, Washington, D.C., 196 pp.

Faanes, C. A., and S. V. Goddard. 1976a. The birds of Pierce and St. Croix counties, Wisconsin. Pass. Pigeon 38(1):19–38.

Faanes, C. A., and S. V. Goddard. 1976b. The birds of Pierce and St. Croix counties, Wisconsin. Pass. Pigeon 38(2):57–71.

Faber, R. A., and J. J. Hickey. 1973. Eggshell thinning, chlorinated hydrocarbons, and mercury in inland aquatic bird eggs. Pestic. Monit. J. 7(1):27–36.

Fargo, G. W., Jr. 1895. Decrease in bluebirds at Kaukauna, Wisconsin. Nidiologist 3:56.

Fassett, N. C. 1976. Spring flora of Wisconsin. Univ. Wis. Press, Madison, 422 pp.

Fawks, E. 1979. Wintering eagles along the Mississippi River. Eagle 8(2):11.

Fawks, E., and T. N. Ingram. 1970. Winter birding along the Mississippi River. Eagle Valley Environmentalists, Apple River, Ill., 13 pp.

Featherstonhaugh, G. W. 1847. A canoe voyage up the Minnay Sotor. 2 vols., R. Bentley, London.

Feeney, W. S. 1941. Forest field notes. Wis. Conserv. Bull. 6(12):4–5.

Fell, S. D. 1952. Photographing the Richardson's Owl. Pass. Pigeon 14(2):51.

Fendry, D., T. A. Andryk, T. Sheafer, R. A. Hunt, and J. Wetzel. 1986. Wisconsin breeding duck populations 1973–1986. Wis. Dep. Nat. Resour. Adm. Rep., 13 pp.

Fernald, M. L. 1950. Gray's manual of botany. American Book Co., New York.

Ficken, M. S. 1968. Bird hybrids in the Kettle Moraine. Univ. Wis.–Milwaukee Field Stn. Bull. 1(2).

Ficken, M. S. 1977. Avian play. Auk 94(3):573–82.

Ficken, M. S., and S. R. Witkin. 1977. Responses of Black-capped Chickadee flocks to predators. Auk 94(1):156–57.

Ficken, M. S., R. W. Ficken, and S. R. Witkin. 1978. Vocal repertoire of the Black-capped Chickadee. Auk 95(1):34–48.

Field, W. H. 1956. Private wildlife management in Wisconsin. Wis. Conserv. Bull. 21(1):20–23.

Finley, R. W. 1951. The original vegetation cover of Wisconsin. PhD diss., Univ. Wis.–Madison, 280 pp.

Finley, R. W. 1975. Geography of Wisconsin. Univ. Wis. Press, Madison, 472 pp.

Flader, S. 1973. The sand country of Aldo Leopold. Sierra Club, San Francisco, 94 pp.; reprinted in part in Wisconsin Alumnus 74(10):8–9, 23.

Fleming, J. H. 1912. The Ancient Murrelet. Auk 29(3):287–88.

Flory, C. M. 1934. Little Blue Heron (Florida caerolea caerolea) in Wisconsin. Auk 51(4):511.

Follen, D. G., Sr. 1966. Hawk Owl at Arpin, Wisconsin. Pass. Pigeon 28(4):149–50.

Follen, D. G., Sr. 1971. Four young in one Barred Owl nest. Pass. Pigeon 33:65–68.

Follen, D. G., Sr. 1975. Harrier production in a central Wisconsin township: A summary. Pass. Pigeon 37(2):91–92.

Follen, D. G., Sr. 1979a. A probable breeding record of Great Gray Owls in Wisconsin. Pass. Pigeon 41(3):53–57.

Follen, D. G., Sr. 1979b. A note on Short-eared Owl production. Pass. Pigeon 41(2):60–61.

Follen, D. G., Sr. 1980. Great Gray Owl study—1979. Pass. Pigeon 42(2):69–70.

Follen, D. G., Sr. 1981a. Saw-whet Owl in a Wood Duck box. Pass. Pigeon 43:47–48.

Follen, D. G., Sr. 1981b. Wisconsin breeding and breeding period records of Saw-whet Owls. Pass. Pigeon 43:113–16.

Follen, D. G., Sr. 1982a. First record of a Boreal Owl in Wood County. Pass. Pigeon 44:68.

Follen, D. G., Sr. 1982b. Great Gray Owl study—1981. Pass. Pigeon 44:69–71.

Follen, D. G., Sr. 1982c. Additional breeding and breeding period records of Saw-whet Owls in Wisconsin. Pass. Pigeon 44:71.

Follen, D. G., Sr. 1983a. Harrier nesting explosion. Pass. Pigeon 45:45–47.

Follen, D. G., Sr. 1983b. Loggerhead Shrikes in Wood County. Pass. Pigeon 45:80.

Follen, D. G., Sr. 1984. Color marked Sandhill Cranes in Wisconsin. Pass. Pigeon 46:136–41.

Follen, D. G., Sr. 1985. Great Gray Owl update. Pass. Pigeon 47:133–35.

Follen, D. G., Sr. 1986a. Harriers, 1984, a reproductive disaster. Pass. Pigeon 48:17–20.

Follen, D. G., Sr. 1986b. Barn Owl in Clark County. Pass. Pigeon 48:21–22.

Follen, D. G., Sr. 1986c. Swainson's Hawks. Pass. Pigeon 48:22–23.

Follen, D. G., Sr. 1987a. Wisconsin Great Gray Owl update. Pass. Pigeon 49:96–98.

Follen, D. G., Sr. 1987b. Black-shouldered Kite 1987: WSO convention highlight. Pass. Pigeon 49:138–39.

Follen, D. G., Sr., and J. C. Haug. 1981. Saw-whet Owl nest in Wood Duck box. Pass. Pigeon 43:47–48.

Foor, L. 1836. Remarks on Indian summers. Am. J. Sci. 30:9–15.

Forbush, E. H. 1913. The last Passenger Pigeon. Bird-Lore 15(2):99–103.

Ford, E. R. 1930. Breeding of Brewer's Blackbird east of its normal summer range. Auk 47(4):565–66.

Ford, E. R. 1936a. Cuban Snowy Plover (Charadrius n. tenuirostris) in Wisconsin. Auk 53(1):79.

Ford, E. R. 1936b. Arkansas Kingbird (Tyrannus verticalis) in Wisconsin. Auk 53(1):83.

Ford, E. R. 1956. Birds of the Chicago region. Chicago Acad. Sci. Spec. Publ. No. 12, Chicago, 117 pp.

Ford, E. R., C. C. Sanborn, and C. B. Coursen. 1934. Birds of the Chicago region. Chicago Acad. Sci. 5(2–3):18–80.

Foster, G. W., Jr. 1956. 1955 in review. Pass. Pigeon 18(2):51–57.

Foster, G. W., Jr. 1969. Sabine's Gulls seen and photographed on Lake Mendota, Dane County. Pass. Pigeon 31(3):294.

Fox, C. P. 1939. The farmer's allies—hawks and owls. Wis. Agric. and Farmer 1939(7 Oct.):5, 15.

Frank, E. J. 1964. We'll try pheasant homes. Wis. Conserv. Bull. 29(3):18–19.

Frank, E. J. 1968. What's new in pheasant homes? Wis. Conserv. Bull. 33(3):5–7.

Frank, E. J., and E. E. Woehler. 1969. Production of nesting and winter cover for pheasants in Wisconsin. J. Wildl. Manage. 33(4):802–10.

Frankowiak, R. J. 1962. The Cattle Egret—habits and identification. Pass. Pigeon 24(3):89–90.

Frautschi, W. A. 1945. Early Wisconsin shooting clubs. Wis. Mag. Hist. 28(4):391–415.

French, G. E., and W. E. Griffee. 1927. Arkansas Kingbirds at Madison, Wisconsin. Auk 44(4):566.

Friends of the Arboretum. 1978. Birds observed in the arboretum in 1978. Friends of the Arboretum (Univ. Wis.–Madison) 4(3):5.

Frister, C., and D. Frister. 1953. A vacation birding trip. Pass. Pigeon 15(2):77–80.

Fruth, K., S. Matteson, C. Gieck, and D. Sample. 1988. Wisconsin endangered, threatened, and nongame birds, performance report—1988. Wis. Dep. Nat. Resour. Wis. Endang. Resour. Rep. No. 45, 9 pp.

Fry, J. E. 1938. Wildlife food patches: Results of four years of observation in southwestern Wisconsin. Trans. North Am. Wildl. Conf. 3:730–35.

Gabrielson, I. N. 1939. American Egrets breed in Wisconsin. Wilson Bull. 51(4):240–41; reprinted in Pass. Pigeon 1(12):165–66.

Gamble, K. E. 1965. Birds and mammals of the Listeman Arboretum, Neillsville, Wis. Pp. 41–44 of appendix in The survey and general management master plan of the Listeman Arboretum, ed. J. E. Purchase. Univ. Wis.–Stevens Point, photocopy.

Gard, R. E. 1972. Wild goose marsh: Horicon stopover. Wisconsin House, Madison, 212 pp.

Gard, R. E. 1975. Wild goose country: Horicon Marsh to Horseshoe Island. Wisconsin House, Madison, 146 pp.

Gates, J. M. 1964. Pheasant bottleneck. Wis. Conserv. Bull. 29(5):12–14.

Gates, J. M. 1965. Duck nesting and production on Wisconsin farmlands. J. Wildl. Manage. 29(3):515–23.

Gates, J. M. 1966a. Crowing counts as indices to cock pheasant populations in Wisconsin. J. Wildl. Manage. 30(4):735–44.

Gates, J. M. 1966b. Renesting behavior in the Ring-necked Pheasant. Wilson Bull. 78(3):309–15.

Gates, J. M. 1970. Recommendations for a scattered wetlands program of pheasant habitat preservation in southeast Wisconsin. Wis. Dep. Nat. Resour. Res. Rep. No. 63, Madison, 24 pp.

Gates, J. M. 1971. The ecology of a Wisconsin pheasant population. PhD diss., Univ. Wis.–Madison, 912 pp.

Gates, J. M. 1972. Red-tailed Hawk populations and ecology in east-central Wisconsin. Wilson Bull. 84(4):421–33.

Gates, J. M. 1973. Gray Partridge ecology in southeast-central Wisconsin. Tech. Bull. 7, Wis. Dep. Nat. Resour., Madison, 8 pp.

Gates, J. M., and J. B. Hale. 1974. Seasonal movement, winter habitat use, and population distribution of an east central Wisconsin pheasant population. Tech. Bull. 76, Wis. Dep. Nat. Resour., Madison, 55 pp.

Gates, J. M., and J. B. Hale. 1975. Reproduction of an east central Wisconsin pheasant population. Tech. Bull. 85, Wis. Dep. Nat. Resour., Madison, 70 pp.

Gates, J. M., and G. M. Ostrom. 1966. Feed grain program related to pheasant production in Wisconsin. J. Wildl. Manage. 30(3):612–17.

Gates, J. M., E. J. Frank, and E. E. Woehler. 1970. Management of pheasant nesting cover on upland sites in relation to cropland diversion programs. Wis. Dep. Nat. Resour. Res. Rep. No. 48, Madison, 22 pp.

Gatterdam, P. C. 1941. Cardinals banded at La Crosse, Wisconsin. IBBA News 13(1):8.

Germain, C. E. 1975. Cedarburg bog. Wis. Conserv. Bull. 40(1):6–9.

Germain, C. E., W. E. Tans, and R. H. Read. 1977. Wisconsin scientific areas 1977. Tech. Bull. 102, Wis. Dep. Nat. Resour., Madison, 52 pp.

Gibbs, E. S. 1901a. A Wisconsin bird paradise. Wilson Bull., o.s., 12(34):9–10.

Gibbs, E. S. 1901b. Evening Grosbeak. Wilson Bull., o.s., 13(34):15.

Gibbs, E. S. 1908. Myrtle Warblers in northern Wisconsin in January. Wilson Bull. 20(3):159.

Gibbs, O., Jr. 1869. Lake Pepin fish-chowder. McIntyre and Co., New York, 141 pp.

Gibbs, R. M. 1894. The small waders of the Great Lakes. Am. Field (Chicago), Nov. 10.

Gibbs, R. M. 1896–1899. The game birds of the Great Lakes. Am. Field (Chicago), series of articles, 27 Dec. 1896–11 Feb. 1899.

Gieck, C. M. 1987. Wisconsin Peregrine Falcon recovery plan. Wis. Dep. Nat. Resour. Wis. Endang. Resour. Rep. No. 27, 38 pp.

Gieck, C. M. 1988. Wisconsin Peregrine Falcon recovery plan. Pass. Pigeon 50:9–13.

Gieck, C. M. 1989. Wisconsin Bald Eagle recovery plan. Pass. Pigeon 51:335–41.

Gigstead, G. 1937. Habits of Wisconsin pheasants. Wilson Bull. 49(1):28–34.

Gilman, W. W. 1890. A Wisconsin heronry. Wis. Nat. 1(2):21–23.

Gilman, W. W. 1919. The American Bittern. Wis. Conserv. 1(5):12–13.

Gilman, W. W. 1920. The nesting of the Ruby-throated Hummingbird in Wisconsin. Wis. Conserv. 2(1):6.

Gilman, W. W. 1921. The Great-Horned Owl. Wis. Conserv. 3(1):11–12.

Glenn, E. 1915. Cardinal at Wyalusing, Wisconsin. Wilson Bull. 27(4):466.

Gluesing, E. A. 1974. Distribution and status of the Greater Sandhill Crane in Wisconsin. MS thesis, Univ. Wis.–Stevens Point, 85 pp.

Goddard, S. V. 1970. Species composition and density of the lower Kinnickinnic River valley. Pass. Pigeon 32(4):151–56.

Goddard, S. V. 1972. Comparisons of breeding bird populations of the lower Kinnickinnic River valley. Pass. Pigeon 34(3):91–95.

Goddard, S. V. 1975. Spring waterfowl utilization of western Wisconsin wetlands. Pass. Pigeon 37(1):32–44.

Godfrey, W. E. 1966. The birds of Canada. Natl. Mus. Can. Bull. 203, Ottawa, 428 pp.

Gordon, R. 1958. The 1958 May migration—a backyard odyssey. Pass. Pigeon 20(3):105–11.

Goss, B. F. 1883. Breeding habits of the Carolina and American Eared Grebes. Ornithol. and Oologist 8(1):1–2.

Goss, B. F. 1885. The Goss collection of birds' eggs. West. Oologist 1(2):3.

Goss, B. F. 1887. Goss collection of N.A. birds. P. 8 in Fifth Annu. Rep. Milwaukee Public Mus.

Goss, B. F. 1895. Notes on nesting habits of Bobwhite, wild pigeons, and Great Horned Owl. Pp. 3, 137, and 378–81, respectively, in Life histories of North American birds, ed. C. Bendire. U.S. Natl. Mus. Spec. Bull. 3, Washington, D.C.

Goss, R. D. 1895. Our boyhood days. Iowa Ornithol. 1:76–79.

Goss, R. D. 1896. Bluebirds and passenger pigeons. Nidiologist 3:87.

Grange, W. B. 1922. Nesting notes from Ladysmith, Wisconsin. Auk 39(4):575–78.

Grange, W. B. 1924a. Palm Warbler summering in northern Wisconsin. Auk 41(1):160–61.

Grange, W. B. 1924b. Ruffed Grouse traits. For. and Stream 94(10):579–81, 620–24.

Grange, W. B. 1930a. The future of the Prairie Chicken. Outdoor Am. 8(8):18–20.

Grange, W. B. 1930b. The Prairie Chicken. Wis. Arbor and Bird Day Annu. 1930:49–53.

Grange, W. B. 1931. Winter feeding of upland game birds. Outdoor Am. 11(6):20–21, 33.

Grange, W. B. 1934. The Goshawks are coming! Game Breeder and Sportsman 38(12):238.

Grange, W. B. 1935a. A study of the Wisconsin game cycle from low to high, and the beginning of the second low, 1928–1934. Dep. Wildl. Ecol., Univ. Wis.–Madison, MS, 32 pp.

Grange, W. B. 1935b. Wild Turkey fail to thrive. Milwaukee J., Sept. 29.

Grange, W. B. 1936. Some observations on the Ruffed Grouse in Wisconsin. Wilson Bull. 48(2):104–10.

Grange, W. B. 1939a. Why not Eastern Sharptails? Game Breeder and Sportsman 43(2):26–31.

Grange, W. B. 1939b. Can we preserve the Prairie Chicken? Game Breeder and Sportsman 43(4):58–59, 62–63.

Grange, W. B. 1939c. Bringing back Ruffed Grouse. Game Breeder and Sportsman 43(10):155–57.

Grange, W. B. 1940a. Ducks need more than water. Game Breeder and Sportsman 44(1):10–11.

Grange, W. B. 1940b. A comparison of the displays and vocal performances of the Greater Prairie Chicken, Lesser Prairie Chicken, Sharp-tailed Grouse and Sooty Grouse. Pass. Pigeon 2(12):127–33.

Grange, W. B. 1941a. Feeding wildlife in winter. Conserv. Bull. 13, U.S. Dep. Inter. Fish and Wildl. Serv., Washington, D.C., 20 pp.

Grange, W. B. 1941b. Acadian Owl in town of Remington, Wood County. Pass. Pigeon 3(6):61.

Grange, W. B. 1941–1942. As leader of Wisconsin grouse management research project, submitted quarterly progress reports from Apr. 1941 through Oct. 1942. Wis. Conserv. Dep., Madison.

Grange, W. B. 1948. Wisconsin grouse problems. Wis. Conserv. Dep. Publ. 328, Madison, 318 pp.

Grange, W. B. 1949. The way to game abundance. Scribner's, New York, 365 pp.

Grange, W. B. 1953. Those of the forest. Flambeau Publ. Co., Babcock, Wis., 314 pp; reprinted, 1955, Faber and Faber, Publ., London; 1967, the Abercrombie and Fitch Libr., Arno Press, New York.

Grant, C. P. 1931. Prairie Plover: An intimate study of the Upland Plover. Outdoor Am. 9(10):8–10.

Grant, C. P. 1932. *Circus hudsonius*: An intimate study of the interesting Marsh Hawk. Outdoor Am. 10(9):13–14.

Grasset, F. 1926. An unusual flight of cormorants at La Crosse. Wilson Bull. 38(4):234–35.

Greeley, F. 1953. Sex and age studies in fall-shot woodcock (*Philohela minor*) from southern Wisconsin. J. Wildl. Manage. 17(1):29–32.

Green, F. C. 1878. Birds of Milwaukee County, Wisconsin. Valley Nat. (St. Louis, Mo.) 1(6):23; 1(7):27.

Green, W. E. 1968–1973. The phenology of the fall migration of Canada geese in Dodge and Fond du Lac counties, Wisconsin, and its relationship to agricultural crops. 6 vols. Prog. Rep. U.S. Fish and Wildl. Serv., Div. Wildl. Refuges, Minneapolis.

Greener. 1886. Hunting Prairie Chicken at Plover, Wis. Am. Field 26(11).

Gregg, L. E. 1969. Probing the woodcock's secrets. Wis. Conserv. Bull. 34(4):18–19.

Gregg, L. E. 1984. Population ecology of Woodcock in Wisconsin. Tech. Bull. 144, Wis. Dep. Nat. Resour., 51 pp.

Gregg, L. E. 1987. Recommendations for a program of sharptail habitat preservation in Wisconsin. Wis. DNR Research Report No. 141.

Gregg, L. E., and J. B. Hale. 1977. Woodcock nesting habitat in northern Wisconsin. Auk 94(3):489–93.

Grimmer, W. F. 1930. Division of game. Pp. 83–96 in Bien. Rep. State Conserv. Comm., Madison.

Grimmer, W. F. 1938a. 1938 experimental game birds. Wis. Conserv. Bull. 3(6):3–6.

Grimmer, W. F. 1938b. General review of the upland and migratory bird seasons. Wis. Conserv. Bull. 3(12):3–5.

Grimmer, W. F. 1940. Food habits of the pheasant in Wisconsin. Wis. Conserv. Bull. 5(4):10–13.

Grimmer, W. F. 1948. Game management in Wisconsin. Wis. Conserv. Bull. 13(6):61–66.

Grindell, A. B. 1890. Snowy Owls. Oologist 7(4):72.

Griscom, L. 1923. Birds of the New York City region. Am. Mus. Nat. Hist. Handb. No. 9

Gromme, O. J. 1922. Collecting for the new school loan groups [Columbia, Fond du Lac, and Sauk counties, Wisconsin]. Milwaukee Public Mus. Yearb. 2:41–47.

Gromme, O. J. 1923. Collecting for the school loan groups [Brown, Oconto, and Shawano counties, Wis.]. Milwaukee Public Mus. Yearb. 3:7–13.

Gromme, O. J. 1924a. Making a three-reel heron picture. Milwaukee Public Mus. Yearb. 4:37–40.

Gromme, O. J. 1924b. On the trail of the Sandhill Crane. Milwaukee Public Mus. Yearb. 4:41–43.

Gromme, O. J. 1925a. Wild life in the Land o'Lakes. Milwaukee Public Mus. Yearb. 5:55–61.

Gromme, O. J. 1925b. Another season with the Sandhill Crane. Milwaukee Public Mus. Yearb. 5:61–65.

Gromme, O. J. 1926. Capturing shore-birds by the aid of a flashlight. Milwaukee Public Mus. Yearb. 6:64–66.

Gromme, O. J. 1927. An unusual flight of Snow Geese in the Lake Winnebago area. Wisconsin. Auk 44(1):96.

Gromme, O. J. 1930a. A Bahama Pintail in Wisconsin. Auk 47(1):73.

Gromme, O. J. 1930b. Egrets and Little Blue Herons in Wisconsin. Auk 47(4):559.

Gromme, O. J. 1930c. The nesting birds of Wisconsin. Wis. Arbor and Bird Day Annu. 1930:34–36.

Gromme, O. J. 1931. Golden Plover in the Lake Winnebago area. Auk 48(3):416.

Gromme, O. J. 1934a. The Mourning Warbler (*Oporornis philadelphia*) nesting in Wisconsin. Auk 51(1):37–38.

Gromme, O. J. 1934b. King Eider (*Somateria spectabilis*) in Wisconsin. Auk 51(3):367.

Gromme, O. J. 1935a. The Goshawk (*Astur atricapillus atricapillus*) nesting in Wisconsin. Auk 52(1):15–20.

Gromme, O. J. 1935b. Further notes on the occurrence of the Hudsonian Godwit (*Limosa haemastica haemastica*) in Wisconsin. Auk 52(1):81.

Gromme, O. J. 1935c. Forster's Tern (*Sterna forsteri*) breeding on the Lake Puckaway Marsh. Auk 52(1):86–87.

Gromme, O. J. 1935d. Unusual water birds in the Lake Winnebago, Wisconsin, area. Auk 52(1):101–2.

Gromme, O. J. 1935e. Status of the birds of prey and herons of Wisconsin. Auk 52(1):132–33.

Gromme, O. J. 1936. Effect of extreme cold on ducks in Milwaukee Bay. Auk 53(3):324–25.

Gromme, O. J. 1938a. Black Gyrfalcon in Wisconsin. Auk 55(2):273–74.

Gromme, O. J. 1938b. Mourning Warbler nesting in Wisconsin. Auk 55(3):543–44.

Gromme, O. J. 1939. Raven killed in Sheboygan County. Pass. Pigeon 1(12):167.

Gromme, O. J. 1940. Arkansas Kingbird nesting in Wisconsin. Pass. Pigeon 2(7):90–91.

Gromme, O. J. 1941a. Several interesting breeding records secured. Pass. Pigeon 3(8):71–72.

Gromme, O. J. 1941b. An open letter to the Society [Wisconsin Society for Ornithology] on the Great Blue Heron. Pass. Pigeon 3(8):72.

Gromme, O. J. 1942a. Breeding status of Connecticut and Mourning Warblers in Wisconsin. Auk 59(1):115–16.

Gromme, O. J. 1942b. Raven nest collected near Crandon. Pass. Pigeon 4(4–6):46–47.

Gromme, O. J. 1957. An open report on the current status of Horicon Marsh as a waterfowl refuge. Pass. Pigeon 19(3):99–106.

Gromme, O. J. 1963. Birds of Wisconsin. Univ. Wis. Press, Madison, 220 pp.

Gromme, O. J. 1973. In memoriam: Herbert Lee Stoddard. Auk 90(4):870–76.

Gross, A. O. 1927. The Snowy Owl's migration of 1926–1927. Auk 44(4):479–93.

Gross, A. O. 1929. The Prairie Chicken of the Wisconsin prairies. Bird-Lore 31(6):383–93.

Gross, A. O. 1930a. Progress report of the Wisconsin Prairie Chicken investigation. Wis. Conserv. Comm., Madison, 112 pp.

Gross, A. O. 1930b. The Wisconsin Prairie Chicken investigation. Trans. Am. Game Conf. 16:87–92.

Gross, A. O. 1930c. The New England Ruffed Grouse and Wisconsin Prairie Chicken investigations. Trans. Am. Game Conf. 17:213–19.

Gross, A. O. 1931. The Snowy Owl migration—1930–1931. Auk 48(4):501–11.

Gross, A. O. 1947. Cyclic migration of the Snowy Owl and the migration of 1945–1946. Auk 64(4):589–601.

Grundtvig, F. L. 1883. The vernal migration of warblers on Wolf River, Outagamie County, Wisconsin. Bull. Nuttall Ornithol. Club 8(2):65–72.

Grundtvig, F. L. 1895. On the birds of Shiocton in Bovina, Outagamie County, Wisconsin, 1881–1883, trans. C. E. Faxon. Trans. Wis. Acad. Sci., Arts, Lett. 10:73–158 + map; revised [one correction] in Auk 1895:173; originally published in 1888 as Meddelelser om Fuglene ved Shiocton i Bovina, Outagamie County, Wisconsin, 1881–1883, in Videns. Medd. naturh. Foren. Kbh. 1887:305–96 + 1 tab.

Guilbert, G. M. 1932. Migratory waterfowl shortage hearings. P. 606 in Hearings of Spec. Comm. Conserv. Wild Life Resour., U.S. Senate, 4–6 Apr. U.S. Government Printing Office, Washington, D.C.

Gundlach, J. J. 1930. A visit to our feathered friends of the marshes. Wis. Arbor and Bird Day Annu. 1930:19–22.

Guse, Mrs. W. 1977. Mute Swan in Waukesha County. Pass. Pigeon 39(1):204.

Gustafson, D. K. 1975a. Species composition and absolute population density of breeding birds obtained by two methods. Univ. Wis.–Milwaukee Field Stn. Bull. 8(1).

Gustafson, D. K. 1975b. Bird population densities derived from transect counts: An evaluation of the Emlen technique. MS thesis, Univ. Wis.–Milwaukee, 52 pp.

Guth, R. W. 1978. Forest and campground bird communities of Peninsula State Park, Wisconsin. Pass. Pigeon 40(4):489–93.

Haasch, S. J. 1979. Ecology of the American Woodcock in central Wisconsin. MS thesis, Univ. Wis.–Stevens Point, 76 pp.

"Hackmetack." 1878. Lake Horicon—Dodge County, Wisconsin. Chicago Field; reprinted in part in 1942, Wis. Conserv. Bull. 7(12):8–11.

Hager, D. 1974. Eagle protection and management in lake states national forests. Pp. 6–15 in Our eagles' future?, ed. T. N. Ingram. Bald Eagle Days Proc. 8–10 Feb. 1974. Eagle Valley Environmentalists, Apple River, Ill.

Hair, J. D. 1984. 1982 midwinter Bald Eagle survey. Pass. Pigeon 46:49–52.

Halazon, G. C., and T. McHugh. 1950. Operation giant grouse. Ford Times 42(10):26–30.

Hale, J. B. 1948. Can we bring back the Prairie Grouse? Wis. Conserv. Bull. 13(11):3–5.

Hale, J. B. 1957. Birds, bugs and jack pines. Pass. Pigeon 19(4):162–65.

Hale, J. B. 1965. Wisconsin ducks: Major minority. Wis. Conserv. Bull. 30(5):12–13.

Hale, J. B. 1970. Waterfowl: A report to the stockholders. Wis. Conserv. Bull. 35(2):14–15.

Hale, J. B. 1989. Sixty years of contributions to ornithology by Wisconsin state agencies. Pass. Pigeon 51:45–56.

Hale, J. B., and R. S. Dorney, 1963. Seasonal movements of Ruffed Grouse in Wisconsin. J. Wildl. Manage. 27(4):648–56.

Hale, J. B., and L. E. Gregg. 1976. Woodcock use of clearcut aspen areas in Wisconsin. Wildl. Soc. Bull. 4(3):111–15.

Hale, J. B., and R. F. Wendt. 1950. Reports on the 1949 Ruffed Grouse season. Wis. Conserv. Bull. 15(3):11–14.

Hale, J. B., and R. F. Wendt. 1951a. Ruffed Grouse hatching dates in Wisconsin. J. Wildl. Manage. 15(2):195–99.

Hale, J. B., and R. F. Wendt. 1951b. Amphibians and snakes as Ruffed Grouse food. Wilson Bull. 63(3):200–201.

Hale, J. B., R. F. Wendt, and G. C. Halazon. 1954. Sex and age criteria for Wisconsin Ruffed Grouse. Tech. Wildl. Bull. 9, Wis. Conserv. Dep., Madison, 24 pp.

Hall, H. M. 1960. A gathering of shorebirds, ed. R. C. Clement. Devon-Adair Co., New York, 242 pp.

Halvorsen, H. H., and B. R. Bacon. 1983. Use of a bluebird nest box trail by Tree Swallows in central Wisconsin. Pass. Pigeon 45:117–23.

Hamerstrom, F. 1942. Dominance in winter flocks of chickadees. Wilson Bull. 54(1):32–42.

Hamerstrom, F. 1950. Range habits and food requirements of the Prairie Chicken. Wis. Conserv. Bull. 15(11):9–11.

Hamerstrom, F. 1962. Winter visitors from the far north. Audubon Mag. 64(1):12–15.

Hamerstrom, F. 1965. A White-tailed Kite in Wisconsin. Pass. Pigeon 27(1):3–8.

Hamerstrom, F. 1969. A harrier population study. Pp. 367–83 in Peregrine Falcon populations: Their biology and decline, ed. J. J. Hickey. Univ. Wis. Press, Madison.

Hamerstrom, F. 1970. An eagle to the sky. Iowa State Univ. Press, Ames, 143 pp.

Hamerstrom, F. 1972. Birds of prey of Wisconsin. Wis. Dep. Nat. Resour., Madison, 64 pp.

Hamerstrom, F. 1977. This raptor keeps a low profile. Natl. Wildl. 15(5):20–25.

Hamerstrom, F. 1979. Effect of prey on predator: Voles and harriers. Auk 96(2):370–74.

Hamerstrom, F. 1980. Strictly for the chickens. Iowa State Univ. Press, Ames, 174 pp.

Hamerstrom, F., and D. D. Berger. 1962. Protective Goshawk trapping. Falconer 4(2):55–57.

Hamerstrom, F., and O. E. Mattson. 1939. Food of central Wisconsin horned owls. Am. Midl. Nat. 22(3):700–702.

Hamerstrom, F., and D. D. Wilde. 1973. Cruising range and roosts of adult harriers. IBBA News 45(4):123–28.

Hamerstrom, F., F. N. Hamerstrom, and J. Hart. 1973. Nest boxes: An effective management tool for kestrels. J. Wildl. Manage. 37(3):400–403.

Hamerstrom, F. N. 1938. Central Wisconsin crane study. Wilson Bull. 50(3):175–84.

Hamerstrom, F. N. 1939. A study of Wisconsin Prairie Chicken and Sharp-tailed Grouse. Wilson Bull. 51(2):105–20.

Hamerstrom, F. N. 1941. A study of Wisconsin prairie grouse (breeding habits, winter foods, endoparasites, and movements). PhD diss., Univ. Wis.–Madison, 179 pp.

Hamerstrom, F. N. 1963. Sharptail brood habitat in Wisconsin's northern pine barrens. J. Wildl. Manage. 27(4):792–802.

Hamerstrom, F. N. 1977. New threat to Buena Vista chickens. Wis. Nat. Resour. 1(1):6–7.

Hamerstrom, F. N., and F. Hamerstrom. 1949. Daily and seasonal movements of Wisconsin Prairie Chickens. Auk 66(4):313–37.

Hamerstrom, F. N., and F. Hamerstrom. 1951. Mobility of the Sharp-tailed Grouse in relation to its ecology and distribution. Am. Midl. Nat. 46(1):174–226.

Hamerstrom, F. N., and F. Hamerstrom. 1955. Population density and behavior in Wisconsin Prairie Chickens (*Tympanuchus cupido pinnatus*). Proc. Internatl. Ornithol. Congr. 11:459–66.

Hamerstrom, F. N., and F. Hamerstrom. 1960. Comparability of some social displays of grouse. Proc. Internatl. Ornithol. Congr. 12:274–93.

Hamerstrom, F. N., and F. Hamerstrom. 1961. Status and problems of North American grouse. Wilson Bull. 73(3):284–94.

Hamerstrom, F. N., and F. Hamerstrom. 1963. Range of the Red-bellied Woodpecker in Wisconsin. Pass. Pigeon 25(4):131–36.

Hamerstrom, F. N., and F. Hamerstrom. 1966. Stove in the popples. Wis. Conserv. Bull. 31(5):3–5.

Hamerstrom, F. N., and F. Hamerstrom. 1972. A male hawk's potential in nest building, incubation and rearing young. Raptor Res. 6(4):144–49.

Hamerstrom, F. N., and F. Hamerstrom. 1973. The Prairie Chicken in Wisconsin: Highlights of a 22-year study of counts, behavior, movements, turnover and habitat. Tech. Bull. 64, Wis. Dep. Nat. Resour., Madison, 52 pp.

Hamerstrom, F. N., F. Hamerstrom, and D. D. Berger. 1961. Nesting of Short-eared Owls in Wisconsin. Pass. Pigeon 23(2):46–48.

Hamerstrom, F. N., F. Hamerstrom, and D. D. Berger. 1965. The effect of mammals on Prairie Chickens on booming grounds. J. Wildl. Manage. 29(3):536–42.

Hamerstrom, F. N., F. Hamerstrom, and O. E. Mattson. 1952. Sharp-tails into the shadows? Wis. Wildl. No. 1, Wis. Conserv. Dep., Madison, 35 pp.

Hamerstrom, F. N., F. Hamerstrom, and O. E. Mattson. 1957. A guide to Prairie Chicken management. Tech. Wildl. Bull. 15, Wis. Conserv. Dep., Madison, 128 pp.

Hamerstrom, F. N., F. Hopkins, and A. J. Rinzel. 1941. An experimental study of browse as a winter diet for the Prairie Chicken. Wilson Bull. 53(3):185–95.

Hampton, O. H. 1894. Wisconsin wanderings [birds]. For. and Stream 43(20):422.

Hampton, O. H. 1895a. Wisconsin wanderings [birds]. For. and Stream 45(16):334.

Hampton, O. H. 1895b. Wisconsin wanderings [grouse]. For. and Stream 45(19):403.

Hampton, O. H. 1896. Wisconsin wanderings [Sharp-tailed Grouse]. For. and Stream 47(13):246.

Hannes, J. L. 1924. Hunting ducks on Butte des Morts. For. and Stream 94(7):416.

Hansen, H. P. 1933. Tamarack bogs of the driftless area of Wisconsin. Milwaukee Public Mus. Bull. 7(2):231–304.

Hanson, H. C. 1943. Wildlife studies at Prairie du Sac. MS thesis, Univ. Wis.–Madison, 81 pp.

Hanson, H. C. 1965. The giant Canada Goose. South Ill. Univ. Press, Carbondale, 224 pp.

Hanson, I. A. 1977. Horicon Marsh: A history of change. Lore 27(2):1–42.

Harris, A. T. 1938. Nesting of the Herring Gull and Common Tern. Oologist 55(9):102–4.

Harris, A. T. 1940. Ring-billed Gull and Caspian Tern. Oologist 57(2):19–21.

Harris, H. J., and J. Trick. 1979. Status and nesting ecology of Forster's Terns (*Sterna forsteri*) in Wisconsin. *In* 1979 Ann. Perf. Rep., Wis. Dept. Nat. Resour., Off. Endangered and Nongame Species.

Harris, H. J., T. R. Bosley, and F. D. Roznik. 1977. Green Bay's coastal wetlands—a picture of dynamic change. Pp. 337–58 *in* Wetlands, ecology, values, and impacts, ed. C. B. DeWitt and E. Solway. Proc. Waubesa Conf. Wetlands, 2–5 June, Madison. Inst. Environ. Stud., Univ. Wis.–Madison.

Harris, J. T. 1977. The migration of cranes. Brolga Bugle 4(1):2–4.

Harris, J. T., and J. Jaeger. 1978. Annotated list of spring birds observed in the Apostle Islands, 1976 and 1977. Pass. Pigeon 40(2):393–405.

Harris, J. T., and S. W. Matteson. 1975a. Gulls and terns on Wisconsin's Lake Superior shore. Pass. Pigeon 37(3):99–110.

Harris, J. T., and S. W. Matteson. 1975b. Gulls and terns as indicators of man's impact upon Lake Superior. Tech. Rep. No. 227, Univ. Wis. Sea Grant Prog., Madison, 45 pp.

Harrison, G. H. 1976. The wild goose chase of 1976. Field and Stream 1976(Sept.):132–39.

Harrison, G. H. 1978. Crane saviors of Baraboo. Audubon Mag. 80(2):25–28.

Hartmeister, F. A., and M. J. Hansen. 1950. Lead shot and waterfowl poisoning. Wis. Coserv. Bull. 15(8):16–18.

Hasbrouck, E. M. 1944. The status of Barrow's Golden-eye in eastern United States. Auk 61(4):544–54.

Hatch, D. 1882. Rough-legged "buzzard" [hawk]. Ornithol. and Oologist 7(15):119.

Hatch, D. 1883. Night herons breeding on the marsh. Ornithol. and Oologist 8(3):23.

Hatch, D. 1889. Destruction of birds by cold. Ornithol. and Oologist 14(8):122.

Hatch, D. 1917. Breeding of the Black-crowned Night Herons in 1880 and 1881. Oologist 34(7):129–31.

Hatch, D. 1920. Oakfield, Wisconsin. Oologist 37(8):98.

Haug, J. C. 1981. Goshawk nest in Juneau County. Pass. Pigeon 43:42–43.

Hawkins, A. S. 1937a. Winter feeding at Faville Grove, 1935–1937. J. Wildl. Manage. 1(3–4):62–69.

Hawkins, A. S. 1937b. Winter feeding at Faville Grove, 1935–1936. Am. Midl. Nat. 18(3):417–25.

Hawkins, A. S. 1937c. Hungarian partridge nesting studies at Faville Grove. Trans. North Am. Wildl. Conf. 2:481–84.

Hawkins, A. S. 1940. A wildlife history of Faville Grove, Wisconsin. Trans. Wis. Acad. Sci., Arts, Lett. 32:29–65.

Hawkins, A. S. 1964. Mississippi Flyway. Pp. 185–207 *in* Waterfowl tomorrow, ed. J. P. Linduska. U.S. Dep. Inter. Fish and Wildl. Serv., Washington, D.C.

Hawkins, A. S. 1970. A "conservation ethic." Wis. Acad. Rev. 16(4):13–14.

Hawkins, A. S., and W. E. Green. 1966. Waterfowl management opportunities in forested areas of the lake states. Proc. Soc. Am. For., Seattle. J. For. 64(1):55–58.

Hayes, M. N. 1955. Mountain Bluebirds visit Wisconsin. Pass. Pigeon 17(2):59.

Heig, V. A. 1970. Corrections for the Schoenebeck collection catalog. Mus. Nat. Hist., Univ. Wis.–Stevens Point, 13 pp. Appendix to Rep. No. 2.

Henderson, D. 1976. A season of birds. Tamarack Press, Madison, 87 pp.

Henderson, D. 1979. Wild things. Tamarack Press, Madison, 94 pp.

Hendrick, D. J. 1962. Wisconsin cardinal populations. Pass. Pigeon 24(1):3–8.

Hendrick, D. J. 1965. A comparison of two Christmas bird counts. Pass. Pigeon 27(4):143–46.

Hendrickson, M. L. 1980. Crane count: An interesting experience. Our Wetlands 3(2):8–9.

Henika, F. S. 1936. Sandhill Cranes in Wisconsin and other lake states. Pp. 644–46 *in* Proc. North Am. Wildl. Conf., Washington, D.C.

Henika, F. S., and G. B. Hanson. 1934. Central Wisconsin marshland survey. U.S. Resettlement Adm., MS, 41 pp.

Henry, W. A. 1881. When the leaves appear. Annu. Rep. Regents Univ. Wis., pp. 35–38.

Henseler, G. 1963. Pine Siskins nest at Appleton. Pass. Pigeon 25(3):102–5.

Herman, E. F. 1941. A faunal survey of Sheboygan Marsh [Wisconsin]. MS thesis, Dep. Zool., Kans. State Coll., Agric. and Appl. Sci., Manhattan, Kans., 89 pp.

Hersey, F. S. 1917. The status of the Black-throated Loon (*Gavia arctica*) as a North American bird. Auk 34(3):283–90.

Hickey, J. J. 1943. A guide to bird watching. Oxford Univ. Press, New York, 262 pp.

Hickey, J. J. 1952. Wildlife in the University of Wisconsin Arboretum. Wis. Gardens 3(5):13.

Hickey, J. J. 1955a. Teal move far and fast, banding work proves. Wis. Conserv. Bull. 20(1):31–32.

Hickey, J. J. 1955b. Some American population research on gallinaceous birds. Pp. 326–96 *in* Recent studies in avian biology, ed. A. Wolfson. Univ. Ill. Press, Champaign.

Hickey, J. J. 1956. Autumnal migration of ducks banded in eastern Wisconsin. Trans. Wis. Acad. Sci., Arts, Lett. 45:59–76.

Hickey, J. J. 1969a. DDT and birds: Wisconsin, 1968. Atlantic Nat. 24(2):86–92.

Hickey, J. J., Ed. 1969b. Peregrine Falcon populations: Their biology and decline. Univ. Wis. Press, Madison, 596 pp.

Hickey, J. J. 1974. Some historical phases in wildlife conservation. Wildl. Soc. Bull. 2(4):164–70.

Hickey, J. J. 1979. Verification on Fork-tailed Flycatcher in Columbia County. Pass. Pigeon 41(3):142.

Hickey, J. J., and L. B. Hunt. 1960a. Initial songbird mortality following a Dutch elm disease control program. J. Wildl. Manage. 24(3):259–65.

Hickey, J. J., and L. B. Hunt. 1960b. Songbird mortality following annual programs to control Dutch elm disease. Atlantic Nat. 15(2):87–92.

Hickey, J. J., J. A. Keith, and F. B. Coon. 1966. An exploration of pesticides in a Lake Michigan ecosystem. J. Appl. Ecol. 3(Suppl.):141–54.

Hickey, M. B. 1960. Migrants at airport ceilometers. Pass. Pigeon 22(1):23–26.

Hill, M. 1986. Sandhill Crane count—1986. Pass. Pigeon 48:99–100.

Hilsenhoff, W. L. 1967. History of Christmas bird counts in Wisconsin. Pass. Pigeon 29(3):55–63.

Hilsenhoff, W. L. 1974. Spring migration of warblers in the vicinity of Madison, Wisconsin. Pass. Pigeon 36(2):55–61.

Hilsenhoff, W. L. 1978. Christmas birds, well done. Wis. Nat. Resour. 2(6):27–29.

Hine, R. L. 1951. Grassland dynasty. Audubon Mag. 53(3):174–83.

Hine, R. L., Comp. 1956. Diseases and parasites in Wisconsin birds and mammals. Proc. Rep., Wis. Conserv. Dep., Madison, 181 pp.

Hine, R. L., Ed. 1960. Research hi-lites. Wis. Conserv. Dep., Madison, 8 pp.

Hine, R. L. 1964a. The wildlife resources of Wisconsin. Pp. 70–225 *in* The natural resources of Wisconsin. Wis. Blue Book, Legis. Reference Bur., Madison; rev. ed., 1967.

Hine, R. L., Ed. 1964b. Wildlife, people and the land. Publ. No. 621, Wis. Conserv. Dep., Madison, 83 pp.

Hine, R. L., Ed. 1970. Man and the environment. Wis. Acad. Rev. 16(4):1–44.

Hine, R. L. 1973a. Endangered birds. Pass. Pigeon 35(4):155–58.

Hine, R. L., Ed. 1973b. Endangered animals in Wisconsin. Wis. Dep. Nat. Resour., Madison, 28 pp.

Hine, R. L. 1975. The case of the vanishing species. Wis. Trails 16(3):22–25.

Hine, R. L., and O. S. Bersing. 1951. Winter feeding for wildlife. Wis. Conserv. Dep., Madison, 22 pp.

Hine, R. L., and C. Schoenfeld, Eds. 1968. Canada Goose management: Current continental problems and programs. Symp. Rep. Dembar Educ. Resour. Serv., Madison, 195 pp.

Hitt, J. 1886. Gift of four dressed Spruce Partridges. Bayfield Press, 20 Nov. 1886.

Hobart, S. D. 1887. Troubadours and trouveres [Wisconsin birds]. For. and Stream 28(15):320.

Hobles, R. G. 1890. A July in Wisconsin. For. and Stream 35(14):272–73.

Hochbaum, H. A. 1955. Travels and traditions of waterfowl. Univ. Minn. Press, Minneapolis, 301 pp.

Hoefler, J. E. 1980. The status and distribution of the Black-crowned Night Heron in Wisconsin. MS thesis, Univ. Wis.–Stevens Point, 70 pp.

Hoefler, J. E., and P. Kooiker. 1983. Eagles vs. cormorants. Pass. Pigeon 45:79.

Hoffman, R. M. 1978. A Ross' Goose at Schoeneberg Marsh, Columbia County. Pass. Pigeon 40(2):414–16.

Hoffman, R. M. 1982. Spring hawk count in southern Sauk County. Pass. Pigeon 44:123–24.

Hoffman, R. M. 1989a. Birds of Wisconsin northern mesic forests. Pass. Pigeon 51:97–110.

Hoffman, R. M. 1989b. Birds of tall shrub communities: Alder thickets and shrub-carr. Pass. Pigeon 51:263–73.

Hoffman, R. M. and D. Sample. 1988. Birds of wet-mesic and wet prairies in Wisconsin. Pass. Pigeon 50:143–52.

Hoffman, W. J. 1896. The Menomini Indians. U.S. Bur. Am. Ethnology, Annu. Rep. 14:3–328.

Hoffmann, E. 1954. Black Terns at Big Muskego. Pass. Pigeon 16(1):3–8.

Hoffmann, P. W. 1926. Nesting of the Black Tern in Wisconsin. Auk 43(1):86–87.

Hoffmann, P. W. 1927. Home life of the Black Tern in Wisconsin. Wilson Bull., o.s., 39(2):78–80.

Hoffmann, P. W. 1937. Feeding habits of the Black Tern. IBBA News 9(4):12.

Hoffmann, P. W. 1938. Banding Forster's Terns at Muskego Lake. IBBA News 10(2):14.

Hoffmann, P. W. 1952. The Yellow-headed Blackbird in southeastern Wisconsin. Pass. Pigeon 14(1):20–21.

Holl, D. G. 1953. Management of the Central Wisconsin Conservation Area. Wis. Conserv. Bull. 18(2):19–22.

Holleback, M. 1974. Behavioral interactions and the dispersal of the family in Black-capped Chickadees. Wilson Bull. 86(4):466–68.

Hollister, N. 1892a. Notes from southern Wisconsin. Oologist 9(5):147–48.

Hollister, N. 1892b. Wisconsin swallows. Taxidermist 1:150–52.

Hollister, N. 1893. Ducks in southern Wisconsin. Ornithol. and Oologist 18(9):128–29.

Hollister, N. 1894. Some winter bird life. Oologist 11(6):207–9.

Hollister, N. 1896a. Notes from southern Wisconsin. Wilson Bull. 8(8):2–3.

Hollister, N. 1896b. Evening Grosbeak in southern Wisconsin. Auk 13(3):259–60.

Hollister, N. 1896c. Recent record of the Passenger Pigeon in southern Wisconsin. Auk 13(4):341.

Hollister, N. 1897. Southern Wisconsin notes. Wilson Bull. 9(12):4–5.

Hollister, N. 1901a. *Helminthophila pinus* [Blue-winged Warbler] in Wisconsin. Wilson Bull. 13(35):30–32.

Hollister, N. 1901b. Capture of Sabine's Gull in Wisconsin. Auk 18(4):392.

Hollister, N. 1902. The Yellow Rail (*Porzana noveboracensis*) in Wisconsin. Auk 19(2):197.

Hollister, N. 1911. New bird records for Delavan, Wisconsin. Bull. Wis. Nat. Hist. Soc. 8(4):187–88.

Hollister, N. 1912. Some erroneous Wisconsin bird records [in A. J. Schoenebeck's (1902) list]. Auk 29(2):397–99.

Hollister, N. 1919a. The systematic position of the Ring-necked Duck. Auk 36(4):460–63.

Hollister, N. 1919b. Some changes in the summer bird life of Delavan, Wisconsin. Wilson Bull. 31(4):103–8.

Hollister, N. 1920a. Relative abundance of wild ducks at Delavan, Wisconsin. Auk 37(3):367–71.

Hollister, N. 1920b. Segregation of male Mallards with regard to migration. Condor 22(1):36–37.

Holmes, A. G. 1911. European Widgeon in Wisconsin. For. and Stream 76(28 Jan.):131.

Holstein-Schoff, G. 1974. Something there is about a crane . . . and the International Crane Foundation. Wis. Acad. Rev. 21(4):22–28.

Hope, L. 1941. Twenty-eight White Pelicans on Mallalieu Lake near Hudson. Pass. Pigeon 3(8):76.

Hopkins, F. 1940. The Wild Turkey problem in Wisconsin. Wis. Conserv. Bull. 5(12):47–48.

Hopkins, R. C. 1940. Notes on the Great Blue Heron. Wis. Conserv. Bull. 5(12):39–40.

Hopkins, R. C. 1947. Waterfowl management research. Wis. Wildl. Resour. Prog. Rep. 5(4):12–33.

Hopkins, R. C. 1948. Report to Wisconsin duck hunters. Wis. Conserv. Bull. 13(9):3–8.

Hopkins, R. C. 1949a. The fate of Mallards banded at Horicon. Wis. Conserv. Bull. 14(10):10–12.

Hopkins, R. C. 1949b. Waterfowl breeding ground survey in Wisconsin. Pp. 184–93 in Waterfowl populations and breeding conditions—summer 1949, ed. U.S. Fish and Wildlife Service. Spec. Sci. Rep. Wildl. No. 2.

Hopkins, R. C. 1951. Waterfowl kill studies, Wisconsin, 1950. Wis. Wildl. Res. 10(1):85–135.

Hopkins, R. C. 1961. Drawdown for ducks. Wis. Conserv. Bull. 27(4):18–19.

Hopkins, R. C. 1972. Damage to scotch pine plantation by Pine Grosbeaks reported. Pass. Pigeon 34(4):161–62.

Hornaday, W. T. 1898. The destruction of our birds and mammals. 2nd Annu. Rep. N.Y. Zool. Soc., New York. (Reference to Wisconsin, pp. 95, 113–114.)

Hough, E. 1889. Chicago and the west. For. and Stream 33(21):407.

Hough, E. 1890a. The Blackhawk Club of Lake Koshkonong. For. and Stream 33(26):514–16.

Hough, E. 1890b. Wisconsin game laws. For. and Stream 34(13): 248–49. (Reference to Game Warden Wentworth.)

Hough, E. 1891. Opening day at Horicon. Part 1, For. and Stream 37(11):205–7; Part 2, For. and Stream 37(12):230–31.

Hough, E. 1892a. Horicon Shooting Club [Diana]. For. and Stream 39(12):246–47.

Hough, E. 1892b. Chicago and the West. For. and Stream 39(18): 381–82.

Hough, E. 1894a. Horicon wins. For. and Stream 42(23):490.

Hough, E. 1894b. A cyclone on Horicon Marsh. For. and Stream 43(14):292.

Hough, E. 1895. Horicon clubs win again. For. and Stream 44(13):245.

Hough, E. 1896. A trip to Koshkonong. For. and Stream 47(23):447.

Hough, E. 1897a. Pelicans in Wisconsin. For. and Stream 49(Oct. 23):327.

Hough, E. 1897b. Wild pigeons in Wisconsin. For. and Stream 49(9):168.

Hough, E. 1898a. Items on spring shooting. For. and Stream 50(14):266.

Hough, E. 1898b. Mongolian Pheasants. For. and Stream 51(23):449.

Hough, E. 1899a. What ails Wisconsin? For. and Stream 52(2):30.

Hough, E. 1899b. Chicago and the West. For. and Stream 53(13):246–58.

Howard, T. J. 1977a. Ecology of the Greater Sandhill Crane in central Wisconsin. MS thesis, Univ. Wis.–Stevens Point, 81 pp.

Howard, T. J. 1977b. The ecology of the Greater Sandhill Crane in central Wisconsin. Pp. 39–47 in Proc. Sandhill Crane Symp., 24–26 Oct., Ind. Wildl. Soc., Michigan City, Ind.

Howard, T. J., and L. E. Nauman. 1975. Sandhill Cranes of central Wisconsin: Habitat and population. Proc. 37th Midwest Fish and Wildl. Conf., 7–10 Dec. 1975, Toronto, Ontario.

Howe, R. W. 1982. Biogeography and ecology of birds in small forest habitat islands. PhD diss., Univ. Wis.–Madison, 314 pp.

Howe, R. W., and G. Jones. 1977. Avian utilization of small woodlots in Dane County, Wisconsin. Pass. Pigeon 39(4):313–20.

Hoy, P. R. 1852. Description of two species of owls, presumed to be new, which inhabit the state of Wisconsin. Proc. Acad. Nat. Sci. Phil. 6:210–11.

Hoy, P. R. 1853a. *Buteo bairdii* [new species]. Proc. Acad. Nat. Sci. Phil. 6:451.

Hoy, P. R. 1853b. Notes on the ornithology of Wisconsin. In Fauna and Flora of Wisconsin, I. E. Lapham. Trans. Wis. State Agric. Soc. 2:341–64; a revision of material originally published in Vol. 6 of the Proc. Acad. Nat. Sci. Phila., 1852 and 1853.

Hoy, P. R. 1860. The Sapsucker. Trans. Wis. State Agric. Soc. 1860, 6(1861):243–48.

Hoy, P. R. 1862a. The Sapsucker: Rare chance for a Bostoner to see the Great West without expense. Wis. Farmer and Northwest. Cultivator 14:184–87.

Hoy, P. R. 1862b. Studies of food habits of woodpeckers. Milwaukee Sentinel 1862(Mar. 29):2.

Hoy, P. R. 1865. The Sap-sucker. Trans. Ill. State Agric. Soc. 5(1861–1864):730–34.

Hoy, P. R. 1869a. Nesting of the Cooper's Hawk. Proc. Boston Soc. Nat. Hist. 12:396–97.

Hoy, P. R. 1869b. Notes on Rough-winged Swallow and Yellow-bellied Flycatcher. Proc. Boston Soc. Nat. Hist. 12:400.

Hoy, P. R. 1871. The mammalia of Wisconsin. Bull. Wis. Acad. Sci., Arts, and Lett. 4(Feb.):62.

Hoy, P. R. 1874. Some of the peculiarities of the fauna near Racine. Trans. Wis. Acad. Sci. Arts, and Lett. 2:120–22; partly reprinted in History of Sauk County, Wisconsin, Western History Co., Chicago, 1880.

Hoy, P. R. 1878. Fauna of Wisconsin. Pp. 153–56 in Historical atlas of Wisconsin, comp. and publ. Snyder, Van Vechten and Co.

Hoy, P. R. 1882. The larger wild animals that have become extinct in Wisconsin. Trans. Wis. Acad. Sci., Arts, and Lett. 5:255–57.

Hoy, P. R. 1885a. Nest and eggs of Golden-winged Warbler (*Helminthophila chrysoptera*). Auk 2(1):102–3.

Hoy, P. R. 1885b. Man's influence on the avifauna of southeastern Wisconsin. Proc. Nat. Hist. Soc. Wis. (Mar. 1885):4–9.

Hoyt, J. W. 1861. Report to the executive committee on the natural resources of Wisconsin, flora and fauna. Trans. Wis. State Agric. Soc., Vol. 6 (1860), Smith and Cullaton, Madison, pp. 46–49.

Hubbard, B. W. 1940. Two Sandhill Cranes seen over state game farm. Pass. Pigeon 2(7):94.

Hubbard, B. W. 1959. The wild one. Wis. Conserv. Bull. 24(8):27–29.

Hughlett, C. A. 1957. Refuge farming practices and Canada Goose management. MS thesis, Univ. Wis.–Madison, 71 pp.

Hummel, P. J. 1962. Gray rock bluebird trail. Pass. Pigeon 24(1):16–17.

Hunt, L. B. 1960. Songbird breeding populations in DDT-sprayed Dutch elm disease communities. J. Wildl. Manage. 24(2):139–46.

Hunt, L. B. 1968. Songbirds and insecticides in a suburban elm environment. MS thesis, Univ. Wis.–Madison, 52 pp.

Hunt, R. A. 1962. The Cattle Egret—observation at Horicon. Pass. Pigeon 24(3):88.

Hunt, R. A. 1964. Hunting Horicon honkers. Wis. Conserv. Bull. 29(5):15–16.

Hunt, R. A. 1966. Lead poisoning wastes waterfowl. Wis. Conserv. Bull. 31(6):18–19.

Hunt, R. A. 1971. Canada Goose management in Wisconsin. Wis. Conserv. Bull. 36(5):18–19.

Hunt, R. A. 1973. Crop depredations by waterfowl in Wisconsin. Pp. 85–101 in Proc. 6th Bird Control Semin. 30 Oct.–1 Nov., Bowling Green State Univ., Ohio.

Hunt, R. A., and H. C. Hanson. 1975. The spring Canada Goose migration in Wisconsin. Wis. Conserv. Bull. 40(2):7–9.

Hunt, R. A., and L. R. Jahn. 1966. Canada Goose breeding populations in Wisconsin. Tech. Bull. 38, Wis. Conserv. Dep., Madison, 67 pp.

Hunt, R. A., J. G. Bell, and L. R. Jahn. 1962. Managed goose hunting at Horicon Marsh. Trans. North Am. Wildl. Conf. 27:91–106.

Hunt, R. A., E. A. Gluesing, and L. E. Nauman. 1976. The Sandhill Crane in Wisconsin: A preliminary report. Wis. Dep. Nat. Resour. Res. Rep. No. 86, 17 pp.

Hunt, R. A., L. R. Jahn, R. C. Hopkins, and G. H. Amelong. An evaluation of artificial Mallard propagation in Wisconsin. Wis. Conserv. Dep. Tech. Wildl. Bull. No. 16, Madison, 79 pp.

Hussong, C. 1941. A large colony of Black-crowned Night Herons. Pass. Pigeon 3(5):41–42.

Hussong, C. 1946. The Clay-colored Sparrow. Pass. Pigeon 8(1):3–7.

Hussong, C. 1953. The Green Bay wildlife sanctuary. Pass. Pigeon 15(2):75–76.

Hussong, C. 1960. Operation Snowy Owl in Green Bay. Pass. Pigeon 22(3):128–30.

Hussong, C. 1961. Bluebird trails, a great success. Pass. Pigeon 23(1):8–9.

Hutchinson, F. K. 1912. Our country life. McClurg and Co., Chicago, 316 pp.

Hutchinson, F. K. 1921. Cardinals at Lake Geneva, Wisconsin. Ill. Audubon Soc. Bull. 1921(Fall):20.

Idzikowski, J. 1985. Winter gulls in Milwaukee County. Pass. Pigeon 47:155–58.

Idzikowsi, J. H. 1989. Trends in the list of Wisconsin birds: A historical perspective. Pass. Pigeon 51:57–65.

Ingold, J. L. 1977. Behavior of adult and juvenile White-breasted Nuthatches at the time of fledging. Pass. Pigeon 39(3):299–300.

Ingram, T. N. 1965a. Wintering Bald Eagles at Guttenberg, Iowa–Cassville, Wisconsin, 1964–65. Iowa Bird Life 35(3):66–78.

Ingram, T. N. 1965b. A field guide for locating Bald Eagles at Cassville, Wisconsin. Southwest. Wis. Audubon Soc., Cassville, Wis., 24 pp.

Ingram, T. N., Ed. 1974. Our eagles' future? Proc. Bald Eagle Days, Feb. 8–10, 1974. Eagle Valley Environmentalists, Apple River, Ill., 80 pp.

Ingram, T. N., Ed. 1975a. Bald Eagle land—preservation and acquisition. Proc. Bald Eagle Days, 31 Jan.–2 Feb. 1975. Eagle Valley Environmentalists, Apple River, Ill., 52 pp.

Ingram, T. N. 1975b. Eagle valley. Pp. 15–20 in Bald Eagle land—preservation and acquisition, ed. T. N. Ingram. Proc. Bald Eagle Days, 31 Jan.–2 Feb. 1975. Eagle Valley Environmentalists, Apple River, Ill.

Ingram, T. N., Ed. 1976. Save the eagle in '76. Proc. Bald Eagle Days, 1976. Eagle Valley Environmentalists, Apple River, Ill., 138 pp.

Ingram, T. N., Ed. 1977. Eagle movements. Proc. Bald Eagle Days, 1977. Eagle Valley Environmentalists, Apple River, Ill., 143 pp.

Ingram, T. N., Ed. 1978a. Learning about eagles. Proc. Bald Eagle Days, 1978. Eagle Valley Environmentalists, Apple River, Ill., 118 pp.

Ingram, T. N. 1978b. Wintering movements and nesting along the Mississippi River. Pp. 115–18 in Learning about eagles, ed. T. N. Ingram. Proc. Bald Eagle Days, 1978. Eagle Valley Environmentalists, Apple River, Ill.

Ingram, T. N., Ed. 1979a. Wintering eagles. Proc. Bald Eagle Days, 1979. Eagle Valley Environmentalists, Apple River, Ill., 196 pp.

Ingram, T. N. 1979b. The environmental challenges of the '80's. Pp. 102–6 in Wintering eagles, ed. T. N. Ingram. Proc. Bald Eagle Days, 1979. Eagle Valley Environmentalists, Apple River, Ill.

Ingram, T. N. 1980a. Wintering Bald Eagles in Wisconsin. Tech. Rep. WBEW-80, Eagle Valley Environmentalists, Apple River, Ill.

Ingram, T. N., Ed. 1980b. Raptor rehabilitation and eagle nesting biology. Proc. Bald Eagle Days, 1980. Eagle Valley Environmentalists, Apple River, Ill., 200 pp.

Ingram, T. N., and H. Koller. 1980. Petenwell eagles. Tech. Rep. PE-80, Eagle Valley Environmentalists, Apple River, Ill., 57 pp.

Institute for Environmental Studies, Univ. Wis.–Madison. 1976. Environmental change related to the Columbia electric generating station. Environ. Stud. Rep. No. 69, Madison, Wis.

Irwin, H. A. 1973. A natural history study of East Marsh of the University of Wisconsin. MS thesis, Univ. Wis.–Madison, 72 pp.

Jackson, G. H. 1975. Ecological aspects of mixed-species bird flocks in southern Wisconsin with emphasis on seasonal shifts in flock range, flock movement and food availability. MS thesis, Univ. Wis.–Madison, 314 pp.

Jackson, H. H. T. 1898. Remarks on return of the birds [Rock county, Wis.]. Oologist 15(3):24.

Jackson, H. H. T. 1904. A ramble in the marsh. Am. Ornithol. 4(1):69–71.

Jackson, H. H. T. 1923. Notes on summer birds of the Mamie Lake region, Wisconsin. Auk 40(3):478–89.

Jackson, H. H. T. 1927. Notes on the summer birds of Door Peninsula, Wisconsin, and adjacent islands. Trans. Wis. Acad. Sci., Arts, Lett. 23:639–65.

Jackson, H. H. T. 1943. Summer birds of northwestern Wisconsin. Wis. Soc. Ornithol., Madison, 36 pp.; reprinted from Pass. Pigeon, Vols. 3–5.

Jackson, H. H. T. 1945. Conserving endangered wildlife species. Smithsonian Rep. 45:247–72.

Jaeger, M. J. 1971. Song-spread perches of male Red-winged Blackbirds. Pass. Pigeon 33(4):201–2.

Jaeger, M. J. 1972. Breeding bird community of a monotypic stand of river bulrush. Pass. Pigeon 34(2):65–69.

Jaeger, M. J. 1980. Breeding songbird association in a southern Wisconsin wetland. Pass. Pigeon 42(2):64–66.

Jaeger, M. J. 1981. Breeding bird distribution along the Bois Brule River. Pass. Pigeon 43(3):97–106.

Jahn, L. R. 1950–1957. Wisconsin waterfowl breeding ground and production surveys for each year, 1950–1957. Published in national or Mississippi Flyway reports by the U.S. Fish and Wildl. Serv.

Jahn, L. R. 1951. Goose hunting: Past, present, future. Wis. Conserv. Bull. 16(4):19–22.

Jahn, L. R. 1952. Helping hand for waterfowl. Wis. Conserv. Bull. 17(9):15–19.

Jahn, L. R. 1955. Waterfowl breeding ground and production survey in Wisconsin (1954). Pp. 242–49 in Waterfowl populations and breeding conditions, summer, 1954. U.S. Fish and Wildl. Service and Can. Wildl. Serv., Washington, D. C., Spec. Sci. Rep. Wildl. No. 27.

670   Bibliography

Jahn, L. R. 1960. The status of waterfowl conservation. Wilson Bull. 73(1):96–106.

Jahn, L. R. 1965. Duck and coot ecology and management in Wisconsin. PhD diss., Univ. Wis.–Madison, 107 pp.

Jahn, L. R. 1968. Summary: Requirements and opportunities for managing geese. Pp. 168–73 *in* Canada Goose management: Current continental problems and programs, ed. R. L. Hine and C. Schoenfeld. Dembar Educ. Resour. Serv., Inc., Madison.

Jahn, L. R., and R. L. Hine. 1952. What about goose refuges? Wis. Conserv. Bull. 17(12):12–13.

Jahn, L. R., and R. A. Hunt. 1956. Waterfowl breeding ground and production survey in Wisconsin (1955). Pp. 226–33 *in* Waterfowl populations and breeding conditions, summer, 1955. U.S. Fish and Wildl. Serv. and Can. Wildl. Serv., Spec. Sci. Rep. Wildl. No. 30. Washington, D.C.

Jahn, L. R., and R. A. Hunt. 1964. Duck and coot ecology and management in Wisconsin. Tech. Bull. 33, Wis. Conserv. Dep., Madison, 212 pp.

Jahn, L. R., L. Gunther, and J. G. Bell. 1954. The managed goose hunt—Horicon Marsh, 1953. Wis. Conserv. Bull. 19(3):6–11.

Jahn, L. R., R. C. Hopkins, and H. C. Jordahl, Jr. 1958. Protection for waterfowl in fall. Wis. Conserv. Bull. 23(9):13–17.

Jenkins, J. H. 1954. No worms here! Pass. Pigeon 16(3):104.

Jenkins, P. B. 1922. Animals and birds of Lake Geneva. Pp. 101–20 *in* The book of Lake Geneva, ed. P. B. Jenkins. Univ. Chicago Press, Chicago.

Jensen, J. 1971. Blue Grosbeak nest in Wisconsin. Pass. Pigeon 33(2):98.

Jibson, N. W. 1922. Bird lore and bird songs of the North American Indian. Oologist 39 (Suppl.).

Johnson, C. D. 1976. Wetland use in Wisconsin; historical perspective and present picture. Wis. Dep. Nat. Resour., 48 pp.

Johnson, D. H. 1979. Modeling Sandhill Crane population dynamics. U.S. Dep. Inter. Fish and Wildl. Serv., Spec. Sci. Rep. Wildl. No. 222, Washington, D.C., 10 pp.

Johnson, L. J. 1949. Bird life on Hay River. Pass. Pigeon 11(2):55–59.

Johnson, R. M. 1976. Incidence of Great Horned Owls nesting in a heron rookery. Pass. Pigeon 38(2):89.

Johnson, T. C. 1951. The American Egret [South Wayne rookery]. Friends of Our Native Landscape 9(28):7; 9(29):5.

Jones, L. 1892a. Report of the committee on bird migration and distribution. Wilson Q. 4(1):23–35.

Jones, L. 1892b. Report of the president for the work of 1891 on the *Fringillidae*. Wilson Q. 4(2):67–84.

Jones, L. 1895. Record of the work of the Wilson Chapter for 1893 and 1894 on the *Mniotiltidae*. Wilson Bull. 7(4):1–21.

Jones, L. 1899. The migration of Killdeer, meadowlark, robin and bluebird. Wilson Bull., o.s., 11(26):33–35, 56–57; n.s., 6(4).

Jones, S. P. 1922. Winter birds of southern Wisconsin. Wilson Bull. 34(1):43–44.

Jones, S. P. 1923. Notes from Waukesha County, Wisconsin. Auk 40(1):137–38.

Jones, S. P. 1927. Starling nesting in Wisconsin. Auk 44(1):104–5.

Jones, S. P. 1930. The identification and study of birds. Wis. Arbor and Bird Day Annu. 1930:12–15.

Jones, S. P. 1938. Holboell's Grebe and American Brant in Wisconsin. Auk 55(4):666.

Jones, W. W. 1978. An analysis of bird population changes resulting from the impact of the Columbia generating station. 12th Semiannu. Rep., Inst. Environ. Stud., Univ. Wis.–Madison.

Jordahl, H. C., Jr. 1958. Wetlands acquisition. Wis. Conserv. Bull. 23(4):3–10.

Jordahl, H. C., Jr., and G. P. Yohann. 1952. The Barron County wildlife development project. Wis. Conserv. Bull. 17(11):3–5.

Jorgensen, A. W. 1954. Wisconsin wildlife. Publ. 613, Wis. Conserv. Dep., Madison, 64 pp.

Jung, C. 1923. The Evening Grosbeak in Wisconsin. Auk 40(1):130–31.

Jung, C. 1927. Additional notes on birds of Vilas County, Wisconsin. Wilson Bull. 39(3):173–74.

Jung, C. 1928. Winter notes from southeastern Wisconsin. Auk 45(3):384–85.

Jung, C. 1930a. Glaucous Gull (*Larus hyperboreus*) in Wisconsin. Auk 47(4):551.

Jung, C. 1930b. Birds of Lake Michigan. Wis. Arbor and Bird Day Annu. 1930:53–56.

Jung, C. 1932. The Western Willet in Wisconsin. Auk 49(4):468.

Jung, C. 1935a. Occurrence of the Least Tern in Wisconsin. Auk 52(1):87.

Jung, C. 1935b. Migration of hawks in Wisconsin. Wilson Bull. 47(1):75–76.

Jung, C. 1936. European Goldfinch (*Carduelis carduelis*) in Wisconsin. Auk 53(3):340–41.

Kabat, C. 1950. The game cycle in Wisconsin. Wis. Conserv. Bull. 15(11):3–8.

Kabat, C. 1955. Wildlife and wetlands: Problems and progress. Wis. Conserv. Bull. 20(11):3–8.

Kabat, C. 1978. Wisconsin pheasants: A bird's eye view. Wis. Nat. Resour. 2(5):18–20.

Kabat, C., and J. B. Hale. 1962. Nesting sites or disaster for pheasants. Wis. Conserv. Bull. 27(1):16–18.

Kabat, C., and R. L. Hine. 1954. Operation wildlife research. Wis. Wildl. No. 2, Game Manage. Div., Wis. Conserv. Dep., Madison, 35 pp.

Kabat, C., and D. R. Thompson. 1960. A program for quail and upland game management. Spec. Wildl. Rep. No. 4, Wis. Conserv. Dep., Madison, mimeo., 41 pp.

Kabat, C., and D. R. Thompson. 1961. A future for quail? Wis. Conserv. Bull. 26(6):16–17.

Kabat, C., and D. R. Thompson. 1963. Wisconsin quail populations, 1834–1962. Tech. Bull. 30, Wis. Conserv. Dep., 136 pp.

Kabat, C., D. R. Thompson, and F. M. Kozlik. 1950. Pheasant weights and wingmolt in relation to reproduction with survival implications. Tech. Bull. 2, Wis. Conserv. Dep., 26 pp.

Kabat, C., R. K. Meyer, G. Flakas, and R. L. Hine. 1956. Seasonal variation in stress resistance and survival in the hen pheasant. Tech. Bull. 13, Wis. Conserv. Dep., Madison, 48 pp.

Kahmann, K. W. 1939. Submitted field observations for Hayward area in February and April. Pass. Pigeon 1(3):42; 1(5):76.

Kahmann, K. W., and O. J. Gromme. 1941. Verify "Montana Junco" from Sawyer County. Pass. Pigeon 3(12):110.

Kangas, F. 1974. Purple Gallinule found near Aurora bridge, Fisher Lake Road, Wis. Pass. Pigeon 36(4):186–87.

Kannenberg, A. P. 1943. A study of birds as food. Pass. Pigeon 5(3):75.

Keating, W. H. 1959. Narrative of an expedition to the source of St. Peter's River, Lake Winnepeek, Lake of the Woods, etc., etc., performed in the year 1823. 2 vols. in one. Ross & Haines, Minneapolis, 706 pp.

Keefer, J. W. 1976. A census estimate of marsh birds obtained from transect counts. MS thesis, Univ. Wis.–Milwaukee, 57 pp.

Keefer, J. W. 1977. A census of marsh birds using transect counts at the Cedarburg Bog. Pass. Pigeon 39(1):207–12.

Keeler, C. A. 1885a. Wisconsin birds. Young Oologist 1(10):144.

Keeler, C. A. 1885b. From Wisconsin. Young Oologist 1(11):147–48; 2(1):17; 2(2):39.

Keeler, C. A. 1888. Notes on some winter birds of Milwaukee. Ornithol. and Oologist 13(1):9–12.

Keeler, C. A. 1890a. The nesting of the loon. Wis. Nat. 1(4):60–62.

Keeler, C. A. 1890b. Wisconsin notes. Auk 7(1):82.

Keeler, C. A. 1890c. An oological half holiday. Wis. Nat. 1(12):178–81.

Keeler, C. A. 1890d. Very late nesting of *Sialia sialis*. Oologist 3(1):12.

Keener, J. M. 1951. Capercaillie in Wisconsin. Wis. Conserv. Bull. 16(12):8–10.

Keir, J. R. 1973. Predation impact on pen-reared pheasants released on shooting preserves and a localized study of Red-tailed Hawks during winter residency and spring migration. MS thesis, Univ. Wis.–Madison, 24 pp.

Keith, J. A. 1966. Reproduction in a population of Herring Gulls (*Larus argentatus*) contaminated by DDT. J. Appl. Ecol. 3:57–70.

Keith, L. B. 1963a. A note on Snowy Owl food habits. Wilson Bull. 75(3):276–77.

Keith, L. B. 1963b. Wildlife's ten-year cycle. Univ. Wis. Press, Madison, 201 pp.

Kellogg, L. P., Ed. 1917. Original narratives of early American history. Scribner's, New York, 382 pp.

Kemper, C. A. 1958a. Destruction at the TV tower. Pass. Pigeon 20(1):3–9.

Kemper, C. A. 1958b. Bird destruction at a TV tower. Audubon Mag. 60(6):270–71.

Kemper, C. A. 1959. More TV tower destruction. Pass. Pigeon 21(4):135–42.

Kemper, C. A. 1964. A tower for TV: 30,000 dead birds. Audubon Mag. 66(2):86–90.

Kemper, C. A. 1973a. Birds of Chippewa, Eau Claire and neighboring counties: An annotated checklist. Pass. Pigeon 35(2):55–91.

Kemper, C. A. 1973b. Birds of Chippewa, Eau Claire and neighboring counties: An annotated checklist. Pass. Pigeon 35(3):107–29.

Kemper, C. A., S. D. Robbins, and A. C. Epple. 1964. The ornithological flood of September 18–20, 1963. Pass. Pigeon 26(4):159–72.

Kendall, J. B. 1941a. The Whistling Swans on Green Bay. Pass. Pigeon 3(3):21–23.

Kendall, J. B. 1941b. Observations on nesting habits of the bluebird. Pass. Pigeon 3(7):63–65.

Kerschbaum, M., and R. E. Kyro. 1972. Paradise on our western border. Wis. Conserv. Bull. 37(4):16–18.

Kiel, W. H., Jr., and A. S. Hawkins. 1953. Status of the coot in the Mississippi Flyway. Trans. North Am. Wildl. Conf. 18:311–22.

Kienitz, A. 1979. Bird banding. Woodland Dunes Duneslett. 16:5.

King, F. Holman. 1941. Golden Plover in Iron County. Pass. Pigeon 3(11):102.

King, F. Holman. 1949. The American Egret in Wisconsin. Pass. Pigeon 11(1):3–17.

King, Franklin H. 1882a. Destruction of birds by the cold wave of May 21st and 22nd. Nuttall Bull. 7(3):185.

King, Franklin H. 1882b. More definite statistics needed in regard to the abundance of birds. Nuttall Bull. 7(3):186–89.

King, Franklin H. 1883. Economic relations of Wisconsin birds. Pp. 441–610, chap. 11, in Geology of Wisconsin, Vol. 1, ed. T. C. Chamberlin. Comm. Public Print., Madison, Wis.

King, Franklin H. 1884a. The industrial relations of our birds. Trans. Wis. State Agric. Soc. 21(1882–1883):261–71.

King, Franklin H. 1884b. Our birds in relation to horticulture. Trans. Wis. State Hortic. Soc. 14(1883–1884):19–29.

King, Franklin H. 1886. Economic relations of Wisconsin birds. Trans. Wis. Agric. Soc. 24:372–480; greatly abridged from 1883 original.

King, Franklin H. 1888. Birds of Buffalo County. Pp. 42–46 in History of Buffalo County, ed. L. Kessinger. Alma, Wis.

King, Franklin H. 1892. The migration and usefulness of our birds. Pp. 5–6 in Wis. Arbor Day Annu.; reprinted in Wis. Arbor and Bird Day Annu. 1899:34–37.

Kinzel, C. 1945. Photographing the Great Horned Owl. Pass. Pigeon 7(2):29–32.

Kinzie, Mrs. J. H. 1856. Wau-Pun, the "early day" in the northwest. Derby and Jackson, New York, 498 pp.

Kirkpatrick, C. M. 1940. Some foods of young Great Blue Herons. Am. Midl. Nat. 24(3):594–601.

Klein, T. J. 1980. Leave the loon alone. Wis. Nat. Resour. 4(3):13–16.

Kleinert, S. J., and P. E. Degurse. 1972. Mercury levels in Wisconsin. Fish and Wildl. Tech. Bull. 52, Wis. Dep. Nat. Resour., Madison, 22 pp.

Kleinhans, J. 1977. The wild goose: Saint or sinner. Wis. Nat. Resour. 1(6):25–27.

Klink, J. 1970a. Reappearance of Red-shafted Flicker. Pass. Pigeon 32(2):54.

Klink, J. 1970b. Flicker in Wisconsin in winter. Pass. Pigeon 32(4):186.

Klopman, R. B., 1956. Certain aspects of the nesting season of Canada Geese (*Branta canadensis interior*). MS thesis, Univ. Wis.–Madison, 45 pp.

Klotz, C. D. 1927. Hudsonian Chickadee in Michigan and Wisconsin. Auk 44(3):427.

Klotz, C. D. 1928. American Hawk Owl in Wisconsin. Auk 45(2):213.

Knoekel, J. M. 1978. Source of variability in the songs of the Yellow-headed Blackbird. MS thesis, Univ. Wis.–Madison, 95 pp.

Knudsen, G. J. 1951. An interesting Wisconsin rookery. Pass. Pigeon 8(4):119–24.

Knudsen, G. J. 1976. Preliminary survey of Turkey Vultures in Wisconsin. Pass. Pigeon 38(3):100–105.

Knudsen, S. J. 1937. Vast game refuge in glacial lake basin. Wis. Outdoors 1(6):3–7.

Knuth, C. C. 1967. Supple Marsh: An open letter. Pass. Pigeon 29(2):43–45.

Knuth, C. C. 1974. Wisconsin's wintering waterfowl. Wis. Sportsman 3(1):22–24.

Knuth, C. C. 1976. The Upland Plover—shorebird of the uplands. Wis. Sportsman 5(4):30–31.

Knuth, R. A. 1967. An unusual goose in Fond du Lac County. Pass. Pigeon 29(3):70–71.

Knuth, R. A. 1970. The birds of Fond du Lac County. O. J. Gromme Ornithol. Assoc., Fond du Lac, Wis., mimeo. 7 pp.

Koenig, E. 1954. The nesting habits of our cardinals. Pass. Pigeon 16(2):56–58.

Koenig, E. 1958. The Purple Finches. Pass. Pigeon 20(2):66–67.

Koenig, E. 1959. More about Purple Finches. Pass. Pigeon 21(3):100–104.

Koenig, E. 1961. Life with the finches. Pass. Pigeon 23(2):43–46.

Kohel, M. E. 1972. Migration and nesting pattern of the Common Loon in Wisconsin. Pass. Pigeon 34(2):55–57.

Kozlik, F. M. 1946. The effects of DDT on birds. Pass. Pigeon 8(4):99–103.

Kozlik, F. M. 1947–1949. Pheasant management research project. Wis. Wildl. Resour. Q. Prog. Reps. 6(3):51–76; 6(4):40–50; 7(1):33–41; 7(4):18–28; 8(1):52–54.

Kozlik, F. M., and C. Kabat. 1949. Why do pheasant populations remain low? Wis. Conserv. Bull. 14(10):7–10.

Kraus, G. V. 1910. Kill the cowbird. Oologist 27(9):108–10.

Krumm, K., and D. G. Schneider. 1974. Possible nesting of Swainson's Hawk in Buffalo County. Pass. Pigeon 36(3):141.

Kruse, H. 1948. The birds of Hickory Hill. Pass Pigeon 10(2):46–55.

Kubisiak, J. F. 1970. Getting the partridge count. Wis. Conserv. Bull. 35(2):16–17.

Kubisiak, J. F. 1971. Experimenting in the popples. Wis. Conserv. Bull. 36(1):20–21.

Kubisiak, J. F. 1977. Mixed aspen—more Ruffed Grouse. Wis. Nat. Resour. 1(5):22–23.

Kubisiak, J. F. 1978. Brood characteristics and summer habitats of Ruffed Grouse in central Wisconsin. Tech. Bull. 108, Wis. Dept. Nat. Resour., Madison, 11 pp.

Kubisiak, J. F. 1984. Ruffed Grouse habitat relationships in aspen and oak forest of central Wisconsin. Tech. Bull. 151, Wis. Dep. Nat. Resour., 22 pp.

Kubisiak, J. F., J. C. Moulton, and K. R. McCaffery. 1980. Ruffed Grouse density and habitat relationships in Wisconsin. Tech. Bull. 118, Wis. Dep. Nat. Resour., Madison, 16 pp.

Kuehn, H. C. 1937. The Passenger Pigeon. Wis. Conserv. Bull. 2(5):8–9.

Kumlien, L. 1876. On the habits of *Steganopus Wilsoni* [Wilson's Phalarope]. Field and For. 2(1):11–12.

Kumlien, L. 1888. Observations on bird migration at Milwaukee. Auk 5(3):325–28.

Kumlien, L. 1891a. A list of the birds known to nest within the boundaries of Wisconsin, with a few notes thereon. Wis. Nat. 1(7):103–5.

Kumlien, L. 1891b. A list of the birds known to nest within the boundaries of Wisconsin, with a few notes thereon. Wis. Nat. 1(8):125–27.

Kumlien, L. 1891c. A list of the birds known to nest within the boundaries of Wisconsin, with a few notes thereon. Wis. Nat. 1(10):146–48.

Kumlien, L. 1891d. A list of the birds known to nest within the boundaries of Wisconsin, with a few notes thereon. Wis. Nat. 1(12):181–83.

Kumlien, L. 1895. A new bird (*Milvulus forficatus*) for Wisconsin. Nidiologist 3(2):19.

Kumlien, L. 1897. Wintering of the Red-headed Woodpecker in Wisconsin. Osprey 2(2):20.

Kumlien, L. 1899. Habits of young Short-eared Owls. Osprey 3(5):69–70.

Kumlien, L., and N. Hollister. 1903. The birds of Wisconsin. Bull. Wis. Nat. Hist. Soc. 3(1–3):1–143; published in same year in one volume with the cooperation of the Board of Trustees of the Milwaukee Public Mus.; reprinted with A. W. Schorger's revisions, Wis. Soc. Ornithol., 1951.

Kumlien, T. 1877. Lake Koshkonong. Pp. 628–31 *in* History of Madison and Dane County. W. J. Park and Co., Madison.

Labanauskas, M., C. Connors, and P. G. Connors. 1969. A Great Gray Owl in the Baraboo hills. Pass. Pigeon 31(2):232.

Labisky, R. F. 1956. Relation of hay harvesting to duck nesting at Horicon refuge, Wisconsin. MS thesis, Univ. Wis.–Madison, 81 pp.

LaMarche, E. D. 1972. Radar monitoring of the departures of *Branta canadensis* from the Horicon Refuge Area—1970 fall migration. MS thesis, Saint Mary's College, Winona, Minn., 55 pp.

Lange, K. I. 1969. The Great Gray Owl in Sauk County. Pass. Pigeon 31(2):233–35.

Lange, K. I. 1972. The Grand River Wildlife Area. Pass. Pigeon 34(4):166–67.

Lange, K. I. 1974. The "Wisconsin desert." Wis. Chap. Nature Conservancy Newslett. 1974 (Spring):1–2, 5–6.

Lange, K. I. 1985. Horicon Marsh in winter. Pass. Pigeon 47:53–59.

Lange, K. I. 1986a. Winter raptors at Devil's Lake State Park, Wisconsin. Pass. Pigeon 48:69–73.

Lange, K. I. 1986b. Bird migration records for the Baraboo hills, Wisconsin. Pass. Pigeon 48:102–18.

Lange, K. I. 1988. The Townsend's Solitaire in Wisconsin. Pass. Pigeon 50:15–20.

Lanyon, W. E. 1953a. Meadowlarks in Wisconsin. Part 1, Historical and ecological aspects of distribution. Pass. Pigeon 15(3):99–112.

Lanyon, W. E. 1953b. Meadowlarks in Wisconsin. Part 2, Wintering, migration, song, and breeding biology. Pass. Pigeon 15(4):150–58.

Lanyon, W. E. 1955. The comparative ethology and ecology of sympatric meadowlarks in Wisconsin and other north-central states. PhD diss., Univ. Wis.–Madison, 152 pp.

Lanyon, W. E. 1957. The comparative biology of the meadowlarks (*Sturnella*) in Wisconsin. Publ. Nuttall Ornithol. Club, 67 pp.

Lapham, I. A. 1852a. A systematic catalogue of the animals of Wisconsin. Pp. 186–95 *in* Journal of Wisconsin Senate, Appendix H. 4th Annu. Rep., Board of Regents Univ. Wis.

Lapham, I. A. 1852b. Fauna and flora of Wisconsin. Trans. Wis. State Agric. Soc. 2:337–419.

Larkin, D. 1946. A letter to my bird friends. Pass. Pigeon 8(1):17–26.

Larkin, D. 1957. A roadside rarity [Painted Bunting]. Pass. Pigeon 19(3):112–13.

Lathrop, S. P. 1852. Meteorological observations and calendar. Trans. Wis. State Agric. Soc. 2:446–48.

Lawson, P. V. 1921. Thure Kumlien biography. Trans. Wis. Acad. Sci., Arts, Lett. 20:663–86.

Laycock. G. 1963. The Prairie Chicken and his friends. Field and Stream 68(5):52–53, 86–89.

Lee, O. B. 1905. English Sparrows vs. swallows at Scandinavia, Wisconsin. Am. Ornithol. 5(1):132.

Leffingwell, W. B. 1890a. Wild fowl shooting. Rand-McNally Co., Chicago, 373 pp.

Leffingwell, W. B. 1890b. Shooting on upland, marsh and stream. Rand-McNally Co., Chicago, 473 pp.

Legler, K., and D. Legler. 1974. Exotic swans at Middleton. Pass. Pigeon 36(4):158–61.

Lemke, C. W. 1952. Sharptails or "chickens"? Wis. Conserv. Bull. 17(8):3–5.

Lemke, C. W. 1957. Hungarian Partridge. Wis. Conserv. Bull. 22(10):19–22.

Lemke, C. W., and H. E. Shine. 1958. Hungarian Partridge census. Wis. Conserv. Bull. 23(11):21–24.

Leopold, A. 1929. Report on a game survey of Wisconsin. Univ. Wis.–Madison Archives, MS, 165 pp.

Leopold, A. 1931a. Report on a game survey of the north central states. Sporting Arms and Ammunition Manufacturers Inst., Madison, 299 pp.

Leopold, A. 1931b. Game methods, the American way. Am. Game 20(2):20, 29–31.

Leopold, A. 1933a. Game management. Scribner's, New York, 481 pp.

Leopold, A. 1933b. The conservation ethic. J. For. 31(6):634–43.

Leopold, A. 1933c. The Mockingbird in Wisconsin. Wilson Bull. 45(3):143.

Leopold, A. 1934. An outline plan for game management in Wisconsin. Reg. Plan Rep., Wis. Reg. Plann. Comm., pp. 243–55, Univ. Wis.–Madison Archives.

Leopold, A. 1935. Wild life research in Wisconsin. Trans. Wis. Acad. Sci., Arts, Lett. 29:203–8.

Leopold, A. 1936a. Franklin J. W. Schmidt [a biography and his writings on Wisconsin wildlife]. Wilson Bull. 48(3):181–86.

Leopold, A. 1936b. Threatened species—a proposal to the Wildlife Conference for an inventory of the needs of near extinct birds and animals. Am. For. 42(3):116–18.

Leopold, A. 1937a. The effect of the winter of 1935–36 on Wisconsin quail. Am. Midl. Nat. 18(3):408–16.

Leopold, A. 1937b. 1936 pheasant nesting study. Wilson Bull. 49(2):91–95.

Leopold, A. 1937c. The Chase Journal; an early record of Wisconsin wildlife. Trans. Wis. Acad. Sci., Arts, Lett. 30:60–76.

Leopold, A. 1937d. Marshland elegy. Am. For. 43(10):472–74.

Leopold, A. 1937e. How to build a game crop? The University sets out to find the answer. Wis. Sportsman 1(5–6):2.

Leopold, A. 1940a. Wisconsin wildlife chronology. Wis. Conserv. Bull. 5(11):8–20; reprinted as Wis. Conserv. Dep. Publ. 301.

Leopold, A. 1940b. Spread of the Hungarian Partridge in Wisconsin. Trans. Wis. Acad. Sci., Arts, Lett. 32:5–28.

Leopold, A. 1941a. Pest hunts. Pass. Pigeon 3(5):42–43.

Leopold, A. 1941b. Wildlife conservation on the farm. Wis. Agric. and Farmer, Racine, leaflet, 24 pp.

Leopold, A. 1943. Spring floods affect wildlife. Pass. Pigeon 5(2):50.

Leopold, A. 1945. Wildlife explorations at Prairie du Sac. Wis. Conserv. Bull. 10(7–8):3–5.

Leopold, A. 1947. On a monument to the Passenger Pigeon. Pp. 3–5 in Silent wings, ed. W. E. Scott. Wis. Soc. Ornithol., Madison.

Leopold, A. 1949. A Sand County almanac and sketches here and there. Oxford Univ. Press, New York, 226 pp.

Leopold, A., and J. Ball. 1931a. British and American grouse cycles. Can. Field-Nat. 45(7):162–67.

Leopold, A., and J. Ball. 1931b. The quail shortage of 1930. Outdoor Am. 9(1):14–15, 17.

Leopold, A., and W. F. Grimmer. 1946. The history and future of the pheasant in Wisconsin. Pp. 15–25 in Wisconsin pheasant populations, ed. I. O. Buss. Wis. Conserv. Dep. Bull. 326, Madison.

Leopold, A., and S. E. Jones. 1947. A phenological record for Sauk and Dane counties, Wisconsin, 1935–1945. Ecol. Monogr. 17(1):81–122.

Leopold, A., and A. W. Schorger. 1930. The decline of the jacksnipe in southern Wisconsin. Wilson Bull. 42(3):183–90.

Leopold, A., O. S. Lee, and H. G. Anderson. 1938. Wisconsin pheasant movement study, 1936–1937. J. Wildl. Manage. 2(1):3–12.

Leopold, A., T. M. Sperry, W. S. Feeney, and J. A. Catenhusen. 1943. Population turnover on a Wisconsin pheasant refuge. J. Wildl. Manage. 7(4):383–94.

Leopold, L. B., ed. 1953. Round river—from the journals of Aldo Leopold. Oxford Univ. Press, New York, 173 pp.

Les, B. L. 1979. The vanishing wild: Wisconsin's endangered wildlife and its habitat. Wis. Dep. Nat. Resour., Madison, 36 pp.

Lesher, F. Z. 1973. Four jaegers on Lake Onalaska. Pass. Pigeon 35(4):197–98.

Lewis, J. C. 1977. Sandhill Crane. Pp. 5–43 in Management of migratory shore and upland game birds in North America, ed. G. C. Sanderson. Internatl. Assoc. Fish and Wildl. Agencies, Washington, D.C.

Lewke, R. E., and J. McGovern. 1981. The birds of Putnam Park: Scientific area number 134. Pass. Pigeon 43:86–96.

Libby, H. J., III. 1972. Ruddy Duck brood distribution in relation to marsh habitat. MS thesis, Univ. Wis.–Madison, 33 pp.

Libby, O. G. 1891. Some Madison winter birds. Wis. Nat. 1(10):155–58; 1(11):168–70.

Libby, O. G. 1899. The nocturnal flight of migrating birds. Auk 16(2):140–46.

Liebherr, H. G. 1953. An unusual visitor. Pass. Pigeon 15(3):121–22.

Lilly, J. H. 1941. The effect of arsenical grasshopper poisons upon pheasants. J. Econ. Entomol. 23(3):501–5.

Lincoln, F. C. 1924a. Banding gulls and terns in Lake Michigan. Wilson Bull., o.s., 36(1):38–41.

Lincoln, F. C. 1924b. Returns from banded birds, 1920 to 1923. U.S. Dep. Agric. Bull. 1268, Washington, D.C., 56 pp.

Lincoln, F. C. 1926. Banding gulls and terns in Lake Michigan: 1924 and 1925. Wilson Bull., o.s., 38(4):240–48.

Lincoln, F. C. 1927. Bird banding in 1927 on Lakes Michigan and Huron. Wilson Bull., o.s., 39(3):178–86.

Lincoln, F. C. 1928. The migration of young North American Herring Gulls. Auk 45(1):49–59.

Lincoln, F. C. 1932. Great Blue Heron in Cuba and Panama. Auk 49(4):457–58.

Lincoln, F. C. 1933. State distribution of returns from banded birds. Bird Banding 4(4):177–89.

Lincoln, F. C. 1936a. Birds of prey. Bird Banding 7(1):38–45.

Lincoln, F. C. 1936b. Returns of banded birds. Bird Banding 7(3):121–28.

Lincoln, F. C. 1936c. Water birds from Latin America. Bird Banding 7(4):139–48.

Lincoln, F. C. 1946. Keeping up with the waterfowl. Audubon Mag. 48(3):194–205; reprinted as Wildlife Leaflet 294, U.S. Dep. Inter. Fish and Wildl. Serv., Washington, D.C., 10 pp.

Lincoln, F. C. 1949. The Mississippi Flyway. Pp. 1–18 in Wildfowling in the Mississippi Flyway, ed. E. V. Connett. Van Nostrand Co., New York.

Lindsay, G. E. 1967. Prairie Chickens died under crusted snow. Pass. Pigeon 29(1):25–28.

Lindsay, G. E. 1976. Early migrants from Iron County. Pass. Pigeon 38(4):164–65.

Lintereur, L. J. 1966. Seagull Bar. Wis. Conserv. Bull. 31(2):22–23.

Livezey, B. C. 1979. Duck nesting in uplands at Horicon National Wildlife Refuge. MS thesis, Univ. Wis.–Madison, 84 pp.

Loiselle, B. A., and J. G. Blake. 1984. Site tenacity of birds on Curtis prairie, Dane County, Wisconsin. Pass. Pigeon 46:16–21.

Long, S. H. 1860. Voyage in a six-oared skiff to the falls of Saint Anthony in 1817. H. B. Ashmead, Philadelphia, 83 pp. (From Collections, Hist. Soc. Minn.)

Loucks, O. L. 1967. Scientific areas in Wisconsin (15 years in review). Wis. Acad. Rev. 14(1):13–16.

Lound, M. 1956. Excitement at Horicon. Pass. Pigeon 18(4):152–54.

Lound, M., and R. H. Lound. 1955. Horicon Marsh field trip. Pass. Pigeon 17(3):116–18.

Lowe, J. L. 1915. The birds of Green Lake County, Wisconsin. Bull. Wis. Nat. Hist. Soc. 13:62–87.

Loyster, E. L. 1939. Collected Hudsonian Curlew at Cedar Grove. Pass. Pigeon 1(4):62.

Loyster, E. L. 1940. Waterfowl banding in southern Wisconsin. Pass. Pigeon 2(8):95–99.

Ludwig, F. E. 1942. Migration of Caspian Terns banded in the Great Lakes area. Bird Banding 13(1):1–9.

Ludwig, F. E. 1943. Ring-billed Gulls of the Great Lakes. Wilson Bull. 55(4):234–44.

Ludwig, J. P. 1962. A survey of the gull and tern populations of Lakes Huron, Michigan and Superior. Jack-Pine Warbler 40(4):104–19.

Ludwig, J. P. 1966. Herring and Ring-billed Gull populations of the Great Lakes, 1960–1965. Great Lakes Res. Div. Publ. 15:80–89.

Ludwig, J. P. 1974. Recent changes in the Ring-billed Gull population and biology in the Laurentian Great Lakes. Auk 91:575–94.

Lukes, R. J. 1976. Once around the sun: A Door County journal. Pine Street Press, Bailey's Harbor, Wis., 216 pp.

Lukes, R. J. 1979. Out on a limb: A journal of Wisconsin birding. Pine Street Press, Bailey's Harbor, Wis., 236 pp.

Lukes, R. J. 1980. Nature-wise. Pass. Pigeon 42:133–34.

Lund, N. F., and G. W. Miner. 1872. Our birds. Trans. Wis. State Hortic. Soc. 2:168.

Lyon, W. I. 1926. Banding gulls and terns on upper Lake Michigan. Wilson Bull., o.s., 38(4):244–48.

Lyon, W. I. 1927. Bird banding in 1927 on Lakes Michigan and Huron. Wilson Bull. 39(3):178–84.

McArthur, H. E. 1947. Gulls and terns on the Great Lakes. IBBA News 19(4):24–25.

McArthur, H. E., and H. C. Wilson. 1951. Banding in the Great Lakes area. IBBA News 23(4):20.

McAsey, M. E. 1979. Aspects of the breeding biology of the Herring Gull (*Larus argentatus*) of Rush Lake. M.S. thesis, Univ. Wis.–Oshkosh, 87 pp.

McAtee, W. L. 1909. Early arrival of Evening Grosbeaks in southern Wisconsin. Bird-Lore 11(6):267.

McAtee, W. L. 1911. Our vanishing shorebirds. U.S. Biol. Surv. Circ. 79, Washington, D.C., 9 pp.

McAtee, W. L. 1943. An obscure Wisconsin bird list. Pass. Pigeon 5(2):58–59.

MacBriar, W. N., Jr. 1959a. Wisconsin's newest bird residents. Explorer's Log, Milwaukee Public Mus., No. 375, 24 Apr. p. 2.

MacBriar, W. N., Jr. 1959b. Strangers at Bank Swallow colonies. LORE, Milwaukee Public Mus. 9(3):96–99.

MacBriar, W. N., Jr. 1959c. Bird fatalities at a "tower" in 1887. Pass. Pigeon 21(3):105–6.

MacBriar, W. N., Jr. 1970. Eight-year-old Bank Swallow (*Riparia riparia*). Bird Banding 41(2):130.

MacBriar, W. N., Jr. 1972. Annual spacing and dispersal movements in the Bank Swallow (*Riparia riparia*) in southeastern Wisconsin. MS thesis, Univ. Wis.–Milwaukee, 58 pp.

MacBriar, W. N., Jr. 1975. First specimen of ground dove from Wisconsin. Auk 92(3):595–96.

MacBriar, W. N., Jr., and D. E. Stevenson. 1976. Dispersal and survival in the Bank Swallow (*Riparia riparia*) in southeastern Wisconsin. Milwaukee Public Mus., Contrib. in Biol. and Geol., No. 10, Aug. 1976, 17 pp.

McCabe, R. A. 1943. Hungarian Partridge (*Perdix perdix* Linn.) studies in Wisconsin. MS thesis, Univ. Wis.–Madison, 96 pp.

McCabe, R. A. 1948. Orchard Oriole nesting at Madison, Wisconsin. Auk 65(3):453–54.

McCabe, R. A. 1949. A ten-year study of a refuge population of Ring-necked Pheasants. PhD diss., Univ. Wis.–Madison, 157 pp.

McCabe, R. A. 1951. The song and song-flight of the Alder Flycatcher. Wilson Bull. 63(2):89–98.

McCabe, R. A. 1954. Wildlife and farm fence rows in Wisconsin. Circ. 469, Univ. Wis. Ext., Coll. Agric., Madison, 8 pp.

McCabe, R. A. 1955. Some data on Wisconsin pheasants obtained by interviewing farmers. J. Wildl. Manage. 19(1):150–51.

McCabe, R. A. 1956. Wetlands and wildlife. Wis. Conserv. Bull. 21(3):24–28.

McCabe, R. A. 1963. Renesting of the Alder Flycatcher. Proc. Internatl. Ornithol. Congr. 13:319–28.

McCabe, R. A. 1965. Wood Duck management and research: Symposium summary. Proc. Midwest Wildl. Conf., Dec. 1965, 27:204–9.

McCabe, R. A. 1978. The Stoughton Faville Prairie Preserve: Some historical aspects. Trans. Wis. Acad. Sci., Arts, Lett. 66:25–49.

McCabe, R. A., and J. B. Hale. 1960. An attempt to establish a colony of Yellow-headed Blackbirds. Auk 77(4):425–32.

McCabe, R. A., and A. S. Hawkins. 1946. The Hungarian Partridge in Wisconsin. Am. Midl. Nat. 36(1):1–75.

McCabe, R. A., R. A. MacMullan, and E. H. Dustman. 1956. Ring-necked Pheasants in the Great Lakes region. Pp. 264–356 *in* Pheasants in North America, ed. D. L. Allen. Stackpole Co., Harrisburg, Pa.

McCarthy, T. J. 1936. Winter birds of the Lake Superior region. Superior Audubon Soc. Bird Notes 1(1):3.

McCollum, C. 1884. Wisconsin Birds [a list]. Young Oologist 1(6):92–94.

McGaffey, E. 1919. The loon, or great northern diver. Wis. Conserv. 1(3):1.

McKee, W. S. 1974. A comparison of two breeding bird censuses on the Prairie Chicken preserve scientific area. Pass. Pigeon 36(2):69–73.

MacQuarrie, G. 1936. A pot-hole rendezvous. Field and Stream 40(10):9–11, 52–55.

Madsen, C. 1974. Bald Eagle nest survey in the Great Lakes states. Pp. 46–48 *in* Our eagles' future?, ed. T. N. Ingram. Proc. Bald Eagle Days. Eagle Valley Environmentalists, Apple River, Ill.

Madura, M. L. 1951–1953. Feathered observations. Pass. Pigeon 13(4):131–32; 14(2):65–68; 14(3):99–102; 15(1):30–32.

Maier, L., and M. Maier. 1973. Our incredible Curve-billed Thrasher. Pass. Pigeon 35(1):37–38.

Main, A. K. 1921. The spring procession—how the birds arrived at the home farm. Wis. Conserv. 3(3):2–3.

Main, A. K. 1925. Bird companions. Richard G. Badger Publ., Boston, 287 pp.

Main, A. K. 1927. The Yellow-headed Blackbirds at Lake Koshkonong and vicinity. Trans. Wis. Acad. Sci., Arts, Lett. 23:631–38.

Main, A. K. 1939. Collecting with Thure Kumlien in 1862. Pass. Pigeon 1(3):29–30, 40–41, 45.

Main, A. K. 1943–1944. Thure Kumlien, Koshkonong naturalist. Wis. Mag. Hist. 27(1):17–39; 27(2):194–220; 27(3):321–43.

Main, A. K. 1945. Studies of ornithology at Lake Koshkonong and vicinity by Thure Kumlien from 1843 to July, 1850. Trans. Wis. Acad. Sci., Arts, Lett. 37:91–109.

Main, J. S. 1926. Brewer's Blackbird nesting at Madison, Wisconsin. Auk 43(4):548–49.

Main, J. S. 1928. Summer birds in Wisconsin. Wis. Mag. 6(8):222.

Main, J. S. 1930a. Some 1930 notes from Madison, Wisconsin. Auk 47(4):578–79.

Main, J. S. 1930b. Census at Madison. Bird-Lore 32(1):46.

Main, J. S. 1931. Some notes on the fall migration of shore birds. Wilson Bull. 43(2):150–51.

Main, J. S. 1932a. The influences of temperature on migration. Wilson Bull. 44(1):10–12.

Main, J. S. 1932b. Migration dates of Yellow-legs and others. Auk 49(1):82–83.

Main, J. S. 1935. Shore birds at Madison, Wisconsin. Auk 52(3):323.

Main, J. S. 1936. Red Phalarope (*Phalaropus fulicarius*) at Madison, Wisconsin. Auk 53(2):212.

Main, J. S. 1937a. The dance of the Prairie Chicken. Wilson Bull. 49(1):37–42.

Main, J. S. 1937b. Lapland Longspurs in Wisconsin in summer. Auk 54(4):546.

Main, J. S. 1938. Relation of temperature to early migrants. Wilson Bull. 50(3):190–93.

Main, J. S. 1939. White-fronted Goose at Madison, Wisconsin. Auk 56(4):471.

Main, J. S. 1940. Notes from Wisconsin. Auk 57(3):424–25.

Main, J. T. 1940. History of the conservation of wild life in Wisconsin. MA thesis, Univ. Wis.–Madison, 104 pp.

Malin, J. 1921. Cardinals at Wyalusing, Wisconsin. Wilson Bull. 33(4):156.

Manci, K. M. 1985. Distribution and annual abundance of waterbirds at Horicon National Wildlife Refuge. MS thesis, Univ. Wis.–Madison, 129 pp.

Manci, K. M., and D. H. Rusch. 1989. Surveying waterbirds from airboats at Horicon Marsh. Pass. Pigeon 51:145–53.

March, J. R. 1969. We band young ducks. Wis. Conserv. Bull. 34(6):16–17.

March, J. R. 1974. Avocets nesting in Dodge County. Pass. Pigeon 36(2):82–84.

March, J. R. 1976. Mallard population and harvest dynamics in Wisconsin. PhD diss., Univ. Wis.–Madison, 312 pp.

March, J. R., and R. A. Hunt. 1968. A survey of open water waterfowl hunting in Wisconsin in 1967. Res. Rep. No. 35, Wis. Dep. Nat. Resour., 12 pp.

March, J. R., and R. A. Hunt. 1978. Mallard population and harvest dynamics in Wisconsin. Tech. Bull. 106, Wis. Dep. Nat. Resour., 67 pp.

March, J. R., G. F. Martz, and R. A. Hunt. 1973. Breeding duck populations and habitat in Wisconsin. Tech. Bull. 68, Wis. Dep. Nat. Resour., Madison, 36 pp.

Martin, L. 1932. The physical geography of Wisconsin. Univ. Wis. Press, Madison, 608 pp.; reprint ed. 1965.

Martin, M. A. 1988. Wisconsin wetlands of importance to migrant waterbirds. Pass. Pigeon 50:213–20.

Martin, S. G. 1972. Bell's and White-eyed Vireos in Wisconsin. Pass. Pigeon 34(4): 143–58.

Martinson, R. K. 1978. Clark bird collection. Wis. Weekend 24(1): 3, 5.

Martz, G. F. 1966. Removal of nesting cover and its effects on breeding waterfowl. MS thesis, Univ. Wis.–Madison, 57 pp.

Mathiak, H. A. 1944. American Egrets nest on Horicon Marsh. Pass. Pigeon 6(4):81.

Mathiak, H. A. 1953. A Mourning Dove banding project. Pass. Pigeon 15(1):7–9.

Matteson, S. W. 1979. Status of breeding gulls and terns on the Wisconsin shore of Lake Superior in 1979. Rep. to U.S. Natl. Park Serv. and Wis Dep. Nat. Resour., 19 pp.

Matteson, S. W. 1982. 1982 survey of the Common Tern, Black Tern, Double-crested Cormorant, and Piping Plover along the Wisconsin shore of Lake Superior. Rep. to Bur. Endangered Resour. of Wis. Dep. Nat. Resour., 20 pp.

Matteson, S. W. 1989. Aldo Leopold's avian phenological observations in Dane and Sauk counties, Wisconsin. Pass. Pigeon 51:369–78.

Matteson, S. W., T. A. Andryk, and J. Wetzel. 1988. Wisconsin Trumpeter Swan recovery plan. Pass. Pigeon 50:119–30.

Mattson, O. E. 1962. The chicken gets a chance. Wis. Conserv. Bull. 27(3):15–17.

Maxson, M. 1949. Banding summary for 1948. IBBA News 21(4):5.

Maxson, M. 1959. Recoveries of interest. IBBA News 31(1):9.

Mead, D. M. 1949. The Dovekie. Pass. Pigeon 11(3):95–97.

Mead, G. S. 1895. The Western Meadowlark at Racine, Wisconsin. Auk 12(3):302–3.

Meier, T. I. 1981. Artificial nesting structures for the Double-crested Cormorant. Tech. Bull 126, Wis. Dep. Nat. Resour., 12 pp.

Meinecke, A. 1877. Gives bird skins to Natural History Society. Milwaukee Sentinel, 10 Oct., p. 8.

Meinel, H. 1956. October 13, 1955, at Cedar Grove, Wisconsin. IBBA News 28(1):11.

Mellish, J. E. 1913. A study of the nesting birds. Wis. Arbor and Bird Day Annu. 1913:88–89.

Melvin, S. M. 1977. Migration studies of Wisconsin Sandhill Cranes. Pp. 27–38 in Proc. Sandhill Crane Symp., Ind. Wildl. Soc., 24–26 Oct., Michigan City, Ind.

Melvin, S. M. 1978. Ecology of non-breeding Wisconsin Sandhill Cranes, with emphasis on crop damage and migration. MS thesis, Univ. Wis.–Stevens Point, 80 pp.

Merkel, K. J. 1989. Wisconsin's first documented nesting of Great Gray Owls. Pass. Pigeon 51:133–43.

Merrill, H. W. 1878. Mud Lake, Fox River. For. and Stream 11(10):214.

Mershon, W. B. 1907. The Passenger Pigeon. Outing Publ. Co., New York, 225 pp.

Meyer, A. F. 1901. A field key to our common birds. Edw. Keogh Press, Milwaukee, 22 pp.

Meyer, J. R. 1973. The post-fledging dispersal of juvenile Black-capped Chickadees. MS thesis, Univ. Wis.–Milwaukee, 79 pp.

Meyers, L. E. 1970. Turkey "transplants": No rejection. Wis. Conserv. Bull. 35(3):26–27.

Meyers, M. 1980. Mississippi Kite in Dane County. Pass. Pigeon 42(1):51.

Miller, L. J. 1976. The effects of an altered photoperiod upon the migratory orientation in the White-throated Sparrow. MS thesis, Univ. Wis.–Milwaukee, 48 pp.

Miller, L. J., and C. M. Weise. 1978. The effects of an altered photoperiod upon the migratory orientation in the White-throated Sparrow, Zonotrichia albicollis. Condor 80(1):94–96.

Miller, R. J., and F. R. Reber. 1962. Farm pond survey: Wildlife to spare. Wis. Conserv. Bull. 27(4):20–21.

Milwaukee Public Museum. 1883–1911. Board of trustees annual reports. (Lists of accessions of unusual Wisconsin bird specimens.)

Mississippi Flyway Council. 1958a. A guide to Mississippi Flyway waterfowl management. St. Paul, Minn., 55 pp.

Mississippi Flyway Council. 1958b. Waterfowl distribution and migration in the Mississippi Flyway. Madison, Wis., 20 pp.

Mississippi Flyway Council. 1970. Lessons from the sixties and challenges of the seventies in the Mississippi Flyway. Lansing, Mich., 63 pp.

Mitchell, E. T. 1943. The Horicon Marsh wildlife area. Wis. Conserv. Bull. 8(6):6–9.

Mitchell, H. P. 1897. Notes from Wisconsin. Wilson Bull. 4(2):17.

Mitchell, Mr. and Mrs. I. N. 1903. Our city farm. Wis. Arbor and Bird Day Annu. 1903:26–28.

Mitchell, Mr. and Mrs. I. N. 1904a. A second list of garden birds. Wis. Arbor and Bird Day Annu. 1904:9–11.

Mitchell, Mr. and Mrs. I. N. 1904b. A bird calendar. Wis. Arbor and Bird Day Annu. 1904:72–74.

Mitchell, Mr. and Mrs. I. N. 1906. Wisconsin bird study bulletin. State Superintendent Public Instruction, Madison, 28 pp.

Mitchell, Mr. and Mrs. I. N. 1906–1913. Birds of Wisconsin in seven series. Wis. Arbor and Bird Day Annu. (Annual summaries of migration arrival dates from statewide network of observers.)

Mitchell, Mr. and Mrs. I. N. 1908a. Our winter birds. Wis. J. Educ. 40(2):63–65.

Mitchell, Mr. and Mrs. I. N. 1908b. The March birds. Wis. J. Educ. 40(3):93–95.

Mitchell, Mr. and Mrs. I. N. 1908c. Our common April birds. Wis. J. Educ. 40(4):123–25.

Mitchell, Mr. and Mrs. I. N. 1908d. The May birds. Wis J. Educ. 40(5):178–80.

Mitchell, Mr. and Mrs. I. N. 1910. A new sparrow record for eastern Wisconsin. Bull. Wis. Nat. Hist. Soc. 8(3):161.

Mitchell, Mr. and Mrs. I. N. 1912. Winter robins in Wisconsin. Bird-Lore 14(3):165–66.

Mitchell, Mr. and Mrs. I. N. 1913. Tufted Titmouse in Wisconsin. Bird-Lore 15(3):176.

Mitchell, Mr. and Mrs. I. N. 1914. Flocking of Purple Martins in Milwaukee. Bird-Lore 16(3):282.

Moe, J. L. 1968. Winter distribution of Red-headed Woodpeckers in Wisconsin. Pass. Pigeon 30(2):72–74.

Moore, E. B. 1937. Studies of food patches for wildlife in southern Wisconsin. MS thesis, Univ. Wis.–Madison, 36 pp.

Morgan, B. B. 1944. Bird mortality, a detailed resume of many known bird diseases. Pass. Pigeon 6(2):27–34.

Morrison, G. A. 1896. Yellow-headed Blackbird in Wisconsin. Nidiologist 3(10–11):114–15.

Morrison, G. A. 1897. Notes on Wisconsin hawks and owls. For. and Stream 50(21):404.

Morrison, G. A. 1898a. Wisconsin game birds nesting. For. and Stream 51(1):4.

Morrison, G. A. 1898b. Colony of herons nesting near Fox Lake. For. and Stream 51(1):25.

Morrison, G. A. 1898c. Notes on raptors of Wisconsin. For. and Stream 51(13):242–43.

Morse, M. E. 1932. Red Crossbills at Viroqua, Wisconsin. Wilson Bull. 44(1):38.

Morse, M. E. 1954. Wisconsin's favorite bird haunts: Genoa. Pass. Pigeon 16:141–42.

Morse, M. E. 1960. Bird banding returns. IBBA News 31(3):32.

Morse, M. E. 1963. Good listening. Pass. Pigeon 25(3):108–13.

Mossman, M. J. 1976. Turkey Vultures in the Baraboo hills, Sauk County, Wisconsin. Pass. Pigeon 38(3):93–99.

Mossman, M. J. 1980a. Turkey Vulture. Wis. Nat. Resour. 4(4):28–31.

Mossman, M. J. 1980b. The second year of Wisconsin's Black Tern survey. In 1980 Ann. Perf. Rep., Wis. Dep. Nat. Resour., Off. Endangered and Nongame Species.

Mossman, M. J. 1981. Historical summary and update of Forster's Tern colonies in Wisconsin. Rep. to Wis. Dep. Nat. Resour. Off. Endangered and Nongame Species, 12 pp.

Mossman, M. J. 1984. Forest bird communities in the Baraboo hills, Wisconsin. MS thesis, Univ. Wis.–Madison, 229 pp.

Mossman, M. J. 1988. Birds of southern Wisconsin floodplain forests. Pass. Pigeon 50:321–37.

Mossman, M. J. 1989. Wisconsin's Forster's Tern recovery plan. Pass. Pigeon 51:171–86.

Mossman, M. J., and K. I. Lange. 1982. Breeding birds of the Baraboo hills, Wisconsin: Their history, distribution and ecology. Wis. Dep. Nat. Resour. and Wis. Soc. Ornithol., Madison, 197 pp.

Mossman, M. J., and R. M. Hoffman. 1989. Birds of southern Wisconsin upland forests. Pass. Pigeon 51:343–58.

Mossman, M. J., S. W. Matteson, A. F. Techlow III, and L. M. Hartman. 1984. 1984 breeding bird survey of Lakes Poygan, Winneconne, and Butte des Morts, Wisconsin. Wis. Dep. Nat. Resour. Wis. Endang. Resour. Rep. No. 10, 25 pp.

Mossman, M. J., A. F. Techlow III, T. J. Ziebell, S. W. Matteson, and K. J. Fruth. 1988. Nesting gulls and terns of Winnebago Pool and Rush Lake, Wisconsin. Pass. Pigeon 50:107–17.

Moulton, J. C. 1968. Ruffed Grouse habitat requirements and management opportunities. Rep. No. 36, Wis. Dep. Nat. Resour., Madison, 32 pp.

Mueller, H. C. 1957. W.S.O. visible migration project. Pass. Pigeon 19(4):166–67.

Mueller, H. C. 1959. Mist-netting: Cedar Grove Ornithological Station in Wisconsin, fall 1958. IBBA News 31(1):1–2.

Mueller, H. C., and D. D. Berger. 1958. Sight record of Prairie Falcon (Falco mexicanus) in Wisconsin. Pass. Pigeon 20(1):28.

Mueller, H. C., and D. D. Berger. 1959a. Some long distance Barn Owl recoveries. Bird Banding 30(3):182.

Mueller, H. C., and D. D. Berger. 1959b. A second Peregrine Falcon banding return from Uruguay. Bird Banding 30(3):182–83.

Mueller, H. C., and D. D. Berger. 1960. The Swainson's Hawk in Wisconsin. Pass. Pigeon 21(4):142–44.

Mueller, H. C., and D. D. Berger. 1961. Weather and fall migration of hawks at Cedar Grove, Wisconsin. Wilson Bull. 73(2):171–92.

Mueller, H. C., and D. D. Berger. 1965. A summer movement of Broad-winged Hawks. Wilson Bull. 77(1):83–84.

Mueller, H. C., and D. D. Berger. 1966. A record of the Gray Vireo in Wisconsin. Auk 83(2):30.

Mueller, H. C., and D. D. Berger. 1967a. Some observations and comments on the periodic invasions of Goshawks. Auk 84(2):183–91.

Mueller, H. C., and D. D. Berger. 1967b. Wind drift, leading lines, and diurnal migrations. Wilson Bull. 79(1):50–63.

Mueller, H. C., and D. D. Berger. 1967c. Observations on migrating Saw-whet Owls. Bird Banding 38(2):120–25.

Mueller, H. C., and D. D. Berger 1967d. Fall migration of Sharp-shinned Hawks. Wilson Bull. 79(4):397–415.

Mueller, H. C., and D. D. Berger. 1967e. The relative abundance of species caught in mist-nets during fall migration at Cedar Grove. Pass. Pigeon 29(4):107–15.

Mueller, H. C., and D. D. Berger. 1968. Sex ratios and measurements of migrant Goshawks. Auk 85(3):431–36.

Mueller, H. C., and D. D. Berger. 1969. Navigation by hawks migrating in spring. Auk 86(1):35–40.

Mueller, H. C., and D. D. Berger. 1972. Irregular migrations of Black-capped Chickadees at Cedar Grove. Pass. Pigeon 34(2):85.

Mueller, H. C., and D. D. Berger. 1973. The daily rhythm of hawk migration at Cedar Grove, Wisconsin. Auk 90(3):591–96.

Mueller, H. C., G. Allez, and D. D. Berger. 1983. Prairie Falcon at Cedar Grove. Pass. Pigeon 45:104.

Mueller, H. C., D. D. Berger, and G. Allez. 1977. The periodic invasions of Goshawks. Auk 94(4):652–63.

Mueller, W. J. 1934. Parasitic Jaeger (Sterconarius parasiticus) in Wisconsin. Auk 51(2):233.

Mueller, W. J. 1935. The magpie (Pica picahudsonia) in Wisconsin. Auk 52(1):90.

Mueller, W. J. 1936. Saw-whet Owl apparently nesting in Wisconsin. Auk 53(4):447–48.

Mueller, W. J. 1942. Hooded Warbler in Wisconsin. Auk 59(1):116.

Muir, J. 1913. The story of my boyhood and youth. Houghton Mifflin, New York, 294 pp.

Munn, C. 1974. Two breeding bird censuses on the Quarry Scientific Area, Wisconsin. Pass. Pigeon 36(2):62–68.

Museum of Natural History (University of Wisconsin–Stevens Point). 1970. Report No. 2. Reports on the fauna and flora of Wisconsin. Part 1, Catalog of North American bird eggs and nests in the August J. Schoenebeck collection; Part 2, Catalog of Wisconsin mounted bird specimens in the August J. Schoenebeck collection, indexed by Sister Mary Alexia. Stevens Point, Wis., 100 pp.

Naeser, C. R. 1931a. A real warbler migration. Oologist 48(5):65–67.

Naeser, C. R. 1931b. Some bird notes of Juneau County, Wisconsin. Oologist 48(10):140–42.

Naeser, C. R. 1931c. Painted Bunting [found at Madison]. Oologist 48(12):176.

Naeser, C. R. 1931d. Black Vulture in Wisconsin. Oologist 48(12):177.

Nehrling, H. 1891. Die nordamerikanische Vogelwelt. G. Brumder, Milwaukee, 637 pp.; trans. as 2 vols. in 1893 and 1896.

Nehrling, H. 1893. Our native birds of song and beauty, Vol. 1. G. Brumder, Milwaukee, 371 pp.

Nehrling, H. 1896. Our native birds of song and beauty, Vol. 2. G Brumder, Milwaukee, 452 pp.

Neidermyer, W. J. 1973. First Monk Parakeet record for Wisconsin. Pass. Pigeon 35(4):170.

Nelson, C. E. 1953. The Cedar Grove field trip. Pass. Pigeon 15(3):124–26.

Nelson, E. W. 1876. Birds of north-eastern Illinois. Bull. Essex Inst. 8(9–12):90–155.

Nelson, E. W. 1920. Conservation of lakes and marshes. Wis. Conserv. 2(3):3.

Nelson, H. K., and W. E. Green. 1962. Wood Duck banding—north central region (1959–1961). Presented to Miss. Flyway Counc. 31 July 1962, mimeo., 28 pp.

Nelson, M. H. 1959. Our back yard in July. Pass. Pigeon 21(1):18–26.

Nelson, M. H. 1965. Barn Swallow observations. Pass. Pigeon 27(4):131–38.

Nero, R. W. 1950. Notes on a Least Bittern nest and young. Pass. Pigeon 12(1):3–8.

Nero, R. W. 1951. Notes on nesting of the Least Bittern. Pass. Pigeon 13(1):5–8.

Nero, R. W. 1956. A behavior study of the Red-winged Blackbird. Wilson Bull. 68(1):5–37; 68(2):129–50.

Nero, R. W. 1980. The Great Gray Owl: Phantom of the northern forest. Smithsonian Inst. Press Books, Washington, D.C. 150 pp.

Nero, R. W., and J. T. Emlen, Jr. 1951. An experimental study of territorial behavior in breeding Red-winged Blackbirds. Condor 53(3):105–16.

Nestel, L. 1975. Wayside wanderings. Country Print, Hayward, Wis., 45 pp.

Newton, R. 1979. Wisconsin project loon watch [1979 field report]. Sigurd Olson Environ. Inst., 1979 annual report, Northland College, Ashland, Wis., pp. 4–9.

Nicholls, T. H. 1962. Food habits of the Long-eared Owl. Pass. Pigeon 24(4):130–33.

Nicholls, T. H. 1968. Wisconsin's 1966–67 Snowy Owl invasion. Pass. Pigeon 30(3):107–12.

Nicklaus, R. H. 1977a. Return of the native—turkey. Wis. Nat. Resour. 1(6):25–27.

Nicklaus, R. H. 1977b. Heron-egret-cormorant rookery directory. Wildl. Tech. Sect., Upper Miss. River Conserv. Comm., Wis. Dep. Nat. Resour., La Crosse, 6 pp.

Nott, E. A. 1923. From a bird-lover's notebook. Bird-Lore 25:313–15.

Oleson, D. 1980. Gulling the birds—how Harold Wilson spent 67 years banding baby gulls. Milwaukee J., 24 Aug., Insight sect., pp. 14–16, 18–19.

Olson, D. L. 1986. The population and distribution of Common Loons (*Gavia immer*) in northern Wisconsin. M.S. thesis. Univ. Minn.–Duluth, 86 pp.

Olson, P. 1962. The Prairie Chicken, a symbol of our land as it used to be. Wis. Tales and Trails 3(1):26–30.

Olson, P. 1963. Five years in review. Prairie Chicken 5(1):1–3.

Olson, P. 1976. Prairie Chicken—and map of Buena Vista Marsh Wildlife Area. Dane Cty. Conserv. League Newslett. 1976 (Nov.):3–10.

Olson, S. F. 1953. Wilderness and the Flambeau. Living Wilderness (Washington, D.C.) 44:3–6.

Olson, S. F. 1964. The St. Croix–Namekagon rivers. Trans. Wis. Acad. Sci., Arts, Lett. 53(Part A):35–39.

Orians, G. 1955. The Red-tailed Hawk in Wisconsin: Range and population study—1954. Pass. Pigeon 17(1):3–10.

Orians, G., and F. Kuhlman. 1956. Red-tailed Hawk and Horned Owl populations in Wisconsin. Condor 58:371–85.

Orians, H. L. 1944. A Marbled Godwit in Milwaukee. Pass. Pigeon 6(4):back cover.

Orians, H. L. 1952. The birds of New Glarus Woods. Pass. Pigeon 14(2):52–55.

Ott, F. L. 1955. Last call for Prairie Chickens. Citizens Nat. Resour. Assoc. Rep. 2(1)24.

Otto, D. 1978. The future of Wisconsin waterfowl. Wis. Sportsman 7(1):11–13.

Palmer, T. S. 1913. Introduction of the Ruffed Grouse on Washington Island, Wisconsin. Auk 30(4):582.

Parmalee, P. W. 1959. Animal remains from the Raddatz Rockshelter, SK 5, Wisconsin. Wis. Archeologist 40:83–90.

Parmalee, P. W. 1960a. Animal remains from the Aztalan Site, Jefferson County, Wisconsin. Wis. Archeologist 41(1):1–10.

Parmalee, P. W. 1960b. Animal remains from the Durst Rockshelter, Sauk County, Wisconsin. Wis. Archeologist 41(1):11–17.

Peabody, P. B. 1934. Yellow Rail. Oologist 51(12):152.

Pearson, H. P. 1974. Bird utilization of a waterfowl management area. MS thesis, Univ. Wis.–Milwaukee, 137 pp.

Peartree, E. W. 1989. Thirty years of bird banding at Honey Creek. Pass. Pigeon 51:253–54.

Peckham, P. 1975. Ferry Bluff eagle roost. Pp. 33–34 *in* Bald Eagle land, ed. T. N. Ingram. Proc. Bald Eagle Days. Eagle Valley Environmentalists, Apple River, Ill.

Peirce, Mrs. W. A. 1956. A Louisiana Heron. Pass. Pigeon 18(1):25.

Pelisek, F. J. 1976. Prairie Grouse! Soc. Tympanuchus Cupido Pinnatus, Milwaukee, 32 pp.

Pelton, C. W. 1912. More Yellow-heads. Oologist 29(1):211.

Pelton, C. W. 1933. Appearance and disappearance of birds. Oologist 50(12):164.

Pericles, E. 1894. Nesting habits of the Passenger Pigeon. Oologist 11(7):237–40.

Perkins, I. J. 1940. Sandhill Cranes in Waukesha County. Pass. Pigeon 2(6)84–85.

Perkins, J. P. 1964–1965. A ship's officer finds 17 flyways over the Great Lakes. Audubon Mag. Part 1, 66(5):294–99; Part 2, 67(1):42–45.

Perrot, N. 1911. The Indian tribes of the upper Mississippi Valley and region of the Great Lakes, trans. E. H. Blair. 2nd ed., Arthur Clark Co., 260 pp.; 1st ed. in French, Arthur Clark Co., 1864.

Personius, R. G. 1974. Managing the marsh: A history of two Horicon Marsh shooting clubs. Wis. Acad. Rev. 21(1):3–7.

Petersen, A. J. 1951. The Red-bellied Woodpecker in Wisconsin. Pass. Pigeon 13(2):51–54.

Petersen, A. J. 1955. The breeding cycle of the Bank Swallow. Wilson Bull. 67(4):235–86.

Petersen, A. J., and H. Young. 1950. A nesting study of the Bronzed Grackle. Auk 67(4):466–76.

Petersen, L. R. 1979. Ecology of Great Horned Owls and Red-tailed Hawks in Wisconsin. Tech. Bull. 111, Wis. Dep. Nat. Resour., 95 pp.

Petersen, L. R. 1980. Status of Barn Owls in Wisconsin, 1979. Res. Rep. 107, Wis. Dep. Nat. Resour., Madison, 17 pp.

Petersen, L. R., M. A. Martin, J. M. Cole, J. R. March, and C. M. Pils. 1982. Evaluation of waterfowl production areas in Wisconsin. Tech. Bull. 135, Wis. Dep. Nat. Resour., 32 pp.

Petersen, U. C. and L. R. Petersen. 1975. A case study of Barn Owls in Wisconsin. Pass. Pigeon 37(4):153–57.

Peterson, A. M. 1943. Your bird sanctuary. Pass. Pigeon 5(4):81–90.

Peterson, A. M. 1947a. The Baltimore Oriole's nest. Pass. Pigeon 9(4):132.

Peterson, A. M. 1947b. Wild Bird neighbors. Wilcox and Follett, Chicago, 298 pp.

Peterson, A. M. 1948. Ten days with the winter birds. Pass. Pigeon 10(3):102–6.

Peterson, A. M. 1951a. The winter robin populations at La Crosse. Pass. Pigeon 13(1):3–5.

Peterson, A. M. 1951b. The Pileated Woodpecker. Pass. Pigeon 13(3):89–92.

Peterson, A. M. 1954. Rare nests at La Crosse. Pass. Pigeon 16(1):17–20.

Peterson, A. M., and M. Peterson. 1956. A Black Rail is seen. Pass. Pigeon 18(4):116–17.

Peterson, M. S. 1986. W.S.O. summer campout at Three Lakes. Pass. Pigeon 48:78–79.

Peterson, M. S., and D. D. Tessen. 1983. Black-throated Sparrow. Pass. Pigeon 45:109.

Peterson, S. R. 1976. The Oldsquaw: Body measurements, food habits and environmental contaminants. PhD diss., Univ. Wis.–Madison, 132 pp.

Peterson, S. R., and R. S. Ellarson. 1975. Incidence of bodyshot in Oldsquaws (*Clangula hyemalis*). J. Wildl. Manage. 29(1):217–19.

Peterson, S. R., and R. S. Ellarson. 1976. Total mercury residues in livers and eggs of Oldsquaws. J. Wildl. Manage. 40(4):704–9.

Peterson, S. R., and R. S. Ellarson. 1977a. Food habits of Old-squaws wintering on Lake Michigan. Wilson Bull. 89(1):81–91.

Peterson, S. R., and R. S. Ellarson. 1977b. P-p'-DDE, polychlorinated biphenyls, and endrin in Oldsquaws in North America, 1969–73. Pesticides Monit. J. 11(4):170–81.

Peterson, S. R., and R. S. Ellarson. 1977c. Bursae, reproductive structures and scapular color in wintering female Oldsquaws. Auk 95(1):115–21.

Peterson, S. R., and R. S. Ellarson. 1979. Changes in Oldsquaw carcass weight. Wilson Bull. 91(2):288–300.

Pettingill, O. S., Jr. 1962. Hawk migrations around the Great Lakes. Audubon Mag. 64(1):44–45.

Pettingill, O. S., Jr. 1977. A guide to bird finding east of the Mississippi. 2nd ed., Oxford Univ. Press, New York, 698 pp.

Pillart, E. E. 1969. Faunal remains from the Millville Site, Grant County, Wisconsin. Wis. Archeologist 50(2):93–108.

Pinney, M. E., and J. F. MacNaughton. 1937. Some early bird records of Wisconsin and neighboring territory to the west and north (1896–1900) and of Indiana (1876–1877). Trans. Wis. Acad. Sci., Arts, Lett. 30:87–116.

Pirnie, M. D. 1934. Wisconsin marshland survey. Wis. Conserv. Dep. Rep. filed in Bur. Res. files, Madison, 120 pp.

Pond, F. E. 1874. Puckaway Lake. Am. Sportsman 5(4):1.

Pond, F. E. 1875a. Duck shooting at Ox Creek, Wisconsin. Am. Sportsman 5(16):243.

Pond, F. E. 1875b. Destruction of game in Wisconsin. Am. Sportsman 5(24):379.

Popov, B. H. 1960. Summary of information on Snow and Blue Goose foods and feeding habits. Spec. Wildl. Rep. 3, Wis. Conserv. Dep., mimeo., 8 pp.

Pospichal, C. E. 1958. Necedah National Wildlife Refuge. Wis. Conserv. Bull. 23(9):18–21.

Postupalsky, S. 1968. The status of the Osprey in the north-central United States, 1967. North Central Audubon Counc. and Detroit Audubon Soc., 10 pp.

Postupalsky, S. 1974. The Bald Eagle in the Great Lakes region: Current population status, research and conservation needs. Pp. 68–78 in Our eagles future? ed. T. N. Ingram. Proc. Bald Eagle Days, 8–10 Feb. 1974, Platteville. Eagle Valley Environmentalists, Apple River, Ill.

Postupalsky, S. 1976. Bald Eagle migration along the south shore of Lake Superior. Jack-Pine Warbler 54(3):98–104.

Postupalsky, S. 1977a. A critical review of problems in calculating Osprey reproductive success. Pp. 1–11 in Trans. North Am. Osprey Res. Conf. U.S. Dep. Inter. Nat. Park Serv.

Postupalsky, S. 1977b. Toxic chemicals and cormorant populations in the Great Lakes. Pp. 197–222 in Proc. Fish-eating Birds of the Great Lakes and Environmental Contaminants Symp. 2–3 Dec. 1976, Hull, Quebec. Can. Wildl. Serv., Toxic Chem. Div. and Ontario Reg., Ottawa.

Postupalsky, S. 1978a. Artificial nesting platforms for Ospreys and Bald Eagles. Chap. 5 in Endangered birds: Management techniques for preserving threatened species, ed. S. A. Temple. Univ. Wis. Press, Madison.

Postupalsky, S. 1978b. The Bald Eagles return. Nat. Hist. 87(7):62–65.

Pratten, H. 1852. Systematic catalogue of birds observed in northern Wisconsin and Minnesota. Pp. 622–23 in Report of a geographical survey of Wisconsin, Iowa and Minnesota, ed. D. D. Owen. Lippincott, Grambo and Co., Philadelphia.

Pugh, B., and W. Pugh. 1966. A three-month visit of Yellow-crowned Night Herons. Pass. Pigeon 28(1):7–8.

Radke, L. 1925. Save Horicon Marsh. Pp. 92–101 in Rep. 3d Annu. Convention Wis. Div. Isaak Walton League of Am., 14–15 Oct., Green Bay, Wis.

Raeth, G. A. 1911. Facts about spring shooting. By the Wayside 12(9):1–2.

Ramharder, B. G. 1976. Habitat selection and movements by Sharp-tailed Grouse (Pediocetes phasianellus) hens during the nesting and brood rearing periods in a fire maintained brush prairie. PhD diss., Univ. Minn.–St. Paul, 78 pp.

Rasmussen, P. W. 1977. Foraging patterns in two species of Wood Warblers. MS thesis, Univ. Wis.–Madison, 104 pp.

Reardon, W. J. 1975. June bird count in the Hayward district, Chequamegon National Forest. Pass. Pigeon 37(2):57–62.

Reese, S. W. 1942a. Spruce Grouse. Wis. Conserv. Bull. 7(2):7–9.

Reese, S. W. 1942b. Mr. Grouse goes a courtin'. Wis. Conserv. Bull. 7(7):7–12.

Reeves, H. M., H. H. Dill, and A. S. Hawkins. 1968. A case study in Canada Goose management: The Mississippi Valley population. Pp. 150–65 in Canada Goose management, ed. R. L. Hine and C. Schoenfeld. Dembar Educ. Res. Stud., Madison, Wis.

Rice, F. L. 1876. The true Brant (Bernicla branta) in Wisconsin. Rod and Gun 8(5 Aug.):293.

Richter, C. H. 1925. The Yellow-headed Blackbird. Oologist 42(6):92.

Richter, C. H. 1926a. More about the Great Horned Owl. Oologist 43(2):20.

Richter, C. H. 1926b. Unintentional destruction of birds. Oologist 43(2):25.

Richter, C. H. 1927a. Snowy Owls numerous. Oologist 44(1):7.

Richter, C. H. 1927b. The Whistling Swan. Oologist 44(7):97.

Richter, C. H. 1927c. A Goshawk caught in the act. Oologist 44(10):141.

Richter, C. H. 1928. Cardinal rare winter visitant in northern Wisconsin. Oologist 45(1):8.

Richter, C. H. 1937. Bonaparte's Gull nesting in Wisconsin: A record. Oologist 54(1):5–7.

Richter, C. H. 1939a. Additions to A. J. Schoenebeck's Birds of Oconto County. Pass. Pigeon 1(8):114–19.

Richter, C. H. 1939b. Additions to A. J. Schoenebeck's Birds of Oconto County. Pass. Pigeon 1(9):124–29.

Richter, C. H. 1948. Breeding birds of Oconto County. Pass. Pigeon 10(1):3–6.

Richter, C. H. 1969. The LeConte's Sparrow in northern Wisconsin. Pass. Pigeon 31(3):275–77.

Robbins, C. S. 1948. Distribution and migration program of the Fish and Wildlife Service. Pass. Pigeon 10(4):150–51.

Robbins, C. S. 1979. Effect of forest fragmentation on bird populations. Pass. Pigeon 41(3):101–19; reprinted from U.S. For. Serv. Tech. Rep. NC-51, North Central For. Exp. Stn., Twin Cities, Minn., pp. 198–212.

Robbins, C. S., and A. J. Erskine. 1975. Population trends in non-game birds in North America. Trans. North Am. Wildl. and Nat. Resour. Conf. 40:288–93.

Robbins, C. S. and W. T. VanVelzen. 1967. The breeding bird survey, 1966. U.S. Fish and Wildl. Serv. Spec. Sci. Rep. Wildl. No. 102, 43 pp.

Robbins, C. S., D. Bystrak, and P. H. Geissler. 1986. The breeding bird survey: Its first fifteen years, 1965–1979. U.S. Fish and Wildl. Serv., Res. Pub. 157. Washington, D.C., 196 pp.

Robbins, S. D. 1942. Christmas bird counts near Madison. Pass. Pigeon 4(3):79–81.

Robbins, S. D. 1943. A review of Wisconsin's bird-life in 1942. Pass. Pigeon 5(1):1–5.

Robbins, S. D. 1946. Reminiscences of Wisconsin birds. Pass. Pigeon 8(3):78–83.

Robbins, S. D. 1947a. 1946 in review. Pass. Pigeon 9(2):48–54.

Robbins, S. D. 1947b. The 1947 nesting season. Pass. Pigeon 9(4):133–37.

Robbins, S. D. 1948. 1947 in review. Pass. Pigeon 10(2):69–77.

Robbins, S. D. 1949a. The 1948 nesting season. Pass. Pigeon 11(1):21–28.

Robbins, S. D. 1949b. 1948 in review. Pass. Pigeon 11(2):66–72.

Robbins, S. D. 1950a. 1949 in review. Pass. Pigeon 12(2):58–63.

Robbins, S. D. 1950b. Three rare stragglers in Wisconsin. Pass. Pigeon 12(4):152–55.

Robbins, S. D. 1951. 1950 in review. Pass. Pigeon 13(2):70–74.

Robbins, S. D. 1956. Black Rail sight records. Pass. Pigeon 18(4):171.

Robbins, S. D. 1958. Another glimpse of Superior-land. Pass. Pigeon 20(4):162–67.

Robbins, S. D. 1959a. Fun with fall warblers. Pass. Pigeon 21(2):57–65.

Robbins, S. D. 1959b. A Ruff in Wisconsin. Pass. Pigeon 21(2):73–74.

Robbins, S. D. 1960. 1959 in review. Pass. Pigeon 22(3):133–39.

Robbins, S. D., ed. 1961. Wisconsin's favorite bird haunts. Wis. Soc. Ornithol., Madison, Wis. 77 pp.

Robbins, S. D. 1962. 1960 in review. Pass. Pigeon 24(3):69–79.

Robbins, S. D. 1964a. Ornithological progress in Wisconsin, 1939–1963. Pass. Pigeon 26(1):3–12.

Robbins, S. D. 1964b. The Groove-billed Ani in Wisconsin. Pass. Pigeon 26(1):26–28.

Robbins, S. D. 1966. Wisconsin's summer bird count: 1961–1965. Pass. Pigeon 28(2):47–62.

Robbins, S. D. 1968. Shorebirds deluxe. Pass. Pigeon 30(1):31–32.

Robbins, S. D. 1969. New light on the LeConte's Sparrow. Pass. Pigeon 31(3):267–74.

Robbins, S. D. 1970. Extreme arrival and departure dates. Pass. Pigeon 32(3):83–137.

Robbins, S. D. 1971. Wisconsin breeding bird survey: 1966–1970. Pass. Pigeon 33(3):115–36.

Robbins, S. D. 1972. A Curve-billed Thrasher visits Buffalo City. Pass. Pigeon 34(1):47–49.

Robbins, S. D. 1973. New light on the Cape May Warbler. Pass. Pigeon 35(4):159–61.

Robbins, S. D. 1974a. New light on the Connecticut Warbler. Pass. Pigeon 36(3):110–15.

Robbins, S. D. 1974b. The Willow and Alder Flycatchers in Wisconsin: A preliminary description of summer range. Pass. Pigeon 36(4):147–52.

Robbins, S. D. 1977. The breeding bird survey in Wisconsin, 1966–1975. Pass. Pigeon 39(2):225–47.

Robbins, S. D. 1982. Wisconsin's breeding bird survey results: 1966–1980. Pass. Pigeon 44:97–120.

Robbins, S. D. 1986. Northern woodpeckers visit Taylor County. Pass. Pigeon 48:122–24.

Robbins, S. D. 1989. WSO: The first fifty years. Pass. Pigeon 51:7–17.

Robbins, S. D., and S. T. Robbins. 1956. A glimpse of Superior-land. Pass. Pigeon 18(2):66–73.

Roberts, T. S. 1932. The birds of Minnesota. 2 vols., Univ. Minn. Press, Minneapolis.

Roberts, T. S. 1938. Logbook of Minnesota bird life, 1917–1937. Univ. Minn. Press, Minneapolis, 355 pp.

Rodgers, R. D. 1979. Ruffed Grouse ecology and factors affecting drumming counts in southwestern Wisconsin. MS thesis, Univ. Wis.–Madison, 74 pp.

Rofritz, D. J. 1972. Ecological investigations on waterfowl wintering in the Milwaukee embayment. MS thesis, Univ. Wis.–Milwaukee, 61 pp.

Rogers, N. M. 1936. Records of unusual birds in eastern Wisconsin. Auk 53(2):229–30.

Rogers, N. M. 1953. Wisconsin's first Green-tailed Towhee. Pass. Pigeon 15(3):120–21.

Rosenfield, R. N. 1978. Attacks by nesting Broad-winged Hawks. Pass. Pigeon 40(2):419.

Rosenfield, R. N. 1979. Broad-winged Hawk preys on Saw-whet Owl. Pass. Pigeon 41(2):60.

Rosenfield, R. N., and R. K. Anderson. 1983. Status of the Cooper's Hawk in Wisconsin. Final Rep., Wis. Dep. Nat. Resour., MS, 41 pp.

Ross, D. A. 1987. Birds of the Petenwell Wildlife Area. Pass. Pigeon 49:140–42.

Ross, D. A. and D. G. Follen Sr. 1988. Bald Eagles wintering at the Petenwell Dam, Wisconsin. Pass. Pigeon 50:99–106.

Rossbach, G. B. 1942–1944. Food habits research. Wis. Wildl. Res. 1(3):91–94; 2(1):32–50; 2(2):77–91; 2(3):33–42; 2(4):26–36; 3(1):22–38; 3(2):9–17; 3(3):14–26; 4(1):19–31.

Rossbach, G. B. 1953. Waterfowl food habits. Pp. 159–76 *in* Final report, federal aid waterfowl research project 6-R, ed. F. R. Zimmerman. Wis. Conserv. Dep., Madison.

Rossman, V. C. 1943. Birds banded at Waukesha, Wisconsin, 1933–1942. IBBA News 15(5):33–34.

Rowan, W. 1933. Fifty years of bird migration. Pp. 51–63 *in* Fifty years' progress of American ornithology—1883–1933. Am. Ornithol. Union, Lancaster, Pa.

Ruegger, D. 1945. Nesting ravens. Pass. Pigeon 7(3):59–60.

Ruggles, D. 1836. Geological and miscellaneous notice of the region around Fort Winnebago, Michigan Territory. Am. J. Sci. (New Haven, Conn.) 30:1–8.

Rusch, A. J. 1961. Ross' Goose discovered in Wisconsin. Pass. Pigeon 23(2):49–51.

Sample, D. W. 1989. Grassland birds in southern Wisconsin; habitat preference, population trends, and response to land use changes. M.S. thesis, Univ. Wis.–Madison, 588 pp.

Sample, D. W., and R. M. Hoffman. 1989. Birds of dry and dry-mesic prairies in Wisconsin. Pass. Pigeon 51:195–208.

Sanborn, C. C. 1921. Some summer birds of the Wisconsin woods. Oologist 38(9):119.

Sandburg, E. H. 1968. A study of Dunn's Marsh near Madison. Pass. Pigeon 30(2):79–83.

Sander, P. 1982. Empty skies. Pass. Pigeon 44:133–37.

Sanderson, G. C., ed. 1977. Management of migratory shore and upland game birds in North America. Internatl. Assoc. Fish and Wildl. Agencies, Washington, D.C., 358 pp.

Sargent, T. D. 1962. A study of homing in the Bank Swallow. Auk 79(2):234–46.

"Scaup." 1882. Destruction of pigeons in Wisconsin. Turf, Field and Farm 34(12 June):379.

Scharf, W. C. 1971. Critical nesting and migration areas. U.S. Great Lakes Basin Comm. 44 pp.

Scharf, W. C., and F. Hamerstrom. 1975. A morphological comparison of two harrier populations. Raptor Res. 9(1–2):27–32.

Scharf, W. C., M. Chamberlin, T. C. Erdman, G. W. Shugart, and I. Shanks. 1979. Nesting and migration areas of birds of the U.S. Great Lakes. FWS/OBS–77/2, U.S. Dep. Inter. Fish and Wildl. Serv., Washington, D.C.

Scheer, F. C. 1939. Two White-winged Scoters taken in Sawyer County. Pass. Pigeon 1(12):166.

Schmidt, F. J. W. 1936. Winter food of the Sharp-tailed Grouse and Pinnated Grouse in Wisconsin. Wilson Bull. 48(3):181–203.

Schoenebeck, A. J. 1902. Birds of Oconto County. Privately printed, Kelley Brook, Wis., 51 pp.; reprinted in Oconto County Reporter, Jan., Feb., and Mar., 1903, and in Pass. Pigeon 1(6):79–88 and 1(7):95–105. (For corrections see Hollister 1912.)

Schoenfeld, C. A. 1938. Predators insignificant compared with farmer's mower. Wis. Sportsman 2(12):5.

Schoenfeld, C. A. 1941. The Upland Plover: A native returns. Sports Afield 1941(July):12–13.

Schoenfeld, C. A. 1961. The lesson of Horicon Marsh. Outdoor Am. 1961(Oct.):17–19, 99.

Schoolcraft, H. R. 1834a. Narrative of an expedition through the upper Mississippi to Itasca Lake. Harper and Bros., New York, 307 pp.

Schoolcraft, H. R. 1834b. Historical and scientific sketches of Michigan [Territory]. S. Wells and G. L. Whitney, Detroit, 189 pp.

Schoolcraft, H. R. 1855. Summary narrative of an exploratory expedition to the sources of the Mississippi River in 1820. Lippincott, Grambo and Co., Philadelphia, 596 pp.

Schorger, A. W. 1912–1971. Field notes, consisting of five volumes of handwritten journal entries recording his observations of birds and other wildlife. MS 388 in State Hist. Soc. Wis. manuscript collections, Madison.

Schorger, A. W. 1914. Unusual occurrences at Madison, Wisconsin. Auk 31(2):256. (Includes LeConte's Sparrow collected.)

Schorger, A. W. 1915a. LeConte's Sparrow in Wisconsin. Auk 32(1):101–2.

Schorger, A. W. 1915b. Blue-gray Gnatcatcher nesting in Wisconsin. Auk 32(1):106.

Schorger, A. W. 1917. Notes from Madison, Wisconsin. Auk 34:219. (Includes Red-throated Loon and Harris' Sparrow.)

Schorger, A. W. 1918. European Widgeon at Madison, Wisconsin. Auk 35(1):74–75.

Schorger, A. W. 1920. Bird notes on the Wisconsin River. Auk 37(1):143–44. (Includes Prothonotary Warbler on the Wisconsin River.)

Schorger, A. W. 1922a. Defense note of a chickadee. Auk 39(3):423–24.

Schorger, A. W. 1922b. Notes on birds of Madison, Wisconsin, and vicinity. Auk 39(4):574–75. (Includes Nelson's Sparrow and as many as 1,000 cormorants.)

Schorger, A. W. 1924a. Notes from Madison, Wisconsin. Auk 40(1):169. (Includes wintering bluebirds, crossbills, and Tufted Titmouse.)

Schorger, A. W. 1924b. White-eyed Vireo at Madison, Wisconsin. Auk 40(2):347.

Schorger, A. W. 1925a. Some summer birds of Lake Owen, Bayfield County, Wisconsin. Auk 42(1):64–70.

Schorger, A. W. 1925b. The Barn Owl (*Tyto pratincola*) breeding at Madison, Wisconsin. Auk 42(1):131.

Schorger, A. W. 1926. Notes from Madison, Wisconsin. Auk 43(4):556–57. (Includes White-winged Scoter, Long-billed Dowitcher, Northern Phalarope, White Pelican.)

Schorger, A. W. 1927a. Notes on the distribution of some Wisconsin birds. Part 1. Auk 44(2):235–40. (Includes Golden-winged Warbler and Mockingbird.)

Schorger, A. W. 1927b. Notes from Madison, Wisconsin. Auk 44(2):261–62. (Includes Stilt Sandpiper, Goshawk, and Long-billed Dowitcher.)

Schorger, A. W. 1928. Notes from Madison, Wisconsin. Auk 45(1):106. (Includes European Widgeon and Northern Phalarope.)

Schorger, A. W. 1929a. Notes from Madison, Wisconsin. Auk 46(2):250. (Includes Saw-whet Owl.)

Schorger, A. W. 1929b. The birds of Dane County, Wisconsin. Trans. Wis. Acad. Sci., Arts, Lett. 24:457–90.

Schorger, A. W. 1930a. Notes from Madison, Wisconsin. Auk 47(3):423.

Schorger, A. W. 1930b. The migration of birds. Wis. Arbor and Bird Day Annu. 1930:56–62.

Schorger, A. W. 1931a. The birds of Dane County, Wisconsin. Trans. Wis. Acad. Sci., Arts, Lett. 26:1–60.

Schorger, A. W. 1931b. Notes from Wisconsin. Auk 48(2):282–83. (Includes American Scoter, Northern Phalarope, Saw-whet Owl, Olive-sided Flycatcher, White-winged Crossbill, and Gambel's Sparrow.)

Schorger, A. W. 1931c. Arkansas Kingbird at Roxbury, Wisconsin. Auk 48(4):603.

Schorger, A. W. 1931d. Prairie Marsh Wren wintering near Madison, Wisconsin. Auk 48(4):614–15.

Schorger, A. W. 1932a. Franklin's Gull at Madison, Wisconsin. Auk 49(2):220.

Schorger, A. W. 1932b. Notes from Madison, Wisconsin. Auk 49:493–94. (Includes Bewick's Wren, Bohemian Waxwing, American Egret, and Louisiana Waterthrush.)

Schorger, A. W. 1934a. Notes from Wisconsin. Auk 51(2):254–55. (Includes American Egret and Mockingbird.)

Schorger, A. W. 1934b. Notes on the distribution of some Wisconsin birds. Part 2, Brewer's Blackbird. Auk 51(4):482–86.

Schorger, A. W. 1934c. Notes from the Madison, Wisconsin, region. Auk 51(4):533–34. (Includes Hudsonian Godwit, Little Blue Heron, and Pigeon Hawk.)

Schorger, A. W. 1937a. Canada Jay breeding in Wisconsin. Auk 54(3):392–93.

Schorger, A. W. 1937b. The great Wisconsin Passenger Pigeon nesting of 1871. Proc. Linnaean Soc., New York, 48:1–26; reprinted *in* Silent wings—a memorial to the Passenger Pigeon, Wis. Soc. Ornithol., Madison, 1947, pp. 26–38.

Schorger, A. W. 1938. The last Passenger Pigeon killed in Wisconsin. Auk 55(3):531–32.

Schorger, A. W. 1939a. A brief bibliography of Wisconsin ornithology. Pass. Pigeon 1(11):151–53.

Schorger, A. W. 1939b. Arkansas Kingbird in Wisconsin. Auk 56(1):86.

Schorger, A. W. 1939c. Spring flight of the Golden Plover at Madison, Wisconsin. Auk 56(4):475.

Schorger, A. W. 1939d. Notes from Wisconsin. Auk 56(4):483. (Includes Holboell's Grebe, Piping Plover, and Richardson's Owl at Hayward.)

Schorger, A. W. 1940. The Arctic Three-toed Woodpecker as a breeding bird in Wisconsin. Wilson Bull. 52(3):209.

Schorger, A. W. 1941a. The Bronzed Grackle's method of opening acorns. Wilson Bull. 53(4):238–40.

Schorger, A. W. 1941b. The crow and raven in early Wisconsin. Wilson Bull. 53(2):103–6.

Schorger, A. W. 1942a. The Wild Turkey in early Wisconsin. Wilson Bull. 54(3):173–82.

Schorger, A. W. 1942b. A clue to Prairie Chicken mortality. Pass. Pigeon 4(3):83.

Schorger, A. W. 1942c. Extinct and endangered mammals and birds of the upper Great Lakes region. Trans. Wis. Acad. Sci., Arts, Lett. 34:23–44; reprinted in part in Pass. Pigeon 5(2):35–39.

Schorger, A. W. 1943. The Prairie Chicken and Sharp-tailed Grouse in early Wisconsin. Trans. Wis. Acad. Sci., Arts, Lett. 35:1–59.

Schorger, A. W. 1944a. Brown Pelican in Wisconsin. Auk 61(2):305.

Schorger, A. W. 1944b. The quail in early Wisconsin. Trans. Wis. Acad. Sci., Arts, Lett. 36:77–103.

Schorger, A. W. 1944c. A list of migrating birds prepared by A. L. Kumlien in 1869. Pass. Pigeon 6(1):13–16.

Schorger, A. W. 1945a. The Ruffed Grouse in early Wisconsin. Trans. Wis. Acad. Sci., Arts, Lett. 37:35–90.

Schorger, A. W. 1945b. The Golden Eagle in Wisconsin. Pass. Pigeon 7(2):48–51.

Schorger, A. W. 1946. Some Wisconsin naturalists—biographies of eight naturalists who made outstanding contributions to Wisconsin's early-day ornithology. Wis. Soc. Ornithol., Madison; reprinted from Pass. Pigeon, Vols. 6–8.

Schorger, A. W. 1947a. Two early Wisconsin bird lists. Pass. Pigeon 9(2):65–67.

Schorger, A. W. 1947b. The introduction of pheasants into Wisconsin. Pass. Pigeon 9(3):101–2; reprinted in Wis. Conserv. Bull. 13(2):10–11.

Schorger, A. W. 1948a. *Pinicola enucleator eschatosus* at Madison, Wisconsin. Auk 65(2):308. (Regarding a Newfoundland-type Pine Grosbeak.)

Schorger, A. W. 1948b. Aldo Leopold obituary. Auk 65(4):648–49.

Schorger, A. W. 1948c. Changing wildlife conditions in Wisconsin. Wis. Conserv. Bull. 13(6):53–60.

Schorger, A. W. 1950. Blue-gray Gnatcatcher, *Polioptial c. caerulea*, in Sawyer County, Wisconsin. Auk 67:394.

Schorger, A. W. 1951a. Revisions for "The Birds of Wisconsin" by L. Kumlien and N. Hollister. Wis. Soc. Ornithol., Madison, 122 pp.; reprinted from Pass. Pigeon, Vols. 10–12.

Schorger, A. W. 1951b. The migration of the Passenger Pigeon in Wisconsin. Pass. Pigeon 13(3):101–4.

Schorger, A. W. 1951c. The migration of the Passenger Pigeon in Wisconsin. Pass. Pigeon 13(4):144–46.

Schorger, A. W. 1954a. A study of road kills. Pass. Pigeon 16(2):53–55.

Schorger, A. W. 1954b. The White Pelican in early Wisconsin. Pass. Pigeon 16(4):136–40.

Schorger, A. W. 1954c. The wintering meadowlarks of Dane County, Wisconsin. Auk 71(1):87–88.

Schorger, A. W. 1954d. Color phases of the Screech Owl between Madison, Wisconsin, and Freeport, Illinois. Auk 71(2):205.

Schorger, A. W. 1955. The Passenger Pigeon—its natural history and extinction. Univ. Wis. Press, Madison, 424 pp.

Schorger, A. W. 1958. Extirpation of a flock of Wild Turkeys in Adams County, Wisconsin. Pass. Pigeon 20(4):170–71.

Schorger, A. W. 1960. Bibliography of Wisconsin ornithology. Pp. 27–32 *in* Wisconsin birds—a checklist with migration graphs, ed. N. R. Barger. 3d ed., Wis. Soc. Ornithol., Madison.

Schorger, A. W. 1962. Wildlife restoration in Wisconsin. Trans. Wis. Acad. Sci., Arts, Lett. 51:21–30.

Schorger, A. W. 1964. The Trumpeter Swan as a breeding bird in Minnesota, Wisconsin, Illinois and Indiana. Wilson Bull. 76(4):331–38.

Schorger, A. W. 1966. The Wild Turkey—its history and domestication. Univ. Okla. Press, Norman, 625 pp.

Schorger, A. W. 1968. Breeding of the Trumpeter Swan at the Madison, Wisconsin, lakes. Wilson Bull. 80(2):228–29.

Schorger, A. W. 1969. Black-throated Gray Warbler (*Dendroica nigrescens*) at Madison, Wisconsin. Auk 86(4):767.

Schultz, T. R. 1987. Some notes on the Milwaukee Mew Gulls. Pass. Pigeon 49:46–48.

Schultz, T. R., and J. L. Baughman. 1985. Thayer's Gull in Milwaukee. Pass. Pigeon 47:151–53.

Scientific Areas Preservation Council. 1975. Breeding bird surveys on scientific areas, 1971–1974. Wis. Dep. Nat. Resour., Madison, 96 pp.

Scott, W. E. 1937–1938. Conservation history [Wisconsin]. Wis. Conserv. Bull. 2(3):10–15; 2(4):14–20; 2(5):23–30; 2(6):27–37; 2(9):26–31; 3(4):26–37.

Scott, W. E. 1939a. Grundtvig's museum specimens. Pass. Pigeon 1(4):57.

Scott, W. E. 1939b. Wisconsin Passenger Pigeon specimens. Pass. Pigeon 1(9):123.

Scott, W. E. 1939c. Recent southern Wisconsin Prairie Chicken reports. Pass. Pigeon 1(9):130–33.

Scott, W. E. 1939d. Spread of the starling in Wisconsin. Pass. Pigeon 1(10):139–43.

Scott, W. E. 1940a. Christmas census [1939] finds 92 different birds in Wisconsin. Pass. Pigeon 2(1):1, 3–11.

Scott, W. E. 1940b. Wildlife protection and restoration in Wisconsin. Outdoors 1940(May):10–11, 34.

Scott, W. E. 1940c. Department begins game research. Wis. Conserv. Bull. 5(10):11–12.

Scott, W. E. 1942. Some Wisconsin bird specimens submitted to the U.S. National Museum. Pass. Pigeon 4(4):103–5.

Scott, W. E. 1943. The Canada Spruce Grouse in Wisconsin. Pass. Pigeon 5(3):61–72.

Scott, W. E., ed. 1947a. Silent wings—a memorial to the Passenger Pigeon. Wis. Soc. Ornithol., Madison, 42 pp.

Scott, W. E. 1947b. The Greater Prairie Chicken. Wis. Conserv. Bull. 12(1):23–27.

Scott, W. E., ed. 1947–1952. Activities progress reports. Wis. Conserv. Dep., Madison.

Scott, W. E. 1948. The public's part in Wisconsin conservation history. Wis. Conserv. Bull. 13(6):84–90.

Scott, W. E. 1955. The management of predacious and fish-eating birds in Wisconsin. Pass. Pigeon 17(2):51–58.

Scott, W. E. 1964. Quarter-century history of the society [Wisconsin Society for Ornithology]. Pass. Pigeon 26(1):28–62.

Scott, W. E. 1967. Conservation's first century in Wisconsin: Landmark dates and people. Pp. 14–42 *in* The quest for quality in Wisconsin., ed. N. C. Camp. Proc. Conservation Centennial Symp. Consumer Educ. Progr. Univ. Wis.–Madison.

Scott, W. E. 1977. Protecting non-game birds in Wisconsin. Pass. Pigeon 39(3):279–84.

Scott, W. E., and G. M. Scott. 1979. Prologue and first 56 years. Pp. 1–76 *in* Wisconsin conservation law enforcement: A centennial chronology. Wis. Dep. Nat. Resour., Madison.

Scott, W. E., R. L. Hine, E. L. Cooper, and A. W. Jorgensen. 1956. The wildlife resource of Wisconsin. Pp. 27–42 *in* Natural resources of Wisconsin, Wis. Conserv. Dep., Madison, Wis.

Semo, L. 1989. The 1988–89 invasion of Great Gray Owls into Wisconsin. Pass. Pigeon 51:331–33.

Sennett, G. B. 1884. Black-throated Auk (*Synthliborhamphus antiquus*) in Wisconsin. Auk 1(1):98–100.

Septon, G. A. 1987. Wisconsin's Peregrine Falcon recovery program—the first year. Pass. Pigeon 49:165–76.

Septon, G. A. and A. Wendt. 1988. A year of firsts and frustrations for Milwaukee's peregrines. Pass. Pigeon 50:297–304.

Sercomb, S. R. 1848. List of birds found in Wisconsin Territory. MS in State Hist. Soc. Wis. manuscript collections, file 1848 Mar., Madison.

Severson, H. P. 1905. The Kentucky Warbler at Winneconne, Wisconsin. Auk 22(3):314.

Sharp, B. 1971. Heavy mortality of migrating birds at Madison's TV towers. Pass. Pigeon 33(4):203–4.

Shaub, B. M., and M. E. Shaub. 1956. The Evening Grosbeak survey. Pass. Pigeon 18(1):3–15.

Sherman, A. R. 1909. Five notes from the upper Mississippi Valley. Wilson Bull. 21(3):155–58.

Sherman, A. R. 1913. The increase of the cardinal in the upper Mississippi Valley. Wilson Bull. 25(3):150–51.

Sherwood, G. A. 1968. Factors limiting production and expansion of local populations of Canada Geese. Pp. 73–85 *in* Canada Goose management, ed. R. L. Hine and C. Schoenfeld. Dembar Educ. Res. Serv., Madison, Wis.

Shiras. G., III. 1921. The wildlife of Lake Superior, past and present. Natl. Geo. Mag. 40(2):113–204.

Shrosbree, G. 1921. Collecting for the museum's new series of bird groups. Milwaukee Public Mus. Yearb. 1:28–36.

Simonds, S. L. 1913. A record of fifty-five bird's nests found near

Beaver Lake, in the summer of 1912. Wis. Arbor and Bird Day Annu. 1913:90–92.

Simpson, J. A. 1955. A Yellow-crowned Night Heron nesting record for Wisconsin. Pass. Pigeon 17(4):152–53.

Simpson, Mrs. M. L. 1914. Harris' Sparrow in Wisconsin. Bird-Lore 16(3):282–83.

Sindelar, C. R., Jr. 1966. A comparison of five consecutive Snowy Owl invasions in Wisconsin. Pass. Pigeon 28(3):103–8.

Sindelar, C. R., Jr. 1968. Mockingbirds nest at Stevens Point. Pass. Pigeon 30(1):18.

Sindelar, C. R., Jr. 1971a. Wisconsin Osprey survey. Pass. Pigeon 33(2):79–88.

Sindelar, C. R., Jr. 1971b. Are we losing the Osprey? Wis. Conserv. Bull. 36(2):20–22.

Sindelar, C. R., Jr. 1977. Reproduction of Wisconsin Ospreys. Pp. 167–73 in Trans. North Am. Osprey Res. Conf., ed. J. C. Ogden. U.S. Dep. Natl. Inter. Park Serv. Ser. 2.

Sindelar, C. R., Jr. 1981. Wisconsin's second recorded Merlin nest. Pass. Pigeon 43(3):107–8.

Sindelar, C. R., Jr. 1985. Wisconsin Bald Eagle breeding survey, 1984. The Eagle 14(1):15–19.

Skavlem, H. L. 1888. Unusual numbers of Goshawks and Barred Owls. Ornithol. and Oologist 14(1):13.

Skavlem, H. L. 1890. Letter on duck shooting—Lake Koshkonong. For. and Stream 34(13):249.

Skavlem, H. L. 1912a. Nature study and bird lore. By the Wayside 13(5):33–35; 13(8):49–51.

Skavlem, H. L. 1912b. Recollections of bird-life in pioneer days. By the Wayside 13(10):57–59.

Small, R. J. 1985. Mortality and dispersal of Ruffed Grouse in central Wisconsin. MS thesis, Univ. Wis.–Madison, 43 pp.

Smith, C. W. 1915. Birds of Wisconsin. Pp. 94–115 in Wisconsin Arbor and Bird Day Manual. Wis. Dep. Public Instruction. Cantwell Print. Co. Madison.

Smith, J. R. 1941. Quail census project completes twelfth consecutive year. Wis. Conserv. Bull. 6(8):42–43.

Smith, J. R. 1942. Horicon Marsh wildlife area. Wis. Conserv. Bull. 7(10):5–10.

Smith, J. R., and H. C. Jordahl. 1959. Two decades on Wisconsin's public hunting and fishing grounds program. Trans. North Am. Wildl. Conf., 2–4 Mar. 24:322–36.

Smith, O. W. 1921. Evening Grosbeaks nesting in Bayfield County, Wisconsin. Bird-Lore 23(2):86–87.

Smith, T. J. 1975. The Wisconsin duck harvest, 1961–1970, as determined from the wing collection surveys. MS thesis, Univ. Wis.–Stevens Point, 351 pp.

Smith, W. M. 1947a. Weather and bird migration. IBBA News 19(1):5–7.

Smith, W. M. 1947b. Orchard Orioles at 44°18′ north, 87°33′42″ west. Pass. Pigeon 9(1):8–16.

Smyth, M. L. 1980. Urban bird populations in Madison, Wisconsin. PhD diss., Univ. Wis.–Madison, 175 pp.

Snyder, L. L. 1943. The Snowy Owl migration of 1941–1942. Wilson Bull. 55(1):8–10.

Snyder, W. E. 1896. Yellow-breasted Chats at Beaver Dam, Wisconsin. Osprey 1(4):53.

Snyder, W. E. 1897. Double-crested Cormorant. Osprey 1(6):82.

Snyder, W. E. 1902. Brief notes on some of the rare birds of Dodge County, Wisconsin. Bull. Wis. Nat. Hist. Soc. 2(2):109–12.

Snyder, W. E. 1905. The Gray Gyrfalcon in Wisconsin. Auk 22(4):413–14.

Snyder, W. E. 1907. The late occurrence of the King Rail (Rallus elegans) in Wisconsin. Auk 24(2):217.

Snyder, W. E. 1913. The Evening Grosbeak in Wisconsin. Auk 30(2):275.

Snyder, W. E. 1925. Blackbirds. Oologist 44:16.

Snyder, W. E. 1927. The Barn Owl in Wisconsin. Auk 44(2):251.

Society of Tympanuchus Cupido Pinnatus, Ltd. 1962. Prairie Grouse! Milwaukee, 20 pp.

Sordahl, T. 1973. Bird life in a boreal sphagnum bog at the Audubon camp, Wisconsin. IBBA News 45(3):97–100.

Soulen, T. K. 1955. May Day at Cedar Grove. Pass. Pigeon 17(1):27–29.

Southern, W. E. 1960a. New breeding locality for LeConte's Sparrow. Pass. Pigeon 22(1):28–29.

Southern, W. E. 1960b. The birds of Hunt Hill Sanctuary. Pass. Pigeon 22(2):59–66.

Southern, W. E. 1962a. Notes on Cerulean Warbler life cycle. Pass. Pigeon 24(1):9–11.

Southern, W. E. 1962b. Distribution of the Blue-winged and Golden-winged Warblers in Wisconsin. Pass. Pigeon 24(1):35–43.

Southern, W. E. 1980. Colonial waterbirds of the Great Lakes region: Population trends and management considerations. Pp. 28–38 in Proc. Ill. Non-game Wildl. Symp. comp. V. M. Kleen, 3 Nov. 1979 Ill. Valley Community Coll., Oglesby. Periodic Rep. 15, Non-game Sect. Div. Wildl. Res., Ill. Dep. Conserv., Springfield, Ill.

Sprunt, A., IV. 1969. Population trends of the Bald Eagle in North America. Pp. 347–51 in Peregrine Falcon populations: Their biology and decline, ed. J. J. Hickey. Univ. Wis. Press, Madison.

Sprunt, A., IV, and R. L. Cunningham. 1962. Continental Bald Eagle project, a progress report. Pass. Pigeon 24(3):63–68.

Sprunt, A., IV, W. B. Robertson, S. Postupalsky, R. J. Hensel, C. E. Knoder, and F. J. Ligas. 1973. Comparative productivity of six Bald Eagle populations. Trans. North Am. Wildl. and Nat. Resour. Conf. 38:96–106.

Starin, D. 1880. The Canvasbacks and Lake Koshkonong. Chicago Field 8(1).

Steele, R. C. 1955. Upper Mississippi River Wildlife and Fish refuge. Minn. Conserv. Volunteer 18(105):28–36.

Steffen, J. F. 1979. 1979 winter bird count. Woodland Dunes Duneslett. 18:6–7.

Steffen, J. F. 1984. Turkey Vultures breeding in unused farm buildings. Pass. Pigeon 46:101.

Stein, R. C. 1963. Isolating mechanisms between populations of Traill's Flycatchers. Proc. Am. Phil. Soc. 107(1):21–50.

Steinke, H. A. 1959. Marsh management. Wis. Conserv. Bull. 24(3):17–20.

Stier, J. C. 1978. The economics of a dual externality: Agriculture and Canada geese in Wisconsin. PhD diss., Univ. Wis.–Madison, 329 pp.

Stierle, J. W. 1913. Great Blue Heron. Oologist 30(9):150–51.

Stierle, J. W. 1915. Long-eared Owls. Oologist 32(1):12.

Stoddard, H. L., Sr. 1917. Notes on a few of the rarer birds of Sauk and Dane counties, Wisconsin. Auk 34(1):63–67.

Stoddard, H. L., Sr. 1921a. The nesting of the Duck Hawk in south-central Wisconsin. Wilson Bull. 33(4):161–65.

Stoddard, H. L., Sr. 1921b. Bird collections of the Milwaukee Public Museum. Wilson Bull. 33(4):197.

Stoddard, H. L., Sr. 1921c. A spring collecting trip to the Wisconsin River. Milwaukee Public Mus. Yearb. 1:36–43.

Stoddard, H. L., Sr. 1922a. Bird notes from southern Wisconsin. Wilson Bull. 34(2):67–79.

Stoddard, H. L., Sr. 1922b. The European Starling in Milwaukee. Milwaukee Public Mus. Yearb. 2:185–86.

Stoddard, H. L., Sr. 1923a. Some Wisconsin shore-bird records. Auk 40(2):319–21.

Stoddard, H. L., Sr. 1923b. The Gyrfalcon in Wisconsin. Auk 40(2):325.

Stoddard, H. L., Sr. 1923c. Notes on a sparrow roost, and the arrival of the starling in Wisconsin. Auk 40(3):537–39.

Stoddard, H. L., Sr. 1931. The Bobwhite quail: Its habits, preservation and increase. Scribner's, New York, 559 pp.

Stoddard, H. L., Sr. 1947. Reminiscences of Wisconsin birding. Pass. Pigeon 9(4):123–29.

Stoddard, H. L., Sr. 1969. Memoirs of a naturalist. Univ. Okla. Press, Norman, 303 pp.

Stoddard, H. L., Sr. 1978. Some Wisconsin original field notes deposited in the manuscript collection of State Historical Society of Wisconsin.

Stokes, A. W. 1950. Breeding behavior of the goldfinch. Wilson Bull. 62(3):106–27.

Stollberg, B. 1949. Competition of American Coots and shoal-water ducks for food. J. Wildl. Manage. 13(4):423–24.

Stollberg, B. 1950. Food habits of shoal-water ducks on Horicon Marsh, Wisconsin. J. Wildl. Manage. 14(2):214–17.

Stollberg, B., and R. L. Hine. 1952. Food habits studies of Ruffed Grouse, pheasant, quail and mink. Tech. Wildl. Bull. No. 4, Wis. Conserv. Dep., Madison, 22 pp.

Stone, N. R., and J. Birkhahn. 1958. Goose management in northern Wisconsin. Wis. Conserv. Bull. 23(5):20–24.

Strehlow, E. W. 1976. Whitnall Park birds. Wehr Nat. Cent. Milwaukee Cty. Park Comm., Hales Corners, Wis., 32 pp.

Strehlow, E. W., T. C. Erdman, J. P. Jacobs, T. Baumann, and I. Baumann. 1978. Brown County birds. Neville Public Mus., Green Bay, Wis., 38 pp.

Strelitzer, C. L. 1952. 1951 in review. Pass. Pigeon 14(3):102–6.

Strelitzer, C. L. 1953. 1952 in review. Pass. Pigeon 15(2):63–67.

Strelitzer, C. L. 1986. House Finch. Pass. Pigeon 48:177–78.

Strohmeyer, D. L. 1976. Wisconsin breeding records of unusual waterfowl species. Pass. Pigeon 38(3):106–8.

Strong, P. I. V. 1988. Changes in Wisconsin's Common Loon population. Pass. Pigeon 50:287–90.

Strong, R. M. 1891. Song Sparrows rearing kingbirds. For. and Stream 36:104–5.

Strong, R. M. 1897. Notes from North Greenfield, Wisconsin. Wilson Bull. 9(16):59–60.

Strong, R. M. 1912. Some observations on the life-history of the Red-breasted Merganser, *Mergus serrator*. Auk 29(4):479–88.

Strong, R. M. 1914. On the habits and behavior of the Herring Gull, *Larus argentatus*. Auk 31(1):22–49; 31(2):178–99.

Strong, R. M. 1915. On the habits and behavior of the Herring Gull. Pp. 470–509 in Smithsonian Rep. for 1914. Washington, D.C.

Strong, R. M. 1923. Further observations on the habits and behavior of the Herring Gull. Auk 40(4):609–21.

Strong, R. M. 1924. Gull and tern banding on the Great Lakes during the season of 1924. Wilson Bull. 36(3):141–43.

Strong, R. M. 1939–1959. A bibliography of birds. Zool. Ser. Field Mus. Nat. Hist., Vol. 25, Parts 1 and 2 (Publ. 442 and 457, 1939); Part 3 (Publ. 581, 1946); Part 4 (Publ. 870, 1959).

Sugden, E. 1943. Some rarer birds seen in Richland County. Pass. Pigeon 5(1):16.

Swanberg, C. D. 1982. Demographic and behavioral characteristics of Redhead ducks nesting in Wisconsin. MS thesis, Univ. Wis.–Madison, 63 pp.

Swengel, A. B. 1987a. Detecting Northern Saw-whet Owls. Pass. Pigeon 49:121–26.

Swengel, A. B. 1987b. The habits of the Northern Saw-whet Owl. Pass. Pigeon 49:127–33.

Swengel, S. R., and A. B. Swengel. 1986. An auditory census of Northern Saw-whet Owls (*Aegolius acadicus*) in Sauk County, Wisconsin. Pass. Pigeon 48:119–21.

Swenk, M. H., and O. A. Stevens. 1929. Harris' Sparrow and the study of it by trapping. Wilson Bull. 41(3):129–77.

Swift, E. F. 1952. Modification of forest practices in the lake states for wildlife habitat betterment. J. For. 51(6):440–43.

Swift, E. F. 1953. The road to wildlife abundance in Wisconsin. Wis. Conserv. Bull. 18(3):14–28.

Taber, R. D. 1947. The Dickcissel in Wisconsin. Pass. Pigeon 9(2):39–46.

Taber, R. D. 1949. Observations on the breeding behavior of the Ring-necked Pheasant. Condor 51(4):153–75.

Tans, W. E. 1976. The presettlement vegetation of Columbia County, Wisconsin, in the 1830's. Tech. Bull. 90, Dep. Nat. Resour., Madison, 19 pp.

Taylor, Mrs. H. J. 1936. Thure Ludwig Theodor Kumlien. Wilson Bull. 48:86–93.

Taylor, J. W., and R. J. Irwin, eds. 1980. Fish and wildlife for the 1980's and beyond. Suppl. to Wis. Nat. Resour. 4(3), 38 pp.

Taylor, W. 1917. Kirtland's Warbler in Madison, Wisconsin. Auk 34(3):343.

Taylor, W. 1919. Further record of the European Widgeon at Madison, Wisconsin. Auk 36(2):277.

Taylor, W. 1920. Some sparrow notes from Madison, Wisconsin. Auk 37(3):299–300.

Taylor, W. 1922a. Some records from the Madison, Wisconsin, region for spring of 1921. Auk 39(2):273–74. (Includes Krider's Hawk, Acadian Flycatcher, Clay-colored, Lark, and Harris' Sparrows, Bewick's Wren, Yellow-breasted Chat, and Duck Hawk nesting sites.)

Taylor, W. 1922b. Two nesting notes for the Madison, Wisconsin, region. Auk 39(4):575. (Includes nesting record of Bell's Vireo and Bewick's Wren.)

Taylor, W. 1923. Some 1922 records of birds of the Madison, Wisconsin, territory. Auk 40(2):339–40. (Includes Holboell's Grebe, Caspian Tern, Marbled Godwit, Smith's Longspur, and Nelson's Sparrow.)

Taylor, W. 1926a. Some records from the Madison, Wisconsin, region, 1923, 1924, and 1925. Auk 43(2):250–51. (Includes Baird's and White-rumped Sandpipers and Western Willet.)

Taylor, W. 1926b. Additional records from the Madison, Wisconsin, region. Auk 43(3):380–83. (Includes Blue-winged and Kentucky Warblers, LeConte's, Nelson's, Harris', and Clay-colored Sparrows, Goshawk, Krider's Hawk, and Peregrine Falcon.)

Temple, S. A., Ed. 1978. Endangered birds: Management techniques for preserving threatened species. Univ. Wis. Press, Madison, 466 pp.

Temple, S. A. 1982. A Wisconsin bird survey based on field checklist information: A W.S.O. research project. Pass. Pigeon 44:56–60.

Temple, S. A., and J. R. Cary. 1987a. Wisconsin birds: A seasonal and geographic guide. Univ. Wis. Press, Madison, 364 pp.

Temple, S. A., and J. R. Cary. 1987b. Climatic effects on year-to-year variations in migration phenology: A W.S.O. research project. Pass. Pigeon 49:70–75.

Temple, S. A., and J. T. Harris. 1985. Birds of the Apostle Islands. Wis. Soc. Ornith., Harland, Wis., 62 pp.

Temple, S. A., and A. J. Temple. 1984. Results of using checklist-records to monitor Wisconsin birds: A W.S.O. research project. Pass. Pigeon 46:61–71.

Temple, S. A., and A. J. Temple. 1986a. Geographic distributions and patterns of relative abundance of Wisconsin birds: A W.S.O. research project. Pass. Pigeon 48:58–68.

Temple, S. A., and A. J. Temple. 1986b. Year-to-year changes in the abundance of Wisconsin birds: Results of the W.S.O. checklist project. Pass. Pigeon 48:158–62.

Temple, S. A., M. J. Mossman, and B. Ambuel. 1979. The ecology and management of avian communities in mixed hardwood-coniferous forests. Pp. 132–53 in Workshop Proc., Management of North Central and Northeastern Forests for Nongame Birds. U.S. Dep. Agric. For. Serv., Gen. Tech. Rep. NC-51, St. Paul, Minn.

Terborgh, J. 1989. Where have all the birds gone? Princeton Univ. Press, Princeton, N.J., 207 pp.

Tessen, D. D., Ed. 1976. Wisconsin's favorite bird haunts. Rev. ed., Wis. Soc. Ornithol., Green Bay, 334 pp.

Tessen, D. D. 1979a. Reflections on a birding weekend. Pass. Pigeon 41(3):120–23.

Tessen, D. D., Ed. 1979b. Wisconsin's favorite bird haunts. Suppl. ed., Wis. Soc. Ornithol., De Pere, pp. 335–424.

Thiel, R. P. 1975. Notes on Short-eared Owl hunting activities. Pass. Pigeon 37(4):184–86.

Thiel, R. P. 1976. Activity patterns and food habits of southeastern Wisconsin Turkey Vultures. Pass. Pigeon 38(4):137–43.

Thiel, R. P. 1977. The status of the Turkey Vulture in southeast Wisconsin. Pass. Pigeon 39(1):213–19.

Thiel, R. P. 1978a. The distribution of the Three-toed Woodpeckers in Wisconsin. Pass. Pigeon 40(4):477–88.

Thiel, R. P. 1978b. Common Loon breeding activity in the Sandhill and Meadow Valley wildlife areas. Pass. Pigeon 40(4):512–13.

Thiel, R. P. 1985. Snow depth affects local abundance of wintering Rough-legged Hawks. Pass. Pigeon 47:129–30.

Thompson, D. H. 1977. Declines in populations of colonial waterbirds nesting within the floodplain of the upper Mississippi River. Pp. 26–37 in Proc., Colonial Waterbird Group Conf. 20–23 Oct. Northern Illinois University Press, DeKalb, Ill.

Thompson, D. H. 1978. Feeding areas of Great Blue Herons and Great Egrets nesting within the floodplain of the upper Mississippi River. Pp. 202–13 in Proc., Colonial Waterbird Group Conf., Oct. Am. Mus. Nat. Hist., New York.

Thompson, D. H., and M. C. Landin, 1978. An aerial survey of waterbird colonies along the upper Mississippi River and their relationship to dredged material deposits. Tech. Rep. D-78-13, U.S. Army Eng. Waterways Exp. Stn., Vicksburg, Miss., 105 pp.

Thompson, D. Q. 1959a. Our investment in the Prairie Chicken. Pass. Pigeon 21(2):51–57.

Thompson, D. Q. 1959b. Biological investigation of the upper Fox River. Spec. Wildl. Rep. No. 2, Wis. Conserv. Dep., Madison, 41 pp.

Thompson, D. Q. 1960. Historic waterways revisited—the upper Fox River. Wis. Acad. Rev. 7(4):145–49.

Thompson, D. R. 1952a. The Bobwhite as a wildlife resource in Wisconsin. Wis. Conserv. Bull. 17(4):7–9.

Thompson, D. R. 1952b. Conservation of the Bobwhite. Pass. Pigeon 14(1):3–6.

Thompson, D. R., and R. D. Taber. 1948. Reference tables for dating events in nesting of Ring-necked Pheasants, Bobwhite quail, and Hungarian Partridge by aging of broods. J. Wildl. Manage. 12(1):14–19.

Thompson, J. B. 1916. Tales of duck and goose shooting. Press of Eastman Bros., Chicago, 167 pp.

Thomsen, H. P. 1944. Ornithological extracts from an ecological survey of the University Bay region, spring, 1943. Pass. Pigeon 6(1):3–13.

Throne, A. L., comp. 1925. Bird field list for the Milwaukee region. Milwaukee Public Mus.

Throne, A. L. 1941. A nesting study of the eastern Hermit Thrush. Pass. Pigeon 3(2):13–16.

Throne, A. L. 1945. A nesting study of the eastern Song Sparrow. Pass. Pigeon 7(4):99–105.

Tilghman, N. G. 1977. Problems in sampling songbird populations in southeastern Wisconsin woodlots. MS thesis, Univ. Wis.–Madison, 150 pp.

Tilghman, N. G. 1979. The search for the Kirtland's Warbler in Wisconsin. Pass. Pigeon 41(1):16–24.

Tilghman, N. G. 1980. The Black Tern survey, 1979. Pass. Pigeon 42(1):1–8.

Toepfer, J. E. 1977. Prairie Chicken reintroduction program in northwestern Wisconsin. Proc. Prairie Grouse Tech. Counc. 13–15 Sept., Pierre, S. Dak. Wis. Dep. Nat. Resour., mimeo., 12 pp.

Trainer, D. O., and G. W. Fischer. 1963. Fatal trematodiasis of coots. J. Wildl. Manage. 27(3):483–86.

Trainer, D. O., and R. A. Hunt. 1965a. Lead poisoning of waterfowl in Wisconsin. J. Wildl. Manage. 29(1):95–103.

Trainer, D. O., and R. A. Hunt. 1965b. Lead poisoning of Whistling Swans in Wisconsin. Avian Dis. 9(2):252–64.

Trainer, D. O., and L. Karstad. 1960. Salt poisoning in Wisconsin wildlife. J. Am. Vet. Med. Assoc. 136(1):14–18.

Trainer, D. O., C. S. Schildt, R. A. Hunt, and L. R. Jahn. 1962. The presence and prevalence of *Leucocytozoon simondi* among some Wisconsin waterfowl. J. Wildl. Manage. 26(2):137–43.

Trost, R. E. 1984. Ecological aspects of Canada Geese and other waterfowl in the Mississippi Flyway. PhD diss., Univ. Wis.–Madison, 95 pp.

Truax, W. C. 1952. Horicon Marsh Wildlife Area—its past—its present—its future. Publ. 350, Wis. Conserv. Dep., Madison. 9 pp.

Truax, W. C., and L. F. Gunther. 1951. The effectiveness of game management techniques employed on Horicon Marsh. Trans. North Am. Wildl. Conf. 16:326–30.

Tuttrup, J. 1939a. Bird watching in towns and villages. Wis. Bull. 1, Work Proj. Adm., 27 pp.

Tuttrup, J. 1939b. Bird watching in farming country. Wis. Bull. 2, Work Proj. Adm., 37 pp.

Tuttrup, J. 1941. Bird watching at Lake Koshkonong. Pass. Pigeon 3(4):33–36.

Tyser, R. W. 1982. Species composition and diversity of bird communities in four wetland habitats of the upper Mississippi River floodplain. Pass. Pigeon 44:16–19.

Tyser, R. W. 1983. Species-area relations of cattail marsh avifauna. Pass. Pigeon 45:125–28.

U.S. Bureau of Sport Fisheries and Wildlife. 1955. Wetlands inventory of Wisconsin. Minneapolis, 33 + 30 pp. append.

U.S. Bureau of Sport Fisheries and Wildlife. 1957. Inventory of permanent water habitat significant to waterfowl in Wisconsin. Minneapolis, 7 pp.

U.S. Bureau of Sport Fisheries and Wildlife. Ca. 1965. Horicon National Wildlife Refuge—a wilderness study summary. Washington, D.C., 19 pp.

U.S. Bureau of Sport Fisheries and Wildllife. 1970. Fish and wildlife as related to water quality of the Lake Superior basin. Spec. Rep., U.S. Dep. Inter. and Wildl. Serv. Washington, D.C., 151 pp.

U.S. Bureau of Sport Fisheries and Wildlife. 1973. Threatened wildlife of the United States. Res. Publ. 114, Washington, D.C., 289 pp.

U.S. Bureau of Sport Fisheries and Wildlife. 1979. Wisconsin ups its protection of native animals and plants. Endangered Species Tech. Bull. 4(1):7–12.

U.S. Fish and Wildlife Service. 1940. Food habits of woodcock, snipe, knot, and dowitchers. Wildl. Res. Bull. No. 1.

U.S. Fish and Wildlife Service. 1964. Upper Mississippi River National Wildlife and Fish Refuge. Refuge Leaflet 90-A, Washington, D.C., 4 pp.

U.S. Fish and Wildlife Service. 1978. Endangered species/Great Lakes region. Twin Cities, Minn., unpaginated (updated periodically with new pages).

U.S. Forest Service (Region 9—Milwaukee). 1973. Birds of the Chequamegon National Forest, checklist. Booklet, 16 pp.

University of Wisconsin Sea Grant College. 1980. The invisible menace—contaminants in the Great Lakes. Madison, 58 pp.

Valentine, R. 1873. Canvas-back Ducks in Wisconsin [Lake Koshkonong]. For. and Stream 1(10):147.

Valentine, R. 1878. Migration notes from Janesville [at Lake Koshkonong]. For. and Stream 10 (14 Mar.):99.

Vanderschaegen, P. V. 1975. Status of Sharp-tailed Grouse in Wisconsin. Res. Rep. 95, Wis. Dep. Nat. Resour., Madison, 6 pp.

Vanderschaegen, P. V. 1981a. Where are the Saw-whet Owls? Pass. Pigeon 43:48–49.

Vanderschaegen, P. V. 1981b. The birds of Forest, Oneida, and Vilas counties, Wisconsin. Pass. Pigeon 43(3):69–85.

Vander Zouwen, W. J. 1983. Waterfowl use and habitat changes of a refuge in southern Wisconsin. PhD diss., Univ. Wis.–Madison, 160 pp.

VanVuren, F. S., and H. M. Mackin. 1927. Wisconsin birds. Milwaukee J. in cooperation with Milwaukee Public Mus., Milwaukee, 87 pp.

Van Winkle, E. 1893. Caspian or Imperial Tern (*Sterna caspia*). Oologist 10(4):114–15.

Vaught, R. W. 1968. Problems and economics of Canada Goose management in the Mississippi Flyway. Pp. 25–30 *in* Canada Goose management, ed. R. L. Hine and C. Schoenfeld. Dembar Educ. Res. Stud., Madison.

Velie, E. D. 1963. Report of a survey of bird casualties at television towers, ceilometers, and other obstructions. Flicker 35(3):79–84.

von Jarchow, B. L. 1940. Some observations on the Wood Duck. Pass. Pigeon 2(7):87–89.

von Jarchow, B. L. 1947. Creating nesting sites for bushnesting birds. Pass. Pigeon 9(1):3–7.

vos Burgh, G. W. H. 1899. Nesting of the American Woodcock in southern Wisconsin. Oologist 16(2):45–46.

vos Burgh, G. W. H. 1901. Wisconsin hash. Oologist 18(7):105–6.

vos Burgh, G. W. H. 1911a. The Marsh Wrens in Columbia County, Wisconsin. Oologist 28(6) 108.

vos Burgh, G. W. H. 1911b. Yellow-headed Blackbirds. Oologist 28(9):148–49.

vos Burgh, G. W. H. 1912a. Some rarities. Oologist 29(6):295.

vos Burgh, G. W. H. 1912b. The herons of south central Wisconsin. Oologist 29(7):313–14.

vos Burgh, G. W. H. 1912c. A letter [regarding the observation of a Little Blue Heron]. Oologist 29(12):402.

vos Burgh, G. W. H. 1913a. The owls of southern Wisconsin. Oologist 30(1):26.

vos Burgh, G. W. H. 1913b. The hawks of southern Wisconsin and northern Illinois. Oologist 30(2):30–32.

vos Burgh, G. W. H. 1914. Series of eggs of the Red-tailed Hawk. Oologist 31(2):22.

vos Burgh, G. W. H. 1915. Nesting of the Black and white Warbler. Oologist 32(1):18.

vos Burgh, G. W. H. 1916. Western Meadowlark in Wisconsin. Oologist 33(6):122.

vos Burgh, G. W. H. 1920. Red-bellied Woodpecker. Oologist 37(5):58–59.

vos Burgh, G. W. H. 1921. Wisconsin notes—1920. Oologist 38(12):173.

vos Burgh, G. W. H. 1923a. Spring arrival dates for Columbus, Wisconsin. Oologist 40(6):100.

vos Burgh, G. W. H. 1923b. A note on the birds of Columbus, Wisconsin. Oologist 40(10):166.

vos Burgh, G. W. H. 1924. Red-bellied Woodpecker. Oologist 41(5):54.

vos Burgh, G. W. H. 1927a. Black Tern. Oologist 44(9):123.

vos Burgh, G. W. H. 1927b. White-tailed Kite. Oologist 44(10):138.

vos Burgh, G. W. H. 1928a. A list of birds found nesting at Columbia County, Wisconsin. Oologist 45(5):67–68.

vos Burgh, G. W. H. 1928b. My first Wilson's Snipe nest. Oologist 45(7):106–7.

vos Burgh, G. W. H. 1929a. Black-crowned Night Herons and Green Herons. Oologist 46(7):96.

vos Burgh, G. W. H. 1929b. Bartramian Sandpiper. Oologist 46(8):108.

vos Burgh, G. W. H. 1929c. Various birds' nests. Oologist 46(8):113.

vos Burgh, G. W. H. 1930. A list of birds observed from a door yard. Oologist 47(3):23.

vos Burgh, G. W. H. 1931. A prolific five acres of marsh pasture. Oologist 48(5):67.

vos Burgh, G. W. H. 1932. Nesting of the Pigeon Hawk in Columbus, Wisconsin. Oologist 49(8):90.

vos Burgh, G. W. H. 1934. Prairie hens—Columbus, Wisconsin. Oologist 51(7):83.

vos Burgh, G. W. H. 1939. Some rare birds I have seen in Wisconsin. Oologist 56(7):77.

vos Burgh, G. W. H. 1941a. A few Wisconsin bird notes. Oologist 58(7):81.

vos Burgh, G. W. H. 1941b. 1940 Wisconsin warblers. Oologist 58(9):107–8.

vos Burgh, G. W. H. 1941c. Wisconsin notes [present compared with 50 years ago]. Oologist 58(11):128.

Vosburgh, J. 1966. Death traps in the flyways. Pp. 364–71 *in* Birds in our lives, ed. A. Stefferud. U.S. Dep. Inter. Fish and Wildl. Serv., Washington, D.C.

Voss, K. S. 1976. Behavior of the Greater Sandhill Crane. MS thesis, Univ. Wis.–Madison, 144 pp.

Wade, D. E. 1937. The Carolina Wren in Wisconsin. Wilson Bull. 49(4):295.

Wade, D. E. 1938. Drouth intensity measurements and the effects of the 1936 drouth on wildlife. Trans. North Am. Wildl. Conf. 3:558–69.

Wagner, F. H. 1953. A Wisconsin Mourning Dove study. MS thesis, Univ. Wis.–Madison, 95 pp.

Wagner, F. H. 1954. Wild Turkeys in Wisconsin. Wis. Conserv. Bull. 19(11):11–14.

Wagner, F. H. 1956. The Mourning Dove in Wisconsin. Wis. Conserv. Bull. 21(8):13–16.

Wagner, F. H. 1961. Role of weather in short-term population fluctuations of Wisconsin pheasants. PhD diss., Univ. Wis.–Madison, 232 pp.

Wagner, F. H., and A. W. Stokes. 1968. Indices to overwinter survival and productivity with implications for population regulation in pheasants. J. Wildl. Manage. 32(1):32–36.

Wagner, F. H., C. D. Besadny, and C. Kabat. 1965. Population ecology and management of Wisconsin pheasants. Tech. Bull. 34, Wis. Conserv. Dep., Madison, 168 pp.

Wagner, G. 1932. Swift banding. IBBA News 3(4):7.

Wagner, G. 1933. Mortality in Marsh Hawks. Bird Banding 4(1):50–51.

Walkinshaw, L. H. 1960. Migration of the Sandhill Crane east of the Mississippi River. Wilson Bull. 72(4):358–84.

Wallace, G. J. 1977. Birds of the Lake Michigan drainage basin. Vol. 14 of Environmental status of the Lake Michigan region. Argonne Natl. Lab., Argonne, Ill., 101 pp.

Ward, H. L. 1906. Notes on the Herring Gull and the Caspian Tern. Bull. Wis. Nat. Hist. Soc. 4(4):113–34.

Ward, H. L. 1907. King Eiders at Milwaukee—a correction. Bull. Wis. Nat. Hist. Soc. 5(2):136–37.

Ward, H. L. 1908a. An addition to the avifauna of Wisconsin. Bull. Wis. Nat. Hist. Soc. 6(1–2):124. (Regarding the Dovekie; also a reference to Wisconsin specimens of the Clarke's Nutcracker and Man-o'-war Bird.)

Ward, H. L. 1908b. Occurrence of a Dovekie at Port Washington, Wisconsin. Auk 25(2):215.

Ward, H. L. 1908c. Clarke's Nutcracker from Wisconsin. Auk 25(3):318.

Ward, H. L. 1912. Townsend's Solitaire in Wisconsin. Bull. Wis. Nat. Hist. Soc. 10(1–2):47–48.

Weaver, J. D. 1966. An efficient method for trapping Long-eared Owls. IBBA News 38:30–31.

Weeks, L. T. 1925. White herons on the upper Mississippi River. Wilson Bull. 37(4):219–20.

Weibe, A. H. 1928. Biological survey of the upper Mississippi River with special reference to pollution. Bull. U.S. Bur. Fish. 1927, Vol. 13, Part 2. Washington, D.C.

Weimer, L., and B. Abbott, Eds. 1973. Earthwatching. Spec. Rep. No. 1, Inst. Environ. Stud., Univ. Wis.–Madison, 221 pp.

Weimer, L., W. Gould, and J. Lang, Eds. 1978. Earthwatching II. Spec. Rep. No. 2, Inst. Environ. Stud., Univ. Wis.–Madison, 281 pp.

Weise, C. M. 1971a. Relative abundance of some small land birds in southeastern Wisconsin. Pass. Pigeon 33(4):173–88.

Weise, C. M. 1971b. Population dynamics of the Black-capped Chickadee. Univ. Wis.–Milwaukee Field Stn. Bull. 4(1).

Weise, C. M. 1973. Breeding birds of the forested portion of Cedarburg Bog. Univ. Wis.–Milwaukee Field Stn. Bull. 6(2).

Weise, C. M., and J. R. Meyer. 1979. Juvenile dispersal and development of site-fidelity in the Black-capped Chickadee. Auk 96(1):40–55.

Weise, C. M., and P. J. Salamun. 1979a. Cliffside Park [Racine County] environmental study. Proj. Rep. Owen Ayres and Assoc., Inc., Sheboygan, Wis., 61 pp.

Weise, C. M., and P. J. Salamun. 1979b. Pigeon River environmental study. Proj. Rep. Owen Ayres and Assoc., Inc., Sheboygan, Wis., 61 pp.

Welch, R. J. 1987. Food habits of the Red-shouldered Hawk in Wisconsin. Pass. Pigeon 49(2):81–92.

Welty, J. C. 1962. The life of birds. W. B. Saunders Co., Philadelphia, 546 pp.

Welty, S. F. 1965. Birds with bracelets: The story of bird banding. Prentice-Hall, Englewood Cliffs, N.J., 72 pp.

Wendt, R. F. 1951. Ruffed Grouse research report. Wis. Wildl. Res. Q. Prog. Rep. 9(4):63–72.

Werner, E., Coord. 1975. Breeding bird surveys on scientific areas, 1971–1974. Sci. Areas Preservation Counc., Wis. Dep. Nat. Resour., Madison, 96 pp.

Westemeier, R. L. 1971. The history and ecology of Prairie Chickens in central Wisconsin. Res. Bull. No. 281, Coll. Agric. Life Sci., Univ. Wis.–Madison, 63 pp.

Wetmore, A. 1941. Some Wisconsin bird specimens submitted to the United States National Museum. Pass. Pigeon 4(4):103–5.

Wetmore, A., and J. Seeley. 1901. A June bird census at North Freedom, Wisconsin. Bird-Lore 2(6):172.

Wheeler, W. E., and J. R. March. 1979. Characteristics of scattered wetlands in relation to duck production in southeastern Wisconsin. Tech. Bull. 116, Wis. Dep. Nat. Resour., Madison, 61 pp.

Wheeler, W. E., R. C. Gatti, and G. A. Bartelt. 1984. Duck breeding ecology and harvest characteristics on Grand River Marsh Wildlife Area. Tech. Bull. 145, Wis. Dep. Nat. Resour., 49 pp.

Wheelock, I. G. 1906. Nesting habits of the Green Heron. Auk 23(4):432–36.

White, K. L. 1953. This marsh is managed for production. Wis. Conserv. Bull. 18(12):21–24.

White, R. P. 1980. Distribution and habitat preference of the Upland Sandpiper in Wisconsin. MS thesis, Univ. Wis.–Madison, 145 pp.

Wiens, J. A. 1965. Behavioral interactions of Red-winged Blackbirds and Common Grackles on a common breeding ground. Auk 82(3):356–74.

Wiens, J. A. 1966. An approach to the study of ecological relationships among grassland birds. PhD diss., Univ. Wis.–Madison, 321 pp.

Wiens, J. A. 1973. Interterritorial habitat variation in Grasshopper and Savannah Sparrows. Ecology 54(4):877–84.

Wiens, J. A., and J. T. Emlen, Jr. 1966. Post-invasion status of the Dickcissel in southern Wisconsin. Pass. Pigeon 28(2):63–69.

Willard, S. W. 1881. The Velvet Scoter at Green Bay, Wisconsin. Nuttall Bull. 6(2):187.

Willard, S. W. 1884. The migration of our winter birds. Auk 1(3):221–23.

Willard, S. W. 1885a. Occurrence of *Chroicocephalus franklini* in Wisconsin. Auk 2(2):222.

Willard, S. W. 1885b. Migration and distribution of North American birds in Brown and Outagamie counties. Trans. Wis. Acad. Sci., Arts, Lett. 6:177–96.

Willard, S. W. 1886. Evening Grosbeak in Wisconsin. Auk 3(4):487.

Williams, R. J. 1957. The Great Blue Heron colonies of Wisconsin. Pass. Pigeon 19(2):51–66.

Wills, R. G. 1958. The dowitcher problem. Pass. Pigeon 20(3):95–105.

Wilson, B. H. 1908. Summer birds at Lake Geneva, Wisconsin. Wilson Bull. 20(1):47–49.

Wilson, H. C. 1926. Work with the gulls on the Sister Islands in Lake Michigan. Wilson Bull., o.s. 38(4):248.

Wilson, H. C. 1927. Studies in the life history of the Herring Gull. Biol. Libr. Univ. Wis.–Madison, 71 pp.

Wilson, H. C. 1933. Report of activities and returns. IBBA News 5(1):7.

Wilson, H. C. 1938. Gull banding—Green Bay area, 1938. IBBA News 10(3):6.

Wilson, H. C. 1939–1942. Bird bander's department [editor's reports]. Pass. Pigeon 1(12):163–64; 2(2):18–20; 2(3):34; 2(4):47; 2(5):66; 2(11):122; 3(3):27; 3(6):55–57; 4(4–6):44; 5(1):12–13.

Wilson, H. C. 1951. Banding Double-crested Cormorants. IBBA News 23(6):37.

Wilson, H. C. 1959. Gull banding in Green Bay, 1959. IBBA News 31(4):39.

Wilson, H. C. 1970. Bird banding in Wisconsin. Wis. Acad. Rev. 17(3):5–7, 11.

Wing, L. W. 1935. The Raven (*Corvus corax*) in Dane County, Wisconsin. Auk 52(4):455.

Wing, L. W. 1937. Further studies of wildlife cycles. Trans. North Am. Wildl. Conf. 2:326–45.

Wing, L. W. 1942. A forty-year summary of the Wisconsin Christmas bird censuses. Pass. Pigeon 4(3):77–79.

Wing, L. W. 1951. Practice of wildlife conservation. John Wiley and Sons, New York, 412 pp.

Wingle, H. P. 1978. Bald Eagle–Osprey survey report. U.S. For. Serv., Eastern Reg. Pass. Pigeon 40(2):424–28.

Winkenwerder, H. A. 1902a. Some recent observations of the migration of birds. Bull., Wis. Nat. Hist. Soc. 2(2):97–107.

Winkenwerder, H. A. 1902b. The migration of birds, with special reference to nocturnal flight. Bull. Wis. Nat. Hist. Soc. 2(4):177–263.

Wisconsin Citizens Natural Resources Association, Inc. 1954. The scandal of the goose refuges, with special reference to the Horicon Marsh Refuge. Mimeo, 40 pp.

Wisconsin Conservation Commission. 1924–1967. Biennial reports; series of 15, each including a section devoted to game management.

Wisconsin Conservation Department. 1965. Wild Turkeys have best year yet! Pass. Pigeon 27(4):157.

Wisconsin Department of Natural Resources. 1968. Wisconsin's outdoor recreation plan. Madison, 397 pp.

Wisconsin Department of Natural Resources. 1970. Operational long-range plan (1971–1982)—Sandhill Wildlife Demonstration Area. Babcock, Wis., MS, 112 pp.

Wisconsin Department of Natural Resources. 1978. Environmental impact statement on proposed Grand Traverse Islands State Park, Door County. Madison, 131 pp.

Wisconsin Department of Natural Resources. 1979. Endangered and threatened species list. Madison, 1 p.

Wisconsin Natural Resources Committee of State Agencies. 1956. The natural resources of Wisconsin. Madison, 159 pp.

Wisconsin Natural Resources Committee of State Agencies. 1973. Managing Wisconsin's natural resources. Madison, 114 pp.

Wisconsin State Planning Board. 1939. The Horicon Marsh. Bull. No. 9, Madison, 38 pp.

Wiswall, Mrs. E. C. 1889. Some peculiar and uncommon birds obtained in Sauk County, Wisconsin. Ornithol. and Oologist 14(3):39.

Wiswall, Mrs. E. C. 1891a. Instances of non-migration of migratory birds. Wis. Nat. 1(8):122–23.

Wiswall, Mrs. E. C. 1891b. Evening Grosbeaks in Sauk County, Wisconsin. Wis. Nat. 1(11):164–66.

Woehler, E. E. 1957. Releases and transplants of Hungarian Partridge in Wisconsin. Pp. 13–15 in Abstracts of Hungarian Partridge Management Papers. Wis. Conserv. Dep., Madison, MS.

Wolf, S. W. 1971. Foraging habits of woodpeckers and nuthatches in southern Wisconsin upland forests. MS thesis, Univ. Wis.–Madison, 42 pp.

Wolfe, L. R., and E. R. Ford. 1933. Photo of a Duck Hawk nest and eggs taken in Wisconsin, April, 1933. Oologist 50(12):159.

Wolff, R. C. 1974. The Northern Raven (Corvus corax principalis). Wis. Conserv. Bull 39(1):24–25.

Wood, L. E. 1978. A comparison of breeding bird communities in northern Wisconsin pine forests. Ms thesis, Univ. Wis.–Madison, 74 pp.

Woodcock, J. 1977. Breeding bird survey—1977. Woodland Dunes Duneslett. 9:13.

Woodruff, F. M. 1918. Notes from the Chicago area. Auk 35(2):234.

Wright, A. H. 1911. Other early records of the Passenger Pigeon. Auk 28(4):427–49.

Wright, C. F. 1923. Swans [Vilas County]. Oologist 40(4):104–5.

Wright, G. E. 1972. Observations of juvenile Brown-headed Cowbirds and an hypothesis on species recognition. MS thesis, Univ. Wis.–Madison, 42 pp.

W.S.O. Records Committee. 1983a. New and additional records of rare or unseasonal birds in Wisconsin, spring 1982 through winter 1982–1983. Pass. Pigeon 45:49–50.

W.S.O. Records Committee. 1983b. Status of the Yellow-billed Loon in Wisconsin. Pass. Pigeon 45:64–65.

W.S.O. Records Committee. 1984a. Reports of rare birds in Wisconsin: Corrigenda fall 1981 through fall 1982. Pass. Pigeon 46:75–77.

W.S.O. Records Committee. 1984b. New and additional records of rare or unseasonal birds in Wisconsin, spring 1983 through winter 1983–1984. Pass. Pigeon 46:77–78.

W.S.O. Records Committee. 1984c. Status and identification of Laughing Gulls in Wisconsin. Pass. Pigeon 46:134–36.

Wurster, D. H., C. F. Wurster, Jr., and W. N. Strickland. 1965. Bird mortality following DDT spray for Dutch elm disease. Ecology 46(4):488–99.

Wydeven, A. P. 1986. Iowa-banded Barn Owl in Waupaca County. Pass. Pigeon 48:79–80.

Wyman, M. 1941. Yellow-crowned Night Heron in Wisconsin. Auk 58(4):569–70.

Young, H. 1946. Further studies of the cardinal. Pass. Pigeon 8(4):104–9.

Young, H. 1949. A comparative study of nesting birds in a five-acre park. Wilson Bull. 61(1):36–47.

Young, H. 1951. Territorial behavior in the Eastern Robin. Proc. Linnaean Soc. N.Y. 58–62:1–37.

Young, H. 1955. Breeding behavior and nesting of the Eastern Robin. Am. Midl. Nat. 53(2):329–52.

Young, H. 1958. The robin's year. Pass. Pigeon 20(2):51–57.

Young, H. 1961a. The Downy and Hairy Woodpeckers in Wisconsin. Pass. Pigeon 23(1):3–6.

Young, H. 1961b. A test for randomness in trapping. Bird Banding 32(3):160–62.

Young, H. 1963a. Age specific mortality in the eggs and nestlings of blackbirds. Auk 80(2):145–55.

Young, H. 1963b. Breeding success of the cowbird. Wilson Bull. 75(2):115–22.

Young, H. 1965. An analysis of Christmas bird counts: Whitebreasted and Red-breasted Nuthatches. Pass. Pigeon 27(1):16–19.

Young, H. 1967. An analysis of Christmas bird counts: The Tufted Titmouse. Pass. Pigeon 29(2):46–49.

Young, H. 1969. Hypotheses on peregrine population dynamics. Pp. 513–19 in Peregrine Falcon populations, ed. J. J. Hickey. Univ. Wis. Press, Madison.

Young, H. 1972. The avifauna of the Pine-Popple watershed. Trans. Wis. Acad. Sci., Arts, Lett. 60:291–302.

Young, H., and R. F. Bernard. 1978. Spring and summer birds of the Pigeon Lake region. Trans. Wis. Acad., Sci., Arts, Lett. 66:130–47.

Young, H., B. Stollberg, and M. Deusing. 1941. The spread of the cardinal through Wisconsin. Pass. Pigeon 3(1):1–4.

Zedler, J. B. 1966. Buena Vista Marsh in historical perspective. MS thesis, Univ. Wis.–Madison, 70 pp.

Zicus, M. C. 1974. A study of the Giant Canada Geese (Branta canadensis maxima) nesting at Crex Meadows, Wisconsin. MS thesis, Univ. Minn.–St. Paul, 116 pp.

Zicus. M. C. 1976. Fall flock behavior of Canada Geese resident at Crex Meadows, Wisconsin. PhD diss., Univ. Minn.–St. Paul, 81 pp.

Zicus, M. C. 1981. Flock behavior and vulnerability to hunting of Canada Geese nesting at Crex Meadows, Wisconsin. J. Wildl. Manage. 45(4):830–41.

Ziebell, T. J. 1985. Breeding ecology of the Black-crowned Night-Heron (Nycticorax nycticorax) on Rush Lake, Winnebago County, Wisconsin. M.S. thesis, Univ. Wis.–Oshkosh, 88 pp.

Zimmer, G. E. 1982. The status and distribution of the Common Loon in Wisconsin. Pass. Pigeon 44:60–66.

Zimmerman, E. H. 1969. Birds of Dunn's Marsh. Arboretum News (Univ. Wis.–Madison) 18(2):12–13.

Zimmerman, F. R. 1938a. Poison effect on wildlife. Wis. Conserv. Bull. 3(6):9–15.

Zimmerman, F. R. 1938b. Waterfowl in Wisconsin. Wis. Conserv. Bull. 3(10):16–39.

Zimmerman, F. R. 1940. The Ruddy Duck in Wisconsin. Pass. Pigeon 2(10):111–16.

Zimmerman, F. R. 1941a. Wisconsin's 1940 waterfowl season. Wis. Conserv. Bull. 6(4):11–14.

Zimmerman, F. R. 1941b. Lesser Scaup breeding at Green Bay. Pass. Pigeon 3(10):94.

Zimmerman, F. R. 1942. Waterfowl management research. Wis. Conserv. Bull. 7(9):15–18.

Zimmerman, F. R. 1943. Water levels in relation to fur bearers and waterfowl in central Wisconsin. Wis. Conserv. Bull. 8(1):23–26.

Zimmerman, F. R. 1944. Wisconsin's 1943 waterfowl season. Wis. Conserv. Bull. 9(1):18–24.

Zimmerman, F. R. 1947. The 1947 spring flight of waterfowl through Wisconsin. Wis. Conserv. Bull. 12(8):18–20. (Includes 1946–1947 Wisconsin winter inventory.)

Zimmerman, F. R. 1948. The 1947 waterfowl season in Wisconsin. Wis. Conserv. Bull. 13(5):26–29.

Zimmerman, F. R. 1948–1952. Short sketches of over 30 Wisconsin game birds [mostly ducks and geese]. Wis. Conserv. Bull., Vols. 13–17.

Zimmerman, F. R. 1951. Waterfowl migrations through Wisconsin. Wis. Conserv. Bull. 16(3):12–13.

Zimmerman, F. R. 1953. Waterfowl habitat surveys and food habit studies, 1940–1943. Wis. Conserv. Dep., Madison, 176 pp.

Zimmerman, F. R. 1961. Spring sex ratios of Wisconsin ducks, 1941–1943, 1947. Pass. Pigeon 23(3):88–91.

Zimmerman, J. H. 1950–1954. Outdoor calendar. Pass. Pigeon, Vols. 12–14, 16.

Zimmerman, J. H. 1952a. The Madison Audubon Society's 1951 summer bird census. Pass. Pigeon 14(2):79–81.

Zimmerman, J. H. 1952b. Wyalusing, 1952. Pass. Pigeon 14(4):127–37, 146–47.

Zimmerman, J. H. 1966. Winter birds. Arboretum News (Univ. Wis.–Madison) 15:1–4.

Zimmerman, J. H. 1969. Summer birds. Arboretum News (Univ. Wis.–Madison) 18(2):1–10, 13; reprinted as Winter and summer birds, Friends of the Arboretum, Madison, booklet, 16 pp.

Zimmerman, J. H. Ed. and Publ. 1972. Proceedings of the Second Midwest Prairie Conference, 18–20 Sept. 1970, Univ. Wis.–Madison and Univ. Wis.–Parkside. Madison, Wis., 242 pp.

Zirrer, F. 1941. Some November notes on Sawyer County birds. Pass. Pigeon 3(12):109–10.

Zirrer, F. 1943. An Audubon's Warbler in Wisconsin. Pass. Pigeon 5(3):73.

Zirrer, F. 1944a. Bittern. Pass. Pigeon 6(2):44–46.

Zirrer, F. 1944b. Wisconsin's smallest owl. Pass. Pigeon 6(3):62–65.

Zirrer, F. 1945a. The Ring-necked Duck. Pass. Pigeon 7(2):41–46.

Zirrer, F. 1945b. The Raven. Pass. Pigeon 7(3):61–67.

Zirrer, F. 1947. The Goshawk. Pass. Pigeon 9(3):79–94.

Zirrer, F. 1951. The Great Blue Heron. Pass. Pigeon 13(3):92–98.

Zirrer, F. 1952. The "great" Pileated Woodpecker. Pass. Pigeon 14(1):9–15.

Zirrer, F. 1956. The Great Horned Owl. Pass. Pigeon 18(3):99–109.

Many years ago, Witmer Stone closed his article "American Ornithological Literature, 1883–1933"* with the following thought, which is pertinent for Wisconsin's present publication: "The more the writer considers his work the more omitted contributions come to mind but he hastens to draw the curtain, or better perhaps close the library door, as he dreads to be considered a bibliographer in view of Dr. Elliott Coues's diagnosis of such an individual. Coues says:

'Bibliography is a necessary nuisance and a horrible drudgery that no mere drudge could perform. It takes a sort of inspired idiot to be a good bibliographer and his inspiration is as dangerous a gift as the appetite of the gambler or dipsomaniac—it grows with what it feeds upon and finally possesses its victim like any other invincible vice.'" To this we add a fervent "Amen!"

*Fifty Years' Progress of American Ornithology—1883–1933. Am. Ornithol. Union, Lancaster, Pa. (1933), 249 pp.

List of Observers

Aberg, William J.
Adams, Robert R.
Ake, Robert
Akeley, Charles E.
Albers, T. W.
Albrecht, James
Albrecht, Marjorie
Allen, Marion
Allen, Ralph W.
Allez, George
Almon, Lois
Alyea, Fred
Anderson, Daniel W.
Anderson, Harry G.
Anderson, Henry
Anderson, James S.
Anderson, Mattie
Anderson, Raymond K.
Andrews, Bernice
Andrich, Nancy
Ansorge, Mrs. Louis E.
Anthes, Clarence A.
Apel, Harold P.
Archibald, George W.
Ashman, Nancy
Ashman, Philip
Ashman, Thomas L.
Atkinson, L.
Auler, Ronald
Aumann, Glenn
Aune, Vernon D.
Axley, A. A.

Babcock, Fred I.
Bacon, Bruce R.
Bailey, Beatrice A.
Baillie, Mark

Bair, William
Baker, Doris G.
Baker, Greg
Baldassarre, Guy A.
Balding, Terry
Baldwin, H.
Baldwin, John H.
Balsom, Ivy N.
Baltus, Karl
Bandekow, Raymond
Baptist, Thomas C.
Barger, Bert A.
Barger, Clara L.
Barger, Norval R.
Barkley, Nancy
Barnard, W. D.
Barndt, Robert J.
Barnes, John W.
Barnett, Cynthia F.
Barrett, Hollis
Barry, A. Constance
Bartel, Karl E.
Bartelt, Gerald A.
Bartonek, James C.
Basten, Elmer L.
Batha, Vince P.
Bauers, Harold A.
Baughman, James E.
Baughman, Jeffrey L.
Bauldry, Vincent M.
Baumann, Ida
Baumann, Ty
Baumgartner, A. Marguerite
Baumgartner, Frederick M.
Beach, Harvey
Beals, Edward W.
Becker, Elmer A.

Becker, George C.
Bednarek, Dorothy
Bednarek, Russell
Beed, Watson E.
Beemer, C. W.
Beer, James R.
Behrens, Richard H.
Beimborn, Donald A.
Bell, James G.
Bell, Thomas E.
Bellrose, Frank C.
Bennett, Alan J.
Bennetts, W. J.
Bentley, Albert
Bentley, Mrs. Albert
Bere, Ruby
Berger, Daniel D.
Bernard, Richard F.
Berner, W.
Bersing, Otis S.
Besadny, C. Dennis
Beske, Alan
Bett, Thomas
Betts, Norman D.
Beule, John
Bickford, Jane
Bielefeldt, John E.
Bielenberg, Warren
Bierbrauer, Emily R.
Bierman, Donald R.
Bintz, Carol
Bintz, Thomas
Bishop, Homer C.
Biss, Richard
Black, Charles T.
Blanchard, Paul D.
Blome, Richard

Bodeman, Cory
Boehmer, Ray F.
Bohn, Mrs. W. J.
Bolduc, Donald
Bond, Richard R.
Bontly, Marilyn
Bowker, Marilyn
Boynton, Paul
Braastad, J. H.
Bradford, Alfred S.
Bradle, Bernard J.
Bradley, Charles C.
Bradley, Nina L.
Bragg, James
Brakefield, Edith
Brandel, Mike
Brandler, Charles
Brasser, David
Brasser, Margaret
Bratley, David A.
Breckinridge, Walter J.
Breitenstein, Gifford
Brenner, John J.
Brigham, Robert L.
Brinker, David F.
Brittingham, Margaret C.
Broerman, F.
Bronson, Jon
Brooks, William S.
Brouchoud, Bernard N.
Brown, Fran
Brown, Keith
Brown, Wilbur D.
Brown, Willard
Brumer, John
Brynildson, Inga V.
Bua, Deborah K.
Bub, Richard A.
Buchanan, Warren
Buckstaff, Ralph N.
Bundy, W. F.
Burbach, Jeannine
Burdick, G. W.
Burgess, Harold H.
Burhans, Patrick
Burns, Stuart
Burrill, Alfred C.
Burtt, Edward H.
Busjaeger, Albert
Buss, Arnold H.
Buss, Irven O.
Bussewitz, Elton E.
Butler, Eugene
Butler, John
Butterbrodt, Mary E.
Butts, Kenneth
Byers, Mark

Cahn, Alvin R.
Caldwell, Helen
Canfield, William H.
Carnes, Even
Carpenter, Anita A.
Carr, Charles F.

Carroll, James M.
Carter, W. D.
Casper, Gary S.
Cederstrom, David
Champion, John
Chase, Arthur
Chase, Samuel P.
Chipman, Irma
Christman, Alvin
Christofferson, Ralph O.
Church, Grace
Chylinski, Julius
Clapp, Howard A.
Clapp, James
Clark, Catherine
Clark, J. N.
Clarke, Arthur C.
Cleary, Edwin D.
Cleek, Richard
Cochran, William W.
Cole, John
Cole, Leon J.
Coleman, Mrs. T. E.
Collias, Nicholas E.
Columban, Brother
Compton, Lester E.
Compton, Olive L.
Connors, Peter G.
Cook, Robert S.
Cooke, May T.
Cooke, Wells W.
Cooper, Lynn
Copeland, Ernest
Cors, Arlene
Cors, Donald
Cory, Charles B.
Cowart, William A.
Cox, David J.
Cox, Hazel
Craven, Scott R.
Crete, Ronald
Crocker, Catherine W.
Crocker, F. S.
Crosby, L.
Cuff, Margarita
Culp, Gaylord M.
Cupertino, Eugene
Curran, George
Curtis, John T.
Curtis, Steven G.
Cuthbert, Nicholas L.
Cutright, Noel J.

Dahlberg, Burton L.
Dahlberg, E. M.
Dahlstrand, Nils P.
Damaske, Norbert E.
David, Guy
Davison, Evron E.
Dayton, Francis S.
De Boer, Gerald A.
De Boer, Stanley G.
De Boor, Thomas
De Briyn, Howard

Decker, Mary E.
Deerwester, Therman
Degerman, John
Degner, Elizabeth
Deignan, H. C.
De Jong, Michael J.
Dennis, Clifford J.
Derleth, August
Dernehl, P. H.
Dery, R. G.
Dettman, Warren P.
Deusing, Murl
Dickson, John G.
Diedrich, John L.
Diers, Richard W.
Dietrich, Helene
Dillon, S. T.
Doane, Gilbert H.
Doll, Mark H.
Donald, Mary F.
Doolittle, Thomas
Dorney, Robert S.
Doty, Spencer N.
Drazkowski, William J.
Drieslein, Robert L.
Dryer, Raymond B.
Dueholm, Keith H.
Duerkson, Barbara F.
Dumke, Robert T.
Dundas, Lester H.

Eckert, Kim R.
Eckstein, Ronald G.
Egelberg, Leo J.
Egger, Karen
Ehlers, Bradley
Eichhorst, Bruce A.
Eisele, Timothy T.
Eisele, Todd
Ela, Janet
Elder, William H.
Ellarson, Robert S.
Ellis, Thomas R.
Emlen, John T.
Engberg, Louise
Engberg, Paul R.
English, H. R.
Epple, Arol C.
Epstein, Eric J.
Erdman, Thomas C.
Erickson, H. A.
Erickson, Laura A.
Erickson, Louise W.
Erickson, Robert G.
Erlach, W.
Errington, Paul L.
Evans, David L.
Evans, J. Harwood
Evanson, Randall M.
Evrard, James O.
Eynon, Alfred E.

Faanes, Craig A.
Faanes, Ruth E.

Fadel, Nora
Fadness, John S.
Fallow, David
Farmer, G. J.
Faust, Marilyn
Feeney, William S.
Fell, Emma
Fell, S. D.
Fenton, Larry M.
Fetterer, Earl
Ficken, Millicent S.
Ficken, Robert W.
Fiehweg, Robert E.
Fisher, Albert K.
Fisher, Eunice
Fisher, S.
Fisk, William
Fitzpatrick, John W.
Flaherty, Roy J.
Flaherty, Mrs. Roy J.
Fleming, Rosemary
Flemming, Mrs. Henry
Flint, Leslie
Flory, C. M.
Folczyk, Dennis
Follen, Don G., Sr.
Follett, Lyle
Foote, Mrs. Charles
Forbes, Walter
Ford, Edward R.
Foster, G. William
Fox, Barbara
Fox, C. P.
Frank, Beth
Frank, James C.
Frankowiak, Robert J.
Franzen, A. J.
Freese, Frank N.
Freitag, Adrian
French, G. E.
Frister, Carl P.
Frister, Dorothy E.
Fuchs, Herman
Fuller, James F.
Fuller, Katherine
Fuller, Pepper

Gable, Fred
Gantenbein, Walter L.
Garber, Richard
Garber, Robert
Gard, Robert E.
Gastrow, Albert
Gates, John M.
Gatterdam, Paul C.
Gauerke, Arthur
Gauerke, Lucy
Gauger, Alvin
Geller, Debbie
Geller, Greg
Germain, Clifford E.
Gibbs, Ella S.
Gilbert, N. C.
Gilles, Walter J.

Gillette, George
Gilmore, Charles L.
Gisness, John
Glassel, Raymond C.
Glenn, Frances
Glueckert, Kevin
Gluesing, Ernest A.
Goddard, Stephen V.
Goers, David
Goff, Alta
Goldsmith, Edna J.
Gordon, G. E.
Gordon, Richard F.
Goss, Benjamin F.
Gralow, William
Grange, Wallace B.
Granlund, Marvin
Grant, Cleveland P.
Gray, Donald E.
Greeley, Frederick
Greeley, Philip H.
Green, Janet C.
Green, William E.
Greenberg, Joel
Greenman, Delbert E.
Greer, Edward
Gregg, Larry E.
Grewe, Alfred H.
Griffee, W. E.
Grimmer, Wiliam F.
Gromme, Owen J.
Gromme, Roy
Grootematt, James E.
Gross, Alfred O.
Grover, Brad
Grundtvig, F. L.
Gundlach, John
Gunther, Lloyd F.
Gustafson, Dennis K.
Gutschow, Ronald P.
Gysendorfer, Richard

Hadow, Herbert H.
Hafemann, Karl E.
Hager, Joseph
Hailman, Jack P.
Hale, James B.
Hale, Karen E.
Hall, George A.
Hall, H. Lowell
Hall, Victor
Hallett, Mary L.
Hallisy, Ray
Halvorsen, Harvey H.
Hamers, James
Hamerstrom, Frances
Hamerstrom, Frederick N.
Hammel, Dorothy
Hammond, Wayne
Hanbury, Don
Hansen, Ellen
Hansen, Kathryn S.
Hanson, Harold C.
Hanson, R. P.

Hardy, Maybelle
Hare, H. P.
Harmer, Dorothy
Harriman, Bettie
Harris, A. Trevenning
Harris, James T.
Harrison, George H.
Hartman, Lisa
Hartmeister, Felix A.
Haseleu, Judy
Hasterlik, Richard A.
Hatch, Delos
Hauerwas, Eugene
Haug, Joseph C.
Haugen, Darrell
Hawkins, Arthur S.
Hayes, Mary N.
Hayssen, Carl G.
Hebard, Eleanor
Hehn, Anna L.
Heidel, Kathleen
Heig, Vincent A.
Heinsohn, L.
Hendrick, Donald J.
Hendrickson, Gary
Henika, F. S.
Hennessy, Fred
Henseler, George
Hernday, Loretta
Hersey, F. Seymour
Hibbard, Richard
Hickey, Joseph J.
Hickey, Margaret B.
Hicks, Lawrence
Higgins, Mabel F.
Hillery, Fred
Hilsenhoff, William L.
Hine, Ruth L.
Hirschy, Robert
Hoefler, James E.
Hoffman, Loraine
Hoffman, Randy M.
Hoffman, Ronald R.
Hoffmann, Emma
Hoffmann, Paul W.
Hofslund, Pershing B.
Holland, W.
Hollister, Ned
Holmes, A. G.
Hoogerheide, John
Hook, Fred L.
Hope, Lawrence
Hopkins, Ralph C.
Hough, Emerson
Howard, T. J.
Howe, Robert W.
Hoy, Philo R.
Hubbard, Ben W.
Huber, Henry
Hudick, Joseph P.
Hull, Ronald
Hulse, Scott
Hummel, Philip J.
Humphrey, Janelle M.

Humphrey, Joan E.
Hunt, L. Barrie
Hunt, Richard A.
Hunter, Eldon
Hunter, Thomas
Hussong, Clara H.
Hussong, Ray P.

Idzikowski, John H.
Idzikowski, Lisa
Ingold, James L.
Ingram, Terrence N.
Ivens, Roy

Jack, Irene
Jackson, Arnold S.
Jackson, Hartley H. T.
Jackson, William B.
Jackson, William F.
Jackson, Mrs. William F.
Jacobs, Eugene
Jacobs, John P.
Jacobsen, Allen K.
Jacobson, Lloyd
Jacoubek, R.
Jaeger, Michael J.
Jahn, Laurence R.
Jankowski, Rufin
Jansen, John
Jarboe, Jean L.
Jelich, Tony
Jenkins, Joseph H.
Jensen, Janice
Jessen, Thomas
Johnson, David
Johnson, James
Johnson, Lawrence J.
Johnson, Lee A.
Johnson, Robbye J.
Johnson, Roy
Jones, Mike
Jones, S. Paul
Jordahl, Harold C.
Jorgenson, Catherine
Jorgenson, Howard
Joslyn, Dorothy
Joslyn, Joy
Juda, John
Judziewicz, Emmet
Juneau, Dorothy
Jung, Clarence S.
Junkin, Francis T.
Jurack, Mary

Kabat, Cyril J.
Kahmann, Karl W.
Kaiman, Bernard D.
Kangas, Frank
Kaspar, John L.
Kaufman, Frank
Kaufman, Irvin
Keefer, James W.
Keeler, Charles A.
Keitt, Alan

Kemper, Charles A.
Kendall, J. B.
Ketchbaw, Larry
Kiel, William H.
Kienitz, Amy
Kinch, Richard
King, F. Holman
King, Franklin H.
Kinnel, Bernard
Kjos, Charles G.
Kjos, Mary A.
Klink, Joann
Klotz, Charles D.
Klugow, Bernard F.
Knudsen, George J.
Knue, A. J.
Knuth, Carl C.
Knuth, Kevin
Knuth, Rockne A.
Koehler, George
Koehler, Luella
Koehn, Charles J.
Kohel, Michael D.
Kohlmeyer, Eugene
Kohn, Bruce
Kooiker, Paul
Koopmann, Harold
Koppenhaver, Al G.
Korducki, Mark
Korotev, Randy
Koslowski, Janet L.
Kossack, Charles W.
Kosterman, David
Kozlik, Frank M.
Krager, Joan M.
Kranich, Lee
Kratzat, Gordon F.
Kraupa, John
Kraus, Glen
Krawczyk, Chester
Kreger, Keith
Krenn, Gordon
Krings, Steven H.
Krombholz, Paul
Krueger, David
Kruger, Allie
Krumm, Kenneth H.
Kruse, Harold C.
Kuehnl, Dorothea
Kuhlman, Frank
Kuhn, Eleanor
Kuhn, H. W.
Kuhn, Kenneth H.
Kumlien, A. Ludwig
Kumlien, Thure L.
Kurtz, John
Kuyava, Gary C.
Kyro, Ray

La Chance, O.
Lang, Stephen J.
Lange, Kenneth I.
Langosch, O.
Lanyon, Wesley E.

Lapham, Increase A.
Larkin, Dixie L.
Larson, Mrs. J. G.
Laws, Bert
Lees, Mary
Legler, Dorothy
Legler, Karl F.
Lemke, Charles W.
Lemke, Oscar R.
Lender, Ruth
Leopold, Aldo
Leppla, Edith M.
Les, Betty L.
Lesher, Frederick Z.
Lewis, Clifford W.
Lewke, Robert E.
Liebherr, Harold G.
Liebherr, Hildegard
Liebmann, Donald F.
Lindberg, Harold L.
Lindsay, Gerald E.
Lindsley, David
Link, Reinhold
Lint, Gertrude
Lintereur, Leroy J.
Lloyd, Charles N.
Loewecke, C.
Logan, Ben
Lohman, Ivar K.
Long, Lymore
Lound, Martha
Lound, Roy H.
Lowe, John L.
Loyster, Earl L.
Ludwig, Frederick E.
Luepke, Janice
Luepke, Kenneth J.
Luetkens, Carol
Lukes, Charlotte M.
Lukes, Roy J.
Lustyk, Jude

MacBriar, Wallace N.
McCabe, Robert A.
McCarthy, T. J.
McCormick, Peter
McGhee, Michael
McKern, E. J.
MacLean, George
McMaster, Leta D.
MacMillan, Frederick N.
McNamara, Evelyn
Macht, Philip
Madsen, E.
Madura, Marilu L.
Maercklein, Robin
Mahlum, Gyda
Maier, Lorena
Maier, Merton
Main, Angie K.
Main, John S.
Mallow, Philip A.
Manz, Kenneth
March, James R.

Marks, Frances A.
Marsh, Lillian
Martin, J. H.
Martin, Mark
Martin, R. E.
Martin, Stephen G.
Martin, Sue
Martz, Gerald F.
Mason, C. N.
Mathews, Ed
Mathiak, Harold A.
Mattern, Leroy
Matteson, Sumner W.
Mattison, Helmer M.
Mattson, Oswald E.
Maul, A. P.
Maurin, Ann
Maxson, Melva T.
Mayer, Winnifred
Mead, Dorothy M.
Mead, G. S.
Meier, Thomas I.
Mello, Kim
Melvin, S. M.
Merchak, Joseph
Merkel, Keith J.
Meyer, H.
Meyer, John R.
Meyer, Steven
Miersch, C. J.
Mihalek, Richard
Miles, Eleanor B.
Miles, Philip E.
Miller, Greg
Miller, William
Minkebige, Dan
Minkebige, Paula
Mitchell, Earl T.
Mitchell, I. N.
Moir, Eric
Monthey, Roger
Morehart, Gary
Morehart, Richard
Morgan, Helen
Morrein, Ronald
Morrison, George A.
Morse, Margarette E.
Morse, Ralph C.
Moss, Bruce A.
Mossman, Michael J.
Moulson, Stan
Moulton, Jack C.
Moye, Wencil O.
Mueller, Helmut C.
Mueller, Walter J.
Mueller, William
Munn, Charles
Myers, Michael

Naeser, Charles R.
Narf, Richard P.
Natzke, Edward A.
Nauman, Lyle E.
Nehrling, Henry

Neidermyer, William J.
Nelson, Alice
Nelson, Charles E.
Nelson, E. W.
Nelson, Mary H.
Nero, Robert W.
Neugebauer, Russell
Nicewander, Walter
Nicholls, Thomas H.
Nicklaus, Ronald H.
Niemi, Gerald J.
Norling, Wayne
Norman, Beatrice
Northup, Helen
Nott, Ethel A.
Nunnemacher, Howard J.

Oar, Jack
Ochsner, Edward D.
Ogden, H. V.
Ogren, Kay
Ohm, Rudy
Olson, Ethel
Olson, Manley E.
Olson, Margaret E.
Orians, Gordon H.
Orians, Howard L.
Orr, Gordon
Osborn, Chandler
Ott, Frederick L.
Otto, Laurie
Otto, N. C.
Overton, George
Overton, Mary J.
Owen, Stella P.

Pabst, Gustav
Paine, George W.
Palmer, Richard
Palmquist, Clarence O.
Parfitt, Bruce
Patek, John
Paul, Steven
Paulson, Edwin O.
Paulson, Martin
Peaks, E.
Pearson, Gary
Peartree, Edward W.
Peckham, G. W.
Pedersen, Gertrude
Pedersen, Mildred
Peirce, Mrs. Walter
Pelton, Charles W.
Pelzer, Walter C.
Pemble, Alice
Pemble, Carl A.
Penning, William
Perala, Julie
Perala, Ronald R.
Perkins, Irving J.
Perkins, Jerry
Perkins, Roy
Perrot, Nicolas
Personius, Robert G.

Petersen, Arnold J.
Petersen, Leroy R.
Petersen, Ursala C.
Peterson, Alvin M.
Peterson, Carl
Peterson, Mrs. Carl
Peterson, Florence
Peterson, Gordon F.
Peterson, Gregory S.
Peterson, Mae
Peterson, Mark S.
Peterson, Robert
Petters, Charles W.
Pickering, Bernard
Pickett, Merle N.
Pillmore, Richard
Pimlott, Douglas H.
Polinski, Daniel
Polk, Janine L.
Poole, Arthur J.
Popov, B. H.
Pospichal, Carl E.
Postupalski, Sergej
Pratt, Dennis
Pratt, Frank
Pratt, Jeranne H.
Priebe, Karl
Prins, Edward B.
Prins, George
Pritash, Robert
Pruski, Kenneth
Pugh, William H.

Quimby, Arelisle

Raasch, Gilbert O.
Radke, W.
Raile, Mary J.
Rankl, Jerome
Ratliff, Francis T.
Ready, Jane A.
Reardon, William J.
Redmond, Kate
Reese, Staber W.
Reich, Mrs. Frank
Reichwaldt, Myron H.
Reindahl, Enoch
Renn, Frank B.
Rensink, Reginald J.
Rice, Joseph
Richards, Stephen H.
Richter, Carl H.
Riegel, Glenn
Rill, Katharine D.
Risch, Leonard
Risch, Timothy
Rispens, Mark
Robbins, Chandler S.
Robbins, Richard A.
Robbins, Samuel D.
Roberts, Harold D.
Roberts, Nancy M.
Roberts, Thomas S.
Roehl, R. R.

Rogers, Nell M.
Rogers, Randy
Rohan, Joan
Rohde, Wayne
Roll, K.
Romig, Paul W.
Rosenfield, Robert N.
Roskos, Thomas C.
Ross, David A.
Rossman, Vernon C.
Rosso, Jerome R.
Roux, George
Roy, Albert J.
Rudy, Carroll E.
Ruegger, George
Ruegger, Sam
Rumpf, E. M.
Rusch, Alan J.
Russell, H.
Russell, John M.
Russell, Robert M.
Russos, Nicki
Ruttman, Cavin

Sacia, Elsie J.
Saetveit, John
Safir, Linda L.
Sanford, Terry
Sayre, Margaret
Schaars, Herman W.
Schaeffer, John
Schimmels, Lynn J.
Schluter, Ernest
Schmide, Harold
Schmidt, David
Schmidt, Franklin J. W.
Schmidt, Norma
Schmidt, Susan
Schmidt, Ted
Schoenebeck, August J.
Schoenebeck, Carl
Schoenfeldt, Clarence A.
Schoolcraft, Henry R.
Schoonmaker, Ralph
Schorger, A. William
Schramm, Ursula
Schraufenbuel, Joseph
Schroeder, Carl
Schulde, Robert
Schultz, Clark
Schultz, Lawrence H.
Schultz, Thomas R.
Schultz, William
Schutz, Nancy
Schwartz, Dennis
Scott, Gertrude M.
Scott, Walter E.
Scott, Warren A.
Searles, Clarence A.
Seevers, Dennis
Seifert, William
Seiling, F.
Sell, Herbert
Semo, Lawrence

Septen, Gregory
Sercomb, Samuel R.
Sharp, Richard
Shea, Allen K.
Shea, Susan
Sheldon, Harry H.
Shepherd, Fred E.
Sheridan, Edith
Sherman, G. H.
Shillinglaw, John
Shine, Harold E.
Sievert, William F.
Simmons, Amelia
Simmons, O. T.
Simonis, John J.
Simpson, J. Allan
Sindelar, Charles R.
Sipe, James P.
Skaar, P. D.
Skavlem, H. L.
Skelly, Chester A.
Skilling, H.
Slepicka, John
Smith, Jerry
Smith, L. P. C.
Smith, Lewis A.
Smith, Nellis F.
Smith, R. Martin
Smith, William A.
Smith, Winnifred M.
Snarski, David J.
Snyder, Charles H.
Snyder, Francis
Snyder, Will E.
Sontag, Charles R.
Soulen, Thomas K.
Southern, William E.
Southwick, C.
Spahn, Robert G.
Spangenburg, Bruce
Sperry, Theodore M.
Springer, Paul F.
Sprunt, Alexander, IV
Spurgeon, Sidney G.
Stabb, Martin
Staege, Mary H.
Starnes, Theodora
Staupe, Thomas R.
Steele, Ray C.
Stefanski, Raymond A.
Steffen, James F.
Stehno, Spencer
Steinbach, Marlin
Steinke, Harold A.
Stephan, Jane
Steuer, Cathryn
Steven, Lee P.
Stierle, John W.
Stock, Emil J.
Stocking, Marion K.
Stoddard, C. H.
Stoddard, Herbert L.
Stoffel, Mardie
Stokes, Allan W.

Stoll, Kenneth
Stollberg, Bruce
Stolzenberg, Thomas
Stone, Norman R.
Stoner, Dwight
Stout, Gary
Stratton, C. G.
Strehlow, Elmer W.
Strelitzer, Carl L.
Strohmeyer, David L.
Strong, Paul I. V.
Strong, Reuben M.
Struckhoff, Norma B.
Studnicka, John
Sugden, Earl
Sunby, Paul
Sundell, Robert A.
Sundell, Roger H.
Sutherland, Mrs. Robert J.
Swedberg, Donald
Swengel, Ann B.
Swengel, Scott R.
Swiderski, Raymond

Taber, Richard D.
Tate, R. C.
Taylor, Warner
Temple, Anita J.
Temple, Stanley A.
Teppen, Terry C.
Te Ronde, Dennis E.
Tessen, Daryl D.
Thiel, Richard P.
Thiessen, Penny
Thiessen, Steven
Thomas, Landon B.
Thomas, Linda J.
Thompson, Daniel Q.
Thompson, David H.
Thompson, Donald R.
Thompson, Richard
Thompson, Robert
Thomsen, Edwin
Throne, Alvin M.
Tiebout, Harry M., III
Tiede, Darwin
Tiews, Lester C.
Tilghman, Nancy G.
Tiller, David
Toepfer, James E.
Tomlinson, Mark
Toppe, Carleton
Trainer, Daniel O.
Treder, Raymond G.
Treichel, George W.
Trick, Joel
Triebensee, Robert
Truax, Wayne C.
Tryggeseth, Gayle O.
Tweet, Peter A.

Underwood, Thomas J.
Urban, Emil K.
Urban, William

Urbanski, Peter

Valen, Terry
Vanderschaegen, Phillip V.
Van Ness, Howard L.
Van Stappen, Mike
Verch, Richard L.
Vig, Cedric
Vincent, Alice C.
Vogelsang, Barbara
Vogelsang, Jerry
Vogt, Linda
Vogt, Vincent
Volkert, William K.
Von Jarchow, B. L.
Vos Burgh, George W. H.
Voss, Edward E.
Voss, Karen S.

Wade, Douglas E.
Wagman, Clarence
Wagner, Frederic H.
Walker, Mary A.
Walkinshaw, Lawrence H.
Wallner, Alfred M.
Ward, Henry L.
Ward, John
Ward, Marilyn K.
Weber, Alice

Weber, Bill
Weber, Viratine E.
Weber, Walter
Wegman, Kim
Weinke, R.
Weise, Charles M.
Wellso, Stanley
Welty, J. Carl
Werner, Evelyn H.
West, Mabel
Wetmore, Alexander
Wheeler, William E.
Whelan, Chris
Whitemarsh, Robyn
Wiens, John A.
Wierzbicki, Melvin M.
Wiita, Clifford
Wilda, Curt L.
Wilde, Jonathan W.
Willard, David E.
Willard, S. W.
Williams, Elsie
Williams, Robert J.
Wills, Richard G.
Wilson, Harold C.
Wing, Leonard W.
Winkenwerder, H. A.
Winkler, Howard A.
Winkler, Peg

Woessner, Warren
Wolf, R.
Wolfe, L.
Wolver, Mary
Wood, Chauncey A.
Woodcock, Archie
Woodcock, John
Woodmansee, Winnie
Woodruff, F. M.
Woodruff, William
Wright, Earl G.
Wydeven, Paula R.
Wyman, Martha

Yeomans, G.
Young, Howard F.

Zehnar, Norma
Zell, Hans
Zicus, Michael C.
Ziebell, Thomas
Zimmer, Gary E.
Zimmerman, Elizabeth H.
Zimmerman, Fred R.
Zimmerman, James H.
Zimmerman, O. B.
Zirrer, Francis

Index of Species

Numbers in boldface designate pages on which species accounts occur.

Accipiter cooperii, 18, 19, 29, 61, 103, **210–211,** 337, 635, 646
  gentilis, 17, 40, 103, **211–212,** 635, 646
  striatus, 52, 103, **208–209,** 621, 635, 646
Actitis macularia, 105, **262,** 628, 630, 631, 637
Aechmophorus clarkii, 102, **607**
  occidentalis, 102, **122,** 607, 649
Aegolius acadicus, 40, 52, 107, 349, **350–351,** 638, 647
  funereus, 106, **348–349,** 647
Agelaius phoeniceus, 4, 38, 39, 61, 84, 88, 111, 407, 442, 443, 459, 460, 558, **576–577,** 582, 585, 586, 629, 633, 644
Aix sponsa, 4, 17, 20, 22, 38, 40, 44, 89, 102, **158–159,** 617, 618, 633, 634, 646
Ajaia ajaja, 102, **146**
Alle alle, 39, 106, **322**
Ammodramus bairdii, 111, **551–552,** 650
  caudacutus, 111, **556–557,** 628, 643
  henslowii, 85, 111, **554,** 643
  leconteii, 88, 111, **555–556,** 628, 643
  savannarum, 19, 27, 30, 84, 85, 111, **552–553,** 643
Amphispiza bilineata, 111, **547–548**
Anas acuta, 102, 161, **164–165,** 171, 172, 635, 646
  americana, 16, 103, 161, **171–172,** 176, 635, 646
  bahamensis, 102, **163**
  clypeata, 40, 103, 161, **167–168,** 171, 172, 635, 646
  crecca, 20, 102, **159–160,** 161, 171, 172, 634, 646
  cyanoptera, 103, **166–167,** 649
  discors, 16, 17, 20, 38, 51, 103, 162, **165–166,** 167, 171, 172, 633, 635, 645

  penelope, 103, **170–171,** 649
  platyrhynchos, 20, 38, 51, 94, 99, 102, 161, **162–163,** 171, 172, 625, 632, 633, 634, 645, 646
  rubripes, 102, **160–161,** 162, 634, 646
  strepera, 16, 103, 161, **169–170,** 171, 172, 635, 646
Anhinga, 102, **127–128,** 649
Anhinga anhinga, 102, **127–128,** 649
Ani, Groove-billed, 106, **332–333,** 650
Anser albifrons, 17, 102, **152–153,** 649
Anthus rubescens, 109, **452,** 611, 650
  spragueii, 109, **611**
Aphelocoma ultramarina, **613**
Aquila chrysaetos, 5, 104, **221–222,** 646
Archilochus colubris, 4, 107, **358–359,** 620, 638
Ardea herodias, 27, 82, 94, 102, **132–133,** 337, 631, 634, 646
Arenaria interpres, 105, **269,** 649
  melanocephala, 105, **270**
Asio flammeus, 52, 88, 106, **347–348,** 638, 646
  otus, 52, 106, **346–347,** 638, 646
Athene cunicularia, 106, **341–342,** 648, 650
Avocet, American, 39, 104, **257,** 649
Aythya affinis, 103, 162, 176, 178, **179–180,** 635, 646
  americana, 17, 103, **175–176,** 635, 646
  collaris, 103, **176–177,** 635, 646
  marila, 103, 162, **178–179,** 180, 646
  valisineria, 103, **173–174,** 176, 646

Bartramia longicauda, 6, 12, 15, 17, 30, 40, 52, 53, 56, 85, 105, **263–264,** 637
Bittern, American, 88, 102, **130–131,** 628, 634, 648
  Least, 38, 102, **131–132,** 629, 634

Blackbird, Brewer's, 17, 18, 40, 53, 111, 582, **583–584,** 644, 647
  Red-winged, 4, 38, 39, 61, 84, 88, 111, 407, 442, 443, 459, 460, 558, **576–577,** 582, 585, 586, 629, 633, 644, 647
  Rusty, 61, 111, **582–583,** 584, 647
  Yellow-headed, 17, 27, 38, 39, 40, 111, **581–582,** 629, 644, 647
Bluebird, Eastern, 19, 20, 37, 82, 89, 90, 108, **432–433,** 558, 621, 624, 628, 641, 647
  Mountain, 108, **434,** 650
Bobolink, 12, 27, 52, 84, 85, 111, 554, **575–576,** 644
Bobwhite, Northern, 3, 12, 16, 20, 21, 26, 27, 41, 85, 104, **238–239,** 623, 636, 645, 646
Bombycilla cedrorum, 48, 109, 224, **454–455,** 641, 645, 647
  garrulus, 109, **453–454,** 645, 647
Bonasa umbellus, 14, 16, 17, 20, 26, 27, 40, 50, 58, 80, 84, 94, 104, **233,** 617, 619, 620, 636, 646
Botaurus lentiginosus, 88, 102, **130–131,** 628, 634, 648
Brant, 102, **155–156,** 649
Branta bernicla, 102, **155–156,** 649
  canadensis, 4, 22, 90, 102, **156–157,** 162, 443, 633, 634, 645, 646
  leucopsis, **613**
Bubo virginianus, 17, 22, 51, 52, 94, 106, **337–338,** 618, 638, 646
Bubulcus ibis, 19, 40, 102, 136, **138–139,** 634, 648
Bucephala albeola, 17, 103, **190–191,** 646
  clangula, 103, **188–189,** 635, 645, 646
  islandica, 103, **189–190,** 646

Bufflehead, 17, 103, **190–191,** 646
Bunting, Indigo, 52, 88, 110, 525, **534–535,** 617, 621, 624, 643
　Lark, 111, **549–550,** 650
　Lazuli, 110, **533**
　Painted, 110, **535–536,** 650
　Snow, 111, 571, **574,** 611, 645, 647
Buteo jamaicensis, 39, 51, 55, 58, 61, 99, 104, **217–218,** 337, 618, 636, 646
　lagopus, 104, **220–221,** 646
　lineatus, 18, 29, 54, 60, 64, 103, **213–214,** 618, 636, 646
　platypterus, 50, 84, 103, 208, **214–215,** 636
　regalis, 104, **219,** 649
　swainsoni, 19, 103, **216–217,** 649
Butorides striatus, 40, 102, **140–141,** 630, 634

Calamospiza melanocorys, 111, **549–550,** 650
Calcarius lapponicus, 111, **570–571,** 574, 611, 645, 647
　ornatus, 111, **573**
　pictus, 111, **572,** 650
Calidris alba, 105, **271–272,** 649
　alpina, 105, **278,** 649
　bairdii, 105, **275–276,** 649
　canutus, 105, **270–271,** 649
　ferruginea, 105, **279,** 649
　fuscicollis, 105, **275,** 649
　himantopus, 19, 105, **280–281,** 649
　maritima, 105, **277–278,** 649
　mauri, 105, **273–274,** 649
　melanotos, 17, 99, 105, **276–277,** 649
　minutilla, 105, **274,** 649
　pusilla, 105, **272–273,** 649
Calypte anna, 107, **359**
Canvasback, 103, **173–174,** 176, 646
Caprimulgus carolinensis, 107, **353–354,** 638
　vociferus, 4, 17, 20, 40, 107, **354–355,** 638
Cardinal, Northern, 16, 17, 18, 27, 40, 88, 89, 94, 110, **527–528,** 626, 632, 643, 647
　Red-crested, **613**
Cardinalis cardinalis, 16, 17, 18, 27, 40, 88, 89, 94, 110, **527–528,** 626, 632, 643, 647
Carduelis carduelis, **613**
　flammea, 112, **598–599,** 600, 645, 647
　hornemanni, 112, **599–600,** 647
　pinus, 112, 592, **600–601,** 644, 647
　psaltria, 112, **612**
　tristis, 88, 112, 592, 598, 600, **602–603,** 612, 624, 632, 644, 647
Carpodacus mexicanus, 19, 90, 112, **594–595,** 600, 644, 647
　purpureus, 112, 588, **593–594,** 621, 644, 647, 648
Casmerodius albus, 15, 19, 27, 29, 39, 40, 94, 102, **134–135,** 136, 634
Catbird, Gray, 4, 12, 56, 88, 108, **446–447,** 624, 641, 645, 647
Cathartes aura, 4, 16, 40, 48, 50, 82, 103, **199–200,** 617, 635
Catharus fuscescens, 52, 55, 108, **436–437,** 586, 625, 641

　guttatus, 40, 53, 60, 108, **440–441,** 621, 641, 645, 647
　minimus, 99, 108, 224, **437,** 648, 650
　ustulatus, 40, 108, 224, 437, **438–439,** 622, 641
Catoptrophorus semipalmatus, 105, **261,** 649
Certhia americana, 54, 108, **417–418,** 618, 640, 647
Ceryle alcyon, 4, 21, 48, 61, 107, **360–361,** 628, 630, 638, 647
Chaetura pelagica, 17, 89, 94, 107, **356–357,** 394, 620, 631, 633, 638
Charadrius alexandrinus, 104, **253**
　melodus, 19, 29, 56, 64, 82, 104, **254,** 633, 637
　semipalmatus, 104, **253,** 377, 649
　vociferus, 19, 85, 104, **255,** 443, 558, 585, 628, 632, 633, 636, 646
Chat, Yellow-breasted, 5, 16, 19, 40, 88, 110, **522–523,** 643
Chen caerulescens, 17, 102, **153–154,** 646
　rossii, 102, **154**
Chickadee, Black-capped, 88, 90, 94, 108, **410–411,** 620, 640, 647
　Boreal, 5, 66, 108, **411–412,** 622, 640, 647
Chicken, Greater Prairie-. *See* Prairie-Chicken, Greater
Chlidonias leucopterus, 106, **320**
　niger, 19, 27, 30, 38, 40, 106, **320–321,** 629, 637
Chondestes grammacus, 17, 40, 52, 64, 111, **546–547,** 628, 643
Chordeiles minor, 4, 20, 49, 64, 89, 107, **352–353,** 628, 633, 638
Chuck-will's-widow, 107, **353–354,** 638
Circus cyaneus, 18, 52, 85, 88, 103, **207–208,** 607, 635, 646
Cistothorus palustris, 38, 108, **426–427,** 629, 633, 640
　platensis, 16, 40, 52, 56, 85, 88, 108, **424–425,** 554, 640
Clangula hyemalis, 54, 103, **183–184,** 645, 646
Coccothraustes vespertinus, 5, 16, 94, 112, 591, 592, **603–604,** 644, 645, 647
Coccyzus americanus, 17, 106, **331,** 638
　erythropthalmus, 106, **330–331,** 586, 637
Colaptes auratus, 4, 19, 61, 90, 107, 363, **372–373,** 459, 639, 647
Colinus virginianus, 3, 12, 16, 20, 21, 26, 27, 41, 85, 104, **238–239,** 623, 636, 645, 646
Columba livia, 69, 90, 106, **324,** 632, 633, 637, 646
Columbina passerina, 106, **328**
Contopus borealis, 40, 52, 107, **375–376,** 622, 639
　sordidulus, 107, **609–610**
　virens, 107, **376–377,** 525, 609, 617, 621, 639
Conuropsis carolinensis, 106, **329**
Coot, American, 38, 104, 176, **247–248,** 636, 646
Coragyps atratus, 103, **198**
Cormorant, Double-crested, 18, 19, 27, 29, 30, 48, 82, 89, 102, **125–126,** 631, 634

Corvus brachyrhynchos, 16, 17, 21, 64, 82, 108, 337, **406–407,** 459, 598, 626, 632, 640, 647
　corax, 4, 16, 19, 40, 48, 53, 54, 81, 108, **408–409,** 640, 647
Coturnicops noveboracensis, 104, **240–241,** 636
Cowbird, Brown-headed, 17, 18, 19, 84, 111, 460, 468, 480, 482, 509, 517, 523, 539, 551, 558, 584, **586–587,** 588, 603, 644, 647
Crane, Sandhill, 16, 27, 38, 39, 51, 52, 89, 90, 104, **249–250,** 637
　Whooping, 16, 104, **250**
Creeper, Brown, 54, 108, **417–418,** 618, 640, 647
Crossbill, Red, 112, 592, **595–596,** 621, 644, 645, 647
　White-winged, 5, 112, 592, **597–598,** 644, 645, 647
Crotophaga sulcirostris, 106, **332–333,** 650
Crow, American, 16, 17, 21, 64, 82, 108, 337, **406–407,** 459, 598, 626, 632, 640, 647
Cuckoo, Black-billed, 106, **330–331,** 586, 637
　Yellow-billed, 17, 106, **331,** 638
Curlew, Eskimo, 15, 105, **264**
　Long-billed, 6, 12, 16, 40, 105, **266,** 649
Cyanocitta cristata, 4, 88, 89, 94, 108, **403–404,** 617, 626, 640, 647
Cygnus buccinator, 16, 22, 30, 89, 102, **149–150**
　columbianus, 39, 102, **148–149,** 644, 646
　olor, 22, 90, 102, **151,** 634, 646

Dendragapus canadensis, 14, 66, 104, **231–232,** 622, 636, 646
Dendrocygna bicolor, 102, **148**
Dendroica caerulescens, 109, **485–486,** 642
　castanea, 109, 485, **498–499,** 650
　cerulea, 5, 110, **501–502,** 642
　coronata, 40, 56, 109, 464, 482, **487–488,** 621, 642, 647, 648
　discolor, 19, 109, **496–497,** 642
　dominica, 30, 109, **492–493,** 642
　fusca, 14, 109, 485, **491,** 621, 642, 650
　kirtlandii, 37, 109, **494–495,** 633, 650
　magnolia, 109, **482–483,** 642
　nigrescens, 109, **488**
　occidentalis, 109, **489**
　palmarum, 52, 109, **497–498,** 622, 642, 648
　pensylvanica, 14, 109, **481–482,** 517, 642
　petechia, 16, 88, 109, **480–481,** 517, 587, 632, 642
　pinus, 84, 109, **493–494,** 621, 642
　striata, 109, **500–501,** 633, 648, 650
　tigrina, 39, 109, **484–485,** 642
　virens, 14, 44, 109, 224, **489–490,** 642
Dickcissel, 17, 19, 27, 30, 39, 40, 84, 85, 110, **536–537,** 643
Dolichonyx oryzivorus, 12, 27, 52, 84, 85, 111, 554, **575–576,** 644
Dove, Common Ground-. *See* Ground-Dove, Common
　Mourning, 15, 39, 67, 85, 89, 106, **325–326,** 621, 628, 632, 637, 646

Dove (*continued*)
    Ringed Turtle-. *See* Turtle-Dove, Ringed
    Rock, 69, 90, 106, **324,** 632, 633, 637,
      646
Dovekie, 39, 106, **322**
Dowitcher, Long-billed, 105, 283, **284–285,** 649
    Short-billed, 105, **283–284,** 285, 649
Dryocopus pileatus, 17, 40, 50, 84, 107, **373–374,** 620, 639, 647
Duck, American Black, 102, **160–161,** 162, 634, 646
    Fulvous Whistling-. *See* Whistling-Duck, Fulvous
    Harlequin, 103, **182,** 646
    Masked, 103, **197**
    Ring-necked, 103, **176–177,** 635, 646
    Ruddy, 17, 40, 103, 174, **196–197,** 635, 646
    Wood, 4, 17, 20, 22, 38, 40, 44, 89, 102, **158–159,** 617, 618, 633, 634, 646
Dumetella carolinensis, 4, 12, 56, 88, 108, **446–447,** 624, 641, 645, 647
Dunlin, 105, **278,** 649

Eagle, Bald, 4, 18, 19, 27, 29, 30, 33, 40, 48, 51, 54, 61, 82, 103, **205–206,** 619, 631, 635, 645, 646
    Golden, 5, 104, **221–222,** 646
Ectopistes migratorius, 3, 4, 15, 16, 17, 20, 82, 106, **326–327**
Egret, Cattle, 19, 40, 102, 136, **138–139,** 634, 648
    Great, 15, 19, 27, 29, 39, 40, 94, 102, **134–135,** 136, 634
    Snowy, 102, **135–136,** 634
Egretta, caerulea, 102, **136–137,** 633, 649
    thula, 102, **135–136,** 634
    tricolor, 102, **137–138,** 633, 649
Eider, Common, 103, **180–181**
    King, 103, **181,** 649
Elanoides forficatus, 5, 16, 39, 106, **202–203**
Elanus caeruleus, 103, **203**
Empidonax alnorum, 40, 107, **380–381,** 382, 384, 609, 639
    flaviventris, 40, 107, **377–378,** 384, 639
    minimus, 40, 107, **383–384,** 639
    traillii, 88, 107, 380, 381, **382–383,** 384, 639
    virescens, 17, 40, 107, **379–380,** 617, 639
Eremophila alpestris, 52, 61, 64, 85, 107, **392–393,** 571, 574, 626, 628, 639, 647
Eudocimus albus, 102, **607**
Euphagus carolinus, 61, 111, **582–583,** 584, 647
    cyanocephalus, 17, 18, 40, 53, 111, 582, **583–584,** 644, 647

Falco columbarius, 104, **224–225,** 622, 636, 646
    mexicanus, 104, **607–608**
    peregrinus, 18, 19, 22, 29, 30, 48, 50, 83, 89, 90, 104, **225–226,** 631, 633, 636
    rusticolis, 104, **227–228,** 646
    sparverius, 61, 69, 85, 104, **222–223,** 624, 628, 632, 633, 636, 646
Falcon, Peregrine, 18, 19, 22, 23, 30, 48, 50, 83, 89, 104, **225–226,** 631, 633, 636
    Prairie, 104, **607–608**

Finch, House, 19, 90, 112, **594–595,** 600, 644, 647
    Purple, 112, 588, **593–594,** 621, 644, 647, 648
    Rosy, 111, **591**
Flicker, Northern, 4, 19, 61, 90, 107, 363, **372–373,** 459, 639, 647
Flycatcher, Acadian, 17, 40, 107, **379–380,** 617, 639
    Alder, 40, 107, **380–381,** 382, 384, 609, 639
    Fork-tailed, 107, **391**
    Great Crested, 84, 107, **386–387,** 525, 617, 639
    Least, 40, 107, **383–384,** 639
    Olive-sided, 40, 52, 107, **375–376,** 622, 639
    Scissor-tailed, 107, **390–391,** 633, 650
    Vermilion, 107, **610**
    Willow, 88, 107, 380, 381, **382–383,** 384, 639
    Yellow-bellied, 40, 107, **377–378,** 384, 639
Fregata magnificens, 102, **129**
Frigatebird, Magnificent, 102, **129**
Fulica americana, 38, 104, 176, **247–248,** 636, 646

Gadwall, 16, 103, 161, **169–170,** 171, 172, 635, 646
Gallinago gallinago, 40, 52, 88, 105, **285–286,** 637, 645, 646
Gallinula chloropus, 38, 40, 104, **246–247,** 636
Gallinule, Purple, 104, **245–246,** 649
Gavia immer, 4, 19, 27, 30, 40, 51, 82, 101, **115–116,** 631, 634, 635
    pacifica, 101, **114–115,** 649
    stellata, 19, 101, **113–114,** 649
Geothlypis trichas, 39, 88, 110, **517–518,** 624, 643, 645
Gnatcatcher, Blue-gray, 18, 40, 94, 108, **431–432,** 618, 640
Godwit, Hudsonian, 17, 105, **267,** 649
    Marbled, 105, **268,** 649
Golden-Plover, Lesser, 6, 15, 17, 104, **252,** 648, 649
Goldeneye, Barrow's, 103, **189–190,** 646
    Common, 103, **188–189,** 635, 645, 646
Goldfinch, American, 88, 112, 592, 598, 600, **602–603,** 612, 624, 632, 644, 647
    European, **613**
    Lesser, 112, **612**
Goose, Barnacle, **613**
    Canada, 4, 22, 90, 102, **156–157,** 162, 443, 633, 634, 645, 646
    Greater White-fronted, 17, 102, **152–153,** 649
    Ross', 102, **154**
    Snow, 17, 102, **153–154,** 646
Goshawk, Northern, 17, 40, 103, **211–212,** 635, 646
Grackle, Common, 19, 61, 89, 111, 407, 442, 459, 460, 582, **585–586,** 617, 632, 644, 647
Grebe, Clark's, 102, **607**
    Eared, 19, 102, **120–121,** 649
    Horned, 101, **118–119,** 634, 646
    Pied-billed, 38, 101, **117–118,** 634, 646

    Red-necked, 19, 29, 40, 89, 102, **119–120,** 634
    Western, 102, **122,** 607, 649
Grosbeak, Black-headed, 110, **530–531,** 647
    Blue, 110, **532–533,** 643
    Evening, 5, 16, 94, 112, 591, 592, **603–604,** 644, 645, 647
    Pine, 5, 111, **592–593,** 645, 647
    Rose-breasted, 40, 84, 110, 525, **529–530,** 617, 621, 632, 643
Ground-Dove, Common, 106, **328**
Grouse, Ruffed, 14, 16, 17, 20, 26, 27, 40, 50, 58, 80, 84, 94, 104, **233,** 617, 619, 620, 636, 646
    Sharp-tailed, 3, 16, 17, 26, 27, 40, 81, 88, 104, **235–236,** 625, 628, 636, 646
    Spruce, 14, 66, 104, **231–232,** 622, 636, 646
Grus americana, 16, 104, **250**
    canadensis, 16, 27, 38, 39, 51, 52, 89, 90, 104, **249–250,** 637
Guiraca caerulea, 110, **532–533,** 643
Gull, Bonaparte's, 105, **299–300,** 637
    Common Black-headed, 19, 105, **298–299,** 649
    Franklin's, 105, **296–297,** 307, 633, 649
    Glaucous, 106, 305, **308–309,** 646
    Great Black-backed, 106, 299, **309–310,** 646
    Herring, 30, 106, **302–303,** 304, 306, 307, 631, 637, 646
    Iceland, 106, **305–306,** 646
    Ivory, 106, **312,** 646
    Laughing, 19, 105, **294–295,** 633, 649
    Lesser Black-backed, 19, 106, **307,** 649
    Little, 19, 105, **297–298,** 637
    Mew, 19, 105, **300**
    Ring-billed, 19, 106, 299, **301–302,** 307, 631, 637, 646
    Sabine's, 106, **311**
    Thayer's, 106, **304–305,** 306, 646
Gyrfalcon, 104, **227–228,** 646

Haliaeetus leucocephalus, 4, 18, 19, 27, 29, 30, 33, 40, 48, 51, 54, 61, 82, 103, **205–206,** 619, 631, 635, 645, 646
Harrier, Northern, 18, 52, 85, 88, 103, **207–208,** 607, 635, 646
Hawk, Broad-winged, 50, 84, 103, 208, **214–215,** 636
    Cooper's, 18, 19, 29, 61, 103, **210–211,** 337, 635, 646
    Ferruginous, 104, **219,** 649
    Harris', **613**
    Red-shouldered, 18, 29, 54, 60, 64, 103, **213–214,** 618, 636, 646
    Red-tailed, 39, 51, 55, 58, 61, 99, 104, **217–218,** 337, 618, 636, 646
    Rough-legged, 104, **220–221,** 646
    Sharp-shinned, 52, 103, **208–209,** 621, 635, 646
    Swainson's, 19, 103, **216–217,** 649
Helmitheros vermivorus, 5, 19, 30, 110, **507–508,** 642
Heron, Black-crowned Night-. *See* Night-Heron, Black-crowned
    Great Blue, 27, 82, 94, 102, **132–133,**

337, 631, 634, 646
  Green-backed, 40, 102, **140–141,** 630,
    634
  Little Blue, 102, **136–137,** 633, 649
  Tricolored, 102, **137–138,** 633, 649
  Yellow-crowned Night-. *See* Night-
    Heron, Yellow-crowned
Himantopus mexicanus, 104, **256**
Hirundo pyrrhonota, 17, 89, 108, 396, **399–
  400,** 401, 631, 633, 639
  rustica, 15, 17, 19, 39, 89, 108, 396, **400–
    401,** 633, 640
Histrionicus histrionicus, 103, **182,** 646
Hummingbird, Anna's, 107, **359**
  Ruby-throated, 4, 107, **358–359,** 620,
    638
  Rufous, 107, **359**
Hylocichla mustelina, 84, 108, **441–442,** 617,
  632, 641

Ibis, Glossy, 102, **144–145,** 146, 649
  White, 102, **607**
  White-faced, 102, 144, **145–146**
Icteria virens, 5, 16, 19, 40, 88, 110, **522–
  523,** 643
Icterus galbula, 18, 61, 83, 111, 363, **589–
  590,** 617, 621, 623, 630, 644
  spurius, 39, 111, **588–589,** 644
Ictinia mississippiensis, 103, **204–205,** 649
Ixobrychus exilis, 38, 102, **131–132,** 629, 634
Ixoreus naevius, 108, **444–445,** 647

Jaeger, Long-tailed, 105, **294**
  Parasitic, 105, **293,** 294, 649
  Pomarine, 105, **292**
Jay, Blue, 4, 88, 89, 94, 108, **403–404,** 617,
    626, 640, 647
  Gray, 5, 40, 56, 66, 108, **402–403,** 622,
    640, 647
  Gray-breasted, **613**
Junco, Dark-eyed, 111, 471, 486, 560, **569–
  570,** 598, 621, 644, 647, 648
Junco hyemalis, 111, 471, 486, 560, **569–
  570,** 598, 621, 644, 647, 648

Kestrel, American, 61, 69, 85, 104, **222–
  223,** 624, 628, 632, 633, 636, 646
Killdeer, 19, 85, 104, **255,** 443, 558, 585,
    628, 632, 637, 646
Kingbird, Cassin's, 107, **610**
  Eastern, 39, 48, 107, 342, 363, **389,** 610,
    639
  Western, 40, 107, **387–388,** 610, 639
Kingfisher, Belted, 4, 21, 48, 61, 107, **360–
  361,** 628, 630, 638, 647
Kinglet, Golden-crowned, 40, 108, **428–
  429,** 622, 640, 645, 647
  Ruby-crowned, 108, **429–430,** 464, 622,
    640, 647
Kite, American Swallow-tailed, 5, 16, 39,
    103, **202–203**
  Black-shouldered, 103, **203**
  Mississippi, 103, **204–205,** 649
Kittiwake, Black-legged, 106, 299, **310–
  311,** 649
Knot, Red, 105, **270–271,** 649

Lagopus lagopus, 22, 104, **232**
Lanius excubitor, 109, **456–457,** 645, 647

  ludovicianus, 19, 27, 29, 109, **457–458,**
    641
Lark, Horned, 52, 61, 64, 85, 107, **392–
  393,** 571, 574, 626, 628, 639, 647
Larus argentatus, 30, 106, **302–303,** 304,
    306, 307, 631, 637, 646
  atricilla, 19, 105, **294–295,** 633, 649
  canus, 19, 105, **300**
  delawarensis, 19, 106, 199, **301–302,** 307,
    631, 637, 646
  fuscus, 19, 106, **307,** 649
  glaucoides, 106, **305–306,** 646
  hyperboreus, 106, 305, **308–309,** 646
  marinus, 106, 299, **309–310,** 646
  minutus, 19, 105, **297–298,** 637
  philadelphia, 105, **299–300,** 637
  pipixcan, 105, **296–297,** 307, 633, 649
  ridibundus, 19, 105, **298–299,** 649
  thayeri, 106, **304–305,** 306, 646
Laterallus jamaicensis, 104, **608**
Leucosticte arctoa, 111, **591**
Limnodromus griseus, 105, **283–284,** 285,
    649
  scolopaceus, 105, 283, **284–285,** 649
Limosa fedoa, 105, **268,** 649
  haemastica, 17, 105, **267,** 649
Longspur, Chestnut-collared, 111, **573**
  Lapland, 111, **570–571,** 574, 611, 645,
    647
  Smith's, 111, **572,** 650
Loon, Common, 4, 19, 27, 30, 40, 51, 82,
    101, **115–116,** 631, 634, 645
  Pacific, 101, **114–115,** 649
  Red-throated, 19, 101, **113–114,** 649
Lophodytes cucullatus, 103, **191–192,** 630,
    635
Loxia curvirostra, 112, 592, **595–596,** 621,
    644, 645, 647
  leucoptera, 5, 112, 592, **597–598,** 644,
    645, 647

Magpie, Black-billed, 108, **405–406,** 650
Mallard, 20, 38, 51, 94, 99, 102, 161,
    162–163, 171, 172, 625, 632, 633, 634,
    645, 646
Martin, Purple, 17, 18, 37, 89, 90, 107,
    394–395, 400, 401, 620, 633, 639
Meadowlark, Eastern, 17, 18, 19, 27, 36,
    38, 52, 61, 84, 85, 111, **578–579,** 580,
    632, 644, 647
  Western, 17, 18, 19, 27, 30, 36, 37, 38,
    40, 52, 61, 84, 85, 111, 578, **579–580,**
    632, 644, 647
Melanerpes carolinus, 17, 18, 27, 40, 54, 60,
    107, **364–365,** 618, 638, 647
  erythrocephalus, 4, 17, 37, 61, 82, 85, 107,
    363–364, 459, 617, 638, 647
  lewis, 107, **362**
Melanitta fusca, 103, **186–187,** 646
  nigra, 103, **184–185,** 649
  perspicillata, 103, **185–186,** 649
Meleagris gallopavo, 3, 4, 16, 21, 89, 104,
    237–238, 617, 636, 646
Melospiza georgiana, 40, 88, 111, 540, **562–
  563,** 643, 647
  lincolnii, 40, 52, 111, 224, 540, **560–561,**
    562, 643
  melodia, 4, 48, 88, 110, 224, 540, 558, **559–
    560,** 562, 624, 632, 643, 647

Merganser, Common, 40, 51, 52, 103,
    193–194, 631, 635, 645, 646
  Hooded, 103, **191–192,** 630, 635
  Red-breasted, 40, 51, 52, 103, **194–195,**
    635, 646
Mergus merganser, 40, 51, 52, 103, **193–
  194,** 631, 635, 645, 646
  serrator, 40, 51, 52, 103, **194–195,** 635,
    646
Merlin, 104, **224–225,** 622, 636, 646
Mimus polyglottos, 5, 16, 108, **447–448,**
    632, 641, 647
Mniotilta varia, 84, 110, 464, 485, **503–504,**
    642
Mockingbird, Northern, 5, 16, 108, **447–
  448,** 632, 641, 647
Molothrus ater, 17, 18, 19, 84, 111, 460, 480,
    482, 509, 517, 523, 539, 551, 558, 584,
    586–587, 588, 608, 644, 647
Moorhen, Common, 38, 40, 104, **246–
  247,** 636
Murrelet, Ancient, 106, **322–323,** 649
Myadestes townsendi, 108, **435,** 647
Mycteria americana, 102, **147**
Myiarchus, crinitus, 84, 107, **386–387,** 525,
    617, 639
Myioborus pictus, 110, **612**

Night-Heron, Black-crowned, 17, 19, 30,
    102, 136, 139, **141–142,** 634
  Yellow-crowned, 17, 19, 30, 102, **142–
    143,** 634
Nighthawk, Common, 4, 20, 49, 64, 89,
    107, **352–353,** 628, 633, 638
Nucifraga columbiana, 108, **404–405**
Numenius americanus, 6, 12, 16, 40, 105,
    266, 649
  borealis, 15, 105, **264**
  phaeopus, 105, **265–266,** 649
Nutcracker, Clark's, 108, **404–405**
Nuthatch, Brown-headed, 108, **416**
  Red-breasted, 17, 58, 108, 224, **414–415,**
    621, 640, 645, 647, 648
  White-breasted, 108, **415–416,** 621, 640,
    647
Nyctanassa violacea, 17, 19, 30, 102, **142–
  143,** 634
Nyctea scandiaca, 106, **338–339,** 645, 646
Nycticorax nycticorax, 17, 19, 30, 102, 136,
    139, **141–142,** 634

Oenanthe oenanthe, 108, **611**
Oldsquaw, 54, 103, **183–184,** 645, 646
Oporornis agilis, 39, 110, **514–515,** 517, 620,
    621, 642
  formosus, 40, 110, **513–514,** 642
  philadelphia, 40, 88, 110, 514, **516–517,**
    620, 625, 643
Oreoscoptes montanus, 108, **448–449**
Oriole, Northern, 18, 61, 83, 111, 363,
    589–590, 617, 621, 623, 630, 644
  Orchard, 39, 111, **588–589,** 644
Osprey, 4, 18, 19, 27, 29, 30, 40, 48, 51,
    82, 89, 103, **201–202,** 619, 631, 635
Otus asio, 83, 106, **336–337,** 632, 638, 646
Ovenbird, 40, 55, 61, 110, **508–509,** 517,
    525, 617, 620, 642
Owl, Barn, 29, 30, 40, 89, 106, **334–335,**
    633, 638, 646

Owl (*continued*)
  Barred, 64, 84, 106, **343**, 618, 638, 646
  Boreal, 107, **348–349**, 647
  Burrowing, 106, **341–342**, 648, 650
  Eastern Screech-. *See* Screech-Owl,
    Eastern
  Great Gray, 5, 16, 106, **344–345**, 638,
    646
  Great Horned, 17, 22, 51, 52, 94, 106,
    337–338, 618, 638, 646
  Long-eared, 52, 106, **346–347**, 638, 646
  Northern Hawk, 5, 16, 106, **340–341**,
    646
  Northern Saw-whet, 40, 52, 107, 349,
    350–351, 638, 647
  Short-eared, 52, 88, 106, **347–348**, 638,
    646
  Snowy, 106, **338–339**, 645, 646
Oxyura dominica, 103, **197**
  jamaicensis, 17, 40, 103, 174, **196–197**,
    635, 646

Pagophila eburnea, 106, **312**, 646
Pandion haliaetus, 4, 18, 19, 27, 29, 30, 40,
    48, 51, 82, 89, 103, **201–202**, 619, 631,
    635
Parabuteo unicinctus, **613**
Parakeet, Carolina, 106, **329**
Paroaria coronata, **613**
Partridge, Gray, 17, 22, 26, 104, **229–230**,
    626, 636, 645, 646
Parula americana, 84, 109, **478–479**, 642
Parula, Northern, 84, 109, **478–479**, 642
Parus atricapillus, 88, 90, 94, 108, **410–411**,
    620, 640, 647
  bicolor, 17, 108, **412–413**, 617, 640, 647
  hudsonicus, 5, 66, 108, **411–412**, 622,
    640, 647
Passer domesticus, 17, 19, 21, 69, 90, 94,
    112, 336, 395, 407, 442, 459, 542, 585,
    598, **605–606**, 644, 647
  montanus, 112, **606**
Passerculus sandwichensis, 84, 111, 540,
    550–551, 554, 643
Passerella iliaca, 111, **558–559**, 647
Passerina amoena, 110, **533**
  ciris, 110, **535–536**, 650
  cyanea, 52, 88, 110, 525, **534–535**, 617,
    621, 624, 643
Pelecanus erythrorhynchos, 3, 4, 17, 39, 102,
    123–124, 633, 648, 649
  occidentalis, 102, **124**
Pelican, American White, 3, 4, 17, 39,
    102, **123–124**, 633, 648, 649
  Brown, 102, **124**
Perdix perdix, 17, 22, 26, 104, **229–230**,
    626, 636, 645, 646
Perisoreus canadensis, 5, 40, 56, 66, 108,
    402–403, 622, 640, 647
Pewee, Eastern Wood-. *See* Wood-Pewee,
    Eastern
  Western Wood-. *See* Wood-Pewee,
    Western
Phalacrocorax auritus, 18, 19, 27, 29, 30, 48,
    82, 89, 102, **125–126**, 631, 634
Phalarope, Red, 105, **290–291**, 649
  Red-necked, 105, **289–290**, 649
  Wilson's, 40, 105, **288**, 637

Phalaropus fulicaria,105, **290–291**, 649
  lobatus, 105, **289–290**, 649
  tricolor, 40, 105, **288**, 637
Phasianus colchicus, 3, 17, 21, 26, 68, 85,
    88, 90, 104, **230–231**, 623, 624, 626,
    636, 645, 646
Pheasant, Ring-necked, 3, 17, 21, 26, 68,
    , 85, 88, 90, 104, **230–231**, 623, 624,
    626, 636, 645, 646
Pheucticus ludovicianus, 40, 84, 110, 525,
    529–530, 617, 621, 632, 643
  melanocephalus, 110, **530–531**, 647
Philomachus pugnax, 105, **282–283**, 649
Phoebe, Eastern, 40, 48, 89, 107, **384–
    385**, 630, 639
  Say's, 107, **385**
Pica pica, 108, **405–406**, 650
Picoides arcticus, 5, 17, 82, 107, **370–371**,
    622, 639, 647
  pubescens, 88, 107, **367**, 638, 647
  tridactylus, 5, 17, 107, **369–370**, 647
  villosus, 84, 107, 367, **368**, 638, 647
Pigeon, Passenger, 3, 4, 15, 16, 17, 20, 82,
    106, **326–327**
Pinicola enucleator, 5, 111, **592–593**, 645,
    647
Pintail, Northern, 102, 161, **164–165,** 171,
    172, 635, 646
  White-cheeked, 102, **163**
Pipilo chlorurus, 110, **538**, 647
  erythrophthalmus, 52, 57, 82, 110, **539–
    540**, 621, 622, 632, 643, 647
Pipit, American, 109, **452**, 611, 650
  Sprague's, 109, **611**
Piranga ludoviciana, 110, **526–527**, 533, 650
  olivacea, 40, 84, 110, **525–526**, 621, 643
  rubra, 110, **524**, 650
Plectrophenax nivalis, 111, 511, **574**, 611,
    645, 647
Plegadis chihi, 102, 144, **145–146**
  falcinellus, 102, **144–145**, 146, 649
Plover, Black-bellied, 99, 104, **251**, 648,
    649
  Lesser Golden-. *See* Golden-Plover,
    Lesser
  Piping, 19, 29, 56, 64, 82, 104, **254,** 633,
    637
  Semipalmated, 104, **253**, 377, 649
  Snowy, 104, **253**
Pluvialis dominica, 6, 15, 17, 104, **252**, 648,
    649
  squatarola, 99, 104, **251**, 648, 649
Podiceps auritus, 101, **118–119**, 634, 646
  grisegena, 19, 29, 40, 89, 102, **119–120**,
    634
  nigricollis, 19, 102, **120–121**, 649
Podilymbus podiceps, 38, 101, **117–118**, 634,
    646
Polioptila caerulea, 18, 40, 94, 108, **431–432**,
    618, 640
Pooecetes gramineus, 16, 18, 19, 27, 67, 84,
    85, 110, **545–546**, 628, 643
Porphyrula martinica, 104, **245–246**, 649
Porzana carolina, 38, 104, **244–245**, 608,
    636
Prairie-Chicken, Greater, 4, 16, 17, 20, 21,
    26, 27, 29, 31, 40, 52, 56, 80, 82, 85, 88,
    89, 99, 104, **234–235**, 625, 636, 646

Progne subis, 17, 18, 37, 89, 90, 107, **394–
    395**, 400, 401, 620, 633, 639
Protonotaria critrea, 40, 110, **506–507**, 630,
    642
Ptarmigan, Willow, 22, 104, **232**
Pyrocephalus rubinus, 107, **610**

Quiscula quiscula, 19, 61, 89, 111, 407, 442,
    459, 460, 582, **585–586**, 617, 632, 644,
    647

Rail, Black, 104, **608**
  King, 17, 19, 40, 104, **241–242**, 636
  Virginia, 38, 104, **242–243**, 608, 636
  Yellow, 104, **240–241**, 636
Rallus elegans, 17, 19, 40, 104, **241–242**, 636
  limicola, 38, 104, **242–243**, 608, 636
Raven, Common, 4, 16, 19, 40, 48, 53, 54,
    81, 108, **408–409**, 640, 647
Recurvirostra americana, 39, 104, **257**, 649
Redhead, 17, 103, **175–176**, 635, 646
Redpoll, Common, 112, **598–599**, 600,
    645, 647
  Hoary, 112, **599–600**, 647
Redshank, Spotted, 104, **609**
Redstart, American, 17, 48, 110, 480, 482,
    485, **504–505**, 617, 630, 642
  Painted, 110, **612**
Regulus calendula, 108, **429–430**, 464, 622,
    640, 647
  satrapa, 40, 108, **428–429**, 622, 640, 645,
    647
Riparia riparia, 108, 396, **398–399**, 628, 639
Rissa tridactyla, 106, 299, **310–311**, 649
Robin, American, 4, 15, 18, 19, 21, 38, 39,
    52, 55, 83, 88, 89, 108, 372, 407, **442–
    443**, 459, 558, 633, 641, 645, 647
Ruff, 105, **282–283**, 649

Sanderling, 105, **271–272**, 649
Sandpiper, Baird's, 105, **275–276**, 649
  Buff-breasted, 105, **281–282**, 649
  Curlew, 105, **279**, 649
  Least, 105, **274**, 649
  Pectoral, 17, 99, 105, **276–277**, 649
  Purple, 105, **277–278**, 649
  Semipalmated, 105, **272–273**, 649
  Solitary, 104, **260**, 649
  Spotted, 105, **262**, 628, 630, 631, 637
  Stilt, 19, 105, **280–281**, 649
  Upland, 6, 12, 15, 17, 30, 40, 52, 53, 56,
    85, 105, **263–264**, 637
  Western, 105, **273–274**, 649
  White-rumped, 105, **275**, 649
Sapsucker, Yellow-bellied, 17, 54, 107,
    365–366, 618, 638, 647
Sayornis phoebe, 40, 48, 89, 107, **384–385**,
    630, 639
  saya, 107, **385**
Scaup, Greater, 103, 162, **178–179**, 180,
    646
  Lesser, 103, 162, 176, 178, **179–180**, 635,
    646
Scolopax minor, 4, 16, 20, 27, 40, 88, 105,
    286–287, 625, 637
Scoter, Black, 103, **184–185**, 649
  Surf, 103, **185–186**, 649
  White-winged, 103, **186–187**, 646

Screech-Owl, Eastern, 83, 106, **336–337,** 632, 638, 646
Seiurus aurocapillus, 40, 55, 61, 110, **508– 509,** 517, 525, 617, 620, 642
  motacilla, 37, 49, 110, 510, **511–512,** 630, 642
  noveboracensis, 37, 52, 110, **510–511,** 512, 630, 642
Selasphorus rufus, 107, **359**
Setophaga ruticilla, 17, 48, 110, 480, 482, 485, **504–505,** 617, 630, 642
Shoveler, Northern, 40, 103, 161, **167–168,** 171, 172, 635, 646
Shrike, Loggerhead, 19, 27, 29, 109, **457– 458,** 641
  Northern, 109, **456–457,** 645, 647
Sialia currucoides, 108, **434,** 650
  sialis, 19, 20, 37, 82, 89, 90, 108, **432– 433,** 558, 621, 624, 628, 641, 647
Siskin, Pine, 112, 592, **600–601,** 644, 647
Sitta canadensis, 17, 58, 108, 224, **414–415,** 621, 640, 645, 647, 648
  carolinensis, 108, **415–416,** 621, 640, 647
  pusilla, 108, **416**
Snipe, Common, 40, 52, 88, 105, **285– 286,** 637, 645, 646
Solitaire, Townsend's, 108, **435,** 647
Somateria mollissima, 103, **180–181**
  spectabilis, 103, **181,** 649
Sora, 38, 104, **244–245,** 608, 636
Sparrow, American Tree, 88, 110, **540– 541,** 546, 598, 644, 647, 648
  Baird's, 111, **551–552,** 650
  Black-throated, 111, **547–548**
  Chipping, 89, 110, 224, **541–542,** 543, 621, 632, 643
  Clay-colored, 18, 40, 64, 110, **542–543,** 621, 622, 643
  Eurasian Tree, 112, **606**
  Field, 16, 85, 110, 540, 543, **544,** 624, 643, 647
  Fox, 111, **558–559,** 647
  Golden-crowned, 111, **565**
  Grasshopper, 19, 27, 30, 84, 85, 111, **552–553,** 643
  Harris', 111, **567–568,** 647
  Henslow's, 85, 111, **554,** 643
  House, 17, 19, 21, 69, 90, 94, 112, 336, 395, 407, 442, 459, 542, 585, 598, **605– 606,** 644, 647
  Lark, 17, 40, 52, 64, 111, **546–547,** 628, 643
  Le Conte's, 88, 111, **555–556,** 628, 643
  Lincoln's, 40, 52, 111, 224, 540, **560– 561,** 562, 643
  Savannah, 84, 111, 540, **550–551,** 554, 643
  Sharp-tailed, 111, **556–557,** 628, 643
  Song, 4, 48, 88, 110, 224, 540, 558, **559– 560,** 562, 624, 632, 643, 647
  Swamp, 40, 88, 111, 540, **562–563,** 643, 647
  Vesper, 16, 18, 19, 27, 67, 84, 85, 110, **545–546,** 628, 643
  White-crowned, 39, 111, **566–567,** 568, 647
  White-throated, 40, 52, 59, 111, 540, 558, **563–564,** 622, 644, 647, 648

Sphyrapicus varius, 17, 54, 107, **365–366,** 618, 638, 647
Spiza americana, 17, 19, 27, 30, 39, 40, 84, 85, 110, **536–537,** 643
Spizella arborea, 88, 110, **540–541,** 546, 598, 644, 647, 648
  pallida, 18, 40, 64, 110, **542–543,** 621, 622, 643
  passerina, 89, 110, 224, **541–542,** 543, 621, 632, 643
  pusilla, 16, 85, 110, 540, 543, **544,** 624, 643, 647
Spoonbill, Roseate, 102, **146**
Starling, European, 17, 19, 69, 90, 109, 395, 407, 442, **459–460,** 585, 598, 620, 632, 633, 641, 647
Stelgidopteryx serripennis, 108, **397–398,** 628, 639
Stercorarius longicaudus, 105, **294**
  parasiticus, 105, **293,** 294, 649
  pomarinus, 105, **292**
Sterna antillarum, 106, **318–319,** 633, 649
  caspia, 106, **313–314,** 631, 637
  dougallii, 106, **609**
  forsteri, 17, 19, 29, 30, 40, 106, 315, 316, **317–318,** 609, 637
  fuscata, 106, **319**
  hirundo, 19, 29, 30, 48, 106, **315–316,** 317, 631, 637
  maxima, 106, **314**
  paradisaea, 106, **316–317,** 649
Stilt, Black-necked, 104, **256**
Stork, Wood, 102, **147**
Streptopelia risoria, **613**
Strix nebulosa, 5, 16, 106, **344–345,** 638, 646
  varia, 64, 84, 106, **343,** 618, 638, 646
Sturnella magna, 17, 18, 19, 27, 36, 38, 52, 61, 84, 85, 111, **578–579,** 580, 632, 644, 647
  neglecta, 17, 18, 19, 27, 30, 36, 37, 38, 40, 52, 61, 84, 85, 111, 578, **579–580,** 632, 644, 647
Sturnus vulgaris, 17, 19, 69, 90, 109, 395, 407, 442, **459–460,** 585, 598, 620, 632, 633, 641, 647
Surnia ulula, 5, 16, 106, **340–341,** 646
Swallow, Bank, 108, 396, **398–399,** 628, 639
  Barn, 15, 17, 19, 39, 89, 108, 396, **400– 401,** 633, 640
  Cliff, 17, 89, 108, 396, **399–400,** 401, 631, 633, 639
  Northern Rough-winged, 108, **397– 398,** 628, 639
  Tree, 37, 89, 107, 363, **395–396,** 397, 400, 401, 624, 639
Swan, Mute, 22, 90, 102, **151,** 634, 646
  Trumpeter, 16, 22, 30, 89, 102, **149–150**
  Tundra, 39, 102, **148–149,** 644, 646
Swift, Chimney, 17, 89, 94, 107, **356–357,** 394, 620, 631, 633, 638
Synthliboramphus antiquus, 106, **322–323,** 649

Tachycineta bicolor, 37, 89, 107, 363, **395– 396,** 397, 400, 401, 624, 639
Tanager, Scarlet, 40, 84, 110, **525–526,** 621, 643

  Summer, 110, **524,** 650
  Western, 110, **526–527,** 533, 650
Teal, Blue-winged, 16, 17, 20, 38, 51, 103, 162, **165–166,** 167, 171, 172, 633, 635, 645
  Cinnamon, 103, **166–167,** 649
  Green-winged, 20, 102, **159–160,** 161, 171, 172, 634, 646
Tern, Arctic, 106, **316–317,** 649
  Black, 19, 27, 30, 38, 40, 106, **320–321,** 629, 637
  Caspian, 106, **313–314,** 631, 637
  Common, 19, 29, 30, 48, 106, **315–316,** 317, 631, 637
  Forster's, 17, 19, 29, 30, 40, 106, 315, 316, **317–318,** 609, 637
  Least, 106, **318–319,** 633, 649
  Roseate, 106, **609**
  Royal, 106, **314**
  Sooty, 106, **319**
  White-winged, 106, **320**
Thrasher, Brown, 12, 17, 94, 109, **449– 450,** 624, 632, 641, 647
  Curve-billed, 109, **450–451**
  Sage, 108, **448–449**
Thrush, Gray-cheeked, 99, 108, 224, **437,** 648, 650
  Hermit, 40, 53, 60, 108, **440–441,** 621, 641, 645, 647
  Swainson's, 40, 108, 224, 437, **438–439,** 622, 641
  Varied, 108, **444–445,** 647
  Wood, 84, 108, **441–442,** 617, 632, 641
Thryomanes bewickii, 17, 19, 39, 40, 108, **420–421,** 640
Thryothorus ludovicianus, 5, 16, 40, 108, **419–420,** 640, 647
Titmouse, Tufted, 17, 108, **412–413,** 617, 640, 647
Towhee, Green-tailed, 110, **538,** 647
  Rufous-sided, 52, 57, 82, 110, **539–540,** 621, 622, 632, 643, 647
Toxostoma curvirostre, 109, **450–451**
  rufum, 12, 17, 94, 109, **449–450,** 624, 632, 641, 647
Tringa erythropus, 104, **609**
  flavipes, 17, 104, **259,** 649
  melanoleuca, 104, **258,** 649
  solitaria, 104, **260,** 649
Troglodytes aedon, 18, 37, 52, 88, 108, **422– 423,** 640
  troglodytes, 38, 40, 50, 108, **423–424,** 640, 647
Tryngites subruficollis, 105, **281–282,** 649
Turdus migratorius, 4, 15, 18, 19, 21, 38, 39, 52, 55, 83, 88, 89, 108, 372, 407, **442– 443,** 459, 558, 633, 641, 645, 647
Turkey, Wild, 3, 4, 16, 21, 89, 104, **237– 238,** 617, 636, 646
Turnstone, Black, 105, **270**
  Ruddy, 105, **269,** 649
Turtle-Dove, Ringed, **613**
Tympanuchus cupido, 4, 16, 17, 20, 21, 26, 27, 29, 31, 40, 52, 56, 80, 82, 85, 88, 89, 99, 104, **234–235,** 625, 636, 646
  phasianellus, 3, 16, 17, 26, 27, 40, 81, 88, 104, **235–236,** 625, 628, 636, 646
Tyrannus forficatus, 107, **390–391,** 633, 650

Tyrannus forficatus (*continued*)
  savana, 107, **391**
  tyrannus, 39, 48, 107, 342, 363, **389**, 610, 639
  verticalis, 40, 107, **387–388**, 610, 639
  vociferans, 107, **610**
Tyto alba, 29, 30, 40, 89, 106, **334–335**, 633, 638, 646

Veery, 52, 55, 108, **436–437**, 586, 625, 641
Vermivora celata, 109, **476–477**, 622, 650
  chrysoptera, 109, **471–472**, 473, 641
  lawrencii, **473–474**
  leucobronchialis, **473–474**
  peregrina, 109, **475–476**, 482, 622, 642
  pinus, 17, 18, 109, **470–471**, 472, 473, 625, 641
  ruficapilla, 17, 40, 52, 53, 59, 60, 109, 464, **477–478**, 621, 622, 642
Vireo, Bell's, 17, 19, 40, 88, 109, **462–463**, 625, 641
  Gray, 109, **463**
  Philadelphia, 109, 224, **467**, 650
  Red-eyed, 14, 55, 109, **468–469**, 525, 617, 621, 641
  Solitary, 109, **464**, 641
  Warbling, 19, 83, 109, **466**, 632, 641
  White-eyed, 19, 109, **461–462**, 641
  Yellow-throated, 40, 83, 109, **465**, 641
Vireo bellii, 17, 19, 40, 88, 109, **462–463**, 625, 641
  flavifrons, 40, 83, 109, **465**, 641
  gilvus, 19, 83, 109, **466**, 632, 641
  griseus, 19, 109, **461–462**, 641
  olivaceus, 14, 55, 109, **468–469**, 525, 617, 621, 641
  philadelphicus, 109, 224, **467**, 650
  solitarius, 109, **464**, 641
  vicinior, 109, **463**
Vulture, Black, 103, **198**
  Turkey, 4, 16, 40, 48, 50, 82, 103, **199–200**, 617, 635

Warbler, Bay-breasted, 109, 485, **498–499**, 650
  Black-and-white, 84, 110, 464, 485, **503–504**, 642
  Black-throated Blue, 109, **485–486**, 642
  Black-throated Gray, 109, **488**
  Black-throated Green, 14, 44, 109, 224, **489–490**, 642

  Blackburnian, 14, 109, 485, **491**, 621, 642, 650
  Blackpoll, 109, **500–501**, 633, 648, 650
  Blue-winged, 17, 18, 109, **470–471**, 472, 473, 625, 641
  Brewster's, **473–474**
  Canada, 52, 110, **521–522**, 643
  Cape May, 39, 109, **484–485**, 642
  Cerulean, 5, 110, **501–502**, 642
  Chestnut-sided, 14, 109, **481–482**, 517, 642
  Connecticut, 39, 110, **514–515**, 517, 620, 621, 642
  Golden-winged, 109, **471–472**, 473, 641
  Hermit, 109, **489**
  Hooded, 110, **519–520**, 643
  Kentucky, 40, 110, **513–514**, 642
  Kirtland's, 37, 109, **494–495**, 633, 650
  Lawrence's, **473–474**
  Magnolia, 109, **482–483**, 642
  Mourning, 40, 88, 110, 514, **516–517**, 620, 625, 643
  Nashville, 17, 40, 52, 53, 59, 60, 109, 464, **477–478**, 621, 622, 642
  Orange-crowned, 109, **476–477**, 622, 650
  Palm, 52, 109, **497–498**, 622, 642, 648
  Parula. *See* Parula, Northern
  Pine, 84, 109, **493–494**, 621, 642
  Prairie, 19, 109, **496–497**, 642
  Prothonotary, 40, 110, **506–507**, 630, 642
  Tennessee, 109, **475–476**, 482, 622, 642
  Wilson's, 110, **520–521**, 650
  Worm-eating, 5, 19, 30, 110, **507–508**, 642
  Yellow, 16, 88, 109, **480–481**, 517, 587, 632, 642
  Yellow-rumped, 40, 56, 109, 464, 482, **487–488**, 621, 642, 647, 648
  Yellow-throated, 30, 109, **492–493**, 642
Waterthrush, Louisiana, 37, 49, 110, 510, **511–512**, 630, 642
  Northern, 37, 52, 110, **510–511**, 512, 625, 642
Waxwing, Bohemian, 109, **453–454**, 645, 647
  Cedar, 48, 109, 224, **454–455**, 641, 645, 647
Wheatear, Northern, 108, **611**
Whimbrel, 105, **265–266**, 649
Whip-poor-will, 4, 17, 20, 40, 107, **354–355**, 638

Whistling-Duck, Fulvous, 102, **148**
Wigeon, American, 16, 103, 161, **171–172**, 176, 635, 646
  Eurasian, 103, **170–171**, 649
Willet, 105, **261**, 649
Wilsonia canadensis, 52, 110, **521–522**, 643
  citrina, 110, **519–520**, 643
  pusilla, 110, **520–521**, 650
Wood-Pewee, Eastern, 107, **376–377**, 525, 609, 617, 621, 639
  Western, 107, **609–610**
Woodcock, American, 4, 16, 20, 27, 40, 88, 105, **286–287**, 625, 637
Woodpecker, Black-backed, 5, 17, 82, 107, **370–371**, 622, 639, 647
  Downy, 88, 107, **367**, 638, 647
  Hairy, 84, 107, 367, **368**, 638, 647
  Lewis', 107, **362**
  Pileated, 17, 40, 50, 84, 107, **373–374**, 620, 639, 647
  Red-bellied, 17, 18, 27, 40, 54, 60, 107, **364–365**, 618, 638, 647
  Red-headed, 4, 17, 37, 61, 82, 85, 107, **363–364**, 459, 617, 638, 647
  Three-toed, 5, 17, 107, **369–370**, 647
Wren, Bewick's, 17, 19, 39, 40, 108, **420–421**, 640
  Carolina, 5, 16, 40, 108, **419–420**, 640, 647
  House, 18, 37, 52, 88, 108, **422–423**, 640
  Marsh, 38, 108, **426–427**, 629, 633, 640
  Sedge, 16, 40, 52, 56, 85, 88, 108, **424–425**, 554, 640
  Winter, 38, 40, 50, 108, **423–424**, 640, 647

Xanthocephalus xanthocephalus, 17, 27, 38, 39, 40, 111, **581–582**, 629, 644, 647
Xema sabini, 106, **311**

Yellowlegs, Greater, 104, **258**, 649
  Lesser, 17, 104, **259**, 649
Yellowthroat, Common, 39, 88, 110, **517–518**, 624, 643, 645

Zenaida macroura, 15, 39, 67, 85, 89, 106, **325–326**, 621, 628, 632, 637, 646
Zonotricia albicollis, 40, 52, 59, 111, 540, 558, **563–564**, 622, 644, 647, 648
  atricapilla, 111, **565**
  leucophrys, 39, 111, **566–567**, 568, 647
  querula, 111, **567–568**, 647